MICROSOFT WINDOWS 98
Comprehensive Concepts and Techniques

Gary B. Shelly
Thomas J. Cashman
Steven G. Forsythe

COURSE TECHNOLOGY
ONE MAIN STREET
CAMBRIDGE MA 02142

an International Thomson Publishing company

CAMBRIDGE • ALBANY • BONN • CINCINNATI • LONDON • MADRID • MELBOURNE
MEXICO CITY • NEW YORK • PARIS • SAN FRANCISCO • TOKYO • TORONTO • WASHINGTON

© 1999 by Course Technology — ITP

Printed in the United States of America

For more information, contact:

Course Technology
One Main Street
Cambridge, Massachusetts 02142, USA

International Thomson Editores
Saneca, 53
Colonia Polanco
11560 Mexico D.F. Mexico

ITP Europe
Berkshire House
168-173 High Holborn
London, WC1V 7AA, United Kingdom

ITP GmbH
Konigswinterer Strasse 418
53227 Bonn, Germany

ITP Australia
102 Dodds Street
South Melbourne
Victoria 3205 Australia

ITP Asia
60 Albert Street, #15-01
Albert Complex
Singapore 189969

ITP Nelson Canada
1120 Birchmount Road
Scarborough, Ontario
Canada M1K 5G4

ITP Japan
Hirakawa-cho Kyowa Building, 3F
2-2-1 Hirakawa-cho, Chiyoda-ku
Tokyo 102, Japan

All rights reserved. This publication is protected by federal copyright laws. No part of this publication may be reproduced, stored in a retrieval system, or transmitted in any form or by any means, electronic, mechanical, photocopying, recording, or otherwise, or be used to make a derivative work (such as translation or adaptation), without prior permission in writing from Course Technology.

TRADEMARKS
Course Technology and the Open Book logo are registered trademarks and CourseKits is a trademark of Course Technology.

ITP The ITP logo is a registered trademark of International Thomson Publishing.

SHELLY CASHMAN SERIES® and **Custom Edition®** are trademarks of International Thomson Publishing. Some of the product names and company names used in this book have been used for identification purposes only and may be trademarks or registered trademarks of their respective manufacturers and sellers. International Thomson Publishing and Course Technology disclaim any affiliation, association, or connection with, or sponsorship or endorsement by, such owners.

DISCLAIMER
Course Technology reserves the right to revise this publication and make changes from time to time in its content without notice.

ISBN 0-7895-4746-5

PHOTO CREDITS: *Project 1, pages WIN 1.4-5* Young Bill Gates, Paul Allen and Bill Gates, Courtesy of Lake Side Middle School; Microsoft Company Photo, Bill Gates, Microsoft Campus, Courtesy of Microsoft Corporation; Intel Microprocessor Chip 4004, Courtesy of Intel Corporation; *Project 2, pages WIN 2.2-3* IBM Personal Computer, Courtesy of International Business Machines Corporation; Xerox Mouse, Courtesy of Xerox PARC; *Project 3, pages WIN 3.2-3* Telephone Booth, ©The Stock Market/Anthony Redpath, 1998; Hard Drive, Courtesy of Seagate Technology; Italian Castle, Courtesy of Corel Professional Photos CD-ROM Image usage; Volkswagen, Courtesy of Volkswagen of America, Inc.; Pentium II Microprocessor, Gordon E. Moore, Chairman of the Board, Intel Corp., Courtesy of Intel Corporation. *Project 4, pages WIN 4.2-3* Screensaver Images, Berkeley Website Images, Man and Woman, Courtesy of Berkeley Systems; Microsoft Screensaver Images, Courtesy of Microsoft Corporation; *Project 5, pages WIN 5.2-3* Briefcase, Book, Photo Elements for House Image, Courtesy of Expert Photo Gallery; Pen, Open Ledger, Cellphone, Courtesy of KPT Metatools; Friends (Girls), Courtesy of Corel Professional Photos CD-ROM Image usage; Pacifier, Alarm Clock, Ladder, Courtesy of Photo Disc Object Sampler; *Project 6, pages WIN 6.2-3* Oscar the Grouch, ©The Children's Television Workshop; File Cabinet, Crumpled Paper, Courtesy of KPT Metatools; Windows and Office Icons, Courtesy of Microsoft Corporation; Other Icons, ©Susan Kare; *Project 7, pages WIN 7.2-3* American flag, pen, stars, Courtesy of PhotoDisc, Inc.; crowded globe, Matterhorn, Courtesy of Digital Stock; Pentagon, Courtesy of U.S. Department of Defense; *Project 8, pages WIN 8.2-3* Policeman, film reel, CD-ROM, Courtesy of PhotoDisc, Inc.; *Project 9, pages WIN 9.2-3* Woman typing, red building, Courtesy of PhotoDisc, Inc.; computer monitors, keyboard, Courtesy of KPT Metatools.

3 4 5 6 7 8 9 10   BC   03 02 01 00

MICROSOFT WINDOWS 98
Comprehensive Concepts and Techniques

CONTENTS

Microsoft Windows 98 — WIN 1.1

● PROJECT ONE
FUNDAMENTALS OF USING MICROSOFT WINDOWS 98

Objectives	WIN 1.3
Introduction	WIN 1.6
Microsoft Windows 98	WIN 1.6
What Is a User Interface?	WIN 1.7
Launching Microsoft Windows 98	WIN 1.8
The Welcome to Windows 98 Screen	WIN 1.9
Closing the Welcome Screen	WIN 1.10
The Desktop as a Work Area	WIN 1.11
Communicating with Microsoft Windows 98	WIN 1.11
Mouse Operations	WIN 1.11
Point and Click	WIN 1.11
Right-Click	WIN 1.14
Double-Click	WIN 1.16
Double-Clicking Errors	WIN 1.17
My Computer Window	WIN 1.18
Minimize Button	WIN 1.19
Maximize and Restore Buttons	WIN 1.21
Close Button	WIN 1.23
Drag	WIN 1.24
Sizing a Window by Dragging	WIN 1.25
Scrolling in a Window	WIN 1.27
Scrolling by Clicking the Scroll Bar	WIN 1.29
Scrolling by Dragging the Scroll Box	WIN 1.30
Resizing a Window	WIN 1.31
Closing a Window	WIN 1.31
Right-Drag	WIN 1.32
Summary of Mouse and Windows Operations	WIN 1.34
The Keyboard and Keyboard Shortcuts	WIN 1.34
The Windows 98 Desktop Views	WIN 1.35
The Classic Style	WIN 1.35
The Internet and World Wide Web	WIN 1.36
The Web Style	WIN 1.37
The Custom Style	WIN 1.39
Launching an Application Program	WIN 1.40
Launching an Application Using the Start Button	WIN 1.40
Launching an Application Using the Quick Launch Toolbar	WIN 1.41
Launching an Application Using an Icon on the Desktop	WIN 1.42
Using Windows Help	WIN 1.43
Contents Sheet	WIN 1.44
Index Sheet	WIN 1.47
Shutting Down Windows 98	WIN 1.49
Project Summary	WIN 1.50
What You Should Know	WIN 1.51
Test Your Knowledge	WIN 1.52
Use Help	WIN 1.55
In the Lab	WIN 1.59
Cases and Places	WIN 1.63

● PROJECT TWO
WORKING ON THE WINDOWS 98 DESKTOP

Objectives	WIN 2.1
Introduction	WIN 2.4
Creating a Document by Launching an Application Program	WIN 2.6
Saving a Document on the Desktop	WIN 2.7
Printing a Document	WIN 2.11
Closing a Document	WIN 2.11
Creating and Naming a Document on the Desktop	WIN 2.12
Naming a Document	WIN 2.14
Entering Data into a Blank Document on the Desktop	WIN 2.14
Closing and Saving a Document	WIN 2.16
Storing Documents in a Folder on the Desktop	WIN 2.17
Opening and Modifying Documents Within a Folder	WIN 2.20
Opening and Modifying a Document Stored in a Folder	WIN 2.21
Opening Multiple Documents	WIN 2.23
Minimizing All Open Windows	WIN 2.25
Closing Multiple Windows	WIN 2.26
Printing a Document from Within a Folder	WIN 2.28
Copying a Folder onto a Disk	WIN 2.30
Opening a Folder on a Floppy Disk	WIN 2.31

Creating Document Shortcuts	WIN 2.34
Placing a Shortcut on the Start Menu	WIN 2.34
Opening a Document from the Start Menu	WIN 2.35
Removing a Shortcut from the Start Menu	WIN 2.37
Creating a Shortcut on the Desktop	WIN 2.39
Opening a Document or Launching an Application Program Using a Shortcut on the Desktop	WIN 2.40
Arranging Icons	WIN 2.41
Deleting Shortcuts, Folders, and Documents on the Desktop	WIN 2.42
Deleting Multiple Files	WIN 2.44
Deleting a Folder	WIN 2.46
Working with the Windows 98 Active Desktop™	**WIN 2.47**
Turning On the Active Desktop	WIN 2.48
Adding an Active Desktop Item to the Active Desktop	WIN 2.49
Displaying Additional Information About a Sporting Event	WIN 2.54
Removing a Desktop Item from the Active Desktop	WIN 2.55
Turning Off the Active Desktop	WIN 2.57
Using Microsoft Support Online	**WIN 2.58**
Shutting Down Windows	WIN 2.62
Project Summary	**WIN 2.62**
What You Should Know	**WIN 2.63**
Test Your Knowledge	**WIN 2.64**
Use Help	**WIN 2.69**
In the Lab	**WIN 2.72**
Cases and Places	**WIN 2.79**

● PROJECT THREE

FILE, DOCUMENT, AND FOLDER MANAGEMENT AND WINDOWS 98 EXPLORER

Objectives	**WIN 3.1**
Introduction	**WIN 3.4**
My Computer Window	**WIN 3.4**
Viewing Icons in the My Computer Window	WIN 3.7
Viewing the Contents of Drives and Folders	WIN 3.9
Opening a Folder Window	WIN 3.10
Opening a Document from a Window	WIN 3.12
Launching an Application Program from a Window	WIN 3.13
Managing Open Windows	**WIN 3.15**
Cascading Windows	WIN 3.15
Making a Window the Active Window	WIN 3.17
Undo Cascade	WIN 3.18
Tiling Open Windows	WIN 3.19
Closing Windows	WIN 3.21
Copying, Moving, and Deleting Files in Windows	**WIN 3.21**
Copying Files from a Folder to a Drive	WIN 3.21
Deleting Files in Windows	WIN 3.25
Windows 98 Explorer	**WIN 3.26**
Launching Windows 98 Explorer	WIN 3.26
Explorer Window	WIN 3.27
Displaying Files and Folders in Windows 98 Explorer	WIN 3.28
Displaying Drive and Folder Contents	WIN 3.28
Expanding a Selected Drive or Folder	WIN 3.29
Opening Folders in Explorer	WIN 3.32
Programs Folder	WIN 3.33
Launching an Application Program from Windows 98 Explorer	WIN 3.34
Closing Folder Expansions	WIN 3.35
Copying, Moving, Renaming, and Deleting Files and Folders in Windows 98 Explorer	**WIN 3.37**
Copying Files in Windows 98 Explorer	WIN 3.37
Displaying the Contents of a Floppy Disk	WIN 3.39
Renaming Files and Folders	WIN 3.40
Deleting Files in Windows 98 Explorer	WIN 3.42
Closing Windows 98 Explorer	WIN 3.44
Summary of Windows 98 Explorer	WIN 3.44
Properties of Objects	**WIN 3.44**
Drive Properties	WIN 3.44
Properties of a Folder	WIN 3.46
Finding Files or Folders	**WIN 3.48**
Finding a File by Name	WIN 3.48
Run Command	**WIN 3.50**
Shutting Down Windows 98	WIN 3.52
Project Summary	**WIN 3.53**
What You Should Know	**WIN 3.53**
Test Your Knowledge	**WIN 3.54**
Use Help	**WIN 3.57**
In the Lab	**WIN 3.58**
Cases and Places	**WIN 3.63**

● PROJECT FOUR

MODIFYING YOUR DESKTOP WORK ENVIRONMENT

Objectives	**WIN 4.1**
Introduction	**WIN 4.4**
Changing Your Desktop Working Environment	**WIN 4.4**
Desktop Properties	WIN 4.5
Changing the Desktop Background	WIN 4.6
Adding Wallpaper to the Desktop	WIN 4.6
Adding a Pattern to the Desktop	WIN 4.9
Changing the Desktop Appearance	WIN 4.11
Adding a Screen Saver	WIN 4.13
Customizing the Taskbar	**WIN 4.15**
Moving the Taskbar	WIN 4.16
Hiding the Taskbar	WIN 4.17
Working with Toolbars on the Taskbar	**WIN 4.20**
Adding a Toolbar to the Taskbar	WIN 4.20
Using the Address Toolbar to Display the Contents of a Folder	WIN 4.21
Using the Address Toolbar to Display a Web Page	WIN 4.22

Using the Address Toolbar to Search for Information on the Internet	WIN 4.23
Resizing the Taskbar	WIN 4.25
Removing a Toolbar and Resizing the Taskbar	WIN 4.26
Customizing a Toolbar	**WIN 4.27**
Placing a Shortcut on a Toolbar	WIN 4.27
Removing a Shortcut from a Toolbar	WIN 4.29
Customizing Folders	**WIN 4.29**
Opening the View Menu in a Folder	WIN 4.30
Adding a Toolbar to a Folder	WIN 4.31
Adding an Explorer Bar to a Folder	WIN 4.32
Adding a Background to a Folder	WIN 4.34
Removing the Toolbar and Explorer Bar from a Folder	WIN 4.37
Displaying a Folder as a Web Page	WIN 4.38
Removing the Background and No Longer Displaying the Folder as a Web Page	WIN 4.39
Windows 98 Desktop Views	**WIN 4.40**
Viewing Web Content in a Folder	WIN 4.42
Displaying Folders as Web Pages	WIN 4.43
Opening Each Folder in the Same Window or in Its Own Window	WIN 4.43
Choosing the Classic Style as the Desktop View	**WIN 4.45**
Viewing the Settings for the Classic Style	WIN 4.47
Choosing the Web Style as the Desktop View	**WIN 4.49**
Viewing the Web Style Settings	WIN 4.51
Desktop View Summary	WIN 4.53
Working with Icons and Windows in the Web Style	**WIN 4.53**
Selecting Icons on the Desktop and Opening Windows in Web Style	WIN 4.53
Selecting an Icon in a Folder Window in Web Style	WIN 4.55
Navigating Folder Windows Using the Back and Forward Buttons	WIN 4.56
Selecting Multiple Files and Copying Files in Web Style	WIN 4.57
Resetting the Desktop View to the Default Custom Style	WIN 4.60
Shutting Down Windows	WIN 4.61
Project Summary	**WIN 4.61**
What You Should Know	**WIN 4.61**
Test Your Knowledge	**WIN 4.62**
Use Help	**WIN 4.65**
In the Lab	**WIN 4.66**
Cases and Places	**WIN 4.71**

● PROJECT FIVE

CUSTOMIZING YOUR COMPUTER USING CONTROL PANEL

Objectives	**WIN 5.1**
Introduction	**WIN 5.4**
The Control Panel Folder	WIN 5.4
Customizing the Keyboard	**WIN 5.6**
Adjusting the Keyboard Repeat Delay	WIN 5.6
Adjusting the Keyboard Repeat Rate	WIN 5.8
Adjusting the Cursor Blink Rate	WIN 5.9
Customizing the Mouse	**WIN 5.11**
Changing the Button Configuration	WIN 5.12
Adjusting the Double-Click Speed	WIN 5.13
Changing the Mouse Pointer Scheme	WIN 5.15
Adjusting the Pointer Speed	WIN 5.16
Displaying Pointer Trails	WIN 5.18
Customizing for Disabilities	**WIN 5.20**
Turning on the MouseKeys Feature	WIN 5.20
Using Bigger Fonts	WIN 5.22
Creating a Desktop Color Scheme Using the New Fonts and Font Sizes	WIN 5.24
Customizing the Date and Time	**WIN 5.24**
Changing the Date, Time, and Time Zone	WIN 5.24
Viewing the Regional Settings	WIN 5.28
Adding New Hardware	**WIN 5.30**
Adding a USB Device	WIN 5.31
Plug and Play Hardware Devices	WIN 5.33
Adding a Non-Plug and Play Device	WIN 5.33
Adding a Printer	WIN 5.33
Solving Hardware Problems Using a Help Troubleshooter	**WIN 5.38**
Viewing Hardware Properties	**WIN 5.41**
Hardware Profiles and System Performance	WIN 5.45
Adding and Removing Programs	**WIN 5.46**
Adding a Program	WIN 5.46
Removing a Program	WIN 5.48
Adding Windows 98 Components and Creating a Startup Disk	WIN 5.49
Project Summary	**WIN 5.49**
What You Should Know	**WIN 5.49**
Test Your Knowledge	**WIN 5.50**
Use Help	**WIN 5.53**
In the Lab	**WIN 5.54**
Cases and Places	**WIN 5.57**

● PROJECT SIX

ADVANCED FILE AND DOCUMENT MANAGEMENT AND MY BRIEFCASE

Objectives	**WIN 6.1**
Introduction	**WIN 6.4**
The Find Command	**WIN 6.4**
Finding Files and Folders on the Hard Drive	**WIN 6.5**
Specifying the Starting Point of the Search	WIN 6.6
Finding a File by Date	WIN 6.8
Finding a File by File Type	WIN 6.10
Finding a File Using a Word or Series of Words in the File	WIN 6.12
Saving a Search	WIN 6.14
Using a Saved Search to Find a File	WIN 6.15

Using Quick View	WIN 6.15
Using the Send To Command	**WIN 6.16**
Adding a Destination to the Send To Menu	WIN 6.17
Deleting a File Using the Send To Menu	WIN 6.19
Removing the Recycle Bin Destination	WIN 6.21
The Recycle Bin	**WIN 6.21**
Viewing the Contents of the Recycle Bin	WIN 6.21
Restoring a Deleted File, Folder, or Shortcut	WIN 6.22
Emptying the Recycle Bin	WIN 6.24
Viewing Recycle Bin Properties	WIN 6.25
Removing the Saved Search File	WIN 6.27
Using the Find Command to Search for Information on the Internet	**WIN 6.27**
Using the Find Command to Search for People on the Internet	**WIN 6.30**
My Briefcase	**WIN 6.32**
Creating the Three Files on the Desktop	WIN 6.33
Dragging the Three Files to My Briefcase	WIN 6.35
Viewing the Contents of My Briefcase	WIN 6.36
Moving My Briefcase to a Floppy Disk	WIN 6.36
Changing the Files on the Office Computer	WIN 6.38
Changing the Robert Moore File	WIN 6.40
Changing the Peter Hollister File	WIN 6.41
Synchronizing the Files	WIN 6.43
Synchronizing the Files Using My Briefcase	WIN 6.44
Opening a Document Using the Documents Command	**WIN 6.47**
Removing the List of Documents from the Documents Submenu	WIN 6.49
Restoring the Desktop to Its Original Configuration	**WIN 6.51**
Power Management	WIN 6.51
Project Summary	**WIN 6.53**
What You Should Know	**WIN 6.54**
Test Your Knowledge	**WIN 6.55**
Use Help	**WIN 6.57**
In the Lab	**WIN 6.58**
Cases and Places	**WIN 6.61**

● PROJECT SEVEN
COMMUNICATING WITH OTHER COMPUTERS

Objectives	**WIN 7.1**
Introduction	**WIN 7.4**
Using a Modem to Communicate with Other Computers	**WIN 7.4**
Accessing an Online Service	**WIN 7.5**
The Microsoft Network (MSN) and the Internet	WIN 7.5
Signing Up to The Microsoft Network	WIN 7.5
Checking The Microsoft Network Connection Settings	WIN 7.6
Signing in to The Microsoft Network	WIN 7.8
Microsoft Outlook Express	WIN 7.10
Launching Outlook Express	WIN 7.10
Opening and Reading E-mail Messages	WIN 7.12
Replying to an E-mail	WIN 7.13
Signing Out from The Microsoft Network	WIN 7.15
Changing the Connection Settings	WIN 7.16
Changing the Backup Telephone Number	WIN 7.21
Resetting the Connection Settings	WIN 7.22
Connecting to the Internet Using an Internet Service Provider	**WIN 7.23**
Setting Up a Connection to an Internet Service Provider	WIN 7.23
Creating a Dial-Up Networking Connection for an Existing ISP Account	WIN 7.31
Dialing an Internet Service Provider	WIN 7.32
Disconnecting from an Internet Service Provider	WIN 7.33
Viewing a Dial-Up Networking Connection Icon	WIN 7.35
Removing a Dial-Up Networking Connection Icon	WIN 7.35
Using a Modem to Communicate Summary	**WIN 7.36**
An Introduction to Networks	**WIN 7.36**
Network Components	**WIN 7.36**
Installing the Network Hardware Component	WIN 7.37
Installing the Network Software Components	WIN 7.38
Viewing Computers and Workgroups on a Network	**WIN 7.45**
Viewing Computers, Workgroups, and Shared Computer Resources on the Network	WIN 7.45
Locating Computers on the Network Using the Find Command	WIN 7.47
Sharing Computer Resources on a Network	**WIN 7.49**
Sharing a Folder	WIN 7.49
Deleting a Shared Folder	WIN 7.51
Sharing a Printer	WIN 7.51
Removing Sharing from a Printer	WIN 7.53
Mapping a Drive Letter to a Network Resource	**WIN 7.54**
Mapping a Drive Letter	WIN 7.54
Accessing a Mapped Network Drive	WIN 7.55
Disconnecting a Mapped Network Drive	WIN 7.56
Project Summary	**WIN 7.57**
What You Should Know	**WIN 7.57**
Test Your Knowledge	**WIN 7.58**
Use Help	**WIN 7.61**
In the Lab	**WIN 7.62**
Cases and Places	**WIN 7.67**

● PROJECT EIGHT
WORKING WITH MULTIMEDIA AND NETMEETING

Objectives	**WIN 8.1**
Introduction	**WIN 8.4**
An Introduction to Multimedia	**WIN 8.4**

Recording and Playing Audio	**WIN 8.5**
Recording and Playing Sound Files Using Sound Recorder	WIN 8.6
Recording a Voice Message Using Sound Recorder	WIN 8.6
Playing a Recorded Voice Message	WIN 8.8
Embedding a Sound File in a Document	WIN 8.9
Playing a Recorded Voice Message	WIN 8.11
Closing the Word and Sound Recorder Windows	WIN 8.11
Deleting the Word Document	WIN 8.12
Changing the Sound Scheme	WIN 8.12
Playing an Audio Compact Disc	WIN 8.15
Creating a Play List Using CD Player	WIN 8.16
Editing the Play List	WIN 8.20
Adjusting the Volume of a Sound Device	WIN 8.23
Ejecting a Compact Disc from the CD-ROM Drive	WIN 8.25
Recording and Playing Videos	**WIN 8.26**
Playing a DVD	WIN 8.26
Changing the Video Window View to Full Screen View	WIN 8.28
To Eject the DVD and Close the Open Windows	WIN 8.28
Playing Multimedia Files	**WIN 8.30**
Playing a Multimedia File Using Media Player	WIN 8.30
Summary of Multimedia Operations	WIN 8.33
Microsoft NetMeeting	**WIN 8.33**
Launching Microsoft NetMeeting	WIN 8.34
Changing the Directory Information	WIN 8.36
NetMeeting Categories and Filters	WIN 8.38
Changing the ILS Server	WIN 8.39
Placing a Call	WIN 8.40
Sending a Text Message Using Chat	WIN 8.42
Drawing a Graphics Image Using Whiteboard	WIN 8.46
Closing the Chat and Whiteboard Windows	WIN 8.48
Sharing an Application	WIN 8.48
Sending a File Using File Transfer	WIN 8.48
Ending a Call and Quitting NetMeeting	WIN 8.51
Project Summary	**WIN 8.52**
What You Should Know	**WIN 8.52**
Test Your Knowledge	**WIN 8.53**
Use Help	**WIN 8.56**
In the Lab	**WIN 8.57**
Cases and Places	**WIN 8.61**

● PROJECT NINE

MAINTAINING AND OPTIMIZING YOUR COMPUTER AND SYSTEM REGISTRY

Objectives	**WIN 9.1**
Introduction	**WIN 9.4**
Backing Up and Restoring Files	**WIN 9.4**
Using Backup to Back Up Selected Files on the Hard Disk	WIN 9.5
Displaying the Contents on a Floppy Disk	WIN 9.13
Restoring the Backup Files to the My Documents Folder	WIN 9.14
The Windows 98 File System and the File Allocation Table (FAT)	**WIN 9.19**
Maintaining the Hard Disk	**WIN 9.20**
Using ScanDisk to Scan a Hard Disk for Errors	WIN 9.20
Using Disk Cleanup to Delete Unnecessary Files on the Hard Disk	WIN 9.24
Using Disk Defragmenter to Defragment Files on the Hard Disk	WIN 9.28
Scheduling Routine Maintenance Using the Maintenance Wizard	**WIN 9.31**
Viewing the Routine Maintenance Tasks Using Task Scheduler	WIN 9.37
Windows Update	**WIN 9.38**
The Product Updates Area	WIN 9.41
Downloading a Component	WIN 9.43
Downloading a Device Driver	WIN 9.46
The Windows 98 System Registry	**WIN 9.46**
Backing Up the System Registry	WIN 9.46
Making a Backup Copy of the System Registry Using Registry Checker	WIN 9.47
Viewing the System Registry Settings Using Registry Editor	WIN 9.50
Modifying the System Registry Settings	WIN 9.54
Modifying the Registered Organization Using Registry Editor	WIN 9.59
Drive Converter (FAT32)	**WIN 9.59**
Additional System Diagnostic Tools	**WIN 9.61**
Project Summary	**WIN 9.61**
What You Should Know	**WIN 9.61**
Test Your Knowledge	**WIN 9.62**
Use Help	**WIN 9.66**
In the Lab	**WIN 9.68**
Cases and Places	**WIN 9.73**
Index	**I.1**

Preface

The Shelly Cashman Series® offers the finest textbooks in computer education. The Microsoft Windows 98 books continue with the innovation, quality, and reliability consistent with this series. We are proud that both our Microsoft Windows 3.1 and Microsoft Windows 95 books were used by more schools and more students than any other series in textbook publishing.

The Windows 98 interface includes a new Quick Launch toolbar on the taskbar, additional toolbars you can add to the taskbar, and a choice of three desktop views (Web style, Classic style, and Custom style). The Web style turns on the Active Desktop™ that places the Internet Explorer Channel bar and constantly changing Web content on the desktop, lets you point to an icon to select it and single-click the icon to open its window, and displays folders that look and respond like Web pages.

In our Microsoft Windows 98 books, you will find an educationally sound and easy-to-follow pedagogy that combines a step-by-step approach with corresponding screens. The Other Ways and More About features offer in-depth knowledge of Windows 98. The all-new project openers provide a fascinating perspective on the subject covered in the project. The Shelly Cashman Series Microsoft Windows 98 textbooks will make your computer applications class exciting and dynamic and one that your students will remember as one of their better educational experiences.

Objectives of This Textbook

Microsoft Windows 98: Comprehensive Concepts and Techniques is intended for a three-unit course that presents Microsoft Windows 98. No computer experience is assumed. The objectives of this book are:

- To teach the comprehensive skills necessary to adequately use Windows 98
- To provide a solid foundation of Windows 98 knowledge upon which students can build
- To expose students to real-world examples and procedures that will prepare them to be skilled users of Windows 98
- To encourage independent study and help those who are working alone in a distance education environment

When students complete the course using this textbook, they will have a working knowledge of Windows 98.

The Shelly Cashman Approach

Features of the Shelly Cashman Series Microsoft Windows 98 books include:

- **Project Orientation:** Related topics are presented using a project orientation that establishes a strong foundation on which students can confidently learn more advanced topics.
- **Screen-by-Screen, Step-by-Step Instructions:** Each task required to complete a project is identified throughout the development of the project. Then, steps to accomplish the task are specified and are accompanied by screens.
- **Thoroughly Tested Projects:** Every screen in the textbook is correct because it is produced by the author only after performing a step, which results in unprecedented quality.

- **Two-Page Project Openers:** Each project begins with a two-page opener that describes an interesting aspect of Windows 98.
- **Other Ways Boxes for Reference:** Microsoft Windows 98 provides a variety of ways to carry out a given task. The Other Ways boxes displayed at the end of most of the step-by-step sequences specify the other ways to do the task completed in the steps. Thus, the steps and the Other Ways box make a comprehensive reference unit.
- **More About Feature:** These marginal annotations provide background information about the topics covered, adding interest and depth to learning.

Other Ways

1. Right-click name in Current Call list, click Send File, select file, click Send
2. Drag file to Current Call list
3. Press CTRL+F, select file, press ENTER

More About

Dial-Up Networking

To determine if Dial-Up Networking is installed on your computer, double-click the My Computer icon on the desktop. If you do not see the Dial-Up Networking folder, then Dial-Up Networking is not installed and can be installed using the Add/Remove Programs icon in the Control Panel window.

Organization of This Textbook

Microsoft Windows 98: Comprehensive Concepts and Techniques consists of nine projects, as follows:

Project 1 – Fundamentals of Using Microsoft Windows 98 In Project 1, students learn about user interfaces and Microsoft Windows 98. Topics include launching Microsoft Windows 98; mouse operations; maximizing, minimizing, moving, sizing, and scrolling windows; describing the Internet and World Wide Web; recognizing the Classic, Web, and Custom styles; launching an application program; using Help; and shutting down Windows 98.

Project 2 – Working on the Windows 98 Desktop In Project 2, students work on the Windows 98 desktop. Topics include creating a document on the desktop by starting an application; creating and naming a document on the desktop; opening, saving, printing, and closing a document on the desktop; storing documents in folders on the desktop; opening, modifying, and printing documents within a folder; copying a folder onto a disk; opening multiple documents; creating shortcuts; deleting documents, shortcuts, and folders; turning on the Active Desktop; adding active desktop items to the desktop; and using Microsoft Support Online.

Project 3 – File, Document, and Folder Management and Windows 98 Explorer In Project 3, students manage windows and files on the desktop and use Windows 98 Explorer. Topics include using My Computer; displaying drive and folder contents; opening a document from a window; launching an application program from a window; cascading and tiling open windows; copying, moving, and deleting files from windows; Windows 98 Explorer; displaying files and folders in Explorer; displaying drive and folder contents; expanding a drive or folder; launching an application from Explorer; copying, moving, renaming, and deleting files in Explorer; displaying object properties; finding files and folders; and the Run command.

Project 4 – Modifying Your Desktop Work Environment In Project 4, students modify desktop properties, personalize the taskbar; customize folders on the desktop, and change the desktop view. Topics include modifying the desktop environment; desktop properties and appearance; screen savers; customizing the taskbar; adding a toolbar to the taskbar; adding a shortcut icon to a toolbar; customizing a folder on the desktop; adding a toolbar to a folder; viewing the desktop in Classic style, Web style, and Custom style; and viewing the settings for the current desktop view.

Project 5 – Customizing Your Computer Using Control Panel In Project 5, students customize the Windows 98 environment using the icons in the Control Panel folder. Topics include customizing the mouse, keyboard, date and time, and desktop fonts; adding a new hardware device and software program; customizing the computer for disabled people; adding a printer and controlling the operation of the printer; using Help Troubleshooters to solve hardware problems; and viewing the hardware properties of the hardware devices attached to the computer.

Project 6 - Advanced File and Document Management and My Briefcase   In Project 6, students use the advanced file and document features and learn to use My Briefcase. Topics include searching for a file based on date, a word or words within the file, or type of file; viewing the contents of a file; copying and deleting a file using the Send To command; recovering a deleted file using the Recycle Bin; opening a document using the Documents command; viewing the properties and emptying the contents of the Recycle Bin; and using My Briefcase, transporting files between two computers; modifying the files on both computers, and updating the files.

Project 7 - Communicating with Other Computers   In Project 7, students use their computers to communicate with other computers. Topics include connecting to The Microsoft Network (MSN) and the Internet; signing in to MSN; starting Outlook Express; opening, reading, and replying to an e-mail message; changing connection settings; signing up for an Internet service provider (ISP) and creating a Dial-Up Networking connection; dialing an ISP; installing a network adapter and software components; viewing and searching for computers on a network; sharing computer resources; and mapping a drive letter and accessing a mapped network drive.

Project 8 - Working with Multimedia and NetMeeting   In Project 8, students explore the multimedia capabilities of the computer and use NetMeeting to communicate with other computer users. Topics include playing and recording an audio file; embedding and playing an audio file in a document; changing the sound scheme of the computer; playing an audio compact disc (CD), creating and editing a play list, adjusting the volume of a sound device; watching a movie on a digital video disc (DVD) player; and using Microsoft NetMeeting to videoconference with, send typed messages to, share an application with, and send a file to other NetMeeting users.

Project 9 - Maintaining and Optimizing Your Computer and System Registry   In Project 9, students learn how to maintain a computer and improve system performance. Topics include backing up files onto a floppy disk; restoring an unusable file; scanning a disk for errors; deleting unnecessary files on the hard disk; defragmenting a hard disk; scheduling routine maintenance; downloading software and device drivers from the Windows Update Web site; making a backup copy of the system registry; and viewing and modifying the system registry settings.

End-of-Project Student Activities

A notable strength of the Shelly Cashman Series Microsoft Windows 98 textbooks is the extensive student activities at the end of each project. Well-structured student activities can make the difference between students merely participating in a class and students retaining the information they learn. These activities include:

- **What You Should Know**   A listing of the tasks completed within a project together with the pages where the step-by-step, screen-by-screen explanations appear. This section provides a perfect study review for students.
- **Test Your Knowledge**   Four activities designed to determine students' understanding of the material in the project. Included are true/false questions, multiple-choice questions, and two other unique activities.
- **Use Help**   Users of Windows 98 must know how to use Help. This book contains extensive Help activities. These exercises alone distinguish the Shelly Cashman Series from any other set of Windows 98 instructional materials.
- **In the Lab**   These assignments require students to make use of the knowledge gained in the project to solve problems on a computer.
- **Cases and Places**   Case studies that allow students to apply their knowledge to real-world situations, and provide subjects for research papers.

Shelly Cashman Series Teaching Tools

A comprehensive set of Teaching Tools accompanies this textbook in the form of a CD-ROM. The CD-ROM includes an electronic Instructor's Manual and teaching and testing aids. The CD-ROM (ISBN 0-7895-5571-9) is available through your Course Technology representative or by calling one of the following telephone numbers: Colleges and Universities, 1-800-648-7450; High Schools, 1-800-824-5179; and Career Colleges, 1-800-477-3692. The contents of the CD-ROM are listed below.

- **Instructor's Manual** The Instructor's Manual consists of Microsoft Word files that include lecture notes, solutions to assignments, and a large test bank. The files allow you to modify the lecture notes or generate quizzes and exams from the test bank using your own word processor. The Instructor's Manual includes the following for each project: project objectives; project overview; detailed lesson plans with page number references; teacher notes and activities; answers to the end-of-project exercises; test bank of 110 questions (50 true/false, 25 multiple-choice, and 35 fill-in-the blank); transparency references; and selected transparencies. The transparencies are available on the Figures in the Book described below. The test bank questions are numbered the same as in Course Test Manager. Thus, you can print a copy of the project and use the printed test bank to select your questions in Course Test Manager.

- **Figures in the Book** Illustrations for every figure in the textbook are available. Use this ancillary to create a slide show from the illustrations for lecture or to print transparencies for use in lecture with an overhead projector.

- **Course Test Manager** Course Test Manager is a powerful testing and assessment package that enables instructors to create and print tests from the large test bank. Instructors with access to a networked computer lab (LAN) can administer, grade, and track tests online. Students also can take online practice tests, which generate customized study guides that indicate where in the textbook students can find more information for each question.

- **Interactive Labs** Eighteen hands-on interactive labs that take students from ten to fifteen minutes to step through help solidify and reinforce computer concepts. Student assessment is available.

Shelly Cashman Online

Shelly Cashman Online is a World Wide Web service available to instructors and students of computer education. Visit Shelly Cashman Online at www.scseries.com. Shelly Cashman Online is divided into four areas:

- **Series Information** Information on the Shelly Cashman Series products.
- **Teaching Resources** Designed for instructors teaching from and using Shelly Cashman Series textbooks and software. This area includes password-protected instructor materials that can be downloaded, course outlines, teaching tips, and much more.
- **Student Center** Dedicated to students learning about computers with Shelly Cashman Series textbooks and software. This area includes cool links, data that can be downloaded, and much more.
- **Community** Opportunities to discuss your course and your ideas with instructors in your field and with the Shelly Cashman Series team.

Acknowledgments

The Shelly Cashman Series would not be the leading computer education series without the contributions of outstanding publishing professionals. First and foremost among them is Becky Herrington, director of production and designer. She is the heart and soul of the Shelly Cashman Series, and it is only through her leadership, dedication, and tireless efforts that superior products are made possible.

Under Becky's direction, the following individuals made significant contributions to these books: Doug Cowley, production manager; Ginny Harvey, series specialist and developmental editor; Ken Russo, graphic designer and Web developer; Mike Bodnar, Stephanie Nance, Mark Norton, Ellana Russo, and Dave Bonnewitz, graphic artists; Jeanne Black, Quark expert; Nancy Lamm, copyeditor; Marilyn Martin, proofreader; Marlo Mitchem, administrative/production assistant; Cristina Haley, indexer; Sarah Evertson of Image Quest, photo researcher; and Susan Sebok contributing writer.

Special thanks go to Jim Quasney, our dedicated series editor; Lisa Strite, senior editor; Lora Wade, associate product manager; Tonia Grafakos, associate Web product manager; Meagan Walsh, editorial assistant; and Kathryn Cronin, product marketing manager. Special mention must go to Becky Herrington for the outstanding book design, Mike Bodnar for the logo designs, and Ken Russo for the cover design and illustrations.

Gary B. Shelly
Thomas J. Cashman
Steven G. Forsythe

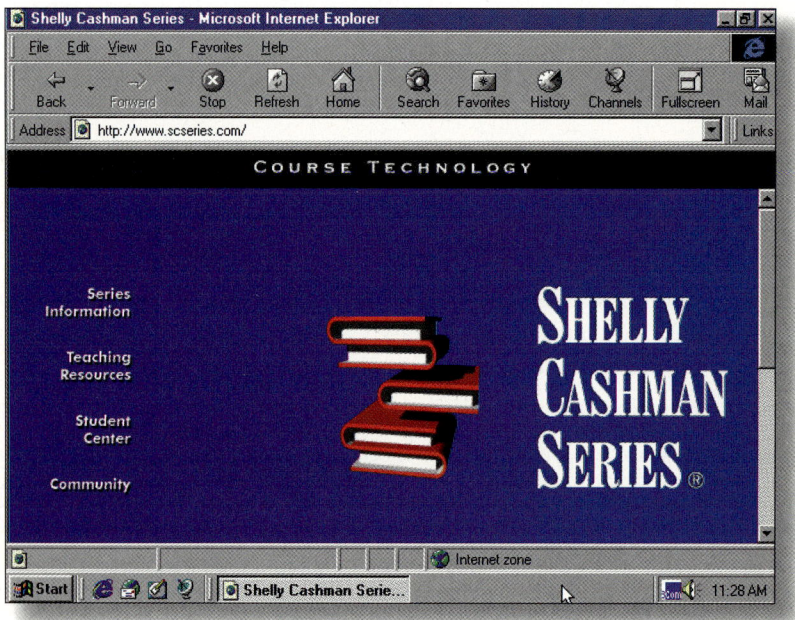

Shelly Cashman Series – Traditionally Bound Textbooks

The Shelly Cashman Series presents the following computer subjects in a variety of traditionally bound textbooks. For more information, see your Course Technology representative or call one of the following telephone numbers: Colleges and Universities, 1-800-648-7450; High Schools, 1-800-824-5179; and Career Colleges, 1-800-477-3692.

COMPUTERS	
Computers	Discovering Computers 98: A Link to the Future, World Wide Web Enhanced
	Discovering Computers 98: A Link to the Future, World Wide Web Enhanced Brief Edition
	Discovering Computers: A Link to the Future, World Wide Web Enhanced
	Discovering Computers: A Link to the Future, World Wide Web Enhanced Brief Edition
	Exploring Computers: A Record of Discovery 2e with CD-ROM
	A Record of Discovery for Exploring Computers 2e
	Study Guide for Discovering Computers: A Link to the Future, World Wide Web Enhanced
	Brief Introduction to Computers 2e (32-page)
WINDOWS APPLICATIONS	
Integrated Packages	Microsoft Office 97: Introductory Concepts and Techniques, Brief Edition (6 projects)
	Microsoft Office 97: Introductory Concepts and Techniques, Essentials Edition (10 projects)
	Microsoft Office 97: Introductory Concepts and Techniques (15 projects)
	Microsoft Office 97: Advanced Concepts and Techniques
	Microsoft Office 95: Introductory Concepts and Techniques (15 projects)
	Microsoft Office 95: Advanced Concepts and Techniques
	Microsoft Works 4* • Microsoft Works 3.0*
Windows	Microsoft Windows 98: Essential Concepts and Techniques
	Microsoft Windows 98: Introductory Concepts and Techniques
	Microsoft Windows 98: Introductory Concepts and Techniques Web Style Edition
	Microsoft Windows 98: Complete Concepts and Techniques
	Microsoft Windows 98: Comprehensive Concepts and Techniques
	Introduction to Microsoft Windows NT Workstation 4
	Microsoft Windows 95: Introductory Concepts and Techniques (96-page)
	Introduction to Microsoft Windows 95 (224-page)
	Microsoft Windows 95: Complete Concepts and Techniques
Word Processing	Microsoft Word 97* • Microsoft Word 7*
	Corel WordPerfect 8 • Corel WordPerfect 7 • WordPerfect 6.1*
Spreadsheets	Microsoft Excel 97* • Microsoft Excel 7* • Microsoft Excel 5* • Microsoft Excel 4
	Lotus 1-2-3 97* • Lotus 1-2-3 Release 5*
Database	Microsoft Access 97* • Microsoft Access 7*
Presentation Graphics	Microsoft PowerPoint 97* • Microsoft PowerPoint 7*
PROGRAMMING	
Programming	Microsoft Visual Basic 6: Complete Concepts and Techniques*
	Microsoft Visual Basic 5: Complete Concepts and Techniques*
	Microsoft Visual Basic 4 for Windows 95* (available with Student version software)
	Microsoft Visual Basic 3.0 for Windows*
	QBasic • QBasic: An Introduction to Programming • Microsoft BASIC
	Structured COBOL Programming (Micro Focus COBOL also available)
INTERNET	
Internet	The Internet: Introductory Concepts and Techniques (UNIX)
Browser	Netscape Navigator 4: An Introduction
	Netscape Navigator 3: An Introduction • Netscape Navigator 2 running under Windows 3.1
	Netscape Navigator: An Introduction (Version 1.1)
	Microsoft Internet Explorer 4: An Introduction
	Microsoft Internet Explorer 3: An Introduction
Web Page Creation	HTML: Complete Concepts and Techniques*
	Microsoft FrontPage 98: Complete Concepts and Techniques*
	Netscape Composer
	JavaScript: Complete Concepts and Techniques*
SYSTEMS ANALYSIS	
Systems Analysis	Systems Analysis and Design, Third Edition
DATA COMMUNICATIONS	
Data Communications	Business Data Communications: Introductory Concepts and Techniques, Second Edition

*Also available as a Double Diamond Edition, which is a shortened version of the complete book

Shelly Cashman Series – Custom Edition® Program

If you do not find a Shelly Cashman Series traditionally bound textbook to fit your needs, the Shelly Cashman Series unique **Custom Edition** program allows you to choose from a number of options and create a textbook perfectly suited to your course. Features of the **Custom Edition** program are:

- Textbooks that match the content of your course
- Windows- and DOS-based materials for the latest versions of personal computer applications software
- Shelly Cashman Series quality, with the same full-color materials and Shelly Cashman Series pedagogy found in the traditionally bound books
- Affordable pricing so your students receive the **Custom Edition** at a cost similar to that of traditionally bound books

The table on the right summarizes the available materials.

For more information, see your Course Technology representative or call one of the following telephone numbers: Colleges and Universities, 1-800-648-7450; High Schools, 1-800-824-5179; and Career Colleges, 1-800-477-3692.

For Shelly Cashman Series information, visit Shelly Cashman Online at www.scseries.com

COMPUTERS	
Computers	Discovering Computers 98: A Link to the Future, World Wide Web Enhanced
	Discovering Computers 98: A Link to the Future, World Wide Web Enhanced Brief Edition
	Discovering Computers: A Link to the Future, World Wide Web Enhanced
	Discovering Computers: A Link to the Future, World Wide Web Enhanced Brief Edition
	A Record of Discovery for Exploring Computers 2e (available with CD-ROM)
	Study Guide for Discovering Computers: A Link to the Future, World Wide Web Enhanced
	Introduction to Computers (32-page)
OPERATING SYSTEMS	
Windows	Microsoft Windows 98: Essential Concepts and Techniques (2-project)
	Microsoft Windows 98: Introductory Concepts and Techniques (3-project)
	Microsoft Windows 98: Introductory Concepts and Techniques Web Style Edition (3-project)
	Microsoft Windows 98: Complete Concepts and Techniques (6-project)
	Microsoft Windows 98: Comprehensive Concepts and Techniques (9-project)
	Microsoft Windows 95: Introductory Concepts and Techniques (96-page)
	Introduction to Microsoft Windows NT Workstation 4
	Introduction to Microsoft Windows 95 (224-page)
	Microsoft Windows 95: Complete Concepts and Techniques
DOS	Introduction to DOS 6 (using DOS prompt)
	Introduction to DOS 5.0 or earlier (using DOS prompt)
WINDOWS APPLICATIONS	
Integrated Packages	Microsoft Works 4*
	Microsoft Works 3.0*
Microsoft Office	Using Microsoft Office 97 (16-page)
	Using Microsoft Office 95 (16-page)
	Microsoft Office 97: Introductory Concepts and Techniques, Brief Edition (396-page)
	Microsoft Office 97: Introductory Concepts and Techniques, Essentials Edition (672-page)
	Object Linking and Embedding (OLE) (32-page)
	Microsoft Outlook 97 • Microsoft Schedule+ 7
	Introduction to Integrating Office 97 Applications (48-page)
	Introduction to Integrating Office 95 Applications (80-page)
Word Processing	Microsoft Word 97* • Microsoft Word 7* • Microsoft Word 6* • Microsoft Word 2.0
	Corel WordPerfect 8 • Corel WordPerfect 7 • WordPerfect 6.1* • WordPerfect 6* • WordPerfect 5.2
Spreadsheets	Microsoft Excel 97* • Microsoft Excel 7* • Microsoft Excel 5* • Microsoft Excel 4
	Lotus 1-2-3 97* • Lotus 1-2-3 Release 5* • Lotus 1-2-3 Release 4*
	Quattro Pro 6
Database	Microsoft Access 97* • Microsoft Access 7* • Microsoft Access 2*
	Paradox 5 • Paradox 4.5 • Paradox 1.0 • Visual dBASE 5/5.5
Presentation Graphics	Microsoft PowerPoint 97* • Microsoft PowerPoint 7* • Microsoft PowerPoint 4*
PROGRAMMING	
Programming	Microsoft Visual Basic 5 • Microsoft Visual Basic 4 for Windows 95* (available with Student version software) • Microsoft Visual Basic 3.0*
	Microsoft BASIC • QBasic
INTERNET	
Internet Browser	The Internet: Introductory Concepts and Techniques (UNIX)
	Netscape Navigator 4: An Introduction • Netscape Navigator 3: An Introduction • Netscape Navigator 2 running under Windows 3.1
	Netscape Navigator: An Introduction (Version 1.1) • Microsoft Internet Explorer 4: An Introduction • Microsoft Internet Explorer 3: An Introduction
Web Page Creation	Netscape Composer
DATA COMMUNICATIONS	
Data Communications	Business Data Communications: Introductory Concepts and Techniques, Second Edition

*Also available as a mini-module

Instructions for Selecting the Default Desktop View Settings

The projects and assignments in this textbook are presented using the default desktop view settings (default Custom style), as chosen by Microsoft Corporation. With the exception of the Open each folder in the same window option, the default settings are those of the Classic style. To ensure your success in completing the projects and assignments, the Windows 98 operating system must be installed on your computer system and the default desktop view settings must be selected. The following steps illustrate how to use the Folder Options dialog box and Custom Settings dialog box to select the default settings.

1. Click the Start button on the taskbar.
2. Point to Settings on the Start menu.
3. Click Folder Options on the Settings submenu to display the Folder Options dialog box (Figure 1a).
4. If necessary, click the General tab in the Folder Options dialog box to display the General sheet.
5. If necessary, click Custom, based on settings you choose to select the option.
6. Click the Settings button in the Folder Options dialog box to open the Custom Settings dialog box (Figure 1b).
7. On a piece of paper, write down the name of each option button that is selected in the Custom Settings dialog box.
8. Click Use Windows classic desktop to select the option.
9. Click Open each folder in the same window to select the option.
10. Click Only for folders where I select "as Web Page" (View menu) to select the option.
11. Click Double-click to open an item (single-click to select) to select the option.
12. Click the OK button in the Custom Settings dialog box.
13. Click the Close button in the Folder Options dialog box.

As a result of selecting the default settings, you can perform the steps and assignments in each project of this book. If, after finishing the steps and assignments, you must reset the desktop view to its original settings, perform steps 1 through 6 above, click the option button of each setting you wrote down in step 7, and then perform steps 12 and 13.

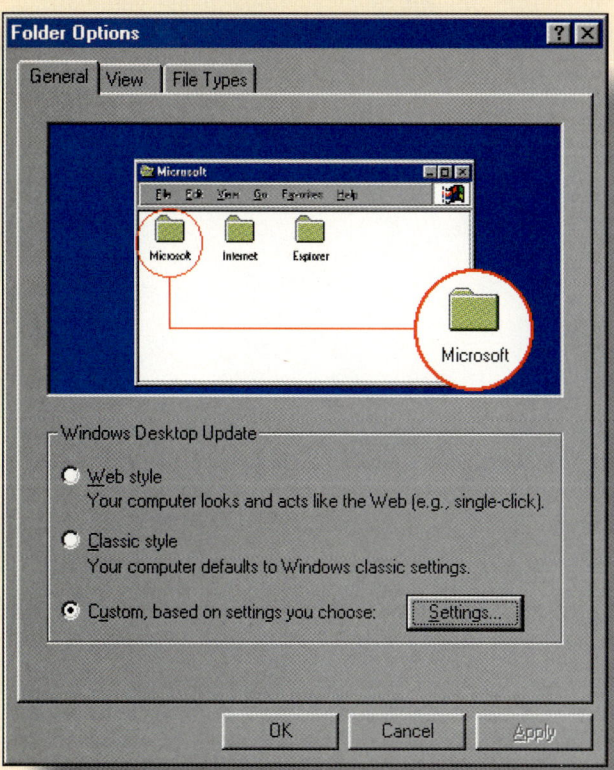

FIGURE 1a

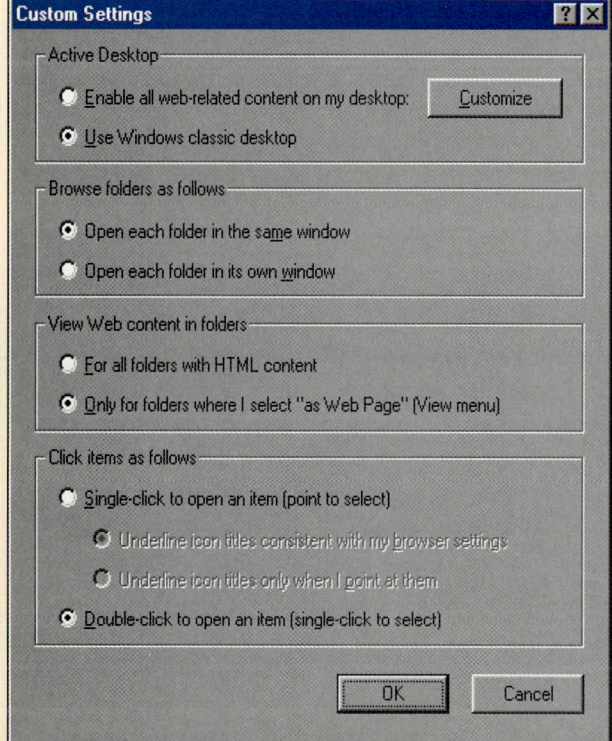

FIGURE 1b

Microsoft Windows 98

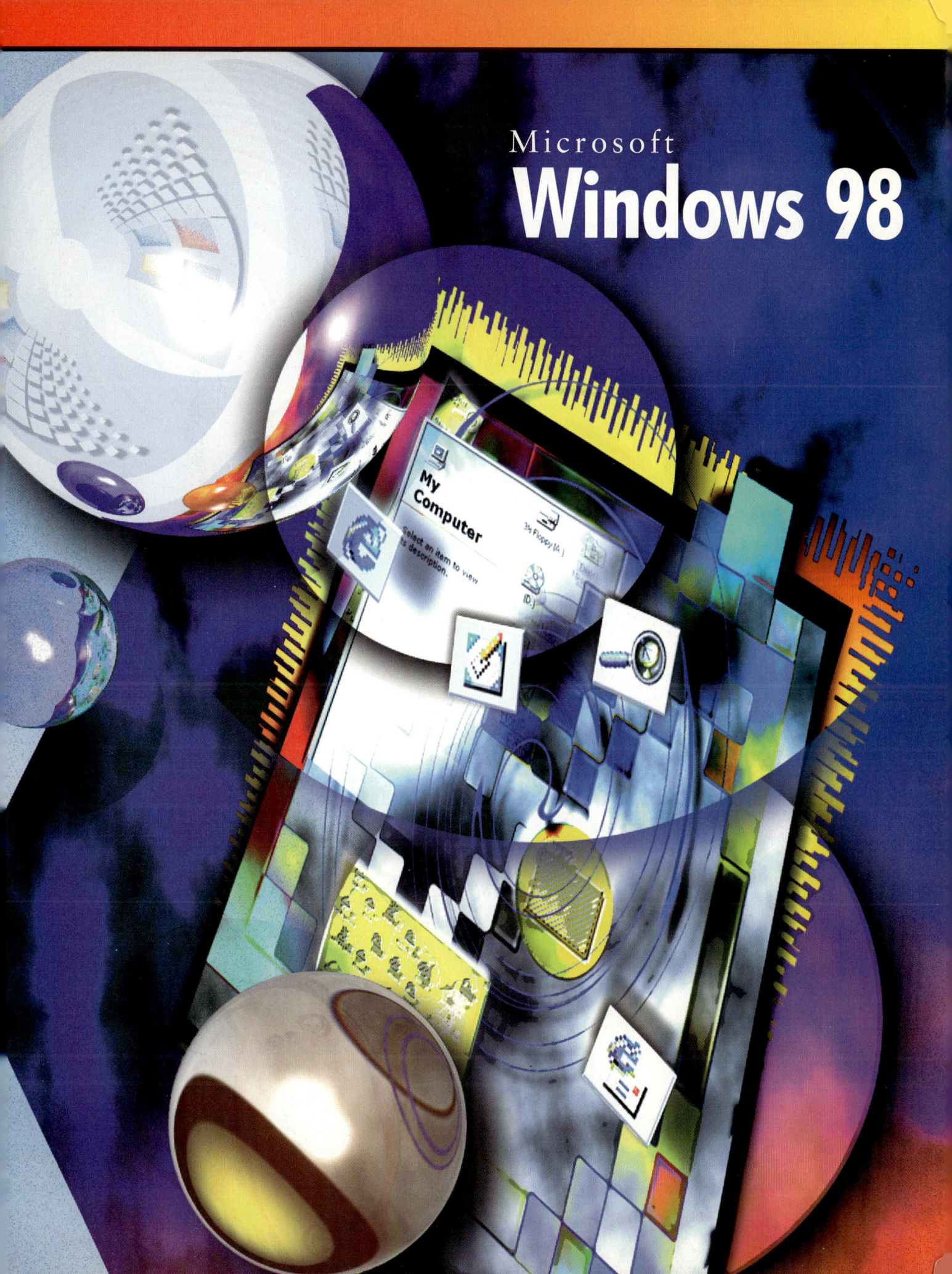

Microsoft Windows 98

Fundamentals of Using Microsoft Windows 98

O B J E C T I V E S

You will have mastered the material in this project when you can:

- Describe Microsoft Windows 98
- Explain a user interface
- Identify the objects on the Microsoft Windows 98 desktop
- Perform the basic mouse operations: point, click, right-click, double-click, drag, and right-drag
- Open, minimize, maximize, and restore a Windows 98 window
- Close a Windows 98 window
- Move and resize a window on the Windows 98 desktop
- Scroll in a window
- Understand keyboard shortcut notation
- Describe the Internet and World Wide Web
- Differentiate between viewing the Windows desktop in Classic style, Web style, and Custom style
- Launch an application program
- Use Windows 98 Contents Help and Index Help
- Shut down Windows 98

Microsoft **Windows 98**

The Best Job In The Whole World

Bill Gates Uses His Leave Wisely

"My job probably is the best job in the whole world." No wonder Bill Gates makes this claim: as founder and CEO of Microsoft, he is the richest person on the planet with a net worth estimated at $50 billion—not bad for a Harvard College student "on leave."

His computing efforts began in grade school when he and a classmate, Paul Allen, learned the BASIC programming language from a manual and programmed a mainframe computer using a Teletype terminal purchased with proceeds from a rummage sale. In 1968, they wrote a program to play tic-tac-toe. Then they developed more complex programs, including one resembling the board game Risk with the objective of world dominance.

In high school, Gates and Allen had a thirst for more computing power than the Teletype terminal could offer. They wrote custom programs for local

businesses during the summer and split their $5,000 salaries between cash and computer time, which cost them about $40 per hour. In addition, they debugged software problems at local businesses in return for computer use. In Gates's sophomore year, one of his teachers asked him to teach his computer skills to his classmates. Also, he boasts that he wrote a program to schedule students in classes and changed a few lines of code so he was the only male in a class full of females.

When Gates was 16 in 1972, he and Allen read a ten-paragraph article in *Electronics* magazine about Intel's first microprocessor chip. They requested a manual from Intel, experimented with pushing the chip to its limits, and formed the Traf-O-Data company. This pursuit involved developing a device about the size of a toaster oven with a rubber hose connected to a metal box containing a paper tape. When a car ran over the hose, the device punched a hole in the tape. They used the Intel chip to analyze the tape and subsequently to determine traffic flow in several cities.

Gates entered Harvard College in 1973, and Allen landed a job programming Honeywell minicomputers in Boston. They continued to scheme about the power of computers. In Gates's sophomore year, they saw a picture of the Altair 8800 computer on the cover of the January 1975 edition of *Popular Electronics*. That computer was about the size of the Traf-O-Data device and contained a new Intel computer chip. For five weeks, they spent sleepless nights writing BASIC for that computer, and Gates says that on some of those days, he did not see anyone or eat.

At that point they formed the world's first microcomputer software company: Microsoft Corporation. They realized they needed to make some sacrifices to achieve their goal of "a computer on every desk and in every home," so Allen quit his job and Gates left Harvard. Gates says he always planned to return to earn his degree, and he considers himself "on a really long leave." In the interim, he has added 25,000 employees to help him achieve yearly net revenues surpassing $11 billion.

Microsoft Windows 98

Fundamentals of Using Microsoft Windows 98

PROJECT 1

CASE PERSPECTIVE

Everyday from locations around the world, millions of Windows 98 users turn on their computers. When the computer starts, the first image on the monitor is the Windows 98 desktop. If these users did not know how to launch an application program, manipulate files and objects on the desktop, send and receive e-mail, and obtain information using the Internet and/or intranet, their computers would be useless.

You have just acquired a computer with the Windows 98 operating system. Your task is to learn the basics of Windows 98 so your computer will be useful to you, and you will be able to assist others who may come to you with questions and requests.

Introduction

An **operating system** is the set of computer instructions, called a computer program, that controls the allocation of computer hardware such as memory, disk devices, printers, and CD-ROM and DVD drives, and provides the capability for you to communicate with your computer. The most popular and widely used operating system for personal computers is **Microsoft Windows**. **Microsoft Windows 98** (called **Windows 98** for the rest of this book), the newest version of Microsoft Windows, allows you easily to communicate with and control your computer.

Windows 98 is easy to use and can be customized to fit individual needs. Windows 98 simplifies the process of working with documents and applications, transferring data between documents, organizing the manner in which you interact with your computer, and using your computer to access information on the Internet and/or intranet. In Project 1, you will learn about Windows 98 and how to use the Windows 98 user interface.

Microsoft Windows 98

Microsoft Windows 98 is an operating system that performs every function necessary for you to communicate with and use your computer. Windows 98 is called a **32-bit operating system** because it uses 32 bits for addressing and other purposes, which means the operating system can address more than four gigabytes of RAM (random-access memory) and perform tasks faster than older operating systems. Windows 98 includes **Microsoft Internet Explorer (IE)**, a software program developed by Microsoft Corporation, that integrates the Windows 98 desktop and the Internet. Internet Explorer allows you to work with programs and files in a similar fashion, whether they are located on your computer, a local network, or the Internet.

Windows 98 is designed to be compatible with all existing **application programs**, which are programs that perform an application-related function such as word processing. To use the application programs that can be executed under Windows 98, you must know about the Windows 98 user interface.

What Is a User Interface?

A **user interface** is the combination of hardware and software that you use to communicate with and control your computer. Through the user interface, you are able to make selections on your computer, request information from your computer, and respond to messages displayed by your computer. Thus, a user interface provides the means for dialogue between you and your computer.

Hardware and software together form the user interface. Among the hardware devices associated with a user interface are the monitor, keyboard, and mouse (Figure 1-1). The **monitor** displays messages and provides information. You respond by entering data in the form of a command or other response using the **keyboard** or **mouse**. Among the responses available to you are responses that specify what application program to run, what document to open, when to print, and where to store data for future use.

The computer software associated with the user interface consists of the programs that engage you in dialogue (Figure 1-1). The computer software determines the messages you receive, the manner in which you should respond, and the actions that occur based on your responses.

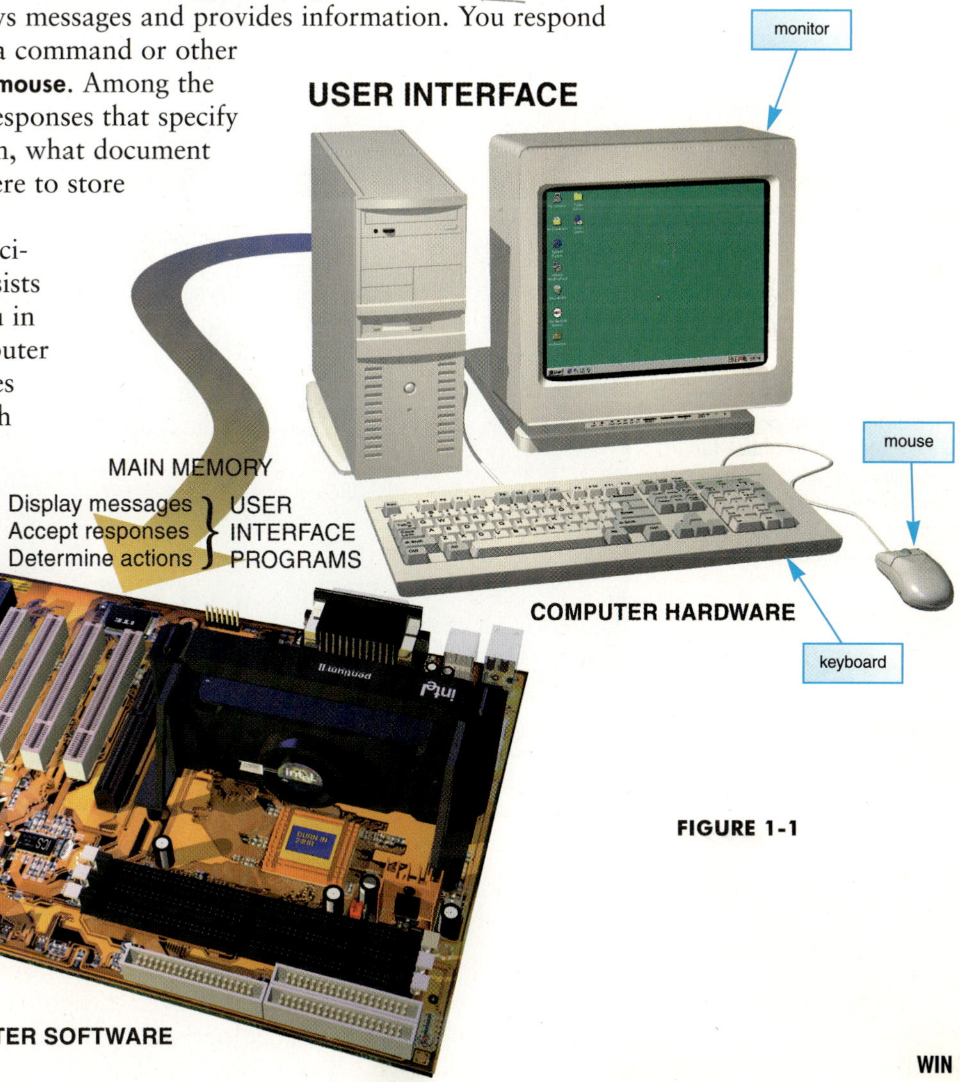

USER INTERFACE

MAIN MEMORY
Display messages
Accept responses } USER INTERFACE PROGRAMS
Determine actions

COMPUTER HARDWARE

monitor
mouse
keyboard

COMPUTER SOFTWARE

FIGURE 1-1

More About

The Windows 98 Interface

The Windows 98 graphical user interface is similar to and an improvement of the Windows 95 graphical user interface. Thousands of hours were spent making improvements to Windows 95. Of tremendous importance were Microsoft's usability labs, where everyone from raw beginners to experts interacted with many different versions of the interface. The Quick Launch toolbar and other significant improvements of the Windows 98 interface emerged from the experiences in these labs.

The goal of an effective user interface is to be **user friendly**, meaning that the software can be used easily by individuals with limited training. Research studies have indicated that the use of graphics can play an important role in aiding users to interact effectively with a computer. A **graphical user interface**, or **GUI** (pronounced gooey), is a user interface that displays graphics in addition to text when it communicates with the user.

The Windows 98 graphical user interface was carefully designed to be easier to set up, simpler to learn, faster and more powerful, and better integrated with the Internet than previous versions of Microsoft Windows.

Launching Microsoft Windows 98

When you turn on your computer, an introductory screen consisting of the Windows logo and Windows 98 name displays on a blue sky and clouds background in the middle of the screen. The screen clears and several items display on a background called the **desktop**. The default color of the desktop background is green, but your computer may display a different color. Your screen will display as shown in Figure 1-2 or Figure 1-3 on page WIN 1.10, depending upon whether you have chosen to display the Welcome screen.

More About

The Windows 98 Desktop

Because Windows 98 is easily customized, the desktop on your computer may not resemble the desktop in Figure 1-2. For example, the icon titles on the desktop may be underlined or objects not shown in Figure 1-2 may display on your desktop. If this is the case, refer to page viii of the Preface of this book for instructions for selecting the default desktop view settings or contact your instructor to change the desktop view.

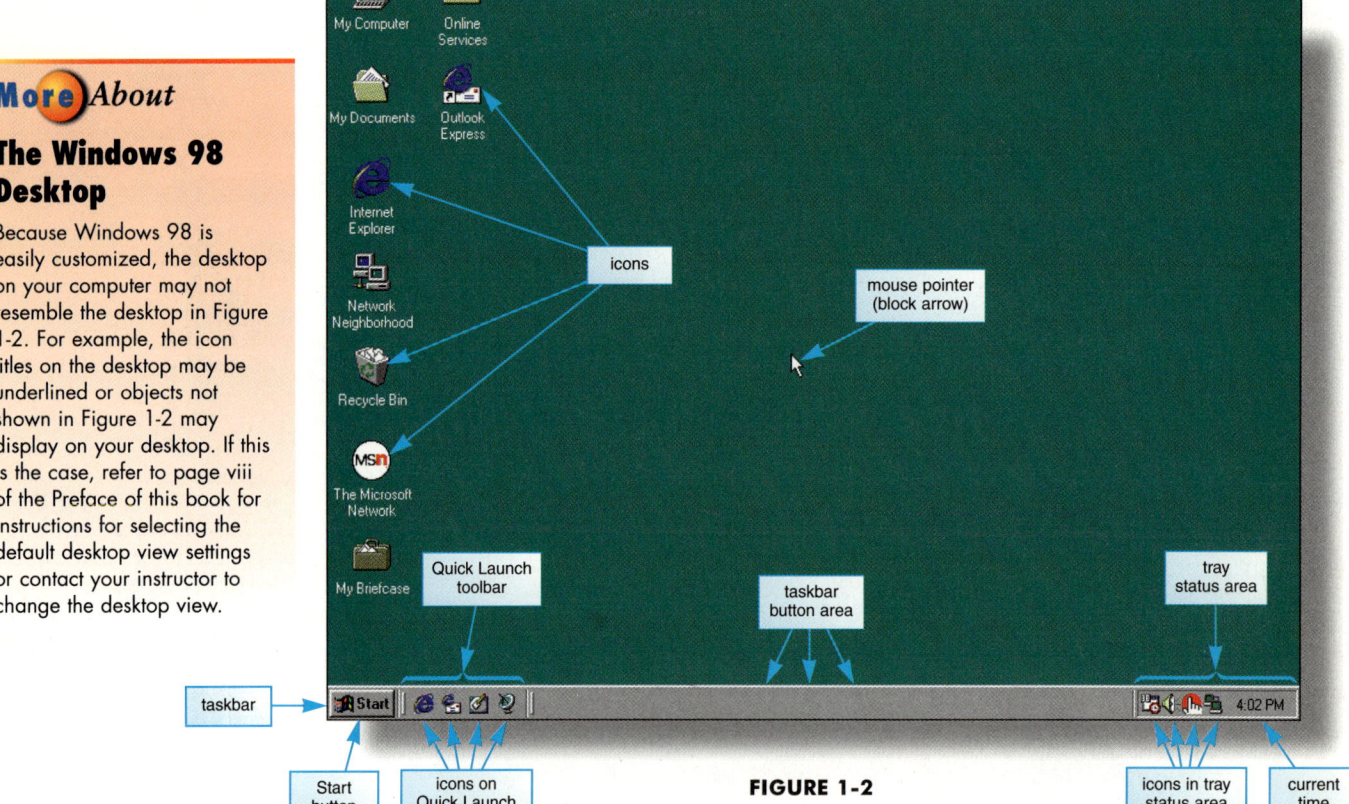

FIGURE 1-2

The items on the desktop shown in Figure 1-2 include nine icons and their titles on the left side of the desktop and the taskbar at the bottom of the desktop. Using the nine **icons,** you can view the contents of your computer (**My Computer**), store documents in one location (**My Documents**), connect to and browse the Internet (**Internet Explorer**), work with other computers connected to your computer (**Network Neighborhood**), discard unneeded objects (**Recycle Bin**), connect to the Microsoft Network online service (**The Microsoft Network**), transfer documents or folders to and from a portable computer (**My Briefcase**), investigate other online services (**Online Services**), and receive and send e-mail (**Outlook Express**). Your computer's desktop might contain more, fewer, or some different icons because the desktop of the computer can be customized.

The **taskbar** at the bottom of the screen in Figure 1-2 contains the Start button, Quick Launch toolbar, taskbar button area, and the tray status area. The **Start button** allows you to launch a program quickly, find or open a document, change your computer's settings, shut down the computer, and perform many more tasks. The **Quick Launch toolbar** contains four icons that allow you to launch Internet Explorer (**Launch Internet Explorer Browser**), launch Outlook Express (**Launch Outlook Express**), view an uncluttered desktop at any time (**Show Desktop**), and view a list of channels (**View Channels**).

The **taskbar button area** contains buttons to indicate which windows are open on the desktop. In Figure 1-2, no windows display on the desktop and no buttons display in the taskbar button area. The **tray status area** contains the **Task Scheduler icon** to schedule daily tasks, a **speaker icon** to adjust the computer's volume level, **The Microsoft Network icon** to connect to The Microsoft Network online service, the **Internet connection icon** to indicate a modem is being used to connect to the Internet, and the current time (4:02 PM). The tray status area on your desktop might contain more, fewer, or some different icons because the contents of the tray status area can be changed.

Nearly every item on the Windows 98 desktop is considered an object. Even the desktop itself is an object. Every **object** has properties. The **properties** of an object are unique to that specific object and may affect what can be done to the object or what the object does. For example, the properties of an object may be the color of the object, such as the color of the desktop. You will learn more about properties in Project 3 of this book.

In the middle of the screen is the mouse pointer. On the desktop, the **mouse pointer** is the shape of a block arrow. The mouse pointer allows you to point to objects on the desktop and may change shape when it points to different objects.

The Welcome to Windows 98 Screen

The Welcome to Windows 98 screen that may display on your desktop when you launch Windows 98 is shown in Figure 1-3 on the next page. The **title bar,** which is dark blue in color at the top of the screen, contains the Windows icon, identifies the name of the screen (Welcome to Windows 98), and contains the Close button, which can be used to close the Welcome to Windows 98 screen.

More About

Desktop Views

You can view the desktop in Classic style, Web style, or you can customize the desktop view by selecting features from both styles. You can choose to single-click or double-click icons, underline all icon titles or underline icon titles only when you point to them, and display the Classic Windows Desktop or the Active Desktop. When you customize the desktop view, the style is referred to as the Custom style.

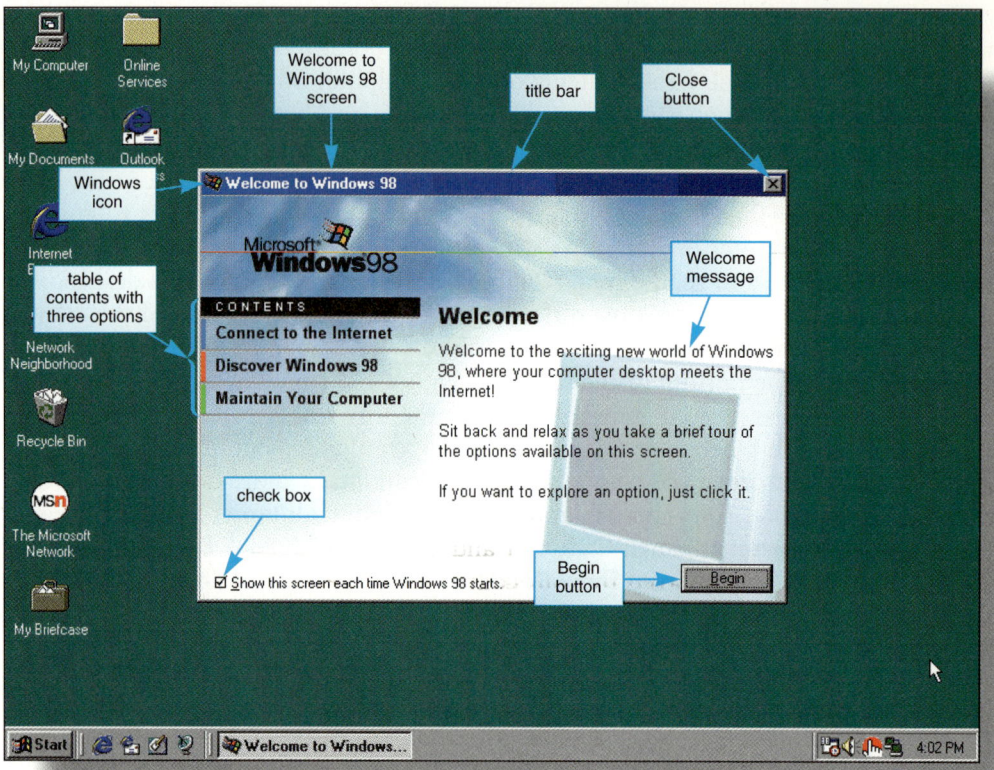

FIGURE 1-3

On the Welcome to Windows 98 screen, a table of contents contains three options (Connect to the Internet, Discover Windows 98, and Maintain Your Computer) and a welcome message (Welcome). The options in the table of contents allow you to perform different tasks such as connecting to the Internet, learning Windows 98 using the Discover Windows 98 tutorial, and improving the performance of your computer. A message to the right of the table of contents welcomes you to the world of Windows 98. Pointing to an option in the table of contents replaces the Welcome message with an explanation of the option. The **Begin button** in the lower-right corner begins the process of connecting to the Internet, and a check mark in the **check box** to the left of the Begin button indicates the Welcome to Windows 98 screen will display each time you start Windows 98.

Closing the Welcome Screen

As noted, the Welcome screen may display when you launch Windows 98. If the Welcome screen does display on the desktop, normally you should close it prior to beginning any other operations using Windows 98. To close the Welcome screen, complete the following step.

TO CLOSE THE WELCOME SCREEN

 Press and hold the ALT key on the keyboard and then press the F4 key on the keyboard. Release the ALT key.

The Welcome to Windows 98 screen closes and the desktop displays as shown in Figure 1-2 on page WIN 1.8.

The Desktop as a Work Area

The Windows 98 desktop and the objects on the desktop were designed to emulate a work area in an office or at home. The Windows desktop may be thought of as an electronic version of the top of your desk. You can move objects around on the desktop, look at them and then put them aside, and so on. In Project 1, you will learn how to interact with and communicate with the Windows 98 desktop.

Communicating with Microsoft Windows 98

The Windows 98 interface provides the means for dialogue between you and your computer. Part of this dialogue involves your requesting information from your computer and responding to messages displayed by your computer. You can request information and respond to messages using either a mouse or a keyboard.

> **More About**
>
> **The Mouse**
>
> The mouse, though invented in the 1960s, was not used widely until the Apple Macintosh computer became available in 1984. Even then, some highbrows called mouse users "wimps." Today, the mouse is an indispensable tool for every computer user.

Mouse Operations

A **mouse** is a pointing device used with Windows 98 that is attached to the computer by a cable. Although not required to use Windows 98, Windows supports the use of the **Microsoft IntelliMouse** (Figure 1-4). The IntelliMouse contains three buttons, the primary mouse button, the secondary mouse button, and the wheel button between the primary and secondary mouse buttons. Typically, the **primary mouse button** is the left mouse button and the **secondary mouse button** is the right mouse button although Windows 98 allows you to switch them. In this book, the left mouse button is the primary mouse button and the right mouse button is the secondary mouse button. The function the **wheel button** and wheel perform depends on the software application being used. If the mouse connected to your computer is not an IntelliMouse, it will not have a wheel button between the primary and secondary mouse buttons.

Using the mouse, you can perform the following operations: (1) point; (2) click; (3) right-click; (4) double-click; (5) drag; and (6) right-drag. These operations are demonstrated on the following pages.

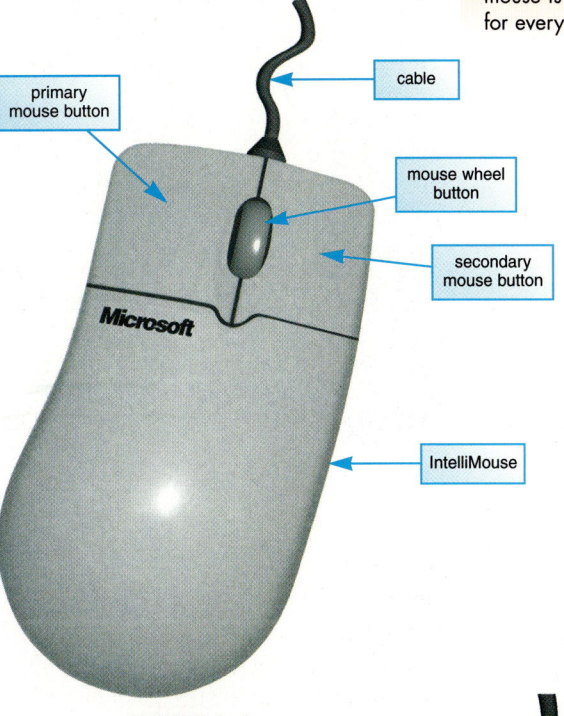

FIGURE 1-4

Point and Click

Point means you move the mouse across a flat surface until the mouse pointer rests on the item of choice on the desktop. As you move the mouse across a flat surface, the movement of a ball on the underside of the mouse (Figure 1-5) is sensed electronically, and the mouse pointer moves across the desktop in the same direction.

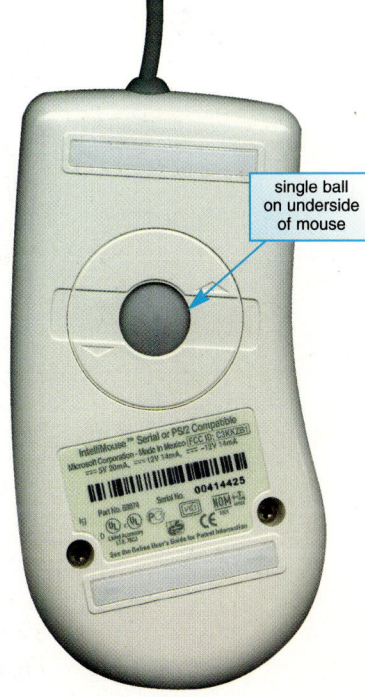

FIGURE 1-5

Click means you press and release the primary mouse button, which in this book is the left mouse button. In most cases, you must point to an item before you click. To become acquainted with the use of the mouse, perform the following steps to point to and click various objects on the desktop.

 To Point and Click

1 **Point to the Start button on the taskbar by moving the mouse across a flat surface until the mouse pointer rests on the Start button.**

The mouse pointer on the Start button displays a **ToolTip** (Click here to begin.) (Figure 1-6). The ToolTip, which provides instructions, displays on the desktop for approximately five seconds. Other ToolTips display on the screen until you move the mouse pointer off the object.

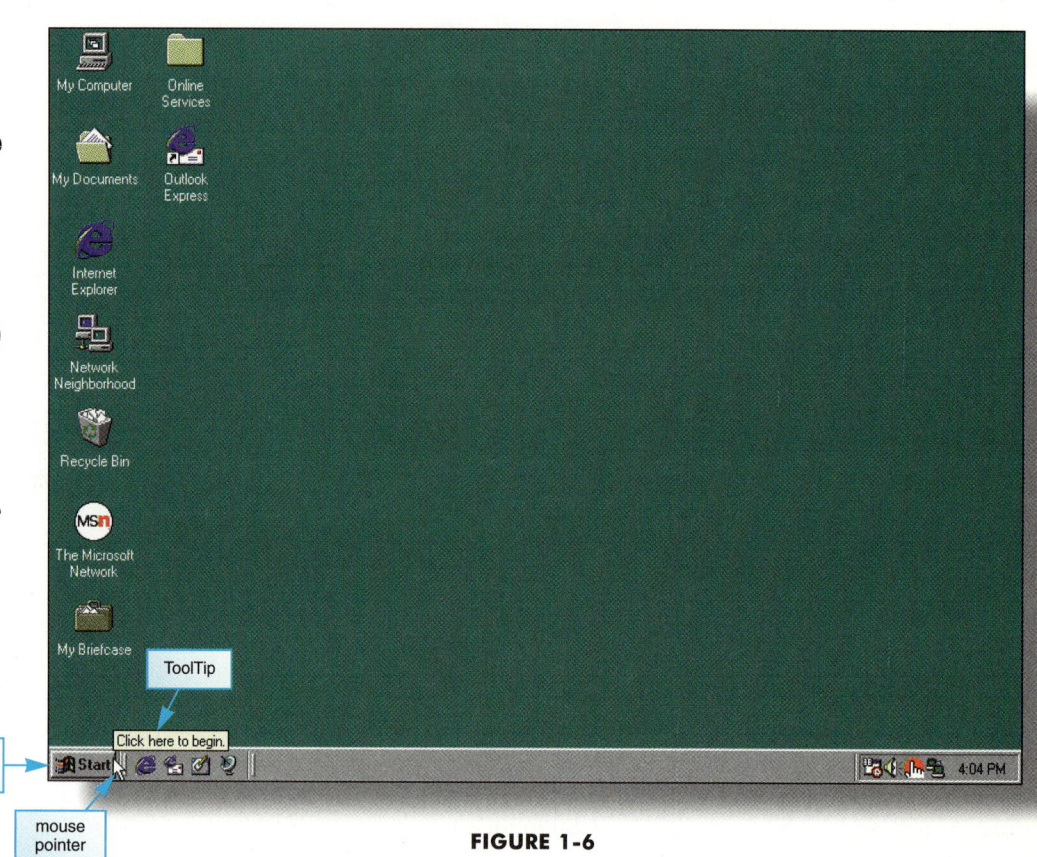

FIGURE 1-6

Communicating with Microsoft Windows 98 • WIN 1.13

2 **Click the Start button on the taskbar by pressing and releasing the left mouse button.**

The *Start menu* displays and the Start button is recessed on the taskbar (Figure 1-7). A **menu** is a list of related commands. A **command** directs Windows 98 to perform a specific action such as shutting down the operating system. Each command on the Start menu consists of an icon and a command name. A **right arrow** follows some commands to indicate pointing to the command will open a submenu. Three commands (Run, Log Off Steven Forsythe, and Shut Down) are followed by an **ellipsis** (...) to indicate more information is required to execute these commands.

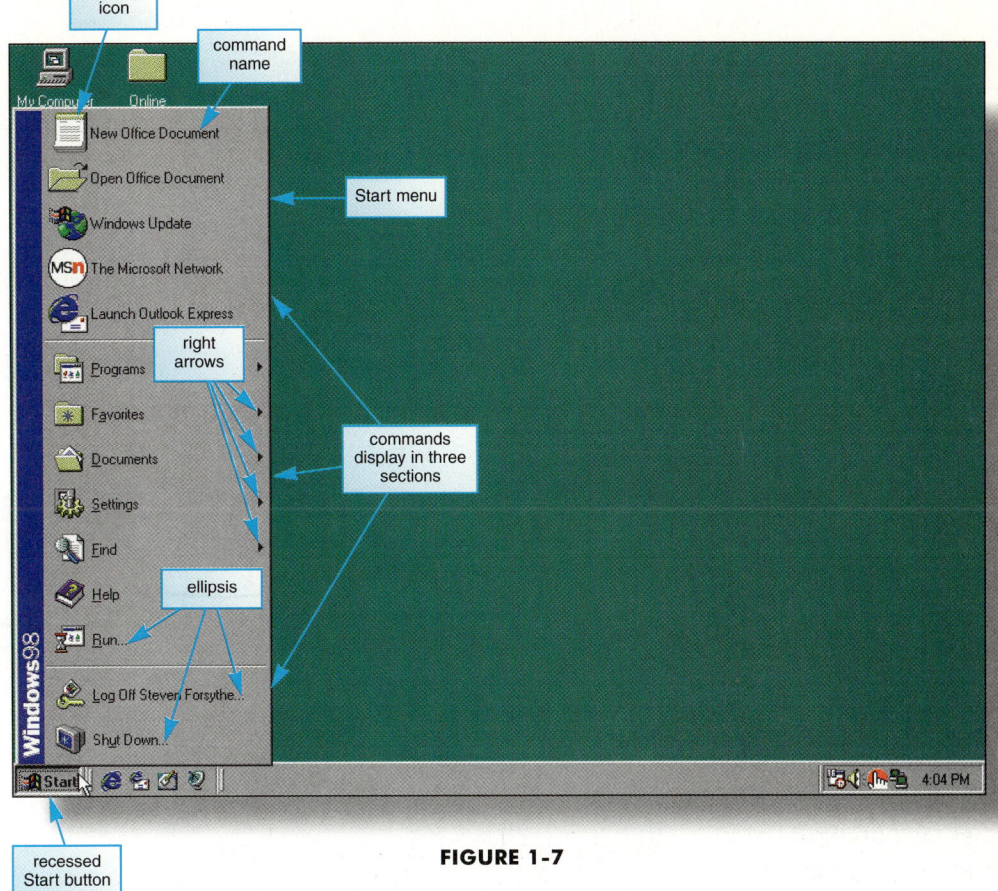

FIGURE 1-7

3 **Point to Programs on the Start menu.**

When you point to Programs, Windows 98 highlights the Programs command on the Start menu and the **Programs submenu** displays (Figure 1-8). A **submenu, or cascading menu,** is a menu that displays when you point to a command that is followed by a right arrow. For example, pointing to the Accessories command on the Programs submenu will display another submenu. Whenever you point to a command on a menu, the command is highlighted.

FIGURE 1-8

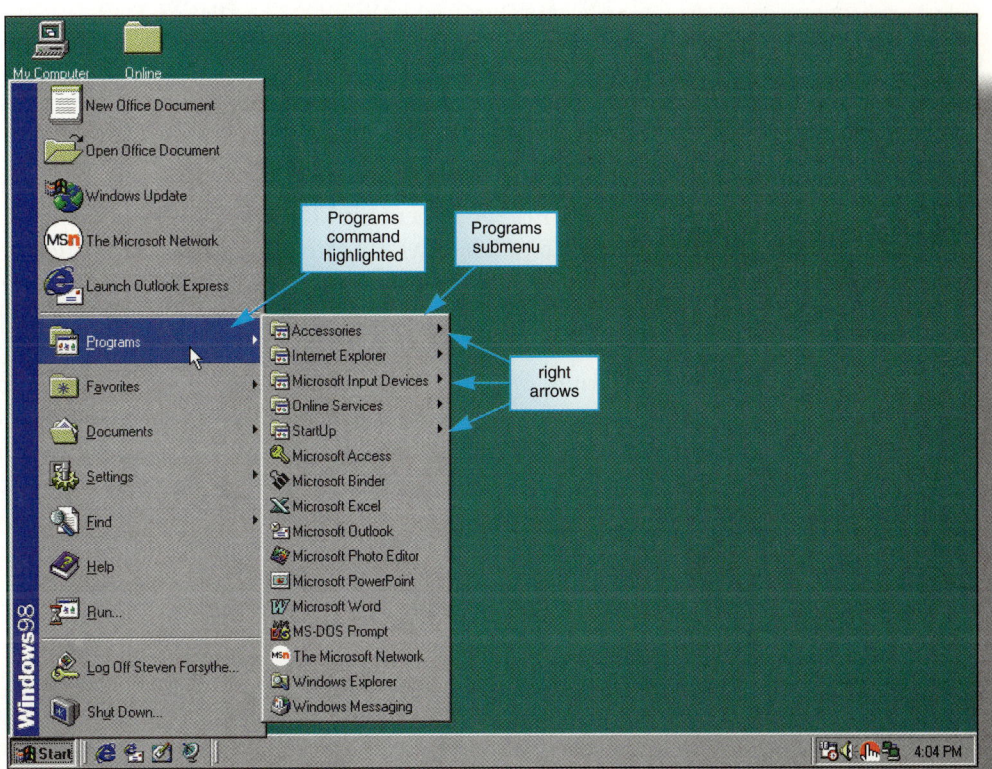

WIN 1.14 • Project 1 • Fundamentals of Using Microsoft Windows 98

Microsoft **Windows 98**

 Point to an open area of the desktop (Figure 1-9).

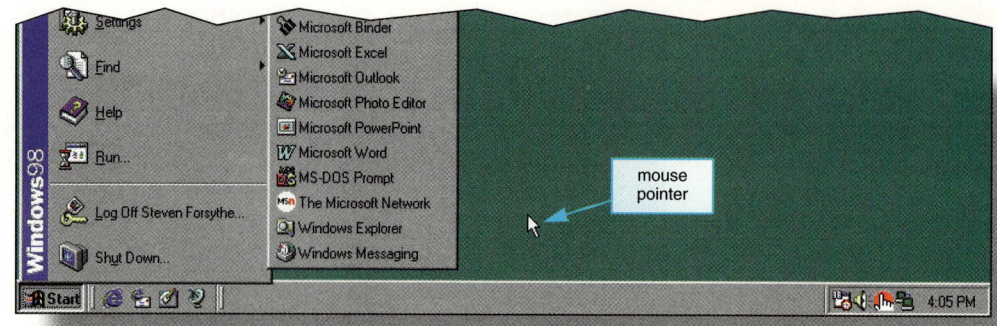

FIGURE 1-9

 **Click the open area of the desktop.**

The Start menu and Programs submenu close (Figure 1-10). The mouse pointer points to the desktop. To close a menu anytime, click any open area of the desktop except on the menu itself. The Start button is no longer recessed.

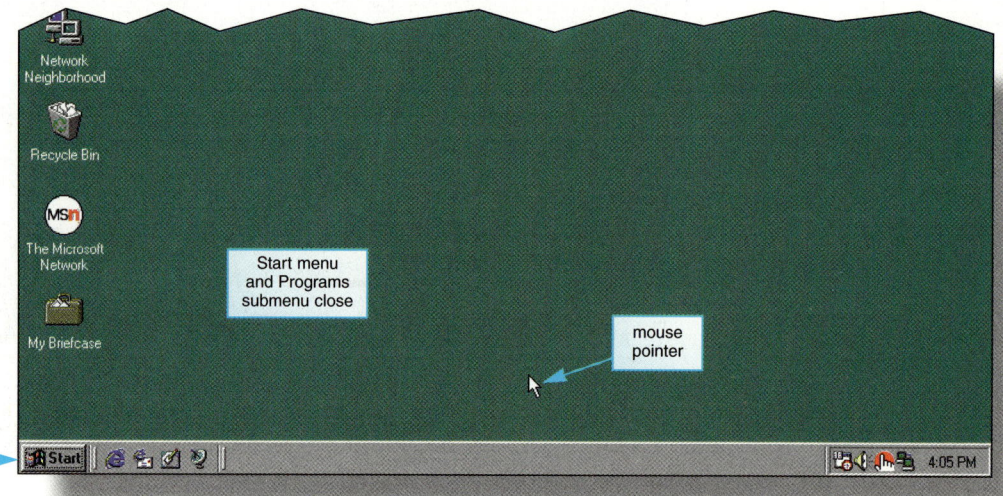

FIGURE 1-10

Buttons

Buttons on the desktop and in programs are an integral part of Windows 98. When you point to them, their function displays in a ToolTip. When you click them, they appear to indent on the screen to mimic what would happen if you pushed an actual button. All buttons in Windows 98 behave in the same manner.

The Right Mouse Button

Earlier versions of Microsoft Windows made little use of the right mouse button. In Windows 98, you will find using the right mouse button essential.

The Start menu in Figure 1-7 on the previous page is divided into three sections. The top section contains commands to create or open a Microsoft Office document (New Office Document and Open Office Document), launch the Windows Update application (Windows Update), connect to The Microsoft Network (The Microsoft Network), and launch the Outlook Express application (Launch Outlook Express); the middle section contains commands to launch an application, work with documents or Web sites, customize options, and search for files or Help (Programs, Favorites, Documents, Settings, Find, Help, and Run); and the bottom section contains basic operating tasks (Log Off Steven Forsythe and Shut Down).

When you click an object such as the Start button in Figure 1-7, you must point to the object before you click. In the steps that follow, the instruction that directs you to point to a particular item and then click is, Click the particular item. For example, Click the Start button means point to the Start button and then click.

Right-Click

Right-click means you press and release the secondary mouse button, which in this book is the right mouse button. As directed when using the primary mouse button for clicking an object, normally you will point to an object before you right-click it. Perform the following steps to right-click the desktop.

Steps: To Right-Click

1 **Point to an open area of the desktop and then press and release the right mouse button.**

A shortcut menu displays (Figure 1-11). The shortcut menu in Figure 1-11 consists of nine commands. Right-clicking an object, such as the desktop, opens a **shortcut menu** that contains a set of commands specifically for use with that object. When a command on a menu appears dimmed, such as the Paste Shortcut command, that command is unavailable.

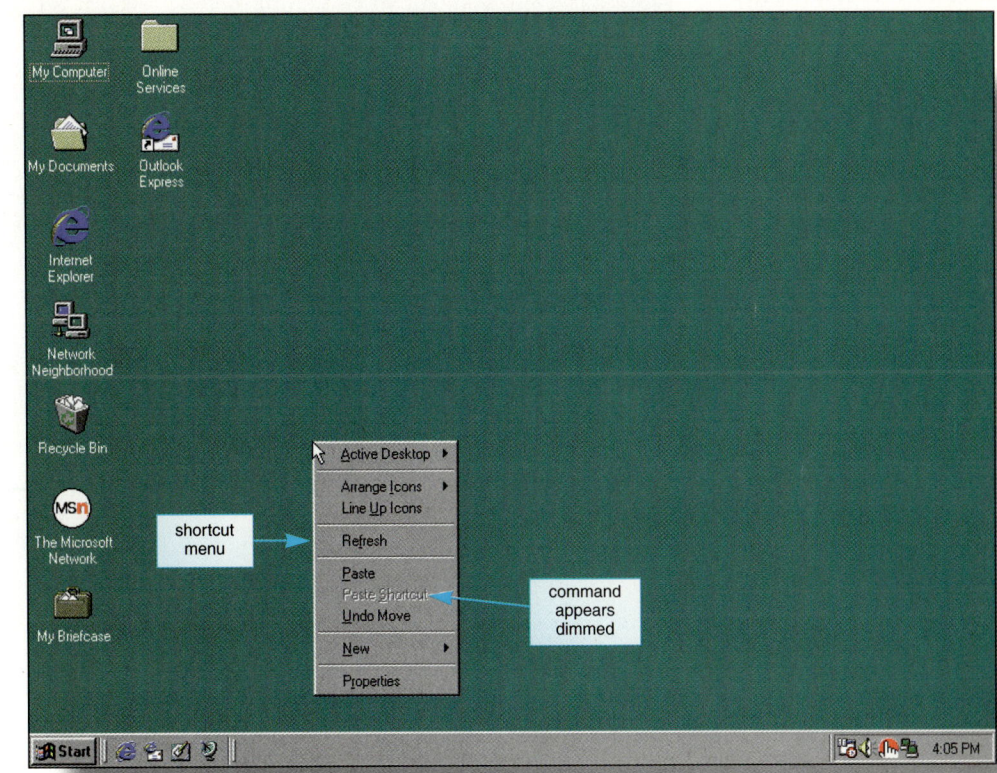

FIGURE 1-11

2 **Point to New on the shortcut menu.**

When you move the mouse pointer to the New command, Windows 98 highlights the New command and opens the New submenu (Figure 1-12). The New submenu contains a variety of commands. The number of commands and the actual commands that display on your computer may be different from those shown in Figure 1-12 because the New submenu lists some of the application programs available on your computer.

FIGURE 1-12

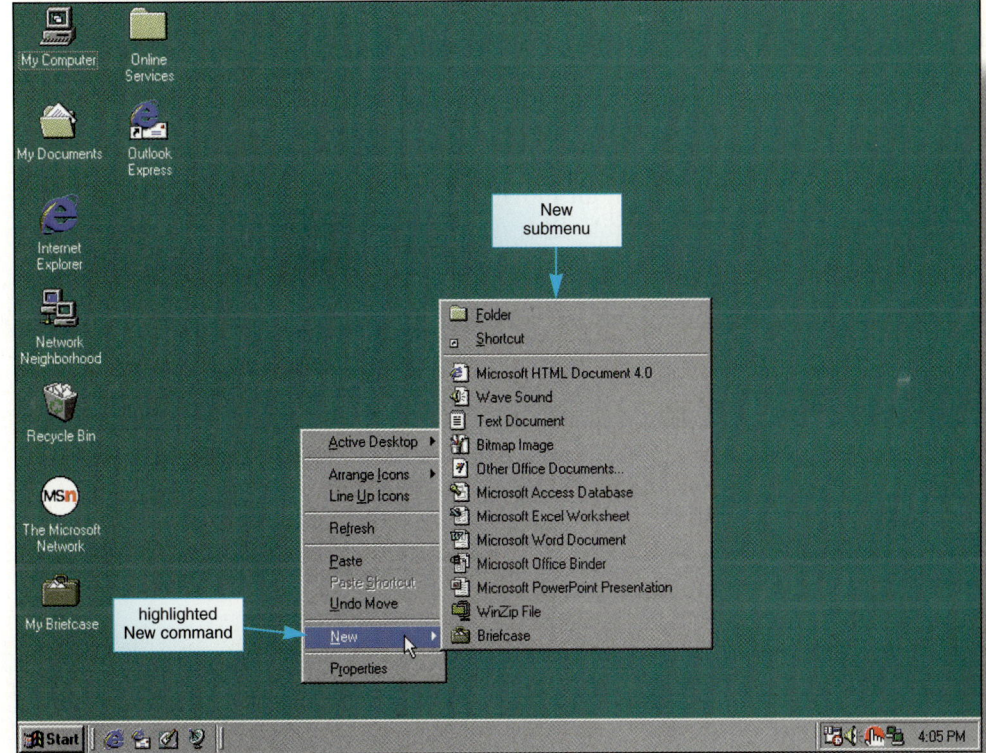

3 **Click an open area of the desktop to remove the shortcut menu and the New submenu.**

The shortcut menu and New submenu close (Figure 1-13). The mouse pointer remains on the desktop.

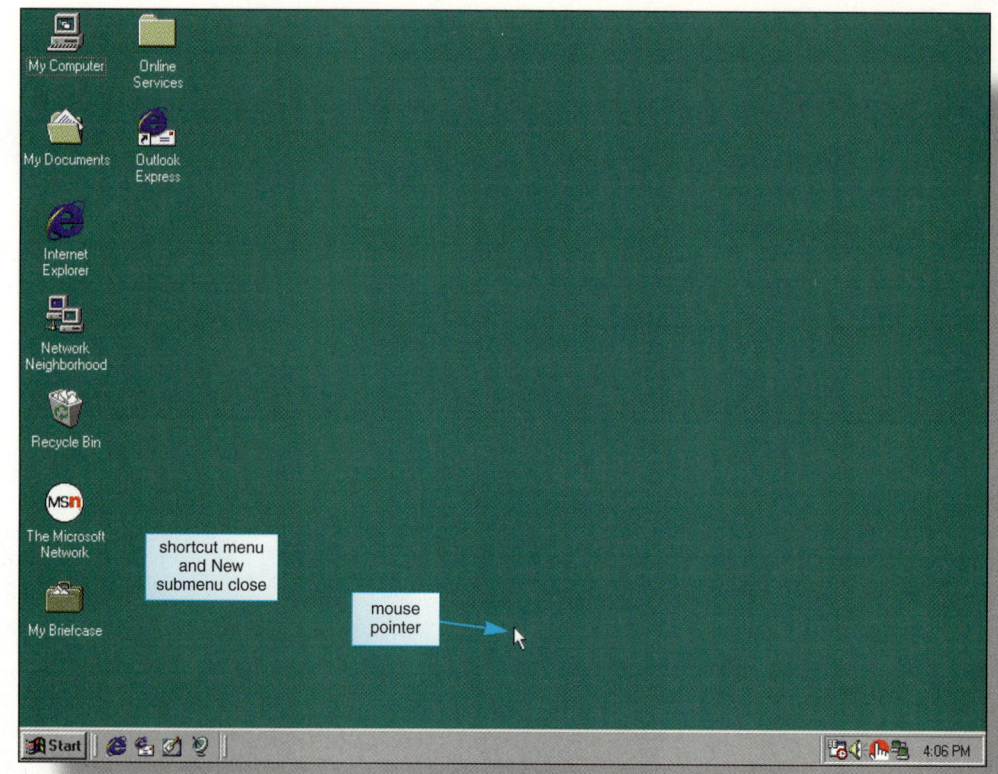

FIGURE 1-13

More About

Right-Clicking

Right-clicking an object other than the desktop will display a different shortcut menu with commands useful to that object. Right-clicking an object is thought to be the fastest method of performing an operation on an object.

More About

Double-Clicking

Double-clicking is the most difficult mouse skill to learn. Many people have a tendency to move the mouse before they click a second time, even when they do not want to move the mouse. You should find, however, that with a little practice, double-clicking becomes quite natural.

Whenever you right-click an object, a shortcut menu (also referred to as an object menu) will display. As you will see, the use of shortcut menus speeds up your work and adds flexibility to your interface with the computer.

Double-Click

Double-click means you quickly press and release the left mouse button twice without moving the mouse. In most cases, you must point to an item before you double-click. Perform the following step to open the My Computer window on the desktop by double-clicking the My Computer icon.

Steps: To Open a Window by Double-Clicking

1 Point to the My Computer icon on the desktop and then double-click by quickly pressing and releasing the left mouse button twice without moving the mouse.

The My Computer window opens (Figure 1-14). The recessed My Computer button is added to the taskbar button area.

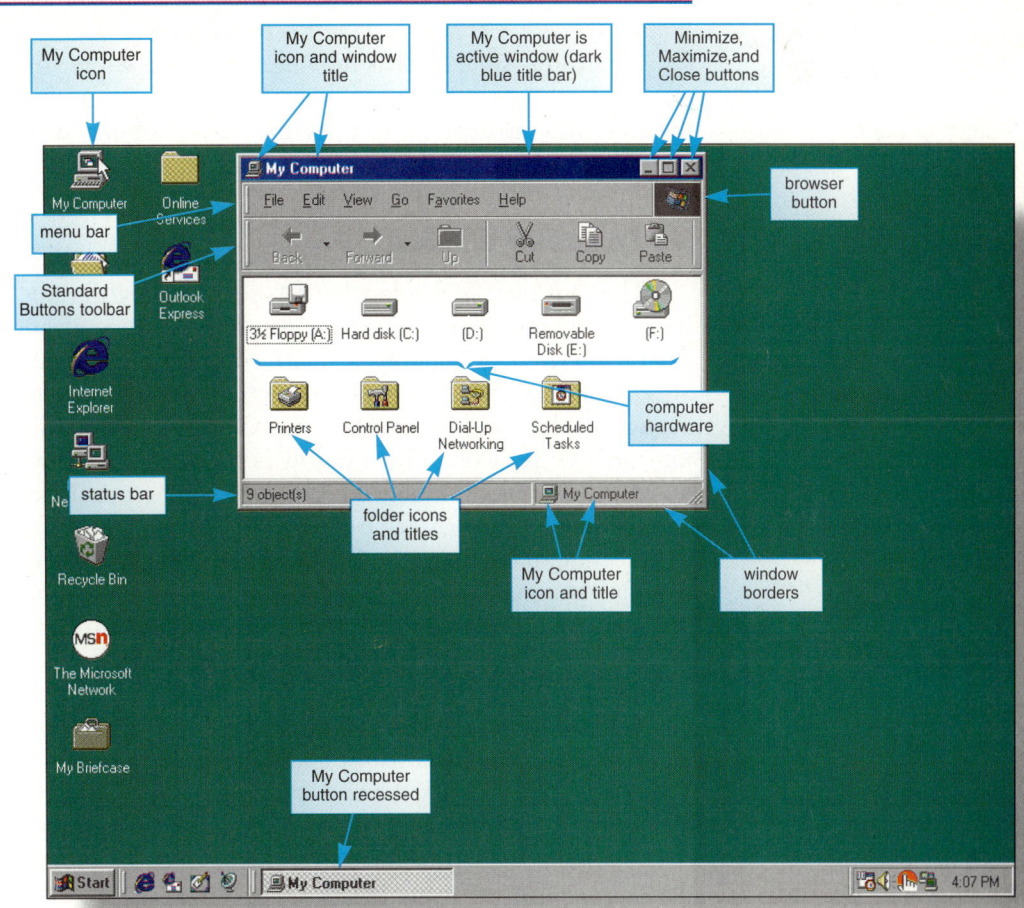

FIGURE 1-14

The My Computer window, the only open window, is the active window. The **active window** is the window currently being used. Whenever you click an object that can be opened, such as the My Computer icon, Windows 98 will open the object; and the open object will be identified by a recessed button in the taskbar button area. The recessed button identifies the active window.

The contents of the My Computer window on your computer may be different from the contents of the My Computer window in Figure 1-14.

Double-Clicking Errors

While double-clicking an object, you easily can click once instead of twice. When you click an object such as the My Computer icon once, the icon becomes the active icon and Windows 98 highlights the icon and its title. To open the My Computer window after clicking the My Computer icon once, double-click the My Computer icon as if you had not clicked the icon at all.

More About

The My Computer Window

Because Windows 98 is easily customized, the My Computer window on your computer may not resemble the window in Figure 1-14. If this is the case, check the commands on the View menu by clicking View on the menu bar. If a check mark precedes the as Web Page command, click the as Web Page command. If a large dot does not precede the Large Icons command, click the Large Icons command.

Another possible error is moving the mouse after you click the first time and before you click the second time. In most cases if you do this, the icon will be highlighted the same as if you click it just one time.

A third possible error is moving the mouse while you are pressing the mouse button. In this case, the icon might actually move on the screen because you have inadvertently dragged it. To open the My Computer window after dragging it accidentally, double-click the icon as if you had not clicked it at all.

My Computer Window

The thin line, or **window border**, surrounding the My Computer window in Figure 1-14 on the previous page determines its shape and size. The **title bar** at the top of the window contains a small icon that is the same as the icon on the desktop and the **window title** (My Computer) that identifies the window. The color of the title bar (dark blue) and the recessed My Computer button in the taskbar button area indicate the My Computer window is the active window. The color of the active window on your computer might be different from the dark blue color shown in Figure 1-14.

Clicking the icon at the left on the title bar will open the **System menu**, which contains commands to carry out the actions associated with the My Computer window. At the right on the title bar are three buttons, the Minimize button, the Maximize button, and the Close button, that can be used to specify the size of the window and close the window.

The **menu bar**, which is the horizontal bar below the title bar of a window (see Figure 1-14), contains a list of menu names for the My Computer window: File, Edit, View, Go, Favorites, and Help. One letter in each menu name is underlined. You can open a menu by clicking the menu name on the menu bar or by typing the corresponding underlined letter on the keyboard in combination with the ALT key. At the right end of the menu bar is a button containing the Windows logo. Clicking this button starts the Microsoft Internet Explorer Web browser and displays one of the Web pages in the Microsoft Web site in the browser window.

Below the menu bar is the **Standard Buttons toolbar** containing buttons that allow you to navigate through open windows on the desktop (Back, Forward, and Up) and copy and move text within a window or between windows (Cut, Copy, and Paste). Additional buttons display when the size of the window is increased. Each button contains a **text label** and an icon describing its function.

The area below the Standard Buttons toolbar contains nine icons. An underlined title below each icon identifies the icon. The five icons in the top row, called **drive icons**, represent a 3½ Floppy (A:) drive, a Hard disk (C:) drive, a different area on the same hard disk (D:), a Removable Disk (E:) drive, and a CD-ROM drive (F:).

The four icons in the second row are folders. A **folder** is an object created to contain related documents, applications, and other folders. A folder in Windows 98 contains items in much the same way a folder on your desk contains items.

The **Printers folder** (see Figure 1-14 on the previous page) allows you to add a new printer or change the settings for an existing printer. The **Control Panel folder** allows you to personalize your computer, such as specifying how you want your desktop to look. The **Dial-Up Networking folder** allows you to access information on other computers. The **Scheduled Tasks folder** allow you to schedule repetitive tasks, such as deleting all unnecessary files, when it is most convenient for you. If you double-click a drive or folder icon, the contents of the drive or folder display in place of the nine icons shown in Figure 1-14.

More About

My Computer

The trade press and media have poked fun at the icon name, My Computer. One wag said no one should use Windows 98 for more than five minutes without changing the name (which is easily done). Microsoft responds that in their usability labs, beginning computer users found the name, My Computer, easier to understand.

A message at the left on the **status bar** located at the bottom of the window indicates the right panel contains nine objects (see Figure 1-14). The My Computer icon and My Computer icon title display to the right of the message on the status bar.

Minimize Button

Two buttons on the title bar of a window, the Minimize button and the Maximize button, allow you to control the way a window displays or does not display on the desktop. When you click the **Minimize button** (see Figure 1-14 on page WIN 1.17), the My Computer window no longer displays on the desktop and the recessed My Computer button in the taskbar button area changes to a non-recessed button. A minimized window is still open but it does not display on the screen. To minimize and then redisplay the My Computer window, complete these steps.

Minimizing Windows

Windows management on the Windows 98 desktop is important in order to keep the desktop uncluttered. You will find yourself frequently minimizing windows and then later reopening them with a click of a button in the taskbar button area.

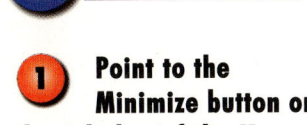 **To Minimize and Redisplay a Window**

1 **Point to the Minimize button on the title bar of the My Computer window.**

The mouse pointer points to the Minimize button on the My Computer window title bar (Figure 1-15). A ToolTip displays below the Minimize button and the My Computer button in the taskbar button area is recessed.

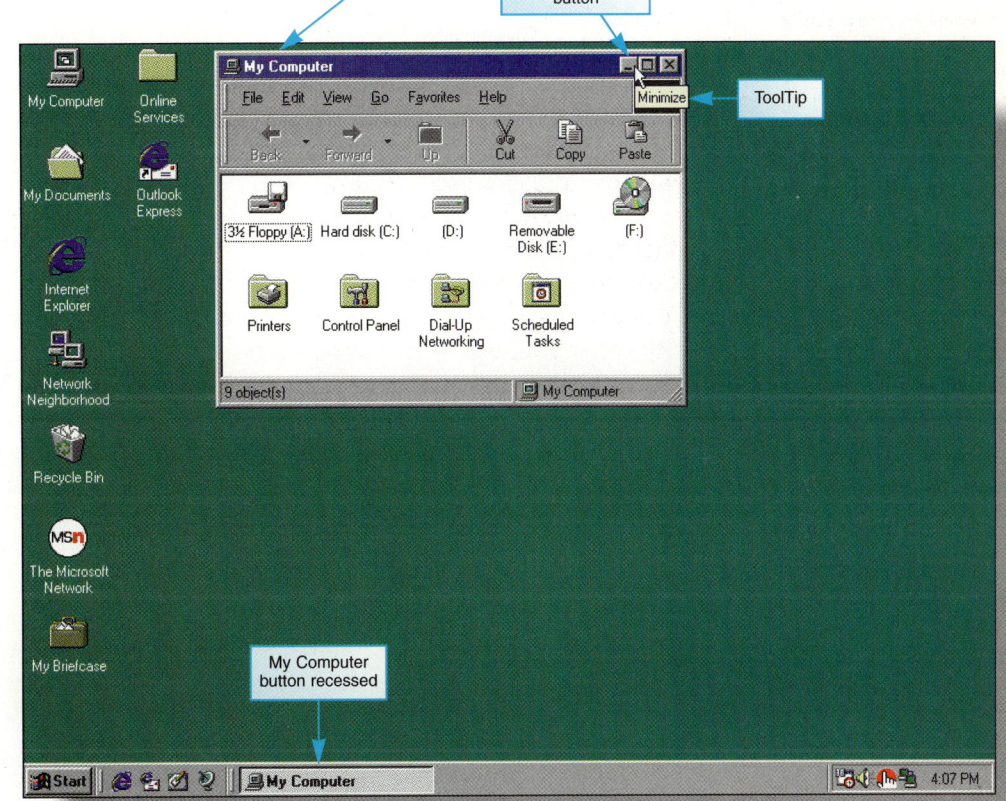

FIGURE 1-15

② Click the Minimize button.

When you minimize the My Compuer window, Windows 98 removes the My Computer window from the desktop and the My Computer button changes to a non-recessed button (Figure 1-16).

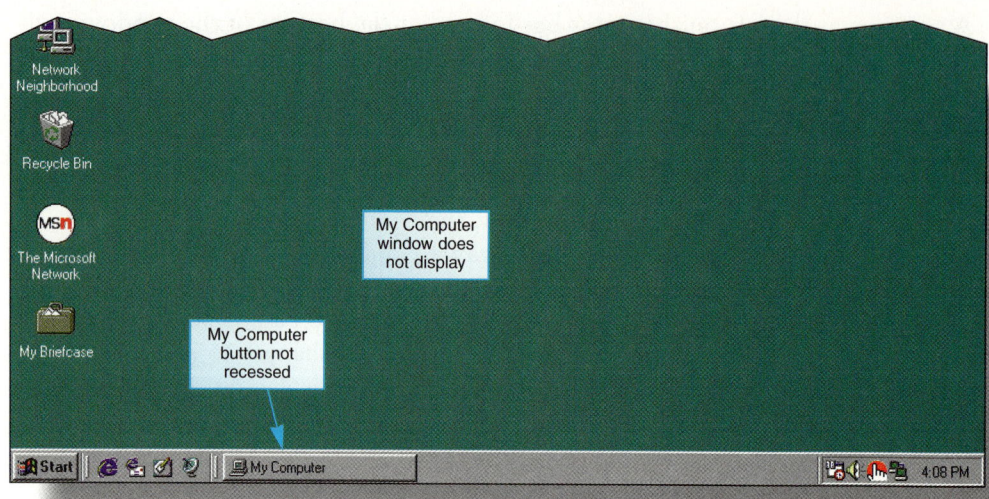

FIGURE 1-16

③ Click the My Computer button in the taskbar button area.

The My Computer window displays on the desktop in the same place and size as it was before being minimized (Figure 1-17). In addition, the My Computer window is the active window because it contains the dark blue title bar, and the My Computer button in the taskbar button area is recessed.

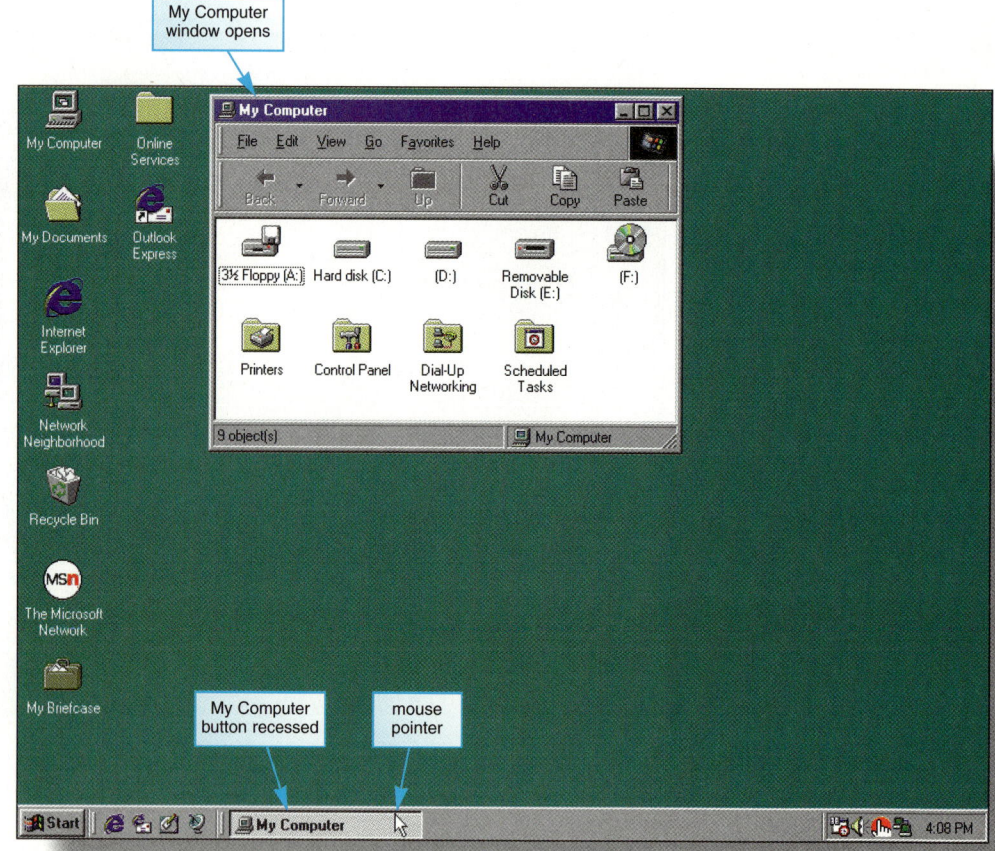

FIGURE 1-17

Whenever a window is minimized, it does not display on the desktop but a non-recessed button for the window does display in the taskbar button area. Whenever you want a minimized window to display and be the active window, click its button in the taskbar button area.

Maximize and Restore Buttons

Sometimes when information is displayed in a window, the information is not completely visible. One method to display the entire contents of a window is to enlarge the window using the **Maximize button**. The Maximize button maximizes a window so the window fills the entire screen, making it easier to see the contents of the window. When a window is maximized, the **Restore button** replaces the Maximize button on the title bar. Clicking the Restore button will return the window to its size before maximizing. To maximize and restore the My Computer window, complete the following steps.

Maximizing Windows

Many application programs run in a maximized window by default. Often you will find that you want to work with maximized windows.

1 **Point to the Maximize button on the title bar of the My Computer window (Figure 1-18).**

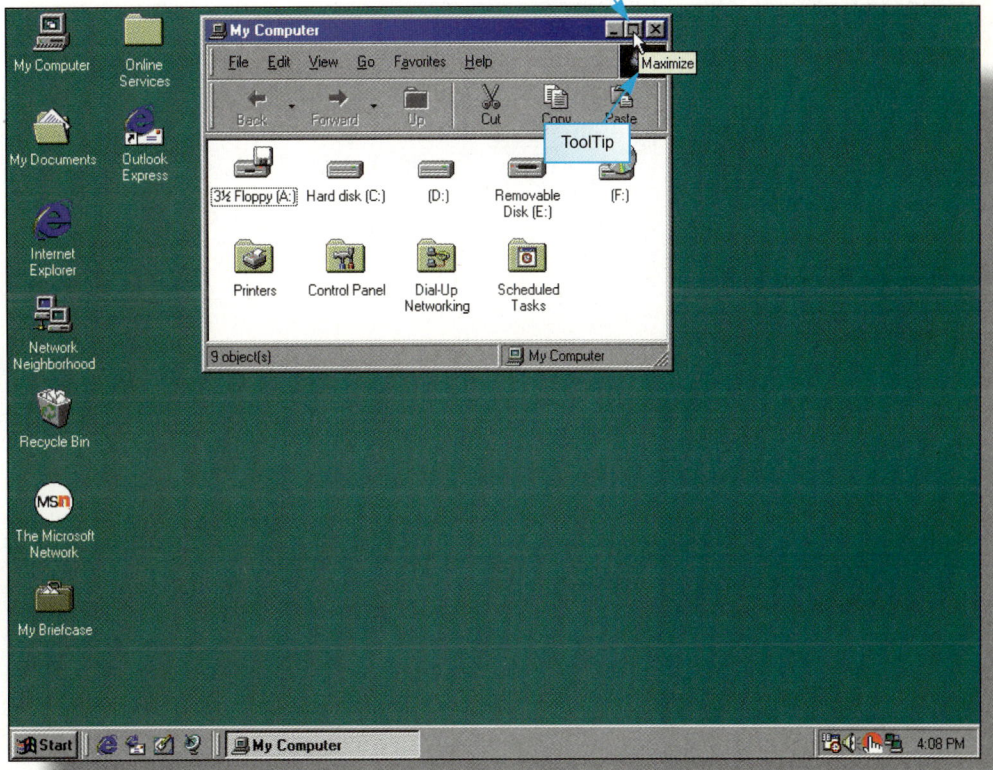

FIGURE 1-18

WIN 1.22 • Project 1 • Fundamentals of Using Microsoft Windows 98

2 Click the Maximize button.

The My Computer window expands so it and the taskbar fill the entire screen (Figure 1-19). The Restore button replaces the Maximize button and the My Computer button in the taskbar button area does not change. The My Computer window is still the active window and additional buttons display on the Standard Buttons toolbar that allow you to undo a previous action (**Undo**), delete text (**Delete**), display the properties of an object (**Properties**), and change the desktop view (**Views**).

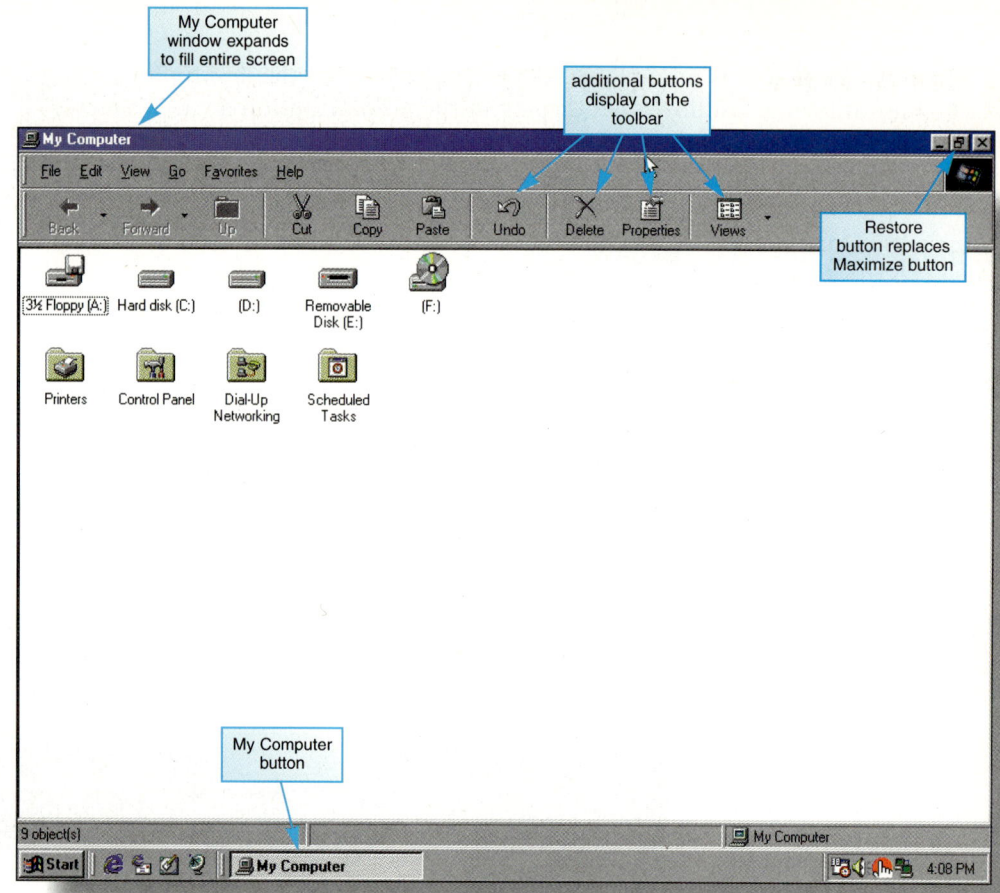

FIGURE 1-19

3 Point to the Restore button on the title bar of the My Computer window (Figure 1-20).

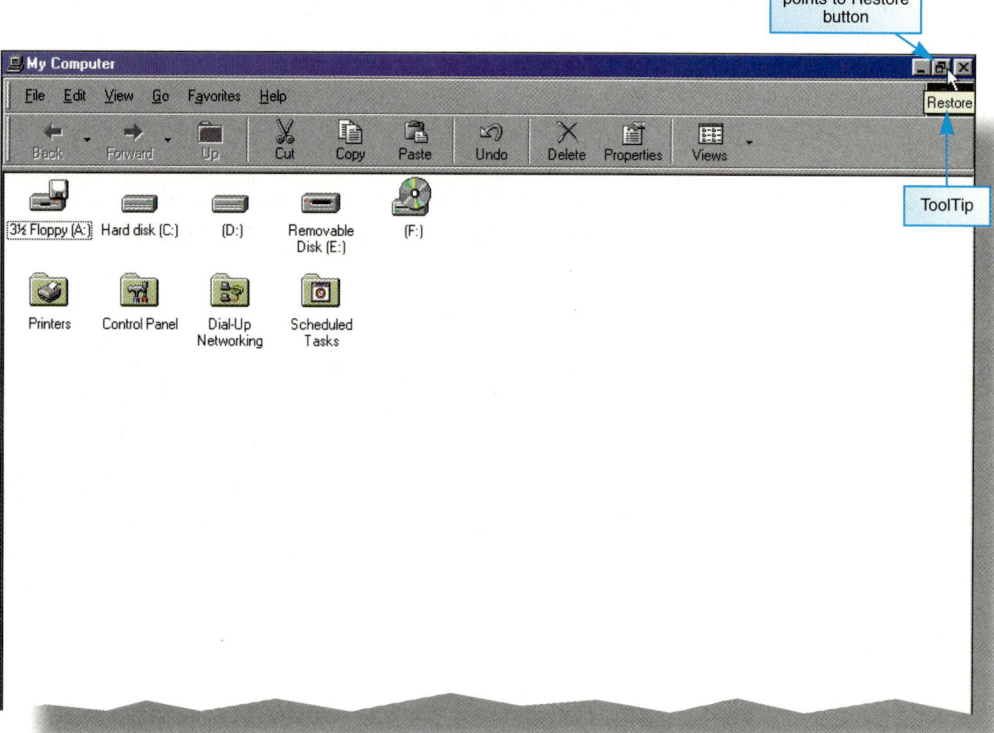

FIGURE 1-20

Communicating with Microsoft Windows 98 • **WIN 1.23**

 Click the Restore button.

The My Computer window returns to the size and position it occupied before being maximized (Figure 1-21). The My Computer button does not change. The Maximize button replaces the Restore button.

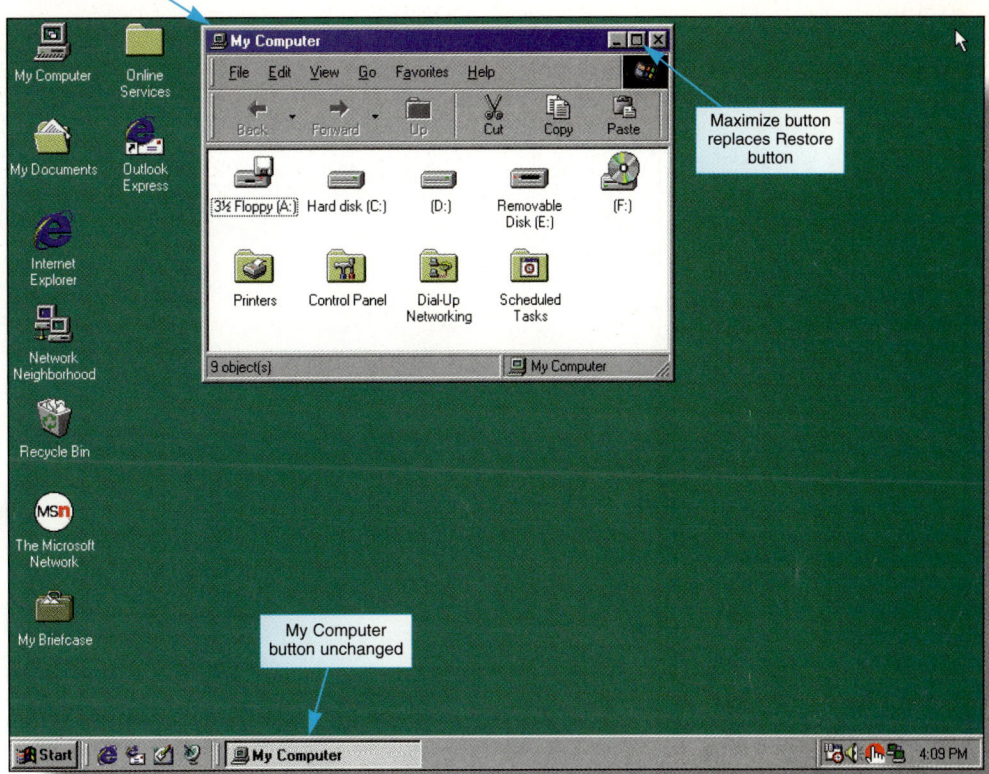

FIGURE 1-21

When a window is maximized, such as in Figure 1-19, you also can minimize the window by clicking the Minimize button. If, after minimizing the window, you click its button in the taskbar button area, the window will return to its maximized size.

Close Button

The **Close button** on the title bar of a window closes the window and removes the window button from the taskbar. To close and then reopen the My Computer window, complete the following steps.

More About

The Close Button

The Close button was a new innovation in the Windows 95 operating system. Before Windows 95, the user either had to double-click a button or click a command on a menu to close the window. As always, the choice of how to perform an operation such as closing a window is a matter of personal preference. In most cases, you will want to choose the method that causes the least amount of work.

 **To Close a Window and Reopen a Window**

 Point to the Close button on the title bar of the My Computer window (Figure 1-22).

FIGURE 1-22

WIN 1.24 • Project 1 • Fundamentals of Using Microsoft Windows 98

 Click the Close button.

The My Computer window closes and the My Computer button no longer displays in the taskbar button area (Figure 1-23).

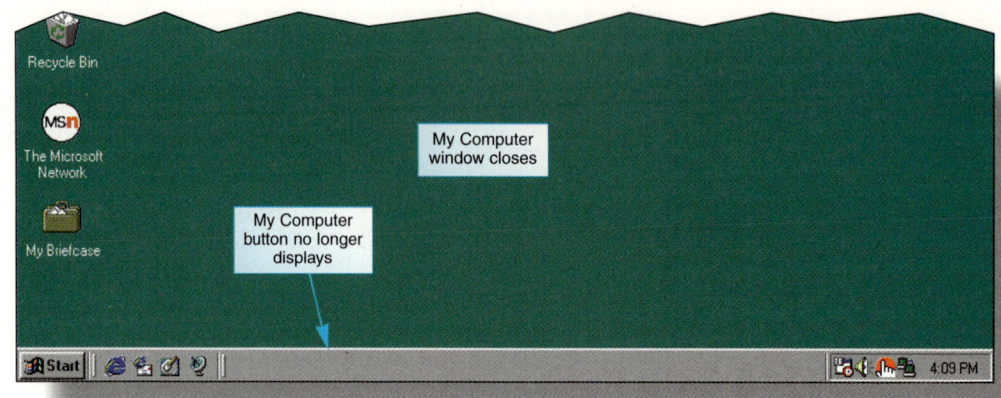

FIGURE 1-23

 **Double-click the My Computer icon on the desktop.**

The My Computer window opens and displays on the screen (Figure 1-24). The My Computer button displays in the taskbar button area.

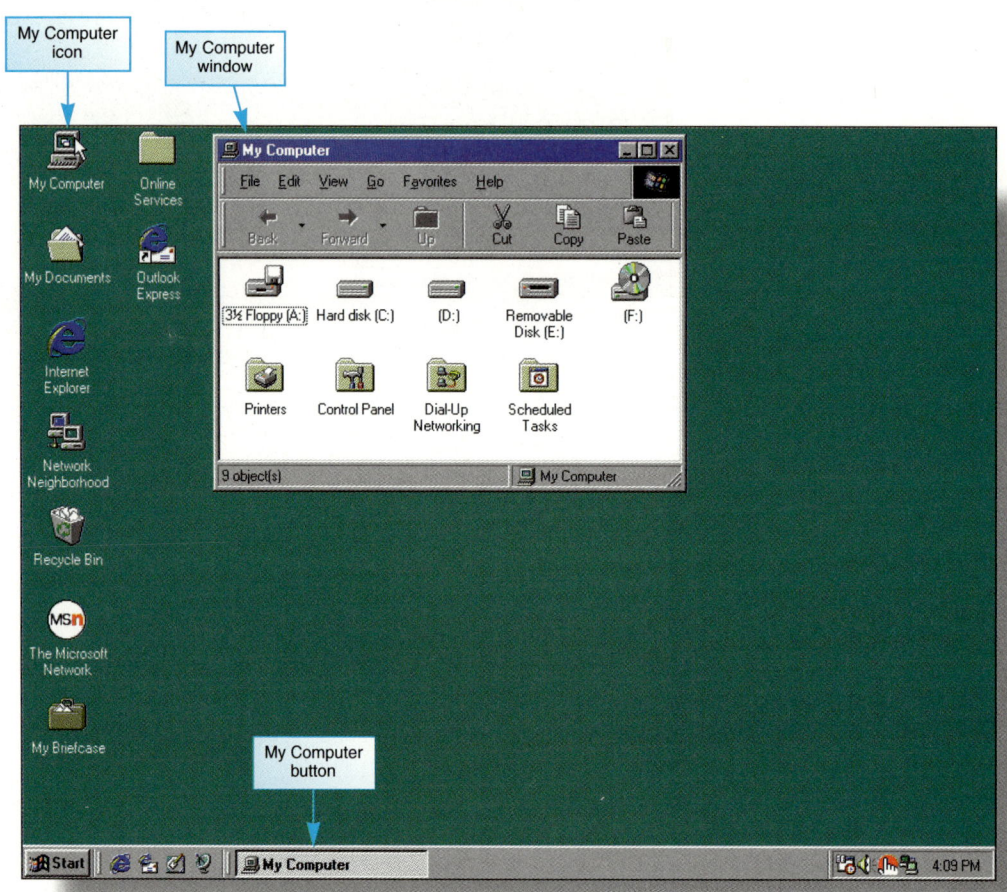

FIGURE 1-24

Dragging

Dragging is the second-most difficult skill to learn with a mouse. You may want to practice dragging a few times so you are comfortable with it.

Drag

Drag means you point to an item, hold down the left mouse button, move the item to the desired location, and then release the left mouse button. You can move any open window to another location on the desktop by pointing to the title bar of the window and dragging the window. To drag the My Computer window to another location on the desktop, perform the following steps.

Communicating with Microsoft Windows 98 • **WIN 1.25**

Steps To Move an Object by Dragging

1 Point to the My Computer window title bar (Figure 1-25).

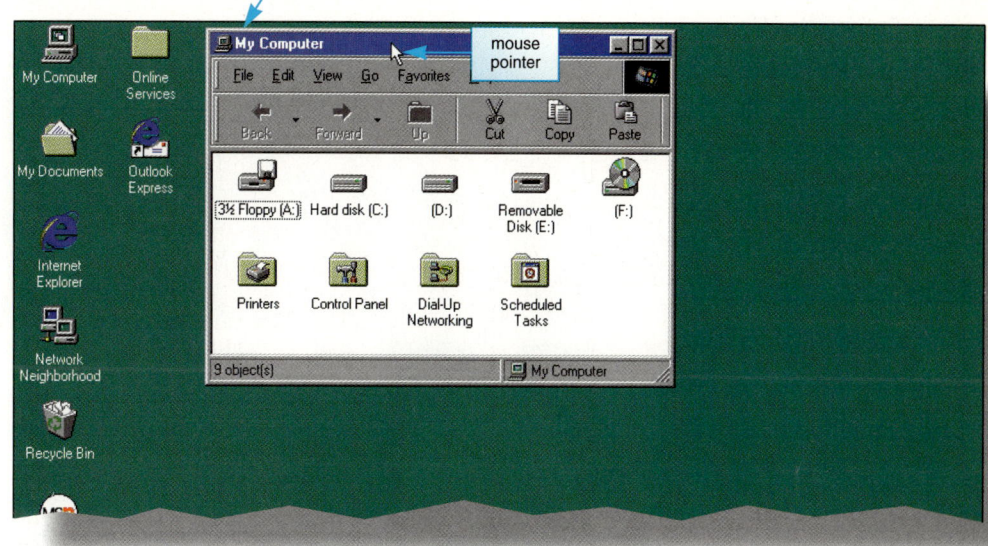

FIGURE 1-25

2 Hold down the left mouse button, move the mouse so the window moves to the center of the desktop, and release the left mouse button.

As you drag the My Computer window, the window moves across the desktop. When you release the left mouse button, the window displays in its new location on the desktop (Figure 1-26).

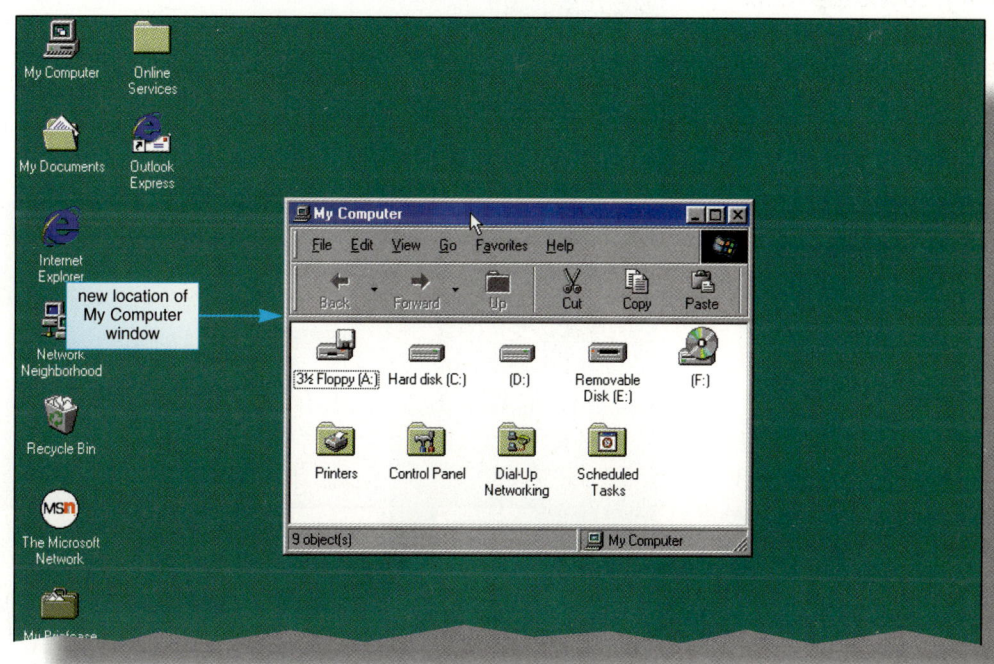

FIGURE 1-26

Sizing a Window by Dragging

As previously mentioned, sometimes when information is displayed in a window, the information is not completely visible. A second method to display information that is not visible is to enlarge the window by dragging the window. For example, you can drag the border of a window to change the size of the window. To change the size of the My Computer window, perform the steps on the next page

Steps To Size a Window by Dragging

1 **Position the mouse pointer over the lower-right corner of the My Computer window until the mouse pointer changes to a two-headed arrow.**

When the mouse pointer is on top of the lower-right corner of the My Computer window, the pointer changes to a two-headed arrow (Figure 1-27).

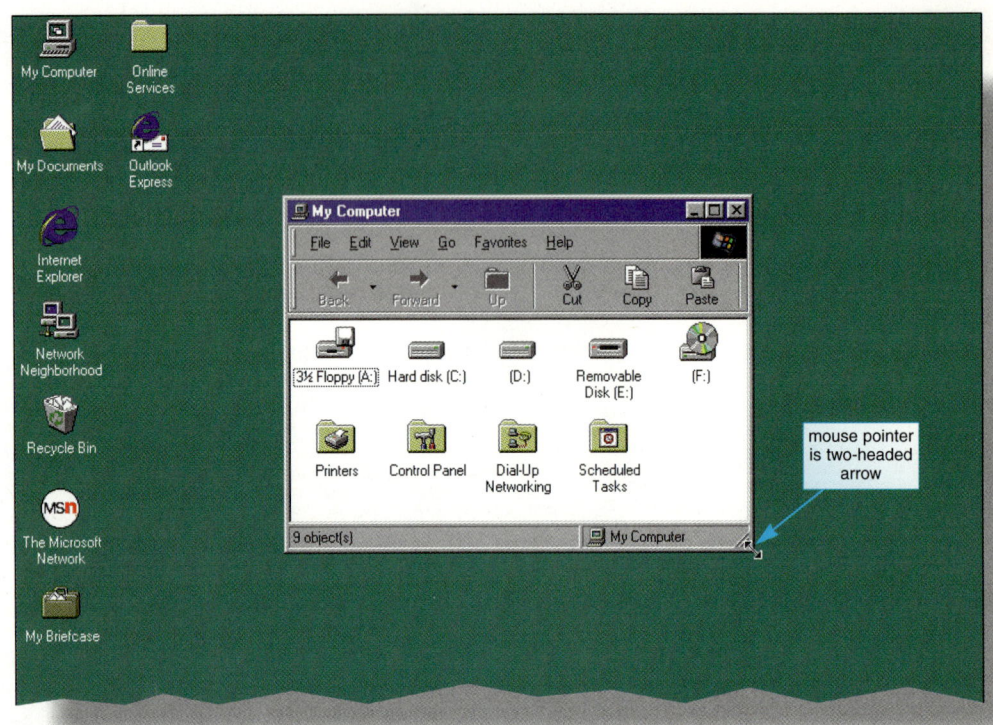

FIGURE 1-27

2 **Drag the lower-right corner upward and to the left until the window on your desktop resembles the window shown in Figure 1-28.**

As you drag the lower-right corner, the My Computer window changes size and a vertical scroll bar displays (Figure 1-28). Only five of the nine icons in the My Computer window are visible in the resized window in Figure 1-28.

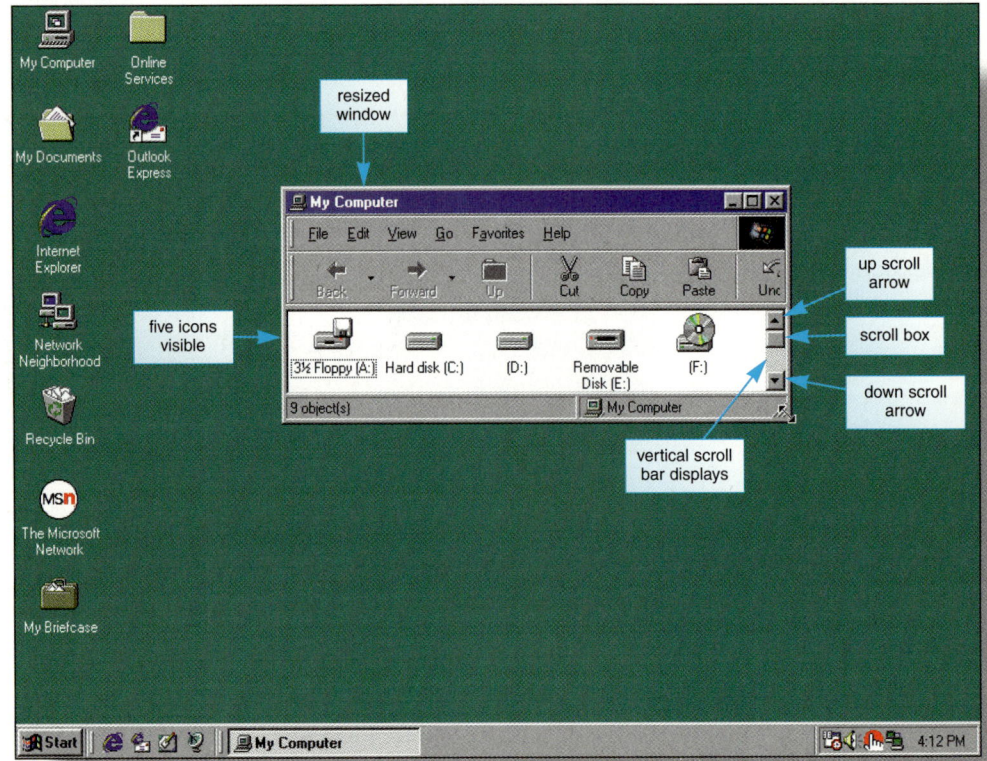

FIGURE 1-28

Communicating with Microsoft Windows 98 • WIN 1.27

A scroll bar is a bar that displays at the right edge and/or bottom edge of a window when the window contents are not completely visible. A vertical scroll bar contains an **up scroll arrow**, a **down scroll arrow**, and a **scroll box** that enable you to view areas of the window not currently visible. A vertical scroll bar displays in the My Computer window shown in Figure 1-28.

The size of the scroll box in any window is dependent on the amount of the window that is not visible. The smaller the scroll box, the more of the window that is not visible. In Figure 1-28, the scroll box occupies approximately half of the scroll bar. This indicates that approximately half of the contents of the window are not visible. If the scroll box were a tiny rectangle, a large portion of the window would not be visible.

In addition to dragging a corner of a window, you also can drag any of the borders of a window. If you drag a vertical border, such as the right border, you can move the border left or right. If you drag a horizontal border, such as the bottom border, you can move the border of the window up or down.

Scrolling in a Window

Previously, two methods were shown to display information that was not completely visible in the My Computer window. These methods were maximizing the My Computer window and changing the size of the My Computer window. A third method uses the scroll bar in the window.

Scrolling can be accomplished in three ways: (1) click the scroll arrows; (2) click the scroll bar; and (3) drag the scroll box. On the following pages, you will use the scroll bar to scroll the contents of the My Computer window. Perform the following steps to scroll the My Computer window using the scroll arrows.

> **More About**
>
> **Window Sizing**
>
> Windows 98 remembers the size of the window when you close the window. When you reopen the window, it will display in the same size as when you closed it.

> **More About**
>
> **Scrolling**
>
> Most people will either maximize a window or size it so all the objects in the window are visible to avoid scrolling because scrolling takes time. It is more efficient not to have to scroll in a window.

Steps To Scroll a Window Using Scroll Arrows

  1 Point to the down scroll arrow on the vertical scroll bar (Figure 1-29).

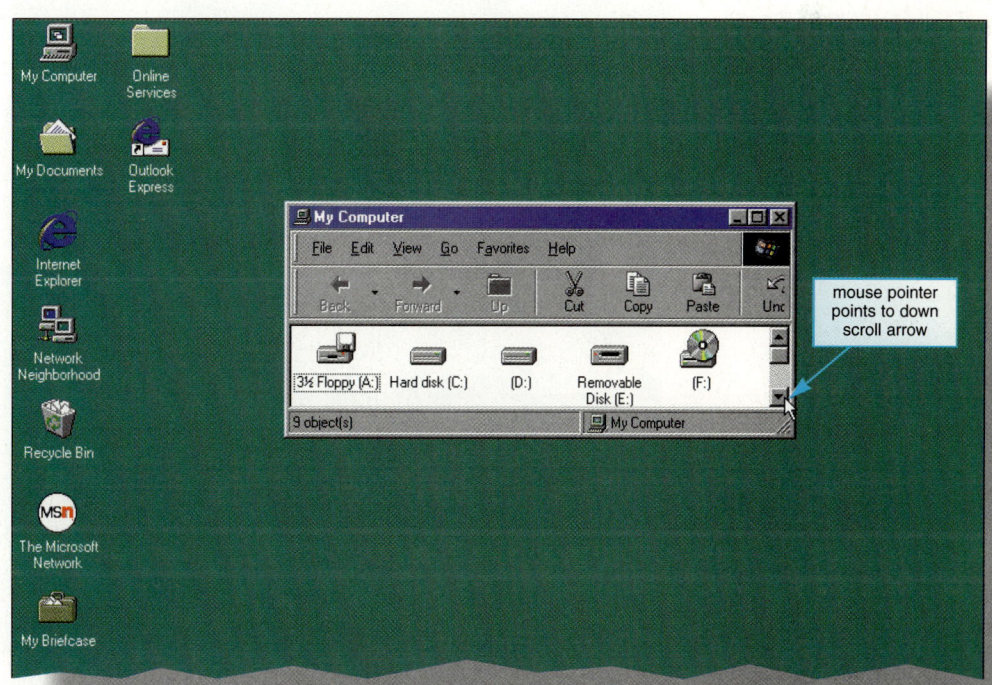

FIGURE 1-29

WIN 1.28 • Project 1 • Fundamentals of Using Microsoft Windows 98

2 **Click the down scroll arrow one time.**

The window scrolls down (the icons move up in the window) and displays the tops of the icons previously not visible (Figure 1-30). Because the window size does not change when you scroll, the contents of the window will change, as seen in the difference between Figure 1-29 on the previous page and Figure 1-30.

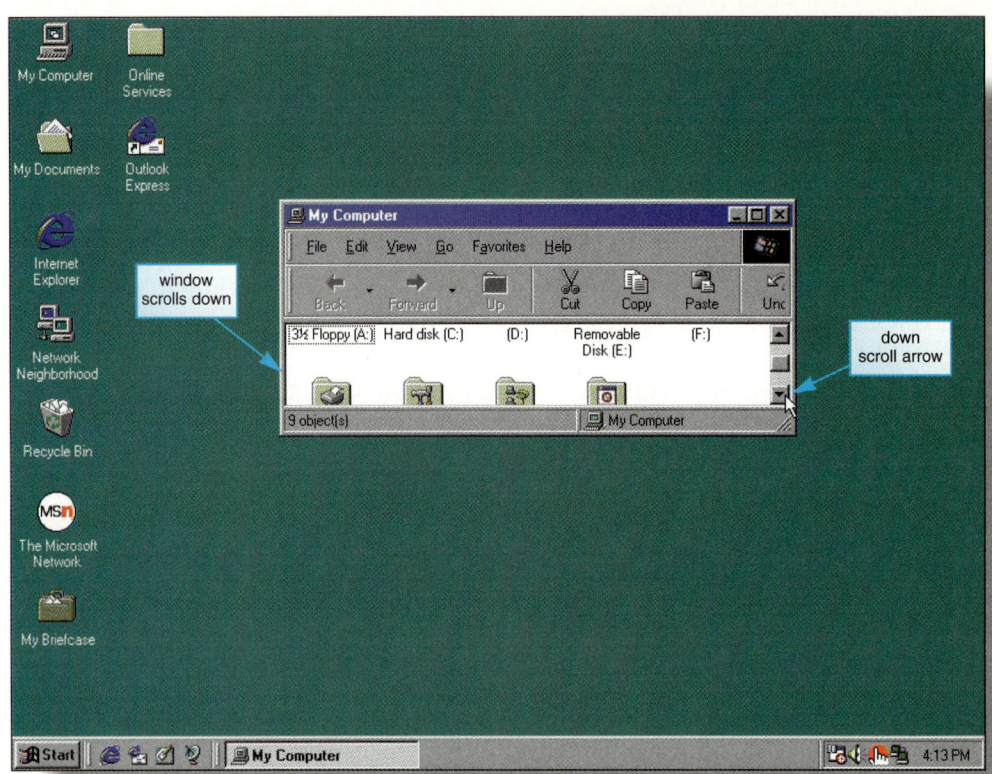

FIGURE 1-30

3 **Click the down scroll arrow two more times.**

The scroll box moves to the bottom of the scroll bar and the remaining icons in the window display (Figure 1-31).

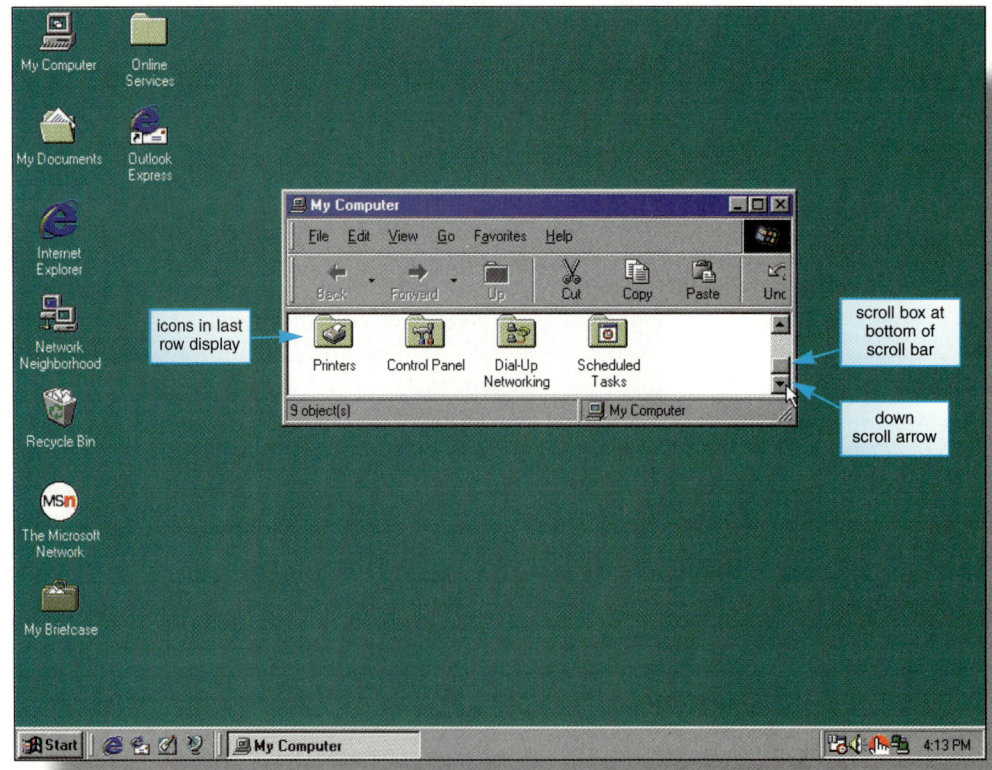

FIGURE 1-31

You can scroll continuously through a window using scroll arrows by pointing to the up or down scroll arrow and holding down the left mouse button. The window continues to scroll until you release the left mouse button or you reach the top or bottom of the window.

Scrolling by Clicking the Scroll Bar

You can also scroll by clicking the scroll bar itself. To scroll to the top of the window by clicking the scroll bar, complete the following steps.

The Scroll Bar

In many application programs, clicking the scroll bar will move the window a full screen's worth of information up or down. You can step through a word processing document screen by screen, for example, by clicking the scroll bar.

 To Scroll a Window Using the Scroll Bar

1 Point to the scroll bar above the scroll box (Figure 1-32).

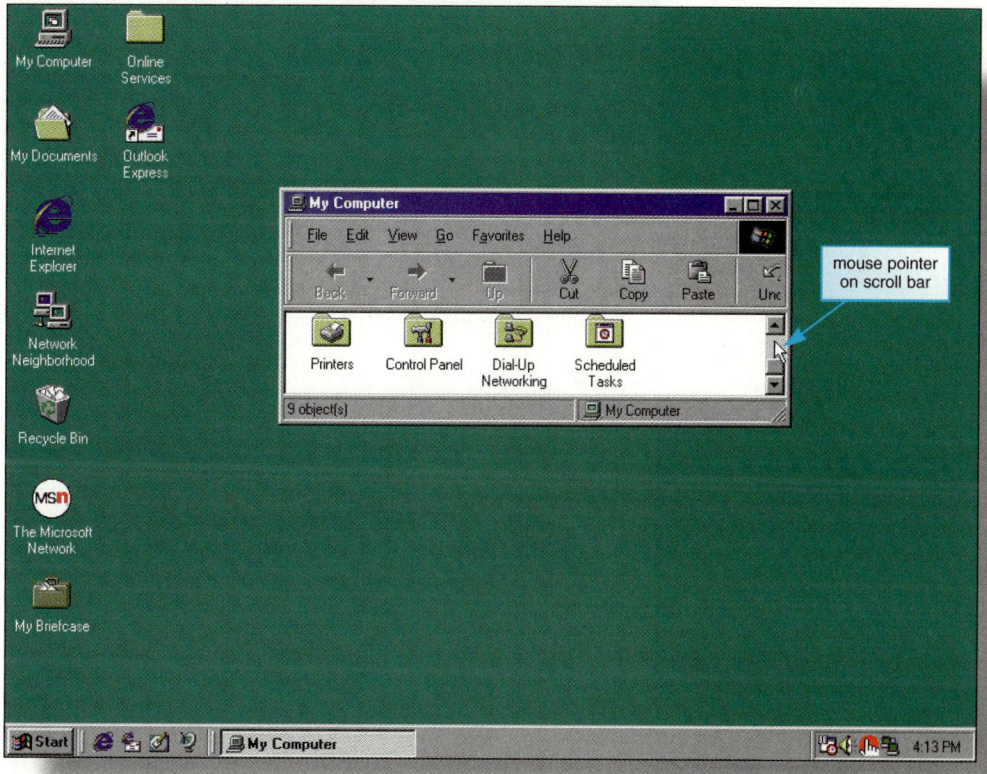

FIGURE 1-32

WIN 1.30 • Project 1 • Fundamentals of Using Microsoft Windows 98

 Click the scroll bar one time.

The scroll box moves toward the top of the scroll bar and a part of the icons at the top of the window display (Figure 1-33).

3 Click the scroll bar one more time to display the top row of icons.

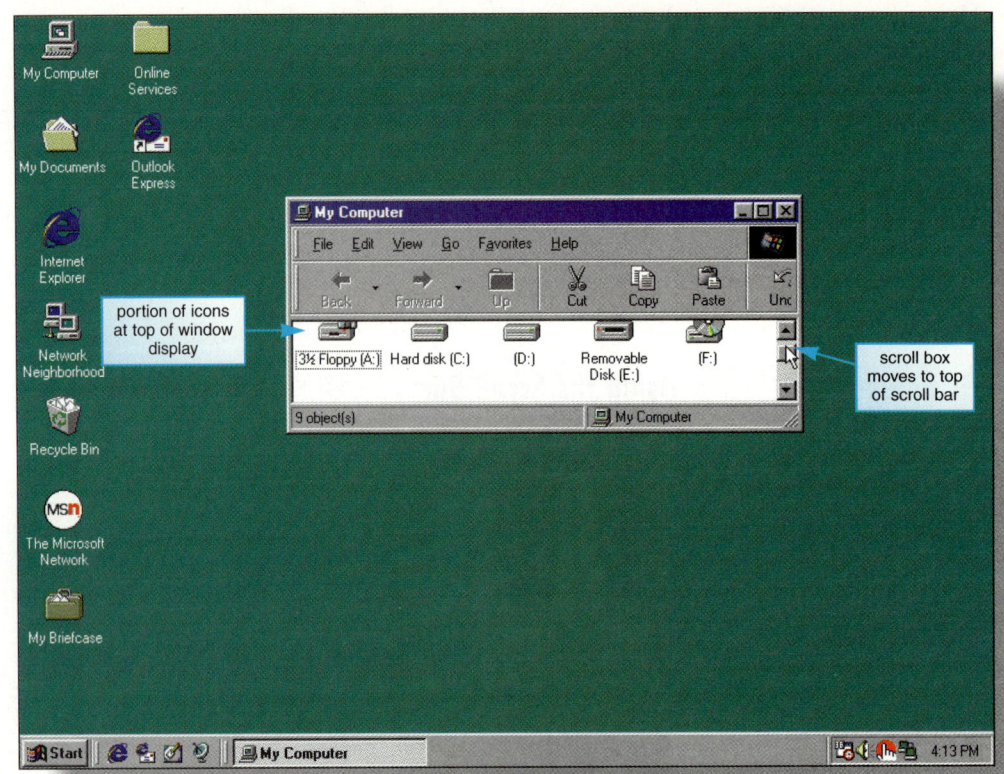

FIGURE 1-33

In the previous steps, you needed to click the scroll bar two times to move the scroll box to the top of the scroll bar and display the contents in the top of the window. In those cases where the scroll box is small and more contents of the window are not visible, you may have to click three or more times to scroll to the top.

Scrolling by Dragging the Scroll Box

The third way in which you can scroll through a window to view its contents is by dragging the scroll box. To view the contents of My Computer window by dragging the scroll box, complete the following step.

The Scroll Box

Dragging the scroll box is the most efficient technique to scroll long distances. In many application programs, such as Microsoft Word, as you scroll using the scroll box, the page number of the document displays next to the scroll box.

Steps To Scroll a Window by Dragging the Scroll Box

1 With the mouse pointer pointing to the scroll box on the scroll bar, drag the scroll box down the scroll bar until the scroll box is about halfway down the scroll bar.

As you drag the scroll box down the vertical scroll bar, the icons move up in the window and additional icons become visible (Figure 1-34). Notice that the icons in the window move as you drag the scroll box.

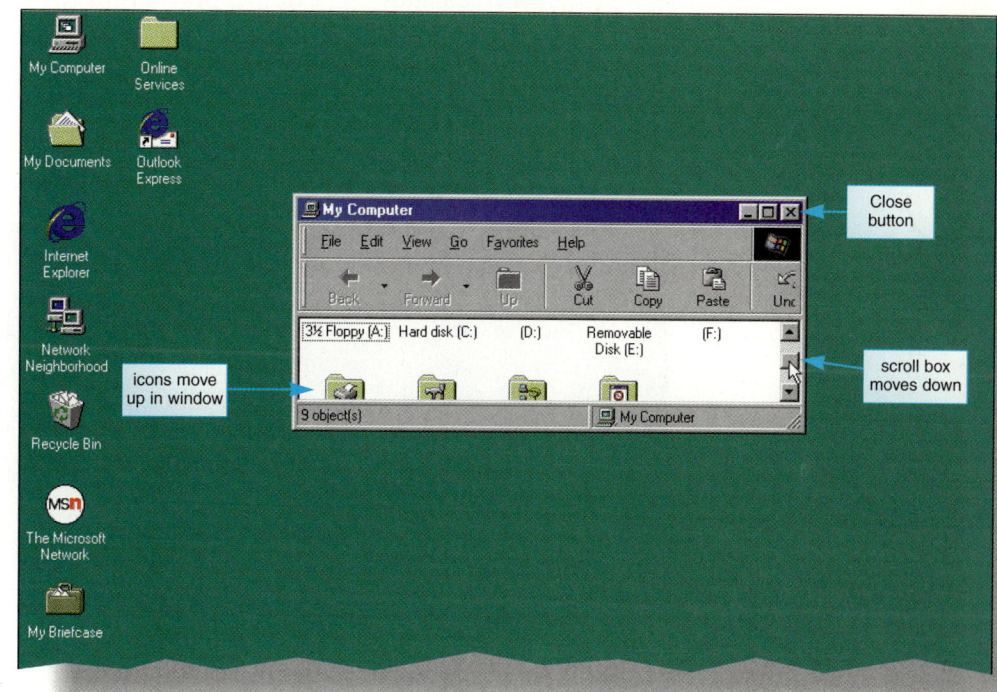

FIGURE 1-34

Being able to view the contents of a window by scrolling is an important Windows 98 skill because in many cases the entire contents of a window are not visible.

Resizing a Window

After moving and resizing a window, you may wish to return the window to approximately its original size. To return the My Computer window to about its original size, complete the following steps.

TO RESIZE A WINDOW

1 Position the mouse pointer over the lower-right corner of the My Computer window border until the mouse pointer changes to a two-headed arrow.

2 Drag the lower-right corner of the My Computer window until the window is the same size as shown in Figure 1-27 on page WIN 1.26, and then release the mouse button.

The My Computer window is approximately the same size as before you made it smaller.

Closing a Window

After you have completed your work in a window, normally you will close the window. To close the My Computer window, complete the steps on the next page.

More About

Scrolling Guidelines

General scrolling guidelines: (1) To scroll short distances (line by line), click the scroll arrows; (2) To scroll one screen at a time, click the scroll bar; and (3) To scroll long distances, drag the scroll box.

TO CLOSE A WINDOW

 Point to the Close button on the right of the title bar in the My Computer window (see Figure 1-34 on the previous page).

 Click the Close button.

The My Computer window closes and the desktop contains no open windows (Figure 1-35). Because the My Computer window is closed, the My Computer button no longer displays in the taskbar button area.

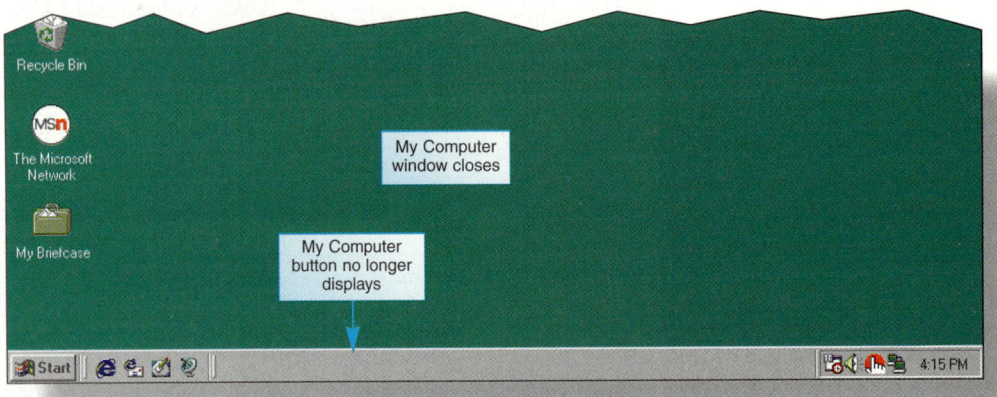

FIGURE 1-35

Right-Dragging

Right-dragging was not available on some earlier versions of Windows, so you might find people familiar with Windows not even considering right-dragging. Because it always produces a shortcut menu, however, right-dragging is the safest way to drag.

Right-Drag

Right-drag means you point to an item, hold down the right mouse button, move the item to the desired location, and then release the right mouse button. When you right-drag an object, a shortcut menu displays. The shortcut menu contains commands specifically for use with the object being dragged. To right-drag the My Briefcase icon to the right of its current position, perform the following steps. If the My Briefcase icon does not display on your desktop, you will be unable to perform Step 1 through Step 4 that follow.

 To Right-Drag

 Point to the My Briefcase icon on the desktop (Figure 1-36).

FIGURE 1-36

 **Hold down the right mouse button, drag the icon to the right toward the middle of the desktop, and then release the right mouse button.**

The dimmed My Briefcase icon and a shortcut menu display in the middle of the desktop (Figure 1-37). The My Briefcase icon remains at its original location on the left of the screen. The shortcut menu contains four commands: Move Here, Copy Here, Create Shortcut(s) Here, and Cancel. The Move Here command in bold (dark) type identifies what would happen if you were to drag the My Briefcase icon with the left mouse button.

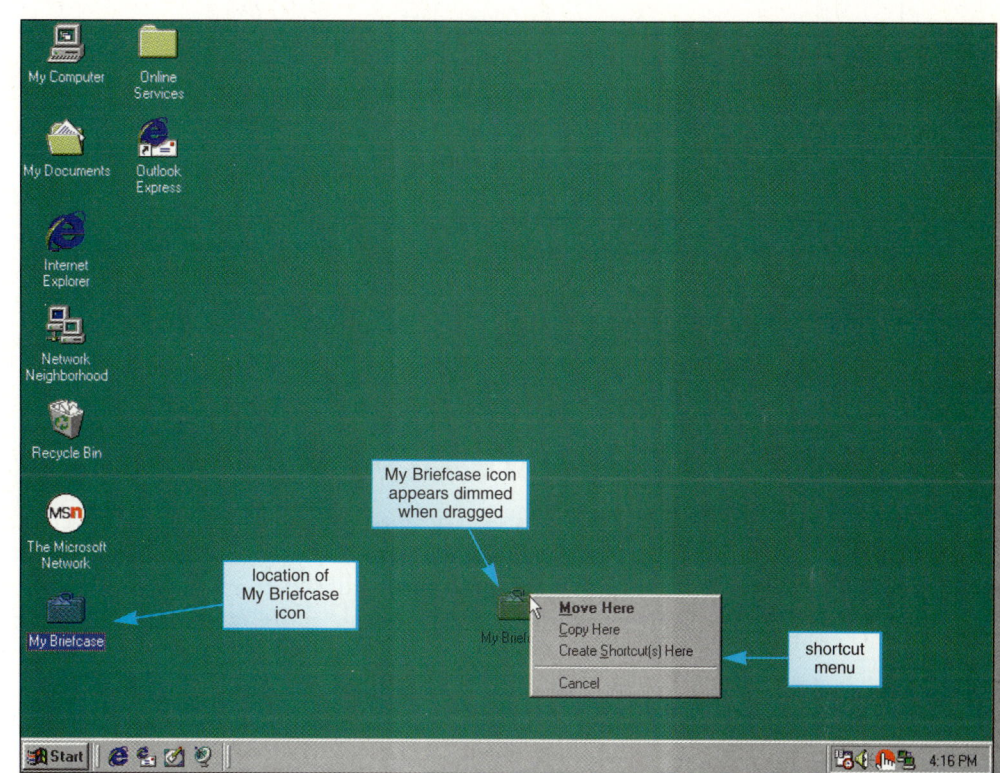

FIGURE 1-37

 Point to Cancel on the shortcut menu.

The Cancel command is highlighted (Figure 1-38).

Click Cancel on the shortcut menu.

The shortcut menu and the dragged My Briefcase icon disappear from the screen.

FIGURE 1-38

Whenever you begin an operation but do not want to complete the operation, you can click Cancel on a shortcut menu or click the Cancel button in a dialog box. The **Cancel** command will reset anything you have done in the operation.

If you click **Move Here** on the shortcut menu shown in Figure 1-38 on the previous page, Windows 98 will move the icon from its current location to the new location. If you click **Copy Here**, the icon will be copied to the new location and two icons will display on the desktop. Windows 98 automatically will give the second icon a different title. If you click **Create Shortcut(s) Here**, a special object called a shortcut will be created. You will learn more about shortcuts in Project 2 of this book.

Although you can move icons by dragging with the primary (left) mouse button and by right-dragging with the secondary (right) mouse button, it is strongly suggested you right-drag because a menu displays and you can specify the exact operation you want to occur. When you drag using the left mouse button, a default operation takes place and the operation may not do what you want.

Summary of Mouse and Windows Operations

You have seen how to use the mouse to point, click, right-click, double-click, drag, and right-drag in order to accomplish certain tasks on the desktop. The use of a mouse is an important skill when using Windows 98. In addition, you have learned how to move around and use windows on the Windows 98 desktop.

The Keyboard and Keyboard Shortcuts

The **keyboard** is an input device on which you manually key, or type, data. Figure 1-39a shows the enhanced IBM 101-key keyboard, and Figure 1-39b shows a Microsoft Natural keyboard designed specifically for use with Windows. Many tasks you accomplish with a mouse also can be accomplished using a keyboard.

To perform tasks using the keyboard, you must understand the notation used to identify which keys to press. This notation is used throughout Windows 98 to identify **keyboard shortcuts**.

More About

The Microsoft Keyboard

The Microsoft keyboard in Figure 1-39(b) not only has special keys for Windows 98, but also is designed ergonomically so you type with your hands apart. It takes a little time to get used to, but several authors on the Shelly Cashman Series writing team report they type faster with more accuracy and less fatigue when using the keyboard.

FIGURE 1-39a

FIGURE 1-39b

Keyboard shortcuts consist of: (1) pressing a single key (example: press the ENTER key); or (2) pressing and holding down one key and pressing a second key, as shown by two key names separated by a plus sign (example: press CTRL+ESC). For example, to obtain Help about Windows 98, you can press the F1 key; to open the Start menu, hold down the CTRL key and then press the ESC key (press CTRL+ESC).

Often, computer users will use keyboard shortcuts for operations they perform frequently. For example, many users find pressing the F1 key to launch Windows 98 Help easier than using the Start menu as shown later in this project. As a user, you probably will find the combination of keyboard and mouse operations that particularly suit you, but it is strongly recommended that generally you use the mouse.

The Windows 98 Desktop Views

Windows 98 provides several ways to view your desktop and the windows that open on the desktop. The three desktop views include the Web style, Classic style, and Custom style. The desktop view you choose will affect the appearance of your desktop, how you open and work with windows on the desktop, and how you work with the files and folders on your computer.

The Classic Style

The **Classic style** causes the desktop and the objects on the desktop to display and function as they did in Windows 95, a previous version of Windows. When you choose the Classic style as your desktop view, the desktop is referred to as the **Classic Windows Desktop**. The Classic Windows Desktop is similar to the desktop shown in Figure 1-2 on page WIN 1.8 and is shown again in Figure 1-40.

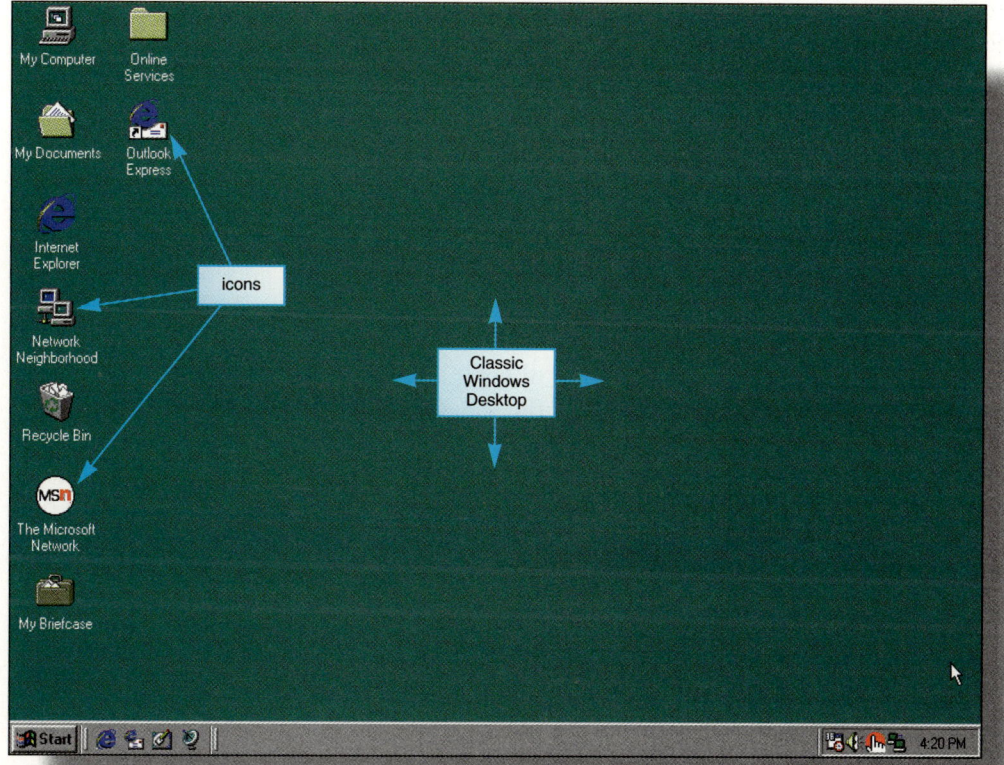

FIGURE 1-40

The icons on the desktop shown in Figure 1-40 on the previous page behave as they did in Windows 95. You double-click an icon to open its window and display its button in the taskbar button area. For example, double-clicking the My Computer icon on the desktop opens the My Computer window and displays the My Computer button in the taskbar button area (Figure 1-41).

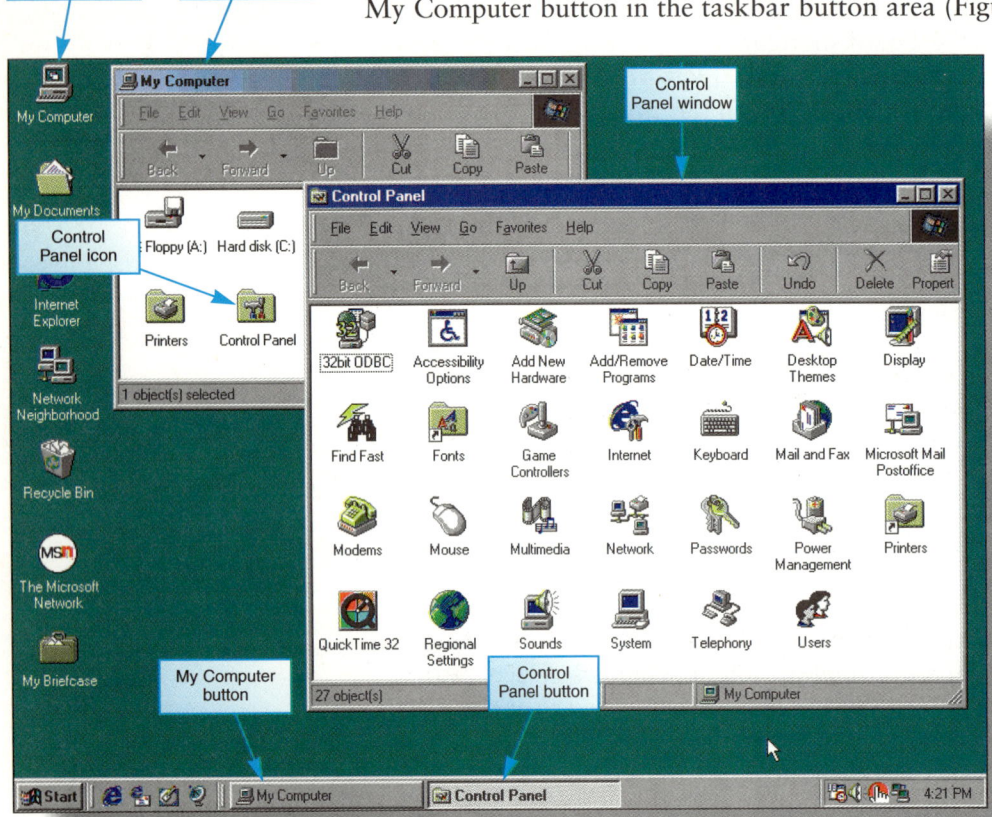

FIGURE 1-41

If, after opening the My Computer window, you want to display the contents of a drive or folder icon in the My Computer window, you double-click the drive or folder icon to open its window and display its taskbar button. For example, you might double-click the Control Panel icon in the My Computer window to open its window and display its taskbar button (Figure 1-41).

Double-clicking the Control Panel icon opens a second window on the desktop (Control Panel window) and places a second button (Control Panel button) in the taskbar button area.

The Internet and World Wide Web

The second desktop view available in Windows 98 is the Web style. The Web style uses the Internet and an area of the Internet called the World Wide Web to retrieve and display information on the desktop.

The **Internet** is a worldwide group of connected computer networks that allows public access to information on thousands of subjects and gives users the ability to send messages and obtain products and services. Computers connected to the Internet deliver information using a variety of computer media, including text, graphics, sound, video clips, and animation. On the Internet, this multimedia capability is called **hypermedia**, which is any variety of computer media. Underlined text, a picture, or an icon used to access hypermedia is called a **hyperlink**, or simply a **link**. Clicking a hyperlink on a computer in Los Angeles could cause a picture stored on a computer in Germany to display on the desktop of the computer in Los Angeles.

The collection of hyperlinks throughout the Internet creates an interconnected network of links called the **World Wide Web**, also referred to as the **Web**. Each computer within the Web that can be referenced by a hyperlink is called a **Web site**. Hundreds of thousands of Web sites around the world can be accessed through the Internet. Graphics, text, and other hypermedia are stored in files called **hypertext documents**, or **Web pages**. Figure 1-42 illustrates one of several Web pages in the Web site operated by ESPN, a popular sports broadcasting company.

The Windows 98 Desktop Views • WIN 1.37

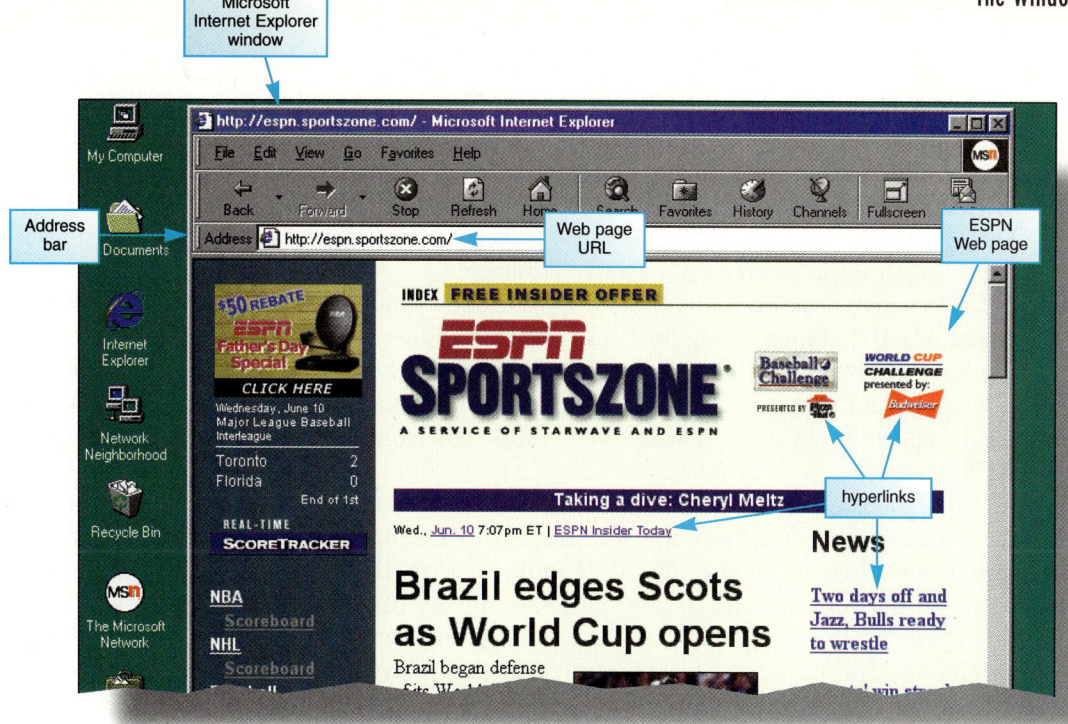

FIGURE 1-42

The Web page shown in Figure 1-42 contains a variety of multimedia (text, graphics, and animation) and hyperlinks. A unique address, called a **Uniform Resource Locator (URL)**, identifies each Web page in a Web site. The URL for the ESPN Web page shown in Figure 1-42, http://espn.sportszone.com, displays in the Address bar at the top of the http://espn.sportszone.com/ – Microsoft Internet Explorer window.

A software tool, called a **Web browser**, allows you to locate a Web page if you know the URL for the Web page. The **Microsoft Internet Explorer 4 Web browser** included with Windows 98 displays the Web page shown in Figure 1-42. Clicking a hyperlink on the Web page causes the browser to locate the associated Web page and display its contents in the same window.

The Web Style

In **Web style**, the icon titles on the desktop are underlined similarly to the hyperlinks in a Web page, and the desktop is referred to as the **Active Desktop™** (Figure 1-43).

FIGURE 1-43

More About

Desktop Views

The Classic style was included in the Windows 98 operating system to allow Windows 95 users to upgrade easily to the newer Windows 98 operating system. Responses from people in the Beta Test program, which is a program designed to test software prior to the public sale of the software, indicated that most Windows 95 users had little difficulty switching to Windows 98, and experienced users liked the Web style and Active Desktop.

The Web style causes the Channel bar to display on the desktop and allows you to place other objects, called **active desktop items**, on the desktop (see Figure 1-43 on the previous page). The **Channel bar** contains twelve **Channel buttons** (channel guide, news & technology, sports, business, entertainment, lifestyle & travel, AOL Preview, The Microsoft Network, MSNBC News, Disney, PointCast, and WB) that assist you in placing desktop items on the Active Desktop.

Two active desktop items (ESPN SportsZone™ and AudioNet Juke Box) display on the desktop shown in Figure 1-43. The **ESPN SportsZone™ item** displays the lastest sports scores from the ESPN SportsZone™ Web site shown in Figure 1-42 on the previous page and updates the scores periodically. The **AudioNet Juke Box item** allows you to select and listen to hundreds of audio CDs from the AudioNet Web site on the Internet.

Unlike the Classic style, the icon titles on the desktop are underlined and you click an icon to open its window and display its taskbar button. When you click an icon on the desktop, such as the My Computer icon, the My Computer window opens on the desktop with a different look and feel than the My Computer window that opens when you double-click its icon in Classic style (Figure 1-44). In Windows terminology, this look and feel is referred to as **displaying a folder as a Web page**.

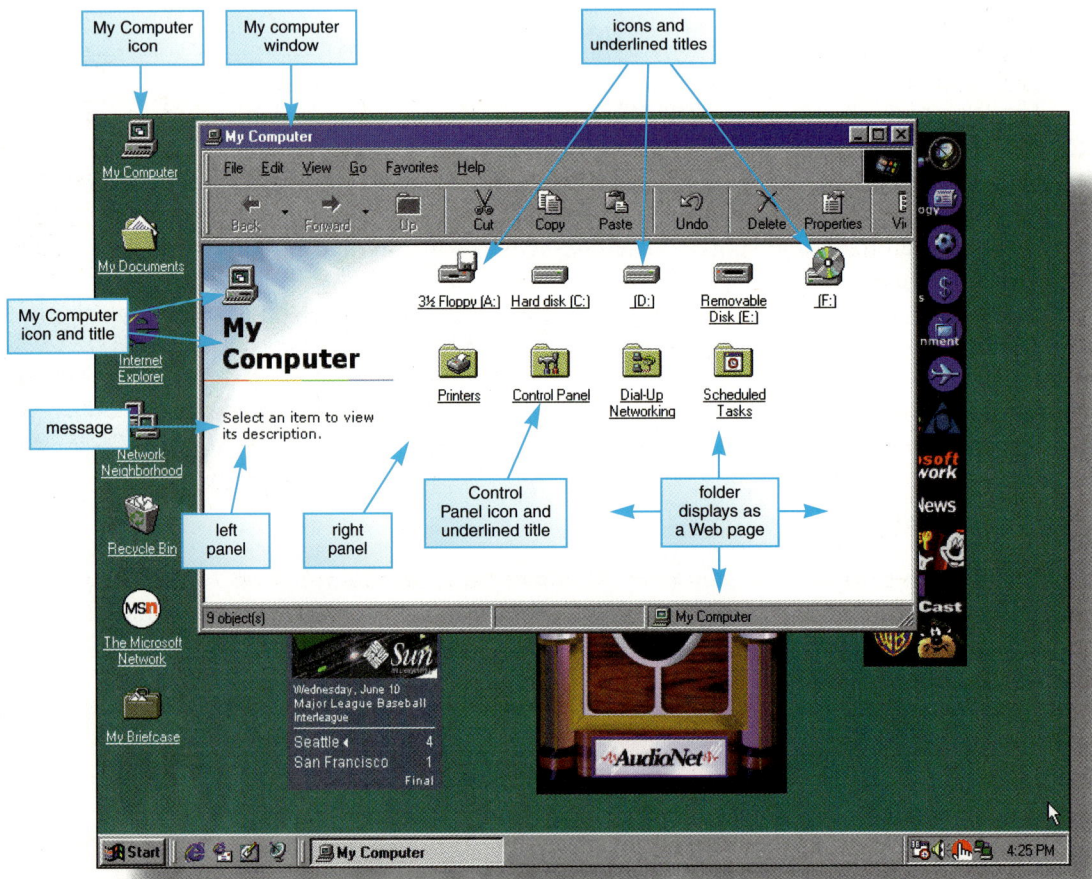

FIGURE 1-44

The My Computer window displays as a Web page with the area below the Standard Buttons toolbar divided into two panels. The My Computer icon and its icon title, My Computer, display at the top of the left panel. The text, Select an item to view its description, displays below the icon and title in the left panel. The right panel of the My Computer window contains nine icons and their underlined titles.

In Classic style, double-clicking the Control Panel icon in the My Computer window opened a second window on the desktop and displayed a second taskbar button (see Figure 1-41 on page WIN 1.36). In Web style, you click instead of double-click a drive or folder icon in the My Computer window to display the contents of the drive or folder. To display the contents of the Control Panel folder, you click the Control Panel icon in the My Computer window (Figure 1-45).

The Control Panel window opens in the same window in which the My Computer window was displayed, and the Control Panel button replaces the My Computer button in the taskbar button area. The Control Panel displays as a Web page with the left panel containing information about the Control Panel and the right panel containing the icons in the Control Panel folder.

If, after displaying the Control Panel window, you again want to display the My Computer window, you can click the Back button on the Standard Buttons toolbar to replace the Control Panel window and taskbar button with the My Computer window and taskbar button.

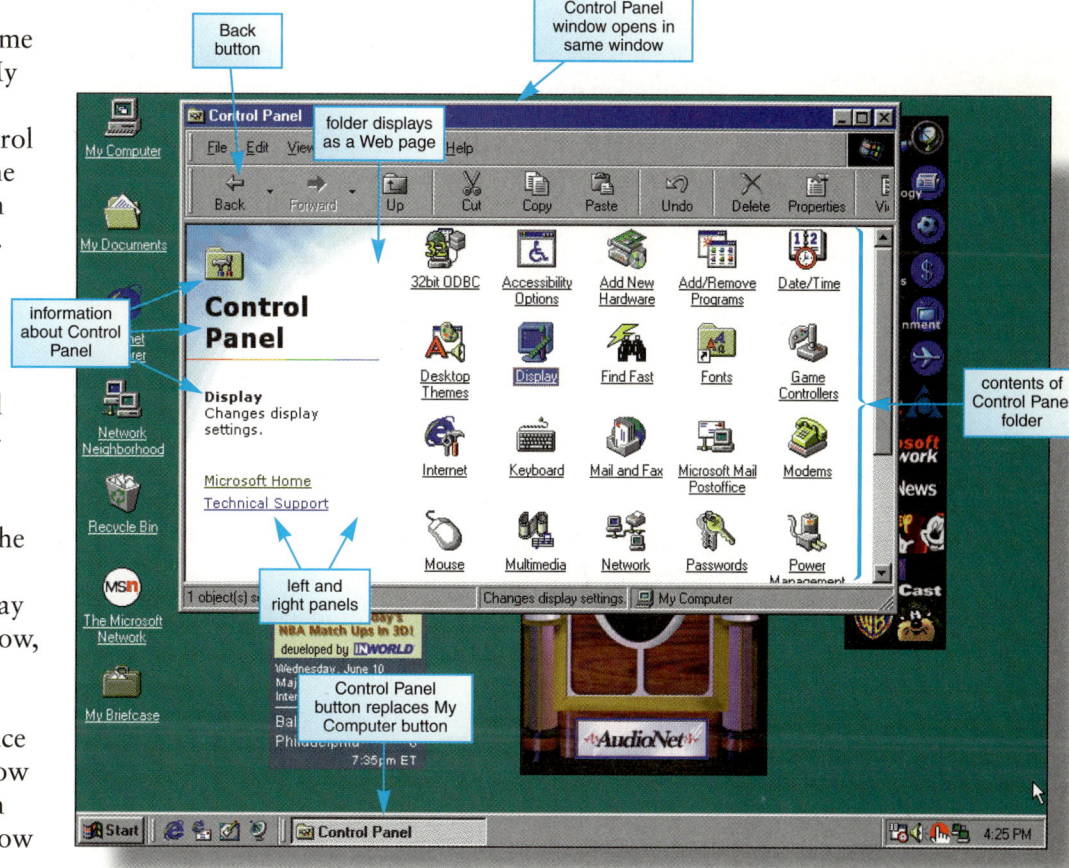

FIGURE 1-45

The Custom Style

The third desktop view available in Windows 98 is the Custom style. The **Custom style** allows you to pick and choose the options you prefer, including a combination of Classic style and Web-style settings. The options include being able to: (1) view the Active Desktop™ or the Classic Windows Desktop; (2) open a folder in the same window or its own window; (3) view Web content in all folders or only in folders you select; and (4) single-click or double-click to open an item.

When Windows 98 is installed on a computer, the desktop view that displays when you launch Windows 98 is the Custom style. The settings that were chosen by Microsoft, referred to as **default settings**, include: (1) viewing the Classic Windows Desktop; (2) opening a folder in the same window; (3) viewing Web content only in folders you select; and (4) double-clicking to open an item. As a result, you view the Classic Windows Desktop on the desktop, folders open in the same window on the desktop, left and right panels do not display in a window, and you double-click an icon to open its window.

The steps and screens you see in this book assume the default settings of the Custom style, as chosen by Microsoft Corporation, are installed on your computer. If you find this not to be the case, refer to the Preface of this book for instructions to switch the desktop view to the default desktop view or contact your instructor to change the desktop view.

More About

Application Programs

Some application programs, such as Internet Explorer, are part of Windows 98. Most application programs, however, such as Microsoft Office, Lotus SmartSuite, and others must be purchased separately from Windows 98.

Launching an Application Program

One of the basic tasks you can perform using Windows 98 is to launch an application program. A **program** is a set of computer instructions that carries out a task on your computer. An **application program** is a program that allows you to accomplish a specific task for which that program is designed. For example, a **word processing program** is an application program that allows you to create written documents; a **presentation graphics program** is an application program that allows you to create graphic presentations for display on a computer; and a **Web browser program** is an application program that allows you to search for and display Web pages.

The most common activity on a computer is to run an application program to accomplish tasks using the computer. You can launch an application program in a variety of ways. When several methods are available to accomplish a task, a computer user has the opportunity to try various methods and select the method that best fits his or her needs.

To illustrate the variety of methods available to launch an application program, three methods will be shown to launch the Internet Explorer Web browser program. These methods include using the Start button; using the Quick Launch toolbar; and using an icon on the desktop.

Launching an Application Using the Start Button

The first method to launch an application program is to use the Start menu. Perform the following steps to launch Internet Explorer using the Start menu and Internet Explorer command.

 To Launch a Program Using the Start Menu

1 **Click the Start button on the taskbar. Point to Programs on the Start menu. Point to Internet Explorer on the Programs submenu. Point to Internet Explorer on the Internet Explorer submenu.**

The Start menu, Programs submenu, and Internet Explorer submenu display (Figure 1-46). The Internet Explorer submenu contains the **Internet Explorer command** to launch the Internet Explorer program. You might find more, fewer, or different commands on the submenus on your computer than those shown in Figure 1-46 because different computers can contain different application programs.

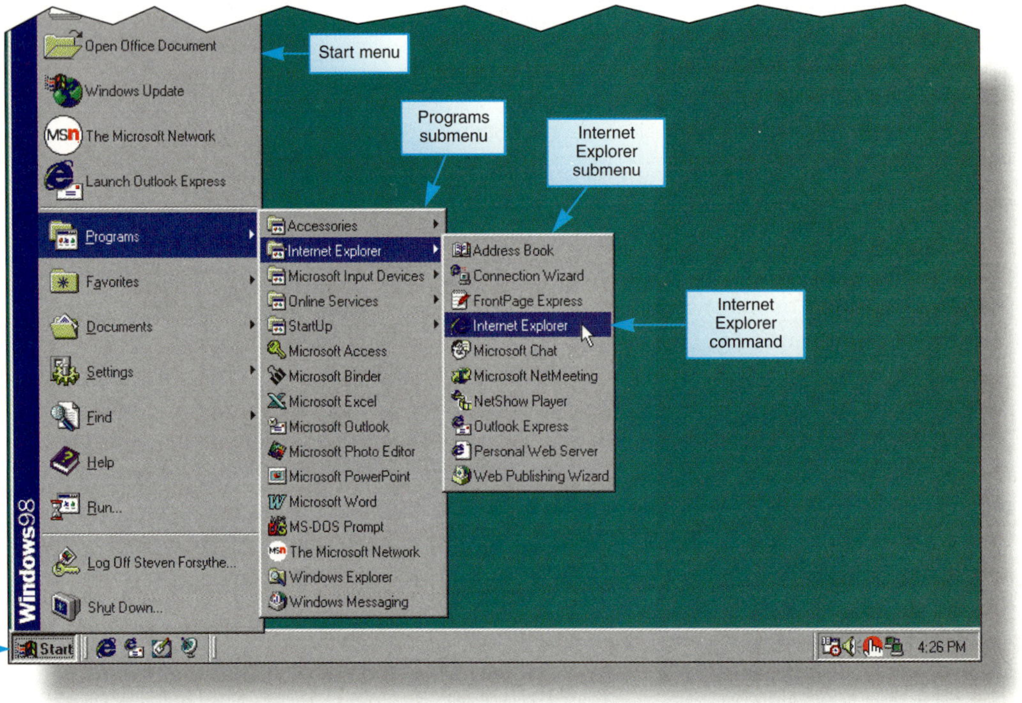

FIGURE 1-46

2 **Click Internet Explorer.**

Windows 98 launches the Internet Explorer program by opening the MSN.COM, Welcome Page – Microsoft Internet Explorer window on the desktop, displaying the Welcome to MSN.COM Web page in the window, and adding a recessed button to the taskbar button area (Figure 1-47). The URL for the Web page displays on the Address bar. Because Web pages are modified frequently, the Web page that displays on your desktop may be different from the Web page in Figure 1-47.

3 **Click the Close button in the Internet Explorer window.**

The Microsoft Internet Explorer window closes.

FIGURE 1-47

After you have launched Internet Explorer, you can use the program to search for and display different Web pages.

Launching an Application Using the Quick Launch Toolbar

The second method to launch an application is to use an icon on the Quick Launch toolbar. Currently, the Quick Launch toolbar contains four icons that allow you to launch Internet Explorer, launch Outlook Express, view an uncluttered desktop at any time, and view a list of channels (see Figure 1-48 on the next page). Perform the steps on the next page to launch the Internet Explorer program using the Launch Internet Explorer Browser icon on the Quick Launch toolbar.

WIN 1.42 • Project 1 • Fundamentals of Using Microsoft Windows 98

 To Launch a Program Using the Quick Launch Toolbar

1 Point to the Launch Internet Explorer Browser icon on the Quick Launch toolbar (Figure 1-48).

2 Click the Launch Internet Explorer Browser icon.

Windows 98 launches the Internet Explorer program as shown in Figure 1-47 on the previous page.

3 Click the Close button in the Internet Explorer window.

Windows 98 closes the Microsoft Internet Explorer window.

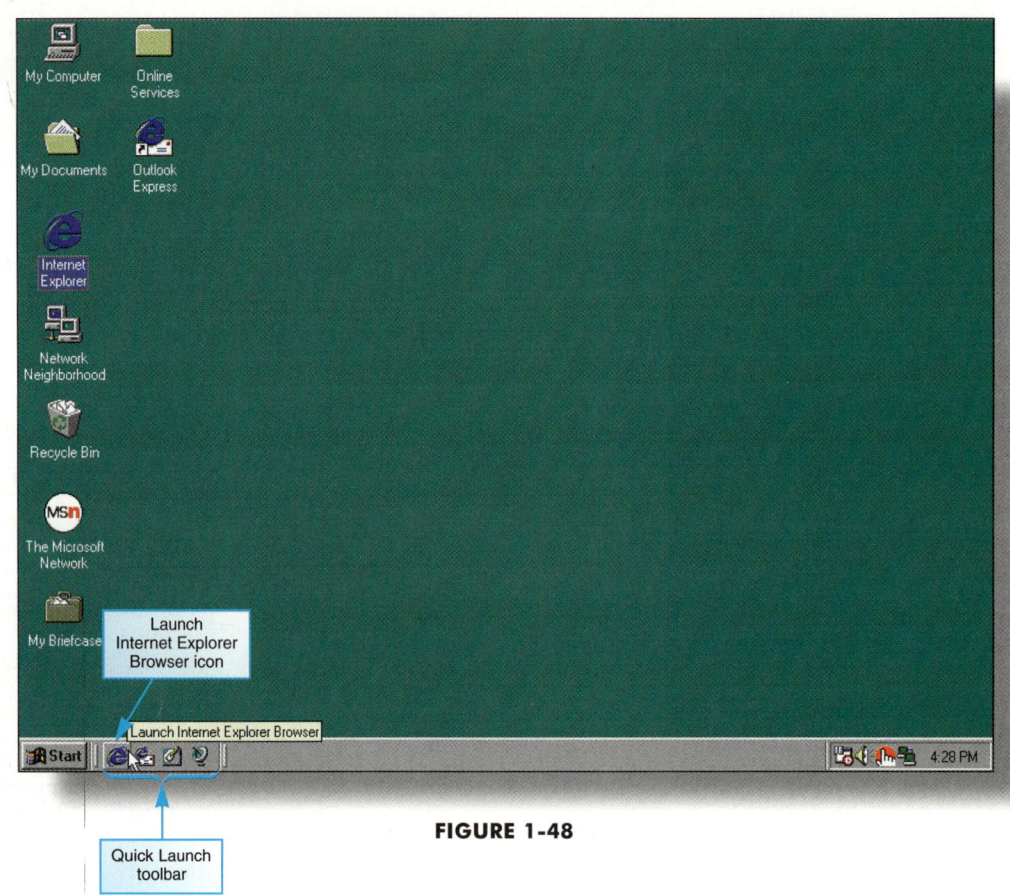

FIGURE 1-48

Launching an Application Using an Icon on the Desktop

The third method to launch an application is to use an icon on the desktop. Perform the following steps to launch the Internet Explorer program using the Internet Explorer icon on the desktop.

Steps To Launch a Program Using an Icon on the Desktop

1 Point to the Internet Explorer icon on the desktop (Figure 1-49).

2 Double-click the Internet Explorer icon.

Windows 98 launches the Internet Explorer program as shown in Figure 1-47 on page WIN 1.41.

3 Click the Close button in the Internet Explorer window.

The Microsoft Internet Explorer window closes.

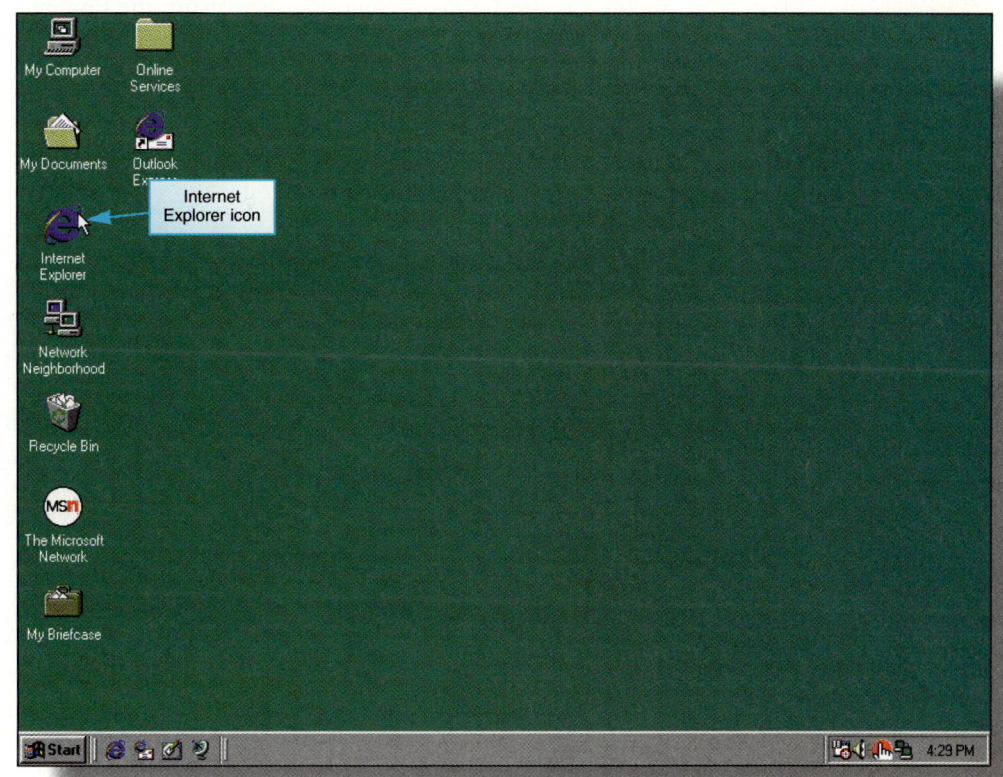

FIGURE 1-49

Windows 98 provides a number of ways in which to accomplish a particular task. Previously, three methods to launch the Internet Explorer program were illustrated. In the remainder of this book, a single set of steps will illustrate how to accomplish a task. Those steps may not be the only way in which the task can be completed. If you can perform the same task using other methods, the Other Ways box specifies the other methods. In each case, the method shown in the steps is the preferred method, but it is important for you to be aware of all the techniques you can use.

Using Windows Help

One of the more powerful application programs for use in Windows 98 is Windows Help. Windows Help is available when using Windows 98, or when using any application program running under Windows 98, to assist you in using Windows 98 and the various application programs. It contains answers to many questions you can ask with respect to Windows 98.

Other Ways

1. In open window, click button at right end of menu bar
2. Click Start button, click Run, type iexplore, click OK button

More About

Windows 98 Help

If you purchased an operating system or application program five years ago, you received at least one, and more often several, thick and heavy technical manuals that explained the software. With Windows 98, you receive a skinny manual less than 100 pages in length. The online Help feature of Windows 98 replaces reams and reams of printed pages in hard-to-understand technical manuals.

Contents Sheet

Windows Help provides a variety of ways in which to obtain information. One method to find a Help topic involves using the **Contents sheet** to browse through Help topics by category. To illustrate this method, you will use Windows Help to determine how to find a topic in Help. To launch Help, complete the following steps.

To Launch Windows Help

1 Click the Start button on the taskbar. Point to Help on the Start menu (Figure 1-50).

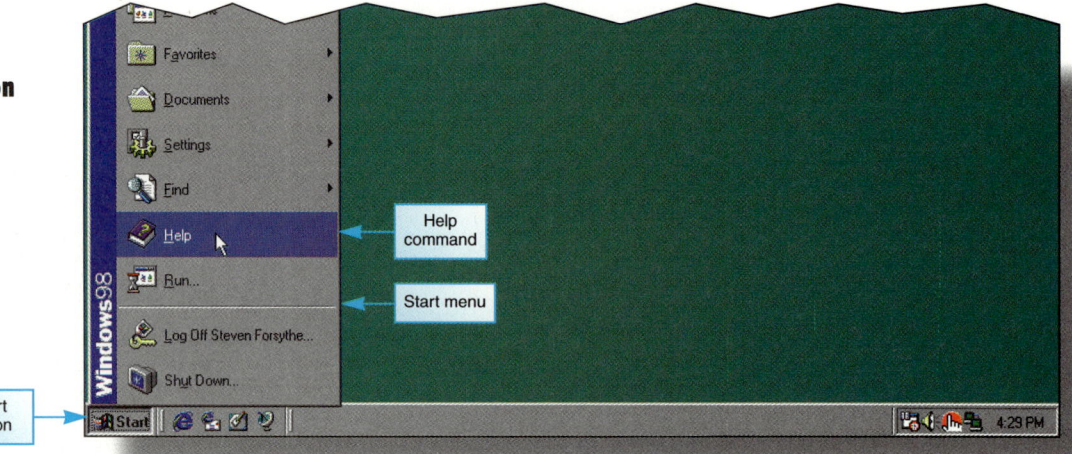

FIGURE 1-50

2 Click Help. Click the Maximize button on the Windows Help title bar. If the Contents sheet does not display, click the Contents tab.

The Windows Help window opens and maximizes (Figure 1-51). The window contains the Help toolbar and two frames. The left frame contains three **tabs** (Contents, Index, and Search). The Contents sheet is visible in the left frame. The right frame contains information about the Welcome to Help topic.

1. Press F1
2. Press WINDOWS+H (WINDOWS key on Microsoft Natural keyboard)

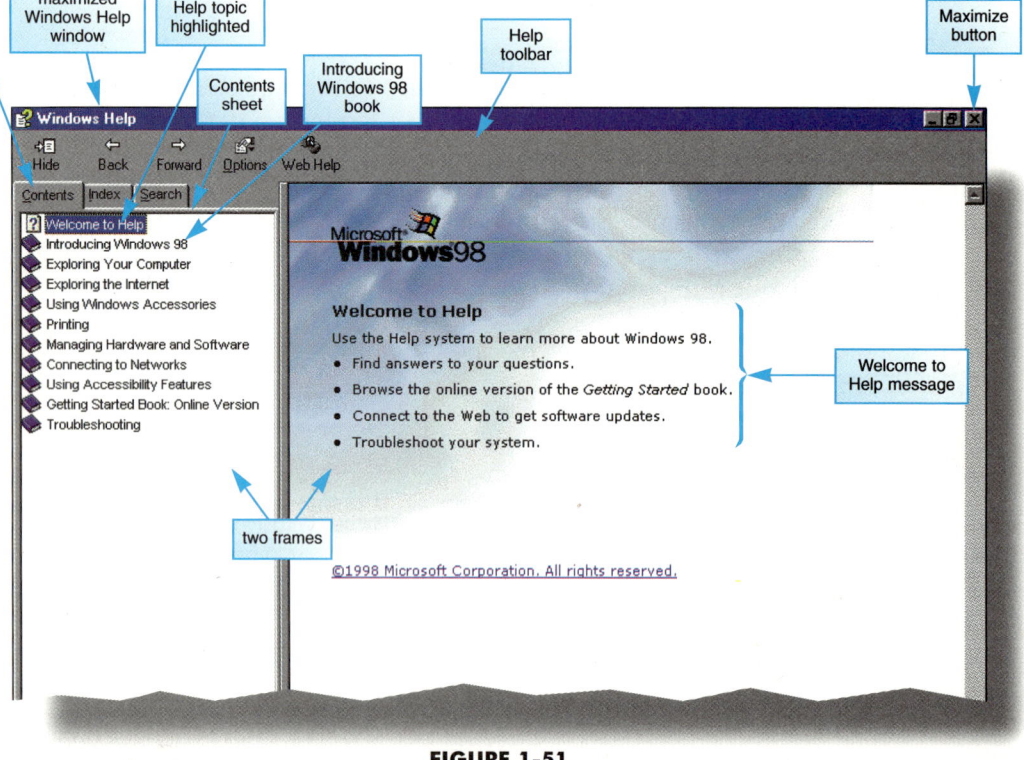

FIGURE 1-51

The Contents sheet contains a **Help topic** preceded by a question mark icon and followed by ten books. Each book consists of a closed book icon followed by a book name. The Help topic, Welcome to Help, is highlighted. In the left frame, the closed book icon indicates that Help topics or more books are contained in the book. The question mark icon indicates a Help topic without any further subdivisions. Clicking either the Index tab or the Search tab in the left frame opens the Index or Search sheet, respectively.

In addition to launching Help by using the Start button, you also can launch Help by pressing the F1 key.

After launching Help, the next step is to find the topic in which you are interested. To find the topic that describes how to find a topic in Help, complete the following steps.

To Use Help to Find a Topic in Help

1 **Point to the Introducing Windows 98 closed book icon.**

The mouse pointer changes to a hand when positioned on the icon and the Introducing Windows 98 book name displays in blue font and underlined (Figure 1-52).

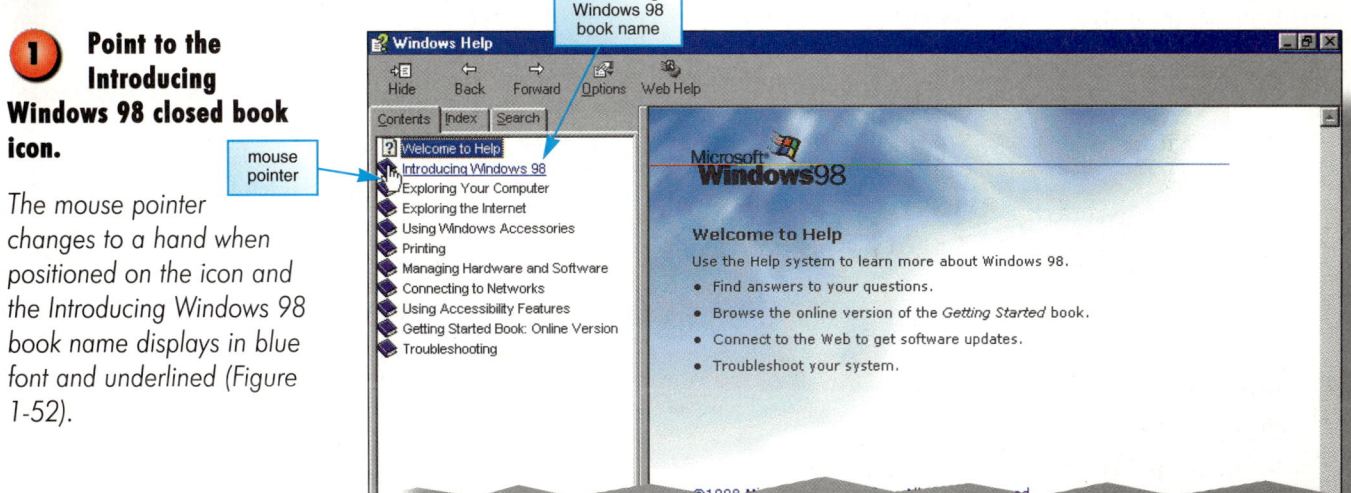

FIGURE 1-52

2 **Click the Introducing Windows 98 closed book icon and then point to the How to Use Help closed book icon.**

Windows 98 opens the Introducing Windows 98 book, changes the closed book icon to an open book icon, highlights the Introducing Windows 98 book name, underlines the How to Use Help book name, and displays the name and underline in blue font (Figure 1-53).

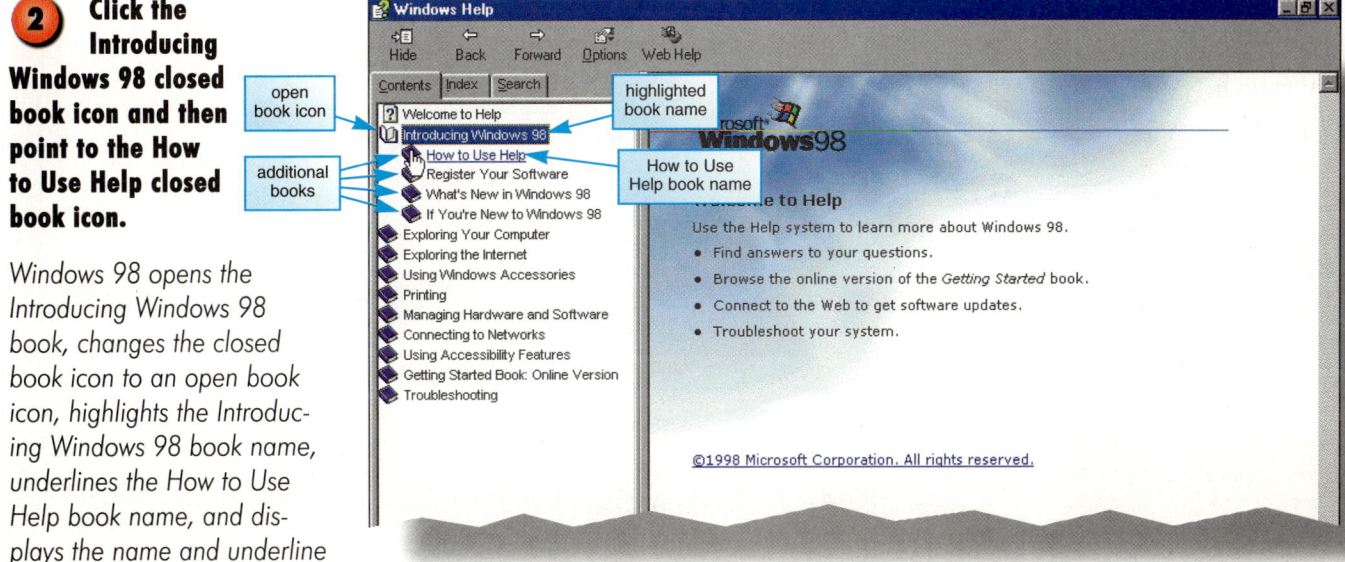

FIGURE 1-53

WIN 1.46 • Project 1 • Fundamentals of Using Microsoft Windows 98

3 **Click the How to Use Help closed book icon and then point to Find a topic in the opened How to Use Help book.**

Windows 98 opens the How to Use Help book and displays several Help topics in the book, changes the closed book icon to an open book icon, highlights the How to Use Help book name, underlines the Find a topic Help topic name, and displays the topic name and underline in blue font (Figure 1-54).

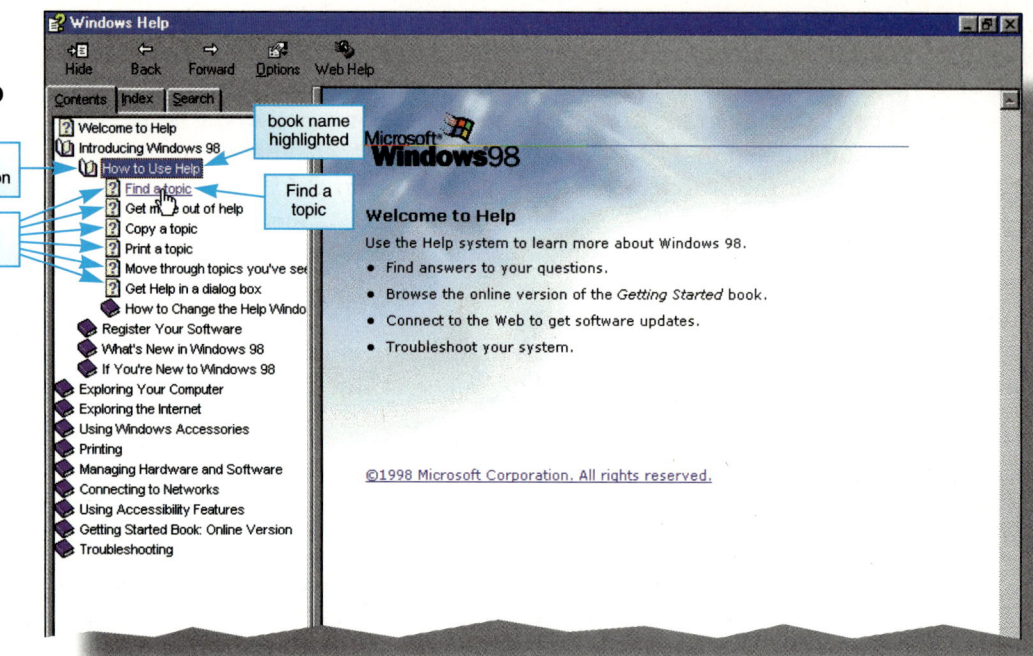

FIGURE 1-54

4 **Click Find a topic. Read the information about finding a Help topic in the right frame of the Windows Help window.**

Windows 98 highlights the Finding a topic Help topic and displays information about finding a Help topic in the right frame of the Windows Help window (Figure 1-55).

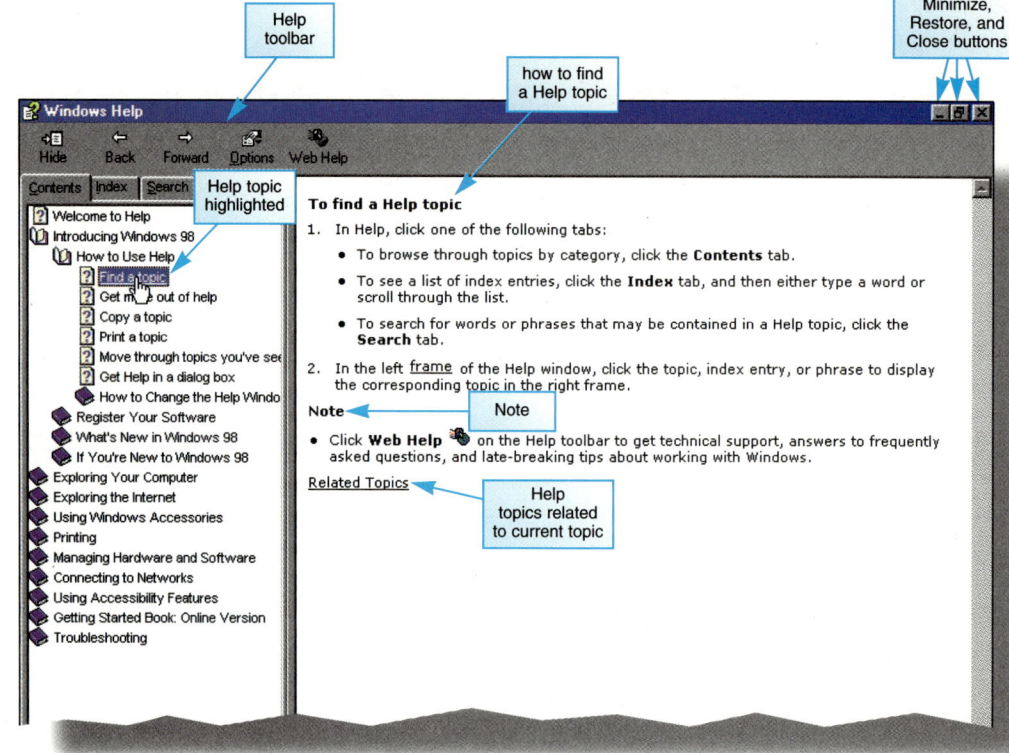

FIGURE 1-55

Other Ways

1. Press DOWN ARROW key until book or topic is highlighted, press ENTER, continue until Help topic displays, read Help topic

Using Windows Help • WIN 1.47

In Figure 1-55, if you click the **Hide button** on the Help toolbar, Windows 98 hides the tabs in the left frame and displays only the right frame in the Windows Help window. Clicking the **Back button** or **Forward button** displays a previously displayed Help topic in the right frame. Clicking the **Options button** allows you to hide or display the tabs in the left frame, display previously displayed Help topics in the right frame, stop the display of a Help topic, refresh the currently displayed Help topic, access Web Help, and print a Help topic. The **Web Help command** on the Options menu and the **Web Help button** on the Help toolbar allow you to use the Internet to obtain technical support, answers to frequently asked questions, and tips about working with Windows 98. Web Help will be explained in Project 2.

Notice also in Figure 1-55 that the Windows Help title bar contains a Minimize button, Restore button, and Close button. You can minimize or restore the Windows Help window as needed and also close the Windows Help window.

The Index Sheet

The Index sheet probably is the best source of information in Windows Help because you can enter the subject you are interested in. Sometimes, however, you will have to be creative to discover the index entry that answers your question because the most obvious entry will not always lead to your answer.

Index Sheet

A second method to find answers to your questions about Windows 98 or application programs running under Windows 98 is the Index sheet. The **Index sheet** lists a large number of index entries, each of which references one or more Help screens. To learn more about the Classic style, complete the following steps.

To Use the Help Index Sheet

1   **Click the Index tab. Type** classic style **(the flashing insertion point is positioned in the text box) in the text box. Point to the Display button at the bottom of the left frame.**

The Index sheet displays in the left frame and includes a list of entries that can be referenced (Figure 1-56). When you type an entry, the list automatically scrolls and the entry you type, such as classic style, is highlighted. To see additional entries, use the scroll bar at the right of the list. To highlight an entry in the list, click the entry.

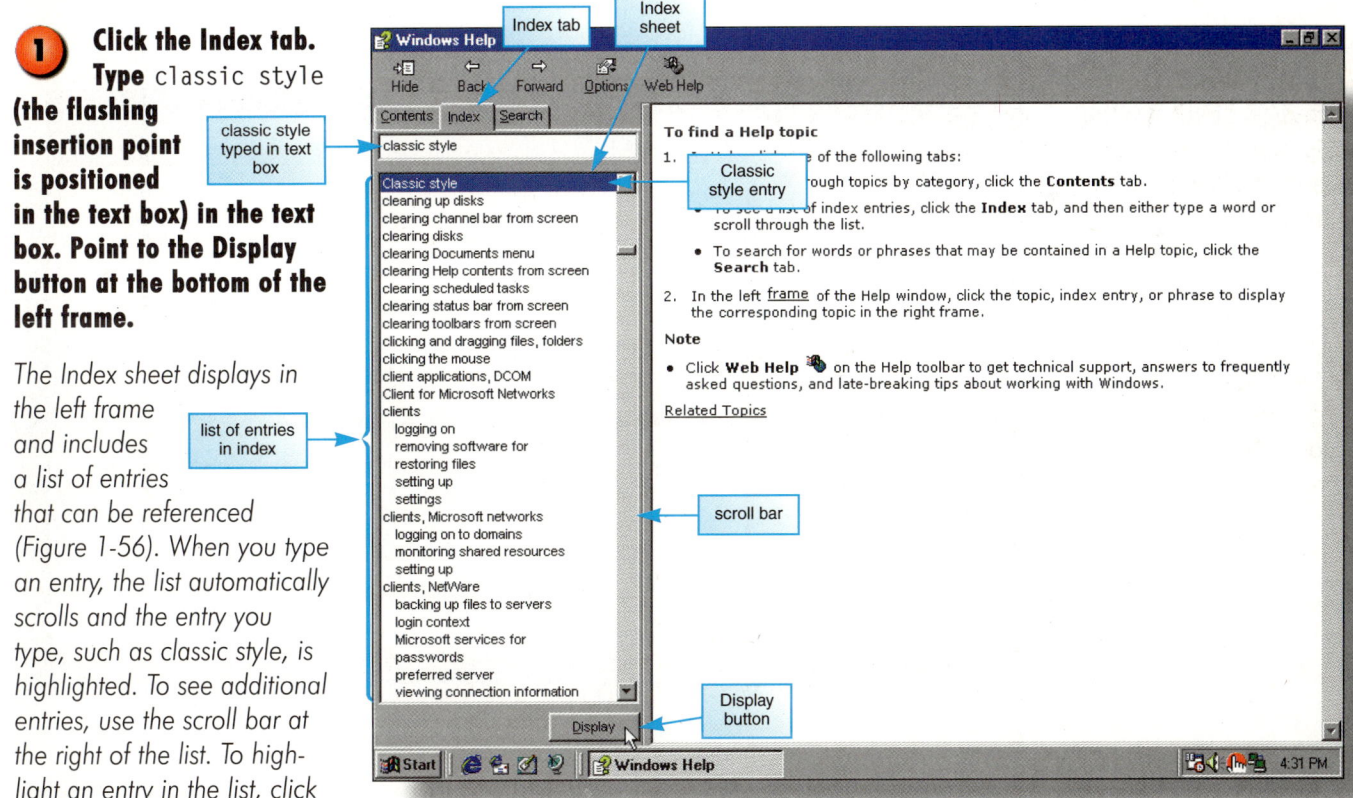

FIGURE 1-56

WIN 1.48 • Project 1 • Fundamentals of Using Microsoft Windows 98

2) Click the Display button in the Windows Help window. Point to the Display button in the Topics Found dialog box.

The Topics Found dialog box displays on top of the Windows Help window and two Help topics display in the dialog box (Figure 1-57). The first topic, choosing Web or Classic style for folders, is highlighted. This topic contains information about the Web and Classic styles.

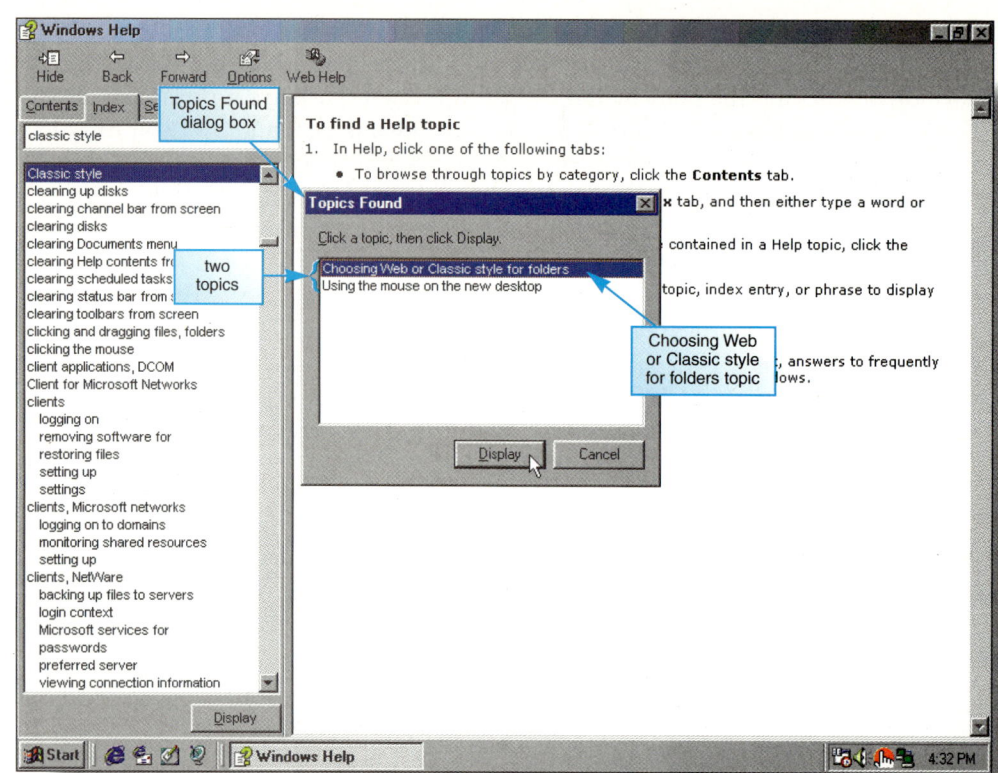

FIGURE 1-57

3) Click the Display button.

Information about the Web and Classic style, several hyperlinks, and one related topic displays in the right frame of the Windows Help window (Figure 1-58).

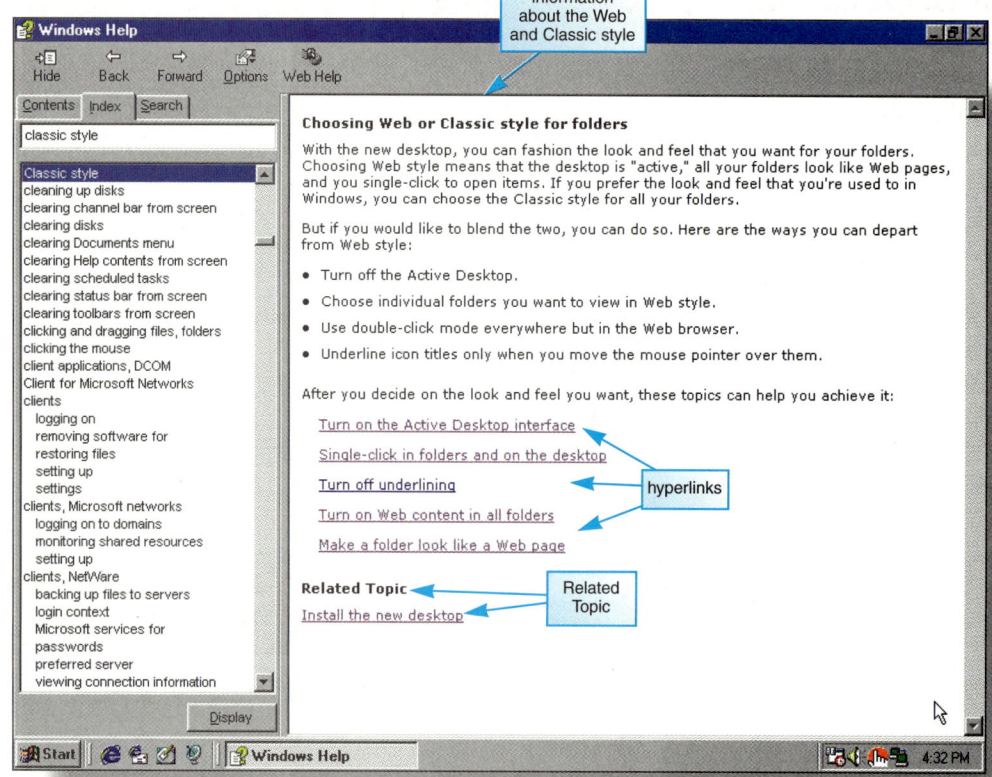

FIGURE 1-58

After viewing the index entries, normally you will close Windows Help. To close Windows Help, complete the following step.

TO CLOSE WINDOWS HELP

1. Click the Close button on the title bar of the Windows Help window.

Windows 98 closes the Windows Help window.

Shutting Down Windows 98

After completing your work with Windows 98, you may want to shut down Windows 98 using the **Shut Down command** on the Start menu. If you are sure you want to shut down Windows 98, perform the following steps. If you are not sure about shutting down Windows 98, read the following steps without actually performing them.

Shut Down Procedures

Some users of Windows 98 have turned off their computers without following the shut down procedure only to find data they thought they had stored on disk was lost. Because of the way Windows 98 writes data on the disk, it is important you shut down Windows properly so you do not lose your work.

 To Shut Down Windows 98

1. **Click the Start button on the taskbar and then point to Shut Down on the Start menu (Figure 1-59).**

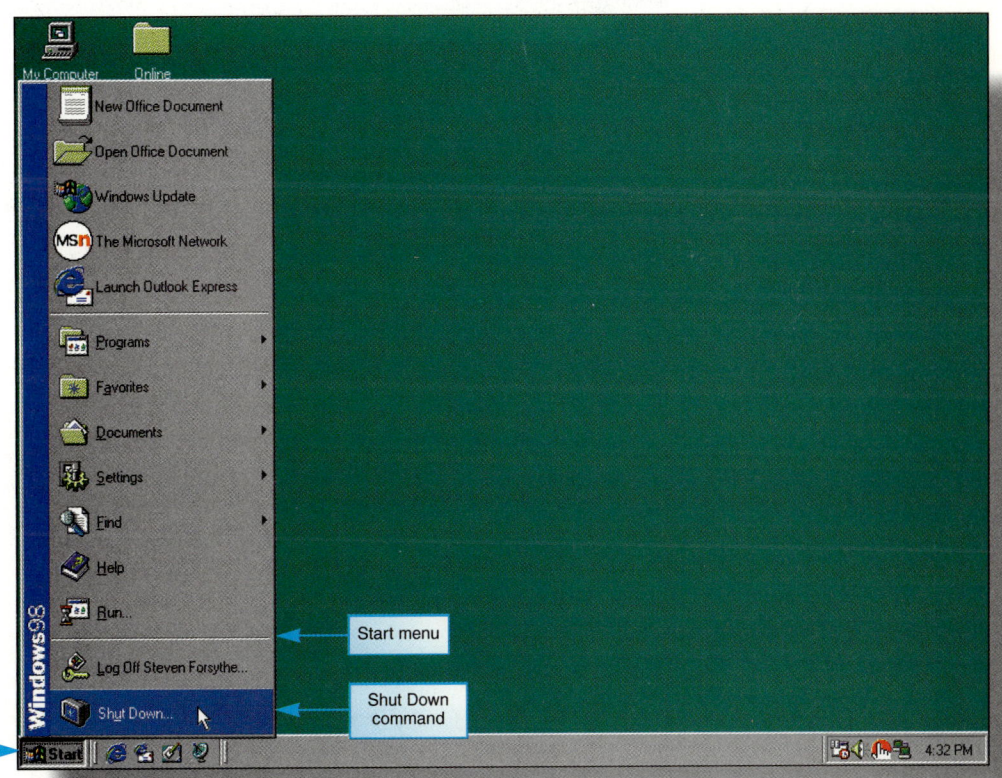

FIGURE 1-59

2 **Click Shut Down. Point to the OK button in the Shut Down Windows dialog box.**

The desktop darkens and the Shut Down Windows dialog box displays (Figure 1-60). A **dialog box** displays whenever Windows 98 needs to supply information to you or requires you to enter information or select among several options. The dialog box contains three option buttons. The selected option button, Shut down, indicates that clicking the OK button will shut down Windows 98.

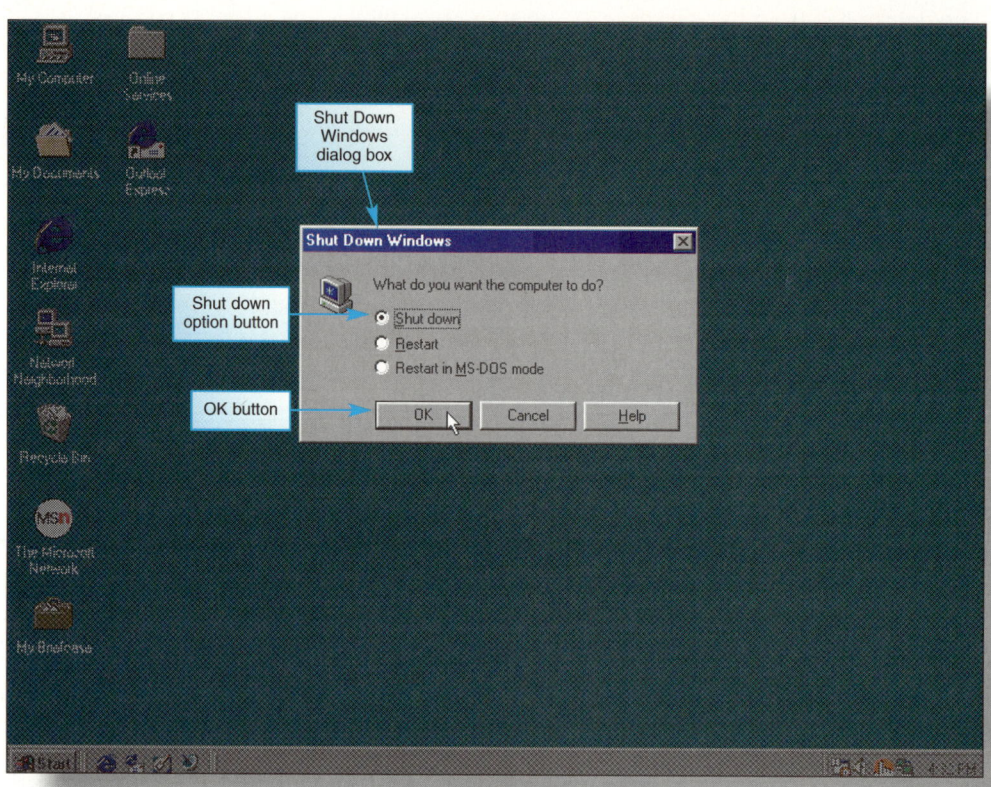

FIGURE 1-60

 **Click the OK button.**

Windows 98 is shut down.

Other Ways

1. Press CTRL+ESC, press U, Press UP ARROW or DOWN ARROW key to select Shut down option button, press ENTER
2. Press ALT+F4, press UP ARROW or DOWN ARROW key to select Shut down option button, press ENTER

Two screens display while Windows 98 is shutting down. The first screen containing the Windows logo, Windows 98 name, and the text, Windows is shutting down, displays momentarily while Windows 98 is being shut down. Then, a second screen containing the text, It's now safe to turn off your computer, displays. At this point you can turn off your computer. When shutting down Windows 98, you should never turn off your computer before these two screens display.

If you accidentally click Shut Down on the Start menu and you do not want to shut down Windows 98, click the Cancel button in the Shut Down Windows dialog box to return to normal Windows 98 operation.

Project Summary

Project 1 illustrated the Microsoft Windows 98 graphical user interface. You started Windows 98, learned the parts of the desktop, and learned to point, click, right-click, double-click, drag, and right-drag. You learned about the Internet World Wide Web, the three desktop views (Classic, Web, and Custom), and launched an application. Using both the Help Content and the Help Index sheets you obtained Help about Microsoft Windows 98. You shut down Windows 98 using the Shut Down command on the Start menu.

What You Should Know

Having completed this project, you now should be able to perform the following tasks:

- Close a Window *(WIN 1.32)*
- Close a Window and Reopen a Window *(WIN 1.23)*
- Close the Welcome Screen *(WIN 1.10)*
- Close Windows Help *(WIN 1.49)*
- Launch a Program Using an Icon on the Desktop *(WIN 1.43)*
- Launch a Program Using the Quick Launch Toolbar *(WIN 1.42)*
- Launch a Program Using the Start Menu *(WIN 1.40)*
- Launch Windows Help *(WIN 1.44)*
- Maximize and Restore a Window *(WIN 1.21)*
- Minimize and Redisplay a Window *(WIN 1.19)*
- Move an Object by Dragging *(WIN 1.25)*
- Open a Window by Double-Clicking *(WIN 1.17)*
- Point and Click *(WIN 1.12)*
- Resize a Window *(WIN 1.31)*
- Right-Click *(WIN 1.15)*
- Right-Drag *(WIN 1.32)*
- Scroll a Window by Dragging the Scroll Box *(WIN 1.31)*
- Scroll a Window Using Scroll Arrows *(WIN 1.27)*
- Scroll a Window Using the Scroll Bar *(WIN 1.29)*
- Shut Down Windows 98 *(WIN 1.49)*
- Size a Window by Dragging *(WIN 1.26)*
- Use Help to Find a Topic in Help *(WIN 1.45)*
- Use the Help Index Sheet *(WIN 1.47)*

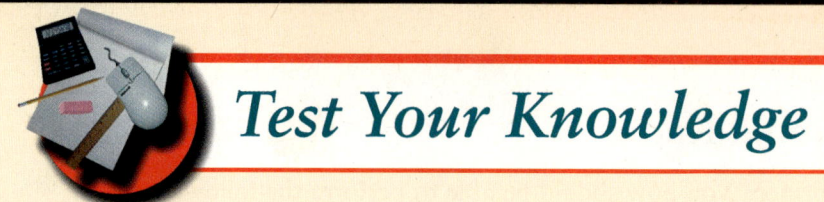

Test Your Knowledge

1 True/False

Instructions: Circle T if the statement is true or F if the statement is false.

T F 1. A user interface is a combination of computer hardware and computer software.
T F 2. The Quick Launch toolbar displays on the taskbar at the bottom of the desktop.
T F 3. Click means press the right mouse button.
T F 4. When you drag an object on the desktop, Windows 98 displays a shortcut menu.
T F 5. Double-clicking the My Computer icon on the desktop opens a window.
T F 6. You can maximize a window by dragging the title bar of the window.
T F 7. Viewing the desktop in Web style causes the desktop and the objects on the desktop to display and function as they did in Windows 95.
T F 8. One of the basic tasks you can perform using the Windows 98 operating system is to launch an application program.
T F 9. You can launch Windows Help by clicking the Start button and then clicking Help on the Start menu.
T F 10. To find an entry in the Windows Help Index, type the first few characters of the entry in the text box in the Contents sheet.

2 Multiple Choice

Instructions: Circle the correct response.

1. Through a user interface, the user is able to _____.
   a. control the computer
   b. request information from the computer
   c. respond to messages displayed by the computer
   d. all of the above
2. A shortcut menu opens when you _____ a(n) _____.
   a. right-click, object
   b. click, menu name on the menu bar
   c. click, submenu
   d. click, recessed button in the taskbar button area
3. In this book, a dark blue title bar and a recessed button in the taskbar button area indicate a window is _____.
   a. inactive
   b. minimized
   c. closed
   d. active

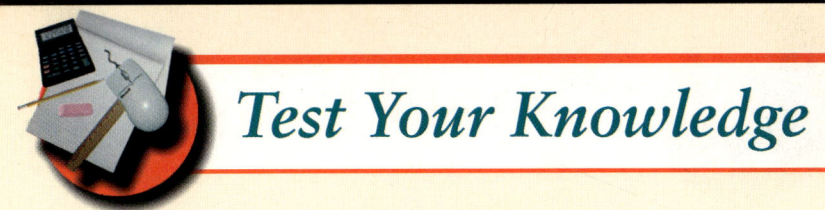

Test Your Knowledge

4. To view the contents of a window that are not currently visible in the window, use the _____.
   a. title bar
   b. scroll bar
   c. menu bar
   d. Restore button

5. _____ is holding down the right mouse button, moving an item to the desired location, and then releasing the right mouse button.
   a. Double-clicking
   b. Right-clicking
   c. Right-dragging
   d. Pointing

6. Text that is underlined in a browser window is called a(n) _____.
   a. uniform resource locator
   b. hyperlink or link
   c. hypertext document → is stored in files
   d. Web page

7. When the desktop is viewed in Web style, the icons on the desktop are _____ and the _____ Desktop displays.
   a. underlined, Active
   b. not underlined, Active
   c. underlined, Classic Windows
   d. not underlined, Classic Windows

8. Which method cannot be used to launch the Internet Explorer application?
   a. Click the Start button, point to Programs, point to Internet Explorer, and click Internet Explorer.
   b. Click the Launch Internet Explorer Browser icon on the Quick Launch toolbar.
   c. Click the Internet Explorer channel button on the Internet Explorer Channel bar.
   d. Click the Internet Explorer icon on the desktop.

9. For information about an index entry on the Index sheet of the Windows Help window, click the Help topic and _____.
   a. press the F1 key
   b. click the Forward button on the toolbar
   c. click the Search tab
   d. click the Display button

10. To shut down Windows 98, _____.
    a. click the Start button, click Shut Down, and click the OK button
    b. click File on the menu bar and then click Shut Down
    c. right-click the taskbar, click Shut down on the shortcut menu, and click the OK button
    d. press the F10 key and then click the OK button

WIN 1.54 • Project 1 • Fundamentals of Using Microsoft Windows 98

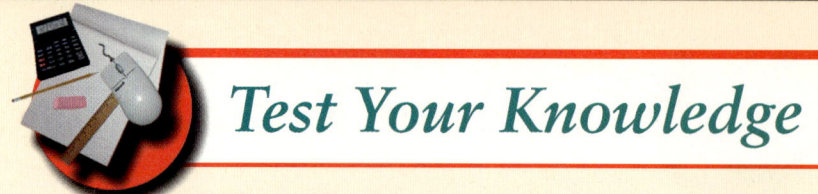

Test Your Knowledge

3 Identifying the Objects on the Desktop

Instructions: On the desktop shown in Figure 1-61, arrows point to several items or objects on the desktop. Identify the items or objects in the spaces provided.

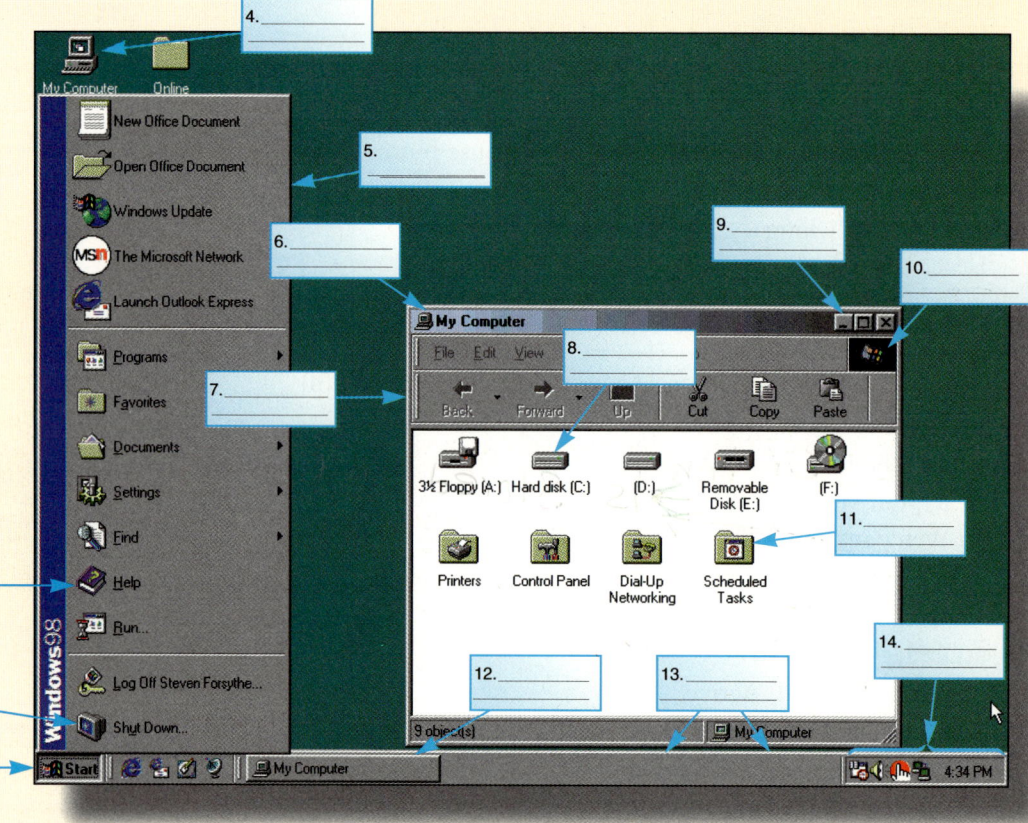

FIGURE 1-61

4 Launching the Internet Explorer Browser

Instructions: In the space provided, list the steps for the three methods used in this project to launch the Internet Explorer browser.

Method 1:

Step 1: _Start_

Step 2: _Program Shout down_

Step 3: _Internet Explorer_

Step 4: _Internet Explore_

Method 2:

Step 1: _____

Method 3:

Step 1: _____

Use Help • WIN 1.55

PROJECT 1

 Use Help

1 Using Windows Help

Instructions: Use Windows Help and a computer to perform the following tasks.

Part 1: *Using the Question Mark Button*

1. If necessary, start Microsoft Windows 98.
2. Click the Start button on the taskbar.
3. Point to Settings on the Start menu.
4. Click Folder Options on the Settings submenu.
5. Click the General tab in the Folder Options dialog box. A dialog box displays whenever Windows 98 needs to supply information to you or requires you to enter information or select among several options.
6. Click the question mark button on the title bar. The mouse pointer changes to a block arrow with question mark (Figure 1-62).
7. Click the preview monitor in the General sheet. A pop-up window displays explaining the contents of the preview monitor. Read the information in the pop-up window.
8. Click an open area of the General sheet to remove the pop-up window.
9. Click the question mark button on the title bar and then click the Web style option button. A pop-up window displays explaining what happens when you select this option. Read the information in the pop-up window.

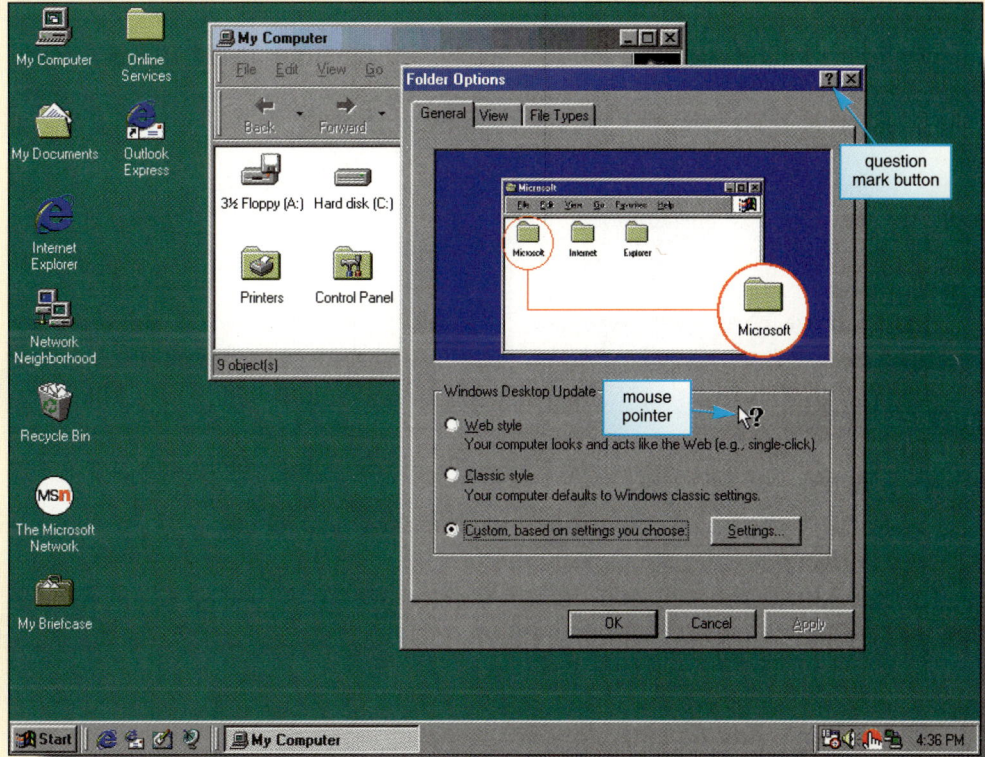

FIGURE 1-62

10. Click the question mark button on the title bar and then click the Classic style option button. A pop-up window displays explaining what happens when you select this option. Read the information in the pop-up window.
11. Click the question mark button on the title bar and then click the Custom style option button. A pop-up window displays explaining what happens when you select this option. Read the information in the pop-up window.
12. Click the question mark button on the title bar and then click the Settings button. A pop-up window displays explaining the function of the button. Read the information in the pop-up window.
13. Click an open area of the General sheet to remove the pop-up window.
14. Summarize the function of the question mark button. _____
15. Click the Close button in the Folder Options dialog box.

(continued)

Use Help

Using Windows Help (continued)

Part 2: *Finding What's New in Windows 98*

1. Click the Start button and then click Help on the Start menu.
2. Click the Maximize button on Windows Help title bar.
3. If the Contents sheet does not display, click the Contents tab. Click the Introducing Windows 98 closed book icon.
4. Click the What's New in Windows 98 closed book icon.
5. Click the True Web integration Help topic. Seven hyperlinks display in the right frame (Figure 1-63).

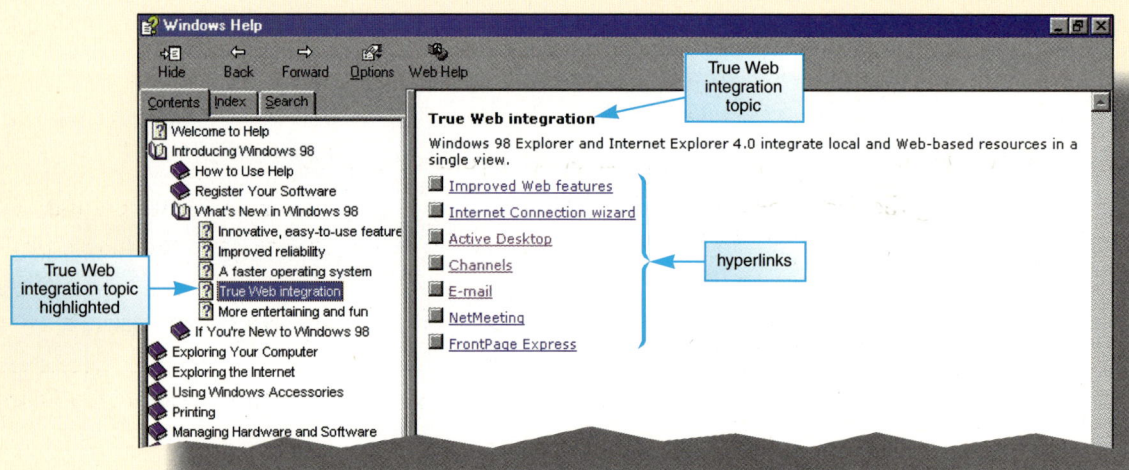

FIGURE 1-63

6. Click the Active Desktop hyperlink in the right frame and read the information about the Active Desktop.
7. Click the Channels hyperlink and read the information about channels.
8. Click the Options button on the Help toolbar to display the Options menu and then click Print.
9. Click the OK button in the Print dialog box to print the True Web integration screen.

Part 3: *Reading About the Online Getting Started Manual*

1. Click the Getting Started Book: Online Version closed book icon in the left frame.
2. Click the Microsoft Windows 98 Getting Started Book Help topic. Read the information Windows 98 displays about the Getting Started Book in the right frame. The *Getting Started Book* is the printed manual for Windows 98.
3. Click the Click here hyperlink in the right frame to open the Getting Started window.
4. If the Contents sheet does not display, click the Contents tab. Click the Introducing Getting Started closed book icon. Click and read each of the four Help topics that display.
5. Click the Welcome closed book icon. Three Help topics and two closed book icons display in the open book. Click and read the Overview, Windows 98 at a Glance, and If You're New to Windows topics.

Use Help

6. Click the Where to Find Information closed book icon.
7. Click the Resources Included with Windows 98 closed book icon. Click and read the Overview topic.
8. Click the Online Tutorial: Discover Windows 98 topic. Read the information about the topic.
9. Click the Troubleshooters topic. Read the information about the topic.
10. Click the Back button on the Help toolbar to display the previous screen (Online Tutorial: Discover Windows 98) in the right frame.
11. Click the Options button on the Help toolbar, click Print, and click the OK button to print the Help topic.
12. Click the Close button in the Getting Started window.
13. Click the Close button in the Windows Help window.

2 Using Windows Help to Obtain Help

Instructions: Use Windows Help and a computer to perform the following tasks.

1. Find Help about viewing the Welcome to Windows 98 screen that displays when you launch Windows 98. Use the search word, welcome, and the Index sheet. Answer the following questions in the spaces provided.
    a. How can you open the Welcome to Windows 98 screen? _____
    b. Open the Welcome to Windows 98 screen. How many entries does the Contents menu contain? _____
    c. Point to Discover Windows 98 on the Contents menu. What are the three choices available in Discover Windows 98? _____
    d. Point to Maintain Your Computer on the Contents menu. How can using Maintain Your Computer benefit your computer? _____
    e. Close the Welcome to Windows 98 screen.
2. Find Help about keyboard shortcuts by looking in the Exploring Your Computer book. Answer the following questions in the spaces provided.
    a. What keyboard shortcut is used to close the current window or quit a program? _____
    b. What keyboard shortcut is used to display the Start menu? _____
    c. What keyboard shortcut is used to display the shortcut menu for a selected item? _____
    d. What keyboard shortcut is used to rename an item? _____
    e. What keyboard shortcut is used to view an item's properties? _____
3. Find Help about changing the Windows Help window by looking in the Introducing Windows 98 book. Answer the following questions in the spaces provided.
    a. How do you hide the Contents, Index, and Search tabs? _____
    b. How do you make the left frame larger? _____
    c. Which software application do you use to change the color or fonts in the Help window? _____

(continued)

Use Help

Using Windows Help to Obtain Help *(continued)*

4. Find Help about the desktop by looking in the Windows Desktop book in the Exploring Your Computer book. Answer the following questions in the spaces provided.
   a. What does the Active Desktop allow you to do? _____
   b. What does the Address toolbar enable you do? _____
   c. What commands do you use to find a person on the Internet? _____

5. Find Help about what to do if you have a problem in Windows 98. The process of solving such a problem is called _____. Answer the following questions in the spaces provided.
   a. What should you check if only part of a document prints on your printer?
      _____
   b. What could the problem be if Windows 98 does not detect that you have a modem connected to your computer?" _____
   c. What could the problem be if the computer restarts each time a sound is played?
      _____

6. Using the Index sheet in the Windows Help window, answer the following questions in the space provided.
   a. How do you get Help in a dialog box? _____
   b. What dialog box do you use to change the appearance of the mouse pointer?
      _____
   c. How do you minimize all open windows? _____
   d. How do you hide the Internet Explorer Channel bar? _____

7. Obtain information on software licensing by answering the following questions. Find and then print information from Windows Help that supports your answers.
   a. How does the law protect computer software? _____
   b. What is software piracy? _____ Why should I be concerned about it?
      _____
   c. What is an EULA (end user licensing agreement)?
   d. Can you use your own software on both your desktop and your laptop computers?
      _____
   e. How can you identify illegal software? _____

8. Your best friend just bought a new computer. Among the software packages she obtained when she received the computer was a NHL hockey game from Microsoft. She has no interest in hockey but she knows you are an avid hockey fan. Answer the following questions and then print the information supporting your answers from Windows Help. Can she legally give this software to you? _____
Can she legally sell this software to you to help recover some of her costs? _____
Can she give you the software and still keep the hockey game on her computer for use by another member of her family? _____

9. Close all open windows.

In the Lab • WIN 1.59

PROJECT 1

In the Lab

1 Improving Your Mouse Skills

Instructions: Use a computer to perform the following tasks:

1. Start Microsoft Windows 98 if necessary.
2. Click the Start button on the taskbar, point to Programs on the Start menu, point to Accessories on the Programs submenu, point to Games on the Accessories submenu, and click Solitaire on the Games submenu.
3. Click the Maximize button in the Solitaire window (Figure 1-64).

FIGURE 1-64

4. Click Help on the Solitaire menu bar and then click Help Topics.
5. If the Contents sheet does not display, click the Contents tab.
6. Review the Playing Solitaire and Choosing a scoring system topics in the Contents sheet.
7. After reviewing the Help topics, close all Help windows.
8. Play the game of Solitaire.
9. Click the Close button on the Solitaire title bar to close the game.

2 Using the Discover Windows 98 Tutorial

Instructions: To use the Discover Windows 98 tutorial you will need a copy of the Windows 98 CD-ROM. If this CD-ROM is not available, skip this lab assignment. Otherwise, use a computer and the CD-ROM to perform the following tasks:

1. Start Microsoft Windows 98 if necessary.
2. Insert the Windows 98 CD-ROM in your CD-ROM drive. If the Windows 98 CD-ROM window displays, click the Close button in the window to close the window.
3. Click the Start button on the taskbar, point to Programs on the Start menu, point to Accessories on the Programs submenu, point to System Tools on the Accessories submenu, and click Welcome to Windows on the System Tools submenu.
4. Click Discover Windows 98 in the Welcome to Windows 98 window to display the Discover Windows 98 Contents.

(continued)

In the Lab

Using the Discover Windows 98 Tutorial *(continued)*

5. Click the Computer Essentials title (hyperlink) in the right panel of the Discover Windows 98 Contents screen (Figure 1-65).

   The Computer Essentials tutorial starts and fills the desktop. The left panel contains a list of lessons. A left arrow to the right of a lesson indicates the current lesson.

FIGURE 1-65

   Pressing the RIGHT ARROW key on the keyboard displays the next screen in the lesson. Pressing the UP ARROW key quits the Computer Essentials tutorial. Clicking the Contents button displays the Table of Contents in the Discover Windows 98 Contents screen.

6. Press the RIGHT ARROW key to begin the Introduction.
7. When appropriate, press the number 1 key to begin the Meeting Your Computer section. Complete this lesson. This lesson takes approximately ten minutes.
8. Click the Contents button to display the Discover Windows 98 Contents screen.
9. If you have experience using Windows 3.0 or Windows 3.1 and are learning to use Windows 98, click the Windows 98 Overview title. Otherwise, go to Step 10. This lesson takes approximately ten minutes.
10. If you have experience using Windows 95 and are learning to use Windows 98, click the What's New title. Otherwise, go to Step 11. Press any key on the keyboard to begin the lesson. Features are organized into five groups. Click each feature (hyperlink) in each group to view a demonstration. When finished, click the Exit button. This lesson takes approximately twenty minutes.
11. If time permits, click the More Windows 98 Resources title. Click the Microsoft Windows 98 Starts Here title (1) and then click the Microsoft Press title (2) to view additional information about Windows 98. Click each the three hyperlinks below the Resources title to explore three Windows-related Web sites. When finished, click the Close button in the Microsoft Internet Explorer window and click the Contents button.
12. Click the Close button in the Discover Windows 98 Contents screen.
13. Click the Yes button in the Discover Windows 98 dialog box.
14. Click the Close button in the Welcome to Windows 98 window.
15. Remove the Windows 98 CD-ROM from your CD-ROM drive.

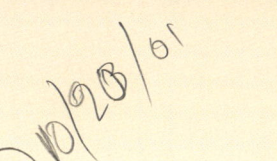 

In the Lab

3 Launching and Using the Internet Explorer Application

Instructions: Perform the following steps to launch the Internet Explorer application.

Part 1: *Launching the Internet Explorer Application*

1. Start Microsoft Windows 98 and, if necessary, connect to the Internet.
2. Click the Internet Explorer icon on the Quick Launch toolbar.
3. If the Address bar does not display below the Standard Buttons toolbar in the Microsoft Internet Explorer window, click View on the menu bar, point to Toolbars, and click Address Bar on the Toolbars submenu.

Part 2: *Entering a URL in the Address Bar*

1. Click the URL in the Address bar to highlight the URL.
2. Type http://www.microsoft.com in the Address bar and press the ENTER key.
3. What URL displays in the Address bar? _____ What window title displays in the title bar? _____
4. Scroll the Web page to view the contents of the Web page. List two topics that are shown on this Web page. _____ List five hyperlinks (underlined text) that are shown on this Web page. _____
5. Click any hyperlink on the Web page. What hyperlink did you click? _____
6. Describe the Web page that displayed when you clicked the hyperlink? _____
7. Click the Print button on the Standard Buttons toolbar to print the Web page.

Part 3: *Entering a URL in the Address Bar*

1. Click the URL in the Address bar to highlight the URL.
2. Type http://www.disney.com in the Address bar and press the ENTER key.
3. What window title displays in the title bar? _____
4. Scroll the Web page to view the contents of the Web page. Do any graphic images display on the Web page? _____ If so, describe two images. _____
5. Pointing to an image on a Web page and having the mouse pointer change to a hand indicates the image is a hyperlink. Does the Web page include an image that is a hyperlink? _____ If so, describe the image. _____
6. Click the hyperlink to display another Web page. What window title displays in the title bar? _____
7. Click the Print button on the Standard Buttons toolbar to print the Web page.

Part 4: *Displaying Previously Displayed Web Pages*

1. Click the Back button on the Standard Buttons toolbar. What Web page displays? _____
2. Click the Back button on the Standard Buttons toolbar twice. What Web page displays? _____
3. Click the Forward button on the Standard Buttons toolbar bar. What Web page displays? _____

Part 5: *Entering a URL in the Address Bar*

1. Click the URL in the Address bar to highlight the URL.
2. Type http://www.scsite.com/WIN98/ in the Address bar and press the ENTER key.
3. Click the Steve's Cool Sites hyperlink on the Web page.
4. Click any hyperlinks that are of interest to you. Which hyperlink did you like the best? _____
5. Use the Back or Forward button to display the Web site you like the best.
6. Click the Print button on the Standard Buttons toolbar to print the Web page.
7. Click the Close button on the Microsoft Internet Explorer title bar.

In the Lab

4 Launching an Application

Instructions:
Perform the following steps to launch the Notepad application using the Start menu, and create the daily reminders list shown in Figure 1-66. **Notepad** is a popular application program available with Windows 98 that allows you to create, save, and print simple text documents.

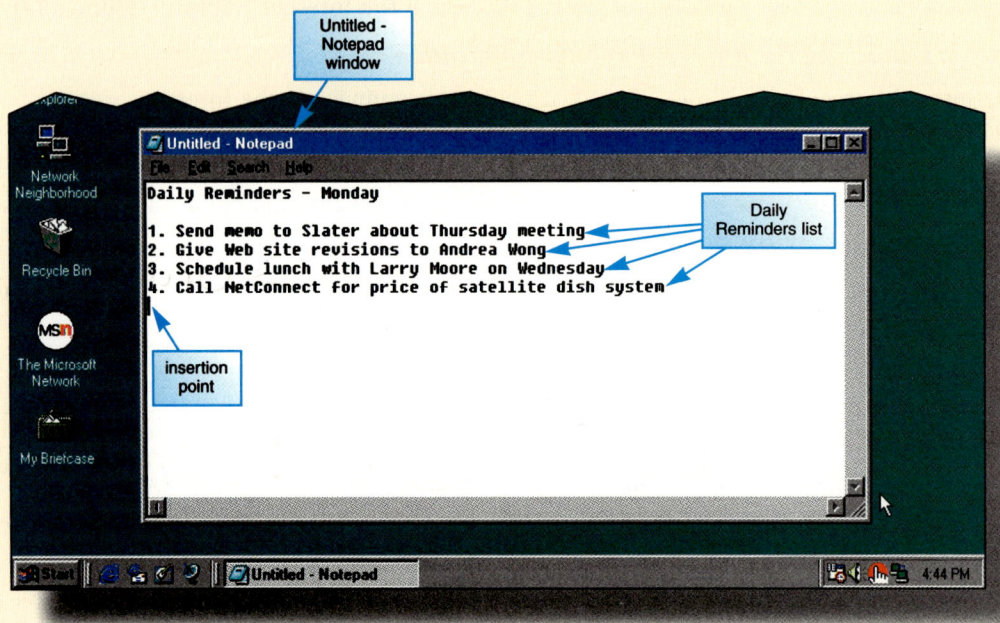

FIGURE 1-66

Part 1: *Launching the Notepad Application*

1. Start Microsoft Windows 98 if necessary.
2. Click the Start button.
3. Point to Programs on the Start menu, point to Accessories on the Programs submenu, and click Notepad on the Accessories submenu. The Untitled - Notepad window displays and an insertion point (flashing vertical line) displays in the blank area below the menu bar.

Part 2: *Creating a Document Using Notepad*

1. Type `Daily Reminders - Monday` and press the ENTER key twice.
2. Type `1. Send memo to Slater about Thursday meeting` and press the ENTER key.
3. Type `2. Give Web site revisions to Andrea Wong` and press the ENTER key.
4. Type `3. Schedule lunch with Larry Moore on Wednesday` and press the ENTER key.
5. Type `4. Call NetConnect about prices for satellite dish system` and press the ENTER key.

Part 3: *Printing the Daily Reminders Document*

1. Click File on the menu bar and then click Print.
2. Retrieve the printed Daily Reminders list from the printer.

Part 4: *Closing the Notepad Window*

1. Click the Close button on the Notepad title bar.
2. Click the No button in the Notepad dialog box to not save the Daily Reminders document.

Cases and Places

The difficulty of these case studies varies:
▶ are the least difficult; ▶▶ are more difficult; and ▶▶▶ are the most difficult.

1 ▶ Using Windows Help, locate the Getting Started Online Manual. Using the Online Manual read about the following ten topics: Connecting to a Network, Customizing Your Desktop, Emergency Startup Disk, FAT32 File, System Explorer Bars, Microsoft NetMeeting, My Documents Folder, OnNow Power Management, TDD Service, and Watching TV. Select five of the ten topics. In a brief report, summarize the five topics you have selected.

2 ▶ Technical support is an important consideration when installing and using an operating system or an application software program. The ability to obtain a valid answer to your question at the moment you have the question can be the difference between a frustrating experience and a positive experience. Using Windows 98 Help, the Internet, or another research facility, write a brief report on the options that are available for obtaining help and technical support while using Windows 98.

3 ▶ Early personal computer operating systems were adequate, but they were not user-friendly and had few advanced features. Over the past several years, however, personal computer operating systems have become increasingly easy to use, and some now offer features once available only on mainframe computers. Using the Internet, a library, or other research facility, write a brief report on two personal computer operating systems. Describe the systems, pointing out their similarities and differences. Discuss the advantages and disadvantages of each. Finally, tell which operating system you would purchase for your personal computer and explain why.

4 ▶▶ Microsoft's decision to make the Internet Explorer 4 Web browser part of the Windows 98 operating system caused many legal problems for Microsoft. Using the Internet, computer magazines and newspapers, or other resources, prepare a brief report on these legal problems. Explain the arguments for and against combining the browser and operating system. Identify the key players on both sides of the legal battle and summarize the final decision. Did the legal process or final decision affect the release date and contents of Windows 98? Do you think computer users benefited from this decision? Explain your answers.

5 ▶▶▶ Software must be compatible with (capable of working with) the operating system of the computer on which it will be used. Visit a software vendor and find the five application packages (word processing, spreadsheet, games, and so on) you would most like to have. List the names of the packages and the operating system used by each. Make a second list of five similar packages that are compatible (meaning they use the same operating system). Using your two lists, write a brief report on how the need to purchase compatible software can affect buying application packages, and even the choice of an operating system.

Cases and Places

6 ▶▶▶ Because of the many important tasks an operating system performs, most businesses put a great deal of thought into choosing an operating system for their personal computers. Interview a person at a local business on the operating system it uses with its personal computers. Based on your interview, write a brief report on why the business chose that operating system, how satisfied it is with it, and under what circumstances it might consider switching to a different operating system.

7 ▶▶▶ In addition to Windows 98, Microsoft also sells the Windows NT operating system. Some say Windows NT will replace Windows 98 in the future. Using the Internet, computer magazines, or other resources, prepare a brief report comparing and contrasting the operating systems. How do their graphical user interfaces compare? What features and commands are shared by both operating systems? Does either operating system have features or commands that the other operating system does not have? Explain whether you think Windows NT could replace Windows 98.

Microsoft Windows 98

PROJECT 2

Working on the Windows 98 Desktop

OBJECTIVES

You will have mastered the material in this project when you can:

- Launch an application, create a text document, and save the document on the desktop
- Create, name, and save a text document on the desktop
- Open and modify a document on the desktop
- Create a folder on the desktop
- Move documents to a folder on the desktop
- Display the contents of a folder
- Modify and print documents in a folder
- Open and modify multiple documents
- Copy a folder from the desktop onto a floppy disk
- Open a folder stored on a floppy disk
- Add and delete shortcuts on the Start menu
- Create and delete shortcuts on the desktop
- Open a document using a shortcut
- Delete shortcut icons and document icons from the desktop
- Turn on and turn off the Active Desktop
- Describe Active Web content and subscriptions
- Add and remove a desktop item from the desktop
- Use Windows Support Online

Microsoft **Windows 98**

Doing Windows

Graphical Computing Clicks with Users

"Doing Windows" has an entirely new meaning since Bill Gates announced plans to add graphical capabilities to the IBM personal computer in 1983. The Microsoft CEO decided to take this step to help current personal computer users work more effectively and entice others to buy systems.

Up until this time, users were typing cumbersome disk operating system (DOS) commands to run their computers. When IBM decided to design a personal computer in 1980, corporate executives approached Gates to develop its new operating system. Gates declined the offer and suggested that IBM contact Gary Kildall at Digital Research, a leading microcomputer software developer. Kildall had

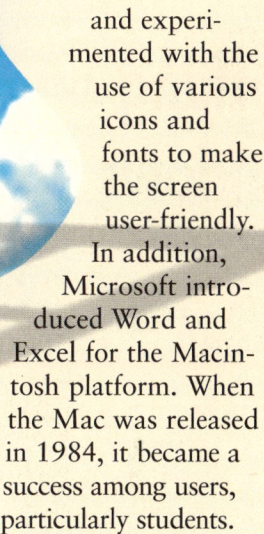

developed a widely used operating system called CP/M.

Kildall, however, decided not to attend the meeting at IBM headquarters. The frustrated IBM executives contacted Gates once again, and this time he reconsidered, even though he knew very little about operating systems. By chance, a neighboring company in Washington named Seattle Computer Products was developing an operating system it called QDOS (QDOS was an acronym for Quick and Dirty Operating System). Bill Gates made a proposal to the company, and in December 1980, Microsoft obtained nonexclusive rights to QDOS. Later, Microsoft acquired all rights for a total purchase price of $1 million, and renamed the system MS-DOS (an acronym for Microsoft Disk Operating System).

Microsoft modified the program, and then shipped it in the first IBM personal computer, the IBM PC, unveiled in August 1981. The sale of millions of IBM PCs and consequently millions of copies of the operating system, propelled Microsoft to the world's largest software company.

Gates's graphical intentions were fueled by work being done at Xerox's Palo Alto Research Center in California. He saw researchers there using an invention they called a mouse to move a pointer instead of using arrow keys on the keyboard to move a cursor.

Then, working with Apple, Microsoft developed software for the Macintosh computer. Combining its original innovations with those of Xerox, Microsoft created the graphical user interface and experimented with the use of various icons and fonts to make the screen user-friendly. In addition, Microsoft introduced Word and Excel for the Macintosh platform. When the Mac was released in 1984, it became a success among users, particularly students.

Microsoft's next step was to develop these applications for the IBM PC and IBM-compatible computers. The company's innovations resulted in the release of Windows 3.1 and Windows 95 prior to Windows 98. Currently more than 100 million computers worldwide use the Windows operating system.

Programmers at Microsoft use a process the corporation calls *continuous reinvention* to constantly add new features to enhance Windows performance. Microsoft also allows anyone to write programs for the Windows platform without requiring prior permission. Indeed, today many of the thousands of Windows-based programs compete with Microsoft's own programs.

Gates predicts his company will continue to release new Windows versions every two or three years. He is convinced that individuals will want to take advantage of user interface enhancements and innovations that make computing easier, more reliable, faster, and integrated with the Internet.

Working on the Windows 98 desktop in this project, you will find out for yourself how these features can help you launch an application, create folders and documents, use shortcuts, and access Windows Support Online.

Microsoft Windows 98

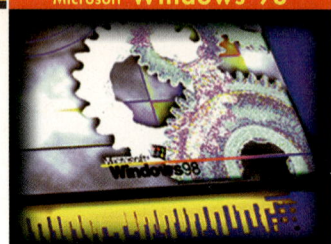

Working on the Windows 98 Desktop

PROJECT 2

CASE PERSPECTIVE

As you work with Windows 98, you will find one of its major features is the ease with which you can access documents and files you use constantly. You also will find that working with multiple documents at the same time is vital to working efficiently. The company where you work has placed you in charge of developing the text documents to keep track of the daily appointments. As you begin the assignment, you ascertain that daily appointments seem to change constantly. If you could work on the Windows 98 desktop, you would save a great deal of time. In this project, you will learn the skills that are essential to your success and gain the knowledge required to work efficiently on the Windows 98 desktop.

Introduction

In Project 1, you learned three methods to launch the Internet Explorer application. To launch Internet Explorer, you used the Start button and Start menu, an icon on the Quick Launch toolbar, and a shortcut icon on the desktop. The ability to accomplish a task, such as launching an application, in a variety of ways is one of Windows 98's most powerful features.

In Project 2, you will learn two methods to create documents on the desktop and discover the intuitive nature of the Windows 98 desktop by creating a folder on the desktop in which to store multiple documents, storing documents in the folder, and moving the folder from the desktop onto a disk. In addition, you will turn on the Active Desktop and add an Active Desktop item to the desktop. An **Active Desktop item** allows you to display the constantly changing content of a Web page directly on the Active Desktop and automatically update the content.

Assume each morning you create two daily appointments lists; one list for Mr. Lopez and a second list for Ms. Parks. Mr. Lopez and Ms. Parks use the lists to remind them of the appointments they have throughout the day. On occasion, you must update the lists as new appointments are made during the day. You decide to use **Notepad**, a popular application program available with Windows 98, to create the daily appointments lists. The finished documents are shown in Figure 2-1.

The name of each document displays at the top of the printed page, the text of the document (the daily appointments) displays below the document name, and a page number displays at the bottom of the page. The first printed document contains a list of Monday's appointments scheduled for Mr. Lopez. The second printed document contains a list of Monday's appointments scheduled for Ms. Parks. The following sections illustrate two methods to create these documents.

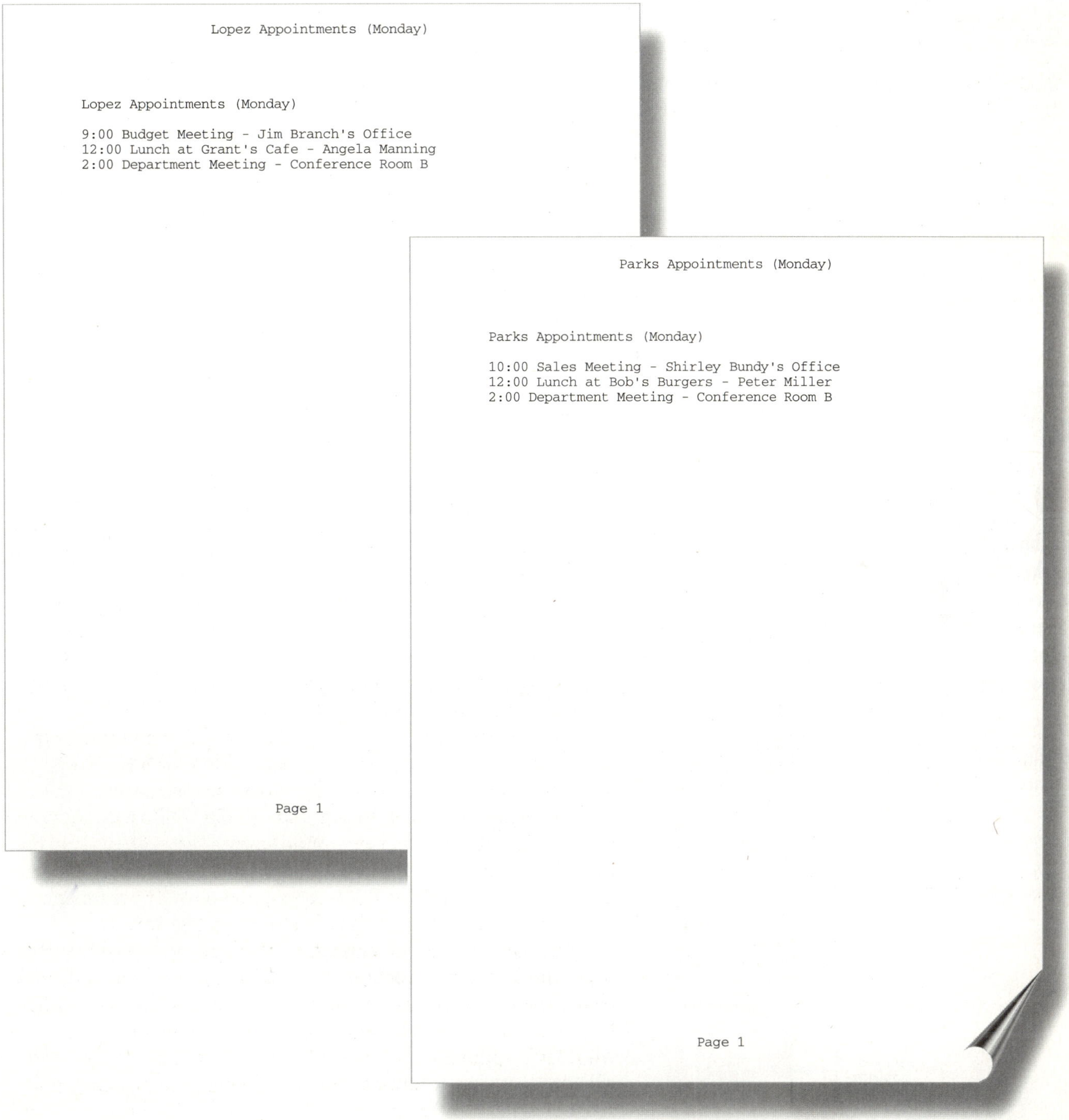

PROJECT 2

```
            Lopez Appointments (Monday)


Lopez Appointments (Monday)

9:00 Budget Meeting - Jim Branch's Office
12:00 Lunch at Grant's Cafe - Angela Manning
2:00 Department Meeting - Conference Room B
```

```
            Parks Appointments (Monday)


Parks Appointments (Monday)

10:00 Sales Meeting - Shirley Bundy's Office
12:00 Lunch at Bob's Burgers - Peter Miller
2:00 Department Meeting - Conference Room B
```

Page 1

Page 1

FIGURE 2-1

WIN 2.5

Creating a Document by Launching an Application Program

As explained in Project 1, a **program** is a set of computer instructions that carries out a task on your computer. An **application program** is a program that allows you to accomplish a specific task for which the program is designed. For example, a **word processing program** is an application program that allows you to create written documents, a spreadsheet program is an application program that allows you to create spreadsheets and charts, and a presentation graphics program allows you to create graphic presentations for display on a computer.

A common activity on a computer is to launch an application program to accomplish tasks using the computer. Three methods to start an application program were illustrated in Project 1. One method used the Start button on the taskbar.

To illustrate the use of an application program to create a written document, you will create the document to contain the daily appointments for Mr. Lopez using **Notepad**, a popular application program available with Windows 98. You will create the document by launching the Notepad application, typing the appointments for Mr. Lopez, and then saving the document on the desktop. In Windows terminology, this method of creating a document is called the **application-centric approach**. Perform the following steps to launch Notepad and enter the appointments for Mr. Lopez.

Application Programs

Some application programs, such as Notepad, are part of Windows 98. Most application programs, however, such as Microsoft Office, Lotus SmartSuite, and others must be purchased separately from Windows 98.

To Launch a Program and Create a Document

1 Click the Start button on the taskbar. Point to Programs on the Start menu. Point to Accessories on the Programs submenu. Point to Notepad on the Accessories submenu.

The Start menu, Programs submenu, and Accessories submenu display (Figure 2-2). The Accessories submenu contains the Notepad command to start the Notepad program.

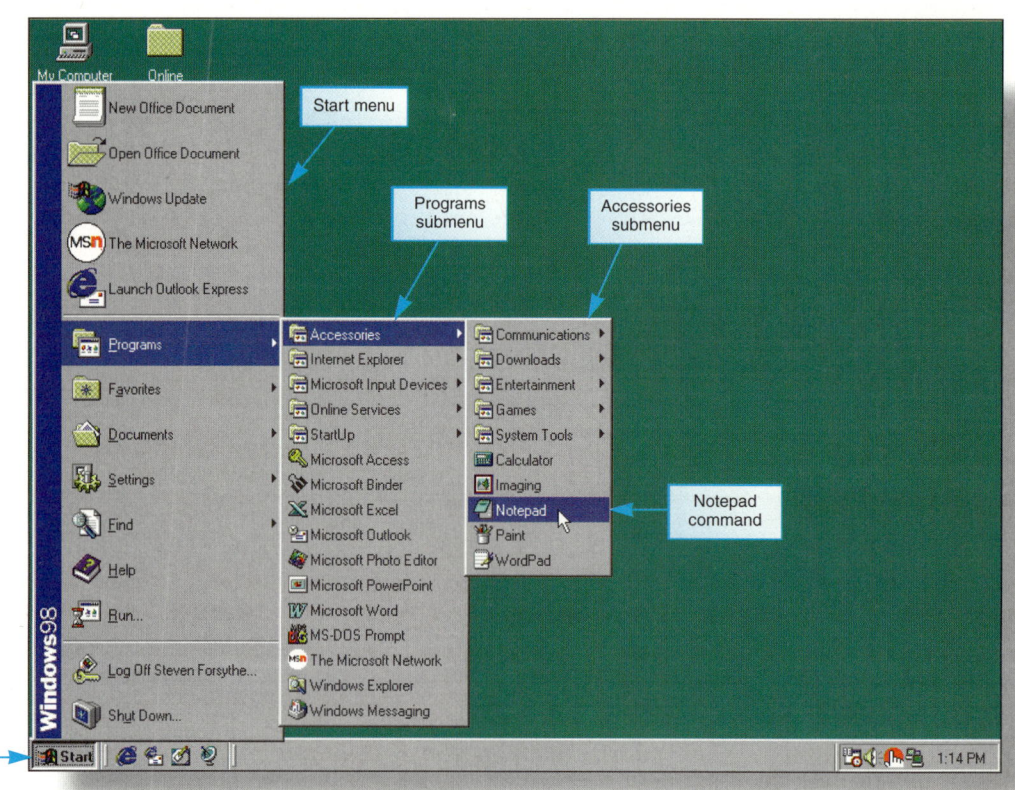

FIGURE 2-2

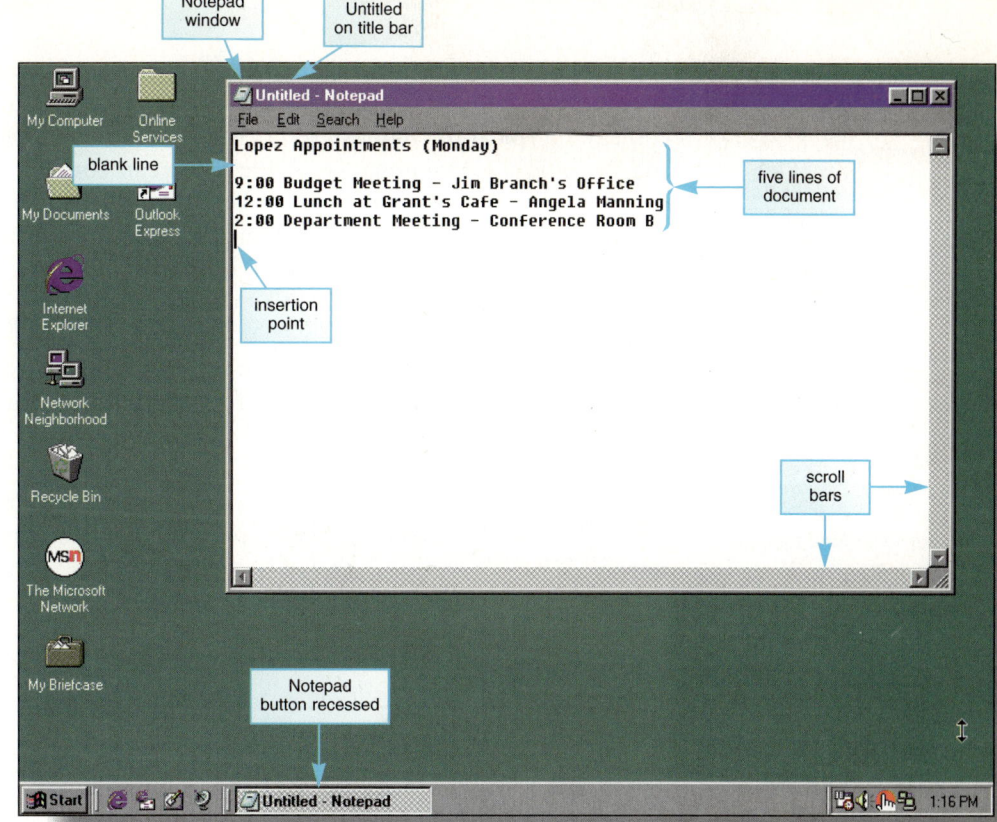

FIGURE 2-3

2 **Click Notepad. Type** Lopez Appointments (Monday) **and then press the ENTER key twice. Type** 9:00 Budget Meeting - Jim Branch's Office **and then press the ENTER key. Type** 12:00 Lunch at Grant's Cafe - Angela Manning **and then press the ENTER key. Type** 2:00 Department Meeting - Conference Room B **and then press the ENTER key.**

The Notepad program starts, the text of the document is entered, and a recessed Notepad button displays in the taskbar button area (Figure 2-3).

In Figure 2-3, the word, Untitled, in the window title bar (Untitled - Notepad) and on the Notepad button indicates the document has not been saved on disk. The area below the menu bar contains the five lines of the document, a blank line, a line containing an insertion point, and two scroll bars. The **insertion point** is a flashing vertical line that indicates the point at which text typed on the keyboard will be displayed. The scroll bars do not contain scroll boxes, indicating the document is not large enough to allow scrolling.

Saving a Document on the Desktop

When you create a document using a program such as Notepad, the document is stored in the main memory (RAM) of your computer. If you close the program without saving the document or if your computer accidentally loses electrical power, the document will be lost. To protect against the accidental loss of a document and to allow you to modify the document easily in the future, you can save the document on a disk (hard disk or floppy disk) or on the desktop. When you save a document on the desktop, a document icon displays on the desktop and the document is stored on the hard disk.

Other Ways

1. Right-click desktop, point to New, click Text Document, double-click New Text Document icon, enter text
2. Click Start button, click Run, type Notepad, click OK button, enter text
3. Press CTRL+ESC, press R, type Notepad, press ENTER key, enter text

More About

Saving a Document

Most people who have used a computer can tell at least one horror story of working on their computer for a long stretch of time and then losing the work because of some malfunction with the computer or even with the operating system or application program. *Be Warned:* Save and save often to protect the work you have completed on your computer.

More About

File Names

Because of the restrictions with Microsoft DOS, some versions of Windows allowed file names of only eight or fewer characters. F56QPSLA and similar indecipherable names were common. When long file names were introduced in Windows 95, Microsoft touted the new feature as a significant breakthrough. Apple Macintosh users, however, shrug and ask, What's the big deal? They have used long file names for years.

When you save a document, you must assign a file name to the document. All documents are identified by a **file name**. A file name should be descriptive of the file you save. Typical file names are Lopez Appointments (Monday), Office Supplies List, and Automobile Maintenance. A file name can contain up to 255 characters, including spaces. Any uppercase or lowercase character is valid when creating a file name, except a backslash (\), slash (/), colon (:), asterisk (*), question mark (?), quotation mark ("), less than symbol (<), greater than symbol (>), or vertical bar (|). File names cannot be CON, AUX, COM1, COM2, COM3, COM4, LPT1, LPT2, LPT3, PRN, or NUL.

To associate a document with an application, Windows 98 assigns an extension of a period and up to three characters to each document. All documents created using the Notepad program are text documents and are saved with the .txt extension.

To save the document you created using Notepad on the desktop of your computer using the file name, Lopez Appointments (Monday), perform the following steps.

 To Save a Document on the Desktop

1 **Click File on the menu bar and then point to Save As.**

The File menu opens in the Notepad window (Figure 2-4). The ellipsis (...) following the Save As command indicates Windows 98 requires more information to carry out the Save As command and will open a dialog box when you click Save As.

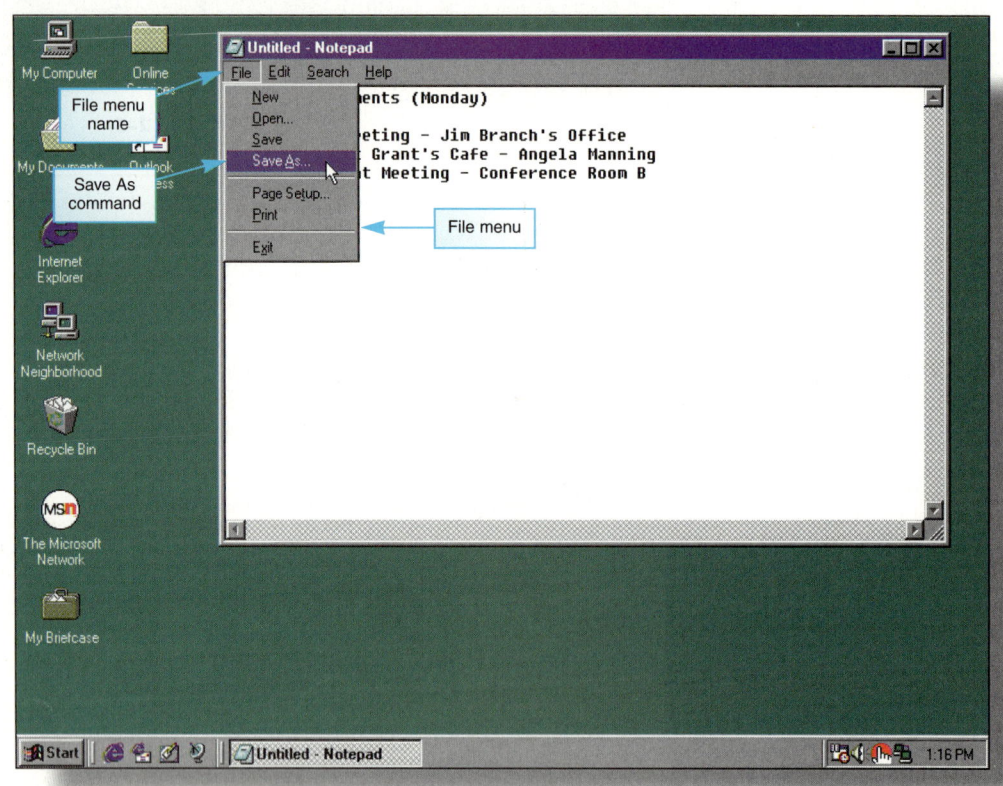

FIGURE 2-4

2 Click Save As. Type Lopez Appointments (Monday) in the File name text box and then point to the Save in box arrow.

The Save As dialog box displays (Figure 2-5). The Save in box contains the My Documents icon and icon title. This entry indicates where the file will be saved. The File name text box contains the document name (Lopez Appointments (Monday)) and the insertion point. When you save this document, Notepad will add the .txt extension to the file name automatically.

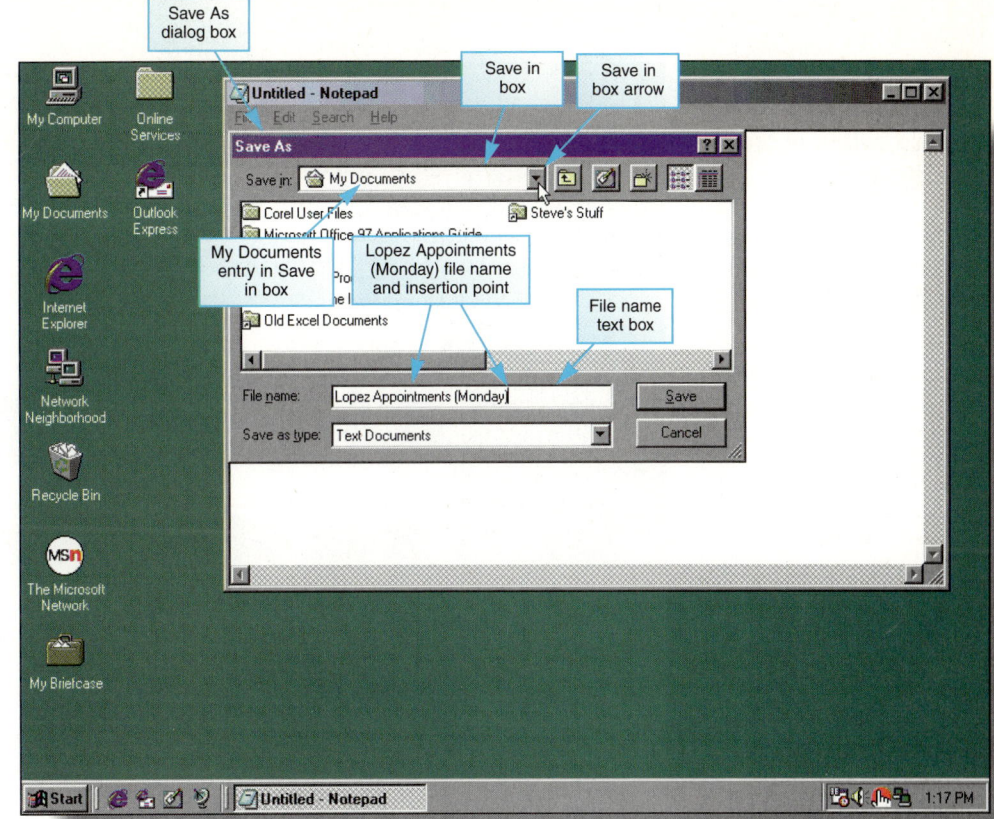

FIGURE 2-5

3 Click the Save in box arrow and then point to the Desktop icon.

The Save in list box displays (Figure 2-6). The list contains various elements of your computer, including the Desktop, My Documents, My Computer, Network Neighborhood, My Briefcase, and Online Services. Within My Computer are 3½ Floppy (A:), Hard disk (C:), (D:), Removable Disk (E:), and (F:). When you point to the Desktop icon, the entry in the list is highlighted. The entries in the Save In list may be different from those on your computer.

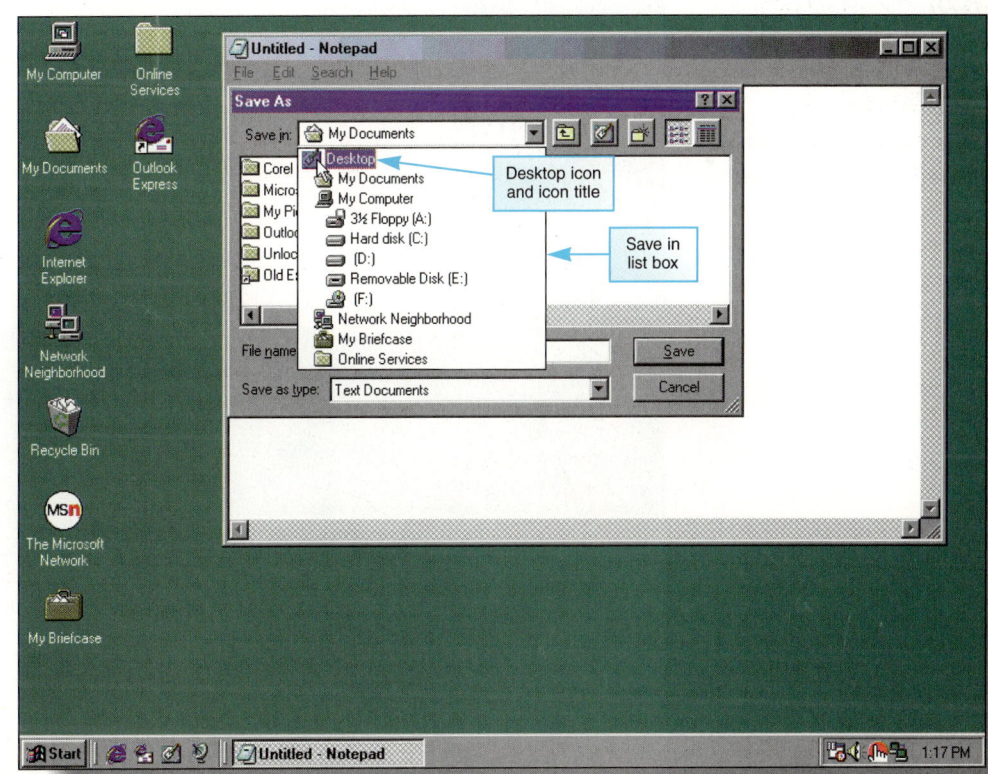

FIGURE 2-6

WIN 2.10 • Project 2 • Working on the Windows 98 Desktop

4 **Click the Desktop icon and then point to the Save button in the Save As dialog box.**

The Desktop entry displays in the Save in box (Figure 2-7). This specifies that the file will be saved on the desktop using the file name contained in the File name text box.

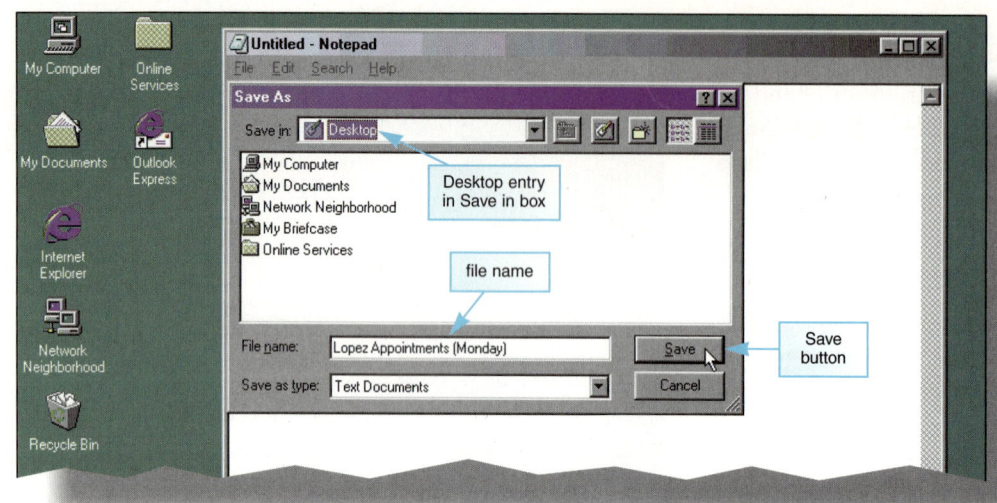

FIGURE 2-7

5 **Click the Save button.**

Windows 98 displays an **hourglass icon** while saving the Lopez Appointments (Monday) document on the desktop. The Save As dialog box closes. The Lopez Appointments (Monday) document icon displays on the desktop, and the file name becomes part of the Notepad window title and button name in the taskbar button area (Figure 2-8).

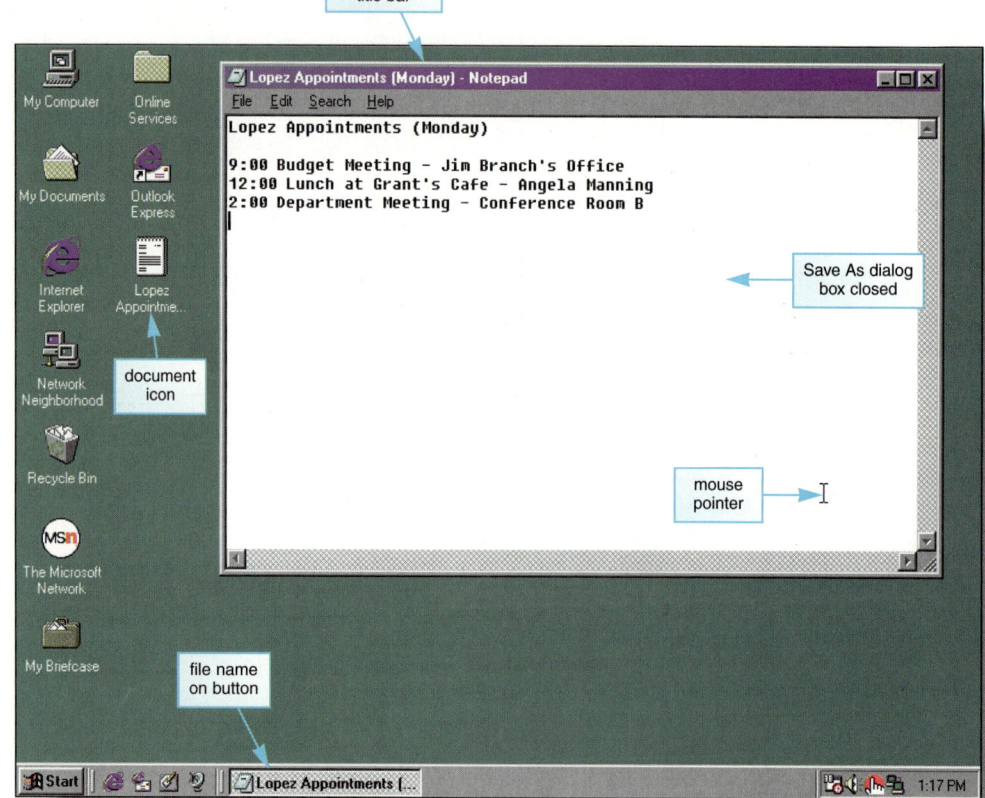

FIGURE 2-8

More About

Menus

Once you have clicked a menu name on the menu bar to open it, you need only point to another menu name on the menu bar to open that menu. To close a menu without carrying out a command, click anywhere on the desktop except on the menu.

Other Ways

1. On File menu click Save, type file name, select Desktop, click Save button
2. Press ALT+F, press A, type file name, select Desktop, click TAB repeatedly to select Save button, press S

In Figure 2-8, the file name on the button in the taskbar button area, (Lopez Appointments (...) contains an ellipsis to indicate the entire button name does not fit on the button. To display the entire button name for a button in the taskbar button area, point to the button. Notice that when the mouse pointer displays within the Notepad text area, it becomes an I-beam.

The method shown in the previous steps for saving a file on the desktop can be used to save a file on a floppy disk or on a hard disk by clicking 3½ Floppy (A:) or Hard disk (C:) in the Save in list.

Printing a Document

Quite often, after creating a document and saving it, you will want to print it. One method to print a document on the desktop is to print it directly from an application program. To print the Lopez Appointments (Monday) document, perform the following steps.

> **More About**
>
> **Printing**
>
> Printing is and will remain important for documents. Many sophisticated application programs, however, are extending the printing capability to include transmitting faxes, sending e-mail, and even posting documents on Web pages of the World Wide Web.

Steps To Print a Document

1   **Click File on the menu bar and point to Print (Figure 2-9).**

2   **Click Print.**

A Notepad dialog box briefly displays with a message indicating the Lopez Appointments document is being printed. The document prints as shown in Figure 2-1 on page WIN 2.5.

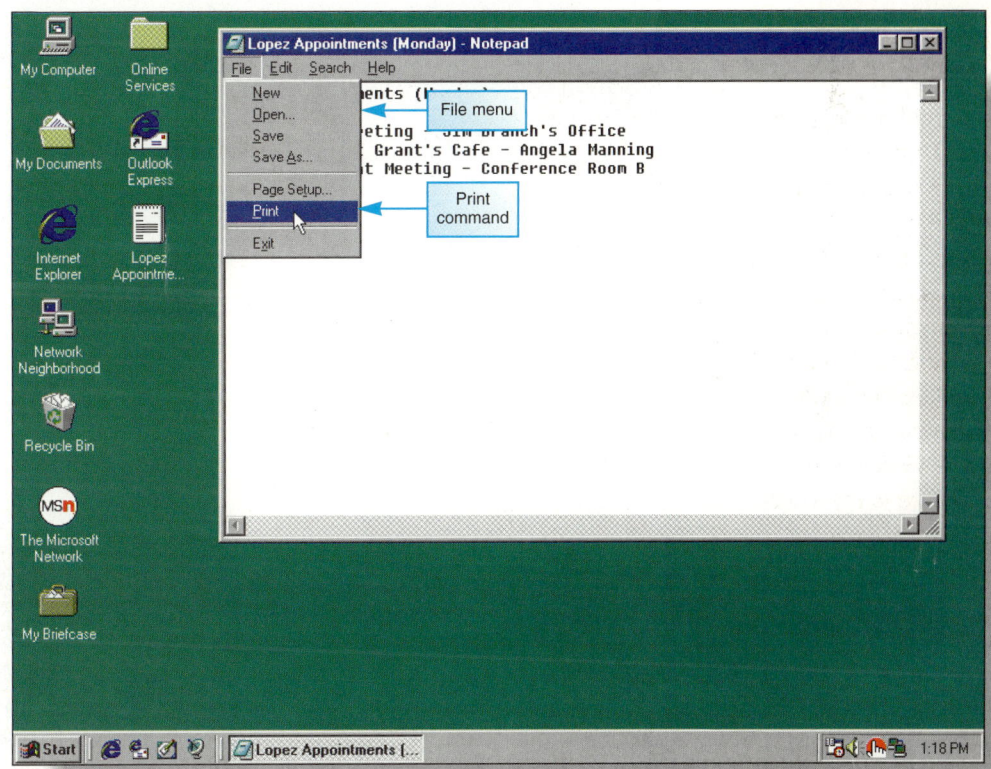

FIGURE 2-9

> **Other Ways**
>
> 1. Right-click document icon on desktop, click Print
> 2. Press ALT+F, press P

Closing a Document

After creating the Lopez Appointments (Monday) document, saving the document, and printing it, your use of the document is complete. Perform the steps on the next page to close the Notepad window containing the document.

Steps To Close a Document

1 Point to the Close button on the Notepad title bar (Figure 2-10).

2 Click the Close button.

The Lopez Appointments (Monday) - Notepad window closes and the Lopez Appointments (Monday) - Notepad button no longer displays.

Other Ways

1. Double-click Notepad logo on title bar
2. Click Notepad logo on title bar, click Close
3. On File menu click Exit
4. Press ALT+F, press X; or press ALT+F4

More About

Document-Centric

The document-centric concept will progress ever further to the point where you neither know nor care what application was used to create a document. For example, when you include a Web page hyperlink in your word processing document, you will not care how the page was created. Only the content of the page is of interest.

More About

Creating Documents on the Desktop

The phrase, creating a document on the desktop, may be confusing. The document you create contains no data. It is blank. In effect you are placing a blank piece of paper with a name on your desktop. The document has little value until you add data.

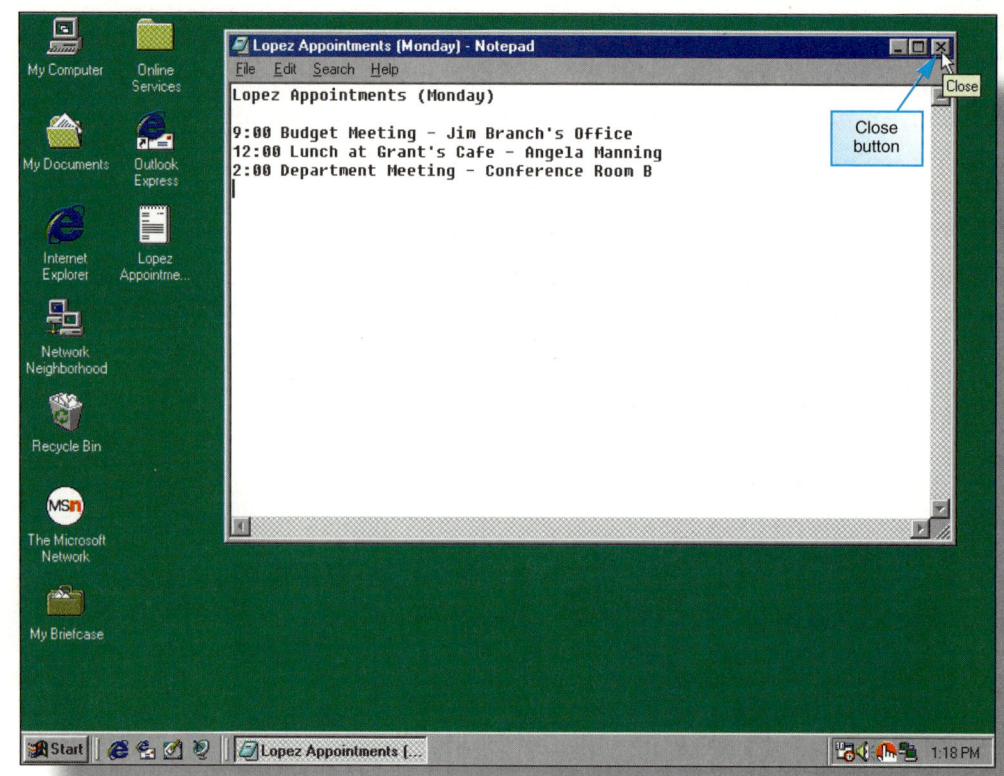

FIGURE 2-10

After completing the appointments list for Mr. Lopez, the next step is to create a similar list for Ms. Parks.

Creating and Naming a Document on the Desktop

Opening an application program and then creating a document (application-centric approach) was the method you used to create the first document. Although the same method could be used to create the second document for Ms. Parks, another method and one that often will be easier and more straightforward, is to create the new document on the Windows 98 desktop without first starting an application program. Instead of launching a program to create and modify a document, you create a blank document directly on the desktop and then use the Notepad program to enter data into the document. This method, called the **document-centric approach**, will be used to create the document to contain the appointments for Ms. Parks.

To create a blank document directly on the desktop, perform the following steps.

Creating and Naming a Document on the Desktop • **WIN 2.13**

PROJECT 2

Steps: To Create a Blank Document on the Desktop

1 **Right-click an open area on the desktop, point to New on the shortcut menu, and then point to Text Document on the New submenu.**

The shortcut menu and New submenu display (Figure 2-11).

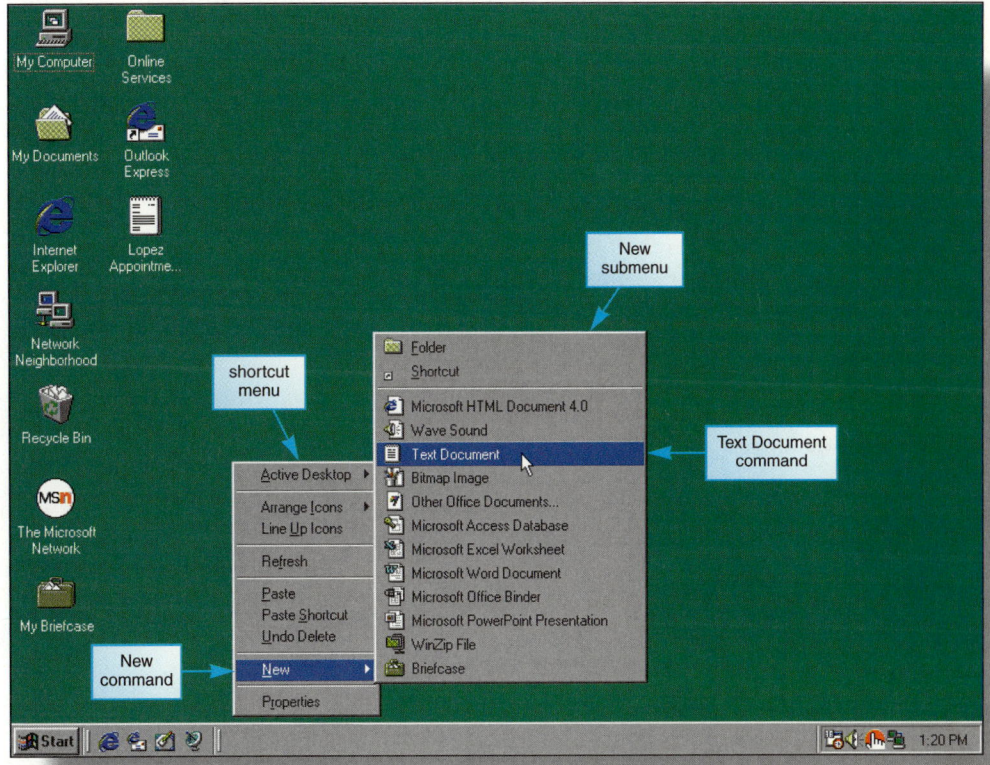

FIGURE 2-11

2 **Click Text Document.**

The shortcut menu and New submenu close, a blank text document with the default name, New Text Document, is created and its icon displays on the desktop (Figure 2-12). The **icon title text box** *below the icon contains the highlighted default file name followed by an insertion point. Whenever text is highlighted in a text box, any characters you type will replace the highlighted text.*

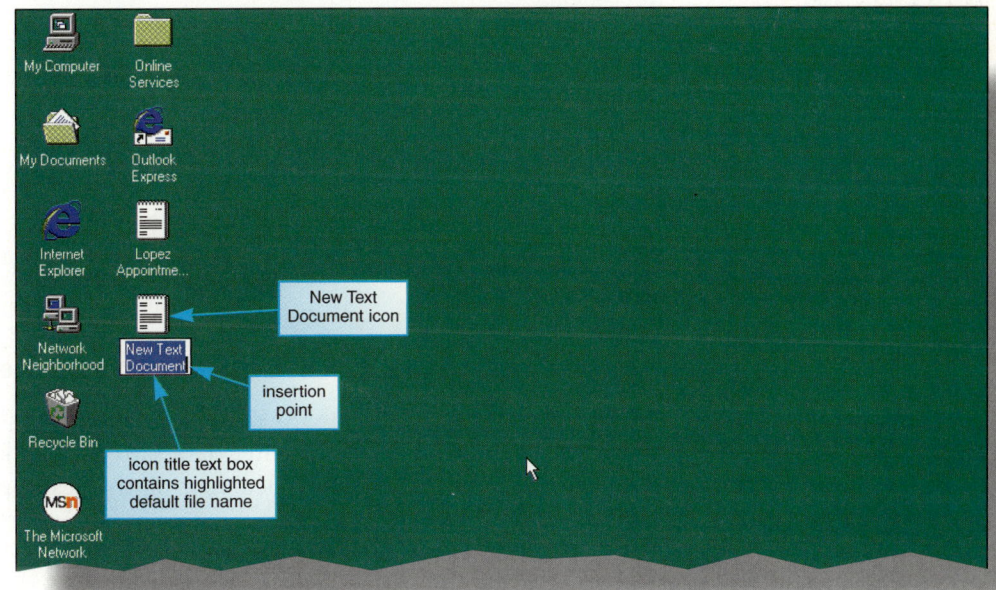

FIGURE 2-12

A blank document has been created on the desktop to contain the daily appointments for Ms. Parks.

Naming a Document

After you create a blank document on the desktop, normally you will name the document so it is easily identifiable. In Figure 2-12 on the previous page, the default file name (New Text Document) is highlighted and the insertion point is blinking, so you can type the new name. To give the name, Parks Appointments (Monday), to the document you just created, complete the step below.

To Name a Document on the Desktop

 **Type** Parks Appointments (Monday) **in the icon title text box and then press the** ENTER **key.**

The file name, Parks Appointments (Monday), displays in the icon title text box, replacing the default name, and the Parks Appointments (Monday) icon is selected (Figure 2-13).

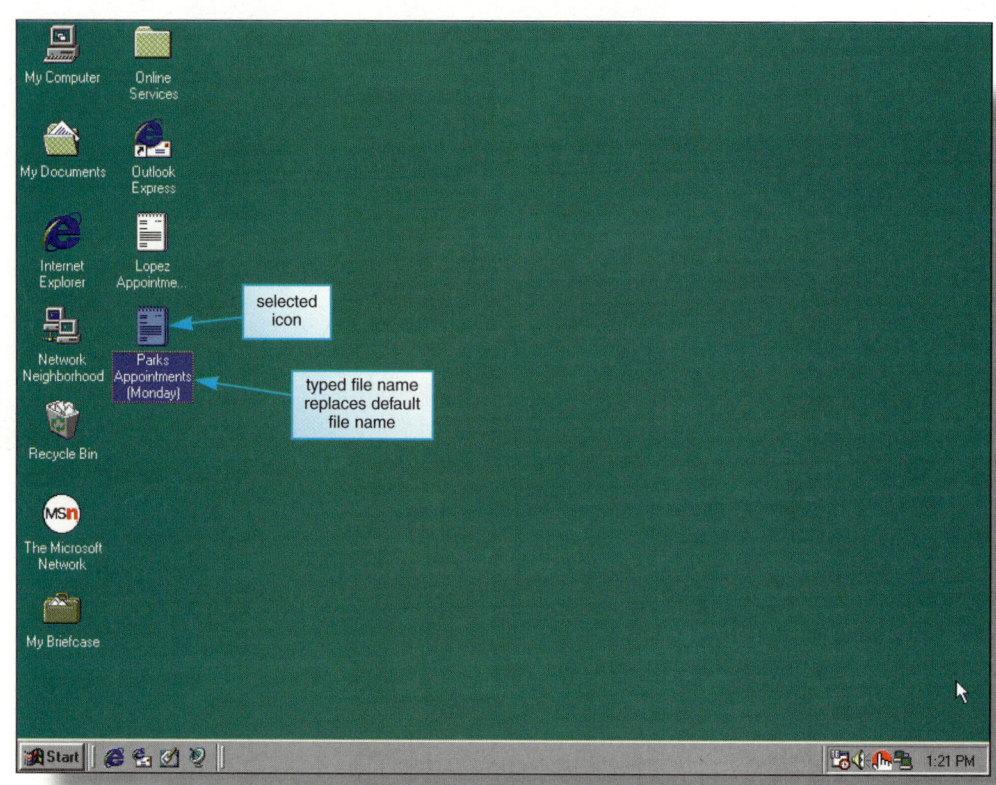

FIGURE 2-13

1. Right-click icon, click Rename, type name, press ENTER
2. Click icon to select icon, press F2, type name, press ENTER

Entering Data into a Blank Document on the Desktop

Although you have created the Parks Appointments (Monday) document, the document contains no data. To enter data into the blank document, you first must open the document. To open a document on the desktop, perform the following steps.

Creating and Naming a Document on the Desktop • **WIN 2.15**

 To Open a Document on the Desktop

1 **Point to the Parks Appointments (Monday) icon on the desktop (Figure 2-14).**

FIGURE 2-14

2 **Double-click the Parks Appointments (Monday) icon.**

The Notepad window opens and the Parks Appointments (Monday) document displays in the Notepad window (Figure 2-15). The document contains no text. The insertion point is located at the beginning of the first line of the document.

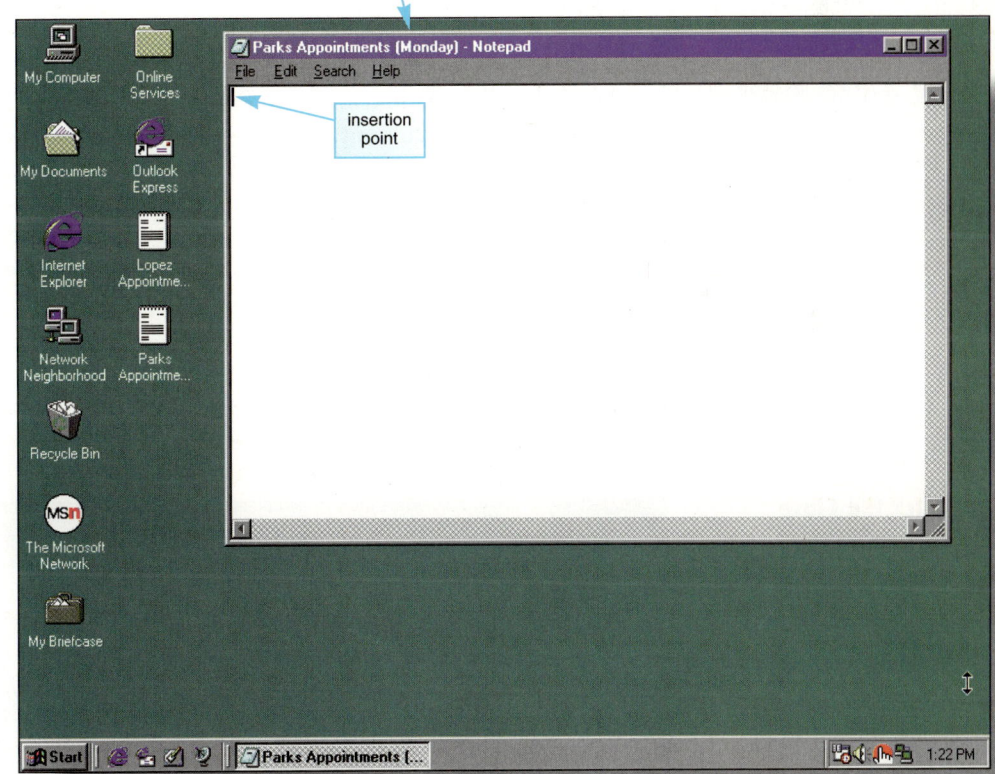

FIGURE 2-15

After the document is open, you can enter the required data by typing the text (the daily appointments) you want in the document. To enter the text for the Parks Appointments (Monday) document, perform the step on the next page.

1. Right-click icon on desktop, click Open on shortcut menu
2. Click icon to select icon, press ENTER

Steps: To Enter Data into a Blank Document

  1 **Type the text shown in Figure 2-16 for the Parks Appointments (Monday) document.**

The text for Parks Appointments (Monday) displays in the document (Figure 2-16).

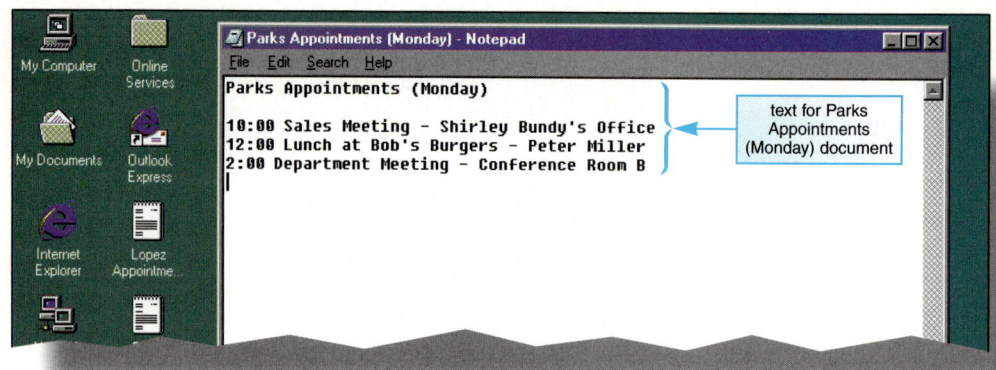

FIGURE 2-16

You can type as many words and lines as necessary for your document. The entry of the text into the Parks Appointments (Monday) document modifies the document resulting in the need to save the document.

Closing and Saving a Document

After entering the text into the Parks Appointments (Monday) document, often you will close the document. You also must save the document so the text you entered will remain part of the document. You could accomplish this by using the Save As command on the File menu as shown earlier in this project. In Windows 98 applications, however, you can close and save a document in one set of steps. To close and save the Parks Appointments (Monday) document, complete the following steps.

> **More About**
> **Saving a Document**
> If you make many changes to a document, you should save the document while you are working on it. To do so, click File on the menu bar and then click Save.

Steps: To Close and Save a Modified Document on the Desktop

  1 **Click the Close button on the Notepad title bar. Point to the Yes button in the Notepad dialog box (Figure 2-18).**

Because the Parks Appointments (Monday) document has been changed, Windows 98 displays the Notepad dialog box asking if you want to save the changes you made in the document (Figure 2-17).

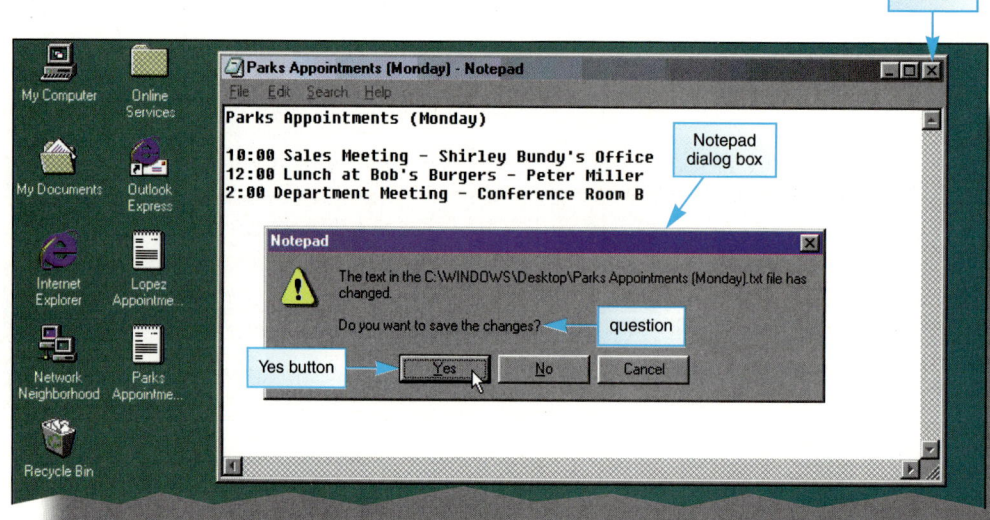

FIGURE 2-17

Click the Yes button.

The Notepad dialog box and Notepad window close and the modified Parks Appointments (Monday) document is saved on the desktop (Figure 2-18).

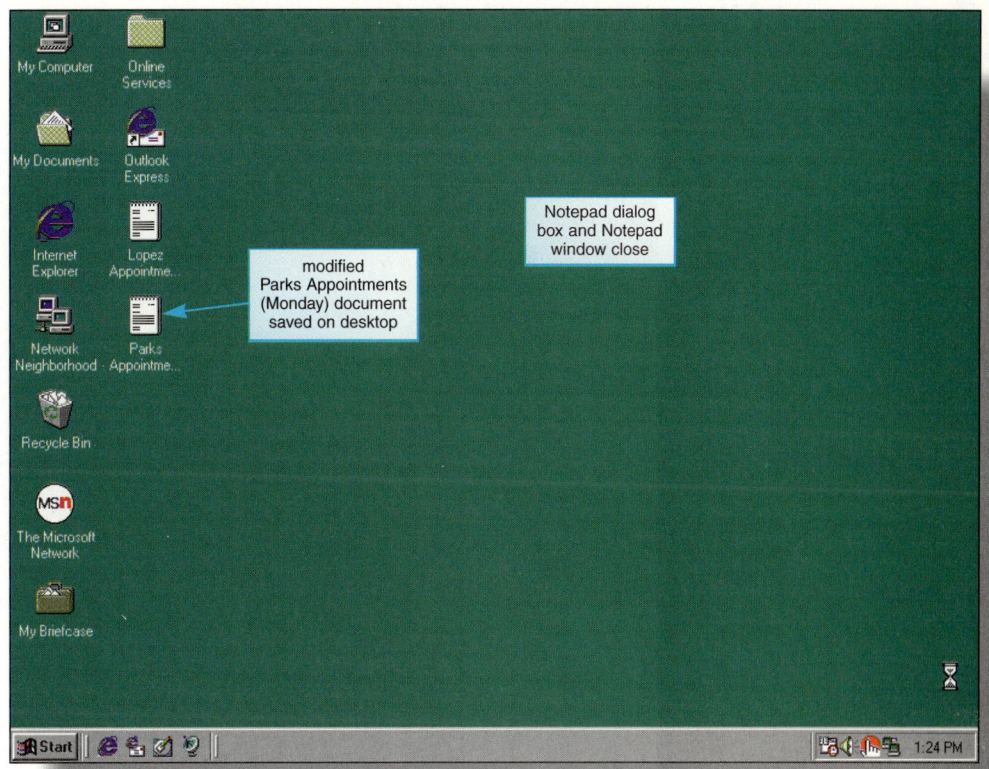

FIGURE 2-18

In most Windows 98 application programs, if you close the program and the document has not been saved since being changed, a dialog box displays asking if you want to save the document before closing the program. This is the way in which Windows 98 ensures you accidentally do not lose work you have completed for a document.

After saving and closing the Parks Appointments (Monday) document, the second document is complete.

Storing Documents in a Folder on the Desktop

When you have created one or more documents on the desktop, you often will want to keep them together so they can be found and referenced easily. Windows 98 allows you to place one or more documents into a folder in much the same manner as you might take a letter written on a piece of paper and place it in a file folder. To place a document in a folder, you must first create the folder. To create and name a folder on the desktop into which you can place the Lopez Appointments (Monday) and Parks Appointments (Monday) documents, complete the steps on the next page.

Other Ways

1. On File menu click Save As, click Save button, click Yes button in Save As dialog box, click Close button
2. Click Notepad icon on title bar, click Close, click Yes button
3. Double-click Notepad icon on title bar, click Yes button
4. Press ALT+F, press S, press ALT+F, press X

The Desktop

The desktop model for interfacing with a computer is quite popular. Critics insist, however, that more efficient and effective models exist. Can you think of any model that would be more efficient for you? What about the interfaces you use for interactive games?

To Create and Name a Folder on the Desktop

1 **Right-click an open area on the desktop, point to New on the shortcut menu, and then point to Folder on the New submenu.**

The shortcut menu and New submenu display (Figure 2-19). Clicking Folder on the New submenu will create a folder using the default folder name, New Folder.

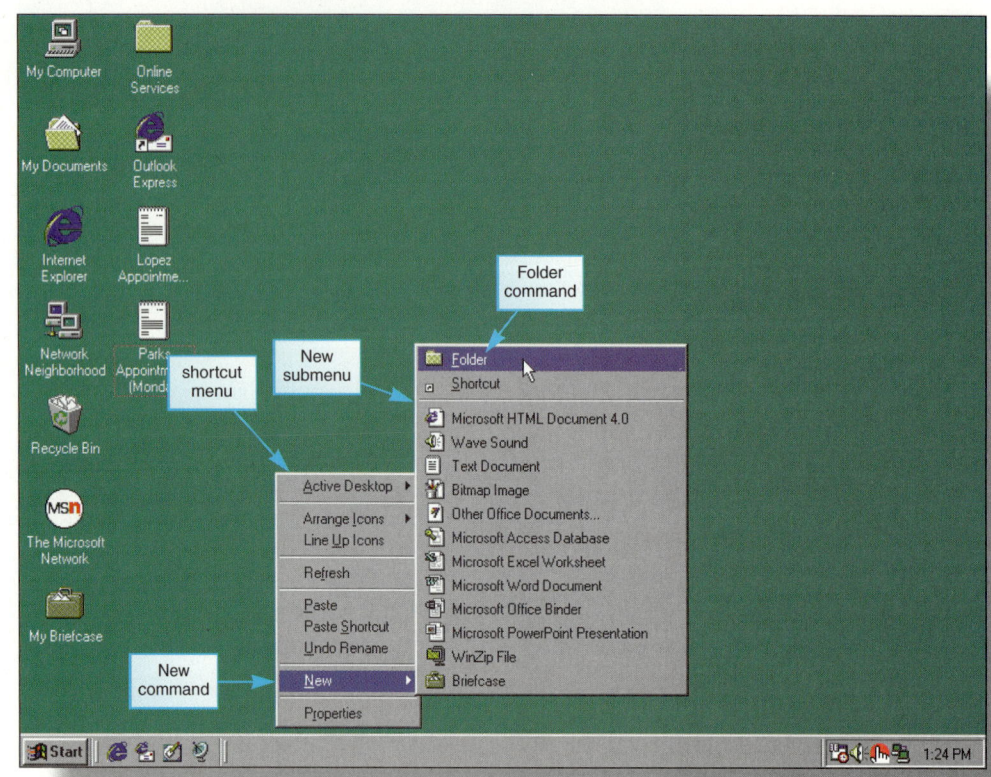

FIGURE 2-19

2 **Click Folder, type** Daily Appointments **in the icon title text box, and press the ENTER key.**

The selected Daily Appointments folder icon displays on the desktop (Figure 2-20). The folder name, Daily Appointments, displays in the icon title text box.

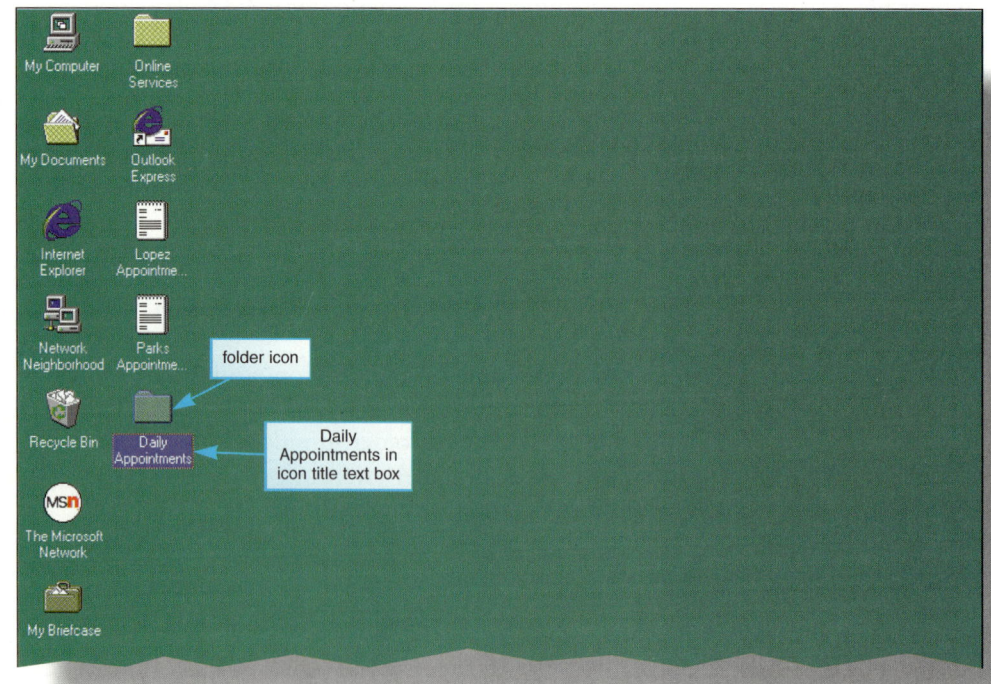

FIGURE 2-20

Storing Documents in a Folder on the Desktop • **WIN 2.19**

After you create a folder on the desktop, normally the next step is to move one or more documents into the folder. For the Daily Appointments folder, you should move the Parks Appointments (Monday) and the Lopez Appointments (Monday) documents into the folder. To accomplish this task, complete the following steps.

Steps: To Move a Document into a Folder

1 **Right-drag the Parks Appointments (Monday) icon on top of the Daily Appointments folder icon and then point to Move Here on the shortcut menu.**

The dimmed Parks Appointments (Monday) icon displays on top of the Daily Appointments folder icon, and a shortcut menu displays (Figure 2-21). The highlighted Parks Appointments (Monday) icon still displays on the desktop.

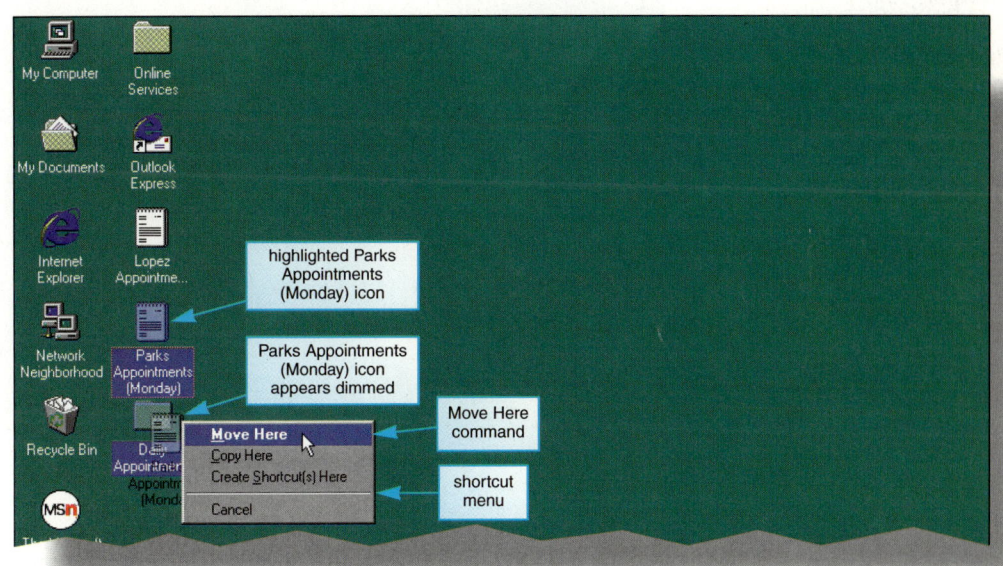

FIGURE 2-21

2 **Click Move Here.**

The Parks Appointments (Monday) document is moved into the Daily Appointments folder, and the Parks Appointments (Monday) icon no longer displays on the desktop (Figure 2-22). Windows 98 rearranges the desktop.

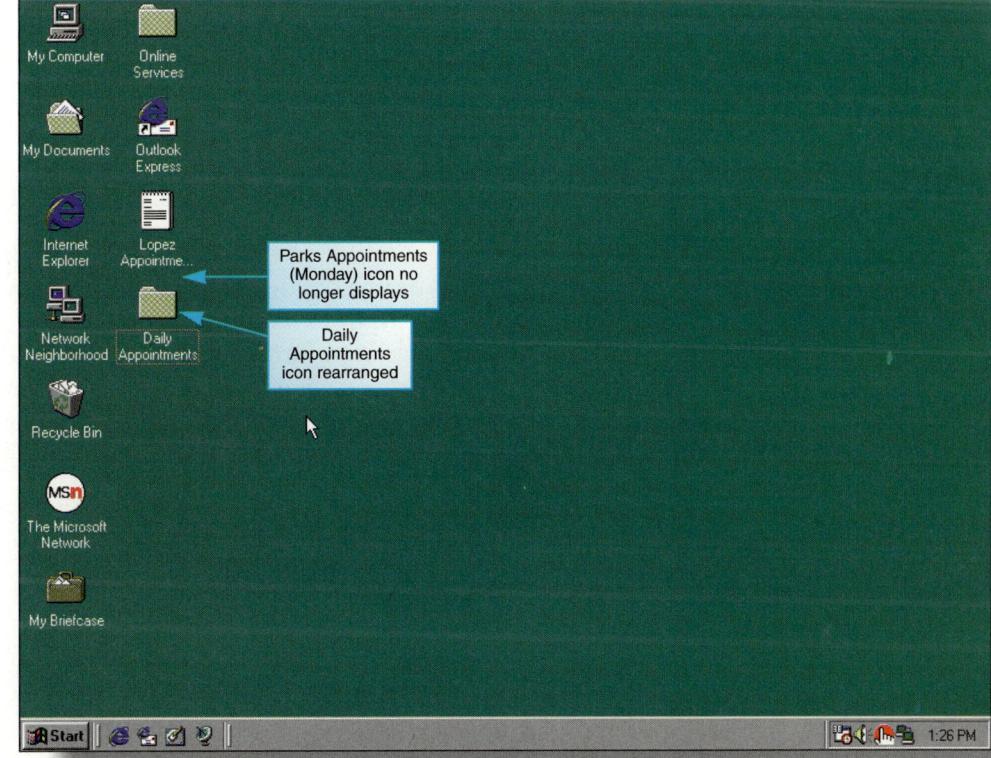

FIGURE 2-22

3 **Right-drag the Lopez Appointments (Monday) icon on top of the Daily Appointments icon. Click Move Here on the shortcut menu.**

The Lopez Appointments (Monday) document is moved into the Daily Appointments folder, and the Lopez Appointments (Monday) icon no longer displays on the desktop (Figure 2-23). Windows 98 rearranges the icons on the desktop.

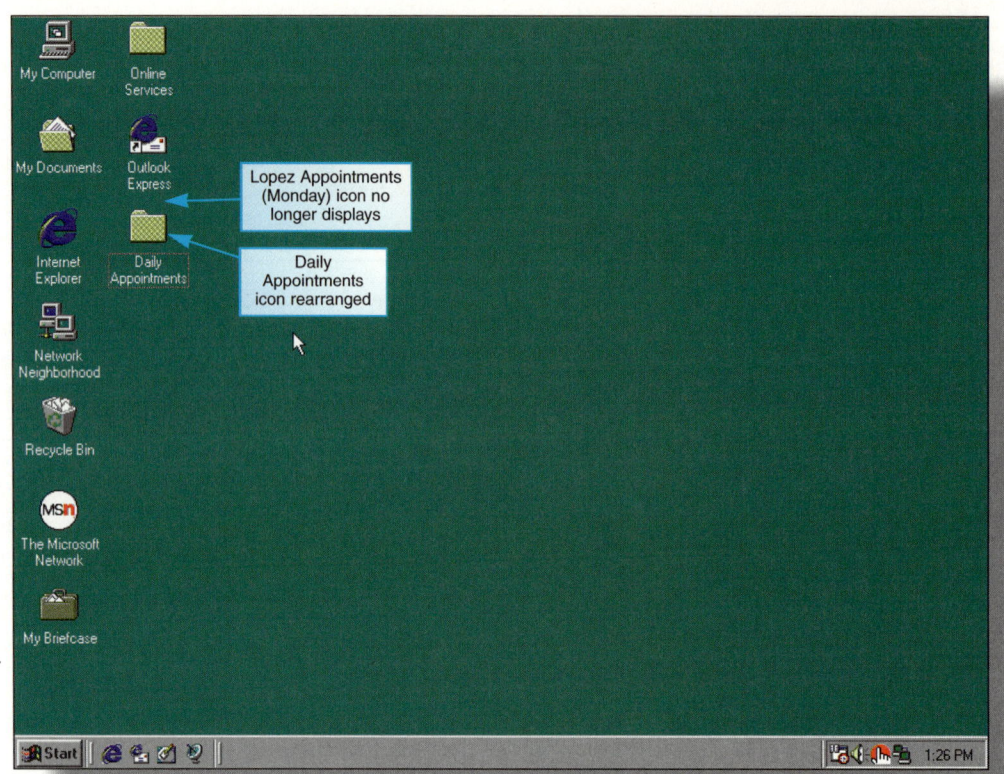

FIGURE 2-23

1. Right-click document icon, click Cut, right-click folder icon, click Paste
2. Drag document icon on top of folder icon

The capability of organizing documents and files within a folder allows you to keep your desktop organized when using Windows 98. Project 3 will discuss the manner in which you can organize your files on your floppy and hard drives.

Opening and Modifying Documents Within a Folder

Documents stored in a folder on the desktop can be modified in much the same way as documents stored on the desktop. First, you must open the folder and then you must open the file you want to modify.

Assume that you received further information about the daily appointments for Mr. Lopez. An Internet meeting with Gary Carney in the Eastern United States has been scheduled at 4:00 p.m. To add this item to the schedule, first you must open the Daily Appointments folder that contains the Lopez Appointments (Monday) document. To do so, complete the following step.

Opening and Modifying Documents Within a Folder • WIN 2.21

 To Open a Folder

1 **Double-click the Daily Appointments folder icon on the desktop. Move and resize the Daily Appointments window to resemble the window shown in Figure 2-24.**

The Daily Appointments window opens and the recessed Daily Appointments button displays in the taskbar button area (Figure 2-24). The Daily Appointments folder icon remains on the desktop. Each of the document icons display within the folder window, indicating they are contained within the folder.

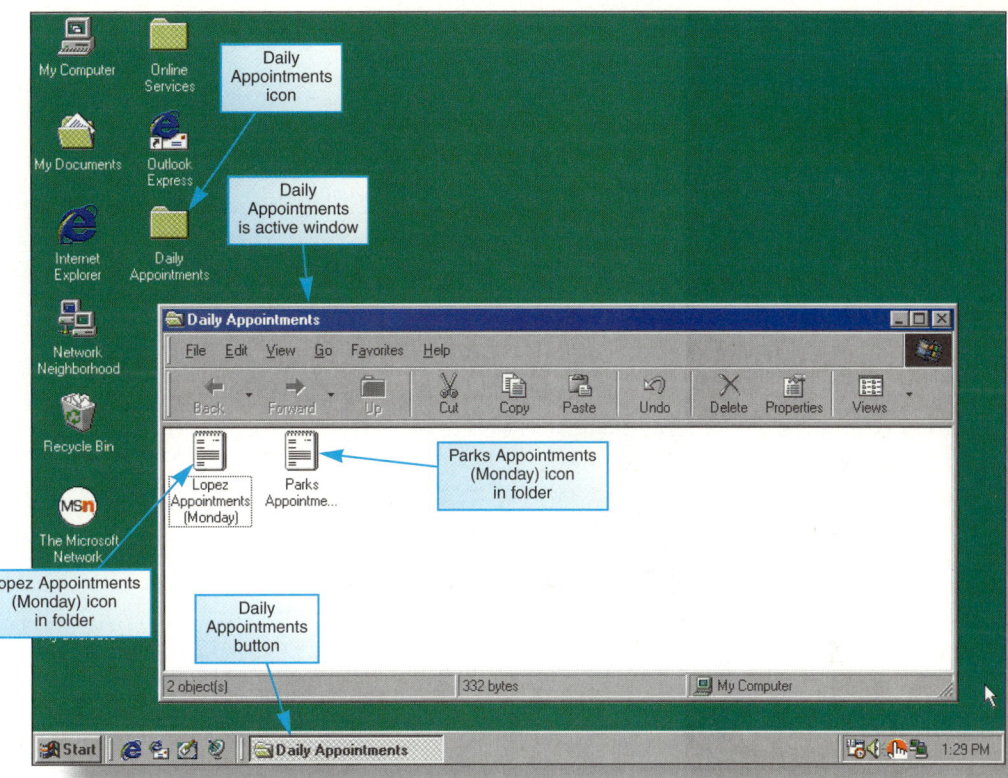

FIGURE 2-24

In Figure 2-24, the color of the Daily Appointments title bar (dark blue) and the recessed button in the taskbar button area indicate the Daily Appointments window is the active window.

Opening and Modifying a Document Stored in a Folder

After opening the folder, you must open the document you want to modify. To open the Lopez Appointments (Monday) document in the Daily Appointments folder and then enter the text about the Internet meeting, complete the steps on the next page.

Other Ways

1. Right-click folder icon, click Open
2. Click folder icon to select icon, press ENTER key

 **Working with Documents**

To modify your document, you are opening the document rather than starting an application program and then opening the document as you did previously in this project. Does this feel more natural? Research has indicated that people feel more at home dealing with documents instead of dealing with application programs and then documents.

WIN 2.22 • Project 2 • Working on the Windows 98 Desktop

 To Open and Modify a Document in a Folder

1 **Double-click the Lopez Appointments (Monday) icon in the Daily Appointments window.**

Notepad starts and the Lopez Appointments (Monday) document displays in the Notepad window. The Lopez Appointments (Monday) - Notepad button is added to the taskbar button area (Figure 2-25). The active Notepad window and the inactive folder window now are open and the Daily Appointments folder button is no longer recessed.

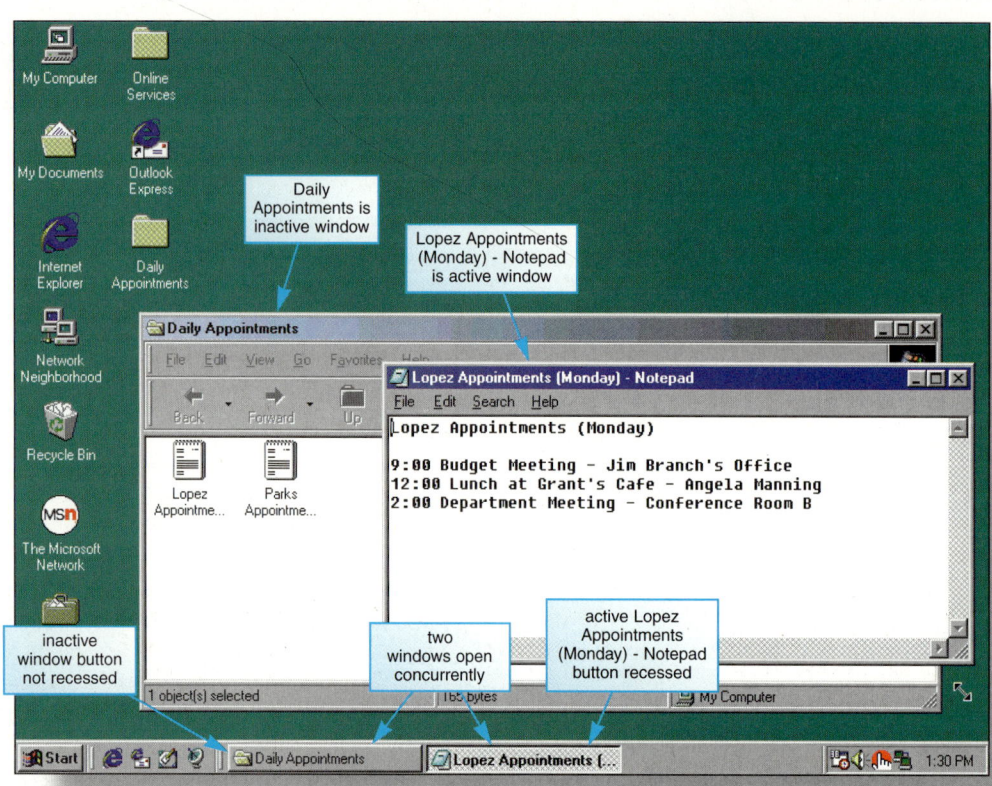

FIGURE 2-25

2 **Press the DOWN ARROW key five times to move the insertion point to the end of the document. Type** `4:00 NetMeeting - Gary Carney` **and then press the ENTER key.**

The insertion point moves to the end of the document and the entry is added to the document (Figure 2-26).

Other Ways

1. Right-click document icon, click Open on shortcut menu
2. Click document icon to select icon, press ENTER key

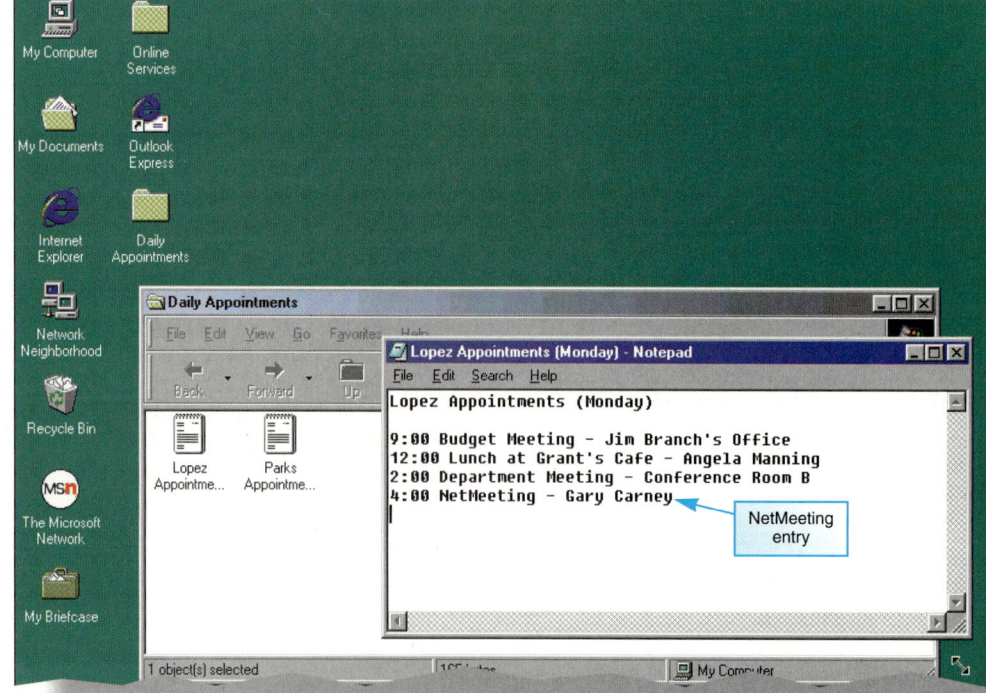

FIGURE 2-26

Opening and Modifying Documents Within a Folder • WIN 2.23

As you can see, it is just as easy to modify a document stored in a folder as it is to modify a document stored on the desktop. The method for opening and modifying a document, regardless of where the document is stored, is the same.

Opening Multiple Documents

Windows 98 allows you to open more than one document and application program at the same time. You then can work on any desired document. The concept of multiple programs running at the same time is called **multitasking**. To illustrate two documents and an application program open at the same time, assume you need to make a change to the Parks Appointments (Monday) document to include a three-way conference call with Brandy Schiller that is scheduled for 4:30 p.m. You do not have to close the Lopez Appointments (Monday) document to do this. Complete the following steps to open the Parks Appointments (Monday) document and make the changes.

  To Open and Modify Multiple Documents

1 **Click the Daily Appointments button in the taskbar button area and then point to the Parks Appointments (Monday) icon in the Daily Appointments window.**

The Daily Appointments window moves on top of the Lopez Appointments document (Figure 2-27). The Daily Appointments window becomes the active window (dark blue title bar) and the inactive Lopez Appointments window is partially visible behind the Daily Appointments window. The Daily Appointments button is recessed, and the Lopez Appointments (Monday) - Notepad button is not recessed.

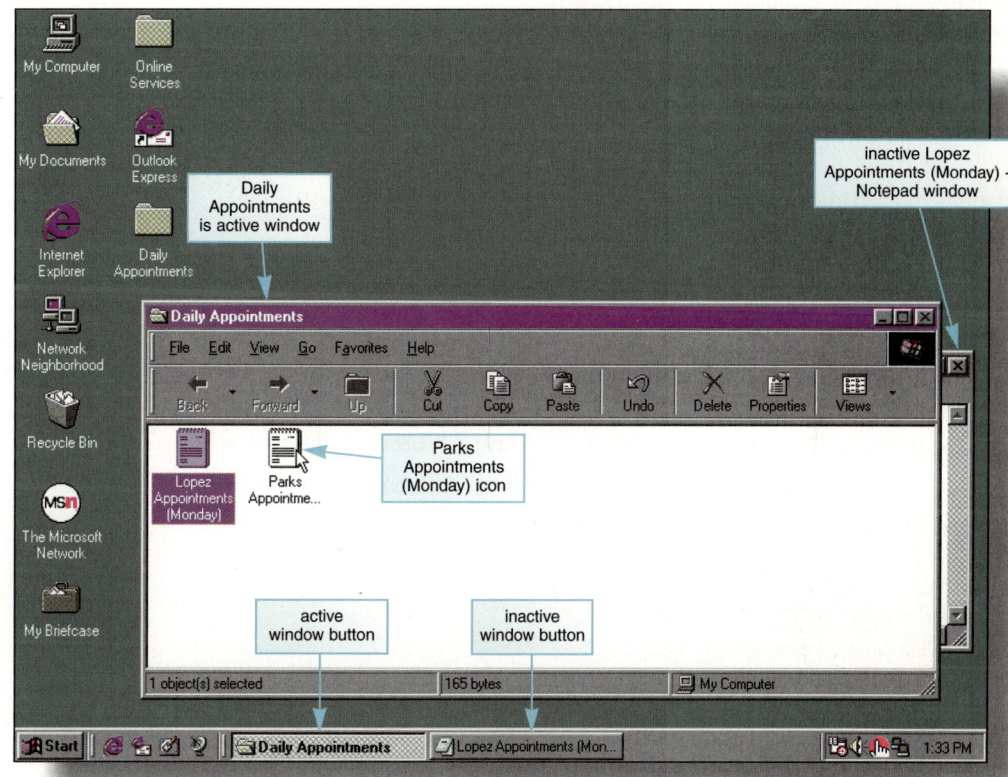

FIGURE 2-27

 **Double-click the Parks Appointments (Monday) icon in the Daily Appointments window. Press the DOWN ARROW key five times to move the insertion point to the end of the document in the Notepad window. Type** 4:30 Conference Call - Brandy Schiller **and then press the ENTER key.**

The Parks Appointments (Monday) - Notepad window opens on top of the other two open windows, the recessed Parks Appointments (Monday) - Notepad button is added to the taskbar button area, and the insertion point moves to the end of the document (Figure 2-28).

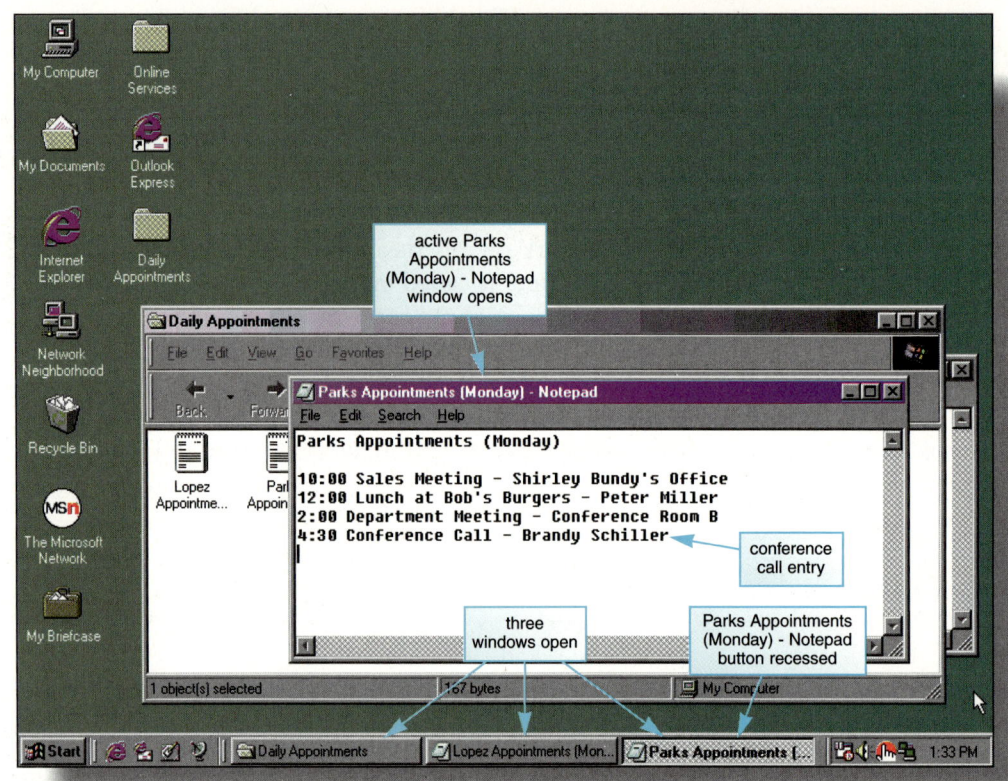

FIGURE 2-28

Other Ways

1. Right-click document icon, click Open on shortcut menu
2. Click to document icon to select icon, press ENTER

More About

Opening Windows

In addition to clicking the taskbar button of an inactive window to make that window the active window, you also may click any open area of the window. Many people routinely click the title bar of a window to activate the window.

After you have modified the Parks Appointments (Monday) document, assume you receive information that a dinner engagement with Sam Goebel has been scheduled for Mr. Lopez at 6:00 p.m. at the London House. You are directed to add this entry to Mr. Lopez's appointments. To do this, you must open the Lopez Appointments (Monday) - Notepad inactive window. To open an inactive window and modify the document, complete the following step.

Opening and Modifying Documents Within a Folder • WIN 2.25

Steps: To Open an Inactive Window

1 Click the Lopez Appointments (Monday) - Notepad button in the taskbar button area. When the window opens, **type** 6:00 Dinner at London House - Sam Goebel **and then press the** ENTER **key.**

The Lopez Appointments (Monday) - Notepad window displays on top of the other windows on the desktop, and the dinner entry is added to the document (Figure 2-29).

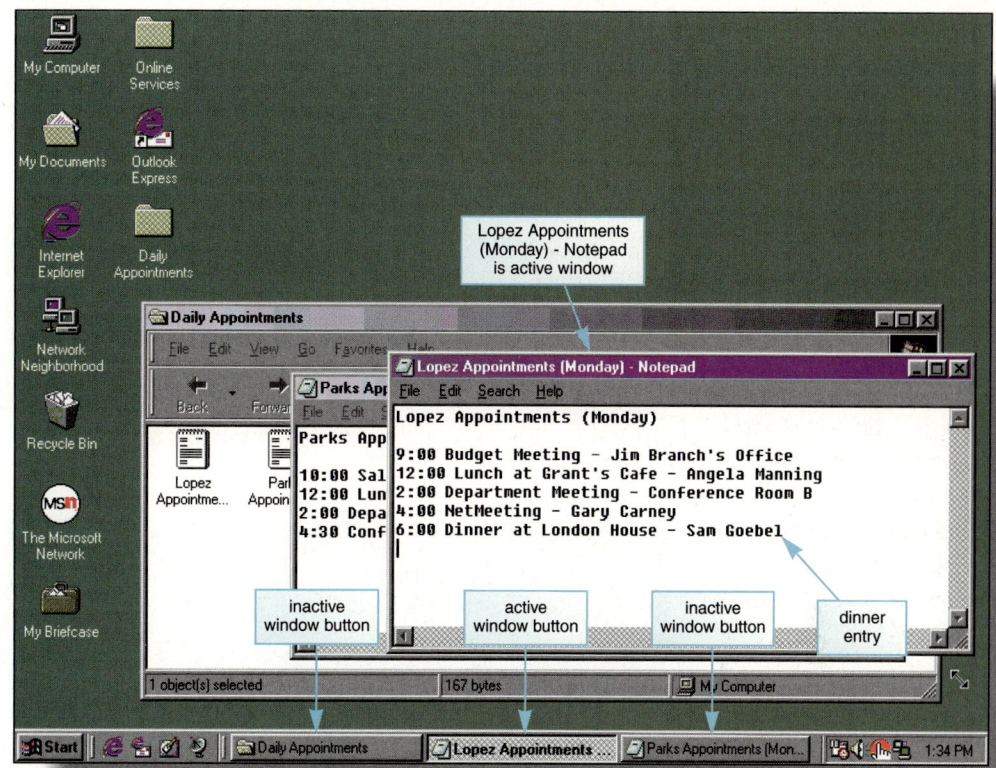

FIGURE 2-29

Other Ways

1. Press ALT+TAB until name of window displays, release keys
2. If visible, click title bar of window

Minimizing All Open Windows

As mentioned earlier, Windows 98 allows you to open multiple windows on the desktop and work within any of the windows by clicking the window button in the taskbar button area. As convenient as it may be to have multiple windows open on the desktop, too many windows or a single maximized window can limit or block your view of the objects on the desktop. To allow you to view the desktop easily without closing all or some of the windows on the desktop, the Quick Launch toolbar contains the Show Desktop icon. The **Show Desktop icon** makes the desktop visible by minimizing all open windows on the desktop.

Currently, the Lopez Appointments (Monday) - Notepad window, Daily Appointments window, and Parks Appointments (Monday) - Notepad window display on the desktop, and a button for each window displays in the taskbar button area (see Figure 2-29). A recessed button displays for the active Lopez Appointments (Monday) - Notepad window and non-recessed buttons for the inactive windows. To minimize the open windows and view the objects on the desktop, perform the steps on the next page.

Steps: To Minimize All Open Windows

1 Point to the Show Desktop icon on the Quick Launch toolbar on the taskbar (Figure 2-30).

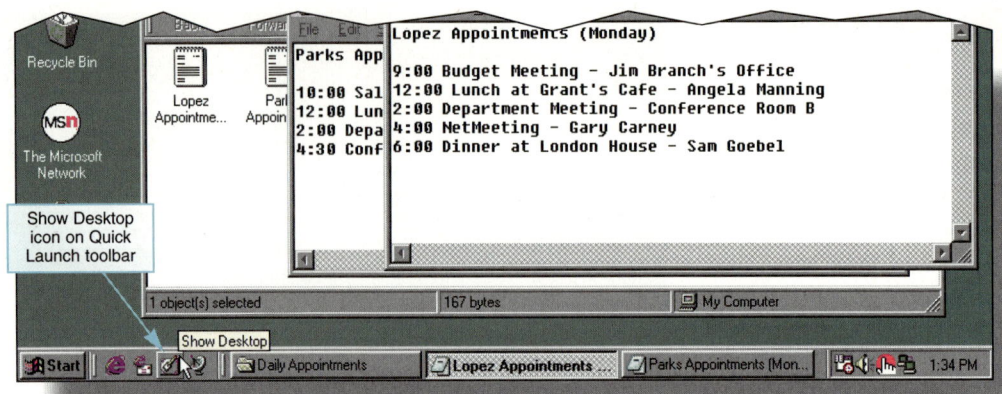

FIGURE 2-30

2 Click the Show Desktop icon.

Windows 98 minimizes all three open windows (Figure 2-31). A button for each minimized window displays in the taskbar button area.

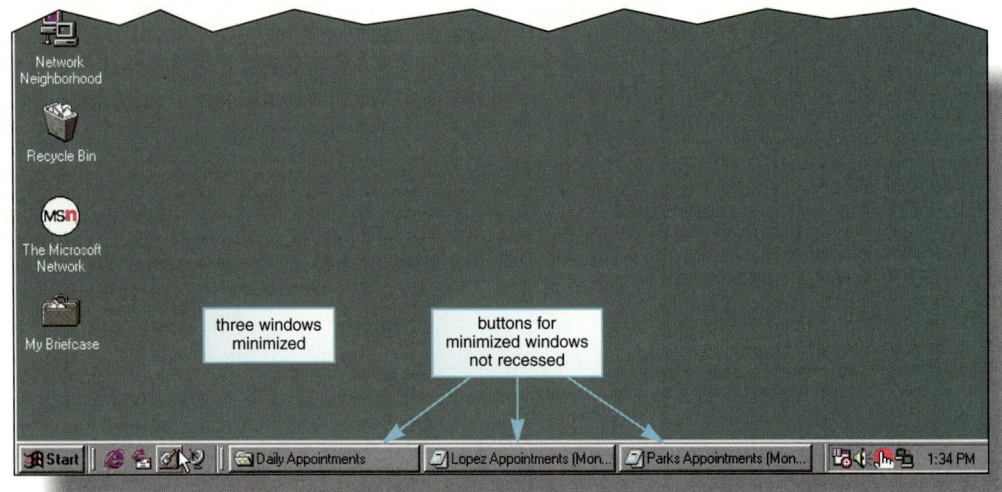

FIGURE 2-31

Other Ways

1. Right-click taskbar, click Minimize All Windows
2. Click the Minimize button on each window

To open one of the three minimized windows and be able to work in that window, click the corresponding button in the taskbar button area. To open all three windows and return the desktop to the way it looked before clicking the Show Desktop icon (see Figure 2-29 on the previous page), click the Show Desktop button a second time.

More About: Closing Windows

The choice of how to close windows is yours. In most cases, you will want to choose the method that causes the least amount of work.

Closing Multiple Windows

When you are finished working with multiple windows, normally you will close them. If the windows are open on the desktop, you can click the Close button on the title bar of each open window to close the windows, as you have done in previous examples. Regardless of whether the windows are open on the desktop or the windows have been minimized using the Show Desktop icon, you also can close the windows using the buttons in the taskbar button area. To close the Lopez Appointments (Monday) - Notepad and Parks Appointments (Monday) - Notepad windows from the taskbar, complete the following steps.

Opening and Modifying Documents Within a Folder • WIN 2.27

Steps: To Close and Save Open Windows from the Taskbar

1 **Right-click the Lopez Appointments (Monday) - Notepad button in the taskbar button area. Point to Close on the shortcut menu.**

A shortcut menu displays containing a variety of commands for the window associated with the button that was clicked (Figure 2-32).

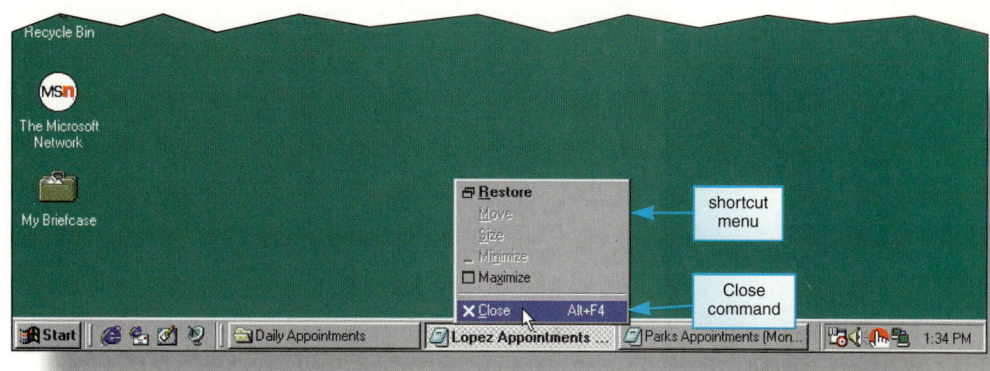

FIGURE 2-32

2 **Click Close. Point to the Yes button.**

The Notepad dialog box displays asking if you want to save the changes (Figure 2-33).

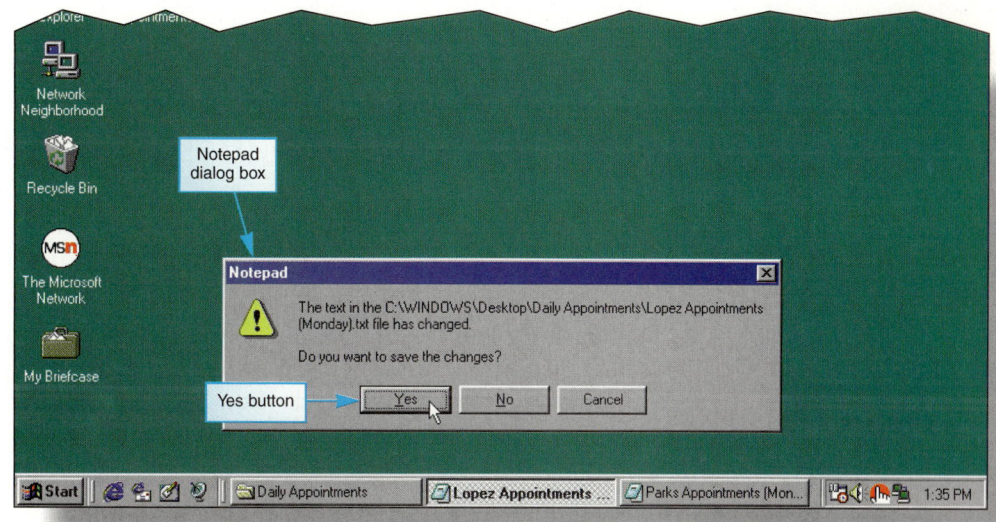

FIGURE 2-33

3 **Click the Yes button. Right-click the Parks Appointments (Monday) - Notepad button in the taskbar button area. Point to Close on the shortcut menu.**

A shortcut menu displays (Figure 2-34). The modified Lopez Appointments (Monday) document is saved in the Daily Appointments folder and its button no longer displays in the taskbar button area.

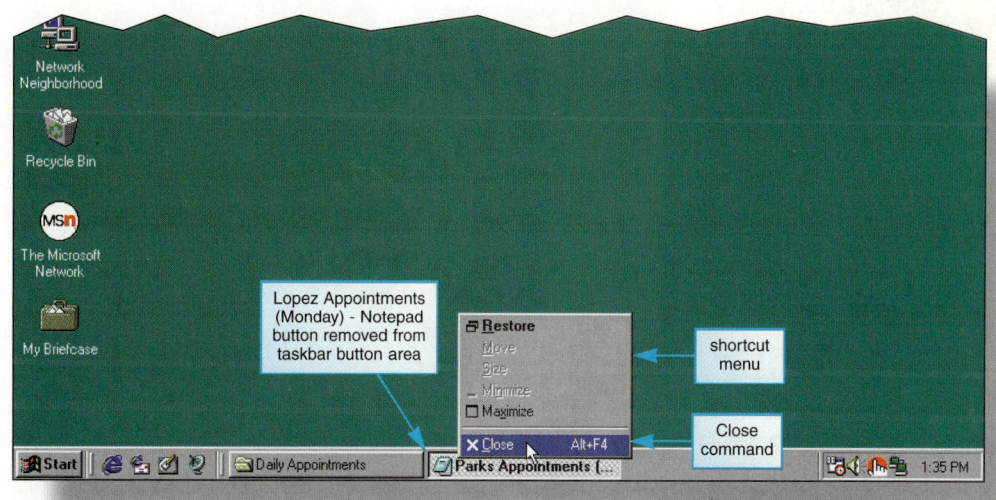

FIGURE 2-34

 **Click Close on the shortcut menu. When the Notepad dialog box displays asking if you want to save the changes, click the Yes button.**

Only the Daily Appointments button remains in the taskbar button area (Figure 2-35).

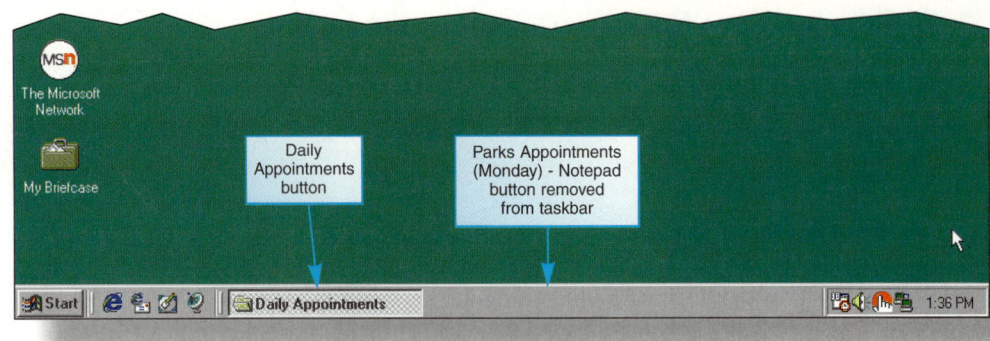

FIGURE 2-35

Other Ways

1. Click taskbar button, on File menu click Save, click Close button
2. Click taskbar button, click Close button on title bar, click Yes button
3. Click taskbar button, on File menu click Exit, click Yes button

The capability of Windows 98 to process multiple documents at the same time and perform multitasking with multiple programs running at the same time is one of the primary features of the operating system.

Printing a Document from Within a Folder

After documents are modified and saved on the desktop, you may wish to print them so you have an updated printed version of the Lopez Appointments (Monday) and the Parks Appointments (Monday) documents. Earlier in this project, you used the Print command from the File menu to print an open document. You also can print documents from a folder without opening the documents, and you can print multiple documents at the same time. To print both the Lopez Appointments (Monday) and the Parks Appointments (Monday) documents from the Daily Appointments folder, perform the following steps.

More About

Printing

Normally it is more efficient to print directly from the document within a folder or on the desktop than to open the document first.

Steps To Print Multiple Documents from Within a Folder

 Click the Daily Appointments button in the taskbar button area. Click the Lopez Appointments (Monday) icon in the Daily Appointments folder to select the icon, hold down the SHIFT key, and click the Parks Appointments (Monday) icon. Release the SHIFT key.

Both icons become selected (Figure 2-36).

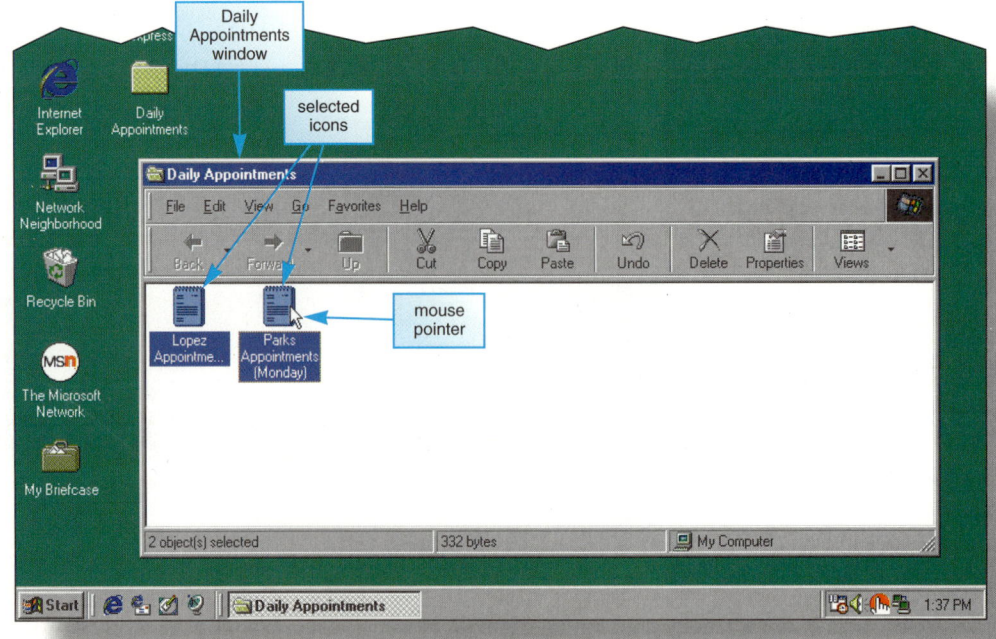

FIGURE 2-36

2 Right-click the Parks Appointments (Monday) icon and then point to Print on the shortcut menu (Figure 2-37).

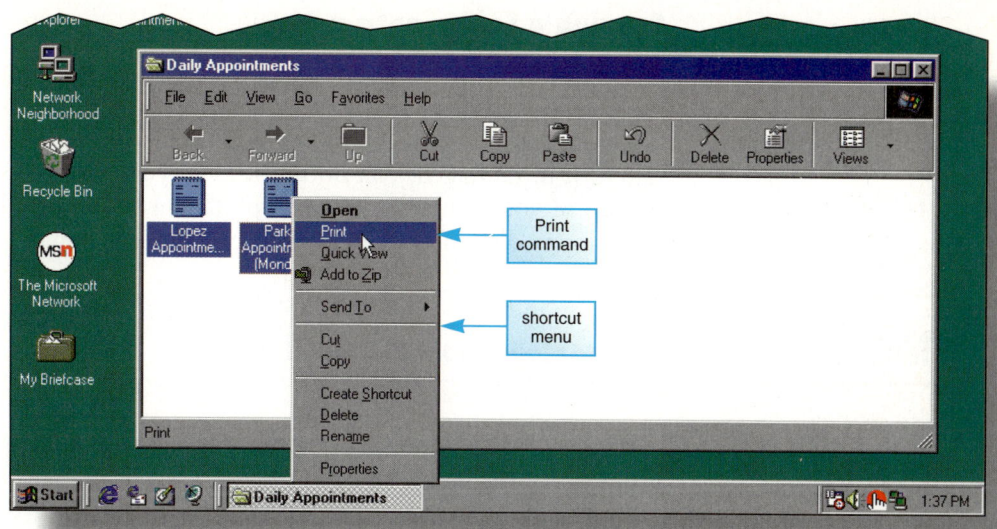

FIGURE 2-37

3 Click Print.

The modified documents print as shown in Figure 2-38.

4 Click the Close button on the Daily Appointments title bar.

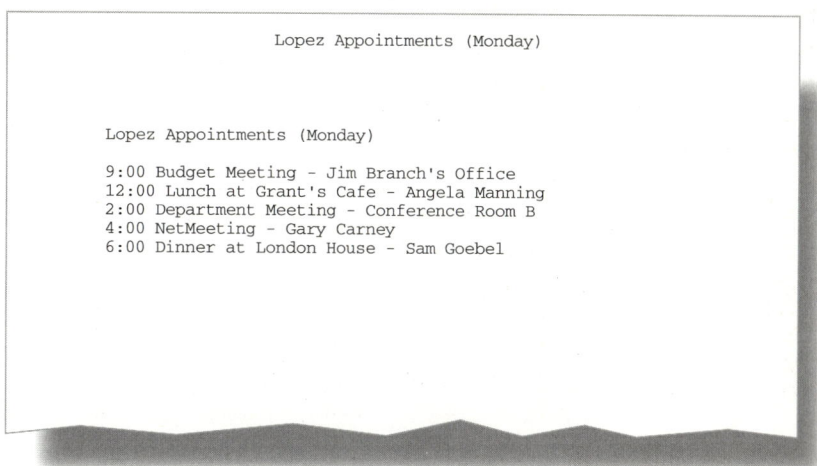

FIGURE 2-38

1. Select document icons, on File menu click Print

Copying a Folder onto a Disk

A folder on the desktop is useful when you are using one or more documents within the folder frequently. It is a good policy, however, to make a copy of a folder and documents within the folder so that in case the folder or its contents are accidentally lost or damaged, you do not lose all your work. This often is called making a **backup** of your folders and files. To make a backup of the Daily Appointments folder on a floppy disk in drive A of your computer, complete the following steps.

To Copy a Folder on the Desktop onto a Floppy Disk

1 Insert a formatted floppy disk into drive A.

2 Right-click the Daily Appointments folder icon on the desktop. Point to Send To on the shortcut menu. Point to 3½ Floppy (A) on the Send To submenu.

The shortcut menu and Send To submenu display (Figure 2-39).

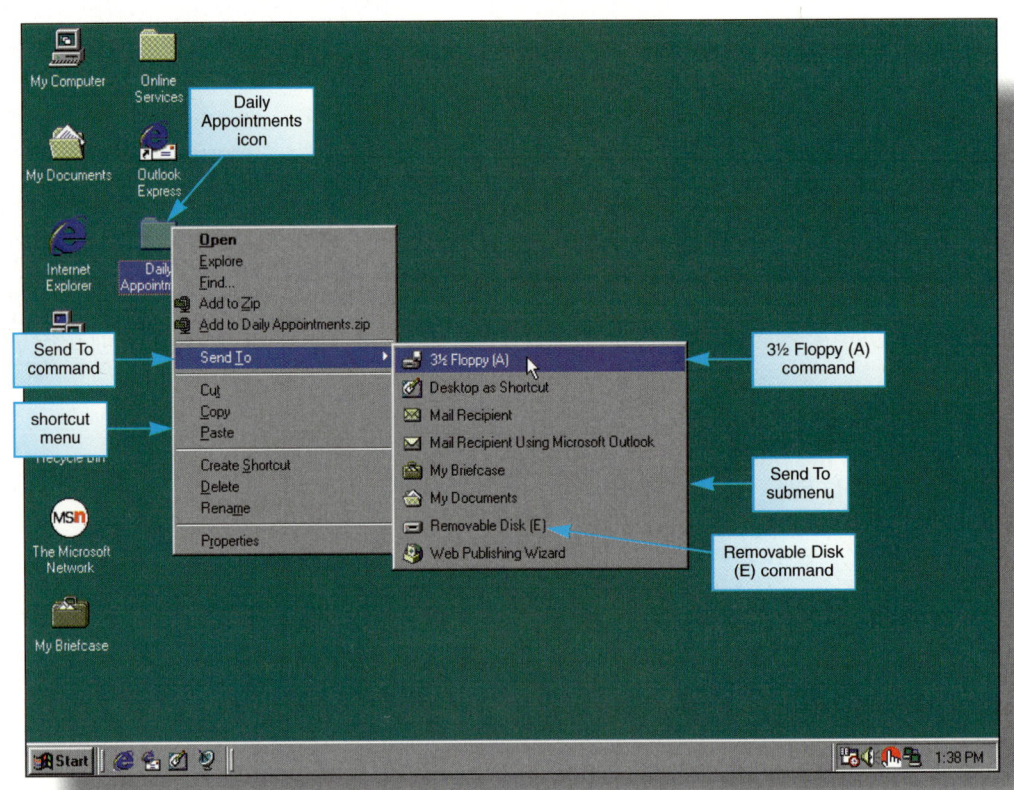

FIGURE 2-39

More About

The Send To Command

Commands can easily be added to and removed from the Send To submenu. Note the Removable Disk (E) command that has been added in Figure 2-39 to allow the user to back up files and folders to a removable disk.

Printing a Document from Within a Folder • **WIN 2.31**

PROJECT 2

 Click 3½ Floppy (A).

While the Daily Appointments folder and the documents within the folder are being copied, the Copying dialog box displays (Figure 2-40).

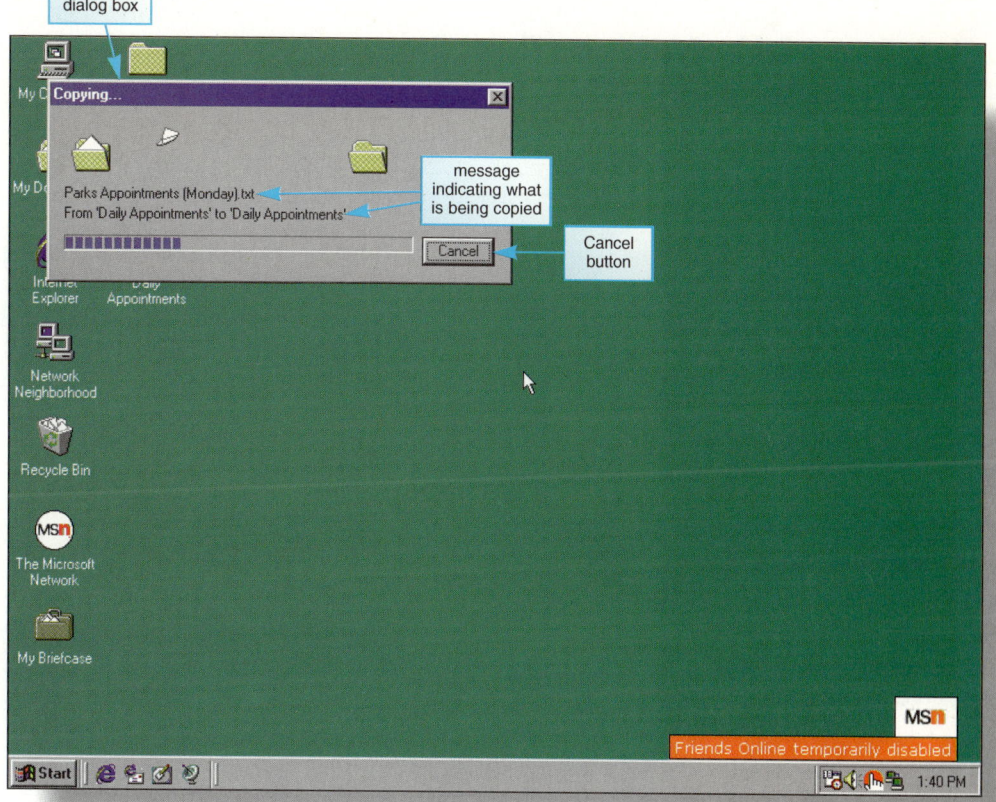

FIGURE 2-40

In Figure 2-40, a message explains which folders and files are being copied, and animated pages fly from one folder to the other in the dialog box. After the folder and all documents have been copied, the Copying dialog box closes. At the conclusion of the copying process, the Daily Appointments folder and the documents in the folder are stored both on the desktop and on the floppy disk in drive A. If you want to stop the copying process, you can click the Cancel button in the Copying dialog box.

Opening a Folder on a Floppy Disk

After copying a folder onto a floppy disk, you may wish to verify that the folder has been copied properly onto the floppy disk; or, you may wish to open a document stored in the folder directly from the floppy disk. To open a folder stored on a floppy disk, complete the steps on the next two pages.

1. Double-click My Computer icon, right-drag folder icon to 3½ Floppy (A:) icon in My Computer window, click Copy Here
2. Double-click My Computer icon, drag folder icon to 3½ Floppy (A:) icon
3. Right-click the folder icon, click Copy, double-click My Computer icon, right-click 3½ Floppy (A:) icon, click Paste

Backups

Copying a file or folder to a floppy disk in drive A is one way to create a backup, but backing up files often is a much more elaborate process. Because floppy disks can contain only 1.44 megabytes of data, most backups are written on tape or portable hard disks that can contain hundreds of megabytes (millions of characters) and even gigabytes (billions of characters).

Steps: To Open a Folder Stored on a Floppy Disk

 Double-click the My Computer icon. Move and resize the window to resemble the My Computer window shown in Figure 2-41. Point to the 3½ Floppy (A:) icon in the My Computer window.

The My Computer window opens and the My Computer button is recessed (Figure 2-41). Notice that the Back and Forward buttons on the toolbar appear dimmed and are unavailable. When the buttons are not dimmed, you can click the buttons to display previously displayed windows.

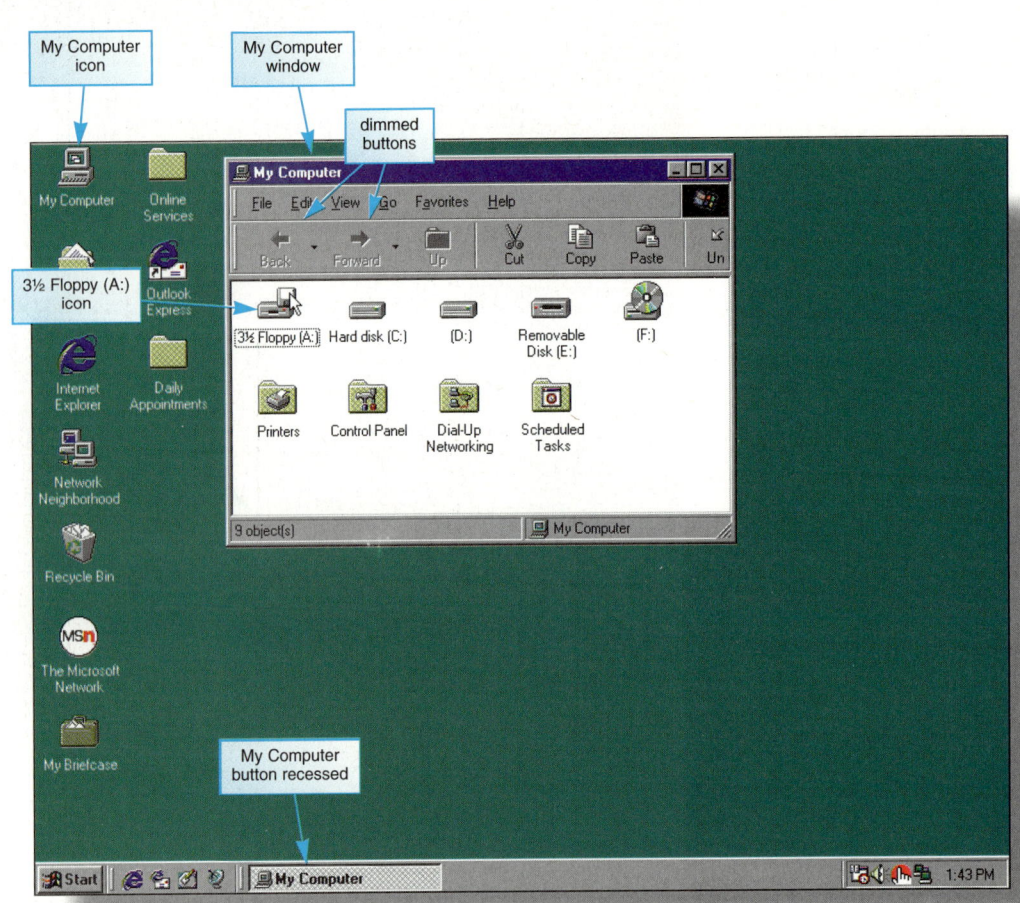

FIGURE 2-41

The Back and Forward Buttons

When the Back and Forward buttons are not dimmed, clicking the Back button displays the last window opened and clicking the Forward button displays the next window in a previously displayed sequence of windows.

Printing a Document from Within a Folder • WIN 2.33

2 **Double-click the 3½ Floppy (A:) icon and then point to the Daily Appointments icon in the 3½ Floppy (A:) window.**

The 3½ Floppy (A:) window opens in the same window in which the My Computer was displayed and the 3½ Floppy (A:) button replaces the My Computer button in the taskbar button area (Figure 2-42). Because the My Computer window was opened prior to opening the 3½ Floppy (A:) window, the Back button on the toolbar no longer is dimmed and is available. Clicking the **Back button** displays the previously displayed window (My Computer window).

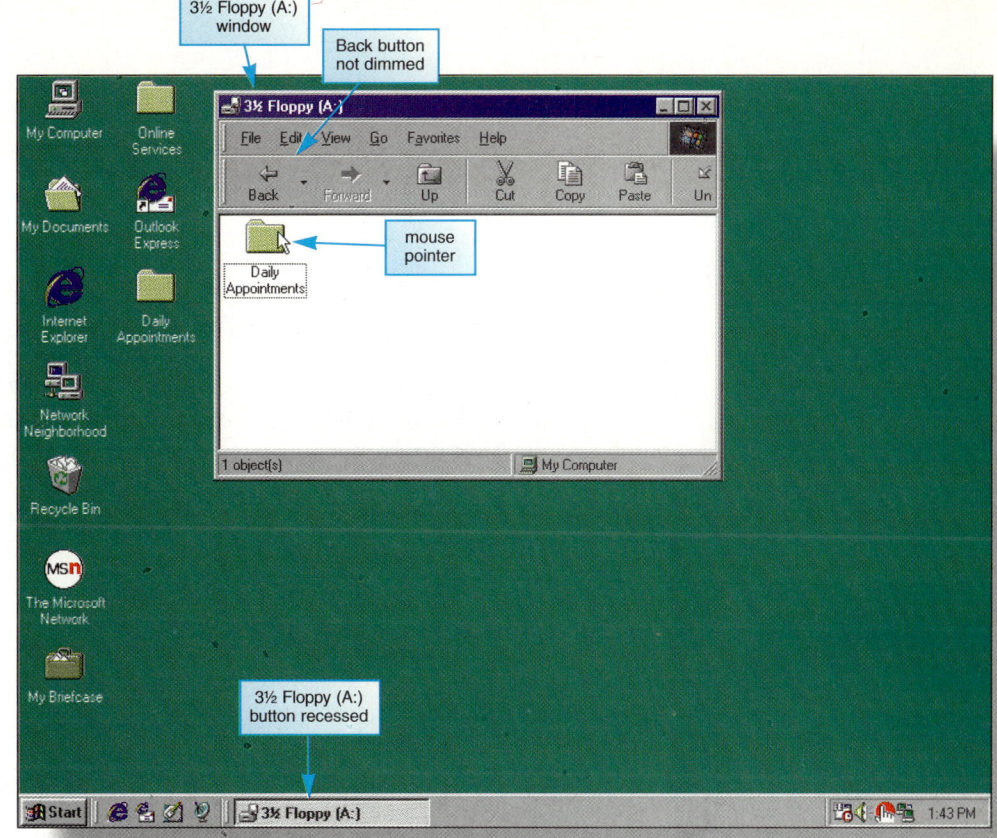

FIGURE 2-42

3 **Double-click the Daily Appointments icon. Point to the Close button on the Daily Appointments title bar.**

The Daily Appointments window opens in the same window in which 3½ Floppy (A:) was displayed and the Daily Appointments button replaces the 3½ Floppy (A:) button (Figure 2-43).

4 **Click the Close button and then remove the floppy disk from drive A.**

The Daily Appointments window closes and the Daily Appointments button no longer displays in the taskbar button area.

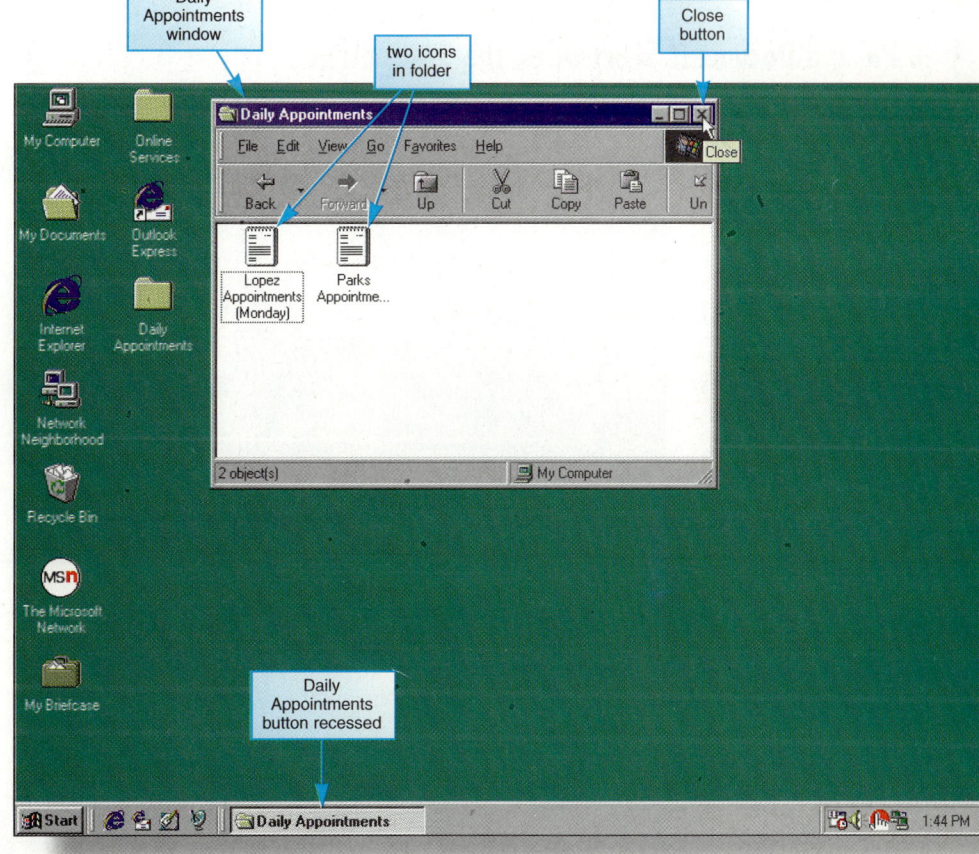

FIGURE 2-43

If you wish to open one of the documents in the folder stored on the floppy disk in drive A as shown in Figure 2-43 on the previous page, use the same procedure as when opening the document from the desktop; that is – double-click the document icon.

Creating Document Shortcuts

> **More About**
>
> **Shortcuts**
>
> A shortcut icon is a pointer that references the location of a document or application on the hard drive. The shortcut icon is not the actual document or application. Thus, when you delete a shortcut icon, you are deleting the shortcut icon and its reference to the document or application. You are not deleting the document or the programs that comprise the application. They remain on the hard drive.

One of Windows 98's most powerful features is its capability of being easily customized. One of the many ways to customize Windows 98 is to use shortcuts to launch application programs and open documents. A **shortcut** is an icon that represents a document or an application program. Placing a shortcut to an application or document on the Start menu or on the desktop can make it easier to launch the application or open the document.

Placing a Shortcut on the Start Menu

One of the ways in which Windows 98 can be customized is to add an application shortcut or a document shortcut to the Start menu that displays when you click the Start button. You do not actually place the application or document on the menu, but instead, you place a shortcut to the document on the menu.

To illustrate this, assume you want to be able to open the Lopez Appointments (Monday) document from the Start menu. To place the Lopez Appointments (Monday) document shortcut on the Start menu, complete the following steps.

To Place a Document Shortcut on the Start Menu

1 **Double-click the Daily Appointments icon to open the folder.**

The Daily Appointments window opens (Figure 2-44). The Lopez Appointments (Monday) and Parks Appointments (Monday) document icons are contained in the folder.

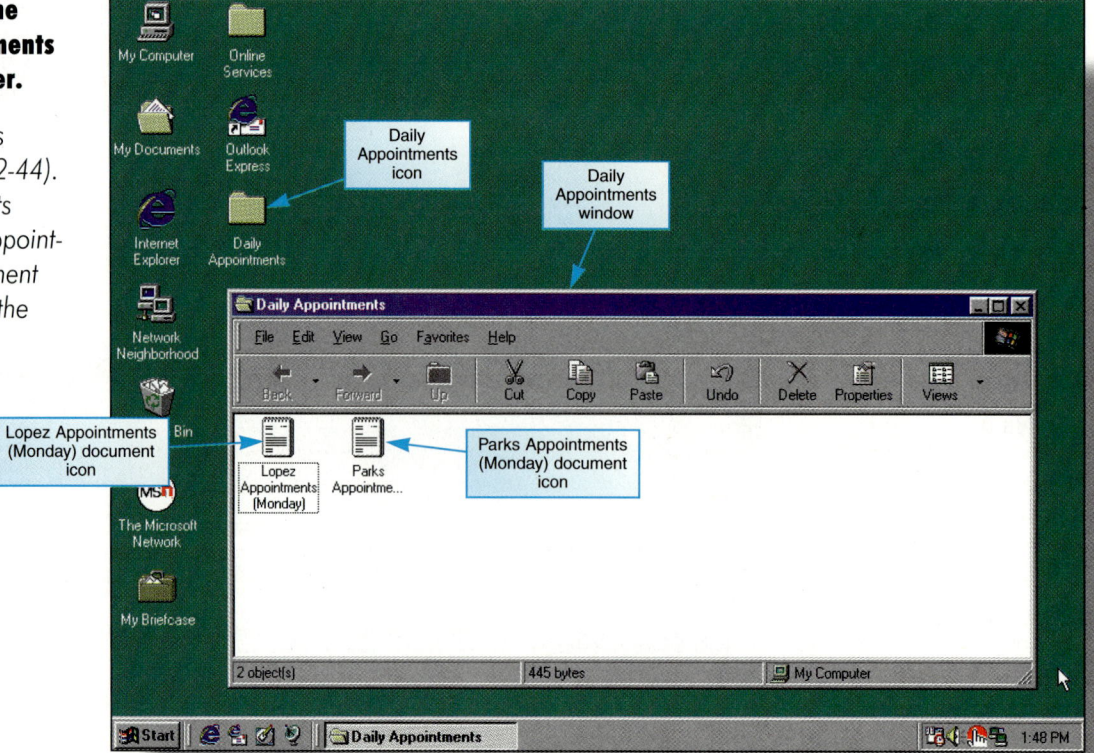

FIGURE 2-44

2 **Drag the Lopez Appointments (Monday) icon on top of the Start button on the taskbar.**

When you drag the icon on top of the Start button, the icon appears dimmed and the Start menu displays (Figure 2-45). When you release the mouse button, the Start menu remains on the desktop.

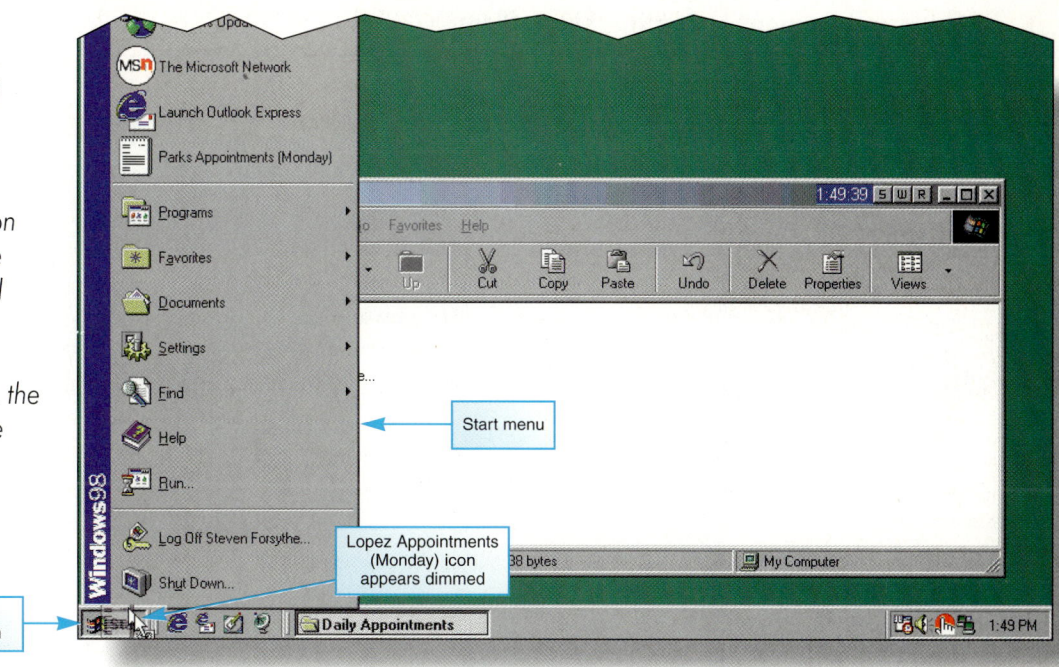

FIGURE 2-45

3 **Click the Start button.**

The Start menu displays (Figure 2-46). The Lopez Appointments (Monday) shortcut displays in the section above the Programs command on the Start menu.

4 **Click an open area of the Daily Appointments window to close the Start menu.**

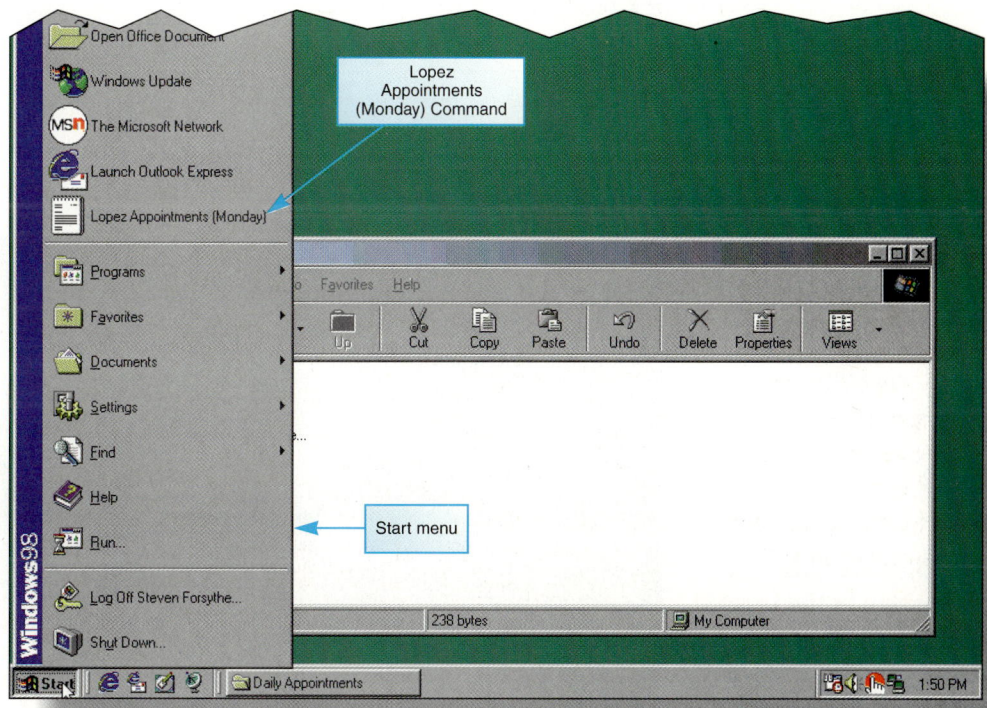

FIGURE 2-46

Opening a Document from the Start Menu

Once you have placed a document or application program shortcut on the Start menu, you can click the Start button and open the document or application program from the Start menu. To open the Lopez Appointments (Monday) document from the Start menu, complete the steps on the next page.

WIN 2.36 • Project 2 • Working on the Windows 98 Desktop

Steps   To Open a Document Using the Start Menu

1 **Click the Start button on the taskbar. Point to Lopez Appointments (Monday) on the Start menu.**

The Start menu displays (Figure 2-47).

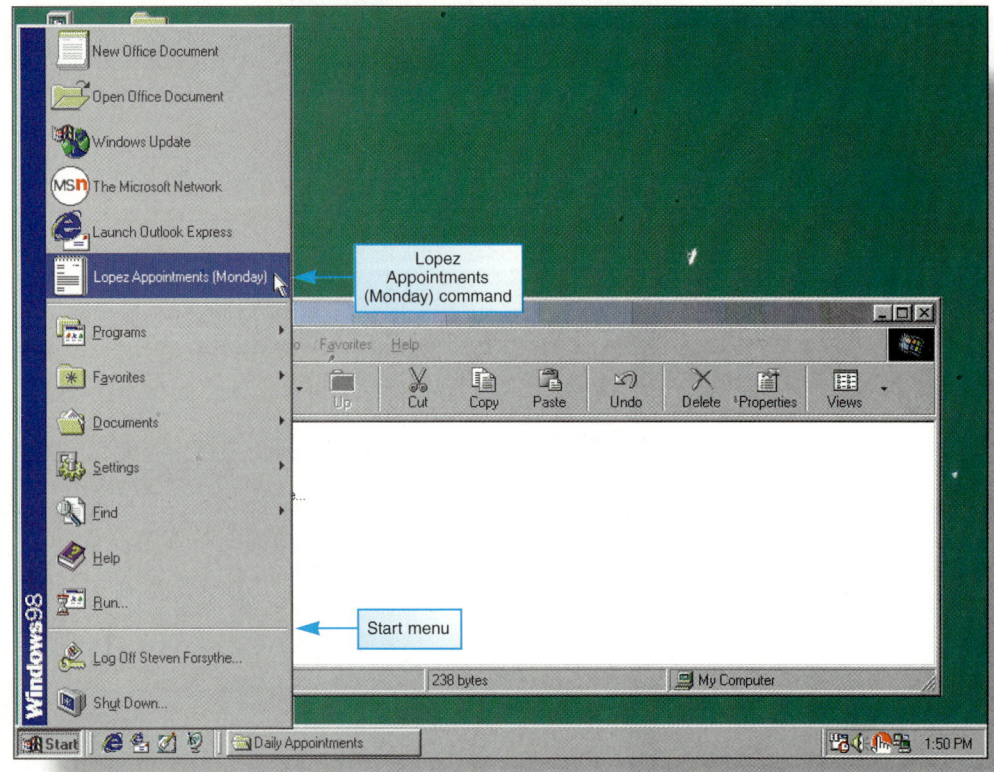

FIGURE 2-47

2 **Click Lopez Appointments (Monday).**

Notepad opens and the Lopez Appointments (Monday) document displays (Figure 2-48).

3 **Click the Close button in the Lopez Appointments (Monday) - Notepad window. Click the Close button in the Daily Appointments window.**

The two windows close.

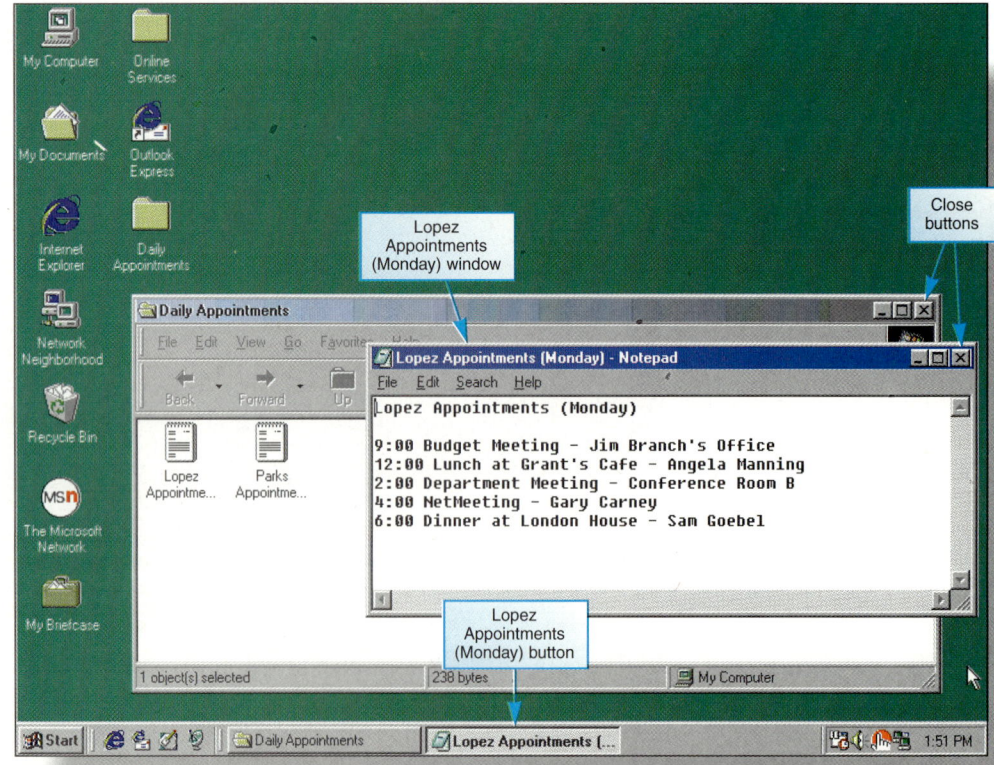

FIGURE 2-48

Creating Document Shortcuts • WIN 2.37

Removing a Shortcut from the Start Menu

Just as you can add document or application program shortcuts to the Start menu, you also can remove them from the Start menu. To remove the Lopez Appointments (Monday) shortcut from the Start menu, complete the following steps.

  To Remove a Shortcut from the Start Menu

1 Click the Start button on the taskbar. Point to Lopez Appointments (Monday) on the Start menu (Figure 2-49).

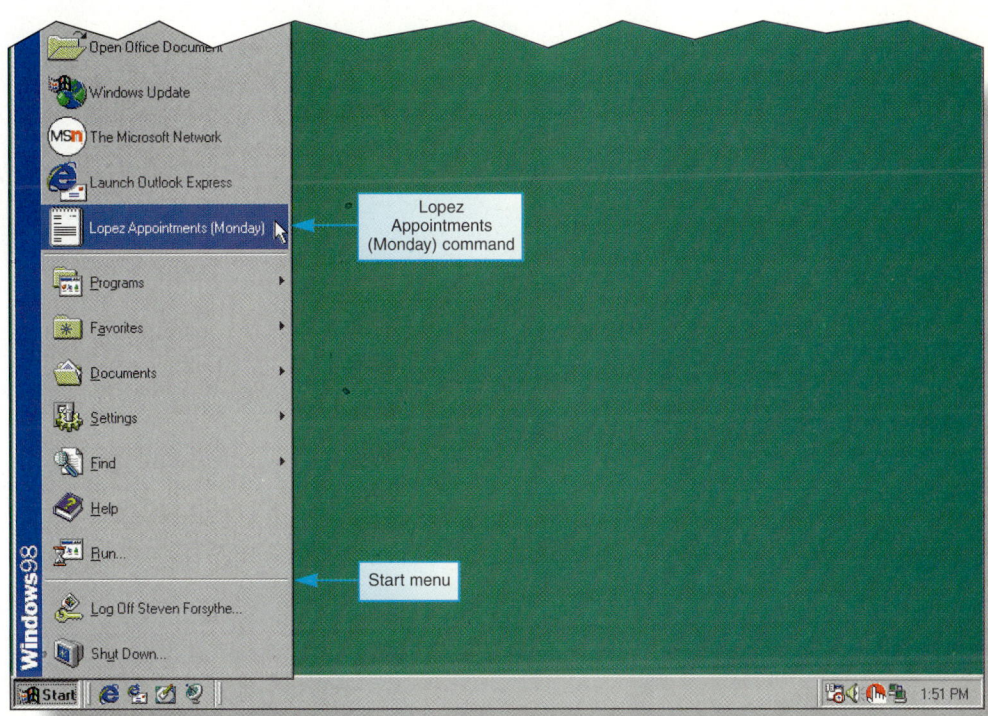

FIGURE 2-49

2 Right-click Lopez Appointments (Monday). Point to Delete on the shortcut menu (Figure 2-50).

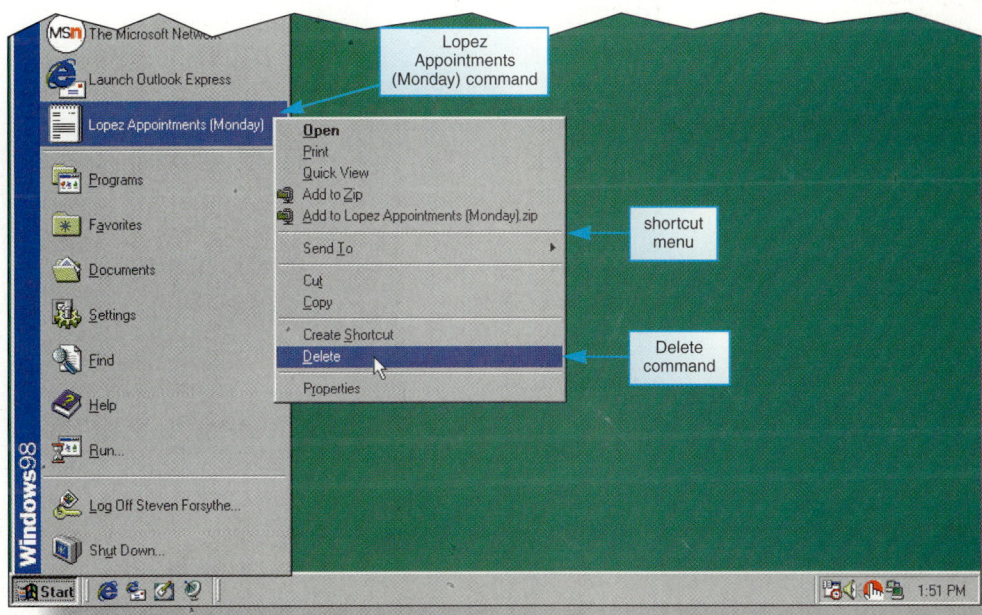

FIGURE 2-50

3 **Click Delete. When the Confirm File Delete dialog box displays, point to the Yes button.**

The Confirm File Delete dialog box displays (Figure 2-51).

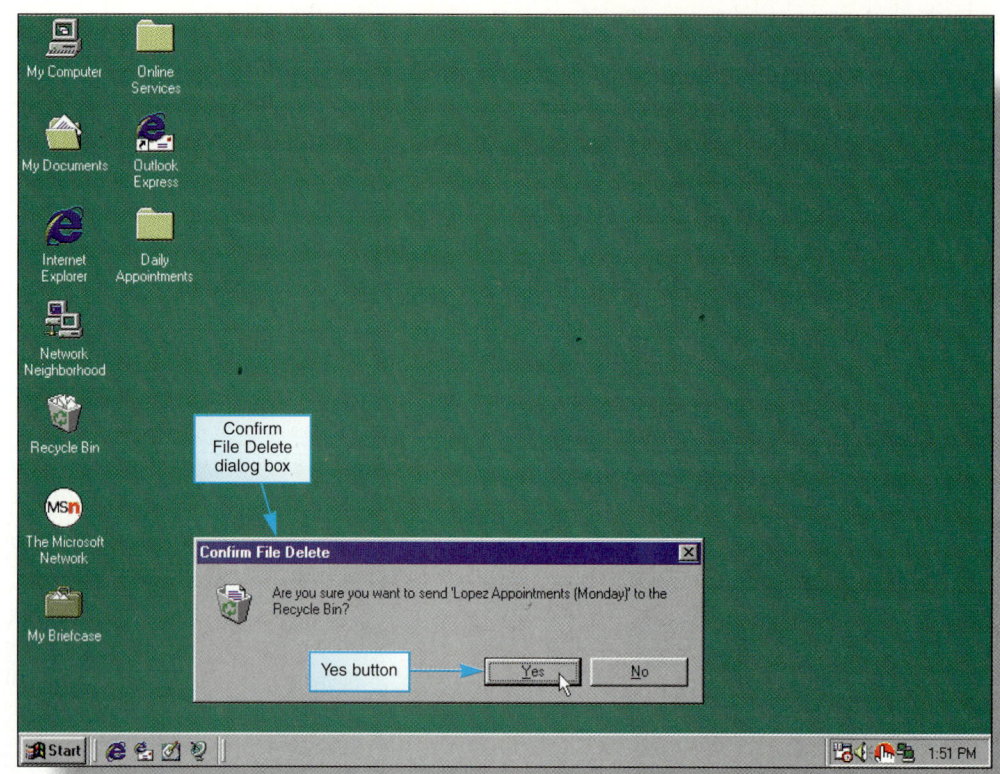

FIGURE 2-51

4 **Click the Yes button. Click the Start button on the taskbar to view the Start menu.**

The Lopez Appointments (Monday) shortcut is removed from the Start menu (Figure 2-52).

5 **Click an open area of the desktop to close the Start menu.**

The Start menu closes.

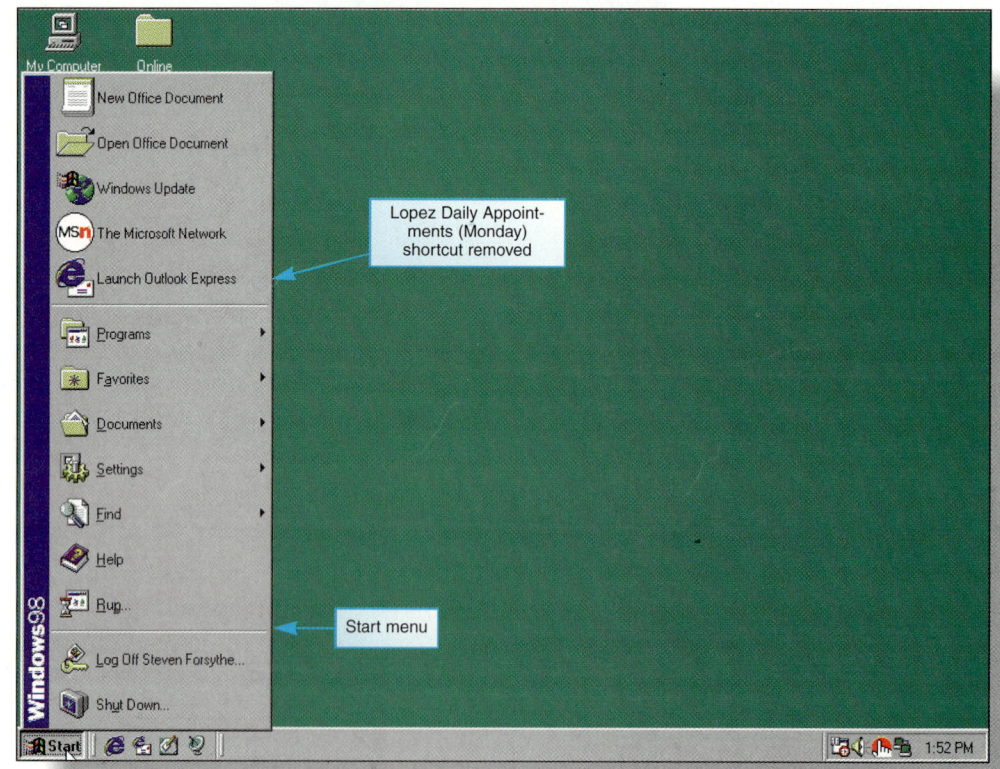

FIGURE 2-52

The capability of adding and removing shortcuts and folders on the Start menu provides great flexibility when customizing your computer.

Creating a Shortcut on the Desktop

You can create document and application program shortcuts directly on the desktop as well as on the Start menu. To create a shortcut for the Parks Appointments (Monday) document, complete the following steps.

To Create a Shortcut on the Desktop

 Double-click the Daily Appointments icon to open the Daily Appointments window. Right-drag the Parks Appointments (Monday) icon from the Daily Appointments window to the desktop. Point to Create Shortcut(s) Here on the shortcut menu.

The Daily Appointments window, a dimmed icon, and a shortcut menu display on the desktop (Figure 2-53).

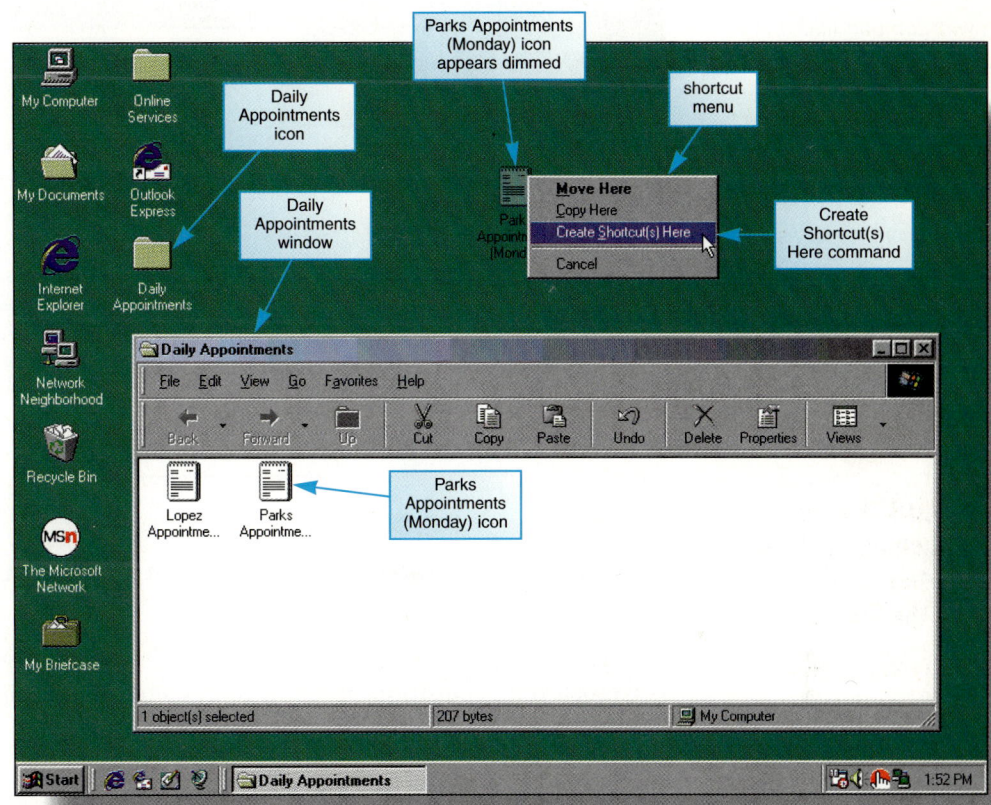

FIGURE 2-53

② Click Create Shortcut(s) Here. If the shortcut does not display on your desktop, move and resize the Daily Appointments window until the shortcut is visible.

Windows 98 creates a shortcut on the desktop (Figure 2-54). The shortcut is identified with an icon title and a small arrow in the bottom-left corner of the icon. The shortcut might display on the desktop where you dragged it or it might display next in line in the columns of icons, depending your computer's settings.

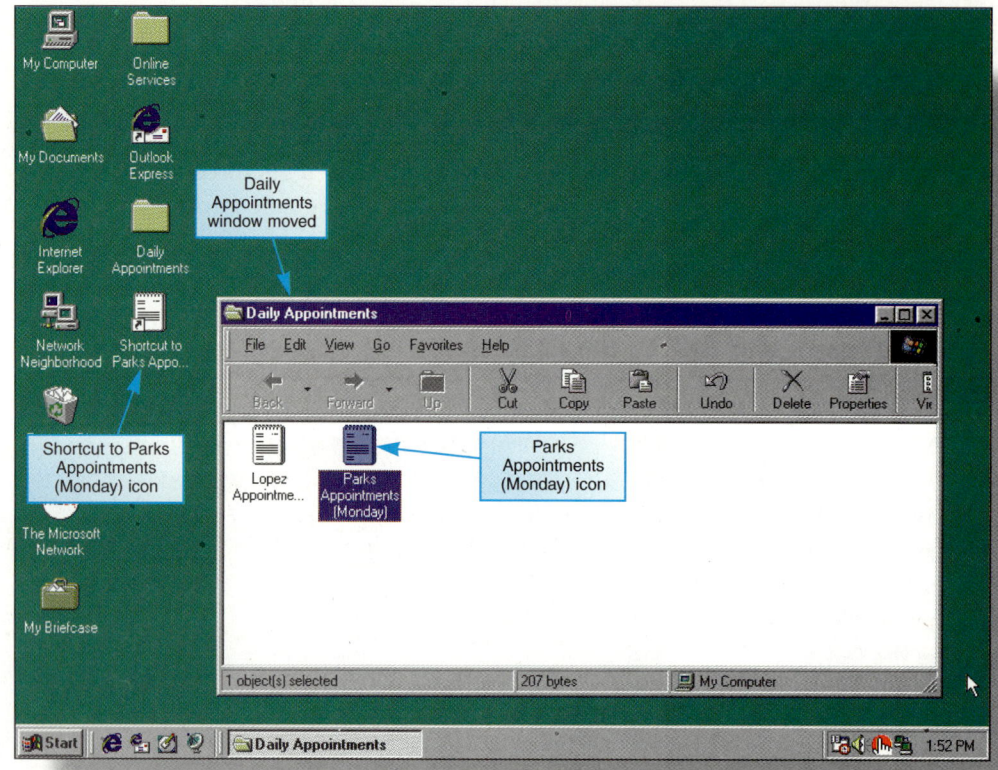

FIGURE 2-54

1. Press CTRL+SHIFT and drag icon to desktop, click Create Shortcut(s) Here

Opening a Document or Launching an Application Program Using a Shortcut on the Desktop

Once the shortcut has been placed on the desktop, you can open the document or launch the application program represented by the shortcut by double-clicking the shortcut. To open the Parks Appointments (Monday) document, complete the following steps.

Creating Document Shortcuts • WIN 2.41

 Steps To Open a Document Using a Shortcut on the Desktop

1 **Double-click the Shortcut to Parks Appointments (Monday) icon.**

Notepad launches and the Parks Appointments (Monday) document displays in the Notepad window (Figure 2-55).

2 **Click the Close button on the Parks Appointments (Monday) - Notepad title bar to close the window. Click the Close button on the Daily Appointments title bar to close the window.**

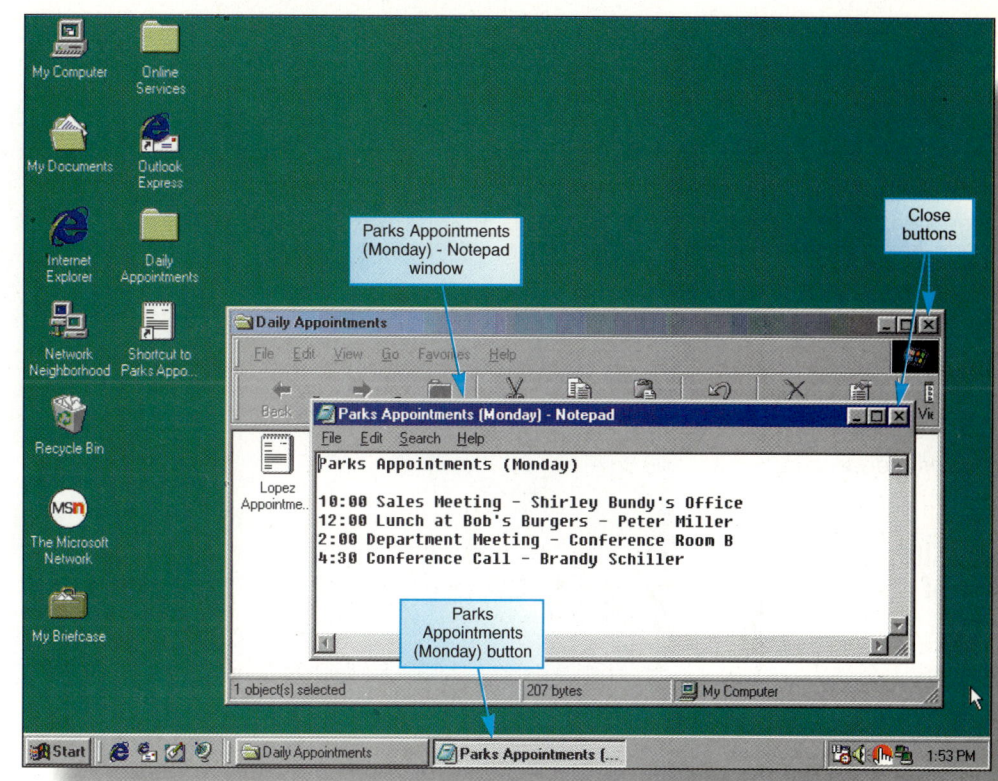

FIGURE 2-55

Shortcuts can be quite useful because they can reference application programs and documents stored on the hard disk. For instance, you can store a document in a folder on your computer's hard disk and create a shortcut to the folder on the desktop. In that manner, you can open the document from the desktop but the document remains stored in its logical place in a folder on your computer's hard disk.

Other Ways

1. Right-click shortcut icon, click Open
2. Click shortcut icon, press ENTER

Arranging Icons

In some instances you may want to control the sequence and arrangement of the icons on the desktop. To arrange the icons, you can use the shortcut menu that displays when you right-click the desktop. To display the shortcut menu and review your capability to arrange icons on the desktop, complete the steps on the next page.

To Display the Arrange Icons Submenu

 Right-click an open area on the desktop and then point to Arrange Icons.

A shortcut menu and the Arrange Icons submenu display (Figure 2-56). A check mark precedes the Auto Arrange command to indicate the Auto Arrange command is selected and Windows 98 will automatically arrange the icons on the desktop.

 Click an open area of the desktop.

The shortcut menu and Arrange Icons submenu no longer display on the desktop.

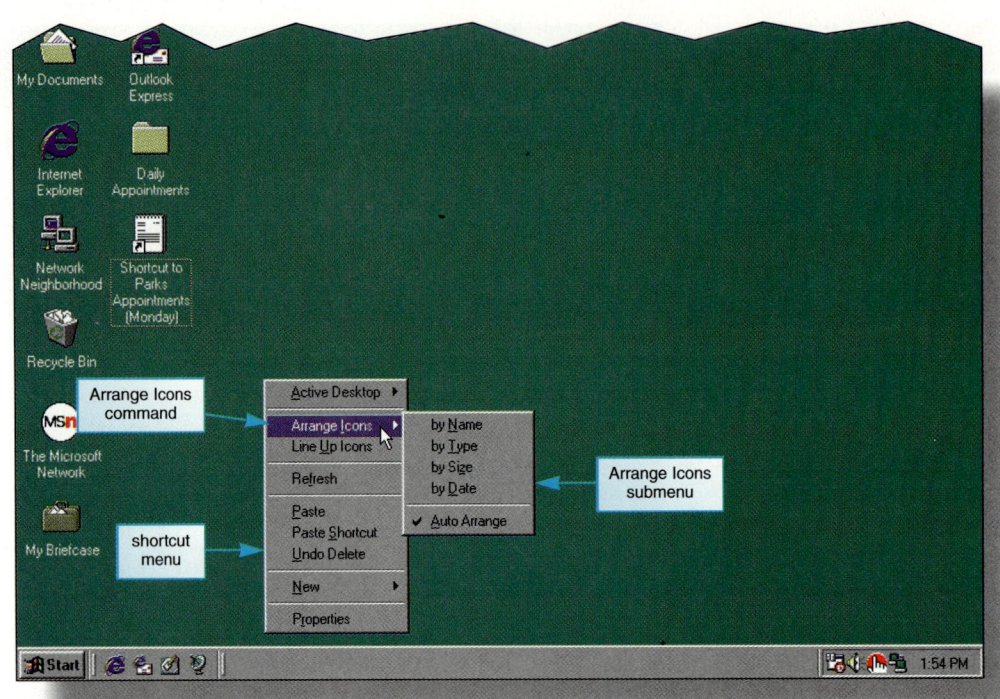

FIGURE 2-56

If the Auto Arrange command is selected, Windows 98 will automatically arrange all icons on the desktop. If an icon is added to the desktop, Windows 98 automatically will place the icon where it belongs in the columns of icons that display on the left side of the desktop. If the Auto Arrange command is not selected, you can place icons anywhere on the desktop you want.

If you click the **by Name command** on the Arrange Icons submenu, the icons you have created on your desktop will be arranged in ascending alphabetical order. The **by Type command** will arrange the icons by the type of file they represent. The **by Size command** arranges the icons from the smallest to the largest file, and the **by Date command** arranges the icons from the newest to the oldest based on when the files were created.

Deleting Shortcuts, Folders, and Documents on the Desktop

In many cases after you have worked with folders and documents on the desktop, at some time you will want to delete the folders and documents from the desktop. Windows 98 offers three different techniques to perform this operation: (1) right-click the object and then click Delete on the shortcut menu; (2) right-drag the object to the Recycle Bin; and (3) drag the object to the Recycle Bin. The steps in this section will demonstrate all three methods.

It is important you realize what you are doing when you delete a folder or document off the desktop, and always be extremely cautious when deleting anything. When you **delete a shortcut** from the desktop, you delete only the shortcut icon and its reference to the document or application program. The document or application program itself, which is stored elsewhere on your hard disk, is not deleted. When you **delete the icon** for a folder, document, or application program on the desktop that is not a shortcut, however, the actual folder, document, or application program is deleted. Therefore, whenever you delete from the desktop, you must be quite cautious and make sure you are deleting exactly what you want to delete.

When you delete a folder, document, or application program from the desktop, Windows 98 places these items in the **Recycle Bin**, which is an area on the hard disk that contains all the items you have deleted not only from the desktop but from the hard disk as well. When the Recycle Bin becomes full, you can empty it. Up until the time you empty the Recycle Bin, you can recover deleted files and application programs. Even though you have this safety net, you should be extremely cautious whenever deleting anything from your desktop or hard disk.

Assume at the end of the week you no longer have a need for the Lopez Appointments (Monday) and the Parks Appointments (Monday) documents. You decide, therefore, that you can delete them safely from the desktop. To accomplish this, you must delete the shortcut to the Parks Appointments (Monday) document, the two documents, and the folder in which the documents are stored. To delete the shortcut, complete the following steps.

To Delete a Shortcut from the Desktop

1 **Right-drag the Shortcut to Parks Appointments (Monday) icon to the Recycle Bin icon on the desktop. Point to Move Here on the shortcut menu.**

The Shortcut to Parks Appointments (Monday) icon appears dimmed on top of the Recycle Bin icon and a shortcut menu with two commands displays (Figure 2-57). The Shortcut to Parks Appointments (Monday) icon remains on the desktop.

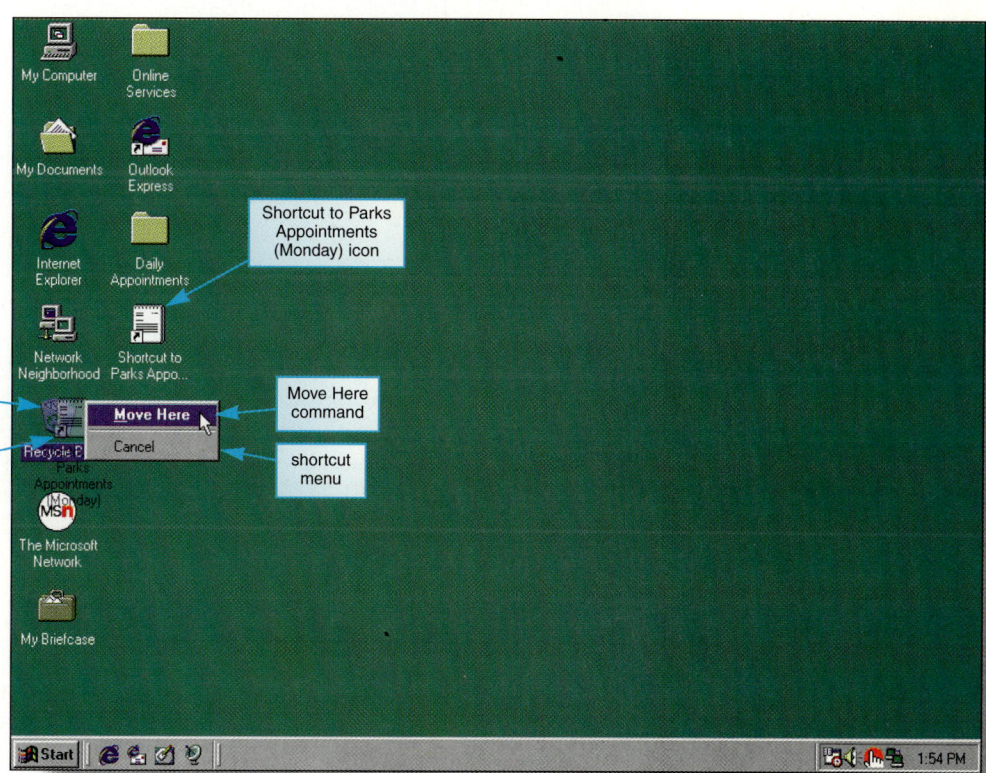

FIGURE 2-57

② **Click Move Here. When the Confirm File Delete dialog box displays, point to the Yes button.**

The Confirm File Delete dialog box displays (Figure 2-58).

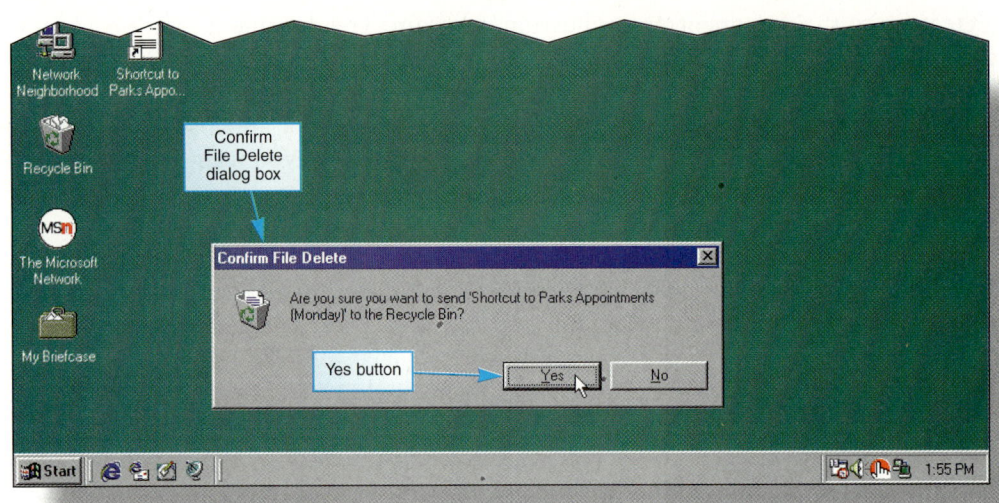

FIGURE 2-58

③ **Click the Yes button.**

The Shortcut to Parks Appointments (Monday) icon no longer displays on the desktop (Figure 2-59). The icon now is contained within the Recycle Bin.

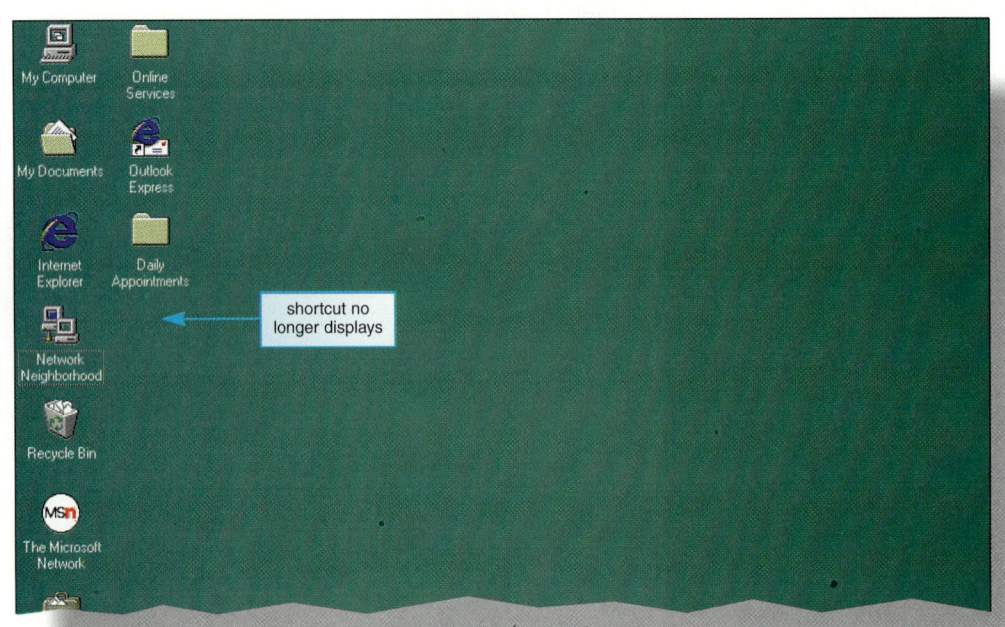

FIGURE 2-59

1. Drag shortcut icon to Recycle Bin, click Yes button
2. Right-click shortcut icon, click Delete, click Yes button

As noted previously, you can recover a shortcut, document, or application program you have moved to the Recycle Bin from the desktop or your hard disk. To do so, you double-click the Recycle Bin icon to open the Recycle Bin window, click the object you want to restore to the desktop, click File on the menu bar, and then click Restore.

Deleting Multiple Files

You can delete multiple files at the same time. Assume you want to delete both the Lopez Appointments (Monday) document and the Parks Appointments (Monday) document. To do so, complete the following steps.

Steps To Delete Multiple Files

1 Double-click the Daily Appointments icon on the desktop. Place the mouse pointer below and to the right of the two document icons in the Daily Appointments window. Drag up and to the left until both icons are selected.

The Daily Appointments window opens, a dotted line surrounds the Lopez Appointments (Monday) and Parks Appointments (Monday) icons and the icons are selected (Figure 2-60).

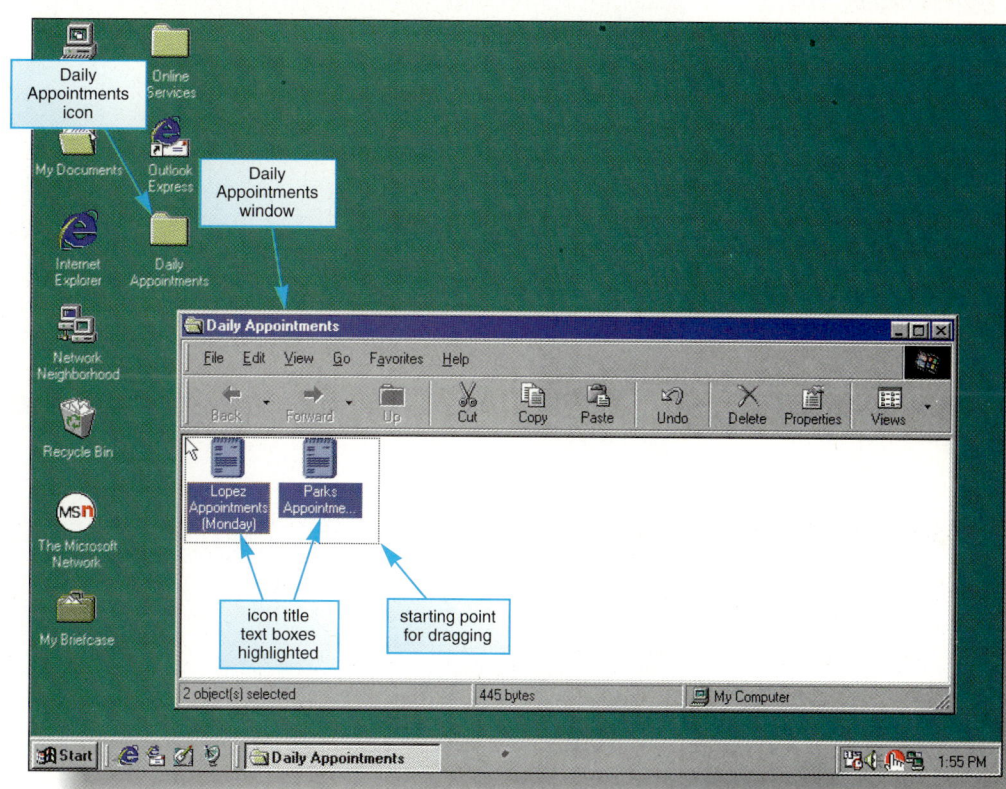

FIGURE 2-60

2 Right-click either icon. Point to Delete on the shortcut menu.

The Lopez Appointments (Monday) icon is right-clicked and a shortcut menu displays (Figure 2-61). Some of the commands on the shortcut menu might be different from those on your computer.

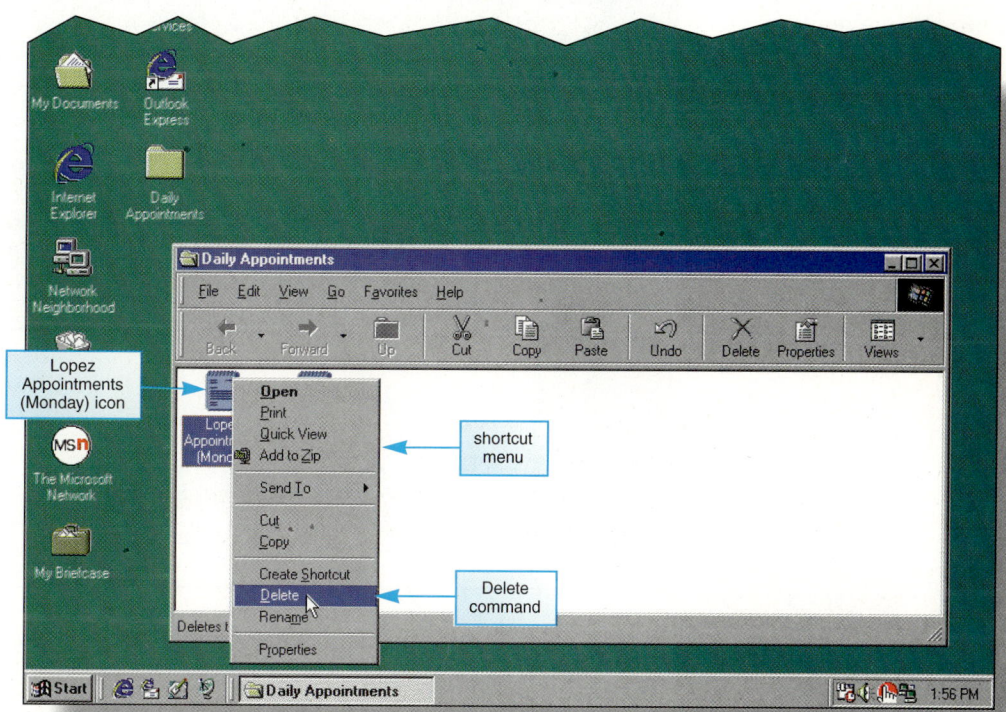

FIGURE 2-61

Click Delete. Point to the Yes button in the Confirm Multiple File Delete dialog box.

The Confirm Multiple File Delete dialog box displays (Figure 2-62). This dialog box ensures that you really want to delete the files. On some computers, this dialog box will not display because a special option has been chosen that specifies not to show this dialog box. If the dialog box does not display on your computer, the documents will be placed directly in the Recycle Bin.

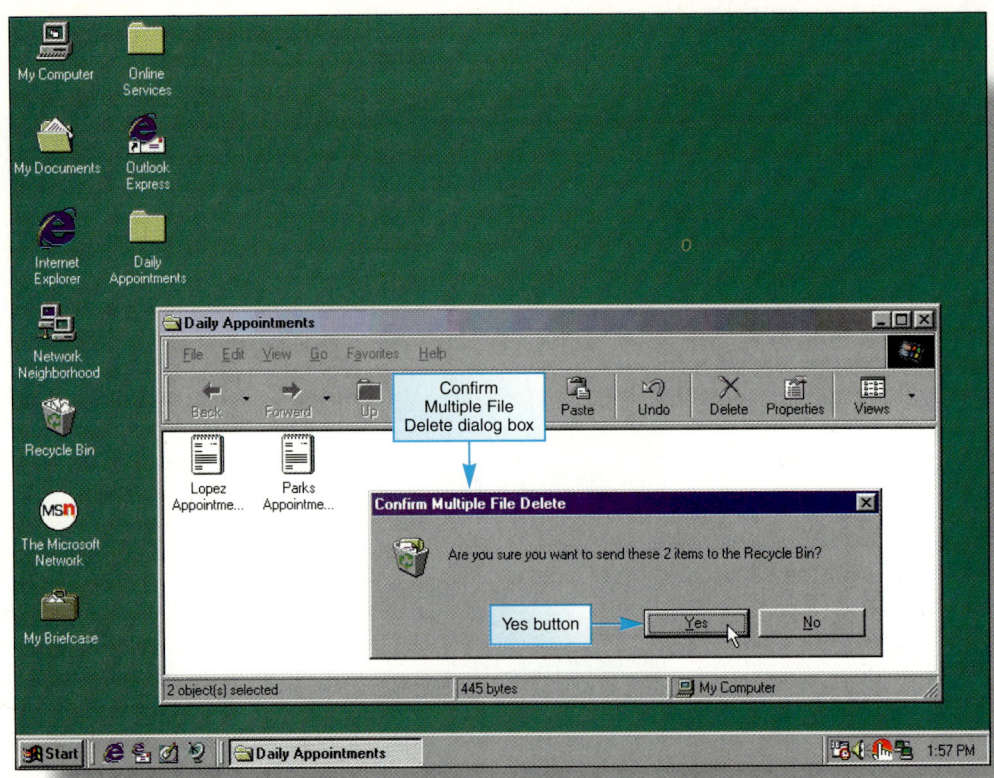

FIGURE 2-62

 Click the Yes button.

The two files are removed from the Daily Appointments window and are placed in the Recycle Bin (Figure 2-63).

 Click the Close button on the Daily Appointments title bar.

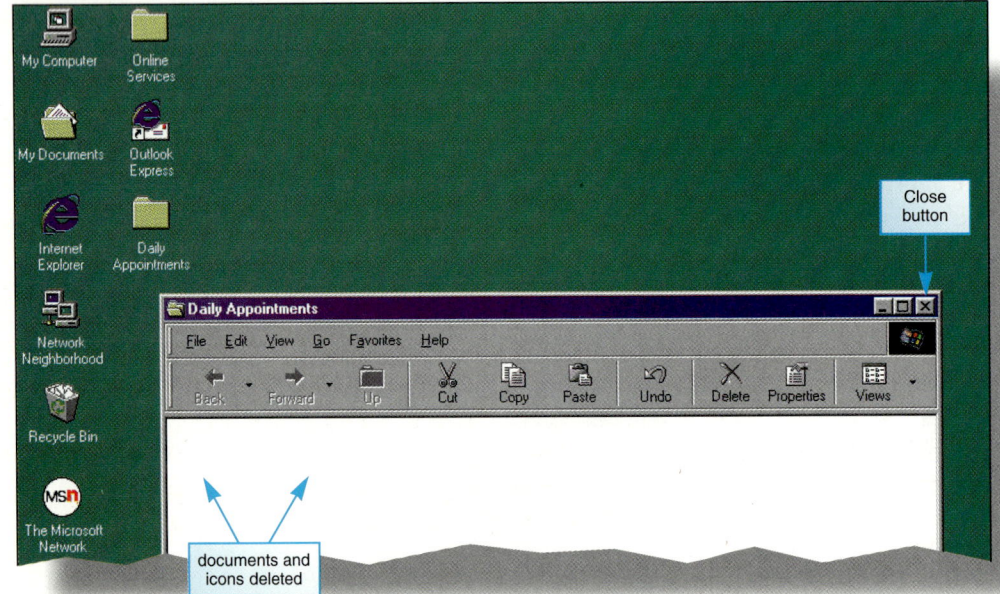

FIGURE 2-63

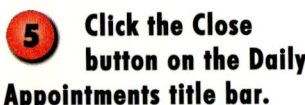

1. Click first document icon, hold down SHIFT key, click other icon, release SHIFT key, right-click either icon, click Delete, click Yes button

Deleting a Folder

Folders also can be deleted from the desktop. To delete the Daily Appointments folder from the desktop, complete the following steps.

Steps To Delete a Folder from the Desktop

1 **Drag the Daily Appointments icon to the Recycle Bin icon.**

When you drag the icon over the Recycle Bin icon, a dimmed icon displays over the Recycle Bin icon (Figure 2-64). When you release the left mouse button, the dimmed icon no longer displays.

2 **Click the Yes button in the Confirm Folder Delete dialog box.**

When you click the Yes button in the dialog box, the folder no longer displays on the desktop.

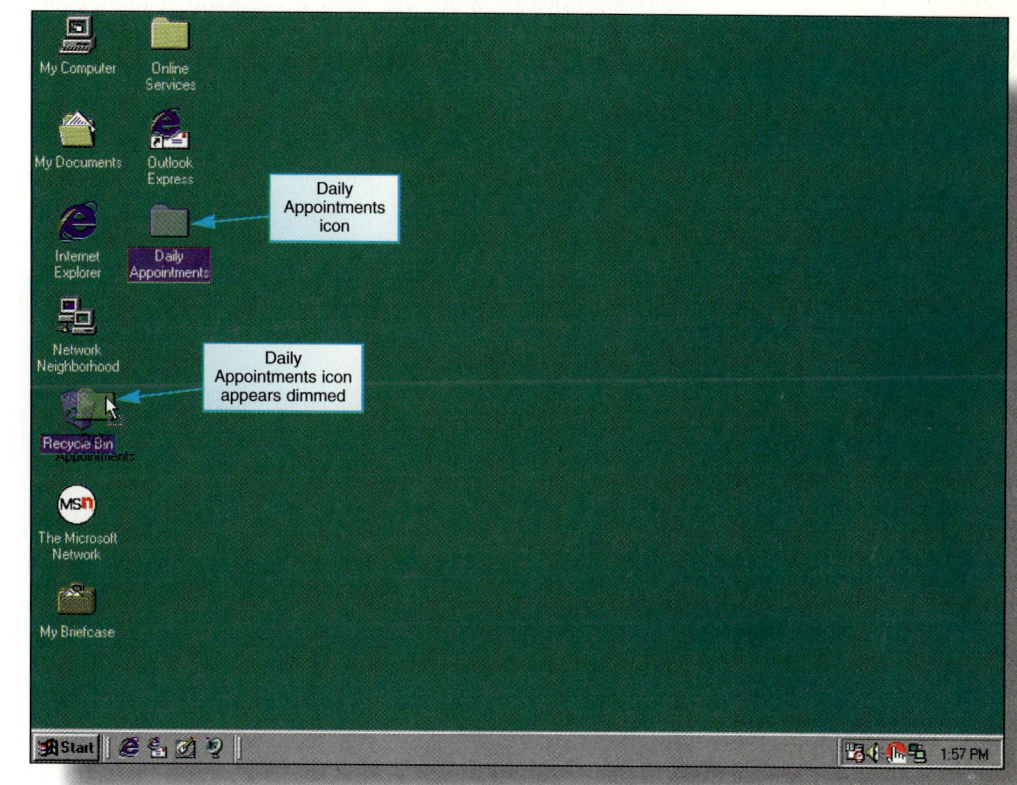

FIGURE 2-64

In summary, you have used three different methods to delete an object from the desktop: (1) right-drag the object to the Recycle Bin; (2) right-click the object and then click Delete on the shortcut menu; and (3) drag the object to the Recycle Bin.

Again, it is important to understand that when you delete a folder icon, you are deleting the folder and its contents from your computer. Therefore, you must be extremely cautious when deleting files.

If after deleting an icon from the desktop, you want to return the icon immediately to the desktop after you delete the icon, you can right-click the desktop and then click the Undo Delete command on the shortcut menu. For example, if you delete the Daily Appointments icon from the desktop, right-click the desktop and click Undo Delete on the shortcut menu. The icon you deleted will be retrieved from the Recycle Bin and placed on the desktop. Multiple deleted icons also can be returned to the desktop in a similar fashion.

Other Ways

1. Right-drag folder icon to Recycle Bin, click Move Here, click Yes button
2. Right-click folder icon, click Delete on shortcut menu, click Yes button

Working with the Windows 98 Active Desktop™

As mentioned in Project 1, the Active Desktop allows you to display the contents of a Web site located on a computer connected to the Internet on your desktop and update that content periodically. This constantly changing content, referred to as **Active Web content**, or **active content**, can be a weather map, a constantly updating stock market ticker of stock quotes, fast-breaking news stories from your favorite online newspaper, or the latest sports scores.

Turning On the Active Desktop™

Before you display active Web content on your desktop, you must turn on the Active Desktop. When the Active Desktop is turned on, the Internet Explorer Channel bar displays on the desktop and the desktop is active. Perform the following steps to turn on the Active Desktop.

Steps: To Turn On the Active Desktop

1 Right-click an open area of the desktop, point to Active Desktop on the shortcut menu, and then point to View As Web Page on the Active Desktop submenu.

A shortcut menu and the Active Desktop submenu display (Figure 2-65). The View As Web Page command on the Active Desktop submenu displays without a check mark preceding the command name to indicate the Active Desktop is turned off.

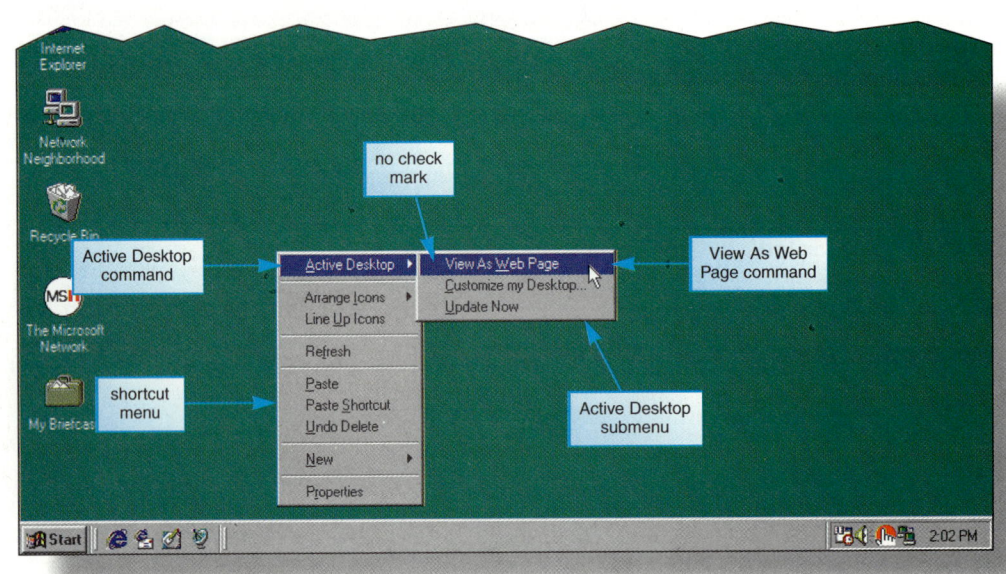

FIGURE 2-65

2 Click View As Web Page.

The Active Desktop is turned on, the Internet Channel bar displays on the desktop, and the shortcut menu and Active Desktop submenu no longer display on the desktop (Figure 2-66). Although not visible in Figure 2-66, a check mark precedes the View As Web Page command on the Active Desktop submenu.

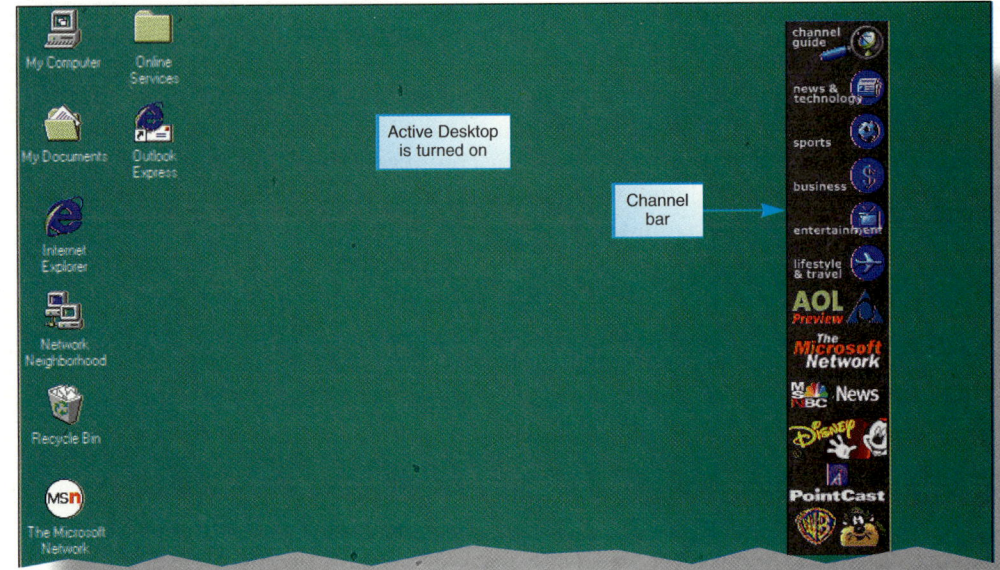

FIGURE 2-66

After turning on the Active Desktop, you can add active content to the Active Desktop.

Adding an Active Desktop Item to the Active Desktop

One method to display Active Web content of the desktop is to use the **Internet Explorer Channel bar** located on the right side of the Active Desktop. The Internet Explorer Channel bar contains **Channel buttons** that allow you to receive active content from Web pages and find new channels. The Channel buttons on the Channel bar in Figure 2-66 have been placed there by Microsoft Corporation to help you understand and use channels. You can customize the Channel bar by removing Channel buttons and adding new channels that are of interest to you.

Another method to display active content on the desktop is to add an Active Desktop item to the desktop. An **Active Desktop item** displays active content from a Web page directly on the Active Desktop and updates the content periodically. Once on the desktop, you can move and resize the item and specify how often you want the active content to be updated.

In the process of adding an Active Desktop item to the desktop, you create a subscription to the channel (Web site) containing the active content. A **subscription** allows the browser (Internet Explorer) to check the Web site to determine if the content has changed and deliver the new content to your desktop. When you **subscribe** to a channel, you have the choice of being notified when new content is available or having the updated content automatically delivered to your desktop. Subscriptions typically are free to the subscriber. Perform the following steps to subscribe to the ESPN SportsZone™ channel and add the ESPN SportsZone™ item to the Active Desktop.

Other Ways

1. Click Start button, point to Settings, point to Active Desktop, click View as Web Page
2. Click Start button, point to Settings, click Folder Options, click Settings button, click Enable all web-related content on my desktop, click OK button, click Close button

More About

The Active Desktop

Windows allows you to view the desktop in three views: Web style, Classic style, and Custom style. When you choose the Web style desktop view, the Active Desktop is automatically turned on, allowing you to view the Channel bar and active content.

 To Subscribe to a Channel and Add an Item to the Active Desktop

1 Right-click an open area on the desktop. Point to Properties on the shortcut menu (Figure 2-67).

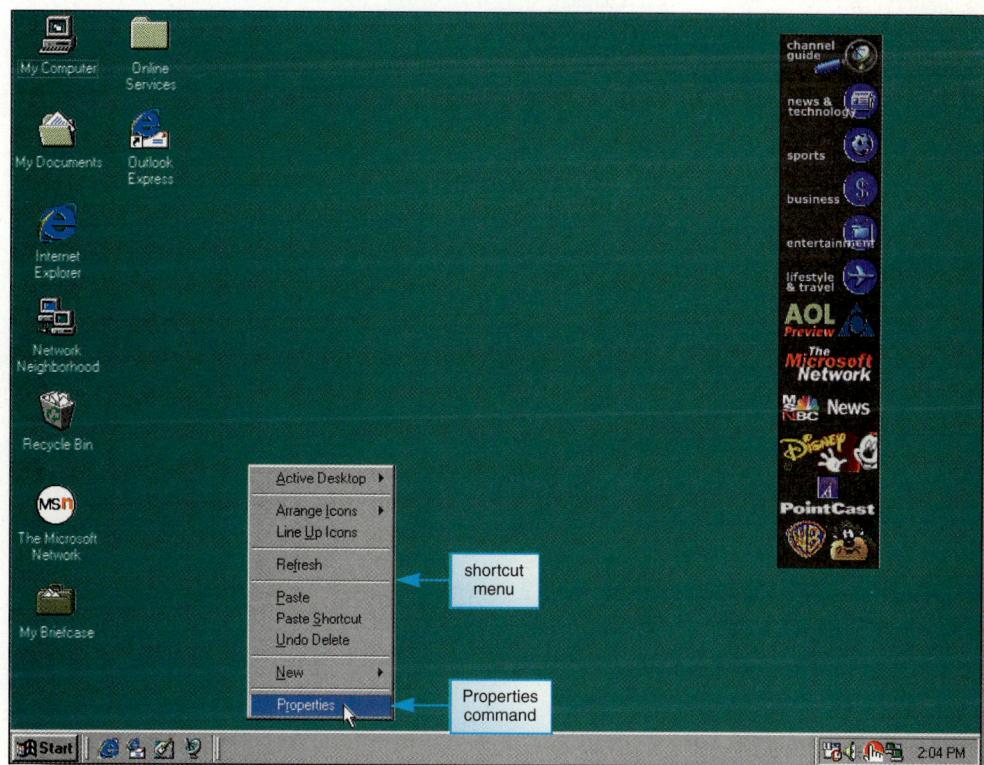

FIGURE 2-67

WIN 2.50 • Project 2 • Working on the Windows 98 Desktop

2 **Click Properties. Point to the Web tab in the Display Properties dialog box.**

The Display Properties dialog box displays (Figure 2-68). Seven tabs (Background, Screen Saver, Appearance, ScreenScan, Web, Effects, and Settings) display in the dialog box. Other tabs may display in the dialog box on your desktop. The Background sheet displays in the dialog box and contains a blank preview monitor, Wallpaper pane, and three command buttons (OK, Cancel, and Apply).

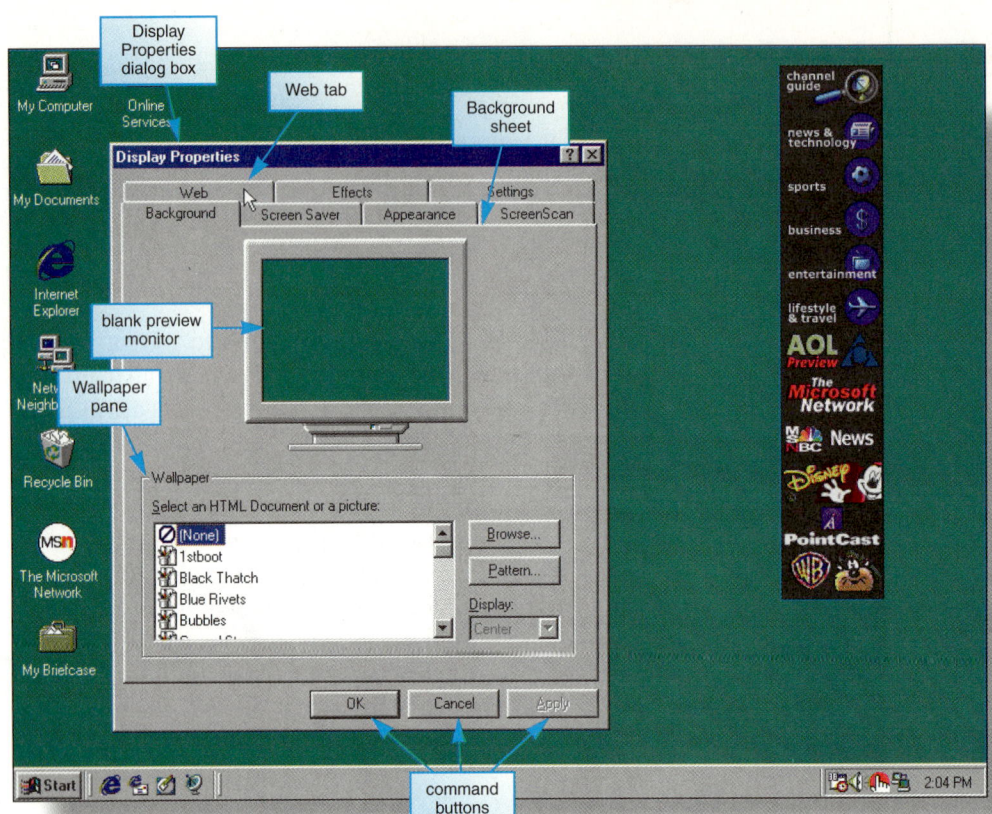

FIGURE 2-68

3 **Click the Web tab. Point to the New button on the Web sheet.**

The Web sheet displays (Figure 2-69). An object (dark blue rectangle) on the monitor illustrates the position of the Internet Explorer Channel bar on the desktop. Below the monitor, the View my Active Desktop as a web page check box is selected indicating the desktop is active. The Internet Explorer Channel bar check box is selected indicating the Channel bar displays on the Active Desktop.

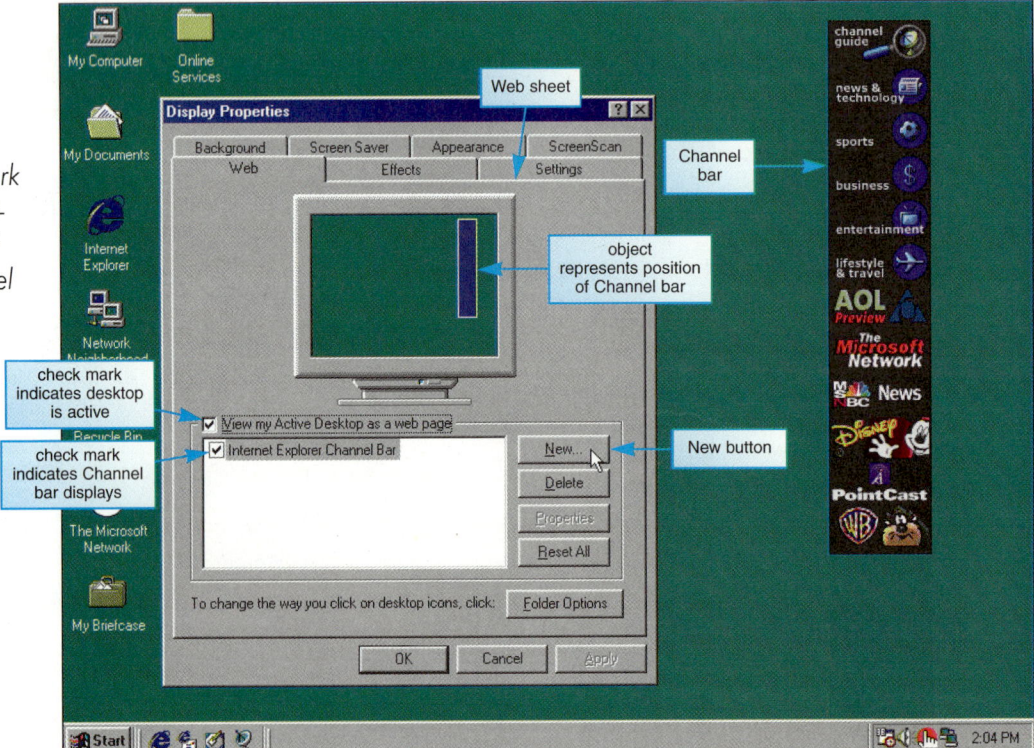

FIGURE 2-69

Working with the Windows 98 Active Desktop™ • WIN 2.51

4 **Click the New button. Point to the Yes button in the New Active Desktop Item dialog box.**

The New Active Desktop Item dialog box displays (Figure 2-70). A message in the dialog box indicates you can visit the **Active Desktop gallery** to preview and add new items to the desktop and you can save and close the Display Properties dialog box. If you click the check box, the dialog box will not display in the future.

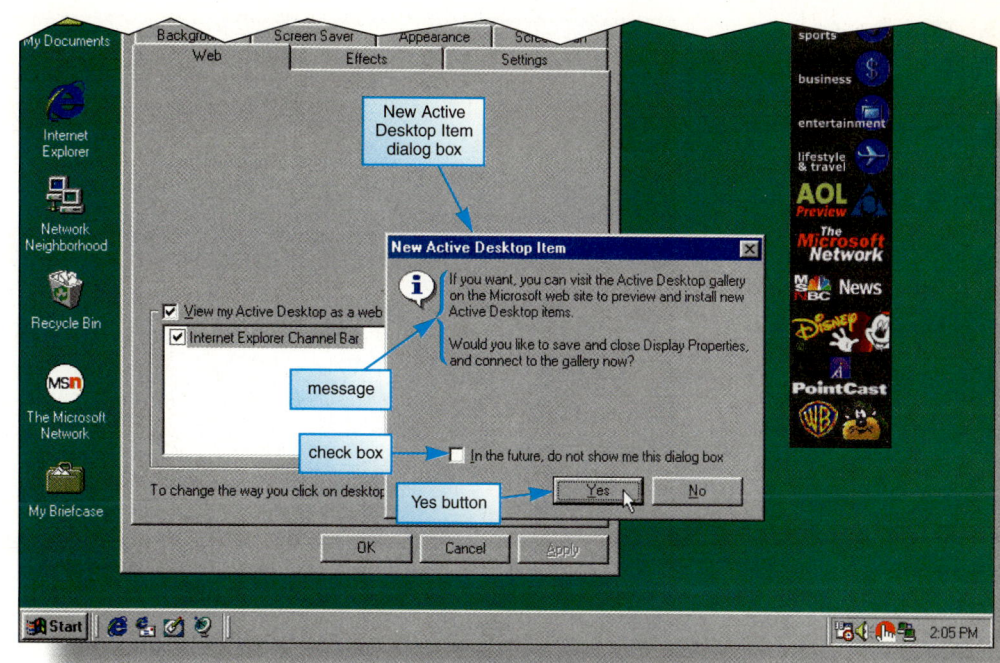

FIGURE 2-70

5 **Click the Yes button. Click the Maximize button in the Desktop Gallery - Microsoft Internet Explorer window. Point to the sports icon in the window.**

Windows 98 launches Microsoft Internet Explorer and displays the maximized Desktop Gallery window (Figure 2-71). The menu bar, Standard Buttons toolbar, and Address bar display at the top of the window. The icons shown in the window represent the categories that contain one or more channels. A message, the Microsoft Investor desktop item, and the Add to Active Desktop button display to the right of the icons.

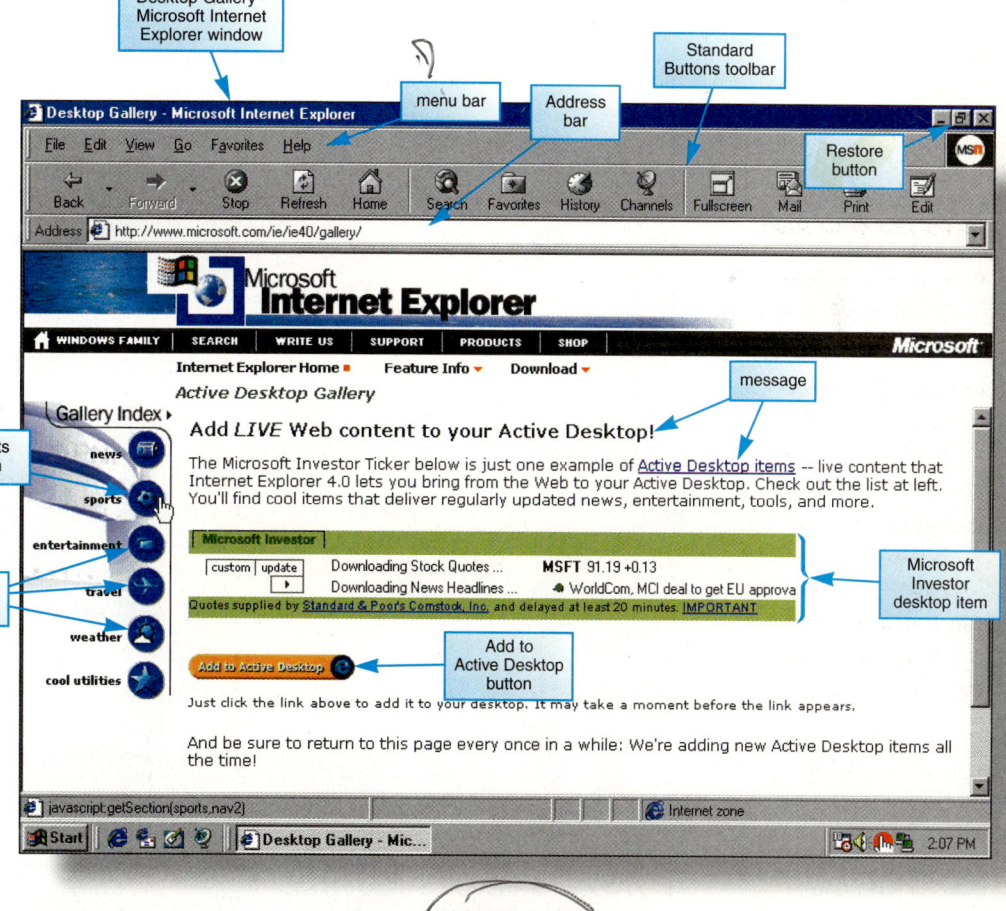

FIGURE 2-71

WIN 2.52 • Project 2 • Working on the Windows 98 Desktop

6 **Click the sports icon. Point to the ESPN SportsZone™ channel name.**

The sports icon is selected. The information that displayed to the right of the category icons has been replaced with the two channel names in the sports category (CBS Sportscenter and ESPN SportsZone™) (Figure 2-72). The ESPN SportsZone™ channel name displays in red text and the mouse pointer changes to a hand indicating it is positioned on a hyperlink.

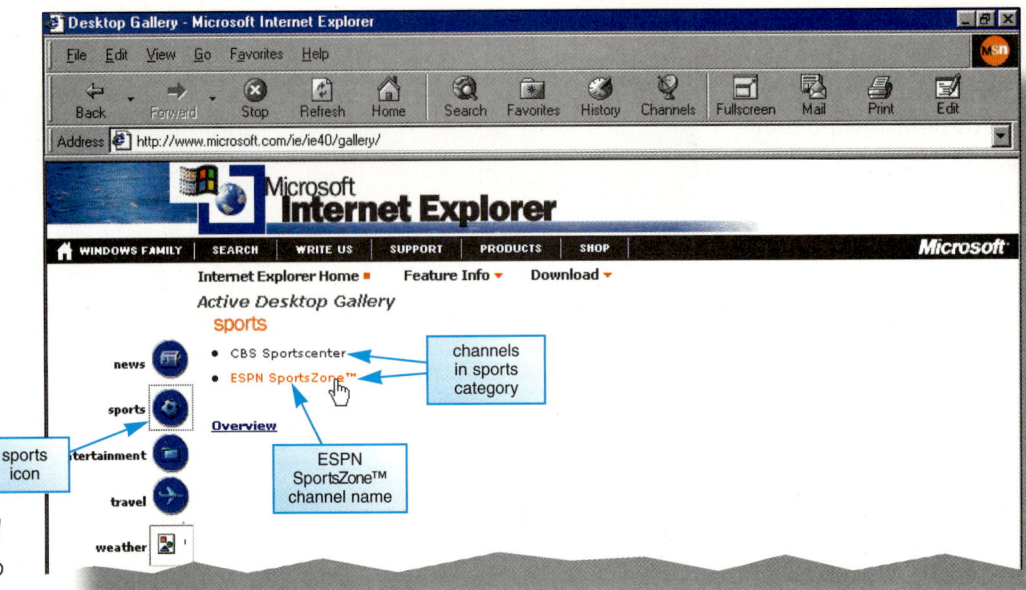

FIGURE 2-72

7 **Click the ESPN SportsZone™ channel name. Point to the Add to Active Desktop button.**

The ESPN SportsZone™ channel name is selected and a sample of the ESPN SportsZone™ desktop item displays (Figure 2-73).

FIGURE 2-73

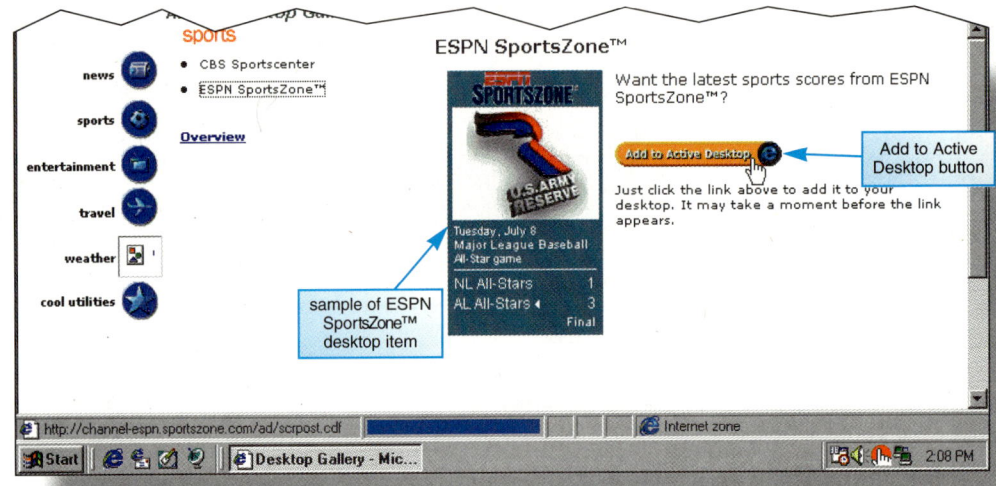

8 **Click the Add to Active Desktop button. Point to the Yes button in the Security Alert dialog box.**

The Security Alert dialog box displays (Figure 2-74). A question asks if you want to add a desktop item to the Active Desktop.

FIGURE 2-74

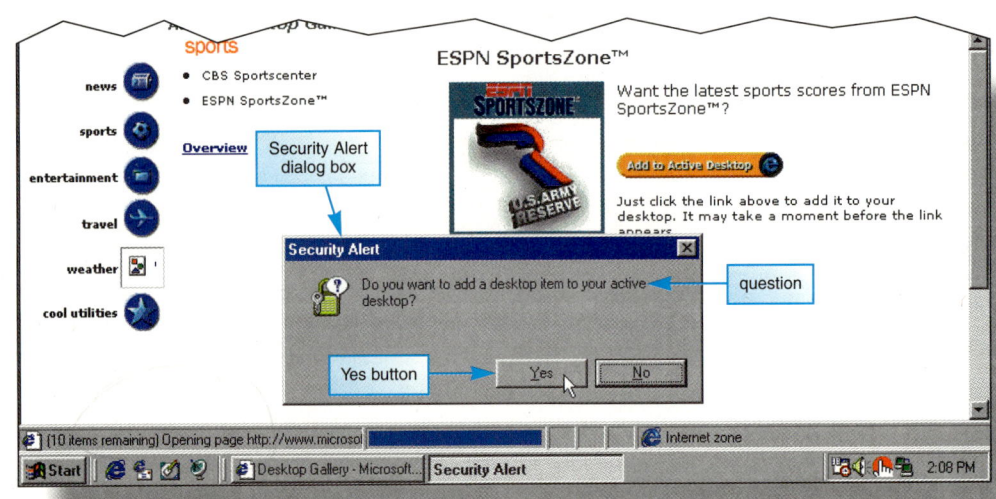

Working with the Windows 98 Active Desktop™ • WIN 2.53

9 **Click the Yes button. Point to the OK button in the Add item to Active Desktop(TM) dialog box.**

The Add item to Active Desktop(TM) dialog box displays (Figure 2-75). The dialog box contains a message that indicates you are about to subscribe to a channel, the channel name (Scorepost: ESPN SportsZone), and the Web page URL of the channel.

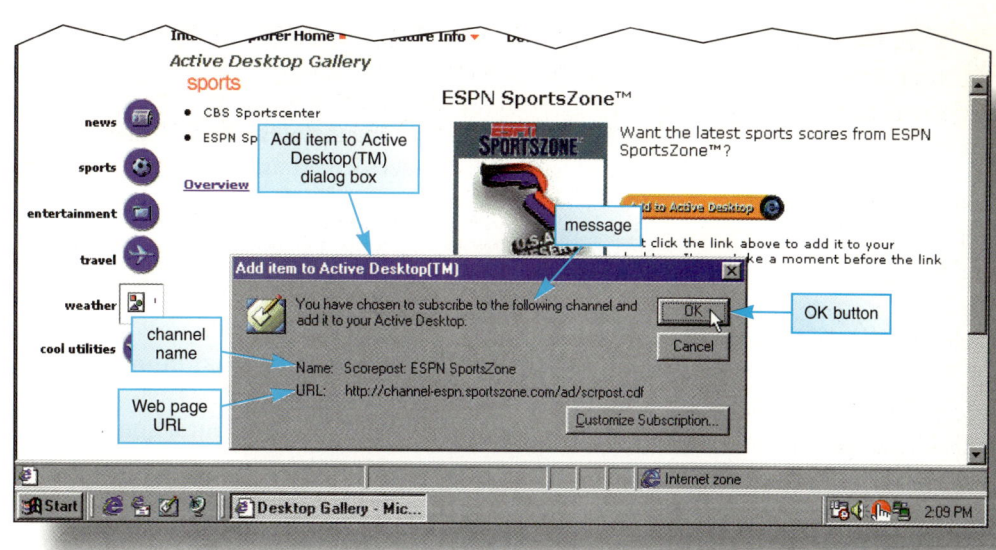

FIGURE 2-75

10 **Click the OK button. Point to the Close button in the Desktop Gallery window.**

The Downloading Subscriptions dialog box displays on top of the Desktop Gallery window while the connection is made to the Scorepost: ESPN SportsZone™ channel. After the connection is made, the dialog box closes and the desktop item can be viewed by clicking the Close button (Figure 2-76).

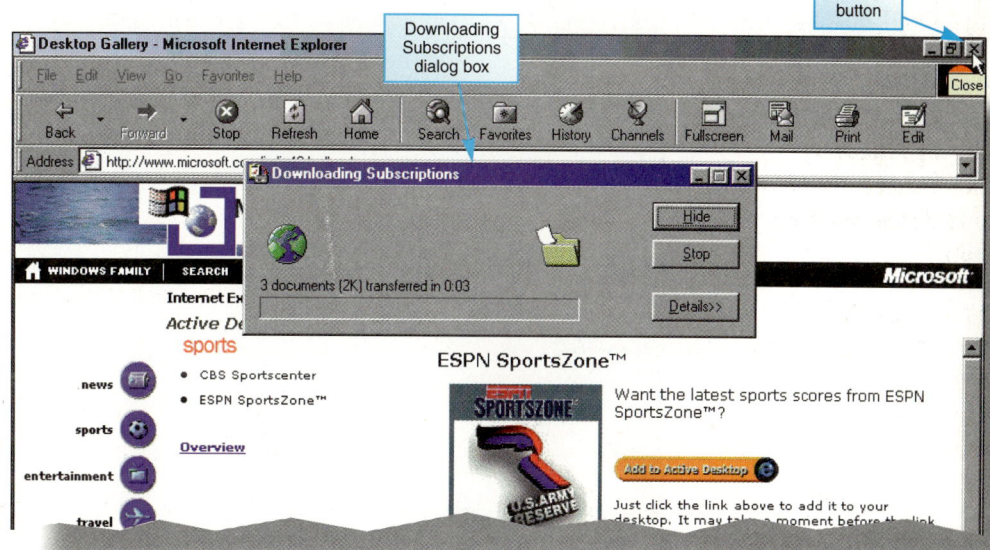

FIGURE 2-76

11 **Click the Close button.**

The Desktop Gallery window closes and the ESPN SportsZone™ item is visible on the desktop (Figure 2-77). The updated sports scores that display at the bottom of the item change approximately every four seconds.

FIGURE 2-77

WIN 2.54 • Project 2 • Working on the Windows 98 Desktop

Other Ways

1. Click Channel button, click channel logo, click Add Active Channel button, click Add to Active Desktop button, click Yes option button, click OK button, click Close button
2. Right-drag sample desktop item from Desktop Gallery (Web page) to desktop, click Create Active Desktop item(s) Here, click Yes button, click OK button

A subscription to the Scorepost: ESPN SportsZone™ channel is established that allows you to view the changing scores of sporting events currently in progress, view the game times of sporting events yet to be played, and obtain additional information about the sporting event that currently displays on the desktop item. Unless changed, updates are performed according to the schedule set by the channel's publisher.

Displaying Additional Information About a Sporting Event

Sometimes, after adding the ESPN SportsZone™ desktop item to the Active Desktop, you may want to display additional information about a sporting event that displays at the bottom of the desktop item. Perform the following steps to display the additional information about a sporting event.

To Display Additional Information About a Sporting Event

1 Point to a score summary at the bottom of the ESPN SportsZone™ desktop item.

The mouse pointer points to the score summary of a baseball game (Figure 2-78).

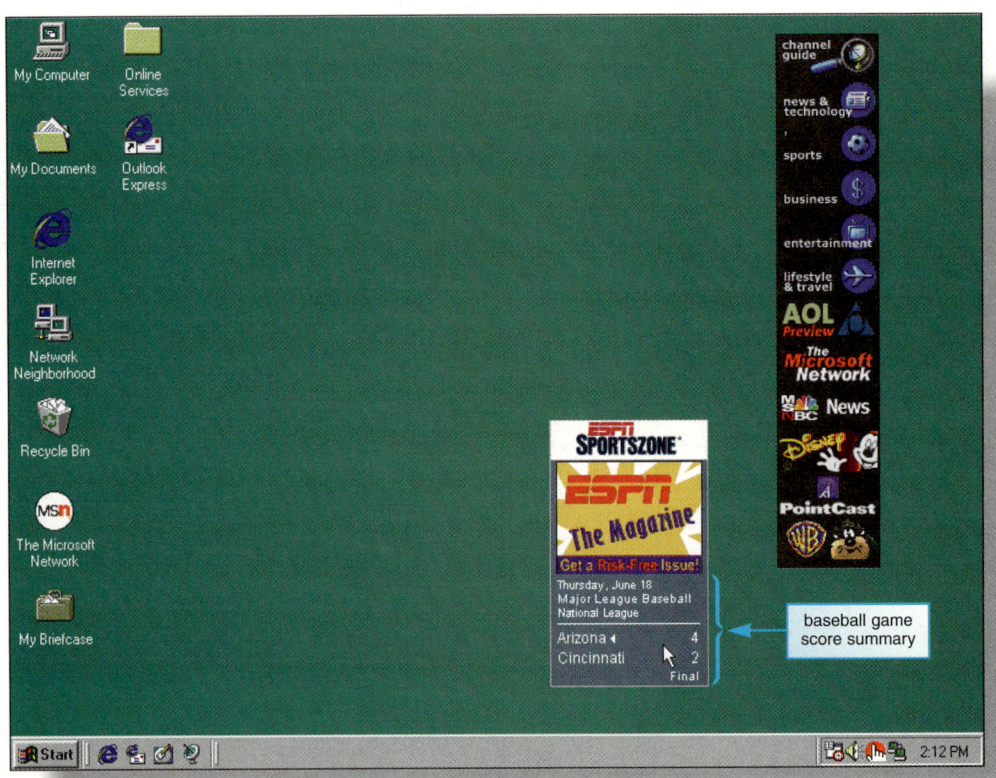

FIGURE 2-78

② Click the score summary. Click the Maximize button in the Microsoft Internet Explorer window.

The Microsoft Internet Explorer window displays and maximizes (Figure 2-79). The window displays additional information about the sporting event.

③ Scroll the window to read the information about the sporting event. When finished, click the Close button in the Microsoft Internet Explorer window to close the window.

The Microsoft Internet Explorer window closes.

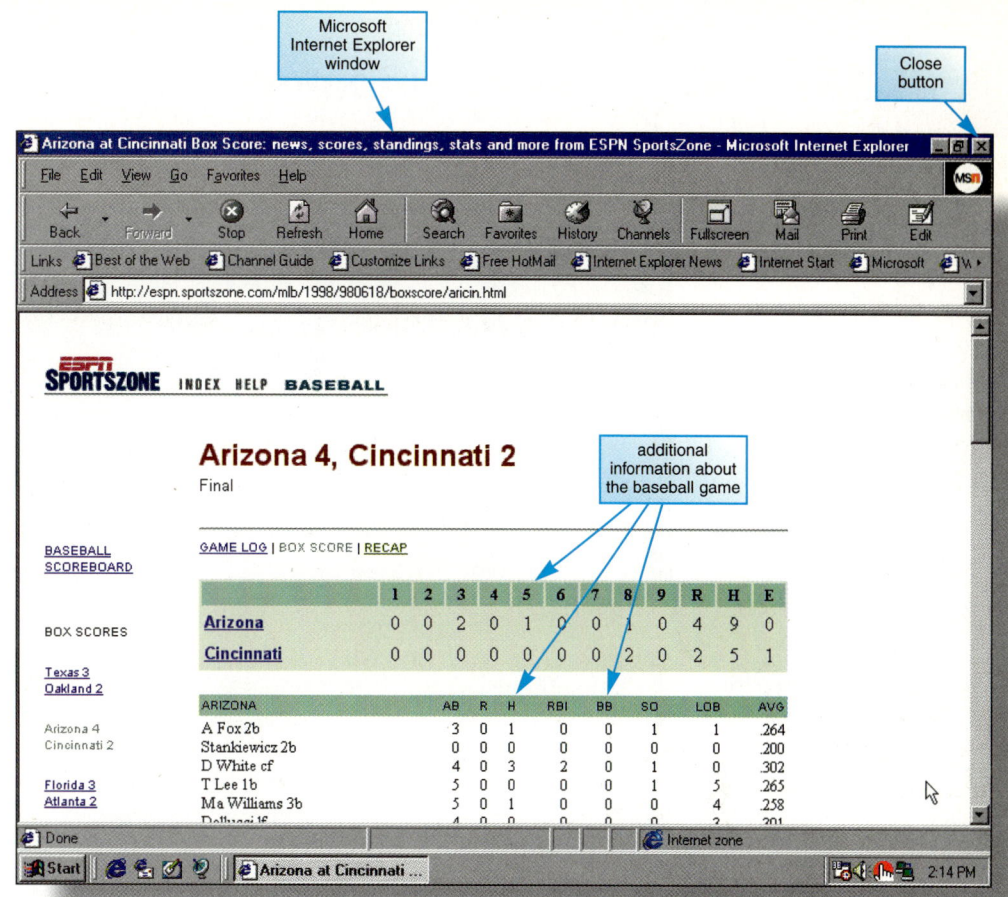

FIGURE 2-79

Removing a Desktop Item from the Active Desktop

When you no longer use a desktop item on the Active Desktop, remove the item from the desktop. In the process of removing the item from the desktop, the subscription to its associated channel also can be canceled. Perform the steps on the next two pages to remove the ESPN SportsZone™ item and cancel the subscription to the Scorepost: ESPN SportsZone™ channel.

More About

The Active Desktop™

After adding an Active Desktop item to the desktop, you can move the item. To move it, point to the desktop item name displayed at the top of the item and then drag the gray bar that displays to a new position on the desktop. Point anywhere off the gray bar to remove the gray bar.

WIN 2.56 • Project 2 • Working on the Windows 98 Desktop

Steps: To Remove a Desktop Item from the Active Desktop and Cancel a Subscription

1 **Right-click an open area on the desktop. Click Properties on the shortcut menu. Click the Web tab in the Display Properties dialog box. Point to the Scorepost: ESPN SportsZone title.**

The Display Properties dialog box displays (Figure 2-80). Check marks in the Internet Explorer Channel Bar and Scorepost: ESPN SportsZone check boxes and the two objects on the monitor indicate the Channel bar and ESPN SportsZone™ items display on the desktop.

FIGURE 2-80

2 **Click Scorepost: ESPN SportsZone to highlight the title. Point to the Delete button.**

The Internet Explorer Channel Bar title no longer is highlighted. The Scorepost: ESPN SportsZone title is highlighted (Figure 2-81).

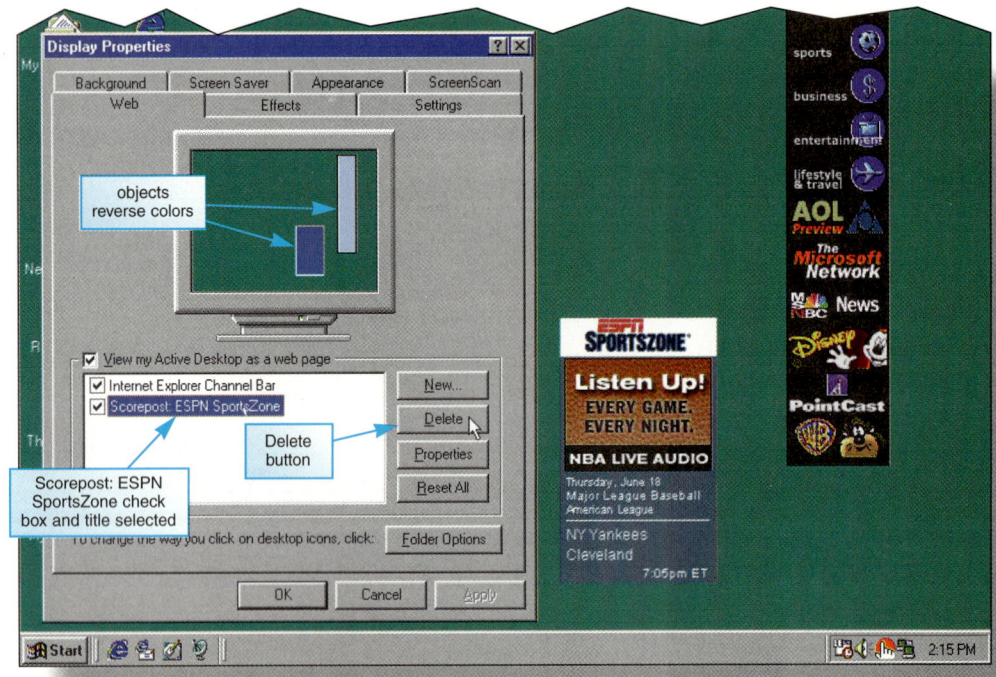

FIGURE 2-81

Working with the Windows 98 Active Desktop™ • **WIN 2.57**

3 **Click the Delete button. Point to the Yes button in the Active Desktop Item dialog box.**

The Active Desktop Item dialog box displays (Figure 2-82). The question, Are you sure you want to delete this item from your Active Desktop?, displays in the dialog box. Clicking the Yes button will terminate the subscription to the Scorepost: ESPN SportsZone channel.

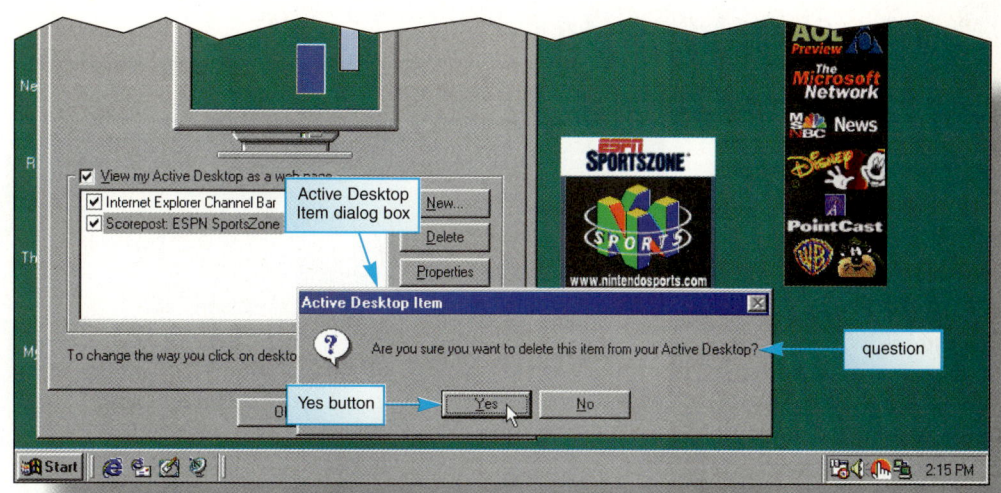

FIGURE 2-82

4 **Click the Yes button. Point to the OK button in the Display Properties dialog box.**

The Scorepost: ESPN SportsZone check box and title and the object that represents it are deleted from the Display Properties dialog box, and the subscription to the Scorepost: ESPN SportsZone channel is canceled (Figure 2-83).

5  **Click the OK button.**

The Scorepost: ESPN SportsZone item no longer displays on the desktop.

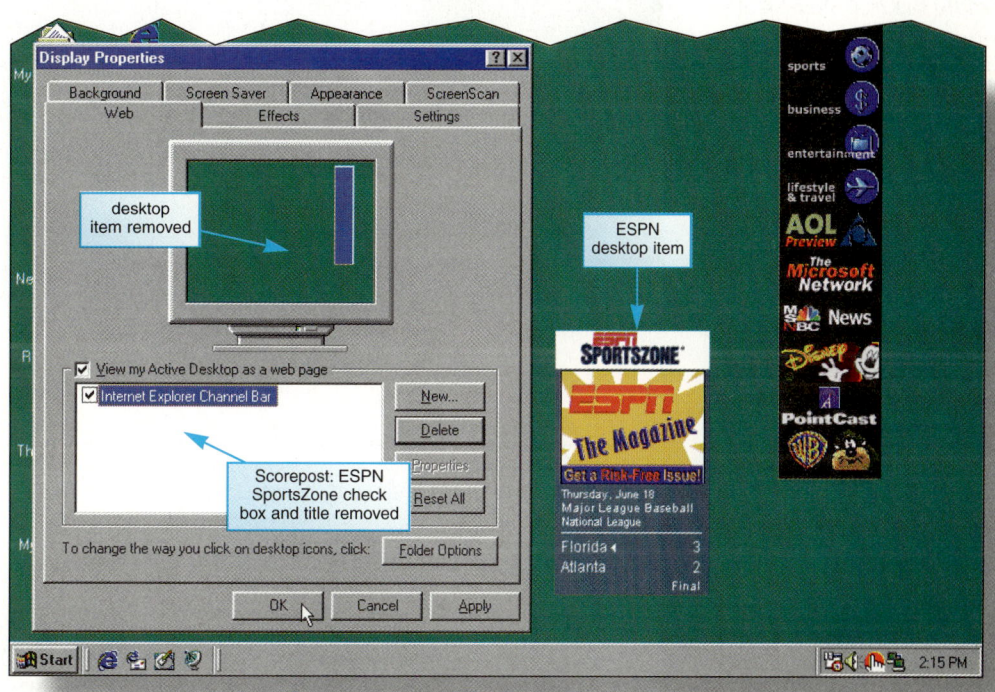

FIGURE 2-83

If after removing a desktop item from the Active Desktop, you wish to return the item to the desktop, follow the steps illustrated on pages WIN 2.49 through WIN 2.53 to add the item to the Active Desktop.

Turning Off the Active Desktop

When you no longer want the Channel bar or active content on the desktop, you can turn off the Active Desktop. When the Active Desktop is turned off, the Internet Explorer Channel bar is removed from the desktop and the desktop no longer is active. Perform the steps on the next page to turn off the Active Desktop.

Other Ways

1. Point to desktop item name on Active Desktop item, click down arrow button on gray bar, click Customize My Desktop, click channel name, click Delete button, click Yes button, click OK button

2. Point to desktop item name on Active Desktop item, click Close button on gray bar

To Turn Off the Active Desktop

 Right-click an open area of the desktop, point to Active Desktop on the shortcut menu, and then point to View As Web Page on the Active Desktop submenu.

A shortcut menu and the Active Desktop submenu display (Figure 2-84). A check mark precedes the View As Web Page command on the Active Desktop submenu to indicate the Active Desktop is turned on.

 Click View As Web Page.

The Active Desktop is turned off and the Internet Channel bar, shortcut menu, and Active Desktop submenu no longer display on the desktop.

Other Ways

1. Click Start button, point to Settings, point to Active Desktop, click View as Web Page
2. Click Start button, point to Settings, click Folder Options, click Settings button, click Use Windows classic desktop, click OK button, click Close button

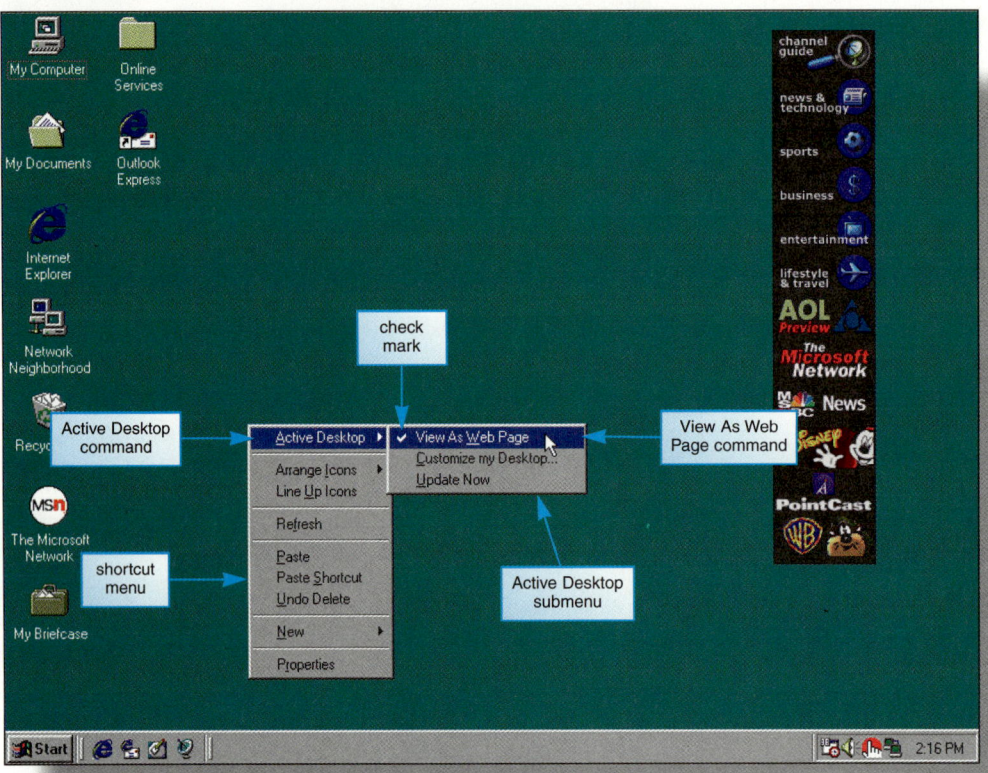

FIGURE 2-84

Using Microsoft Support Online

Windows Help provides a variety of ways in which to obtain information. In Project 1, you browsed through Help topics by category using the Contents sheet. Next, you found answers to questions about Windows 98 by searching entries in the Index sheet and viewing Help screens.

Another way to obtain information about Windows 98 is to use Microsoft Support Online. **Microsoft Support Online** allows you to use the Internet to search for Help about Windows 98 using the **Microsoft Windows Update Web site**. Because the information on the Internet can be easily updated, the information you obtain using Microsoft Support Online is more current than the information contained in the Windows Contents and Index sheets.

To obtain Help using **Microsoft Support Online**, you select the Microsoft product about which you want information and then construct a search inquiry. You can use a keyword, or Boolean, search or a natural language search to find the information. A **keyword**, or **Boolean**, **search** can consist of a single word (desktop), or a phrase (active desktop), while a **natural language search** uses keywords (How do I save changes to a document?). Words such as save, change, and document are keywords. Windows Support Online searches its collection of information, called the **Knowledge Database**, and displays a list of articles that relate to your search inquiry. The following table lists types of searches, examples of search inquiries, and the results of searching using the inquiries.

In this project, you will use Windows Support Online and the Internet to obtain Help about Windows Update. **Windows Update** is an application included with Windows 98 that allows you to keep the Windows 98 operating system on your computer up to date by obtaining current system information from the Microsoft Support Online site. The search inquiry to obtain help about Windows Update consists of the natural language question, What is Windows Update? Perform the following steps to obtain help about Windows Update.

Table 2-1

SEARCH TYPE	SEARCH INQUIRY	SEARCH RESULTS
Word	desktop	Articles containing the word, desktop
Phrase	active desktop	Articles containing the phrase, active desktop
Wild card (*)	hyper*	Articles containing words with the same first characters (hyperlink, hypertext, hypermedia)
Wild card (*.*)	close*.*	Articles containing all forms of the word (close, closing, closed, closes)
AND Boolean operator	open AND maximize	Articles containing both words (open, maximize)
NEAR Boolean operator	open NEAR maximize	Articles in which the two words are located closest to each other are listed first in the list of articles
AND NOT Boolean operator	close AND NOT a window	Articles containing the first word (close) but not the phrase (close a window)
Knowledge Database article number	Q155353	Articles identified by the Knowledge Database characters, Q155353
Natural language	How do I save changes to a document?	Articles containing the keywords in the search inquiry (save, change, document)

Steps: To Use Windows Support Online

1 **Click the Start button on the taskbar. Click Help on the Start menu. Point to the Web Help button on the Help toolbar.**

The Windows Help window opens (Figure 2-85).

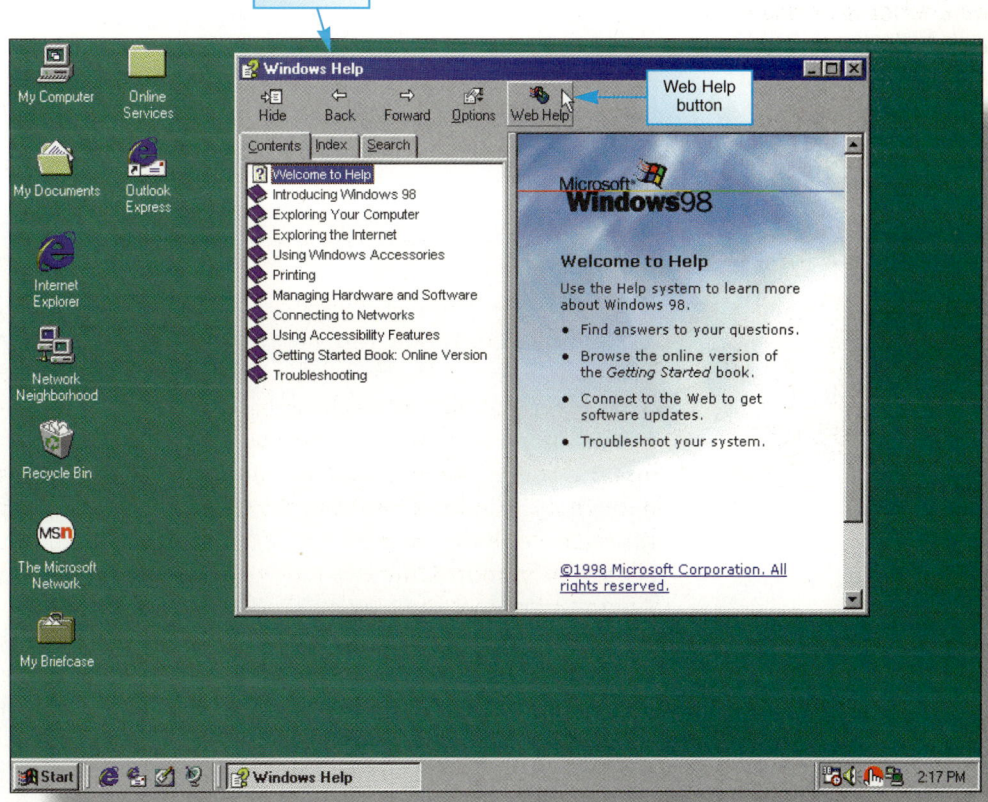

FIGURE 2-85

WIN 2.60 • Project 2 • Working on the Windows 98 Desktop

2 **Click the Web Help button. Point to the Support Online hyperlink in the right frame.**

Information about Support Online displays in the right frame of the Windows Help window (Figure 2-86).

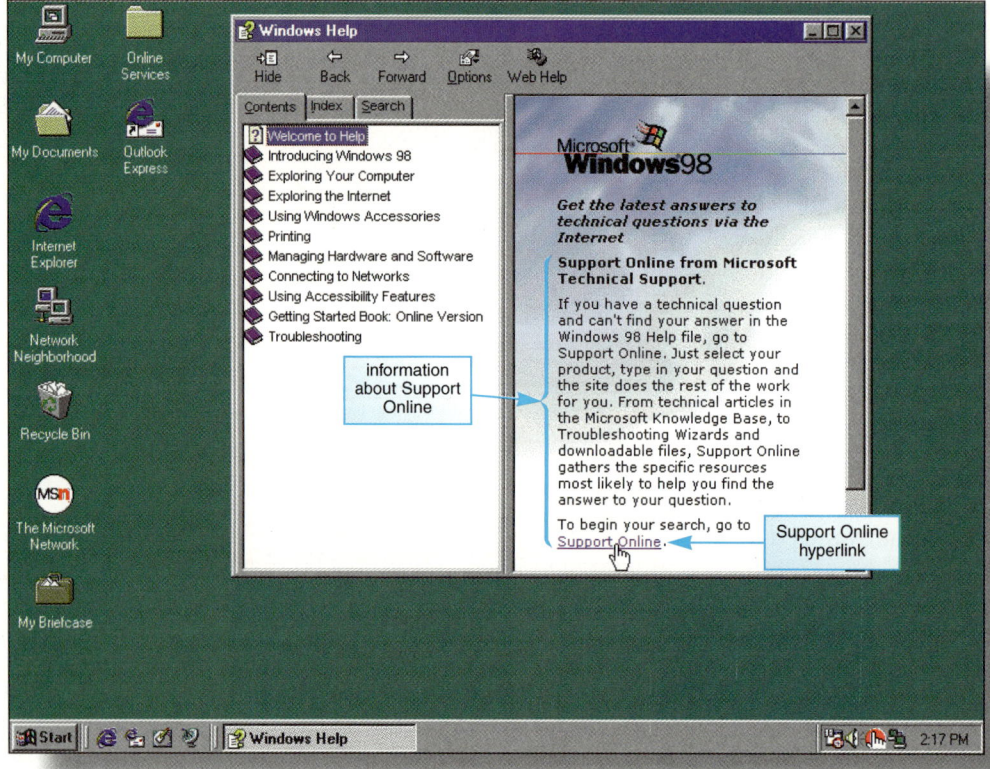

FIGURE 2-86

3 **Click Support Online. Click the Asking a question using Natural Language Search option button. Type** What is Windows Update? **in the My question is text box. Point to the find button.**

The Support Online window displays (Figure 2-87). A menu displays in the left frame and Advanced View options display in the right frame. Windows 98 displays in the My search is about box, the Asking a question using Natural Language Search option button is selected, and the My question is text box contains the search inquiry. The URL of the Web page displays in the Address bar.

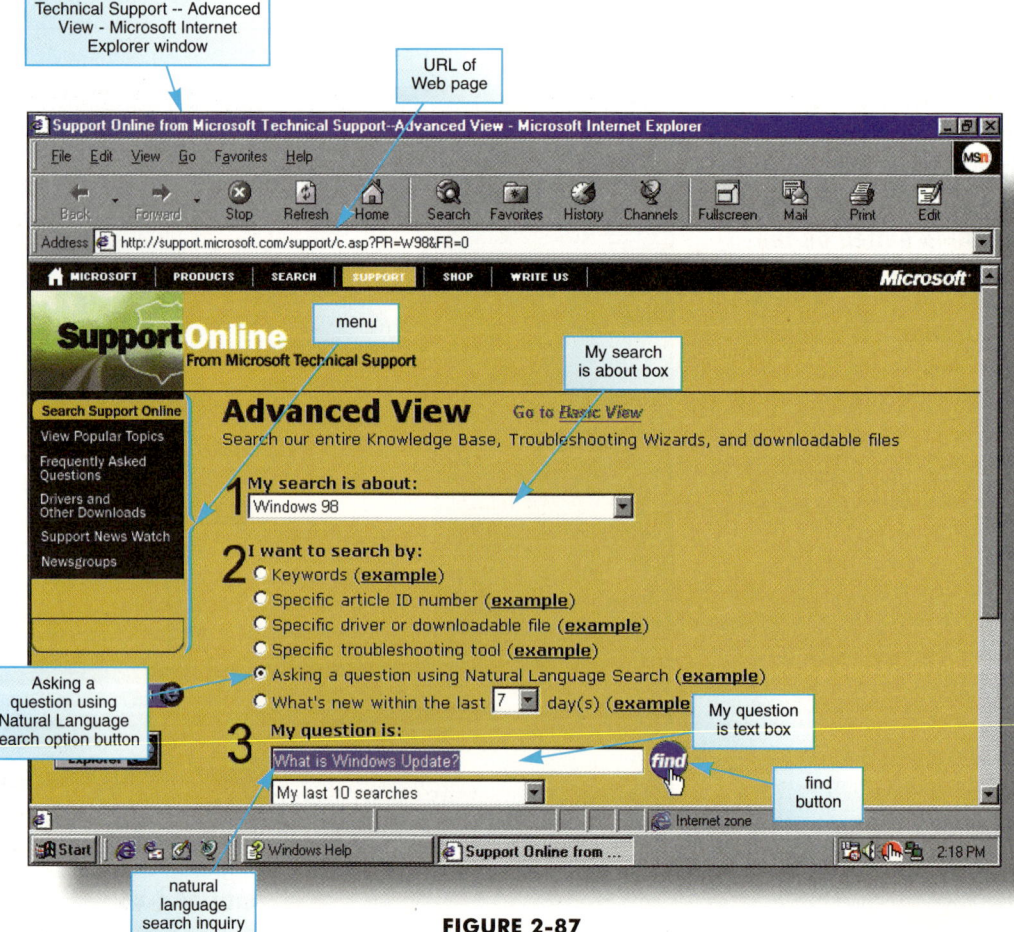

FIGURE 2-87

Using Microsoft Support Online • WIN 2.61

④ **Click the find button. If necessary, scroll to display the Windows Update article. Point to the Windows Update article name. If this article name does not display, point to another article name.**

Windows 98 searches the database of information about Windows 98 and displays a list of article names in the window (Figure 2-88). The URL changes to reflect the current Web page. Because information on the Internet can change frequently, the list of article names on your computer may be different.

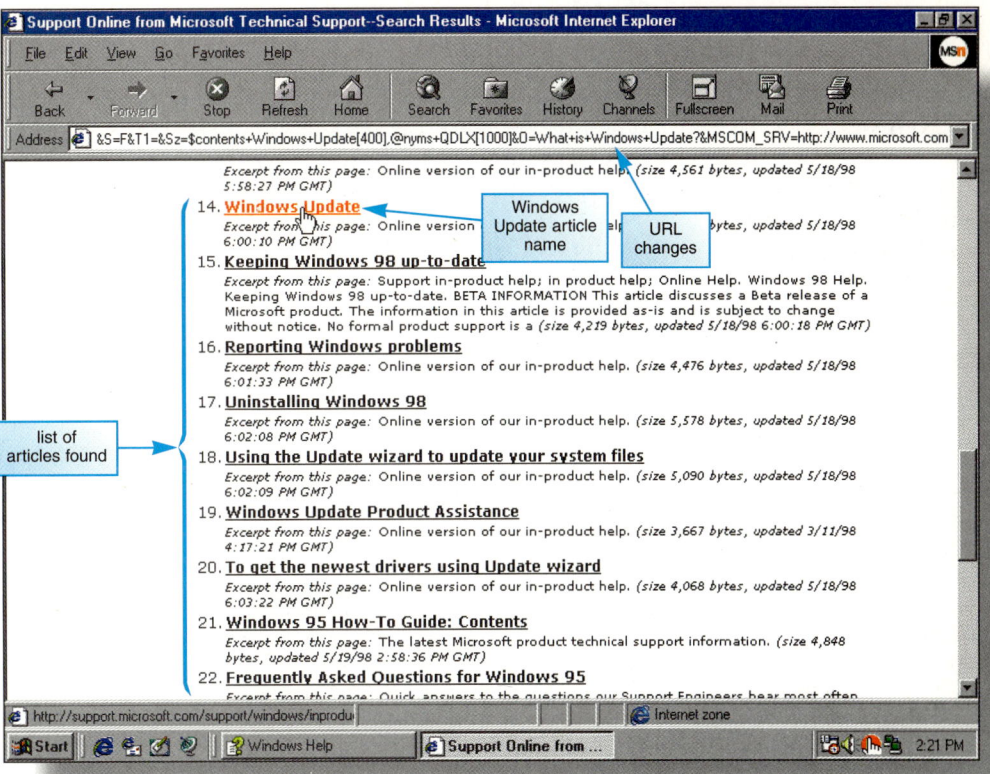

FIGURE 2-88

⑤ **Click Windows Update. If necessary, scroll the window to read the information about Windows Update. Point to the Close button in the window.**

The content of the Windows Update article displays in the window (Figure 2-89). The URL changes to reflect the current Web page.

⑥ **Click the Close button. Click the Close button in the Windows Help window.**

The Windows Update and Windows Help windows close.

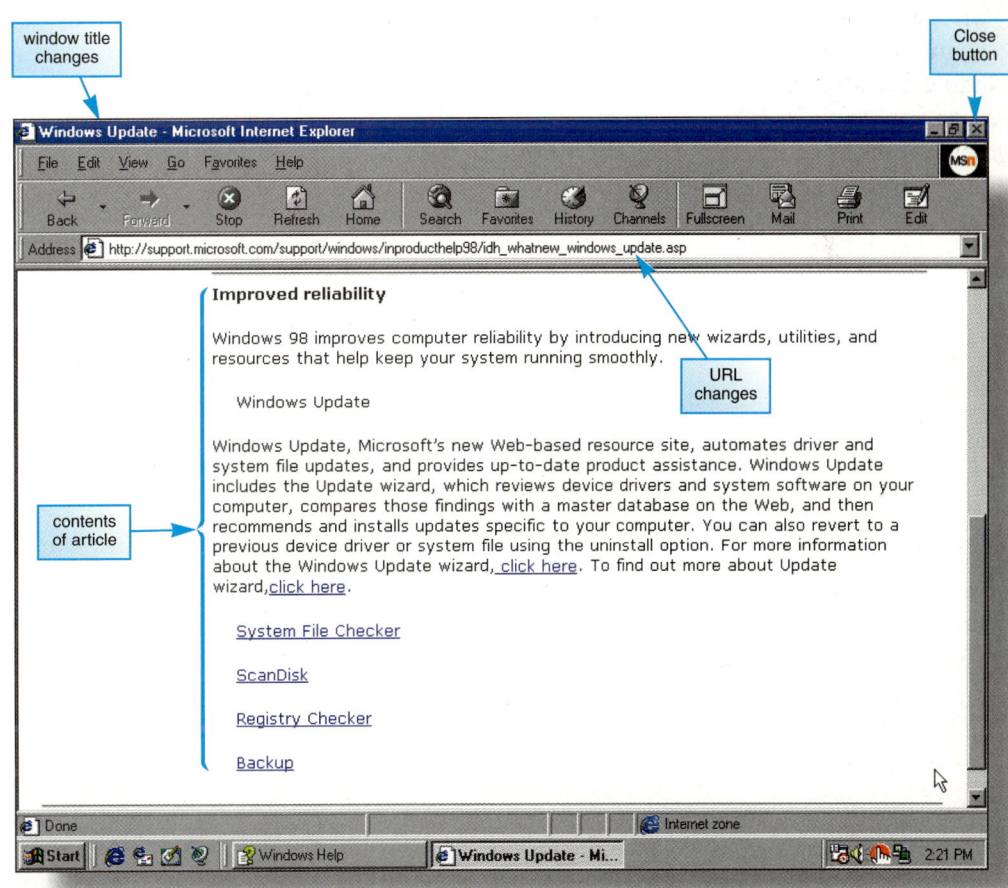

FIGURE 2-89

Shutting Down Windows

After completing your work, you may wish to shut down Windows 98 using the Shut Down command on the Start menu. If you are sure you want to shut down Windows 98, perform the following steps. If you are not sure about shutting down Windows 98, read the following steps without actually performing them.

TO SHUT DOWN WINDOWS 98

1. Click the Start button on the taskbar and then point to Shut Down on the Start menu.
2. Click Shut Down and then click the OK button in the Shut Down Windows dialog box.

If you accidentally click Shut Down on the Start menu and you do not want to shut down Windows 98, click the Cancel button in the Shut Down Windows dialog box.

Windows 98 Web Help

Microsoft Support Online was not available in previous versions of Windows. Microsoft Support Online replaces the need for lengthy, hard-to-understand technical manuals. Because the Help information in Microsoft Support Online can be updated quickly by Microsoft, it provides the most up-to-date technical information, answers to frequently asked questions, and late-breaking tips about working with Windows 98.

Project Summary

In this project you used the application-centric approach and document-centric approach to create two text documents on the desktop and then modified and printed these documents. Using a shortcut menu, you created a folder on the desktop and then placed the documents in the folder and copied the folder onto a floppy disk in drive A. You worked with multiple documents open at the same time. You placed a document shortcut on both the Start menu and desktop and removed the shortcuts. Using various methods, you deleted shortcuts, documents, and a folder from the desktop. You learned about the Active Desktop, turned on the Active Desktop, added an item to the Active Desktop, displayed additional information about a sporting event, removed the item, and turned off the Active Desktop. Finally, you used Windows Support Online to search for Help about Windows 98.

What You Should Know

Having completed this project, you now should be able to perform the following tasks:

- Close a Document *(WIN 2.12)*
- Close and Save a Modified Document on the Desktop *(WIN 2.16)*
- Close and Save Open Windows from the Taskbar *(WIN 2.27)*
- Copy a Folder on the Desktop onto a Floppy Disk *(WIN 2.30)*
- Create a Blank Document on the Desktop *(WIN 2.13)*
- Create a Shortcut on the Desktop *(WIN 2.39)*
- Create and Name a Folder on the Desktop *(WIN 2.18)*
- Delete a Folder from the Desktop *(WIN 2.47)*
- Delete a Shortcut from the Desktop *(WIN 2.43)*
- Delete Multiple Files *(WIN 2.45)*
- Display Additional Information About a Sporting Event *(WIN 2.54)*
- Display the Arrange Icons Submenu *(WIN 2.42)*
- Enter Data into a Blank Document *(WIN 2.16)*
- Launch a Program and Create a Document *(WIN 2.6)*
- Minimize All Open Windows *(WIN 2.26)*
- Move a Document into a Folder *(WIN 2.19)*
- Name a Document on the Desktop *(WIN 2.14)*
- Open a Document on the Desktop *(WIN 2.15)*
- Open a Document Using a Shortcut on the Desktop *(WIN 2.41)*
- Open a Document Using the Start Menu *(WIN 2.36)*
- Open a Folder *(WIN 2.21)*
- Open a Folder Stored on a Floppy Disk *(WIN 2.32)*
- Open an Inactive Window *(WIN 2.25)*
- Open and Modify a Document in a Folder *(WIN 2.22)*
- Open and Modify Multiple Documents *(WIN 2.23)*
- Place a Document Shortcut on the Start Menu *(WIN 2.34)*
- Print a Document *(WIN 2.11)*
- Print Multiple Documents from Within a Folder *(WIN 2.28)*
- Remove a Desktop Item from the Active Desktop and Cancel a Subscription *(WIN 2.56)*
- Remove a Shortcut from the Start Menu *(WIN 2.37)*
- Save a Document on the Desktop *(WIN 2.8)*
- Shut Down Windows 98 *(WIN 2.62)*
- Subscribe to a Channel and Add an Item to the Active Desktop *(WIN 2.49)*
- Turn on the Active Desktop *(WIN 2.48)*
- Turn off the Active Desktop *(WIN 2.58)*
- Use Windows Support Online *(WIN 2.59)*

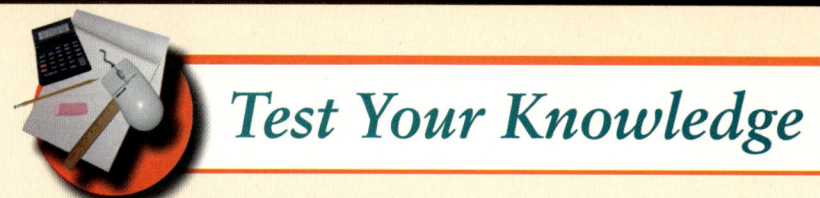

Test Your Knowledge

1 True/False

Instructions: Circle T if the statement is true or F if the statement is false.

T F 1. Application-centric means a user thinks in terms of the application program used to create a document rather than the document itself.

T F 2. To create a text document directly on the desktop, right-click the desktop, point to New on the shortcut menu, and click Text Document on the New submenu.

T F 3. To open a document stored on the desktop, click the Start button, point to Programs, and then click the document name on the Programs submenu.

T F 4. To create a folder on the desktop, right-click the desktop and then click Folder on the shortcut menu.

T F 5. When you drag a document into a folder on the desktop, you must click Move Here on the shortcut menu to place the document in the folder.

T F 6. To open a folder stored on the desktop, double-click the folder icon.

T F 7. The concept of multiple programs running at the same time is called multitasking.

T F 8. You can create a shortcut on both the desktop and Start menu.

T F 9. One way to view Active Web content on your desktop is to add an Active Desktop item to your desktop.

T F 10. The Help information you obtain while using Windows Support Online is located on the Internet.

2 Multiple Choice

Instructions: Circle the correct response.

1. A(n) _____ is a program that allows you to accomplish a specific task for which the program is designed.
   a. document
   b. operating system
   c. user interface
   d. application

2. To create a text document on the desktop, _____.
   a. click the desktop, click Text Document
   b. right-click the desktop, point to New, click Text Document
   c. click the desktop, point to Document, and click Text Document
   d. right-click the desktop, point to New, click Document

3. To open an inactive window, _____.
   a. click the inactive window's button in the taskbar button area
   b. press ALT+TAB until the name of the window displays, and then release the keys
   c. click the inactive window's button on the Start menu
   d. both a and b

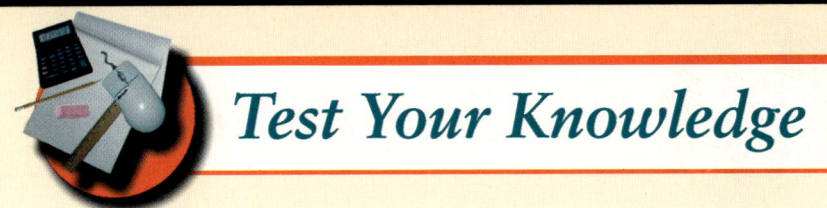

Test Your Knowledge

4. To select two documents within a folder, _____.
   a. right-drag any single document
   b. click File on the menu bar and then click Select All
   c. click one document icon, hold down the SHIFT key, and click the other document icon
   d. click the folder title bar

5. A shortcut is _____.
   a. a program that makes your work easier and faster
   b. an icon that represents a document or an application program
   c. any icon found in an open window
   d. another name for a button in the taskbar button area

6. To open a document using the Start menu, _____.
   a. double-click the document name on the Start menu
   b. click the document name on the Start menu
   c. right-click the document name on the Start menu
   d. point to the document name on the Start menu

7. When you delete a shortcut from the desktop, _____.
   a. the shortcut is deleted permanently
   b. Windows 98 will display an error message in a dialog box because you cannot delete a shortcut from the desktop
   c. the shortcut and the related file are placed in the Recycle Bin
   d. the shortcut is placed in the Recycle Bin

8. Which of the following is not a way to delete an object from the desktop? _____.
   a. Right-drag the object to the Recycle Bin.
   b. Drag the object to the Recycle Bin.
   c. Click the object and then click Delete on the shortcut menu.
   d. Right-click the object and then click Delete on the shortcut menu.

9. Using the words, Start menu, as a search inquiry would result in the articles containing _____ to display.
   a. the phrase, Start menu
   b. both the word, Start, and the word, menu
   c. the word, Start, but not the word, menu
   d. Q155353

10. When you add an Active Desktop item to the Active Desktop, you also _____ to a _____.
    a. add a button, toolbar
    b. add active content, window
    c. subscribe, channel
    d. move a window, new location

WIN 2.66 • Project 2 • Working on the Windows 98 Desktop

Test Your Knowledge

3 Working with Folders and Documents

Instructions: The open Business Documents folder displays on the desktop shown in Figure 2-90. The Address Book and Daily Appointments documents are stored in the Business Documents folder. In the spaces below, write the steps to accomplish the tasks indicated.

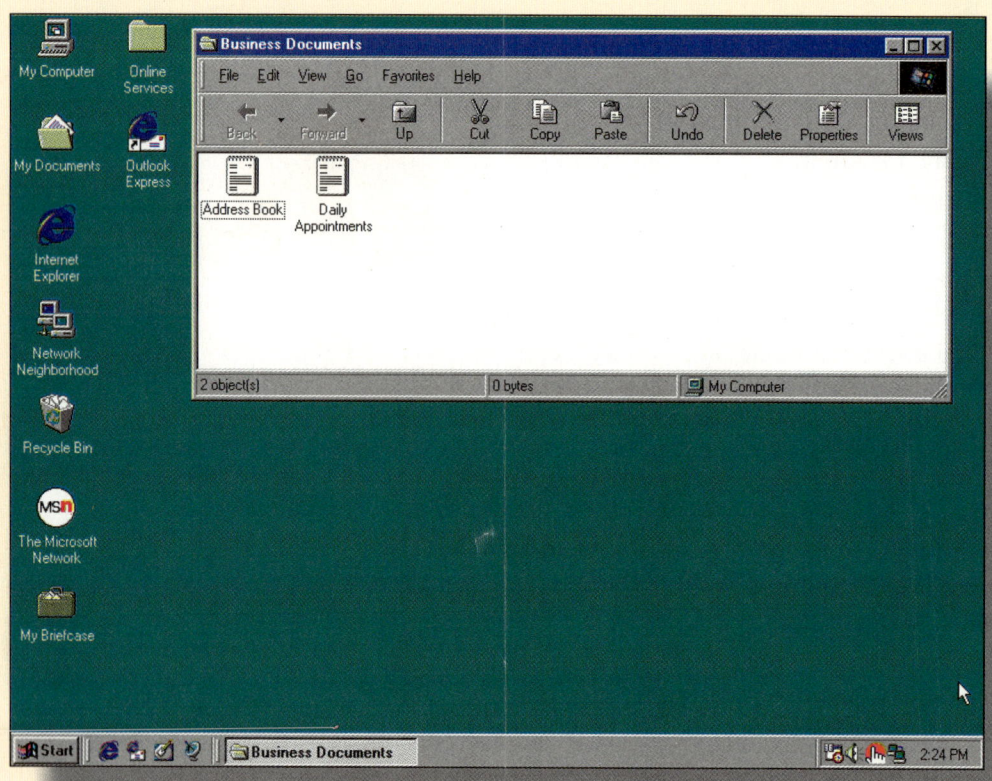

FIGURE 2-90

To Print the Address Book document

Step 1: _____

Step 2: _____

To Copy the Daily Appointments document to the desktop

Step 1: _____

Step 2: _____

To Delete the Address Book document from the Business Documents folder

Method 1:

Step 1: _____

Step 2: _____

Test Your Knowledge

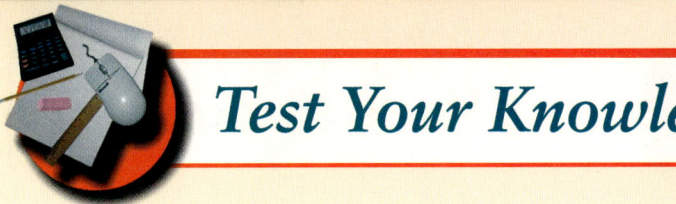

Method 2:

Step 1: _____

Step 2: _____

Step 3: _____

Method 3:

Step 1: _____

To Delete the Business Documents folder from the desktop

Method 1:

Step 1: _____

Step 2: _____

Method 2:

Step 1: _____

Step 2: _____

Step 3: _____

Method 3:

Step 1: _____

4 Working with Document Shortcuts

Instructions: The closed Sales Document folder on the desktop contains the Monthly Sales document. In the spaces provided below, write the steps to accomplish the tasks indicated.

To place a document shortcut for the Monthly Sales document on the Start menu

Step 1: _____

Step 2: _____

To open the Monthly Sales document from the Start menu

Step 1: _____

Step 2: _____

To remove the Monthly Sales shortcut from the Start menu

Step 1: _____

Step 2: _____

Step 3: _____

Step 4: _____

WIN 2.68 • Project 2 • Working on the Windows 98 Desktop

Microsoft **Windows 98**

Test Your Knowledge

5 Adding a Desktop Item to the Active Desktop

Instructions: List the steps in the spaces provided to add the ESPN SportsZone™ desktop item to the Active Desktop.

Step 1: _____

Step 2: _____

Step 3: _____

Step 4: _____

Step 5: _____

Step 6: _____

Step 7: _____

Step 8: _____

Step 9: _____

Step 10: _____

Step 11: _____

Use Help

1 Finding Terms and Definitions in the Windows Glossary

Instructions: Use a computer and Windows Help to perform the following tasks.

Part 1: *Creating a Document on the Desktop*
1. Start Windows 98 and connect to the Internet if necessary.
2. Create a text document on the desktop. Name the document Windows Definitions.
3. Double-click the Windows Definitions document icon to open the document. Maximize the Windows Definitions - Notepad window.

Part 2: *Launching Windows Help and Using the Glossary*
1. Click the Start button on the taskbar.
2. Click Help on the Start menu.
3. Click the Web Help button on the Help toolbar.
4. Click the Support Online hyperlink in the right frame of the Windows Help window.
5. Click the View Popular Topics command in the menu in the left frame.
6. Click the Choose a Popular Topic box arrow and then click Glossary in the list.
7. Click the go button.
8. If the Security Alert dialog box displays, click the Yes button.
9. If the Internet Redirection dialog box displays, click the Yes button. The title, Glossary, and the letters of the alphabet display in the window (Figure 2-91).

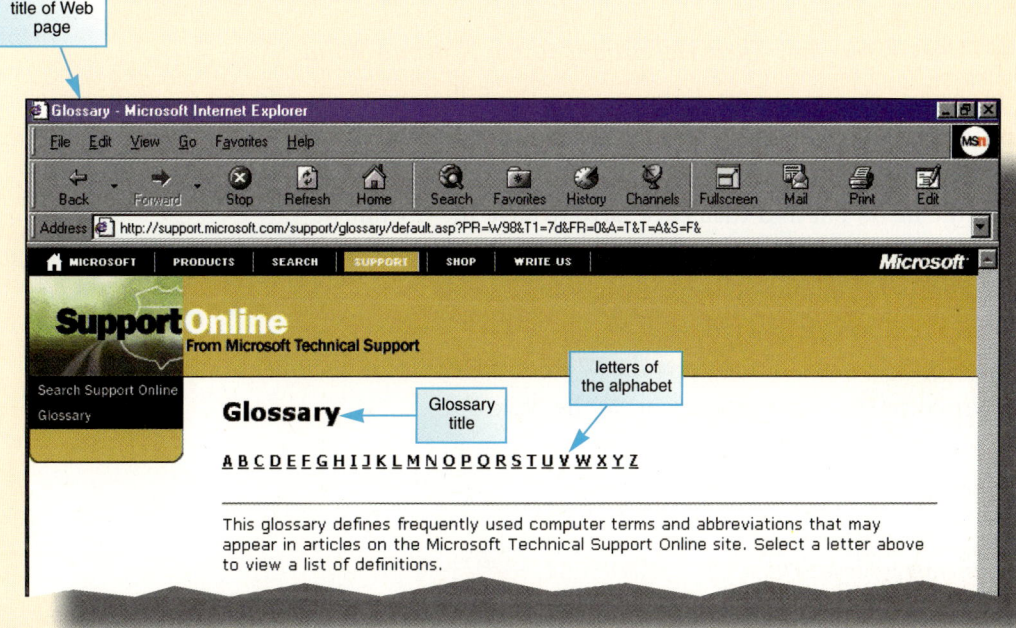

FIGURE 2-91

(continued)

Use Help

Finding Terms and Definitions in the Windows Glossary *(continued)*

Part 3: *Copying a Term and Its Definition from the Glossary to the Notepad Window*

1. Click the first letter (A) in the list. A list of the terms beginning with the letter A and their definitions display.
2. Scroll the window to make the term, application-centric, and its definition visible.
3. Highlight the term and its definition by dragging.
4. Right-click the highlighted definition to display a shortcut menu.
5. Click Copy on the shortcut menu.
6. Click the Windows Definitions button in the taskbar button area to display the Windows Definitions - Notepad window.
7. Right-click the text area of the Notepad window to display a shortcut menu.
8. Click Paste on the shortcut menu. The term and definition display in the window. Click the Home button on the keyboard.
9. Position the insertion point between two words at the right side of the window and then press the ENTER key to move the text to the right of the insertion point to the next line in the document. Repeat this procedure until the entire definition is visible in the window.
10. Insert a blank line in the document following the definition.
11. Click File on the menu bar and then click Save to save the document.
12. Click the Glossary - Microsoft Internet Explorer button in the taskbar button area to display the Glossary - Microsoft Internet Explorer window.
13. Click the Back button on the Standard Buttons toolbar to display the alphabet list.

Part 4: *Copying Other Terms and Their Definitions to the Notepad Window*

1. Using the procedure shown in Part 3 above, copy the following terms and their definitions from the Glossary to the Notepad window: bit map, document-centric, and operating system. The definition for each term should be visible in the Notepad window.
2. Click File on the menu bar and then click Save to save the document.
3. Click File on the menu bar and then click Print to print the document.
4. Close the Windows Definition - Notepad window.
5. Close all open Windows Help windows.
6. Insert a floppy disk in drive A and copy the Windows Definition document onto the disk.
7. Delete the Windows Definition document on the desktop.

2 Performing Searches Using Windows Support Online

Instructions: Use Windows Support Online and a computer to perform the following tasks.

1. Design a search inquiry to search for articles about launching Notepad. List the names of the first three articles found in the spaces provided. Select an article that answers your inquiry and print the article.

   _____
   _____
   _____

2. Design a search inquiry to search for articles about creating a shortcut on the desktop. List the names of the first three articles found in the spaces provided. Select an article that you feel answers your inquiry and print the article.

   _____
   _____
   _____

3. Design a search inquiry to search for articles about Support Online. List the names of the first three articles found in the spaces provided. Select an article that you feel answers your inquiry and print the article.

   _____
   _____
   _____

4. Design a search inquiry to search for articles about retrieving a deleted shortcut. List the names of the first three articles found in the spaces provided. Select an article that you feel answers your inquiry and print the article.

   _____
   _____
   _____

In the Lab

1 Launching an Application, Creating a Document, and Modifying a Document

Instructions: Your boss asks you to create an office supplies shopping list for your department. You decide to use the application-centric approach to create the shopping list. Complete the following steps to accomplish this task.

Part 1: *Launching the Notepad Application*

1. Start Microsoft Windows 98 if necessary.
2. Click the Start button.
3. Point to Programs on the Start menu.
4. Point to Accessories on the Programs submenu.
5. Click Notepad on the Accessories submenu.
6. Enter the text shown in Figure 2-92.

Part 2: *Saving the Document onto a Floppy Disk and Printing the Document*

1. Insert a formatted floppy disk in drive A of your computer.
2. Click File on the menu bar and then click Save As to display the Save As dialog box.
3. Type Office Supplies Shopping List in the File name text box.

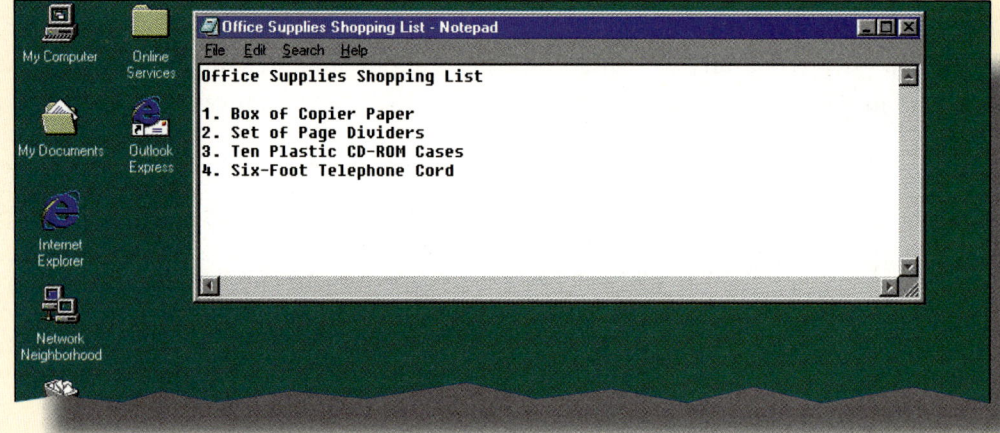

FIGURE 2-92

4. Click the Save in box arrow.
5. Click the 3½ Floppy (A:) icon.
6. Click the Save button in the Save As dialog box.
7. Click File on the menu bar and click Print.
8. Click the Close button on the Notepad title bar.
9. If you are not completing Part 3 of this assignment, remove your floppy disk from drive A.

Part 3: *Modifying a Document*

1. Click the Start button, point to Programs, point to Accessories, and then click Notepad.
2. Click File on the menu bar and then click Open.
3. Click the Look in box arrow and then click the 3½ Floppy (A:) icon.
4. Click Office Supplies Shopping List in the list.
5. Click the Open button in the Open dialog box.
6. Press the DOWN ARROW key six times.
7. Type 5. Crystal Clear Glaze (4 Ounce Bottle) and then press the ENTER key.

In the Lab

8. Click File on the menu bar and then click Save.
9. Click File on the menu bar and then click Print.
10. Click the Close button on the Notepad title bar.
11. Remove the floppy disk from drive A.

2 Creating, Saving, and Printing Windows 98 Seminar Announcement and Schedule Documents

Instructions: A two-day Windows 98 seminar will be offered to all teachers at your school. You have been put in charge of developing two text documents for the seminar. One document announces the seminar and will be sent to all teachers. The other document contains the schedule for the seminar. Complete the following steps to prepare the documents using Notepad.

Part 1: *Creating the Windows 98 Seminar Announcement Document*

1. Start Microsoft Windows 98 if necessary.
2. Create a blank text document on the desktop. Name the document Windows 98 Seminar Announcement.
3. Enter the text shown in Figure 2-93.

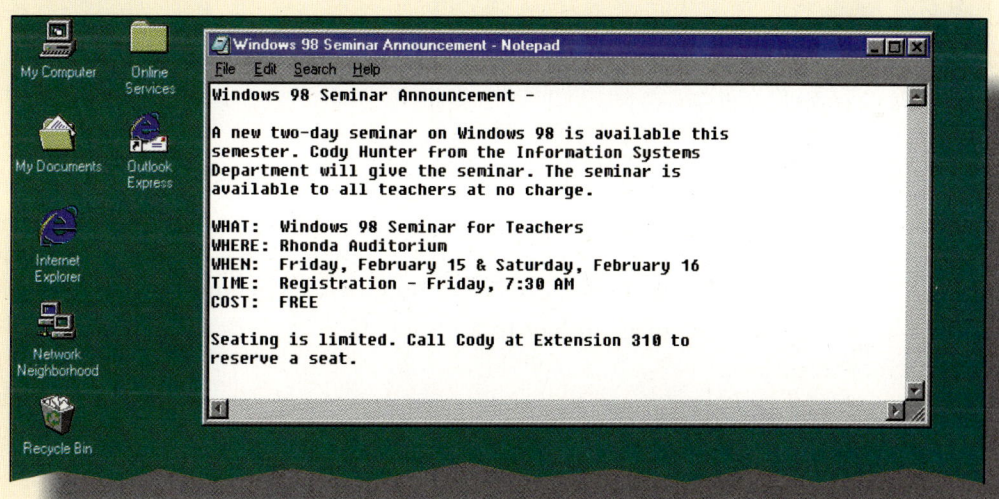

FIGURE 2-93

4. Save the document on the desktop.
5. Print the document.
6. Create a folder on the desktop called Windows 98 Seminar Documents.
7. Place the Windows 98 Seminar Announcement document in the Windows 98 Seminar Documents folder.

(continued)

In the Lab

Creating, Saving, and Printing Windows 98 Seminar Announcement and Schedule Documents *(continued)*

Part 2: *Creating the Windows 98 Seminar Schedule Document*

1. Create a blank text document on the desktop. Name the document Windows 98 Seminar Schedule.
2. Enter the text shown in Figure 2-94.

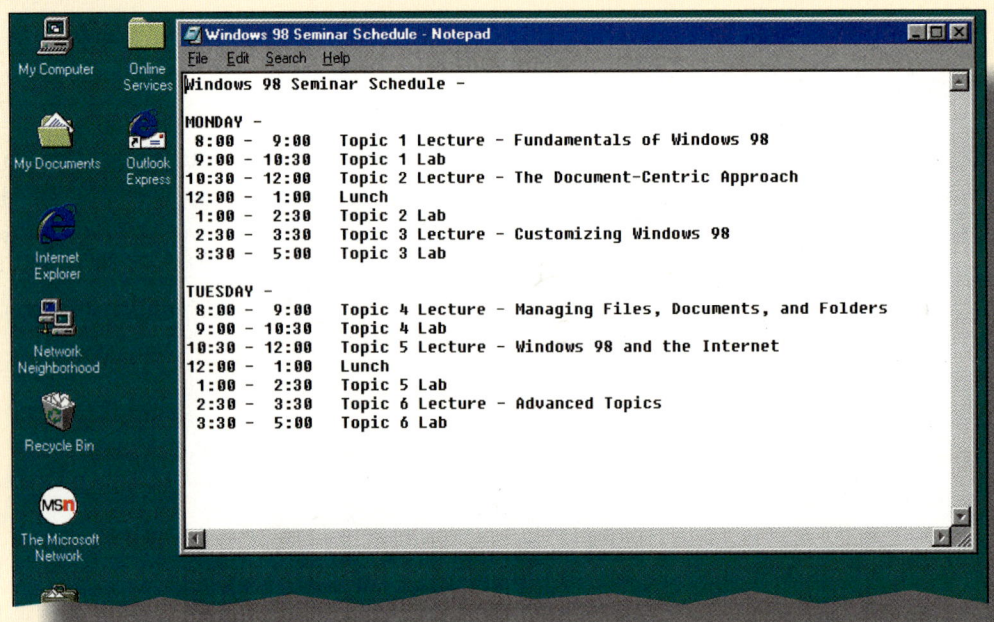

FIGURE 2-94

3. Save the document on the desktop.
4. Print the document.
5. Place the Windows 98 Seminar Schedule document in the Windows 98 Seminar Documents folder.
6. Move the Windows 98 Seminar Documents folder to a floppy disk.

3 Creating, Saving, and Printing Automobile Information Documents

Instructions: For almost a year, you have accumulated data about your 1999 Pontiac automobile. You have written some of the information on pieces of paper, while other information is in the form of receipts. Now you have decided to organize all this information on your computer. Create all documents using the document-centric approach. Complete the following steps to accomplish this task.

Part 1: *Creating the Automobile Information Document*

1. Start Microsoft Windows 98 if necessary.
2. Create a text document on the desktop. Name the document Automobile Information.
3. Enter the text shown in Figure 2-95.

In the Lab

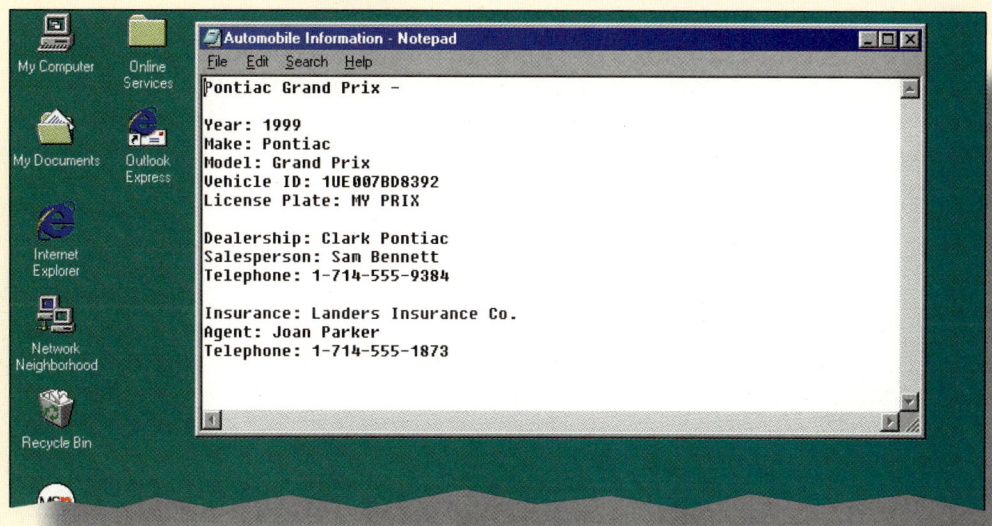

FIGURE 2-95

4. Save the document on the desktop.
5. Print the document.
6. Create a folder on the desktop called Automobile Documents.
7. Place the Automobile Information document in the Automobile Documents folder.

Part 2: *Other Automobile Documents*

1. Create the Phone Numbers document (Figure 2-96), the Automobile Gas Mileage document (Figure 2-97 on the next page), and the Automobile Maintenance document (Figure 2-98 on the next page).
2. Save each document on the desktop.
3. Print each document.
4. Place each document in the Automobile Documents folder.
5. Move the Automobile Documents folder to a floppy disk.

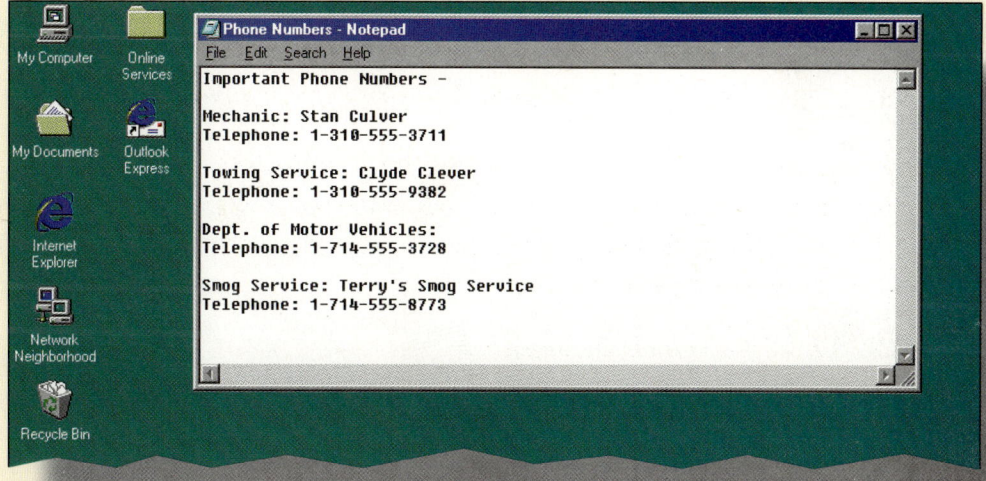

FIGURE 2-96

(continued)

In the Lab

Creating, Saving, and Printing Automobile Information Documents (continued)

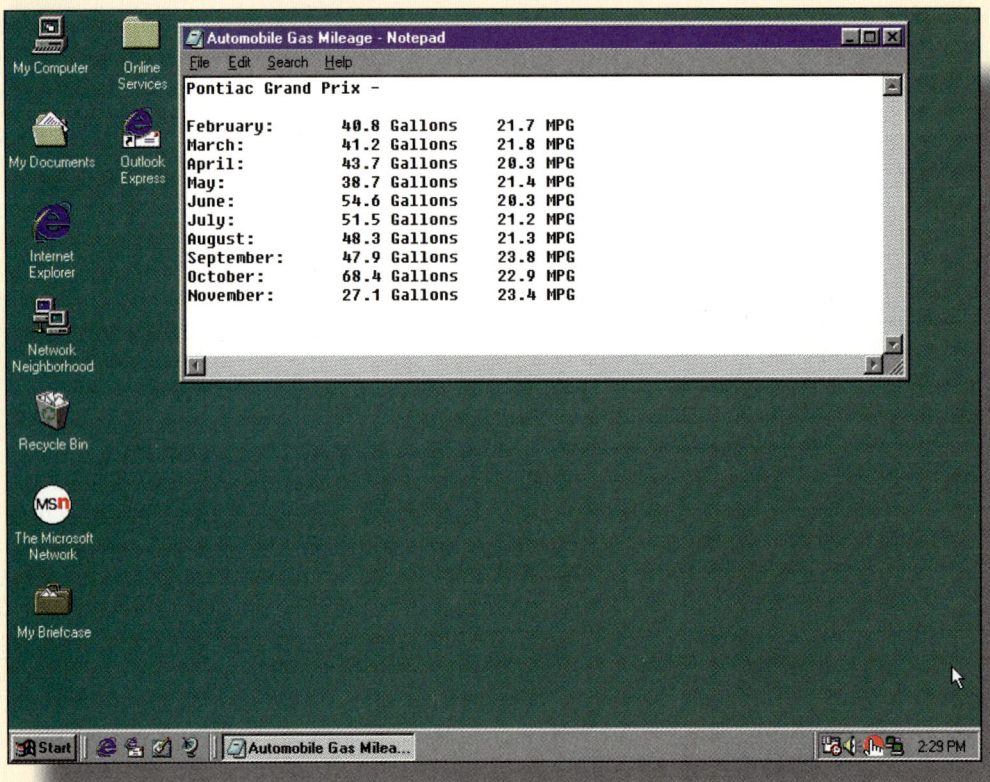

FIGURE 2-97

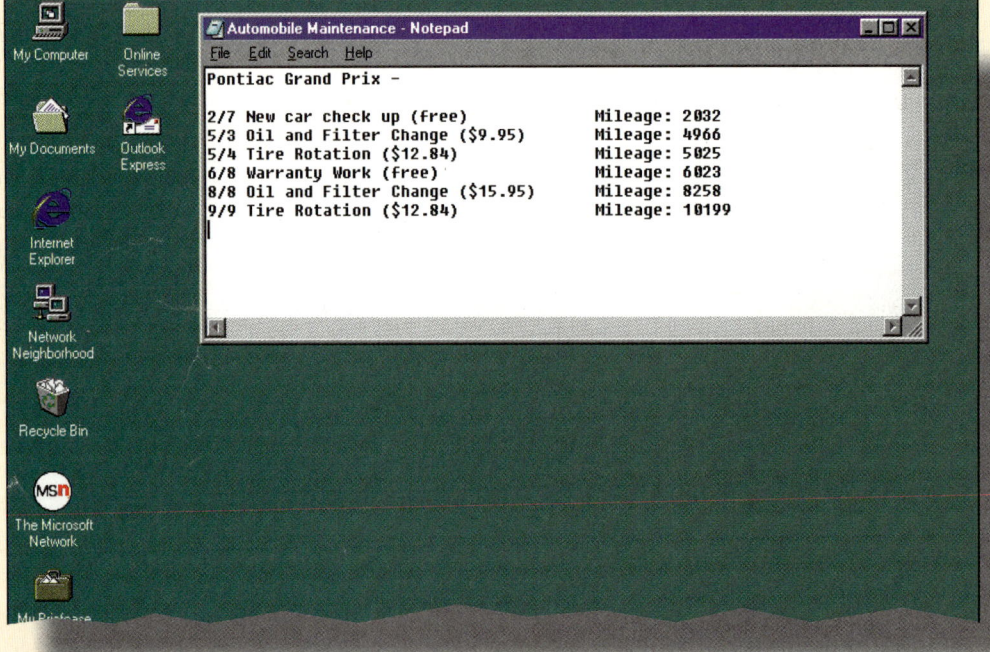

FIGURE 2-98

In the Lab

4 Adding a Desktop Item to the Active Desktop

Instructions: Perform the following steps to add a desktop item to the desktop, move the item on the desktop, display additional information about a news story, and remove the item from the desktop.

Part 1: *Adding a Desktop Item to the Desktop*

1. Start Microsoft Windows 98 and connect to the Internet if necessary.
2. Right-click an open area on the desktop.
3. Click Properties on the shortcut menu.
4. Click the Web tab in the Display Properties dialog box and then click the New button.
5. Click the Yes button in the New Active Desktop Item dialog box.
6. Click the Maximize button in the Desktop Gallery window.
7. Click the travel icon in the Desktop Gallery window. Two channel names display in the window (Figure 2-99).

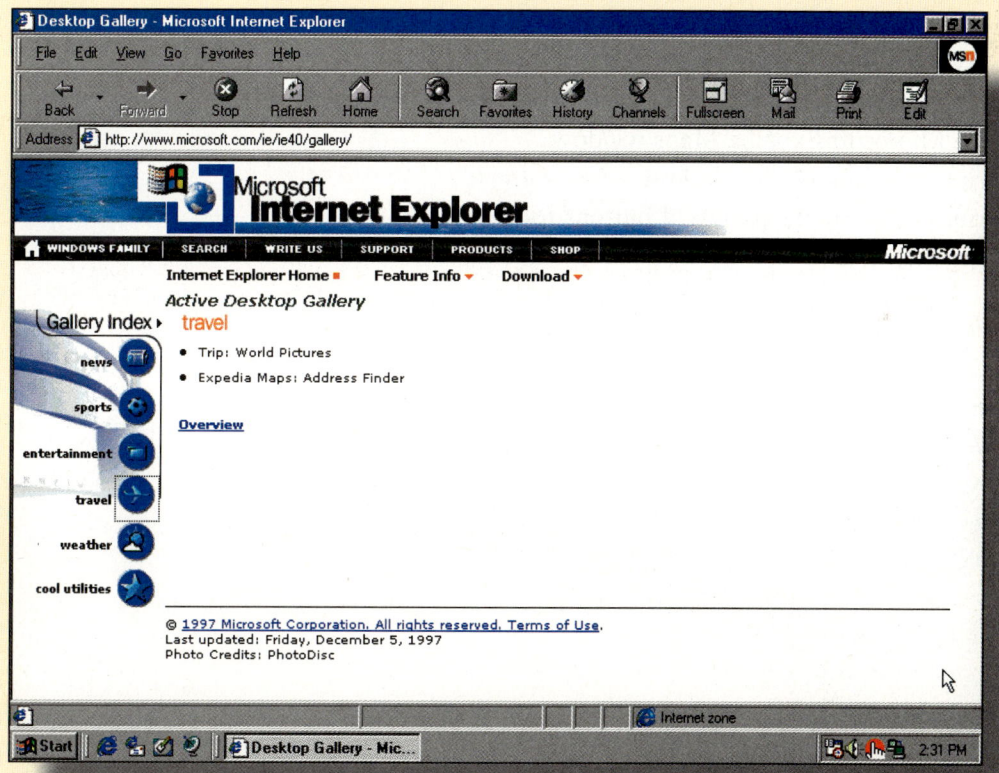

FIGURE 2-99

8. Click the Expedia Maps: Address Finder channel name.
9. Click the Add to Active Desktop button.

(continued)

In the Lab

Adding a Desktop Item to the Active Desktop *(continued)*

10. Click the Yes button in the Security Alert dialog box.
11. Click the OK button in the Add item to Active Desktop dialog box.
12. Click the Close button in the Desktop Gallery window.

Part 2: Sizing the Desktop Item

1. Point to the bottom window border to change the mouse pointer to a double-headed arrow.
2. Drag the border down until the Address, City, State, and ZIP boxes are visible.

Part 3: Displaying and Printing a Map

1. Click the Address text box and then type your street address in the text box.
2. Click the City text box and then type your city name in the text box.
3. Click the State box arrow. Click your state name in the list.
4. Click the ZIP text box and type your Zip code in the text box.
5. Click the Find button.
6. If the Security Alert dialog box displays, click the Yes button.
7. If the Internet Redirection dialog box displays, click the Yes button.
8. Maximize the Microsoft Expedia Maps window.
9. Click the Print hyperlink in the window.
10. Click the Print button on the Standard Buttons toolbar to print the map.
11. Close the browser window.

Part 4: Removing a Desktop Item on the Desktop

1. Right-click an open area on the desktop.
2. Click Properties on the shortcut menu.
3. Click the Web tab in the Display Properties dialog box.
4. Click the Expedia Address Finder check box title to highlight it and then click the Delete button.
5. Click the Yes button in the Active Desktop Item dialog box.
6. Click the OK button.

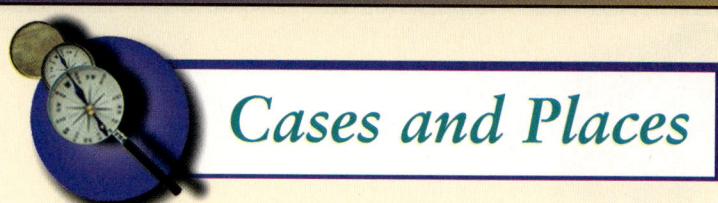
Cases and Places

The difficulty of these case studies varies:
▶ are the least difficult; ▶▶ are more difficult; and ▶▶▶ are the most difficult.

1 ▶ Your employer is concerned that some people in the company are not thoroughly researching software purchases. She has prepared a list of steps she would like everyone to follow when acquiring software (Figure 2-100).

You have been asked to use WordPad to prepare a copy of this list that can be posted in every department. Use the concepts and techniques presented in this project to create a WordPad document on the desktop. Save and print the document. After you have printed one copy of the document, try experimenting with different WordPad features to make the list more eye-catching. If you like your changes, save and print a revised copy of the document. If WordPad is not available on your computer, use Notepad.

Steps in Software Acquisitions

1. Summarize your requirements
2. Identify potential vendors
3. Evaluate alternative software packages
4. Make the purchase

FIGURE 2-100

2 ▶▶ You volunteer to show your friend how to add desktop items to the Active Desktop. After explaining the concept of channels and showing several desktop items to your friend, he decides he would like for you to show him how to add the ESPN SportsZone™, CNET, and Microsoft Ticker Tape items. Add these three desktop items to your desktop. Move and size the desktop items on the desktop to make each item visible. Click a sporting event in the ESPN SportsZone™ item and print the event. Click a news story in the CNET item and print the story. Click a stock quote in the Microsoft Ticker Tape item and print the quote.

3 ▶▶ Document-centric versus application-centric: prepare a brief report about the two approaches. Explain what each approach means to the computer user, summarize the advantages and disadvantages of each approach, and indicate which is the better approach for you and why. Do you think one approach will be more popular in the future? Will future operating systems emphasize one approach over the other? Support your opinions with information from computer magazines, articles on the Internet, and other resources.

Cases and Places

4 ▶▶ Microsoft touts Windows 98 as an intuitive operating system. Webster's dictionary defines *intuitive* as knowing or perceiving by immediate apprehension or cognition. Using current computer magazines or other resources, prepare a brief report on the intuitive nature of Windows 98. Describe the features of Windows 98 that Microsoft feels help people instantly understand the operating system. Discuss the opinions that reviewers had about learning and using Windows 98. Finally, from your research and your own experience, explain whether you believe Windows 98 is an intuitive operating system.

5 ▶▶▶ Microsoft Corporation offers many ways to obtain information about its software products. In addition to Windows 98 Help, the Microsoft Web site (www.microsoft.com) contains helpful information about Microsoft products. Products include operating systems (Windows 3.1, Windows 95, Windows 98, and Windows NT), application software (Office, Word, Excel, Access, PowerPoint, NetMeeting, Bookshelf, and Outlook Express), and an online service (MSN). Using any two operating systems and any four application programs just mentioned and the online service, write a brief report summarizing each product's function. Write a single paragraph about each product.

6 ▶▶▶ Registering for classes can be a daunting task for incoming college freshmen. As someone who has gone through the process, prepare a guide for students who are about to register for the first time next semester. Your guide should be two or more documents and include a calendar and/or schedule of key dates and times, a description of the registration procedure, and suggestions for how students can make registration easier. Give the documents suitable names and save them in a folder on the Windows 98 desktop. Print each document.

7 ▶▶▶ In the course of a year, a typical business might save hundreds of document files. These files must be organized so they can be located and retrieved efficiently. Windows 98 provides an easy way to work with document files on personal computers. How are document files organized with other operating systems used by businesses? Visit a business that uses personal computers with an operating system different from Windows 98. Find out how document files are saved, organized, and accessed. Write a brief report describing the way document files are stored. Explain how the same files might be kept using Windows 98. Based on what you have learned, decide which operating system can be used to organize document files more effectively and explain why.

Microsoft Windows 98

PROJECT 3

File, Document, and Folder Management and Windows 98 Explorer

OBJECTIVES

You will have mastered the material in this project when you can:

- Display icons in various views in a window
- Open a folder, document, and application program from a window
- Cascade and tile open windows on the desktop
- Copy, move, and delete files from open windows
- Launch Windows 98 Explorer
- Display files and folders in Explorer
- Expand drives and folders in Explorer
- Open a drive and folder in Explorer
- Launch an application program from Explorer
- Close folder expansions
- Copy, move, rename, and delete files in Explorer
- Close Explorer
- Display drive and folder properties
- Find files or folders using Find on the Start menu
- Use the Run command

MOORE AND More Storage

Cramming Data in Small Places

Is it any doubt that you are an expert when it comes to cramming? You cram for final exams, cram books into heavy backpacks, and cram clothes into tiny closets. Only a few decades ago, college students held contests to see how many people could cram into telephone booths and Volkswagen Beetles. About the same time, Gordon Moore, a semiconductor engineer, realized cramming was a good thing when it came to computer chips.

In 1965, Moore observed a trend when he was drawing an illustration for a speech: every 18 to 24 months a new memory chip was being released with double the number of transistors as its predecessor. He predicted that this growth would continue exponentially, and he was correct. Today's Pentium II processor has 7.5 million transistors, which is nearly 3,200 times more than the 2,300 transistors found on a chip released in 1971.

7.5 MILLION

His theory became known as Moore's Law. In 1968, Gordon Moore became a cofounder of Intel Corporation, one of the world's largest microprocessor manufacturers.

Hard disk capacity has grown to impressive densities in recent years. In 1956, IBM's first hard drive stored five megabytes (five million bytes) of data. Subsequent drive capacity doubled every 30 months until 1991. At that time, IBM introduced new technology that doubled capacity every 18 months. IBM needed a truck to deliver that refrigerator-sized first hard drive, which consisted of fifty 24-inch disks, called platters, and cost more than $1 million, at the value of today's dollars. The hard drive in your computer probably has two 3½-inch platters, stores at least four gigabytes (four billion bytes), and costs less than $300.

With such increased disk capacity, computers store more data, programs, and files than ever before. Consider how in this project, you will manage and organize files and documents using tools supplied with Windows 98. You will master the operations of copying, moving, renaming, and deleting files stored on your computer's floppy disk and then display your computer's hard disk properties. Do you wonder how all the data files and programs fit on those disks?

Engineers use the term, *areal density,* when referring to capacity, which is a combination of the disk's magnetic properties, read/write head movement, and electronic principles. As the hard disk's platters whirl at 3,600 to 7,200 revolutions per minute, read/write heads attached to access arms move to the correct position on a particular platter and retrieve or record bits of data.

Technology gurus predict that Moore's Law for silicon chips will hold true until 2020. At that time, they will be forced to use new methods and materials, such as the optical technique of holography. As for disk drives, capacity may max out in 2010, when densities will reach 70 to 100 gigabytes per square inch, as compared with today's one gigabyte per square inch. Engineers are investigating holographic storage, which will hold 1,000 gigabytes per square inch, but they have set their sights on technologies that could lead to capacities of one million gigabytes per square inch.

With that capacity in your computer, just think of how many programs and data files you will be able to cram into that space. Be forewarned: you probably will need every bit (or byte) of this space to hold the progressive applications planned for the next decade and beyond.

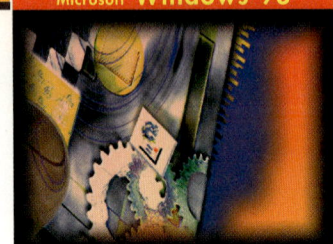

Microsoft Windows 98

File, Document, and Folder Management and Windows 98 Explorer

PROJECT 3

CASE PERSPECTIVE

Your organization has decided to switch to Windows 98 from Windows 95. Your supervisor has read in computer magazines that to use Windows 98 effectively, people must be able to control and manage windows on their Windows 98 desktop, and their proficient use of Windows 98 Explorer will be critical in the successful implementation of Windows 98. Although almost everyone is excited about the change, those who have little experience using Windows 95 are apprehensive about having to learn about file and window management. You have been asked to teach a class with an emphasis on file and desktop management to any employees who are not experienced Windows users. Your goal in Project 3 is to become competent using these features of Windows 98 so that you can teach the class.

Introduction

In Project 2, you used Windows 98 to create documents and store them on both a floppy disk and the desktop, and you created folders in which to place the documents. Windows 98 also allows you to examine the documents, files, and folders on your computer in a variety of ways, depending on the easiest and most accessible manner during your work on the computer. The two major ways for you to work with files and documents are using the My Computer window and Windows 98 Explorer, which is an application program provided with Windows 98. This project will illustrate how to manage and organize files and documents using the tools supplied by Windows 98.

My Computer Window

As noted in previous projects, the My Computer icon displays in the upper-left corner of the Windows 98 desktop. The **My Computer icon** represents a window that displays all the hardware components on your computer (disk drives, CD-ROM drives, and DVD drives) and system folders (Printers, Control Panel, Dial-Up Networking, and Scheduled Tasks). To open and maximize the My Computer window and view the components of your computer, complete the steps on the next two pages.

Steps To Open and Maximize the My Computer Window

1 Double-click the My Computer icon on the desktop. Point to the Maximize button in the My Computer window.

The My Computer window opens (Figure 3-1).

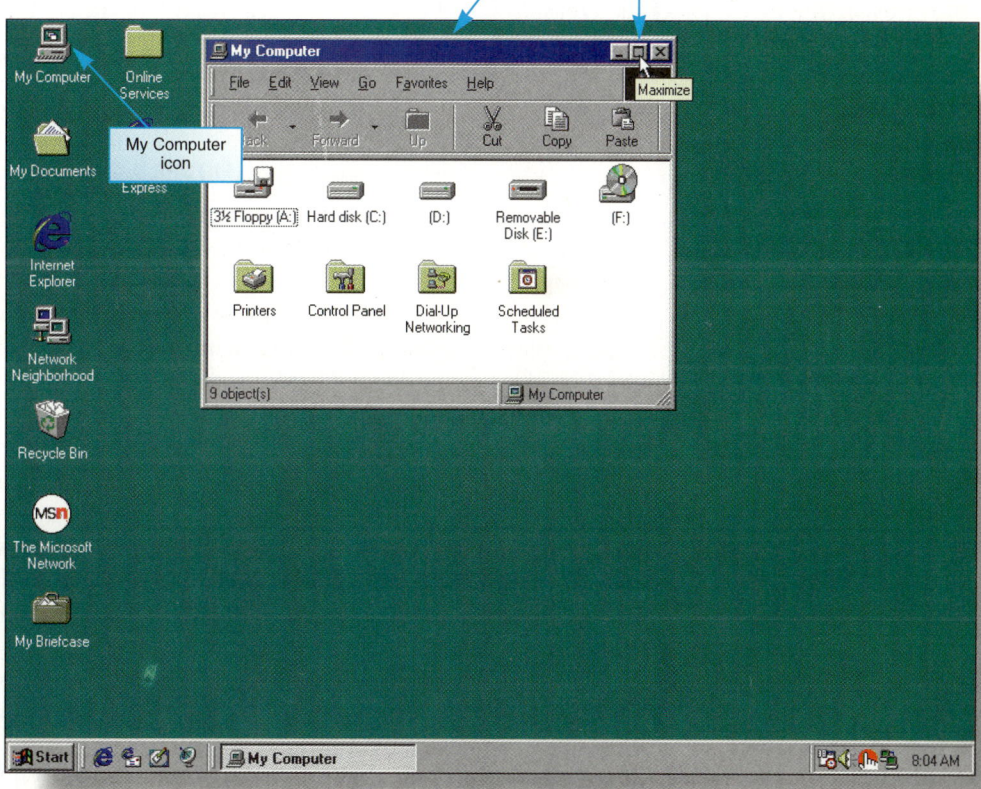

FIGURE 3-1

WIN 3.6 • Project 3 • File, Document, and Folder Management and Windows 98 Explorer

② **Click the Maximize button.**

The My Computer window is maximized (Figure 3-2).

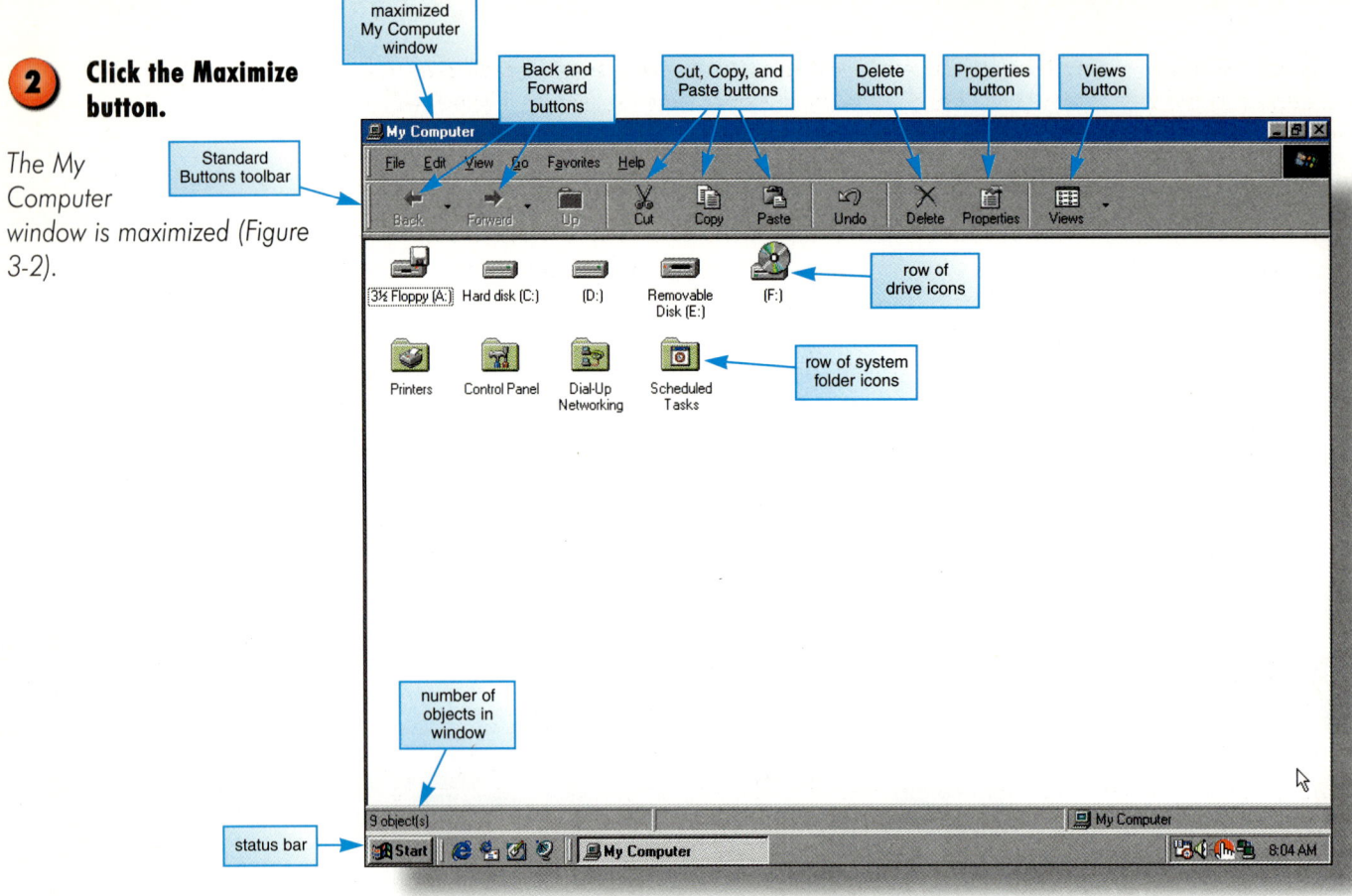

FIGURE 3-2

The Standard Buttons toolbar shown in Figure 3-2 contains buttons you will use in this project to navigate between windows (Back and Forward), copy and move files (Cut, Copy, and Paste buttons), delete files (Delete icon), display object properties (Properties), and change the appearance of the icons in a window (Views button).

The area below the Standard Buttons toolbar contains a row of drive icons (3½ Floppy (A:) icon, Hard disk (C:) icon, (D:) icon, Removable Disk (E:) icon, and (F:) icon) and a row of system folder icons (Printers icon, Control Panel icon, Dial-Up Networking icon, and Scheduled Tasks icon). The icons on your computer may be different and may display in a different format than the ones shown in Figure 3-2.

The **Hard disk (C:) icon** shown in Figure 3-2 represents the hard disk on your computer. The **hard disk** is where you can store files, documents, and folders if it is not necessary for you to transport them from one computer to another. Storing data on a hard disk often is more convenient than storing it on a floppy disk in drive A because using a hard disk is faster, and generally more storage room is available on a hard disk than on a floppy disk. Your computer always will have at least one hard disk drive, normally designated as drive C. On the computer represented by the My Computer window in Figure 3-2, the hard disk has been given a **disk label**, or title (*Hard disk*). The label is not required. Later in this project you will see how to give a drive a name.

Some computers may have additional hard drives or have a single hard drive that has been subdivided into two or more areas by the operating system. In Figure 3-2, the Hard disk (C:) icon and (D:) icon refer to different areas of the same hard drive. The Hard disk (C:) icon represents the area of the hard drive that contains the programs required by the operating system and the files, folders, and programs you want to save. The **(D:) icon** represents an area on the hard drive where additional files, folders, or programs can be stored. Some computers may have a separate second hard drive or a removable hard drive, such as the removable hard drive represented by the **Removable Disk (E:) icon** shown in Figure 3-2. Removable disk drives, such as a Jaz drive or a Zip drive, allow you to store large files or a large number of files on a cartridge that can be removed from the disk drive.

The **(F:) icon** is a CD-ROM drive. In Figure 3-2, the label for the drive is blank because the drive does not contain a CD-ROM. If you insert a CD-ROM in the drive, such as an **audio CD** containing music, then Windows 98 changes the label to reflect the type of CD in the drive and musical notes are added to the icon.

The status bar at the bottom of the My Computer window indicates the window contains nine objects.

Viewing Icons in the My Computer Window

The icons in the My Computer window shown in Figure 3-2 are displayed in a format called **Large Icons**, which means the icons are relatively large. The icons can, however, display in other formats. Complete the following steps to display icons in all the different formats available in the My Computer window.

 To Change the Format of the Icons in a Window

 **Point to the Views button on the Standard Buttons toolbar (Figure 3-3).**

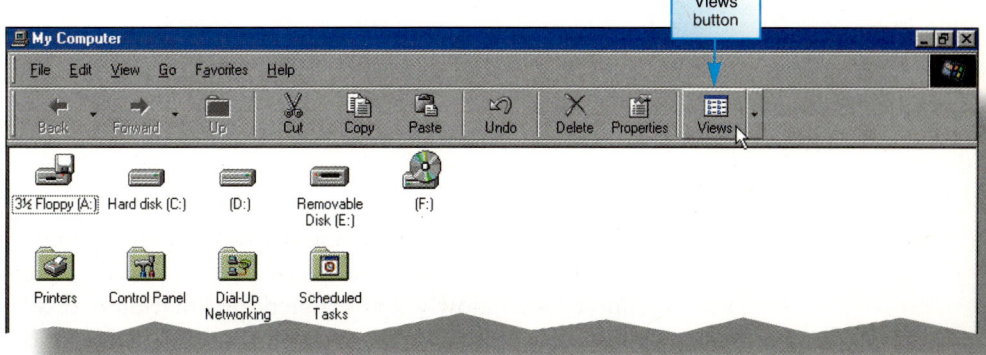

FIGURE 3-3

Click the Views button.

The icons display in Small Icons format with the icon title adjacent to the icon (Figure 3-4). The icons display in five columns.

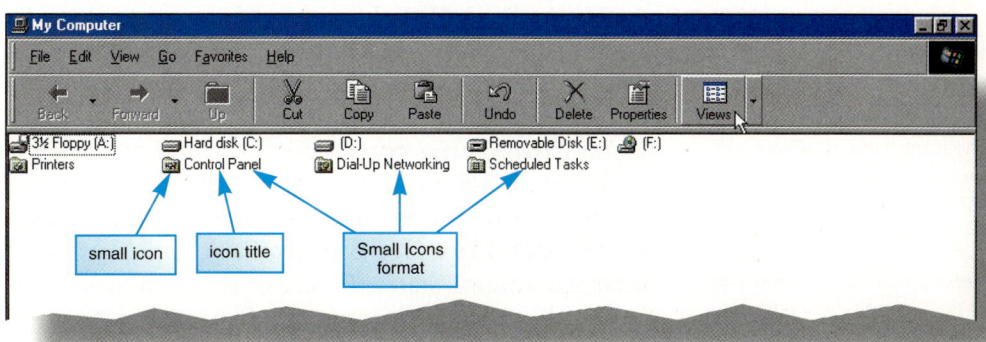

FIGURE 3-4

3 Click the Views button.

The icons display in the window in List view using the Small Icons format (Figure 3-5). The **List view** places the drive and folder icons in a list.

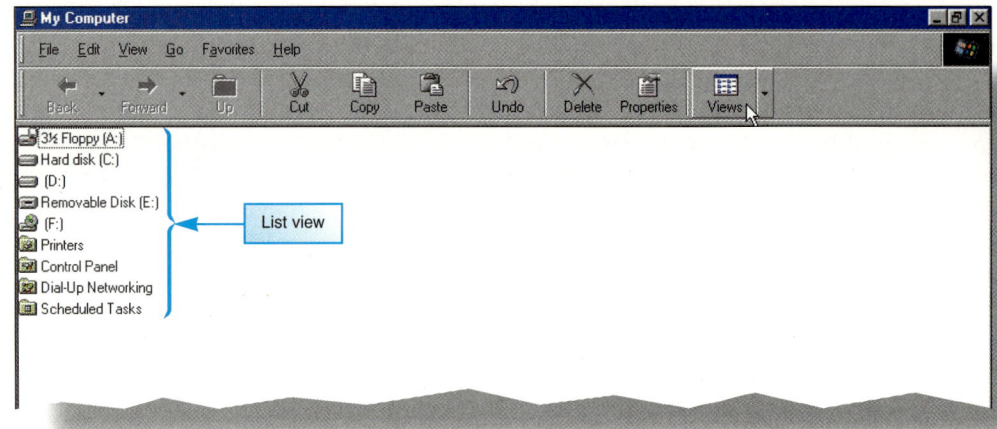

FIGURE 3-5

4 Click the Views button.

The icons display in a list in Details view using the Small Icons format (Figure 3-6). The **Details view** provides detailed information about each drive or folder

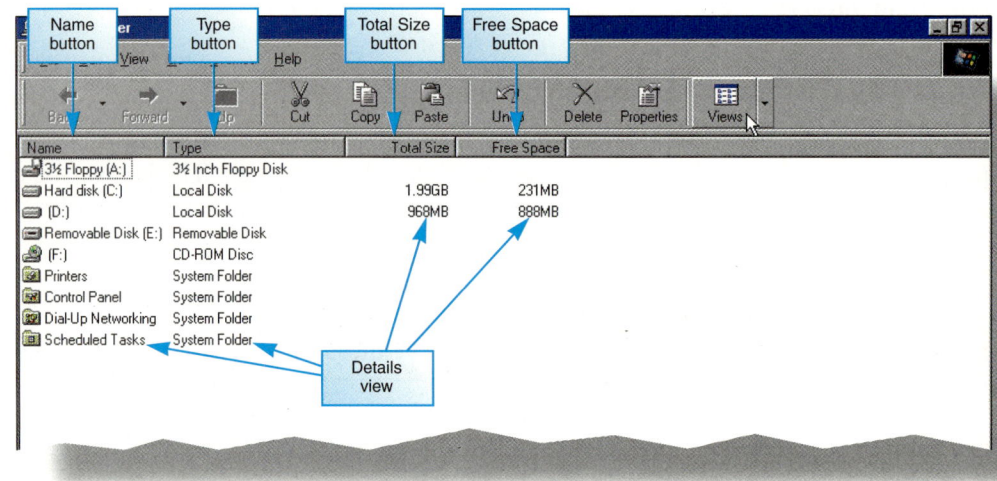

FIGURE 3-6

Other Ways

1. Right-click open area of My Computer window, point to View, click icon format
2. On Views button, click down arrow, click icon format
3. On View menu click icon format
4. Press ALT+V, select icon format

More About

Viewing Icons

The icons in any window can be displayed as large icons, small icons, in a list, or with details. You also can increase the size of the icons on the desktop and decrease the size of the icons on the Start menu. For detailed instructions for making these changes, consult Windows 98 Help.

The manner in which you display folder contents in the My Computer window is a matter of personal preference. You also can sequence the icons in the My Computer window when detailed information is displayed using the buttons below the Standard Buttons toolbar. If you click the **Name button**, the items will display in alphabetical sequence by name either in ascending or descending sequence. If you click the Name button again, the alphabetical sequence is reversed. If you click the **Type button**, the items will display in alphabetical sequence by type. Although only two entries have the total size and free space values displayed, you also can sequence the icons by total size and free space. Clicking the **Total Size button** causes the items to display in size sequence, from the smallest to the largest or from largest to smallest, while clicking the **Free Space button** causes items to display from smallest to largest based on free space.

In Figure 3-6, the Type column tells you the type of object for each icon. The first five objects are 3½ Inch Floppy Disk, Local Disk, Local Disk, Removable Disk, and CD-ROM Disc, respectively. Each of the last four items is a system folder. The Total Size column states the size of the hard disks (1.99GB and 968MB) and the Free Space column states the amount of space that is not being used on the disks (231MB and 888MB). The values for the total size and free space may be different on your computer.

My Computer Window • WIN 3.9

The view you use to display icons in a window is a matter of personal preference. The Windows 98 default setting for viewing the icons in a window is the Large Icons view. When you close a window, Windows 98 remembers the format of the icons in the window and uses that format to display the icons the next time you open the window. For example, if you close the My Computer wiindow shown in Figure 3-6 (Details view) and then open the window, the icons in the window will display in Details view.

Viewing the Contents of Drives and Folders

In addition to the contents of My Computer, the contents of drives and folders also can be viewed. In previous projects, you have seen both windows for folders and windows for floppy drive A. In fact, the contents of any folder or drive on your computer can display in a window.

The default option for opening drive and folder windows, called the **single window option**, uses the same window to display the contents of a newly opened drive or folder. Because only one window displays on the desktop at a time, the single window option eliminates the clutter of multiple windows on the desktop. To illustrate the single window option and view the contents of hard drive C, complete the following step.

Icons

In many cases, you may not recognize a particular icon because hundreds of icons are developed by software vendors to represent their products. Each icon is supposed to be unique and eye-catching. You can purchase thousands of icons on floppy disk or CD-ROM that you can use in documents you create.

Steps To View the Contents of a Drive

1 Point to the Hard disk (C:) icon in the My Computer window.

2 Double-click the Hard disk (C:) icon.

The maximized Hard disk (C:) window opens in the same window as My Computer was displayed (Figure 3-7). The objects in the window display in the Large Icons format. The button on the taskbar is now for the Hard disk (C:) window, not for the My Computer window.

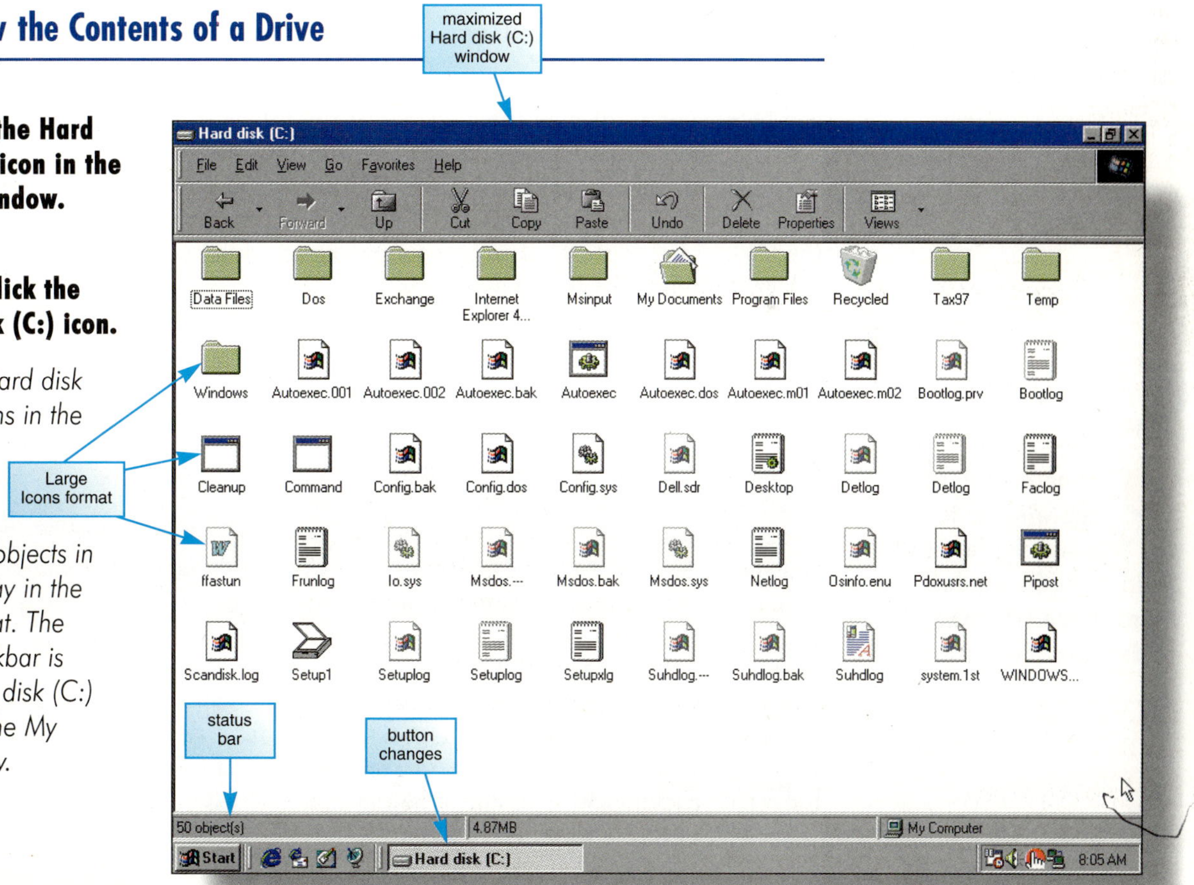

FIGURE 3-7

Other Ways

1. Right-click Hard disk (C:) icon, click Open
2. Click Hard disk (C:) icon, press ENTER

A yellow folder icon represents each folder in the Hard disk (C:) window. Application programs and documents are represented by icons unique to the application program or to the application program that can open the document.

The contents of the hard disk window you display on your computer can differ considerably from the contents shown in Figure 3-7 on the previous page because each computer has its own application programs and documents. The manner in which you interact with and control the programs and documents in Windows 98 is the same, however, regardless of the actual programs or documents.

The status bar in Figure 3-7 contains information about the folders, programs, and documents displaying in the window. Fifty objects (folders, programs, and documents) display in the window.

The designation, 4.87MB, on the status bar in Figure 3-7 indicates the objects in the window consume 4.87 megabytes on the hard disk. This number does not include the contents of any of the folders displayed in Figure 3-7. Recall from Figure 3-6 on page WIN 3.8 that the entire drive C, which is 1.99 gigabytes in size, has only 231 megabytes free. Therefore, considerably more storage space is used on drive C than 4.87 megabytes.

If the My Computer window in Figure 3-6 was not maximized before double-clicking the Hard disk (C:) icon, the Hard disk (C:) window would display in the same physical window as My Computer, be the same size, and be located at the same place on the desktop.

Opening a Folder Window

In Figure 3-7 on the previous page, ten folder icons display. Each of the folders can be opened to display the contents of the folder. One folder in the Hard disk (C:) window, the **Windows folder**, contains programs and files necessary for the operation of the Windows 98 operating system. As such, caution should be exercised when working with the contents of the Windows folder because changing the contents of the folder may cause your programs to stop working correctly. To open the Windows folder, complete the following steps.

More About

Hidden Files

Sometimes the status bar will indicate that a folder contains hidden files. Hidden files usually are placed on your hard disk by software vendors such as Microsoft and often are critical to the operation of the software. Rarely will you designate a file as hidden. You should almost never delete a hidden file.

 To Open a Folder Window

1 If necessary, scroll the window to view the Windows folder in the Hard disk (C:) window. Point to the Windows folder icon (Figure 3-8).

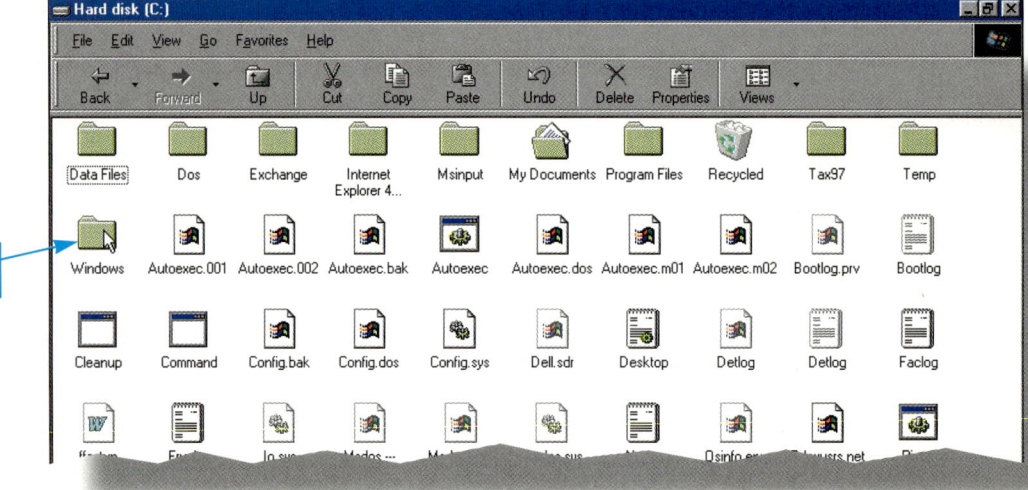

FIGURE 3-8

Double-click the Windows folder.

The maximized Windows window opens in the same window that contained the Hard disk (C:) window, and the Hard disk (C:) button in the taskbar button area is replaced with the Windows button (Figure 3-9). The window displays folder and file icons but the scroll box in the window is small, indicating many more objects are contained within the window. The status bar indicates the objects in the window consume 51.7 megabytes.

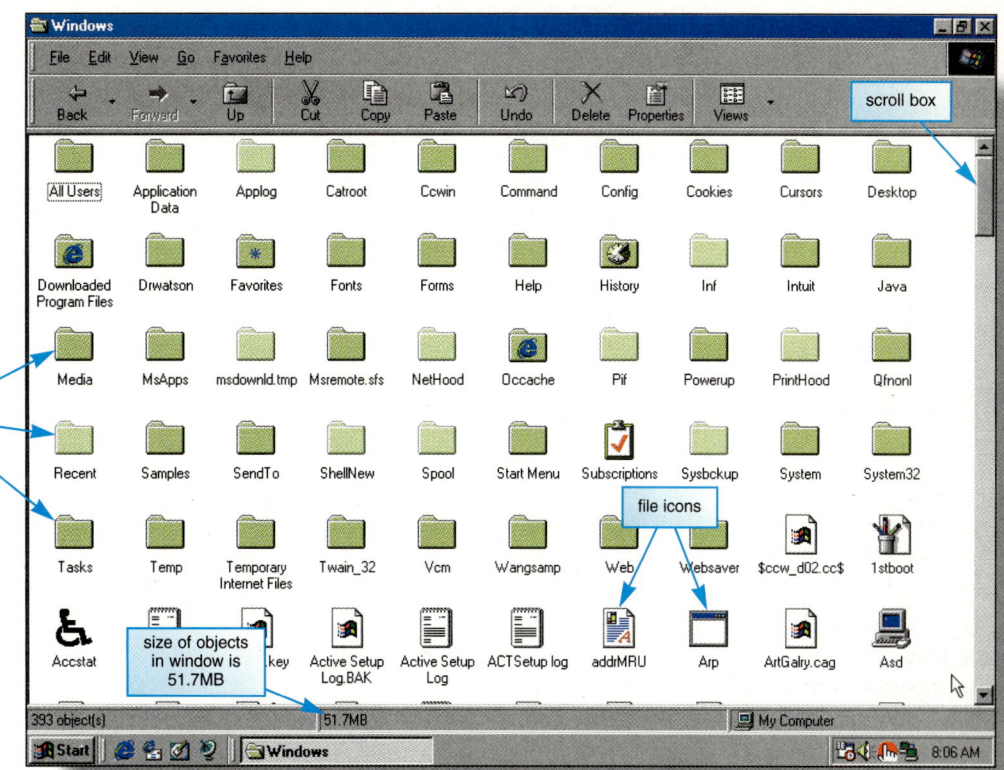

FIGURE 3-9

The majority of objects shown in Figure 3-9 are folder icons. As you can see, folder icons always display first in the window. File icons display after the folders. As with every window you will see in the steps within this book, the contents of the windows on your computer may be different. Every effort has been made, however, to ensure that the files used in the steps within this book also will be found on any computer you are using.

1. Right-click Windows icon, click Open
2. Click Windows icon, press ENTER

Opening a Document from a Window

In Project 2, you created a text document on the desktop and then opened the document by double-clicking the document icon on the desktop. In addition to opening a text document on the desktop, you can open a Paint document in a folder in a similar fashion. Paint documents contain graphics images, called **bitmap images**, and are created using the **Paint program**, which is a program that is supplied with Windows 98. Several Paint documents are included with Windows 98 and stored in the Windows folder on the hard drive. A Paint icon identifies each Paint document. To open a Paint document from the Windows window, complete the following steps.

Steps   To Open a Document from a Window

  Scroll down the Windows window until the Forest icon displays. Point to the Forest icon. If your computer does not contain the Forest icon, find and point to one of these Paint icons: Gold Weave, Leaves, Tartan, and Winlogo, or any other Paint icon.

The mouse pointer points to the Forest icon (Figure 3-10). This icon, called a Paint icon, is associated with all document files that can be opened by the Paint application program. Thus, you can identify all Paint documents because they all are represented by this icon.

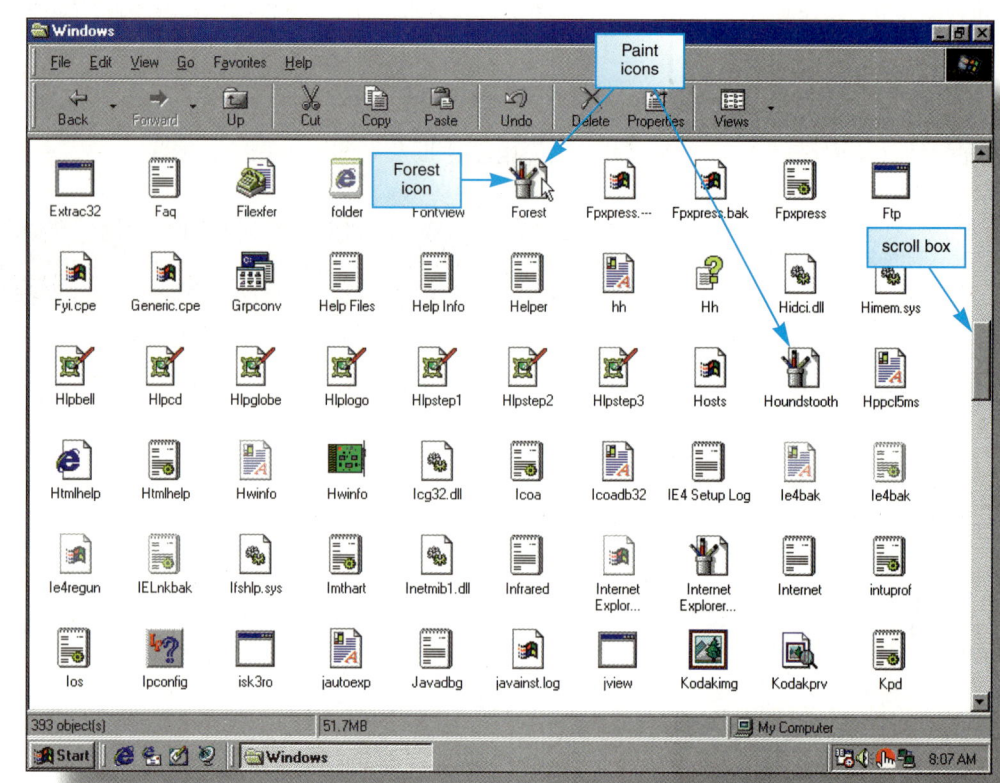

FIGURE 3-10

② **Double-click the Forest icon. If the Forest - Paint window is maximized, click the Restore button and then size the window to approximately the size shown in Figure 3-11.**

Windows 98 launches the Paint application program, the Paint window containing the Forest document opens on top of the Windows window, and the recessed Forest - Paint button displays in the taskbar button area (Figure 3-11).

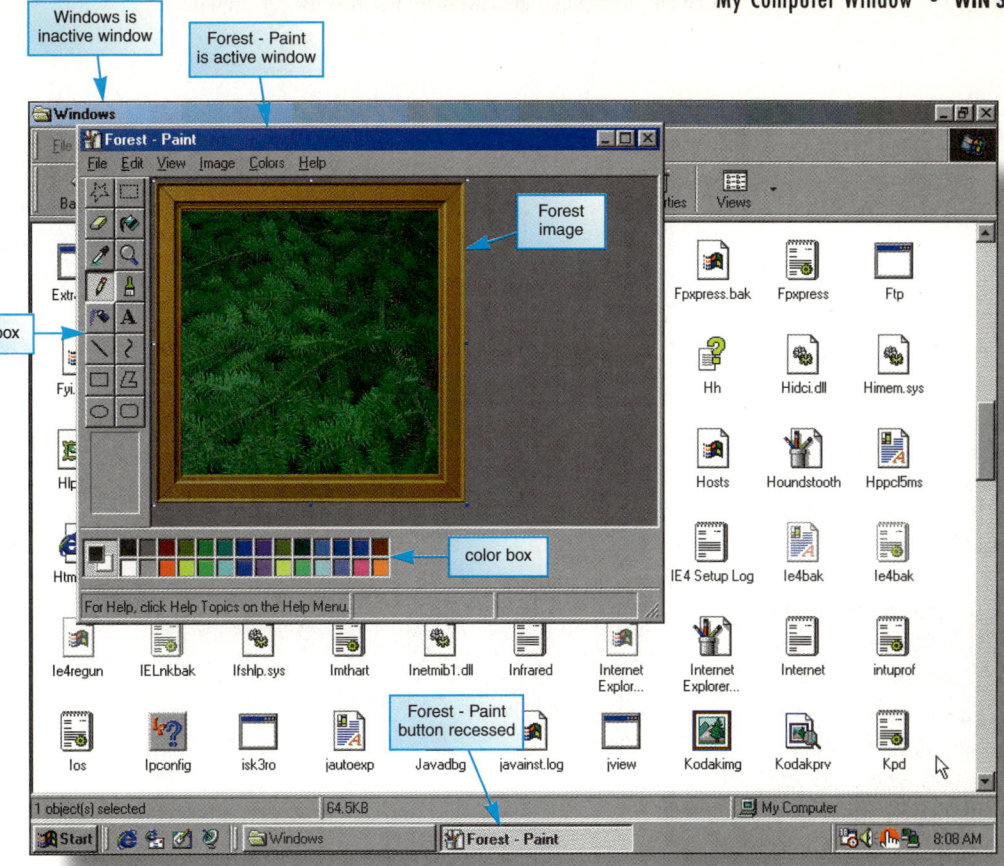

FIGURE 3-11

The Forest - Paint window displays on top of the Windows window on the desktop. The Forest - Paint window consists of a title bar and menu bar. On the left of the window is the **tool box**, which contains tools used to create images. At the bottom of the window is the **color box**, where colors can be selected for an image. The Forest - Paint window is the active window and the Windows window is the inactive window. Currently, a folder window and a document window are open on the desktop.

Launching an Application Program from a Window

In addition to opening a document from a window, you also can launch an application program from a window. To launch the Notepad application program, complete the steps on the next page.

1. Right-click document icon, click Open
2. Click document icon, press ENTER

The Paint Program

An image with color usually has more impact than one without color. The Paint program allows you to create color images. To learn about the Paint program, click Help on the menu bar in the Paint window, click Help Topics, and use the Contents or Index sheet to read about the features of Paint.

WIN 3.14 • Project 3 • File, Document, and Folder Management and Windows 98 Explorer

Microsoft **Windows 98**

 Steps **To Launch an Application Program from a Window**

1 **Click the Windows button in the taskbar button area. When the maximized Windows window displays, scroll until the Notepad icon displays in the window. Point to the Notepad icon.**

The maximized Windows window displays as the active window and its button is recessed in the taskbar button area (Figure 3-12). You can switch between one open window and another open window by clicking the button in the taskbar button area.

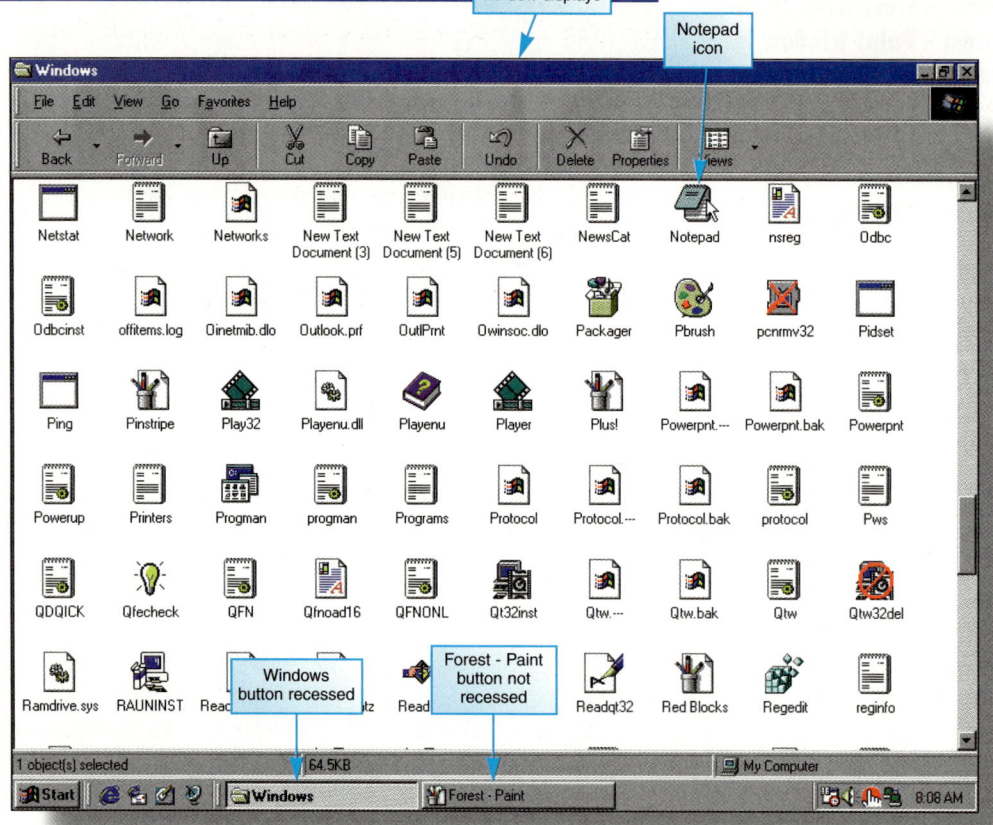

FIGURE 3-12

 Double-click the Notepad icon.

Windows 98 launches the Notepad application program (Figure 3-13). The Untitled - Notepad button in the taskbar button area is recessed, indicating it is active. Three windows now are open on the desktop. Although, the Forest - Paint window is not visible on the desktop, its button displays in the taskbar button area.

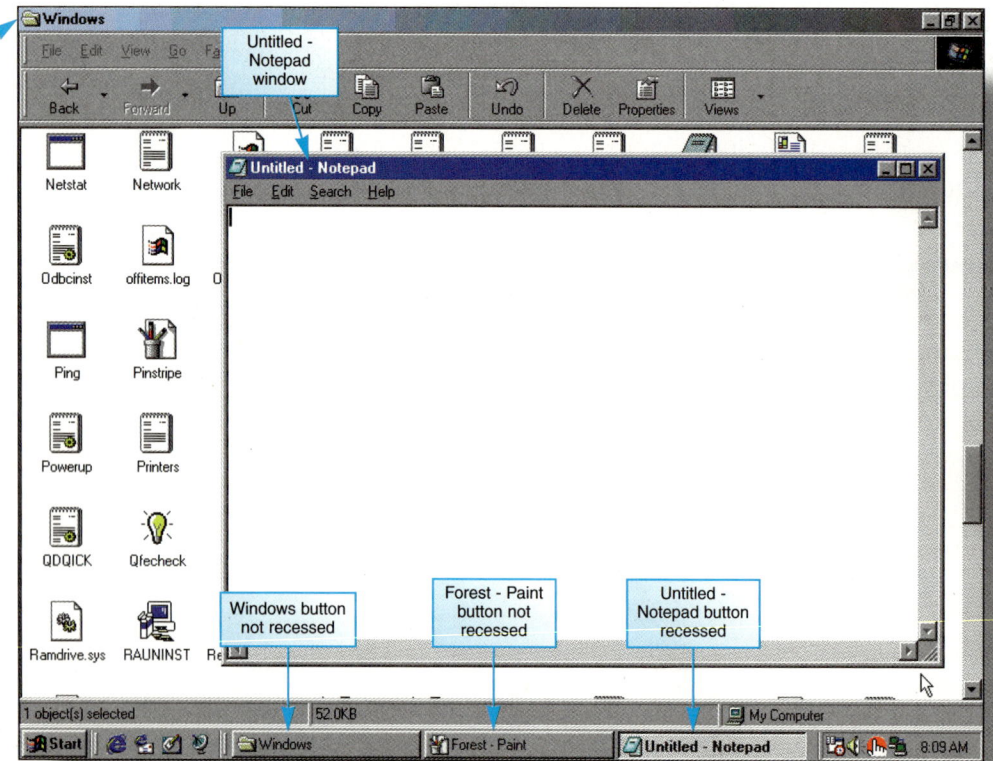

FIGURE 3-13

As seen in Figure 3-12, whenever you click a button for an open window in the taskbar button area, the window displays and becomes the active window. Windows 98 provides another method to switch between windows, as mentioned in the Other Ways box. If you press and hold the ALT key and then press the TAB key, a box showing an icon for each open window displays on the screen, together with the name of the active window. If you continue to hold the ALT key, each time you press the TAB key the name of the next open window will display and the associated icon in the box will be highlighted by a colored square. When you release the ALT key, the window associated with the highlighted icon will become the active window.

In this section, you have opened the My Computer window, the Hard disk (C:) window, a folder window (Windows), a document window (Forest - Paint), and an application program window (Notepad).

> **Other Ways**
>
> 1. Click Windows button or press ALT+TAB until Windows displays in box on screen, right-click Notepad icon, click Open
> 2. Click Windows button or press ALT+TAB until Windows displays in box on screen, click Notepad icon, press ENTER

Managing Open Windows

In Figure 3-13, three windows are open. Windows 98 allows you to open many more windows, depending on the amount of RAM you have on your computer. As you can see in Figure 3-13, however, many open windows on the desktop can be cluttered and difficult to use. Therefore, Windows 98 provides some tools with which to manage open windows. You already have used one tool — the capability of maximizing a window. When a window is maximized, it occupies the entire screen and cannot be confused with other open windows.

In some cases, however, it is important that multiple windows display on the desktop. Windows 98 allows you to arrange the windows in specific ways. The following sections describe the ways in which you can manage open windows.

Cascading Windows

One way to organize windows on the desktop is to **cascade** them, which means they are displayed on top of each other in an organized manner. To cascade the open windows on the desktop shown in Figure 3-13, complete the steps on the next page.

> **More About**
> **ALT+TAB**
>
> In Windows 3.1, a previous version of Windows, the most convenient way to switch between open windows was pressing the ALT+TAB keys. Microsoft discovered that most users either did not know about this method or were wary about using it. Therefore, few people were using the multitasking capabilities of Windows 3.1. Microsoft tried to solve the problem by placing the buttons of open windows on the taskbar.

> **More About**
> **Managing Windows**
>
> Probably the most intimidating aspect of the Windows operating system is multiple windows open on the desktop. In addition to the techniques shown in this section, always remember that if you maximize a window, it is the only window you will see on the desktop. Then, if you want to switch to another open window, merely click its button in the taskbar button area and maximize it. Many people find working with one maximized window at a time the easiest way to contend with window clutter.

WIN 3.16 • Project 3 • File, Document, and Folder Management and Windows 98 Explorer

Microsoft **WINDOWS 98**

Steps: To Cascade Open Windows

  1 **Right-click an open area on the taskbar. Point to Cascade Windows on the shortcut menu.**

A shortcut menu displays (Figure 3-14). The commands on the menu apply to the open windows on the desktop. The Notepad window no longer is the active window (light blue title bar and button not recessed).

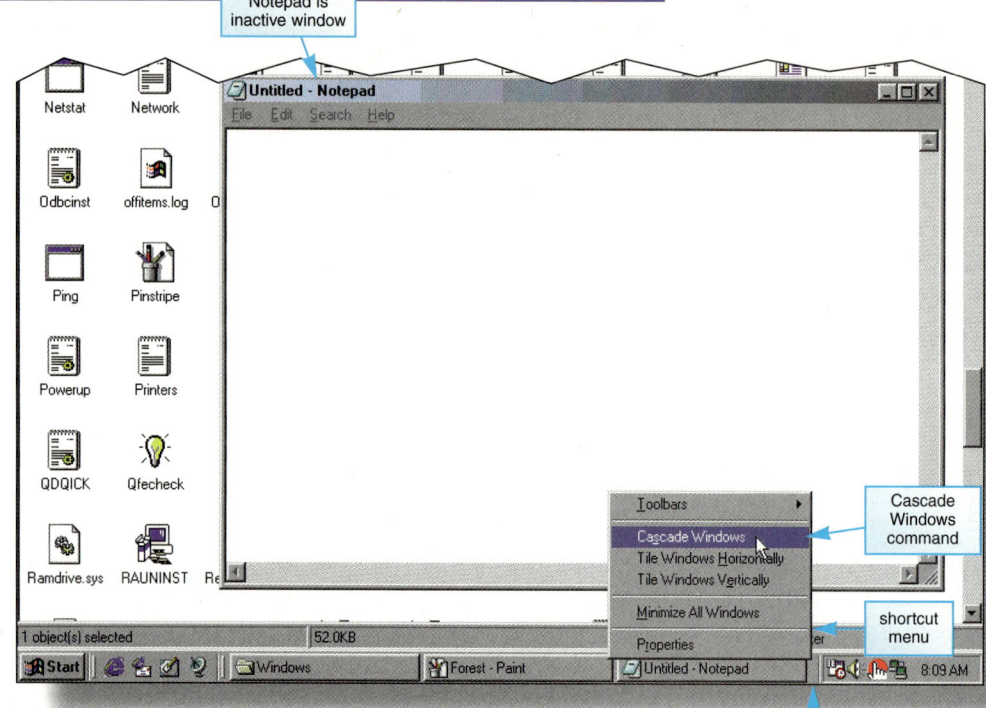

FIGURE 3-14

 **2** **Click Cascade Windows.**

The open windows display cascaded on the desktop (Figure 3-15). You can see the title bar of each window and the top two windows are moved slightly to the right. None of the windows is the active window (all light blue title bars and no recessed buttons).

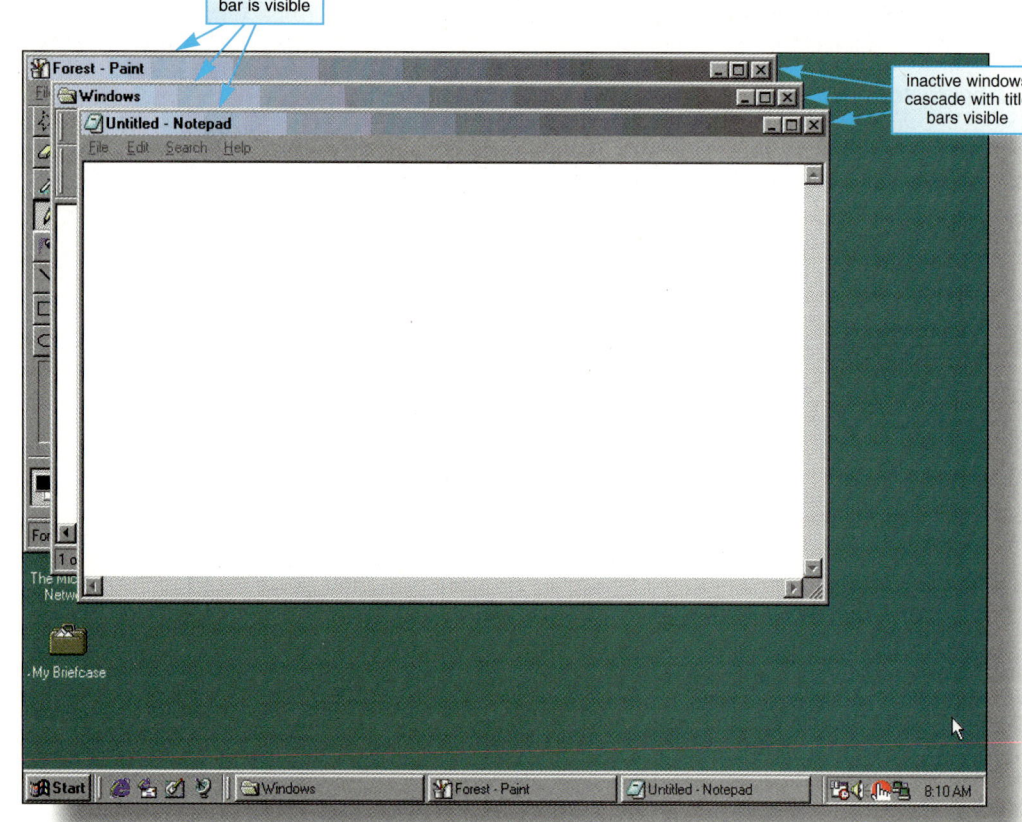

FIGURE 3-15

Other Ways

1. Right-click open area on taskbar, press s

Windows 98 cascades only windows that are open. Windows that are minimized or closed will not be cascaded on the desktop. When you cascade the open windows, the windows are resized for cascading. In Figure 3-15, all windows have been resized to be the same size.

Making a Window the Active Window

When windows are cascaded as shown in Figure 3-15, they are arranged so you see them easily, but you must make one of the windows the active window in order to work in the window. To make the Forest - Paint window the active window, complete the following step.

> **More About**
>
> **The Taskbar**
>
> When you cascade windows, you must right-click an open area of the taskbar to display a shortcut menu. Sometimes it is difficult to find an open area on the taskbar. If so, try right-clicking the area to the left or right of the taskbar buttons in the taskbar button area, the area to the left of the first icon on the Quick Launch toolbar, or a blank area in the status tray area.

Steps: To Make a Window the Active Window

1 Point to the Forest - Paint window title bar.

2 Click the Forest - Paint window title bar.

The Forest - Paint window moves to the top of the desktop indicating it is active (dark blue title bar) and the Forest - Paint button is recessed in the taskbar button area (Figure 3-16).

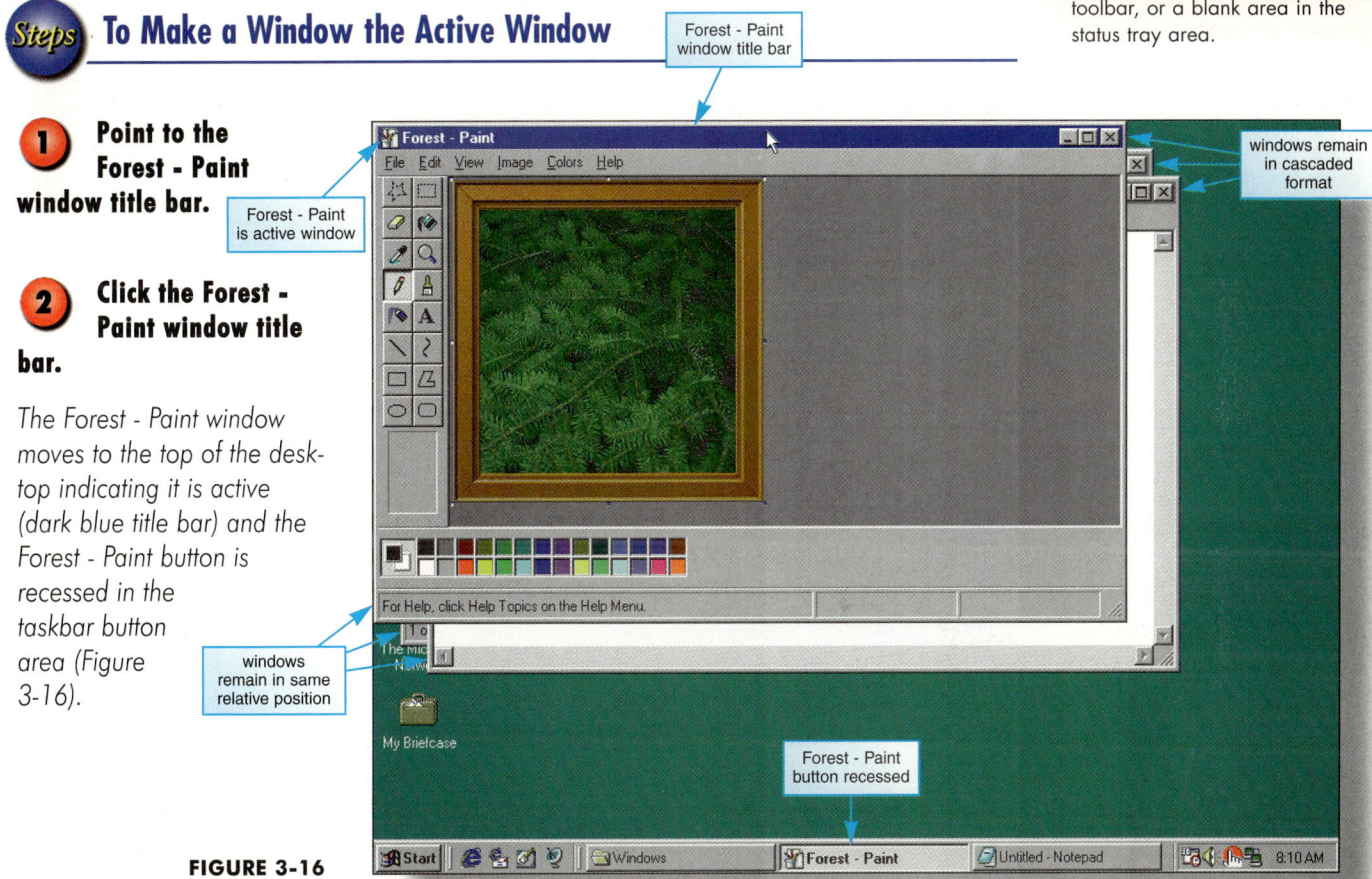

FIGURE 3-16

The size of the Forest - Paint window in Figure 3-16 does not change and the other windows remain in a cascaded format. The Forest - Paint window title bar remains just above the Windows title bar, which is in the same relative position as it was when it was not the active window (see Figure 3-15).

To make a window the active window, you clicked the title bar of the window. You also can click the button in the taskbar button area of the window you want to make active, or you can click anywhere in the window that you want to be active. You do not necessarily have to click the title bar of the window.

> **Other Ways**
>
> 1. Click Forest - Paint button in taskbar button area
> 2. Press ALT+TAB until Forest - Paint displays in box, release ALT key
> 3. Click anywhere in window to make it active

Undo Cascade

Sometimes after you have cascaded the windows, you may want to undo the cascade operation and return the windows to their size and location before cascading. To undo the previous cascading, complete the following steps.

Steps: To Undo Cascading

 Right-click an open area on the taskbar. Point to Undo Cascade on the shortcut menu (Figure 3-17).

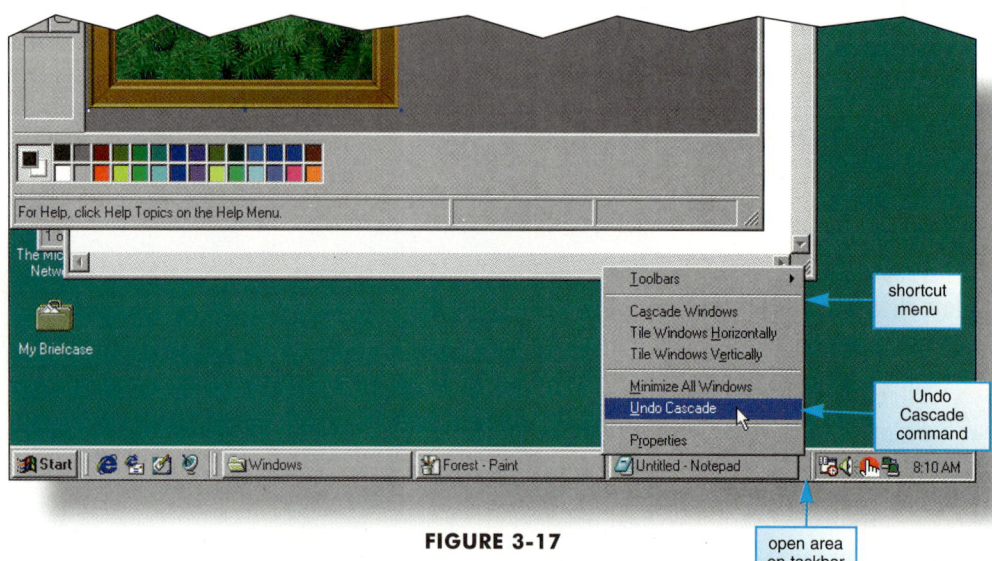

FIGURE 3-17

 **Click Undo Cascade.**

The maximized Windows window displays on top of the other windows on the desktop (Figure 3-18). Although not visible in Figure 3-18, the windows on the desktop display as if they had never been cascaded. The only difference is the maximized Windows window remains on top instead of placing Notepad on top as before the windows were cascaded (see Figure 3-13 on page WIN 3.14 for the desktop prior to cascading).

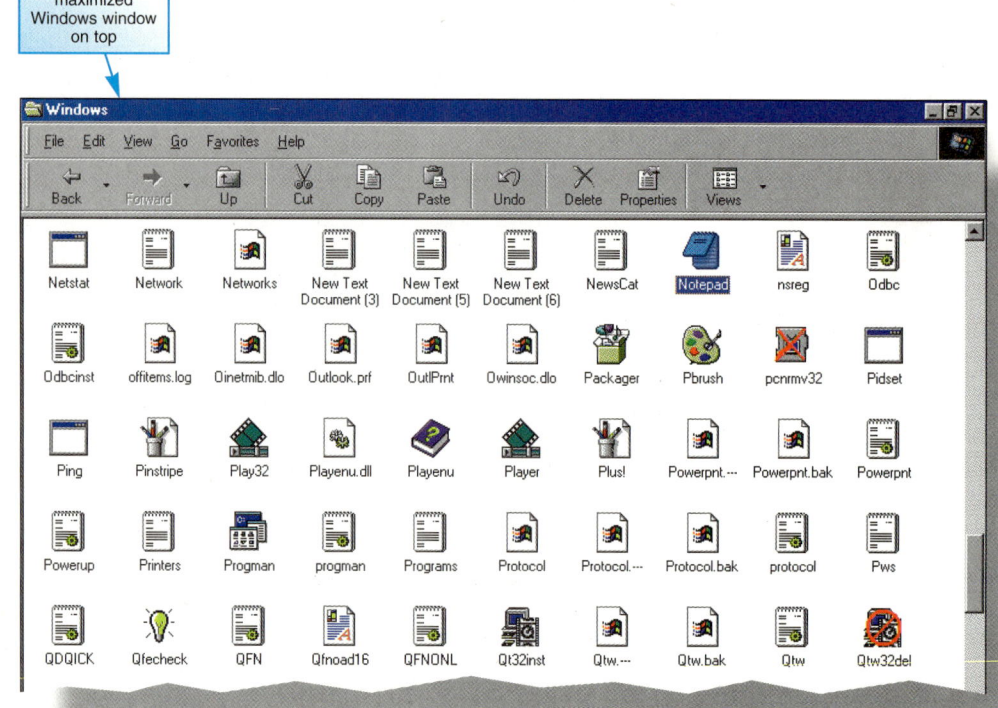

FIGURE 3-18

1. Right-click open area on taskbar, press U

Tiling Open Windows

While cascading arranges the windows on the desktop so each of the title bars in the windows is visible, it is impossible to see the contents of each window. Windows 98 also can **tile** the open windows, which allows you to see partial contents of each window. To tile the open windows in Figure 3-18, complete the following steps.

Steps: To Tile Open Windows

  Right-click an open area on the taskbar. Point to Tile Windows Vertically on the shortcut menu (Figure 3-19).

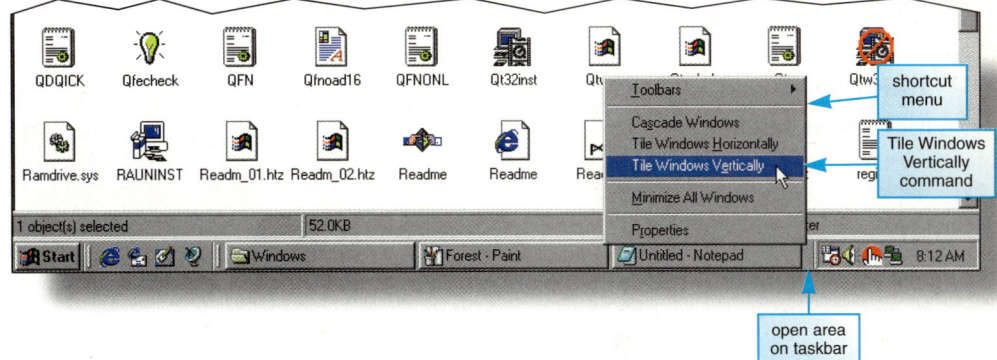

FIGURE 3-19

Click Tile Windows Vertically.

The three open windows are arranged in a tile format (Figure 3-20). The Paint window takes a slightly larger portion of the space in the middle because of the color box and covers the title bar of the Notepad window. None of the windows is active (no recessed buttons).

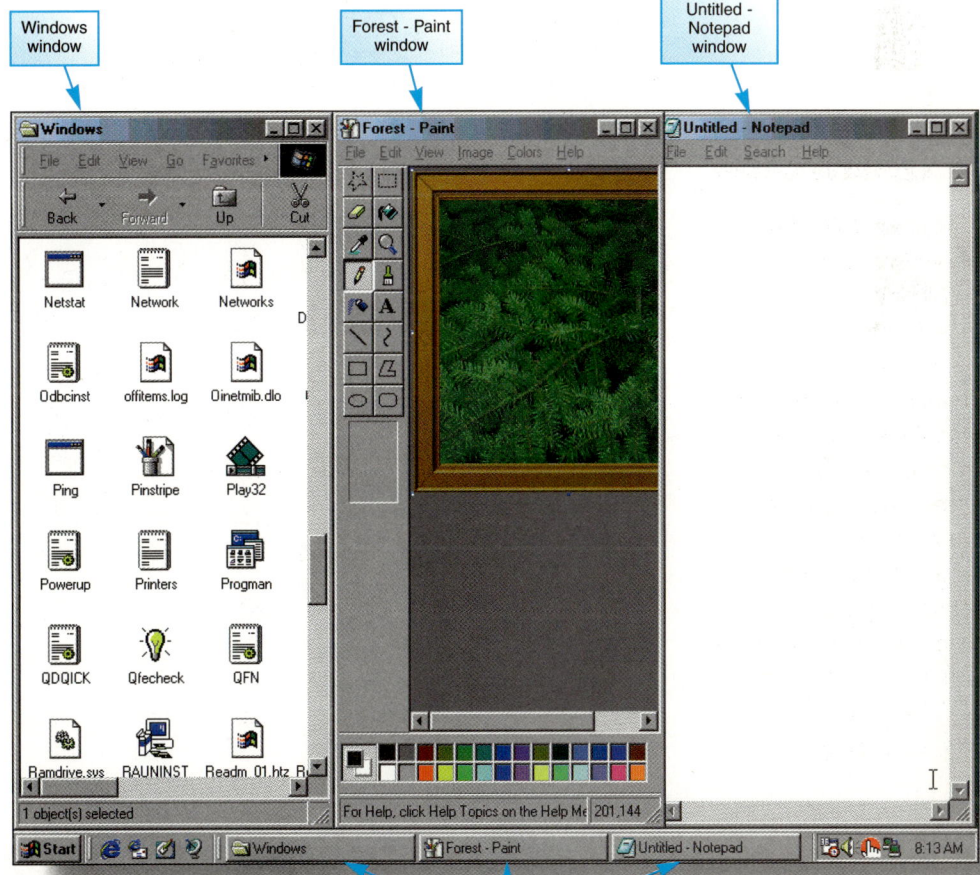

FIGURE 3-20

Other Ways

1. Right-click open area on taskbar, press E

While the windows shown in Figure 3-20 on the previous page are arranged so you can view all of them, it is likely that the size of each one is not useful for working. You can undo the tiling operation if you want to return the windows to the size and position they occupied prior to tiling. If you want to work in a particular window, you may want to click the Maximize button in that window to maximize the window.

To undo the tiling operation and return the windows to the format shown in Figure 3-18 on page WIN 3.18, complete the following steps.

Steps: To Undo Tiling

1 **Right-click an open area on the taskbar. Point to Undo Tile (Figure 3-21).**

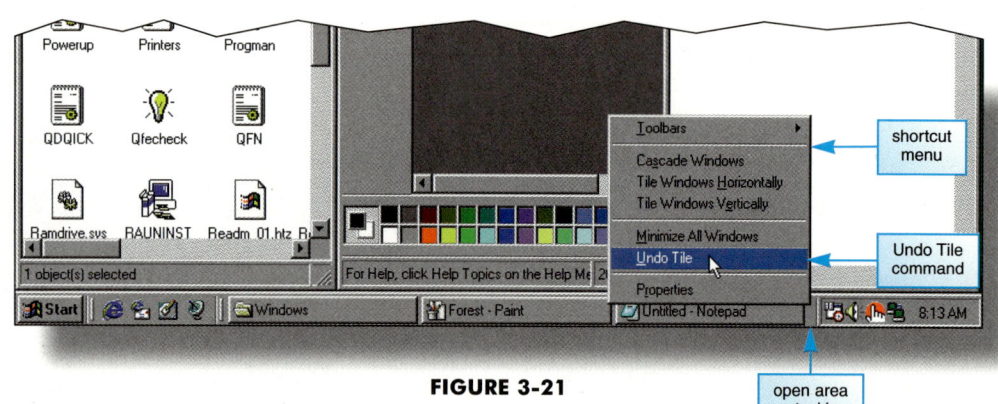

FIGURE 3-21

2 **Click Undo Tile.**

The windows no longer are tiled and display as if they had never been tiled (Figure 3-22). The maximized Windows window displays on top of the other windows on the desktop.

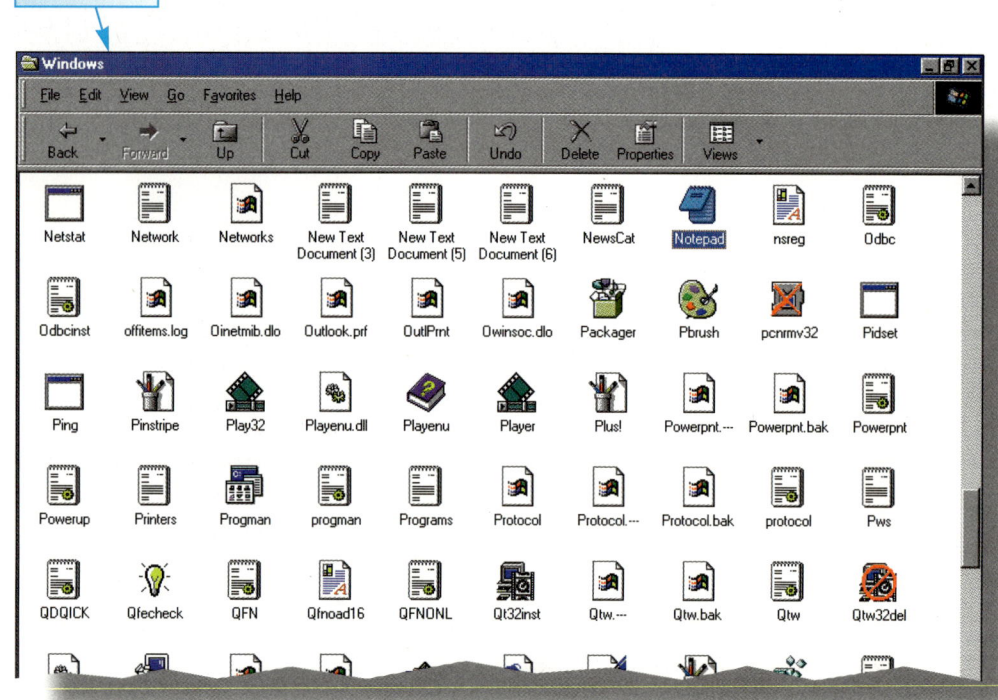

FIGURE 3-22

Other Ways

1. Right-click open area on taskbar, press U

Closing Windows

When you have finished working with windows, normally you should close the windows so your desktop remains as uncluttered as possible. To close the three open windows, complete the following steps.

TO CLOSE OPEN WINDOWS

1. Click the Close button in the Windows window.
2. Click the Close button in the Untitled - Notepad window.
3. Click the Close button in the Forest - Paint window.

All the windows are closed and the buttons no longer display in the taskbar button area (Figure 3-23).

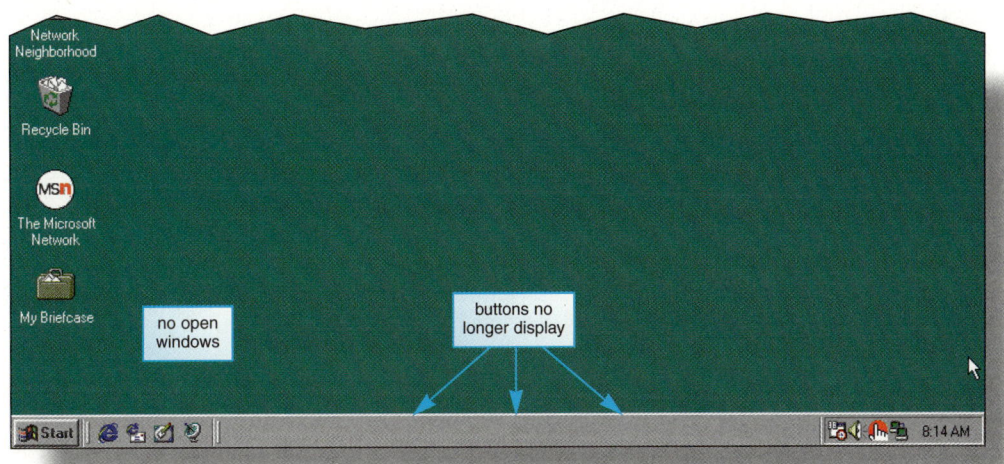

FIGURE 3-23

Copying, Moving, and Deleting Files in Windows

In Project 2, you learned how to move and copy document files on the desktop to a folder on the desktop, how to copy a folder from the desktop onto a floppy disk, and how to delete files from the floppy disk. Another method you can use to copy a file or folder is called the **copy and paste method**. To copy a document file from a folder to another folder or drive, open the window containing the file, point to the file to copy, and then click the Copy button on the Standard Buttons toolbar to place a copy of the file in a storage area of the computer called the **Clipboard**. Then, open the folder or drive window to contain the file, and click the Paste button on the Standard Buttons toolbar to copy the file from the Clipboard to the window. The following section explains how to perform these tasks.

Copying Files from a Folder to a Drive

Assume you want to copy three files, Black Thatch, Bubbles, and Carved Stone, from the Windows folder onto the floppy disk in drive A. To copy from a folder, the folder window must be open on the desktop. To open the Windows window on drive C and display in the window the icons for the files to be copied, complete the steps on the next page.

> **More About**
>
> **Copying and Moving**
>
> "Copying, moving, it's all the same to me," you might be tempted to say. They are not the same at all! When you copy a file, it will be located in two different places: the place to which it was copied and the place from which it was copied. When a file is moved, it will be located in only one place, the location to which it was moved. Many users have been sorry they did not distinguish the difference when a file they thought they had copied was moved instead.

TO OPEN A FOLDER WINDOW

1. Double-click the My Computer icon on the desktop.

2. Double-click the Hard disk (C:) icon in the My Computer window.

3. Double-click the Windows icon in the Hard disk (C:) window.

4. Scroll down in the Windows window until the icons for the Black Thatch, Bubbles, and Carved Stone files are visible in the window. If one or more of these icons is not in the Windows window on your computer, display any other icons.

The Black Thatch, Bubbles, and Carved Stone icons are visible in the Windows window (Figure 3-24). The Back button does not appear dimmed and this indicates more than one window has been opened. The Forward button appears dimmed indicating it is not available.

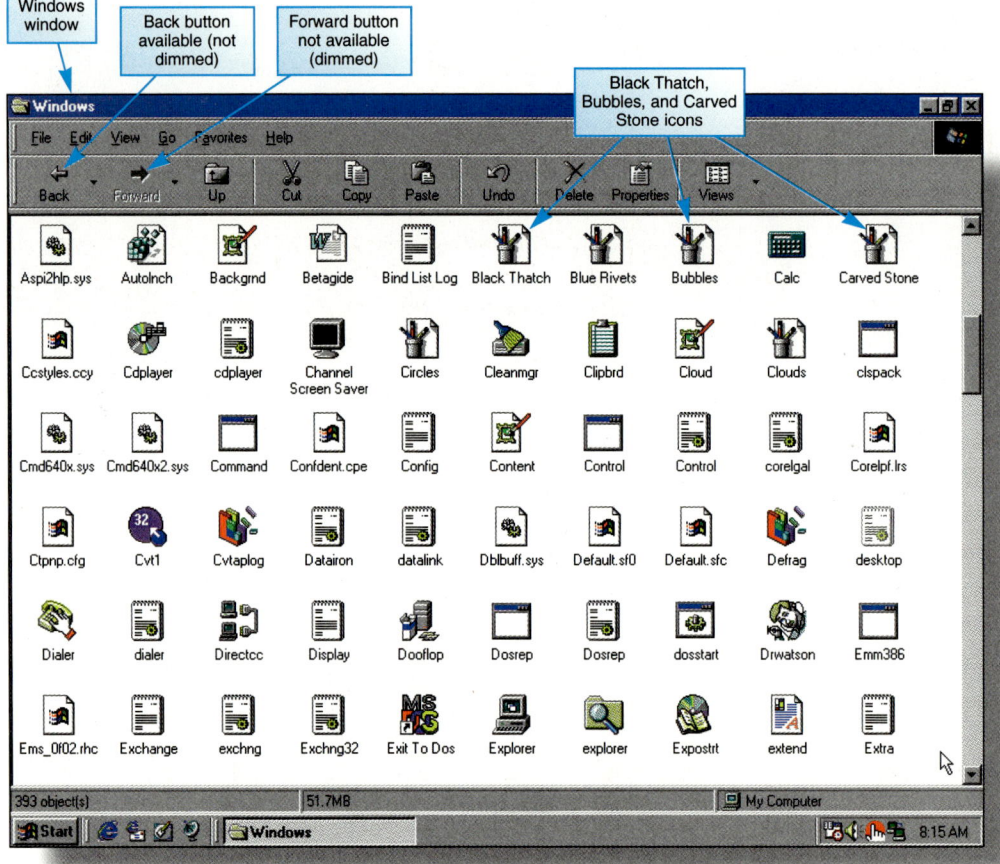

FIGURE 3-24

Once you have opened the folder window and the icons for the files to be copied display, you can select the files and then copy them. To copy the Black Thatch, Bubbles, and Carved Stone files onto the floppy disk in drive A, complete the following steps.

Steps To Copy Files from a Folder onto a Floppy Disk

1 Insert a formatted floppy disk in drive A of your computer.

2 Press and hold the CTRL key and click the Black Thatch icon, Bubbles icon, and Carved Stone icon. Release the CTRL key. Point to the Copy button on the Standard Buttons toolbar.

The Black Thatch, Bubbles, and Carved Stone icons are selected (Figure 3-25).

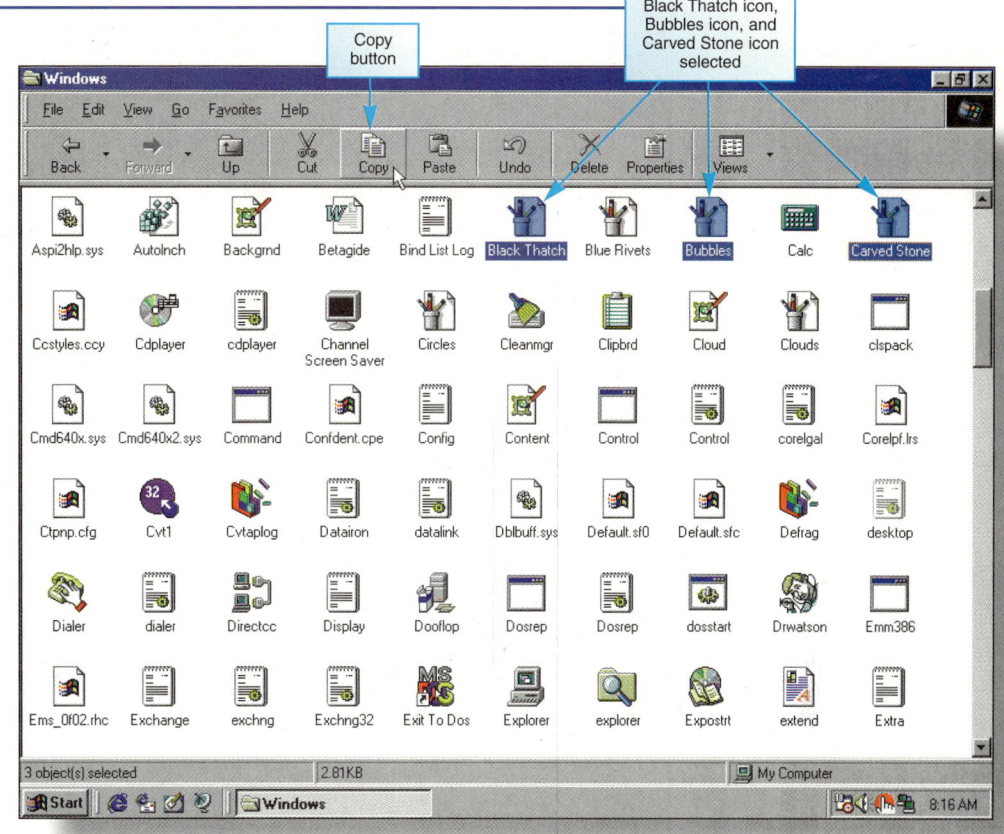

FIGURE 3-25

3 Click the Copy button. Point to the Back button arrow on the Standard Buttons toolbar (Figure 3-26).

Windows 98 copies the three files to the Clipboard. The Back button and arrow become three-dimensional.

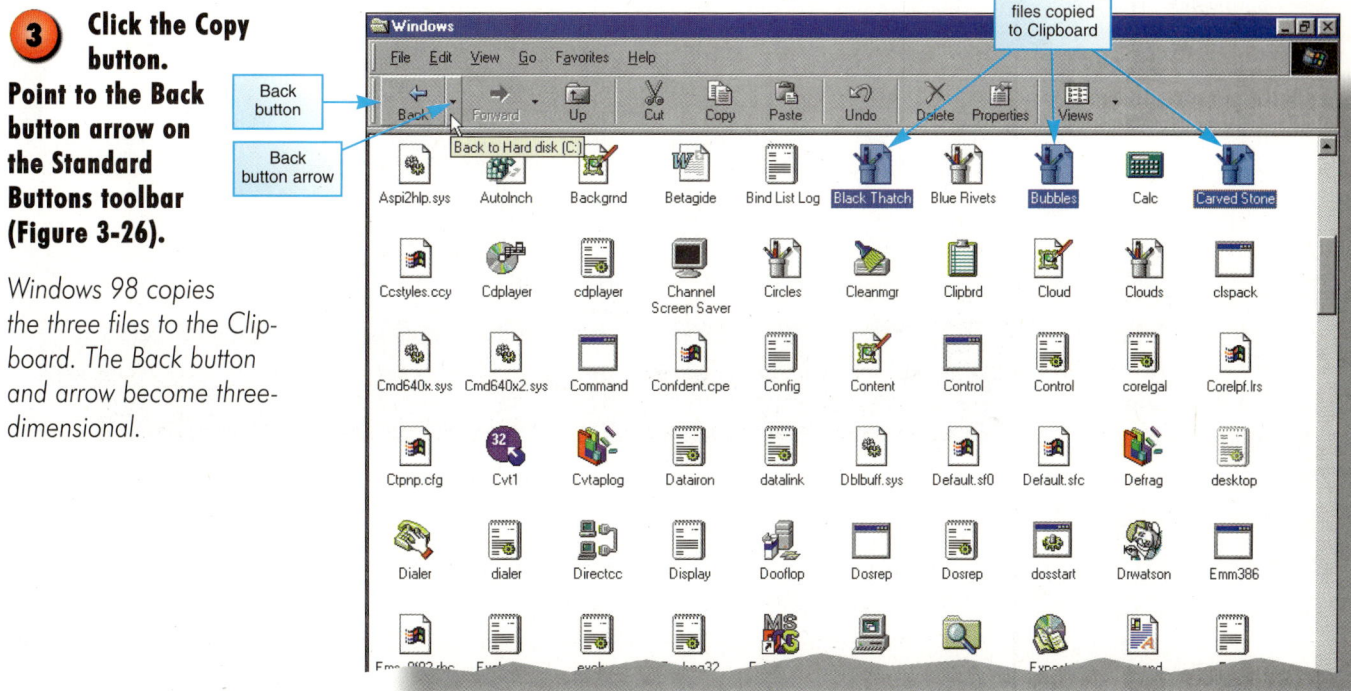

FIGURE 3-26

WIN 3.24 • Project 3 • File, Document, and Folder Management and Windows 98 Explorer

4 **Click the Back button and then point to My Computer.**

The Back button menu displays containing the names of the previously opened windows (Hard disk (C:) and My Computer) (Figure 3-27).

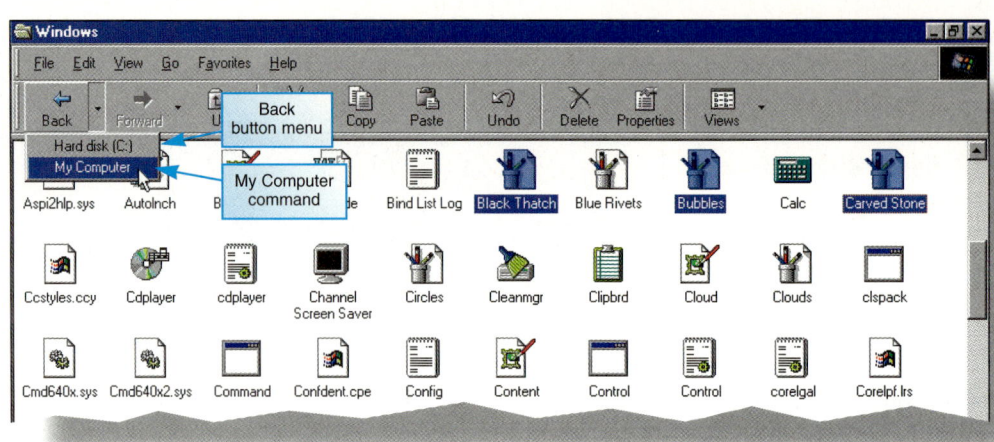

FIGURE 3-27

5 **Click My Computer. Point to the 3½ Floppy (A:) icon in the My Computer window.**

The My Computer window opens (Figure 3-28). The Back button appears dimmed indicating the My Computer window was the first window opened. The Forward button no longer appears dimmed.

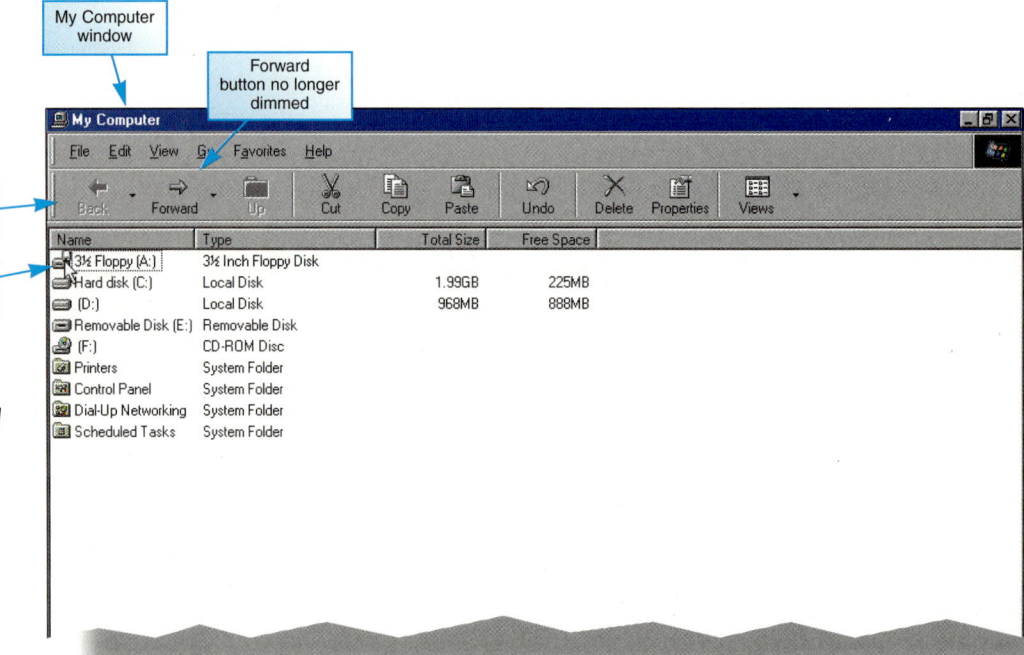

FIGURE 3-28

6 **Double-click the 3½ Floppy (A:) icon. Point to the Paste button on the Standard Buttons toolbar.**

The 3½ Floppy (A:) window opens (Figure 3-29).

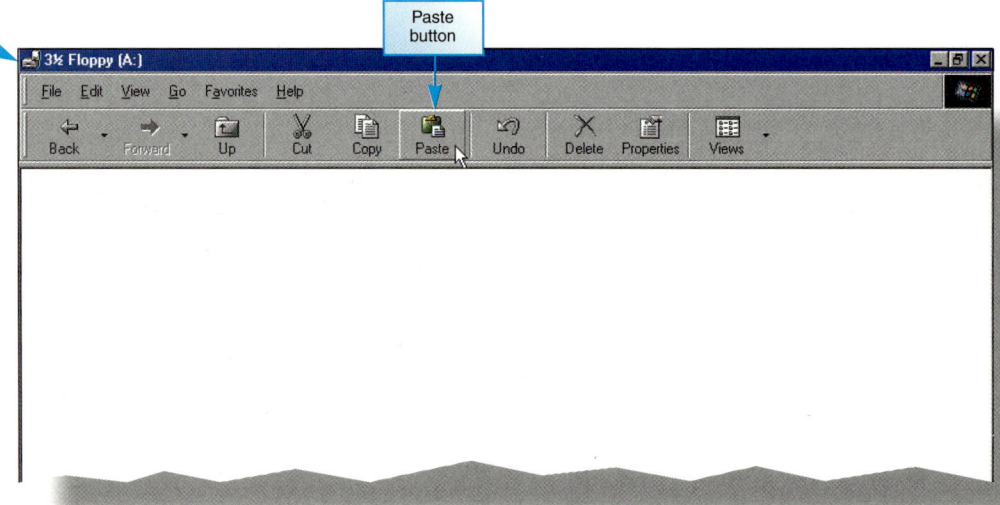

FIGURE 3-29

Copying, Moving, and Deleting Files in Windows • **WIN 3.25**

 Click the Paste button.

While the files are being copied, the Copying dialog box displays indicating the files are being copied from the Windows folder to the disk in drive A (Figure 3-30). The dialog box contains the name of the file being copied, where the file is from, and to where the file is being copied. If you wish to terminate the copying process before it is complete, you can click the Cancel button.

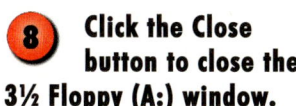 **Click the Close button to close the 3½ Floppy (A:) window.**

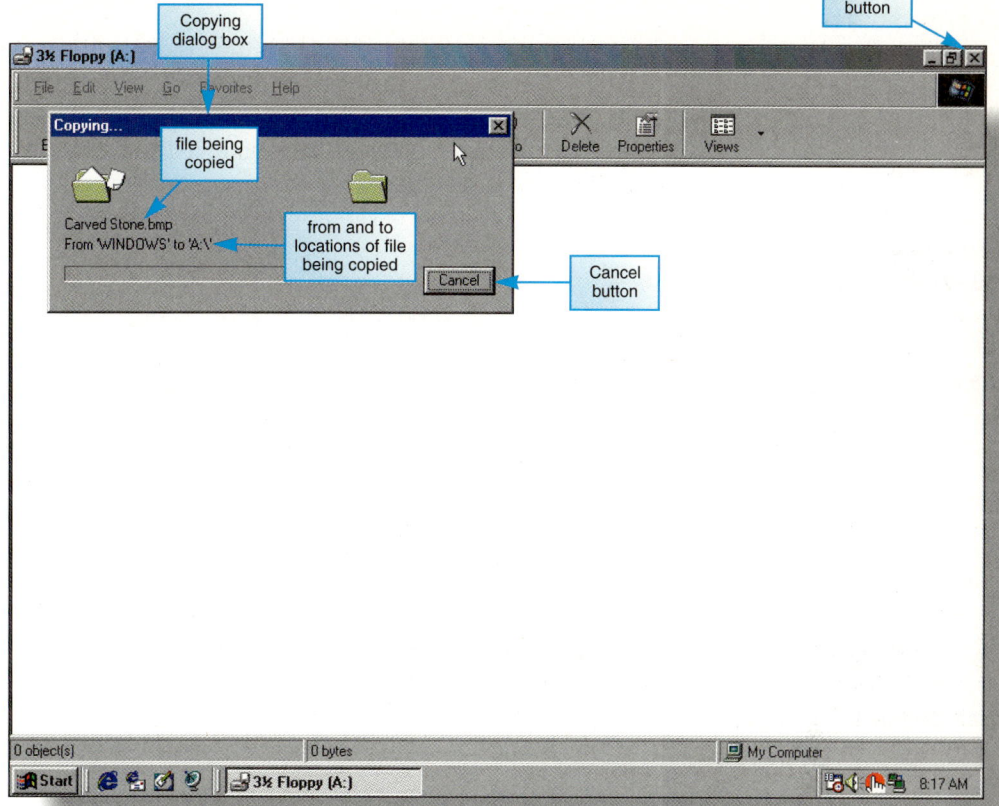

FIGURE 3-30

After copying the three files onto the floppy disk, the files are stored on both the floppy disk and in the Windows folder on drive C. If you want to move a file instead of copy a file, use the **Cut button** on the Standard Buttons toolbar to move the file to the clipboard and the Paste button to copy the file from the Clipboard to the new location. When the move is complete, the files are moved onto the floppy disk and are no longer stored in the Windows folder.

Moving and copying files is a common occurrence when working in Windows 98 and should be understood. Later in this project, you will see how to accomplish these same tasks using a Windows 98 program called Explorer.

Deleting Files in Windows

In Project 2, you saw how to delete shortcuts, folders, and files from the desktop. You can use the same techniques when deleting shortcuts, folders, and files from an open window. To review, the methods are: (1) right-drag the object (shortcut icon, folder icon, or file icon) to the Recycle Bin and then click Move Here on the shortcut menu; (2) right-click the object, click Delete on the shortcut menu, and then click the Yes button in the Confirm File Delete dialog box; and (3) drag the object to the Recycle Bin and then click the Yes button in the Confirm File Delete dialog box. A fourth method is available when deleting shortcuts, folders, or files from an open window: (4) click the object to be deleted, click File on the menu bar, click Delete, and then click the Yes button in the Confirm File Delete dialog box.

Other Ways

1. Select icons of file(s) to be copied, right-click an icon, click Copy, display window to contain file(s), right-click window, click Paste
2. Select icons of file(s) to be copied, on Edit menu click Copy, display window to contain file(s), on Edit menu click Paste
3. Select icons of file(s) to be copied, press CTRL+C, display window to contain file(s), press CTRL+V

Deleting Files

Someone proposed the Delete command be removed from operating systems after an employee, who thought he knew what he was doing, deleted an entire database, which cost the company millions of dollars. The Delete command should be considered a dangerous weapon.

More About

Windows 98 Explorer

For those familiar with Windows 3.1, Windows 98 Explorer bears some resemblance to File Manager. With the introduction of Windows 95, Microsoft made significant improvements and changed the basic way the program works. Those who passionately disliked File Manager found Explorer a better way to perform file maintenance.

Copying, moving, and deleting shortcuts, folders, and files is an important part of using Windows 98. You should be completely comfortable with all these operations. In addition, your ability to manage windows on the Windows 98 desktop can make the difference between an organized approach to dealing with multiple windows and a disorganized, confusing mess of windows on your desktop.

Windows 98 Explorer

Windows 98 Explorer is another program that is part of Windows 98. It allows you to view the contents of your computer, including drives, folders, and files, in a hierarchical format. In Explorer, you also can move, copy, and delete files in much the same manner as you can when working with open windows. The following section explains how to work with Windows 98 Explorer.

Launching Windows 98 Explorer

As with many operations, Windows 98 offers a variety of ways in which to launch Explorer. To launch Explorer using the My Computer icon, complete the following steps.

Steps: To Launch Explorer

1 **Right-click the My Computer icon and then point to Explore on the shortcut menu.**

A shortcut menu displays (Figure 3-31). The **Explore command** will launch Windows 98 Explorer.

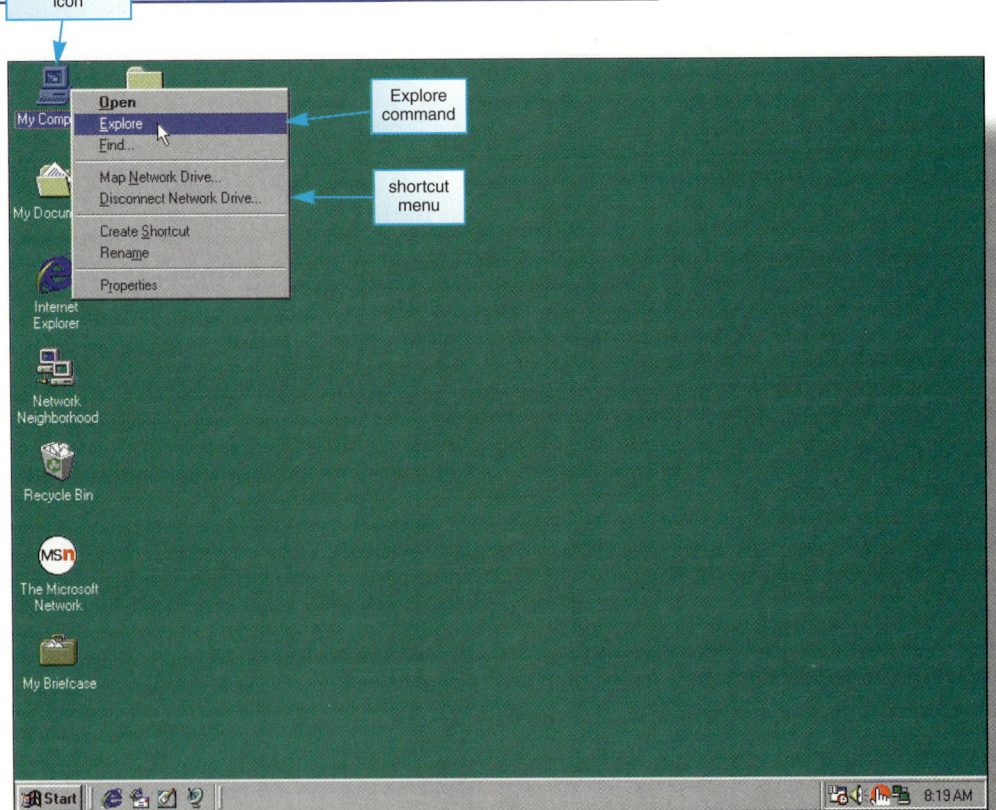

FIGURE 3-31

2 Click Explore. If necessary, maximize the Exploring - My Computer window.

The maximized Exploring - My Computer window displays (Figure 3-32).

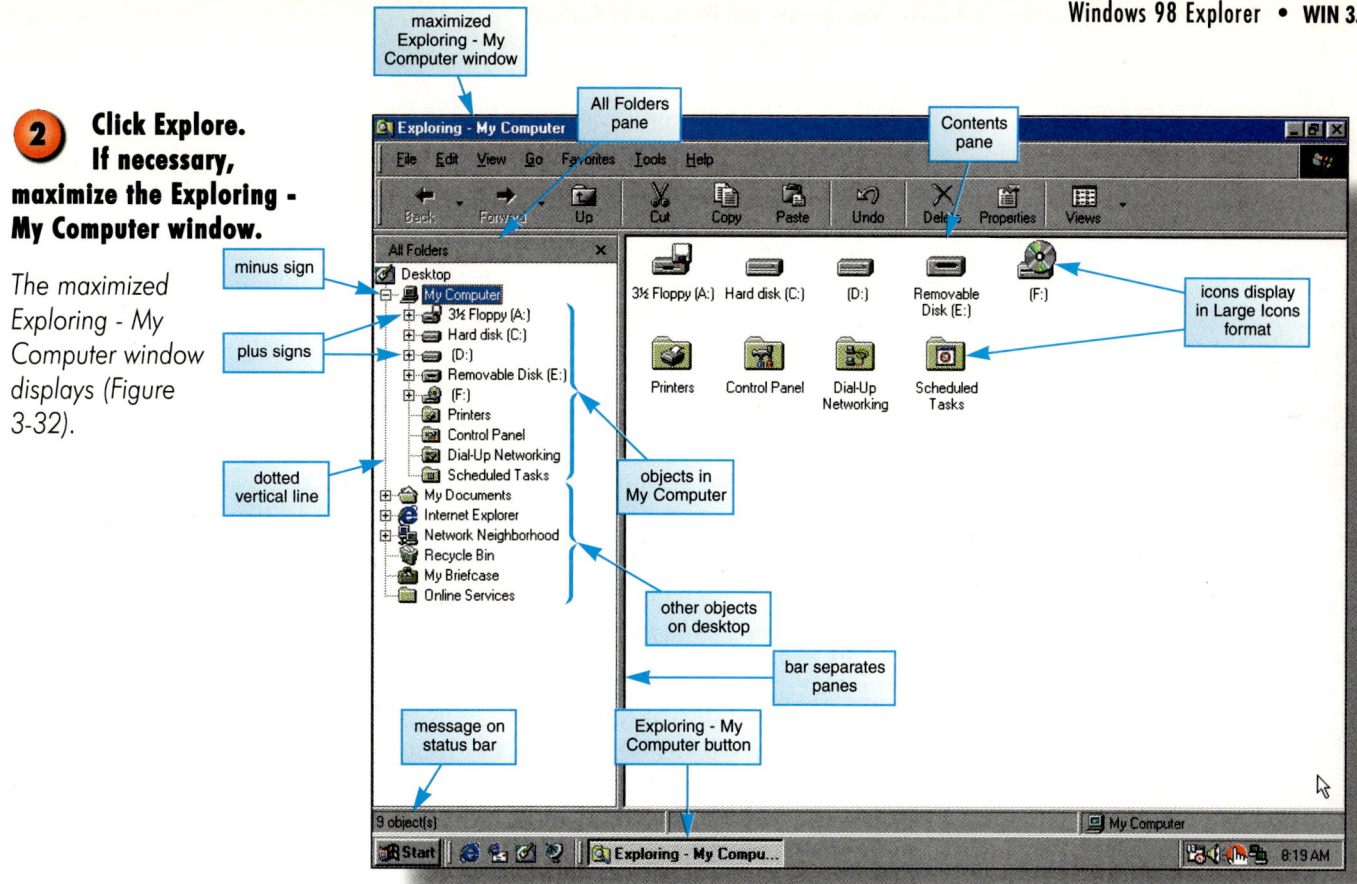

FIGURE 3-32

Explorer Window

The Exploring window in Figure 3-32 contains a number of elements, some of which should be familiar and some of which are new. The title bar in the window is the same as seen in other windows, and the menu bar contains the File, Edit, View, Go, Favorites, Tools, and Help menu names. The use of some of these menus will be explained later in this project. The Standard Buttons toolbar displays below the menu bar.

The main window is divided into two panes – the All Folders pane on the left and the Contents pane on the right. A bar separates the panes. You can drag the bar left or right to change the size of the two panes.

In the **All Folders pane**, Explorer displays, in a **hierarchical structure**, the icons and titles on the computer. The highest level in the hierarchy is the Desktop. Connected by a dotted vertical line below the Desktop are the My Computer, My Documents, Internet Explorer, Network Neighborhood, Recycle Bin, My Briefcase, and Online Services icons. These icons are found on the desktop. Your computer may have other icons.

Other Ways

1. Right-click Start button, click Explore on shortcut menu
2. Click Start button, point to Programs, click Windows Explorer
3. Right-click any icon on desktop (except The Microsoft Network icon and Outlook Express icon) or any button on Channel bar, click Explore on shortcut menu
4. Right-click Start button or any icon on desktop (except The Microsoft Network icon and Outlook Express icon) or any button on Channel bar, press E

More About

Large Icons

Research by Microsoft Corporation indicates that the Large Icons format is easier to work with and less confusing than the other icon formats. For this reason, the files and folders in the Exploring - My Computer window in Figure 3-32 display in the Large Icons format.

More About

A Hierarchy

One definition of hierarchy in *Merriam Webster's Collegiate Dictionary Tenth Edition* is a division of angels. While no one would argue angels have anything to do with Windows 98, some preach that working with a hierarchical structure as presented by Explorer is less secular (of or relating to the world) and more spiritual (of or relating to supernatural phenomena) than the straightforward showing of files in windows. What do you think?

To the left of the My Computer icon and title is a minus sign in a small box. The **minus sign** indicates that the drive or folder represented by the icon next to it, in this case My Computer, contains additional folders or drives and these folders or drives are displayed below the icon. Thus, below the My Computer icon, again connected by a dotted vertical line, are the 3½ Floppy (A:) icon, Hard disk (C:) icon, (D:) icon, Removable Disk (E:) icon, (F:) icon, and the Printers, Control Panel, Dial-Up Networking, and Scheduled Tasks folder icons. These drives and folders are contained within the My Computer window, as seen in previous examples.

The 3½ Floppy (A:) icon, Hard disk (C:) icon, (D:) icon, Removable Disk (E:) icon, and (F:) icon each have a small box with a plus sign next to it. The **plus sign** indicates that the drive or folder represented by the icon has more folders within it but the folders are not displayed in the All Folders pane of the Exploring window. As you will see shortly, clicking the box with the plus sign will display the folders within the drive or folder represented by the icon. If an item contains no folders, such as Recycle Bin and My Briefcase, no hierarchy exists to display and, therefore, no small box displays next to the icons.

The **Contents pane** in the Exploring window is identical to the My Computer window (see Figure 3-1 on page WIN 3.5). The Contents pane contains the 3½ Floppy (A:) icon, Hard disk (C:) icon, (D:) icon, Removable Disk (E:) icon, (F:) icon, and the Printers, Control Panel, Dial-Up Networking, and Scheduled Tasks folder icons. These icons may be different and may display in a different format on your computer. A message on the left of the status bar located at the bottom of the window indicates the Contents pane contains nine objects.

Windows 98 Explorer displays the drives and folders on the computer in hierarchical structure. This arrangement allows you to move and copy files and folders using only the Exploring - My Computer window. In the following sections, you will learn how to accomplish these tasks.

Displaying Files and Folders in Windows 98 Explorer

You can display files and folders in the Contents pane of the window as large icons, small icons, a list, or with details. Currently, the files and folder in the Contents pane display in Large Icons format. The manner in which you display folder contents in the Contents pane largely is a matter of personal preference.

Displaying Drive and Folder Contents

Explorer is used to display both the hierarchy of items in the All Folders pane of the window and the contents of drives and folders in the Contents pane of the window. To display the contents of a drive or folder, you need only click the drive or folder icon in the All Folders pane of the window. To display the contents of the Hard disk (C:) drive, complete the following step.

To Display the Contents of a Drive

1 Click the Hard disk (C:) icon in the All Folders pane.

The Contents pane of the Exploring window contains the contents of drive C (Figure 3-33). Notice that all the folder icons display first and then the file icons display.

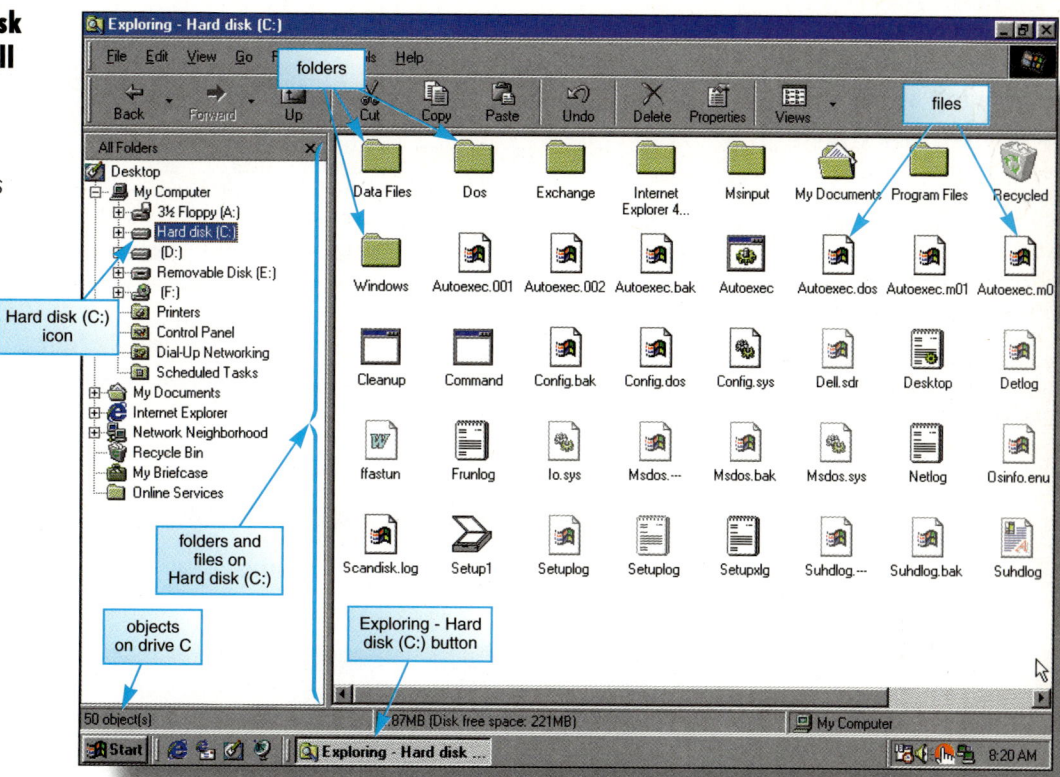

FIGURE 3-33

The status bar shown in Figure 3-33 contains information about the folders and files displaying in the window. Fifty folders and files display in the window.

Expanding a Selected Drive or Folder

When a plus sign in a small box displays to the left of a drive or folder icon in the All Folders pane of the window, the drive or folder can be expanded to show all the folders it contains. To expand drive C and view the folders on drive C, complete the steps on the next page.

Other Ways

1. Double-click Hard disk (C:) icon in Contents pane
2. Press TAB to select any drive icon in All Folders pane, press DOWN ARROW or UP ARROW to select drive C icon in Contents pane
3. Press TAB to select any drive icon in Contents pane, press DOWN ARROW or UP ARROW to select drive C icon in Contents pane, press ENTER

WIN 3.30 • Project 3 • File, Document, and Folder Management and Windows 98 Explorer

Steps: To Expand a Drive

1 Point to the plus sign in the small box to the left of the Hard disk (C:) icon (Figure 3-34).

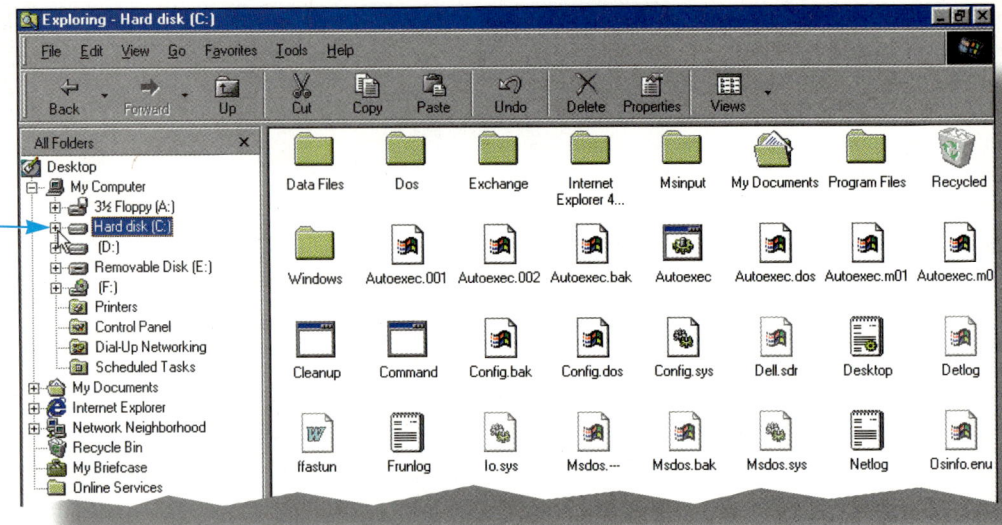

FIGURE 3-34

2 Click the plus sign.

The hierarchy below the Hard disk (C:) icon expands to display folders contained on drive C (Figure 3-35). A dotted vertical line connects these folders. A folder without a plus sign to the left of it contains no more folders. A folder with a plus sign to the left of it contains more folders. The minus sign to the left of the Hard disk (C:) icon indicates the drive has been expanded.

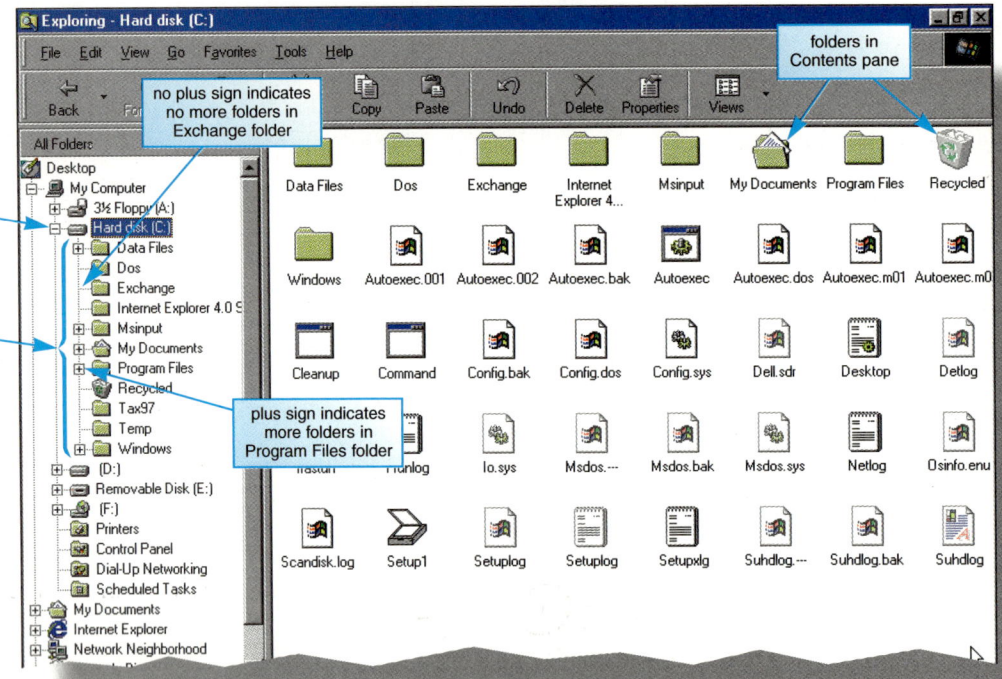

FIGURE 3-35

Other Ways

1. Double-click highlighted drive icon in All Folders pane
2. Select drive to expand, press PLUS on numeric keyboard
3. Select drive to expand, press RIGHT ARROW

With a drive or folder expanded, folders contained within the expanded drive or folder display in the All Folders pane of the window. You can continue this expansion to view further levels of the hierarchy. To expand the Windows folder, complete the following steps.

Windows 98 Explorer • **WIN 3.31**

PROJECT 3

 To Expand a Folder

1 Point to the plus sign in the small box to the left of the Windows icon (Figure 3-36).

FIGURE 3-36

2 Click the plus sign.

The Windows icon displays at the top of the All Folders pane and the Windows folder expands (Figure 3-37). Some of the folders in the Windows folder contain more folders and others do not. The minus sign to the left of the Windows folder indicates it is expanded.

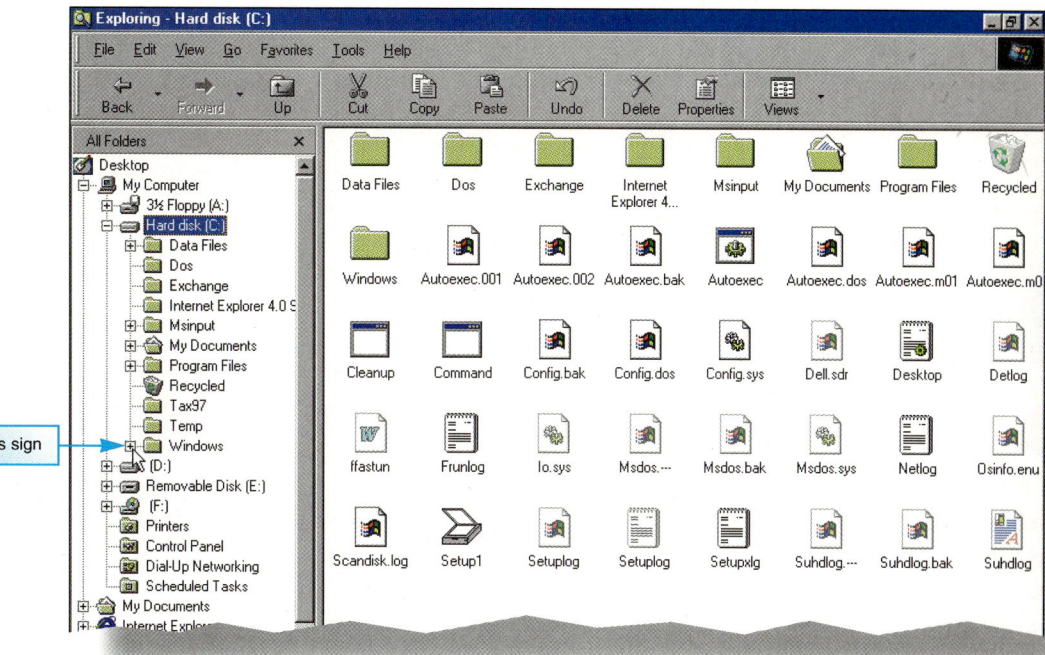

FIGURE 3-37

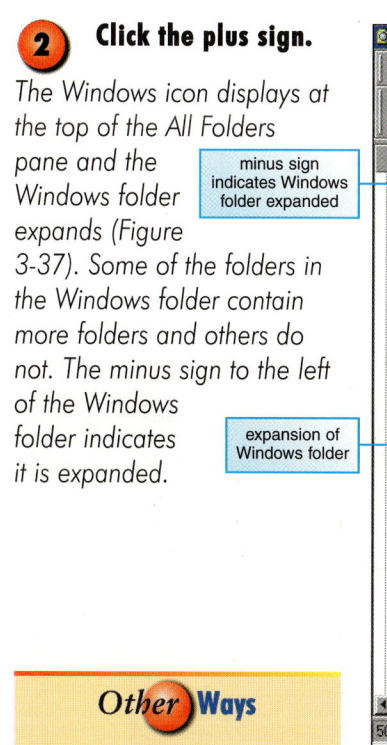

1. Double-click highlighted folder icon in All Folders pane
2. Select folder to expand, press PLUS
3. Select folder to expand, press RIGHT ARROW

WIN 3.32 • Project 3 • File, Document, and Folder Management and Windows 98 Explorer

Explorer

In Figure 3-37 on the previous page, the Windows folder is expanded but the Contents pane of the window still contains the contents of Hard disk (C:) because the Windows folder was not opened. It was expanded but not opened by clicking the plus sign next to the Windows icon.

Opening Folders in Explorer

Whenever you display folders and files in the Contents pane of the Exploring window, you can open these folders and files in a separate window on the desktop. For example, to open the Programs window, complete the following steps.

 To Open a Folder Window in Explorer

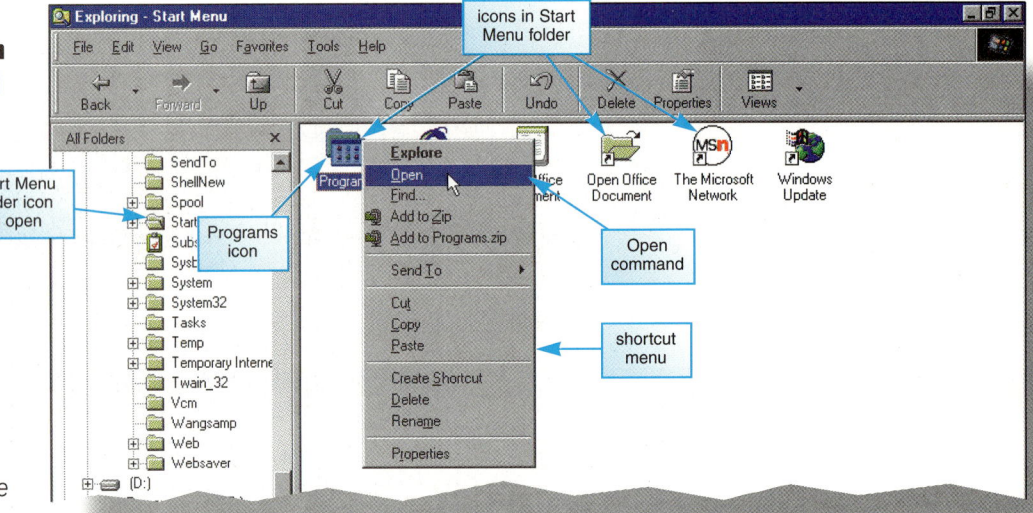

1 If the Start Menu icon is not visible in the All Folders pane, scroll to make the icon visible. Click the Start Menu icon. Right-click the Programs icon in the Contents pane of the window. Point to Open on the shortcut menu.

The open Start Menu icon displays in the All Folders pane and a shortcut menu displays in the Contents pane (Figure 3-38).

FIGURE 3-38

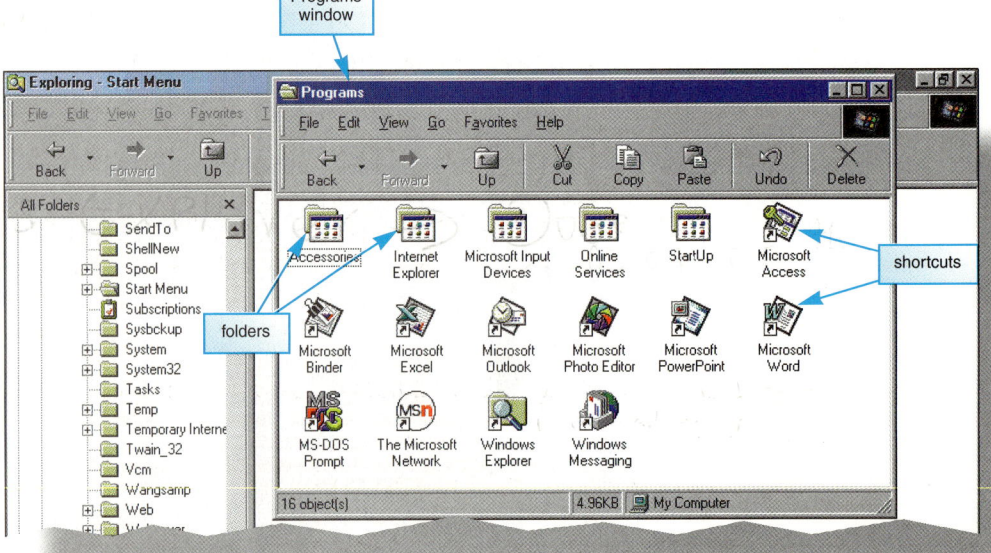

 Click Open.

The Programs window opens on top of the Exploring window (Figure 3-39). The Programs window contains folders and shortcuts.

FIGURE 3-39

Other Ways

1. Right-click Programs icon in Contents pane, press O

In Figure 3-38, the Explore command on the shortcut menu is in bold (dark) font. This means Explore is the default command on the shortcut menu. If you double-click the Programs icon in the Contents pane of the Exploring window, the Explore command will be executed. When it is, the contents of the Programs folder will display in the Contents pane of the Exploring window.

Programs Folder

The **Programs folder** contains all the folders and shortcuts found on the Programs submenu when you click the Start button and point to Programs. Figure 3-40 illustrates the Programs submenu and the corresponding objects in the Programs folder. Notice that Accessories on the Programs submenu corresponds to the Accessories folder in the Programs window. Similarly, the Internet Explorer, StartUp, and Microsoft Outlook folders and shortcut correspond to the entries on the Programs submenu. Thus, you can see that the entries on the Programs submenu actually are folders and shortcuts in the Programs folder.

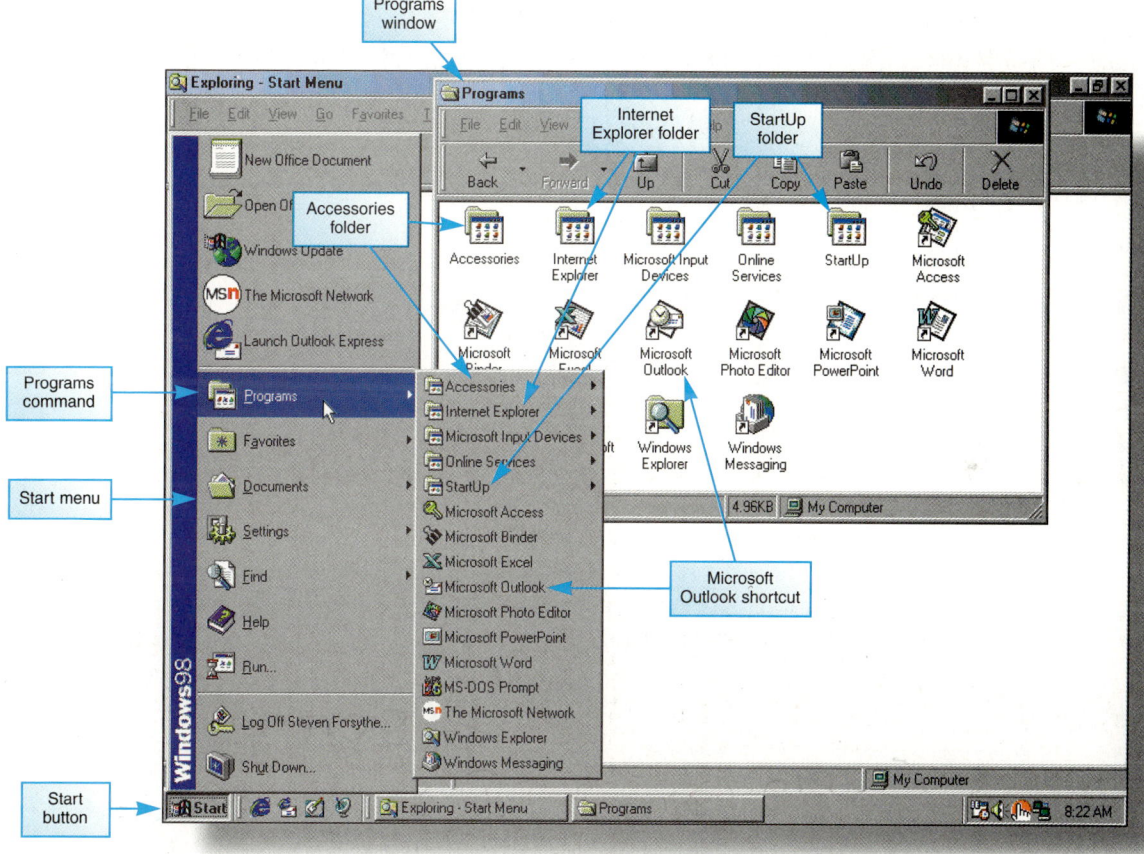

FIGURE 3-40

The Programs window shown in Figure 3-39 must be closed. To close the Programs window, complete the following step.

TO CLOSE A WINDOW

 Click the Close button on the Programs window title bar.

The Programs window closes and the Start menu no longer displays.

Launching an Application Program from Windows 98 Explorer

You can launch an application program from the Contents pane of the Exploring window using the same techniques you used for launching an application program from an open window earlier in this project (see Figure 3-12 and Figure 3-13 on page WIN 3.14). To launch the Internet Explorer program stored in the Internet Explorer folder from the Contents pane of the Exploring window, complete the following steps.

To Launch an Application Program from Explorer

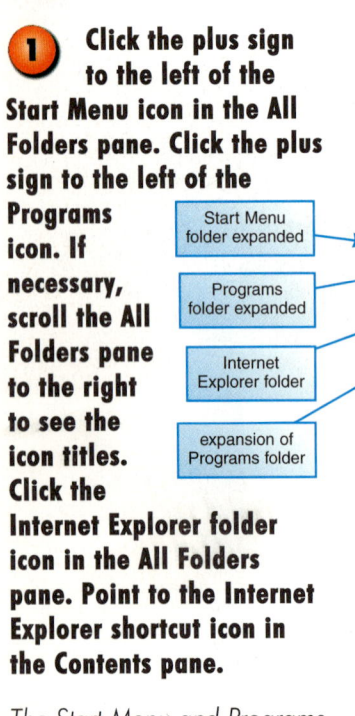

1 Click the plus sign to the left of the Start Menu icon in the All Folders pane. Click the plus sign to the left of the Programs icon. If necessary, scroll the All Folders pane to the right to see the icon titles. Click the Internet Explorer folder icon in the All Folders pane. Point to the Internet Explorer shortcut icon in the Contents pane.

The Start Menu and Programs folders are expanded and the contents of the Internet Explorer folder display in the Contents pane (Figure 3-41).

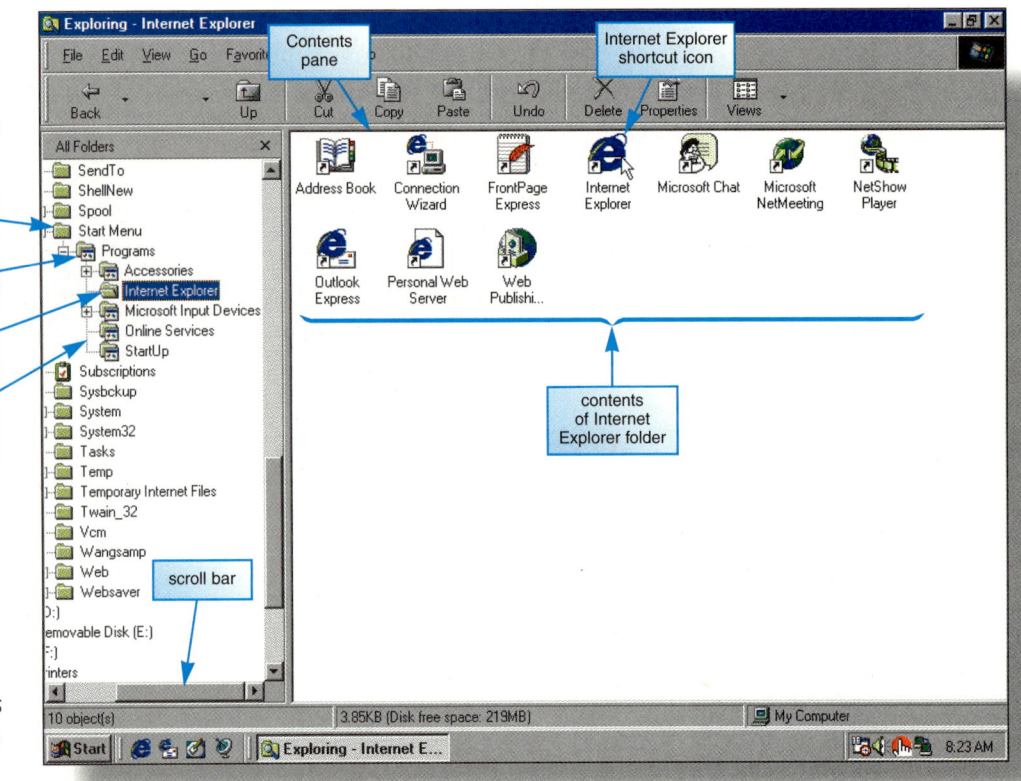

FIGURE 3-41

Double-click the Internet Explorer shortcut icon.

Windows 98 launches the Internet Explorer program. The MSN.COM, Welcome Page - Microsoft Internet Explorer window opens and the Welcome to MSN.COM page displays (Figure 3-42). Because Web pages are modified frequently, the Web page that displays on your desktop may be different from the Web page in Figure 3-42. The URL for the Web page displays in the Address bar.

FIGURE 3-42

You can use the Internet Explorer program for any purpose you want, just as if you had launched it from the desktop or Quick Launch toolbar. When you are finished with the Internet Explorer program, you should close the program. To close the Internet Explorer program, complete the following step.

TO CLOSE AN APPLICATION PROGRAM

 Click the Close button on MSN.COM, Welcome Page - Microsoft Internet Explorer title bar.

Closing Folder Expansions

Sometimes, after you have completed work with expanded folders in Explorer, you will want to close the expansions while still leaving Explorer open. To close the open folders shown in Figure 3-41, complete the steps on the next two pages.

1. Right-click Internet Explorer shortcut icon, click Open
2. Click Internet Explorer shortcut icon, press ENTER

Launching Programs in Explorer

Usually, people find starting application programs from the Start menu or from a window easier and more intuitive than starting programs from Explorer. In most cases, you will not be launching programs from Explorer.

WIN 3.36 • Project 3 • File, Document, and Folder Management and Windows 98 Explorer

 To Close Expanded Folders

1 If necessary, scroll to the left in the All Folders pane so the Programs and Start Menu icons are visible. Click the minus sign to the left of the Programs icon. Click the minus sign to the left of the Start Menu icon.

The expansion of both folders close (Figure 3-43). The minus sign to the left of the Start Menu icon changes to a plus sign. When you close the expansion of a folder by clicking the minus sign, the contents of the folder display in the Contents pane of the Exploring window, so the contents of the Start Menu folder display in the Contents pane.

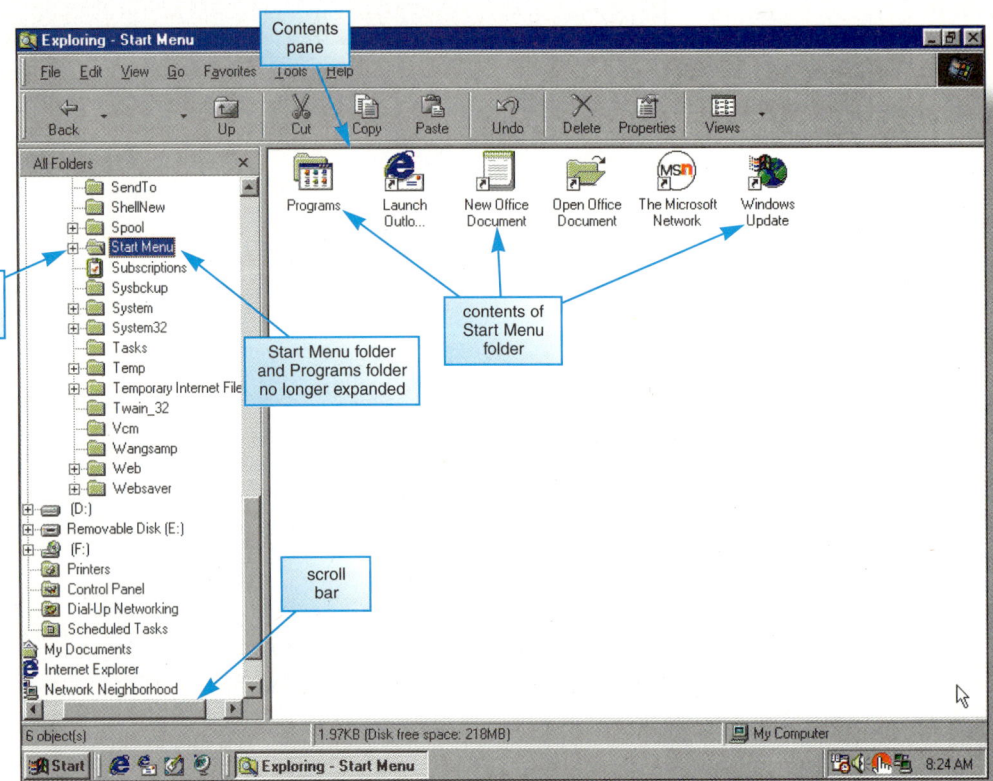

FIGURE 3-43

2 Scroll up in the All Folders pane so the Windows folder is visible. Point to the minus sign in the small box to the left of the Windows icon.

The Windows icon displays in the All Folders pane (Figure 3-44). The minus sign indicates the Windows folder is expanded.

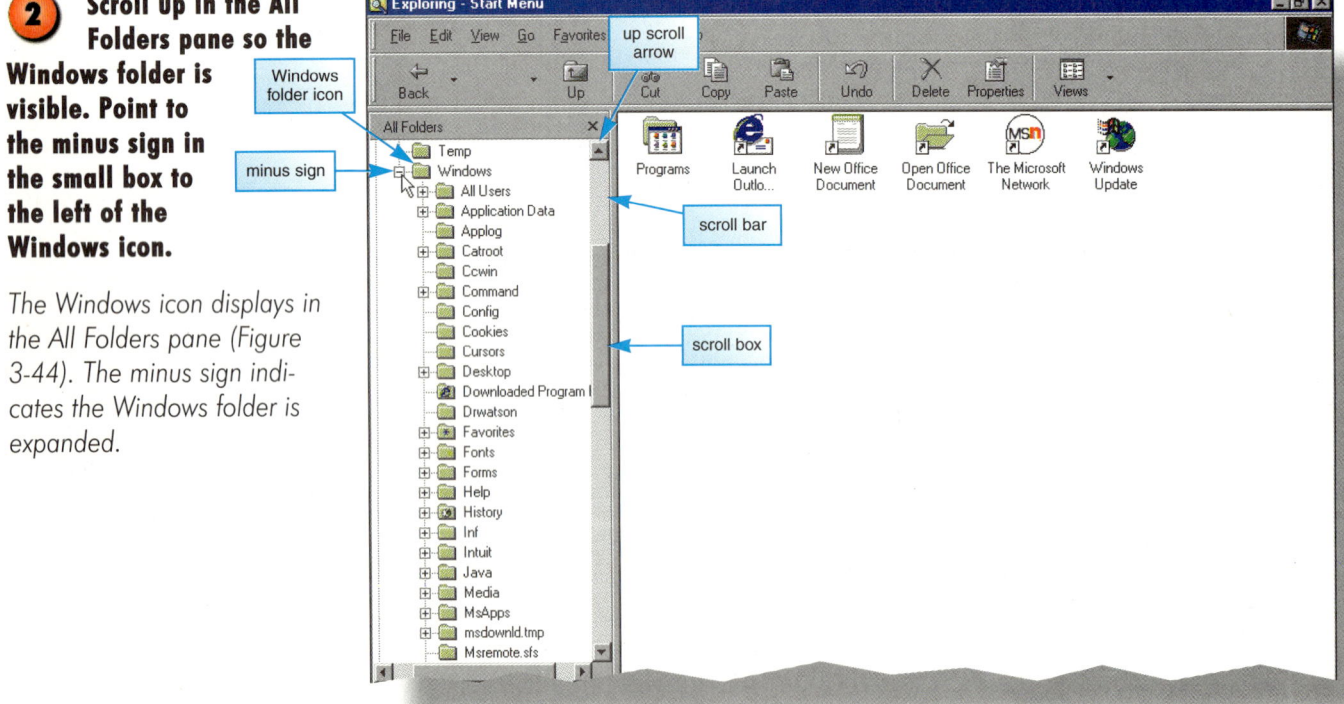

FIGURE 3-44

3 Click the minus sign

The expansion of the Windows folder closes (Figure 3-45). The minus sign changes to a plus sign to indicate the Windows folder is not expanded. The Windows entry in the All Folders pane is highlighted and the contents of the Windows folder display in the Contents pane of the window. The button in the taskbar button area and the open Windows icon reflect this.

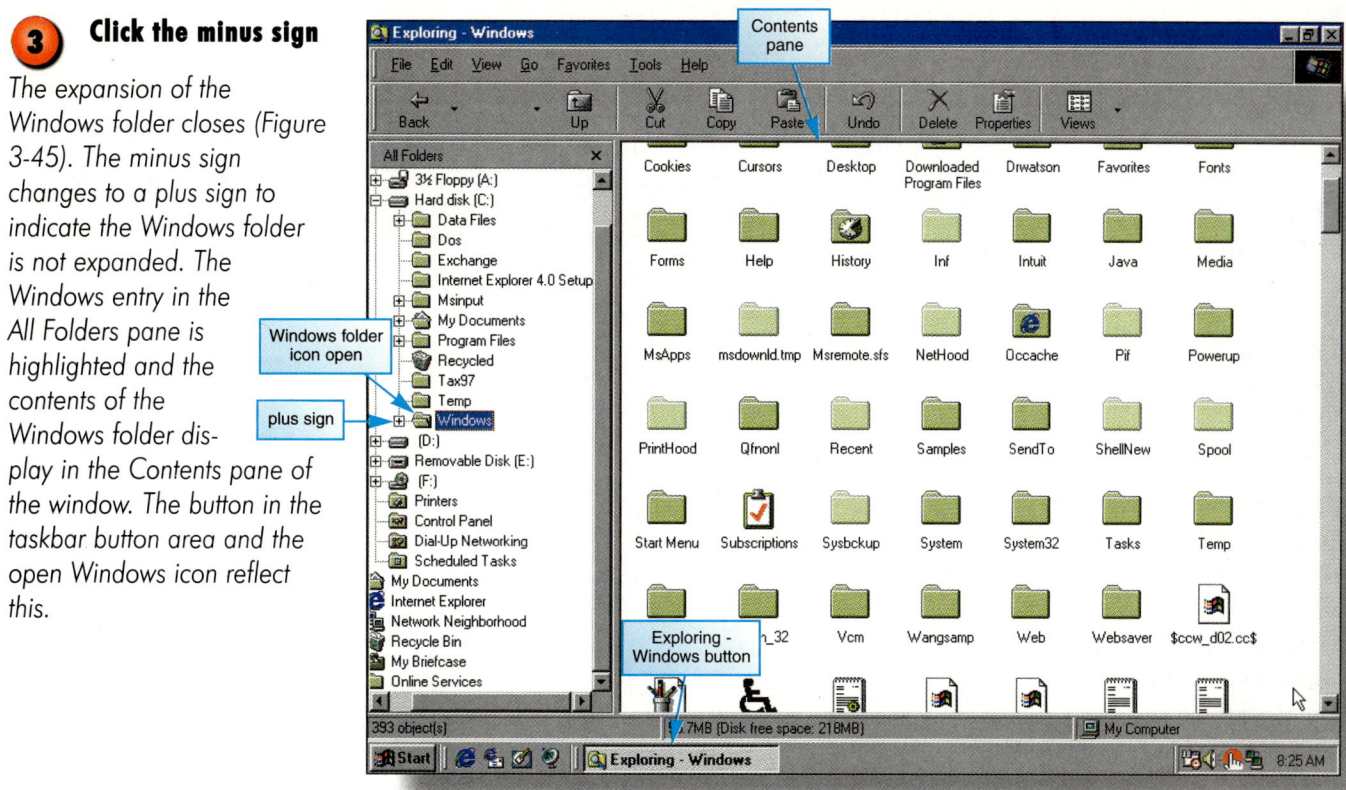

FIGURE 3-45

Moving through the All Folders and Contents panes of the Exploring window is an important skill because you will find that you use Explorer to perform a significant amount of file maintenance on your computer.

Other Ways

1. Click expanded folder icon, press MINUS SIGN
2. Click expanded folder icon, press LEFT ARROW
3. Click expanded folder icon, double-click folder icon

Copying, Moving, Renaming, and Deleting Files and Folders in Windows 98 Explorer

You can copy, move, rename, and delete files and folders in Windows 98 Explorer using essentially the same techniques as when working in folder windows. To a large extent, whether you perform these activities in folder windows, in Explorer, or in a combination of the two is a personal preference. Nonetheless, it is important for you to understand the techniques used in both cases so you can make an informed decision about how you want to perform file maintenance when using Windows 98.

Copying Files in Windows 98 Explorer

In previous examples of copying files, you used the copy and paste method to copy a document file from a folder to a drive. Although you could use the copy and paste method to copy files in Windows 98 Explorer, another method of copying a file is to right-drag a file (or folder) icon from the Contents pane to a folder or drive icon in the All Folders pane. To copy the Circles bitmap image file from the Windows folder onto a floppy disk in drive A of your computer, complete the steps on the next two pages.

WIN 3.38 • Project 3 • File, Document, and Folder Management and Windows 98 Explorer

Microsoft **Windows 98**

 Steps To Copy a File in Explorer by Right-Dragging

1 Insert a formatted floppy disk in drive A of your computer.

2 Scroll down the Contents pane until the Circles icon displays. If the Circles bitmap image file is not on your computer, scroll the Contents pane to display any other bitmap image file icon. If necessary, scroll the All Folders pane until the 3½ Floppy (A:) icon displays.

The Circles icon displays in the Contents pane and the 3½ Floppy (A:) icon displays in the All Folders pane (Figure 3-46).

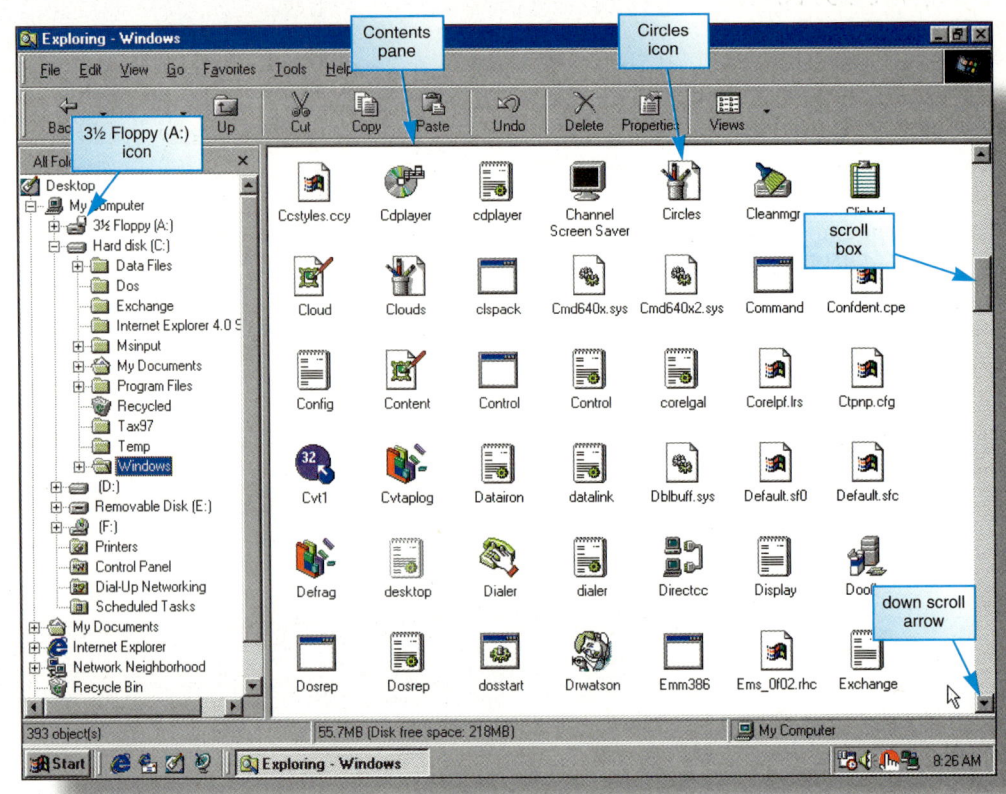

FIGURE 3-46

3 Right-drag the Circles icon on top of the 3½ Floppy (A:) icon. Point to Copy Here on the shortcut menu.

The dimmed image of the Circles icon displays on top of the 3½ Floppy (A:) icon and a shortcut menu displays (Figure 3-47).

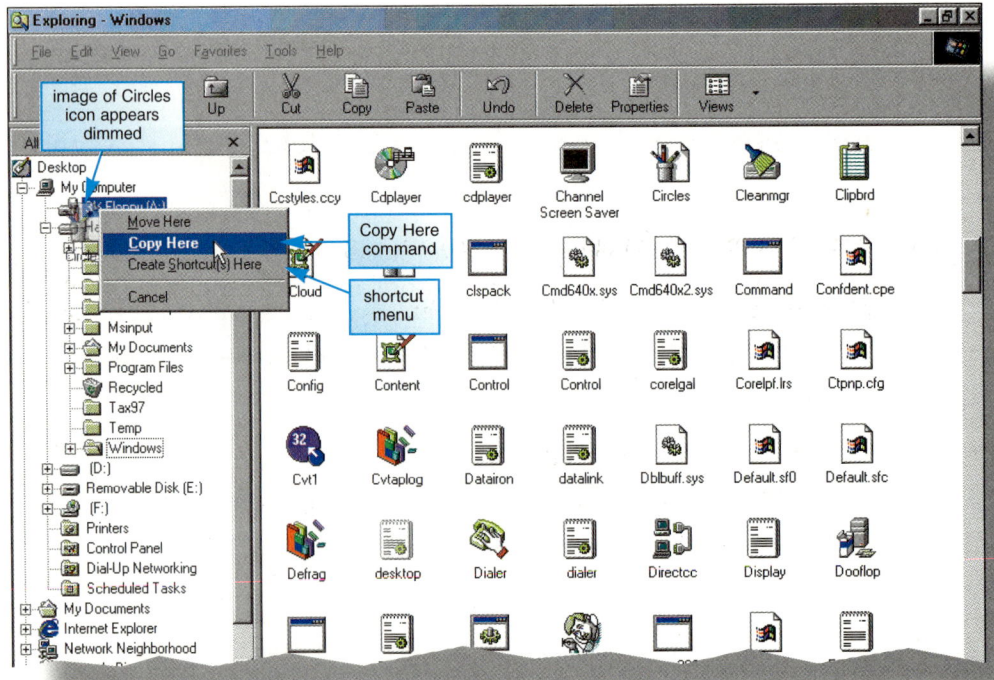

FIGURE 3-47

Click Copy Here.

The Copying dialog box displays while the file is being copied (Figure 3-48). The file being copied (Circles.bmp) and the from (WINDOWS) and to (A:\) locations are identified in the dialog box. After the file is copied, it is stored on the floppy disk in drive A.

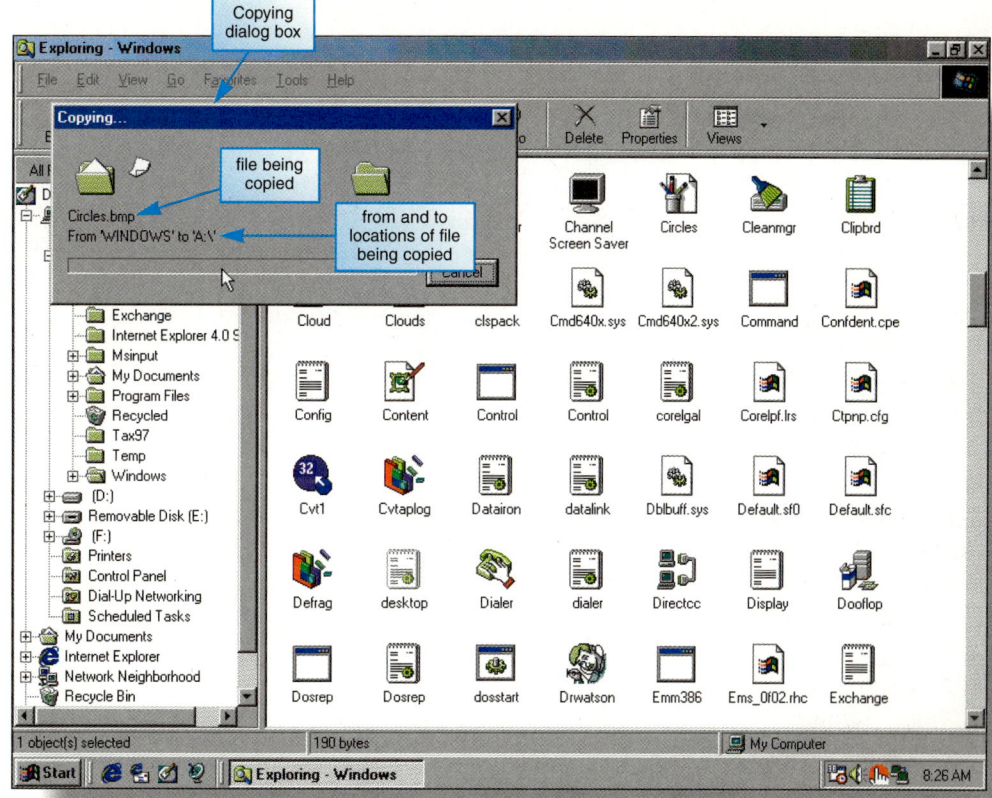

FIGURE 3-48

Other Ways

1. Right-click file to copy, click Copy, right-click 3½ Floppy (A:) icon, click Paste
2. Drag file to copy on top of 3½ Floppy (A:) icon
3. Click file to copy in Contents pane, on Edit menu click Copy, click 3½ Floppy (A:) icon, on Edit menu click Paste
4. Select file to copy in Contents pane, press CTRL+C, select 3½ Floppy (A:) icon, press CTRL+V

Files can be moved using the same techniques just discussed except that you click **Move Here** instead of Copy Here on the shortcut menu (see Figure 3-47). The difference between a move and a copy, as mentioned previously, is that when you move a file, it is placed on the destination drive or in the destination folder and is removed from its current location. When a file is copied, it is placed on the destination drive or in the destination folder as well as remaining stored in its current location. Use caution when moving a file so that you will not remove it from a location where you want to keep it.

In general, you should right-drag or use the copy and paste method to copy or move a file instead of merely dragging a file. If you drag a file from one folder to another on the same drive, Windows 98 moves the file. If you drag a file from one folder to another on a different drive, Windows 98 copies the file. Because of the different ways this is handled, it is strongly suggested you right-drag or use copy and paste when moving or copying files.

Displaying the Contents of a Floppy Disk

After copying a file, you might want to examine the folder or drive where the file was copied to ensure it was copied properly. To see the contents of the floppy disk in drive A, complete the step on the next page.

WIN 3.40 • Project 3 • File, Document, and Folder Management and Windows 98 Explorer

To Display the Contents of a Floppy Disk

1 Click the 3½ Floppy (A:) icon in the All Folders pane.

The contents of the floppy disk in drive A display in the Contents pane (Figure 3-49). The Circles file is stored on the floppy disk. If you have additional files and/or folders on the floppy disk you are using, their icons and titles also will display.

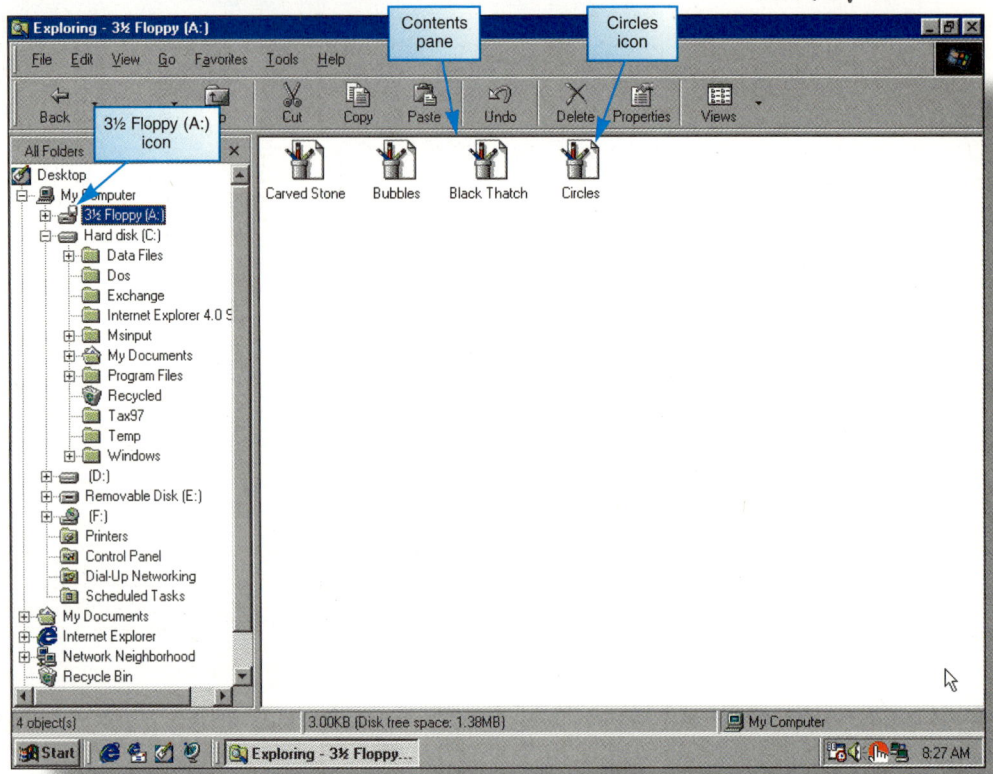

FIGURE 3-49

Other Ways

1. Right-click 3½ Floppy (A:) icon, click Explore

Renaming Files and Folders

In some circumstances you may want to **rename** a file or a folder. This could occur when you want to distinguish a file in one folder or drive from a copy, or if you decide you need a better name to identify a file. To change the name of the Circles file on the floppy disk to Blue Circles, complete the following steps.

Copying, Moving, Renaming, and Deleting Files and Folders in Windows 98 Explorer • **WIN 3.41**

 To Rename a File

1 **Right-click the Circles icon in the Contents pane. Point to Rename on the shortcut menu.**

The Circles icon is selected and a shortcut menu displays (Figure 3-50).

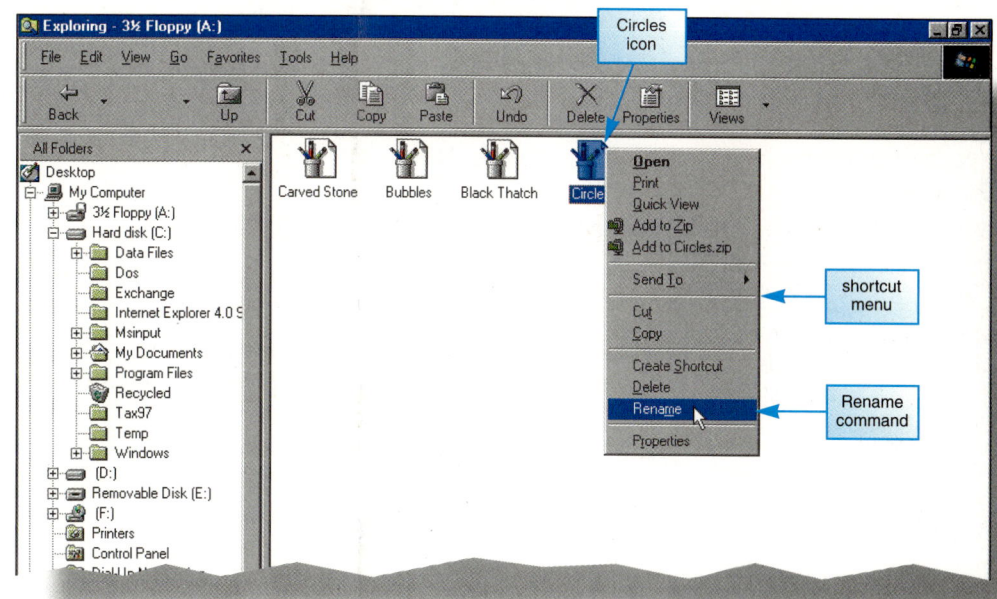

FIGURE 3-50

2 **Click Rename. Type** Blue Circles **and then press the ENTER key.**

The file is renamed Blue Circles (Figure 3-51). Note that the file on the floppy disk in drive A is renamed, but the original file in the Windows folder on drive C is not renamed.

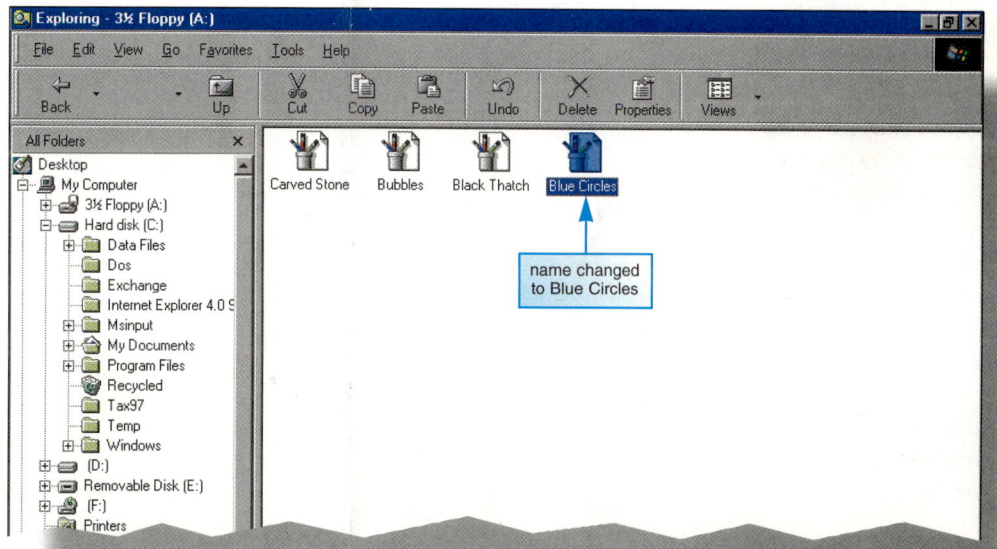

FIGURE 3-51

Renaming files in the manner shown above also can be achieved in other windows. For example, if you open the My Computer window and then open the 3½ Floppy (A:) window, you can rename any file stored on the floppy disk using the technique just shown.

Other Ways

1. Right-click icon in Contents pane, press M, type name, press ENTER
2. Click icon in Contents pane, press F2, type name, press ENTER
3. Click icon, on File menu click Rename, type name, press ENTER
4. Select icon, press ALT+F, press M, type name, press ENTER

More About

Deleting Files

Warning! This is your last warning! Be EXTREMELY careful when deleting files. Hours and weeks of hard work can be lost with one click of a button. If you are going to delete files or folders from your hard disk, consider making a backup of those files to ensure that if you inadvertently delete something you need, you will be able to recover.

You also can rename files on a hard disk using the techniques shown, but you should use caution when doing so. If you inadvertently rename a file that is associated with certain programs, the programs may not be able to find the file and, therefore, may not execute properly.

If you change a file name for which a shortcut exists on a menu, in a folder, or on the desktop, Windows 98 will update the shortcut link so the shortcut points to the renamed file. The name of the shortcut, however, is not changed to reflect the name change of the linked file.

Deleting Files in Windows 98 Explorer

A final function that you may want to use in Windows 98 Explorer is to delete a file. As has been mentioned, you should exercise extreme caution when deleting a file or files. When you delete a file from a floppy disk, the file is gone once you delete it. If you delete a file from a hard disk, the deleted file is stored in the Recycle Bin where you can recover it until you empty the Recycle Bin. Nevertheless, be very careful when deleting files, whether from a floppy disk or from a hard disk.

Assume you have decided to delete all four files from the floppy disk in drive A. To delete the files, complete the following steps.

Steps: To Delete Files from a Floppy Disk

1 Click the Carved Stone icon in the Contents pane. Press and hold the SHIFT key and then click the Blue Circles icon. Point to the Delete button on the Standard Buttons toolbar.

The four icons are selected (Figure 3-52). Holding the SHIFT key and then pointing to a second icon selects all the icons between the two you have clicked.

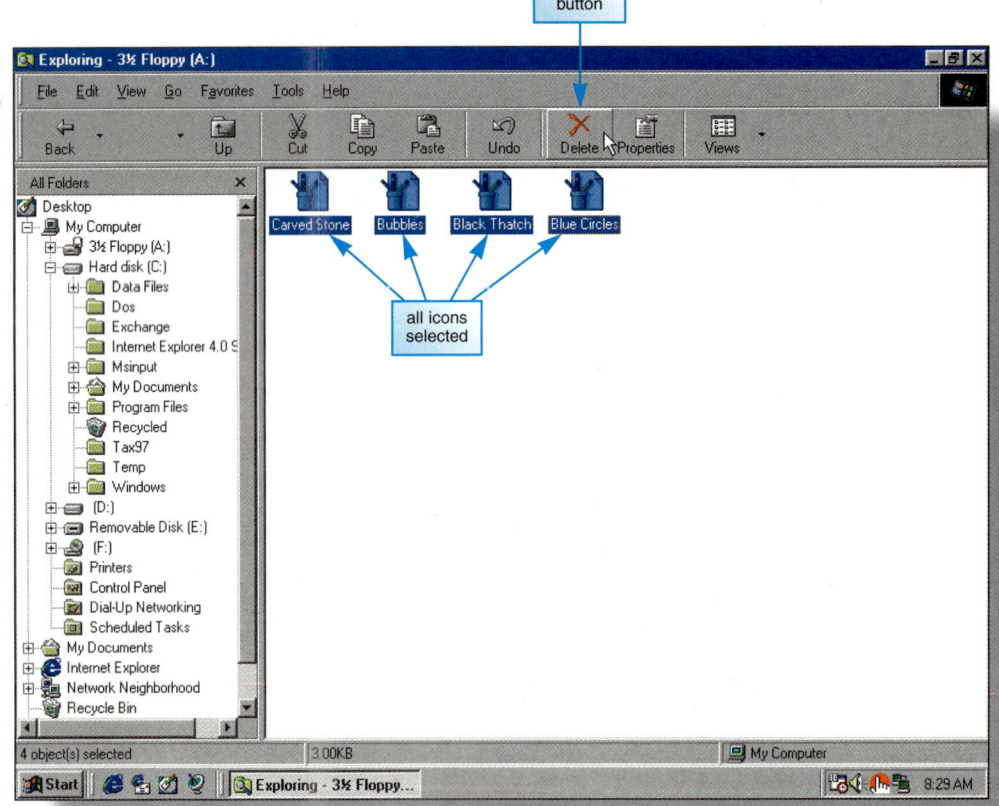

FIGURE 3-52

Copying, Moving, Renaming, and Deleting Files and Folders in Windows 98 Explorer • WIN 3.43

2 **Click the Delete button. Point to the Yes button.**

The Confirm Multiple File Delete dialog box displays (Figure 3-53). The dialog box asks if you are sure you want to delete the four items.

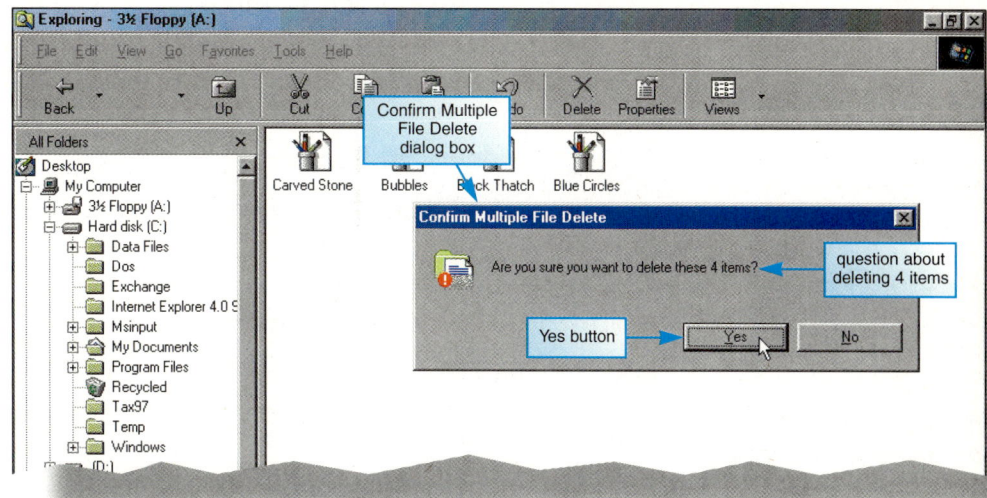

FIGURE 3-53

3 **Click the Yes button.**

A Deleting dialog box displays while the four files are being deleted (Figure 3-54). The Deleting dialog box indicates the file being deleted (Black Thatch.bmp) and where the file is being deleted from (A:\). If you wish to terminate the deleting process before it is complete, you can click the Cancel button.

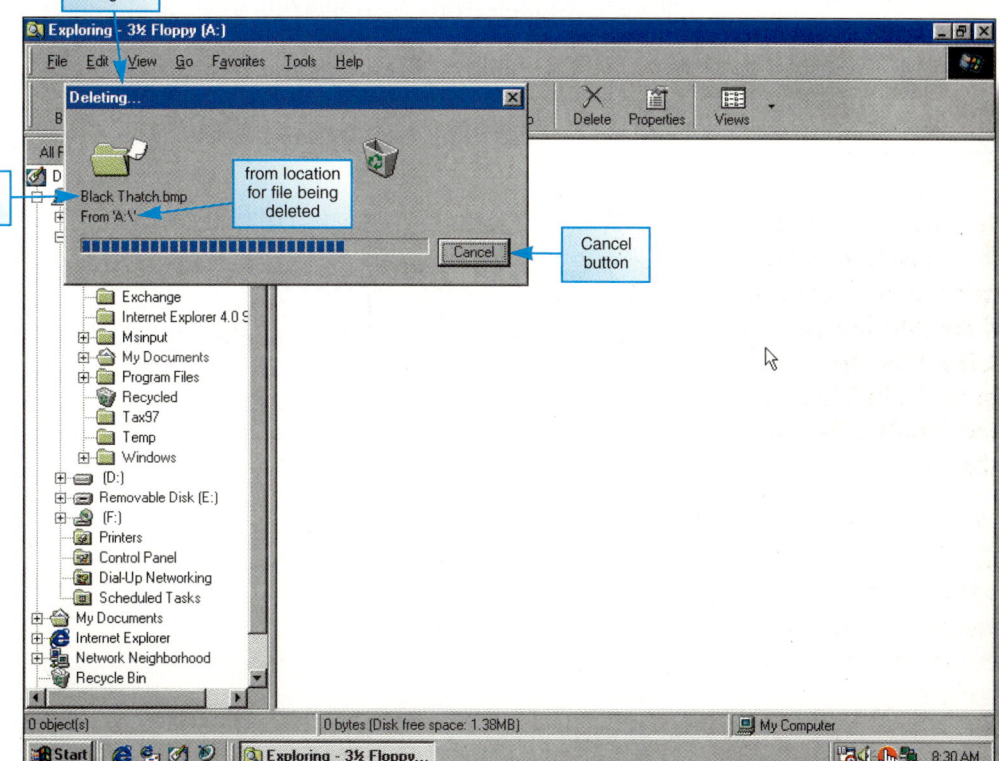

FIGURE 3-54

Other Ways

1. Right-drag icon to Recycle Bin, click Move Here, click Yes button
2. Drag icon to Recycle Bin, click Yes button
3. Right-click icon, click Delete, click Yes button.
4. Click icon, on File menu click Delete, click Yes button
5. Select icon, press ALT+F, press D, press Y

You can use the same methods just specified to delete folders from a floppy disk or a hard disk. Again, however, you should use extreme caution when deleting folders and files to ensure you do not delete something you may not be able to recover.

Closing Windows 98 Explorer

When you are finished with file maintenance, normally you will close the Exploring window. To close the Exploring window, complete the step below.

TO CLOSE THE EXPLORING WINDOW

 Click the Close button on the Exploring window title bar.

Windows 98 closes the Exploring window.

Summary of Windows 98 Explorer

Windows 98 Explorer gives you the capability of performing file maintenance in a single window without displaying additional windows or worrying about windows management on the desktop. In addition, it provides a hierarchical view of all drives, folders, and files on your computer. Whether you choose to use Explorer or My Computer to perform file maintenance is a personal choice. You may find that some tasks are easier using Explorer and others are easier using My Computer.

More About

Properties

Properties are something new with Windows 95 and Windows 98. The Properties dialog boxes allow you to customize not only your desktop and working environment, but also control how devices respond and operate. They provide useful information as well. Right-click/Properties is a sequence you should become familiar with in Window 98.

Properties of Objects

Every object in Windows 98 has **properties**, which describe the object. In some cases, you can change the properties of an object. Each drive, folder, file, and program in Windows 98 is considered an object and, therefore, has properties. In the following section, the properties of objects will be shown.

Drive Properties

Each drive on your computer has properties. To display the properties for drive C, complete the following steps.

Steps To Display Hard Disk Properties

1 Double-click the My Computer icon on the desktop. Click the Hard disk (C:) icon in the My Computer window. Point to the Properties button on the Standard Buttons toolbar.

The My Computer window opens on the desktop (Figure 3-55).

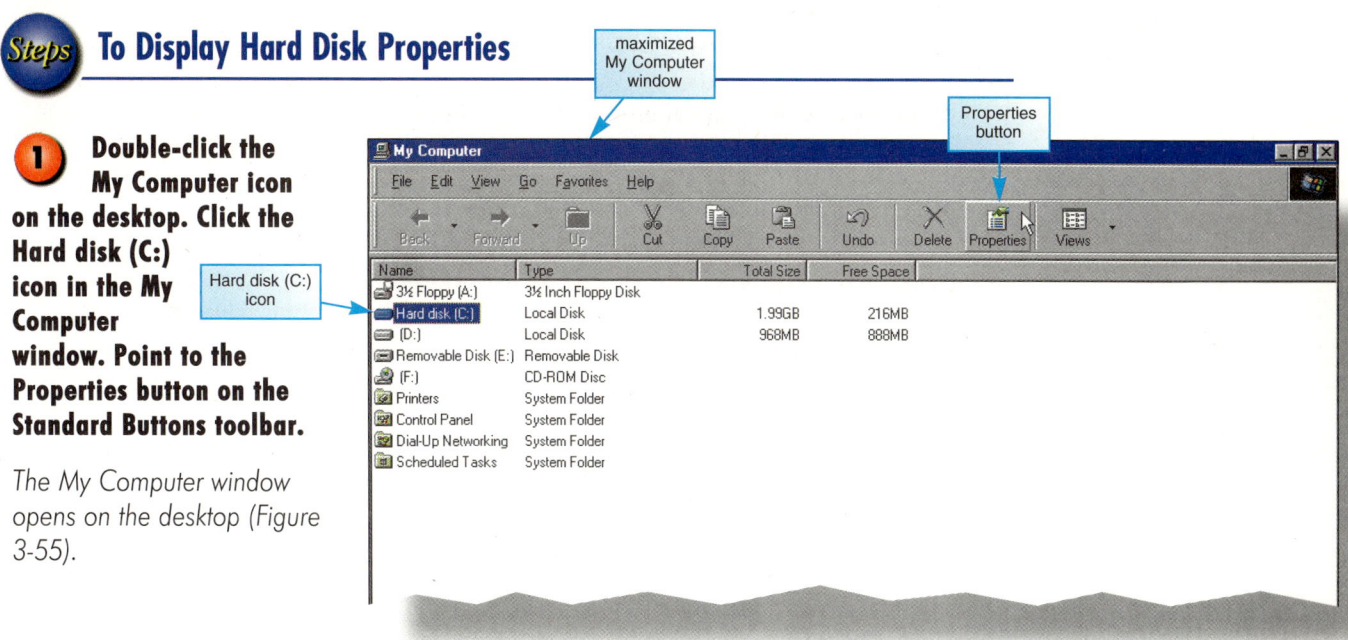

FIGURE 3-55

2 Click the Properties button. Point to the Cancel button.

*The Hard disk (C:) Properties dialog box displays with the General sheet on top (Figure 3-56). On the **General sheet**, the Label text box allows you to change the label name given to the drive (HARD DISK). The name on your computer may be different. The type of drive (Local Disk) and File system (FAT) display below the Label text box. The used space on the drive (dark blue box) is the space on the disk holding files and folders. The free space (magenta box) is the space available for more folders and files. The total capacity of the disk is specified and a pie chart graphically represents the used and free space on the disk.*

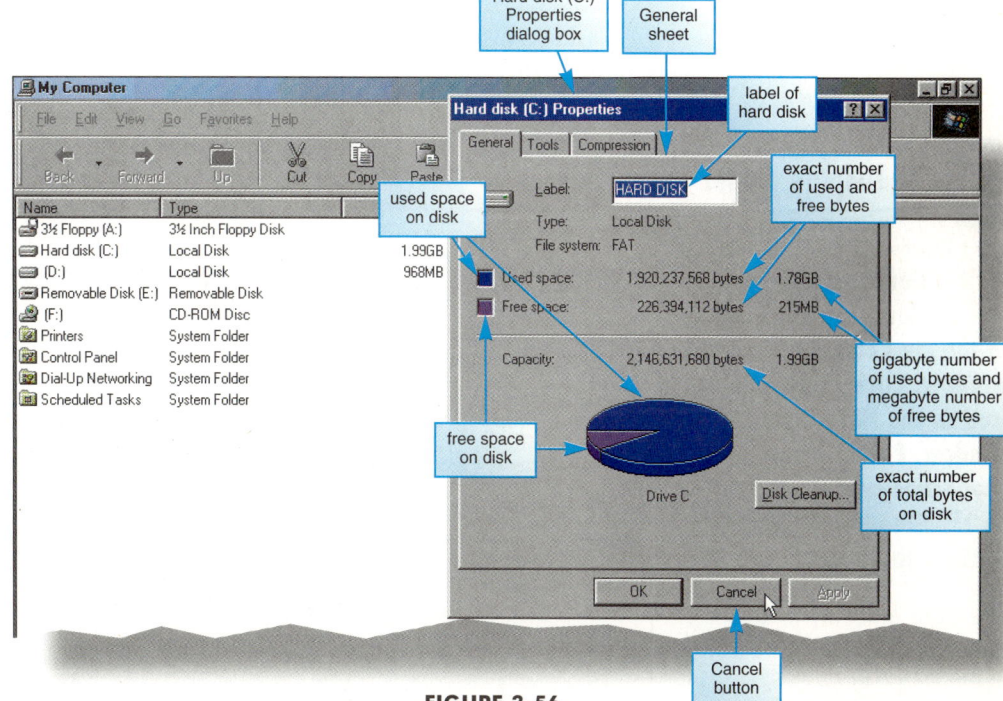

FIGURE 3-56

3 Click the Cancel button.

The Hard disk (C:) dialog box no longer displays.

Other Ways

1. Right-click drive icon, click Properties, click Cancel button
2. Click drive icon, on File menu click Properties, click Cancel button
3. Select drive icon, press ALT+ENTER, press ESC

The **Tools sheet** in the Hard disk (C:) Properties dialog box in Figure 3-56 on the previous page, accessible by clicking the Tools tab, allows you to check errors on the hard disk, back up the hard disk, or defragment the hard disk. The **Compression sheet**, accessible by clicking the Compression tab, allows you to increase free space on the hard disk by compressing the hard disk or creating a new compressed drive.

In Figure 3-56, you might think the number of bytes specified for used space and for free space do not correspond with the megabyte or gigabyte specification shown, but in fact they do. A **gigabyte of RAM** or disk space is not exactly one billion characters, or bytes. Because addresses are calculated on a computer using the binary number system, a gigabyte of RAM or disk space actually is 1,073,741,824 bytes, which is equal to 2^{30}. In Figure 3-56, if you multiply 1.78 times 1,073,741,824, the answer is just less than 1,920,237,568, which is shown as the total number of bytes of used space on drive C. Therefore, 1.78 GB is the closest estimate, expressed as gigabytes, for the total amount of unused space on drive C.

The same is true of the megabyte specification for free space. A **megabyte of RAM** or disk space is 1,048,576 bytes and not exactly one million bytes, which is equal to 2^{20}. In Figure 3-56, if you multiply 215 times 1,048,576, the answer is just less than 226,394,112, which is shown as the total number of bytes of free space on drive C. Therefore, 215 MB is the closest estimate, expressed as megabytes, for the total amount of free space on drive C.

Properties of a Folder

Folders also have properties. To display the properties of the Windows folder, complete the following steps.

Steps: To Display Folder Properties

1 Double-click the Hard disk (C:) icon in the My Computer window. Click the Windows icon in the Hard disk (C:) window. Point to the Properties button on the Standard Buttons toolbar.

The Hard disk (C:) window opens and the Windows icon is selected (Figure 3-57).

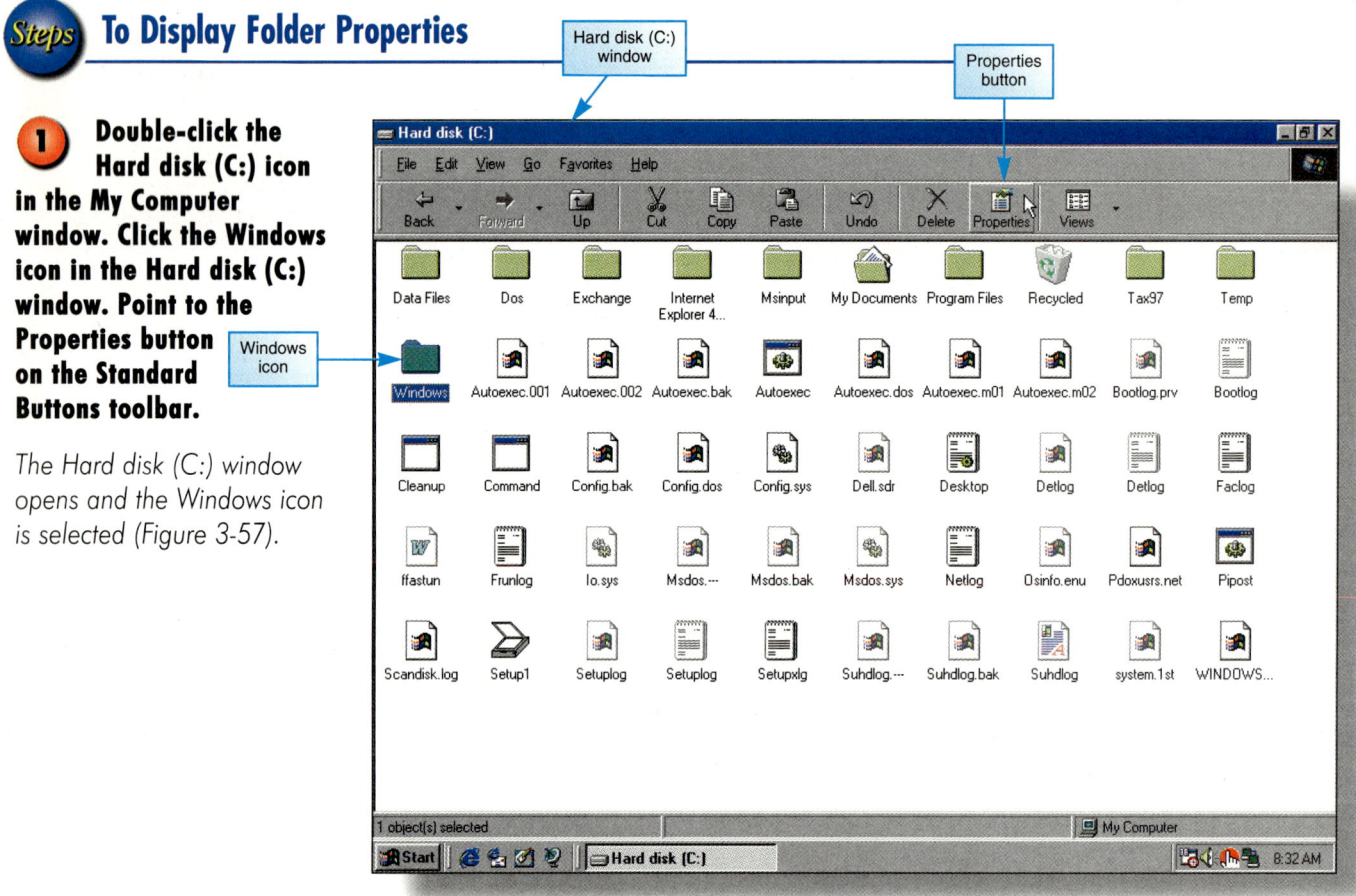

FIGURE 3-57

Properties of Objects • WIN 3.47

PROJECT 3

② Click the Properties button. Point to the Cancel button.

The Windows Properties dialog box displays (Figure 3-58). The Windows folder name displays near the top of the dialog box. The type, File Folder, is specified. The location of the folder is shown. The size in megabytes and actual bytes displays. The Windows folder contains 8,686 files and 186 folders. These values may be different on your computer. The MS-DOS name (WINDOWS) is the name used for the folder in Microsoft DOS, an operating system available before Windows.

③ Click the Cancel button and then close all open windows.

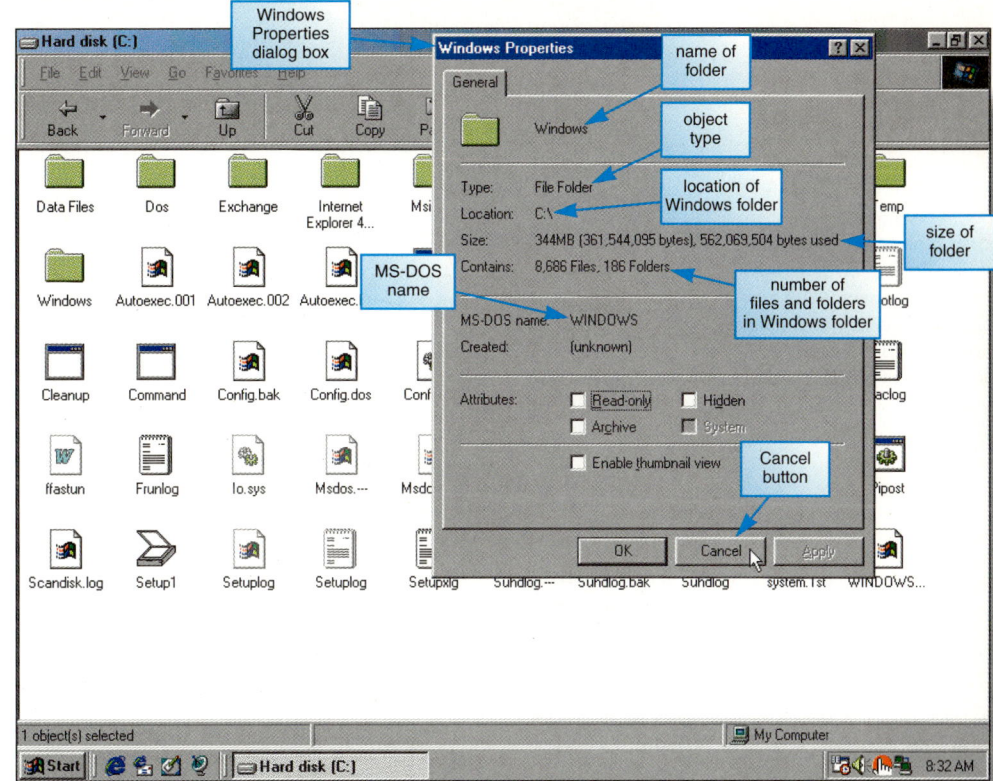

FIGURE 3-58

In the examples of drive and folder properties, you opened windows, pointed to the object, and then clicked the Properties button on the Standard Buttons toolbar. These same steps can be performed in Windows 98 Explorer. Thus, if you have Explorer open and want to display the properties of drive C, point to the drive C icon and then click the Properties button on the Standard Buttons toolbar.

Files and programs also have properties, although these properties are different from the properties for a hard disk and the properties for a folder. As you can see, each object on the desktop and in folder windows has properties.

Other Ways

1. Right-click folder icon, click Properties, click Cancel button
2. Click folder icon, on File menu click Properties, click Cancel button
3. Select folder icon, press ALT+ENTER, press ESC

More About

Find

Some would argue that Find is the handiest Windows 98 tool. If an application program is not represented by an icon on the desktop or on the Start menu, many people use Find to display the icon in the Find dialog box and then double-click the icon to launch the program.

Finding Files or Folders

The Windows folder shown in Figure 3-58 on the previous page contains 8,686 files in 186 folders. Your entire computer, however, will contain many more files and folders. In many instances, you will know the location of files you use often and can open the folder that contains them. In some cases, however, you might know you have a certain file on your computer but you have no idea in what folder it is located. To manually search every folder on your computer to find the file would be time-consuming and, perhaps, impossible. Fortunately, Windows 98 provides a **Find command** that allows you to find the location of a file if you know its name or even if you know some text that is included in the file.

Finding a File by Name

If you know the name or partial name of a file, you can use Find to locate the file. Assume, for example, you know a wallpaper bitmap image file named blue rivets exists somewhere on your computer. You want to open the file to see what the image looks like. To find the file, complete the following steps.

 To Find a File by Name

1 **Click the Start button on the taskbar. Point to Find on the Start menu. Point to Files or Folders on the Find submenu.**

The Start menu and Find submenu display (Figure 3-59).

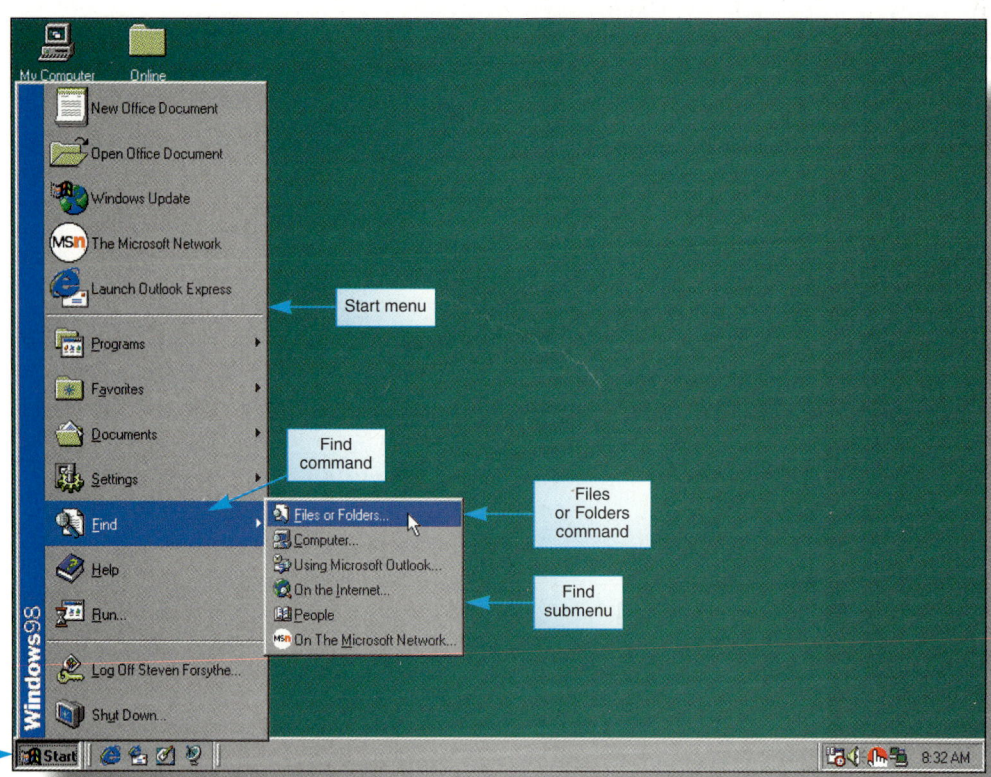

FIGURE 3-59

Finding Files or Folders • WIN 3.49

 Click Files or Folders. Type blue rivets **in the Named text box and then point to the Find Now button.**

The Find: All Files window opens (Figure 3-60). On the Name & Locations sheet, the words you typed and a blinking insertion point display in the Named text box. The Look in box specifies where the search will take place (all of drive C will be examined).

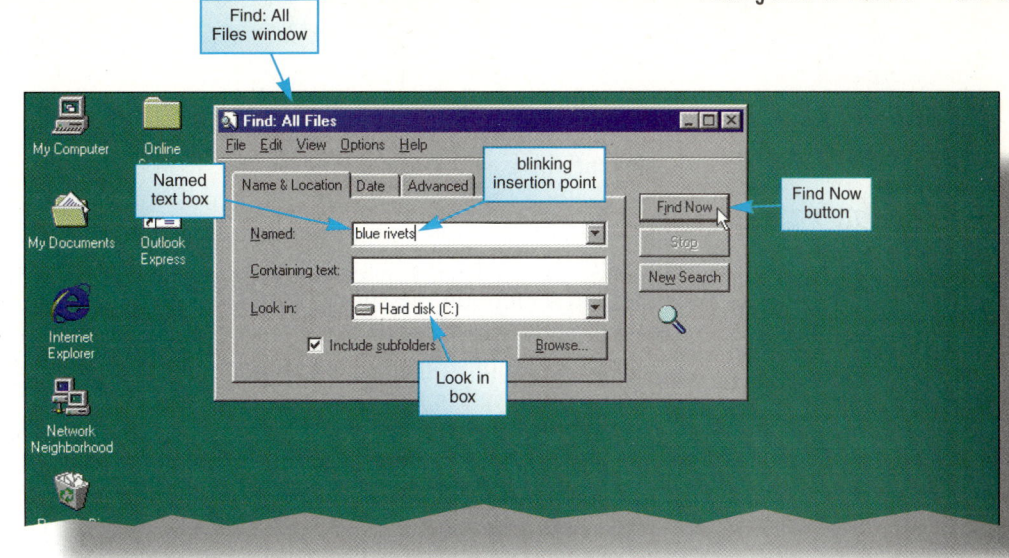

FIGURE 3-60

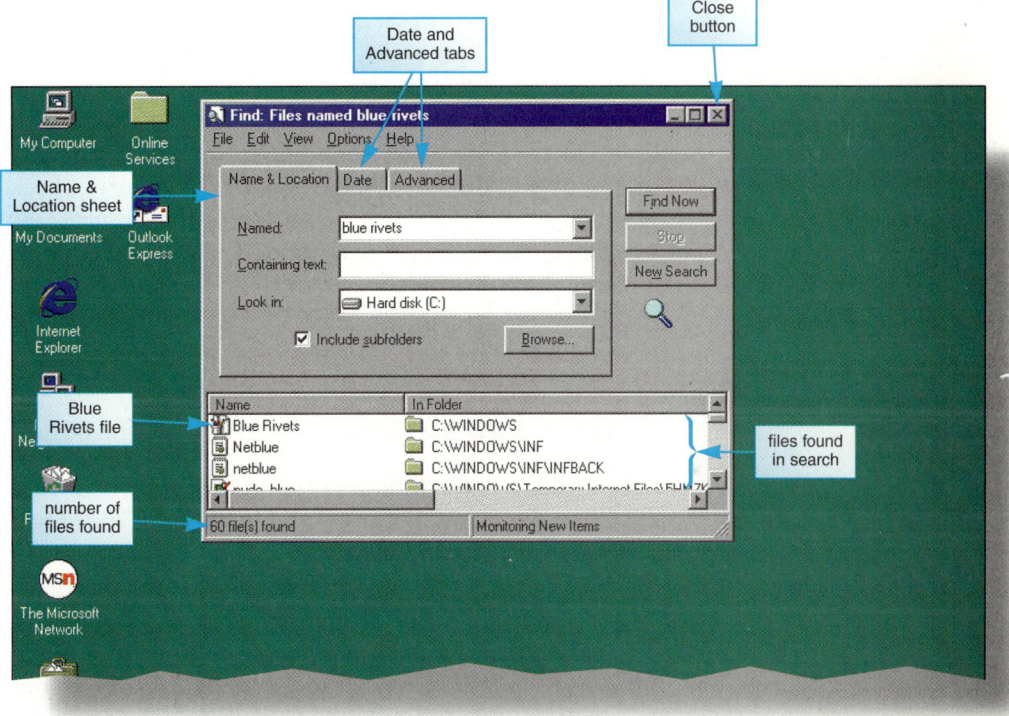

Click the Find Now button.

Windows 98 searches all of drive C looking for files with the term, blue, or the term, rivets, in their names. Any files that are found are listed in the window. Several files were found in this search (Figure 3-61). The first file in the list is named Blue Rivets. The Find window displays the names of the files, the folder where the file is located, the size of the file, the type of files, and the date and time the files were last modified. The file sizes, files types, and modified dates and times are not visible in the dialog box shown in Figure 3-61.

FIGURE 3-61

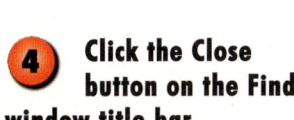 **Click the Close button on the Find window title bar.**

1. Right-click Start button, click Find, type file name, click Find Now button, click Close button
2. Right-click drive icon in All Folders pane, click Find, type file name, click Find Now button, click Close button
3. Press F3 (or CTRL+ESC, press F, press F), type file name, press ENTER

In the Find window in Figure 3-61 on the previous page, after the search is complete you can work with the files found in any manner desired. For example, you can open the file by double-clicking the file icon or by right-clicking the file icon and then clicking Open on the shortcut menu. You can print the file by right-clicking the file icon and then clicking Print on the shortcut menu. You can create a shortcut on the desktop by right-dragging the file icon to the desktop and then clicking Create Shortcut(s) Here on the shortcut menu. You can copy or move the file in the same manner shown for files in My Computer or in Explorer. In summary, any operation you can accomplish from My Computer or from Explorer can be accomplished on the files displayed in the Find window.

If the file you are searching for is an executable program file, such as Notepad, you can launch the program by double-clicking the file icon in the Find window in the same manner as when you double-click the file icon in a window on the desktop.

If you know only a portion of a file's name, you can use an asterisk in the name to represent the remaining characters. For example, if you know a file starts with the letters MSP, you can type msp* in the Named text box. All files that begin with the letters msp, regardless of what letters follow, will display.

The Date and Advanced tabs identify sheets that provide different criteria for a search. On the **Date sheet**, you can specify you want to display all files that were created or modified before or after a certain date. On the **Advanced sheet**, you can specify that you want to find all files that contain the text you enter. If no files are found in the search, the window is empty and the message, 0 file(s) found, displays on the status bar. In this case, you might want to check the file name you entered or examine a different drive to continue your search.

The Find capability of Windows 98 can save much time when you need to locate a file on your computer.

Run

You often will use the Run command with programs stored on a floppy disk that you run one time but do no save on your hard disk. Run has its origins from text-based operating systems such as MS-DOS where the only way to cause a program to execute was to type the name of the program and press the ENTER key.

Run Command

You have seen how to launch programs by double-clicking the program icons in a window or on the desktop, and by clicking the shortcut icons on the Programs submenu or other submenus. Windows 98 also offers the **Run command**, located on the Start menu, to launch programs. The Run command is particularly useful when you are installing new software on your computer.

For example, assume you just purchased a new piece of software from Microsoft. Often, on the CD-ROM or floppy disk containing the software, the instructions will state something such as, Click Start button, click Run, type a:\setup, and click OK. These instructions are common when you buy an application program.

To use the Run command to launch the Paint program (the actual name of the program is MSPAINT), complete the following steps.

Run Command • WIN 3.51

PROJECT 3

 To Launch a Program Using the Run Command

1 **Click the Start button on the taskbar and then point to Run.**

Windows 98 displays the Start menu (Figure 3-62).

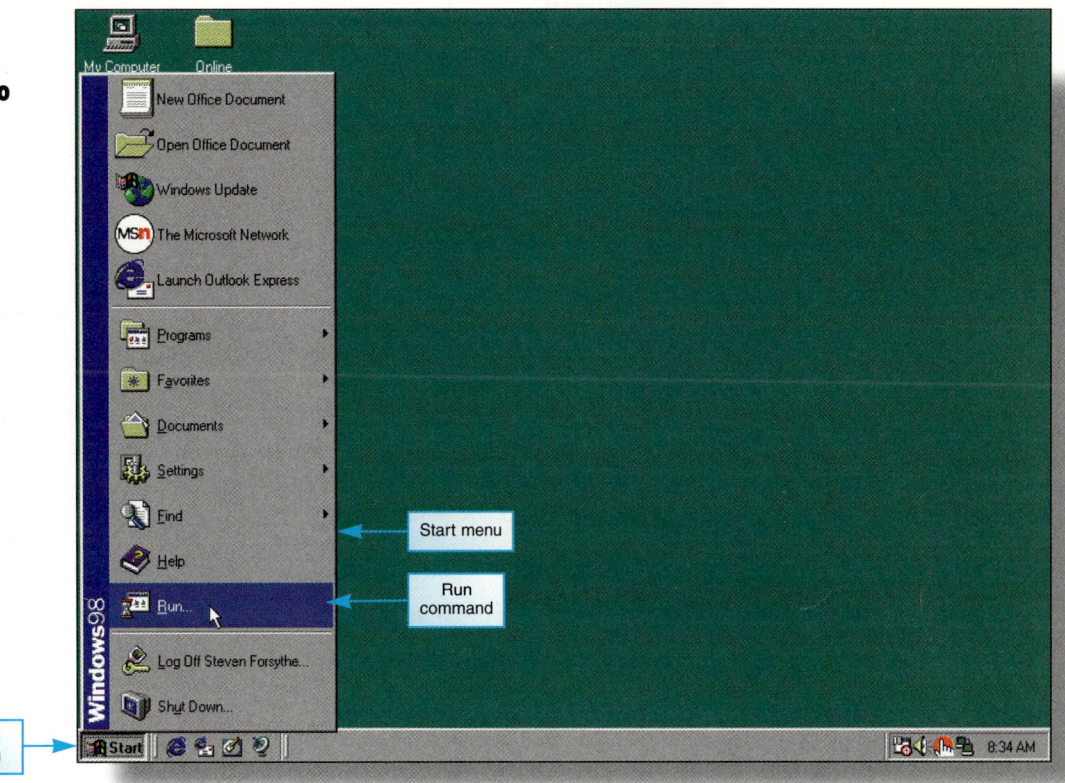

FIGURE 3-62

2 **Click Run. Type** `mspaint` **in the Open text box and then point to the OK button.**

The Run dialog box displays (Figure 3-63). The entry, mspaint, displays in the Open text box.

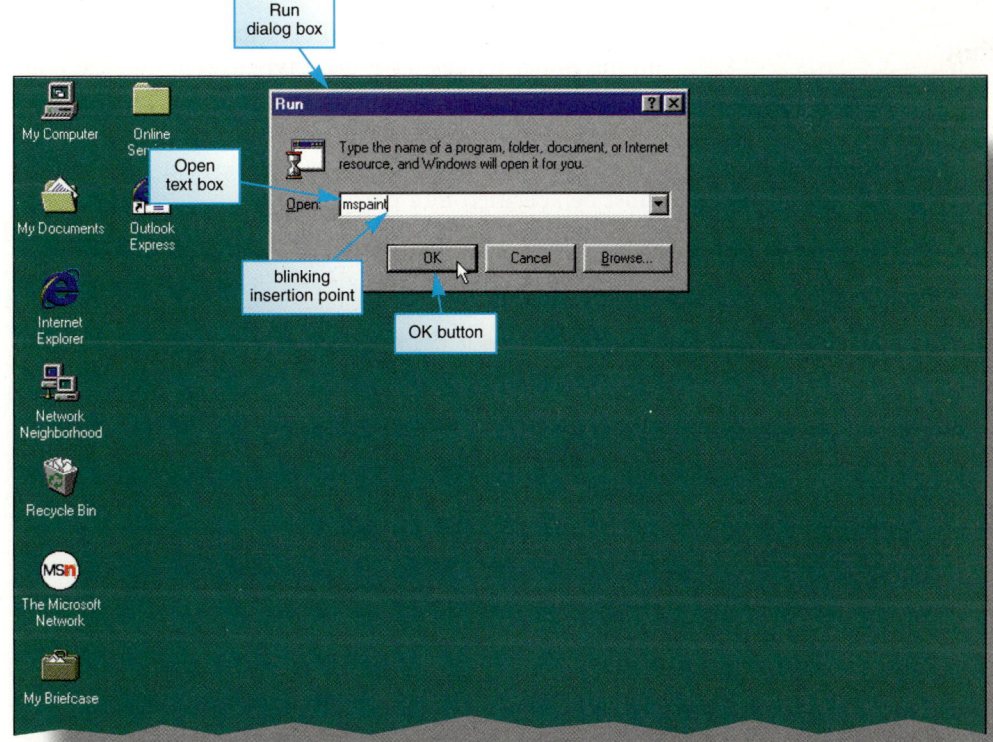

FIGURE 3-63

WIN 3.52 • Project 3 • File, Document, and Folder Management and Windows 98 Explorer

 Click the OK button.

Windows 98 launches the mspaint program (Figure 3-64). You can perform any activities you want with the Paint program.

 Click the Close button on the Paint window title bar.

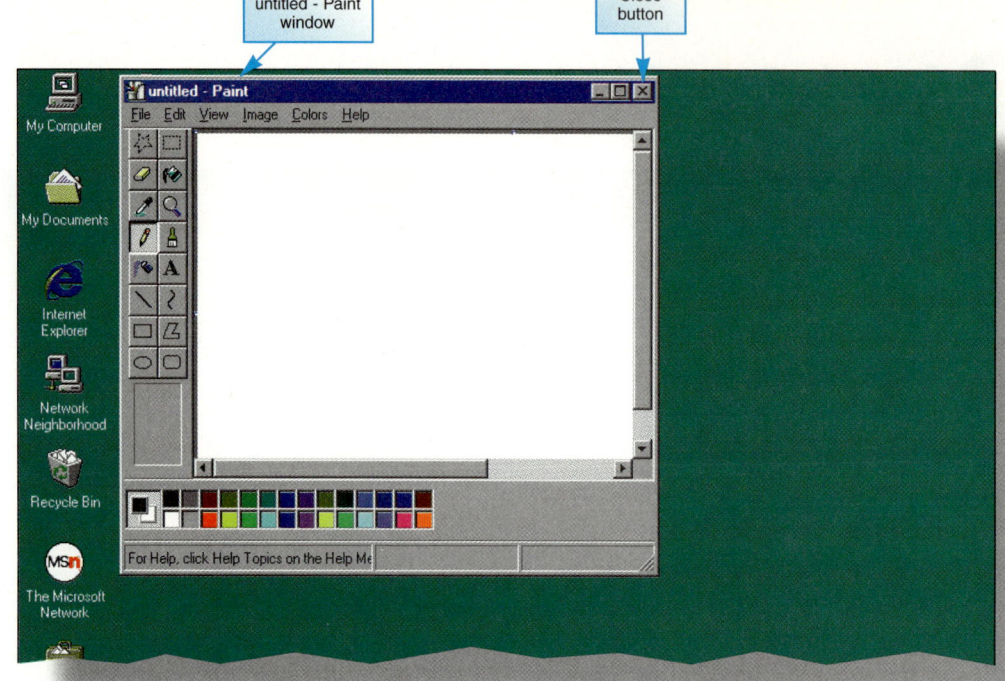

FIGURE 3-64

1. Press CTRL+ESC, press R, type program name, press ENTER

Paths

Paths are left over from MS-DOS and the manner in which you had to identify where a file was stored for access. In Windows 98, you merely need to open a window or, in Explorer, open the folder to access the file. You normally will not be concerned about paths, although you will see them specified often.

You can use the Run command to open folders and files as well as executable programs. If the program, file, or folder is located in the Windows folder, you simply type the name of the program, file, or folder. If the file is located elsewhere, you must type the path for the file. A **path** is the means of navigating to a specific location on a computer or network. To specify a path, you must type the drive letter, followed by a colon (:) and a backslash (\). Then type the name of the folders and subfolders that contain the file. A backslash should precede each folder name. After all the folder names have been typed, type the file name. The file name should be preceded by a backslash. For example, the path name for the Bubbles bitmap image file stored in the Windows folder on drive C is: C:\WINDOWS\BUBBLES.BMP. The file extension (.bmp) identifies the file as a bitmap image file. File extensions always must be specified in a path name.

The Run command is useful to open programs. It also can be used to open files and folders.

Shutting Down Windows 98

After completing your work with Windows 98, you may wish to shut down Windows 98 using the Shut Down command on the Start menu. If you are sure you want to shut down Windows 98, perform the following steps. If you are not sure about shutting down Windows 98, read the steps without actually performing them.

TO SHUT DOWN WINDOWS 98

1. Click the Start button on the taskbar.
2. Click Shut Down on the Start menu.
3. Click the OK button in the Shut Down Windows dialog box.

If you accidentally click Shut Down on the Start menu and you do not want to shut down Windows 98, click the Cancel button in the Shut Down Windows dialog box.

Project Summary

In this project, you viewed icons in windows in different formats. After opening a document and launching an application program, you learned to manage windows on the desktop. Next, you saw how to copy, move, and delete files from an open window. You gained knowledge of Windows 98 Explorer, both in how to display drives, folders, and files, and how to copy, move, rename, and delete files. Finally, you learned about the Find and Run commands.

What You Should Know

Having completed this project, you now should be able to perform the following tasks:

- Cascade Open Windows *(WIN 3.16)*
- Change the Format of the Icons in a Window *(WIN 3.7)*
- Close a Window *(WIN 3.33)*
- Close an Application Program *(WIN 3.35)*
- Close Expanded Folders *(WIN 3.36)*
- Close Open Windows *(WIN 3.21)*
- Close the Exploring Window *(WIN 3.44)*
- Copy a File in Explorer by Right-Dragging *(WIN 3.38)*
- Copy Files from a Folder onto a Floppy Disk *(WIN 3.23)*
- Delete Files from a Floppy Disk *(WIN 3.42)*
- Display Folder Properties *(WIN 3.46)*
- Display Hard Disk Properties *(WIN 3.45)*
- Display the Contents of a Drive *(WIN 3.29)*
- Display the Contents of a Floppy Disk *(WIN 3.40)*
- Expand a Drive *(WIN 3.30)*
- Expand a Folder *(WIN 3.31)*
- Find a File by Name *(WIN 3.48)*
- Launch a Program Using the Run Command *(WIN 3.51)*
- Launch an Application Program from a Window *(WIN 3.14)*
- Launch an Application Program from Explorer *(WIN 3.34)*
- Launch Explorer *(WIN 3.26)*
- Make a Window the Active Window *(WIN 3.17)*
- Open a Document from a Window *(WIN 3.12)*
- Open a Folder Window *(WIN 3.10, WIN 3.22)*
- Open a Folder Window in Explorer *(WIN 3.32)*
- Open and Maximize the My Computer Window *(WIN 3.5)*
- Rename a File *(WIN 3.41)*
- Shut Down Windows 98 *(WIN 3.53)*
- Tile Open Windows *(WIN 3.19)*
- Undo Cascading *(WIN 3.18)*
- Undo Tiling *(WIN 3.20)*
- View the Contents of a Drive *(WIN 3.9)*

Test Your Knowledge

1 True/False

Instructions: Circle T if the statement is true or F if the statement is false.

T (F) 1. A floppy disk generally is faster and has more storage capacity than the hard disk on your computer.
(T) F 2. To open a folder, double-click the folder icon.
(T) F 3. You can open documents from a window, but to launch an application program you must click the Start button and use the Programs submenu.
T (F) 4. After you cascade or tile windows, you must restart Windows 98 in order for the windows to display as they did before you cascaded or tiled them.
(T) F 5. A major feature of Windows 98 is that more than one window can be open at the same time.
(T) F 6. You can copy files from a folder on the desktop onto a floppy disk, but you cannot copy files from the floppy disk into a folder on the desktop.
(T) F 7. The best way to open Windows 98 Explorer is to right-click the My Computer icon and then click Explore.
T F 8. To display the contents of drive C on your computer in the Contents pane of the Exploring window, click the plus sign in the small box next to the drive C icon.
T F 9. After you expand a drive or folder, the information displayed in the Contents pane of the Exploring window is the same as the information displayed below the drive or folder icon in the All Folders pane.
T F 10. To find a file by its name, you can use the Find command on the Start menu.

2 Multiple Choice

Homework 11-08-01

Instructions: Circle the correct response.
1. To display within a folder window the details of the files found in the folder, _____.
   a. click View on the menu bar and then click List
   b. click Edit on the menu bar and then click Details
   c. right-click the folder, point to View, and click Details
   d. click View on the menu bar
2. To cascade all the open windows on the desktop, _____.
   a. click File on the menu bar and then click Cascade Windows
   b. right-click the taskbar, click Cascade Windows on the shortcut menu
   c. right-click the Start button, click Properties, click Cascade Windows, and click the OK button
   d. right-click the desktop, click Cascade Windows on the shortcut menu
3. When using the single window option to browse windows, _____.
   a. clicking the BACK button will display one window back from the window you are currently viewing
   b. you increase the probability of window clutter on your desktop
   c. you cannot use the copy and paste method
   d. the window size changes depending on the number of files and folders you want to display

Test Your Knowledge

4. To select multiple icons in a folder at one time, _____.
   a. right-click each icon
   b. press and hold the SHIFT key and point to each icon you want to select
   c. press and hold the CTRL key and double-click each icon you want to select
   d. press and hold the CTRL key and click each icon you want to select

5. When you right-click an icon and a shortcut menu displays, the command in bold means _____.
   a. this command cannot be used at the current time
   b. this command will be executed if you double-click the icon
   c. this is the only command you can use at this time
   d. this is the preferred command to use and if you click another command, Windows 98 may not be able to carry out the command successfully

6. To display the contents of a folder in the Exploring window, _____.
   a. click the plus sign next to the folder icon
   b. right-click the folder icon in the All Folders pane of the window
   c. point to the folder icon in the Contents pane of the window
   d. click the folder icon in the All Folders pane of the window

7. The Programs folder contained within the Start menu folder contains _____.
   a. all the programs available on the computer
   b. all shortcuts and folders found on the Programs submenu
   c. programs you can execute only if you have a special password
   d. only programs placed on your computer when Windows 98 was loaded onto your computer

8. When you close an expanded folder in the All Folders pane of the Exploring window, _____.
   a. the expansion closes in the All Folders pane and the contents of the folder display in the Contents pane
   b. the Exploring window closes
   c. the computer beeps at you because you cannot perform this activity
   d. the My Computer window displays

9. Before you can copy a file from one folder to another folder in Windows Explorer by right-dragging, you must _____.
   a. display the icon for the file you want to copy in the Contents pane of the Exploring window
   b. display the icon for the file you want to copy in the All Folders pane of the Exploring window
   c. open the My Computer window to display the folder where you want to copy the file
   d. display the folder where you want to copy the file in the Contents pane.

10. The Run command on the Start menu _____.
    a. can be used only when no other way to launch a program is available
    b. is most useful when you are not sure of the actual name of the program
    c. is useful when installing new software on your computer
    d. must be used if the program is stored with a specific path on your hard disk

WIN 3.56 • Project 3 • File, Document, and Folder Management and Windows 98 Explorer

Microsoft **Windows 98**

Test Your Knowledge

3 Understanding the Exploring Window

Instructions: In Figure 3-65, arrows point to several items in the Exploring window. Identify the items or objects in the spaces provided.

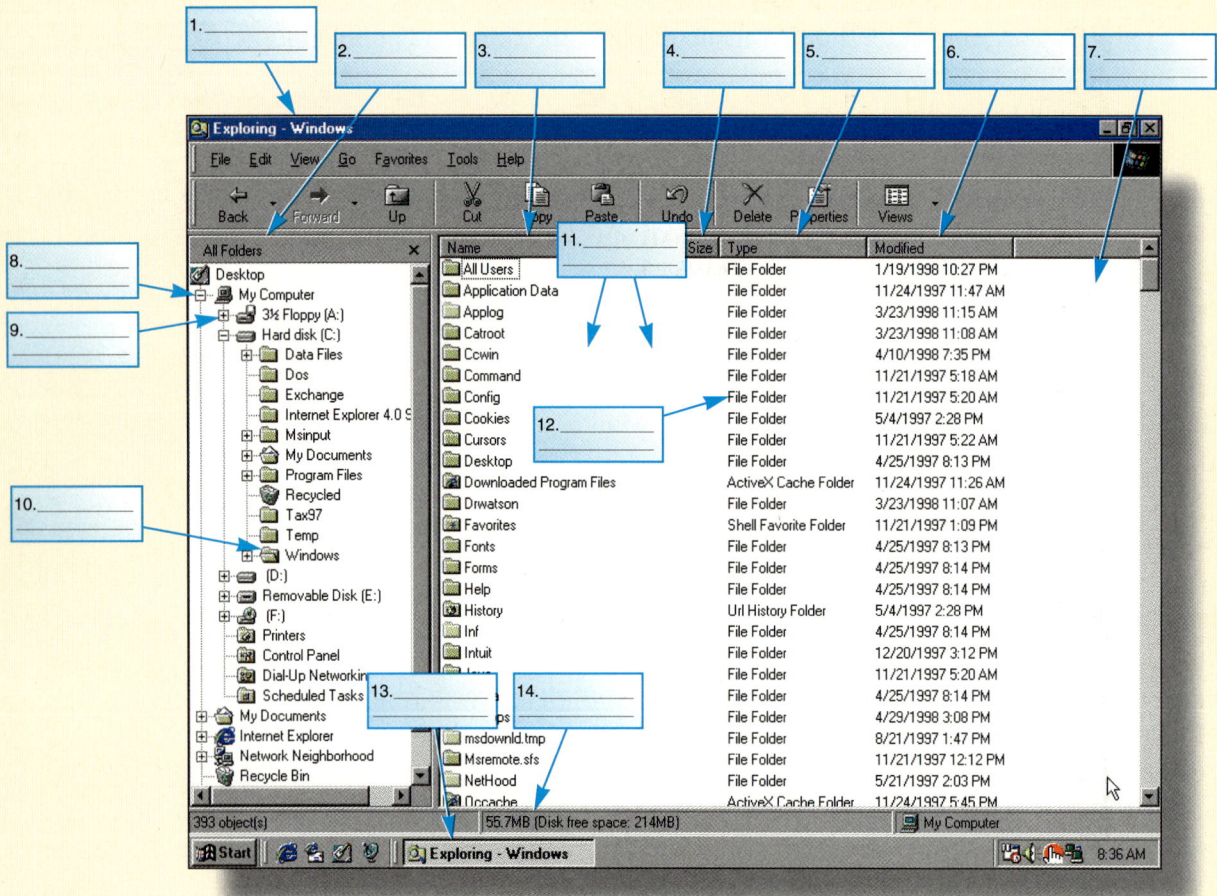

FIGURE 3-65

4 Copying Files

Instructions: Copy the Blue Rivets file shown in Figure 3-66 onto a floppy disk in drive A. In the space below, list all the methods you can use to copy the file and write the specific steps for each method.

_____
_____
_____
_____

Use Help • WIN 3.57

Test Your Knowledge

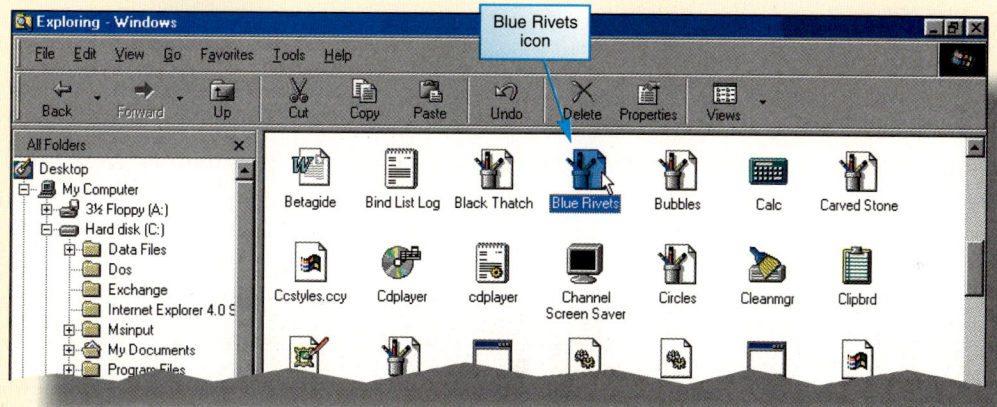

FIGURE 3-66

 Use Help

1 Using Windows Help

Instructions: Use Windows Help and a computer to perform the following tasks.

1. Start Microsoft Windows 98 if necessary.
2. Answer the following questions about paths.
   a. What is a path? _____
   b. What can a path include? _____
   c. How do you specify a path? _____
   d. Specify the path for a file named Harriet's Research Paper that is stored in the My Files folder within the Office folder within the Program Files folder on drive C of your computer. _____
3. Open Windows Help. In the Help Topics: Windows Help dialog box, click the Index tab if necessary, and then type windows explorer in the text box. Answer the following questions about Windows Explorer.
   a. How do you create a folder in Windows Explorer? _____
   b. How do you copy a disk in Windows Explorer? _____
   c. How do you display the full path of a file in the title bar? _____
   d. How do you print an unopened file from Windows Explorer? _____

(continued)

Use Help

Using Windows Help *(continued)*

4. You have recently written a business letter to a manager named Laura Chaney. You explained DVD drives to her. You want to see what else you said in the letter, but you cannot remember the name of the file or where you stored the file on your computer. You read something in your Windows 98 manual that said the Find command could be used to find lost files. Using Help, determine what you must do to find your letter. Write those steps in the spaces provided.

   Step 1: _____
   Step 2: _____
   Step 3: _____
   Step 4: _____

5. You and a friend both recently bought computers. She was lucky and received a color printer as her birthday gift. You would like to print some of your more colorful documents on her color printer. You have heard that for a reasonable cost you can buy a network card and some cable and hook up your computers on a network. Then, you can print documents stored on your computer on her color printer. Using Windows Help, determine if you can share her printer. If so, what must you do in Windows 98 to make this become a reality? Print the Help pages that document your answer.

6. You can hardly believe that last week you won a laptop computer at a charity dance. The application programs on the laptop are the same as those on your desktop computer. The only trouble is that when you use your laptop computer to modify a file, you would like the same file on your desktop also to be modified. In that way, you can work on the file either on your desktop computer or on your laptop computer. A friend mentioned that the My Briefcase feature of Windows 98 allows you to do what you want to do. Using Windows Help, find out all you can about My Briefcase. Print the Help pages that specify how to keep files on both your desktop and laptop computers synchronized with each other.

In the Lab

1 File and Program Properties

Instructions: Use a computer to perform the following tasks and answer the questions.

1. Start Microsoft Windows 98 if necessary.
2. Double-click the My Computer icon. Double-click the drive C icon.
3. Double-click the Windows icon.

In the Lab

4. Scroll until the Blue Rivets icon is visible (Figure 3-67). If the Blue Rivets icon does not display on your computer, find another Paint icon.

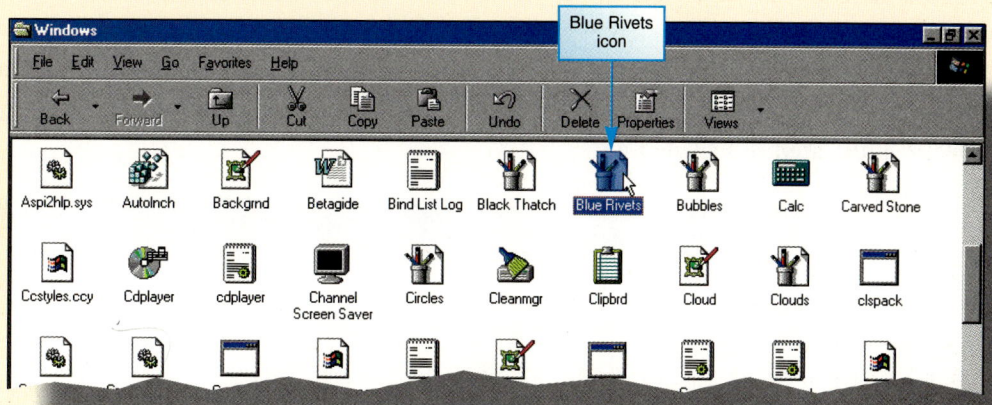

FIGURE 3-67

5. Right-click the Blue Rivets icon. Click Properties on the shortcut menu.
6. Answer the following questions about the Blue Rivets file:
   a. What type of file is Blue Rivets? __bitmap__
   b. What is the path for the location of the Blue Rivets file? __C:\Windows__
   c. What is the size (in bytes) of the Blue Rivets file? __194 bytes__
   d. What is the MS-DOS name of the Blue Rivets file? __BLUERI~1.BMP__ The tilde (~) character is placed in the MS-DOS file name when the Windows 98 file name is greater than eight characters. Windows 98 uses the first six characters of the long file name, the tilde character, and a number to distinguish the file from other files that might have the same first six characters.
   e. When was the file created? __4/23/99__
   f. When was the file last modified? __4/23/99__
   g. When was the file last accessed? __11/7/2000__
7. Click the Cancel button in the Blue Rivets Properties dialog box.
8. Scroll in the Windows window until the Notepad icon displays.
9. Right-click the Notepad icon. Click Properties on the shortcut menu.
10. Answer the following questions:
    a. What type of file is Notepad? __Application__
    b. What is the path of the Notepad file? __C:\WINDOWS__
    c. How big is the Notepad file? __52.0KB__
    d. What is the file extension of the Notepad file? What does it stand for? __exe executable__
    e. What is the file version of the Notepad file? __4.10.1998__
    f. What is the file's description? __Windows Notepad Application File__
    g. Who is the copyright owner of Notepad? __Microsoft__
    h. What language is Notepad written for? __English US__
11. Click the Cancel button in the Notepad Properties dialog box.
12. Close all open windows.

WIN 3.60 • Project 3 • File, Document, and Folder Management and Windows 98 Explorer

In the Lab

2 My Computer

Instructions: Use a computer to perform the following tasks.

1. Start Microsoft Windows 98.
2. Double-click the My Computer icon. Double-click the drive C icon. Double-click the Windows icon.
3. Double-click the Notepad icon in the Windows window to start the Notepad application program. Create the text document illustrated in Figure 3-68.
4. Perform the following steps to save the Notepad document in the My Documents folder using the name, Big Ten Tournament Results. Click File on the menu bar and then click Save As. When the Save As dialog box displays, type Big Ten Tournament Results in the File name text box, verify that My Documents displays in the Save in box, and click the Save button in the Save As dialog box.

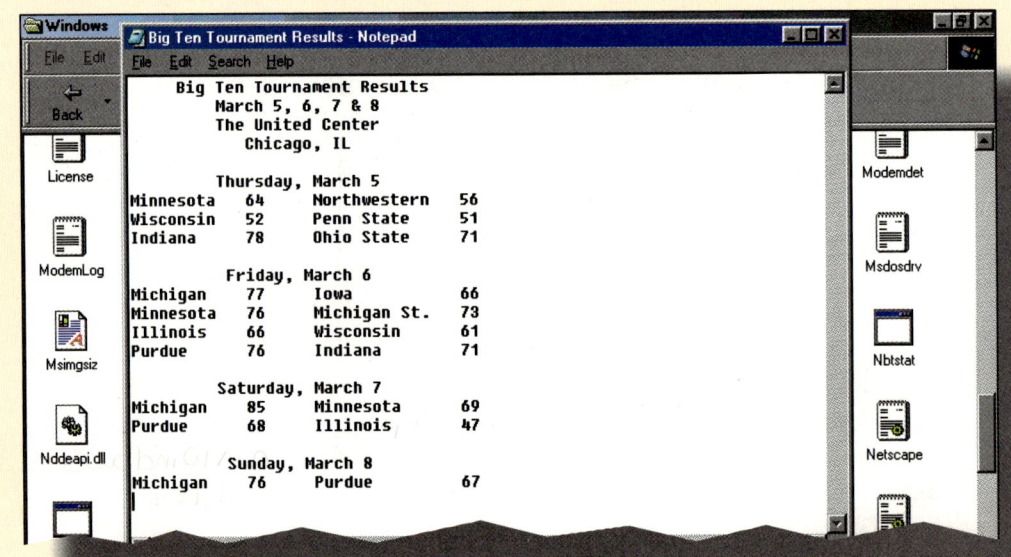

FIGURE 3-68

5. Click the Close button in the Notepad window. Click the Close button in the Windows window.
6. Double-click the My Documents icon on the desktop. Is the Big Ten Tournament Results icon in the My Documents folder? _____
7. Double-click the Big Ten Tournament Results icon to open its window.
8. Right-click the taskbar and click Tile Windows Horizontally on the shortcut menu. What does the desktop look like? _____
9. Click the Big Ten Tournament Results - Notepad button on the taskbar. Using the DOWN ARROW key, move the insertion point to the end of the document. Press the ENTER key. Type Tournament MVP: Robert Traylor and then press the ENTER key.
10. Save the modified document. Print the modified document.
11. Close the Big Ten Tournament Results - Notepad window.
12. Click the My Documents icon on the taskbar.
13. Insert a formatted floppy disk in drive A of your computer.
14. Double-click the My Computer icon on the desktop. Double-click the 3½ Floppy (A:) icon. Are the two windows tiled on the desktop? _____

In the Lab

15. Right-click the taskbar and then click Tile Windows Horizontally on the shortcut menu.
16. Right-drag the Big Ten Tournament Results icon in the My Documents window to an open area of the 3½ Floppy (A:) window. Click Move Here on the shortcut menu. What window(s) contains the Big Ten Tournament Results icon?
17. Close all open windows on the desktop.

3 Windows Explorer

Homework 11-08-01

* Type file JPEG Image
* Last modified Tuesday November 13, 2001, 10:18:58 A
* the size file 116 KB (118,797 bytes) 119,296 bytes used

Instructions: Use a computer to perform the following tasks:

1. Start Microsoft Windows 98.
2. Right-click the Start button on the taskbar, click Explore on the shortcut menu, and maximize the Exploring - Start Menu window (Figure 3-69).

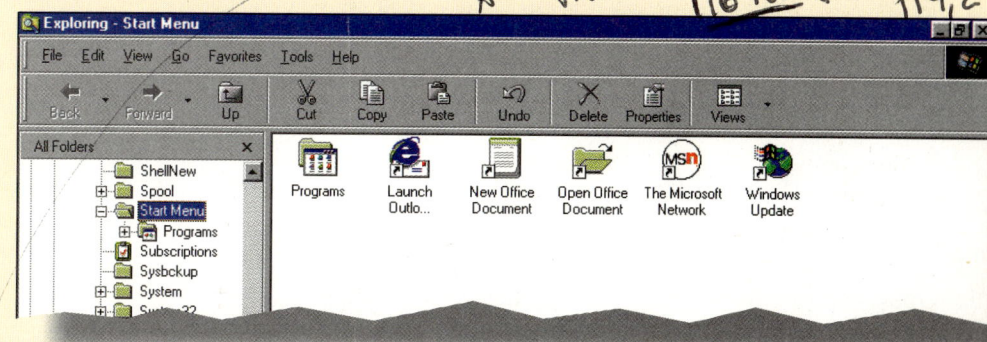

FIGURE 3-69

3. If necessary, scroll to the left in the All Folders pane so the Start Menu and Programs icons are visible. Click the plus sign in the small box to the left of the Programs icon.
4. Click the Internet Explorer icon in the All Folders pane.
5. Double-click the Internet Explorer icon in the Contents pane to launch the Internet Explorer application. What is the URL of the Web page that displays in the Internet Explorer window? _____
6. Click the URL in the Address bar in the Internet Explorer window to select it. Type www.scsite.com/win98 and then press the ENTER key.
7. Right-click the Space Needle clip art image on the Web page, click Save Picture As on the shortcut menu, and click the Save button in the Save Picture dialog box to save the image in the My Documents folder.
8. Click the Close button in the Microsoft Internet Explorer window.
9. Click the minus sign to the left of the Programs folder.
10. Scroll the All Folders pane to make the Windows folder visible and click the minus sign to the left of the Windows folder.
11. Scroll to the top of the All Folders pane to make the 3½ Floppy (A:) icon and My Documents icon visible.
12. Click the My Documents folder.
13. Right-click the Space Needle icon and click Properties.
    What type of file is the Space Needle file? _____ 150,528 bytes 147 KB
    1307 136 bytes 1.24 mB
    When was the file last modified? _____ Capacity 1457 664 byte 1.38 mB
    What is the size of the file? _____ Capacity 1457,664 byte 1.38 mB
14. Click the Cancel button in the Space Needle Properties dialog box.

(continued)

WIN 3.62 • Project 3 • File, Document, and Folder Management and Windows 98 Explorer

In the Lab

Windows Explorer *(continued)*

15. Insert a formatted floppy disk in drive A of your computer.
16. Right-drag the Space Needle icon over the 3½ Floppy (A:) icon. Click Move Here on the shortcut menu. Click the 3½ Floppy (A:) icon in the All Folders pane. Is the Space Needle file stored on drive A? _To d_
    To drive A
17. Click Tools on the menu bar, point to Find, and click People on the Find submenu.
18. Click the Look in box arrow and then click MSN in the Look in list box.
19. Click the Name text box and then type Steven Forsythe in the text box. Click the Find Now button. How many entries are listed for Steven Forsythe? _____
    What is the first e-mail address listed for Steven Forsythe? _____
20. Click the Close button in the Find People dialog box.
21. Click the Close button in the Exploring - 3½ Floppy (A:) window.

4 Windows Toolbars

Instructions: Use a computer to perform the following tasks.

1. Open and maximize the My Computer window.
2. Display the icons in the My Computer window using the Large Icons format
3. Click View on the menu bar and then point to Toolbars (Figure 3-70).

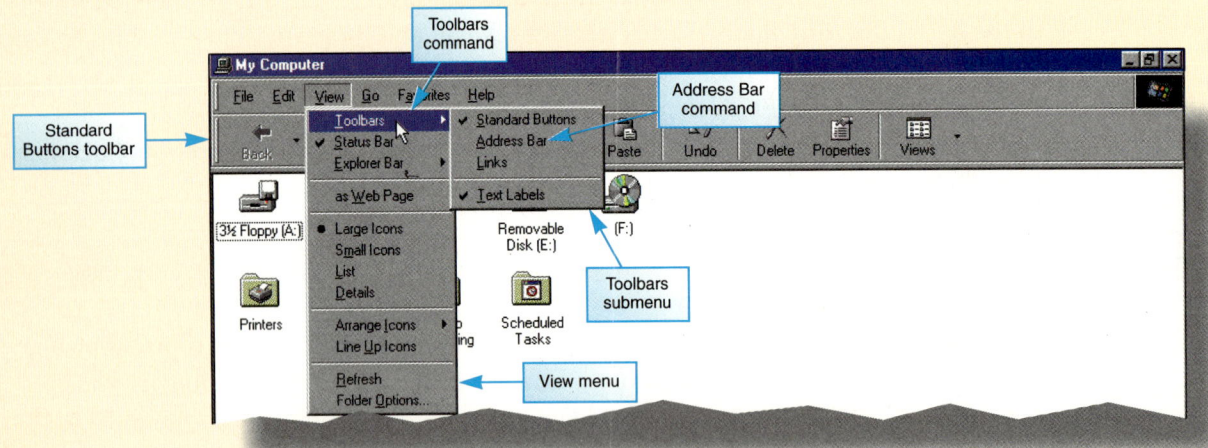

FIGURE 3-70

4. If a check mark does not display to the left of the Address Bar command on the Toolbars submenu, click Address Bar. The Address bar displays in the My Computer window.
5. Click the Address bar arrow.
6. Click the drive C icon in the Address list box. How did the window change? _____
   _____
7. Double-click the Windows icon. What happened? _____
   _____

In the Lab

8. In the Windows window, if the Standard Buttons toolbar does not display, click View on the menu bar, point to Toolbars, and then click Standard Buttons on the Toolbars submenu.
9. Scroll down if necessary until the Black Thatch icon displays in the window. If the Black Thatch icon does not display on your computer, find another Paint icon. Click the Black Thatch icon and then click the Copy button on the Standard Buttons toolbar.
10. Insert a formatted floppy disk in drive A of your computer.
11. Click the Address bar arrow.
12. Click the 3½ Floppy (A:) icon in the Address bar list box. What happened? _____
_____
13. In the 3½ Floppy (A:) window, click the Paste button on the Standard Buttons toolbar. The Black Thatch icon displays in the 3½ Floppy (A:) window (Figure 3-71).
14. Click the Black Thatch icon in the 3½ Floppy (A:) window to select the icon, click the Delete button on the Standard Buttons toolbar, and then click the Yes button in the Confirm File Delete dialog box.
15. In the 3½ Floppy (A:) window, return the toolbar status to what it was prior to step 4.
16. Close the 3½ Floppy (A:) window.

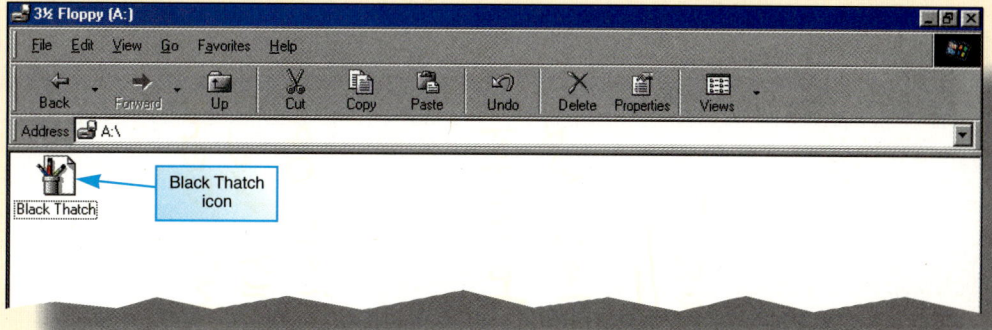

FIGURE 3-71

The difficulty of these case studies varies:
▶ are the least difficult; ▶▶ are more difficult; and ▶▶▶ are the most difficult.

1 ▶ Your seven-year old brother is a graphics nut. He cannot get enough of the graphics that display on computers. Lately, he has been hounding you to show him all the graphics images that are available on your computer. You have done your best to put him off but finally have agreed to show him. Using techniques you learned in Project 3, display the icons for all the graphics image files that are stored on your computer (*Hint*: Many graphics files on Windows 98 computers contain a file extension of .bmp. Others may have a file extension of .pcx, .tif, or .gif). Once you have found the graphics files, display all of them and then print the three you like best.

Cases and Places

2 ▸ Your employer suspects that the computer you use normally has been used by someone else during off-hours for non-company business. She has asked you to search your computer for all files that have been created or modified during the last ten days. When you find the files, determine if any of them are Notepad files or Paint files that you did not create or modify. If so, summarize the number of them and the date on which they were created or modified in a brief report to your employer.

3 ▸▸ Backing up files is an important way to protect data and ensure it is not lost or destroyed accidentally. File backup on a personal computer can use a variety of devices and techniques. Using the Internet, a library, personal computer magazines, or other resources, determine the types of devices used to store backed up data, the schedules, methods, and techniques for backing up data, and the consequences of not backing up data. Write a brief report of your findings.

4 ▸▸ A hard disk must be maintained to be used most efficiently. This maintenance includes deleting old files, defragmenting a disk so it is not wasteful of space, and from time to time, finding and attempting to correct disk failures. Using the Internet, a library, Windows 98 Help, or other research facilities, determine the maintenance that should be performed on hard disks, including the type of maintenance, when it should be performed, how long it takes to perform the maintenance, and the risks, if any, of not performing the maintenance. Write a brief report on the information you obtain.

5 ▸▸ The quest for more and faster disk storage continues as application programs grow larger and create sound and graphics files. One technique for increasing the amount of data that can be stored on a disk is disk compression. Disk compression programs, using a variety of mathematical algorithms, store data in less space on a hard disk. Many companies sell software you can load on your computer to perform the task. Windows 98 has disk compression capabilities as part of the operating system. Visit a computer store and find two disk compression programs you can buy. Write a brief report comparing the two packages to the disk compression capabilities of Windows 98. Discuss the similarities and differences between the programs and identify the program that claims to be the most efficient in compressing data.

6 ▸▸▸ Some in the computer industry think the Windows 98 operating system is deficient when it comes to ease of file management. Therefore, they have developed and marketed software that augments the operating systems to provide different and, they claim, improved services for file management. Visit a computer store and inquire about such products for Windows 98. Try a few of the activities in Project 3 using some of these products. What do you think? Write a brief report comparing the products you tested with Windows 98. Explain which you prefer and why.

7 ▸▸▸ Data stored on disk is one of a company's more valuable assets. If that data were to be stolen, lost, or compromised so it could not be accessed, the company literally could go out of business. Therefore, companies go to great lengths to protect their data. Visit a company or business in your area. Find out how it protects its data against viruses, unauthorized access, and even against such natural disasters as fire and tornadoes. Prepare a brief report that describes the company's procedures. In your report, point out any areas where you see the company has not protected its data adequately.

Microsoft Windows 98

PROJECT 4

Modifying Your Desktop Work Environment

OBJECTIVES

You will have mastered the material in this project when you can:

- Open the Display Properties dialog box
- Add wallpaper or a pattern to the desktop
- Change the desktop appearance
- Add a screen saver
- Move, hide, and resize the taskbar
- Add and remove a toolbar on the taskbar
- Add and remove a shortcut on a toolbar
- Add and remove a toolbar in a folder
- Add an Explorer bar and background to a folder
- Display a folder as a Web page
- Choose the Classic style, Web style, and default Custom style as the desktop view
- View the settings of the current desktop view
- Work with icons, windows, and folders in Web style

Microsoft **Windows 98**

Lions and Tigers and Toast—Oh My!

Screen Savers to Suit Your Taste

Do you like your toast light or dark? With strawberry jam or grape jelly? Served on a plate or flying on your monitor? Toast no longer is a simple breakfast item. For the past decade, it has found its way to desktops all over the world, thanks to Berkeley Systems's After Dark. This set of unique screen savers includes Flying Toasters, which generates capricious multicolored cartoon images of the appliance and toast, complete with wings that float across the screen.

Berkeley Systems's roots stem back to 1987 when three developers received a federal grant to write software to assist visually impaired computer users. At that time, computer monitors were plagued with phosphor burnt-in images that developed when the same form

stayed in one place on the screen for a long period of time. Two years later, the company developed the After Dark screen saver utility to move images to various locations on the screen when the computer was idle.

Today, more than three million After Dark products have been sold worldwide, and several monitor manufacturers include a mini-After Dark edition with their products. Along with the Flying Toasters, other After Dark pop-culture icons are Bad Dog, Mowin' Man, and Boris the Kitten.

The After Dark images, however, have permeated more than desktops. The products have been seen in the movies, *The Net*, *Malice*, and *Copy Cat*, and on the television shows, *Seinfeld*, *The X-Files*, and *Beverly Hills 90210*. Their likenesses also appear on clothing, ranging from neckwear to underwear.

The designers at Berkeley Systems, which is named after its Berkeley, California, location, work in an environment maximized for creativity. For example, they can take the slide instead of the stairs from the second to the first floor. Lunchtime equates to playtime when they can play Mortal Kombat in the kitchen and then go outside to play Ultimate Frisbee, basketball, or croquet.

More than one million people get their monthly fill of toaster mania by visiting Toasted, the Berkeley Website (www.toasted.com), which debuted in 1995. Its self-proclaimed toastmaster milks the toaster concept by featuring Toast Opera, a comedy program resembling the good old days of radio. The U and UR Toaster Gallery features photos submitted by people from around the world holding their prized toasters and favorite pieces of toast.

After Dark set the stage for innovative screen savers, but many other developers have produced unique products. Thousands of screen saver utilities are available, both in the commercial and shareware flavors. In Project 4, you will explore Microsoft's offerings included in Windows 98. Several companies have created ergonomic utilities that exercise tired eyes and help alleviate muscle strain. Others feature The Simpsons, tropical reefs, and rain forests. Animals abound – from actual aardvarks and zebras to virtual pets and fish requiring feeding and attention. You even can create a personalized screen saver to display your prized wedding, honeymoon, children, and pet photos.

Certainly this array of custom products allows you to find a screen saver that modifies your desktop and adds personality to your work environment.

Microsoft Windows 98

Modifying Your Desktop Work Environment

PROJECT 4

CASE PERSPECTIVE

Several months ago, you installed Windows 98 on your computer. Since then, you have spent most of your time learning to communicate with Windows 98, starting programs and creating documents, exploring Windows Help, working on the desktop, and learning file and desktop management. Because you spend so much time interacting with your computer, the manner in which you interact with the desktop and the objects on the desktop are important to you. You want to modify the properties of your desktop display, including changing some colors you find undesirable. You want to personalize the objects on the desktop (taskbar, toolbars, and folder windows) and change the desktop view. Your assignment in this project is to customize your desktop work environment to suit your needs.

Introduction

In Project 1, you viewed the desktop in the Classic style and Web style. In Project 2, you worked with documents and folders on the desktop, minimized the open windows on the desktop, created shortcuts on the desktop, turned on the Active Desktop™, and added an active desktop item to the desktop. In Project 3, you managed the windows on the desktop by cascading and tiling the windows.

In addition to learning about and working on the desktop, you also should be able to modify the desktop on which you work. In this project, you will learn more about the properties of the desktop, modify the desktop by changing the desktop background, modify the desktop appearance, and add a screen saver to the desktop. You will customize the taskbar by changing the position of the taskbar, hiding the taskbar, adding a toolbar to the taskbar, and adding shortcuts to a toolbar. In addition, you will learn how to change the desktop view to the Classic style, Web style, and Custom style.

Changing Your Desktop Working Environment

Windows 98 provides a variety of tools that allow you to modify the screen desktop on which you work. As mentioned in Project 1, most items on the desktop, including the desktop itself, are considered objects. Every object in Windows 98 has **properties**, which describe the object. In many cases, an object's properties can be changed to fit your needs.

Desktop Properties

A beginning point to modify your desktop working environment is to change, if necessary, the properties of the desktop display. These properties include the color and design of the desktop, the settings of the desktop that determine size and color of the images on the desktop, the appearance of open windows on the desktop, and the screen saver.

To make changes to the desktop display, first you must open the Display Properties dialog box. To open the Display Properties dialog box, complete the following steps.

More About

The Desktop

You might be surprised at the many different preferences people have for their computer desktops. Some like quiet, cool colors, while others like bright, glittery schemes. No single correct way exists — everyone is an individual. That's why Microsoft and other operating system designers give you the capability of customizing your computer desktop.

 To Open the Display Properties Dialog Box

1 **Right-click an open area of the desktop. Point to Properties on the shortcut menu.**

A shortcut menu displays (Figure 4-1).

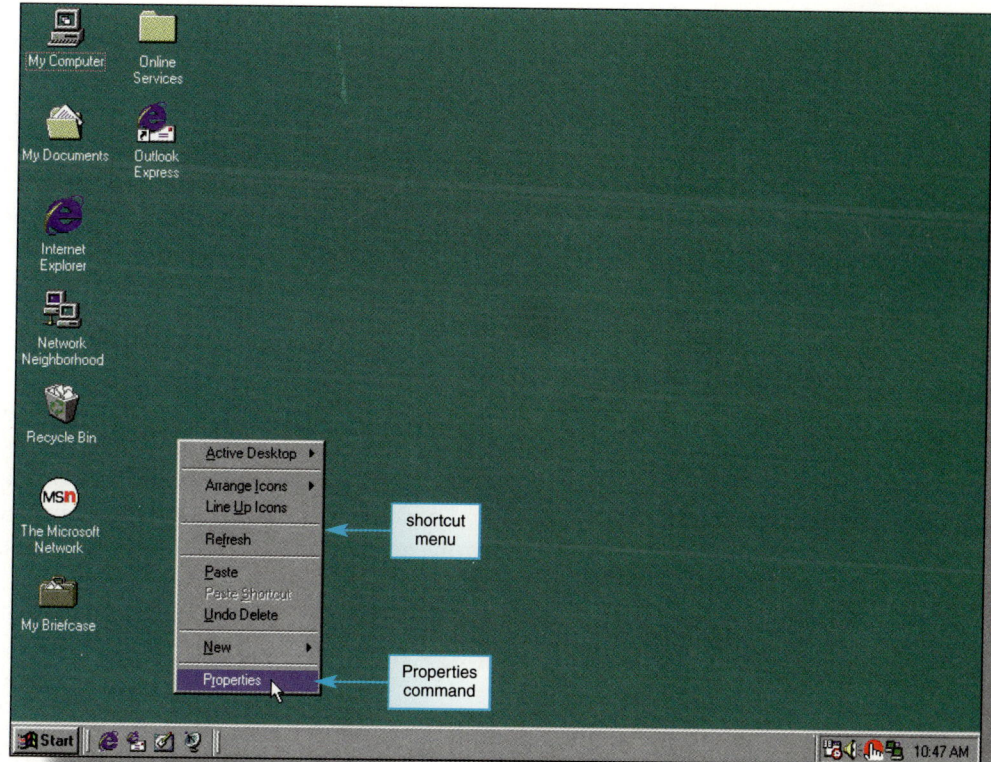

FIGURE 4-1

WIN 4.6 • Project 4 • Modifying Your Desktop Work Environment

2 Click Properties. If necessary, click the Background tab.

The Display Properties dialog box and the Background sheet display (Figure 4-2). Seven tabs display in the dialog box. The Display Properties dialog box may display differently on your desktop.

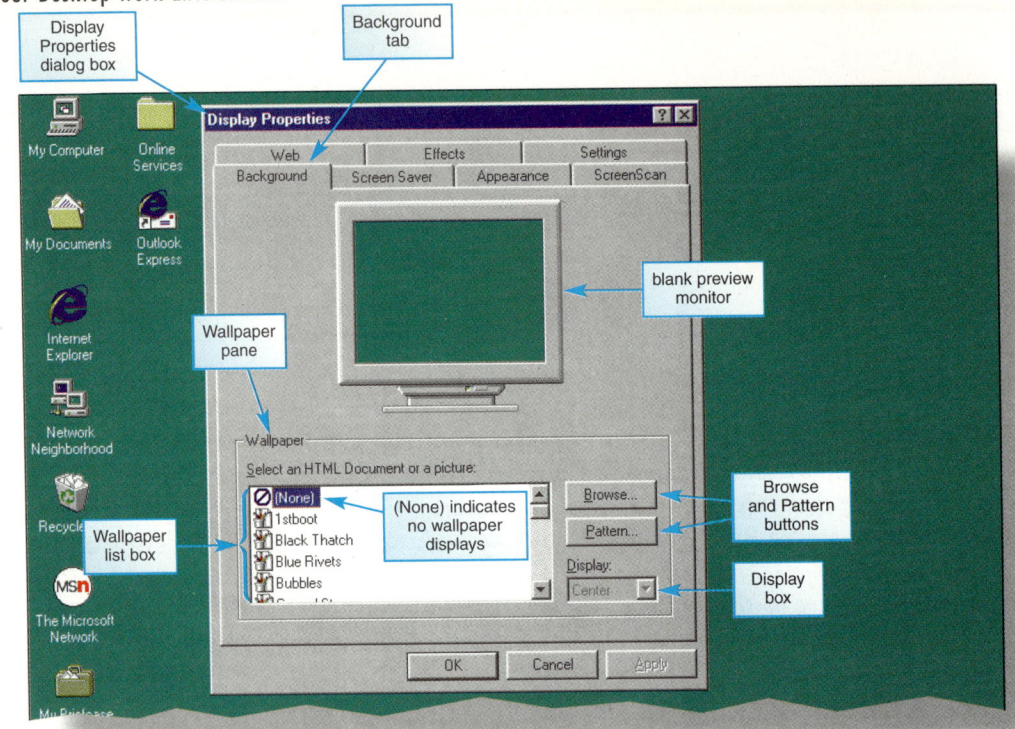

FIGURE 4-2

Other Ways

1. Double-click My Computer icon, double-click Control Panel icon, double-click Display icon
2. Click Start button, point to Settings on Start menu, click Control Panel on submenu, double-click Display icon

More About

The Desktop Background

When you are working in Windows 98 and not with a maximized application, the desktop background is the singlemost dominant feature of your computer screen. You should choose the background carefully because your choice can affect your mood, the ease of using your computer, and even others who work nearby.

In Figure 4-2, the Background sheet in the Display Properties dialog box contains a blank preview monitor, a Wallpaper pane, and three buttons (OK, Cancel, and Apply). The Wallpaper pane contains a list box, two buttons (Browse and Pattern), and the Display box. The Wallpaper list box is identified by the text, Select an HTML Document or a picture, and contains a list of the available wallpapers you can use to decorate the desktop. When a wallpaper name is selected in the list box, the entry in the Display box controls how the wallpaper will display on the desktop (tiled, stretched, or centered).

Changing the Desktop Background

You can change the desktop background by adding a pattern or wallpaper to the desktop. In the following steps, it is important to realize that you should not actually change the permanent desktop on which you are working unless you are using your own computer and wish to make the changes. The instructions within the steps in the next two sections are organized so that you will make no permanent changes to your desktop background.

Adding Wallpaper to the Desktop

One method to modify your desktop background is to add wallpaper. The image or pattern that displays as a background on your desktop is called **wallpaper**. You can use most graphic files (bitmaps (.bmp), GIF files (.gif) and JPEG files (.jpeg)) or HTML documents (Web pages) as wallpaper. Several graphic files that can be used as wallpaper are included with Windows 98, or you can use one of your own files as your wallpaper. Currently, the highlighted (None) name in the Wallpaper list box (see Figure 4-2) indicates no wallpaper displays on the desktop.

When you click a wallpaper name in the list box, a preview of how the wallpaper will look displays in the preview monitor. As mentioned earlier, the wallpaper

Changing Your Desktop Working Environment • WIN 4.7

displays on the desktop as tiled, stretched, or centered, depending on the current setting in the Display box. The **Tile setting**, designed for use with small images, repeats an image across the desktop. The **Stretch setting** enlarges an image to fill the desktop. The **Center setting** displays an image in the center of the desktop.

To see how to change the desktop background by adding wallpaper, complete the following steps.

 To Add a Wallpaper to the Desktop

1 Write down on a piece of paper the name in the Wallpaper list box and the display option in the Display box on your computer.

2 Scroll the wallpaper list until Clouds displays. Click Clouds. If Clouds is not in the Wallpaper list on your computer, click another wallpaper name. Point to the Display box arrow.

Depending on the option in the Display box, the Clouds picture will be tiled, centered, or stretched on the desktop in the preview monitor (Figure 4-3). In Figure 4-3, the Clouds image is centered on the desktop because the word, Center, displays in the Display box.

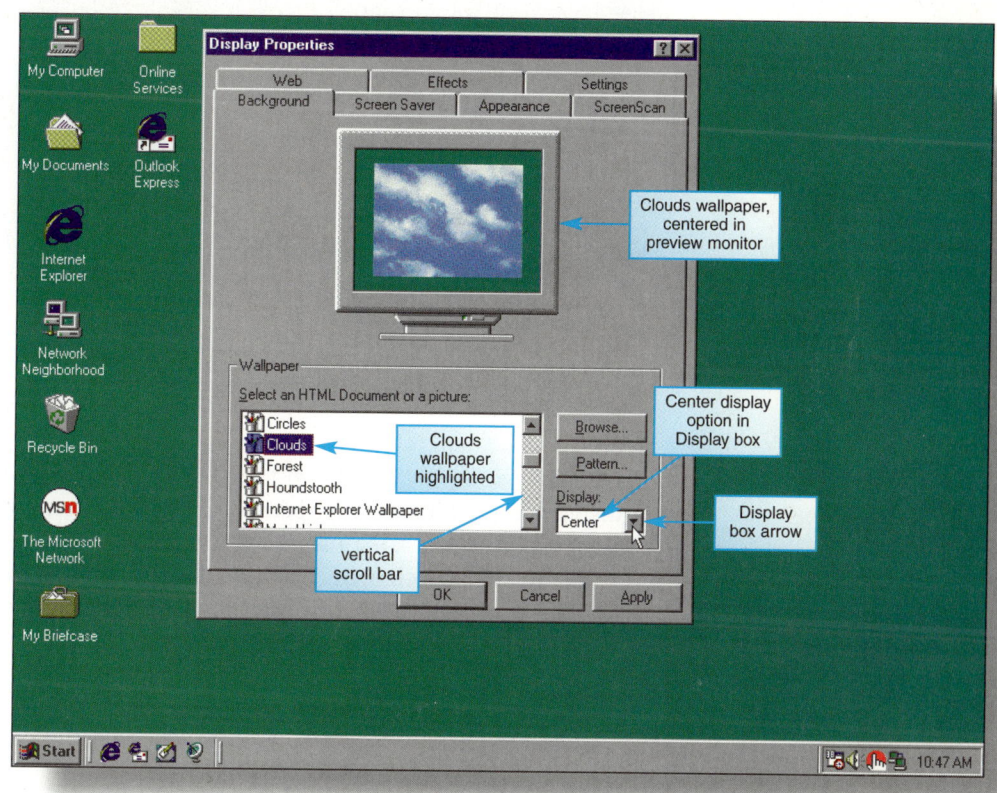

FIGURE 4-3

3  Click the Display box arrow and then point to Stretch.

The Display list box displays with the Stretch option highlighted (Figure 4-4).

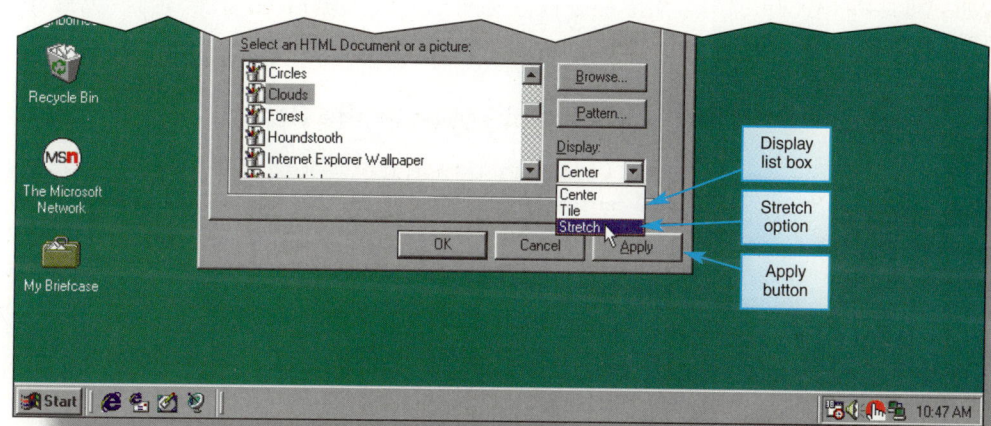

FIGURE 4-4

WIN 4.8 • Project 4 • Modifying Your Desktop Work Environment

  Click Stretch. Click the Apply button.

When you click Stretch in the Display list box, the Clouds wallpaper stretches to cover the desktop in the preview monitor. When you click the Apply button, the Clouds wallpaper covers the desktop on your computer and the Display Properties dialog box remains open on the desktop (Figure 4-5).

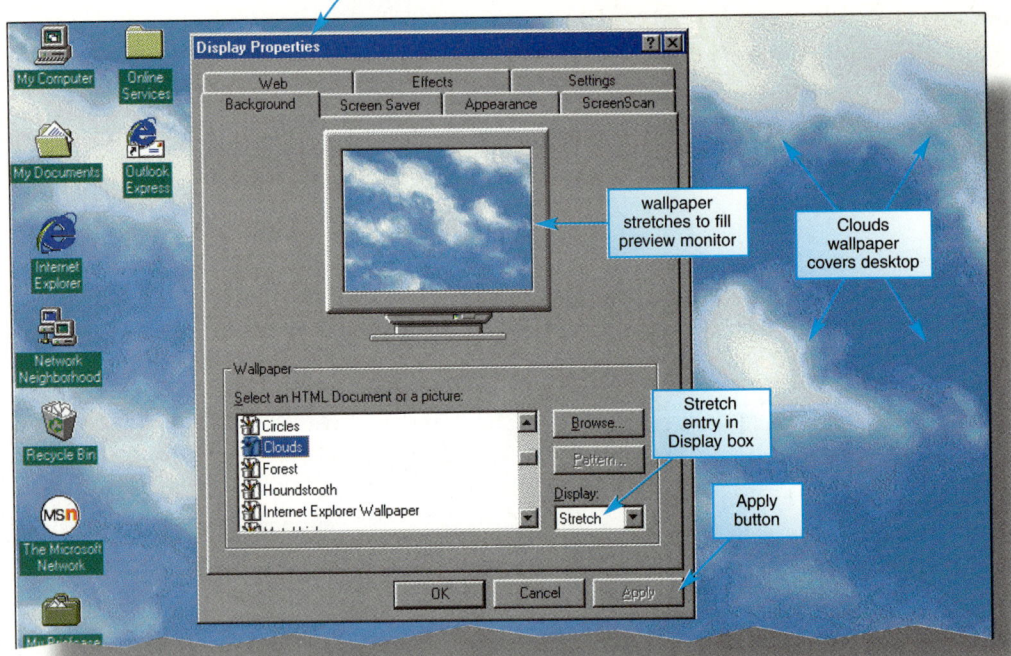

FIGURE 4-5

1. Press TAB until name in Wallpaper list box is highlighted, press DOWN ARROW until wallpaper name highlighted, press TAB until entry in Display box is highlighted, press LEFT ARROW or RIGHT ARROW to highlight Tile, Center, or Stretch, press ALT+A

Clicking the Apply button in the Display Properties dialog box shown in Figure 4-5 displays the Clouds wallpaper on the desktop on your computer and the Display Properties dialog box remains open. This allows you to see the effect of your change and to make another change. Clicking the OK button in the dialog box, displays the Clouds wallpaper on the desktop and closes the Display Properties dialog box.

TO REMOVE WALLPAPER

1. Click the Display box arrow and then click the display option you wrote down in Step 1 on the previous page.

2. Scroll the Wallpaper list box until the name of the wallpaper you wrote down in Step 1 on the previous page displays, click the wallpaper name, and click the Apply button.

The display option and wallpaper name are returned to their original settings in the Display Properties dialog box, and the Clouds wallpaper is removed from the preview monitor and the desktop (Figure 4-6).

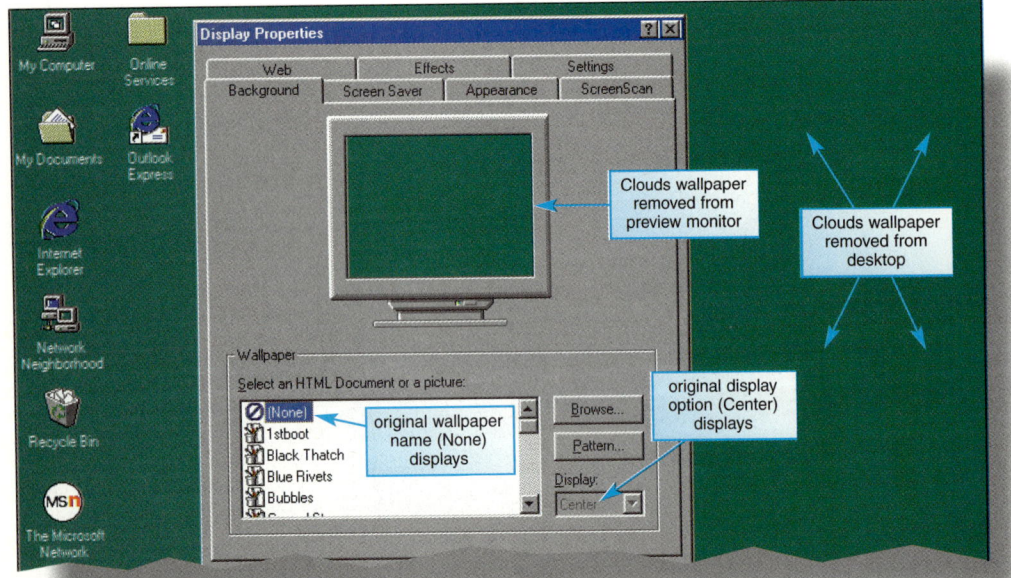

FIGURE 4-6

Adding a Pattern to the Desktop

Another method to modify your desktop background is to add a pattern to the desktop. A **pattern** is a design you can use to decorate your desktop. You can add one of the patterns included with Windows 98 to the desktop or modify an existing pattern and add it to the desktop. Perform the following steps to add the Circuit pattern to the desktop.

Steps: To Add a Pattern to the Desktop

1 Click the Pattern button in the Display Properties dialog box. Write down on a piece of paper the Pattern name in the Pattern list box on your computer. Point to Circuits in the Pattern list box.

The Pattern dialog box displays (Figure 4-7). The Pattern dialog box contains a message about choosing a pattern, the Pattern list box, the Preview pane, and three buttons. The Pattern list box contains a list of available patterns. Currently, (None) displays in the list box and the preview pane does not display a pattern. The Edit Pattern button is dimmed.

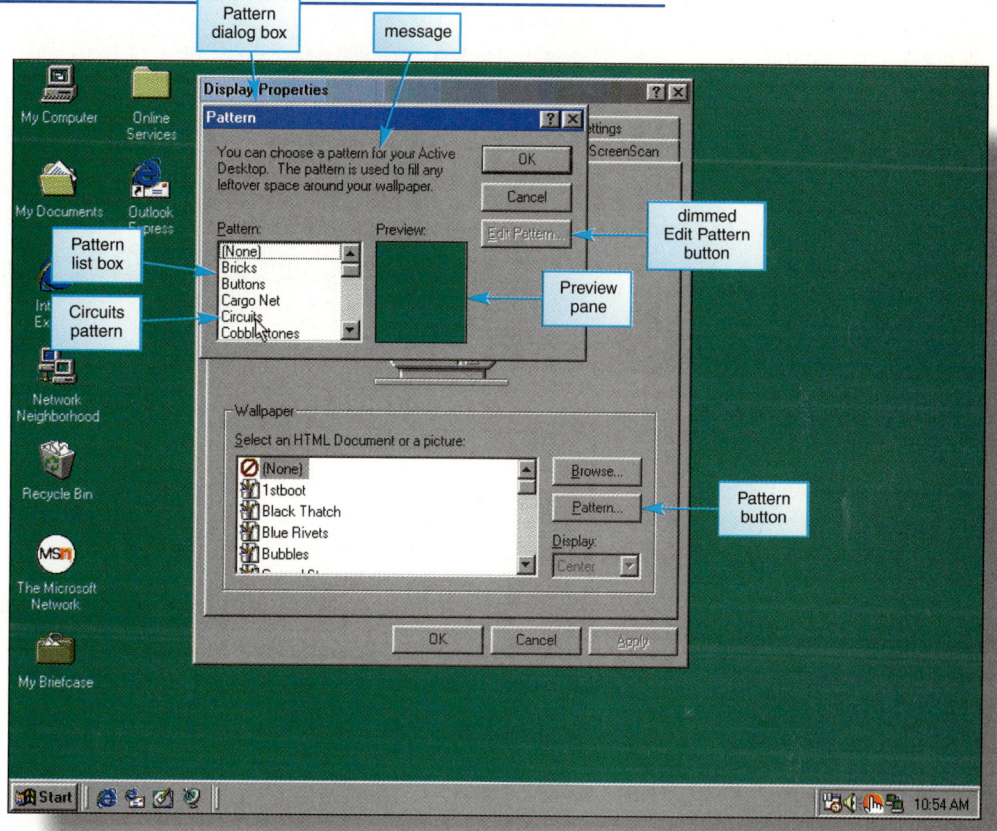

FIGURE 4-7

2 Click Circuits. Point to the OK button in the Pattern dialog box.

The Circuits pattern is highlighted in the list box and displays in the Preview pane. The Edit Pattern button no longer appears dimmed (Figure 4-8).

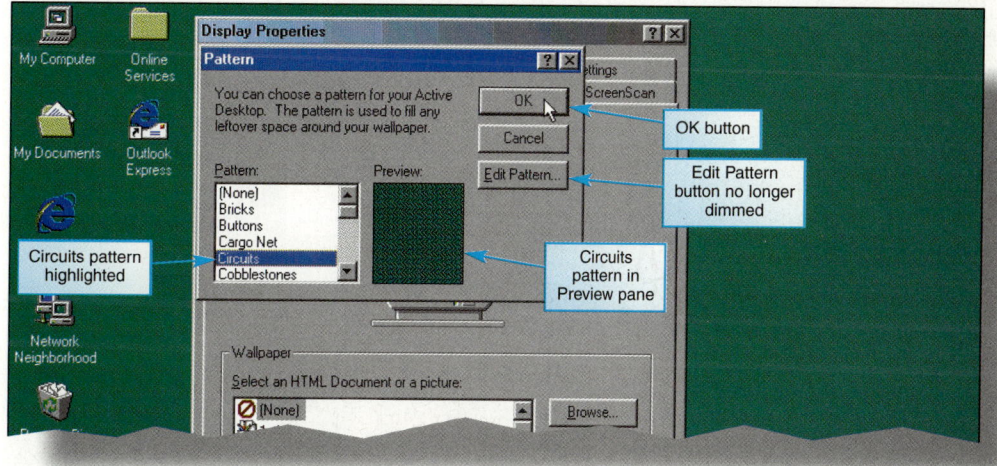

FIGURE 4-8

WIN 4.10 • Project 4 • Modifying Your Desktop Work Environment

③ Click the OK button in the Pattern dialog box. Click the Apply button in the Display Properties dialog box.

When you click the OK button, the Pattern dialog box closes and the Circuits pattern displays in the preview monitor. When you click the Apply button, the Circuits pattern displays on the desktop (Figure 4-9).

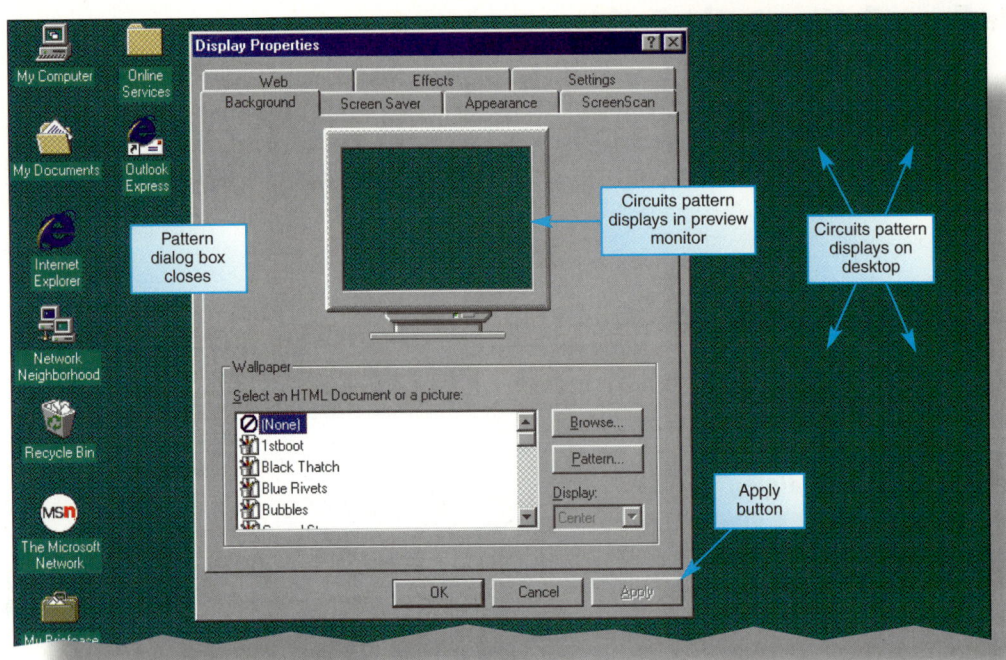

FIGURE 4-9

Other Ways

1. Press TAB until Pattern button selected, press ENTER, press DOWN ARROW to select pattern name in Pattern list box, press ENTER, press ALT+A

TO REMOVE A PATTERN

① Click the Pattern button.

② Scroll the Pattern list box until the name of the pattern you wrote down in Step 1 on the previous page displays.

③ Click the pattern name in the Pattern list box.

④ Click the OK button in the Pattern dialog box.

⑤ Click the Apply button in the Display Properties dialog box.

The pattern is returned to its original setting and the pattern is removed from the desktop (Figure 4-10).

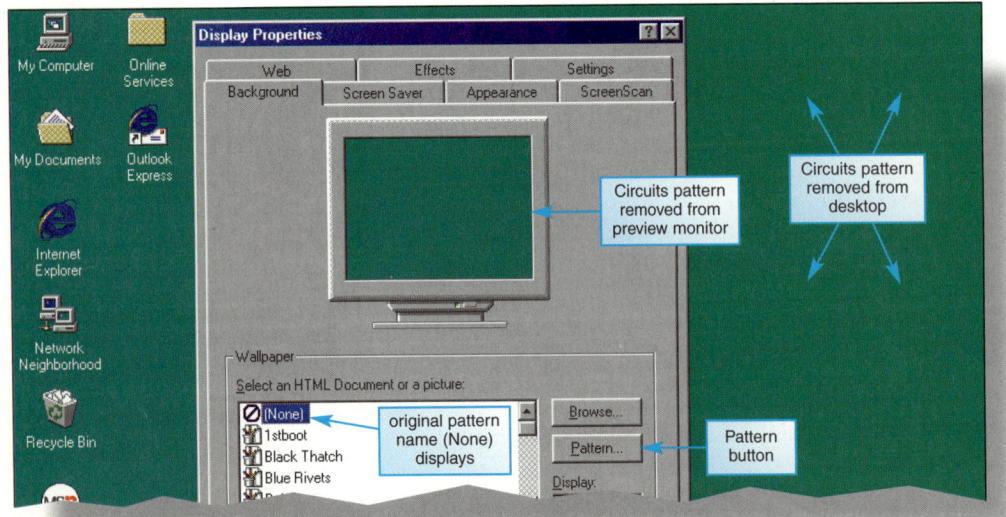

FIGURE 4-10

If no wallpaper is selected when you select a desktop pattern, the pattern fills the entire desktop. If you select a wallpaper and then select either Tile or Stretch in the Display list (see Figure 4-4 on page WIN 4.7), no pattern will display on the desktop. If you select a wallpaper and then select Center, the pattern will display around the outside of the wallpaper design.

Changing Your Desktop Working Environment • WIN 4.11

Changing the Desktop Appearance

The **Appearance sheet** in the Display Properties dialog box allows you to change the appearance of windows and other objects that display on the desktop. Again, in the following examples, you should revert to the current settings of your desktop appearance at the end of the steps unless you are working on your own computer and want to make the changes in the steps. To learn how to change your desktop appearance, perform the following steps.

Steps: To Change the Desktop Appearance

1 Click the Appearance tab in the Display Properties dialog box. Write down the scheme name shown in the Scheme list box on your computer.

The Appearance sheet displays in the Display Properties dialog box (Figure 4-11). The Scheme box specifies a color scheme that controls the colors that display on the screen. The preview pane above the Scheme box shows the colors currently in use. You can click any of the named items in the pane to see its color.

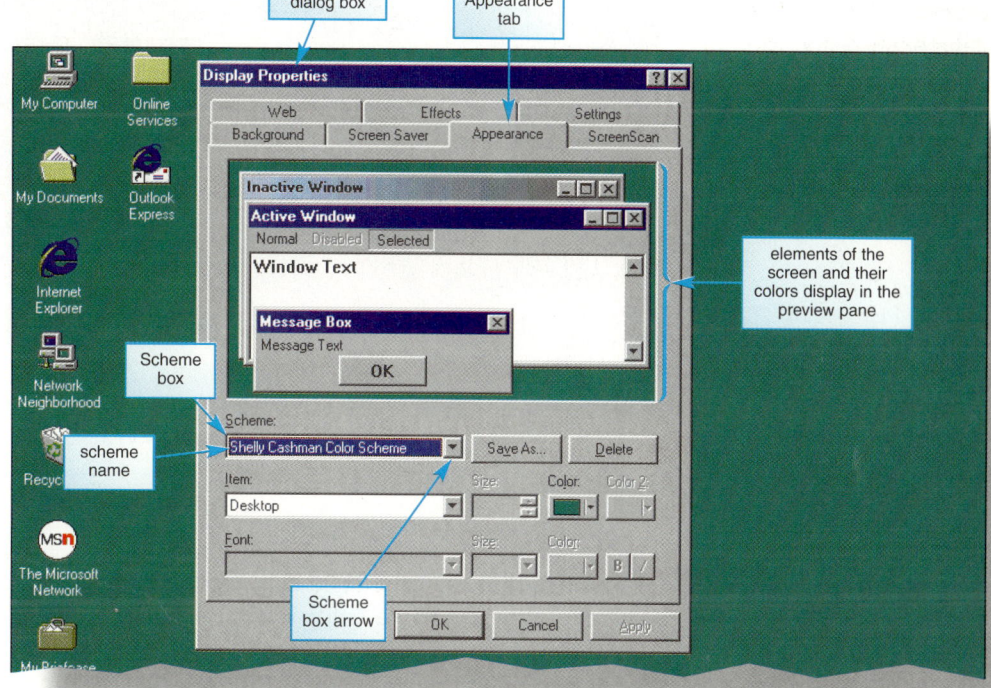

FIGURE 4-11

2 Click the Scheme box arrow. Scroll up or down until Desert displays in the list. Point to Desert.

The Scheme list box displays (Figure 4-12). The Scheme list box contains a list of color schemes you can apply to the desktop elements.

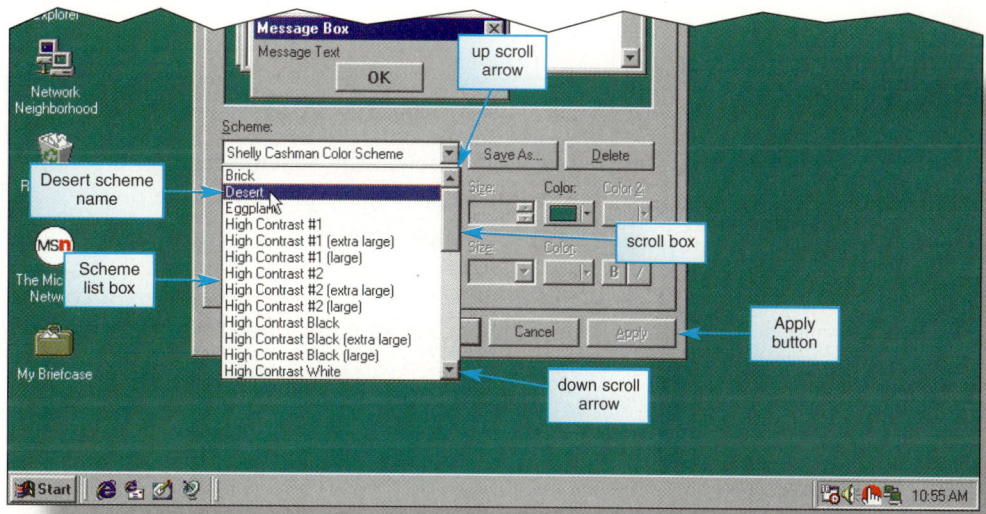

FIGURE 4-12

WIN 4.12 • Project 4 • Modifying Your Desktop Work Environment

 Click Desert. Click the Apply button.

When you click Desert, the elements in the preview pane are colored according to the Desert scheme and the Apply button is no longer dimmed. When you click the Apply button, the desktop and all the elements on the desktop display in the Desert scheme and the Apply button is dimmed (Figure 4-13).

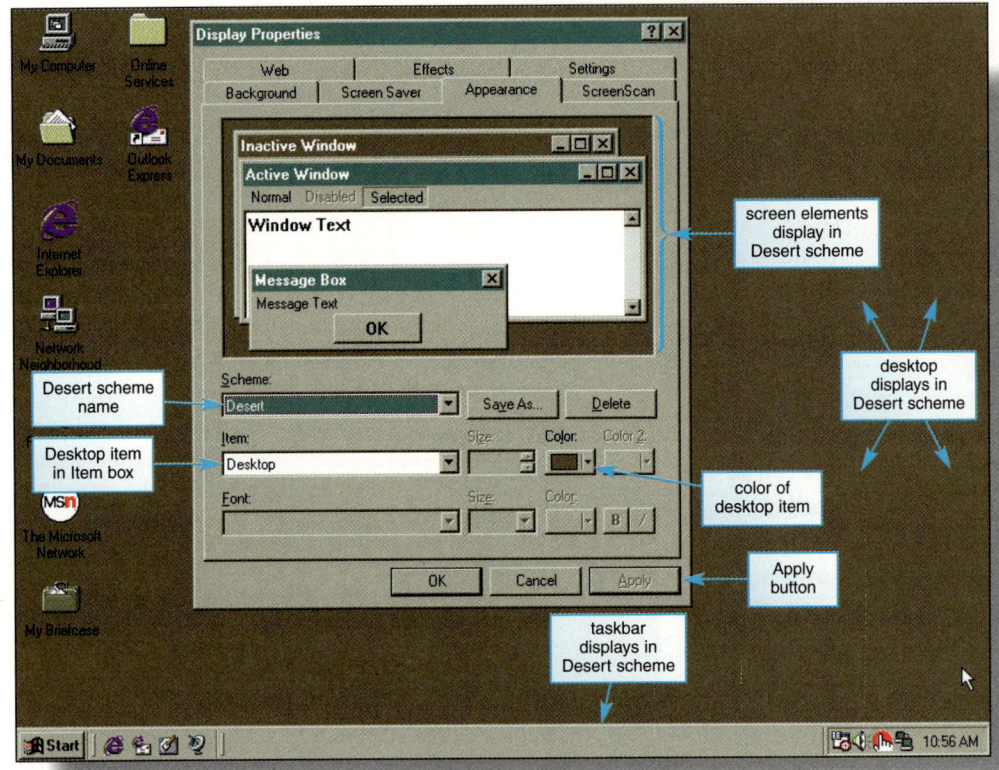

FIGURE 4-13

Other Ways

1. Press TAB until Background tab selected, press RIGHT ARROW until Appearance sheet displays, press ALT+S, press UP ARROW or DOWN ARROW to select scheme, press ALT+A

Notice that even the taskbar shown in Figure 4-13 is colored according to the scheme. If you display a color scheme while a tiled or stretched wallpaper displays on the desktop of your computer, the wallpaper continues to display on the desktop and the color of the wallpaper is not affected by the change. If you change the color scheme while a pattern displays on the desktop, the pattern continues to display on the desktop but the background color of the pattern changes to the color of the desktop in the new color scheme.

More About

Desktop Appearance

Desktop themes also allow you to change the desktop appearance. A desktop theme displays a desktop background and the objects on the desktop consistent with a theme, such as Baseball, Dangerous Creatures, Jungle, Nature, Science, Space, Sports, and Underwater. To select a desktop theme, click the Start button, point to Settings, click Control Panel, and then double-click Desktop Themes.

TO RESET THE DESKTOP APPEARANCE

 Click the Scheme box arrow.

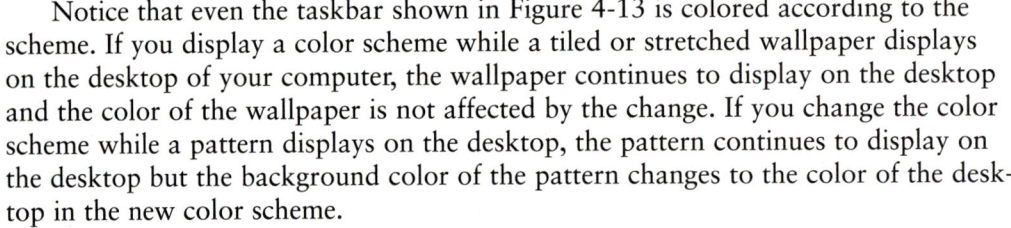 If necessary, scroll the Scheme list box until the name of the scheme you wrote down in Step 1 on the previous page displays and then click the scheme name.

 Click the Apply button.

The desktop appearance is reset to the original color scheme and the Display Properties dialog box remains open on the desktop (Figure 4-14).

Changing Your Desktop Working Environment • WIN 4.13

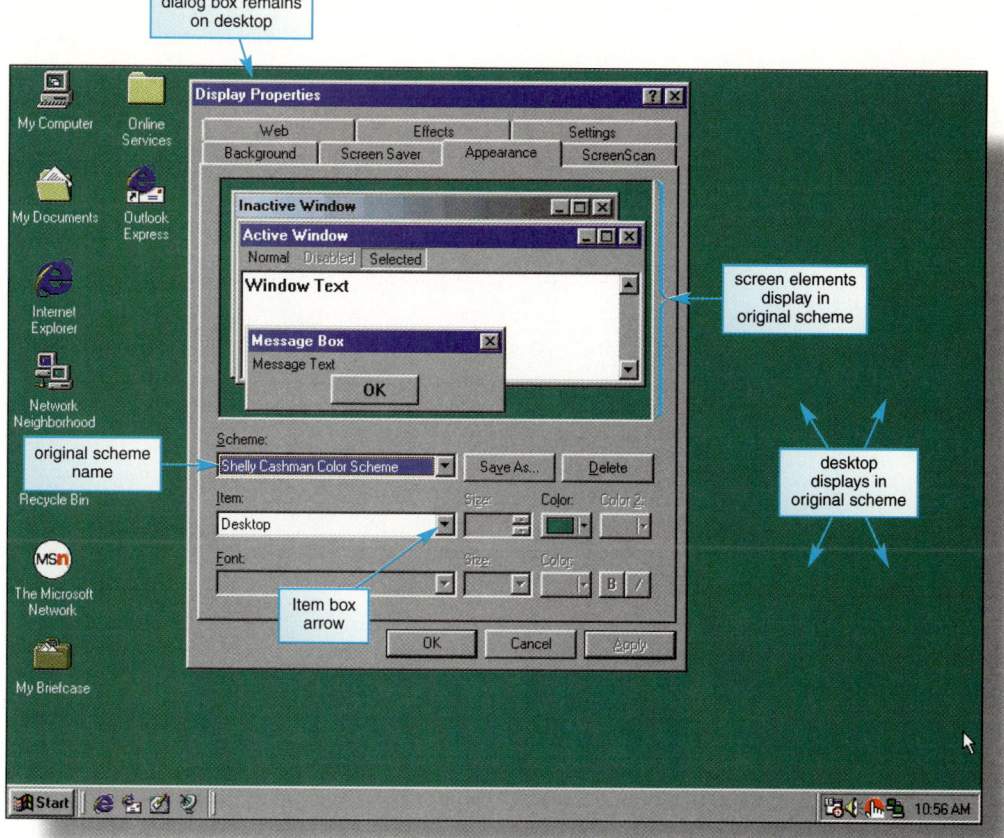

FIGURE 4-14

In addition to changing an entire color scheme, you also can change individual elements of the desktop to your liking. If you click any labeled element in the preview pane within the Display Properties dialog box, such as Inactive Window, Active Window, or Selected, the same element name will display in the Item box (see Figure 4-13). Then, you can click the Color box arrow and Color 2 box arrow and select the colors for the element from a color palette. You also can click the Item box arrow, click any of the items in the list, and select a color for that particular item. In addition, you can choose the font and font size for elements.

Windows 98 provides tools to customize your desktop in any manner you see fit.

Adding a Screen Saver

Originally, a **screen saver** was a program that prevented the problem of *ghosting* (a dim version of an image permanently etched on the monitor screen because the same image is displayed for a long time) by continually changing your monitor screen. Today, the changes are animations, designs, and other entertaining or fascinating activities on the screen. A screen saver begins operation after a given period of time has passed without any computer activity. It stops execution if you press a key on the keyboard or move the mouse.

Windows 98 provides a variety of screen savers you can choose. To see the screen savers, complete the steps on the next page.

Screen Savers

Berkeley Software, developers of After Dark screen saver software, has created innovative screen savers that play music, act out stories and animations, and thoroughly entertain, while at the same time generating millions of dollars in revenue. Screen savers today vary from cartoons to ever-changing masterpieces of art.

WIN 4.14 • Project 4 • Modifying Your Desktop Work Environment

Steps To Add a Screen Saver

1 Click the Screen Saver tab in the Display Properties dialog box.

The Screen Saver sheet displays and contains a preview monitor, Screen Saver pane, and Energy saving features of monitor pane (Figure 4-15). The preview monitor shows how each screen saver will display. The Energy saving features of monitor pane may or may not display in the dialog box on your computer.

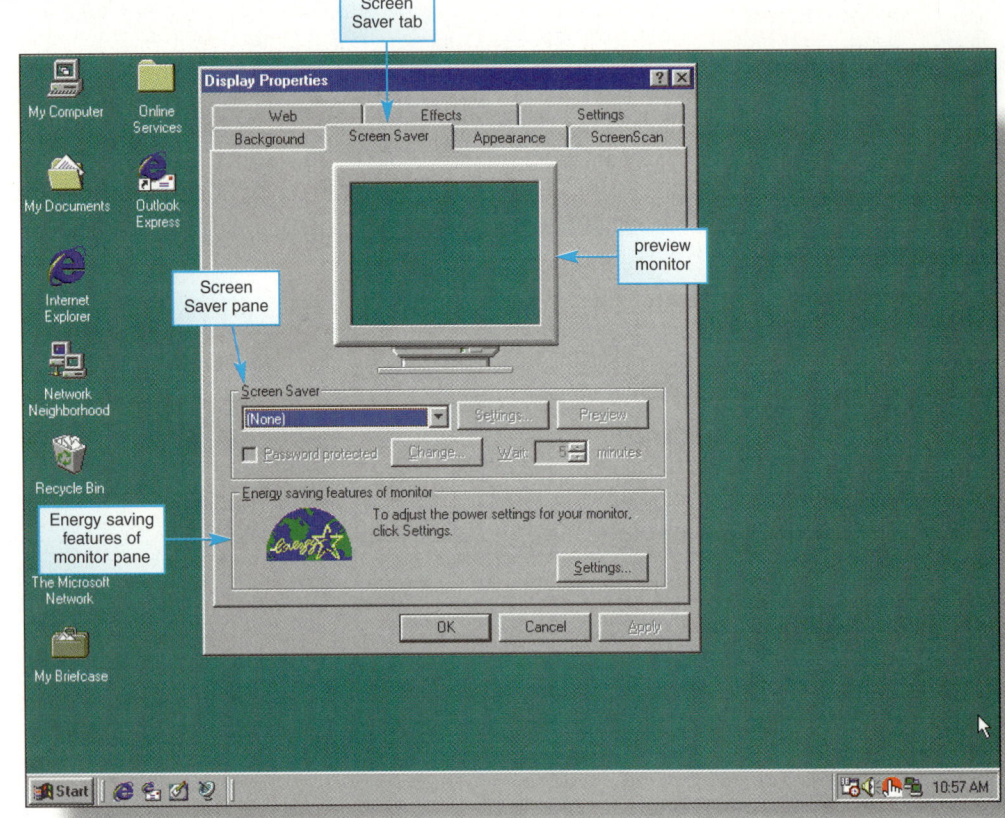

FIGURE 4-15

2 Click the Screen Saver box arrow. Point to 3D Flower Box in the list box.

A list of screen savers displays (Figure 4-16). Your computer may contain more screen savers than displayed in Figure 4-16, and you may have to scroll to see 3D Flower Box in the list.

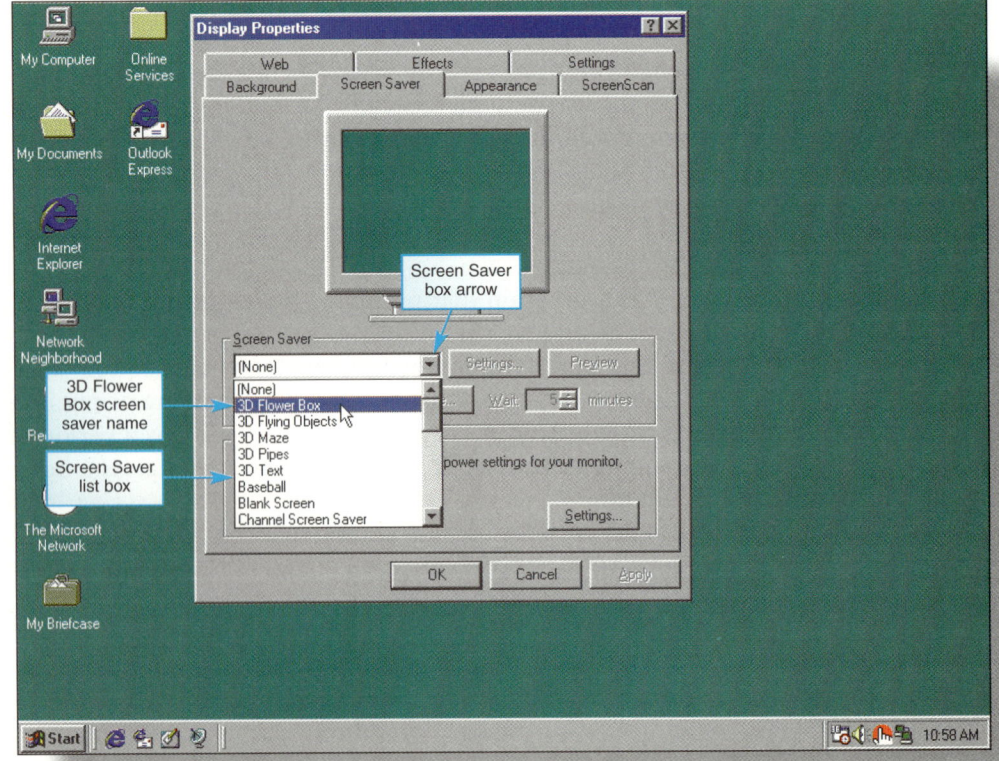

FIGURE 4-16

Customizing the Taskbar • **WIN 4.15**

3 **Click 3D Flower Box.**

The 3D Flower Box screen saver plays in the preview monitor and 3D Flower Box displays in the Screen Saver box, indicating it is the selected screen saver (Figure 4-17).

4 **Select other screen savers in the Screen Saver list box to view them. Then, click the Cancel button in the Display Properties dialog box.**

The Display Properties dialog box disappears and the desktop displays.

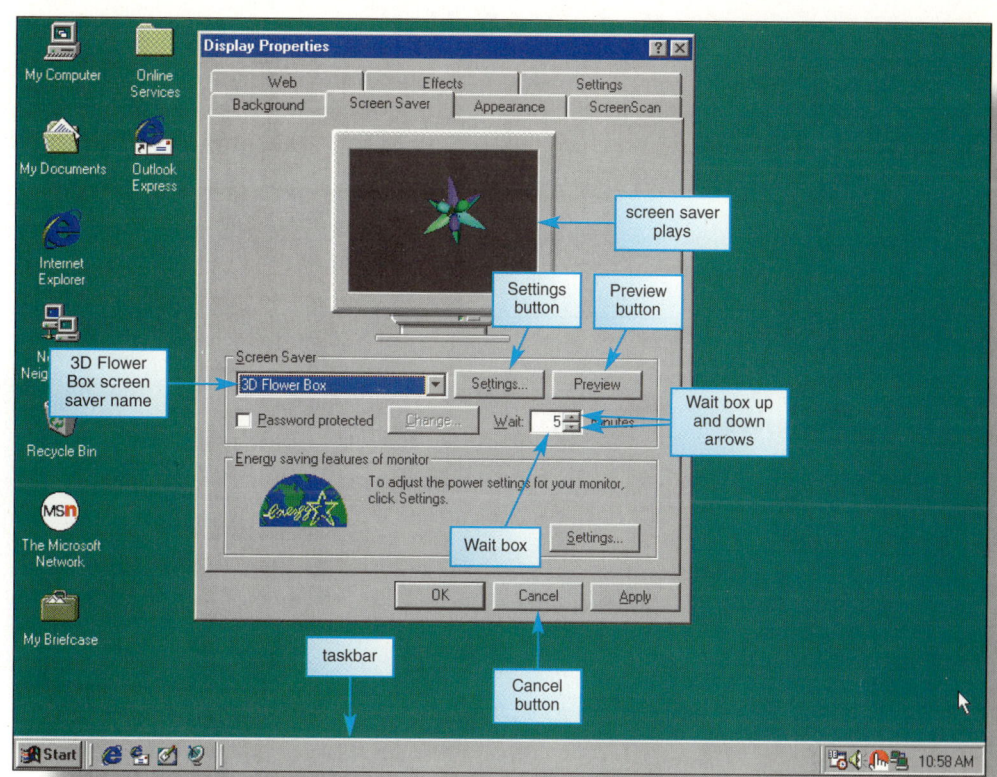

FIGURE 4-17

Clicking the **Settings button** in the Screen Saver pane shown in Figure 4-17 allows you to change the color, shape, and size of the image that displays in the 3D Flower Box screen saver. If you click the **Preview button**, Windows 98 displays the screen saver on the whole screen. To stop the screen saver when it is being previewed, move the mouse or press a key on the keyboard. To set the number of minutes of computer inactivity to wait until the screen saver displays, click the Wait box up or down arrow. The number of minutes to wait is set at five in Figure 4-17.

Customizing the Taskbar

Another method to customize your desktop work environment is to customize the taskbar at the bottom of the desktop. The taskbar shown in Figure 4-17 contains the Start button, Quick Launch toolbar, and tray status area.

You can customize the taskbar and the objects on the taskbar. For example, you can move, resize, and hide the taskbar; add toolbars and remove toolbars on the taskbar; add folders and remove folders on the taskbar; change the appearance of the taskbar; and change the taskbar properties. In addition, you can customize the toolbars on the taskbar by adding applications and removing applications on the toolbars. The steps in the next sections will show you how to customize the taskbar and the toolbars on the taskbar.

Other Ways

1. Press TAB until Background tab is highlighted, press RIGHT ARROW until Screen Saver tab is highlighted, press TAB to select current screen saver, press UP ARROW or DOWN ARROW to select screen saver, press ESC to cancel

More About

Display Properties

Additional desktop properties can be changed using other tabbed sheets in the Display Properties dialog box. The Web sheet controls whether the Active Desktop™ is active. The Effects sheet allows you to change the size of icons and icon titles on the desktop. The Settings sheet allows you to change the color settings and resolution of the desktop.

Moving the Taskbar

The default placement of the taskbar is at the bottom of the desktop, but it can be placed on any of the four sides of the desktop by dragging. To move the taskbar to the top, left side, and right side of the desktop and then back to the bottom, complete the steps below.

 To Move the Taskbar

1. **Point to an open area on the taskbar** (Figure 4-18)

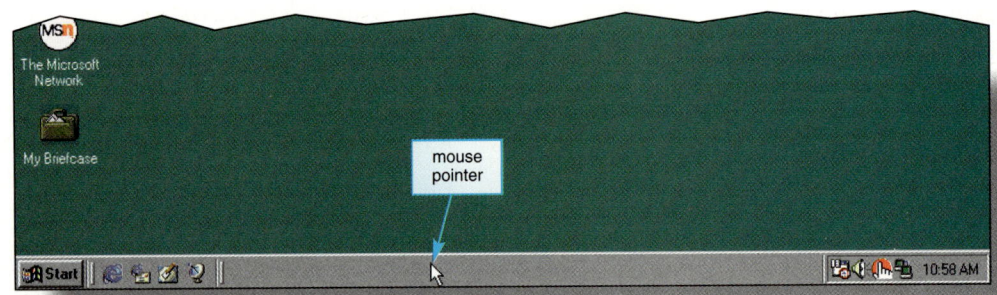

FIGURE 4-18

2. **Drag the taskbar to the top of the desktop.**

As you drag the taskbar to the top of the desktop, the taskbar remains at the bottom of the desktop until the mouse pointer approaches the center of the desktop and then it moves to the top of the desktop, displaying on top of any icons at the top of the desktop. When you release the mouse button, the icons on the desktop move downward on the desktop (Figure 4-19).

3. **Drag the taskbar to the left side and then the right side of the desktop. Drag the taskbar back to the bottom of the desktop.**

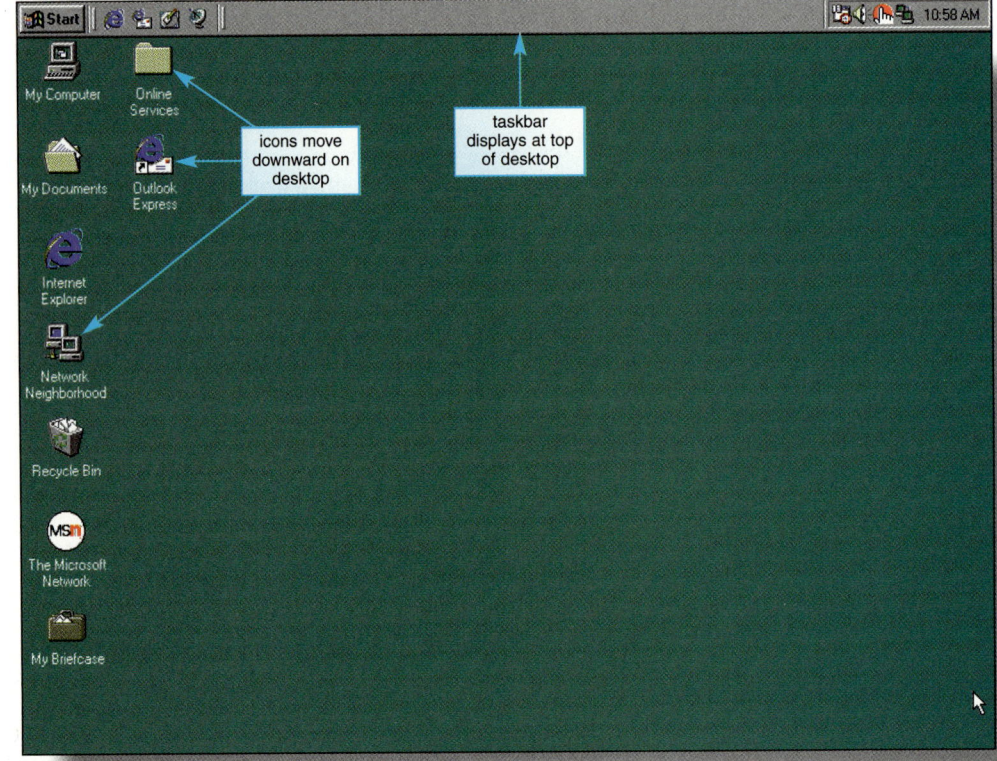

FIGURE 4-19

Placement of the taskbar is an individual preference, but the default for Windows 98 is on the bottom and most people prefer the taskbar to display at the bottom of the desktop.

Hiding the Taskbar

Another way to customize the taskbar is to hide the taskbar so only its top edge is visible at the bottom of the desktop. After hiding the taskbar, pointing to the top edge again displays the taskbar on the desktop. Complete the following steps to hide and then redisplay the taskbar.

To Hide and Redisplay the Taskbar

 Right-click an open area of the taskbar. Point to Properties on the shortcut menu.

A shortcut menu displays (Figure 4-20).

FIGURE 4-20

Click Properties. Point to Auto hide.

*The Taskbar Properties dialog box and Taskbar Options sheet display (Figure 4-21). The **Taskbar Options sheet** contains a preview pane and four check boxes. The preview pane contains the Start menu, an open window, and the taskbar. Check marks display in the Always on top and Show clock check boxes indicating they are selected.*

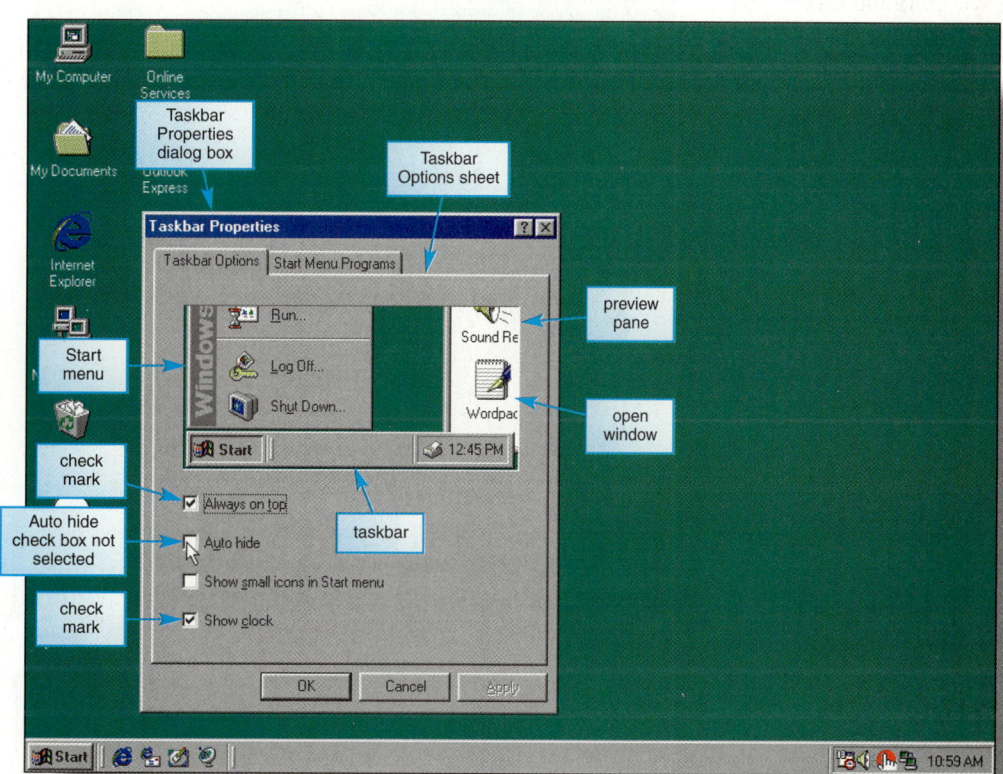

FIGURE 4-21

③ If a check mark does not display in the Auto hide check box, click Auto hide to select it. Point to the Apply button.

A check mark displays in the Auto hide check box and a gray rectangle replaces the taskbar in the preview pane (Figure 4-22).

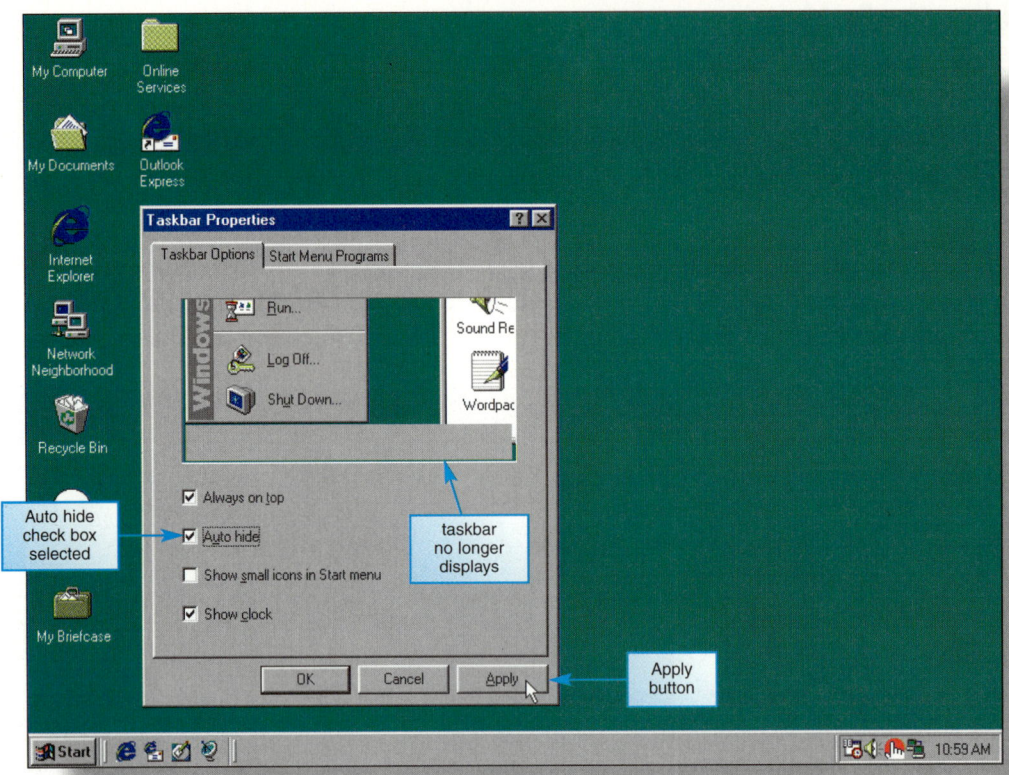

FIGURE 4-22

④ Click the Apply button.

The Apply button appears dimmed, the top edge (thin horizontal line) of the taskbar displays at the bottom of the desktop, and the Taskbar Properties dialog box remains open (Figure 4-23). Clicking the OK button instead of the Apply button hides the taskbar and closes the dialog box.

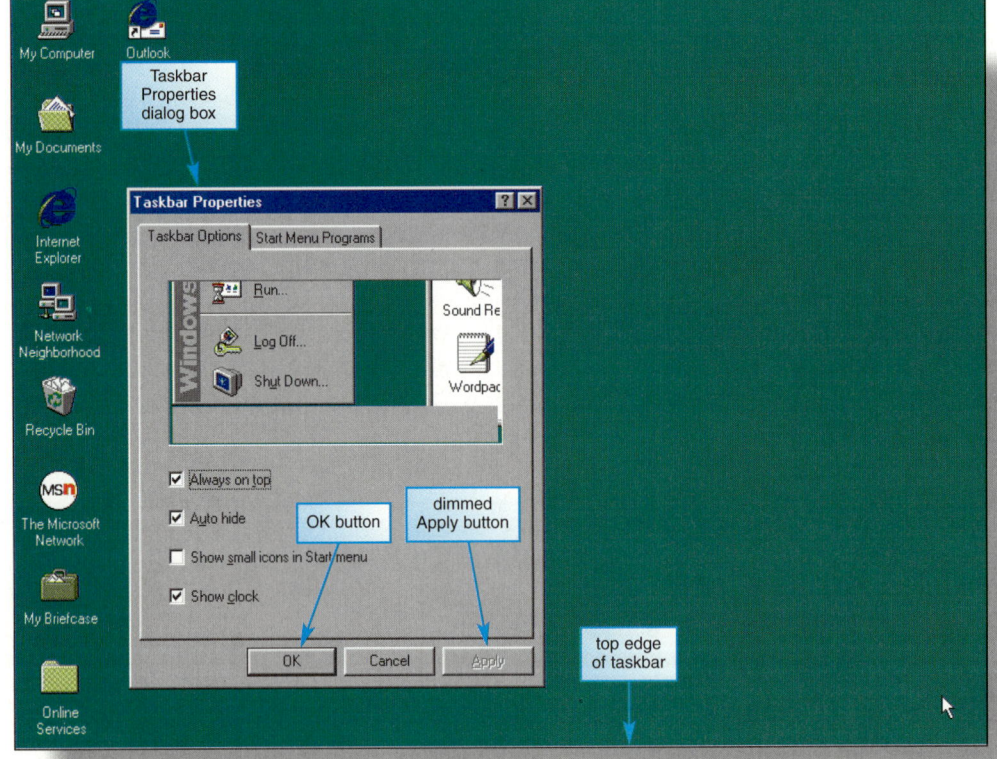

FIGURE 4-23

Customizing the Taskbar • **WIN 4.19**

⑤ Point to the top edge (thin horizontal line) of the taskbar to display the taskbar again.

When the mouse pointer points to the top edge of the taskbar, the taskbar displays again (Figure 4-24). The taskbar remains on the desktop as long as the mouse pointer points to the taskbar.

⑥ Click Auto hide to remove the check mark from the check box. Click the OK button to close the Taskbar Properties dialog box.

The check mark is removed from the check box, the taskbar displays in the preview pane, and the Taskbar Properties dialog box is removed from the desktop. The desktop displays as shown before hiding the taskbar.

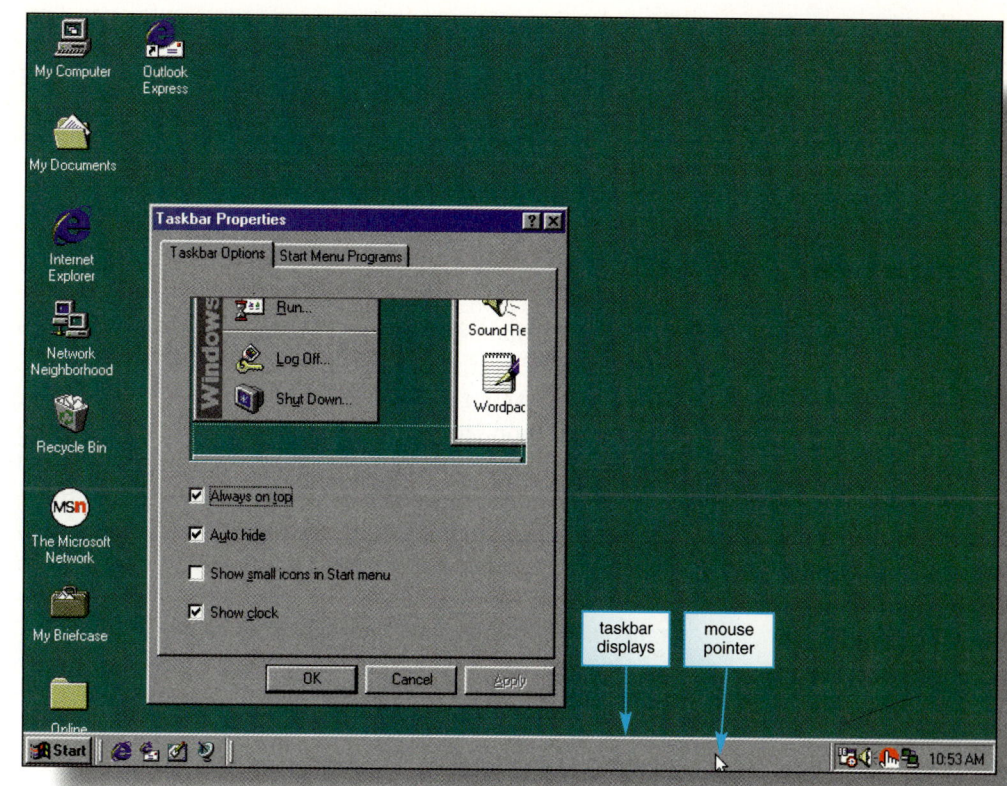

FIGURE 4-24

Other Ways

1. Click Start button, point to Settings, click Taskbar & Start Menu, click check box, click Apply button
2. Point to top edge of taskbar to display two-headed arrow, drag edge downward until taskbar is hidden

In the Taskbar Options sheet in the Taskbar Properties dialog box shown in Figure 4-21 on page WIN 4.17, check marks display in the Always on top and Show clock check boxes. The **Always on top option** allows you to change whether the taskbar displays on top of any other objects on the desktop. A check mark in the Always on top check box causes the taskbar to display on top of all objects on the desktop and the taskbar in the preview pane to display on top of the open window. The **Show clock option** allows you to display or remove the digital clock that displays in the tray status area on the taskbar. When the Show clock option button is selected, the clock displays in the tray status area on the taskbar and in the tray status area in the preview pane. The **Show small icons in Start menu option** allows you to change the size of the icons (small or large) preceding the commands on the Start menu. Smaller icons make the Start menu display smaller on the desktop.

Working with Toolbars on the Taskbar

Windows 98 allows you to add, remove, move, and resize a toolbar on the taskbar and add a shortcut to a toolbar. The following sections illustrate how to perform these operations.

Adding a Toolbar to the Taskbar

As explained earlier in this project, the Quick Launch toolbar provides shortcuts to several frequently used features: the Web browser (Launch Internet Explorer Browser icon), an e-mail program (Launch Outlook Express icon), the desktop (Show Desktop icon), and channels (View Channels icon). In addition to the Quick Launch toolbar, Windows 98 provides three other toolbars that you can add to the taskbar. The **Address toolbar** allows you to search for a Web page, launch an application program, open a document, open a folder window, and search for information on the Internet. The **Links toolbar** allows you to use shortcuts to go to a favorite Web site without first launching the Internet Explorer browser. The **Desktop toolbar** contains all of the shortcuts that display on your desktop.

In addition to the four toolbars included with Windows 98, you also can create your own toolbar. For example, you might create a Current Projects toolbar that contains the icons for all the applications and documents with which you are currently working.

To illustrate how to add a toolbar to the taskbar, perform the following steps to add the Address toolbar to the taskbar.

To Add a Toolbar to the Taskbar

1 **Right-click an open area of the taskbar. Point to Toolbars on the shortcut menu. Point to Address on the Toolbars submenu.**

A shortcut menu and the Toolbars submenu display (Figure 4-25). A check mark precedes Quick Launch on the Toolbars submenu to indicate that the Quick Launch toolbar is the only toolbar that displays on the taskbar. The three other toolbar names (Address, Links, and Desktop) are not preceded by check marks.

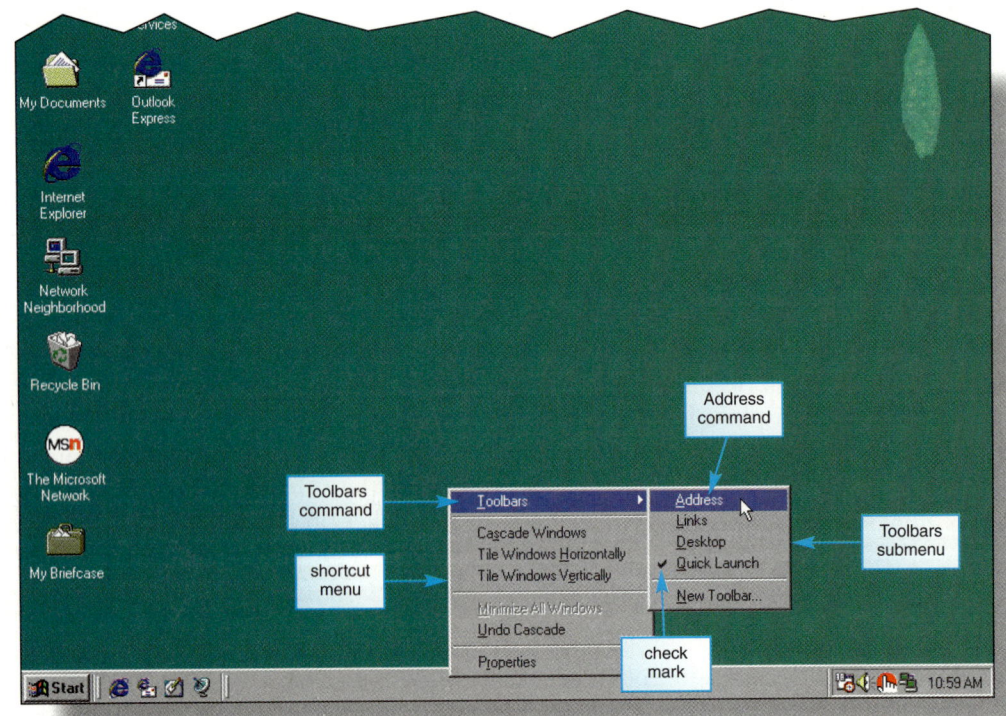

FIGURE 4-25

Click Address.

The Address toolbar displays on the taskbar (Figure 4-26). Although not visible in Figure 4-26, a check mark precedes Address on the Toolbars submenu.

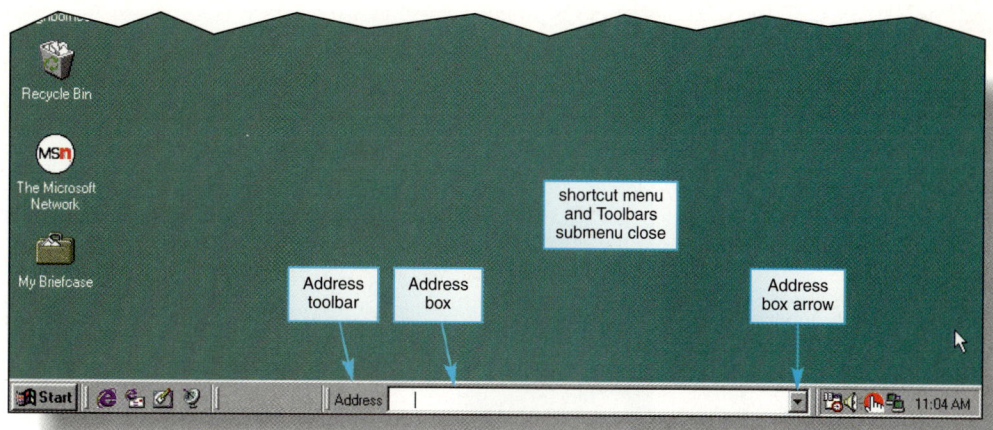

FIGURE 4-26

After adding the Address toolbar to the taskbar, you can use the Address box to type an address (URL) and display the associated Web page, type an application program name to launch a program, type a folder location (path) to open a folder window, type a document name to launch an application and display the document in the application window, and type a keyword or phrase (search inquiry) to display Web pages containing the keyword or phrase. These operations are illustrated in the following sections.

Using the Address Toolbar to Display the Contents of a Folder

To display the contents of a folder using the Address toolbar, you must type the path of the folder and then press the ENTER key. A **path** is the means of navigating to a specific location on a computer or network. To specify a path, you must type the drive letter, followed by a colon (:), a backslash (\), and the folder name. For example, the path for the Windows folder on drive C is: C:\WINDOWS.

Perform the following steps to type the path of the Windows folder and display the contents of the Windows folder.

 **To Display the Contents of a Folder Using the Address Toolbar**

 Type c:\windows **in the Address box.**

The path of the Windows folder displays in the Address box (Figure 4-27).

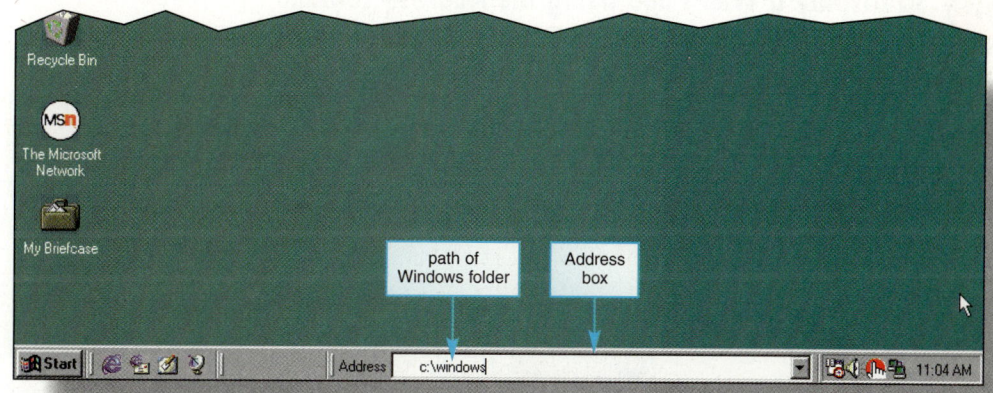

FIGURE 4-27

> **More About**
>
> **Adding a Toolbar to the Taskbar**
>
> After adding a toolbar to the taskbar, you can move the toolbar to the desktop by dragging the toolbar on the taskbar to an open area of the desktop. A box with the toolbar name in the title bar displays on the desktop. Then, you can move and resize the box to your preference.

WIN 4.22 • Project 4 • Modifying Your Desktop Work Environment

② Press the ENTER key.

A folder icon and the Windows path display in the Address box and the Windows window containing the contents of the Windows folder opens on the desktop (Figure 4-28).

③ Click the Close button in the Windows window.

The Windows window closes.

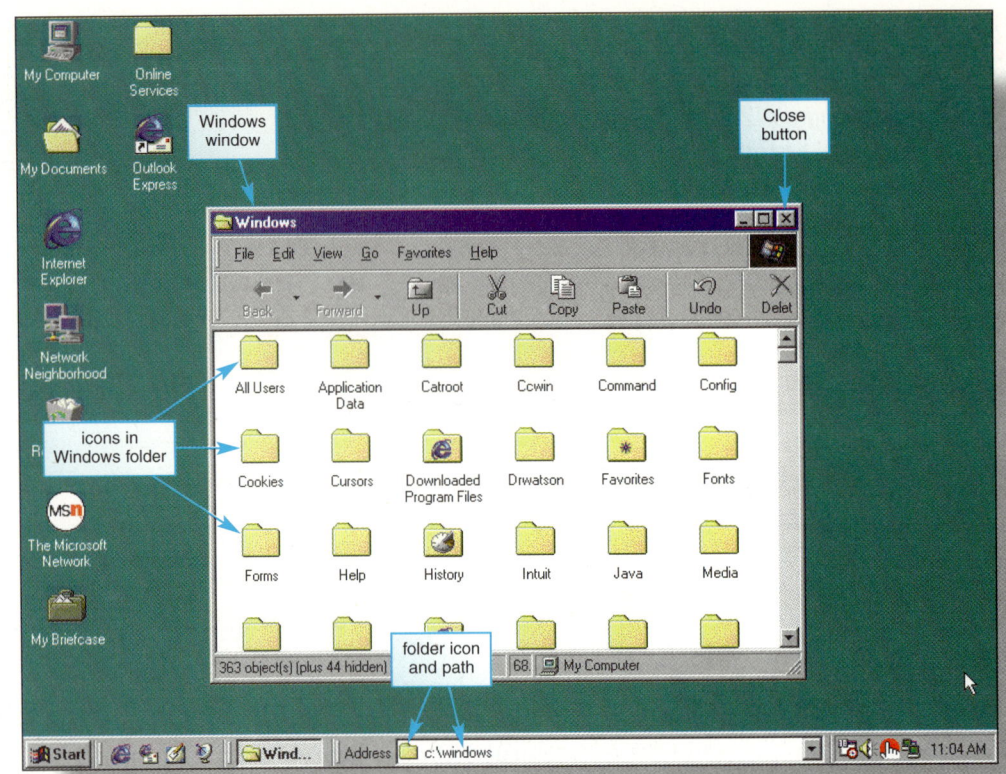

FIGURE 4-28

Using the Address Toolbar to Display a Web Page

To search for and display a Web page using the Address toolbar, you must type an address, or Uniform Resource Locator (URL), and then press the ENTER key. A unique URL identifies each Web page in a Web site. For example, the URL for the ESPN SportsZone Web page is www.espn.sportszone.com.

Perform the following steps to type the URL of the ESPN SportsZone Web page in the Address box, launch the Internet Explorer browser, and display the ESPN SportsZone Web page in the browser window.

 To Display a Web Page Using the Address Toolbar

 Click the Address box and then type www.espn.sportszone.com **in the Address box.**

The URL for the ESPN Web page displays in the Address box (Figure 4-29).

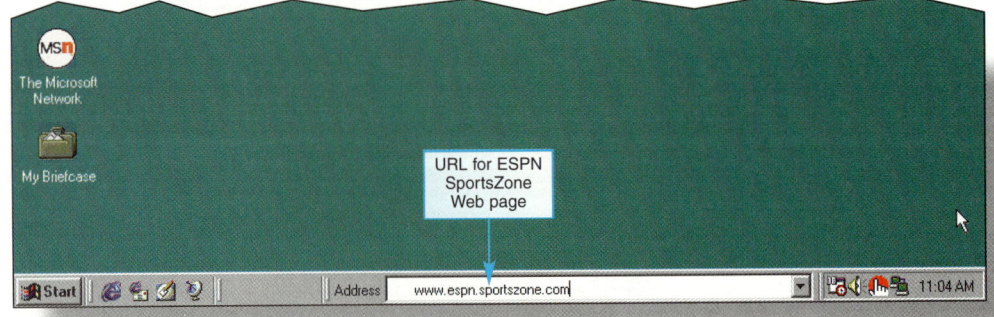

FIGURE 4-29

2 **Press the ENTER key.**

The URL for the ESPN SportsZone Web page displays in the Address box. The Internet Explorer Web browser launches, and the ESPN Web page displays in the ESPN SportsZone - Microsoft Internet Explorer window (Figure 4-30).

3 **Click the Close button in the ESPN SportsZone - Microsoft Internet Explorer window.**

The ESPN SportsZone - Microsoft Internet Explorer window closes.

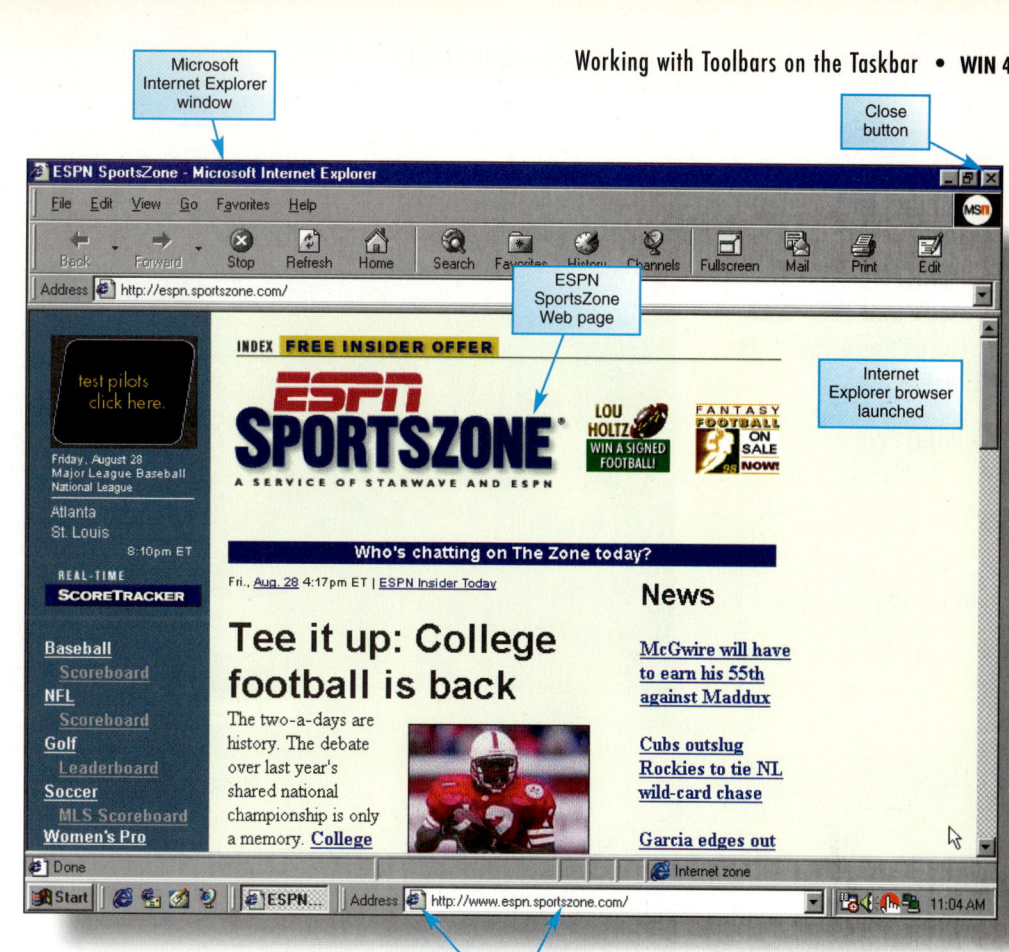

FIGURE 4-30

Using the Address Toolbar to Search for Information on the Internet

To search for information on the Internet using the Address toolbar, you must type a keyword or phrase and then press the ENTER key. For example, you might enter the phrase, national weather, enclosed in quotation marks, to search for and display the hyperlinks of all Web pages that contain the phrase, national weather. Entering the phrase without quotation marks will result in displaying Web pages that contain either word (national or weather) instead of the phrase, national weather.

Perform the steps on the next page to type the phrase, "national weather", in the Address box, launch the Internet Explorer browser, and display all Web pages containing the phrase, national weather.

WIN 4.24 • Project 4 • Modifying Your Desktop Work Environment

Steps: To Search for Information on the Internet Using the Address Toolbar

 **Click the Address box and then type** "national weather" **in the Address box.**

The phrase, "national weather", displays in the Address box (Figure 4-31).

FIGURE 4-31

 Press the ENTER key.

The Internet Explorer icon, Web page URL, and search inquiry display in the Address box and the Internet Explorer Autosearch – Microsoft Internet Explorer window opens (Figure 4-32). The window contains several hyperlinks to other Web pages containing information about the national weather.

Click the Close button in the Internet Explorer Autosearch - Microsoft Internet Explorer window.

The Internet Explorer Autosearch - Microsoft Internet Explorer window closes.

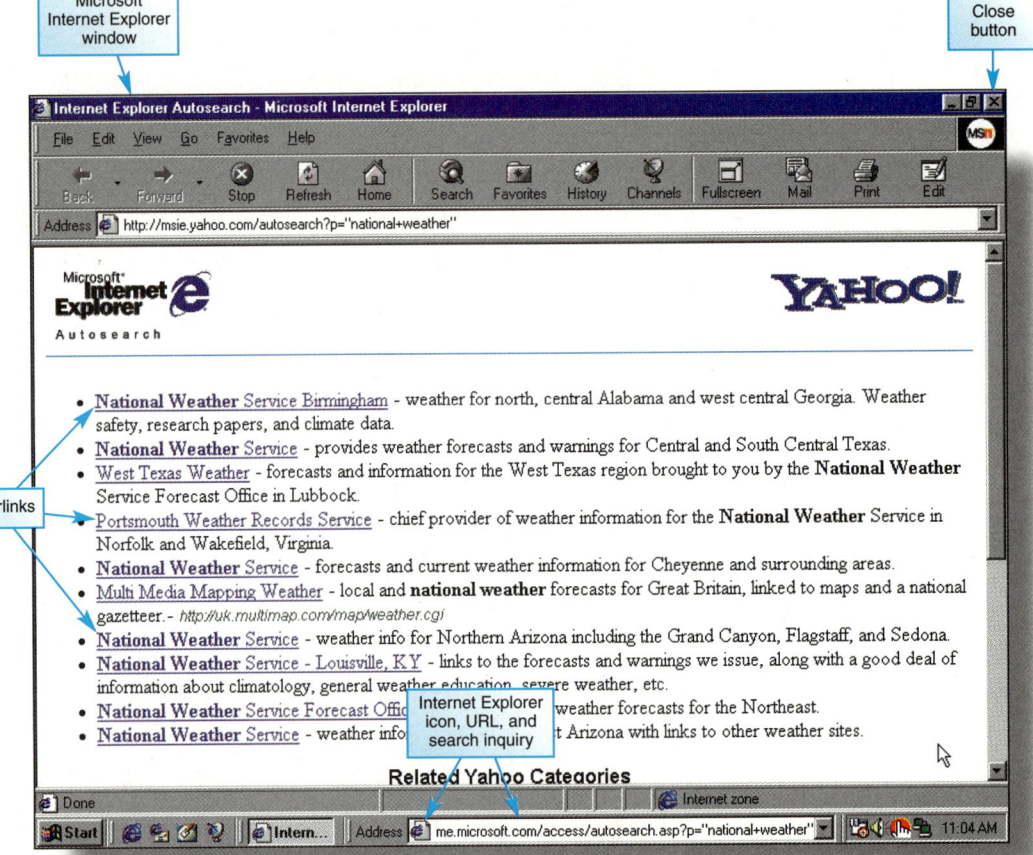

FIGURE 4-32

In addition to using the Address toolbar to display a Web page, display the contents of a folder, and search for information on the Internet, you also can use the Address toolbar to launch a program and open a document. To launch an application, such as the Notepad application, you type the application name (Notepad) in the Address box and then press the ENTER key. The Untitled - Notepad window will open on the desktop. To display a document, such as the Tips.txt document, you type the document name (Tips.txt) in the Address box and then press the ENTER key. The Tips document will display in the Tips - Notepad window.

Resizing the Taskbar

The taskbar shown in Figure 4-31 contains the Start button, Quick Launch toolbar, taskbar button area, Address toolbar, and tray status area. As you add more toolbars to the taskbar and open more windows on the desktop, the taskbar may become cluttered with buttons and toolbars. To make it easier to read the button names and toolbar contents, you can resize the taskbar by pointing to the top border of the taskbar and dragging the border upward toward the top of the desktop. Perform the following steps to resize the taskbar.

To Resize the Taskbar

1 **Point to the top edge of the taskbar until a two-headed arrow displays.**

When the mouse pointer points to the top edge of the taskbar, it changes to a two-headed arrow (Figure 4-33).

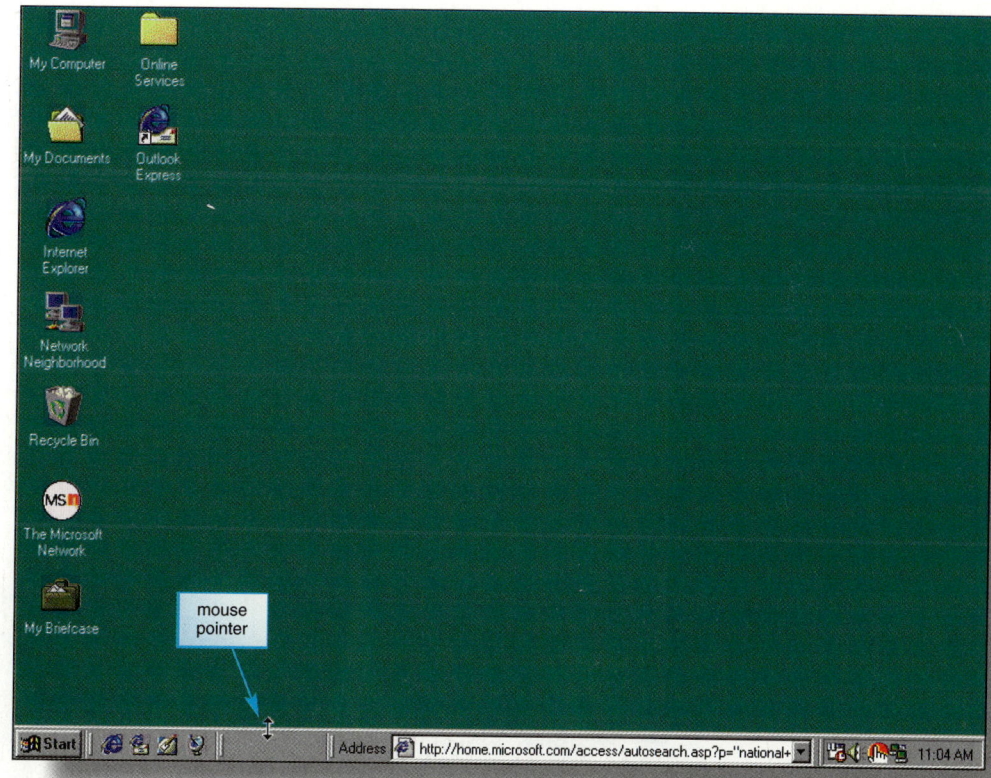

FIGURE 4-33

2 Drag the top edge of the taskbar toward the top of the desktop until the taskbar on your desktop resembles the taskbar in Figure 4-34.

The taskbar is resized and its contents are rearranged (Figure 4-34).

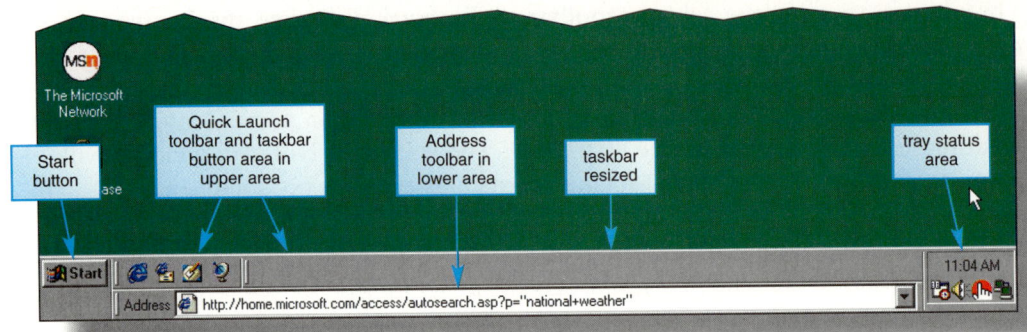

FIGURE 4-34

More About

Toolbar Icons

You can change the appearance of a toolbar by displaying larger icons, toolbar title, and icon titles. Right-click the toolbar to display a shortcut menu and then click Show Text or Show Title to display the toolbar title or icon titles. Point to the View command on the shortcut menu and then click Large Icons to display larger icons.

In Figure 4-34, the Start button displays at the left side of the taskbar and the tray status area (time and icons rearranged) displays at the right side of the taskbar. The area between the Start button and tray status area is divided into two areas. The upper area contains the Quick Launch toolbar and taskbar button area. The lower area contains the Address toolbar.

The taskbar often is resized to make it easier to view its contents after adding toolbars to the taskbar.

Removing a Toolbar

When you no longer want a toolbar on the taskbar, you can remove the toolbar easily. Perform the following steps to remove the Address toolbar from the taskbar.

TO REMOVE A TOOLBAR FROM THE TASKBAR

1 Right-click an open area on the taskbar.

2 Point to Toolbars on the shortcut menu.

3 Click Address on the Toolbars submenu.

The Address toolbar is removed from the taskbar and the contents of the taskbar are rearranged (Figure 4-35). The Quick Launch toolbar displays in the upper area and the taskbar button area displays in the lower area. The Start button and tray status area remain unchanged.

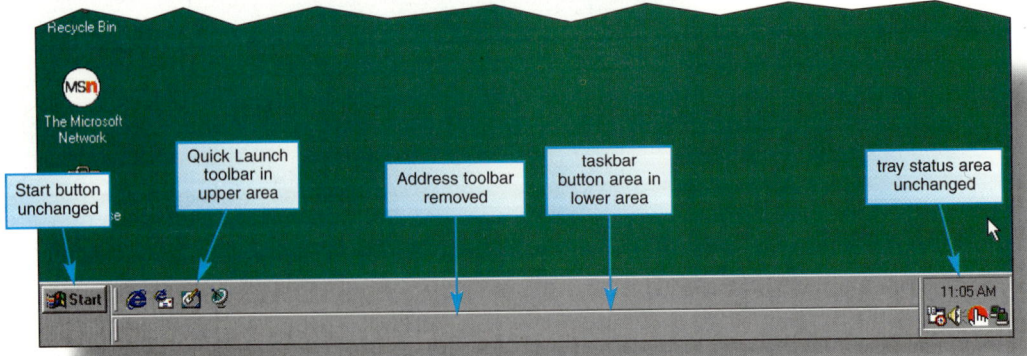

FIGURE 4-35

Although not visible in Figure 4-35, the check mark preceding the Address command on the Toolbars submenu is removed.

Customizing a Toolbar

In addition to customizing the taskbar, you also can customize a toolbar by placing a shortcut on the toolbar. Among the shortcuts you can place on a toolbar are shortcuts to a file, folder, program, subscription, or Web page.

Placing a Shortcut on a Toolbar

In this section, you will place a shortcut on a toolbar by adding the Control Panel folder to the Quick Launch toolbar. The Control Panel folder is located in the My Computer folder. The **Control Panel folder** contains icons that allow you to customize the mouse, keyboard, date and time, desktop fonts, add new hardware and software to your computer, make a computer more usable by disabled people, add and control the operation of a printer, use Help troubleshooters to solve hardware problems, and view the properties of your hardware devices. Project 5 will explain how to use these icons to further customize your computer.

Perform the following steps to place a shortcut to the Control Panel folder on the Quick Launch toolbar.

To Place a Shortcut on a Toolbar

1 Double-click the My Computer icon on the desktop. If necessary, click the Restore button in the My Computer icon to restore the window to its original size. Point to the Control Panel icon.

The My Computer window displays (Figure 4-36).

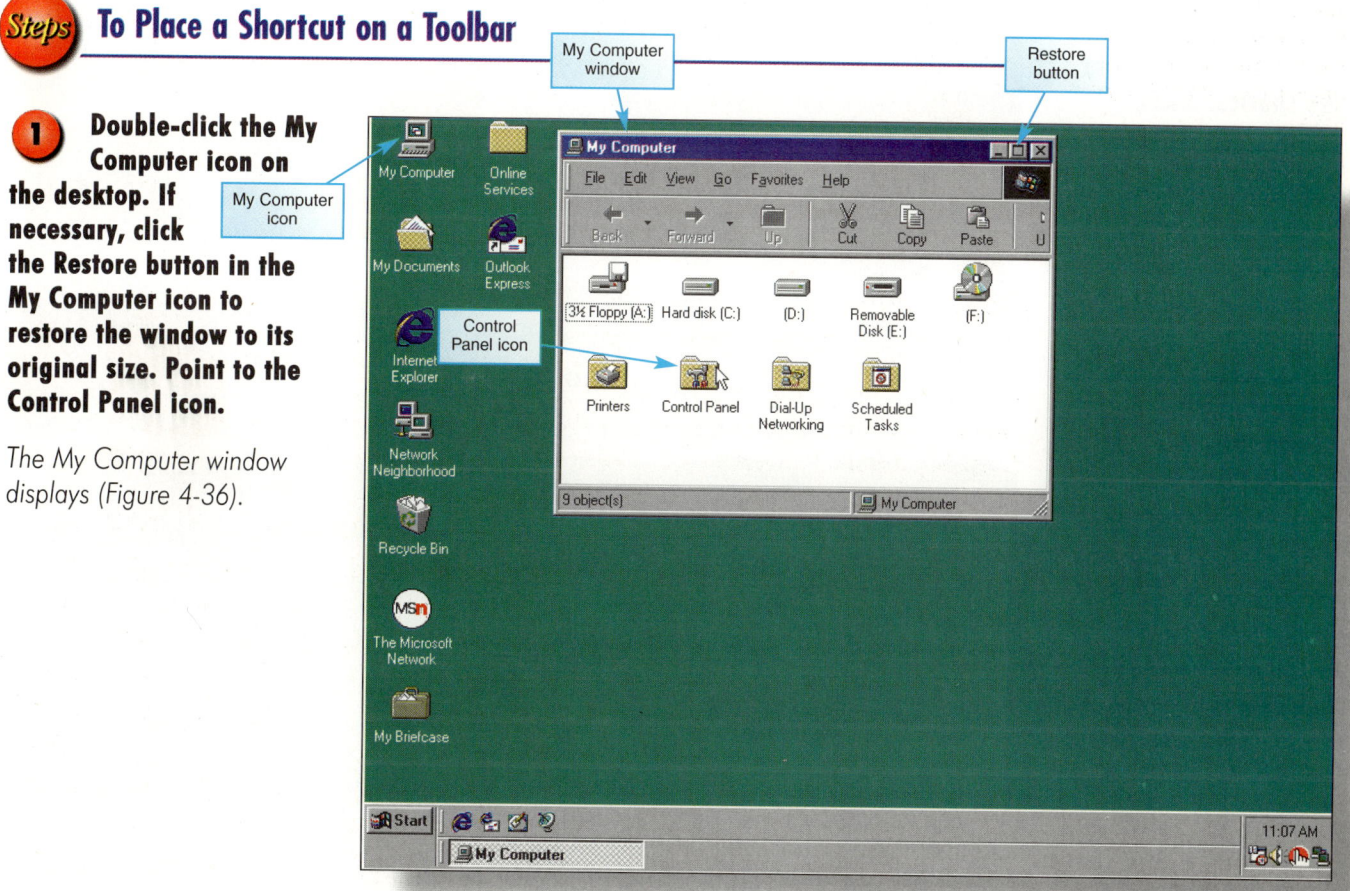

FIGURE 4-36

WIN 4.28 • Project 4 • Modifying Your Desktop Work Environment

2 Hold down the right mouse button and right-drag the Control Panel icon to the Quick Launch toolbar until a vertical divider line displays. Without releasing the right mouse button, position the divider line to the right of the View Channels icon on the toolbar.

A divider line displays to the right of the icons on the toolbar, a dimmed Control Panel icon displays, and a shortcut icon displays as part of the mouse pointer, indicating a shortcut is being placed on the toolbar (Figure 4-37).

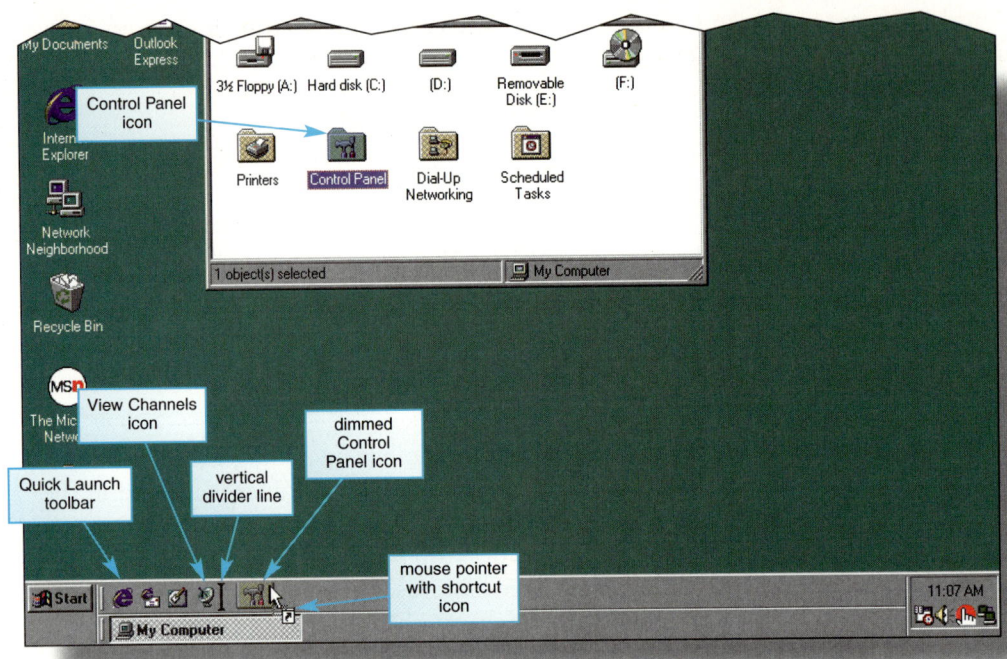

FIGURE 4-37

3 Release the right mouse button. Point to Create Shortcut(s) Here on the shortcut menu.

The dimmed Control Panel icon disappears, the vertical divider line remains on the toolbar, and a shortcut menu displays (Figure 4-38).

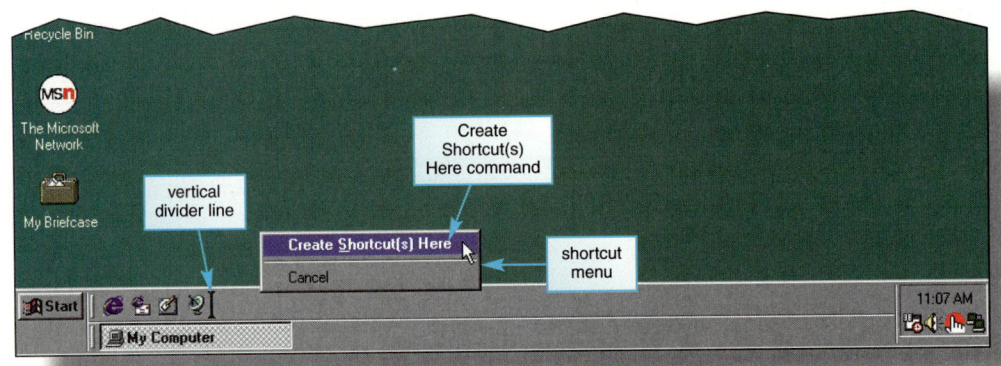

FIGURE 4-38

4 Click Create Shortcut(s) Here. Click the Close button in the My Computer window.

The Control Panel shortcut icon displays on the Quick Launch toolbar (Figure 4-39).

FIGURE 4-39

1. Drag folder icon to toolbar, click Yes button

After adding the Control Panel shortcut icon to the Quick Launch toolbar, you can open the Control Panel window by clicking the Control Panel icon on the toolbar.

Removing a Shortcut from a Toolbar and Resizing the Taskbar

After changing the size of the taskbar and adding a shortcut to the Quick Launch toolbar, remove the shortcut from the toolbar and return the toolbar to its original size by performing the following steps.

TO REMOVE A SHORTCUT FROM A TOOLBAR AND RESIZE THE TASKBAR

1. Right-click the Control Panel icon on the Quick Launch toolbar to display a shortcut menu.

2. Click Delete on the shortcut menu.

3. Click the Yes button in the Confirm File Delete dialog box.

4. Point to the top edge of the taskbar.

5. Drag the top edge of the taskbar downward until the taskbar on your desktop resembles the taskbar shown in Figure 4-40.

The shortcut to the Control Panel is removed from the Quick Launch toolbar and the taskbar is resized (Figure 4-40). The Start button, Quick Launch toolbar, taskbar button area, and tray status area display in their original positions on the taskbar.

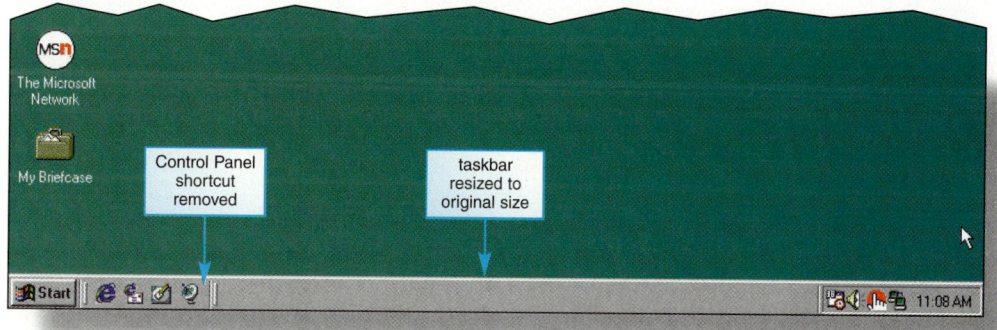

FIGURE 4-40

Customizing Folders

In addition to customizing the desktop, taskbar, and toolbars on the taskbar, you also can customize the folders that display on the desktop. You can customize a folder by adding a toolbar, an Explorer bar, or background to the folder, and you can display a folder as a Web page. The following sections use the My Documents folder to demonstrate how to customize a folder on your desktop. The **My Documents folder** allows you to store documents you create using a variety of application programs in one folder on the desktop.

Opening the View Menu in a Folder

To customize a folder you must open the folder and display the View menu in the folder window. Complete the following steps to open the My Documents folder and display the View menu in the folder.

 To Open a Folder and Display the View Menu

1 Point to the My Documents icon on the desktop (Figure 4-41).

FIGURE 4-41

2 Double-click the My Documents icon. If necessary, click the Maximize button to maximize the My Documents window. Click View on the menu bar.

The My Documents window opens and maximizes on the desktop and the View menu displays (Figure 4-42). Folder and document icons display in the My Documents window. The folders and files in the My Documents window on your computer may be different.

 **3** Click anywhere off the View menu to close the View menu.

The View menu closes.

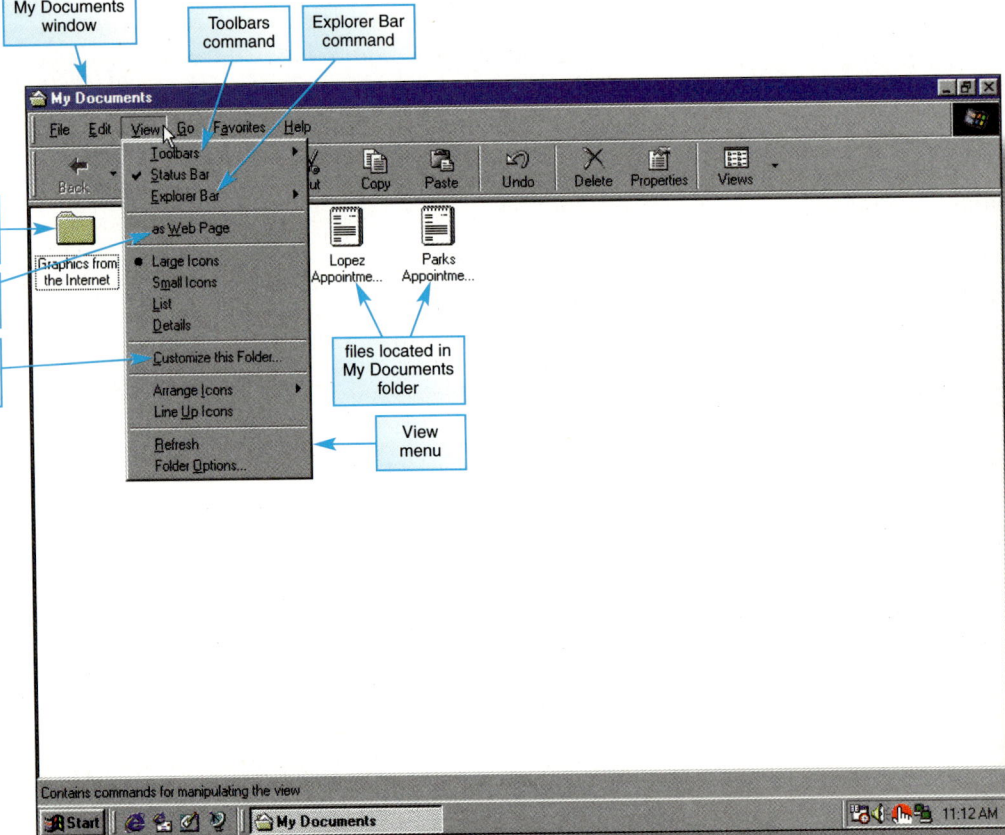

FIGURE 4-42

1. Click icon on desktop, press ENTER, press ALT+V

Among the commands on the View menu shown in Figure 4-42 are the commands to add a toolbar (Toolbars), add an Explorer Bar (Explorer Bar), display the folder as a Web page (as Web Page), and add a background (Customize this Folder).

Adding a Toolbar to a Folder

One method to customize a folder is to display additional toolbars (Address Bar or Links) in the folder window. The Standard Buttons toolbar already displays in all folder windows. When you add a toolbar to a folder window, the toolbar displays below the Standard Buttons toolbar in the folder window and displays in all folder windows you open in the future.

The **Address Bar toolbar** allows you to search for a Web page, launch an application program, display a document, open a folder window, and search for information on the Internet. The **Links toolbar** contains shortcuts to important Web pages that you click to display the associated Web pages in the folder window.

When you add a toolbar to any folder window, the toolbar displays in all open folder windows. Perform the following steps to add a second toolbar, the Address Bar toolbar, to the folder window.

Steps: To Add a Toolbar to a Folder

1 Click View on the menu bar, point to Toolbars, and point to Address Bar on the Toolbars submenu.

The View menu and Toolbars submenu display (Figure 4-43). The Address Bar command is highlighted on the Toolbars submenu and a check mark precedes the Standard Buttons command, indicating the Standard Buttons toolbar displays in the folder window.

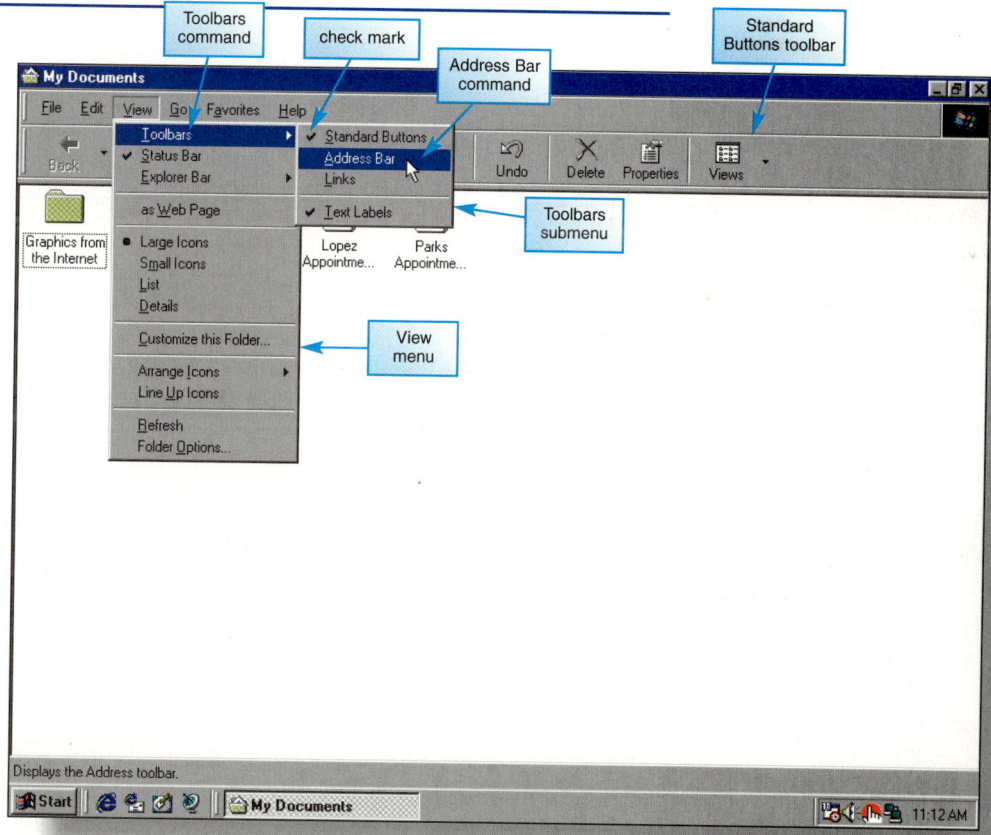

FIGURE 4-43

 **Click Address Bar.**

The Address Bar toolbar displays in the folder window (Figure 4-44). The Address box contains the My Documents icon and title, and all the folder and document icons in the My Documents folder are visible in the window.

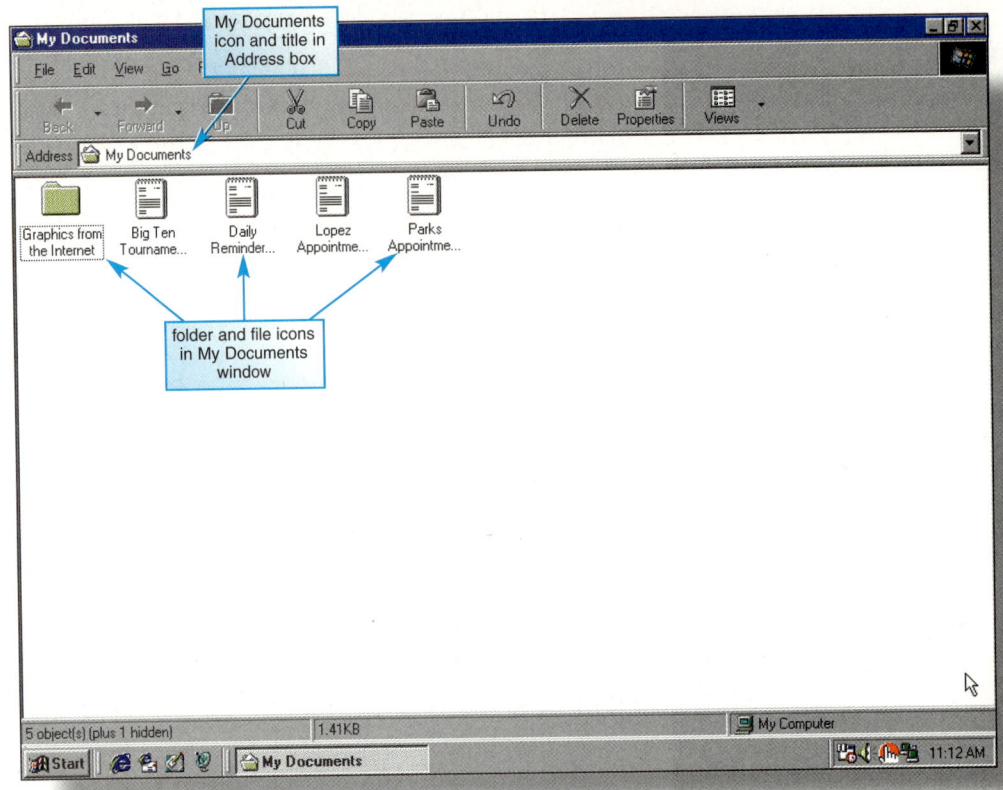

FIGURE 4-44

Other Ways

1. Press ALT+V, press T, press A
2. Right-click open area of menu bar or toolbar, click toolbar name

After adding the Address Bar toolbar to the folder, you can use the toolbar to type an address (URL) and display the associated Web page, type an application program name to launch a program, type a folder location (path) to open a folder window, type a document name to launch an application and display the document in the application window, and type a keyword or phrase (search inquiry) to display Web pages containing the keyword or phrase.

Adding an Explorer Bar to a Folder

Another method of customizing a folder is to add one of the four Explorer bars (Search, Favorites, History, and Channels) to the folder window. When you add an Explorer bar, two frames display in the folder window. The left frame contains the Explorer bar and the right frame contains the icons in the folder. The Explorer bar displays in the folder window until you close the window.

The **Search bar** allows you to search the World Wide Web for a word or phrase using a Search engine (MSN, AltaVista, Infoseek, Excite, Deja-News) that you select. A **Search engine** is a software tool that allows you to enter a **keyword** (a word or phrase) about a topic in which you are interested, searches for Web pages on the World Wide Web that contain the keyword, and then displays a list of hyperlinks that you can click to display the associated Web pages. The results of the search are displayed in the right frame of the folder window when you use the Search bar.

The **Favorites bar** displays a list of your favorite Web sites in the right frame of the folder window, the **History bar** displays a list of Web sites you previously have visited, and the **Channels bar** displays a list of channels. Perform the following steps to add the Search bar to the folder window.

More About

The Search Bar

Every search engine has its own rules for entering a search inquiry. For example, placing the word, AND, between two words (application AND software) finds only Web pages containing both the word, application, and the word, software. To learn the rules, look for a Tips or other hyperlink and then click the hyperlink for help.

Customizing Folders • WIN 4.33

PROJECT 4

Steps: To Add an Explorer Bar to a Folder

1 **Click View on the menu bar, point to Explorer Bar, and point to Search on the Explorer Bar submenu.**

The View menu and Explorer Bar submenu display (Figure 4-45). The Search command is highlighted and a large dot precedes the None command on the Explorer Bar submenu, indicating no Explorer bars display in the My Documents window.

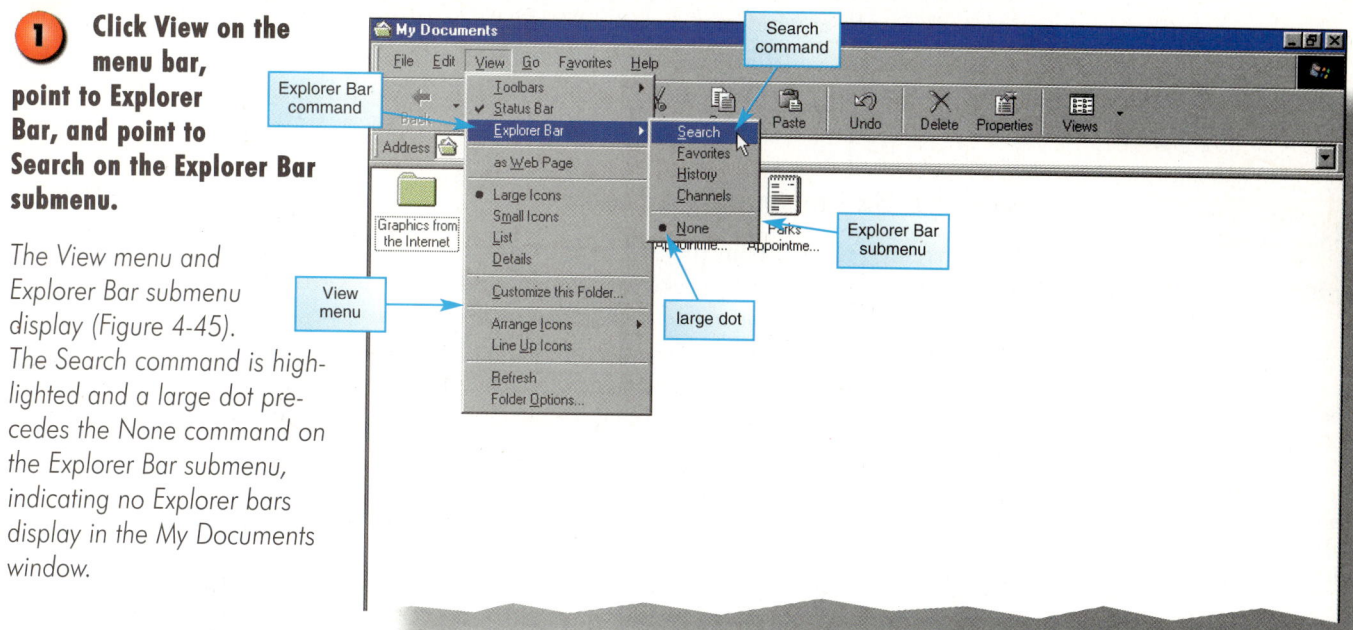

FIGURE 4-45

2 **Click Search.**

The Search bar displays in the left frame and the items in the My Document folder display in the right frame of the window (Figure 4-46). The Infoseek option button is selected to indicate the Infoseek search engine will be used to search the World Wide Web.

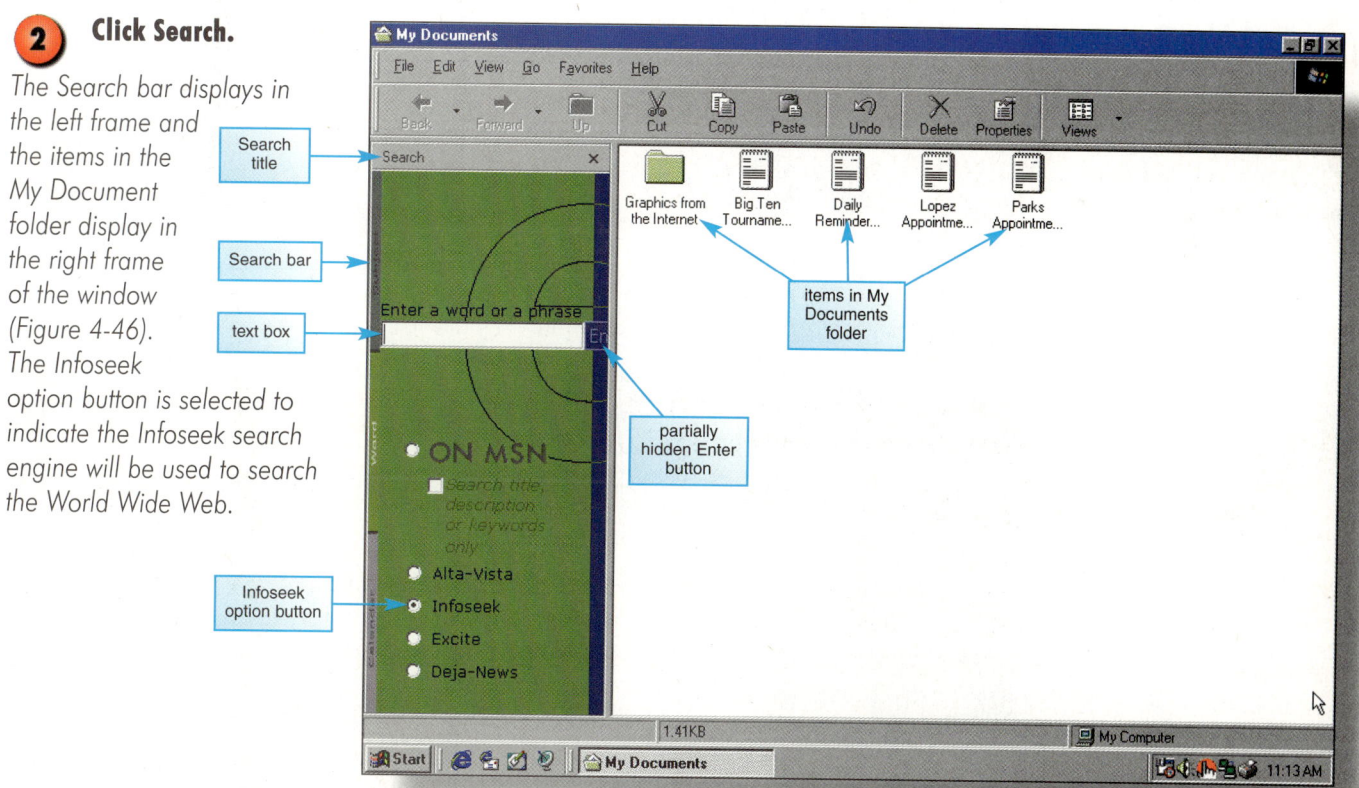

FIGURE 4-46

Other Ways

1. Press ALT+V, press E, press S

In Figure 4-46 on the previous page, you can search the World Wide Web for a word or phrase by typing a keyword (word or phrase) into the text box and clicking the partially hidden Enter button in the left frame. The selected search engine (Infoseek search engine) searches the World Wide Web for Web pages containing the keyword and then displays a list of hyperlinks for the Web pages found in the right frame of the folder window. Clicking a hyperlink displays the corresponding Web page in the right frame of the window.

Adding a Background to a Folder

Currently, the icons in the My Documents folder window display on a white background. You can customize a folder by adding a background to the window. The background can consist of a graphics image (picture) or an HTML document (Web page) and you also can select the color of the text and text background. When you add a background to a folder window, the background displays in the folder window until you remove it. A background cannot be added to the My Computer window.

To simplify the process of adding a background to a folder, Windows 98 allows you to use the Customize this Folder wizard. A **wizard** makes a difficult process easier by guiding you through the process step by step. The **Customize this Folder wizard** assists you in changing the appearance of a folder by adding a background. Perform the following steps to add a background consisting of the Clouds.bmp picture to the My Documents folder.

> **More About**
>
> **Folder Backgrounds**
>
> A background can be added to a folder using the Customize this Folder wizard when the folder is opened using My Computer or Windows Explorer. A background cannot be added to the My Computer window or any Windows Explorer window.

To Add a Background to a Folder

1 Click View on the menu bar and then point to Customize this Folder.

The View menu displays and the highlighted Customize this Folder command displays (Figure 4-47).

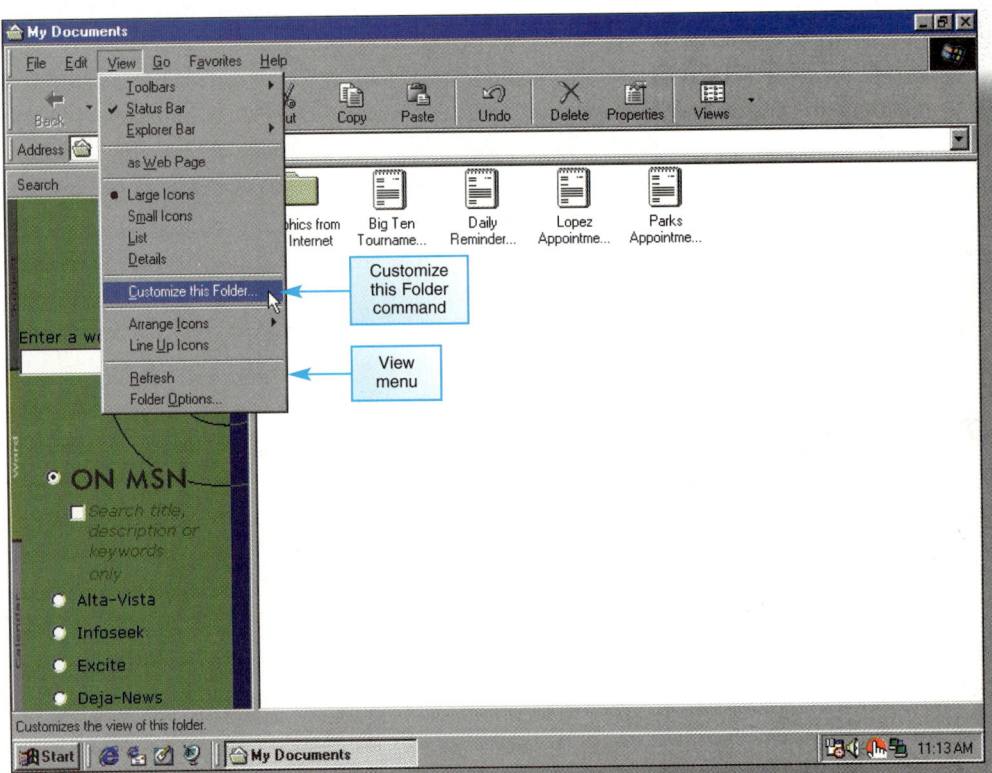

FIGURE 4-47

Customizing Folders • WIN 4.35

2 Click Customize this Folder. Click Choose a background picture in the Customize this Folder dialog box. Point to the Next button.

The Customize this Folder dialog box displays (Figure 4-48). The dialog box contains a preview pane containing a picture, message, question, three option buttons and their explanations, and two command buttons (Next and Cancel). The Choose a background picture option button is selected.

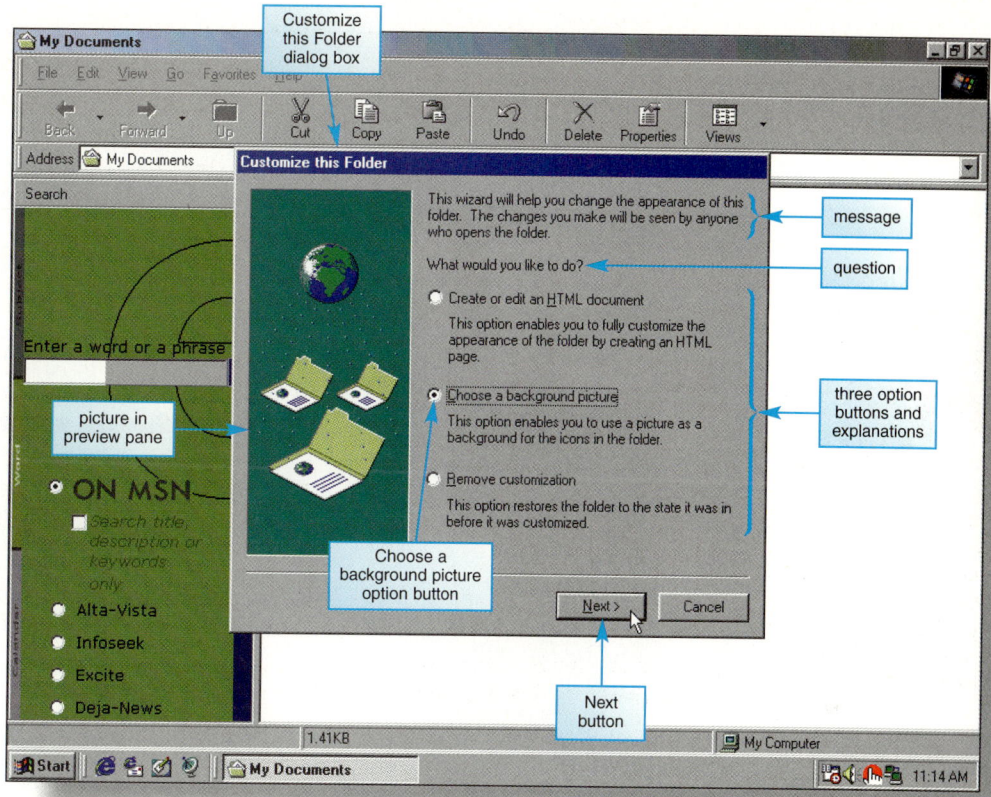

FIGURE 4-48

3 Click the Next button. Point to Clouds.bmp in the list box.

The contents of the Customize this Folder dialog box change (Figure 4-49). The picture in the preview pane is replaced with a vertical scroll bar, and the dialog box contains a message explaining how to choose a background picture, a Browse button, a list box of background picture file names, the Icon caption colors pane, and a Back button.

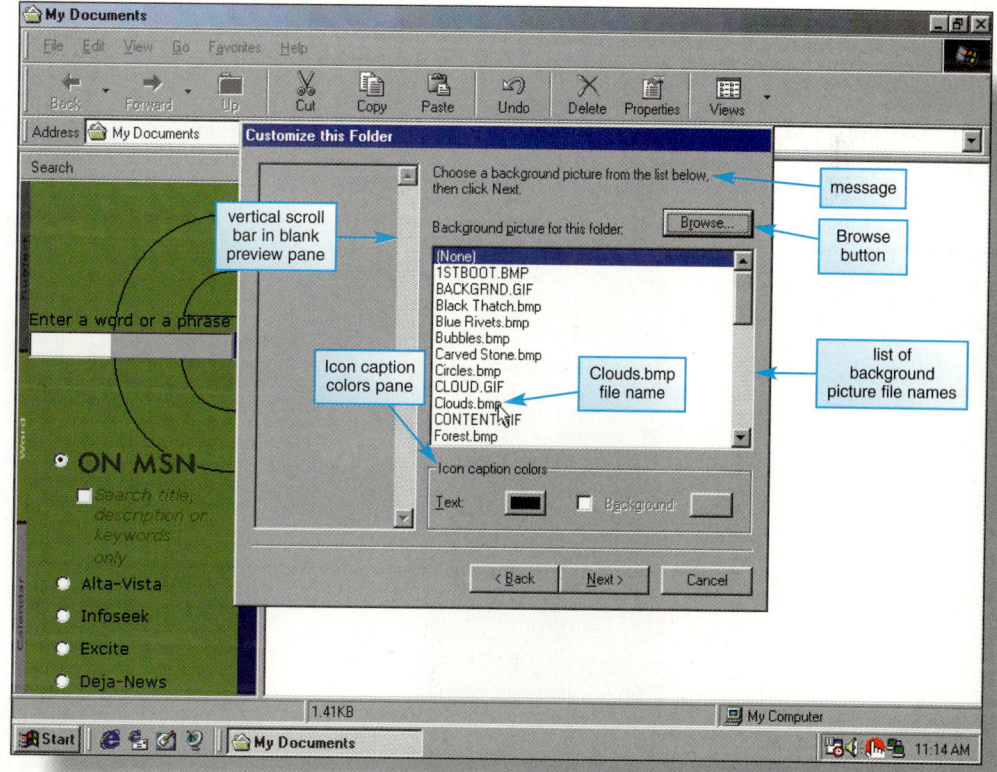

FIGURE 4-49

WIN 4.36 • Project 4 • Modifying Your Desktop Work Environment

4 **Click Clouds.bmp in the list box. Point to the Next button.**

The Clouds.bmp entry is highlighted in the list box, and the Clouds image displays in the preview pane (Figure 4-50).

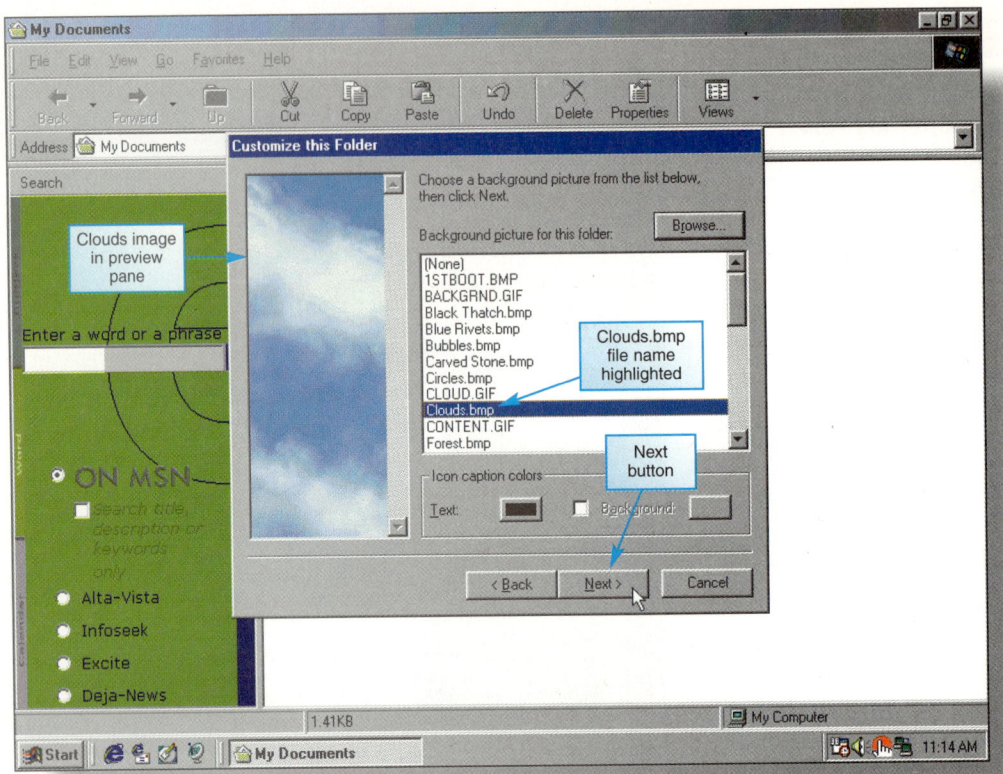

FIGURE 4-50

5 **Click the Next button. Point to the Finish button.**

The Customize this Folder dialog box changes to contain a message and a summary of the changes being made to the folder background, and the graphics image in the preview pane changes (Figure 4-51).

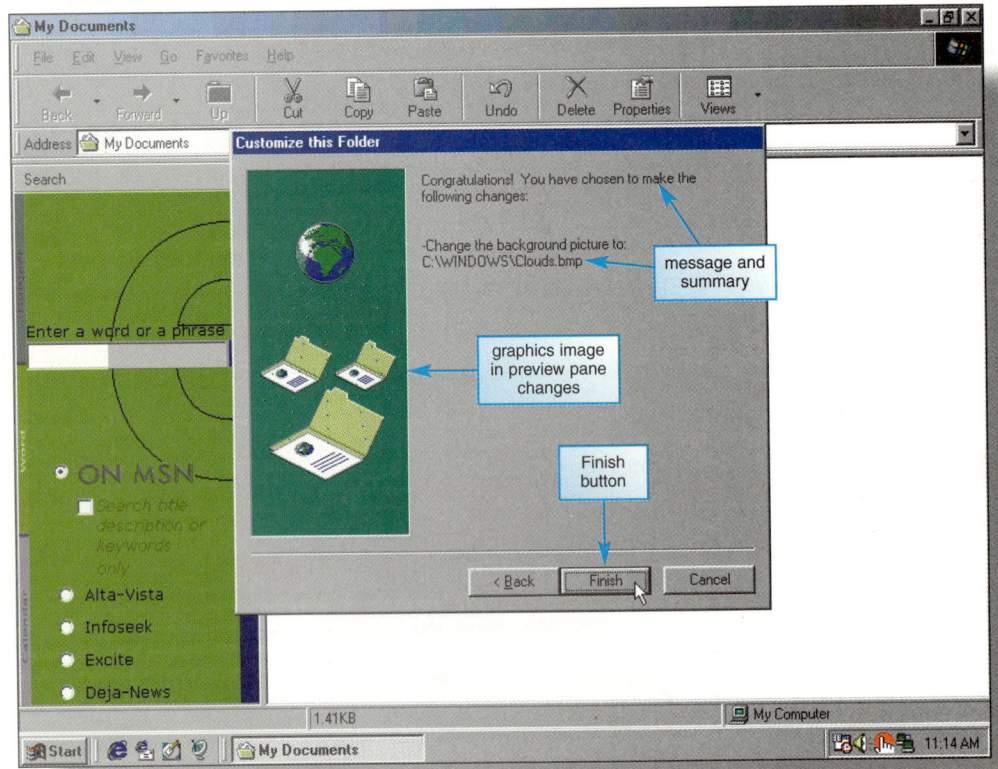

FIGURE 4-51

Click the Finish button.

The Customize this Folder dialog box closes and the Clouds background displays in the right frame of the My Documents window (Figure 4-52).

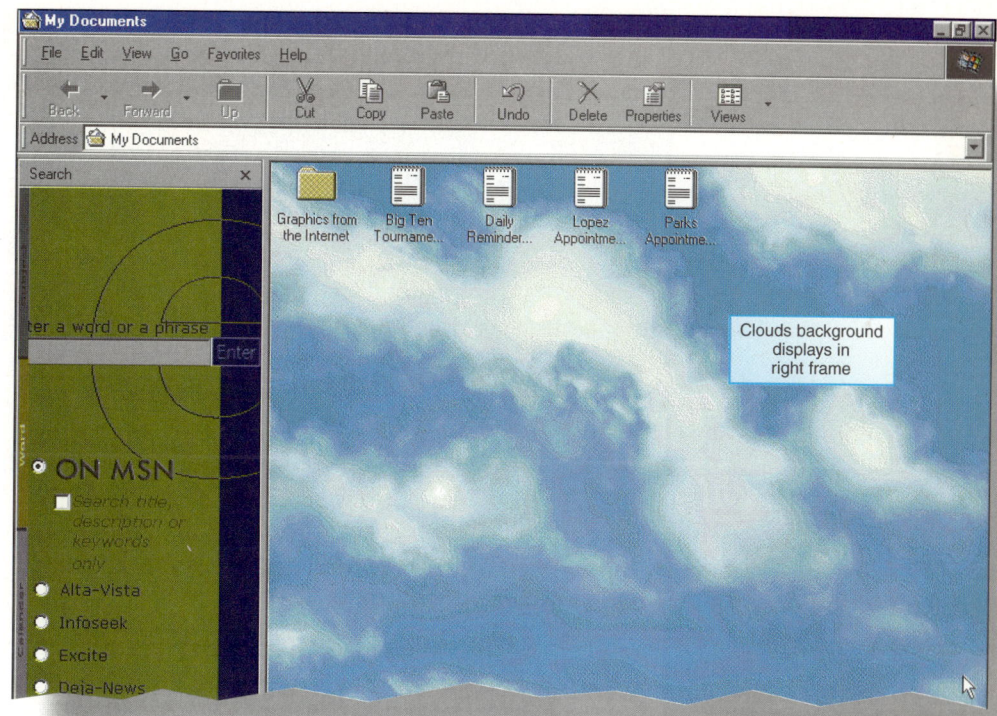

FIGURE 4-52

Removing the Toolbar and Explorer Bar from a Folder

Previously in this project you added the Address bar toolbar, Explorer bar, and a background to the My Documents folder window. In the next section, you will customize the folder by displaying the folder as a Web page. Prior to customizing the folder, remove the Address bar toolbar and Explorer bar from the folder window so only the background displays in the window. Perform the following steps to remove the Address bar toolbar and Explorer bar from the My Documents folder window.

TO REMOVE A TOOLBAR AND EXPLORER BAR FROM A FOLDER

1. Click View on the menu bar, point to Toolbars, and click Address Bar on the Toolbars submenu.
2. Click View on the menu bar, point to Explorer Bar, and click None on the Explorer Bar submenu.

The Address bar toolbar and Explorer bar are removed from the My Documents window (Figure 4-53 on the next page). The Clouds background fills the area below the Standard Buttons toolbar in the folder window.

> **Other Ways**
>
> 1. Right-click open area of folder window, click Customize this Folder, click Choose a background picture, click Next button, select background picture, click Next button, click Finish button

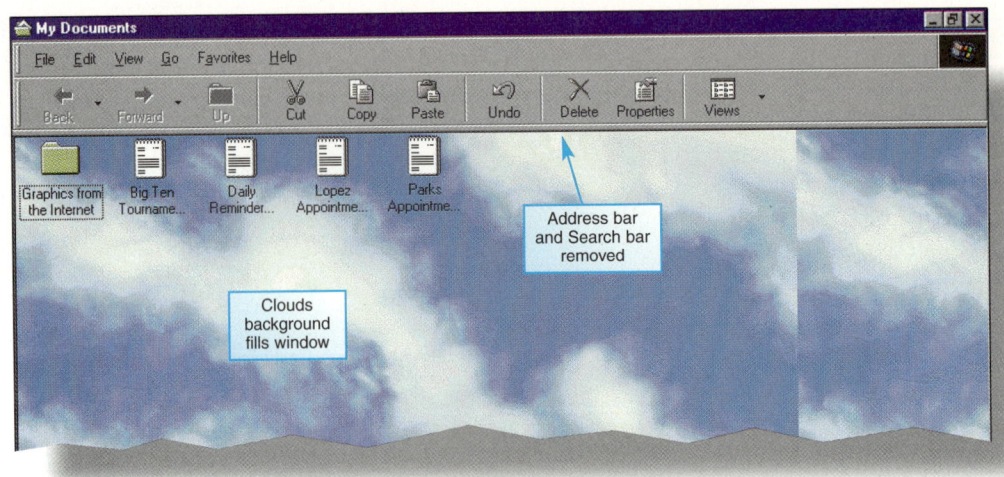

FIGURE 4-53

More About

Displaying a Folder as a Web Page

To display all folders as Web pages, open the My Computer window, click View on the menu bar, click Folder Options, click the General tab, click Custom, based on settings you choose, click the Settings button, click For all folders with HTML content, and click the OK button.

Displaying a Folder as a Web Page

When you display a folder as a Web page (see Figure 4-55), the area below the Standard Buttons toolbar is divided into a left and right panel. The **left panel** contains the folder icon, folder title, and information about the folder. The **right panel** contains the icons in the folder. In Windows terminology, this is referred to as **displaying a folder as a Web page.**

You display a folder as a Web page by clicking the **as Web page command** on the View menu. After displaying a folder as a Web page, the folder continues to display as a Web page until you click the as Web Page command again. Perform the following steps to display the My Documents folder as a Web page.

 To Display a Folder as a Web Page

1. **Click View on the menu bar and then point to as Web Page.**

   The View menu displays (Figure 4-54).

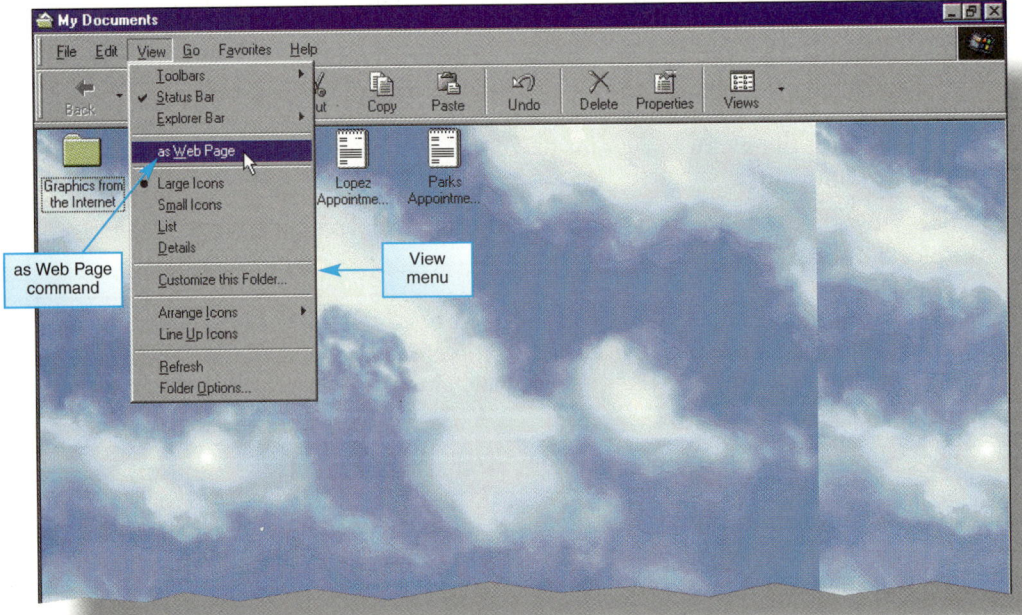

FIGURE 4-54

2 **Click as Web Page.**

Two panels now display in the My Document window (Figure 4-55). Although not visible, a check mark precedes the as Web Page command on the View menu.

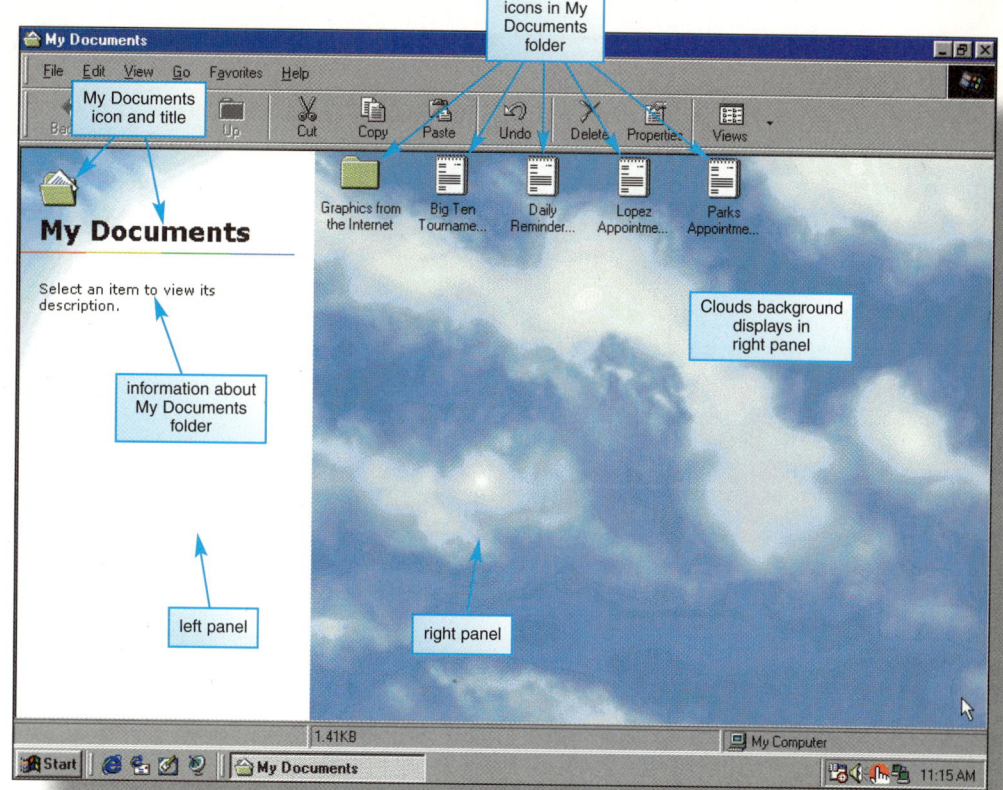

FIGURE 4-55

In Figure 4-48, the left panel contains the My Document icon and icon title and the text, Select an item to view its description. In the right panel, the icons in the My Document folder display on the Clouds background.

Removing the Background and No Longer Displaying the Folder as a Web Page

To remove the background from the My Documents folder and no longer display the folder as a Web page, perform the following steps.

TO REMOVE THE BACKGROUND AND NO LONGER DISPLAY A FOLDER AS A WEB PAGE

1 Click View on the menu bar and then click Customize this Folder.

2 Click Remove customization and then click the Next button in the Customize this Folder dialog box.

3 Click the Next button and then click the Finish button in the Customize this Folder dialog box.

4 Click View on the menu bar and then click as Web Page.

The Clouds background is removed from the My Documents window and the My Documents folder no longer displays as a Web page (Figure 4-56 on the next page).

1. Click ALT+V, press W

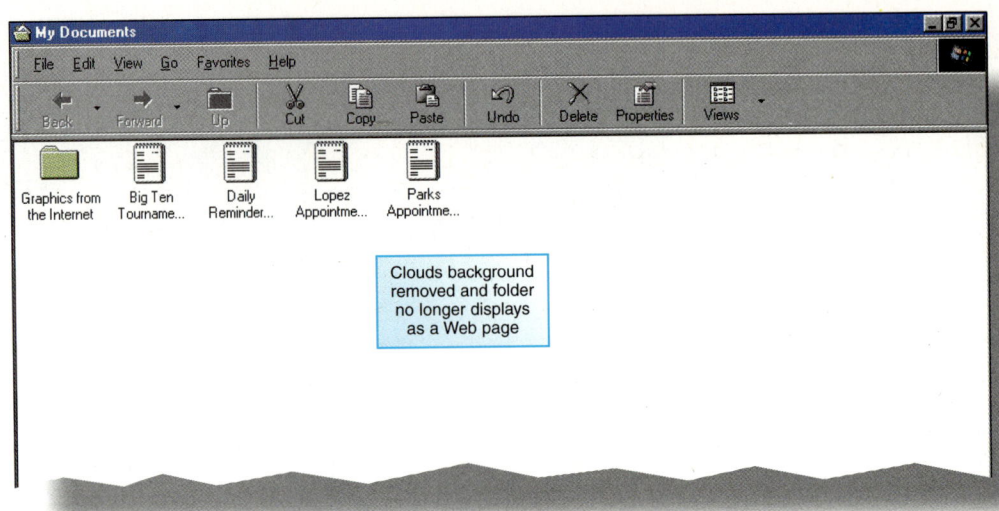

FIGURE 4-56

Windows 98 Desktop Views

The desktop view you choose affects the appearance of the desktop, how you open and work with icons and windows on the desktop, and how you work with files and folders on your computer. The desktop can be viewed in three styles: Classic style, Web style, and Custom style. When you choose the **Classic style** as the desktop view, the desktop and the objects on the desktop display and function as they did in Windows 95, a previous version of Windows. The icon titles of the icons on the desktop are not underlined, you must double-click icons to open their windows, and the desktop is referred to as the **Classic Windows Desktop**. (Figure 4-57a).

A second desktop view available in Windows 98 is the Web style. When you choose the **Web style** as the desktop view, the icon titles of the icons on the desktop are underlined, you must single-click (click) icons to open their windows, and the desktop is referred to as the Active Desktop™. The **Active Desktop™** causes the Internet Explorer Channel bar to display on the desktop and allows you to display other objects, called **active desktop items**, on the desktop (Figure 4-57b). Underlined icon titles, such as those shown with the icons on the desktop in Figure 4-57b, resemble the underlined hyperlinks found on most Web pages. In Windows terminology, the Active Desktop™ enables all Web-related content on the desktop and causes the desktop to display as a Web page.

The third desktop view is the Custom style. The **Custom style** allows you to pick and choose the options you prefer, including a combination of Classic style and Web style settings. When Windows 98 is installed on a computer, the desktop view that displays when you launch Windows 98 is predetermined by Microsoft to be the Custom style. Because the settings for the Custom style are set by Microsoft, the desktop view that displays when you launch Windows 98 is referred to as the default Custom style. When the **default Custom style** is the desktop view, the icon titles of the icons on the desktop are not underlined, you must double-click icons to open their windows, the Classic Windows Desktop displays, and the Internet Explorer Channel bar and active desktop items do not display on the desktop (Figure 4-57c). The desktop shown in Figure 4-57c is identical to the desktop that displays when the desktop view is the Classic style (see Figure 4-57a).

Desktop Views

The Classic style was included in the Windows 98 operating system to allow Windows 95 users to upgrade easily to the newer Windows 98 operating system. Responses from people in the Beta Test program, which is a program designed to test software prior to the public sale of the software, indicated that most Windows 95 users had little difficulty switching to Windows 98, and experienced users liked the Web style and Active Desktop™.

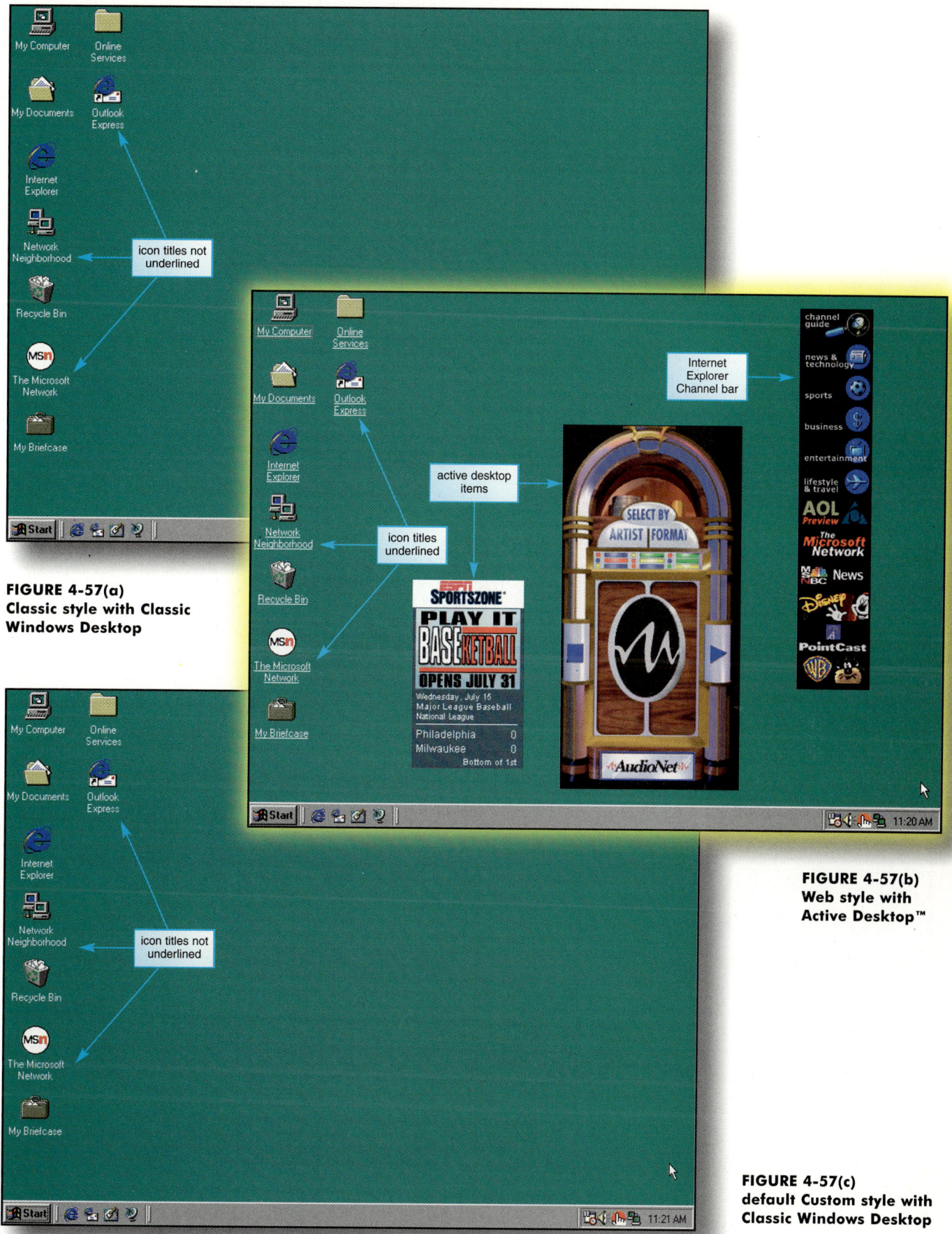

FIGURE 4-57(a)
Classic style with Classic Windows Desktop

FIGURE 4-57(b)
Web style with Active Desktop™

FIGURE 4-57(c)
default Custom style with Classic Windows Desktop

As shown in Figure 4-57 on the previous page, the desktop view you choose determines what objects display on the desktop and how the objects on the desktop look. Depending upon your choice of a desktop view, the Channel bar and active desktop items may or may not display on the desktop and the icon titles of the icons on the desktop may or may not be underlined.

Viewing Web Content in a Folder

The desktop view you choose also affects the manner in which the contents of a folder display in an open window. Figure 4-58 illustrates the results of opening the My Computer window when the desktop view is the Classic style or Web style.

When the desktop view is the Classic style and you open the My Computer window, the nine icons in the My Computer folder display in the open area below the Standard Buttons toolbar (Figure 4-58a). The My Computer window shown in Figure 4-58a displays when you open the My Computer window and the desktop view is the default Custom style.

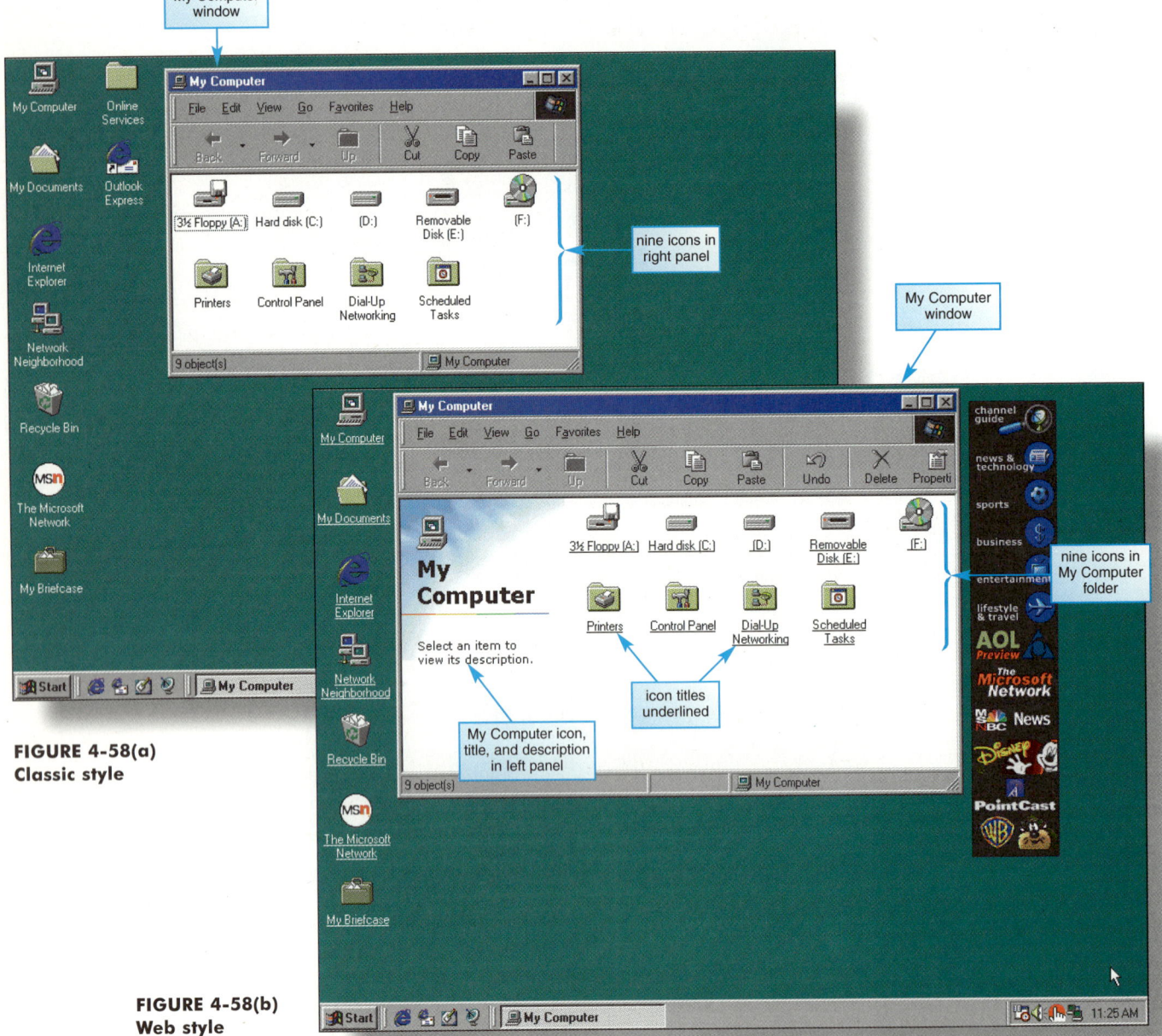

FIGURE 4-58(a)
Classic style

FIGURE 4-58(b)
Web style

Displaying Folders as Web Pages

Previously in this project, you displayed a folder (the My Documents folder) as a Web page by clicking the as Web Page command on the View menu in the folder window (see Figures 4-54 and 4-55 on pages WIN 4.38 and WIN 4.39). When the desktop view is the Web style, all folders display as Web pages. When you open the My Computer window, the My Computer icon and icon title, My Computer, display at the top of the left panel (Figure 4-58b). The text, Select an item to view its description, displays below the icon and title in the left panel. The right panel contains the nine icons in the My Computer folder and each icon title in the right panel is underlined.

As shown in Figure 4-58, the desktop view you choose determines whether a folder displays as a Web page or not. Depending upon your choice of a desktop view, the area below the Standard Buttons toolbar may contain only the icons in a folder, or it may contain a left and right panel with information about the folder and the icons in the folder.

Opening Each Folder in the Same Window or in Its Own Window

The desktop view you choose also affects how folder windows display on the desktop. Figure 4-59 illustrates the results of opening the My Computer and Control Panel windows when the desktop view is the Classics style or the Web style.

When the desktop view is the Classic style and you open the My Computer window and then open the Control Panel window, two windows display on the desktop and two buttons display in the taskbar button area (Figure 4-59a). The My Computer window is partially hidden behind the Control Panel window. To view the contents of the My Computer window, you click the My Computer title bar to move the My Computer window on top of the Control Panel window.

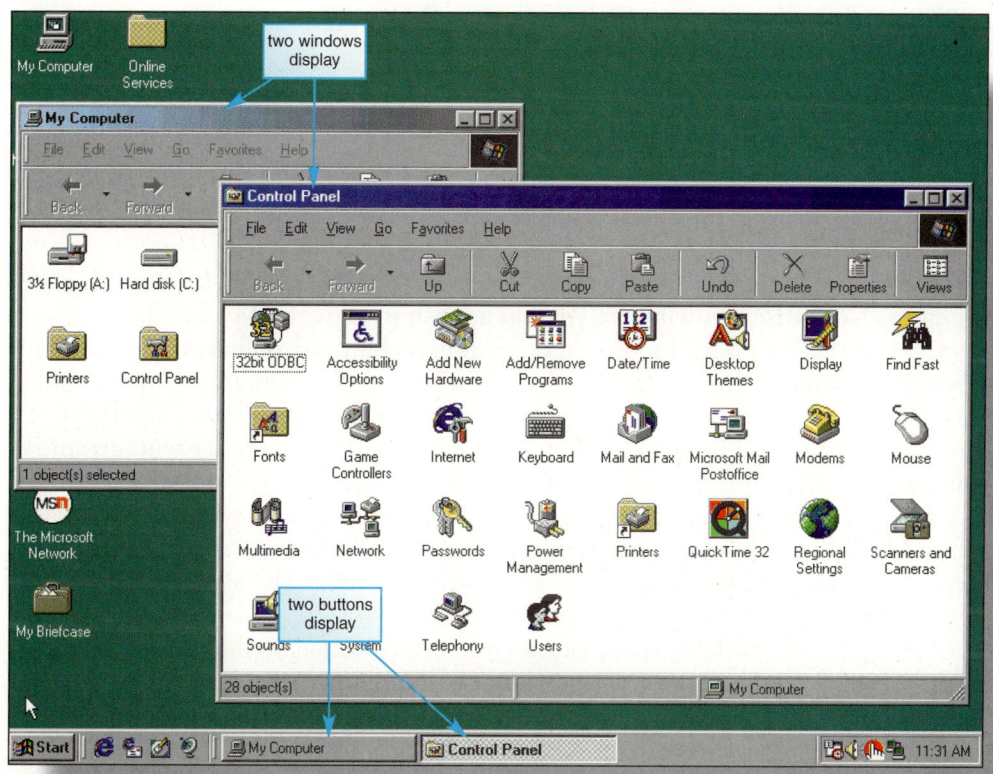

FIGURE 4-59(a)
Classic style

When the desktop view is the Web style and you open the My Computer window, a single window displays on the desktop. When you click the Control Panel icon in the My Computer window, the Control Panel window opens in the same window in which the My Computer window was displayed, and the Control Panel button replaces the My Computer button in the taskbar button area (Figure 4-59b). The Control Panel folder displays as a Web page with the left panel containing information about the Control Panel and the right panel containing the icons in the Control Panel folder.

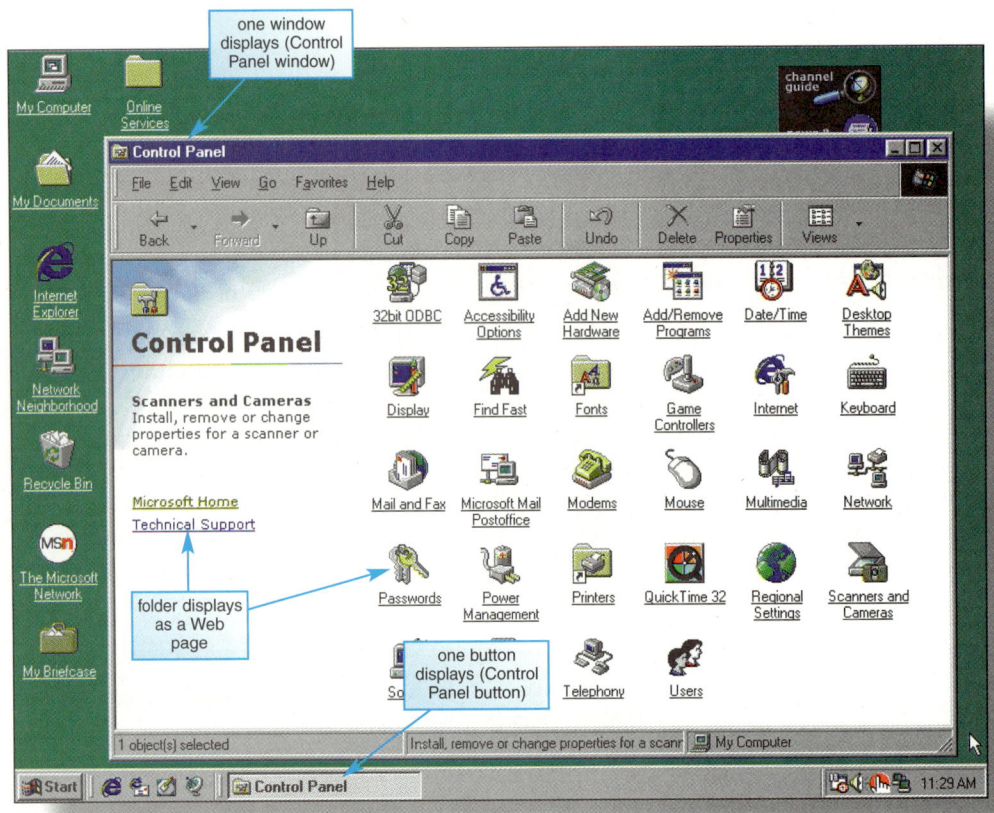

**FIGURE 4-59(b)
Web style**

The contents of the My Computer folder are not visible on the desktop. If, after opening the Control Panel window, you again wish to view the My Computer window, you can click the Back button on the Standard Buttons toolbar to replace the Control Panel window and its taskbar button with the My Computer window and its taskbar button. At this point, if you wish to view the Control Panel window again, you can click the Forward button to replace the My Computer window and its taskbar button with the Control Panel window and its taskbar button.

A single window, such as the Control Panel window shown in Figure 4-59b, also displays when you open the My Computer window and then open the Control Panel window when the desktop view is the default Custom style. The icons in the Control Panel window are not underlined, however.

As shown in Figure 4-59, the desktop view you choose determines how folder windows display on the desktop. Depending on your choice of a desktop view, a folder may open in the same window or in its own window on the desktop.

Choosing the Classic Style as the Desktop View

You easily can change the desktop view from the default Custom style to the Classic style or Web style. If you have worked with and are familiar with Windows 95, a previous version of Windows, you may prefer to change the desktop view to the Classic style. In the Classic style, the desktop and the objects on the desktop display and function as they did in Windows 95. You choose the Classic style as the desktop view using the Start menu and the Folder Options dialog box. Perform the following steps to choose the Classic style as the desktop view.

To Choose the Classic Style as the Desktop View

1 **Click the Start button, point to Settings on the Start menu, and then point to Folder Options on the Settings submenu.**

The Start menu and Settings submenu display (Figure 4-60).

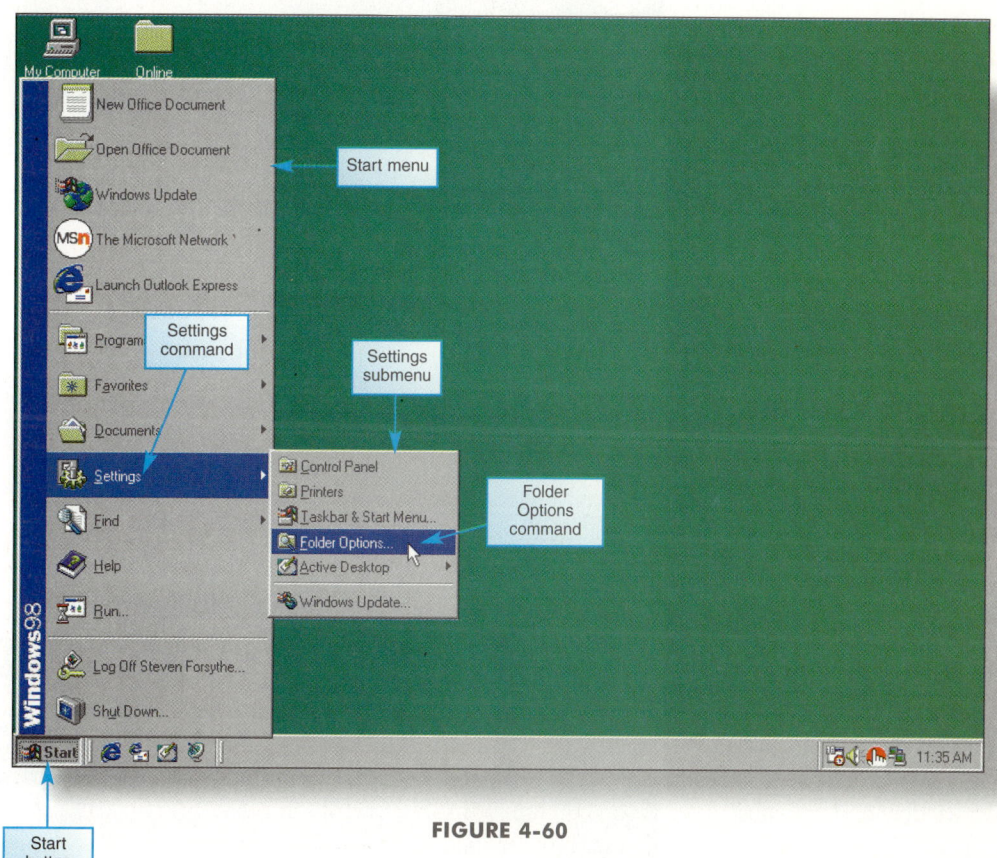

FIGURE 4-60

2 Click Folder Options and then point to Classic style in the Folder Options dialog box.

The Folder Options dialog box and General sheet display (Figure 4-61). The Windows Desktop Update pane contains three option buttons. The Custom, based on settings you choose option button is selected. The preview pane contains a single window in which the icon titles are not underlined. As such, the preview pane illustrates that in the default Custom style, each folder opens in the same window and you must double-click an icon to open its window.

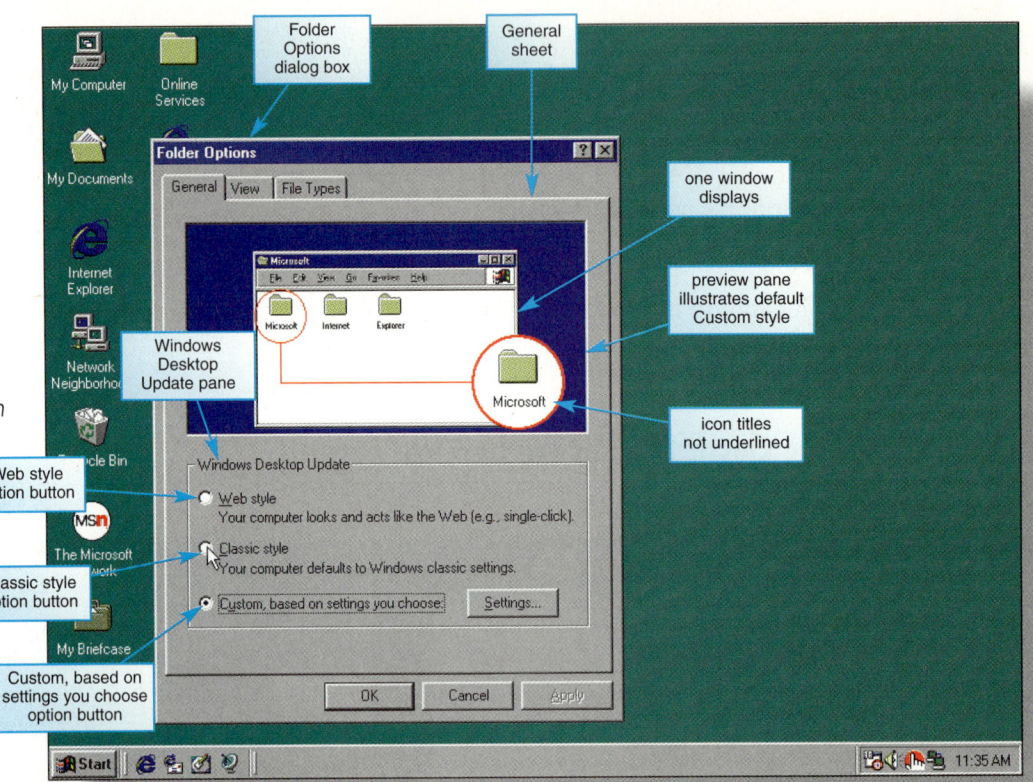

FIGURE 4-61

3 Click Classic style and then point to the OK button.

The Classic style option button is selected (Figure 4-62). The preview pane contains two windows in which the icon titles are not underlined. As such, the preview pane illustrates that in the Classic style, each folder opens in its own window and you must double-click an icon to open its window.

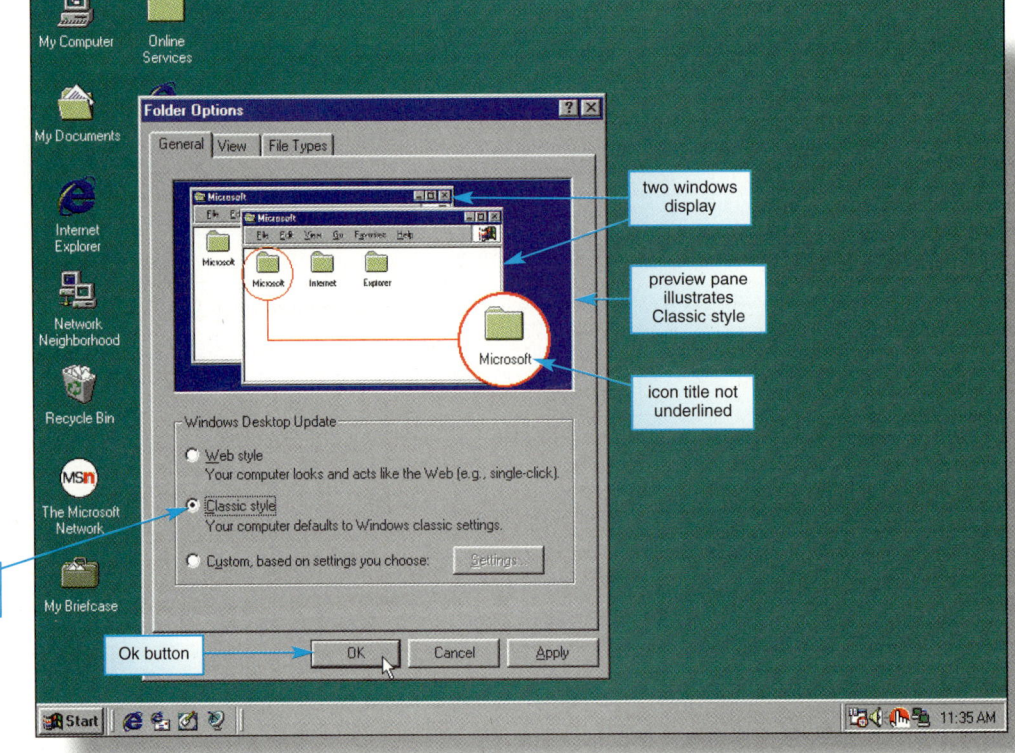

FIGURE 4-62

Choosing the Classic Style as the Desktop View • WIN 4.47

 Click the OK button.

When you click the OK button, the Folder Options dialog box closes and the desktop view changes to the Classic style (Figure 4-63). If you click the Apply button, the desktop view changes to the Classic style but the Folder Options dialog box remains open, allowing you to see the effect of the change and to make another change.

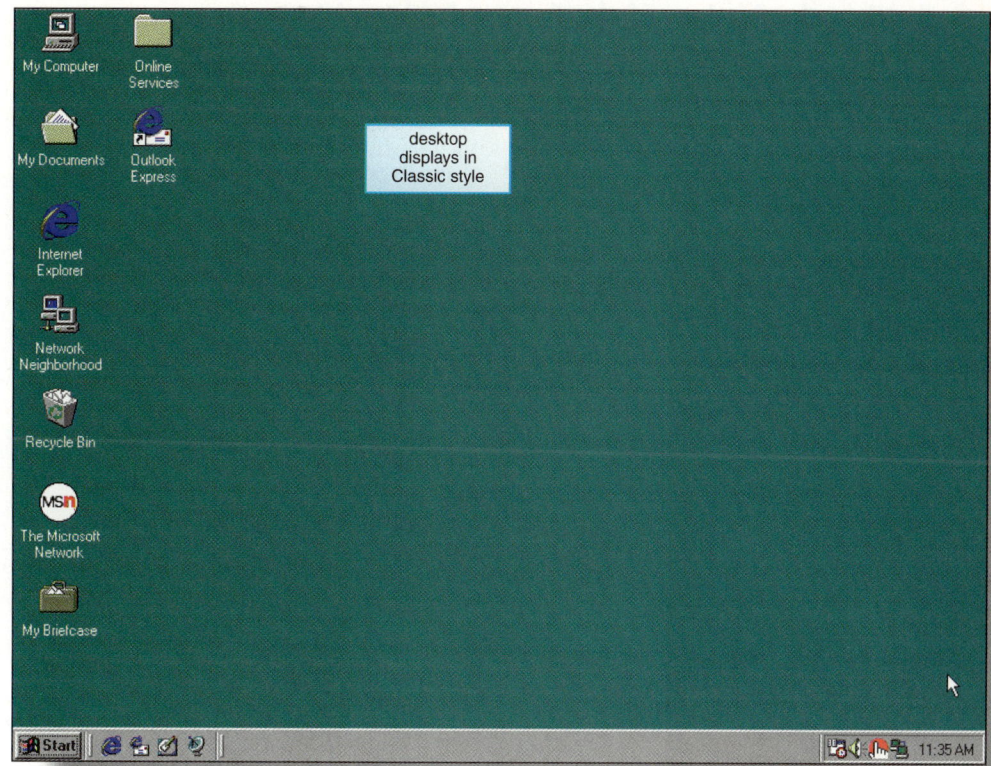

FIGURE 4-63

When you choose the Classic style as the desktop view, the desktop displays as it did when the default Custom style was the desktop view. The only difference between the default Custom style and the Classic style is the manner in which windows open on the desktop. In default Custom style, each folder opens in the same window. In Classic style, each folder opens in its own window.

Viewing the Settings for the Classic Style

After choosing the Classic style as the desktop view, you can view the settings for the current desktop view (Classic style) in the Folder Options dialog box. Perform the steps on the next page to view the settings for the current desktop view (Classic style).

1. Double-click My Computer icon, on View menu click Folder Options, click Classic style, click OK button
2. Right-click desktop, click Properties, click Web tab, click Folder Options, click Yes button, click Classic style, click OK button

WIN 4.48 • Project 4 • Modifying Your Desktop Work Environment

 Steps **To View the Settings of the Current Desktop View**

1 Click the Start button, point to Settings on the Start menu, click Folder Options on the Settings submenu, click Custom, based on settings you choose in the Folder Options dialog box, and then point to the Settings button.

The Folder Options dialog box displays and the Custom, based up settings you choose option button is selected (Figure 4-64).

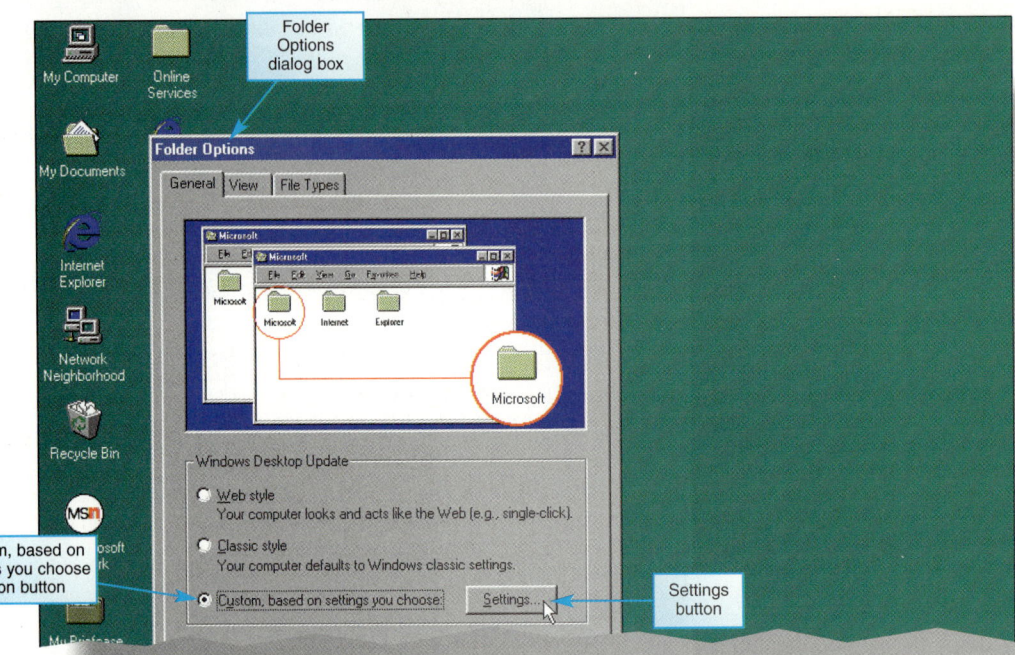

FIGURE 4-64

2 Click the Settings button.

The Custom Settings dialog box displays (Figure 4-65). The four selected option buttons in the dialog box define the settings for the Classic style.

3 Click the Cancel button in the Custom Settings dialog box. Click the Cancel button in the Folder Options dialog box.

The Custom Settings dialog box and Folder Options dialog box close.

 **Other Ways**

1. Press TAB to select option button, press UP ARROW or DOWN ARROW to select Custom style option button, press RIGHT ARROW to select Settings button, press ENTER

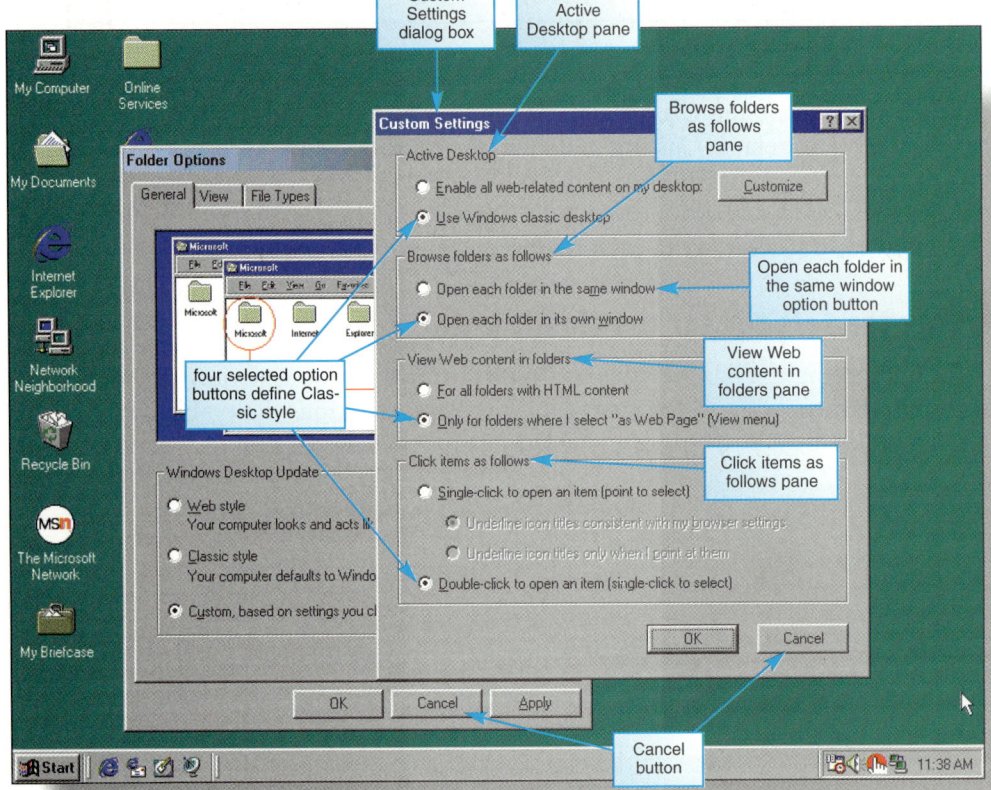

FIGURE 4-65

The Custom Settings dialog box shown in Figure 4-65 contains four panes (Active Desktop, Browse folders as follows, View Web content in folders, and Click items as follows). The **Use Windows classic desktop option button** is selected in the Active Desktop pane, the **Open each folder in its own window option button** is selected in the Browse folders as follows pane, the **Only for folders where I select "as Web Page" (View menu) option button** is selected in the View Web content in folders pane, and the **Double-click to open an item (single-click to select) option button** is selected in the Click items as follows pane.

Collectively, the four selected option buttons define the settings for the Classic style. The settings indicate that in Classic style, the Windows Classic Desktop displays, each folder opens in its own window, only folders that you select display as Web pages, and you must double-click an icon to open its window and single-click to select the icon.

The settings for the Classic style are similar to the settings for the default Custom style. By selecting the Open each folder in the same window option button in the Browse folders as follows pane instead of the Open each folder in its own window option button, the resulting four selected option buttons define the default Custom style. Thus, the only difference between the Classic style and the default Custom style is whether a folder opens in the same window or in its own window.

Choosing the Web Style as the Desktop View

In the previous section, you changed the desktop view from the default Custom style to the Classic style. You also can change the desktop view to the Web style. The appearance of the desktop in the Web style and the settings that define the Web style are noticeably different from the desktop and settings of the default Custom style and Classic style. In Web style, the icon titles of the icons on the desktop are underlined, you must single-click icons to open their windows, the Channel bar displays on the desktop, and active desktop items may display on the desktop. Perform the steps on the next page to choose the Web style as the desktop view.

WIN 4.50 • Project 4 • Modifying Your Desktop Work Environment

Microsoft **Windows 98**

 To Choose the Web Style as the Desktop View

1 Click the Start button, point to Settings on the Start menu, click Folder Options on the Settings submenu, click Web style in the Folder Options dialog box, and point to the OK button.

The Folder Options dialog box displays and the Web style option button is selected (Figure 4-66). The preview pane contains a single window with underlined icons and the Channel bar. This illustrates the Web style opens each folder in the same window, an icon is single-clicked to open its window, and all Web-related content (Channel bar and active desktop items) display on the desktop.

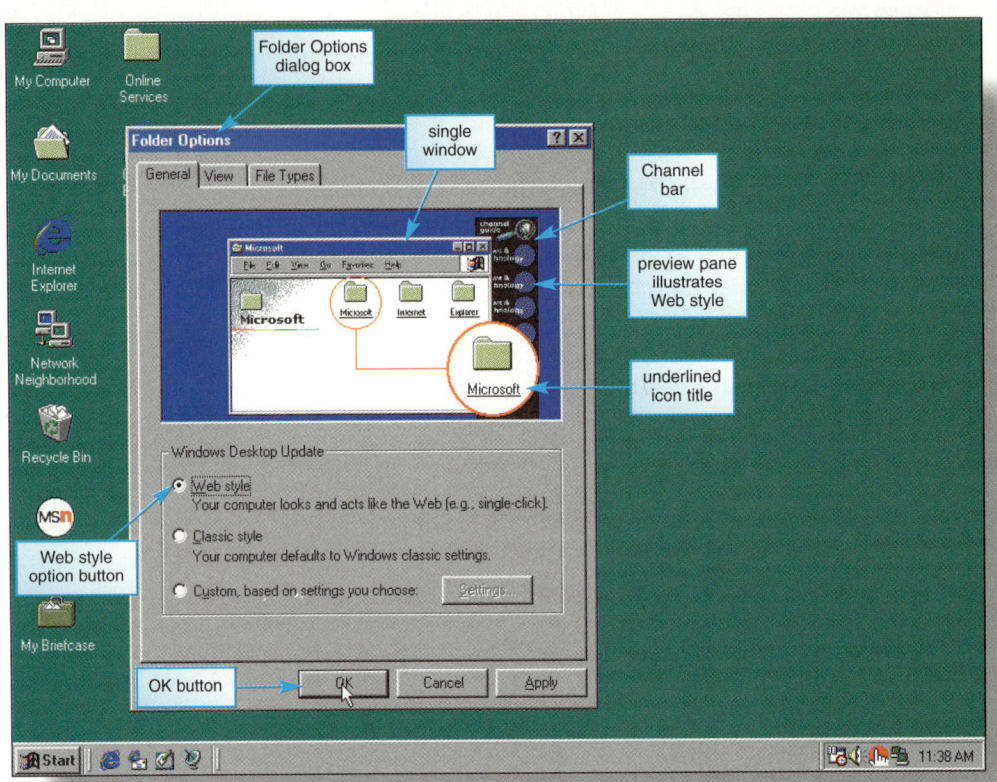

FIGURE 4-66

 Click the OK button.

The desktop view changes to the Web style (Figure 4-67).

Other Ways

1. Double-click My Computer icon, on View menu click Folder Options, click Web style, click OK button
2. Right-click desktop, click Properties, click Web tab, click Folder Options, click Yes button, click Web style, click OK button

FIGURE 4-67

When the desktop view is changed to the Web style, icon titles of the icons on the desktop are underlined. As such, you single-click an icon to open its window and display its button in the taskbar button area and point to an icon to select the icon. In this sense, the icons of the desktop behave in a similar fashion to hyperlinks on a Web page. Also, the Active Desktop™ displays, allowing you to view the Internet Explorer Channel bar and add active desktop items to the desktop.

Viewing the Web Style Settings

After choosing the Web style as the desktop view, view the individual settings of the Web style by performing the following steps.

TO VIEW THE SETTINGS OF THE CURRENT DESKTOP VIEW

1. Click the Start button and then point to Settings on the Start menu.
2. Click Folder Options on the Settings submenu.
3. Click Custom, based on settings you choose in the Folder Options dialog box.
4. Click the Settings button.

The Folder Options dialog box and Custom Settings dialog box display on the desktop (Figure 4-68).

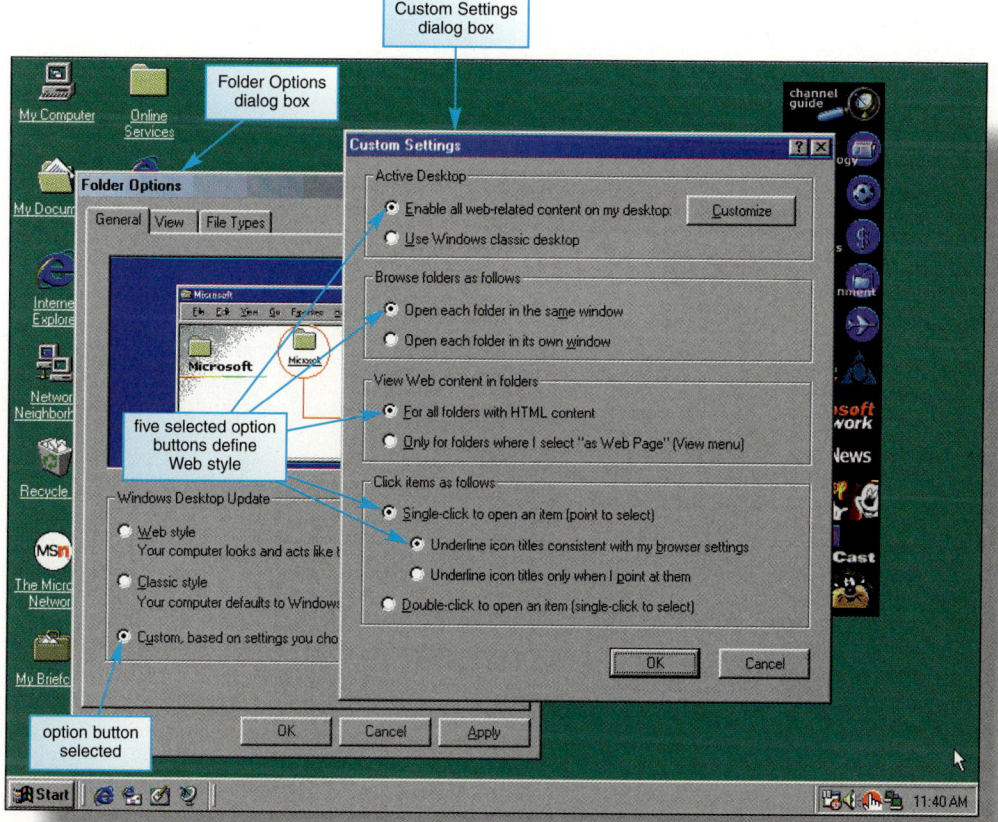

FIGURE 4-68

The selected option buttons in the Custom Settings dialog box in Figure 4-68 on the previous page show the settings for the Web style. The **Enable all web-related content on my desktop option button** is selected in the Active Desktop pane, the **Open each folder in the same window option button** is selected in the Browse folders as follows pane, the **For all folders with HTML content** option button is selected in the View Web content in folders pane, and the **Single-click to open an item (point to select) option button** is selected in the Click items as follows pane. Two additional buttons are indented and display below the Single-click to open an item (point to select) option button. The **Underline icon titles consistent with my browser settings option button** is selected.

Collectively, the five selected option buttons define the settings for the Web style. The settings indicate that in Web style, all Web-related content (Channel Bar and active desktop items) displays on the desktop, each folder opens in the same window, all folders are viewed with HTML content (as Web pages), and you must single-click an icon to open its window and point to an icon to select the icon.

After viewing the settings for the Web style, close the Custom Settings dialog box and Folder Options dialog box by performing the following steps.

TO CLOSE THE CUSTOM SETTINGS AND FOLDER OPTIONS DIALOG BOXES

1. Click the Cancel button in the Custom Settings dialog box.

2. Click the Cancel button in the Folder Options dialog box.

The Custom Settings dialog box and Folder Options dialog box close (Figure 4-69).

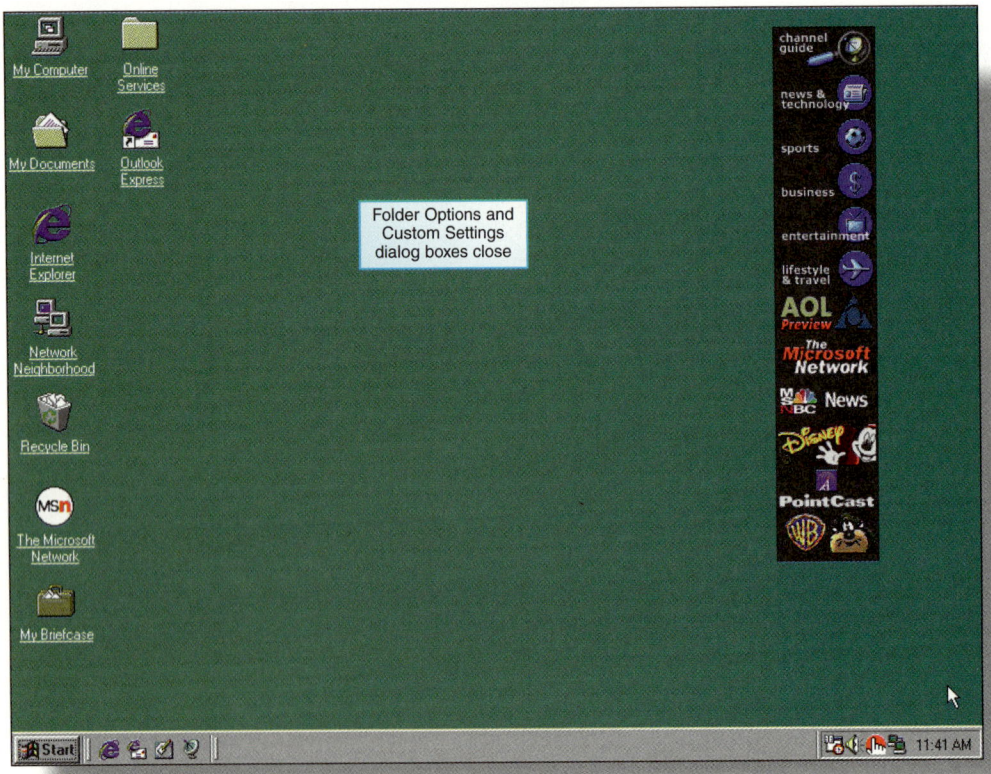

FIGURE 4-69

Desktop View Summary

Windows 98 allows you to view the desktop in the Classic style, Web Style, or Custom style. The desktop view you choose affects the appearance of the desktop, how you open and work with icons and windows on the desktop, and how you work with files and folders on your computer. As shown in this project, a combination of settings defines each desktop view. The table below summarizes the settings for the Classic style, Web style, and default Custom style. The X signifies the setting to be selected.

Table 4-1

CUSTOM SETTINGS	CLASSIC STYLE	WEB STYLE	DEFAULT CUSTOM STYLE
Enable all web-related content on my desktop		X	
Use Windows classic desktop	X		X
Open each folder in the same window		X	X
Open each folder in its own window	X		
For all folders with HTML content		X	
Only for folders where I select "as Web page" (View menu) (View menu)	X		X
Single-click to open an item (point to select)		X	
Double-click to open an item (single-click to select)	X		X

Working with Icons and Windows in the Web Style

Currently, the desktop view is the Web style (see Figure 4-69). Several differences exist when working with icons and windows in the Web style and in the default Custom style or Classic style. To understand these differences, the following section presents sequences of steps so that you can practice the techniques for selecting a single icon, opening a folder window, navigating folder windows, and selecting and copying multiple files using the Web style.

Selecting Icons on the Desktop and Opening Windows in Web Style

When the desktop view is the default Custom style or Classic style, you click an icon to select an icon and double-click an icon to open its window. In contrast, when the desktop view is the Web style, you point to an icon to select the icon and click an icon to open its window. The window that opens when you click an icon displays as a Web page with the area below the Standard Buttons toolbar divided into two panels. Perform the steps on the next page to select the My Computer icon on the desktop and then open the My Computer window.

WIN 4.54 • Project 4 • Modifying Your Desktop Work Environment

 To Select an Icon on the Desktop and Open Its Window in Web Style

1 **Click an open area of the desktop. Point to the My Computer icon on the desktop.**

When you point to the My Computer icon, the mouse pointer changes to a hand (indicating you are pointing to a hyperlink), the My Computer icon is selected, and a ToolTip displays (Figure 4-70). In Windows 98 terminology, the process of pointing to an object that results in the selection of that object is referred to as **hovering**.

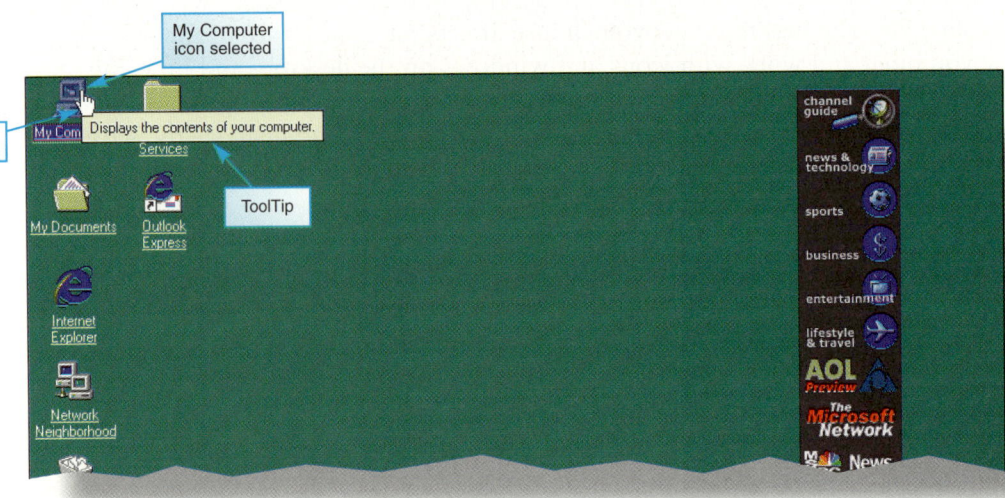

FIGURE 4-70

2 **Click the My Computer icon. Click the Maximize button on the My Computer title bar.**

The My Computer window opens and maximizes (Figure 4-71). The recessed My Computer button displays in the taskbar button area.

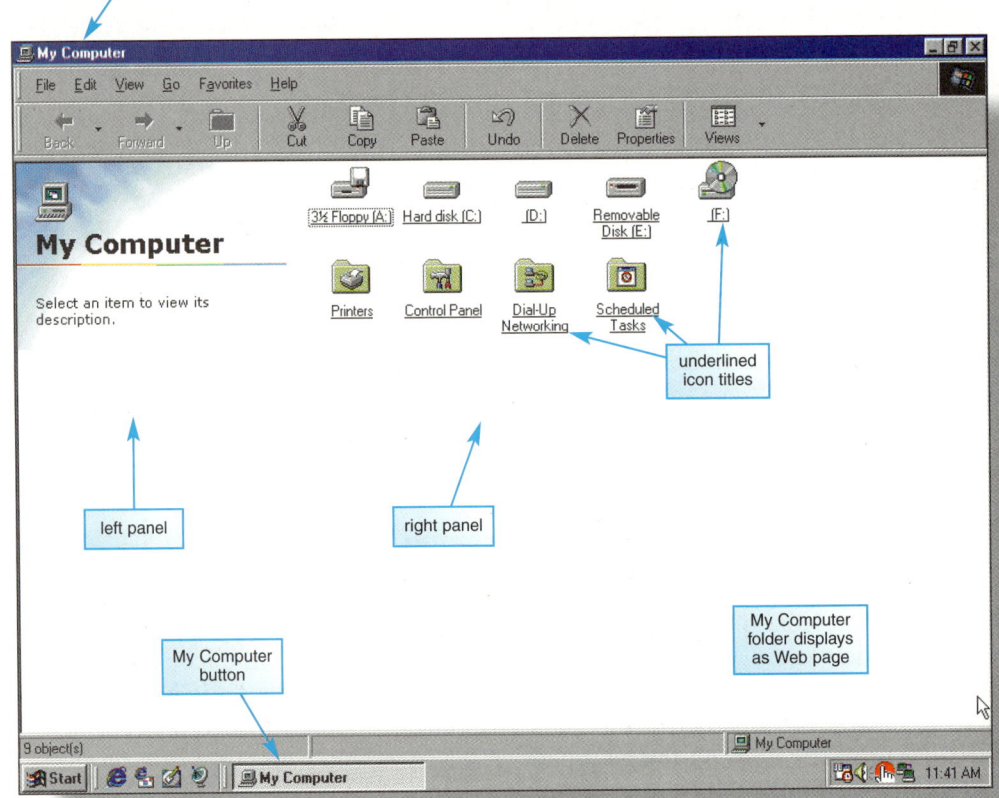

FIGURE 4-71

1. Right-click icon, click Open
2. Point to icon, press ENTER

The My Computer folder shown in Figure 4-71 displays as a Web page with the area below the Standard Buttons toolbar divided into two panels. The My Computer icon and icon title display at the top of the left panel. The text, Select an item to view its description, displays below the icon and title in the left panel. The right panel of the My Computer window contains the contents of the My Computer folder (nine icons). The icon title of each icon is underlined.

Selecting an Icon in a Folder Window in Web Style

When you point to an object in the right panel of the My Computer window, information about the object displays in the left panel of the window. Perform the following step to select the Control Panel icon in the right panel and display information about the Control Panel folder in the left panel.

Steps: To Select an Icon in a Folder and Open its Window in Web Style

1 Point to the Control Panel icon in the My Computer window.

When you point to the Control Panel icon, the mouse pointer changes to a hand, the selected Control Panel icon displays in the right panel, and information about the Control Panel folder displays in the left panel (Figure 4-72).

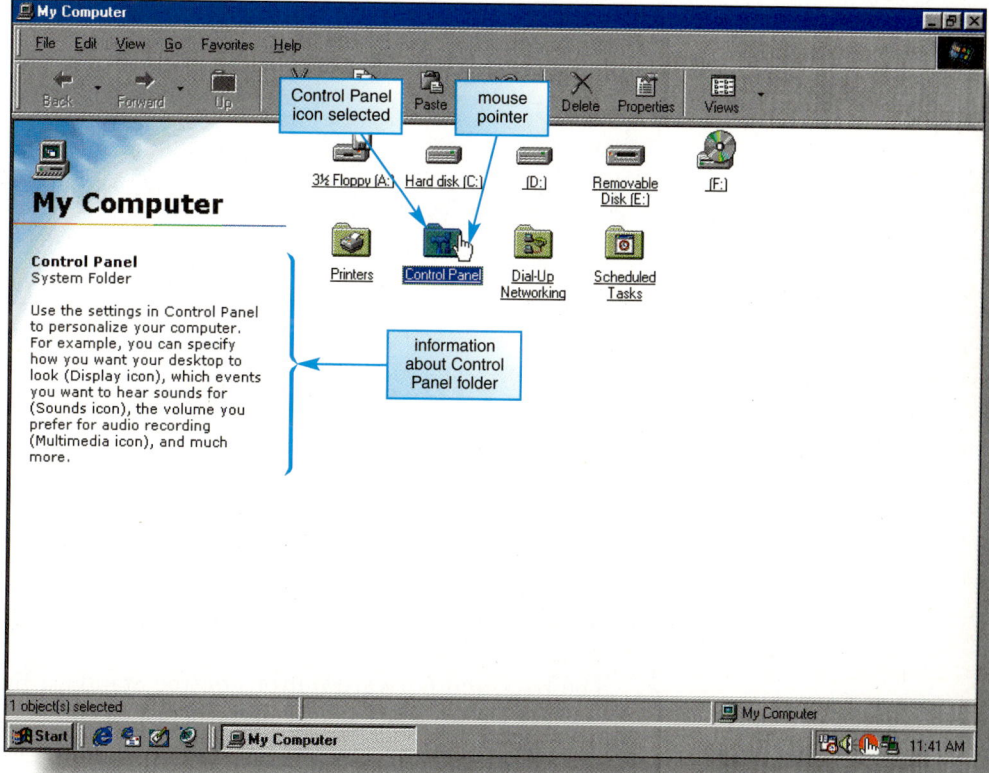

FIGURE 4-72

WIN 4.56 • Project 4 • Modifying Your Desktop Work Environment

 Click the Control Panel icon.

The Control Panel folder opens in the same window and the Control Panel button replaces the My Computer button in the taskbar button area (Figure 4-73). The Control Panel folder displays as a Web page with the left panel containing information about the Control Panel and the right panel containing the icons in the Control Panel folder.

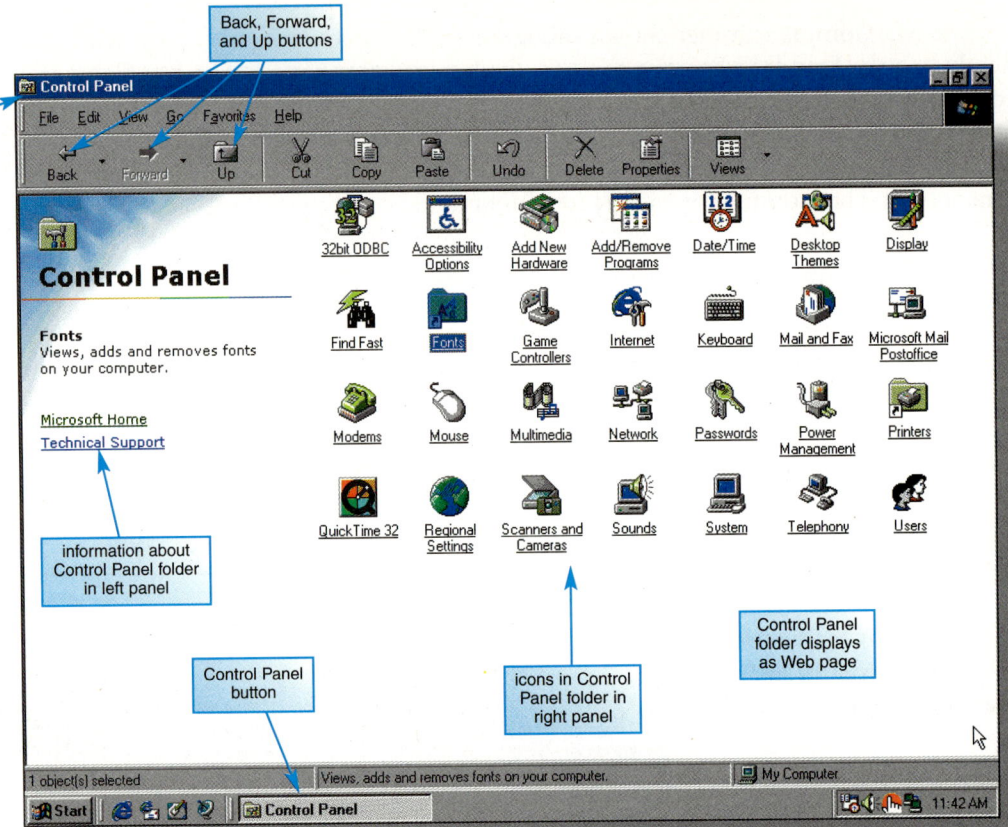

FIGURE 4-73

1. Right-click icon, click Open
2. Point to icon, press ENTER

Navigating Folder Windows Using the Back and Forward Buttons

In Web style, each folder you open displays in the same window on the desktop. Windows 98 maintains a list of folder names and adds the folder name of the previously displayed folder to the list each time you open a new folder. Because you opened the My Computer folder (Figure 4-71 on page WIN 4.54) and then opened the Control Panel folder (Figure 4-73), the list consists solely of the My Computer folder name. Opening another folder would cause the Control Panel folder name to be added to the list.

The Back and Forward buttons on the Standard Buttons toolbar (see Figure 4-73) allow you to navigate through the list of folders. Clicking the **Back button** displays the window of the previous folder name in the list (My Computer). Similarly, clicking the **Forward button** will display the window of the next folder name in the list. To view the list, you can click the Back button arrow or Forward button arrow.

Perform the following steps to use the Back button to display the My Computer folder in the window on the desktop.

To Display a Previously Displayed Folder

1 Point to the Back button on the Standard Buttons toolbar.

A ToolTip (Back to My Computer) displays below the Back button (Figure 4-74). Clicking the Back button will display the My Computer folder in the window on the desktop.

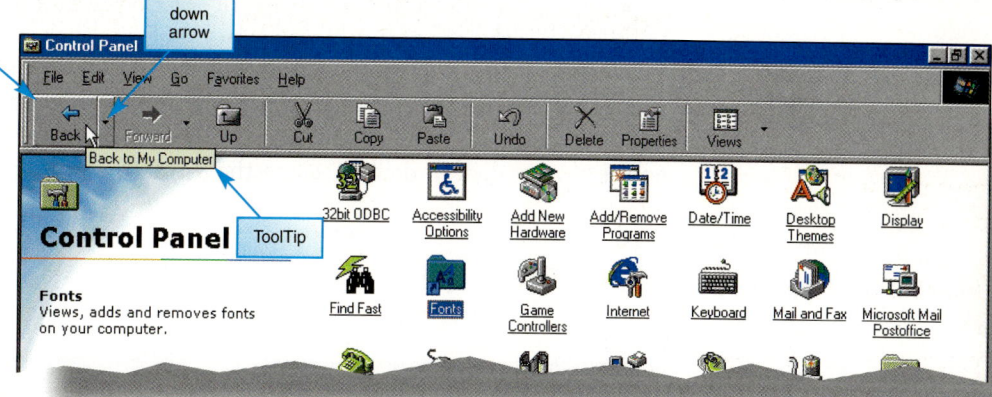

FIGURE 4-74

 Click the Back button.

The My Computer folder opens in the same window in which the Control Panel Folder was displayed, and the My Computer button replaces the Control Panel button in the taskbar button area (Figure 4-75).

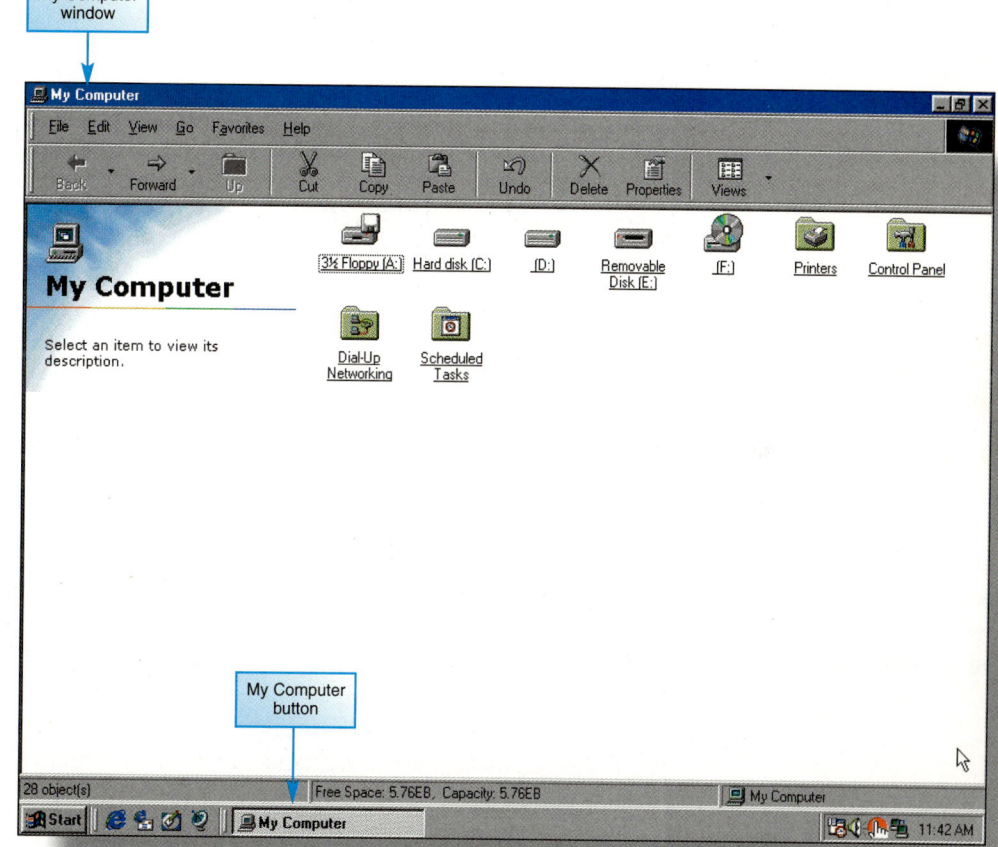

FIGURE 4-75

Using the Back, Forward, and Up buttons on the Standard Buttons toolbar, you can display any previously displayed folder.

1. Point to Back button arrow, click Back to My Computer
2. Press BACKSPACE

Selecting Multiple Files and Copying Files in Web Style

While copying document icons from a folder to a floppy disk in Project 3, you selected three document icons in the Windows folder (Black Thatches, Bubbles, and

More About

The Windows Folder

The Windows window containing the warning message and Show Files hyperlink in Figure 4-72 does not display if the desktop view is the Classic style or Custom style.

Carved Stone) and right-dragged the icons to the floppy disk in drive A. The technique to select the multiple files was to press and hold down the CTRL key and then click each document icon. This technique works in the Classic and default Custom styles.

In Web style, the technique to select multiple files is slightly different. To select multiple files you point to one of the document icons, hold down the CTRL key, point to each of the other document icons, and release the CTRL key. Perform the following steps to select and copy the Black Thatch icon, Bubbles icon, and Carved Stone icon on the floppy disk in drive A using the Send To command.

To Select and Copy Multiple Files in Web Style

1 Insert a formatted floppy disk in drive A.

2 Point to the Hard disk (C:) icon in the My Computer window.

The Hard disk (C:) icon is highlighted in the right panel and information about drive C displays in the left panel (Figure 4-76).

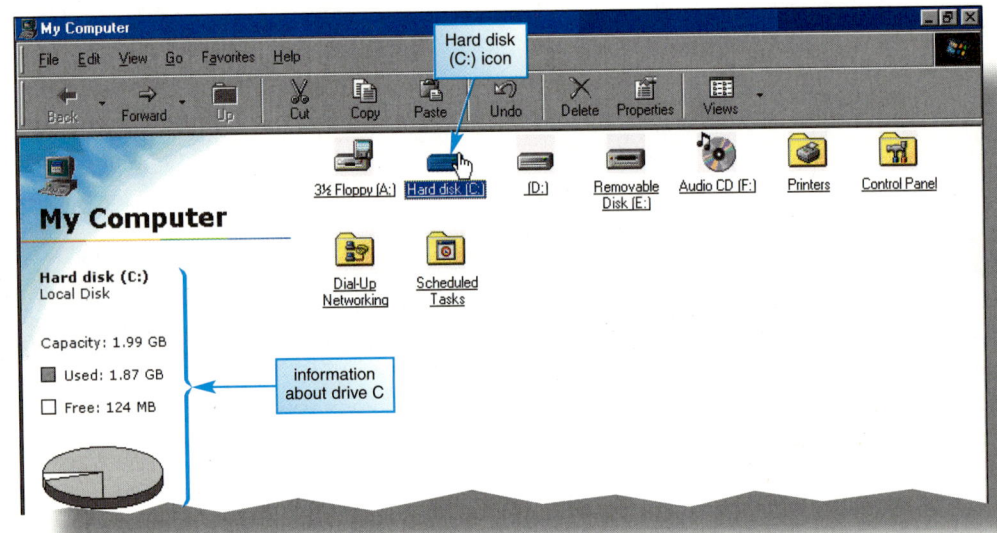

FIGURE 4-76

3 Click the Hard disk (C:) icon in the My Computer window, click the Windows icon in the Hard disk (C:) window, and point to the Show Files hyperlink in the Windows window.

The maximized Windows window displays on the desktop and the Windows button displays in the taskbar button area (Figure 4-77). The left panel contains information about the Windows folder, including a warning message. The right panel contains the Windows 98 logo, name, and graphics.

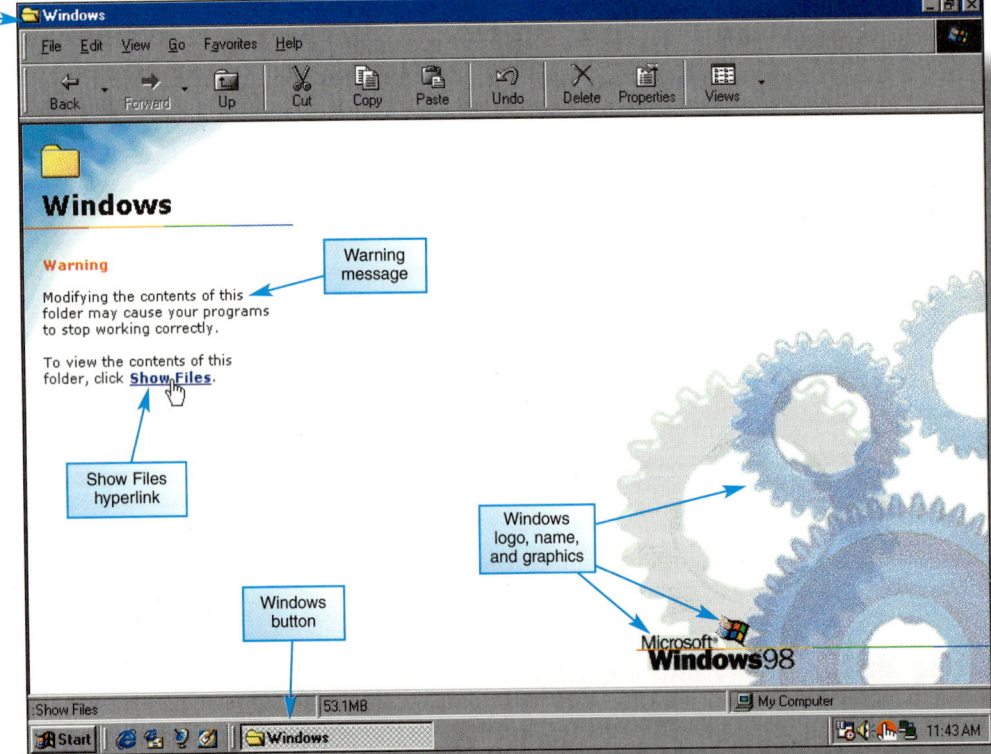

FIGURE 4-77

4 Click the Show Files hyperlink. Scroll down in the Windows window until the icons for the Black Thatch, Bubbles, and Carved Stone files are visible in the window.

The objects in the Windows folder display in the right panel and the message in the left panel changes (Figure 4-78). The Black Thatch, Bubbles, and Carved Stone icons are visible in the Windows window.

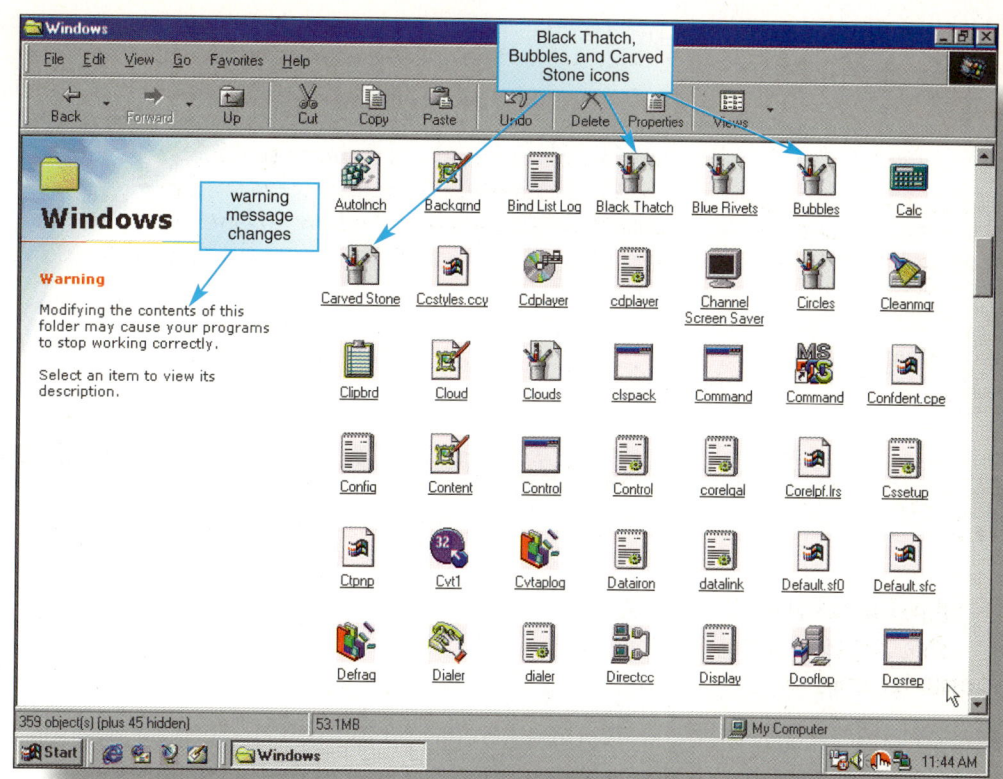

FIGURE 4-78

5 Press and hold the CTRL key and then point to the Black Thatch icon, Bubbles icon, and Carved Stone icon. Release the CTRL key. Right-click the Carved Stone icon to display a shortcut menu, point to Send To on the shortcut menu, and then point to 3½ Floppy (A) on the Send To submenu.

The Black Thatch, Bubbles, and Carved Stone icons are selected. A shortcut menu and the Send To submenu display (Figure 4-79). The information in the left panel changes to facts about the selected icons (number of items selected, total size of items, and file names).

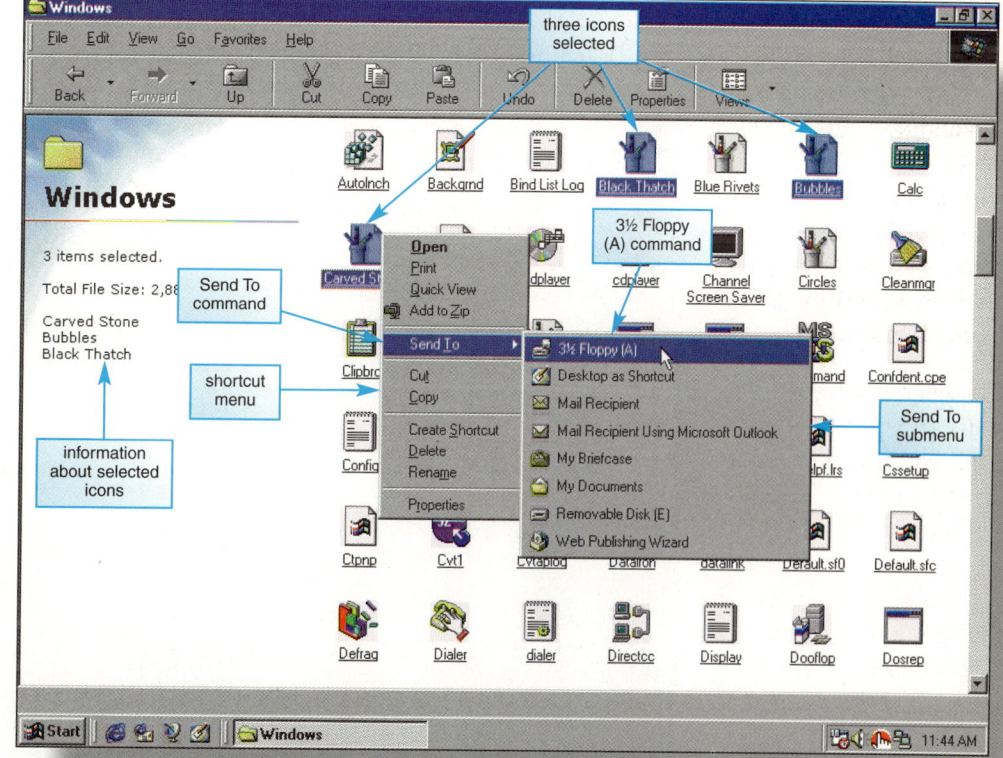

FIGURE 4-79

WIN 4.60 • Project 4 • Modifying Your Desktop Work Environment

 Click 3½ Floppy (A).

The Copying dialog box displays while copying the three files to the floppy disk in drive A (Figure 4-80).

 Click the Close button to close the Windows window.

Remove the floppy disk from drive A.

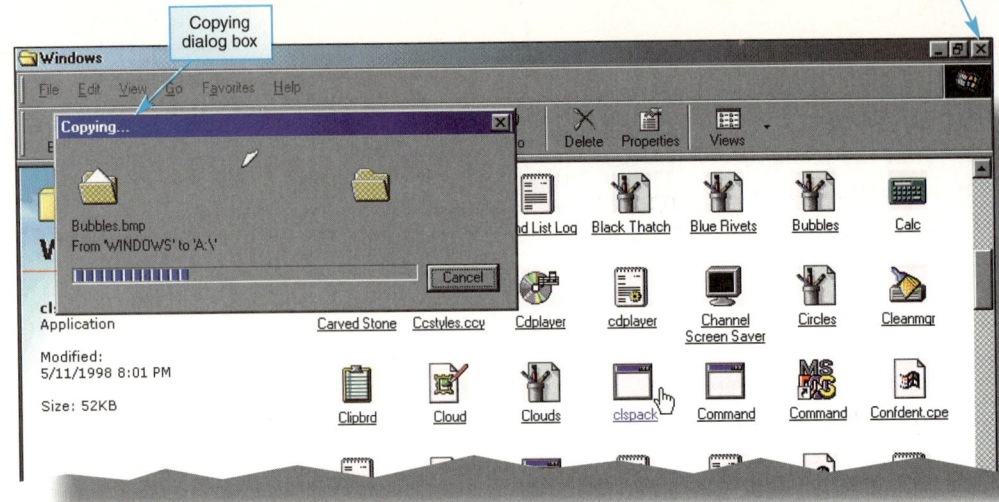

FIGURE 4-80

Other Ways

1. Select icons of file(s) to be copied, click Copy button on Standard Buttons toolbar, display 3½ Floppy (A:) window, click Paste button on Standard Buttons toolbar
2. Select icons of file(s) to be copied, right-click an icon, click Copy, display 3½ Floppy (A:) window, click Paste
3. Select icons of file(s) to be copied, on Edit menu click Copy, display 3½ Floppy (A:) window, on Edit menu click Paste
4. Select icons of file(s) to be copied, press CTRL+C to display 3½ Floppy (A:) window, press CTRL+V

Resetting the Desktop View to the Default Custom Style

Previously in this project you changed the desktop view to the Classic style and then changed the desktop view to the Web style. After making these changes, you should restore the desktop view to the default Custom style. Perform the following steps to return the desktop view to the default Custom style.

TO RESET THE DESKTOP VIEW TO THE DEFAULT CUSTOM STYLE

1. Click the Start button, point to Settings on the Start menu, click Folder Options on the Settings submenu.
2. Click Custom, based on settings you choose in the Folder Options dialog box and then click the Settings button.
3. Click Use Windows classic desktop in the Active Desktop pane.
4. Click Only for folders where I select "as Web Page" (View menu) in the View Web content in folders pane.
5. Click Double-click to open an item (single-click to select) in the Click items as follows pane and then click the OK button in the Custom Settings dialog box.
6. Click the Close button in the Folder Options dialog box.

The desktop view returns to the default Custom style (Figure 4-81).

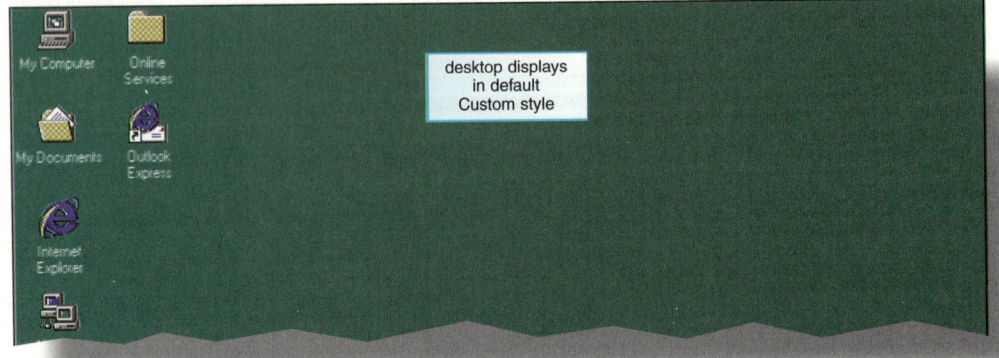

FIGURE 4-81

Shutting Down Windows

After completing your work, you might want to shut down Windows 98 using the Shut Down command on the Start menu. If you are sure you want to shut down Windows 98, perform the following steps. If you are not sure about shutting down Windows 98, read the following steps without actually performing them.

TO SHUT DOWN WINDOWS 98

1. Click the Start button on the taskbar and then point to Shut Down.
2. Click Shut Down and then click the OK button in the Shut Down Windows dialog box.

If you accidentally click Shut Down on the Start menu and you do not want to shut down Windows 98, click the Cancel button.

Project Summary

In this project, you modified desktop properties by changing the background, appearance, and screen saver properties. You personalized the taskbar by moving, resizing, and hiding the taskbar; adding a toolbar to the taskbar; and adding a shortcut icon to a toolbar. You customized a folder on the desktop by adding an Explorer bar, a toolbar, and background to a folder. Finally, you viewed the desktop using the Classic style, Web style, and Custom style.

What You Should Know

Having completed this project, you now should be able to perform the following tasks:

- Add a Background to a Folder *(WIN 4.34)*
- Add a Pattern to the Desktop *(WIN 4.9)*
- Add a Screen Saver *(WIN 4.14)*
- Add a Toolbar to a Folder *(WIN 4.31)*
- Add a Toolbar to the Taskbar *(WIN 4.20)*
- Add a Wallpaper to the Desktop *(WIN 4.7)*
- Add an Explorer Bar to a Folder *(WIN 4.33)*
- Change the Desktop Appearance *(WIN 4.11)*
- Choose the Classic Style as the Desktop View *(WIN 4.45)*
- Choose the Web Style as the Desktop View *(WIN 4.50)*
- Close the Custom Settings and Folder Options Dialog Boxes *(WIN 4.52)*
- Display a Folder as a Web Page *(WIN 4.38)*
- Display a Previously Displayed Folder *(WIN 4.57)*
- Display a Web Page Using the Address Toolbar *(WIN 4.22)*
- Display the Contents of a Folder Using the Address Toolbar *(WIN 4.21)*
- Hide and Redisplay the Taskbar *(WIN 4.17)*
- Move the Taskbar *(WIN 4.16)*
- Open a Folder and Display the View Menu *(WIN 4.30)*
- Open the Display Properties Dialog Box *(WIN 4.5)*
- Place a Shortcut on a Toolbar *(WIN 4.27)*
- Remove a Pattern *(WIN 4.10)*
- Remove a Shortcut from a Toolbar and Resize the Taskbar *(WIN 4.29)*
- Remove a Toolbar and Explorer Bar from a Folder *(WIN 4.37)*
- Remove a Toolbar from the Taskbar *(WIN 4.26)*
- Remove Wallpaper *(WIN 4.8)*
- Remove the Background and No Longer Display a Folder as a Web Page *(WIN 4.39)*
- Reset the Desktop Appearance *(WIN 4.12)*
- Reset the Desktop View to the Default Custom Style *(WIN 4.60)*
- Resize the Taskbar *(WIN 4.25)*
- Search for Information on the Internet Using the Address Toolbar *(WIN 4.24)*
- Select an Icon in a Folder and Open its Window in Web Style *(WIN 4.55)*
- Select an Icon on the Desktop and Open Its Window in Web Style *(WIN 4.54)*
- Select and Copy Multiple Files in Web Style *(WIN 4.58)*
- Shut Down Windows 98 *(WIN 4.61)*
- View the Settings of the Current Desktop View *(WIN 4.48, WIN 4.51)*

WIN 4.62 • Project 4 • Modifying Your Desktop Work Environment

Test Your Knowledge

Homework 12-06-01

1 True/False

Instructions: Circle T if the statement is true or F if the statement is false.

- **T** F 1. The color of the desktop and the screen saver are considered desktop properties.
- T F 2. You can change the desktop background by adding a pattern or wallpaper to the desktop.
- T **F** 3. The 3D Flower Box is an example of a color scheme.
- **T** F 4. When you hide the taskbar, only the top edge of the taskbar is visible at the bottom of the desktop.
- **T** F 5. You can use the Desktop toolbar to search for and display a Web page if you know the URL of the Web page.
- **T** F 6. A graphics image (or picture) can be used as the background in a folder.
- **T** F 7. A left and right panel display below the Standard Buttons toolbar when you display a folder as a Web page.
- T **F** 8. The icon titles are not underlined when the desktop view is the Web style.
- **T** F 9. A folder opens in its own window when the desktop view is the Classic style.
- **T** F 10. You double-click an icon to open its window when the desktop view is the Classic style.

2 Multiple Choice

1K2SS2b

Instructions: Circle the correct response.

1. To open the Display Properties dialog box, _____.
   - **a.** right-click the taskbar and then click Properties on the shortcut menu
   - b. click the Start button, point to Settings on the Start menu, click Taskbar & Start menu on the Settings submenu
   - c. right-click the My Computer icon, click Open on the shortcut menu, click the Control Panel folder, and click the Display icon
   - d. right-click the desktop and then click Properties on the shortcut menu

2. _____ changes the desktop background on your computer.
   - a. Changing the desktop appearance
   - **b.** Adding a wallpaper
   - c. Displaying a screen saver
   - d. Selecting a power scheme

3. When only the top edge of the taskbar is visible at the bottom of the desktop, the taskbar has been _____.
   - a. moved
   - b. resized
   - c. removed
   - **d.** hidden

4. Which taskbar option displays in the Taskbar Properties dialog box?
   - a. Single-click to open an item
   - **b.** Auto hide
   - c. Double-click to open an item
   - d. Show desktop

Test Your Knowledge

5. The _____ toolbar allows you to type a Web page address (URL) and view the associated Web page in the Microsoft Internet Explorer window.
   a. Quick Launch
   b. Address
   c. Links
   d. Desktop

6. To place a shortcut to a folder on a toolbar, locate the folder icon, _____, and _____.
   a. right-drag the icon to the toolbar, click Create Shortcut(s) Here on the shortcut menu
   b. right-click the icon, click Send To Toolbar on the shortcut menu
   c. drag the icon to the toolbar, click Move Here on the shortcut menu
   d. point to the icon to select the icon, drag the icon to the toolbar

7. When you add the Search bar to a folder, you use the _____.
   a. View menu
   b. Display Properties dialog box
   c. Views button on the Standard Buttons toolbar
   d. Folder Options dialog box

8. The Internet Channel bar and active desktop items display when the _____ style is the desktop view.
   a. Web
   b. Classic
   c. Classic and Custom
   d. Web and Classic

9. Many open windows may display on the desktop when you use the _____ custom setting.
   a. Enable all web-related content on my desktop
   b. Open each folder in its own window
   c. Single-click to open an item (point to select)
   d. Underline icon titles only when I point at them

10. Using the _____ custom setting results in icon titles that display without underlines.
    a. Open each folder in the same window
    b. Single-click to open an item (point to select)
    c. Use Windows classic desktop
    d. Double-click to open an item (single-click to select)

3 Understanding the Folder Options and Custom Settings Dialog Boxes

Instructions: Arrows point to several objects in the Folder Options dialog box in Figure 4-82 on the next page. Identify the five objects (numbered 1 through 5) in the Folder Options dialog box in the spaces provided. In the Custom Settings dialog box, each setting is identified by a number (numbers 6 through 15). Indicate the five settings that define the Web style and the four settings that define the Classic style in the spaces that follow.

(continued)

WIN 4.64 • Project 4 • Modifying Your Desktop Work Environment

Test Your Knowledge

Understanding the Folder Options and Custom Settings Dialog Boxes (continued)

Web Style Settings

_____
_____
_____
_____

Classic Style Settings

_____
_____
_____
_____

FIGURE 4-82

4 Modifying Display Properties

Instructions: When you sit down at a computer, you see the Windows 98 desktop shown in Figure 4-83. While it is interesting, you know it would be difficult to work on this desktop for any period of time. In the spaces below, list the steps required to remove the Bricks pattern and change the color scheme to the Windows Standard color scheme.

Step 1: _____
Step 2: _____
Step 3: _____
Step 4: _____
Step 5: _____
Step 6: _____
Step 7: _____
Step 8: _____
Step 9: _____
Step 10: _____

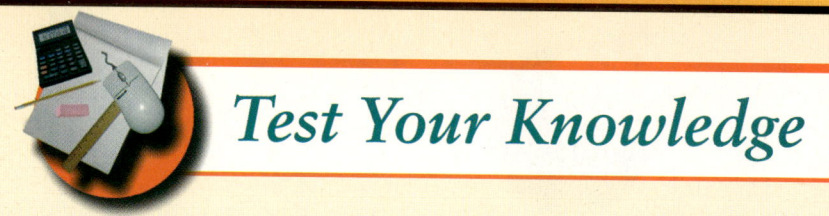

Test Your Knowledge

FIGURE 4-83

1 Using Windows Help

Instructions: Use Windows Help and a computer to perform the following tasks. Answer all questions in the space provided.

1. If necessary, start Microsoft Windows 98.
2. Right-click the desktop and then click Properties on the shortcut menu to display the Display Properties dialog box.
3. Click the Screen Saver tab.
4. Answer the following questions about energy management using the Question Mark button in the Display Properties dialog box.
   a. What is the Energy Star™ program? _____
   b. Who administers the Energy Star™ program? _____
   c. What dialog box does the Settings button open? _____
5. Click the Settings button.
6. Answer the following questions about energy management using the Question Mark button in the Power Management dialog box.
   a. What is a power scheme? _____
   b. What power scheme displays in the Power Schemes pane? _____
   c. What does the entry in the Turn off monitor box indicate? _____
   d. What does the entry in the Turn off hard disks box indicate? _____

(continued)

Use Help

Using Windows Help *(continued)*

7. Click the Cancel button in the Power Management Properties dialog box.
8. Click the Cancel button in the Display Properties dialog box.
9. Click the Start button, point to Settings, and click Folder options.
10. Click the View tab in the Folder Options dialog box.
11. Answer the following questions about file and folder settings using the Question Mark button in the Folder Options dialog box.
    a. What does the Reset All Folders button do?_____
    b. What advanced settings are active (a check mark in a box indicates an active setting)?
    _____
    _____
    c. Which setting is active for hidden files (a selected option button indicates an active setting)?
    _____
    _____
    d. What does the Restore Defaults button do? _____
12. Click the Cancel button in the Folder Options dialog box.

1 Creating and Saving a Color Scheme

Instructions: Your friend showed you a creative color scheme she created for her desktop. You return home and decide to create your own color scheme for your desktop. Perform the following steps to create a color scheme.

Part 1: *Change to the Windows Standard Scheme*

1. Right-click the desktop and then click Properties on the shortcut menu to open the Display Properties dialog box.
2. Click the Appearance tab.
3. On a piece of paper, write down the name of the color scheme in the Scheme box.
4. Click the Scheme box arrow to display the Scheme list box.
5. Scroll the list to make the Windows Standard scheme name visible. Click the Windows Standard scheme name.

In the Lab

Part 2: *Set the Size and Color of the Inactive Window Title Bar Text*

1. Click the Inactive Window title bar (gray title bar) in the preview pane. The Item box contains the Inactive Title Bar name, the Size box contains the value 18, and the Color and Color 2 buttons to the right of the Size box are dark gray. These settings control the color and size of the inactive window title bar.
2. The Font box contains the MS Sans Serif (Western) font name, the Size box contains the value 8, and the Color button is light gray. These settings control the font, size, color, and attributes of the text in the inactive window title bar. The recessed B (bold) button indicates the text is bold.
3. Click the font Size box arrow. Click 12 in the Size list box. The font size of the text in the Inactive Window title bar in the preview pane increases.
4. Click the light gray Color button to open a color palette. Click the black color box (row 1, column 2). The color of the text in the Inactive Window title bar in the preview pane changes to black.

Part 3: *Set the Size and Color of the Active Window Title Bar*

1. Click the Active Window title bar (dark blue title bar) in the preview pane. The Item box contains the Active Title Bar name, the Size box contains the value 22, and the Color and Color 2 buttons to the right of the Size box are dark blue. These settings control the color and size of the active window title bar.
2. Click the Color button to open a color palette. Click the black color box (row 1, column 2). Click the Color 2 button to open a color palette. Click the black color box (row 1, column 2). The color of the Active Window title bar and Message Box title bar in the preview pane change to black.

Part 4: *Set the Size and Color of the Selected Text*

1. Click Selected on the Active Window menu bar in the preview pane. The Item box contains the Selected Items name, the Size box contains the value 18, and the Color button to the right of the Size box is dark blue. These settings control the color and size of selected, or highlighted, text.
2. Click the Color button to open a color palette. Click the black color box (row 1, column 2). The color of the selected text on the Active Window menu bar in the preview pane changes to black.
3. The Font box contains the MS Sans Serif (Western) font name, the Size box contains the value 8, and the Color button is white. These settings control the font, size, and color of the selected text.
4. Click the font Size box arrow. Click 10 in the Size list box. The size of the selected text on the Active Window menu bar increases.

Part 5: *Set the Color and Font Size of the Message Box Text*

1. Click the words, Message Text, in the preview pane. The Item box contains the Message Box name. The Size box and the Color and Color 2 buttons appear dimmed. The Font box contains the MS Sans Serif (Western) font name, the Size box contains the value 8, and the Color button is black. These settings control the font, size, and color of the text in message boxes (dialog boxes, error message boxes, and so on.)
2. Click the font Size box arrow. Click 10 in the Size list box. The size of the text in the Message Box in the preview pane increases.

(continued)

In the Lab

Creating and Saving a Color Scheme *(continued)*

Part 6: Save the Color Scheme

1. Click the Save As button. Change the name in the Save Scheme dialog box to Windows Standard - Easy to Read and then click the OK button in the Save Scheme dialog box.
2. Click the OK button in the Display Properties dialog box.
3. Double-click the My Computer icon on the desktop to view the new color scheme.
4. Click the Close button in the My Computer window.

Part 7: Remove the Color Scheme

1. Right-click the desktop and then click Properties on the shortcut menu.
2. If necessary, click the Appearance tab.
3. Verify the Windows Standard - Easy to Read scheme name displays in the Scheme box and then click the Delete button.
4. Click the Scheme box arrow to display the Scheme list.
5. Scroll the Scheme list to make the scheme name you wrote down in Step 3 of Part 1 visible. Click the scheme name and then click the OK button.

2 Working with the Classic Style and Web Style

Instructions: Perform the following steps to switch the desktop view between Web style and Classic style and then turn off the Active Desktop™. Answer all questions in the space provided.

Part 1: Recording the Current Desktop Settings

1. If necessary, start Microsoft Windows 98.
2. Click the Start button, point to Settings on the Start menu, and click Folder Options on the Settings submenu.
3. If the Custom, based on settings you choose option button is not selected, click the option button.
4. Click the Settings button.
5. On a separate piece of paper, record which option buttons in the Custom Settings dialog box are selected.
6. Click the Cancel button in the Custom Settings dialog box.

Part 2: Choosing the Classic Style as the Desktop View

1. Click Classic style in the Folder Options dialog box.
2. Click the OK button. In which style does the desktop currently display? _____

Part 3: Opening Dialog Boxes in Classic Style

1. Double-click the My Computer icon.
2. Double-click the Control Panel icon. Does the Control Panel window open in its own window? _____
3. Double-click the Display icon in the Control Panel window.
4. Click the Web tab in the Display Properties dialog box. Does the View my Active Desktop as a web page check box contain a check mark? _____ Does the Internet Explorer Channel Bar check box contain a check mark? _____ Why is the Channel bar not displaying on the desktop? _____

In the Lab

5. Click the Cancel button in the Display Properties dialog box.
6. Click the Close button in the Control Panel window.
7. Click the Close button in the My Computer window.

Part 4: Choosing the Web as the Desktop View

1. Double-click the My Computer icon of the desktop.
2. Click View on the menu bar and then click Folder Options.
3. Click Web style in the Folder Options dialog box and then click the OK button.
4. Click the Close button in the My Computer window. How does the desktop change? _____

Part 5: Turning Off the Active Desktop in Web Style

1. Right-click an open area on the desktop.
2. Point to Active Desktop on the shortcut menu. A check mark should display preceding the View As Web Page command in the Active Desktop submenu.
3. Click View As Web Page to remove the check mark. How does the desktop change? _____ Are the icon titles underlined? _____
4. Click the My Computer icon on the desktop.
5. Does the My Computer window display as a Web page?
6. In the My Computer window, click View on the menu bar and then click Folder Options.
7. In the Folder Options dialog box, what option button is selected in the Windows Desktop Update pane? _____ Why is this button selected? _____
8. Click the Web style option button and then click the OK button.
9. Click the Close button in the My Computer window. How does the desktop change? _____

Part 6: Resetting the Desktop Settings

1. Click the Start button, point to Settings on the Start menu, and then click Folder Options on the Settings submenu.
2. If Custom, based on settings you choose is not selected, click the option button.
3. Click the Settings button.
4. Click the option buttons in the Custom Settings dialog box that correspond to the settings you recorded in Step 5 of Part 1 and then click the OK button.
5. Click the Close button in the Folder Options dialog box.

3 Customizing the Desktop View

Instructions: Use a computer to perform the following tasks and answer the questions.

Part 1: Recording the Current Desktop Settings

1. If necessary, start Microsoft Windows 98.
2. Click the Start button, point to Settings on the Start menu, and click Folder Options on the Settings submenu.

(continued)

In the Lab

Customizing the Desktop View (continued)

3. If Custom, based on settings you choose is not selected, click the option button.
4. Click the Settings button.
5. On a separate piece of paper, record which option buttons in the Custom Settings dialog box are selected.
6. Click the Cancel button in the Custom Settings dialog box.
7. Click the Cancel button in the Folder Options dialog box.

Part 2: Customizing the Desktop View

1. Double-click the My Computer icon on the desktop. Click View on the menu bar and then click Folder Options.
2. If Web Style is not selected, click the option button and then click the Apply button.
3. Click Custom, based on settings you choose.
4. Click the Settings button.
5. Click the Enable all web-related content on my desktop option button.
6. Click the Open each folder in its own window option button.
7. Click the Only for Folders where I select "as Web Page" (View menu) option button.
8. Click the Single-click to open an item (point to select) option button.
9. Click the Underline icon titles only when I point at them option button.
10. Click the OK button in the Custom Settings dialog box.
11. Click the Close button in the Folder Options dialog box.
12. Click the Close button in the My Computer window.

Part 3: Working with the Custom Style

1. Point to the My Computer icon on the desktop. What happens when you point to the icon? _____ _____ Which custom setting is responsible for what happened? _____
2. Click the My Computer icon on the desktop. Describe the appearance of the icons in the My Computer window? _____ Does the window display as a Web page? _____ _____ Which custom setting is responsible for what happened? _____
3. Click the View menu in the My Computer window. Click the as Web Page command. Describe the appearance of the My Computer window? _____ Does the window display as a Web page? _____ Why? _____
4. Click the Control Panel icon in the My Computer window. Does the window display as a Web page? _____ Which custom setting is responsible for what happened? _____ How many windows display on the screen? _____ Which custom setting is responsible for how the windows display? _____
5. Close the Control Panel window. Click the My Computer icon on the desktop.
6. In the My Computer window, click View on the menu bar and then click as Web page. Close the My Computer window.

Part 4: Resetting the Desktop Settings

1. Click the Start button, point to Settings on the Start menu, and then click Folder Options on the Settings submenu.

In the Lab

2. If Custom, based on settings you choose is not selected, click the option button.
3. Click the Settings button.
4. Click the option buttons in the Custom Settings dialog box that correspond to the settings you recorded in Step 5 of Part 1.
5. Click the OK button in the Custom Settings dialog box.
6. Click the Close button in the Folder Options dialog box.

4 Using the Desktop Properties Dialog Box

Instructions: You have been appointed by your boss to design the Windows 98 desktop that will be used by all employees within your company. Experiment with all the options in the Display Properties dialog box until you have decided on the perfect pattern, wallpaper, scheme, and screen saver. Write down all settings so that everyone can set their machines to the standard. Make sure after this exercise that you reset your computer to its settings before you made the changes.

Cases and Places

The difficulty of these case studies varies: ▶ are the least difficult; ▶▶ are more difficult; and ▶▶▶ are the most difficult.

1 ▶ Although several screen savers are included with Windows 98, many more are available at local retail computer stores for purchase, and other screen savers are given away by various organizations. This year, the Anaheim Angels baseball team and Edison International teamed up to give away a free Angels screen saver. The screen saver contains player information, a season schedule, the dates and times of the next games, fun facts and sports trivia, energy-saving facts and tips, and links to the Angels Web page (www.angelsbaseball.com). Locate five free screen savers. In a brief report, describe each screen saver, state the source from whom you can obtain the screen saver, and the contents of the screen saver.

2 ▶ In Project 3, you copied multiple files while the desktop view was the default Custom style. You used the My Computer window and Windows Explorer and the cut and paste, drag, and right-drag methods to copy the files. In this project, you copied multiple files while the desktop view was the Web style. Experiment with file copying in the default Custom style and the Web style. Prepare a brief report comparing the process of copying files in the default Custom style and Web style. In your opinion, which desktop view makes it easier to copy files?

Cases and Places

3 ▶▶ Colors, patterns, and the arrangement of the workplace can have a significant effect on worker productivity. These factors might draw attention to some objects, deemphasize others, speed the completion of tasks, and even promote desirable moods and attitudes. Visit the Internet, a library, or other research facility to find out how colors, patterns, and arrangement can impact a work environment. Using what you have learned, together with the concepts and techniques presented in this project, create the Windows 98 desktop that you think would help you work most efficiently. Write a brief report describing your desktop and explaining why you feel it would enhance your productivity.

4 ▶▶ Microsoft's beta testing program allowed computer users to examine pre-retail copies of Windows 98, called *beta copies*, before Windows 98 was released for sale to the public. Between the last beta copy (Beta 3) and the release of the retail copy, Microsoft changed the default desktop view from the Web style to the default Custom style shown in this book. Using the Internet, Windows Help, computer articles, and your own opinions, write a brief report detailing what features were changed, what you think caused Microsoft to make these changes, and how the changes affected the look and feel of Windows 98.

5 ▶▶▶ The taskbar is a central part of the Windows 98 desktop. As such, it is important to organize the taskbar and the toolbars on the taskbar to best fit your individual needs. Interview a friend, relative, teacher, businessperson, or other individual to determine what activities he or she performs from their desktop. Based on your interview, design the taskbar and toolbars to meet the individual's needs and customize the taskbar. Write a brief report summarizing your experience.

6 ▶▶▶ The custom settings that define the Classic style, Web style, and default Custom style can be confusing to a beginning computer user. Using Table 4-1 on page WIN 4.53 and your experience, prepare a ten-minute presentation that illustrates the three desktop views, shows how to change each desktop view, explains the custom settings, and illustrates how the desktop and the objects on the desktop change when you select each custom setting. Give this presentation to someone who is familiar with Windows but has not used Windows 98. Develop an outline to use while you make your presentation, and write a brief report describing the presentation and the individual's reaction to your presentation and the desktop views.

7 ▶▶▶ A key component of Windows 98 is the capability of customizing the desktop or computer screen to suit the user. Do other operating systems offer the same capability? Visit a computer vendor and try another operating system or environment. Find out what changes can be made to the computer screen and how these alterations are accomplished. Prepare a brief report comparing the operating system you tried to Windows 98. Contrast the general look of the screens, the ways they are customized, and their potential effects on users. Finally, on the basis of screen appearance alone, tell which operating system you prefer and why.

Microsoft Windows 98

Customizing Your Computer Using Control Panel

OBJECTIVES

You will have mastered the material in this project when you can:

- Open the Control Panel folder
- Adjust the keyboard repeat delay, keyboard repeat rate, and cursor blink rate
- Change the button configuration and mouse pointer scheme
- Adjust the double-click and pointer speeds and display pointer trails
- Turn on accessibility features
- View fonts and font sizes
- Change the date, time, and time zone and the date and time format
- Add and remove a USB hardware device
- Add a printer using a wizard
- Solve a hardware problem using Help troubleshooters
- View the properties of a hardware device
- Add and remove a program

Look at All the Changes!

Customizing for Optimum Fulfillment

As time flies and the moments tick away, your life continues to change. If you are attending college and also are employed, you may find it a difficult task to balance your time among school, job, family, and friends. Good time-management skills can be enhanced by your

ability to customize your life yourself, and your computer desktop. Computers and the Internet can help you explore a variety of topics and stretch your imagination in search of the ideal car, personal style, home, and working environment.

Every automobile manufacturer has a presence on the Web. You can view the exterior and interior of particular models, watch videos, choose options, examine performance statistics, and check the total cost and monthly payments. Once you design your ideal vehicle, you can jump to Edmund's (www.edmunds.com) or other sites to zero in on the dealer's costs for the base vehicle and options. Then you can strap on your negotiating cap and head to the nearest virtual or actual car lot. Many dealers have Web sites, so you can check inventory without setting foot in a showroom.

While you are out negotiating, you might want an updated look to match those new wheels. Cruise over to the Ray-Ban® site (www.ray-ban.com) and try on a new pair of cybershades. On the Ray-Ban® Virtual Preview Web page, a new, advanced technology makes trying on sunglasses from your home a virtual reality. The process is simple. You scan a photo of your face (or you can send a picture to the Ray-Ban® headquarters), and Ray-Ban® issues you an access code vial e-mail so you can virtually try on any sunglass style.

Next stop, for men or women, the cyber hair salon. Again, by scanning your photo or sending one to an online salon, you can check out your new appearance. Technology allows you to change the color or length of your hair and even experiment with the color of your eyes. Men can see how they would look in a mustache, and women can preview a new hair style.

Now, on to a new house for that new car and the new you. Home improvement software packages allow you to design a new home, deck, kitchen, and bathroom and see three-dimensional views of your creations. Then, visualize your landscaping dreams by planting virtual perennials and ornamental grasses and by installing sprinklers, lights, and a brick walkway.

Customization seemingly is taking over the way individuals think about and respond to their day-to-day tasks. This variety adds an element of fun to what otherwise might be humdrum activities. As you have been exploring the concepts in this textbook, you have learned that Windows 98 offers a myriad of opportunities to change your desktop. You can resize and tile windows, copy, rename, and delete files and folders, create shortcuts, customize the taskbar, and arrange icons. In this project, you will use the Control Panel to customize the keyboard, mouse and monitor, add a printer, and view hardware properties. These changes allow you to tailor your computer working conditions to your liking.

Yes, time may change you. But you can adapt to these changes and make the best use of your time by customizing your life and your Windows 98 environment.

Microsoft Windows 98

Customizing Your Computer Using Control Panel

PROJECT 5

CASE PERSPECTIVE

Several months ago, you installed Windows 98 on your computer. Since then, you have spent most of your time learning to communicate with Windows 98, starting programs and creating documents, exploring Windows Help, learning about desktop views and the Active Desktop™, learning file and desktop management, and working on and modifying the desktop.

Taking a friend's advice, you subscribed to several computer magazines. As a result of learning Windows 98 and reading many of the articles in the magazines, you decide to customize your computer using the icons in the Control Panel folder. You also recently purchased a mouse, printer, and speech recognition program. You intend to customize the mouse and keyboard operations, set the date and time, and add the new hardware and software to your computer. Your goal is to customize the Windows 98 environment using Control Panel and add the new hardware and software.

Introduction

In Project 4, you customized the Windows 98 desktop by changing the desktop background and appearance, implementing a screen saver, customizing the taskbar, and customizing folders. The desktop and the items on the desktop are considered objects and every object in Windows 98 has properties, which describe the object. In Project 4, you customized the manner in which you interacted with the Windows 98 environment by changing the properties of objects.

The **Control Panel folder** contains icons that allow you to change the properties of an object and thus customize the Windows 98 environment. In Project 5 you will use the icons in the Control Panel folder to customize the mouse, keyboard, date and time, and desktop fonts. In addition, you will learn how to add a new hardware device to your computer, add a program (software), make a computer more usable by disabled people, add a printer to your computer, use Help troubleshooters to solve hardware problems, and view the hardware properties of the hardware devices attached to the computer.

The Control Panel Folder

To use Control Panel to change an object's properties, click the Start button, point to Settings on the Start menu, click Control Panel on the Settings submenu, and double-click the icon of the object you wish to change. Perform the following steps to open the Control Panel folder and view the icons in the Control Panel window.

To Open the Control Panel Folder

 Click the Start button on the taskbar, point to Settings on the Start menu, and then point to Control Panel on the Settings submenu.

The Start menu and Settings submenu display (Figure 5-1).

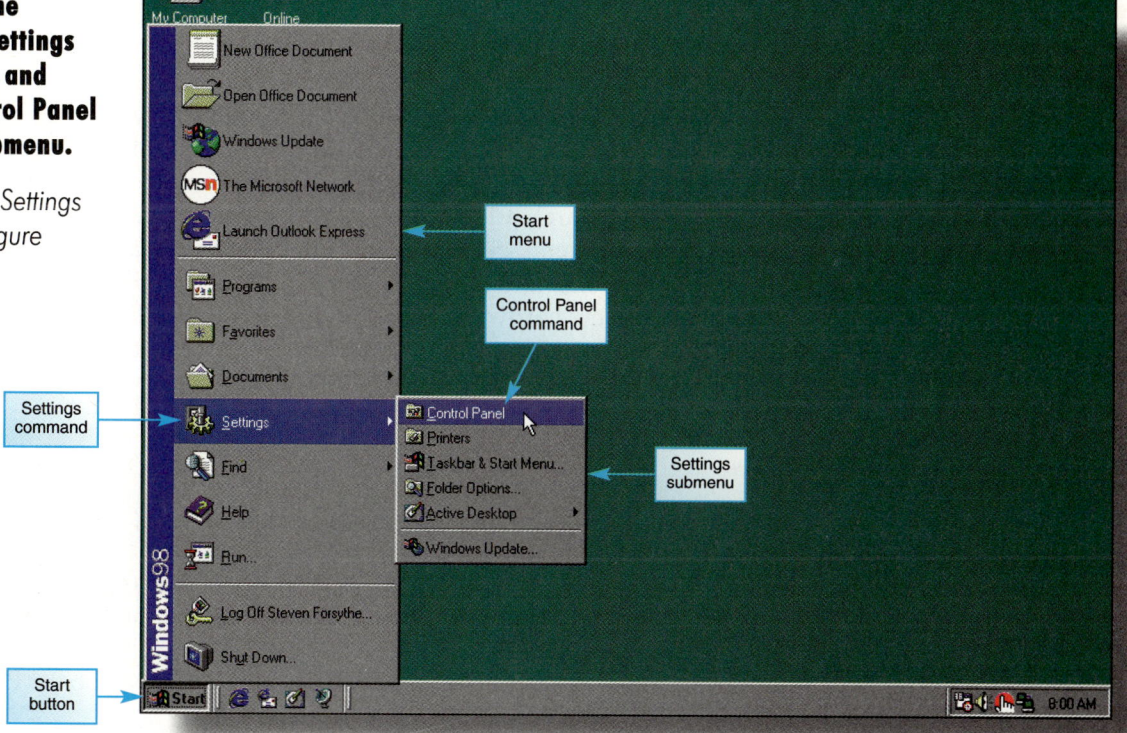

FIGURE 5-1

2 Click Control Panel on the Settings submenu.

The Control Panel window opens (Figure 5-2).

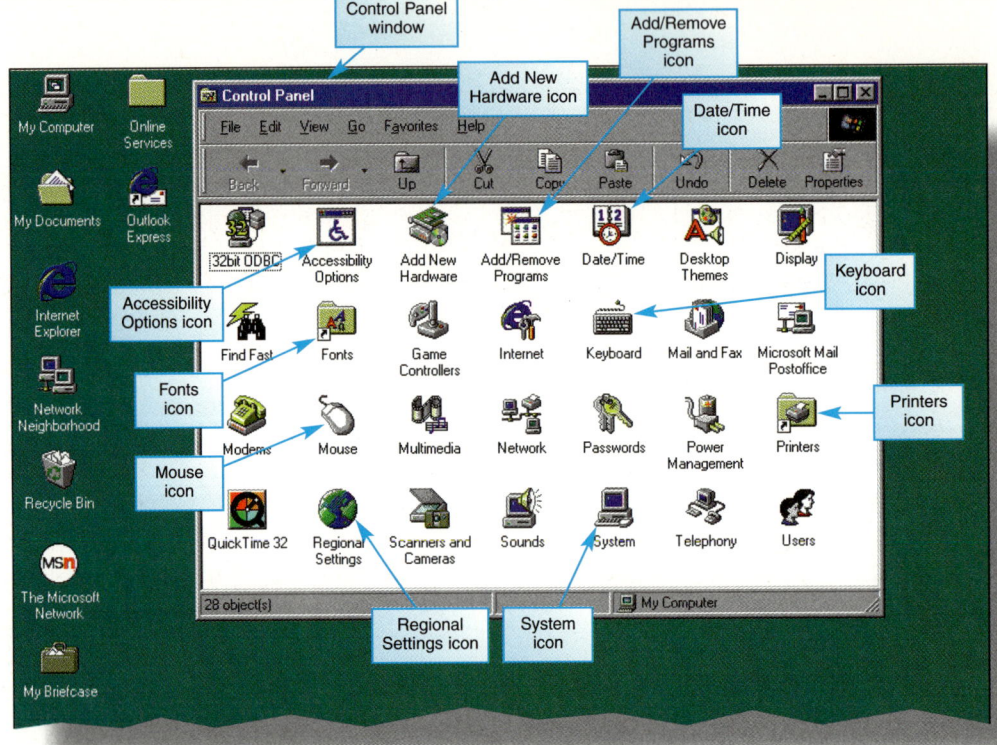

FIGURE 5-2

Other Ways

1. Double-click My Computer icon, double-click Control Panel icon
2. Click Start button, click Run, type control.exe, click OK button
3. Press CTRL+ESC, S, C

Among the icons in the Control Panel window shown in Figure 5-2 are the icons to change the properties of the keyboard (Keyboard), mouse (Mouse), and the date and time (Date/Time). In addition, the window contains icons to add new hardware (Add New Hardware), add and remove a program (Add/Remove Programs), work with printers (Printers), customize the computer for disabled people (Accessibility Options), view fonts and font sizes (Fonts), change regional settings (Regional Settings), and view hardware properties (System). The Fonts and Printers icons are shortcut icons. To change properties using the icons in the Control Panel window, double-click the appropriate icon in the Control Panel window.

More About

Customizing

Computer users learn to customize their computers in a variety of ways. Some customize their computers based on their prior use of a computer, a magazine article they read, or the recommendation of a friend. The purpose of Control Panel is to allow computer users to customize their computers based on their desires and preferences.

Customizing the Keyboard

Windows 98 allows you to customize the way you use the keyboard by changing its properties. Among the properties you can change are the keyboard repeat delay, keyboard repeat rate, and cursor (or insertion point) blink rate. Double-clicking the **Keyboard icon** in the Control Panel window opens the Keyboard Properties dialog box that allows you to change these properties.

Adjusting the Keyboard Repeat Delay

The **keyboard repeat delay** is the amount of time that elapses between holding down a key on the keyboard and seeing the character repeated across the screen. The Repeat delay slider and test box in the Keyboard Properties dialog box (see Figure 5-3) are used to set the keyboard repeat delay. Dragging the Repeat delay slider to the left or right lengthens or shortens the keyboard repeat delay. You use the test box to test the adjustment in the keyboard repeat delay. Perform the following steps to adjust the keyboard repeat delay.

Steps To Adjust the Keyboard Repeat Delay

1 Double-click the Keyboard icon in the Control Panel window. If necessary, click the Speed tab to display the Speed sheet. Point to the Repeat delay slider in the Character repeat pane.

The Keyboard Properties dialog box and Speed sheet display (Figure 5-3). The **Speed sheet** contains the Character repeat and Cursor blink rate panes. The Character repeat pane contains the Repeat delay slide and slider, Repeat rate slide and slider, and test box.

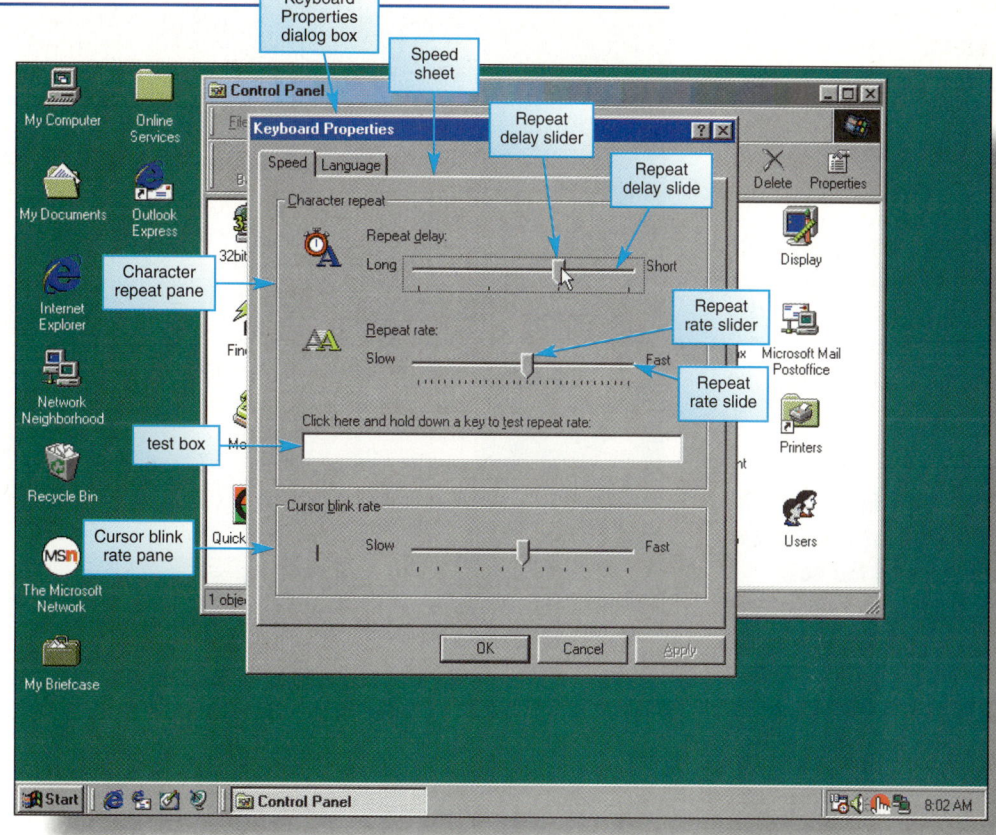

FIGURE 5-3

2 Drag the Repeat delay slider to the left end of the slide, click the test box, and then hold down the x key on the keyboard to test the repeat delay.

The slider is located at the left end of the Repeat delay slide (Figure 5-4). The first x character displays in the test box. After a long delay, the remaining x's display.

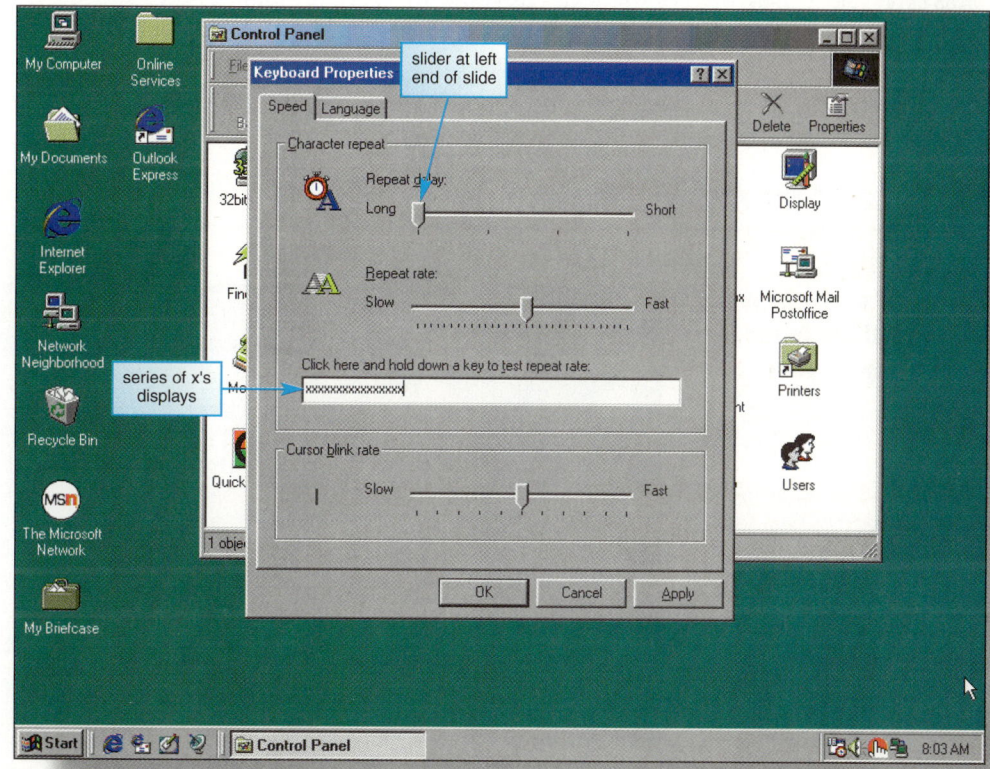

FIGURE 5-4

WIN 5.8 • Project 5 • Customizing Your Computer Using Control Panel

3 Drag the Repeat delay slider to the right end of the slide, click the test box, remove the x's in the box, and then hold down the x key to test the repeat delay.

The slider is located at the right end of the Repeat delay slide (Figure 5-5). The first x character displays in the test box. After a short delay, the remaining x's display.

4 Experiment with the Repeat delay slider until you find the best keyboard repeat delay for you.

Other Ways

1. Right-click Keyboard icon, click Open, click Speed tab, drag Repeat delay slider
2. Click Start button on taskbar, click Help, click Index tab, type delay, click Display button, click Display button, click Click here link, click Speed tab, drag Repeat delay slider

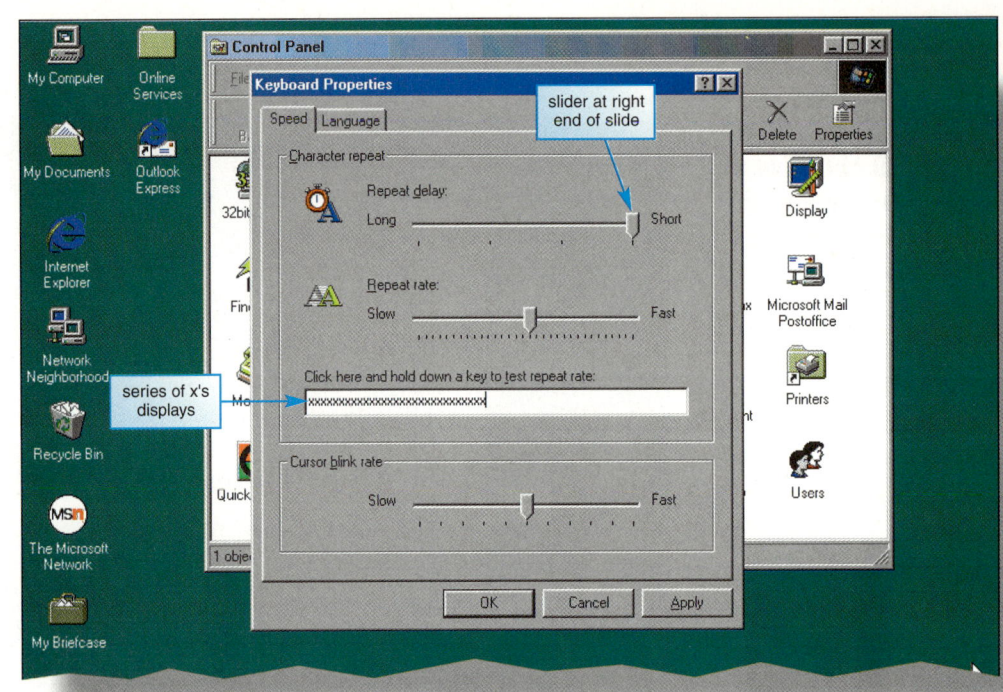

FIGURE 5-5

Adjusting the Keyboard Repeat Rate

The **keyboard repeat rate** is the speed at which a character repeats across the screen when you hold down a key on the keyboard. The Repeat rate slider and test box in the Keyboard Properties dialog box (see Figure 5-6) are used to set the keyboard repeat rate. Dragging the slider to the left or right decreases or increases the keyboard repeat rate. You use the test box to test the adjustment in the keyboard repeat rate. Perform the following steps to adjust the keyboard repeat rate.

 To Adjust the Keyboard Repeat Rate

1 Point to the Repeat rate slider in the Character repeat pane (Figure 5-6).

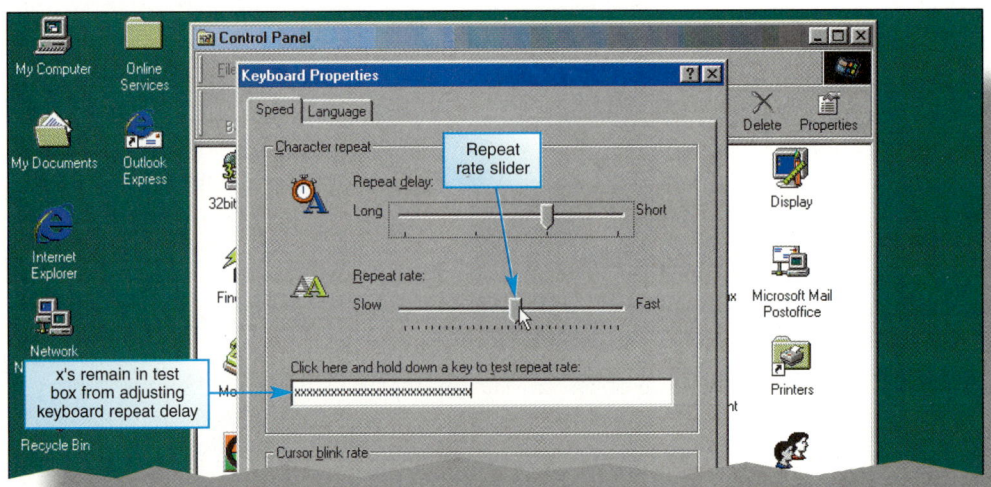

FIGURE 5-6

Customizing the Keyboard • **WIN 5.9**

2 **Drag the Repeat rate slider to the left end of the slide, click the test box, remove the x's, and then hold down the z keyboard key to test the repeat rate.**

The Repeat rate slider is located at the left end of the Repeat rate slide (Figure 5-7). The z character is repeated slowly across the test box.

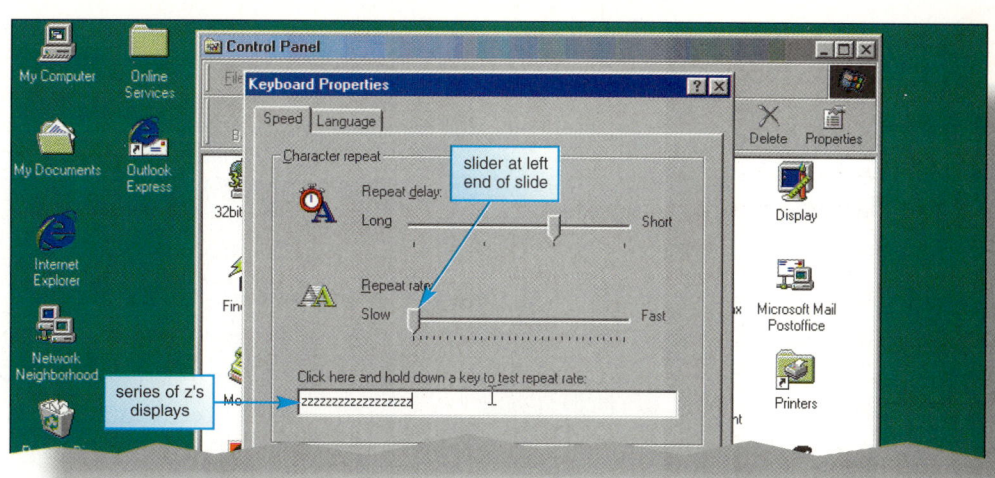

FIGURE 5-7

3 **Drag the Repeat rate slider to the right end of the slide, click the test box, remove the z's in the box, and then hold down the z keyboard key to test the repeat rate.**

The Repeat rate slider is located at the right end of the Repeat rate slide and the z character is repeated quickly across the test box (Figure 5-8).

4 **Experiment with the Repeat rate slider until you find the best keyboard repeat rate for you.**

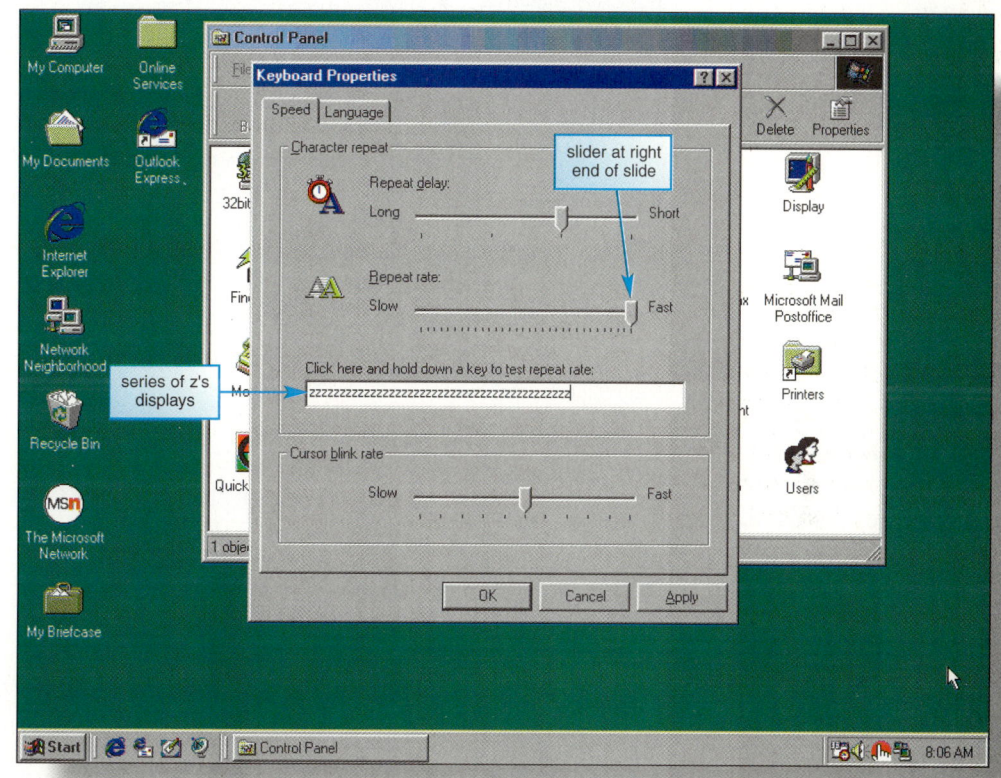

FIGURE 5-8

Adjusting the Cursor Blink Rate

The **cursor blink rate** is the speed at which the cursor (insertion point) blinks. Adjusting the cursor blink rate can make it easier to see the insertion point on the desktop. The Cursor blink rate slider and a blinking insertion point in the Keyboard Properties dialog box (see Figure 5-9 on the next page) are used to set the cursor blink rate. Dragging the slider to the left or right decreases or increases the cursor blink rate. Perform the steps on the next page to adjust the cursor blink rate.

Other Ways

1. Right-click Keyboard icon, click Open, click Speed tab, drag Repeat rate slider
2. Click Start button on taskbar, click Help, Click Index tab, type repeat rate, click Display button, click Display button, click Click here link, click Speed tab, drag Repeat rate slider

WIN 5.10 • Project 5 • Customizing Your Computer Using Control Panel   Microsoft **Windows 98**

 To Adjust the Cursor Blink Rate

① Point to the Cursor blink rate slider in the Cursor blink rate pane (Figure 5-9).

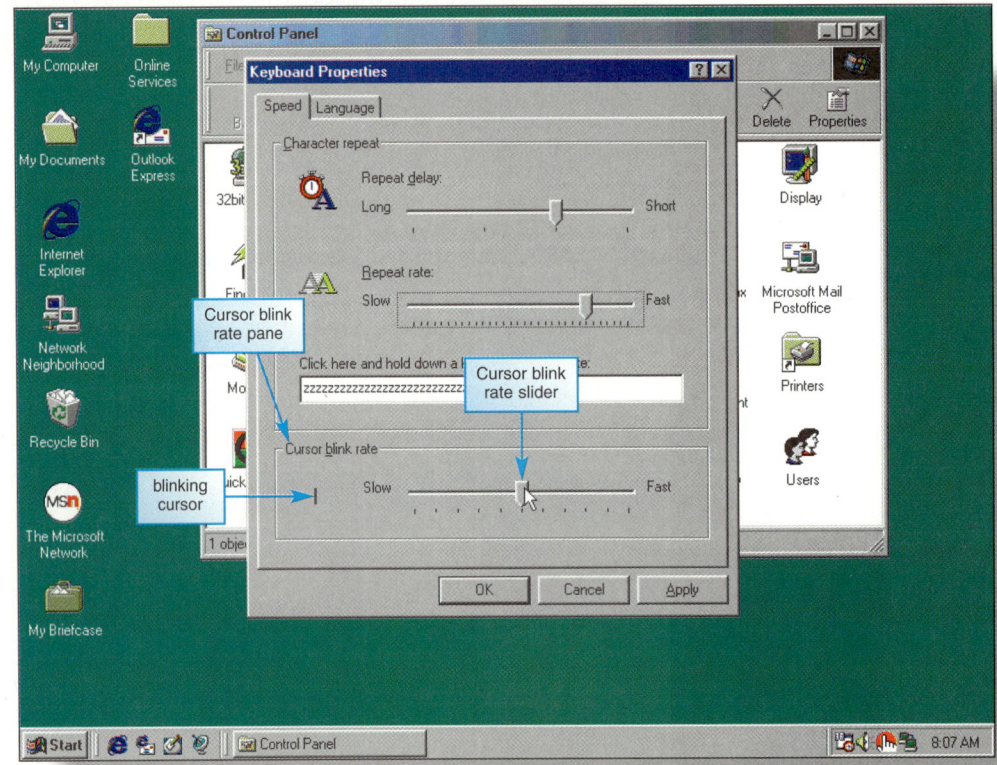

FIGURE 5-9

② Drag the Cursor blink rate slider to the left end of the slide.

The slider is located at the left end of the Cursor blink rate slide (Figure 5-10). The blinking insertion point to the left of the Cursor blink rate slide blinks slowly.

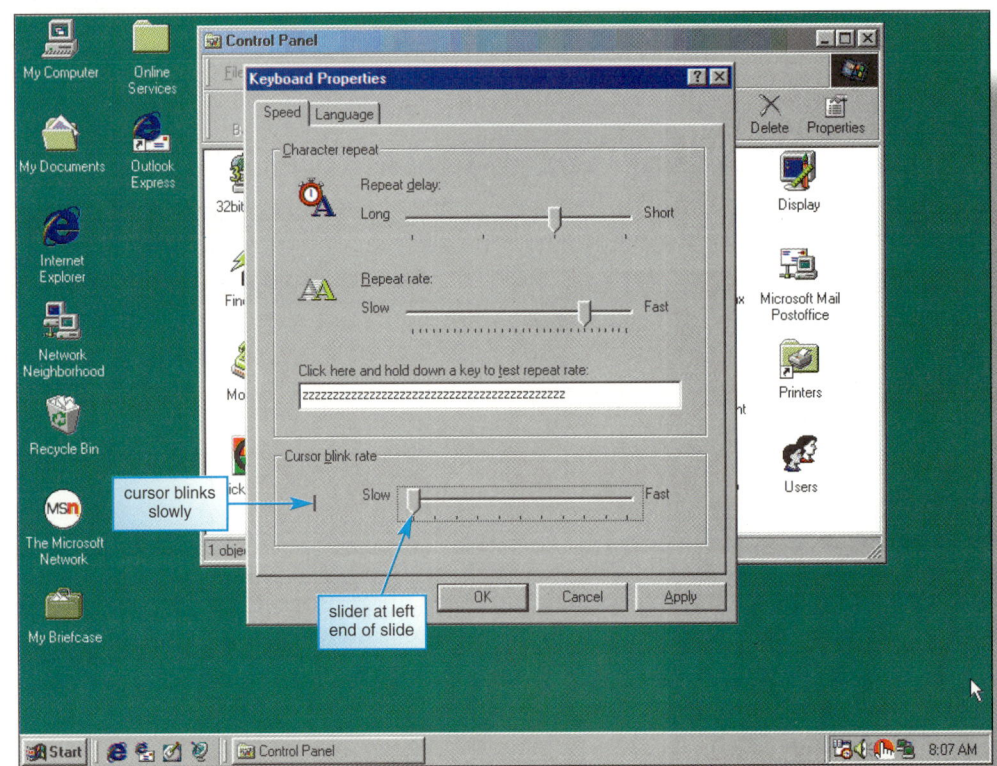

FIGURE 5-10

3) **Drag the Cursor blink rate slider to the right end of the slide.**

The slider is located at the right end of the Cursor blink rate slide (Figure 5-11). The blinking insertion point to the left of the Cursor blink rate slide blinks faster.

4) **Experiment with the Cursor blink rate slider until you find the best cursor blink rate for you.**

5) **Click the OK button.**

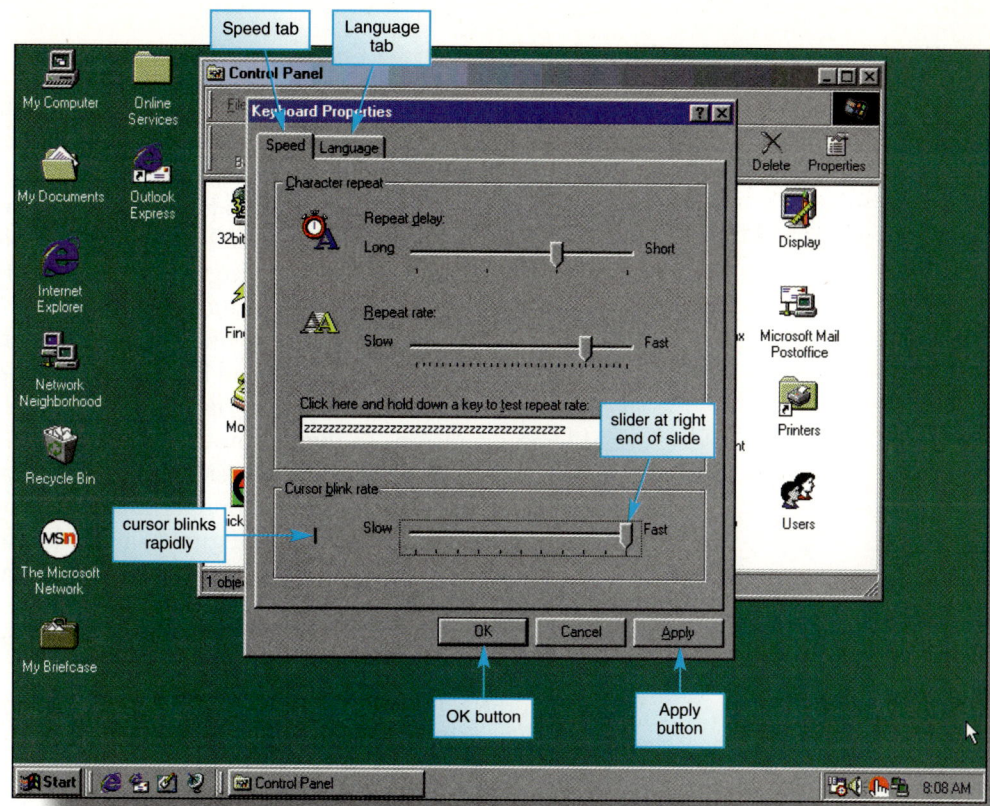

FIGURE 5-11

The Keyboard Properties dialog box shown in Figure 5-11 contains the Apply button. Usually, when you click the Apply button, the requested adjustment takes place and the dialog box remains open. This allows you to see the effect of the adjustment and to make another change. Because the keyboard repeat rate, keyboard repeat delay, and cursor blink rate adjustments are made immediately upon moving the slider, it is not necessary to use the Apply button.

Two tabs (Speed and Language) display in the Keyboard Properties dialog box. As illustrated earlier, the Speed sheet allows you to change the keyboard repeat delay, keyboard repeat rate, and cursor blink rate. The **Language sheet** allows you to select a different keyboard language or keyboard layout and easily switch among languages or layouts.

Customizing the Mouse

The mouse is another hardware device that Windows 98 allows you to customize. Among the mouse properties you can change are the function of the left and right mouse buttons, double-click speed, mouse pointer speed, pointer trails, and mouse pointer scheme. Double-clicking the Mouse icon in the Control Panel window opens the Mouse Properties dialog box that allows you to change these properties.

Other Ways

1. Right-click Keyboard icon, click Open, click Speed tab, drag Cursor blink rate slider
2. Click Start button on taskbar, click Help, click Index tab, type cursor blink speed, click Display button, click Click here link, click Speed tab, drag Cursor blink rate slider

More About

Keyboard Layouts

Changing the keyboard layout to accommodate its use with other languages may cause the characters that display on your screen to no longer correspond to the characters that are printed on your keyboard's keys. If you experience this problem, remember that changing the keyboard layout may be the solution.

Changing the Button Configuration

As mentioned in Project 1, the mouse contains a primary and secondary mouse button. If you are right-handed, the primary mouse button typically is the left mouse button and the secondary mouse button typically is the right mouse button. This button configuration, called the **Right-handed button configuration**, assigns the mouse operations of selecting (Normal Select) and dragging (Normal Drag) to the left mouse button and the mouse operations of right-clicking (Context Menu) and right-dragging (Special Drag) to the right mouse button.

If you are left-handed, you may find it more convenient to use the Left-handed button configuration. The **Left-handed button configuration** assigns the Normal Select and Normal Drag operations to the right mouse button and the Context Menu and Special Drag operations to the left mouse button.

If you are using the **Microsoft IntelliMouse™** a wheel and wheel button is positioned between the primary and secondary mouse buttons. As with the two-button mouse, the right-handed button configuration and left-handed button configuration also are valid with the IntelliMouse. The procedures that follow assume a two-button mouse is attached to your computer and not the IntelliMouse. If you have an IntelliMouse mouse attached to your computer, the instructions will be slightly different.

Perform the following steps to change the button configuration to the Left-handed configuration, and then change the button configuration back to the Right-handed configuration.

 To Change the Mouse Button Configuration

1 **Double-click the Mouse icon in the Control Panel window. If necessary, click the Buttons tab. Point to the Left-handed option button in the Button configuration pane.**

The Mouse Properties dialog box and Buttons sheet display (Figure 5-12). The selected Right-handed option button indicates the Right-handed configuration is being used. The highlighted left mouse button in the mouse illustration indicates the left mouse button is the primary button. The button operations display on either side of the illustration.

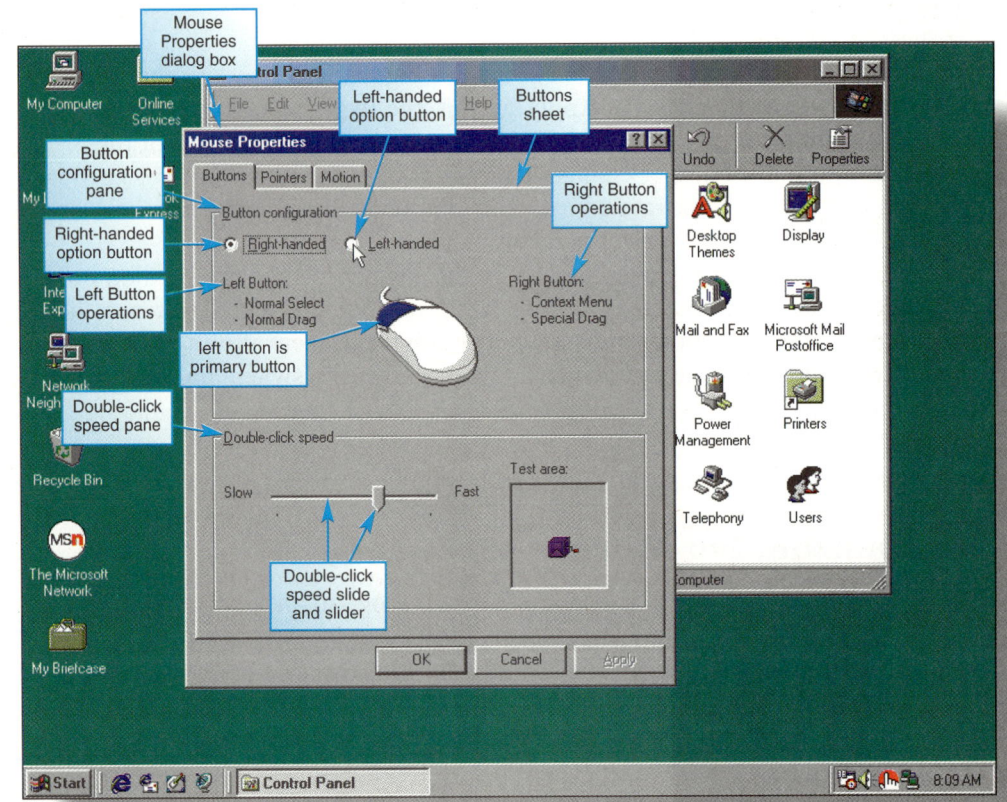

FIGURE 5-12

② Click Left-handed. Click the Apply button.

The Left-handed option button is selected (Figure 5-13). The button configuration changes to the Left-handed configuration, the primary button in the mouse illustration changes to the right mouse button, and the mouse operations associated with the left and right buttons switch.

③ Experiment with the left and right mouse buttons until you are comfortable with the Left-handed configuration.

④ Using the right mouse button, click Right-handed in the Button configuration pane, and then click the Apply button.

The button configuration changes to the Right-handed configuration.

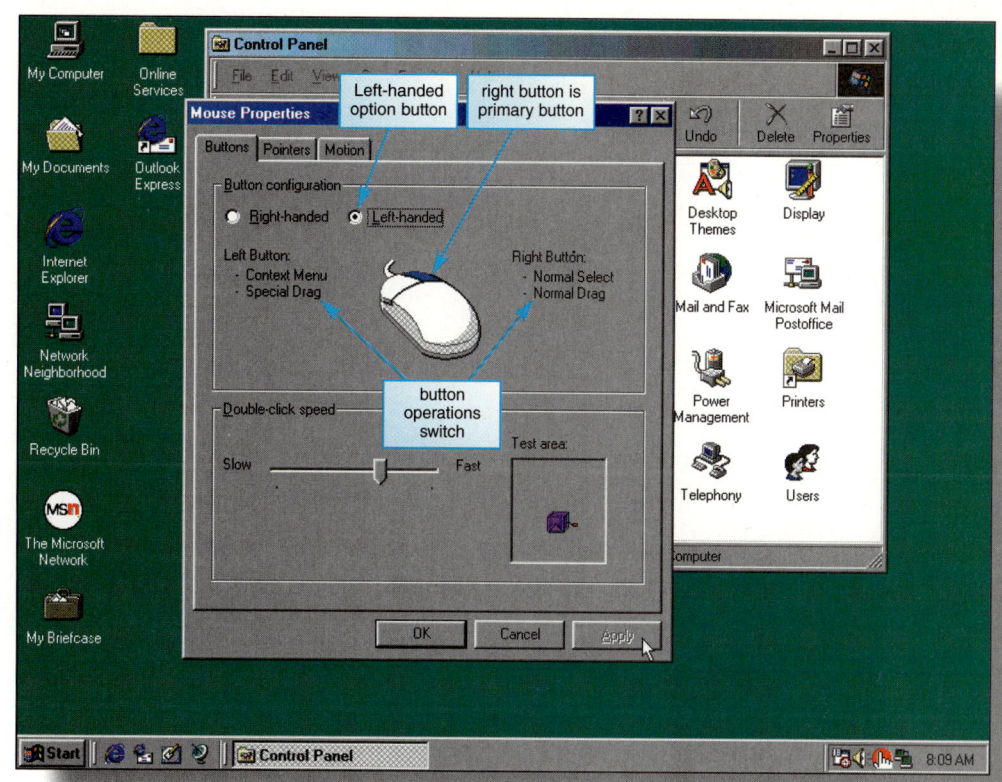

FIGURE 5-13

Adjusting the Double-Click Speed

As explained in Project 1, clicking means pressing a mouse button and double-clicking means quickly pressing and releasing a mouse button twice. Windows 98 measures the amount of time between clicking the mouse button once and clicking the same button again. This time interval, called **double-click speed**, determines whether Windows 98 recognizes clicking the mouse button twice as a double-click or two single clicks.

If you click a mouse button and do not click the button again within the time interval, Windows 98 determines that the mouse was *clicked*. If you click a mouse button and click the button again within the time interval, Windows 98 determines that the mouse was *double-clicked*. To increase or decrease the double-click speed, move the Double-click speed slider (see Figure 5-14 on the next page) to the left or right along the Double-click speed slide.

After adjusting the double-click speed, test the new speed by double-clicking the Test area (see Figure 5-14 on the next page). If you double-click the Test area within the specified time interval, a jack-in-the-box emerges from the box to indicate that Windows 98 recognized your double-click. If the jack-in-the-box does not emerge from the box, the double-click speed is set too fast and should be reduced. Double-clicking within the specified time interval when the jack-in-the-box has already emerged from the box will cause it (if necessary) to return to the box.

Other Ways

1. Right-click Mouse icon, click Open, click Buttons tab, click option button
2. Click Start button on taskbar, click Help, Click Index tab, type left-handed, click Display button, click Click here link, click Buttons tab, click option button

More About

Double-Click Speed

Setting the double-click speed to its fastest speed may make it impossible to double-click an object. If this happens, open the Mouse Properties dialog box without double-clicking, use the TAB key to select the Double-click speed slide and the LEFT ARROW key on the keyboard to reduce the speed, and then click the Apply button.

WIN 5.14 • Project 5 • Customizing Your Computer Using Control Panel

Perform the following steps to adjust and test the double-click speed.

Steps: To Adjust the Double-Click Speed

1 Drag the Double-click speed slider to the right end of the slide. Double-click the Test area.

The Double-click speed slider displays at the right end of the Double-click speed slide (Figure 5-14). Although the Test area is double-clicked, a jack-in-the-box does not emerge from the box.

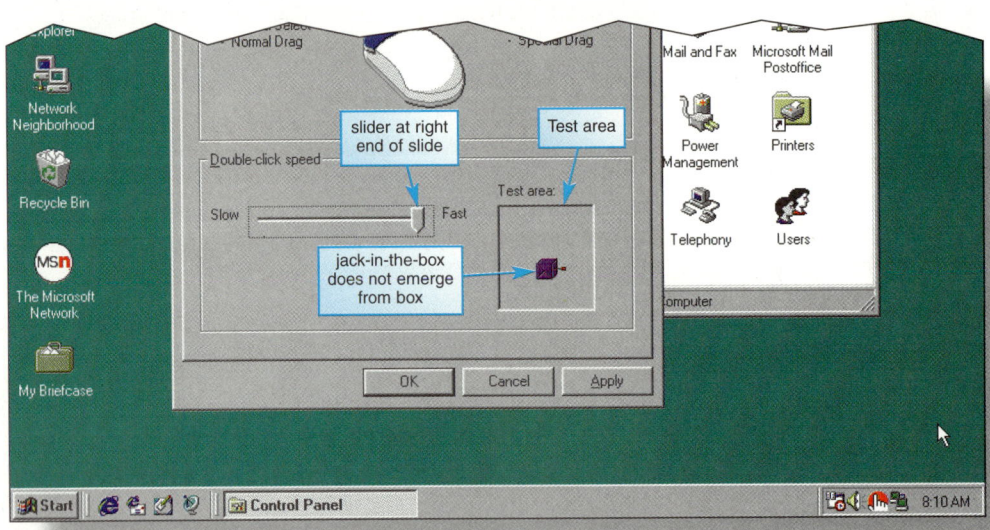

FIGURE 5-14

2 Drag the Double-click speed slider to the left along the slide until the jack-in-the-box emerges from the box when you double-click the Test area.

The Double-click speed slider is moved so that when you double-click the Test area, the jack-in-the box emerges from the box (Figure 5-15). This is your best double-click speed.

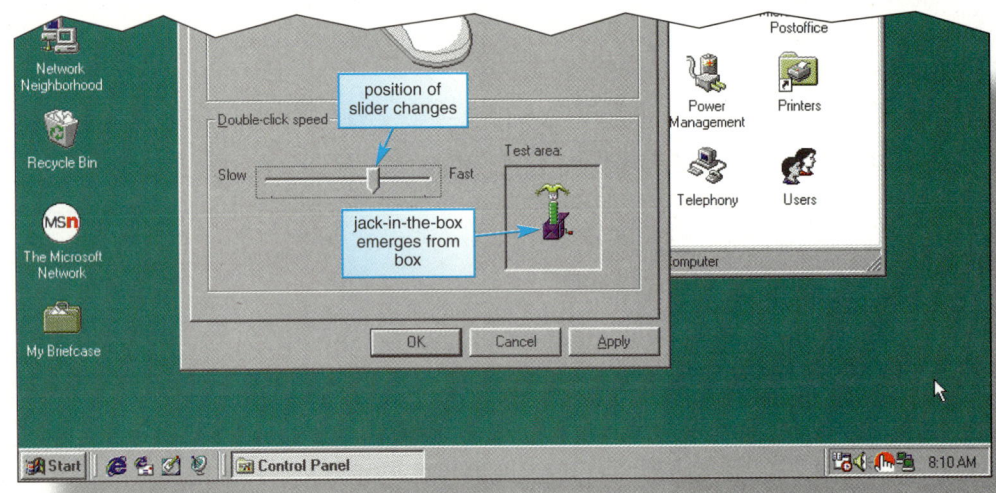

FIGURE 5-15

Other Ways

1. Right-click Mouse icon, click Open, click Buttons tab, drag Double-click speed slider
2. Click Start button on taskbar, click Help, click Index tab, type double-click speed, click Display button, click Display button, click Click here link, click Buttons tab, drag Double-click speed slider

Changing the Mouse Pointer Scheme

The shape the mouse pointer takes when you point to an area of the desktop (block arrow), wait for an operation to be completed (hourglass), point to the border or corner of a window (two-headed arrow), enter text in a word processor (I-beam), or draw in a graphics program (pencil) is determined by the mouse pointer scheme you select. To change the mouse pointer scheme, complete the following steps.

Steps: To Change the Mouse Pointer Scheme

1 **Click the Pointers tab. Write down on a piece of paper the mouse pointer scheme name displayed in the Scheme box on your computer. Point to the Scheme box arrow.**

The Pointers sheet displays (Figure 5-16). The current mouse pointer scheme, (None), is highlighted in the Scheme box. A partial list of the mouse pointers that make up the current scheme display in the list box. The Normal Select mouse pointer is highlighted in the list box and its mouse pointer displays in the preview box.

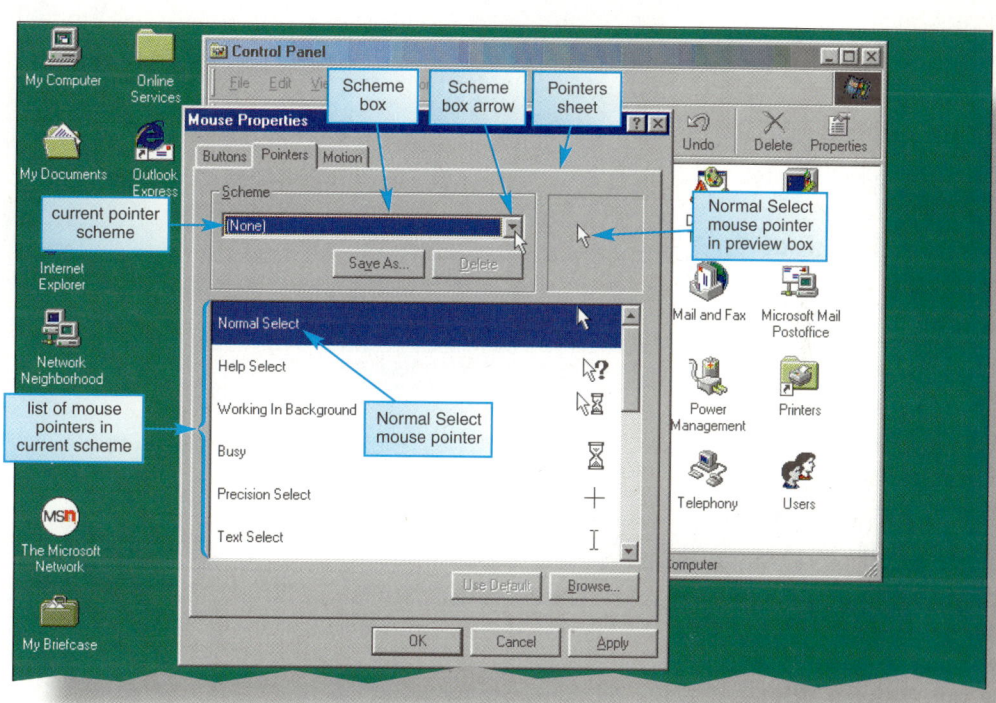

FIGURE 5-16

2 **Click the Scheme box arrow. Point to the Animated Hourglasses scheme name in the Scheme list box.**

The Scheme list box displays and the Animated Hourglasses scheme name is highlighted (Figure 5-17).

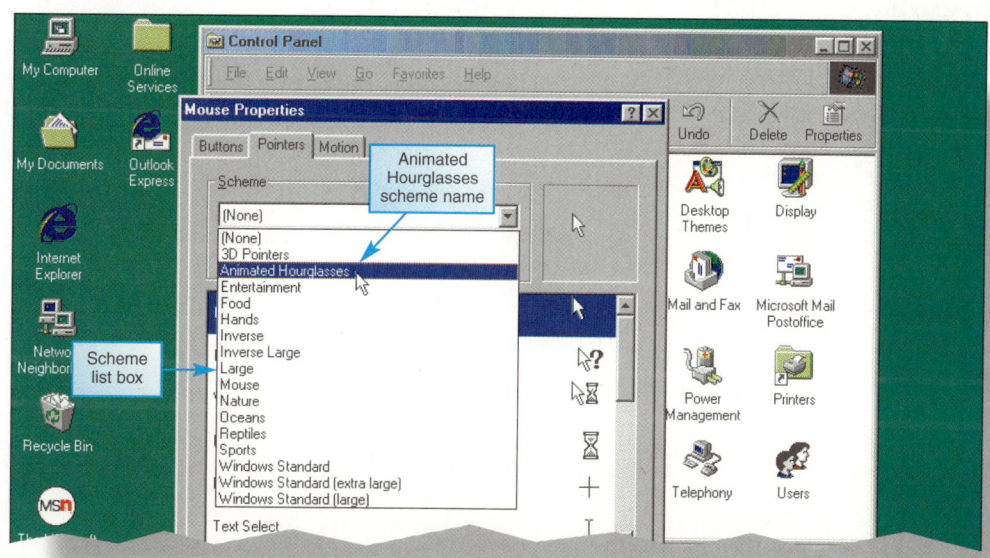

FIGURE 5-17

WIN 5.16 • Project 5 • Customizing Your Computer Using Control Panel

3 **Click the Animated Hourglasses scheme name. Click Busy in the list box to view the Busy mouse pointer in the preview box.**

The mouse pointer scheme changes to the Animated Hourglasses scheme, the Busy entry is highlighted, and the animated Busy mouse pointer displays in the preview box (Figure 5-18).

4 **Click other entries in the list box to view the different mouse pointers in the Animated Hourglasses scheme.**

5 **Click the Scheme box arrow and then click the mouse pointer scheme name you wrote down in Step 1 on the previous page.**

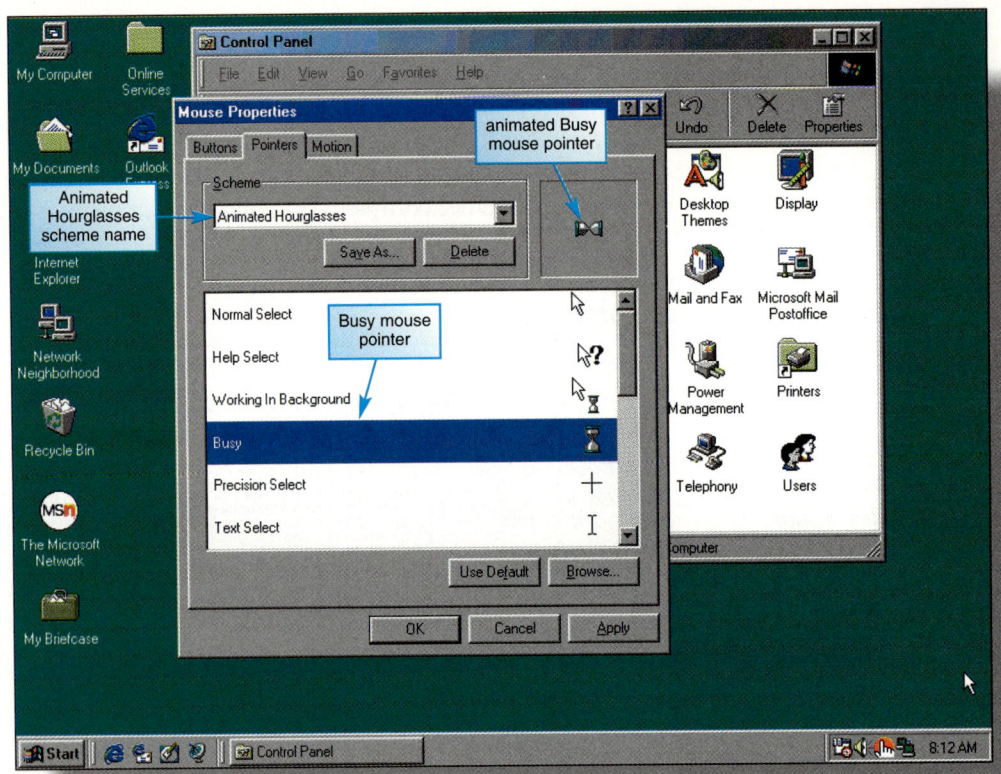

FIGURE 5-18

Other Ways

1. Right-click Mouse icon, click Open, click Pointers tab, click Scheme box arrow, click mouse scheme, click Apply button
2. Click Start button on taskbar, click Help, click Index tab, type mouse pointer, click appearance, changing topic, click Display button, click Display button, click Click here link, click Pointers tab, click Scheme box arrow, click mouse scheme, click Apply button

If your display supports animation, the animated Busy mouse pointer shown in Figure 5-18 inverts itself each time the sand finishes running out of the top part of the hourglass.

Adjusting the Pointer Speed

The **pointer speed** is the speed at which the mouse pointer travels across the desktop when you move the mouse across a flat surface. Perform the following steps to adjust the pointer speed.

To Adjust the Pointer Speed

1. **Click the Motion tab in the Mouse Properties dialog box. Drag the Pointer speed slider to the left end of the slide. Click the Apply button.**

   The Motion sheet displays and the Pointer speed slider displays at the left end of the Pointer speed slide (Figure 5-19). Clicking the Apply button makes the adjustment to the pointer speed and dims the Apply button.

2. **Move the mouse pointer to the lower-left corner of the desktop. Then, quickly move the mouse so the mouse pointer moves toward the upper-right corner of the desktop.**

   The mouse pointer moves slowly toward the upper right corner of the desktop.

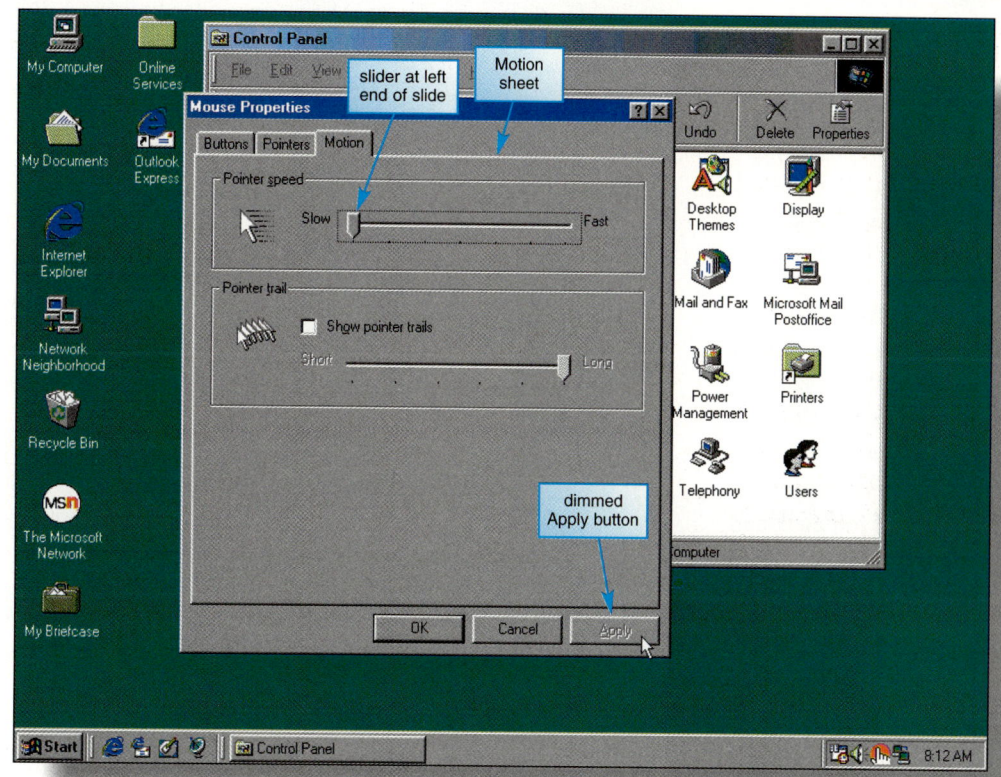

FIGURE 5-19

3 **Drag the Pointer speed slider to the right end of the slide. Click the Apply button.**

The Pointer Speed slider moves to the right end of the Pointer Speed slide (Figure 5-20). The adjustment to the pointer speed is made.

4 **Move the mouse pointer to the lower-left corner of the desktop. Then, quickly move the mouse so the mouse pointer moves toward the upper right corner of the desktop.**

The mouse pointer moves quickly toward the upper right corner of the desktop.

5 **Experiment with the pointer speed until you find the best pointer speed for you.**

Other Ways

1. Right-click Mouse icon, click Open, click Motion tab, drag Pointer speed slider, click Apply button
2. Click Start button on taskbar, click Help, click Index tab, type pointer, click speed, changing topic, click Display button, click Click here link, click Motion tab, drag Pointer speed slider, click Apply button

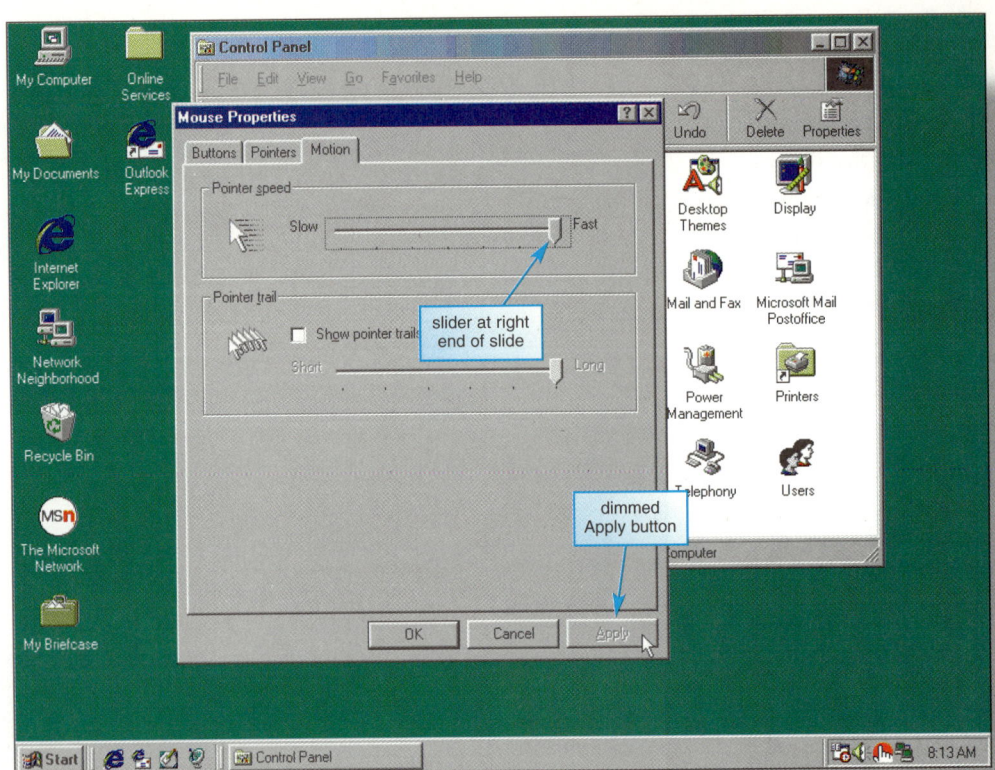

FIGURE 5-20

Displaying Pointer Trails

Sometimes when the mouse pointer moves across the desktop, it is difficult to see the position it occupies on the desktop. To improve the visibility of the mouse pointer, you can display a **pointer trail**, or trail of mouse pointers, on the desktop as you move the mouse. In addition, you can control whether the pointer trail consists of a few mouse pointers or many mouse pointers. Perform the following steps to display a pointer trail.

Customizing the Mouse • **WIN 5.19**

 **To Display a Pointer Trail**

1 Click Show pointer trails check box in the Pointer trail pane.

The Show pointer trails check box is selected (Figure 5-21). The Pointer trail slider displays at the right end of the slide to indicate the pointer trail will consist of many mouse pointers.

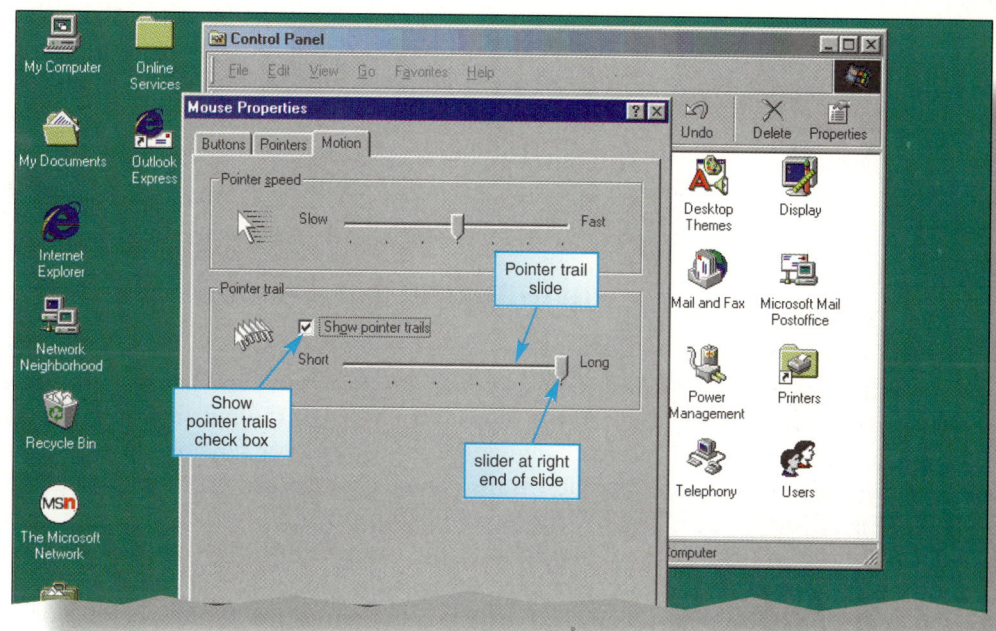

FIGURE 5-21

2 Move the mouse across a flat surface and watch the mouse pointer as it moves across the desktop.

A series of mouse pointers displays on the desktop (Figure 5-22). The pointer trail disappears when you stop moving the mouse.

3 Experiment with the length of the pointer trail by dragging the Pointer trail slider until you find the best length for you.

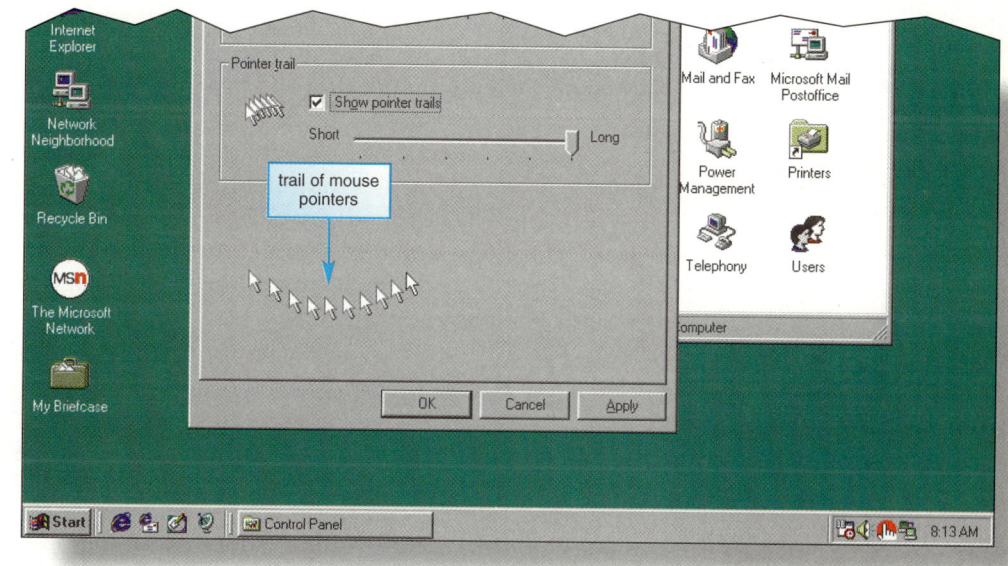

FIGURE 5-22

4 When you have finished viewing the pointer trail, click Show pointer trails to remove the pointer trails. Click the OK button.

1. Right-click Mouse icon, click Open, click Motion tab, click Show pointer trails
2. Click Start button on taskbar, click Help, click Index tab, type `trail`, click Display button, click Click here link, click Motion tab, click Show pointer trails

As illustrated earlier, the **Buttons sheet** allows you to change the button configuration and adjust the double-click speed. On the **Pointers sheet**, you can change the mouse pointer scheme. The **Motion sheet** permits you to adjust the pointer speed, display pointer trails, and adjust the length of the pointer trails.

The Mouse Properties dialog box shown in Figure 5-12 on page WIN 5.12 contains the Buttons, Pointers, and Motion tabs. If you have an IntelliMouse connected to your computer, additional tabs may display in the dialog box and additional features are available.

More About

Accessibility Options

If accessibility options are not available on your computer, you can make them available by double-clicking the Add/Remove Programs icon, clicking the Windows Setup tab, clicking the Accessibility Options check box, clicking the OK button, and following the instructions to install the option.

Customizing for Disabilities

In the previous sections, you customized the keyboard by adjusting the keyboard repeat delay, keyboard repeat rate, and cursor blink rate. In addition, you customized the mouse by changing the button configuration, adjusting the double-click speed, changing the mouse pointer scheme, adjusting the pointer speed, and displaying pointer trails. These changes are designed to make it easier for everyone to work in the Windows 98 environment.

In addition to the changes just mentioned, Windows 98 also provides additional features, called **accessibility features**, that make it easier for people who are mobility, hearing, or visually impaired to use Windows 98. For example, people who have restricted movement and cannot move the mouse (**mobility impaired**) have the option of using the **MouseKeys feature** that allows them to use the numeric keypad to move the mouse pointer, click, double-click, and drag.

People who are deaf or hard-of-hearing (**hearing impaired**) have the **Sound Sentry feature** that generates visual warnings when the computer makes a sound and the **ShowSounds feature** that causes an application program to display captions when a program speaks or makes sounds.

In addition to some of the changes shown earlier in this project (displaying pointer trails and adjusting the cursor blink rate), people who have difficulty seeing the screen (**visually impaired**) have the High Contrast feature. The **High Contrast feature** changes the desktop color scheme to the High Contrast Blank (Large) color scheme. This color scheme increases the size of text on the desktop, which improves a person's ability to read the text.

Turning on the MouseKeys Feature

To illustrate the use of an accessibility feature, perform the steps on the following pages to turn on the MouseKeys feature, and then use the MouseKeys feature to turn off the MouseKeys feature.

When the MouseKeys feature is turned on, the numeric keys on the numeric keypad can be used to move the mouse pointer across the desktop. Pressing the 2, 4, 6, or 8 key moves the mouse pointer left, up, right, or down, respectively. Pressing the 1, 3, 7, or 9 key moves the mouse pointer diagonally down and to the left, down and to the right, up and to the left, or up and to the right, respectively. Pressing the 5 key selects the object to which the mouse pointer points.

Customizing for Disabilities • WIN 5.21

 To Turn on the MouseKeys Feature

1 Double-click the Accessibility Options icon in the Control Panel window and then point to the Mouse tab.

The Accessibility Properties dialog box and Keyboard sheet display (Figure 5-23). The dialog box contains five tabbed sheets. In the Keyboard sheet, you can turn on the StickyKeys, FilterKeys, and ToggleKeys features.

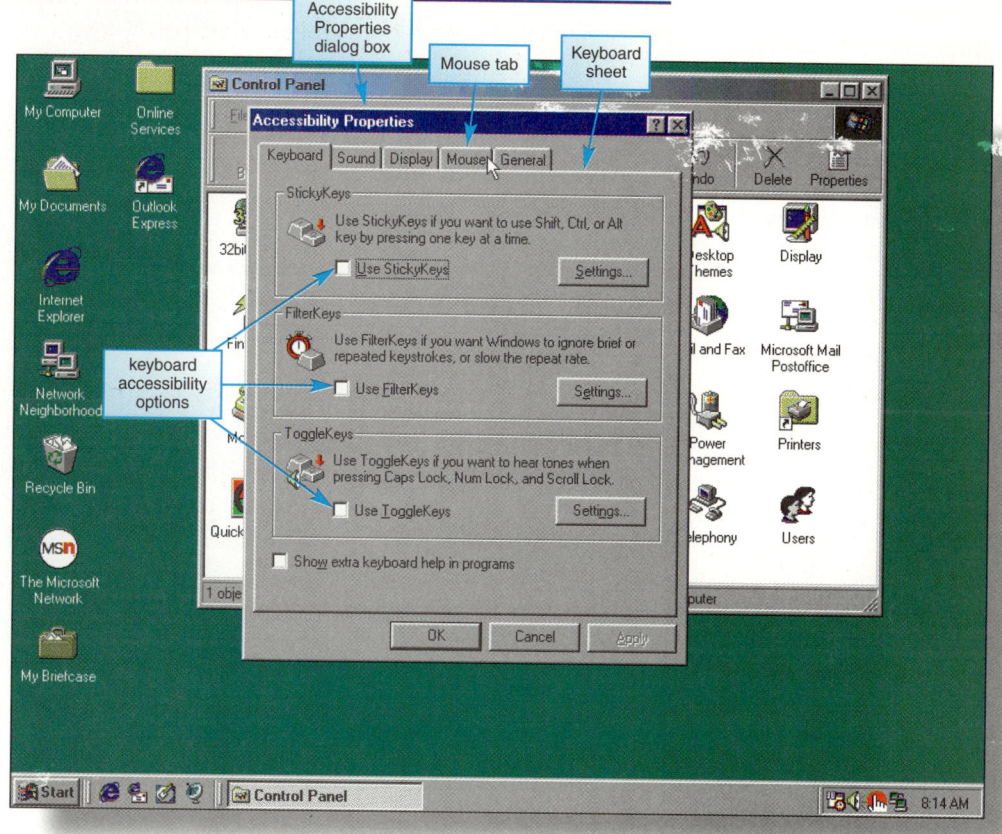

FIGURE 5-23

2 Click the Mouse tab. Click Use MouseKeys and then click the Apply button.

The Mouse sheet displays and the MouseKeys check box is selected, which turns on the MouseKeys feature. A mouse icon displays in the tray status area (Figure 5-24).

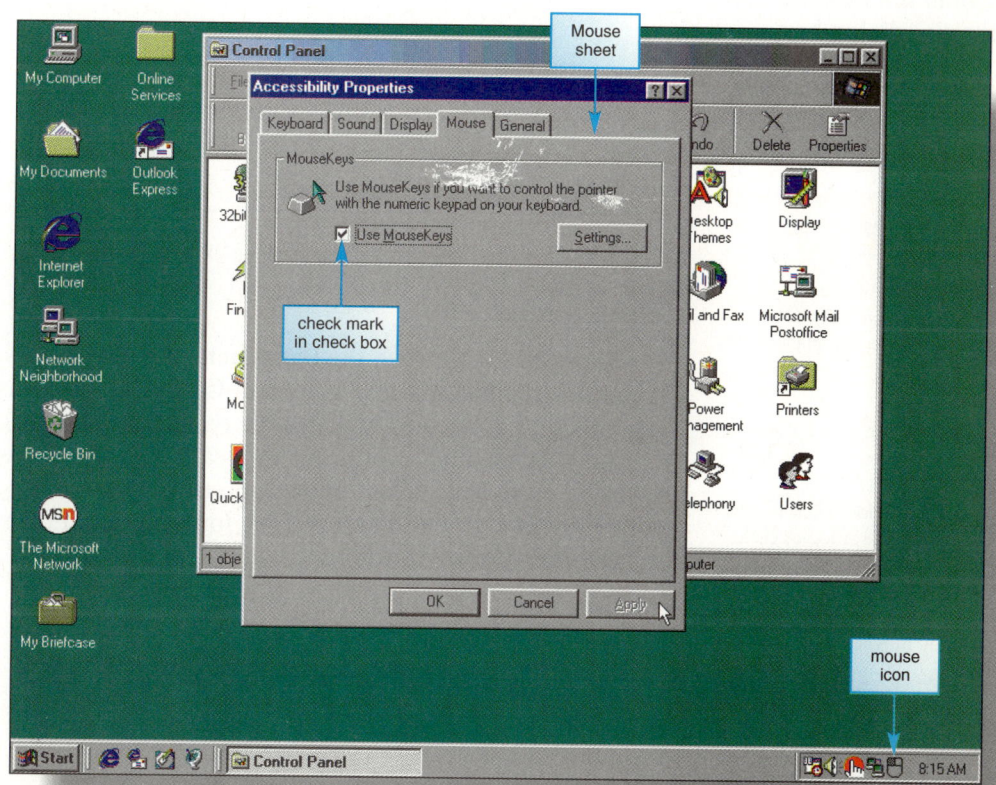

FIGURE 5-24

③ If a circle with a slash symbol displays over the mouse icon in the tray status area, press the NUM LOCK key. Use the 1, 2, 3, 4, 6, 7, 8, and 9 numeric keys on the numeric keypad to move the mouse pointer to the Use MouseKeys check box, and then press the 5 key to remove the check mark from the check box.

The mouse pointer points to the MouseKeys check box, and the check mark no longer displays in the check box (Figure 5-25).

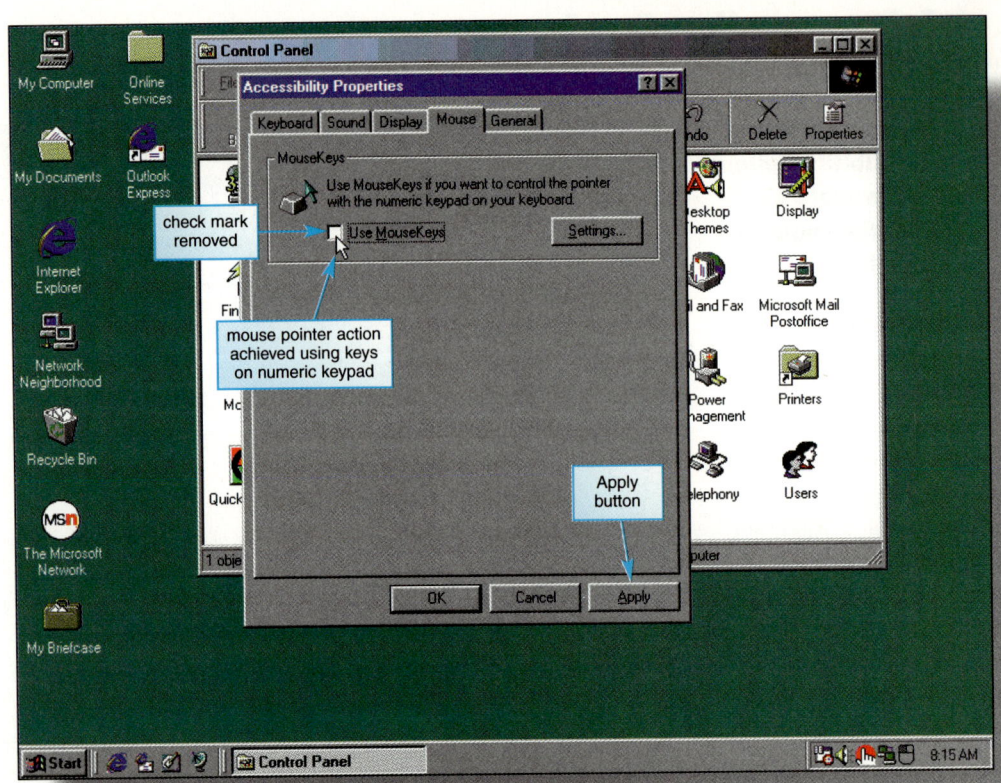

FIGURE 5-25

④ Using the numeric keys on the numeric keypad, move the mouse pointer to the Apply button and then click the button to turn off the MouseKeys feature. Click the OK button in the Accessibility Properties dialog box.

The MouseKeys feature turns off and the Accessibility Properties dialog box closes.

Other Ways

1. Right-click Accessibility Options icon, click Open, click Mouse tab, click Use MouseKeys, click Apply button
2. Click Start button on taskbar, click Help, click Index tab, type mousekeys, click Display button, click To turn on MouseKeys topic, click Display button, click Click here link, click Mouse tab, click Use MouseKeys, click Apply button

Using Bigger Fonts

As mentioned earlier, the **High Contrast feature** is designed for use by individuals who are visually impaired. The High Contrast feature uses the High Contrast Black (Large) color scheme to improve the readability of text on the desktop.

Another method to improve the readability of text is to use different fonts and font sizes. The **Fonts folder** allows you to view the fonts and fonts sizes available on your computer and add and remove fonts. Perform the steps on the following pages to view different fonts and font sizes.

Customizing for Disabilities • WIN 5.23

PROJECT 5

 To View Fonts and Font Sizes

1 **Double-click the Fonts icon in the Control Panel window. Point to the Arial icon in the Fonts window.**

The Fonts window opens (Figure 5-26). The Fonts window contains a large icon for each available font. The TT entry on the Arial icon indicates that the Arial font is part of a collection of fonts called **TrueType** fonts.

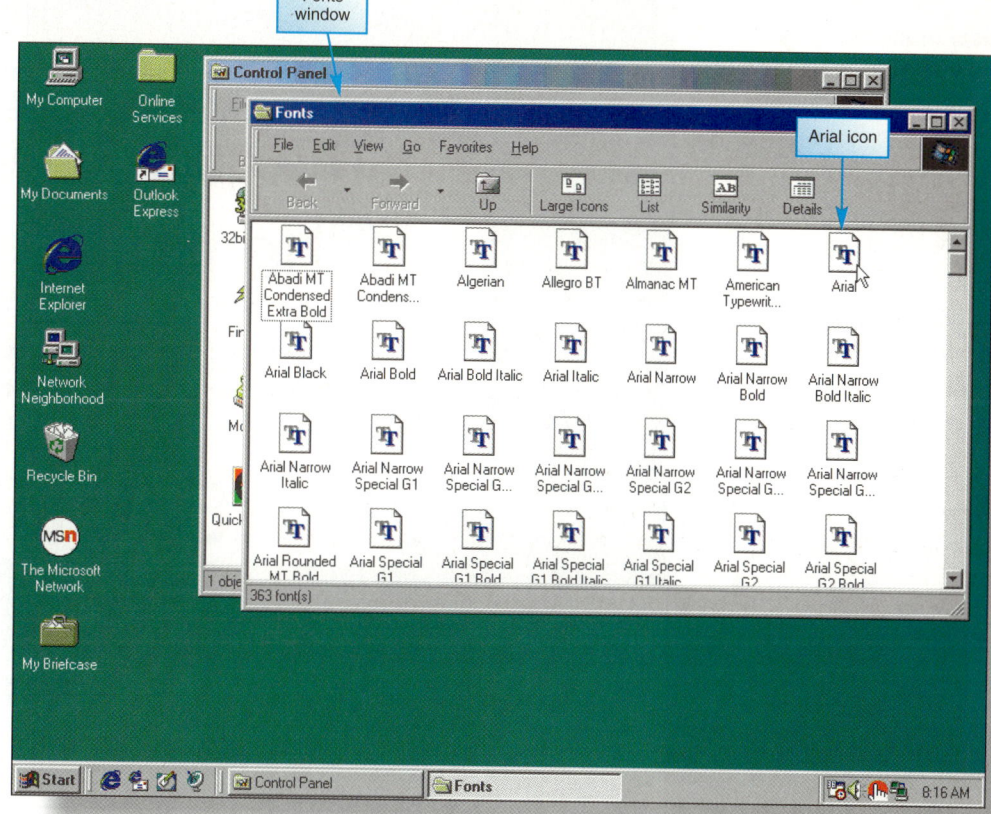

FIGURE 5-26

2 **Double-click the Arial icon.**

The Arial (TrueType) window opens (Figure 5-27). The window displays the Arial font name, and lists the Typeface name, File size, Version, and copyright notices. A sample of the Arial font in various font sizes also displays.

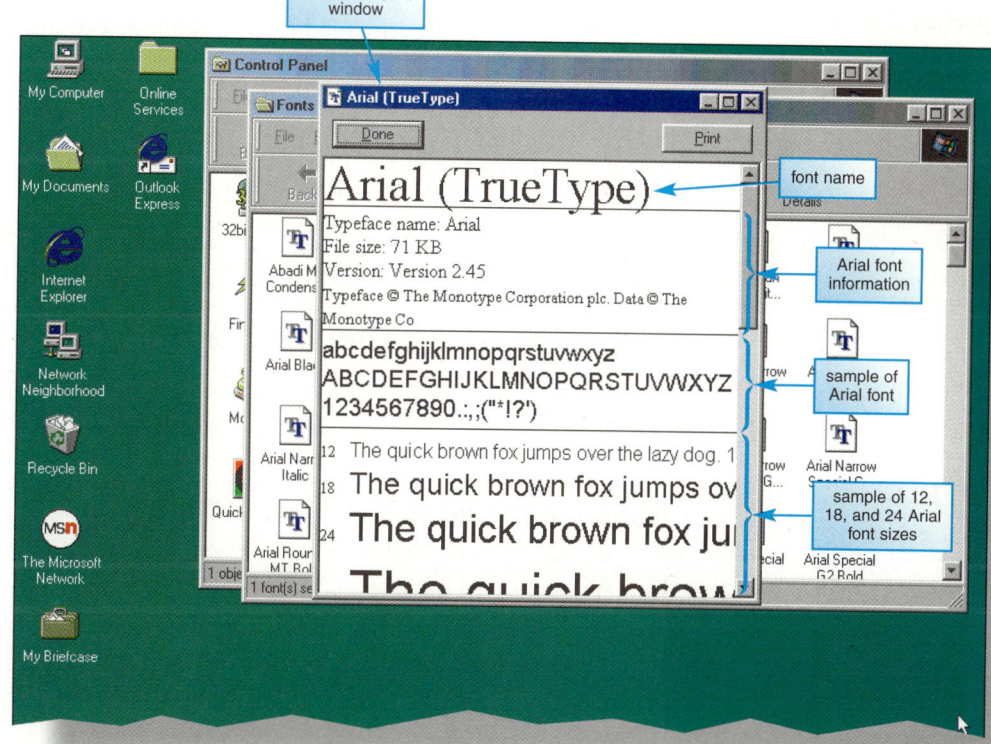

FIGURE 5-27

3 **Scroll the Arial (TrueType) window to view other font sizes. When you have finished, point to the Done button.**

Additional font sizes display in the Arial (TrueType) window (Figure 5-28).

4 **Click the Done button and then click the Close button to close the Fonts window.**

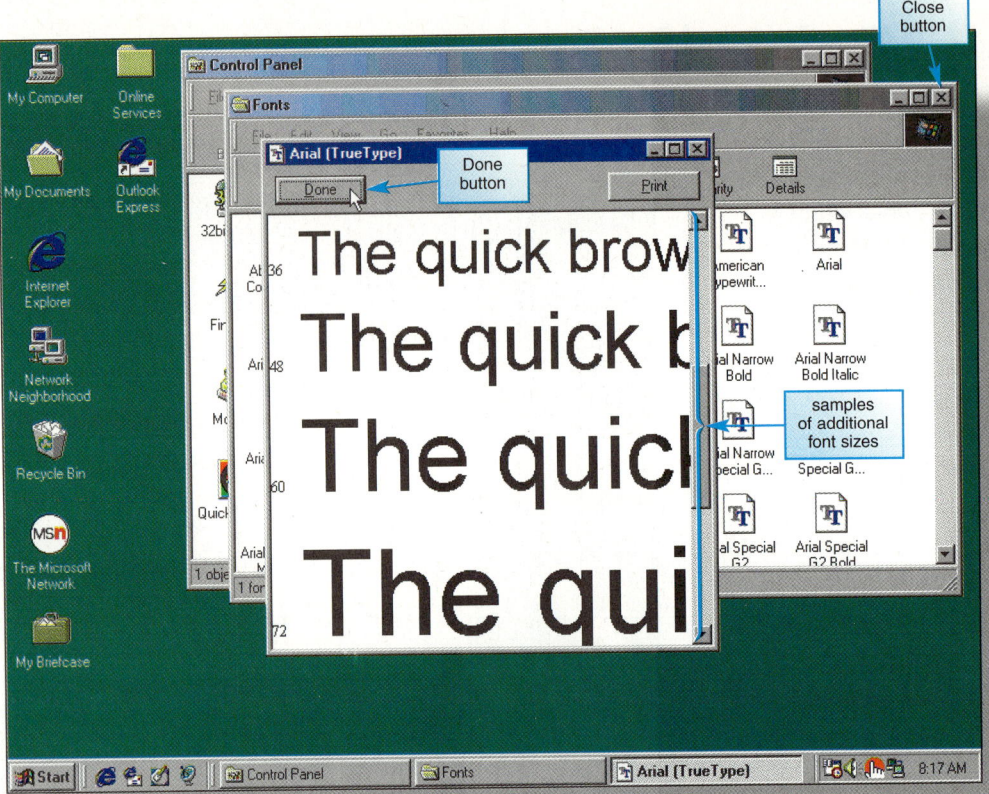

FIGURE 5-28

OtherWays

1. Double-click Fonts icon, right-click any font icon, click Open
2. Right-click Fonts icon, click Open, double-click any font icon

Creating a Desktop Color Scheme Using the New Fonts and Font Sizes

In Project 4, you performed steps to change the desktop color scheme to the Desert color scheme (pages WIN 4.11 and 4.12). Earlier in this project, you determined which fonts and fonts sizes you like. Now you can create a new desktop color scheme that includes those font and size choices. For practice in creating a color scheme, perform the In the Lab Exercise 1 (Creating and Saving a Color Scheme) on page WIN 4.66 at the end of Project 4.

Customizing the Date and Time

Previously, you changed the properties of the mouse and keyboard. You also can change the properties and format of the date and time.

Changing the Date, Time, and Time Zone

Changes to the date, time, and time zone are made by double-clicking the Date/Time icon in the Control Panel window and changing the individual date, time, and time zone settings. After changing these settings, it is important to cancel the changes and return these settings to their original settings. Perform the following steps to change the date, time, and time zone, and then cancel the changes.

To Change the Date, Time, and Time Zone

1 **Double-click the Date/Time icon in the Control Panel window. If necessary, click the Date & Time tab. Point to the month box arrow.**

The Date/Time Properties dialog box and Date & Time sheet display (Figure 5-29). The **Date pane** contains the month box with the current month, the year box with the current year, and a monthly calendar with the current day highlighted. The **Time pane** contains an analog clock and the current time. The current time zone displays below the Date and Time panes. The date, time, and time zone may be different on your computer.

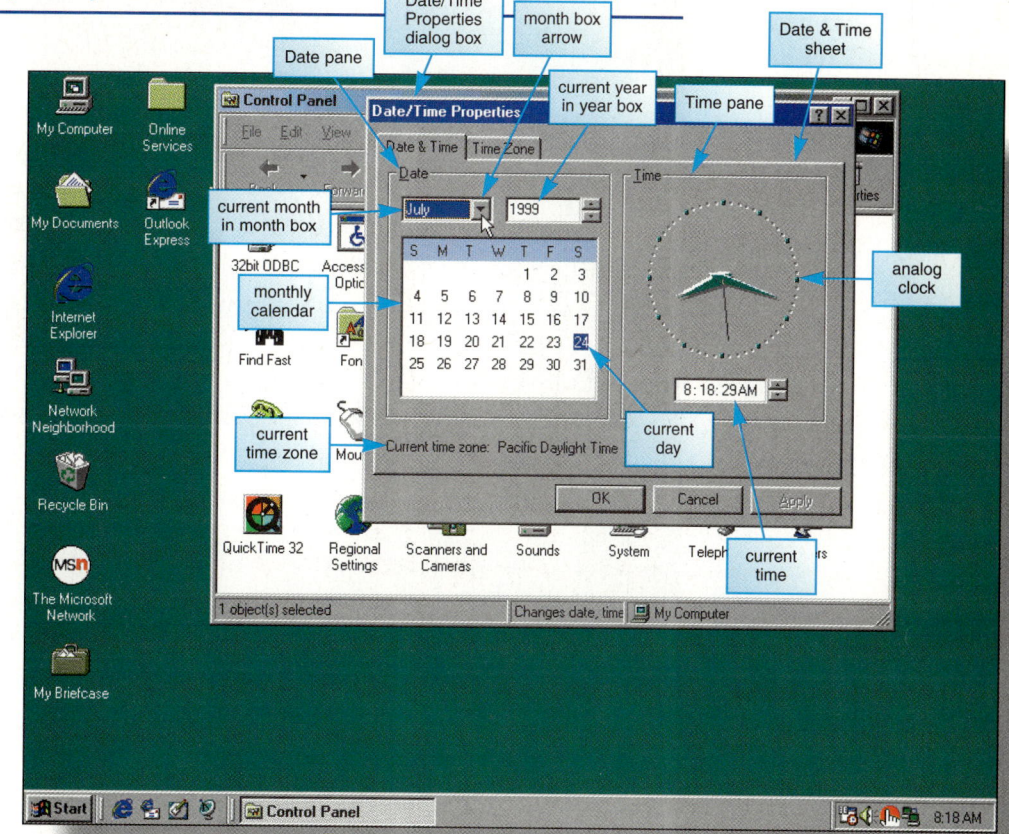

FIGURE 5-29

2 **Click the month box arrow. Point to October.**

The month list box displays (Figure 5-30).

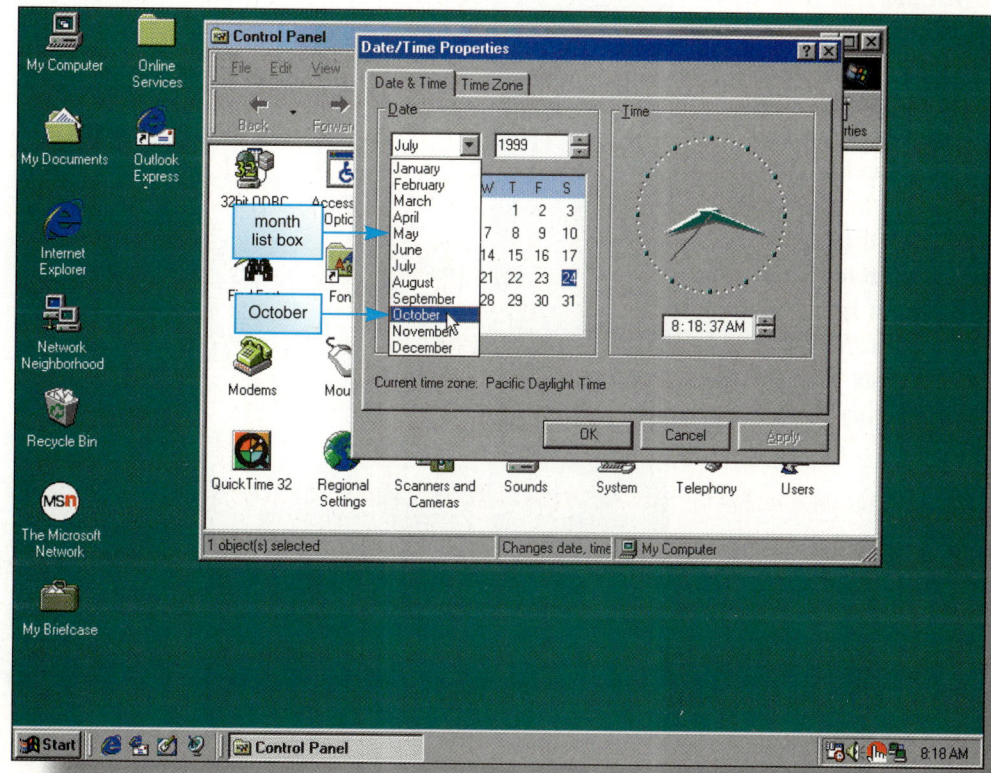

FIGURE 5-30

3 **Click October. Click the year box up or down arrow until 2001 displays. Click the number 15 in the monthly calendar.**

The month box contains the October entry, the year box contains the 2001 entry, and the number 15 is highlighted in the monthly calendar (Figure 5-31).

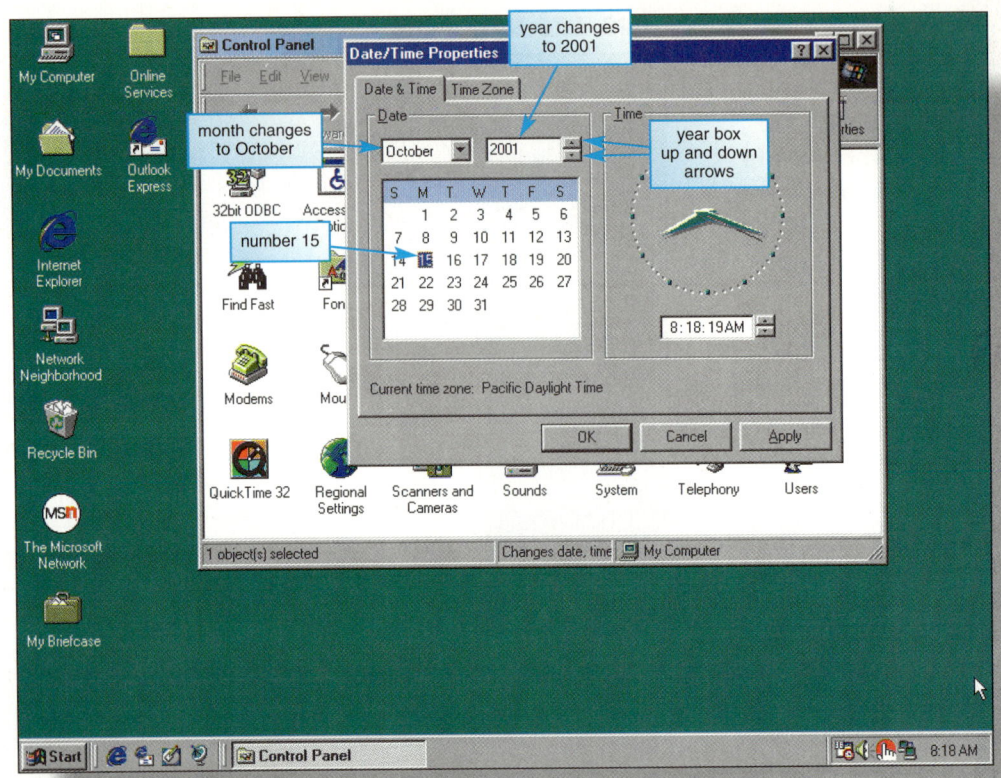

FIGURE 5-31

4 **Double-click the hour value in the time text box and then type 11 as the new value. Double-click the minute value in the time text box and then type 00 as the new value. Double-click the second value in the time text box and then type 00 as the new value. If the PM entry displays in the time text box, click the PM entry, and then click the up arrow to display the AM entry.**

The new time displays in the time box and on the analog clock (Figure 5-32).

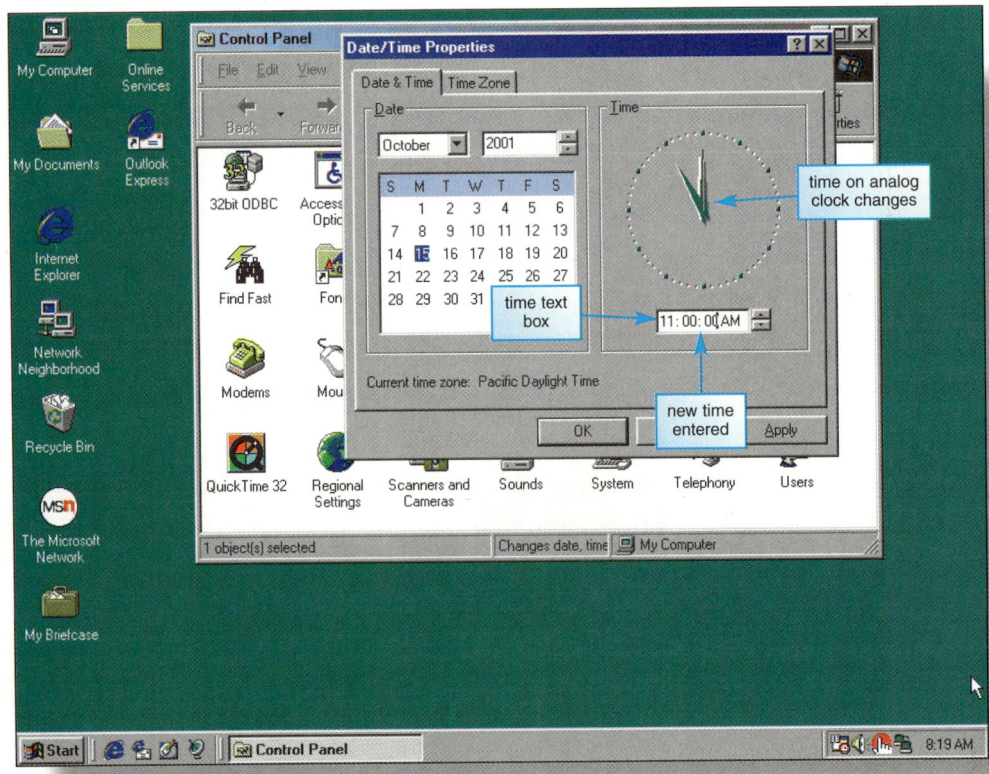

FIGURE 5-32

5 Click the Time Zone tab. Point to the Time Zone box arrow.

The Time Zone sheet displays (Figure 5-33). The **Time Zone sheet** contains the Time Zone list box containing the current time zone, a world map, and the selected Automatically adjust clock for daylight saving changes check box.

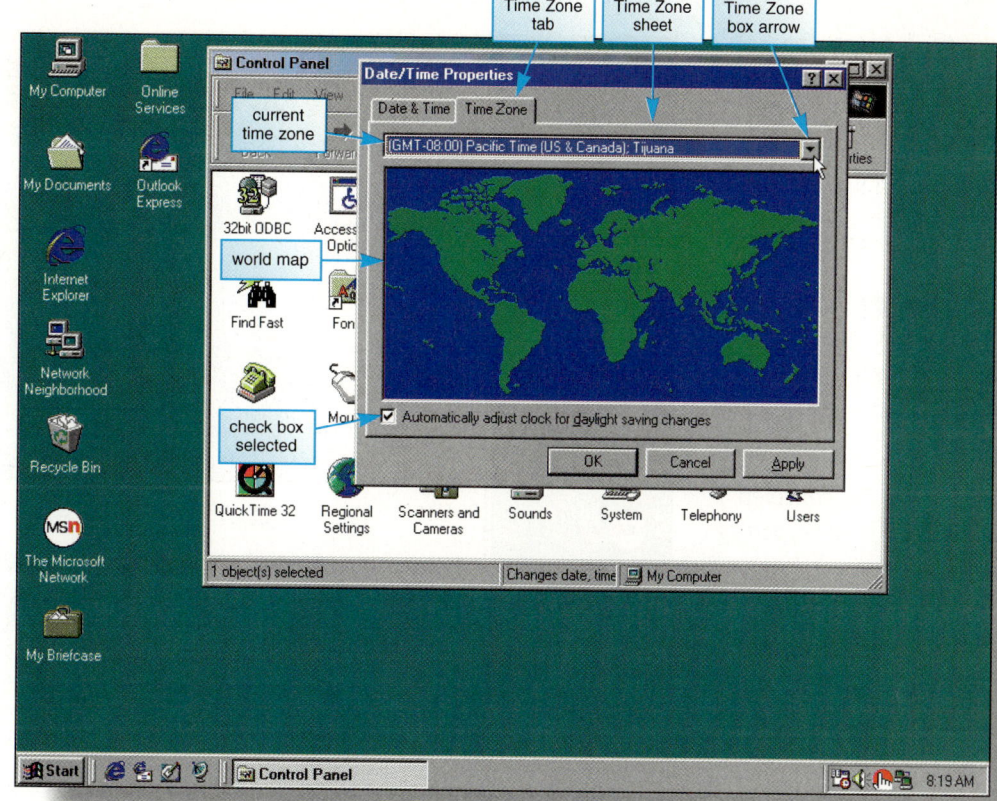

FIGURE 5-33

6 Click the Time Zone box arrow. Point to the (GMT –03:30) Newfoundland entry in the Time Zone list box.

The Time Zone list box displays containing a list of time zones (Figure 5-34). The (GMT –03:30) Newfoundland entry is highlighted in the list.

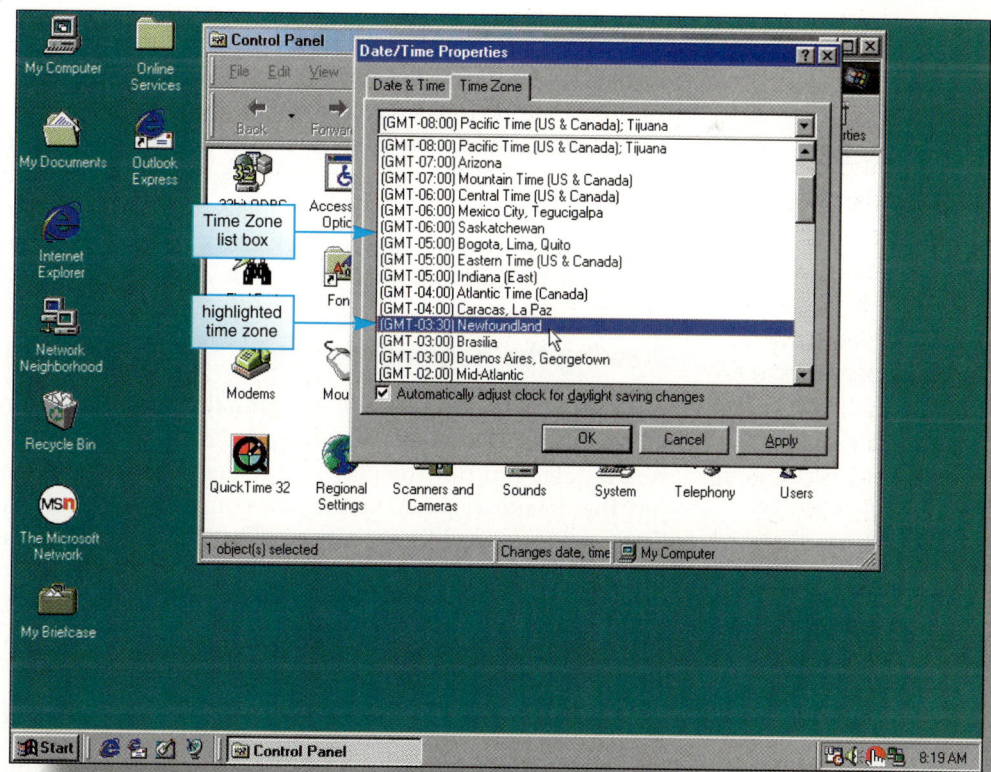

FIGURE 5-34

Click (GMT -03:30) Newfoundland.

The selected time zone displays in the Time Zone box (Figure 5-35).

 **Click the Cancel button to cancel the date, time, and time zone changes.**

The date, time, and time zone changes are canceled and the Date/Time Properties dialog box closes.

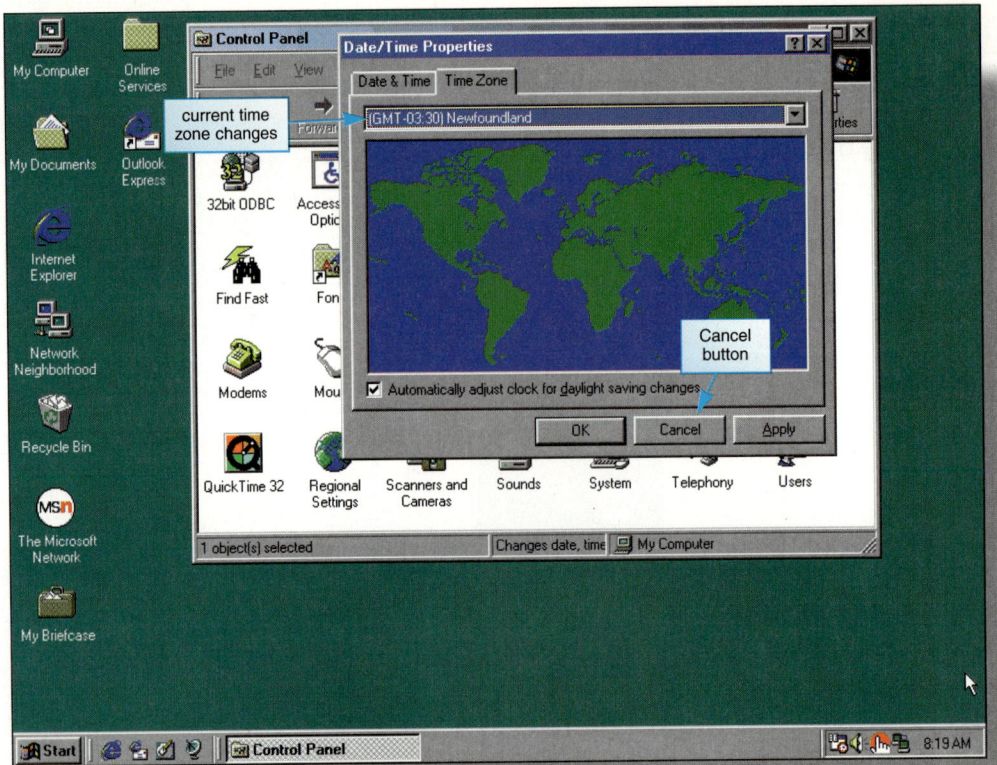

FIGURE 5-35

Other Ways

1. Double-click time in tray status area on taskbar
2. Right-click time in tray status area on taskbar, click Adjust Date/Time

Below the world map in the Date/Time Properties dialog box shown in Figure 5-33 on the previous page is the Automatically adjust clock for daylight saving changes check box. **Daylight Saving Time (DST)** is a one-hour time adjustment made in the spring and fall to provide more usable hours of daylight for outdoor activities in the late afternoon and evening. Clocks are set ahead one hour in the spring and set back one hour in the fall. A check mark in the check box causes the computer to adjust the time automatically when daylight saving time changes.

Viewing the Regional Settings

Every computer sold has a regional setting that is preset by the manufacturer of the computer. The **regional setting** determines the manner in which numbers, currency, date, and time display on the desktop and on printed documents. For example, the default regional setting for computers manufactured and sold in the United States is the United States setting. The **United States setting** causes numbers, currency, date, and time to display in a format that is familiar in the United States. Computers sold in other countries of the world have a default regional setting that is familiar in those countries.

Although each computer comes with a default regional setting, you can change the format of the numbers, currency, date, and time of a region using the **Regional Settings icon** in the Control Panel window. While you change the actual date and time using the Date/Time icon in the Control Panel window, you change the format of the date and time when you use the Regional Settings icon. Perform the following steps to view the default regional settings on your computer.

Steps To View the Time and Date Formats

1 **Double-click the Regional Settings icon in the Control Panel window.**

The Regional Settings Properties dialog box and Regional Settings sheet display (Figure 5-36). The default regional setting in the box is English (United States). Changing the regional setting in the box will change the number, currency, time, and date format to the format of the region selected.

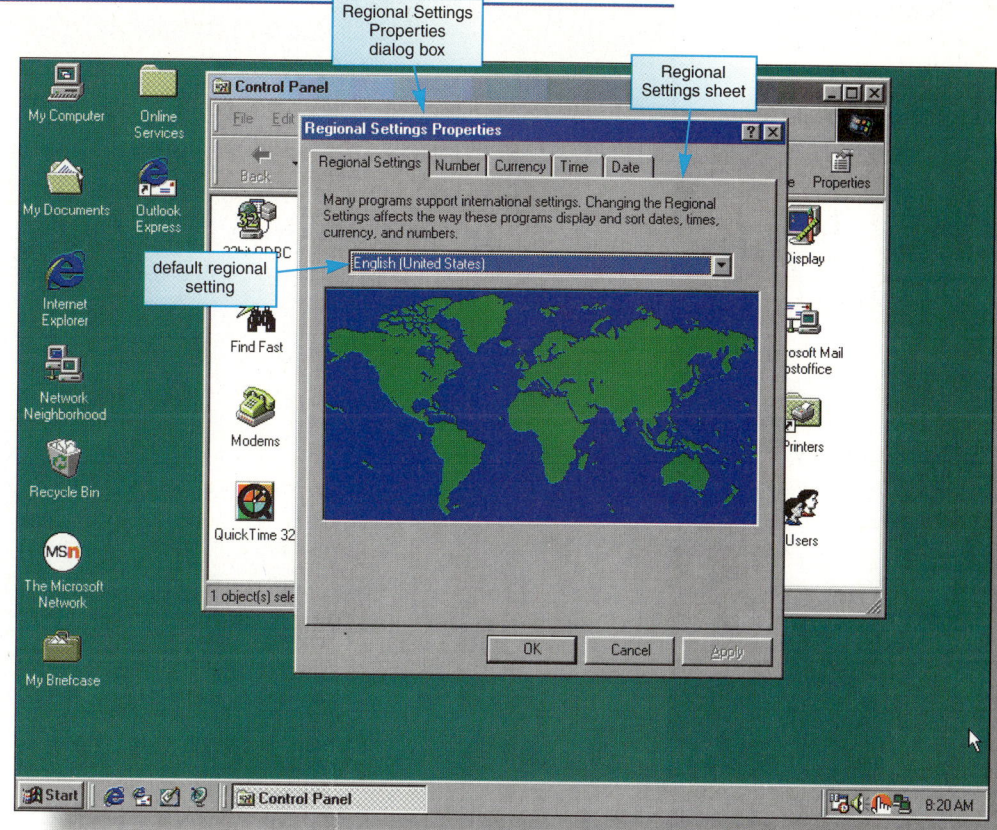

FIGURE 5-36

2 **Click the Time tab.**

The Time sheet displays (Figure 5-37). The **Time sheet** contains the Appearance pane and the AM symbol and PM symbol boxes. The Appearance pane contains a time sample (8:20:05 AM), time style (h:mm:ss tt), and time separator (:). The h:mm:ss tt style indicates the time will be in 12-hour time (h) followed by either the AM or PM entry (tt). The time style and time separator can be changed.

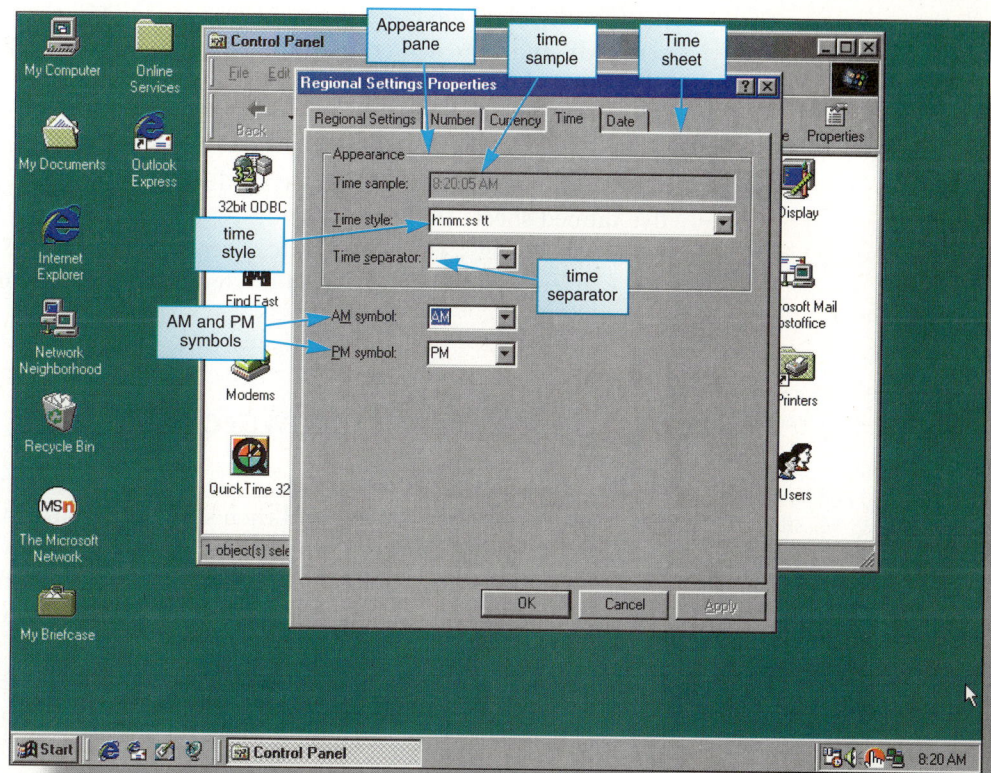

FIGURE 5-37

3 Click the Date tab.

The *Date sheet* displays (Figure 5-38). The Calendar pane contains the dimmed calendar type (Gregorian Calendar), which cannot be changed, and year interval. The Short date pane contains the Short date sample (7/24/1999), Short date style (M/d/yyyy), and date separator (/). The Long date pane contains the Long date sample (Saturday, July 24, 1999) and Long date style (dddd, MMMM dd, yyyy).

4 Click the OK button in the Regional Settings Properties dialog box.

1. Right-click Regional Settings icon, click Open
2. Click Start button on taskbar, click Help, click Index tab, type `regional settings`, click Display button, click Display button, click Click here link

Adding New Hardware

Adding new hardware was a difficult task prior to the emergence of USB and Plug and Play devices. These devices have facilitated adding hardware by making it possible for users with little hardware experience to add hardware and eliminating the expense of having to hire computer professionals to perform costly installations. Although Plug and Play devices have existed since the release of Windows 95, Windows 98 is the first operating system to allow you to install USB devices.

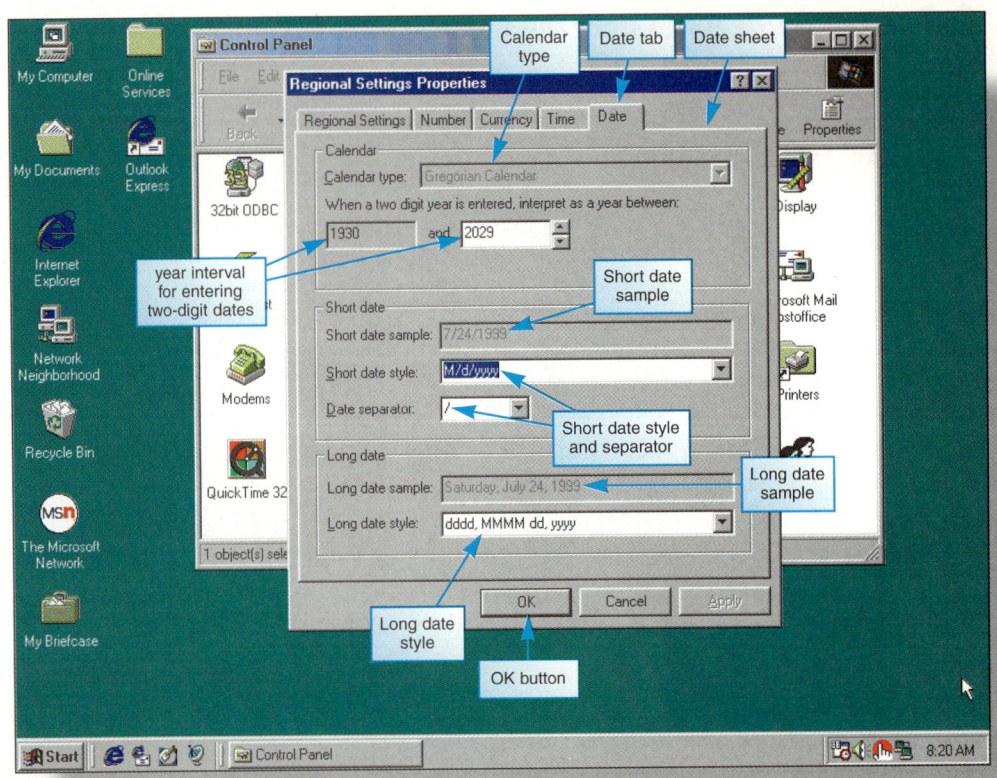

FIGURE 5-38

In the Date sheet shown in Figure 5-38, the short date style (M/d/yyyy) indicates the month value will contain no leading zeros (M), the day will contain no leading zeros (d), and year will contain four digits (yyyy). The long date style (dddd, MMMM dd, yyyy) indicates the date will contain the full name of the day (dddd), full name of month (MMMM), and a four-digit year (yyyy). The date will display with leading zeros (dd). Both the short date and long date settings can be changed.

The Regional Settings Properties dialog box in shown Figure 5-38 contains five tabbed sheets (Regional Settings, Number, Currency, Time, and Date). The Regional Settings, Time, and Date sheets were explained previously. The Number and Currency sheets can be used to change the format of numbers and currency.

Adding New Hardware

When you purchase hardware for your computer, you must physically install the hardware on your computer and then set up the hardware so Windows 98 recognizes the new hardware. Installing the hardware often will involve following the hardware manufacturer's instructions to connect the new hardware or its components to the computer. Setting up the hardware involves detecting the presence of the new hardware and associating a device driver with the hardware. A **device driver** is a program used by the operating system to control the hardware device. The device driver for a new hardware device may be located in the Windows folder on your hard disk, on a 3½ floppy disk packaged with the hardware device, or located on the Windows 98 CD-ROM.

Windows 98 allows you to install three types of hardware devices: USB devices, Plug and Play devices, and devices that are not Plug and Play devices. The following section illustrates how to install a USB (universal serial bus) device.

Adding a USB Device

Many hardware devices require that you install the hardware by shutting down Windows, removing the cover from the system unit, adding a circuit board to the computer, replacing the cover, and restarting Windows. In addition, the number of hardware devices you can add to your computer is limited by the number of spaces available inside the system unit. In most cases, only two or three boards can be added.

In response to this problem, computer hardware manufacturers built hardware devices, called **USB (universal serial bus) devices,** according to the USB specifications; computer manufacturers added a special port, called the **USB port**, to their computers; and Microsoft added support for USB devices to the Windows 98 operating system. With one USB port, you can install as many as 127 USB devices without having to add a single circuit board to your computer or restart your computer. In addition, the electrical power for a USB device comes through the USB port, making an electrical power cord unnecessary.

To install a USB device, you plug the cord from the USB device into the USB port of your computer. Windows 98 installs the device, finds the correct device driver for the USB device, and associates the driver with the USB device. If the device driver for the USB device is located on the hard drive, only two dialog boxes display on the desktop. The first dialog box states that Windows 98 has found new hardware and the second dialog box states that Windows 98 is locating the software (device driver) for the device. If the device driver is not located on the hard disk, Windows 98 may search the Windows 98 CD-ROM or a 3½ floppy disk supplied by the device manufacturer for the device driver.

To illustrate how to add a USB hardware device, you will add the Storm Technology PageScan USB device to your computer. If you do not have a PageScan USB device, the Windows 98 CD-ROM, or are not allowed to set up hardware devices on the computer you are working on, read the following steps without performing them.

> **More About**
>
> **USB Technology**
>
> Most new computers are manufactured with a USB port for connecting serial devices to your computer. The dimensions of the port are approximately 1 mm by 7 mm. The 1394 port, similar to the USB port, measures 1 mm by 5 mm, and allows you to connect faster serial devices to your comuputer. You cannot plug a USB device into a 1394 port, and vice versa.

Steps: To Add a USB Device

  Connect the PageScan USB device to the USB port on your computer.

The PageScan USB is plugged into the USB port on the computer (Figure 5-39).

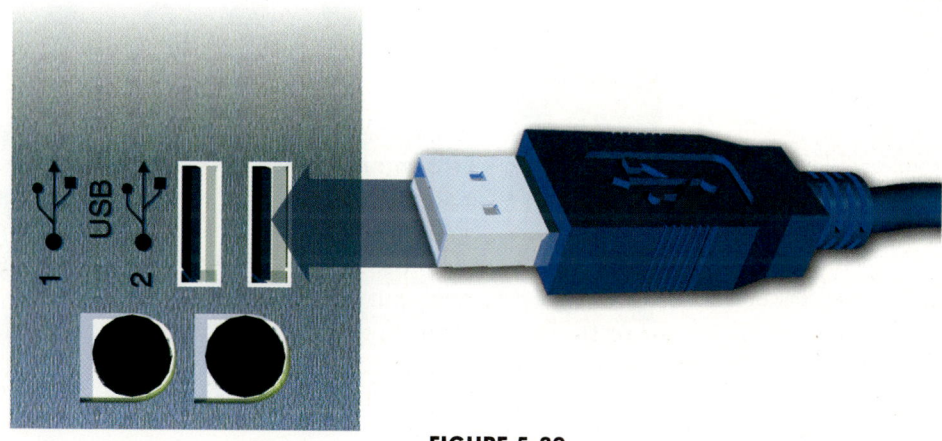

FIGURE 5-39

WIN 5.32 • Project 5 • Customizing Your Computer Using Control Panel

Microsoft **WINDOWS 98**

2 **Windows detects the addition of a new device.**

The New Hardware Found dialog box displays momentarily on the desktop (Figure 5-40). The dialog box contains a circuit board/CD ROM icon and two messages. The Unknown Device message indicates an unknown hardware device is being added and the second message (Windows has found new hardware and is locating the software for it.) indicates Windows recognizes the device and will try to locate the device driver for the new device.

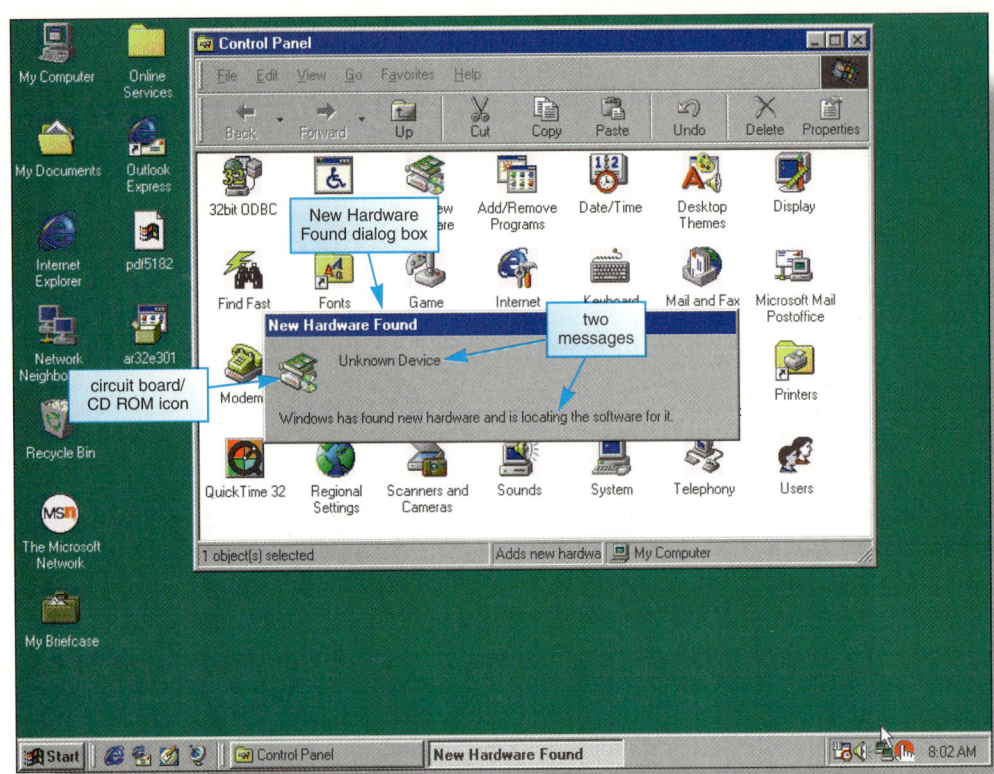

FIGURE 5-40

3 **Windows searches for the device driver for the PageScan USB device.**

The first New Hardware Found dialog box closes and a second New Hardware Found dialog box displays (Figure 5-41). The dialog box contains a scanner/camera icon and two messages. The Storm Technology - Logitech PageScan USB message indicates the PageScan USB device was recognized, and the second message (Windows is installing the software for your new hardware.) indicates Windows is trying to locate the device driver for the new device.

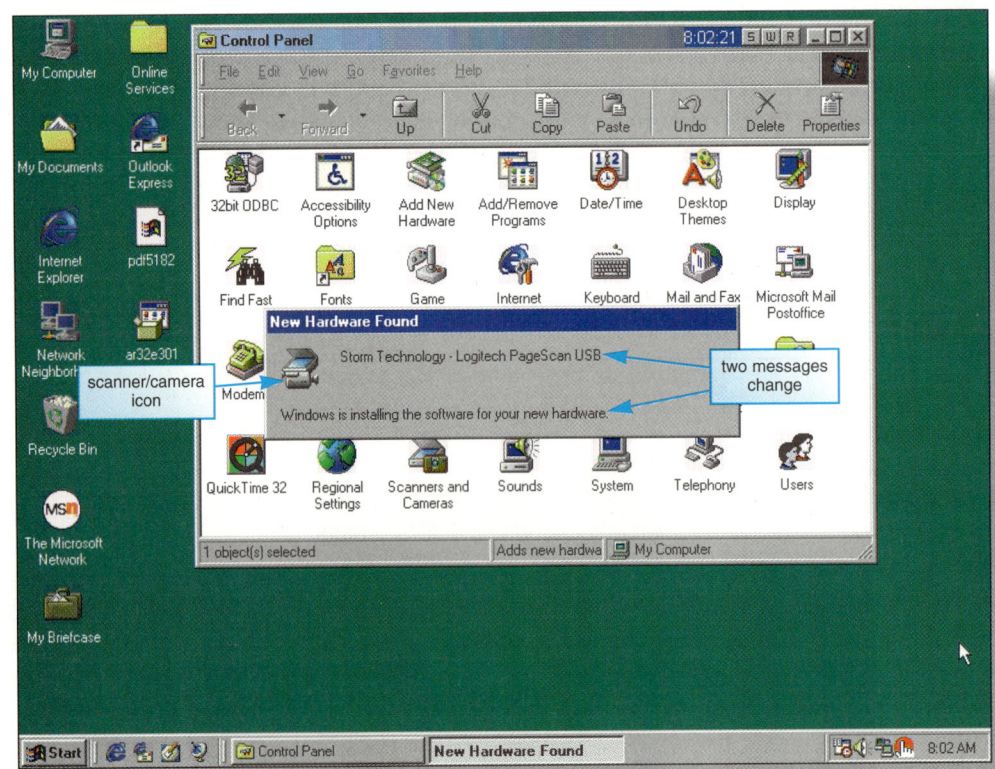

FIGURE 5-41

Often, after installing and setting up a new hardware device, additional software supplied with the new hardware device also must be installed. With the PageScan USB device, a 3½ floppy disk supplied with the device contains the software that allows the user to work with documents and graphics images scanned using the PageScan USB device. This software also must be installed on the hard drive. The instructions for installing this software are located in the manual that accompanies the PageScan USB device and include inserting the 3½ floppy disk in drive A, clicking the Start button, clicking the Run command, typing a:\setup.exe in the Open text box, and clicking the OK button.

Plug and Play Hardware Devices

A second type of hardware device that Windows 98 allows you to install is a Plug and Plug device. The **Plug and Play (PNP) technology** allows the operating system to detect the presence of a new hardware device and set up the hardware automatically with little or no user intervention. Plug and Play is a design philosophy, or industry standard, developed by a group of hardware and software development companies to make it easier to add new hardware devices to a computer. The box in which the Plug and Play hardware device is packaged identifies the device as Plug and Play. As such, Windows 98 can use the Plug and Play technology to set up the hardware device.

When installing a Plug and Play device, you turn off the power to the computer, connect the device to your computer according to the manufacturer's instructions, and then turn on the computer. Windows will detect the new Plug and Play device and install the necessary software automatically. In some cases, you may not be required to turn off and then turn on the computer.

More About

Plug and Play Devices

Many hardware devices sold today still do not use the Plug and Play technology. The Windows 95 operating system allowed you to use the Add New Hardware wizard to install these devices. Information in Windows Help instructs you to use the Add New Hardware wizard only for devices that are not plug and play.

Adding a Non-Plug and Play Device

A third type of hardware device that Windows 98 allows you to install is a device that is not a Plug and Plug device. Many devices sold today are not USB devices and some are not manufactured according to the Plug and Play specifications. To install these devices, you should use the Add New Hardware wizard. A **wizard** is a computer tool that walks you through the steps of a complex task. The **Add New Hardware wizard** is designed to walk you through the steps to set up a hardware device that is not designated as a Plug and Play device. The Add New Hardware wizard should not be used to install USB devices or Plug and Play devices.

You first must connect the hardware to the computer according to the manufacturer's instructions. After installing the device, you start the Add New Hardware wizard by clicking the Start button, pointing to Settings, clicking Control Panel, and then double-clicking the Add New Hardware icon in the Control Panel window. The Add New Hardware wizard locates the software required to operate the hardware device and copies the software to the correct location on the hard drive.

Adding a Printer

In Project 2, you printed a document from within an application using the Print command on the File menu and then printed multiple documents from within a folder using the Print command on a shortcut menu. The Printers folder contains programs to add a printer and control the printers attached to the computer. In the following section, you will use the Add Printer icon in the Printers folder to add a printer to the computer.

Previously in this project, you added a hardware device (PageScan USB) to the computer. To illustrate how easy it is to add a printer and also to illustrate the use of a wizard, you will add a printer to the computer. The **Add Printer wizard** allows you easily to add a printer to your computer.

More About

Adding a Printer

If your computer is connected to a network and you want to use the network printer, you can set up the printer quickly by using the Network Neighborhood icon on the desktop to browse for the printer icon, right-clicking the printer icon, and then clicking Install on the shortcut menu.

To add a printer, you must know the port to use to connect the printer to the computer and decide whether the printer should be the default printer. Recall that a **port** is a socket on the back of a computer used to connect a hardware device to the system unit. The **LPT1 printer port** typically is used to connect a printer to the system unit. The **default printer** is the printer to which all printed documents are sent. Most likely, a printer already is attached to the computer on which you are working and the printer is designated as the default printer. The HP printer you add to your computer in the following steps, therefore, should not be designated as the default printer.

The following steps add the Hewlett-Packard DeskJet 1600C printer to the computer using the LPT1 printer port and do not select the printer as the default printer. Perform these steps even though you do not have a Hewlett-Packard DeskJet 1600C printer.

Steps: To Add a Printer

Double-click the Printers icon in the Control Panel window and then point to the Add Printer icon in the Printers window.

The Printers window displays (Figure 5-42).

FIGURE 5-42

Double-click the Add Printer icon. Point to the Next button in the Add Printer Wizard dialog box.

The Add Printer wizard dialog box displays (Figure 5-43). Instructions indicate that the wizard will help you install a printer.

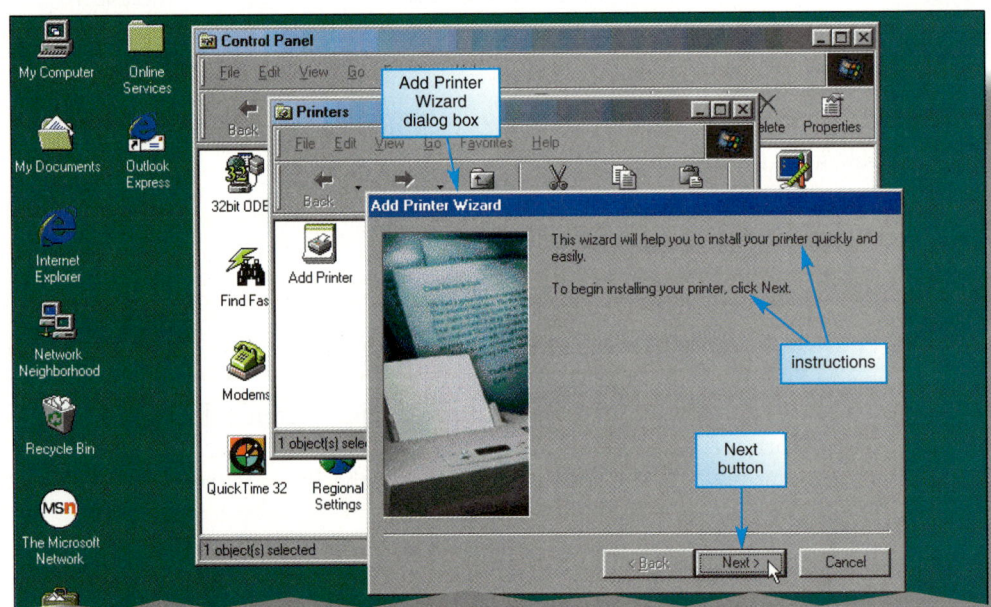

FIGURE 5-43

Adding New Hardware • WIN 5.35

3 **Click the Next button.** If necessary, click Local printer and then point to the Next button. If your computer is not connected to a network, the instructions and option buttons shown in Figure 5-44 will not display, and you should proceed to Step 5 on the next page.

The instructions change and the Local printer and Network printer option buttons display (Figure 5-44). The Local printer option button is selected.

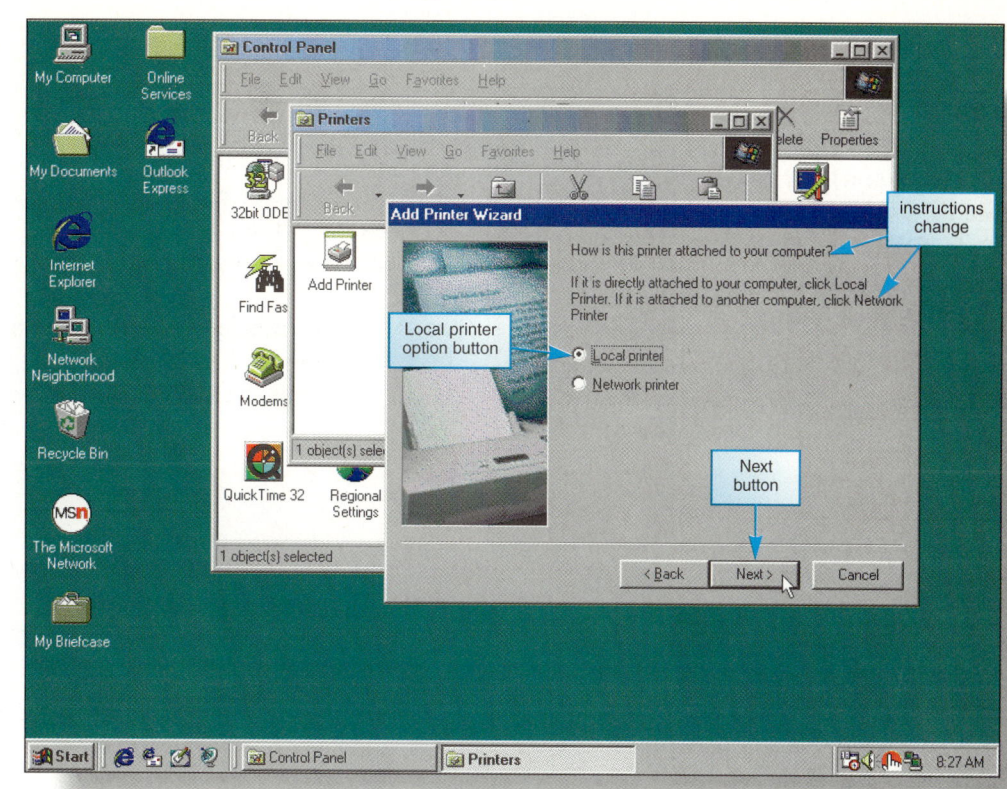

FIGURE 5-44

4 **Click the Next button.**

The contents of the dialog box change and the instructions and the Manufacturers and Printers list boxes display (Figure 5-45). The Agfa and AGFA-AccuSet 1000 names are highlighted in the list boxes. Different printer names and manufacturers may be highlighted on your computer.

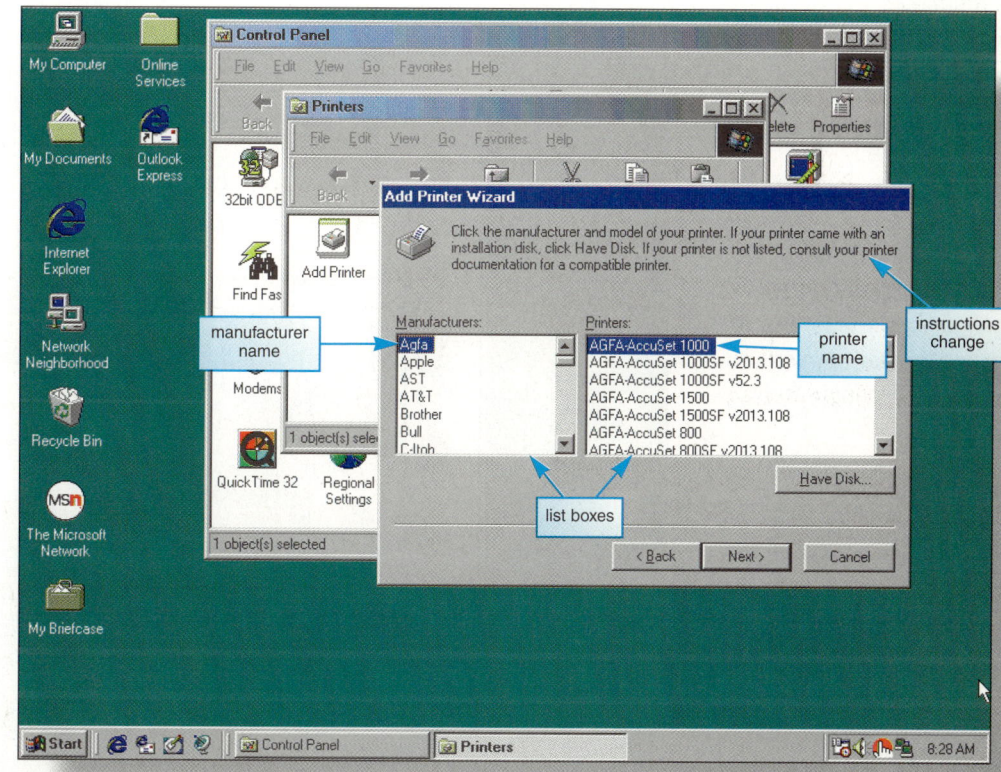

FIGURE 5-45

5 **Scroll the Manufacturers list box so the HP name is visible and then click HP. Scroll the Printers list box so the HP DeskJet 1600C name is visible and then click HP DeskJet 1600C. Point to the Next button.**

The HP and the HP DeskJet 1600C names are highlighted (Figure 5-46).

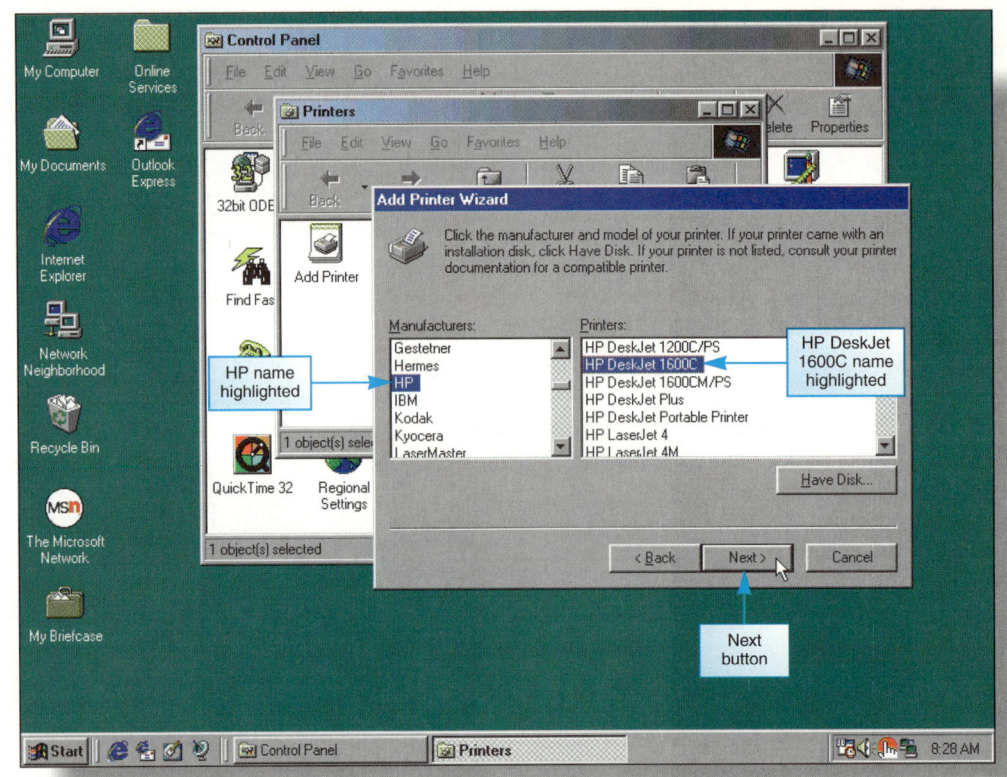

FIGURE 5-46

6 **Click the Next button. Point to the Next button in the Available ports list box.**

The dialog box contains instructions and the Available ports list box (Figure 5-47). The LPT1: Printer Port entry is highlighted in the list box to indicate the new printer will use the LPT1 printer port.

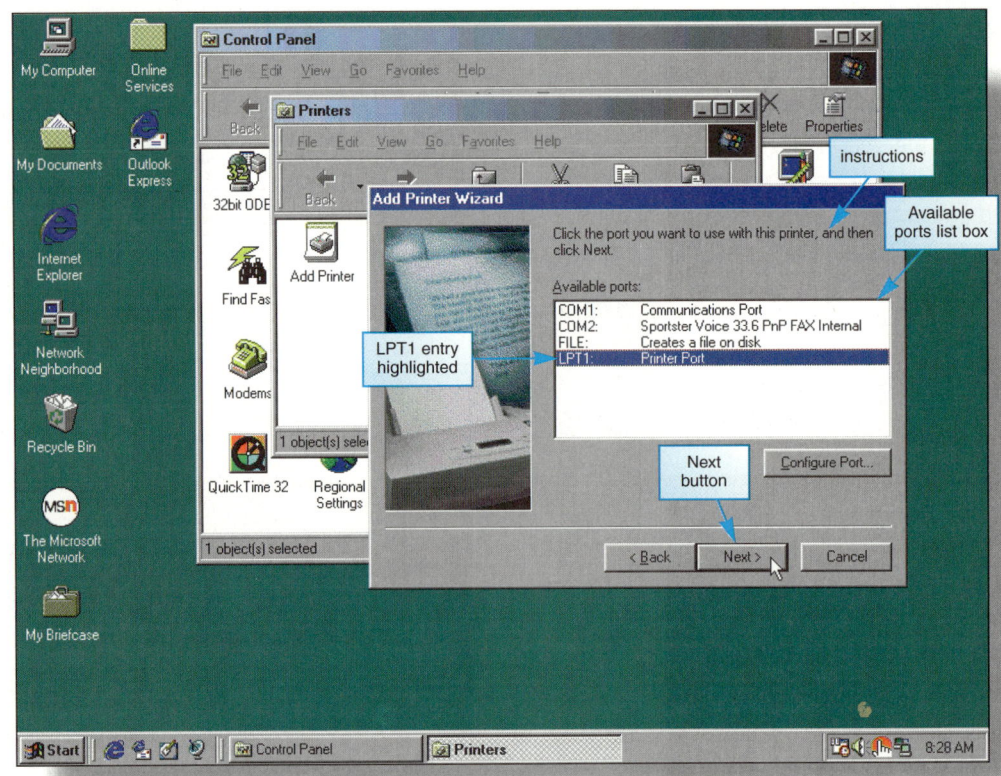

FIGURE 5-47

Adding New Hardware • WIN 5.37

7 **Click the Next button. Click No and then point to the Next button.**

The highlighted HP DeskJet 1600C printer name displays in the Printer name text box and the No option button is selected (Figure 5-48), indicating that the new printer will not be the default printer.

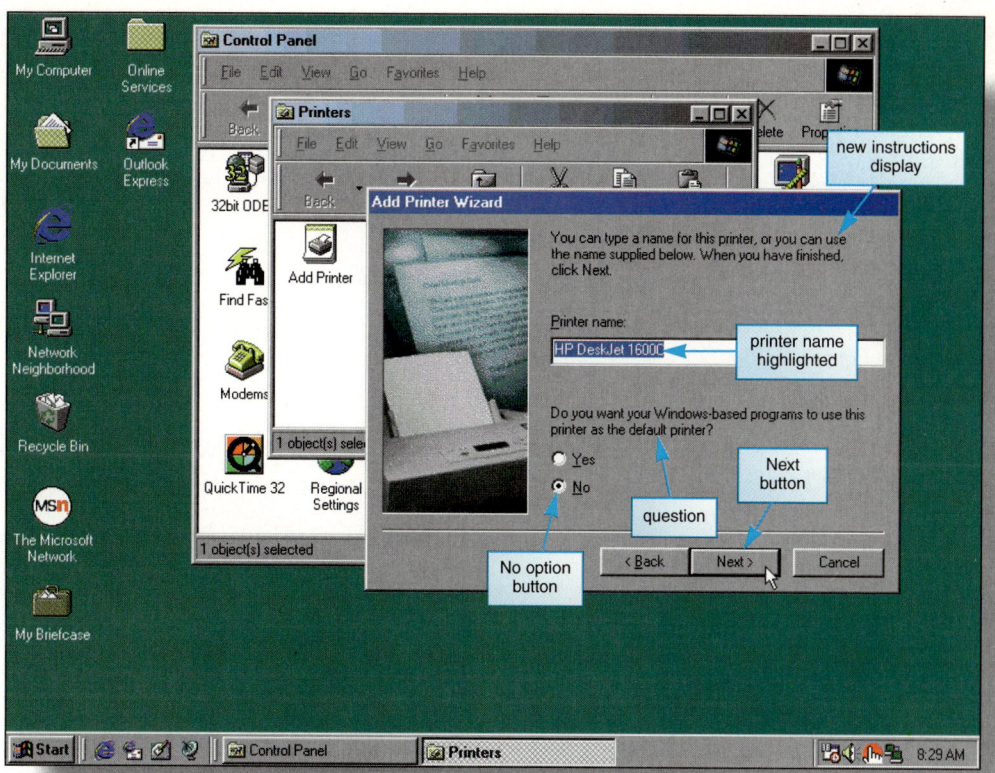

FIGURE 5-48

8 **Click the Next button. If necessary, click No and then point to the Finish button.**

Instructions and a question in the window indicate that Windows can print a test page to confirm the printer is set up properly and the No option button is selected (Figure 5-49). Because you are adding a printer without having installed the printer, the No option button should be selected to not print a test page.

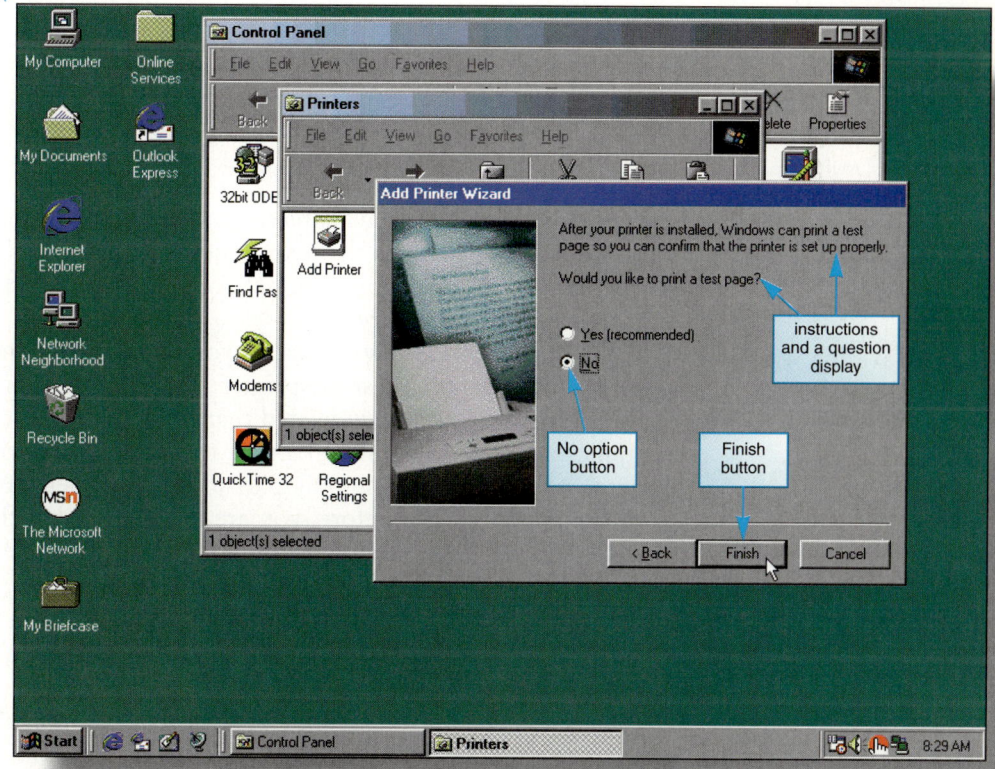

FIGURE 5-49

Click the Finish button.

The Copy Files dialog box may display as the printer device driver is located and copied to the Windows folder, the Add Printer Wizard dialog box closes, and the HP DeskJet 1600C Printer icon is added to the Printers folder (Figure 5-50).

 **Click the Close button in the Printers window.**

The Printers window closes.

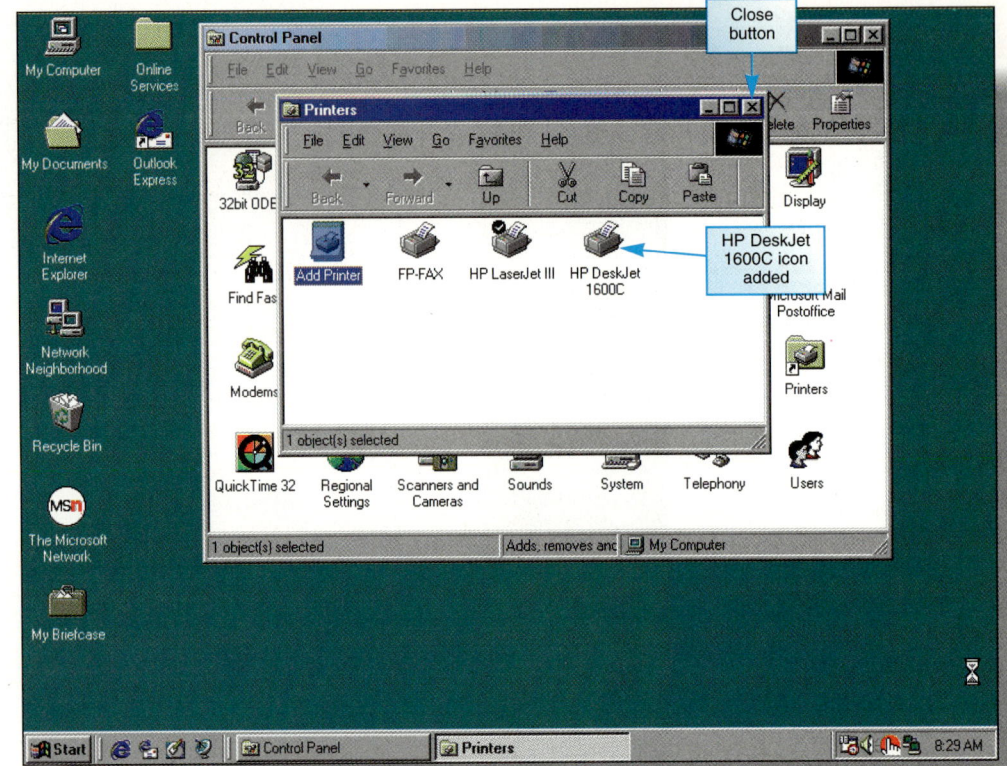

FIGURE 5-50

1. Double-click My Computer icon, double-click Printers icon, double-click Add Printer icon
2. Double-click My Computer icon, right-click Printers icon, click Open, double-click Add Printer icon
3. Click Start button on taskbar, point to Settings, click Printers, double-click Add Printer icon
4. Press CTRL+ESC, S, P, double-click Add Printer icon

Troubleshooting

Help Troubleshooters allow you investigate and solve a problem while simultaneously following a set of instructions in the Windows Help window. This process is introduced in Windows 95 Help and has been expanded and improved in Windows 98.

Solving Hardware Problems Using a Help Troubleshooter

A **Help Troubleshooter** is available if you encounter problems when using Windows 98. Among the problems that can be solved using a Help Troubleshooter are problems with starting Windows 98, networks, printing, lack of memory, using a modem, and adding new hardware.

You just added a new printer to your computer using the Add Printer wizard. Suppose you decide to test the printer by printing a word processing file that a friend gave to you. Your friend indicated that it is a large file containing several large graphics images and would take time to print. While printing the document, the printer stops after printing only part of the document. Because it is a new printer and you have never used it before, you are unsure of what the problem is and would like to use the Help Troubleshooter to investigate the problem. Perform the following steps to solve the problem of not being able to print the full document on the printer. Perform these steps even if you did not add a printer in the previous section.

Steps To Solve a Problem Using a Help Troubleshooter

1 Click the Start button on the taskbar. Click Help on the Start menu. If necessary, click the Contents tab. Click the Maximize button in the Windows Help window. Click the Troubleshooting book to open the book and then click the Windows 98 Troubleshooters book to open the book. Point to the Print topic.

The Contents sheet displays in the maximized Windows Help window and the Troubleshooting book and Windows 98 Troubleshooters book open (Figure 5-51).

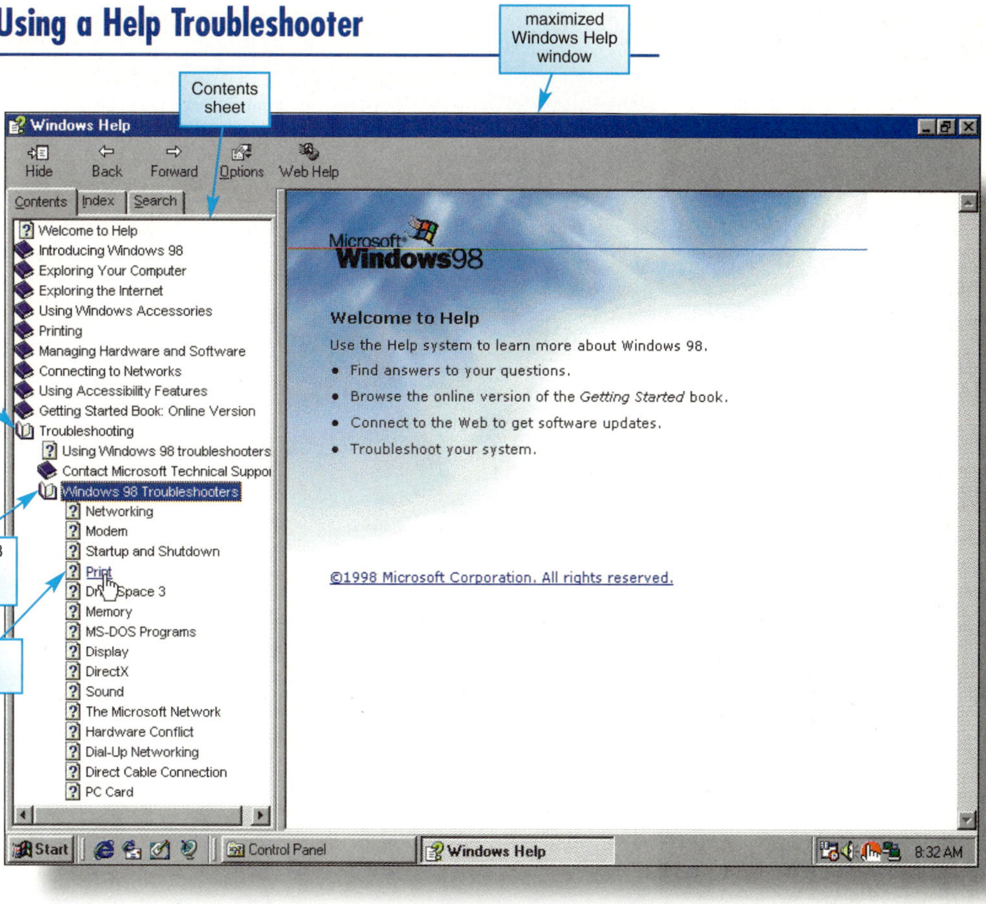

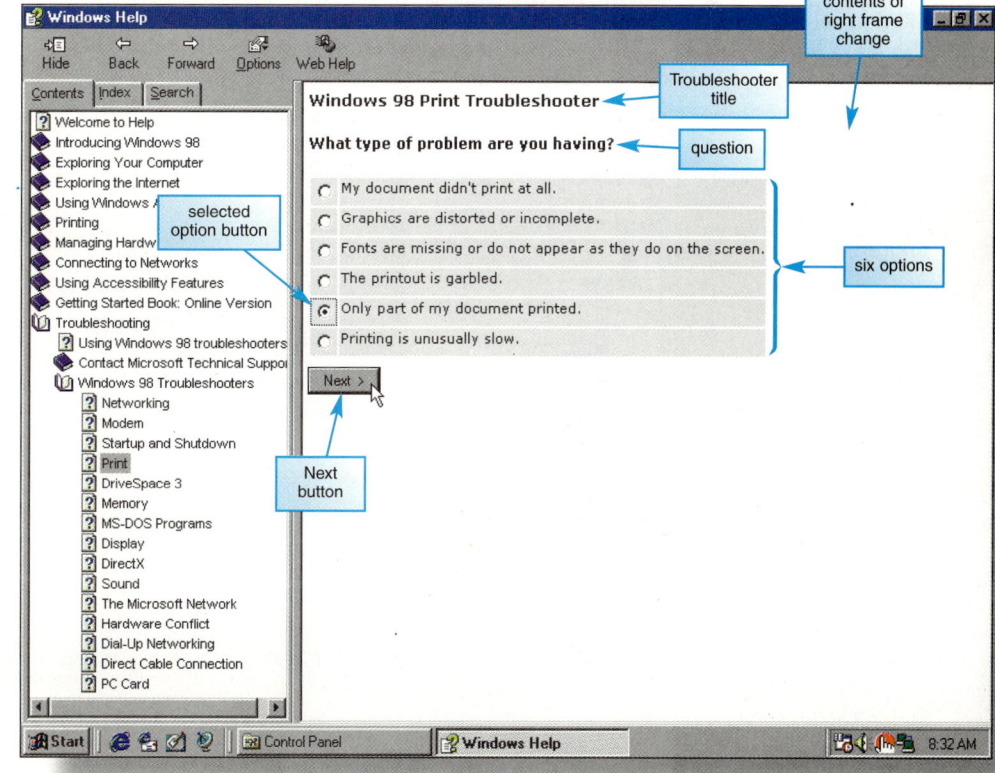

FIGURE 5-51

2 Click the Print topic. Click the Only part of my document printed option button. Point to the Next button.

The Windows 98 Print Troubleshooter displays in the right frame of the Windows Help window (Figure 5-52). The Troubleshooter consists of a question, six option buttons, and the Next button.

FIGURE 5-52

3 **Click the Next button. Read the text in the right frame and then try printing a smaller document.**

The contents of the right frame change (Figure 5-53). The Troubleshooter consists of a question, information about how to determine whether the problem is with printer memory, and three option buttons. You print the smaller document and the document prints without a problem.

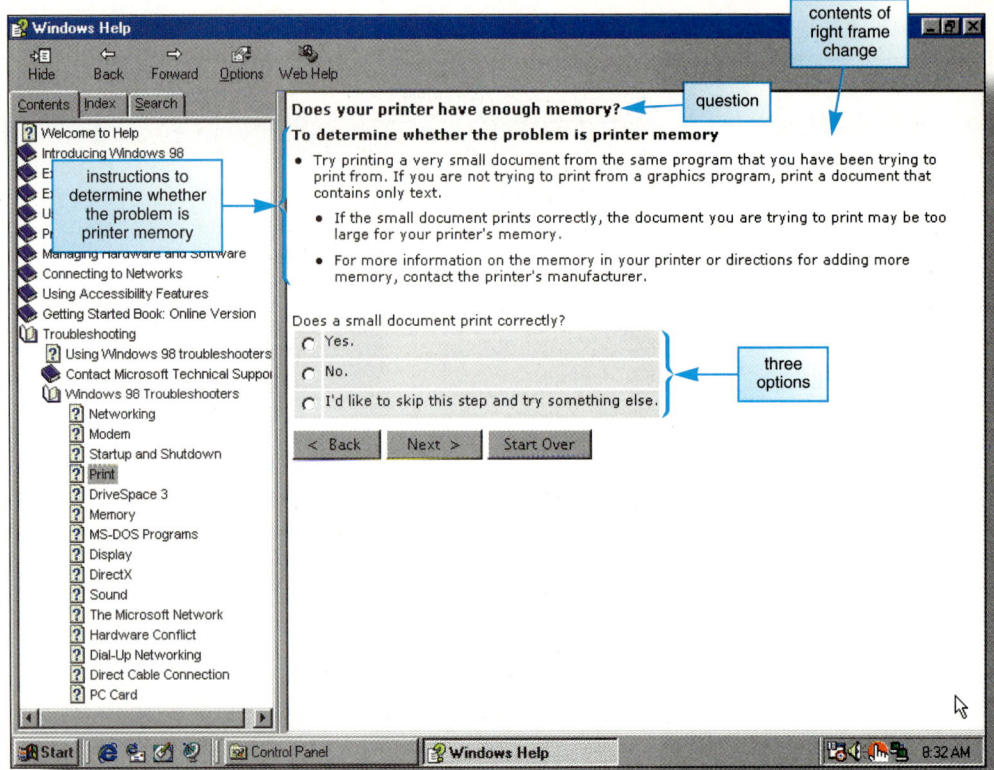

FIGURE 5-53

4 **After determining the problem does not occur when printing a small document, click Yes. Point to the Next button.**

The problem is determined to be that the printer does not have enough memory to print documents containing large graphics images (Figure 5-54).

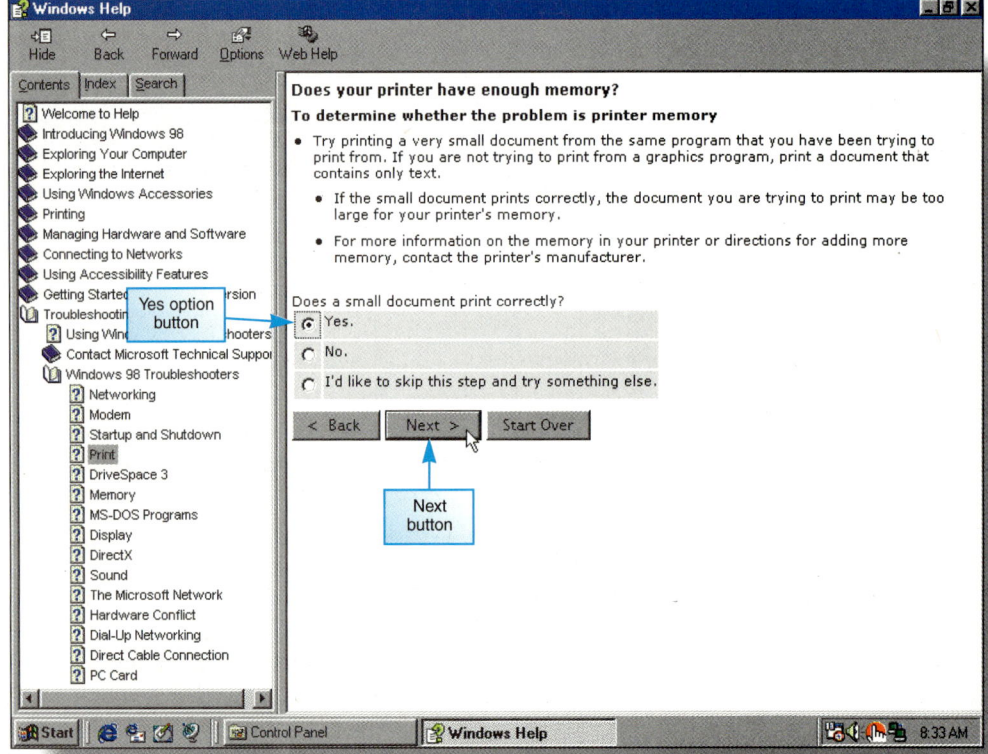

FIGURE 5-54

5 **Click the Next button.**

The contents of the right frame change. The Troubleshooter consists of a thank you message and the Back and Start Over buttons (Figure 5-55).

 6 **Click the Close button in the Windows Help window.**

The Windows Help window closes.

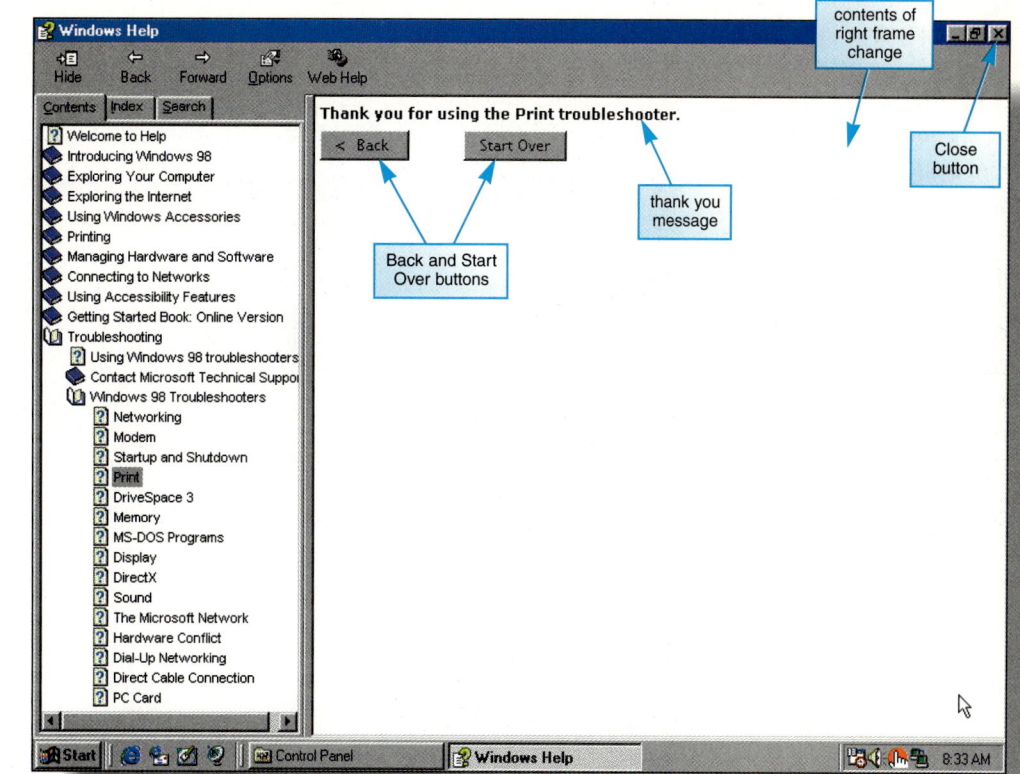

FIGURE 5-55

Viewing Hardware Properties

During the process of setting up new hardware, the operating system detects the presence of a hardware device and associates a device driver with the hardware device. The hardware detection and assignment of a device driver are handled by the operating system. The device driver is one property of the newly installed hardware device.

Some hardware devices require computer resources to function properly. **Computer resources** include computer memory and interrupt requests. An **interrupt request (IRQ)** is a signal that indicates the transmission of data between computer memory and a hardware device is complete. Each hardware device that requires an interrupt request is assigned a unique interrupt request by the operating system. Hardware devices that require computer memory are assigned a unique location within memory by the operating system. The operating system is careful to assign a different area of computer memory and a different interrupt request to each hardware device. The computer resources used by a hardware device also are properties of the hardware device.

Using the **System icon** in the Control Panel, you can view a list of the hardware categories on your computer and view the properties of each hardware device in each category. To view a list of the hardware categories on your computer, perform the steps on the next page to view the properties of a modem.

Viewing Hardware Properties

An X through an icon in the Device Manager sheet in the System Properties dialog box indicates the hardware has been disabled. A circled exclamation point through the icon means the hardware has a problem. The problem can be viewed by clicking the hardware name and then clicking the Properties button.

To View Hardware Properties

1 Double-click the System icon in the Control Panel window. If necessary, click the General tab.

The System Properties dialog box displays (Figure 5-56). The General sheet contains information about the operating system, registered owner, and computer.

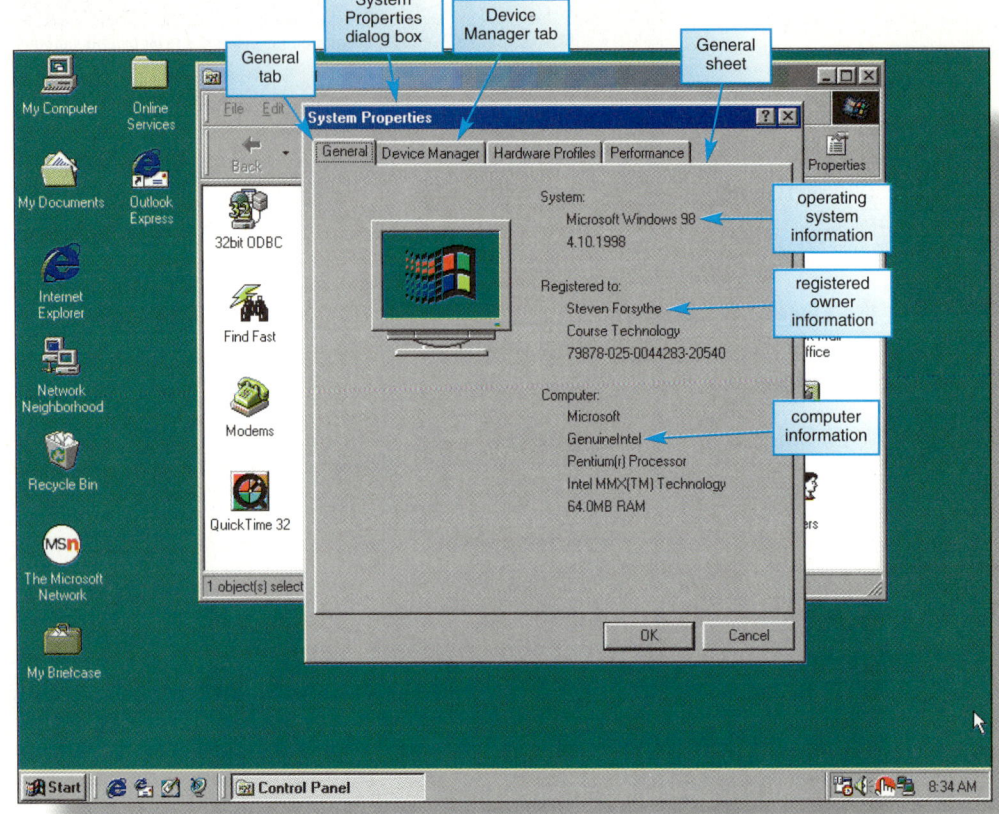

FIGURE 5-56

2 Click the Device Manager tab. Point to the plus sign in the box to the left of the Modem category.

The Device Manager sheet displays (Figure 5-57). The names of the hardware categories on the computer are shown in the hierarchical structure. The highest level in the hierarchy is the Computer. Connected by a dotted vertical line below Computer are the hardware categories, with each preceded by a plus sign in a box. The selected View Devices by type option button indicates the devices are listed by hardware category.

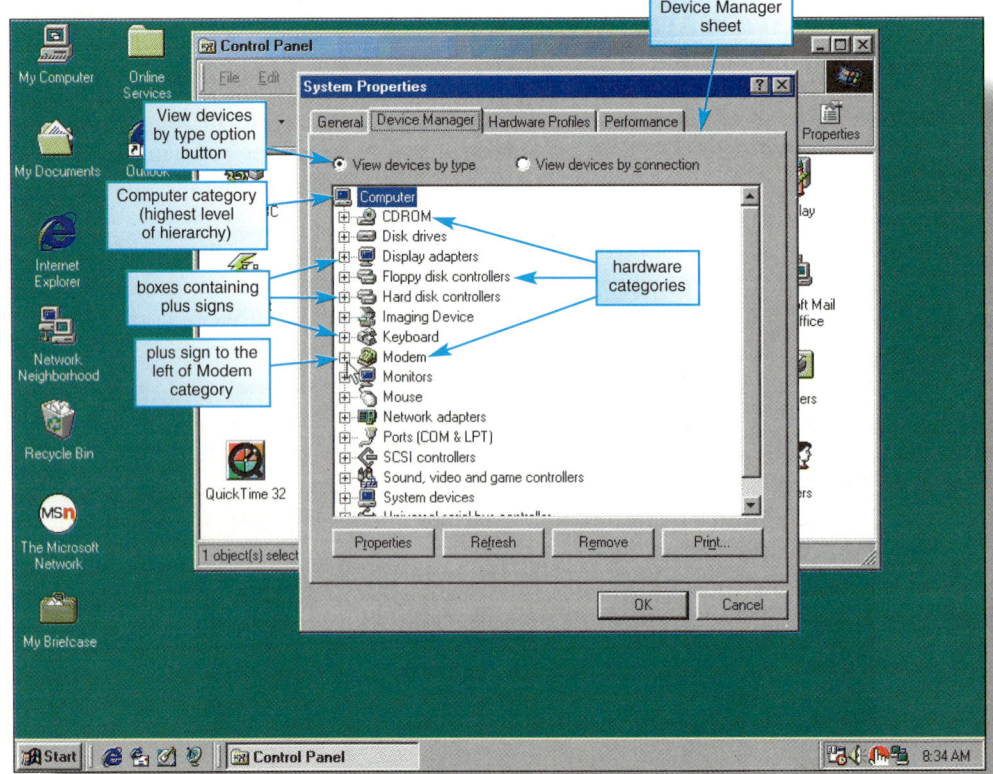

FIGURE 5-57

③ **Click the plus sign to the left of the Modem category and then point to the Sportster Voice 33.6 PnP FAX Internal device name. If the modem device name on your computer is different, point to another modem device name.**

The Modem category expands, the plus sign changes to a minus sign, and the Sportster Voice 33.6 PnP FAX Internal hardware device in the Modem category displays (Figure 5-58). Different or additional hardware devices may display on your computer.

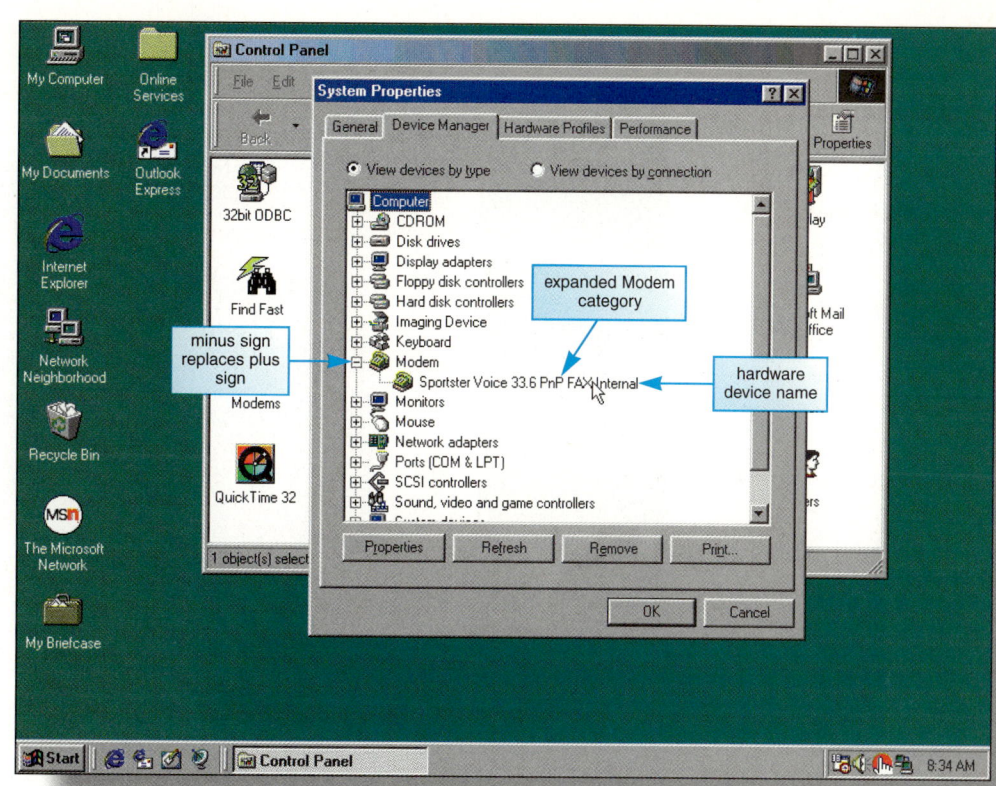

FIGURE 5-58

④ **Double-click the Sportster Voice 33.6 PnP FAX Internal device name. When the Sportster Voice 33.6 PnP FAX Internal Properties dialog box opens, click the General tab.**

*The Sportster Voice 33.6 PnP FAX Internal Properties dialog box and the General sheet display (Figure 5-59). The **General sheet** contains information about the modem, its status, and usage. This information may be different on your computer.*

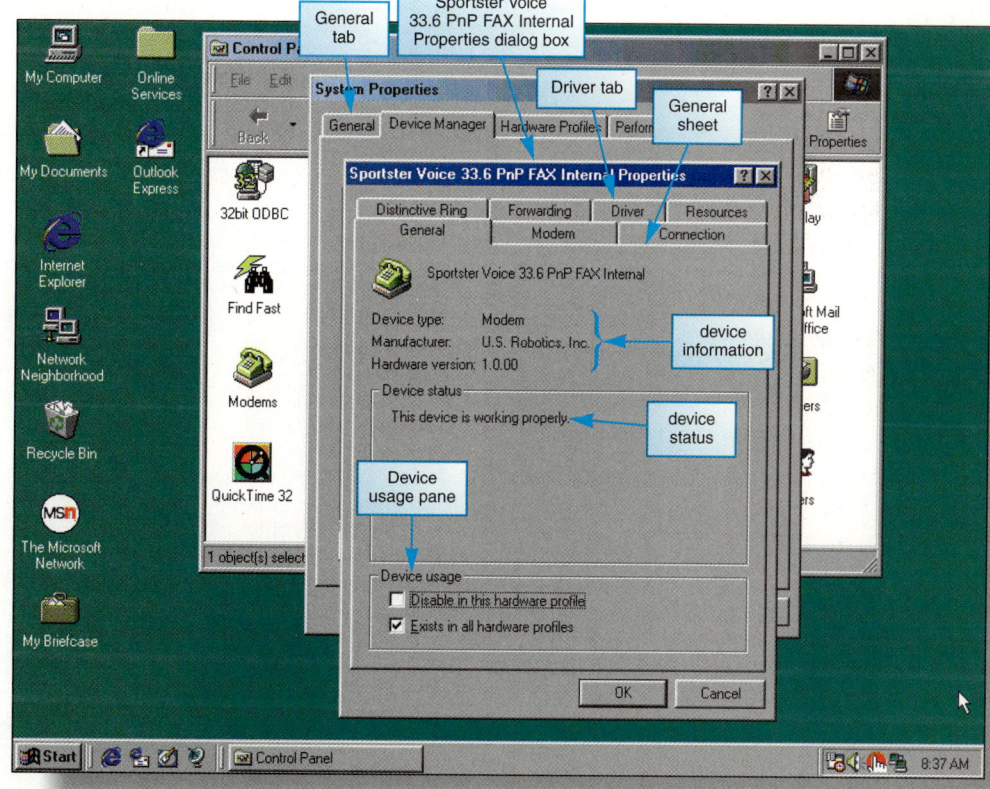

FIGURE 5-59

WIN 5.44 • **Project 5** • Customizing Your Computer Using Control Panel

5) Click the Driver tab. Point to the Driver File Details button.

The Driver sheet displays (Figure 5-60). The Driver sheet contains driver information and the Driver File Details and Update Driver buttons.

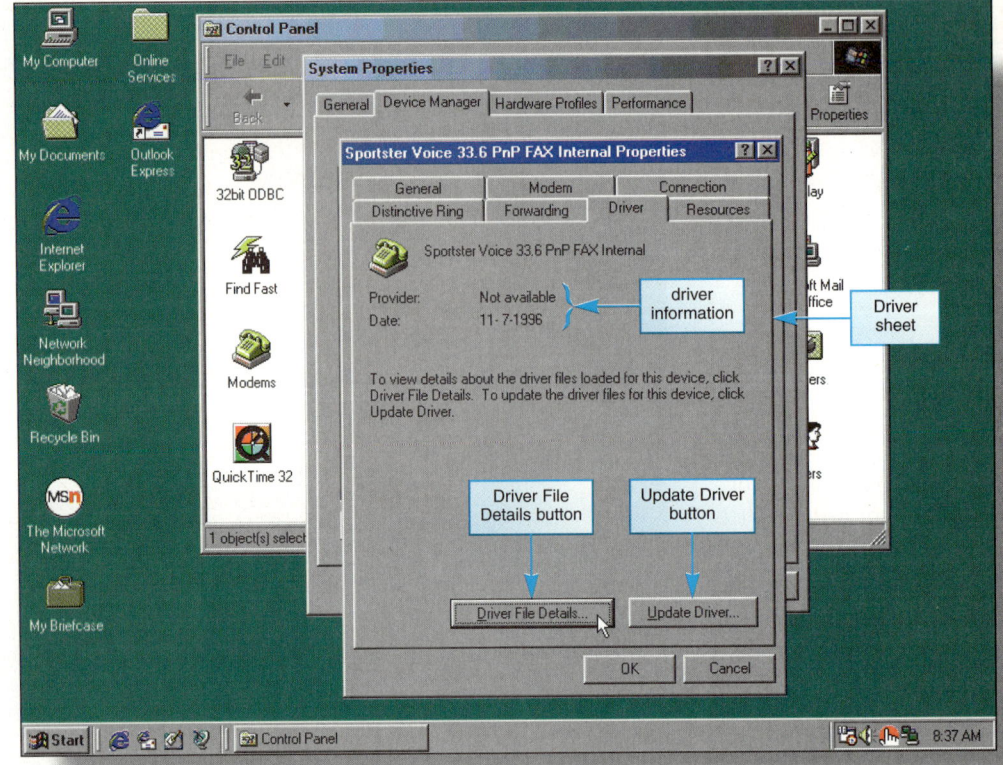

FIGURE 5-60

6) Click the Driver File Details button. Point to the OK button in the Driver File Details dialog box.

The Driver File Details dialog box contains a list of device driver files currently being used by the modem and file details about the highlighted driver file (Figure 5-61).

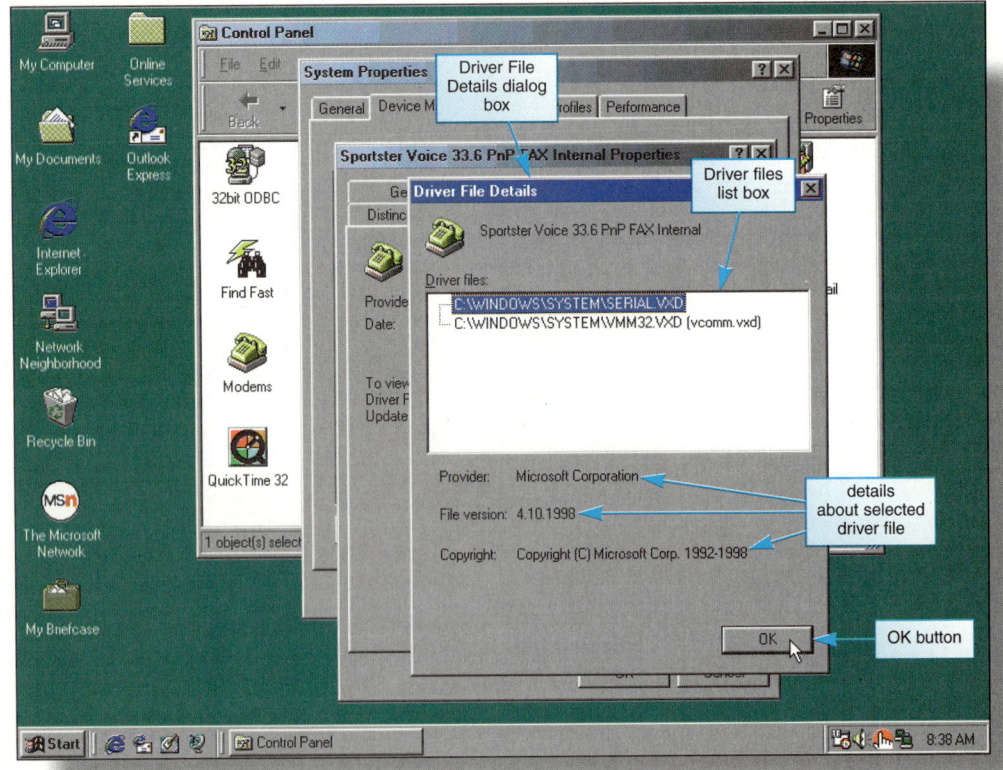

FIGURE 4-61

⑦ **Click the OK button. Click the Resources tab in the Sportster Voice 33.6 PnP FAX Internal Properties dialog box. Point to the OK button in the Sportster Voice 33.6 PnP FAX Internal Properties dialog box.**

The Resources sheet displays in the Sportster Voice 33.6 PnP FAX Internal Properties dialog box (Figure 5-62). The **Resources sheet** *contains the Use automatic settings check box, resource type and settings for the modem, and Conflicting device list. The modem has been assigned the Input/Output Range 02F8-02FF and Interrupt Request 03. No hardware conflicts exist with other hardware devices.*

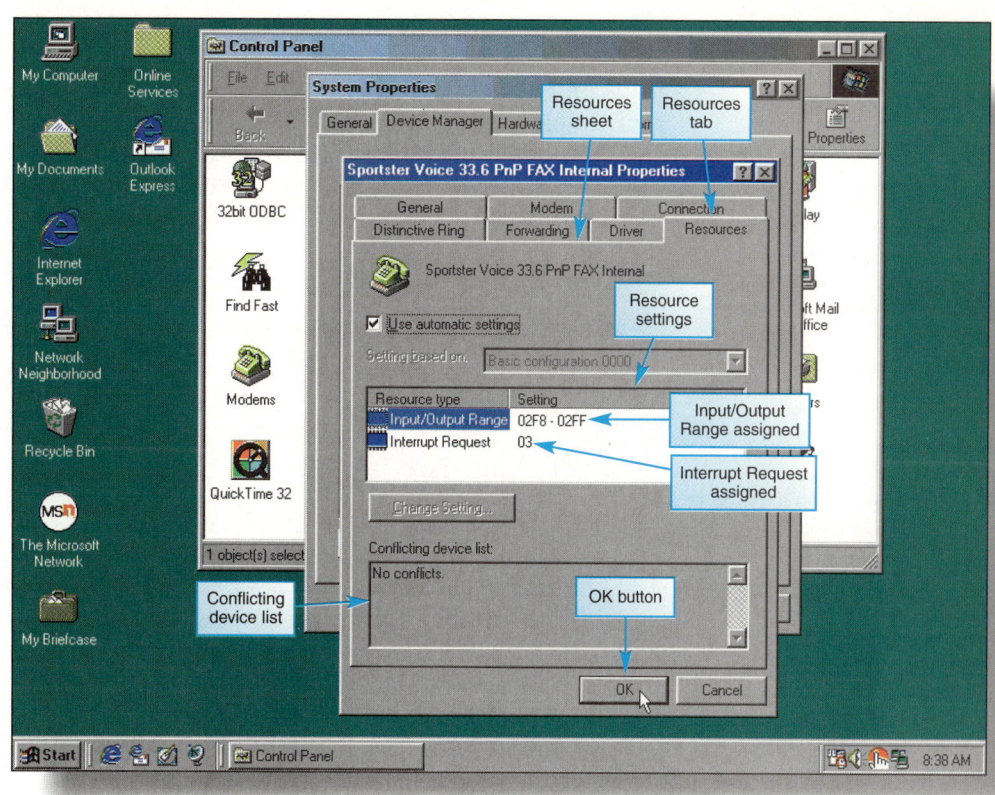

FIGURE 5-62

⑧ **Click the OK button in the Sportster Voice 33.6 PnP FAX Internal Properties dialog box. Click the OK button in the System Properties dialog box.**

The two dialog boxes close.

When you double-click a device name in the Systems Properties dialog box, the dialog box that opens for the hardware device may have additional tabs. For example, the Modem dialog box has the Modem tab and Connection tab to view information about modem and connection settings (see Figure 5-59 on page WIN5.43). The properties of a printer, which cannot be viewed using the System Properties dialog box, can be seen by double-clicking the Printers folder in the Control Panel window, right-clicking the printer icon, and clicking Properties on the shortcut menu.

Hardware Profiles and System Performance

In addition to the General and Device Manager tabs in the Systems Properties dialog box, two other tabs (Hardware Profiles and Performance) are available (see Figure 5-56 on page WIN 5.42). The **Hardware Profiles sheet** allows you to create a hardware profile for each person who uses the computer. Each profile then can be customized to contain access to only the hardware devices that the user requires.

> **Other Ways**
>
> 1. Right-click System icon, click Open, click Device Manager tab, click plus sign to left of hardware category, click hardware device name, click Properties button
> 2. Click Start button, click Help, click Index tab, type system properties, click Display button, scroll and click To view or change resource settings for a hardware device topic, click Display button, click Click here link, click Device Manager tab, click plus sign to left of hardware category, double-click hardware device name

Adding and Removing Programs

When you start Windows 98 after having created a new hardware profile, you are prompted to select the hardware profile in which to start Windows 98. Windows 98 loads only the device drivers for those hardware devices that have been chosen in the profile you select. The **Performance sheet** allows you to view the amount of RAM on your computer, percentage of free system resources available, and information about the file system, virtual memory, disk compression, and PC cards on your computer.

Removing Programs

Only programs that were designed for Windows 98 can be removed using the Add/Remove Programs Properties dialog box. For all other programs, you should check the program's documentation to determine which files should be removed and then remove only those files.

Previously, you added a page scanner and printer to the computer. In addition to adding hardware, Windows 98 also makes it easy to add and remove programs (software).

Adding a Program

The procedure to add a program is to double-click the **Add/Remove Programs icon** in the Control Panel window, follow the instructions to locate the installation program that accompanies the program you wish to install, and install the program by following the installation instructions. Perform the following steps to install NaturallySpeaking™, which is a speech recognition program. If you do not have a copy of NaturallySpeaking or are not allowed to install software on the computer you are using, read the following steps without performing them.

 To Add a Program

1 Double-click the Add/Remove Programs icon in the Control Panel window. If necessary, click the Install/Uninstall tab. Point to the Install button.

The Add/Remove Programs Properties dialog box and the Install/Uninstall sheet display (Figure 5-63). The **Install button** *allows you to install a new program. Using the list box and the* **Add/Remove button***, you can remove an existing program.*

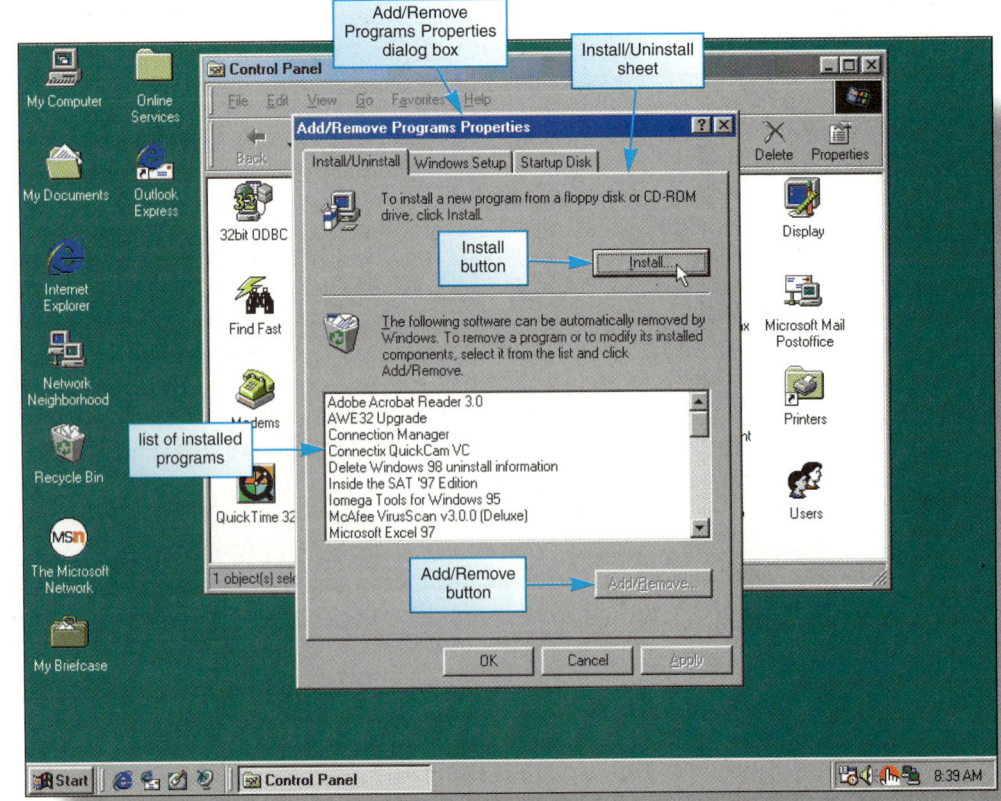

FIGURE 5-63

Adding and Removing Programs • WIN 5.47

PROJECT 5

2 **Click the Install button. When the Install Program From Floppy Disk or CD-ROM dialog box displays, read the instructions, insert the NaturallySpeaking CD-ROM into the CD-ROM drive, and point to the Next button.**

The Install Program From Floppy Disk or CD-ROM dialog box displays (Figure 5-64).

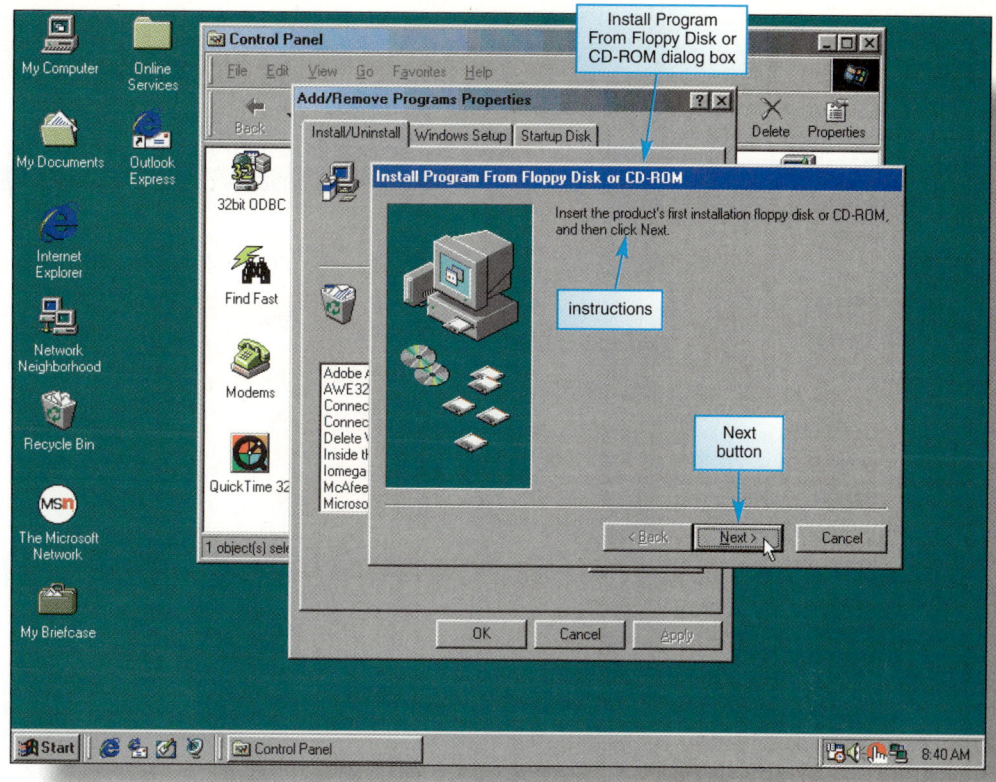

FIGURE 5-64

3 **Click the Next button. When the Run Installation Program dialog box opens, read the instructions and then point to the Finish button.**

The Run Installation Program screen displays (Figure 5-65). The Command line for installation program text box contains the name and location of the installation program on the NaturallySpeaking CD-ROM.

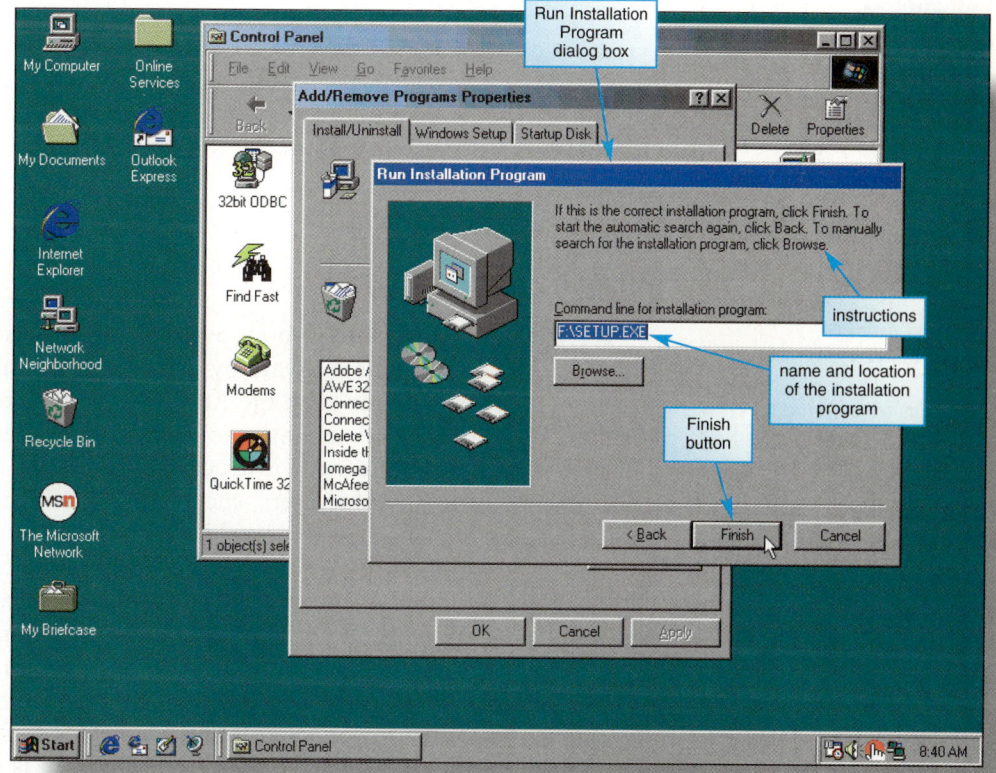

FIGURE 5-65

WIN 5.48 • Project 5 • Customizing Your Computer Using Control Panel

4. **Click the Finish button. When the installation screen containing the Dragon NaturallySpeaking Setup Wizard - Step 1 of 5 dialog box displays, click the Next button and follow the instructions on the screen to begin the installation of the NaturallySpeaking program.**

   The NaturallySpeaking installation screen displays (Figure 5-66). The Dragon NaturallySpeaking Setup Wizard steps you through the installation of the software.

5. **Remove the NaturallySpeaking CD-ROM from the CD-ROM drive. Click the Close button in the Control Panel window.**

   The installation of NaturallySpeaking is complete.

FIGURE 5-66

Other Ways

1. Insert CD-ROM into CD-ROM drive, follow instructions to install software
2. Click Start button, click Run, click Browse button, locate installation program, click Open
3. Click Start button, click Run, type f:\setup.exe (installation location and program), click OK button

Removing a Program

Several methods exist to remove a program. Some software manufacturers allow you to remove their software by using an Uninstall button on the installation screen. In this case, double-click the Add/Remove Programs icon in the Control Panel, follow the instructions until the installation screen displays, and then click the Uninstall button and follow the instructions to remove the software.

Other software manufacturers, such as the manufacturers of NaturallySpeaking, do not have an Uninstall button on the installation screen (see Figure 5-65 on the previous page). Instead, a menu command is available that you can use to uninstall the software. In this case, click the Start button, point to Programs, point to Dragon NaturallySpeaking on the Programs submenu, click Uninstall on the Dragon NaturallySpeaking submenu, and follow the instructions.

Other software must be removed by deleting the files that comprise the software. To remove the software, you can right-click the My Computer icon on the desktop, click Explore, make the folder in which the program is stored visible in the All Folders pane of the Exploring - My Computer window, and drag the folder to the Recycle Bin. Dragging the folder deletes the folder and the contents of the folder.

Adding Windows 98 Components and Creating a Startup Disk

The Add/Remove Program Properties dialog box shown in Figure 5-63 on page WIN 5-46 contains three tabbed sheets. The **Install/Uninstall sheet** allows you to install and uninstall a new program. The **Windows Setup sheet** allows you to add or remove Windows 98 components. Components that can be added or removed include the Accessibility Options, Accessories, Communications, Internet Tools, Microsoft Outlook Express, Multimedia, and System tools. Adding new components requires the floppy disk or CD-ROM that accompanies Windows 98. The **Startup Disk sheet** allows you to create a startup disk for Windows 98. In the event that Windows 98 will not start, you can use the startup disk to start Windows 98, run diagnostics to determine why Windows 98 will not start, and fix the problem.

Project Summary

Project 5 introduced you to the icons in the Control Panel folder that allow you to customize your computer system. In this project, you used icons in the Control Panel folder to customize the mouse, keyboard, date and time, and desktop fonts. In addition, you learned how to add a new hardware device, add a program (software), customize the computer for disabled people, add a printer, use Help troubleshooters to solve hardware problems, and view the hardware properties of the hardware devices attached to the computer.

What You Should Know

Having completed this project, you now should be able to perform the following tasks:

- Add a Printer *(WIN 5.34)*
- Add a Program *(WIN 5.46)*
- Add a USB Device *(WIN 5.31)*
- Adjust the Cursor Blink Rate *(WIN 5.10)*
- Adjust the Double-Click Speed *(WIN 5.14)*
- Adjust the Keyboard Repeat Delay *(WIN 5.7)*
- Adjust the Keyboard Repeat Rate *(WIN 5.8)*
- Adjust the Pointer Speed *(WIN 5.17)*
- Change the Date, Time, and Time Zone *(WIN 5.25)*
- Change the Mouse Button Configuration *(WIN 5.12)*
- Change the Mouse Pointer Scheme *(WIN 5.15)*
- Display a Pointer Trail *(WIN 5.19)*
- Open the Control Panel Folder *(WIN 5.5)*
- Solve a Problem Using a Help Troubleshooter *(WIN 5.39)*
- Turn On the MouseKeys Feature *(WIN 5.21)*
- View Fonts and Font Sizes *(WIN 5.23)*
- View Hardware Properties *(WIN 5.42)*
- View the Time and Date Formats *(WIN 5.29)*

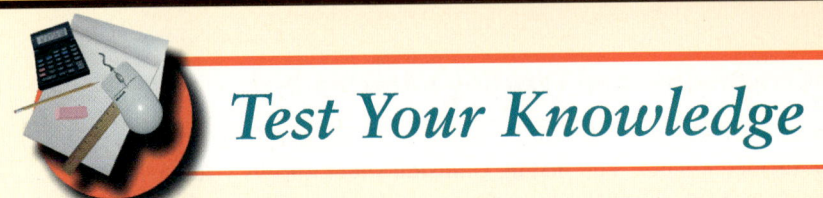

Test Your Knowledge

1 True/False

Instructions: Circle T if the statement is true or F is the statement is false.

T F 1. The Printers folder contains icons that allow you to change the properties of an object.
T F 2. The keyboard repeat delay is the speed at which a character repeats across the screen when you hold down a key on the keyboard.
T F 3. The cursor blink rate is the speed at which the insertion point blinks.
T F 4. The Left-handed button configuration assigns the mouse operations of normal select and normal drag to the left mouse button.
T F 5. To adjust and test the double-click speed, drag the Double-Click Speed slider along its slide and double-click the Test area.
T F 6. One method to improve the visibility of the mouse pointer is to remove pointer trails.
T F 7. Accessibility features make it easier for people who are mobility, hearing, or visually impaired to use Windows 98.
T F 8. If you have a problem adding new hardware, you must call Microsoft Corporation for technical support.
T F 9. To add a USB hardware device, use the Add New Hardware wizard.
T F 10. To display a list of hardware categories for your computer, click the Device Manager tab in the Systems Properties dialog box.

2 Multiple Choice

Instructions: Circle the correct response.

1. _____ is the speed at which a character repeats across the screen when you hold down a key on the keyboard.
   a. Keyboard repeat delay   c. Keyboard repeat rate
   b. Cursor blink rate   d. Double-click speed
2. To customize the mouse, double-click the _____ icon in the _____ window.
   a. Customize, Control Panel   c. Mouse, Customize Mouse
   b. Mouse, Control Panel   d. Customize Mouse, Mouse Properties
3. _____ is the amount of time between clicking the mouse button once and clicking the same button again.
   a. Double-click speed   b. Cursor blink rate   c. Keyboard repeat delay   d. Keyboard repeat rate
4. The _____ sheet is used to change the button configuration.
   a. Language   b. Mouse   c. General   d. Buttons
5. The regional settings determine the _____.
   a. time   c. date
   b. format of the time   d. format of the time and date
6. The MouseKeys feature is designed for individuals who are _____ impaired.
   a. mobility   b. hearing   c. visually   d. none of the above

Test Your Knowledge

7. A _____ is a program used by the operating system to control an input or output device.
   a. wizard   b. computer resource   c. device driver   d. interrupt request
8. When you have problems adding a hardware device, you should _____.
   a. cancel the hardware setup process and start again
   b. click the Hardware Help button
   c. ask a friend who has experience in adding hardware
   d. use Help troubleshooters
9. Which of the following is not a method to delete a software program? _____
   a. Using the Uninstall button on the installation screen.
   b. Using a menu command.
   c. Using the Uninstall wizard.
   d. Deleting the files that comprise the software.
10. The _____ icon in the Control Panel window allows you to view the properties of various hardware devices.
    a. Printers   b. Mouse   c. System   d. Add New Hardware

3 Identifying Icons and Their Properties Using the Control Panel Folder

Instructions: The Control Panel window displays on the desktop in Figure 5-67. In Part 1 on the next page, in the spaces provided, list the icon name corresponding to the circled number shown in Figure 5-67 and then list three properties you can change using the icon. In the spaces provided in Part 2 on the next page, list the icon name corresponding to the circled number shown in Figure 5-67 and then describe what function you can perform using the icon.

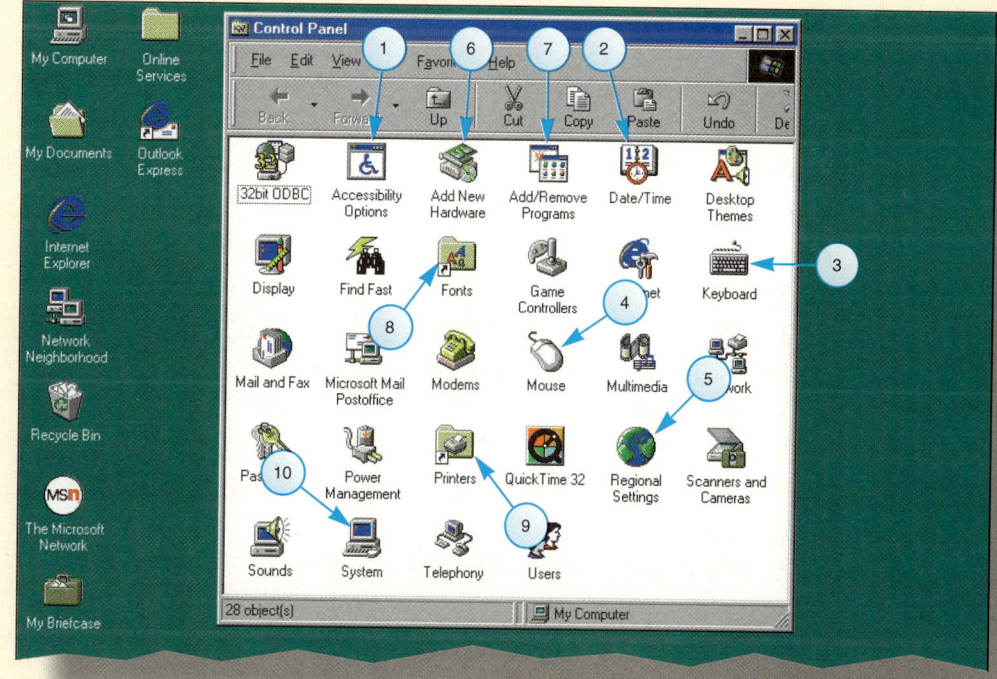

FIGURE 5-67

(continued)

Test Your Knowledge

Identifying Icons and Their Properties Using the Control Panel Folder *(continued)*

Part 1: *Identifying Properties*

ICON NAME	PROPERTIES
1. _____	_____ _____ _____
2. _____	_____ _____ _____
3. _____	_____ _____ _____
4. _____	_____ _____ _____
5. _____	_____ _____ _____

Part 2: *Identifying Functions*

ICON NAME	FUNCTION
6. _____	_____
7. _____	_____
8. _____	_____
9. _____	_____
10. _____	_____

4 Identifying Computer Resources

Instructions: Use the Device Manager in the System Properties dialog box to view the computer resources of each hardware device listed below. In the spaces provided, list the computer memory (memory range or input/output range) and interrupt request assigned to each device. Some devices may not be assigned computer memory or an interrupt request.

HARDWARE DEVICE	COMPUTER MEMORY	INTERRUPT REQUEST
Display Adapters	_____	_____
Keyboard	_____	_____
Mouse	_____	_____
Hard Disk Controllers (Primary)	_____	_____
Modem	_____	_____
Communication Port (COM1)	_____	_____
Printer Port (LPT1)	_____	_____

Test Your Knowledge • WIN 5.53

PROJECT 5

Use Help

1 Using Windows Help to Troubleshoot Hardware Problems

Instructions: Use Windows 98 Troubleshooters to answer the following questions.

1. You are having problems printing a document. The document you want to print did not print at all. What is the first thing the troubleshooter suggests doing to fix the problem? _____

2. You do not hear sounds when using a flight simulator program. What does the troubleshooter suggest you do? _____

3. You are having trouble using your modem because Windows 98 does not detect your modem. What does the troubleshooter suggest you do? _____

4. Your computer does not respond when you try to start Windows 98. In what mode does the troubleshooter suggest you start Windows? _____
   Using Windows Help, explain the purpose of this mode. _____

5. A hardware conflict results when two hardware devices are using the same computer resources (memory range or interrupt request). If you have a single hardware device connected to the computer but two entries are shown for the device in the Device Manager, what three steps does the troubleshooter suggest you perform?
   1) _____
   2) _____
   3) _____

2 Describing the Function of Other Control Panel Folder Icons

Instructions: Use Windows 98 Help and/or double-click the appropriate icon in the Control Panel window to determine the function of the icons listed below. In the spaces provided, list the function of each icon.

ICON	FUNCTION
Multimedia	_____
Internet	_____
Power Management	_____
Network	_____
Passwords	_____
Sounds	

In the Lab

1 Using the Add New Hardware Wizard to Add a Printer

Instructions: In the past, you have added a new printer to your computer using the Add Printer wizard. A friend recently informed you that you also can use the Add New Hardware wizard. You decide to take your friend's advice and add your new Epson AP-3000 printer using the Add New Hardware wizard. Perform the following steps to add the printer and answer several questions about the printer's properties.

Part 1: Install the Epson AP-3000 Printer

1. If necessary, start Windows 98.
2. Click the Start button, point to Settings, and click Control Panel.
3. Double-click the Add New Hardware icon in the Control Panel window.
4. Click the Next button in the Add New Hardware Wizard dialog box.
5. When the instructions in the Add Hardware Wizard change, click the Next button.
6. When the instructions in the Add New Hardware Wizard window change, click No so that Windows does not search for your new hardware, and then click the Next button.
7. When the Hardware types list box displays, scroll the list to make the Printer entry visible, click the Printer entry, and click the Next button.
8. When the Add Printer Wizard dialog box displays, click Local printer, and then click the Next button.
9. Scroll the Manufacturers list box so the Epson name is visible and then click the Epson name. Scroll the Printers list box so the Epson AP-3000 name is visible and then click the Epson AP-3000 name. Click the Next button.
10. When the Available ports list box displays, click the Next button.
11. When the Printer name text box and the Yes and No option buttons display, click No, and then click the Next button.
12. Click No so a test page will not print, and then click the Finish button.

Part 2: Display the Properties of the Epson AP-3000 Printer

1. Double-click the Printers icon in the Control Panel window.
2. Is the Epson AP-3000 icon in the Printers window? _____
3. Right-click the Epson AP-3000 icon and then click Properties on the shortcut menu to open the Epson AP-3000 Properties dialog box.
    a. To which port does the printer print? _____
    b. What is the Transmission retry setting? _____
    c. What is Transmission retry? _____
    d. What is the orientation of the paper? _____
    e. What is the paper size? _____
    f. What is the resolution of the printer? _____
    g. What is the print quality? _____
4. Click the OK button.

In the Lab

Part 3: Delete the Epson AP-3000 Icon

1. Right-click the Epson AP-3000 icon.
2. Click Delete on the shortcut menu to delete the Epson AP-3000 icon.
3. Click the Yes button in the Printers dialog box.
4. If the Epson AP-3000 dialog box displays, click the Yes button in the Epson AP-3000 dialog box to delete the files used only for this printer.
5. Click the Close button in the Printers dialog box to close the dialog box.
6. Click the Close button in the Control Panel window.

2 Controlling the Print Queue

Instructions: You recently read an article in a computer magazine entitled, "Take Control of Your Print Queue." The article defines the **print queue** as an area of memory reserved for the storage of documents waiting to be printed and states that the operating system creates a separate print queue for each printer. After reading the article, you decide to learn more about controlling the print jobs in the print queue. Perform the following steps to practice controlling the print queue.

Part 1: Open the Default Printer's Window

1. Click the Start button, point to Settings, and click Control Panel.
2. Double-click the Printers icon in the Control Panel window.
3. If multiple printer icons display in the Printers window, determine which printer is the default printer by right-clicking each icon to open a shortcut menu. A check mark precedes the Set as Default command in the shortcut menu if the printer is the default printer. Use the default printer for the remainder of this exercise.
4. Right-click the default printer icon to open a shortcut menu. Click Pause Printing on the shortcut menu to pause the default printer.
5. Double-click the default printer icon to open a window with the default printer's name in the title bar. This window displays the contents of the print queue for the default printer. Position this window across the top of the desktop so the My Computer icon is visible.

Part 2: Print Documents Using My Computer

1. Right-click the My Computer icon, click Explore on the shortcut menu. Arrange the Exploring - My Computer window so the default printer window is visible on the desktop.
2. Click the plus sign to the left of the Hard drive [C:] entry in the All Folders pane, scroll the All Folders pane to make the Windows folder visible, and click the Windows folder.
3. Scroll the Contents pane to make the Forest file name visible. Right-click the Forest file name and then click Print on the shortcut menu. The Forest icon displays in the print queue.
4. Scroll the Contents pane to make the Carved Stone file name visible. Right-click the Carved Stone file name and then click Print on the shortcut menu to send the Carved Stone file to the print queue.
5. Scroll the Contents pane to make the Houndstooth file name visible. Right-click the Houndstooth file name and then click Print on the shortcut menu to send the Houndstooth file to the print queue.

(continued)

In the Lab

Controlling the Print Queue *(continued)*

6. Scroll the Contents pane to make the Sandstone file name visible. Right-click the Sandstone file name and then click Print on the shortcut menu to send the Sandstone file to the print queue.
7. Scroll the Contents pane to make the Stitches file name visible. Right-click the Stitches file name and then click Print on the shortcut menu to send the Stitches file to the print queue.
8. Click the Close button in the Exploring - Windows window.
9. Five file names display in the default printer window.

Part 3: *Control the Print Jobs*

1. Drag the Sandstone print job above the first file name in the print queue. The Sandstone print job should display first in the print queue. What print job is in the third position in the print queue? _____
2. Drag the Stitches print job above the first file name in the print queue. The Stitches print job should display first in the print queue. What print job is in the third position? _____
3. Right-click the Forest icon and then click the Cancel Printing command to cancel the printing of the Forest print job and remove the Forest icon from the print queue. What print job is in the third position? _____
4. Right-click the Houndstooth icon and then click Cancel Printing to cancel the printing of the Houndstooth print job and remove the Houndstooth icon from the print queue. What print job is in the second position in the print queue? _____
5. Right-click the Stitches icon and then click Pause Printing to pause the printing of the Stitches print job. What entry displays under the Status heading? _____ What three documents are in the print queue? _____ What position does the Stitches print job occupy? _____ Which print job is paused in the print queue? _____
6. Right-click an open area of the window and then click Pause Printing to restart the paused print queue and print the documents in the print queue.
Which documents print on the printer? _____
Which print job remains in the print queue? _____
7. Right-click an open area of the window and click Purge Print Documents to cancel the printing of all print jobs. How many print jobs remain in the print queue? _____

Part 4: *Close the Default Printer Window and Printers Window*

1. Click the Close button in the default printer window.
2. Click the Close button in the Printers window.
3. Click the Close button in the Control Panel window.

In the Lab

3 Using the Accessibility Options to Design a Personalized Desktop

Instructions: You have been appointed by your boss as the person who will design a single Windows 98 desktop that can be used by employees within your company who are both hearing and visually impaired. Experiment with the accessibility features until you have determined the best combination of features. Then, write down all settings so you can personalize each employee's computer to the standard. Make sure after this exercise that you reset your computer to its settings prior to your making changes.

Cases and Places

The difficulty of these case studies varies:
▶ are the least difficult; ▶▶ are more difficult; and ▶▶▶ are the most difficult.

1 ▶ A friend of yours recently purchased a new computer. She would like to customize the mouse and keyboard. She wants to change the mouse pointer to look three-dimensional and have mouse trails to make it easier to see the mouse pointer on the desktop, and slow down the cursor blink rate to make it easier to see the insertion point while word processing. She is left-handed and has trouble using the left mouse button, so she asks if you also would write down the instructions for these changes so that she can make the changes herself. You agree to word process the instructions using Notepad and print a copy for her.

2 ▶ You purchased and then installed a new Epson ActionLaser 1600 on your computer. You had no problem installing the printer by following the manufacturer's instructions or adding the new printer to your computer using the Add Printer Wizard. You are frustrated, however, because it takes an unusually long time to print a document, and while the document is printing, the application program is unavailable to perform other tasks. Instead of calling technical support, you decide to use the Windows 98 Troubleshooters. Determine the problem and write a brief summary describing how to fix the problem.

3 ▶▶ You currently have a Hewlett-Packard LaserJet 6P printer to use to print black and white documents. The HP LaserJet 6P is set up as the default printer. You recently purchased a used Hewlett-Packard DeskJet 650C printer. You add the HP DeskJet 650C printer to the computer so you can print color documents from the same computer. Summarize in writing the procedure you must follow to print the document on the HP DeskJet 650C when the default printer is the HP LaserJet 6P.

Cases and Places

4 ▶▶ Your friend with a disability asks you to help him set up his computer and customize the keyboard to his specific needs. He is unable to hold the ALT, CTRL, or SHIFT key while pressing another key and would prefer to use the keyboard instead of the mouse. He also would like to control the mouse pointer using the keys on the numeric keypad. List the two accessibility options that could be used to help your friend. Summarize each accessibility option, including how the keyboard is used with and without the option.

5 ▶▶▶ Windows 98 is the first Windows operating system to support the use of USB hardware devices. Using the Internet, computer magazines, or other resources, collect information about the USB hardware devices. Prepare a detailed report describing how USB devices work, who developed the USB specifications, and the problems that were solved with the new devices. Include what USB devices are currently available for sale, the cost of the devices, and where they can be purchased. If time permits, compare and contrast the USB technology to the IEEE 1394 technology.

6 ▶▶▶ Windows 98 allows you to add application programs to your computer easily when you use the Add/Remove Programs feature. In addition, the same feature allows you to remove a program. Although this feature works well with application programs written for Windows 98, many computers have application programs written for previous operating systems (Windows 3.1 or DOS) that cannot be removed using the Add/Remove Programs feature. Several programs have been developed and marketed that remove, or uninstall, non-Windows application programs. Using the Internet or computer magazines or visiting a computer store, obtain information about these products. Write a brief report listing the programs available and comparing and contrasting their features.

7 ▶▶▶ Many companies maintain a *Standards and Procedures Manual* that outlines the standards for using a company computer. Topics often include the procedures for adding new hardware, adding and removing application programs, and customizing a company computer. Visit a small, medium, and large company in your area. Find out if, and how, each company handles employee standards and procedures. Prepare a brief report summarizing the standards and procedures developed for each company. Include the procedures for adding new hardware, adding and removing application programs, and customizing the computer. In the report, make recommendations for each company based on what you found.

Microsoft Windows 98

PROJECT 6

Advanced File and Document Management and My Briefcase

OBJECTIVES

You will have mastered the material in this project when you can:

- Begin a new search, save a search, and find a file using a saved search
- Find a file by specifying the starting point, date, or file type of the search, or knowing a word or series of words in the file
- View a document using Quick View
- Copy and delete a file using the Send To menu
- Add and remove a destination on the Send To menu
- View the contents and properties of the Recycle Bin
- Empty the Recycle Bin
- Find Web content and information about a person on the Internet
- Open My Briefcase and drag a file to My Briefcase
- Move My Briefcase between a floppy disk and the desktop
- Synchronize files using My Briefcase
- Open a document using the Documents menu
- Clear the contents of the Documents menu
- View the power management settings for a computer

Microsoft **Windows 98**

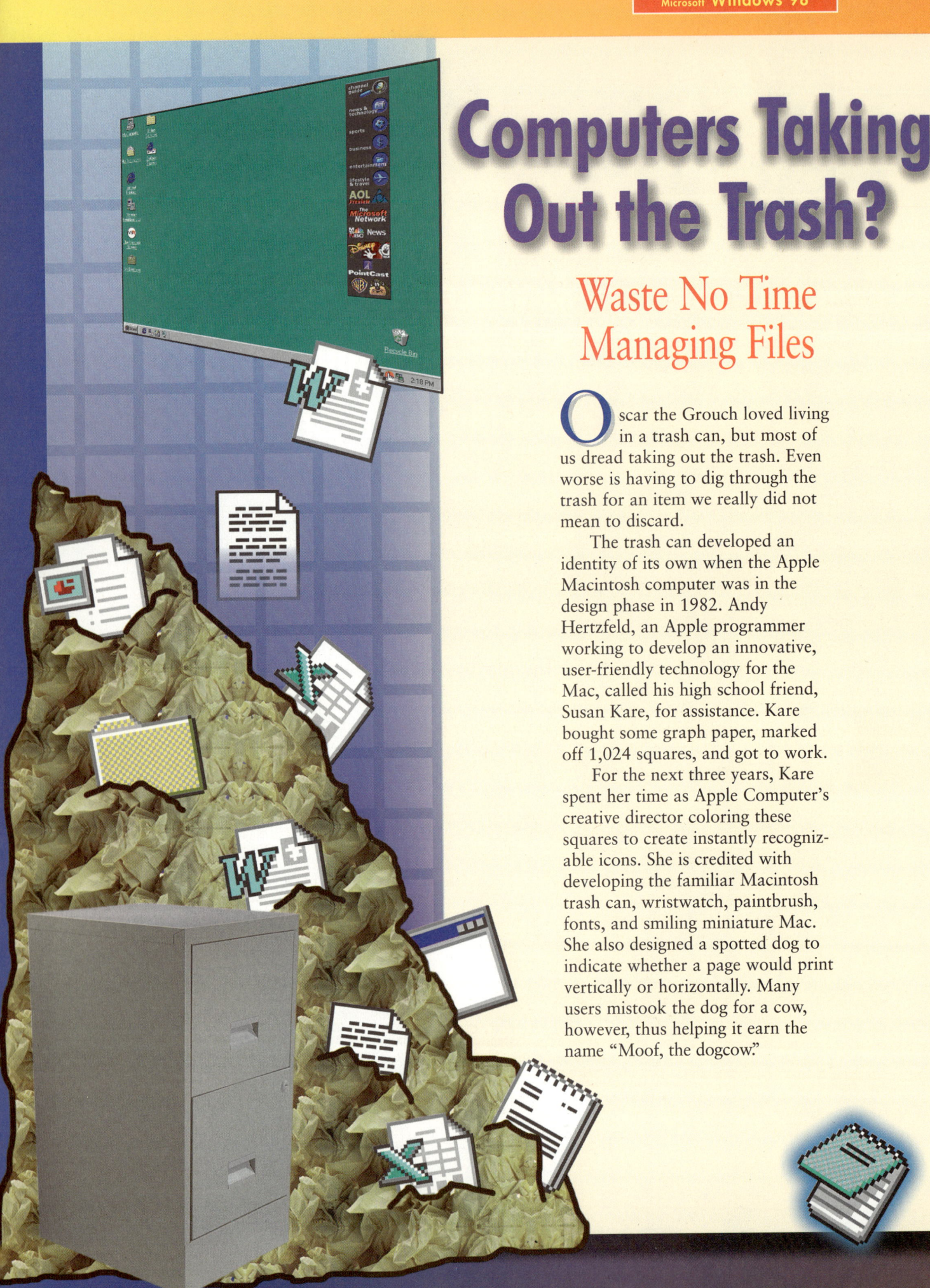

Computers Taking Out the Trash?

Waste No Time Managing Files

Oscar the Grouch loved living in a trash can, but most of us dread taking out the trash. Even worse is having to dig through the trash for an item we really did not mean to discard.

The trash can developed an identity of its own when the Apple Macintosh computer was in the design phase in 1982. Andy Hertzfeld, an Apple programmer working to develop an innovative, user-friendly technology for the Mac, called his high school friend, Susan Kare, for assistance. Kare bought some graph paper, marked off 1,024 squares, and got to work.

For the next three years, Kare spent her time as Apple Computer's creative director coloring these squares to create instantly recognizable icons. She is credited with developing the familiar Macintosh trash can, wristwatch, paintbrush, fonts, and smiling miniature Mac. She also designed a spotted dog to indicate whether a page would print vertically or horizontally. Many users mistook the dog for a cow, however, thus helping it earn the name "Moof, the dogcow."

Microsoft recruited Kare in 1988 to design the icons and buttons for Windows 3.0 and most of the original solitaire cards. While developing icon ideas, she considered using a trash truck, plastic and aluminum trash cans, and fires. You can view samples of Kare's work at her Web site (www.kare.com).

In this project, you will learn to use the Recycle Bin by viewing its contents, restoring a deleted file, folder, or shortcut, emptying the Recycle Bin, and viewing its properties. You also will use advanced file management features including the Find command to search for files if you know only when the file was created, a few words located in the file, or the type of file, such as a Microsoft Word or a JPEG image file.

In addition, you will use the Quick View feature to view the contents of a file, the Send To command to copy and delete a file, and the Documents command to open a document.

Living in a mobile society dictates the need to keep files updated when you use two computers, such as a networked computer at work and your laptop computer. Windows 98 eases that chore with My Briefcase, a program you will learn to use in this project. You select the files you will want to use on the secondary computer and copy them on a floppy disk. Then you work on the files from your laptop, and when you reconnect to your desktop computer, you click Update All and allow My Briefcase to synchronize, or update, the original copies of the files.

The advanced file and document management features in Windows 98 make storing, retrieving, and modifying files fast and easy. If you put a file in a folder and then forget where you put it, Windows will help you find it. If you delete a file and then realize you need it, you can dig through the trash with ease. Even Oscar the Grouch would approve.

Microsoft Windows 98

Advanced File and Document Management and My Briefcase

PROJECT 6

CASE PERSPECTIVE

Your organization has been using Windows 98 for several months. Most people in the organization feel comfortable with simple file operations such as copying, moving, renaming, and deleting. Many people have found that being able to use the Find command to search for a file knowing only the file name is a timesaving feature. Your boss has used Windows Help and has found, however, that the employees do not know of the additional methods to search for a file. He wants the employees to learn these methods. In addition, the company purchased several laptop computers. Your boss wants everyone in the organization to be trained to use the laptop computers so they can telecommute from time to time or work while away from the office on business.

Your goal is to learn more about the advanced features of the Find command and how to transport files between computers so you can conduct a training seminar for the people in the organization.

Introduction

In Project 2, you used Windows 98 to create documents and store them on both a floppy disk and the desktop; and you deleted files from the desktop. In Project 3, you learned to manage and organize files and documents using My Computer and Windows Explorer. Using My Computer, you opened a document and copied files from a folder to a drive and disk. Using Windows Explorer, you copied, renamed, and deleted files and searched for a file name using the Find command.

Project 6 presents the use of the advanced features of the Find command to search for files when the information you know about the files is limited. You will search the Internet to locate Web content and search for information about people on the Internet. You will use Quick View to view the contents of a file, copy and delete a file using the Send To command, add to and remove destinations from the Send To command, and open documents using the Documents command. You will recover a deleted file from the Recycle Bin, view the properties, and empty the Recycle Bin. In addition, you will use My Briefcase to transport files between two computers, update the changes made to those files, and check the power settings for a laptop computer.

The Find Command

Using the **Find command**, you can find files and folders on your hard drive knowing only the time and date the file was created, a word or words within the file, or the type of file. On the Internet, you can locate content using a Web browser and find information on people with the Find command. The following sections illustrate the various ways to use the Find command.

Finding Files and Folders on the Hard Drive

As mentioned in Project 3, it is easy to locate files and folders on your computer. One method to find a file is to browse through the folders on your computer using My Computer. If you want to find a file quickly, however, you use the Find command on the Start menu. In Project 3, you used Find to locate a file on the hard disk knowing only the name of the file. It is common after saving a file on the hard disk to forget its file name. In this case, the Find command allows you to search for a file by file type, creation or modification date, or knowing a word or series of words in the file name. To make the search quicker, you can specify the folder in which to begin the search. Perform the following steps to begin a search.

> **More About**
>
> **The Find Command**
>
> Some would argue that the Find command is the handiest tool in Windows 98. If an application program is not represented by an icon on the desktop or on the Start menu, many people use the Find command to display the icon in the Find window, and then double-click the icon to start the program.

 To Begin a Search

1 **Click the Start button, point to Find on the Start menu, and point to Files or Folders on the Find submenu.**

The Start menu and Find submenu display and the Files or Folders command is highlighted (Figure 6-1). Other commands on the Find submenu allow you to find computers on your network (Computer), find Web content on the Internet (On the Internet), find people on the Internet (People), and find information on The Microsoft Network (On The Microsoft Network).

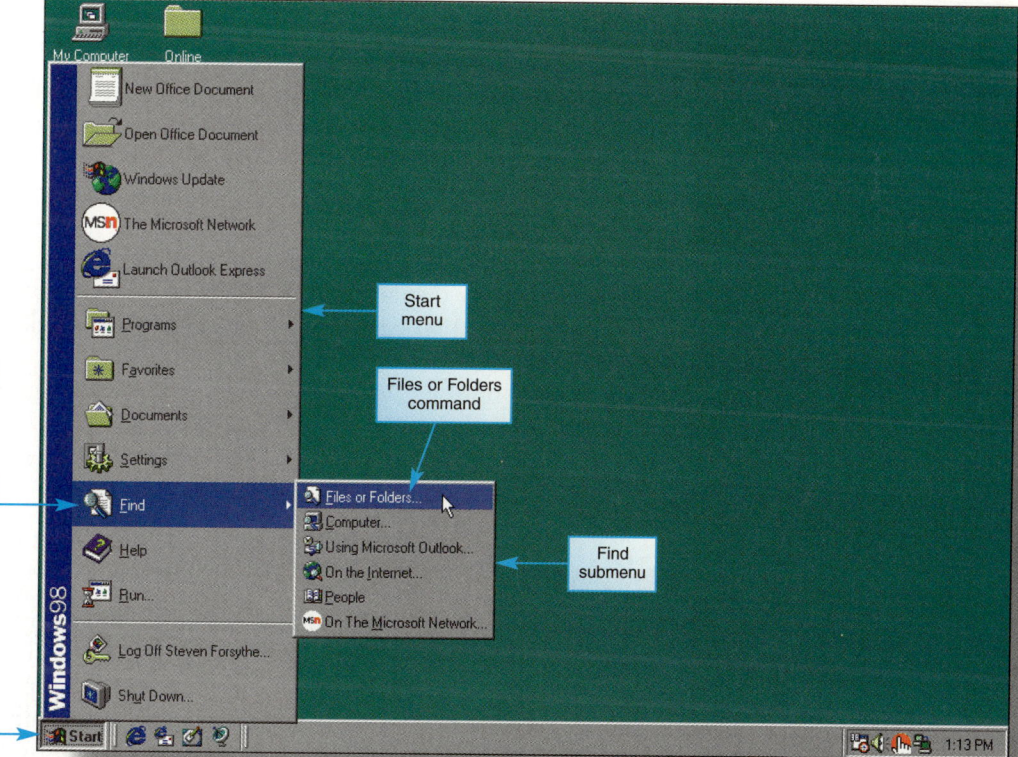

FIGURE 6-1

 **Click Files or Folders. If the Hard disk (C:) entry does not display in the Look in box, click the Look in box arrow and then click Hard disk (C:).**

The Find: All Files window opens and the Name & Location sheet displays (Figure 6-2). The Hard disk (C:) entry in the Look in box indicates the starting point of the search, the Named box and Containing text text box are empty, and the Include subfolders check box is selected.

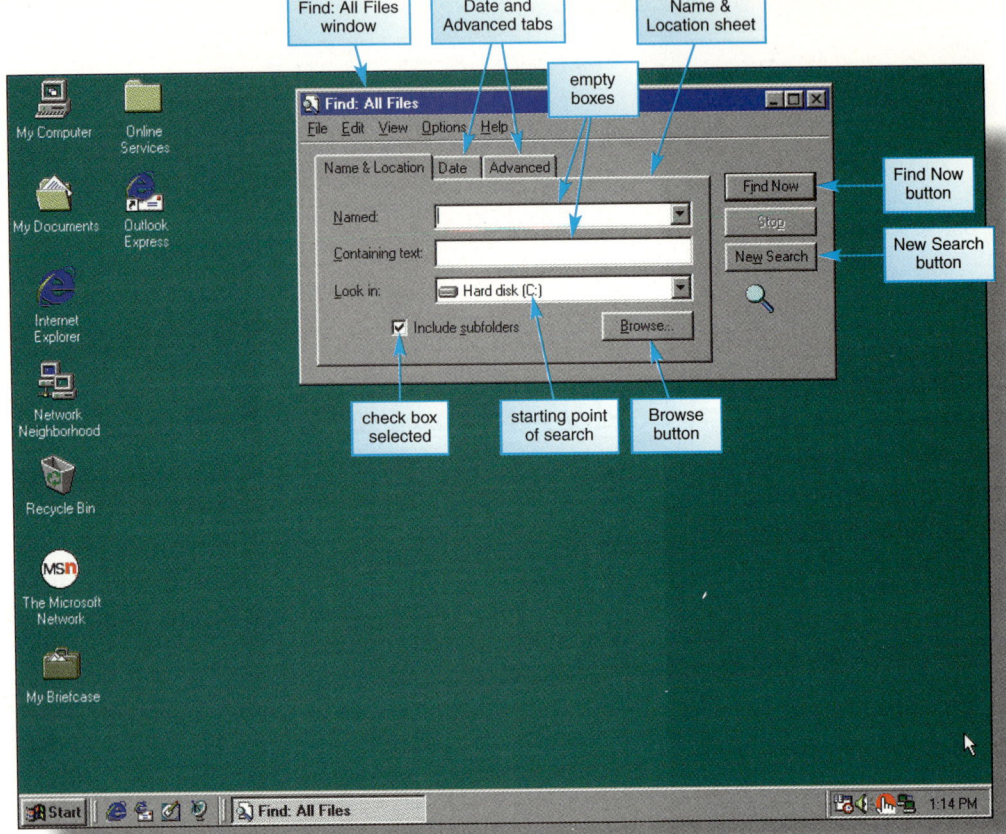

FIGURE 6-2

Other Ways

1. Click New Search button in Find: All Files window, click OK button
2. Right-click Network Neighborhood icon, click Find Computer on shortcut menu
3. Right-click Online Services icon or My Computer icon, click Find on shortcut menu
4. Right-click Start button, click Find on shortcut menu

The Named box in the Name & Location sheet in the Find: All Files window shown in Figure 6-2 allows you to specify the name of a file or files to search for. The Containing text text box allows you to search for files containing a word or series of words. The text box is empty to indicate the contents of the files will not be examined during the search.

The Look in box indicates the starting point for the search. In Figure 6-2, the Hard disk (C:) entry displays in the box to indicate the starting point is the hard drive and the check mark in the Include subfolders check box indicates all subfolders on the hard drive will be searched.

The Browse button allows you to specify a new starting point for the search. The Find Now button starts the search and the New Search button cancels the current search and begins a new search. The Date sheet and Advanced sheet allow you to further define the search criteria you use to search for a file or files.

Specifying the Starting Point of the Search

The Find: All Files Window

When you close the Find: All Files window, Windows 98 retains the entry in the Look in box and displays that entry the next time you open the window. If the Hard disk (C:) entry does not display in the Look in box, you can display it by clicking the Look in box arrow and clicking Hard disk (C:) in the list box.

If you know which folder a file is stored in but do not know the name of the file, you can decrease the search time to find the file by specifying the folder in which Windows 98 should begin its search. Assume, for example, you want to search for a file you know is located in the Windows folder or the subfolders in the Windows folder. Perform the following steps to specify the Windows folder as the starting point of the search and to include the subfolders in the Windows folder in the search.

Finding Files and Folders on the Hard Drive • WIN 6.7

To Specify the Starting Point of a Search

1 Click the Browse button. When the Browse for Folder dialog box displays, point to the plus sign in the small box to the left of the Hard disk (C:) icon.

The Browse for Folder dialog box displays (Figure 6-3). The list box displays a hierarchical structure with the names and icons of items on the computer. The highest level in the hierarchy is the Desktop, and the My Computer folder name is highlighted.

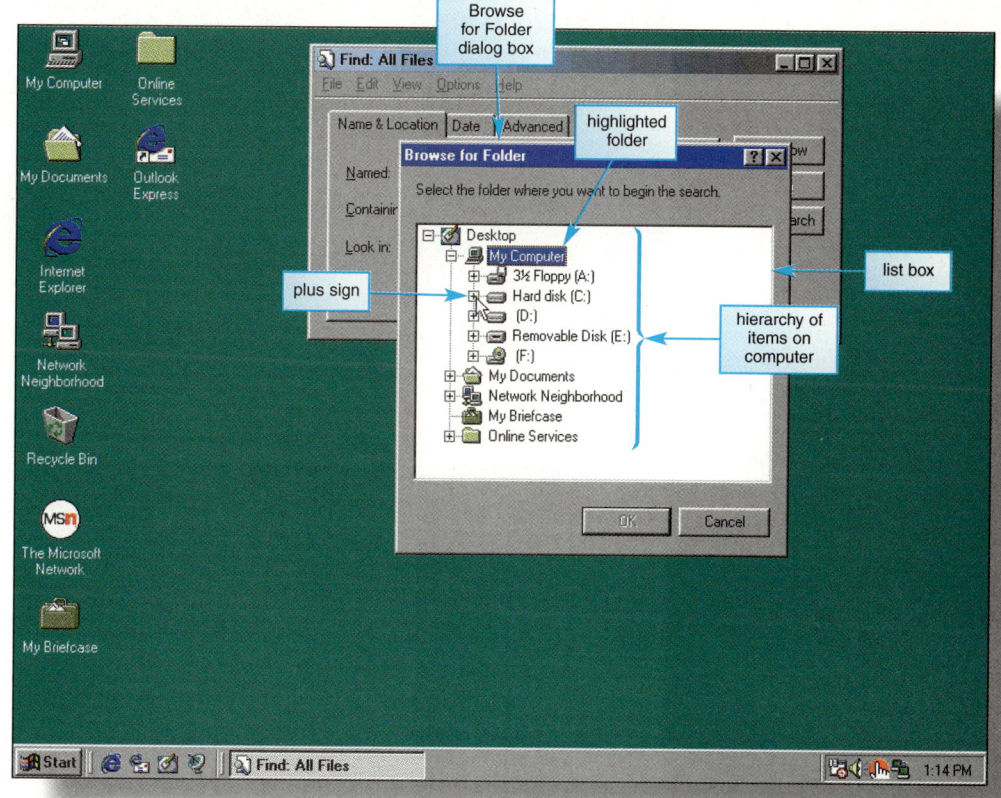

FIGURE 6-3

2 Click the plus sign. Scroll the list box until the Windows folder name is visible in the list box. Click the Windows folder name. Point to the OK button.

The Hard disk (C:) entry expands to display a partial list of the folders contained on the hard disk (drive C), and the Windows folder name is highlighted (Figure 6-4).

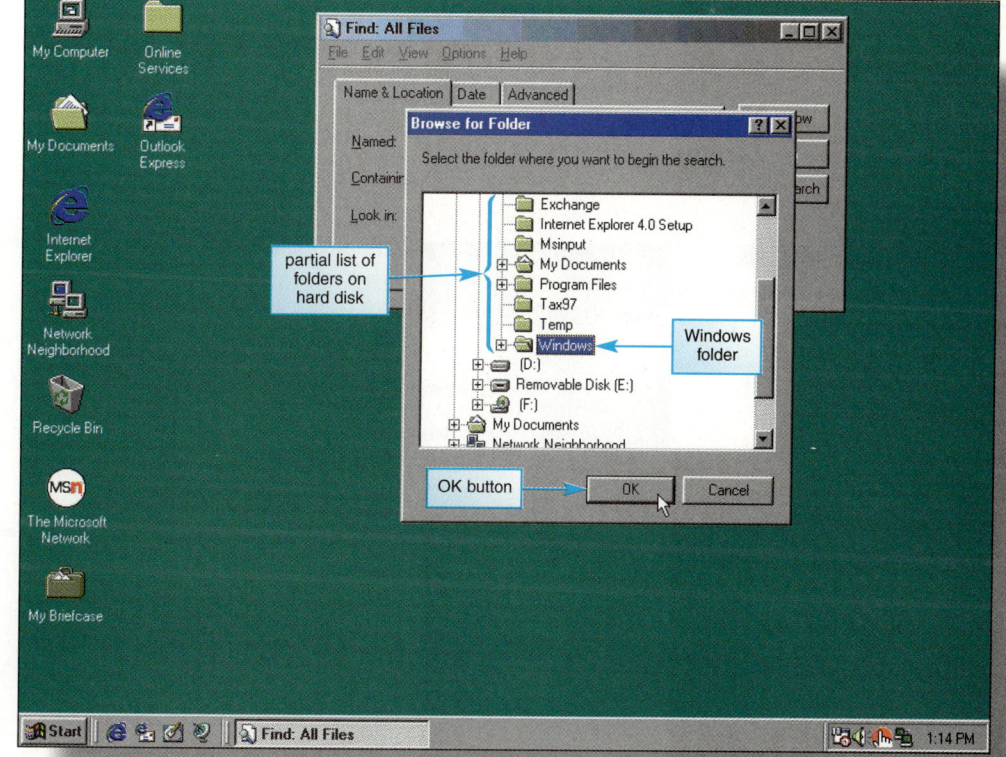

FIGURE 6-4

WIN 6.8 • Project 6 • Advanced File and Document Management and My Briefcase

 Click the OK button.

A folder icon and the location and name of the Windows folder (C:\WINDOWS) display in the Look in box (Figure 6-5). The Include subfolders check box is selected, indicating the search will include all subfolders in the Windows folder.

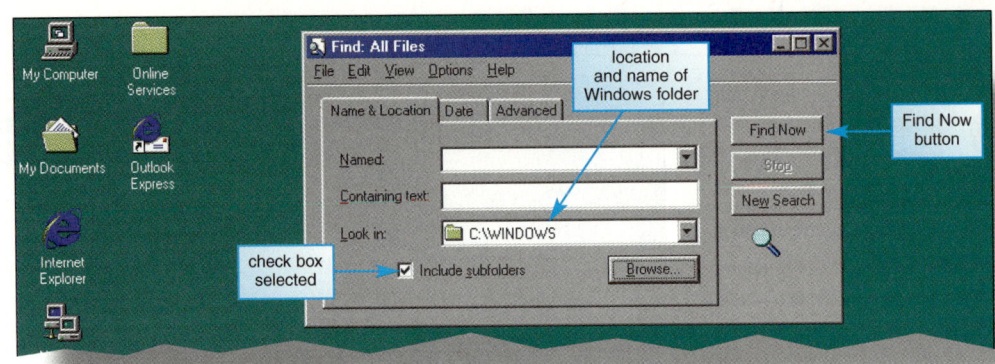

FIGURE 6-5

Other Ways

1. Click Name & Location tab, click Look in box, type location and folder name
2. Click Name & Location tab, click Look in box arrow, click desired entry in Look in list box

Unless you change the starting point of the search, clicking the Find Now button will search the Windows folder and its subfolders. In addition to specifying the starting point of a search, you can further define the search criteria. For example, you can change the search criteria to search for a file created or modified within a specified time period, a specific type of file (application file, bitmap image file, text file, and so on), a word or series of words contained in a file, or the size of a file. Methods to further define the search criteria are explained in the following sections.

Finding a File by Date

If you know a file was created or modified before or after a certain date, you can specify a time interval in which to search for the file using the options on the Date sheet. Assume, for example, if you have forgotten the name of a file that you know is located in the Windows folder or its subfolders and that was modified within the last two days. The following steps search for all files in the Windows folder and its subfolders that were created or modified within the last two days.

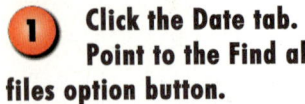 **To Find a File by Date**

 Click the Date tab. Point to the Find all files option button.

The Date sheet displays on top of the other sheets (Figure 6-6). The All files option button is selected, indicating all files in the Windows folder and its subfolders, regardless of creation or modification date, will be examined.

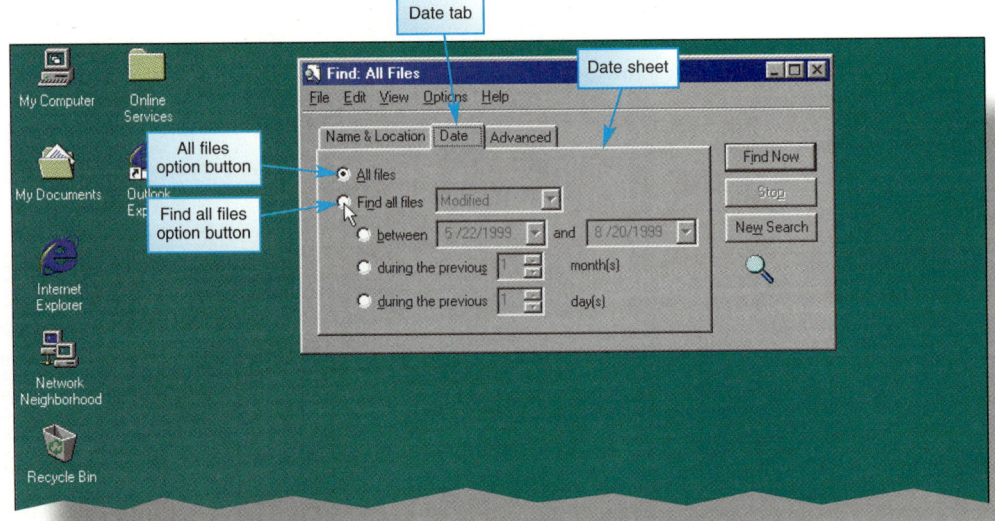

FIGURE 6-6

Finding Files and Folders on the Hard Drive • **WIN 6.9**

② Click Find all files. Click during the previous day(s), and then click the text box up arrow to the right of the option button to display the value 2 in the text box. Point to the Find Now button.

The All files option button is deselected, the Find all files option button and during the previous day(s) option button are selected, the word, Modified, displays in the Find all files box and the value 2 displays in the text box (Figure 6-7).

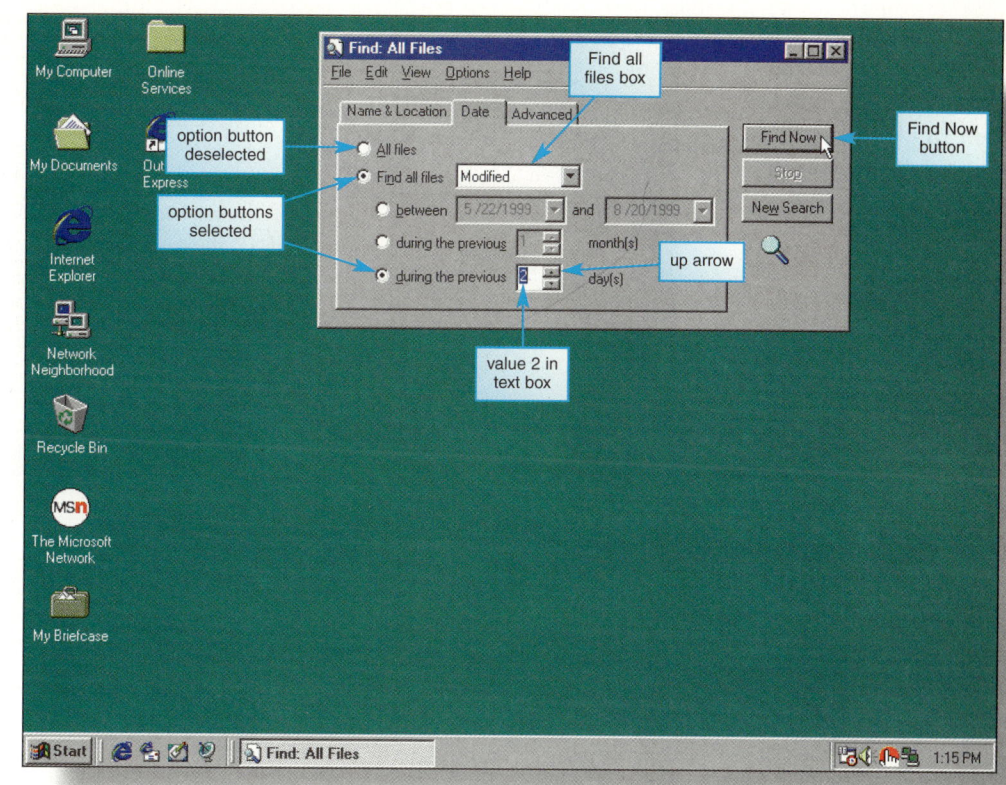

FIGURE 6-7

③ Click the Find Now button.

A partial list of the files in the Windows folder or its subfolders created or modified within the previous two days display in the list box (Figure 6-8). Column headers identify the file name (Name), location (In Folder), size (Size), type (Type), and date and time modified (Modified) of each file. Only the Name and In Folder headers are visible in the list. Different files may display in the list box on your computer and more headers may be visible.

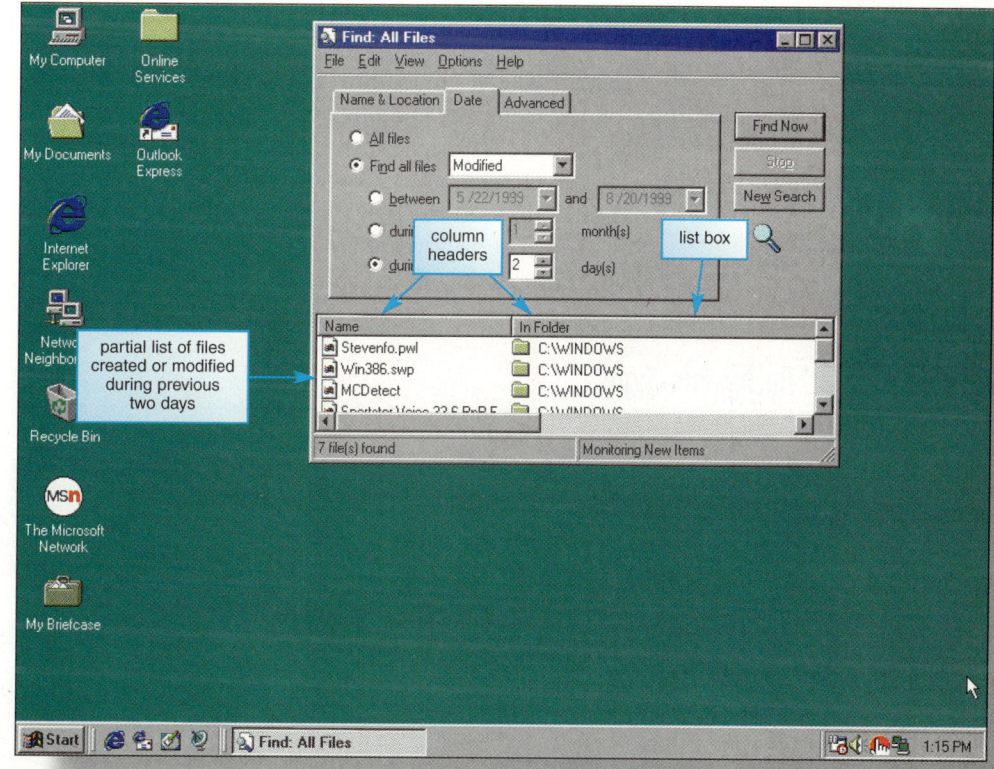

FIGURE 6-8

WIN 6.10 • Project 6 • Advanced File and Document Management and My Briefcase

Microsoft **Windows 98**

4 **In preparation for the next search, click the All files option button so all files will be examined regardless of creation or modification date.**

The All files option button is selected (Figure 6-9). Subsequent searches will search for and display all files in the Windows folder and its subfolders, regardless of creation or modification dates.

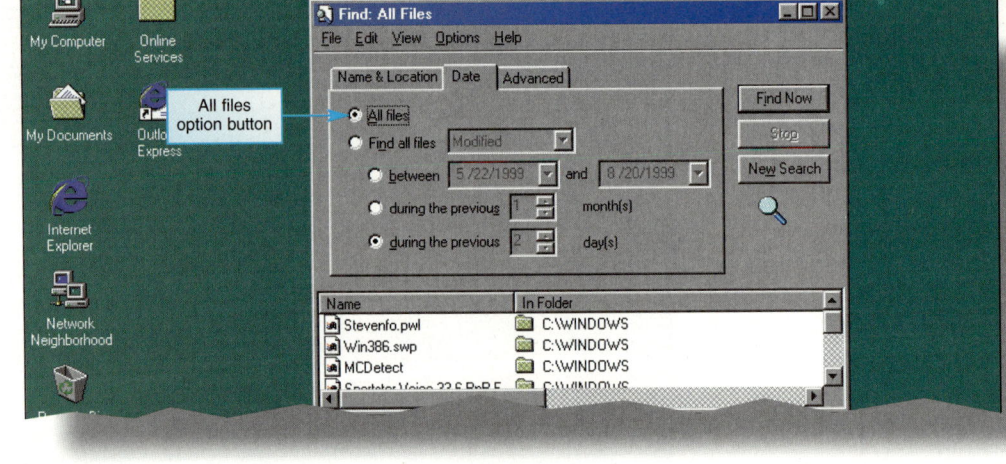

FIGURE 6-9

Other Ways

1. Click Date tab, click during the previous months, click text box up or down arrow to select number of months, click Find Now button
2. Click Date tab, click between, type beginning date, type ending date, click Find Now button

More About

File Types

File types are determined by file name extensions, a period, and up to three characters added to the end of a file name. The Find command uses the extension when searching.

After completing a search, you can work with the files you found in any manner desired. For example, if a file can be opened, you can open it by double-clicking the file icon or right-clicking the file icon and then clicking Open on the shortcut menu. In addition, you can print the file, create a shortcut to the file, rename or delete the file, and copy or move the file using commands on the shortcut menu. If the file you find is an executable program file, you can start the program by double-clicking the file icon.

Finding a File by File Type

If you want to search for a specific type of file, you can specify the type of file to search for using the options on the Advanced sheet. Among the file types you can search for are application files (.exe extension), bitmap image files (.bmp extension), device driver files (.dll extension), and text files (.txt extension). Assume, for example, that you want to find all the text document files in the Windows folder and its subfolders. The following steps search for only text document files in the Windows folder and its subfolders.

 To Find a File by File Type

1 **Click the Advanced tab. Point to the Of type box arrow.**

The Advanced sheet displays (Figure 6-10). The Of type box contains the All Files and Folders entry, indicating that all files will be examined during the search. The Size is boxes allow you to search for files of a certain size.

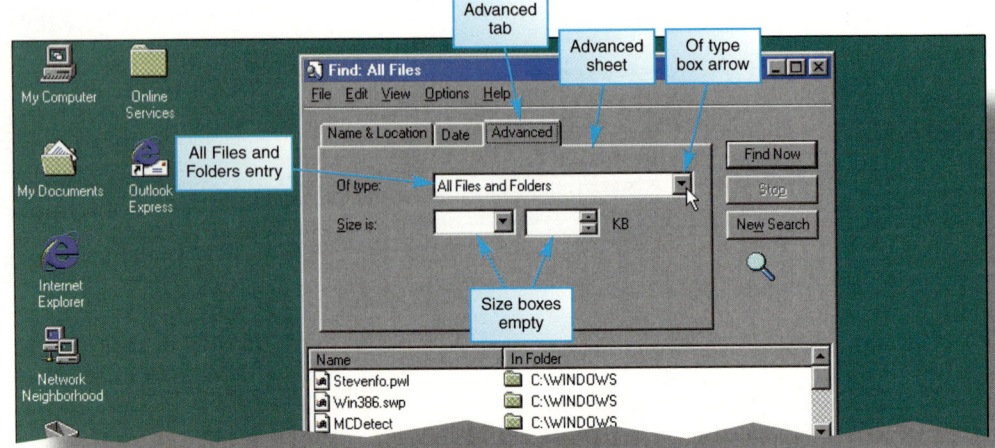

FIGURE 6-10

2 Click the Of type box arrow. Scroll the Of type list box until the Text Document file type is visible and then point to the Text Document file type.

The Of type list box displays (Figure 6-11). The Text Document file type is highlighted.

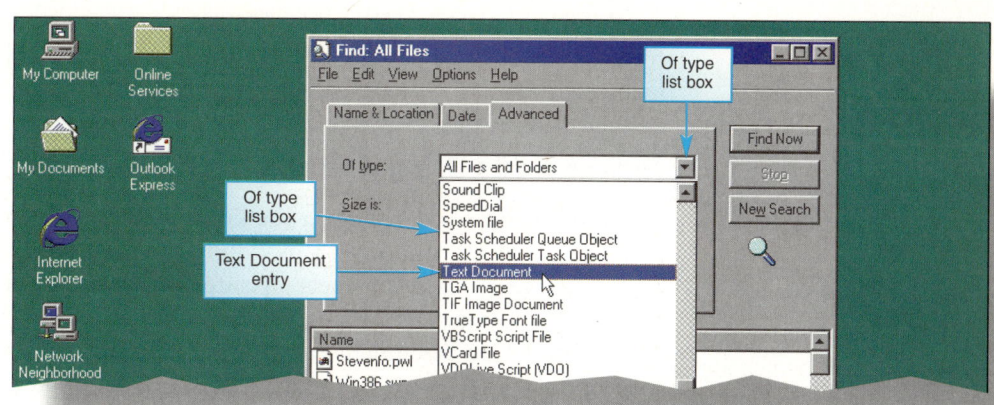

FIGURE 6-11

3 Click Text Document. Point to the Find Now button.

Text Document displays highlighted in the list box (Figure 6-12).

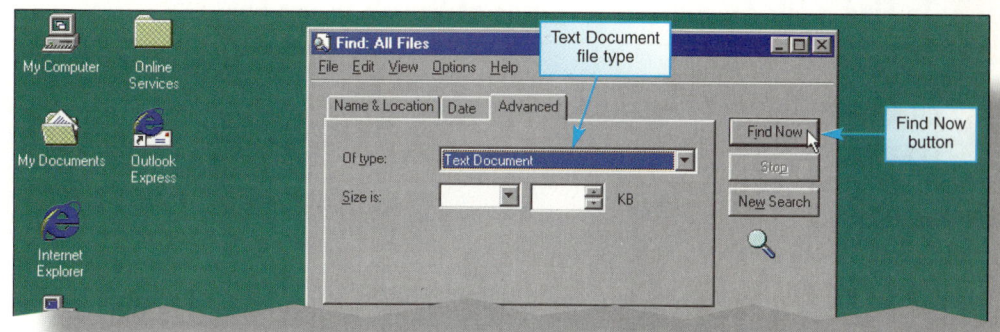

FIGURE 6-12

4 Click the Find Now button.

The window title changes to reflect the change in search criteria and a partial list of the document files in the Windows folder or its subfolders displays in the Advanced sheet list box (Figure 6-13). The icon below the Name column header identifies each file as a text document. Different files may display in the list box on your computer.

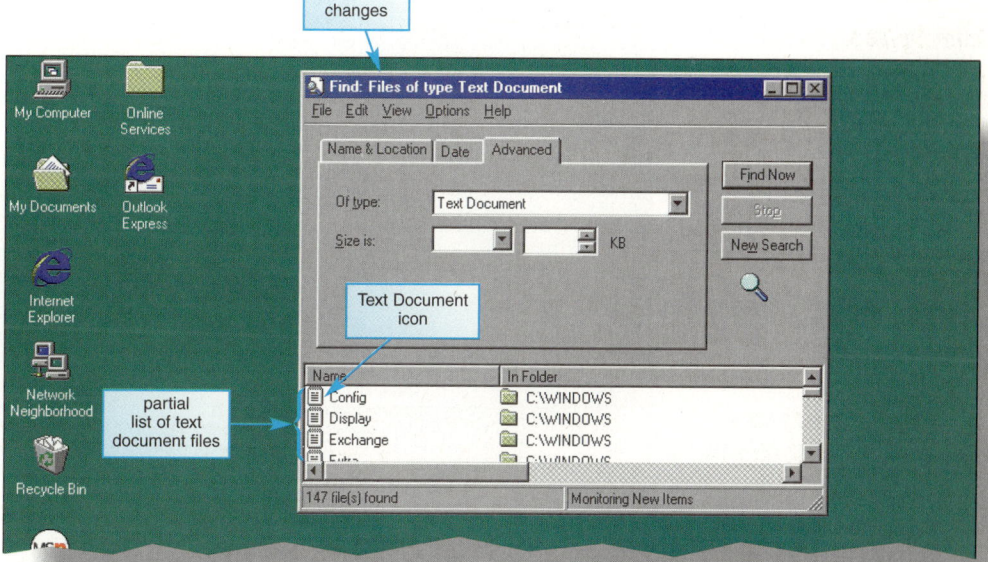

FIGURE 6-13

Other Ways

1. Click Advanced tab, click Of type box arrow, use arrow keys to select file type, press ENTER

After completing a search by file type, you can perform many operations on the file by right-clicking the file icon and then clicking a command on the shortcut menu.

Finding a File Using a Word or Series of Words in the File

If you want to search for a file knowing only a word or series of words in the file, you can perform a search by typing the word(s) in the Containing text text box on the Name & Location sheet. Assume you want to find all text document files in the Windows folder and its subfolders containing the words, technical support. Because the Text Document entry displays in the Of type list box (see Figure 6-12 on the previous page), you will search for only text document files containing the words, technical support. Perform the following steps to perform the search.

To Find a File by a Word or Series of Words in the File

1 **Click the Name & Location tab. Click the Containing text text box. Type** technical support **and then point to the Find Now button.**

The words, technical support, display in the Containing text text box (Figure 6-14). Although not visible, the Text Document file type continues to display in the Of type list box in the Advanced sheet.

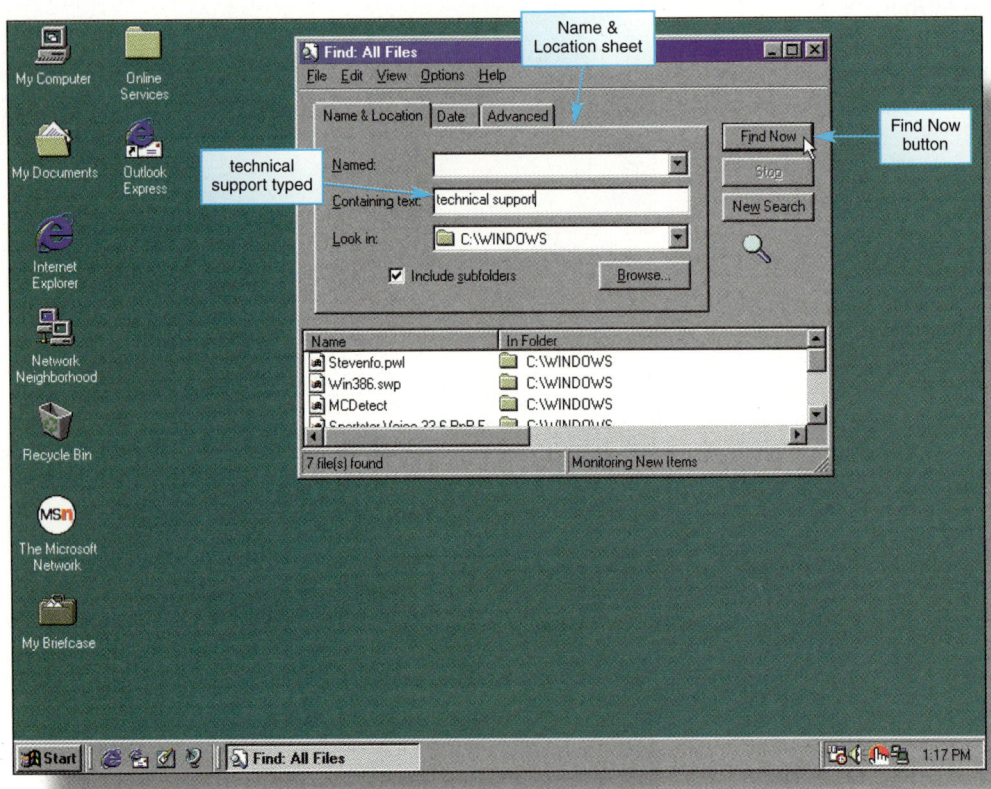

FIGURE 6-14

Finding Files and Folders on the Hard Drive • **WIN 6.13**

2 Click the Find Now button. Point to the Support file icon in the list box. If the Support file icon does not display, point to another file icon in the list box.

The window title changes to reflect the change in search criteria and a partial list of the text document files containing the words, technical support, in the Windows folder or its subfolders displays in the list box (Figure 6-15). The Support file icon displays in the list box. Different files may display on your computer.

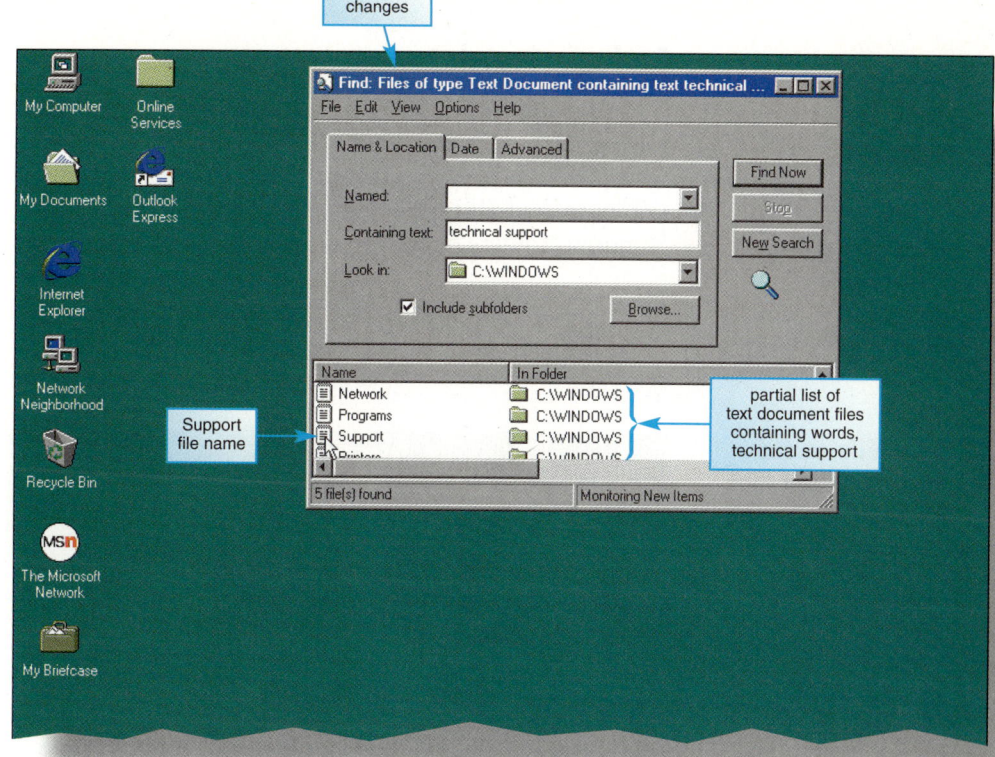

FIGURE 6-15

3 Double-click the Support file icon.

The Support – Notepad window opens, and the Support document displays in the window (Figure 6-16).

4 Scroll the Support document to find the words, technical support, and then read the information you find. Click the Close button to close the Support – Notepad window.

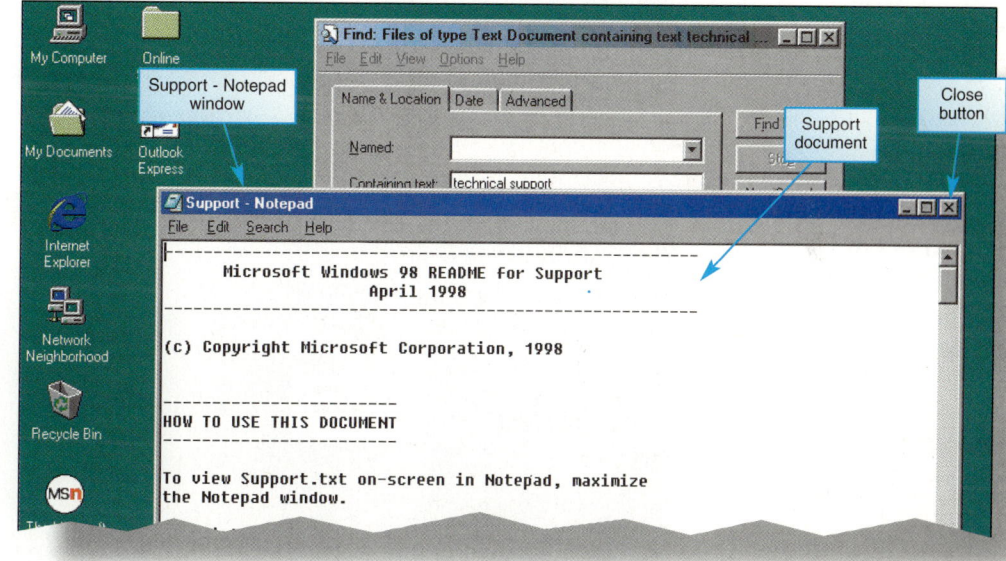

FIGURE 6-16

After finding all text documents in the Windows folder or its subfolder that contain the words, technical support, and opening the Support document, you scrolled the document to find occurrences of the words, technical support. Another method to search for the words, technical support, in the Support document is to click Search on the menu bar, click Find, type `technical support` in the Find what text box, and then click the Find Next button. The first occurrence of the word will display in the Notepad window. To search for additional occurrences, press the Find Next button again.

WIN 6.14 • Project 6 • Advanced File and Document Management and My Briefcase

Saving a Search

After defining a search criteria, you can use the Save Search command on the File menu to save the search. In the future, you can find a file using the saved search instead of having to recreate the search. Perform the following steps to save the search to find all text documents containing the words, technical support, in the Windows folders or its subfolders.

To Save a Search

1 Click File on the menu bar and then point to Save Search (Figure 6-17).

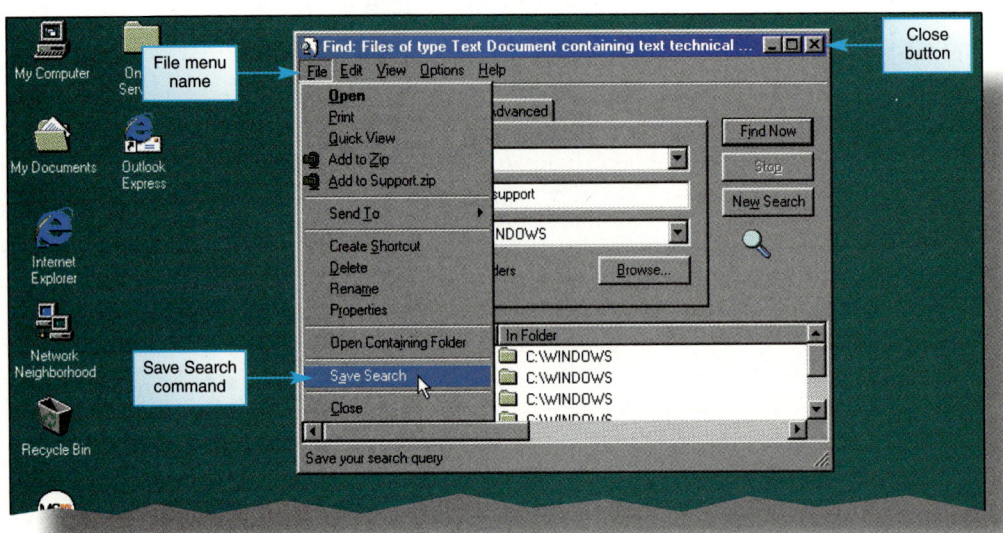

FIGURE 6-17

2 Click Save Search. Click the Close button in the Find: Files of type Text Document window.

The search is saved in a file on the desktop named Files of type Text Document (Figure 6-18).

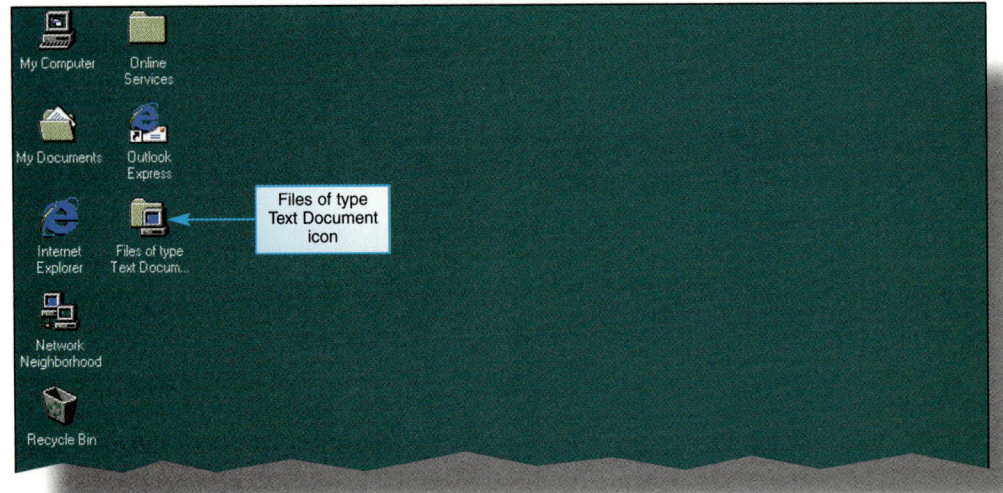

FIGURE 6-18

More About

Saving a Search

The Save Search command saves the search criteria in a file on the desktop. If you click Save Results on the Options menu, the search results and search criteria are saved together.

After saving the search, double-clicking the Files of type Text Document icon displays the Find: Files of type Text Document window and allows you to use the saved search to find all text documents containing the words, technical support, in the Windows folder or its subfolders.

Using a Saved Search to Find a File

After saving the search and creating an icon on the desktop, perform the search to find all text documents containing the words, technical support, in the Windows folder or its subfolders by performing the following step.

Steps: To Find a File Using a Saved Search

1 Double-click the Files of type Text Document icon on the desktop. When the Find: Files of type Text Document window displays, click the Find Now button to begin the search.

The Find: Files of type Text Document window opens and then a search for all text documents containing the words, technical support, in the Windows folder or its subfolders is performed (Figure 6-19). The same files display in the list box as were shown in Figure 6-15 on page 6.13.

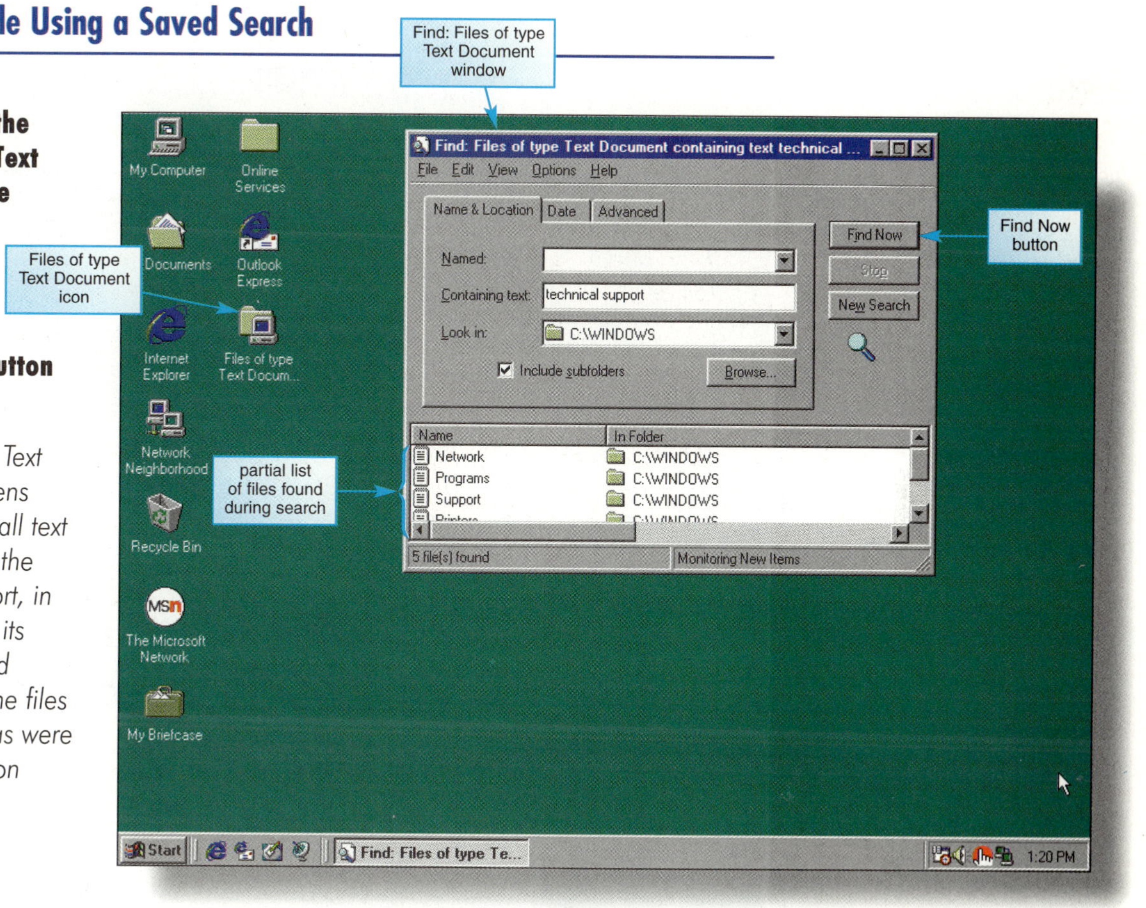

FIGURE 6-19

Other Ways

1. Right-click icon on desktop, click Open on shortcut menu, click Find Now button

Using Quick View

Quick View allows you to view documents that were created with a Windows application program without first starting the program. For example, you may want to look quickly at the contents of a document you found while using My Computer, Windows Explorer, or the Find command. To look quickly at the contents of the Support document found while performing a search for files containing the words, technical support, perform the steps on the next page.

More About

Quick View

Clicking Quick View on the shortcut menu allows you to view the contents of a document in the Quick View window. While the Quick View window is open, you can view the contents of another document by dragging its icon to the open Quick View window.

To View a Document Using Quick View

1 **Right-click the Support file name in the Name & Location sheet list box. Point to Quick View on the shortcut menu.**

The Support file name is highlighted in the list box, and a shortcut menu displays (Figure 6-20).

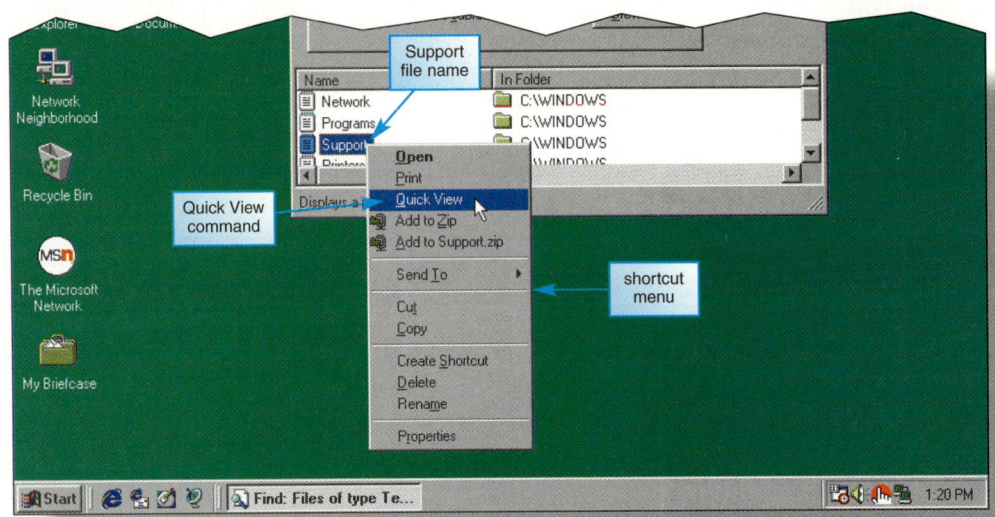

FIGURE 6-20

2 **Click Quick View.**

The Support - Quick View window opens and the Support document displays in the window (Figure 6-21).

3 **Click the Close button in the Support - Quick View window.**

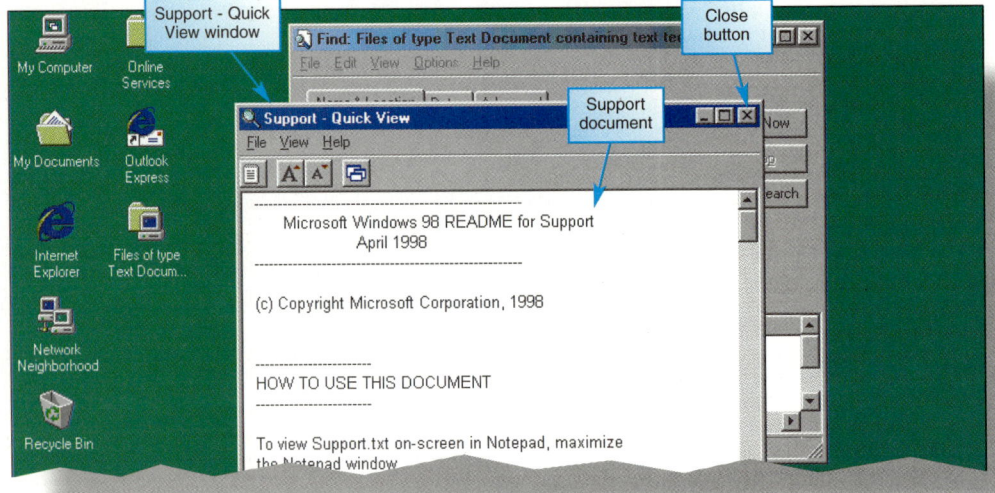

FIGURE 6-21

Other Ways

1. Right-click an icon on desktop, click Quick View on shortcut menu
2. Right-click an icon in My Computer or Windows Explorer, click Quick View on shortcut menu

Other documents can be viewed in a similar manner using Quick View.

Using the Send To Command

Right-clicking any object displays a shortcut menu containing commands related to that object. When you right-click a file or folder icon and point to the Send To command on the shortcut menu, the Send To menu displays. The commands on the Send To menu allow you to copy (send) a file or folder to one of several destinations. In Project 3, you used the Send To command to copy the Daily Appointments folder on the floppy disk in drive A.

In addition, you can add new destinations to the Send To menu. To review the procedure to copy a file to a floppy disk using the Send To command, perform the following steps to copy the Support file from the Name & Location sheet list box onto a floppy disk in drive A.

TO COPY A FILE USING THE SEND TO COMMAND

1. Insert a formatted floppy disk into drive A of your computer.
2. Right-click the Support file name and then point to Send To on the shortcut menu.
3. Click 3½ Floppy (A) on the Send To submenu.
4. Click the Close button in the Find: Files of type Text Document dialog box.
5. Remove the floppy disk from drive A of your computer.

After performing Steps 1 and 2, the shortcut menu and Send To submenu display (Figure 6-22). The commands, or destinations, on the Send To menu are 3½ Floppy (A), Desktop as Shortcut, Mail Recipient, Mail Recipient Using Microsoft Outlook, My Briefcase, My Documents, Removable Disk (E:), and Web Publishing Wizard. The destinations on the Send To menu on your computer may be different. After completing the first four steps, the Support file is copied to the floppy disk in drive A.

Adding a Destination to the Send To Menu

In addition to the destinations on the Send To menu shown in Figure 6-22, new destinations can be added to the Send To menu. You can customize the Send To menu by adding shortcuts to the destinations to which you send files most frequently. One destination that might be useful is the Recycle Bin. As mentioned in previous projects, the Recycle Bin is an area of the hard disk reserved for files that have been deleted. Adding a shortcut to the Recycle Bin to the Send To menu allows you to delete a file using the Send To menu. Perform the steps on the next page to add the Recycle Bin destination to the Send To menu.

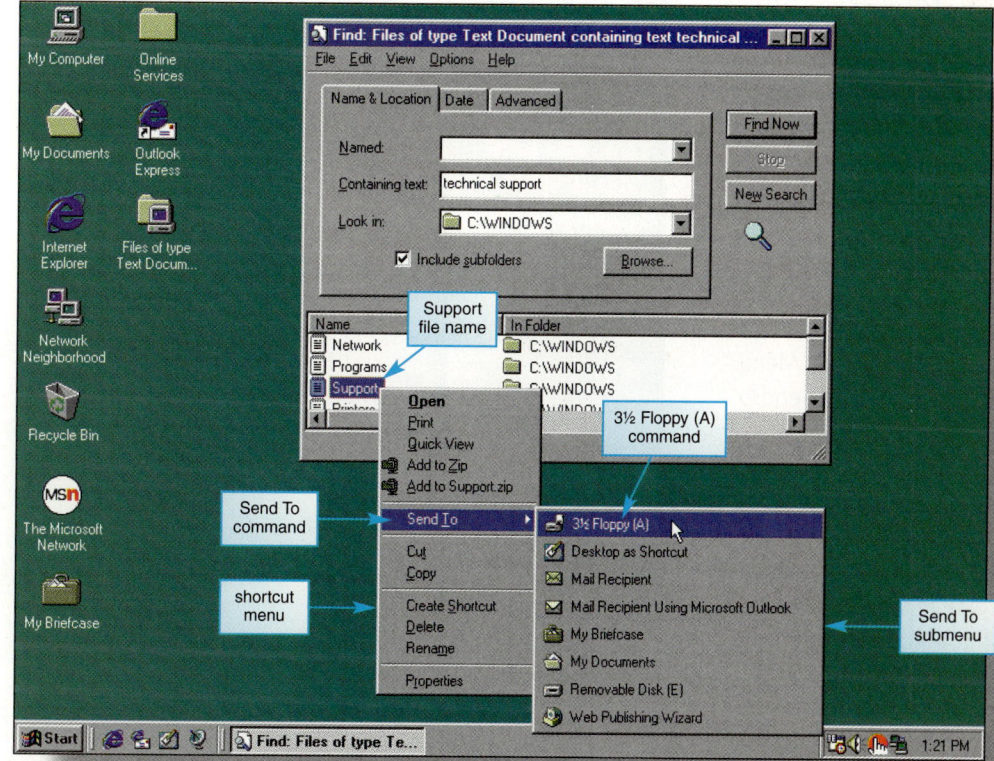

FIGURE 6-22

WIN 6.18 • Project 6 • Advanced File and Document Management and My Briefcase

Steps: To Add a Destination to the Send To Menu

1 Right-click the Start button on the taskbar. Point to Explore on the shortcut menu.

A shortcut menu displays (Figure 6-23).

FIGURE 6-23

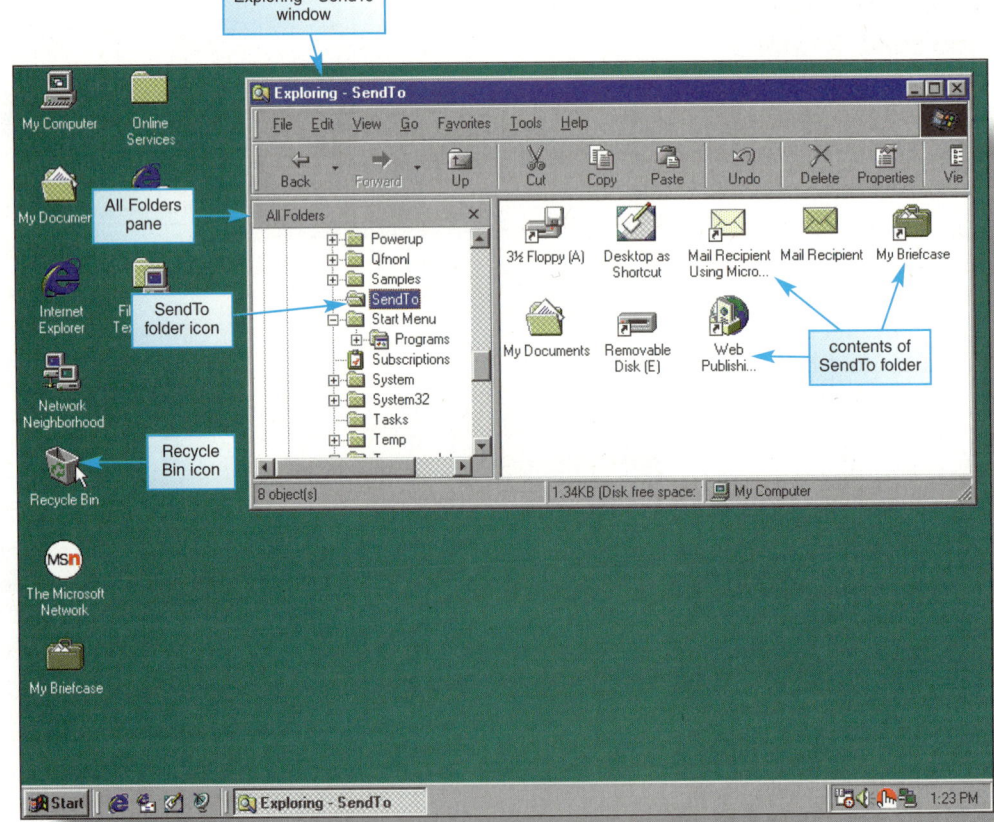

2 Click Explore. If necessary, scroll the All Folders pane to display the SendTo folder name. Click SendTo in the All Folders pane of the Exploring - Start Menu window. Point to the Recycle Bin icon on the desktop.

The Exploring - Start Menu window opens, the SendTo folder name is highlighted in the All Folders pane, the window title changes to Exploring - SendTo, and the contents of the SendTo folder display in the Contents pane of the window (Figure 6-24).

FIGURE 6-24

Using the Send To Command • WIN 6.19

3 **Right-drag the Recycle Bin icon to the Contents pane of the Exploring - SendTo window. Release the right mouse button. Click Create Shortcut(s) Here on the shortcut menu.**

The Shortcut to Recycle Bin icon is added to the Contents pane of the Exploring - SendTo window (Figure 6-25). To be consistent with the other icon names in the SendTo folder, the icon name (Shortcut to Recycle Bin) should be shortened to Recycle Bin.

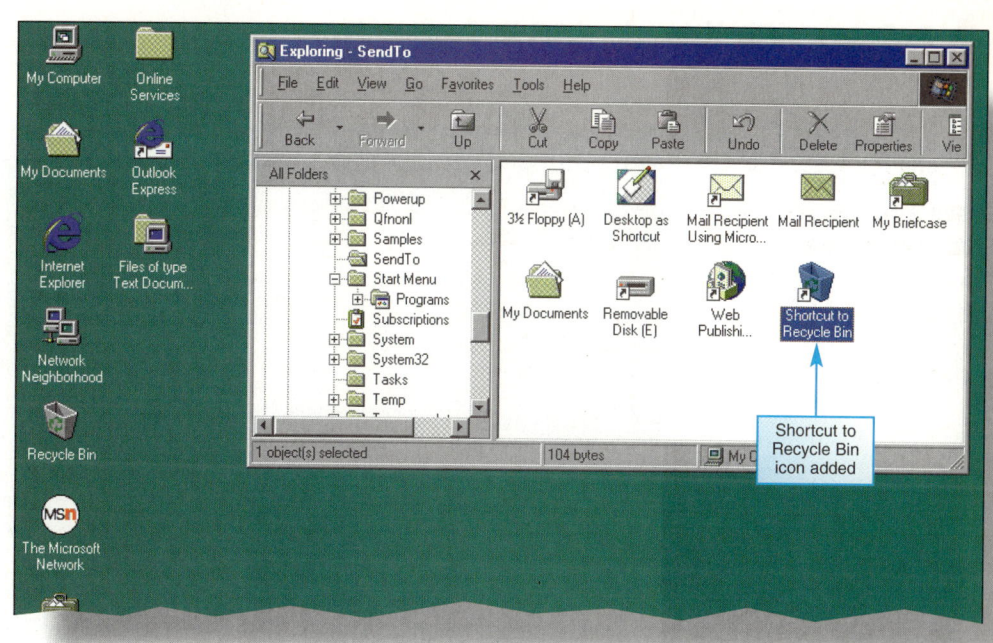

FIGURE 6-25

4 **Click the Shortcut to Recycle Bin icon twice (do not double-click the icon). Type** Recycle Bin **and then press the ENTER key.**

The shortcut is renamed Recycle Bin (Figure 6-26).

5 **Click the Close button in the Exploring - SendTo window to close the window.**

The Exploring - SendTo window closes.

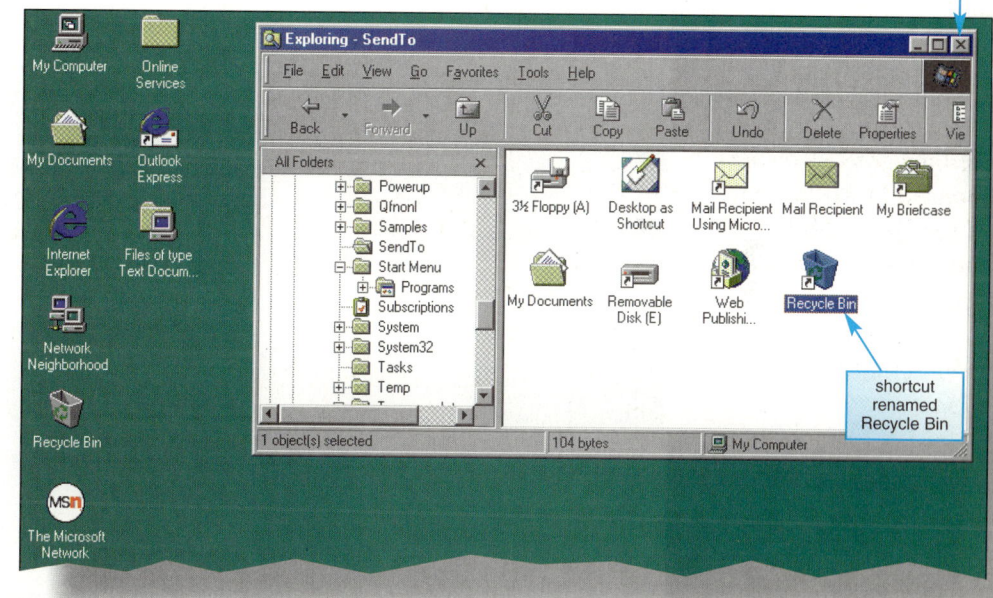

FIGURE 6-26

Deleting a File Using the Send To Command

After adding the Recycle Bin destination to the Send To menu, delete the Files of type Text Document file on the desktop using the Send To command. Perform the steps on the next page to delete the file.

Other Ways

1. Drag icon to Contents pane of Exploring – SendTo window, click Yes button
2. Right-click My Computer, click Explore, click plus sign to left of Hard disk (C:) entry in All Folders pane, click plus sign to left of Windows entry, click SendTo folder in All Folders pane, right-drag icon to Contents area, click Create Shortcut(s) Here

To Delete a File Using the Send To Command

1 **Right-click the Files of type Text Document file on the desktop. Point to Send To on the shortcut menu and then point to Recycle Bin.**

The shortcut menu and Send To submenu display (Figure 6-27).

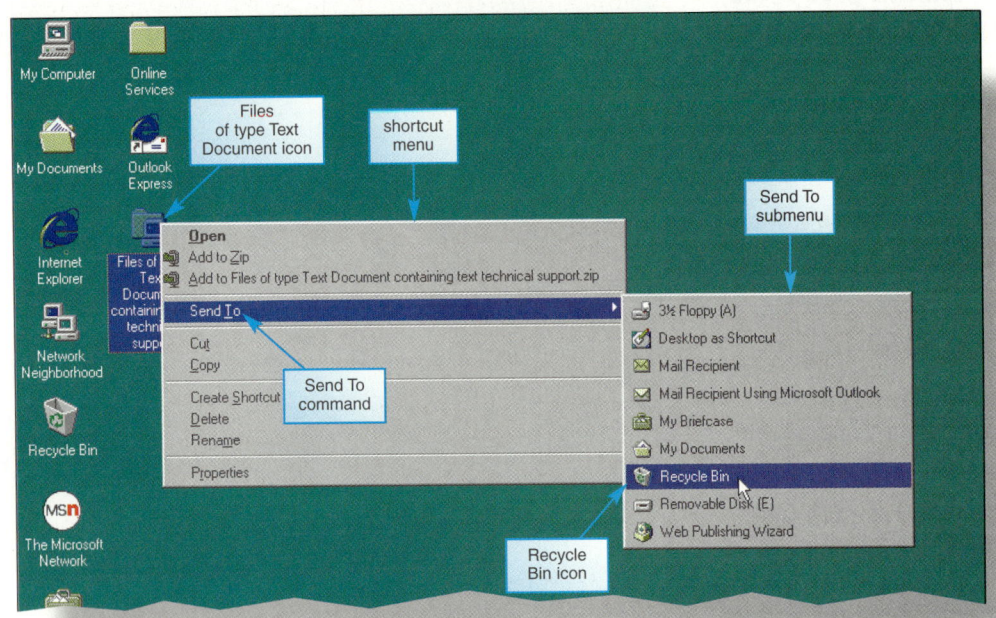

FIGURE 6-27

2 **Click Recycle Bin. Point to the Yes button in the Confirm File Delete dialog box.**

The Confirm File Delete dialog box displays (Figure 6-28).

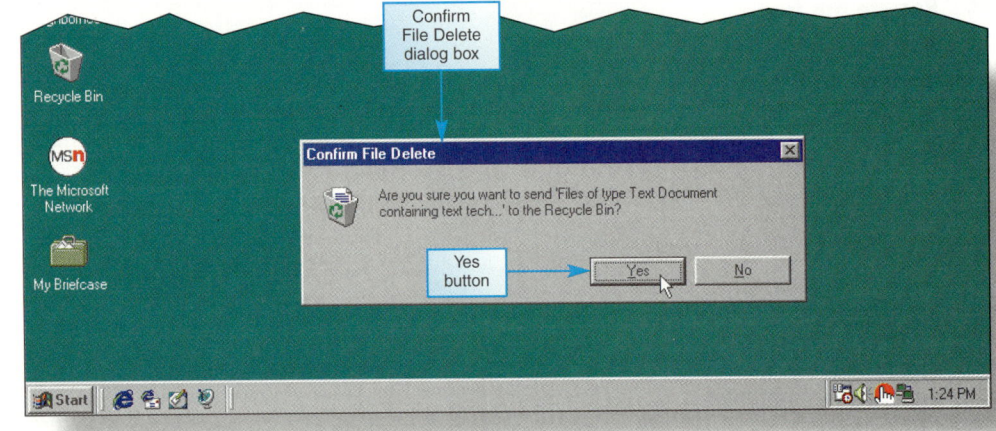

FIGURE 6-28

 **Click the Yes button.**

The Files of type Text Document file icon is removed from the desktop and placed in the Recycle Bin folder (Figure 6-29).

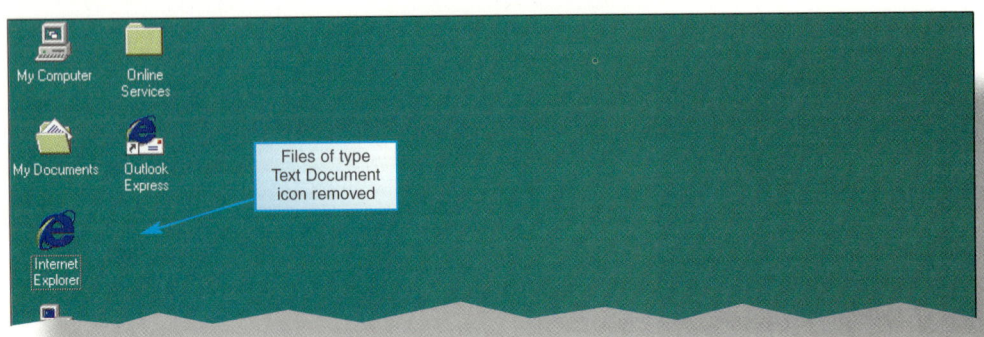

FIGURE 6-29

Removing the Recycle Bin Destination

After adding the Recycle Bin destination to the Send To menu, you should restore the Send To menu to its original configuration. Perform the following steps to remove the Recycle Bin destination from the Send To menu.

TO REMOVE A DESTINATION FROM THE SEND TO MENU

1. Right-click the Start button.
2. Click Explore on the shortcut menu.
3. If necessary, scroll the All Folders pane to display the SendTo folder and then click the SendTo folder icon.
4. Right-click the Recycle Bin icon in the Contents pane.
5. Point to Send To on the shortcut menu.
6. Click Recycle Bin on the Send To submenu.
7. Click the Yes button in the Confirm File Delete dialog box.
8. Click the Close button in the Exploring - SendTo window.

The Recycle Bin destination is removed from the Send To menu.

The Recycle Bin

When Windows 98 is installed, the amount of hard disk space reserved for the Recycle Bin is set at ten percent (10%) of the total size of the hard disk. For example, if the size of the hard disk is two gigabytes (2,000 megabytes), the amount of disk space reserved for the Recycle Bin is approximately 200 megabytes (200 megabytes = 2,000 megabytes × .10). The amount of disk space reserved is a property of the Recycle Bin and can be changed to make more or less disk space available for the Recycle Bin. In addition to changing the size of the Recycle Bin, the entire contents of the Recycle Bin can be emptied to make more disk space available.

Other properties of the Recycle Bin allow you to restore a file that has been deleted in error to its original location, choose to delete a file without first sending the file to the Recycle Bin, and cause no confirmation dialog box to display when a file is deleted. Prior to changing the properties of the Recycle Bin, it is important to be able to view the contents of the Recycle Bin.

Viewing the Contents of the Recycle Bin

To view a list of the deleted files displayed in Details view, including the Files of type Text Document file that was deleted previously in this project, perform the steps on the next page to view the contents of the Recycle Bin.

To View the Contents of the Recycle Bin

1 Double-click the Recycle Bin icon to display the Recycle Bin window. Click View on the menu bar and then click Details. If all five column headers are not visible in the Recycle Bin window, resize the window to view all five headers.

The Recycle Bin window opens with five column headers below the menu bar (Figure 6-30). The Files of type Text Document and Recycle Bin entries display below the Name header. Each entry consists of the deleted file's name, original location, deletion date, file type, and file size. The file entries on your computer may be different.

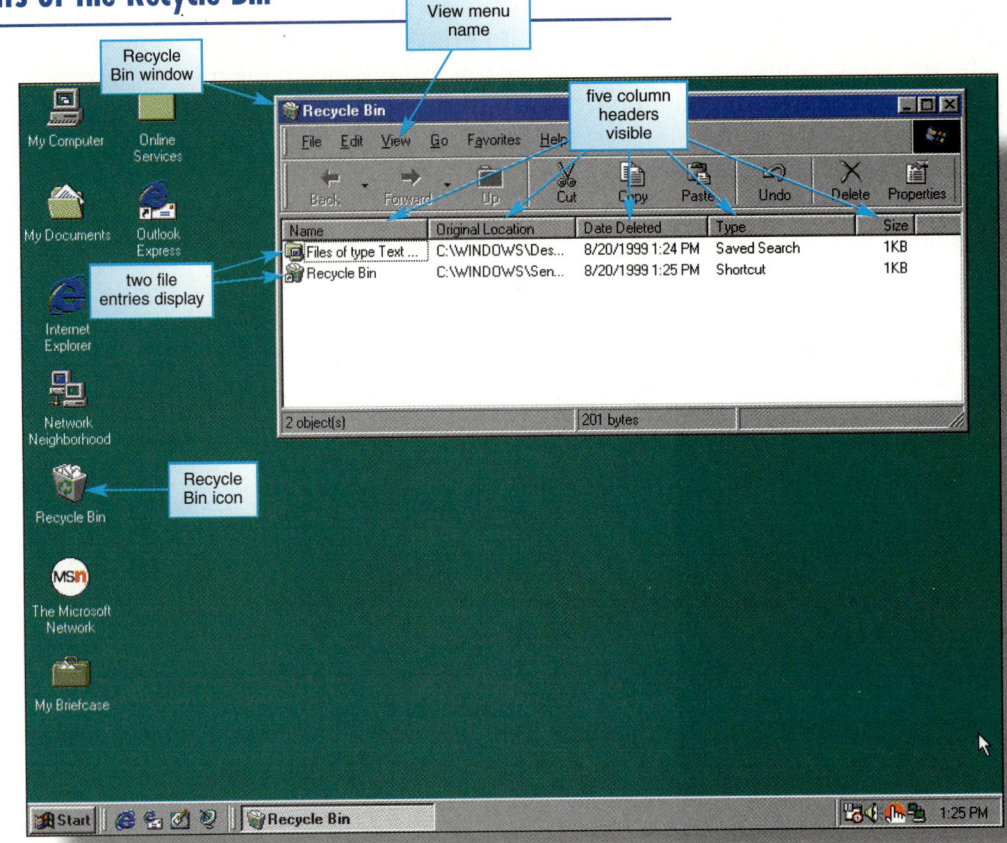

FIGURE 6-30

Restoring a Deleted File, Folder, or Shortcut

Files, folders, or shortcuts deleted in error can be recovered using the Recycle Bin. When you delete a file or shortcut and then restore the deleted file or shortcut, the Recycle Bin restores the file or shortcut to its original location. When you delete a folder, only the files within that folder display in the Recycle Bin. If you restore a file that originally was located in a deleted folder, Windows recreates the folder, and then restores the file to the folder. Perform the following steps to restore the Files of type Text Document file that was deleted previously in this project to its original location on the desktop.

The Recycle Bin • WIN 6.23

Steps: To Restore a Deleted File Using the Recycle Bin

1 If necessary, scroll the window to make the Files of type Text Document file name visible. Right-click the Files of type Text Document file name in the Recycle Bin window. Point to Restore on the shortcut menu.

A shortcut menu displays (Figure 6-31).

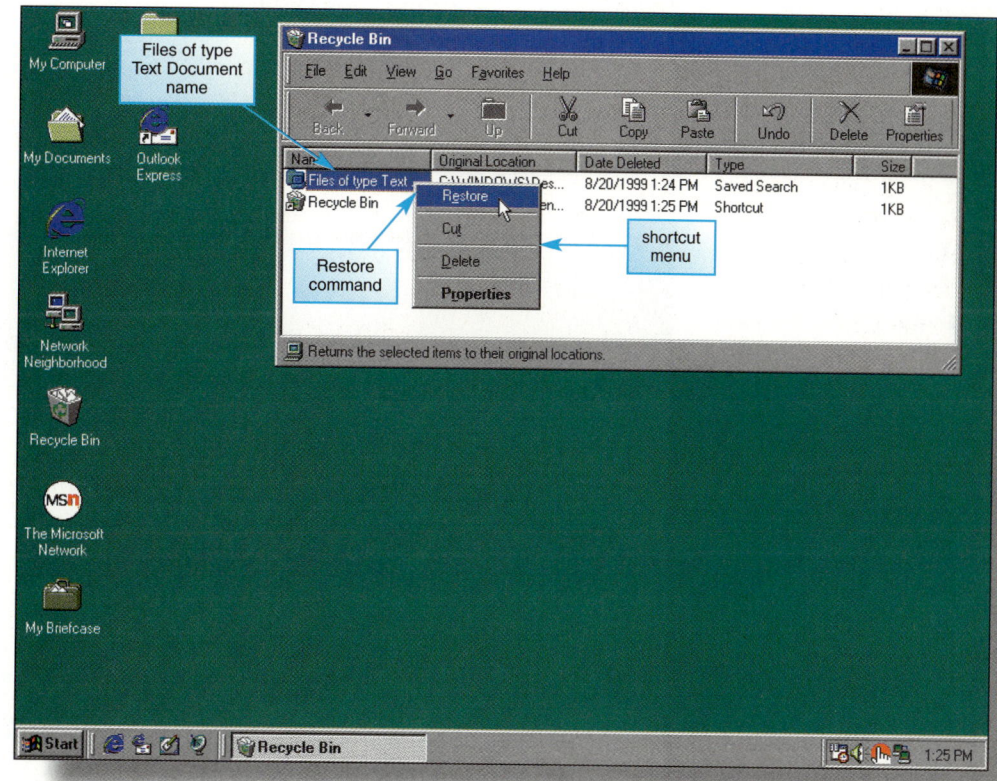

FIGURE 6-31

2 Click Restore.

The Files of type Text Document icon is removed from the Recycle Bin window and the file's icon displays in its original location on the desktop (Figure 6-32).

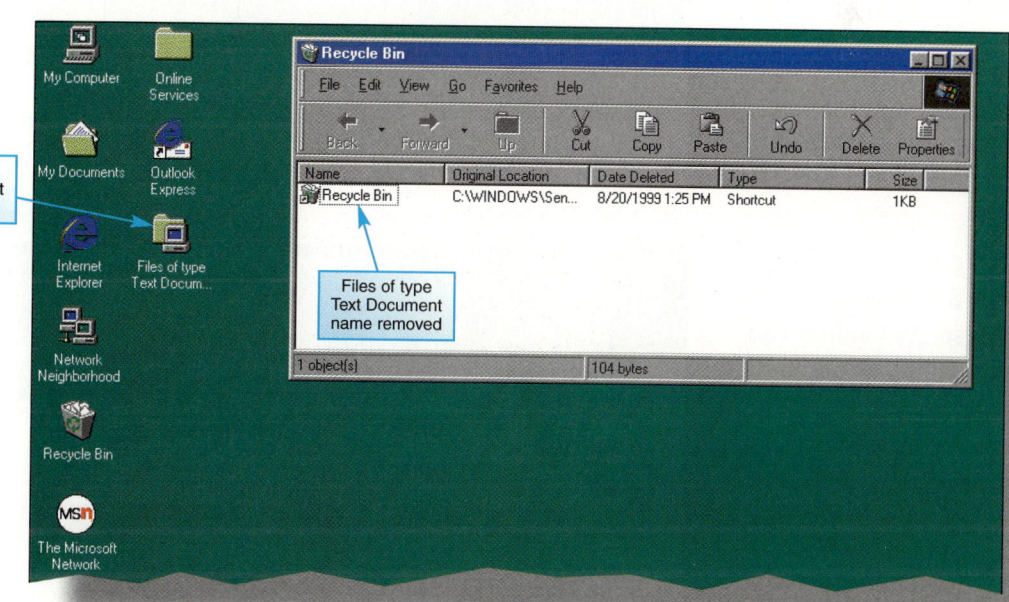

FIGURE 6-32

Other Ways

1. Click file name in Recycle Bin window, on File menu click Restore

WIN 6.24 • Project 6 • Advanced File and Document Management and My Briefcase

Emptying the Recycle Bin

When the Recycle Bin is full or when the files in the Recycle Bin are no longer needed, you should empty the contents of the Recycle Bin. Perform the following steps to empty the Recycle Bin.

 To Empty the Recycle Bin

1 **Right-click the Recycle Bin icon on the desktop. Point to Empty Recycle Bin on the shortcut menu.**

A shortcut menu displays (Figure 6-33).

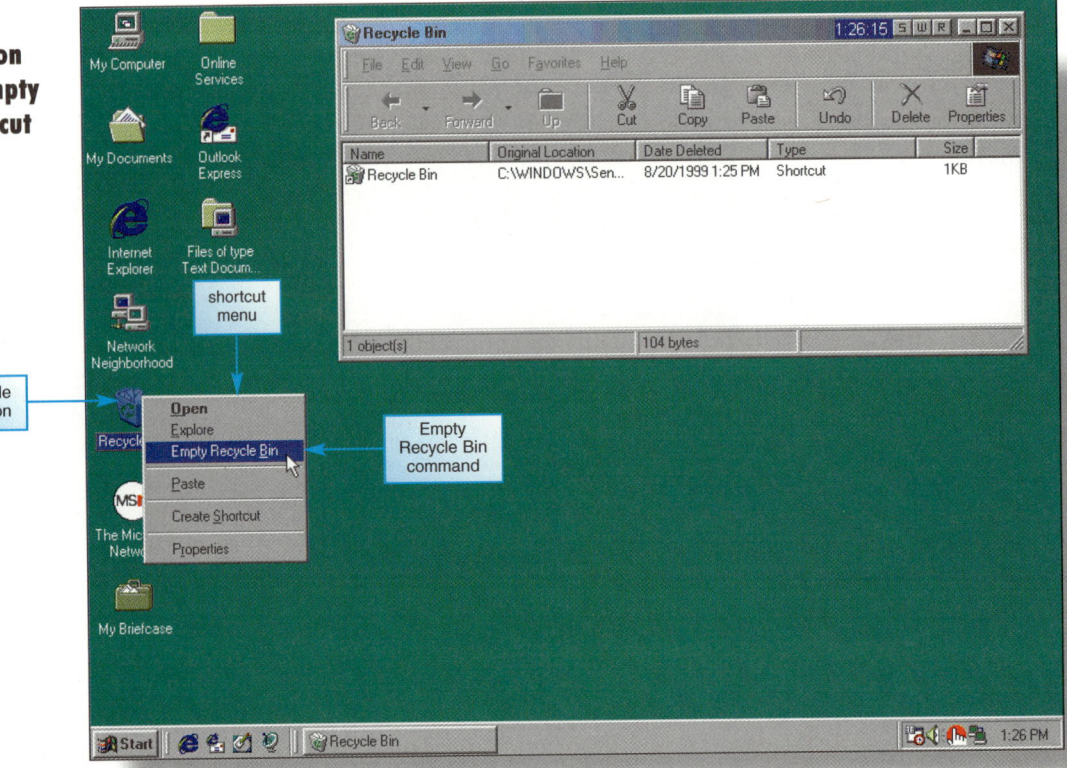

FIGURE 6-33

2 **Click Empty Recycle Bin. Point to the Yes button in the Confirm File Delete dialog box.**

The Confirm File Delete dialog box displays (Figure 6-34). If the Recycle Bin contains multiple files, the Confirm Multiple File Delete dialog box displays instead of the Confirm File Delete dialog box.

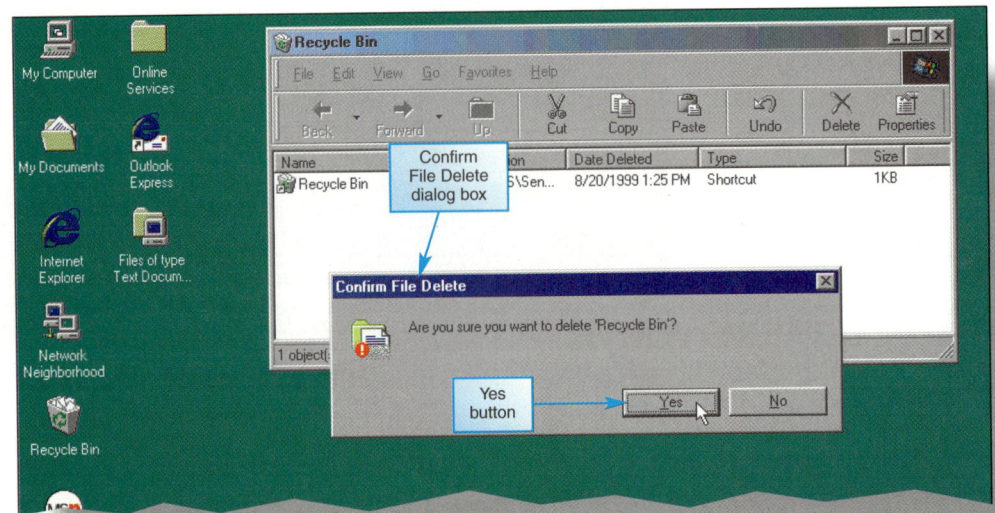

FIGURE 6-34

3 **Click the Yes button.**

The contents of the Recycle Bin are removed (Figure 6-35).

4 **Click the Close button in the Recycle Bin window.**

The Recycle Bin window closes.

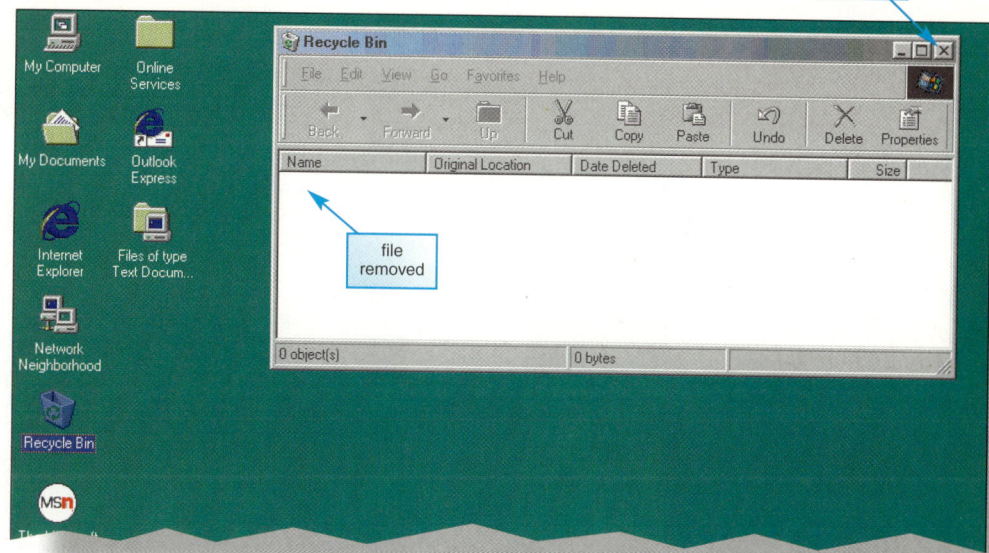

FIGURE 6-35

Other Ways

1. In Recycle Bin window, on File menu click Empty Recycle Bin, click Yes button
2. Right-click My Computer icon, click Explore, right-click Recycle Bin icon, click Empty Recycle Bin on shortcut menu, click Yes button
3. Right-click Start button, click Explore, right-click Recycle Bin icon, click Empty Recycle Bin on shortcut menu, click Yes button

Viewing Recycle Bin Properties

As mentioned previously, changing the properties of the Recycle Bin allows you to choose to delete files without first sending them to the Recycle Bin, choose to display or not display a confirmation dialog box when a file is deleted, and change the amount of disk space reserved by the Recycle Bin. Perform the following steps to view the Recycle Bin properties.

To View the Recycle Bin Properties

1 **Right-click the Recycle Bin icon on the desktop. Point to Properties on the shortcut menu.**

A shortcut menu displays (Figure 6-36).

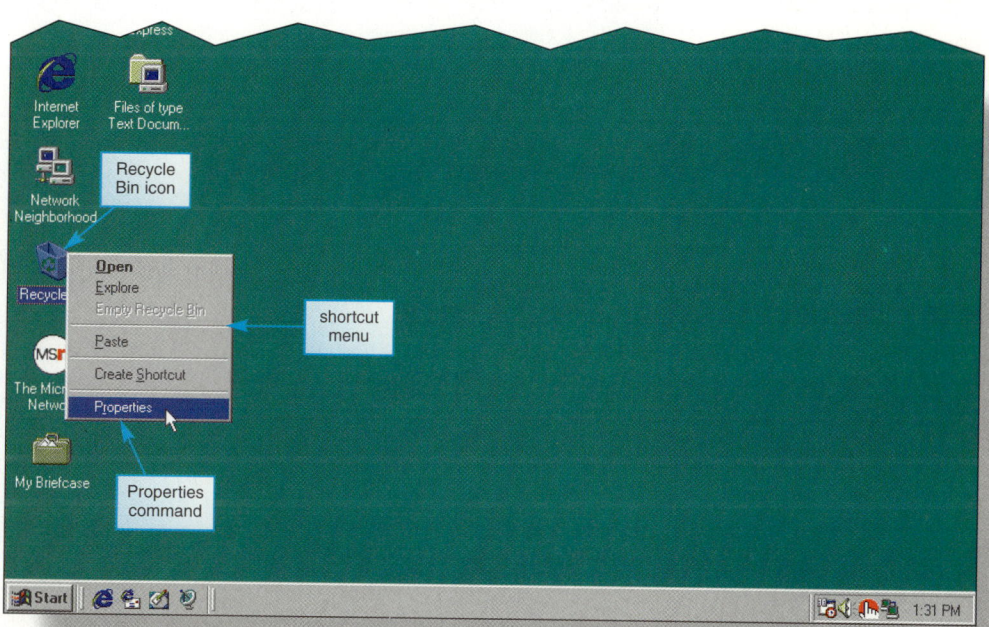

FIGURE 6-36

2 Click Properties. If necessary, click the Global tab.

The Recycle Bin Properties dialog box and Global sheet display (Figure 6-37). The Use one setting for all drives option button is selected, the maximize size of the Recycle Bin is set to 10%, a slider allows you to select the size of the Recycle Bin, and the Display delete confirmation dialog check box is selected. This dialog box may display additional tabbed sheets.

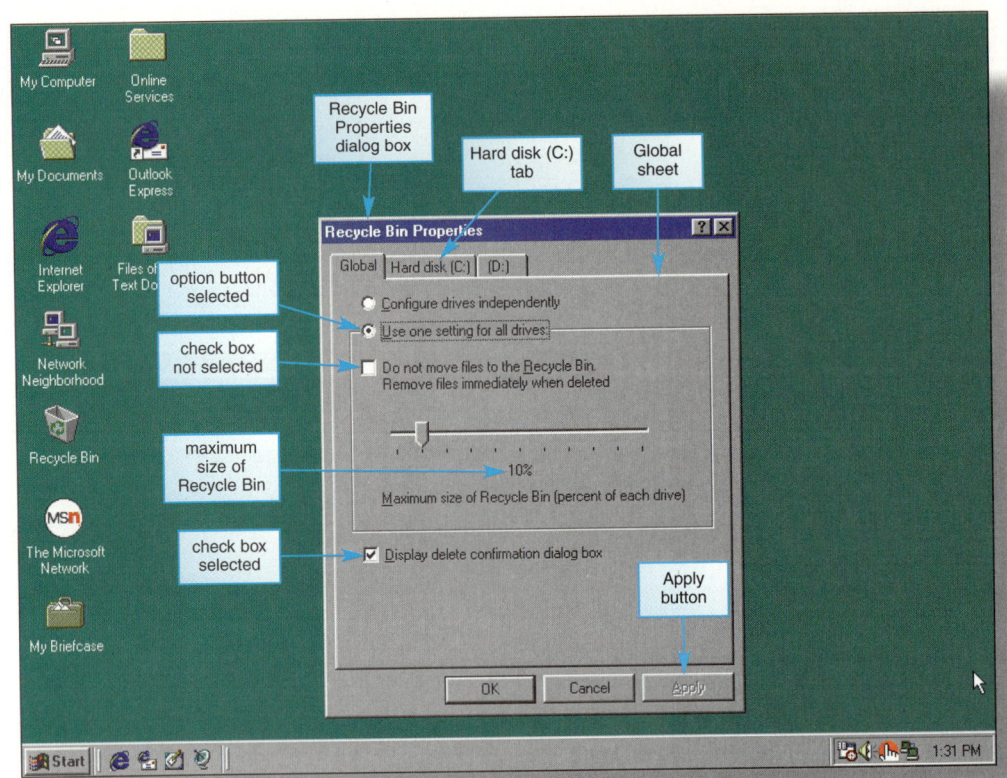

FIGURE 6-37

3 Click the Hard disk (C:) tab.

The Hard disk (C:) sheet indicates the size of the first area on the hard disk (1.99GB) and the space reserved for the Recycle Bin (204MB) (Figure 6-38). The settings on the Global sheet cause the check box and slider to display dimmed.

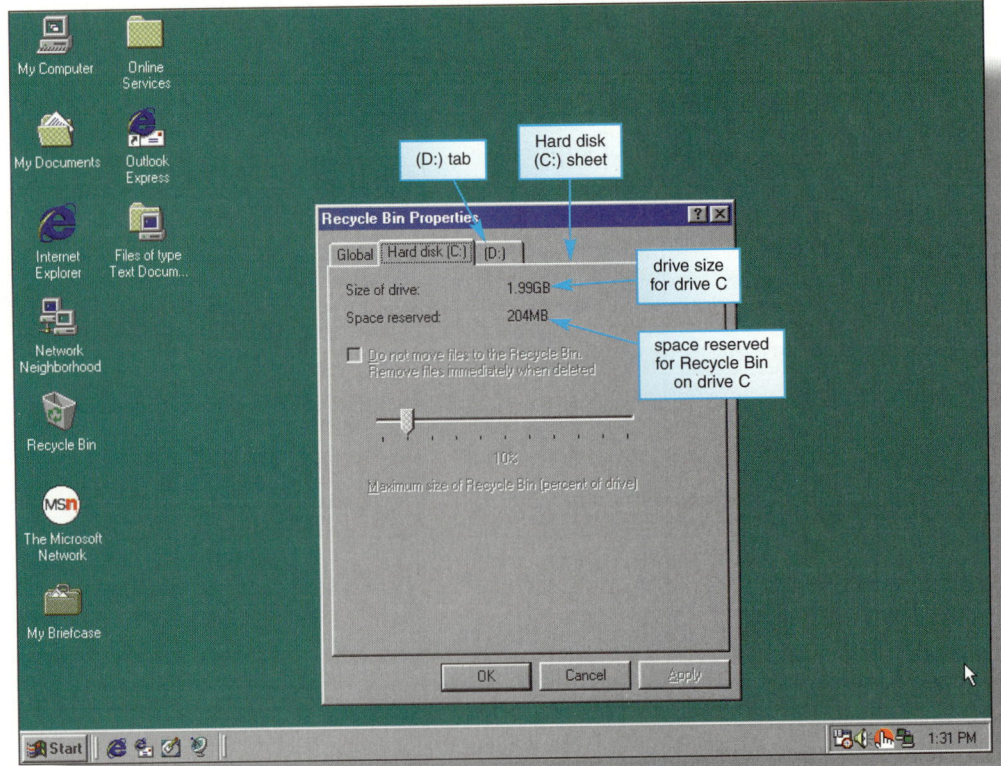

FIGURE 6-38

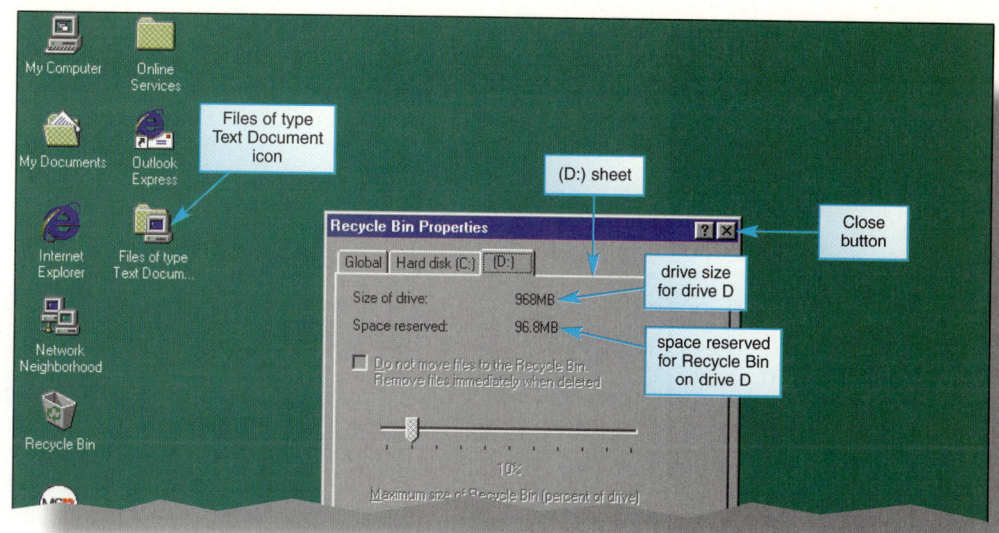

4 If the (D:) tab displays in your Recycle Bin Properties dialog box, click the (D:) tab.

The (D:) sheet indicates the size of the second area on the hard disk (968MB) and the space reserved for the Recycle Bin (96.8MB) (Figure 6-39).

5 Click the Close button.

FIGURE 6-39

In Figure 6-37, Use one setting for all drives is selected instead of Configure drives independently because only one disk drive is connected to the computer (drive C and drive D are two areas on the same physical disk drive). The check box below the option buttons is not selected, which indicates all deleted files are sent to the Recycle Bin. The maximum size of the Recycle Bin is set at 10% of the disk drive. The Display delete confirmation dialog box is selected, indicating that a confirmation dialog box displays whenever a file is deleted. To change the amount of disk space the Recycle Bin requires, you must drag the slider to the desired amount and then click the Apply button.

Removing the Saved Search File

The Files of type Text Document icon remains on the desktop (see Figure 6-39). To restore the desktop to its original configuration, remove the Files of type Bitmap Image icon by performing the following steps.

TO REMOVE THE SAVED SEARCH FILE

1 Drag the Files of type Text Document icon to the Recycle Bin icon.

2 Click the Yes button in the Confirm File Delete dialog box.

The Files of type Text Document file is removed from the desktop.

Using the Find Command to Search for Information on the Internet

The Find command also allows you to search for information on the Internet using a search service. A **search service** allows you to enter a **keyword** (a word or phrase) about a topic in which you are interested, searches for Web pages on the World Wide Web that contain the keyword, and then displays a list of hyperlinks that you can click to display the associated Web pages.

This section uses the **Alta-Vista search service** to search the Internet for information. Perform the following steps to use Alta-Vista to search the Internet for information about the 1976 Presidential Election.

To Find Information on the Internet

1 If necessary, connect to the Internet. Click the Start button, point to Find, and then point to On the Internet.

The Start menu and Find submenu display (Figure 6-40).

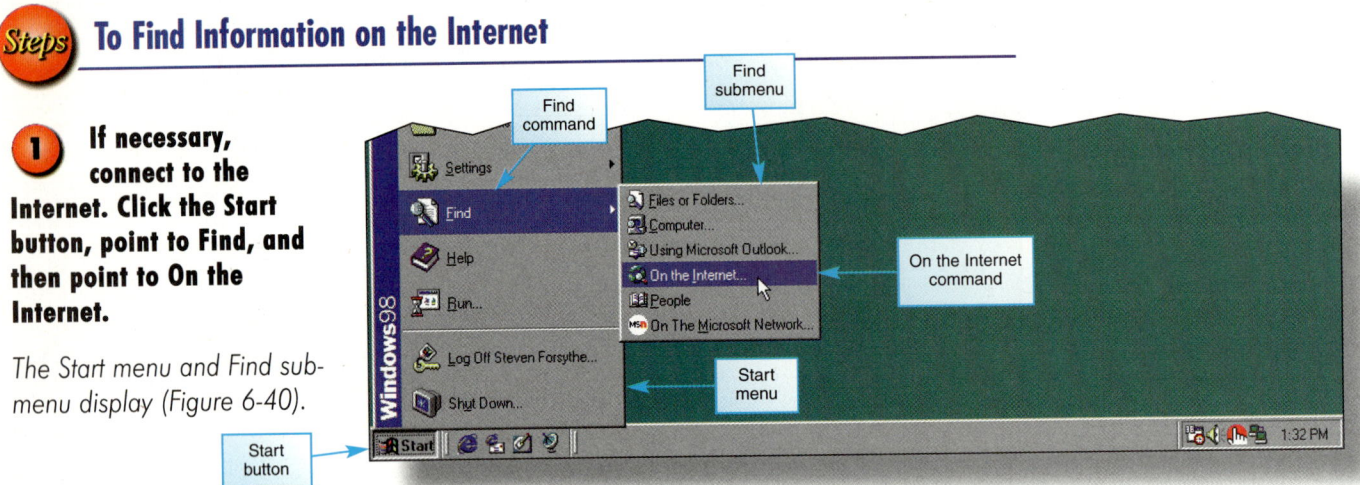

FIGURE 6-40

2 Click On the Internet. If necessary, maximize the Find – Microsoft Internet Explorer window. Click the Alta-Vista option button to select it. Click the white editbox, type 1976 Presidential Election in the white editbox, and point to the Enter button.

Internet Explorer starts, the maximized Find – Microsoft Internet Explorer window displays, and the URL for the Web page displays in the Address bar (Figure 6-41). The Web page consists of three headings (Subject, Word, and Calendar), the white editbox containing the keywords 1976 Presidential Election, the Enter button, and a list of search services (On MSN, Alta-Vista, Infoseek, Excite, and Deja-News). The subject heading and Alta-Vista button are selected.

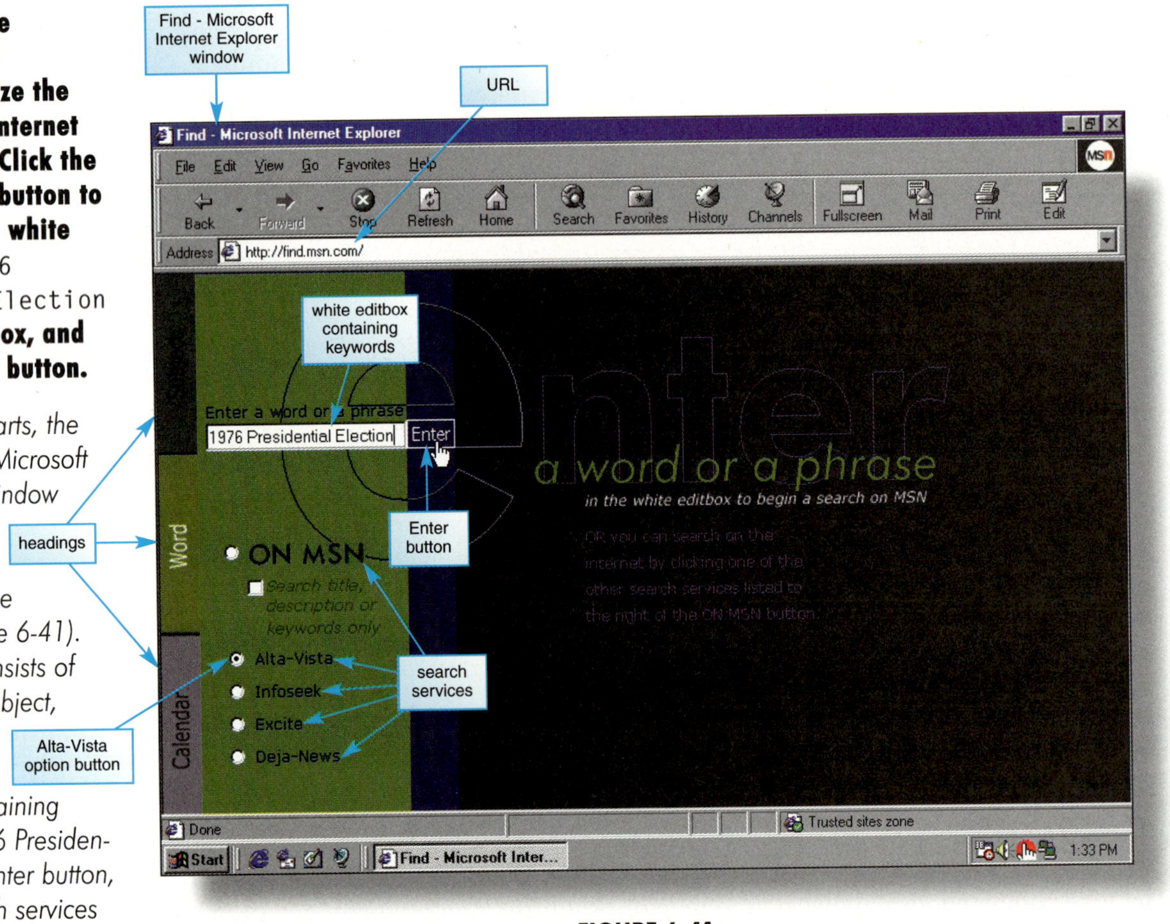

FIGURE 6-41

3 **Click the Enter button. If the Security Alert dialog box displays, click the Yes button. If necessary, scroll the window to display the Presidential Election History – 1976 hyperlink and then point to the hyperlink. If this hyperlink does not display on your computer, point to another hyperlink in the window.**

Alta-Vista searches for and finds 407,127 matches (Figure 6-42). The window title and URL change and the Presidential Election History – 1976 hyperlink displays. Because information on the Internet changes frequently, the hyperlinks that display on your computer may be different.

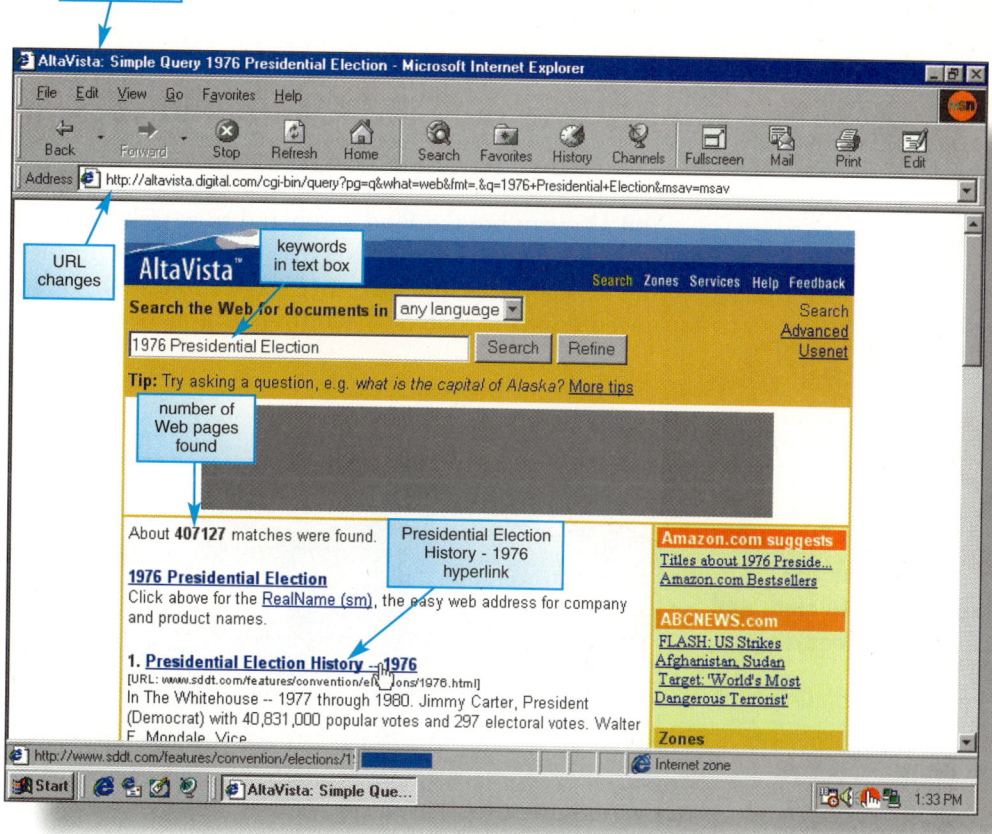

FIGURE 6-42

4 **Click the Presidential Election History – 1976 hyperlink.**

Information about the 1976 presidential election displays in the Microsoft Internet Explorer window (Figure 6-43).

5 **Scroll the window to read the article about the 1976 election. When finished, click the Close button in the Microsoft Internet Explorer window.**

The Microsoft Internet Explorer window closes.

1. Click Start button on taskbar, point to Find, click On the Microsoft Network, click search service, type word or phrase, click Enter button

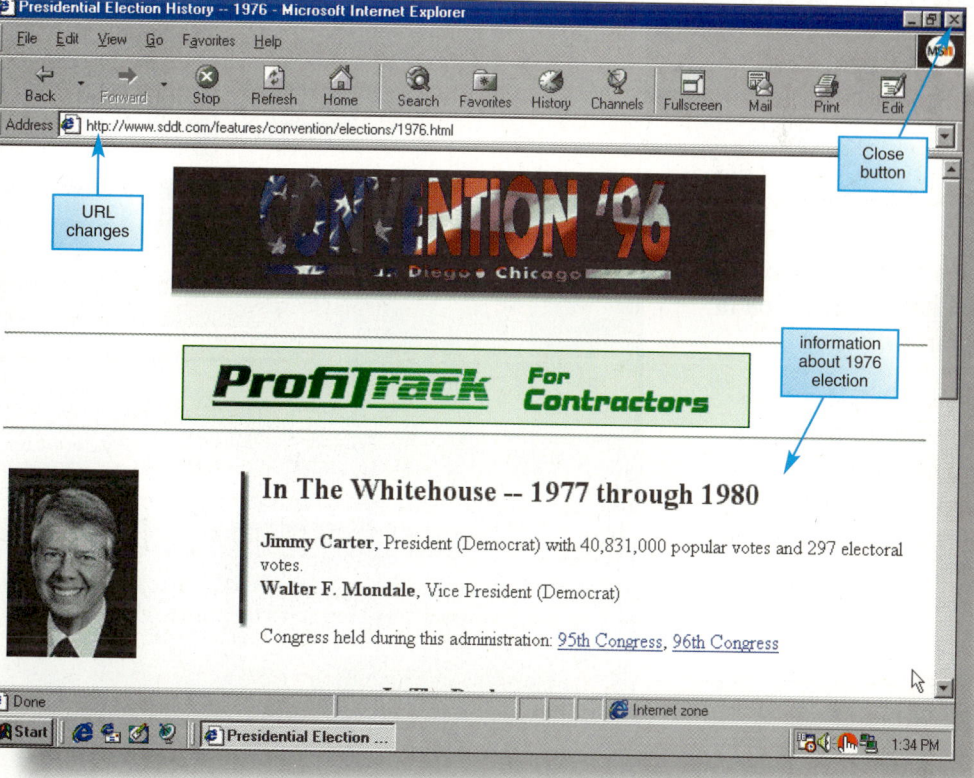

FIGURE 6-43

Using the Find Command to Search for People on the Internet

You also can use the Find command to search for information about an individual whose name or e-mail address you know. Perform the following steps to use the Yahoo! People Search directory service to search the Internet for information about Steven Forsythe, one of the authors of this book.

To Find Information About a Person

1) Click the Start button on the taskbar, point to Find, and then point to People.

The Start menu and Find sub-menu display (Figure 6-44).

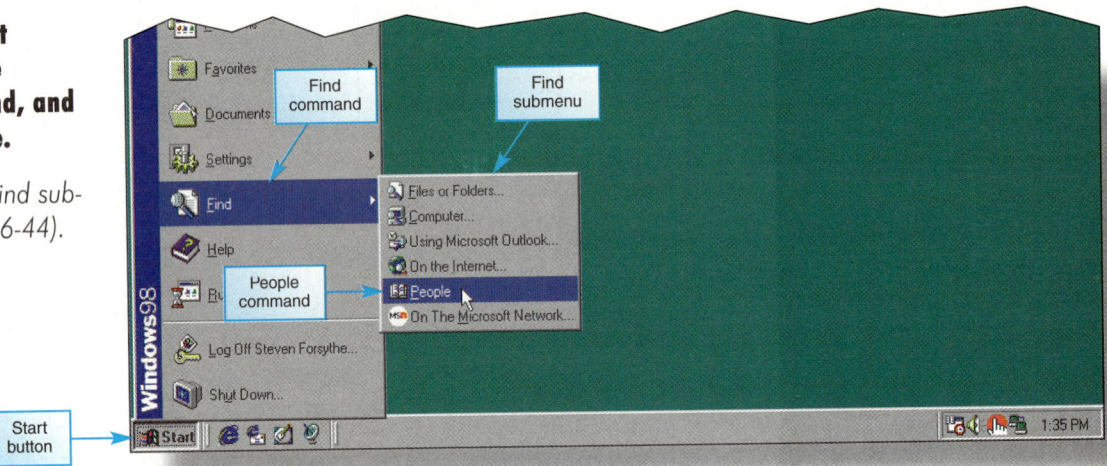

FIGURE 6-44

2) Click People. Type `Steven Forsythe` **in the Name text box and then point to the Look in box arrow.**

The Find People window opens (Figure 6-45). The Look in box contains the WhoWhere directory service name and the Name text box in the People sheet contains the name, Steven Forsythe. The entry in the Look in box may be different on your computer.

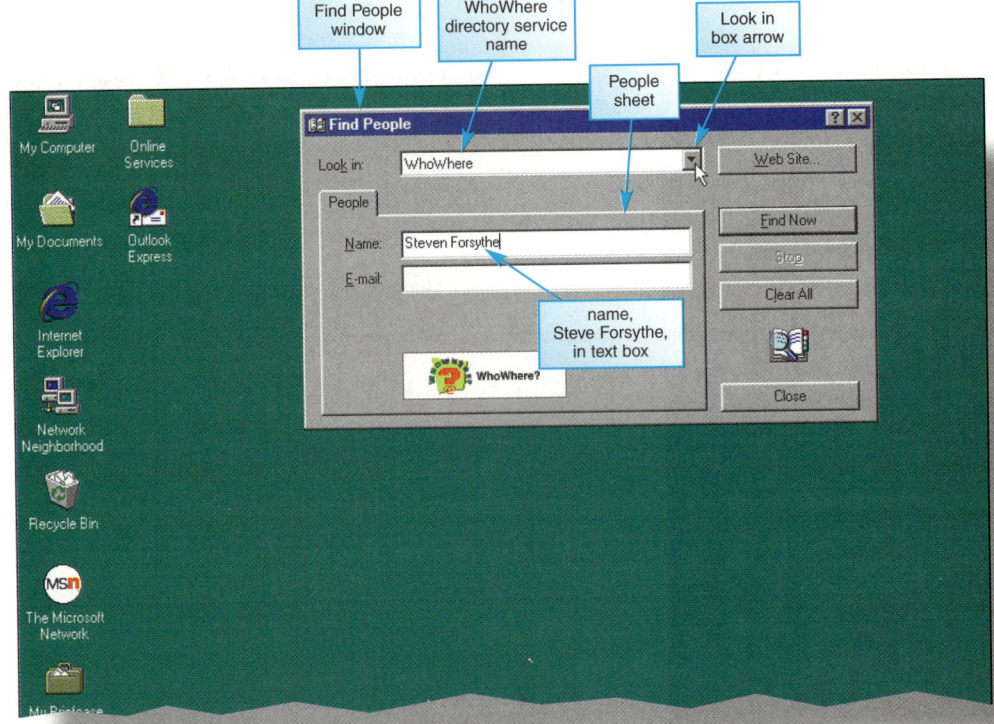

FIGURE 6-45

Using the Find Command to Search for People on the Internet • WIN 6.31

3 **Click the Look in box arrow and then point to Yahoo! People Search.**

The Look in list box displays and the Yahoo! People Search entry is highlighted in the list box (Figure 6-46).

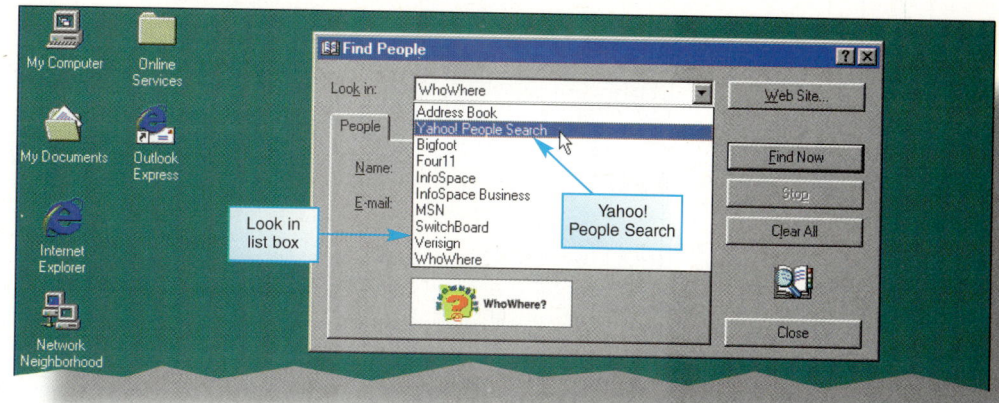

FIGURE 6-46

4 **Click Yahoo! People Search in the list box and then point to the Find Now button.**

The highlighted Yahoo! People Search entry displays in the Look in box (Figure 6-47).

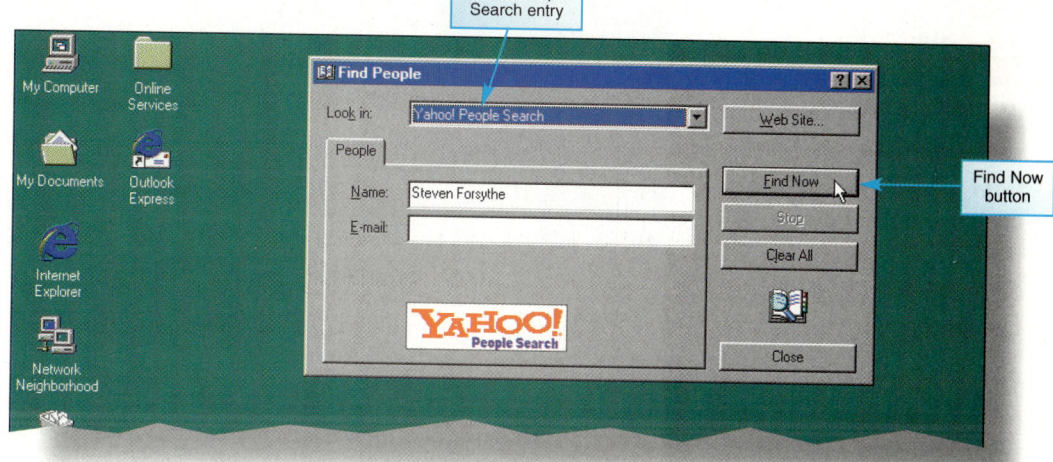

FIGURE 6-47

5 **Click the Find Now button. Click the Steven George Forsythe name preceding the StevenForsythe@msn.com e-mail address and then point to the Properties button.**

A partial list of names and e-mail addresses displays in the People sheet list box (Figure 6-48). The highlighted entry contains the name and e-mail address for Steven Forsythe, the author.

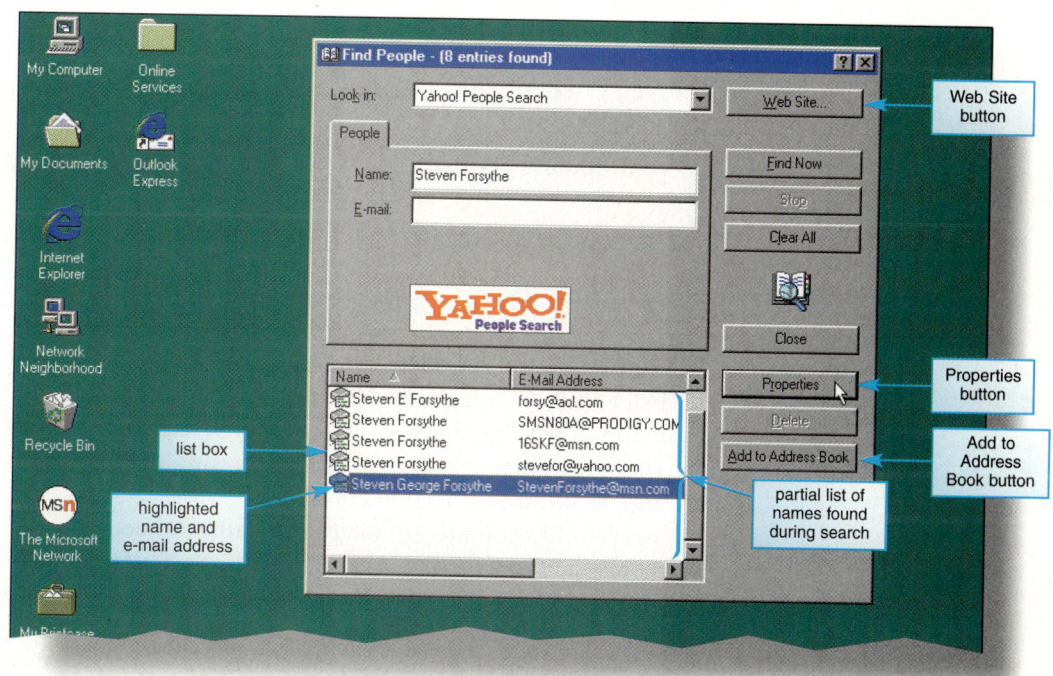

FIGURE 6-48

WIN 6.32 • Project 6 • Advanced File and Document Management and My Briefcase

 Click the Properties button.

The Steven George Forsythe Properties dialog box displays (Figure 6-49). The Personal sheet contains personal information about Steven Forsythe. Additional tabbed sheets (Home, Business, Other, NetMeeting, and Digital IDs) contain additional information about the individual.

 **When finished viewing the information, click the Close button in the Steven George Forsythe Properties dialog box and then click the Close button in the Find People – (8 entries found) window.**

The Steven George Forsythe and Find People dialog boxes close.

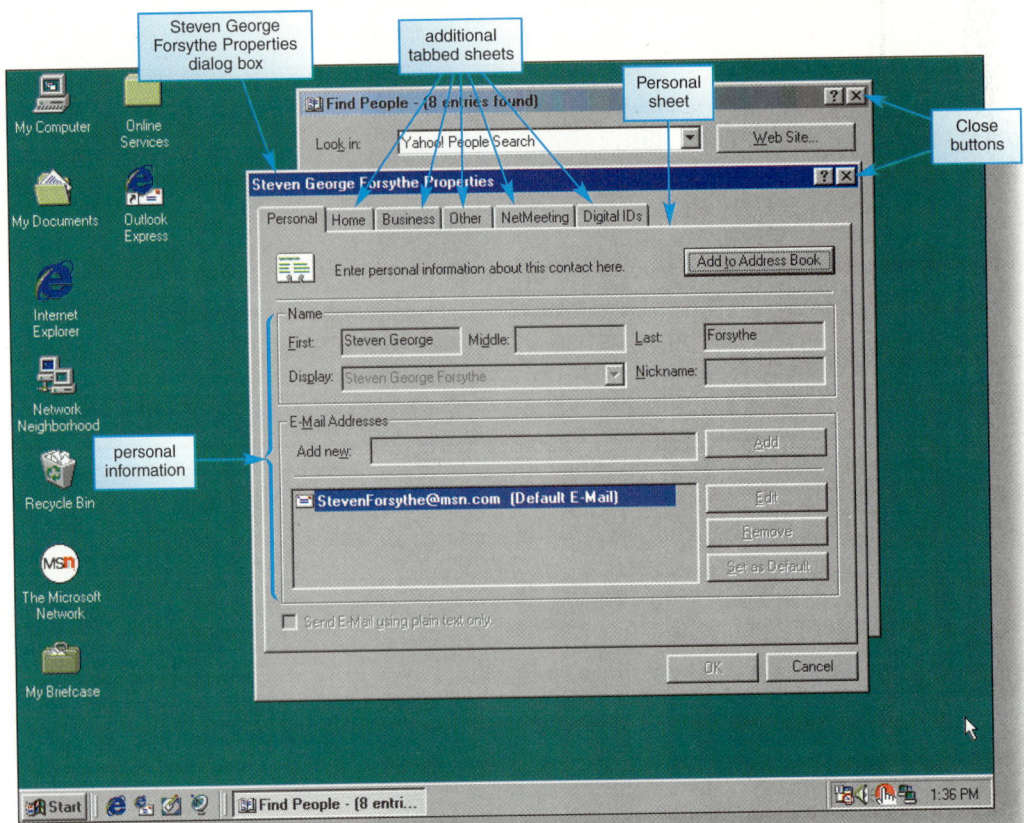

FIGURE 6-49

More About

Searching for People on the Internet

Yahoo! gathers information about people from many sources. For example, telephone data is gathered from local telephone companies. People who do not have a listing with their local telephone company or who have an unpublished telephone number are not listed.

In Figure 6-48 on the previous page, clicking a name in the list box and then clicking the Properties button displays personal and business information about a person. Clicking the Web Site button starts Microsoft Internet Explorer and displays the Yahoo Web site. Clicking the Add to Address Book button adds this entry to your address book and then you may use it to send e-mail messages to that person.

My Briefcase

My Briefcase was designed to allow a computer user to work on the same file on more than one computer and update the original file automatically when changes are made to the file on the other computer. You can use My Briefcase when working with two different computers, two computers on the same network, or a computer and a laptop or portable computer.

Assume you are an insurance claims adjuster and must visit three clients today to assess damages to their homes or offices. Three files, one for each client, are located on the desktop of your office computer. Each file contains the policy number, name, address, telephone number, and description of the damage. When you leave the office to visit the three clients, you want each client's file on your laptop computer.

Before leaving the office, you copy the three files on the desktop of your office computer to the My Briefcase icon on the desktop and move the My Briefcase icon to the laptop computer using either a 3½-inch floppy disk or a direct cable connection. While visiting a client, you open My Briefcase on the laptop computer and make any necessary changes or additions to the client's file. After visiting all three clients, you return to the office and move the My Briefcase icon from the laptop computer to the office computer using the 3½-inch floppy disk or direct cable connection. Next, you use My Briefcase to update the original files on the office computer with the changes made to the files on the laptop computer.

Before you leave the office, your secretary creates three new files on the desktop of your office computer, one file for each client you must visit. Use the steps and techniques that follow to create these files on the desktop.

> **More About**
>
> **My Briefcase**
>
> Windows 98 allows you to have more than one My Briefcase icon on the desktop. To create a second icon, right-click the desktop, point to New on the shortcut menu, and click Briefcase on the New submenu. Windows names the newly created icon, New Briefcase, thus eliminating any confusion between the two icons.

Creating the Three Files on the Desktop

The first file to create is for Robert Moore. The document contains his policy number, name, address, telephone number, and a summary of the damage. Perform the following steps to create the file on the desktop, open the file, enter client information, and save the file on the desktop.

TO CREATE THE ROBERT MOORE FILE ON THE DESKTOP

1. Right-click an open area on the desktop. Point to New on the shortcut menu and then click Text Document on the New submenu.

2. Type Robert Moore in the object name text box and then press the ENTER key.

3. Double-click the Robert Moore icon to display the Robert Moore - Notepad window.

4. Type HP 3550966 06 (policy number) and then press the ENTER key twice.

5. Type Robert Moore and then press the ENTER key.

6. Type 113 Pacific Drive and then press the ENTER key.

7. Type Dana Point, CA 92629 and then press the ENTER key.

8. Type (714) 555-8354 and then press the ENTER key twice.

9. Type Description: water damage - master bath and then press the ENTER key.

10. Click File on the menu bar and then click Save.

11. Click the Close button in the Robert Moore - Notepad window.

The second file to create is for Carol Young. The file contains her policy number, name, address, telephone number, and description of the damage. Perform the steps on the next page to create the file for Carol Young.

TO CREATE THE CAROL YOUNG FILE ON THE DESKTOP

1. Right-click an open area on the desktop. Point to New on the shortcut menu and then click Text Document on the New submenu.
2. Type `Carol Young` in the object name text box and then press the ENTER key.
3. Double-click the Carol Young icon to display the Carol Young - Notepad window.
4. Type `HP 2719803 30` (policy number) and then press the ENTER key twice.
5. Type `Carol Young` and then press the ENTER key.
6. Type `1785 Central Drive` and then press the ENTER key.
7. Type `Redondo Beach, CA 90277` and then press the ENTER key.
8. Type `(714) 555-6102` and then press the ENTER key twice.
9. Type `Description: concrete damage from earthquake` and then press the ENTER key.
10. Click File on the menu bar and then click Save.
11. Click the Close button in the Carol Young - Notepad window.

The third file to create is for Peter Hollister. The file contains the same information as the previous two files. Perform the following steps to create the file for Peter Hollister.

TO CREATE THE PETER HOLLISTER FILE ON THE DESKTOP

1. Right-click an open area of the desktop. Point to New on the shortcut menu and then click Text Document on the New submenu.
2. Type `Peter Hollister` in the object name text box and then press the ENTER key.
3. Double-click the Peter Hollister icon to display the Peter Hollister - Notepad window.
4. Type `HP 2698013 12` (policy number) and then press the ENTER key twice.
5. Type `Peter Hollister` and then press the ENTER key.
6. Type `987 Arbor Avenue` and then press the ENTER key.
7. Type `Huntington Beach, CA 92647` and then press the ENTER key.
8. Type `(714) 555-1324` and then press the ENTER key twice.
9. Type `Description: broken garage door` and then press the ENTER key.
10. Click File on the menu bar and then click Save.
11. Click the Close button in the Peter Hollister - Notepad window.

Three files, one for each client, have been created and arranged on the desktop (Figure 6-50).

FIGURE 6-50

Dragging the Three Files to My Briefcase

Prior to leaving the office, you will copy the three files on the desktop of your office computer to My Briefcase by dragging their icons. Then you should verify that they were copied prior to leaving for the client appointments. Follow the steps below to drag the three icons to the My Briefcase icon.

TO DRAG THE THREE FILES TO THE MY BRIEFCASE ICON

1. Drag the Robert Moore icon to the My Briefcase icon.
2. Drag the Carol Young icon to the My Briefcase icon.
3. Drag the Peter Hollister icon to the My Briefcase icon.

The Copying dialog box displays momentarily while each file is copied to My Briefcase. The original Robert Moore, Carol Young, and Peter Hollister files, called **synchronized copies**, remain on the desktop and a copy of each file is moved to My Briefcase (Figure 6-51).

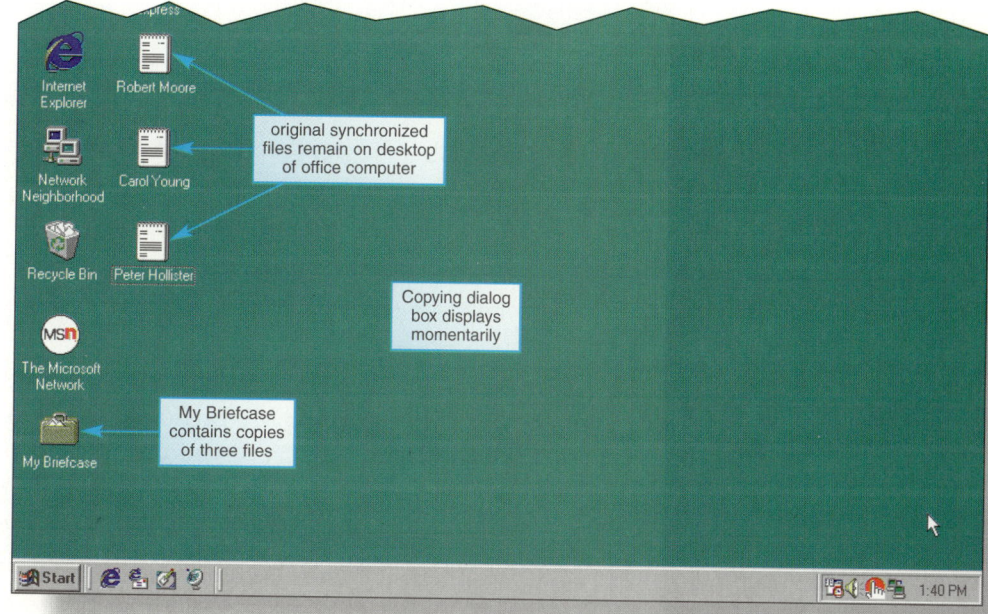

FIGURE 6-51

Viewing the Contents of My Briefcase

After copying the Robert Moore, Carol Young, and Peter Hollister files to My Briefcase, perform the following steps to view the files in the My Briefcase window and verify the files were copied correctly.

To View the Contents of My Briefcase

1 **Double-click the My Briefcase icon. Click View on the menu bar and then click Details.**

The My Briefcase window opens. The window consists of six column headers below the menu bar (Figure 6-52). If all six headers are not visible, you can resize the window to make the headers visible. The Carol Young, Peter Hollister, and Robert Moore names display below the Name header. Each entry includes a file name along with the location of the synchronized file copy, file status, file size, file type, and date and time of last modification.

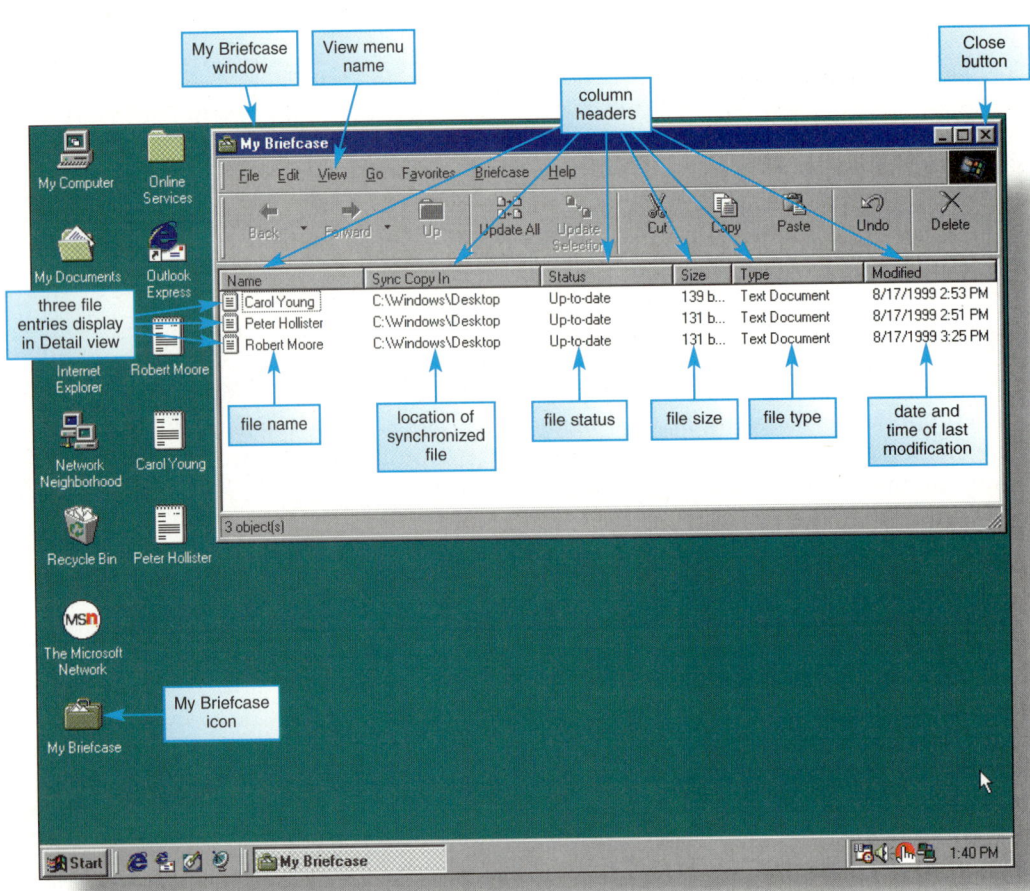

2 **Click the Close button in the My Briefcase window.**

The My Briefcase window closes.

FIGURE 6-52

Moving My Briefcase to a Floppy Disk

After copying the files to the My Briefcase icon, you must move My Briefcase to a formatted floppy disk in drive A so you can transport the files in My Briefcase to the laptop computer. Perform the following steps to move My Briefcase to a floppy disk.

My Briefcase • WIN 6.37

PROJECT 6

 To Move My Briefcase to a Floppy Disk

1 Insert a formatted floppy disk in drive A of your computer.

2 Right-click the My Briefcase icon and then point to Send To on the shortcut menu. Point to 3½ Floppy (A).

A shortcut menu and Send To submenu display (Figure 6-53).

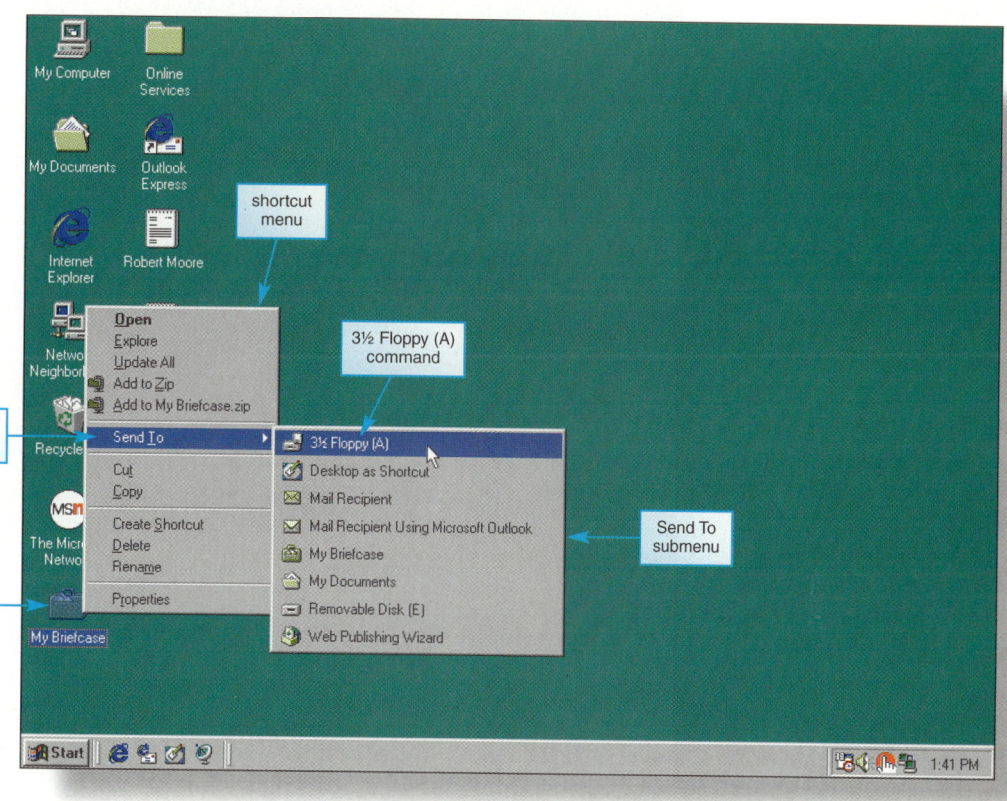

FIGURE 6-53

3 Click 3½ Floppy (A).

A Moving dialog box displays as the My Briefcase icon and the contents of My Briefcase are moved from the desktop to the floppy disk in drive A (Figure 6-54). In Figure 6-54, the Robert Moore file is being moved.

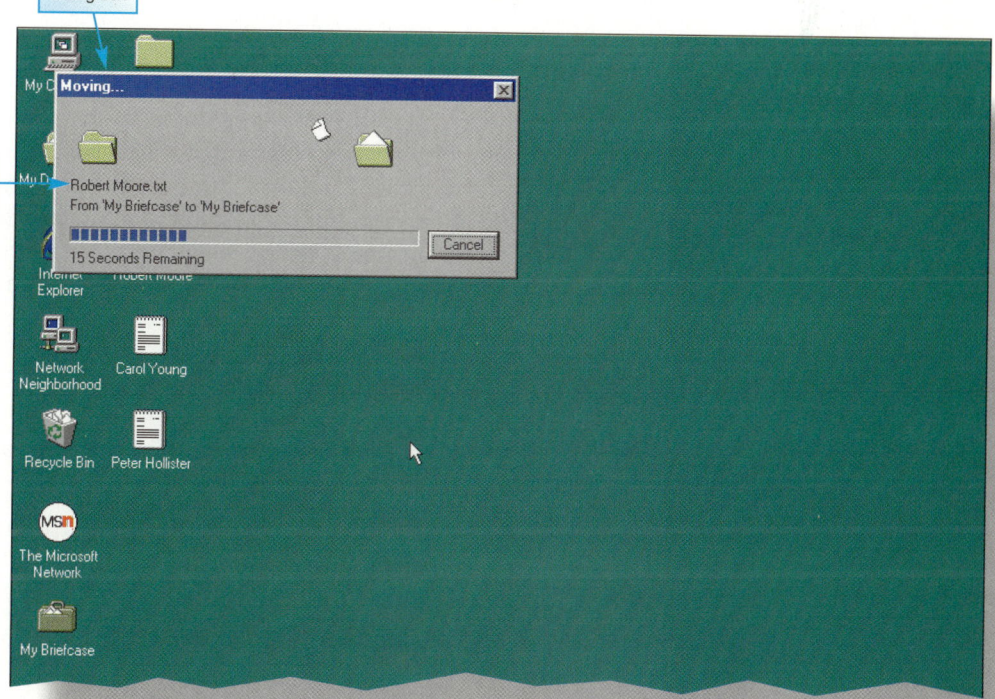

FIGURE 6-54

④ Remove the floppy disk from drive A of your computer.

After the Move operation is complete, the Moving dialog box closes and the My Briefcase icon is removed from the desktop (Figure 6-55). The original three files remain on the desktop.

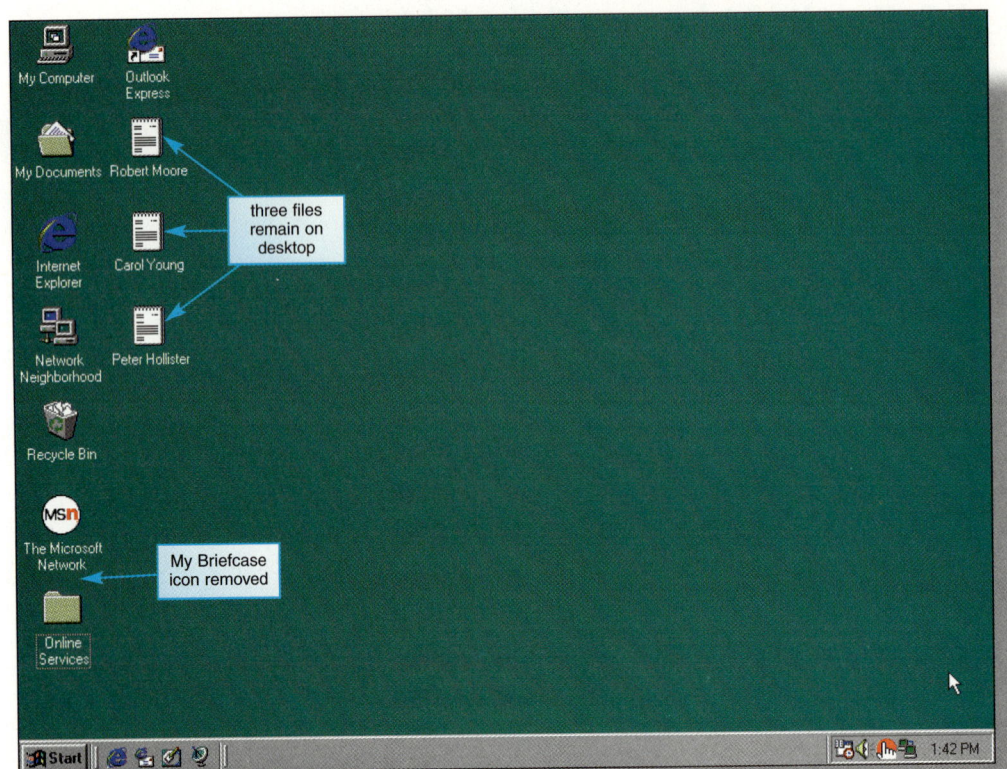

FIGURE 6-55

After moving My Briefcase containing the three files to the floppy disk, you leave the office to visit Robert Moore, Peter Hollister, and Carol Young.

Changing the Files on the Office Computer

After you leave the office, Peter Hollister calls and informs your secretary that his telephone number has been changed to 555-1342. In addition, your secretary realizes the policy number for Carol Young's policy is incorrect in the file on the desktop of your office computer. The policy number, incorrectly recorded as HP 2719803 30, should be HP 2719803 03. Your secretary makes the changes for you.

The following steps change the telephone number in the Peter Hollister file on the desktop of your office computer.

TO CHANGE THE PETER HOLLISTER FILE

① Double-click the Peter Hollister icon on the desktop to display the Peter Hollister - Notepad window.

② Type 555-1342 as the new telephone number.

③ Click File on the menu bar and then click Save.

④ Click the Close button in the Peter Hollister - Notepad window to close the window.

The change made to the Peter Hollister file on the desktop after performing Step 2 is shown in Figure 6-56.

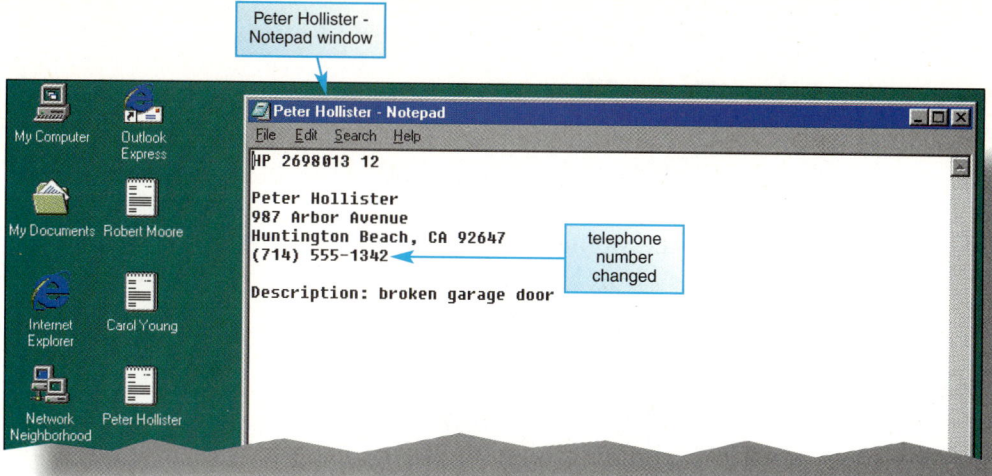

FIGURE 6-56

Changing the Peter Hollister file on the desktop causes the contents of the Peter Hollister file on the desktop and the Peter Hollister file in My Briefcase on the laptop computer to be different. The copy on the desktop contains the most current information.

Next, Carol Young's policy number should be changed to HP 2719803 03. The following steps change the policy number in the Carol Young file on the desktop of your office computer.

TO CHANGE THE CAROL YOUNG FILE

1. Double-click the Carol Young icon to display the Carol Young - Notepad window.

2. Type HP 2719803 03 as the new policy number.

3. Click File on the menu bar and then click Save.

4. Click the Close button in the Carol Young - Notepad window to close the window.

The change made to the Carol Young file on the desktop after performing Step 2 is shown in Figure 6-57.

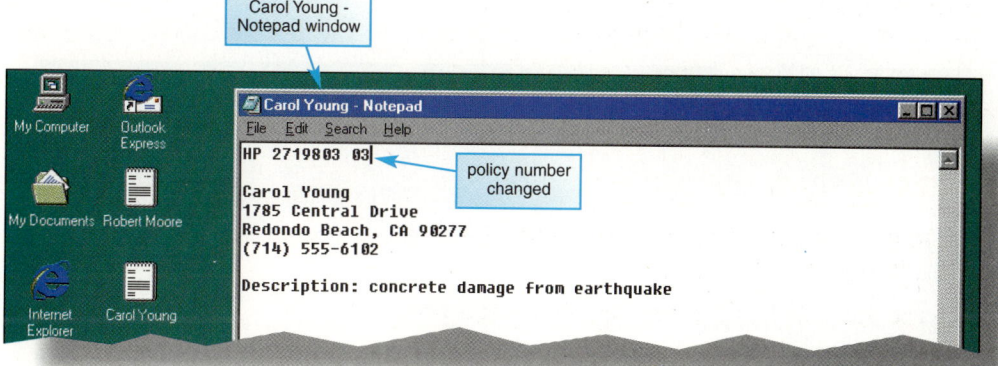

FIGURE 6-57

Changing the Carol Young file on the desktop causes the contents of the Carol Young file on the desktop and the Carol Young file in My Briefcase on the laptop computer to be different. The copy on the desktop contains the most current information.

Changing the Robert Moore File

After leaving the office, your first stop is Robert Moore's business office. You assess the water damage and determine the repair costs to be $1,375. You decide to add the comment, Cost to repair: $1,375.00, to the end of the Robert Moore file while at Robert Moore's business office. Perform the following steps to make the changes to the Robert Moore file in My Briefcase on the laptop computer.

 To Change the Robert Moore File

1 Turn on the laptop computer (or a second computer that is available). Start Windows 98. Insert the floppy disk from the office computer into drive A.

2 Double-click the My Computer icon on the desktop. Double-click the 3½ Floppy (A:) icon in the My Computer window. Double-click the My Briefcase icon in the 3½ Floppy (A:) window to display the My Briefcase window. Point to the Robert Moore icon.

The My Briefcase window opens (Figure 6-58).

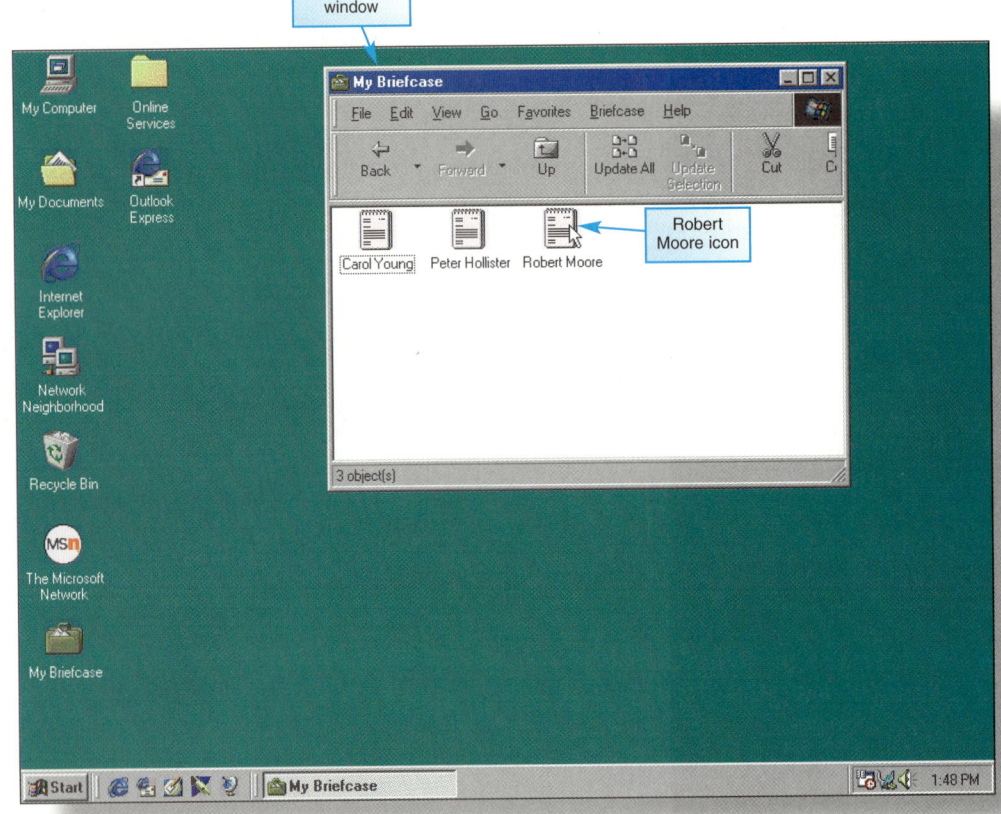

FIGURE 6-58 Desktop of Laptop Computer

3 Double-click the Robert Moore icon to open the document. Use the arrow keys to move the insertion point to the end of the document, type Cost to repair: $1,375.00 and then press the ENTER key.

The Robert Moore document displays with the comment added (Figure 6-59).

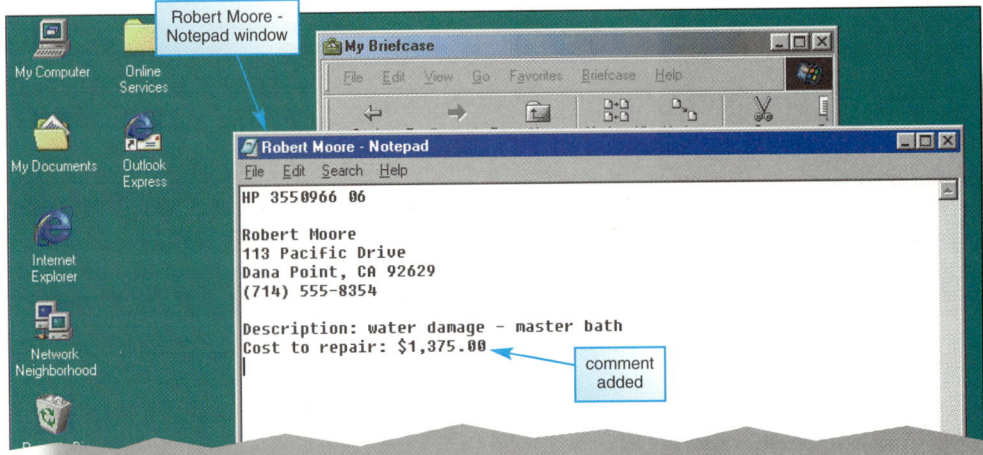

FIGURE 6-59 Desktop of Laptop Computer

④ **Click File on the menu bar and then click Save to save the changes to the document. Click the Close button in the Robert Moore window to close the window. Click the Close button in the My Briefcase window.**

The changes to the Robert Moore file are saved and the Robert Moore – Notepad and My Briefcase windows close (Figure 6-60).

⑤ **Remove the floppy disk from drive A. Quit Windows 98.**

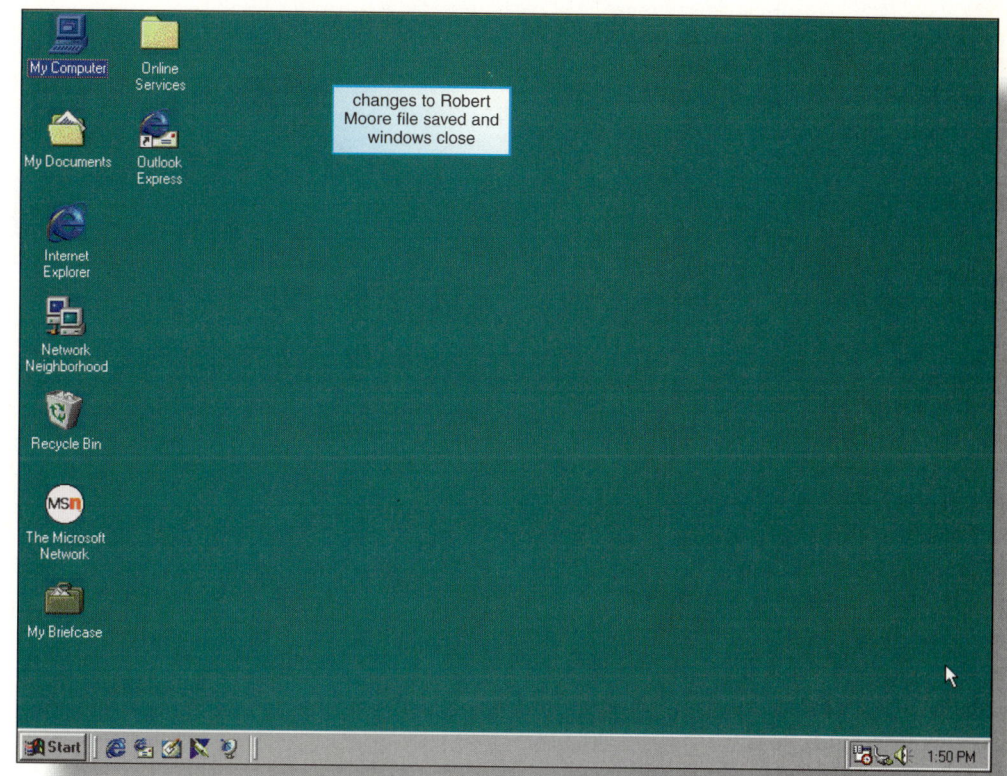

FIGURE 6-60 Desktop of Laptop Computer

Changing the Robert Moore file in My Briefcase causes the contents of the Robert Moore file in My Briefcase on the laptop computer and the Robert Moore file on the desktop of the office computer to be different. The copy of the file in My Briefcase contains the most current information.

Changing the Peter Hollister File

Next, you leave Robert Moore's office and drive to Peter Hollister's house. In your conversation, Peter tells you that he called your office and gave his new telephone number to your secretary, but the number he gave your secretary was incorrect. The correct telephone number is 555-1344. In addition, you assess damage to the broken garage door and determine the repair costs to be $500. You decide to make the telephone number change and add the comment, Cost to repair: $500.00, to the end of the Peter Hollister file while at Peter Hollister's house. Perform the steps on the next page to change the telephone number and add a comment to the end of the file on the laptop computer.

WIN 6.42 • Project 6 • Advanced File and Document Management and My Briefcase

Steps   To Change the Peter Hollister File

1 **Turn on the laptop computer (or a second computer that is available). Start Windows 98. Insert the floppy disk from the office computer into drive A.**

2 **Double-click the My Computer icon on the desktop. Double-click the 3½ Floppy (A:) icon in the My Computer window. Double-click the My Briefcase icon. Double-click the Peter Hollister icon. Type** 555-1344 **as the new telephone number. Position the insertion point at the end of the document, type** Cost to repair: $500.00 **and then press the ENTER key.**

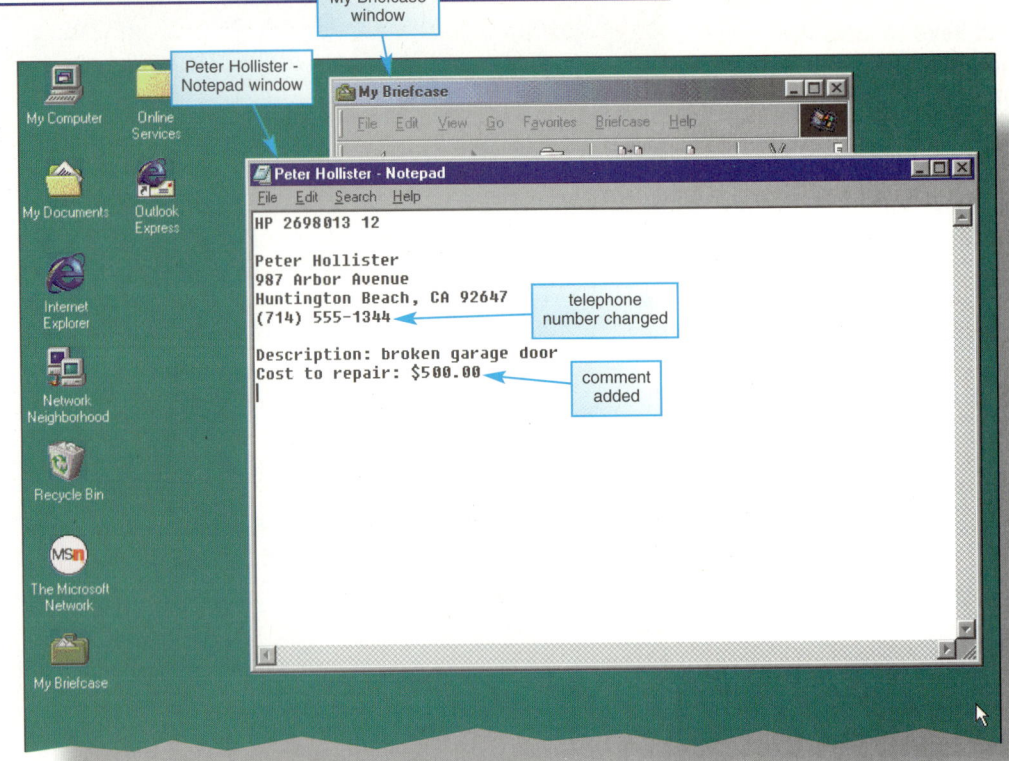

FIGURE 6-61 Desktop of Laptop Computer

The My Briefcase and Peter Hollister - Notepad windows open (Figure 6-61). The Peter Hollister document displays with the new telephone and a comment added.

3 **Click File on the menu bar and then click Save. Click the Close button in the Peter Hollister - Notepad window. Click the Close button in the My Briefcase window.**

The changes to the Peter Hollister file are saved and the two windows close (Figure 6-62).

4 **Remove the floppy disk from drive A. Quit Windows 98.**

FIGURE 6-62 Desktop of Laptop Computer

Previously, an incorrect telephone number (555-1342) was entered in the Peter Hollister file on the desktop on the office computer by your secretary. The Peter Hollister file in My Briefcase on the laptop computer contains the correct number (555-1344). Your last stop is Carol Young's house. In this case, you determine that the damage is not covered by her insurance policy and, therefore, no change is required to the Carol Young file. You return to the office. Previously, the policy number in the Carol Young file was changed on the desktop of the office computer by your secretary. As a result, the Carol Young file in My Briefcase on the laptop computer and the Carol Young file on the desktop are different. The copy of the file on the desktop of the office computer contains the most current information.

Synchronizing the Files

Upon returning to the office, you move My Briefcase from the floppy disk to the desktop of the office computer and synchronize the files. **Synchronizing**, or updating, involves checking each file in My Briefcase against the corresponding synchronized file (original file) on the desktop and updating the files on the desktop if necessary. You synchronize the file using the **Update All button** on the Standard Buttons toolbar in the My Briefcase window. Perform the following steps to move My Briefcase from the floppy disk to the desktop of the office computer.

 To Move My Briefcase to the Desktop of the Office Computer

1 Insert the floppy disk into drive A of the office computer.

2 Double-click the My Computer icon to open the My Computer window. Double-click the 3½ Floppy (A:) icon in the My Computer window to open the 3½ Floppy (A:) window. Point to the My Briefcase icon in the 3½ Floppy (A:) window.

The 3½ Floppy (A:) window displays (Figure 6-63). The three synchronized files display on the desktop of the office computer.

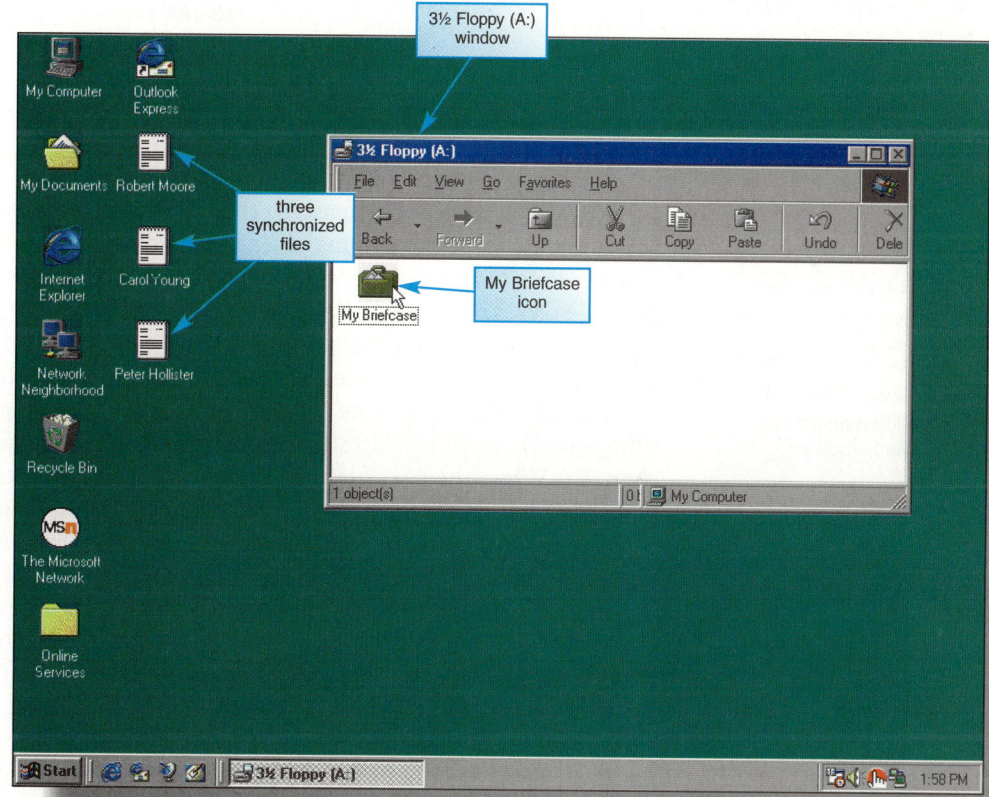

FIGURE 6-63

3 **Drag the My Briefcase icon from the 3½ Floppy (A:) window to the desktop.**

A Moving dialog box displays as the My Briefcase icon is moved from the 3½ Floppy (A:) window to the desktop. After the move operation, the My Briefcase icon displays on the desktop and the My Briefcase icon is removed from the 3½ Floppy (A:) window (Figure 6-64).

4 **Click the Close button in the 3½ Floppy (A:) window and then remove the floppy disk from drive A of the office computer.**

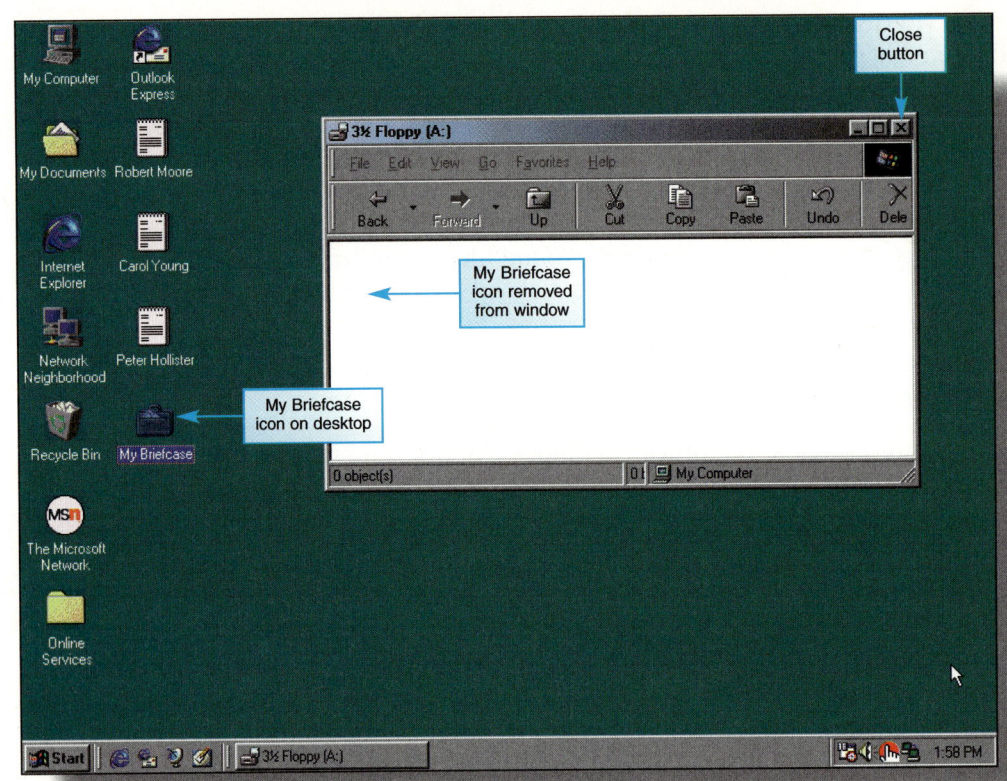

FIGURE 6-64

Synchronizing Files

When a decision must be made as to which file should be replaced while synchronizing files, My Briefcase determines which file to replace based on the date and time the files were modified.

Synchronizing the Files Using My Briefcase

After moving My Briefcase to the desktop, you now must synchronize the files in My Briefcase with the original files on the desktop.

Previously, a comment was added to the Robert Moore file in My Briefcase (Cost to repair: $1,375.00), but the Robert Moore file on the desktop of the office computer was not changed. When the files are synchronized, the Robert Moore file on the desktop must be replaced with the Robert Moore file in My Briefcase.

The policy number was changed in the Carol Young file on the desktop of the office computer (HP 2719803 03), but the Carol Young file in My Briefcase was not changed. When the two files are synchronized, the Carol Young file in My Briefcase will be replaced with the Carol Young file on the desktop.

The telephone number in the Peter Hollister file in My Briefcase and the Peter Hollister file on the desktop of the office computer were both changed. The telephone number in the document on the desktop contains an incorrect number (555-1324). The number in the Peter Hollister document in My Briefcase contains the correct number (555-1344). In addition, a comment was added to the Peter Hollister file in My Briefcase (Cost to repair: $500.00). When the two files are synchronized, the decision to replace the Peter Hollister document on the desktop with the Peter Hollister document in My Briefcase must be made.

Perform the following steps to synchronize the files.

My Briefcase • WIN 6.45

 **To Synchronize the Files Using My Briefcase**

1 **Double-click the My Briefcase icon on the desktop. Point to the Update All button on the Standard Buttons toolbar.**

The My Briefcase window opens (Figure 6-65). The My Briefcase window contains the Carol Young, Peter Hollister, and Robert Moore files. According to the entries under the Status header, all three files require updating.

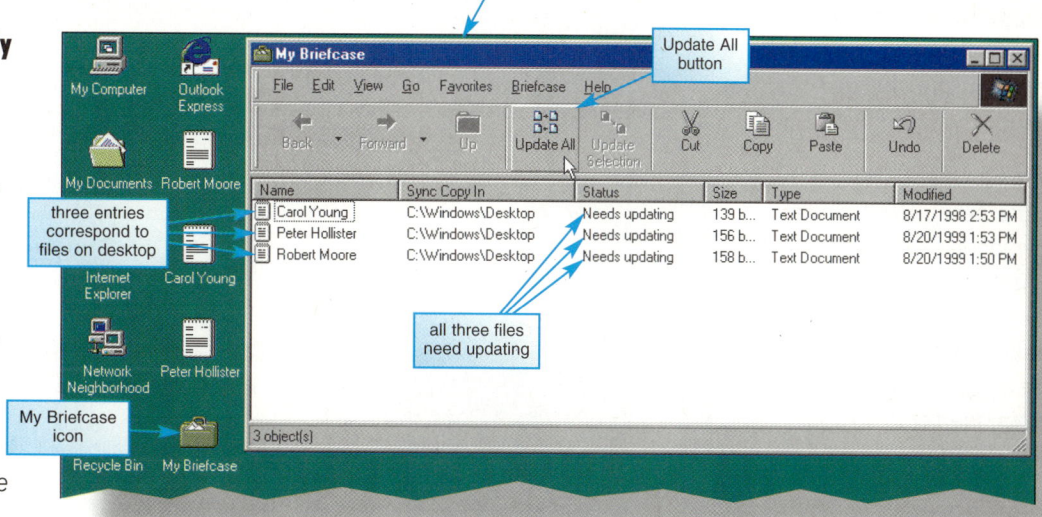

FIGURE 6-65

2 **Click the Update All button. Point to the red down arrow to the right of the Peter Hollister icon.**

The Update My Briefcase dialog box displays, the files in My Briefcase are compared with the synchronized copies on the desktop, and the files that need to be replaced are indicated (Figure 6-66). The Carol Young file in My Briefcase is unmodified, the file on the desktop has been modified, and the file on the desktop should replace the file in My Briefcase (**green left arrow**). Both Peter Hollister files have been modified and a decision must be made as to which file should be replaced (**red down arrow**). The Robert Moore file in My Briefcase has been modified, the file on the desktop is unmodified, and the file in My Briefcase should replace the file on the desktop (**green right arrow**).

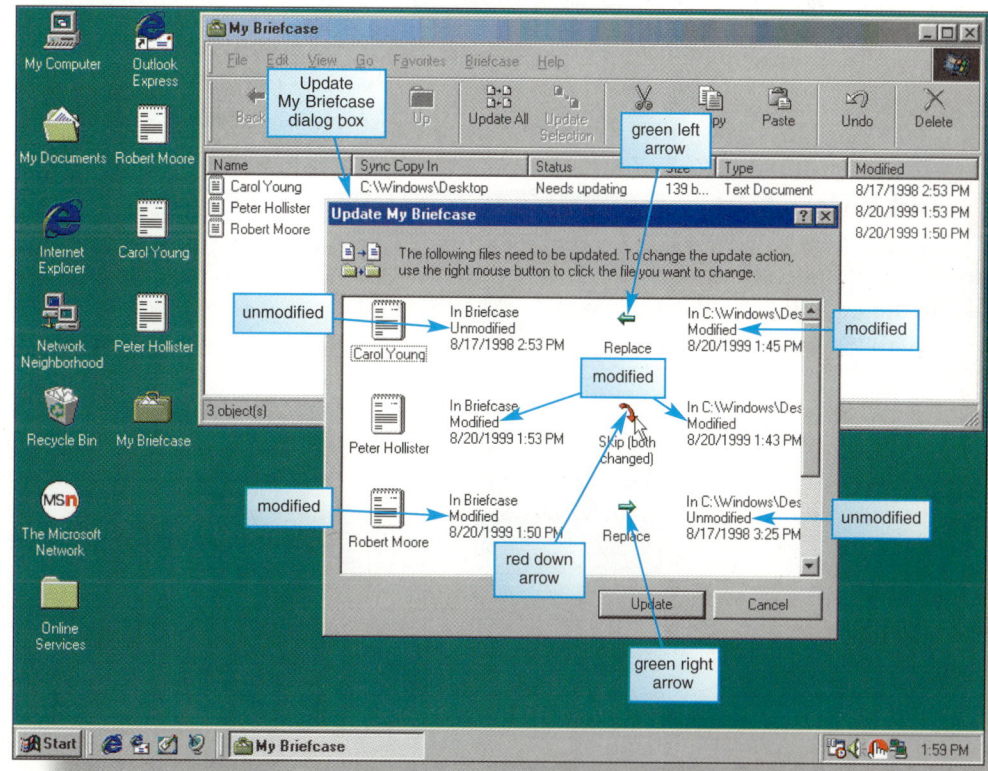

FIGURE 6-66

WIN 6.46 • Project 6 • Advanced File and Document Management and My Briefcase

Microsoft **Windows 98**

③ **Right-click the red down arrow and then point to Replace, identified by the green left arrow, on the shortcut menu.**

A shortcut menu displays (Figure 6-67). Because the information in the Peter Hollister file in My Briefcase is accurate (correct telephone number and a comment added), this file should replace the Peter Hollister file on the desktop.

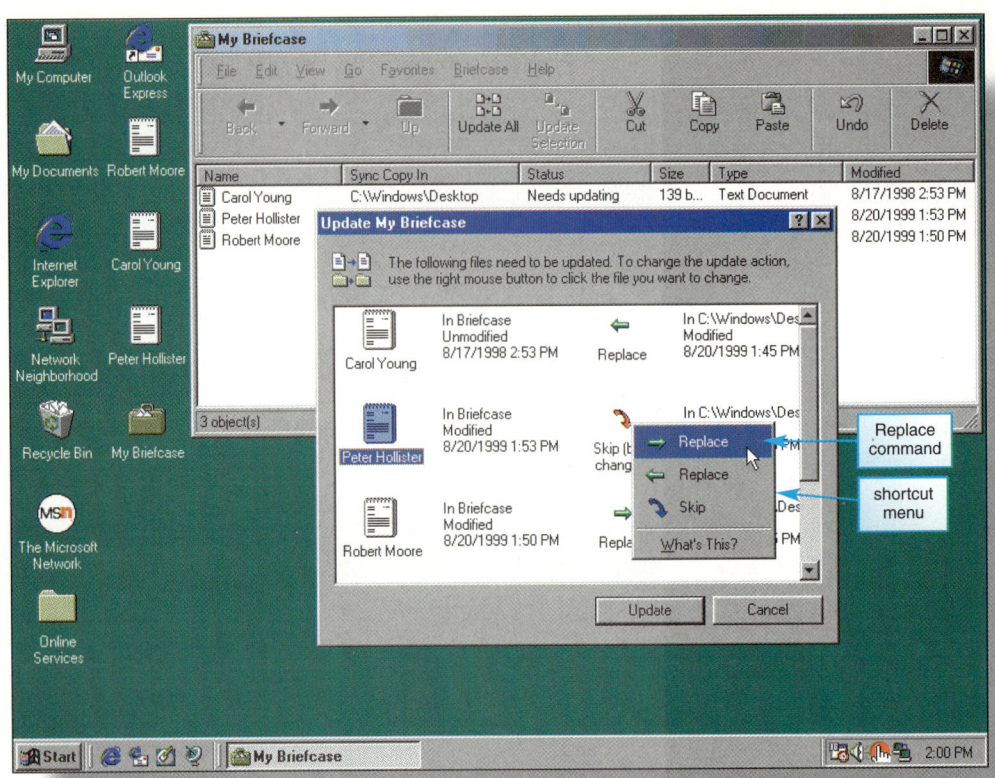

FIGURE 6-67

④ **Click Replace. Point to the Update button in the Update My Briefcase dialog box.**

The red down arrow changes to a green right arrow to indicate the file in My Briefcase will replace the file on the desktop (Figure 6-68).

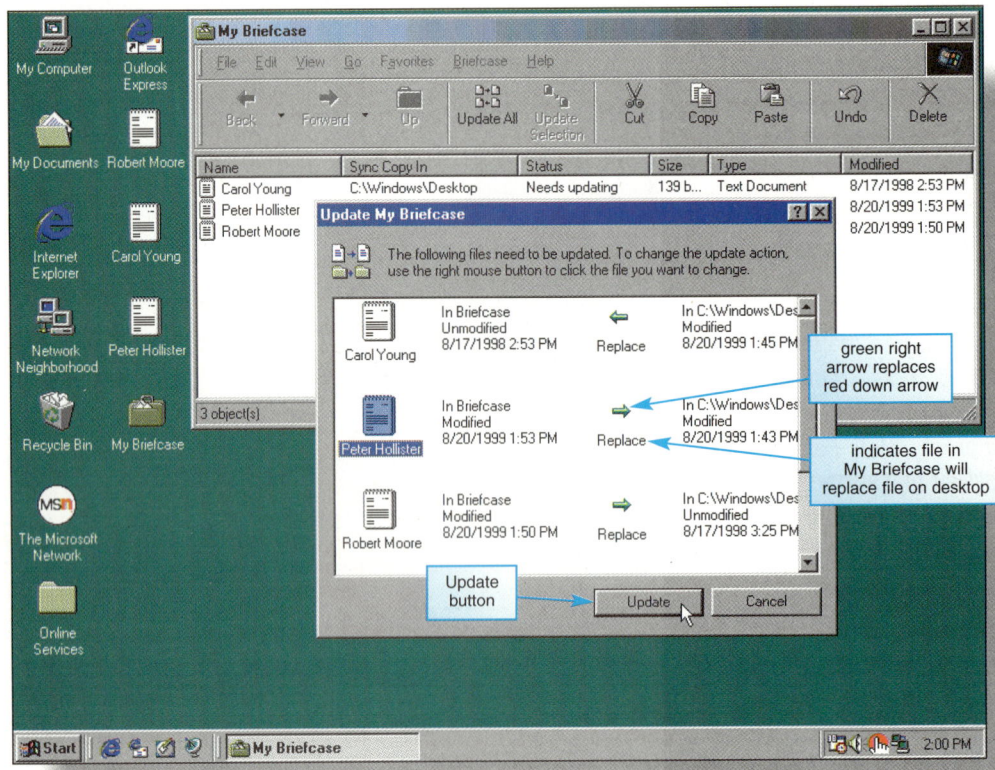

FIGURE 6-68

My Briefcase • WIN 6.47

5 **Click the Update button.**

The Updating Briefcase dialog box displays momentarily while the files are synchronized and then the Update My Briefcase dialog box closes. The entries below the Status header in the My Briefcase widow indicate that each file currently is Up-to-date (Figure 6-69).

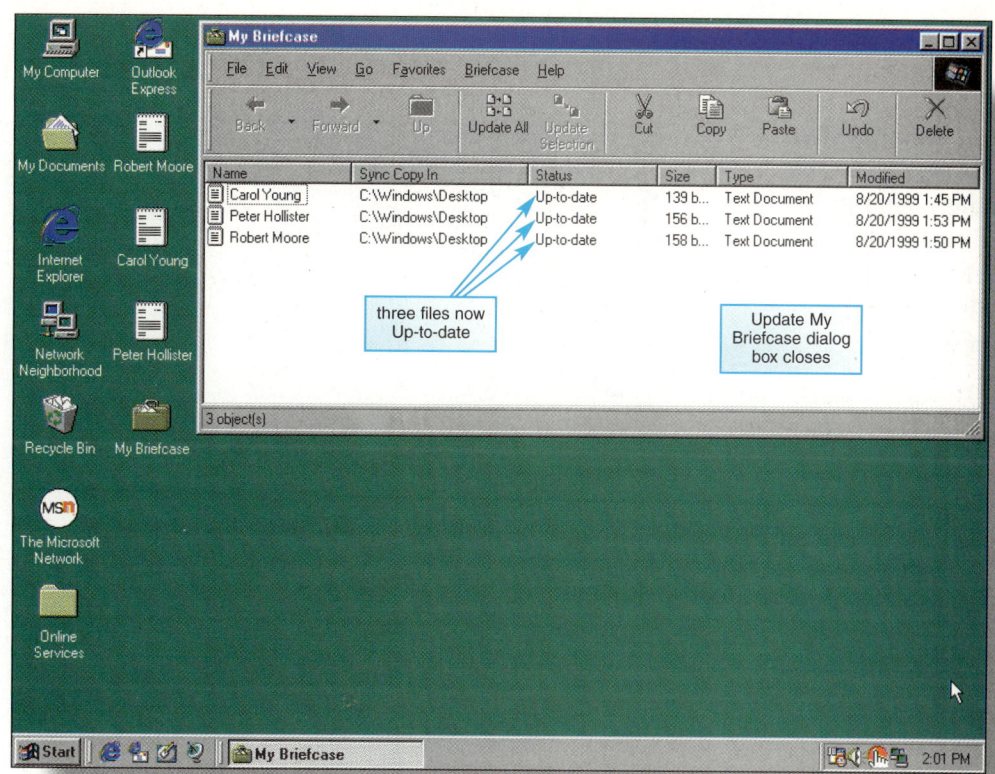

FIGURE 6-69

TO DELETE THE FILES IN MY BRIEFCASE AND CLOSE THE WINDOW

1. Select all the file names in the My Briefcase window.
2. Right-click a highlighted file name.
3. Click Delete on the shortcut menu.
4. Click the Yes button in the Confirm Multiple File Delete dialog box.
5. Click the Close button in the My Briefcase window.

The three files from the My Briefcase window are removed and the window closes.

Opening a Document Using the Documents Command

Throughout this project, you have created and worked with several documents. Each time you open a document, the application associated with the document saves the name and location of the document and adds an entry to the Documents submenu. If you want to work with a document you have previously opened, you can open the document quickly by clicking the document name on the Documents submenu. Perform the steps on the next page to open the Support document.

More About

Opening a Document

Some application programs cannot add document names to the Documents submenu. If the document you want to open is not listed on the Documents submenu, use the Find command and the techniques for finding documents illustrated earlier in this project to find the document.

To Open a Document Using the Documents Command

1 Click the Start button on the taskbar, point to Documents on the Start menu, and point to Support on the Documents submenu.

The Start menu and Documents submenu display (Figure 6-70). The Documents submenu is divided into two areas. The upper area contains the My Documents icon and title and the lower area contains a list of documents that have been previously opened.

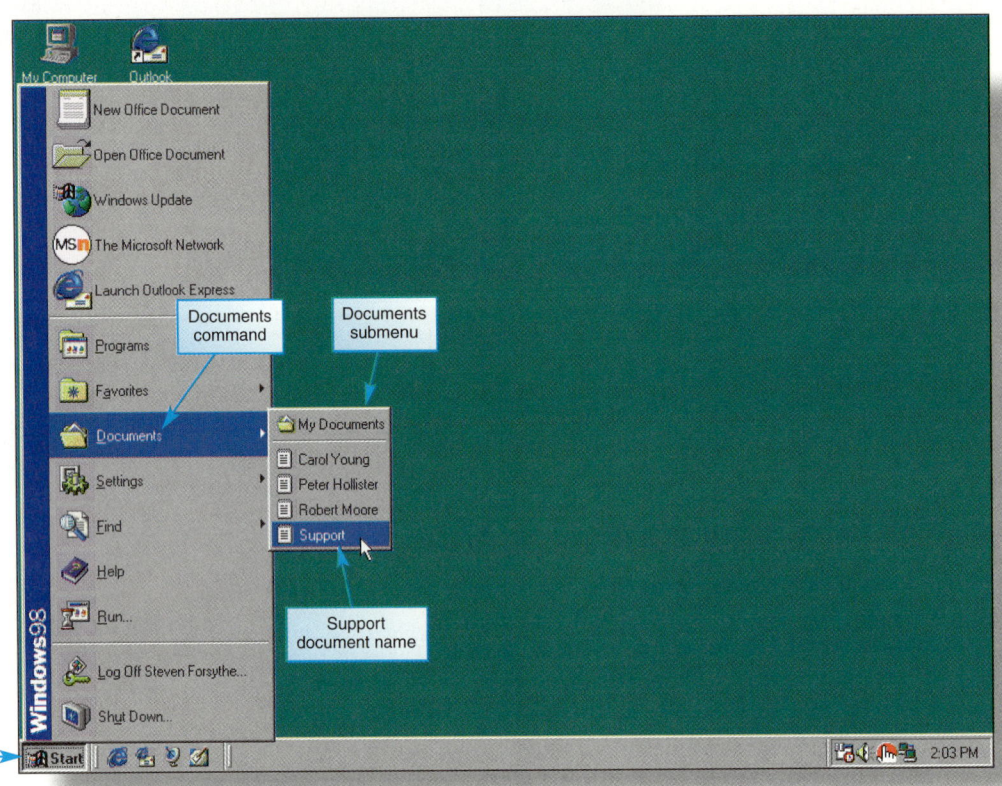

FIGURE 6-70

2 Click Support.

Notepad is launched, the Support - Notepad window opens, and the Support document displays in the window (Figure 6-71). After opening the document, you may modify or otherwise use the document as required.

3 Click the Close button in the Support - Notepad window.

The Support - Notepad window closes.

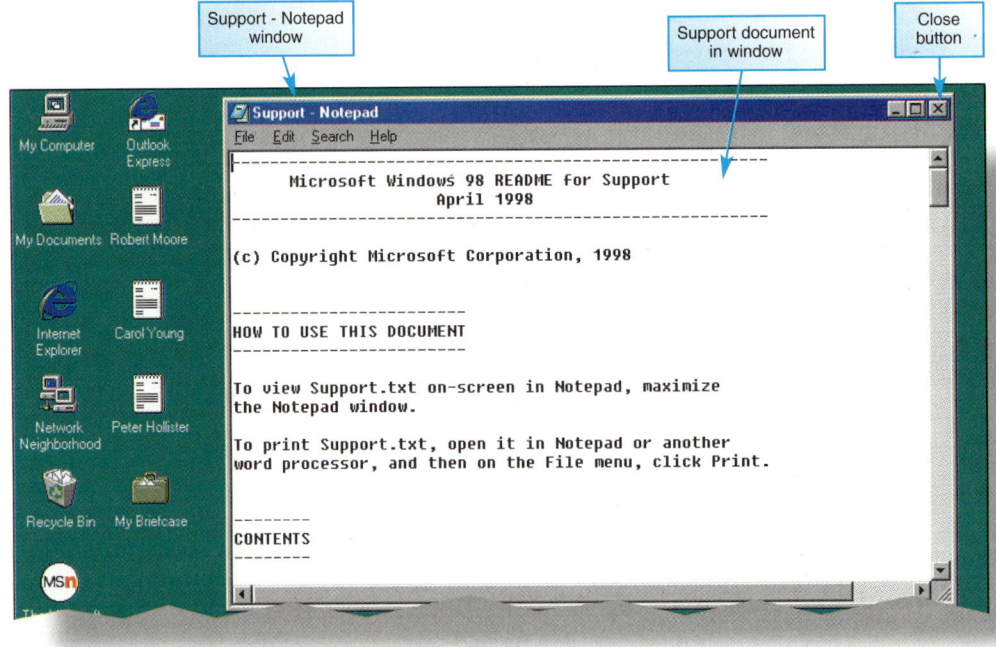

FIGURE 6-71

1. Press CTRL+ESC, D, click document name

Removing the List of Documents from the Documents Submenu

When you open a document, a document name is added to the list of document names in the Documents submenu. After opening many documents, it becomes slower to locate and open a document using the Documents command. To remove the list of documents from the Documents submenu and leave only the My Documents command, perform the following steps.

To Remove the List of Documents from the Documents Submenu

1 **Right-click an open area on the taskbar and then point to Properties on the shortcut menu.**

A shortcut menu displays (Figure 6-72).

FIGURE 6-72

2 **Click Properties. Click the Start Menu Programs tab, and then point to the Clear button in the Documents menu pane.**

The Taskbar Properties dialog box displays and the Start Menu Programs sheet displays in the dialog box (Figure 6-73).

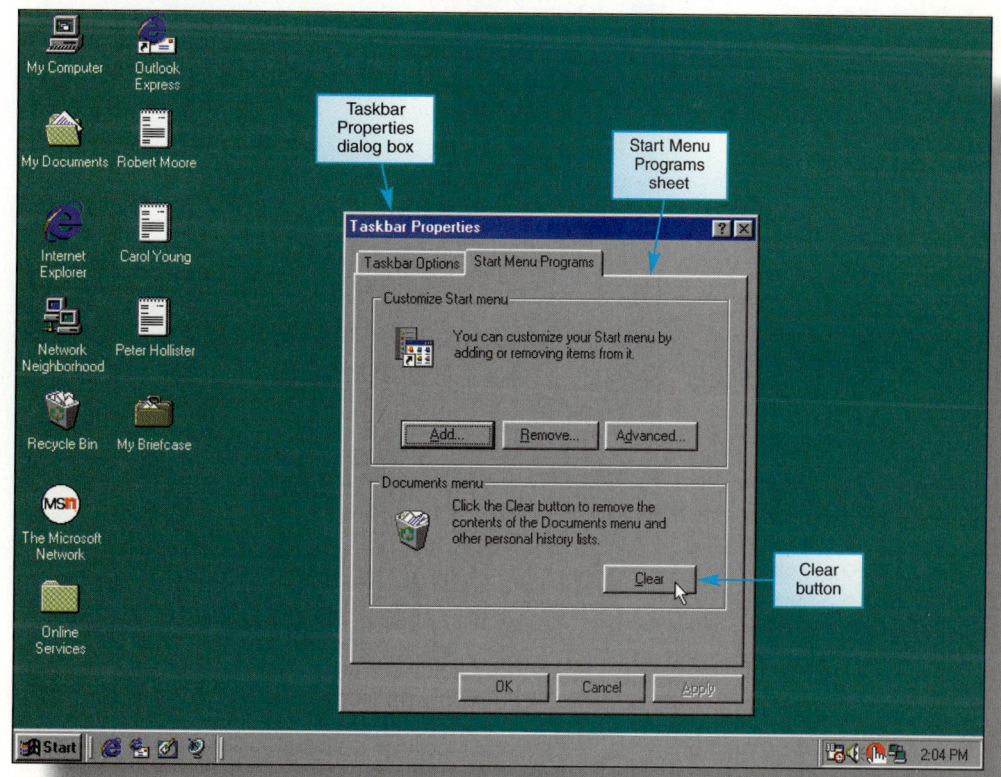

FIGURE 6-73

WIN 6.50 • Project 6 • Advanced File and Document Management and My Briefcase

3 **Click the Clear button and then point to the OK button.**

The Clear button dims to indicate the contents of the Documents submenu have been cleared (Figure 6-74).

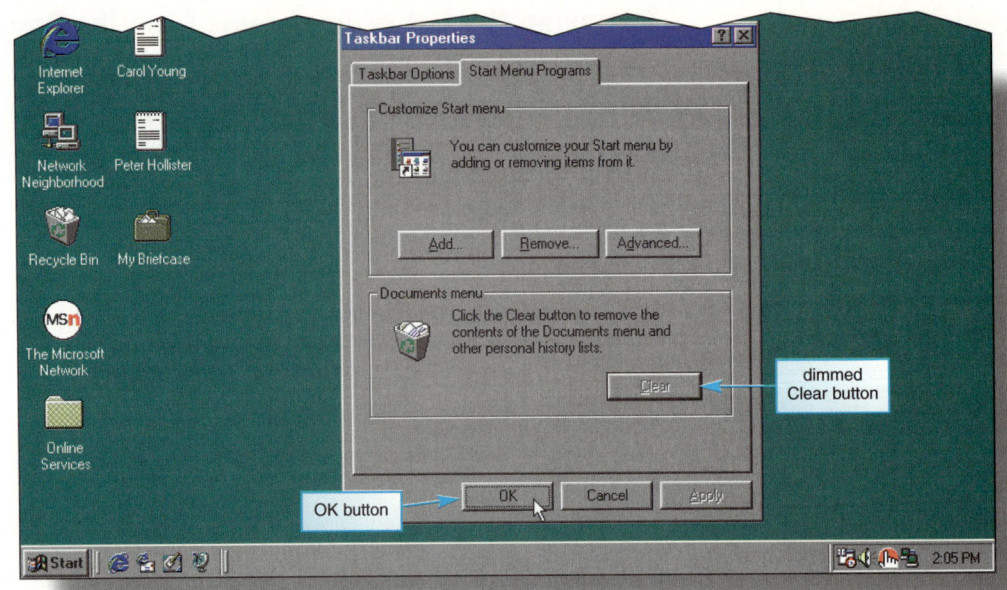

FIGURE 6-74

4 **Click the OK button.**

The Taskbar Properties dialog box closes.

5 **Click the Start button on the taskbar and then point to Documents on the Start menu.**

The Start menu and Documents submenu display (Figure 6-75). The Documents submenu contains the My Documents folder icon and title and no documents. On some computers the (empty) entry may display below the My Documents entry on the Documents submenu.

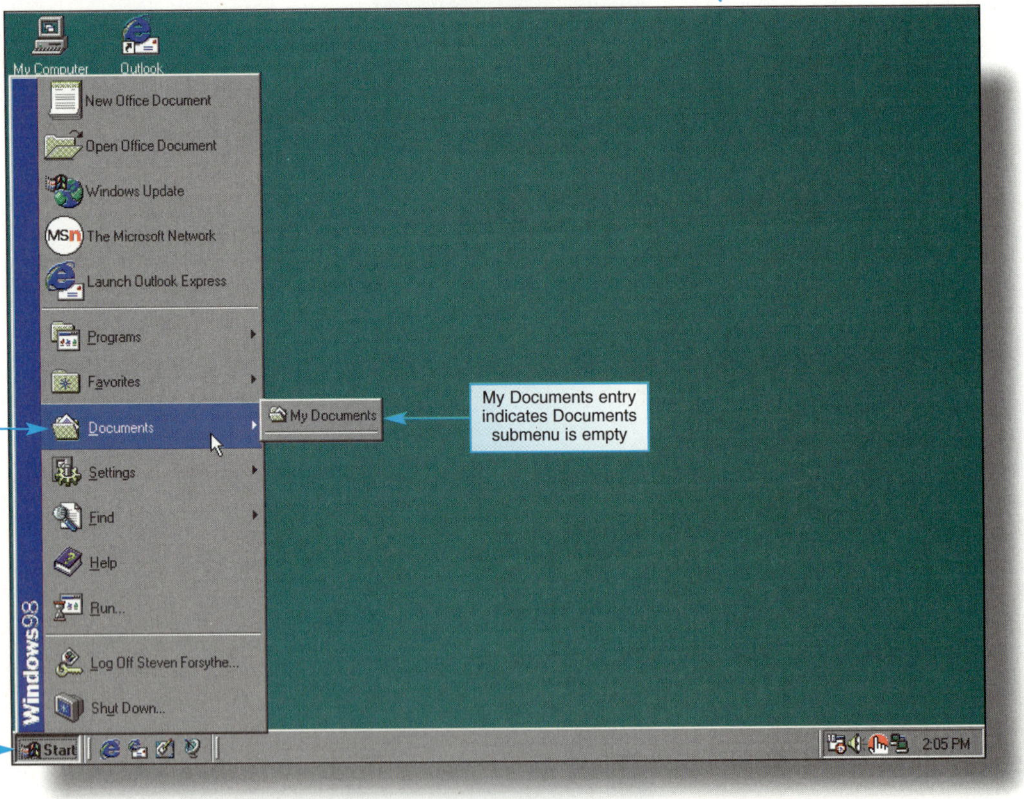

FIGURE 6-75

6 **Click an open area on the desktop to remove the Start menu and Documents submenu.**

Other Ways

1. Click Start button on the taskbar, point to Settings, click Taskbar & Start Menu on the Settings submenu, click Start Menu Programs tab, click Clear button, click OK button

Restoring the Desktop to Its Original Configuration

After creating the Robert Moore, Carol Young, and Peter Hollister files on the desktop, restore the desktop to its original configuration by deleting each of the files and then emptying the contents of the Recycle Bin. Perform the following to accomplish this.

TO RESTORE THE DESKTOP AND EMPTY THE RECYCLE BIN

1. Drag the Robert Moore icon to the Recycle Bin and then click the Yes button in the Confirm File Delete dialog box.
2. Drag the Carol Young icon to the Recycle Bin and then click the Yes button in the Confirm File Delete dialog box.
3. Drag the Peter Hollister icon to the Recycle Bin and then click the Yes button in the Confirm File Delete dialog box.
4. Right-click the Recycle Bin icon and then click Empty Recycle Bin.
5. Click the Yes button in the Confirm Multiple File Delete dialog box.

The Robert Moore, Carol Young, and Peter Hollister documents are removed from the desktop and the Recycle Bin is emptied.

Power Management

Power management allows you to reduce the power consumption of your computer devices (monitor, hard drives, and so on) or your entire system. Power Management is useful particularly to reduce the consumption of battery power on a portable computer. Although power management requires you to have a computer that is set up by the manufacturer to support power management, most new computers now support power management.

Power management allows you to put your computer into standby or hibernation mode. **Standby mode** turns off your monitor and hard disks causing your computer to use less power. Standby mode is particularly useful for conserving battery power in portable computers and is used when you plan to be away from your computer for a short period of time. When you want to use the computer again, you move the mouse or press a keyboard key and the desktop displays as it did before entering standby mode.

Hibernation mode turns off your monitor and hard disks, saves everything in memory on disk, and turns off your computer. You should use hibernation mode when you plan to be away from your computer for extended periods of time, such as several hours or overnight. To leave hibernation mode, you restart your computer and the desktop displays as it did before entering hibernation mode.

You use power management by selecting a **power scheme**, which is a collection of settings that manages the power usage of your computer. In addition, you can adjust the individual settings in a power scheme to turn off your monitor and hard disks automatically to save power, or put the computer in standby mode or hibernation mode. To view your power management settings, perform the steps on the next page.

WIN 6.52 • Project 6 • Advanced File and Document Management and My Briefcase

Steps: To View the Power Management Settings on a Laptop Computer

1 Turn on the laptop computer. Start Windows 98. Click the Start button on the taskbar, point to Settings, and then click Control Panel. Point to the Power Management icon in the Control Panel window

The Control Panel window opens (Figure 6-76).

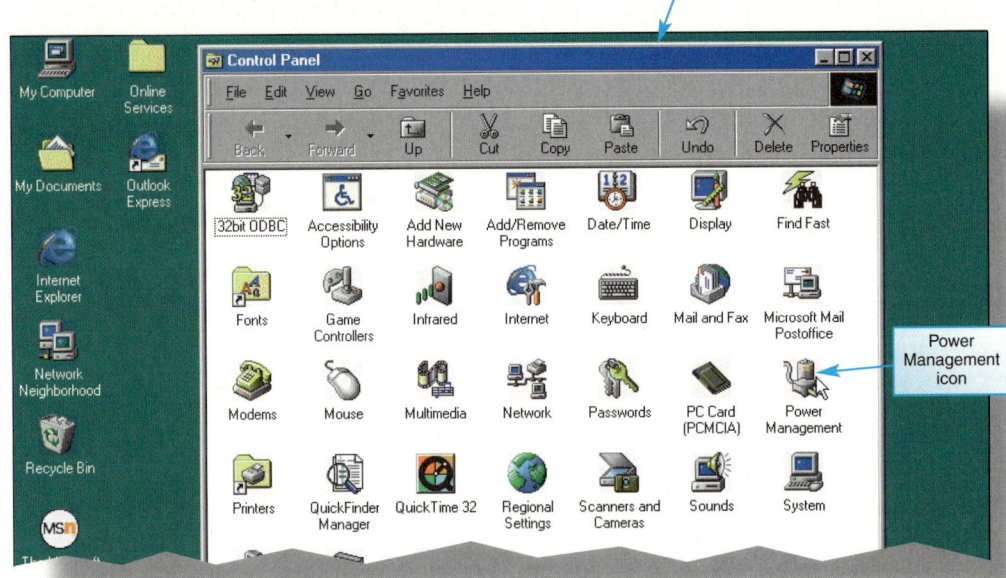

FIGURE 6-76 Desktop of Portable Computer

2 Double-click the Power Management icon.

The Power Management Properties dialog box and Power Schemes sheet display (Figure 6-77). The Power schemes box in the Power Schemes pane contains the highlighted power scheme (Portable/Laptop) for the laptop computer. The Settings for Portable/Laptop power scheme pane contains the system standby and monitor settings for operating the portable/laptop with AC power or battery power.

3 When you have finished viewing the Power Management Properties dialog box, click the OK button.

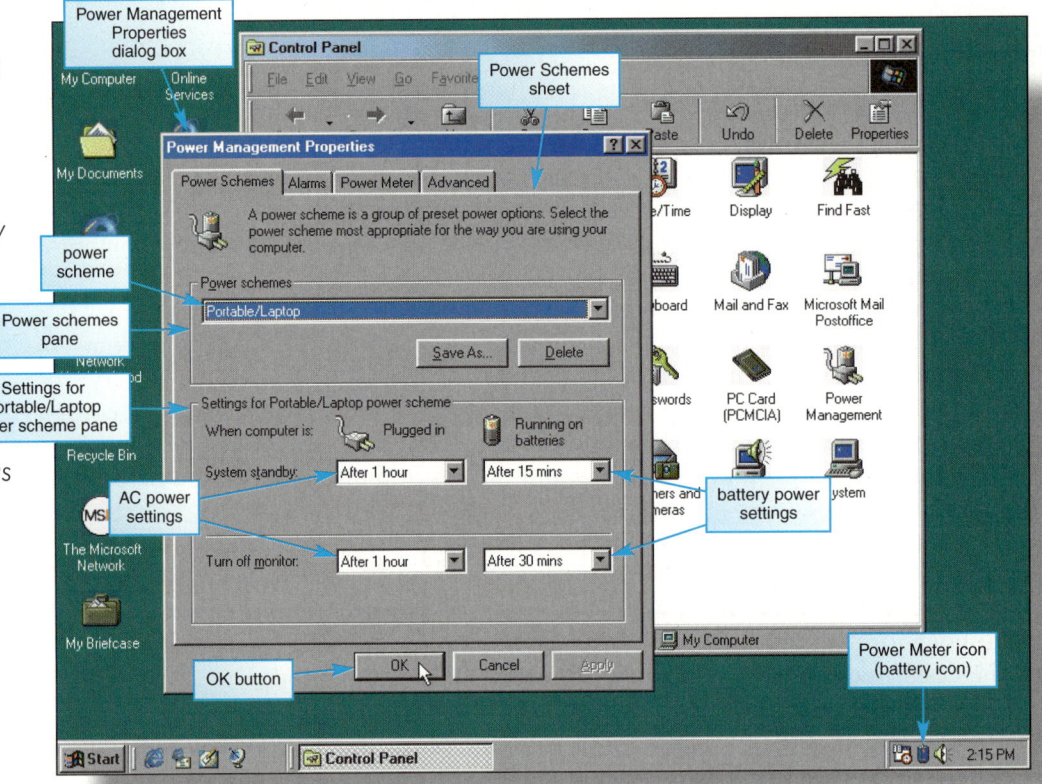

FIGURE 6-77 Desktop of Portable Computer

When using battery power, the default system standby setting is After 15 mins, the turn off monitor setting is After 30 mins, and the Power Meter icon (a battery icon) displays in the tray status area (see Figure 6-77) to indicate the computer is running on battery power. After 15 minutes of inactivity, the power management feature puts the computer into standby mode and after 30 minutes turns off the computer monitor. Pointing to the Power Meter icon displays a ToolTip that indicates what percentage the battery is charged and double-clicking the Power Meter icon displays the Power Meter dialog box that displays the current power source (Batteries) and total battery power remaining, and allows you to remove the Power Meter icon from the tray status area.

When using AC power, the default system standby setting and turn off monitor setting is After 1 hour. After one hour of inactivity, the power management feature puts the portable/laptop computer into standby mode and turns off the monitor and hard disks, and the Power Meter icon (power cord and plug) displays in the tray status area to indicate the computer is running on AC power.

To leave standby mode, move the mouse or press a keyboard key. The desktop displays as it did before entering standby mode.

The Power Management Properties dialog box may have fewer or more tabs on your computer than those shown in Figure 6-77. If available, the Alarms sheet, identified by the Alarms tab, allows you to set two different audible alarms that warn you when the battery is 10% charged and 3% charged, respectively. The 10% and 3% values can be changed to your preference. If available, the Power Meter sheet, identified by the Power Meter tab, indicates the current power source (AC or battery) and the total battery power remaining. This information also is available by double-clicking the Power Meter in the tray status area. The Advanced sheet, identified by the Advanced tab, contains a check box that allows you to display or not display the Power Meter icon in the tray status area on the taskbar.

The Hibernation sheet, identified by the Hibernation tab (not shown in the Power Management Properties dialog box in Figure 6-77), allows you to turn on or turn off the hibernation mode.

Power Management features also can be used on your desktop computer. In a similar fashion, you can turn off the monitor and hard disk to save electricity. The default time setting for the monitor and hard disks on a desktop computer is 20 minutes.

Project Summary

This project introduced you to additional techniques for working with files, folders, and documents. Using the Find command, you searched for files based on a date, a word or words within the file, and the type of file; for Web content on the Internet; and for people on the Internet. You used Quick View to view the contents of a file; the Send To command to copy and delete a file; the Recycle Bin to recover a deleted file; and the Documents command to open a document. In addition, you viewed the properties of the Recycle Bin, emptied the Recycle Bin, and used My Briefcase to transport files between two computers. Then, you modified the files on both computers and updated the files. In addition, you learned about the power management features.

What You Should Know

Having completed this project, you now should be able to perform the following tasks:

- Add a Destination to the Send To Menu *(WIN 6.18)*
- Begin a Search *(WIN 6.5)*
- Change the Carol Young File *(WIN 6.39)*
- Change the Peter Hollister File *(WIN 6.38, WIN 6.42)*
- Change the Robert Moore File *(WIN 6.40)*
- Copy a File Using the Send To Command *(WIN 6.17)*
- Create the Second File for Carol Young File on the Desktop *(WIN 6.34)*
- Create the Third File for Peter Hollister File on the Desktop *(WIN 6.34)*
- Create the First File for Robert Moore File on the Desktop *(WIN 6.33)*
- Delete a File Using the Send To Command *(WIN 6.20)*
- Delete the Files in My Briefcase and Close the Window *(WIN 6.47)*
- Drag the Three Files to the My Briefcase Icon *(WIN 6.35)*
- Empty the Recycle Bin *(WIN 6.24)*
- Find a File by a Word or Series of Words in the File *(WIN 6.12)*
- Find a File by Date *(WIN 6.8)*
- Find a File by File Type *(WIN 6.10)*
- Find a File Using a Saved Search *(WIN 6.15)*
- Find Information About a Person *(WIN 6.30)*
- Find Information on the Internet *(WIN 6.28)*
- Move My Briefcase to the Desktop of the Office Computer *(WIN 6.43)*
- Move My Briefcase to a Floppy Disk *(WIN 6.37)*
- Open a Document Using the Documents Command *(WIN 6.48)*
- Remove a Destination from the Send To Menu *(WIN 6.21)*
- Remove the List of Documents from the Documents Submenu *(WIN 6.49)*
- Remove the Saved Search File *(WIN 6.27)*
- Restore a Deleted File Using the Recycle Bin *(WIN 6.23)*
- Restore the Desktop and Empty the Recycle Bin *(WIN 6.51)*
- Save a Search *(WIN 6.14)*
- Specify the Starting Point of a Search *(WIN 6.7)*
- Synchronize the Files Using My Briefcase *(WIN 6.45)*
- View a Document Using Quick View *(WIN 6.16)*
- View the Contents of My Briefcase *(WIN 6.36)*
- View the Contents of the Recycle Bin *(WIN 6.22)*
- View the Power Management Settings on a Laptop Computer *(WIN 6.52)*
- View the Recycle Bin Properties *(WIN 6.25)*

Test Your Knowledge

1 True/False

Instructions: Circle T if the statement is true or F is the statement is false.

T (F) 1. The Find command allows you to find a file based on knowing the deletion date of the file.
(T) F 2. You can speed up a search by specifying the folder in which to begin the search.
(T) F 3. Clicking the Browse button in the Find: All Files window allows you to specify the starting point of a search.
T (F) 4. After completing a search, you can open a file that was found by clicking the file icon in the list of files found during the search.
(T) F 5. Quick View allows you to view documents without first starting the program associated with the document.
(T) F 6. The Send To menu allows you to copy a file onto a floppy disk.
T (F) 7. Only destinations currently on the Send To submenu can be used to copy a file.
T (F) 8. You cannot change the amount of disk space reserved for the Recycle Bin.
T (F) 9. Synchronizing a file involves dragging the My Briefcase icon to a floppy disk destination.
(T) F 10. Hibernation mode should be used when you plan to be away from your computer for extended periods of time.

2 Multiple Choice

Instructions: Circle the correct response.

1. To find a file using the Find command, click the ____b____ button, point to _____, and click the Files or Folders command.
   a. Find Now, Search   b. Start, Find   c. Find, Search   d. Start, Find Now
2. To specify a starting point for a search, click the ____c____ button.
   a. Starting Point   b. New Search   c. Browse   d. Find Now
3. You use the ____d____ sheet to find a file based on file type.
   a. Name & Location   b. Date   c. File Type   d. Advanced
4. To find a file in the Windows folder or its subfolders that is a text document file, you use the _____ and _____ sheets.
   a. Name & Location, Advanced   c. Name & Location, Date
   b. All Files & Folders, Advanced   d. Look In, Date
5. To save a search for future use, click _____.
   a. the Save Search button in the Find: All Files window
   b. Save Search on the File menu
   c. the New Search button in the Find: All Files window
   d. Save on the Search menu
6. You can view a document using Quick View by _____.
   a. right-clicking the document icon and then clicking Quick View on the shortcut menu
   b. double-clicking the document icon with the right mouse button
   c. dragging the document icon to the Quick View icon on the desktop
   d. clicking Quick View on the File menu

(continued)

Test Your Knowledge

Multiple Choice (continued)

7. You can use the Send To menu to copy a document to _____.
   a. a 3½ floppy disk   b. My Briefcase   c. Recycle Bin   d. all of the above
8. _____ to restore a document that was deleted in error.
   a. Double-click the document icon in the Recycle Bin window
   b. Right-click the document icon in the Recycle Bin window and then click Restore
   c. Drag the document icon to the Recycle Bin icon on the desktop
   d. Right-click the document icon and then click Recycle Bin on the shortcut menu
9. If _____, you might want to empty the Recycle Bin.
   a. the Recycle Bin is full
   b. the files in the Recycle Bin are no longer needed
   c. more disk space is needed
   d. all of the above
10. My Briefcase allows you to work with _____.
    a. multiple documents on the same computer
    b. the same document on two computers
    c. only documents on a laptop computer
    d. both a and c

3 Finding Documents Based on File Type and Content

Instructions: The Find: All Files window is illustrated in Figure 6-78 below. In the spaces provided below the figure, list the steps to search the entire hard disk to find all text document files containing the words, Windows Help.

Step 1: _____
Step 2: _____
Step 3: _____
Step 4: _____
Step 5: _____

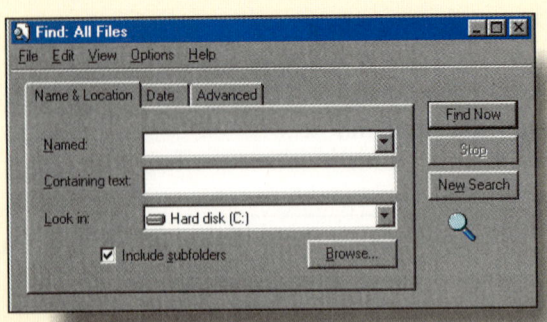

FIGURE 6-78

Test Your Knowledge

4 Using My Briefcase to Synchronize Files

Instructions: A file on the desktop was copied to My Briefcase, moved onto a floppy disk, and modified on another computer. The My Briefcase icon containing the modified file was moved back to the desktop of the original computer. In the spaces provided, list the steps needed to synchronize the files.

Step 1: _____
Step 2: _____
Step 3: _____
Step 4: _____
Step 5: _____

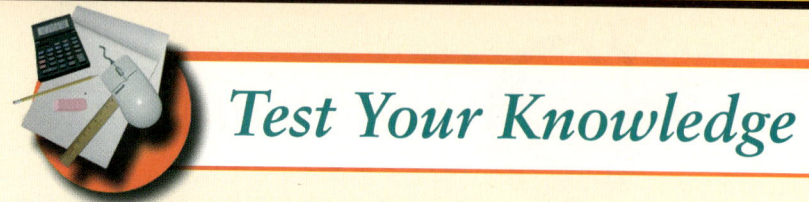

Use Help

1 Using Windows Help

Instructions: Use Windows Help and a computer to perform the following tasks.

1. If necessary, start Microsoft Windows 98.
2. Click the Start button. Click Help on the Start menu. If necessary, click the Index tab.
3. Type `case-sensitive` in the text box.
4. Double-click the case-sensitive searches entry in the list box.
    a. What do you do to make a search case-sensitive? _____
5. Type `search results` in the text box.
6. Double-click the search results entry.
7. Double-click the To save the results of a search for files or folders entry.
    a. How do you save only the search criteria? _____
    b. How do you save the search criteria and the results of a search? _____
    c. What appears on the desktop when the search criteria and results are saved? _____
    d. How do you display the search criteria and results of a search after saving them? _____
    e. How do you reinitiate the search or update the search results? _____
8. Type `power management` in the text box.
9. Double-click the system standby entry in the list box.
10. Double-click the To manually put your computer on standby entry.
    a. How do you manually put your computer on standby? _____
    _____

(continued)

Use Help

Using Windows Help (continued)

11. Type briefcase in the text box.
12. Double-click the Briefcase entry in the list box.
13. Double-click the Using My Briefcase entry in the list box.
14. Follow the instructions in the right frame of the Windows Help window.
15. What are the four easy steps you can use to help you organize and keep your documents up to date between two computers?
    _____ _____
    _____ _____
16. Double-click the Briefcase entry again in the list box.
17. Double-click the To create a new Briefcase folder entry in the list box.
18. Click the Close button in the Windows Help window.

In the Lab

1 Using the Find Command to Search for Files

Instructions: To familiarize yourself with the Find command, you would like to search for files based on date, file type, content, and name. Perform the following steps to search for various files using the Find command.

Part 1: *Searching for Files Based on Date*

1. If necessary, Start Windows 98.
2. Use Find to search the entire hard drive for all files or folders created on 5/11/98. How many files or folders were found? _____
3. Use Find to search the entire hard drive for all files or folders created on your last birthday. How many files or folders were found? _____
4. Use Find to search the entire hard drive for all files or folders created or modified within the previous month. How many files or folders were found? _____

Part 2: *Searching for Files Based on File Type*

1. Use Find to search the entire hard drive for Screen Saver files.
2. List the first three Screen Saver files found during the search.
   _____
   _____
   _____

In the Lab

3. Scroll to make the Curves and Colors icon visible, right-click the Curves and Colors icon, and then click Test on the shortcut menu. What happens when you click Test? _____
_____
4. Scroll to make the Scrolling Marquee icon visible and then double-click the Scrolling Marquee icon. What happens when you double-click? _____
5. Use Find to search the entire hard drive for Midi Sequence files. How many files or folders were found? _____. Double-click one of the files found. What do you hear? _____
_____
6. Use Find to search the Windows folder and its subfolders for Video Clip files. How many files or folders were found? _____. Double-click one of the Video Clip file icons. What is demonstrated? _____
7. Use Find to search the Windows folder and its subfolders for Wave Sound files. How many files or folders were found? _____. Double-click one of the Wave Sound file icons. What do you hear? _____

Part 3: Searching for Files Based on Content or File Name

1. Use Find to search the entire hard drive for all text documents containing the word, Microsoft. How many files or folders were found? _____
2. Use Find to search the entire hard drive for files or folders with the .bat extension (*Hint*: Type *.bat in the Named box in the Name & Location sheet). What type of files were found? _____
_____
3. Close the Find: Files named *.bat window. Quit Windows 98.

2 Using the Find Command to Search for Folders and Applications

Instructions: You would like to be able to print the contents of a folder on the printer. You are aware that one method to do it is to use Find to search for the folder you want to print, open the folder, press the ALT and PRINT SCREEN keys on the keyboard to capture a picture of the window, and then use Paint to open and print the window. Perform the following steps to print the contents of the Send To folder on the printer.

Part 1: Searching for Folders in the Windows Folder

1. If necessary, Start Windows 98.
2. Use Find to search ONLY the Windows folder for Folders file types. (*Hint*: Specify Windows as the starting point of the search and do not include its subfolders. Then, select the Folder entry in the Of type list box in the Advanced sheet.)

Part 2: Capturing a Picture of the SendTo Folder

1. Scroll the list box to make the SendTo folder visible and then double-click the SendTo icon to display the SendTo window.
2. Minimize the Find: Files of type Folder window.
3. Hold down the ALT key and then press the PRINT SCREEN key on the keyboard. A copy of the window is placed on the Clipboard.

(continued)

In the Lab

Using the Find Command to Search for Folders and Applications *(continued)*

Part 3: Printing the SendTo Folder Window
1. Click the Find: Files of type Folder button on the taskbar.
2. Use Find to search for Application file types. (*Hint*: In the Advanced sheet, select the Application entry in the Of type list box to search only for all Application file types.)
3. Scroll the list box to make the Pbrush icon visible.
4. Double-click the Pbrush icon to start the Paint application and then maximize the Paint window.
5. Click Edit on the menu bar and then click Paste to copy the image on the Clipboard into the Paint window.
6. If the Paint window opens and the message, The image in the clipboard is larger than the bitmap. Would you like the bitmap enlarged?, displays in the window, click the Yes button.
7. Click File on the menu bar, click Print, and click the OK button.
8. Click the Close button in the Paint window. Click the No button in the Paint dialog box. Click the Close button in the Find: Files of type Application window and then click the Close button in the SendTo window.
9. Quit Windows 98.

3 Using My Briefcase

Instructions: You want to create a document containing your class schedule. While creating the document on your home computer, you are interrupted and cannot complete the document. You decide to move the document to your laptop and enter the remainder of the document at school. After completing the document at school and returning home, you synchronize the files. Perform the following steps to create and save the document containing your class schedule.

Part 1: Creating and Saving a New Text Document
1. Create a new text document on the desktop.
2. Name the new document, School Schedule.
3. Open the School Schedule document.
4. Enter the following classes and their schedules:
   ```
   8:00 a.m. to 8:50 a.m. Spanish Room A-113 Ms. Tirado
   9:00 a.m. to 9:50 a.m. Math Room B-374 Mr. Powers
   10:00 a.m. to 10:50 a.m. History Room B-233 Mr. Sanders
   11:00 a.m. to 11:50 a.m. Literature Room C-356 Mr. Bennington
   12:00 p.m. to 12:25 p.m. Lunch Cafeteria
   ```
5. Print a copy of the document.
6. Save the document on the desktop and close the School Schedule - Notepad window.

Part 2: Transporting the Document
1. Drag the School Schedule document to the My Briefcase icon.
2. Insert a formatted floppy disk into drive A of your computer.
3. Move the My Briefcase icon to the disk in drive A using the Send To command.
4. Remove the formatted floppy disk from drive A.

In the Lab

Part 3: *Changing the School Schedule Document*

1. Insert the floppy disk containing the My Briefcase icon into a second computer.
2. Display the contents of My Briefcase on the floppy disk.
3. Open the School Schedule document.
4. Enter the following class information at the end of the document:
   ```
   12:30 p.m. to 1:25 p.m. Computer Room A-122 Ms. Anderson
   1:30 p.m. to 2:25 p.m. Science Room D-103 Mr. Flanders
   ```
5. Print a copy of the document. Save the document and close all open windows.
6. Remove the floppy disk from drive A.

Part 4: *Synchronizing the Briefcase Files*

1. Insert the floppy disk into drive A of the original computer.
2. Open the My Computer window. Open the 3½ Floppy (A:) window.
3. Drag the My Briefcase icon to the desktop.
4. Close the 3½ Floppy (A:) window.
5. Remove the floppy disk from drive A.
6. Display the contents of My Briefcase.
7. Update the School Schedule document.
8. Delete the document in the My Briefcase window.
9. Close the My Briefcase window. Open the School Schedule document.
10. Print a copy of the document on the printer.
12. Close the School Schedule – Notepad window.
13. Delete the School Schedule document. Quit Windows 98.

Cases and Places

The difficulty of these case studies varies: ▸ are the least difficult; ▸▸ are more difficult; and ▸▸▸ are the most difficult.

1 ▸ You help your friend Alicia buy a new computer. Late one night, she calls and is frantic because she cannot find a document on the computer. The document contains a big project for her Science class that she created using Microsoft Word and is due tomorrow. She cannot remember what file name she used to save the file but does remember the document contains her teacher's name, Ms. Lipton. To help her remember how to search for a file containing a word or series of words, write down the steps to find the file and give or e-mail her a copy.

Cases and Places

2 ▸ You are in the process of moving old text and bitmap documents on the desktop to the My Documents folder on the desktop where you keep all your documents when a friend walks in. He sees that you are sending documents to the My Documents folder using the Send To command. Your friend does not know how to use the Send To command to send a document to a folder on the desktop. You quickly show him how to add a destination to the Send To menu, but he complains that you did it so quickly he could not see what you did. Using Notepad, write down the steps to add a folder (destination) to the Send To menu and the steps to move a file to a folder using the Send To command. Print a copy for your friend.

3 ▸ In the past, you have written notes to yourself on pieces of paper and put them in your briefcase while on business trips. Because you frequently lose these notes and because these notes are important and often result in increased sales, you purchase a laptop computer to take on business trips. You ask a business partner to help you organize your notes using My Briefcase. He shows you how to create a New Briefcase icon on your desktop. To help you remember, you create a text document on the desktop, type the steps to follow to create a New Briefcase icon in the document, create the New Briefcase icon, and then move the text document to the New Briefcase icon. If you have forgotten how to create a New Briefcase icon on the desktop, use Help to refresh your memory.

4 ▸▸ Wildcard characters often are used in a file name to locate a group of files using the Find command. For example, to locate all files with the Business file name regardless of the file name extension, an entry (Business.*) containing the asterisk wildcard character would be used. Using the Internet, computer magazines, or any other resources, develop a guide to using wildcards. Summarize what a wildcard character is, what the valid wildcard characters are, and give several examples to explain their use.

5 ▸▸▸ Windows is not the first operating system to contain a Recycle Bin. Many Apple computers have had a similar item, called the Trash Can, for years. Find an Apple computer that has the Trash Can. Have someone else show you how to use the Trash Can or experiment with the Trash Can yourself. Compare and contrast the procedures used to delete a file, restore a file, and empty the contents of the Recycle Bin with the procedures used with the Trash Can. How similar are the Recycle Bin and Trash Can?

6 ▸▸▸ Visit two companies in your area that supply their employees with laptop computers. Interview two laptop users at each company to determine how they use their laptops, how they transfer files and folders between their laptops and main computers, and whether or not they use My Briefcase. Prepare a brief report summarizing what you found. If you find a laptop user who does not use My Briefcase, be prepared to demonstrate how My Briefcase works.

7 ▸▸▸ You get a summer job working at a local insurance office. The sales staff at the insurance office recently has received laptop computers but few know how to use My Briefcase to transfer files between their laptops and main computers. Your first project is to train the sales staff. Create an outline of the major points and then prepare a fifteen-minute presentation demonstrating how to use My Briefcase. Create any documents you will need during the presentation. Hand out the outline and give your presentation to the sales staff (or the students in your class). If you are familiar with Microsoft PowerPoint (a presentation program), use PowerPoint to give your presentation.

Microsoft Windows 98

PROJECT 7

Communicating with Other Computers

OBJECTIVES

You will have mastered the material in this project when you can:

- Use a modem to communicate with other computers
- Check and change the connection settings for The Microsoft Network
- Sign in and sign out from The Microsoft Network
- Launch Outlook Express, open and read an e-mail message, and reply to an e-mail
- Sign up for an Internet service provider account using the Internet Connection wizard
- Create a Dial-Up Networking connection using the Internet Connection wizard
- Dial and disconnect from an Internet service provider
- View and remove a Dial-Up Networking connection
- Install a network adapter, client, service, and protocol
- View computers and workgroups on a network
- Locate a computer on the network
- Share a folder and printer over a network
- Remove sharing from a folder and printer
- Map and access a network drive

Microsoft **Windows 98**

Genius at Work
The Amazing Success of the Web

"A revolutionary communications system requiring minimal technical understanding." That is how the John D. and Catherine T. MacArthur Foundation described the World Wide Web while awarding a $270,000 *genius grant* to Tim Berners-Lee in 1998 for his pioneering efforts developing this system.

The impetus for the Internet occurred when Russia launched the first artificial Earth satellite, *Sputnik*, in 1957. In response, U.S. Department of Defense officials became alarmed about a possible nuclear attack. The Pentagon's Advanced Research Projects Agency developed ARPANET, a decentralized computer system that could reroute data if some transmission lines among the country's military, defense contractors, and research universities became obstructed. Four of these computers were networked in 1969; this number grew to fifteen two years later and to thirty-seven the following year.

Nonmilitary users connected to ARPANET in the 1970s, and some networks offered to allow the public to connect to the system in the 1980s. The Department of Defense then decided to create another private network for its nonclassified information. The department moved its files to its new military side, MILNET, and left ARPANET in place. More and more networks added information to ARPANET, which earned the new name, Internet, to reflect this community of connected computers.

At this point, Berners-Lee began his magic. When he was working as a scientist at the European Laboratory for Particle Physics in Geneva, Switzerland, he proposed the initial idea for the system that ultimately would evolve into the Web that would serve individuals in all parts of the world. He also set up the Internet's first Web server.

His creation, the World Wide Web, contains sites filled with text, graphics, audio, and video. Internet users can navigate from one site to another by clicking hypertext links, which connect the sites to each other. "I didn't know it was going to succeed the way it has," Berners-Lee said. Indeed, the size of the Web is expanding by an estimated one percent daily. Although it is impossible to count the number of people actually connected, some researchers theorize more than three million people in 200 countries use the Web. These numbers are expected to grow at a rate of ten percent monthly.

In this project, you will learn to communicate with other computers using a modem, telephone lines, and connecting to a network. People all over the world communicate via networks using online services for sharing information on computers and workgroups. Windows features such as the Internet Connection Wizard and Dial-Up Networking will guide you through the steps to get connected.

Online services make it possible for you to send and receive electronic mail, talk to others in a chat room, access the latest news, sports, weather, and financial information, and access the Internet. Outlook Express, allows you to receive and store incoming e-mail messages, compose and send e-mail messages, and read and post messages to Internet newsgroups.

Everyday individuals and businesses set up networks of varying sizes in their own homes, office sites, and across the country. In this project, you will see how Windows can help you install the network hardware and software components so you can communicate with other computers and connect to the Internet. After completing the project, you will join the millions of others worldwide sharing networked information.

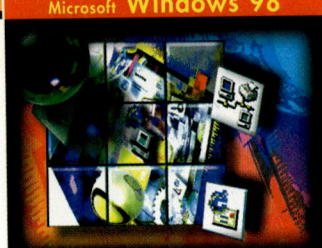

Microsoft Windows 98

Communicating with Other Computers

PROJECT 7

CASE PERSPECTIVE

The father of a friend of yours who lives down the street is the owner of a computer company that installs networks. He has set up a network in their house so his children can do their homework, connect to online services, send and receive e-mail, play video games, and access the Internet. While visiting their house, you and your friend, Sally, have used her computer many times. Previously, when visiting the house you stood behind Sally while she logged on to the network, signed in to The Microsoft Network, accessed the Internet, and surfed the World Wide Web. Occasionally, you followed her instructions to access the Internet and surf the World Wide Web and are beginning to understand more about communicating with other computers.

You understand that Sally's father hires a few students to work at his company during the summer. You think his company would be a great place to work so you decide you need to know more about networks and communicating with other computers. Your goal is to learn more about using a computer to communicate with other computers so you may obtain a summer job and work with Sally's father.

Introduction

Two popular methods exist to use a computer to communicate with other computers. One method uses a modem to connect to other computers. In this project, you will use a modem to access an online service and the Internet. An **online service**, such as The Microsoft Network, America Online, Prodigy, and CompuServe, allows you to connect to the service using a modem. While connected to an online service, you can send and receive electronic mail (e-mail) from other computers; talk to other groups of members in a chat room; and read the latest news, sports, weather, and financial information.

A second method of communicating with other computers is to connect a computer to a network of computers. In this project, you learn about networks and network components, setting up a computer to connect to a network, and logging on to the network. In addition, you will share computer resources (files, folders, printers, and so on) with other computers on the network.

Using a Modem to Communicate with Other Computers

One method to communicate with other computers is to use a modem. A **modem** is a communications device that converts signals to and from the computer so that they can travel over telephone lines to other computers. Today, most computers sold by retail stores contain a modem that is installed inside the computer (internal modem). You can use the modem to access information on the Internet using an online service or Internet service provider (ISP).

Accessing an Online Service

One popular method of communicating using a modem involves accessing an online service, such as The Microsoft Network (MSN). **The Microsoft Network (MSN)** is one of many online services available to computer users. Unlike the other online services, access to MSN is a feature of Windows 98.

The **services** available on MSN include sending and receiving electronic mail (e-mail); talking to other groups of members in a chat room; access to the latest news, sports, weather, and financial information; access to the Internet, and more. Services change frequently and new services are added regularly, making it possible that MSN may be different each time you sign in.

The Microsoft Network (MSN) and the Internet

The **Internet** is a collection of networks, each of which is composed of a collection of smaller networks. A **network** is a communication system, composed of hardware and software, which allows users to share data and computer resources (files, folders, printers, and so on).

With the addition of new networks and computers on those networks, the Internet is constantly growing. Since its creation in the 1960s, it has grown exponentially and millions of people around the world use the Internet. Once you are connected to the Internet, you can access a large amount of information, including news and weather information, software, and games. In addition, you can view price and product information from a wide variety of companies and corporations, order products and pay for them using a credit card, and send and receive electronic mail throughout the world.

Windows 98 provides two methods to connect to the Internet. You can connect using an online service or an Internet service provider. The following pages illustrate how to connect to the Internet using MSN (an online service), receive e-mail messages, and reply to e-mail messages.

Signing Up to The Microsoft Network

The first connection to MSN is a process called **signing up**. At sign up, you provide MSN with the personal and credit card information necessary to open an account and pay the monthly fee and then select a user name and password. The **user name** is the name other MSN users will see when you send e-mail or use a chat room. Once you have chosen a user name and MSN has approved it, you cannot change it. The user name is a unique online identification. A **password** is a code you select to prevent unwanted access to the Internet using your MSN account. After connecting to MSN for the first time, connecting involves signing in. To prevent others from signing in using your password and possibly incurring charges on your account, you should keep your password secret. You can, however, change a password at any time.

> **More About**
>
> **Other Online Services**
>
> The software necessary to sign up for and use The Microsoft Network icon on the desktop is included in Windows 98. The software you need to use other online services (America Online, AT&T WorldNet, CompuServe, and Prodigy) is contained on the Windows 98 CD-ROM. To install the software, double-click the Online Services folder on the desktop and double-click the icon of the selected service.

Checking The Microsoft Network Connection Settings

Each time you sign in to MSN, Windows 98 uses previously chosen connection settings. The **connection settings** include a telephone number to connect to MSN, a backup telephone number to connect to MSN if the first telephone is not operational, and dialing properties. The **dialing properties** include the settings for the location from which you are dialing (country name and area code) and any special instructions to dial a local or long distance call. Before signing in to MSN, check the connection settings to guarantee they are correct. Perform the following steps to check the MSN connection settings.

 To Check the MSN Connection Settings

1 **Right-click The Microsoft Network icon on the desktop and then point to Connection Settings on the shortcut menu.**

A shortcut menu, containing the highlighted Connection Settings command, displays (Figure 7-1).

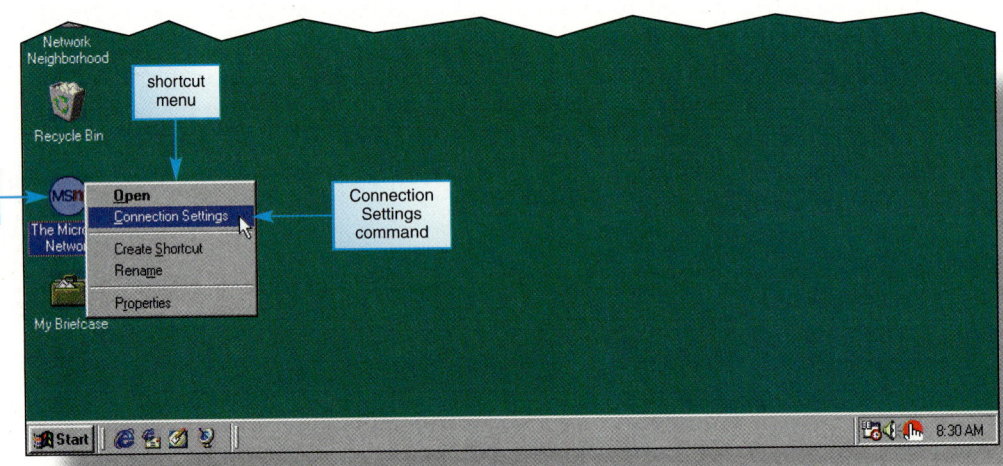

FIGURE 7-1

2 **Click Connection Settings and then point to the Dialing Properties button.**

The Connection Settings dialog box displays (Figure 7-2). The dialog box contains information about the telephone number and backup telephone number, two Phone Book buttons, a Dialing Properties button, and the modem name.

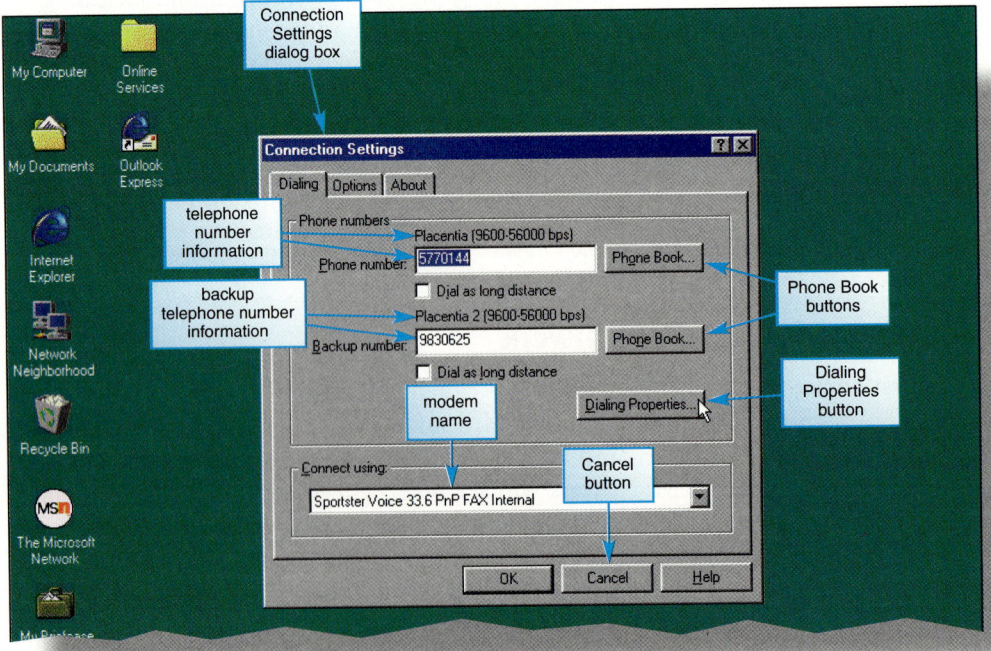

FIGURE 7-2

Accessing an Online Service • **WIN 7.7**

PROJECT 7

 **Click the Dialing Properties button and then point to the Cancel button in the Dialing Properties dialog box.**

The Dialing Properties dialog box displays (Figure 7-3). The dialing location name (Default Location) displays in the I am dialing from box, the country name (United States of America) displays in the I am in this country/region box, the area code number (714) displays in the Area code text box, the Tone dial option button is selected, and the telephone number (5770144) displays.

 **Click the Cancel button in the Dialing Properties dialog box. Click the Cancel button in the Connection Settings dialog box.**

The Dialing Properties and Connection Settings dialog boxes close.

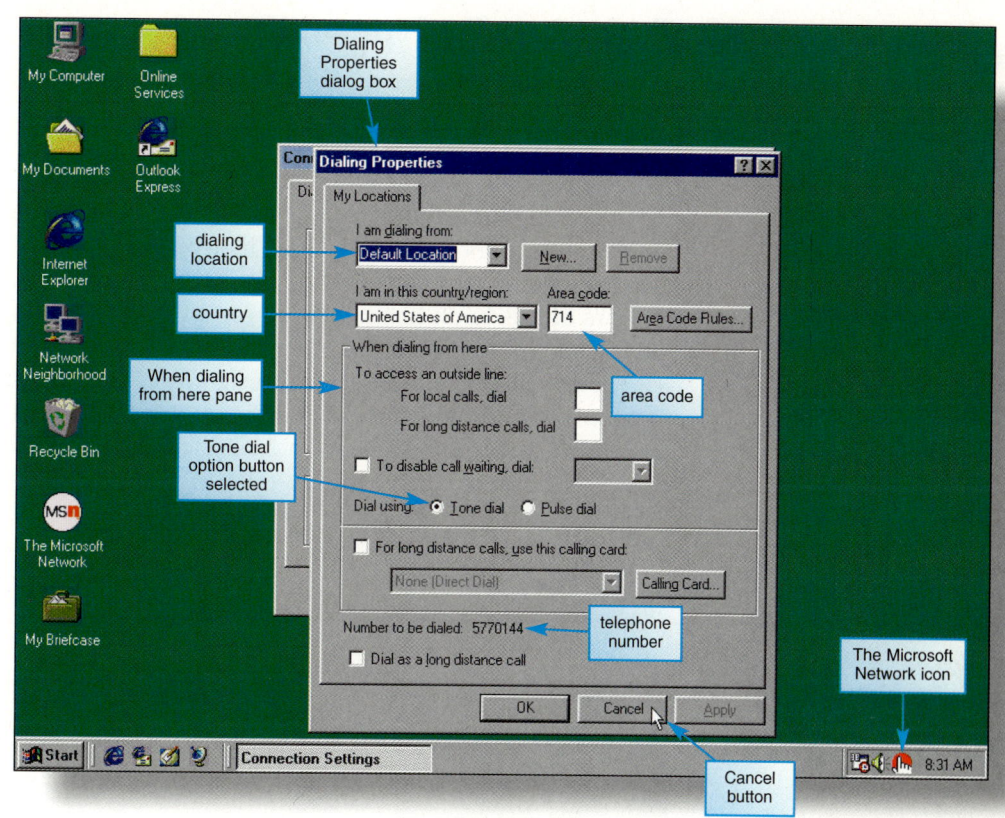

FIGURE 7-3

> **Other Ways**
> 1. Click The Microsoft Network icon in tray status area, point to MSN Options, click Connection Settings
> 2. Double-click The Microsoft Network icon, click Settings button in MSN - Sign-In window

---

In Figure 7-2, the telephone number (5770144) is located in the city of Placentia (Placentia) and is designed for modems that transmit data in a certain bits per second (bps) range (9600-56000 bps). The backup telephone number (9830625) also is located in the city of Placentia (Placentia 2) and is designed for modems that transmit in the same range (9600-56000 bps). In addition, the two Phone Book buttons that display to the right of the telephone numbers allow you to change the telephone number and backup telephone number, respectively.

In Figure 7-3, the When dialing from here pane contains the settings for the special settings for dialing local and long distance telephone calls. As indicated by the four blank text boxes in the pane, an outside line for local or long distance calls is not used, call waiting is enabled, and a credit card is not required for long distance calls.

It is common to create several sets of communication settings. For example, you may want to create one group of communication settings to connect to an online service from a computer located at your business location. You may want to create another set if you must stay in a motel in another city and want to connect to an online service using a laptop computer. This set may contain a different area code, telephone numbers, and special instructions for dialing local and long distance telephone calls. A method to create a new set of communication settings by changing the existing settings is illustrated later in this book.

More About

Telephone Numbers

Local telephone companies may charge you to dial a local telephone number if they use calling zones to determine the cost of a telephone call. To determine the exact cost, call the telephone company, give them the telephone number, and ask for the cost of the first and subsequent minutes.

Signing In to The Microsoft Network

Each time you want to use MSN, you must sign in. During the sign in process, Windows 98 dials a telephone number to contact MSN. Because MSN has local nodes in many cities and towns, and local nodes allow you to dial a local telephone number to connect to MSN, many MSN users save the expense of dialing a long distance telephone number.

Because MSN is a feature of Windows 98, you can sign in easily by double-clicking The Microsoft Network icon on the desktop. Assume that one of the authors of this book has signed up for an MSN account and the StevenForsythe user name and GoBlue password were chosen during that process. The following steps use the user name and password to sign in. If you do not have an account with MSN or cannot sign in with the computer you are using, read the following steps without performing them. If you have an MSN account, perform the following steps using your user name and password.

 To Sign In to The Microsoft Network

1 Double-click The Microsoft Network icon on the desktop.

The MSN - Sign-In window displays (Figure 7-4). The User name text box contains a user name (StevenForsythe) and the Password text box contains the insertion point. The Connection status pane contains a message to remind you to type your password.

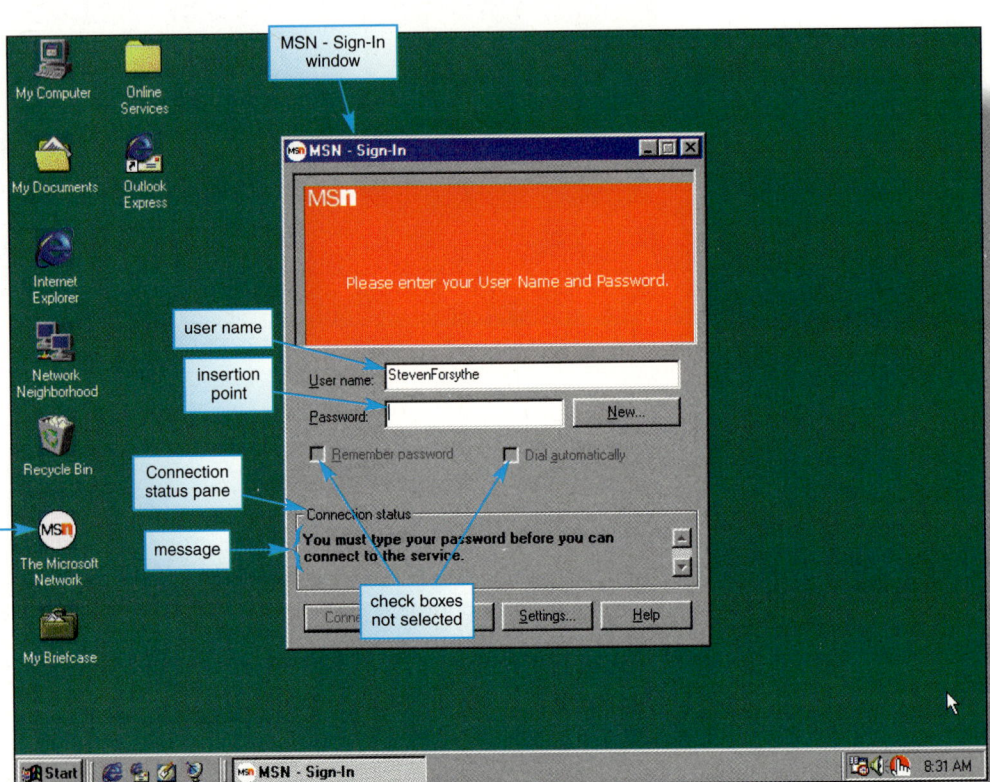

FIGURE 7-4

Other Ways

1. Click The Microsoft Network icon in tray status area, click Connect to MSN
2. Double-click My Computer icon, double-click Dial-Up Networking icon, double-click MSN icon
3. Click Start button, point to Programs, point to Accessories, point to Communications, click Dial-Up Networking, double-click MSN icon

Accessing an Online Service • WIN 7.9

② **Type** `GoBlue` **in the Password text box and then point to the Connect button.**

For security purposes, an asterisk for each character of the password (******) displays in the Password text box (Figure 7-5).

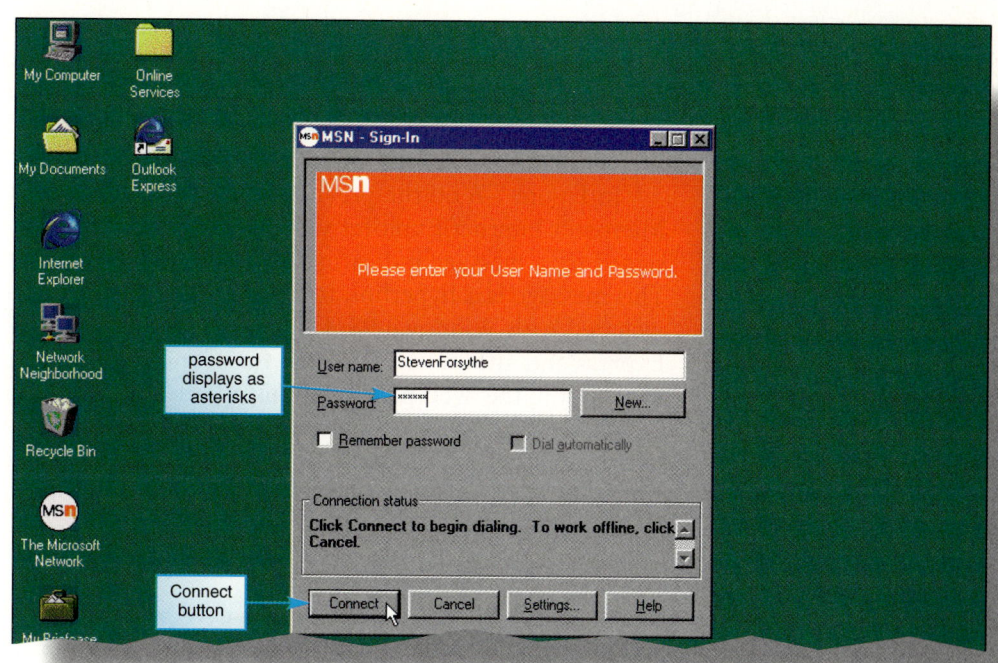

FIGURE 7-5

③ **Click the Connect button.**

Various messages display in the Connection status pane in the MSN - Sign-In window as the modem dials the telephone number, the online service verifies the user name and password, and the computer connects to MSN. When the connection is complete, the Sign-In window closes, Internet Explorer launches, the MSN On Stage - Microsoft Internet Explorer window displays, and the Internet connection icon displays in the tray status area (Figure 7-6).

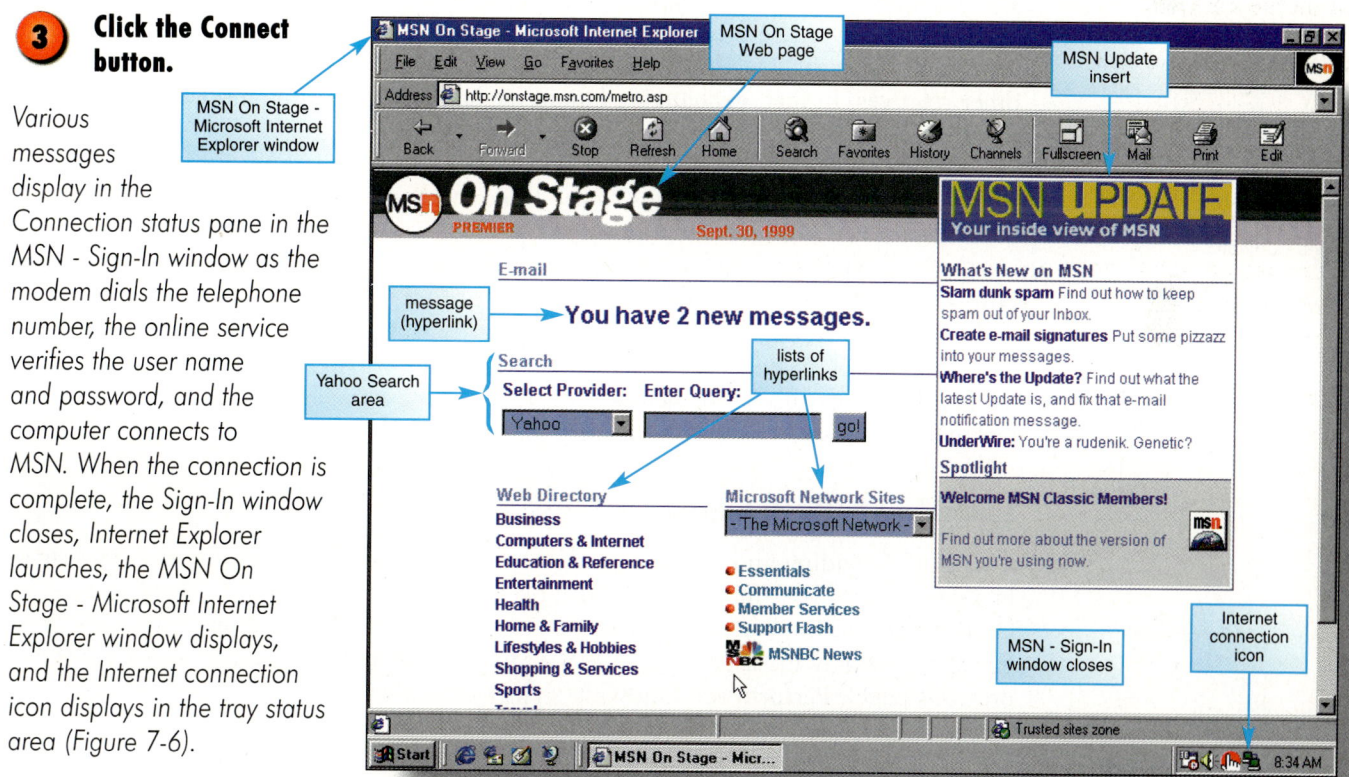

FIGURE 7-6

In Figure 7-4 on page WIN 7.8, the Remember password check box is not selected. Although not recommended for security reasons, clicking the Remember password check box allows you to sign in without entering a password. In addition, clicking the Dial automatically check box allows other application programs to connect to the Internet without your intervention.

In Figure 7-6 on the previous page, the MSN On Stage Web page displays in the Microsoft Internet Explorer window. If you have received new mail since you last signed in, a message indicating the number of new messages displays in the window. This message is a hyperlink to Microsoft Outlook Express, the e-mail program included with Windows 98. Clicking the message launches Microsoft Outlook Express and allows you to check for new e-mail messages and send e-mail messages. In addition, the Web page contains an area to perform a search using the Yahoo Search service, two lists containing hyperlinks, and the MSN UPDATE insert containing links to new features of MSN. Because Web pages change frequently, the MSN On Stage Web page that displays on your desktop may be different from the Web page shown in Figure 7-6.

Microsoft Outlook Express

> **More About**
>
> **Outlook Express**
>
> Outlook Express allows you to change how an e-mail looks by using special type faces, changing the background graphic, attaching files and pictures, and adding a hyperlink to a Web page. Many schools and businesses, however, still use older, less sophisticated mail programs that do not recognize these newer additions.

Electronic mail (e-mail) has become an important means of exchanging messages and files between business associates and friends. Businesses find that using e-mail to send documents electronically saves both time and money. Parents with students away at college or relatives who are scattered across the country find that exchanging e-mail messages is a cheap and easy way to stay in touch with their children or other relatives. In fact, exchanging e-mail messages is one of the more widely used features of the Internet.

Besides exchanging e-mail messages, another popular method of exchanging information among individuals is to use Internet newsgroups. An **Internet newsgroup** contains articles and messages about many varied and interesting topics.

Outlook Express allows you to receive and store incoming e-mail messages, compose and send e-mail messages, maintain a list of frequently used e-mail addresses, and read and post messages to Internet newsgroups. Outlook Express displays all incoming e-mail messages, regardless of whether the e-mail comes from other MSN members, Internet users, or members of other online services. Outlook Express is included with Windows 98.

Launching Outlook Express

Prior to sending and receiving e-mail messages and reading and posting messages in a newsgroup, you must launch Outlook Express. Although many ways exist to launch Outlook Express, the easiest way is to click the message (hyperlink) indicating you have new messages on the MSN On Stage Web page (see Figure 7-6 on the previous page). Perform the following steps to launch Outlook Express.

Microsoft Outlook Express • WIN 7.11

 Steps **To Launch Outlook Express**

1 **Point to the You have 2 new messages hyperlink in the MSN On Stage - Microsoft Internet Explorer window (Figure 7-7).**

The number of e-mail messages (2) in the hyperlink may be different on your computer.

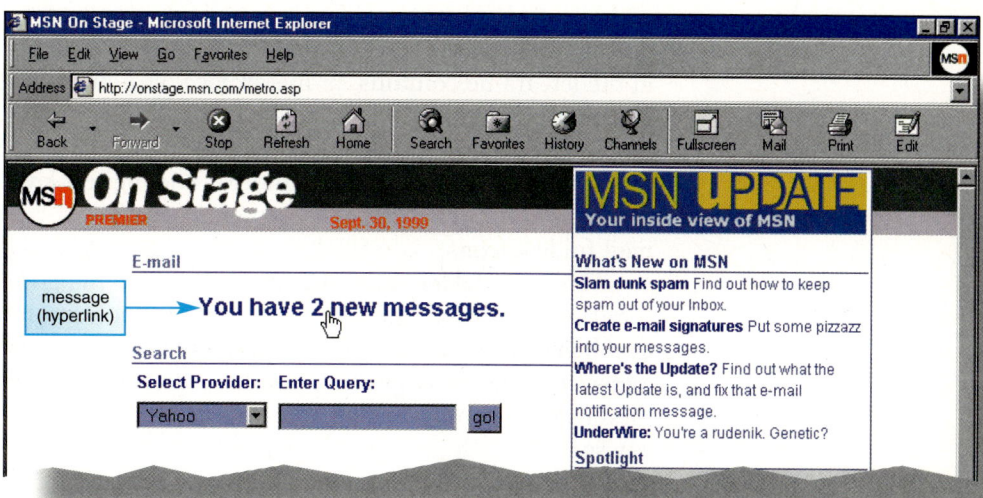

FIGURE 7-7

2 **Click the hyperlink. If necessary, maximize the Inbox - Outlook Express window.**

The Outlook Express introductory screen displays momentarily while Outlook Express launches and then the Inbox - Outlook Express window displays (Figure 7-8). The window contains the folder list, message list, and preview pane.

 **Other Ways**

1. Double-click Outlook Express icon on desktop
2. Click Launch Outlook Express icon on Quick Launch toolbar
3. Click Start button, click The Microsoft Network, click Connect, click You have 2 new messages
4. Click Start button, point to Programs, point to Internet Explorer, click Outlook Express

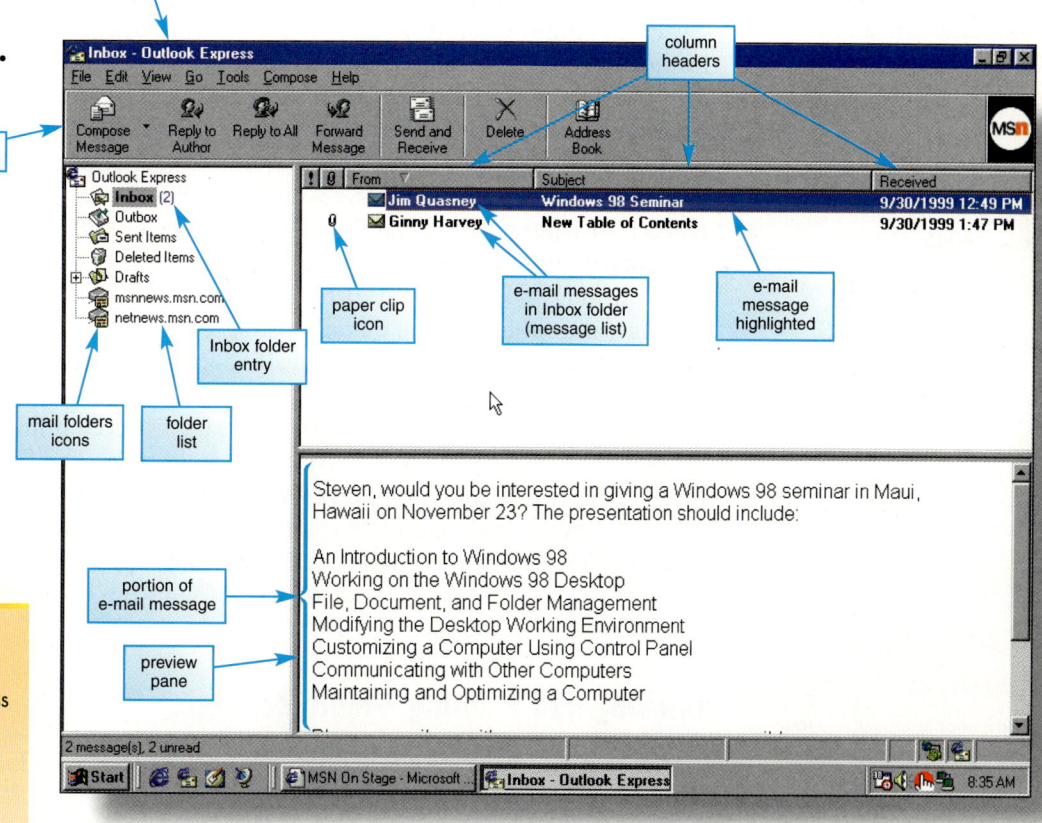

FIGURE 7-8

The Inbox - Outlook Express window shown in Figure 7-8 on the previous page contains a number of elements. Below the title bar and menu bar is a toolbar containing buttons specific to Outlook Express (Compose Message, Reply to Author, and so on).

The Inbox - Outlook Express window is divided into three frames. The folder list in the left frame contains, in hierarchical structure, seven mail folders. Five standard mail folders (Inbox, Outbox, Sent Items, Deleted Items, and Drafts) display when you first launch Outlook Express. Although, you cannot rename or delete these folders, you can create additional folders. The highest level in the hierarchy is Outlook Express. Connected by a dotted vertical line below the Outlook Express icon are the mail folders icons.

The **Inbox folder** is the destination for incoming mail. The **Outbox folder** temporarily holds messages you send until Outlook Express delivers the messages. The **Sent Items folder** retains copies of messages that you have sent. The **Deleted Items folder** contains messages that you have deleted. The **Drafts folder** retains copies of messages that you are not yet ready to send. The last two folders contain lists of newsgroups.

Folders can contain e-mail messages, faxes, files created in other Windows applications, and messages from online services, such as The Microsoft Network, America Online, Prodigy, and CompuServe. Folders in bold type and followed by a number in parentheses (**Inbox** (2)) indicate the number of messages in the folder that have not been opened. Other folders may display on your computer instead of or in addition to the folders shown in Figure 7-8 on the previous page.

Five column headers display above the message list at the top of the upper-right frame of the window. An exclamation point icon (Importance) identifies the first header and a paper clip icon (Attachment) identifies the second header. An exclamation point icon in the column below the first header indicates the e-mail message is important and you should read it immediately. A paper clip icon in the column below the second header indicates the e-mail message contains an attachment (file or object). In Figure 7-8 on the previous page, the e-mail message from Ginny Harvey contains an attachment. Entries in the columns below the third header (From), fourth header (Subject), and fifth header (Received) indicate who sent the e-mail message, the subject of the e-mail message, and the date and time Outlook Express received the e-mail message. An envelope icon identifies each message as an e-mail message.

Below the column headers is the message list containing the two e-mail messages in the Inbox folder. New mail displays in bold type. The first new e-mail message (in bold type) is highlighted and from Jim Quasney. The second new e-mail message (in bold type) is from Ginny Harvey. Other e-mail messages may display on your computer instead of these messages. The lower-right frame contains a preview pane containing a portion of the text associated with the highlighted e-mail message (Jim Quasney) in the message list.

Reading E-mail messages

Many people launch Outlook Express when they turn on their computer and then minimize the Inbox - Outlook Express window. When they receive a new e-mail message, Outlook displays an envelope icon in the tray status area and plays the sound of a telephone ringing. Outlook removes the envelope icon when they open the e-mail message.

Opening and Reading E-mail Messages

In Figure 7-8 on the previous page, the highlighted Jim Quasney message displays in the message list, and a portion of the message displays in the preview pane. If you wish to view the e-mail message in a separate window, you must open the e-mail message. To open and read an e-mail message, double-click the envelope icon associated with the message in the message list. Perform the following step to open the e-mail message from Jim Quasney.

Steps To Open an E-mail Message

1 **Double-click the envelope icon associated with the Jim Quasney message and then scroll the preview pane to read the message. If this envelope icon does not display, double-click another envelope icon.**

The Windows 98 Seminar window displays and the subject displays in the window title bar (Figure 7-9). The upper frame contains identifying information about the e-mail message and the lower frame contains the e-mail message.

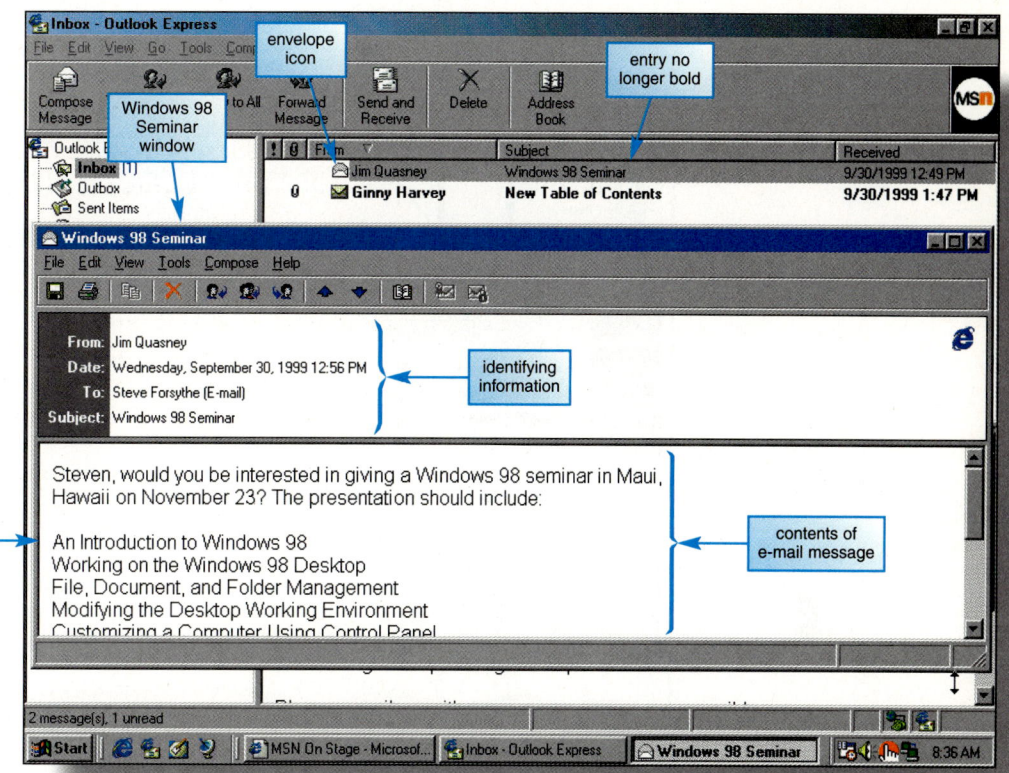

FIGURE 7-9

In Figure 7-9, the Jim Quasney message in the message list is no longer bolded, indicating you have opened the e-mail message. Although this e-mail was received by an MSN member, anyone with an MSN account can send e-mail to and receive e-mail from a member of another online service or any individual with an Internet service provider account. In addition, you can maximize the Windows 98 Seminar window to make it easier to view the message.

Replying to an E-mail

Each time Outlook Express receives an e-mail message, business and personal information about the sender (name, address, telephone number, e-mail address, and so on) is added to an Address Book. The **Address Book** is a central location for the storage of business and personal information about those individuals you contact frequently. Outlook Express uses the information in the Address Book to reply to an e-mail message, compose a new e-mail message, and quickly find information about an individual.

After reading the e-mail message from Jim Quasney, you decide to compose and send an e-mail reply to Jim Quasney. The Reply to Author button on the toolbar allows you to reply quickly to an e-mail message by using the e-mail address stored in the Address Book. Perform the steps on the next page to reply to Jim Quasney.

Other Ways

1. Right-click envelope icon, click Open
2. Click envelope icon, on File menu click Open
3. Press CTRL+O

WIN 7.14 • Project 7 • Communicating with Other Computers

To Reply to an E-mail Message

1 Point to the Reply to Author button on the toolbar in the Windows 98 Seminar window (Figure 7-10).

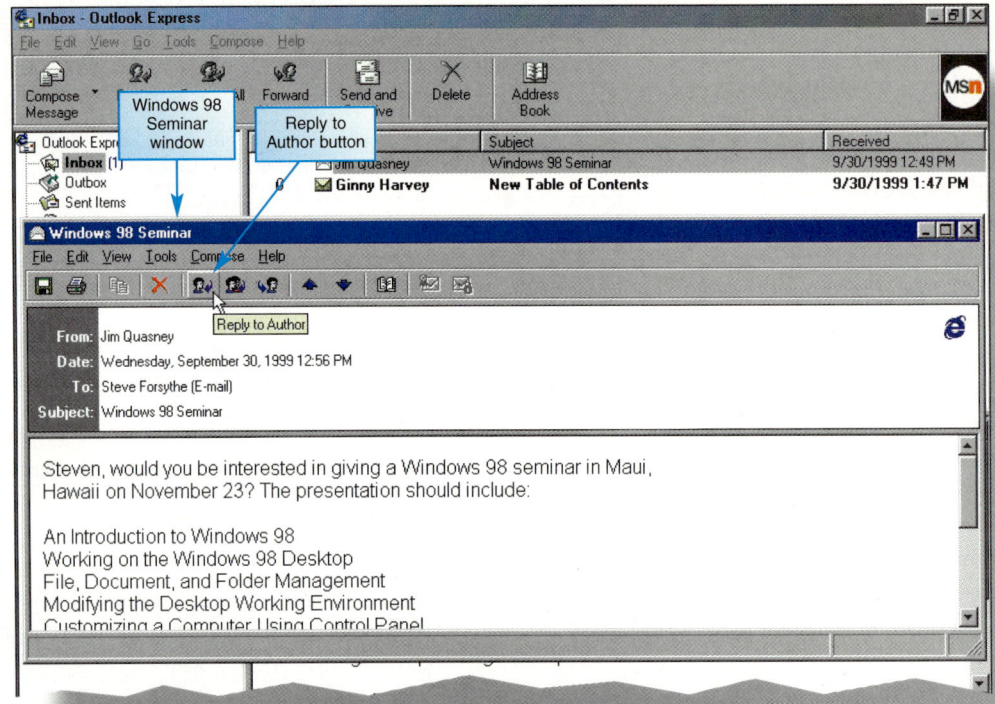

FIGURE 7-10

2 Click the Reply to Author button. Type the e-mail reply as shown in Figure 7-11 and then point to the Send button on the toolbar.

The window title bar includes the Re: entry and the contents of the two frames change (Figure 7-11). In the upper frame, the To entry consists of the underlined Jim Quasney name and Re: is added to the Subject entry. The e-mail reply displays in the lower frame.

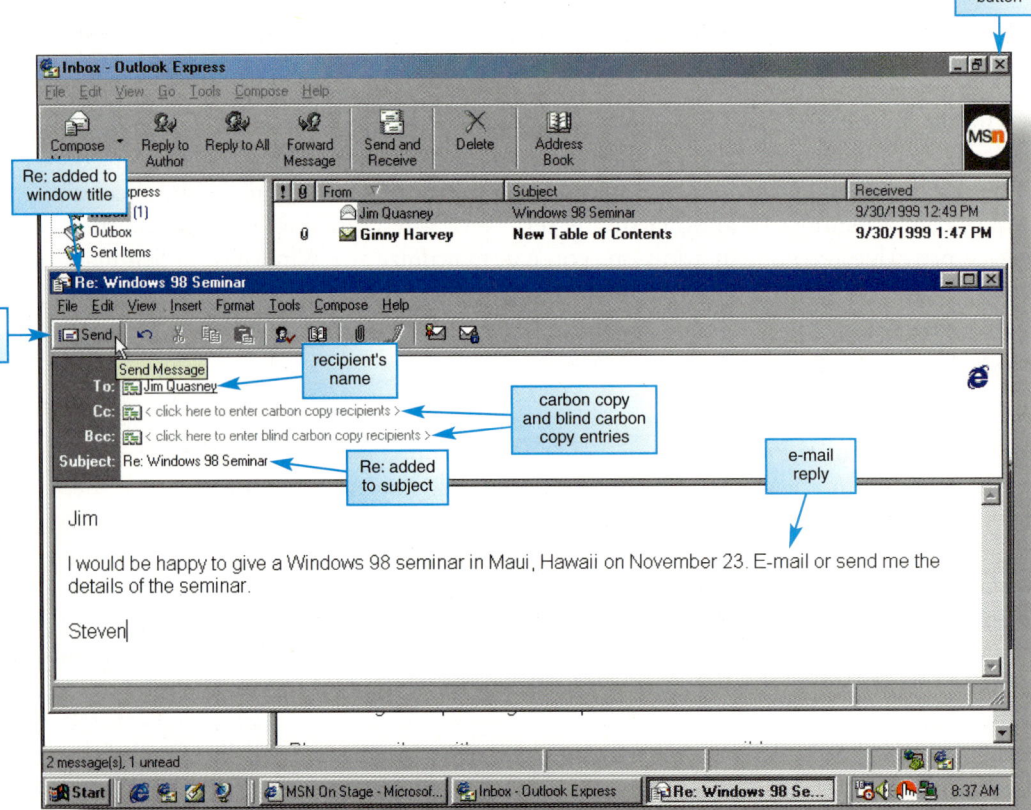

FIGURE 7-11

3 | Click the Send Message button. Click the Close button in the Inbox - Outlook Express window.

The Re: Windows 98 Seminar window closes, Outlook Express stores the reply e-mail message in the Outbox folder while it sends the message and then moves the message to the Sent Items folder (Figure 7-12). The Inbox - Outlook Express window closes and the message hyperlink in the MSN On Stage - Microsoft Internet Explorer window indicates there are no new e-mail messages.

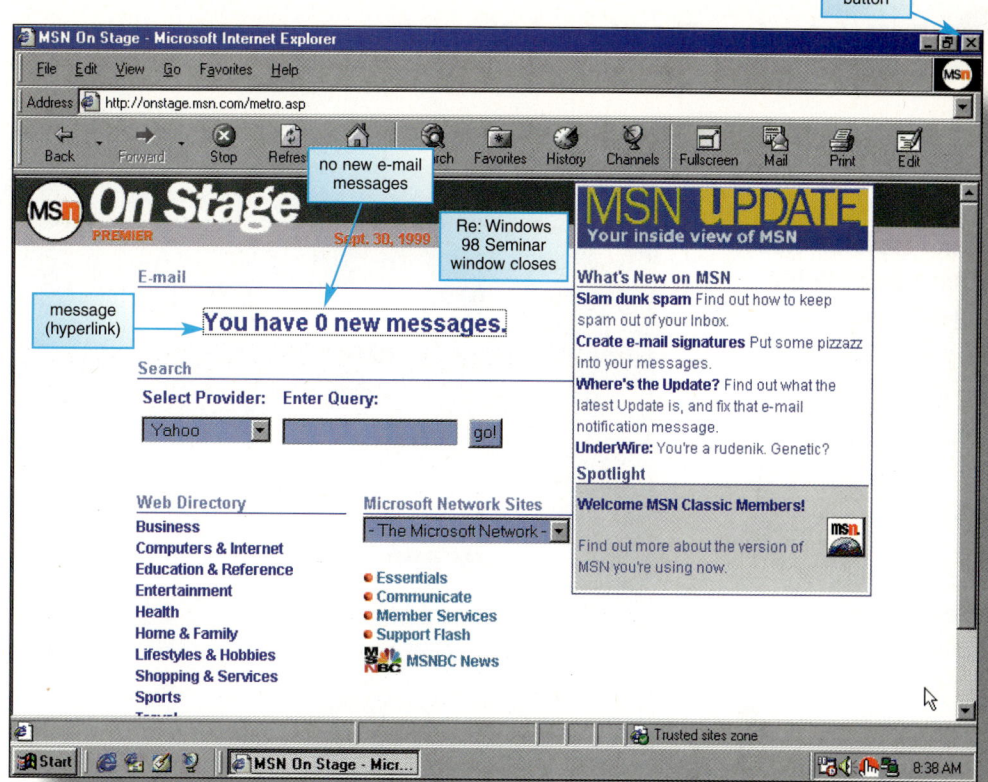

FIGURE 7-12

After replying to an e-mail message, you may want to delete the original e-mail message from the message list by selecting the e-mail message and clicking the Delete button on the toolbar.

Signing Out from The Microsoft Network

After checking for new e-mail messages and responding to an e-mail message, disconnect from MSN by performing the steps on the next page.

Other Ways

1. Right-click envelope icon, click Reply to Author
2. Click envelope icon, click Reply to Author button
3. On Compose menu click Reply to Author
4. Press CTRL+R

WIN 7.16 • Project 7 • Communicating with Other Computers

 Steps: To Sign Out from The Microsoft Network

1 **Click the Close button in the MSN On Stage - Microsoft Internet Explorer window and then point to the Hang-up Now button in the MSN - Disconnect dialog box.**

The MSN On Stage - Microsoft Internet Explorer window closes and the MSN - Disconnect dialog box displays (Figure 7-13). A message and the seconds left until being disconnected (25 seconds) display.

 Click the Hang-up Now button.

The MSN - Disconnect dialog box closes and the Internet connection icon is removed from the tray status area.

Other Ways

1. On File menu click Close, click Hang-up Now
2. Click MSN logo in tray status area, click Disconnect from MSN, click Hang-up Now

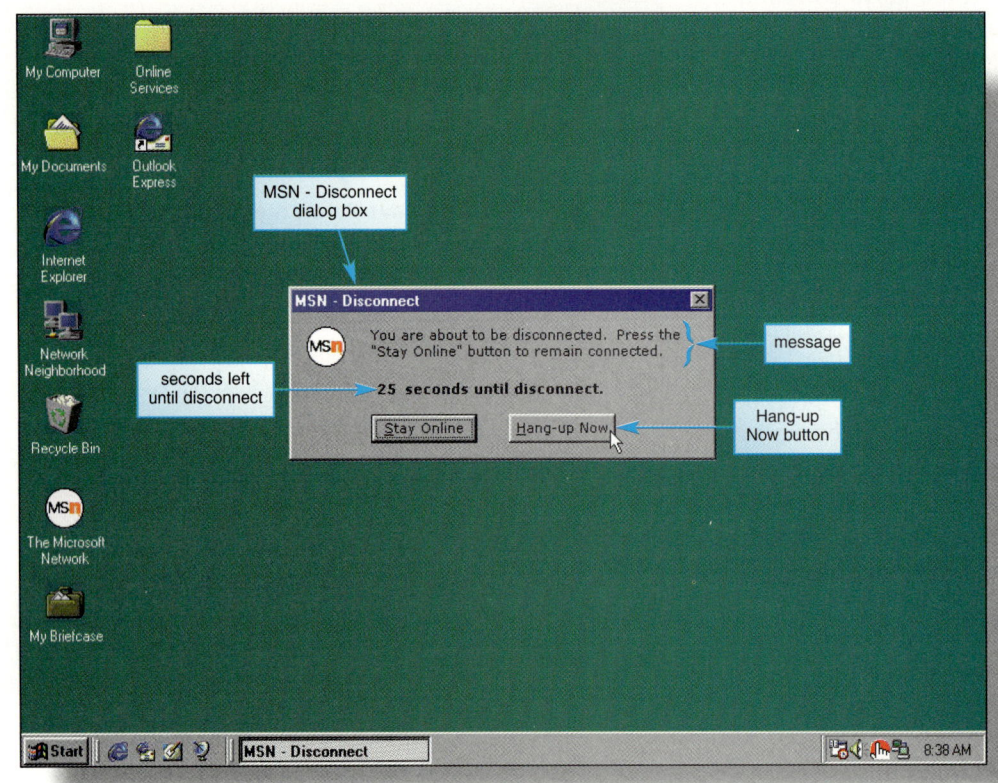

FIGURE 7-13

Changing the Connection Settings

Previously, you checked the connection settings and then signed in to The Microsoft Network using the existing telephone number, backup telephone number, and default dialing properties. These telephone numbers and dialing properties are for use in the city in which the computer is located.

If you had to move the computer to a location that requires new telephone numbers or special dialing instructions, you would have to change the connection settings. Similarly, if you use a laptop computer at work or at home, you would use one set of connection settings. If you travel to another city to attend a business meeting and stay in a motel, you would have to change the connection settings on the laptop computer before connecting to MSN. The new connection settings may consist of a different area code and telephone numbers, and special instructions for dialing local and long distance telephone calls from the motel.

For example, assume the connection settings on your laptop computer are set so you can use your laptop computer in Placentia, California. In Placentia, the area code is 714, the telephone number is 577-0144, and the backup telephone number is 983-0625. These connection settings were shown in Figures 7-2 and 7-3 on pages WIN 7.6 and WIN 7.7.

Microsoft Outlook Express • WIN 7.17

Assume that you have to stay at the Holiday Motel in Ann Arbor, Michigan and would like to use your laptop computer to connect to The Microsoft Network from your motel room. Upon checking into the motel, you determine the area code in Ann Arbor is 734 and you must dial the digit 8 when making a local telephone call. You do not know what telephone numbers to use to connect to The Microsoft Network. After connecting the laptop to the telephone line in the motel room, you must change the connection settings so you can sign in to MSN. Perform the following steps to change the connection settings.

> ### More About
> ### Connection Settings
> Changing the connection settings allows you to use the same computer from several locations. Locations may include a home with call waiting, an office with a dial-prefix, and a hotel with the ability to pay using a credit card.

 To Change the Connection Settings

1 **Right-click The Microsoft Network icon on the desktop and then point to Connection Settings.**

A shortcut menu displays (Figure 7-14).

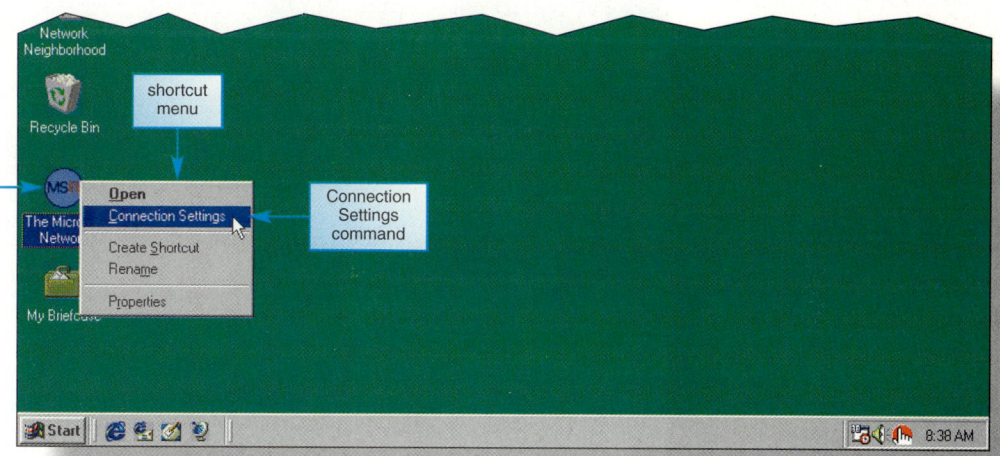

FIGURE 7-14

2 **Click Connection Settings and then point to the Dialing Properties button.**

The Connection Settings dialog box displays (Figure 7-15). The telephone number and backup telephone number (5770144 and 9830625) allow you to sign in from the city of Placentia. The telephone numbers in your dialog box may be different.

3 **Write down on a piece of paper the city name and telephone number, city name and backup telephone number, and state name associated with the two city names.**

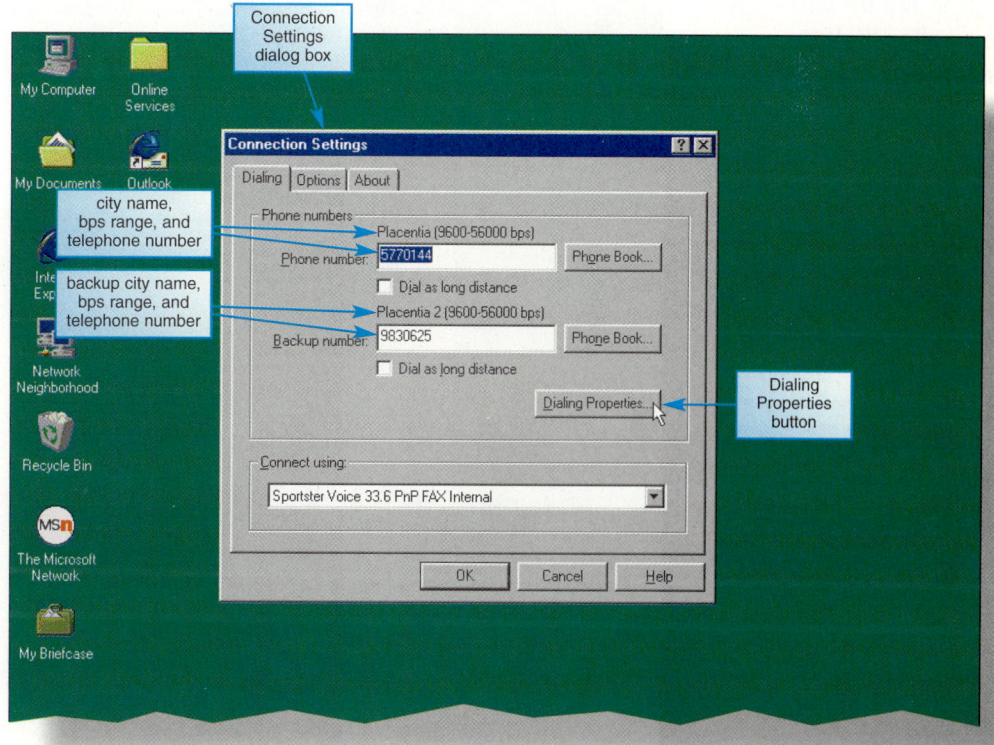

FIGURE 7-15

WIN 7.18 • Project 7 • Communicating with Other Computers

4 **Click the Dialing Properties button and then point to the New button in the Dialing Properties dialog box.**

The Dialing Properties dialog box displays (Figure 7-16). The current location (Default Location) is highlighted in the I am dialing from box and the current area code (714) displays in the Area code text box.

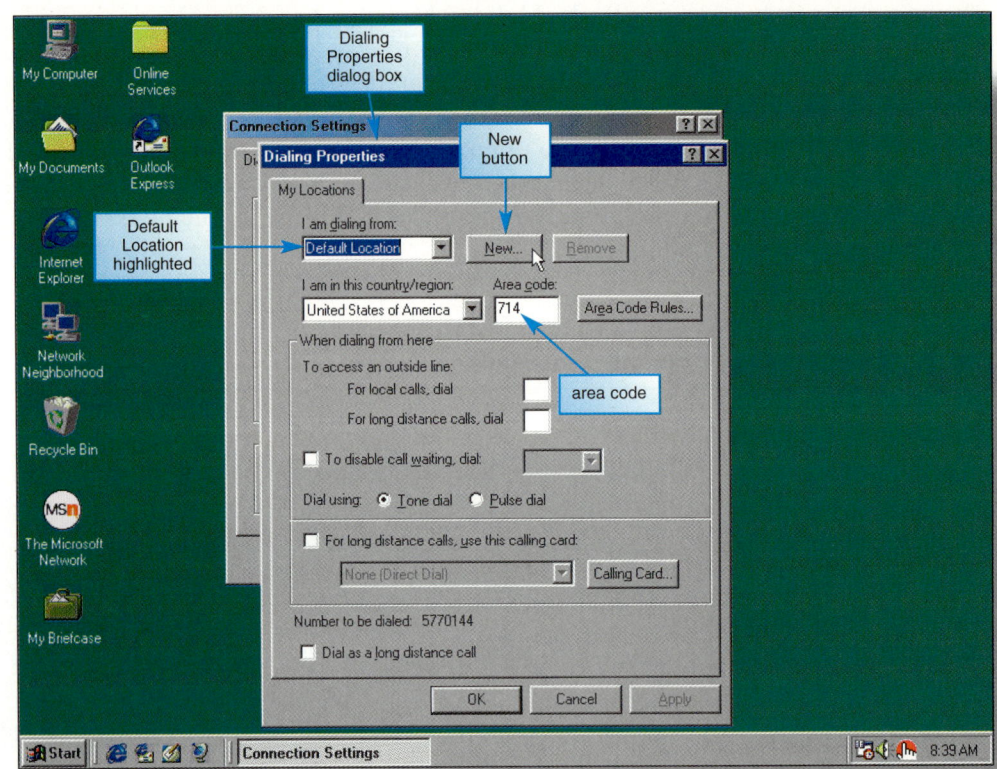

FIGURE 7-16

5 **Click the New button and then point to the OK button in the smaller Dialing Properties dialog box.**

A second, smaller Dialing Properties dialog box containing a message and the OK button displays (Figure 7-17). The default New Location name (New Location) displays in the I am dialing from box in the larger Dialing Properties box.

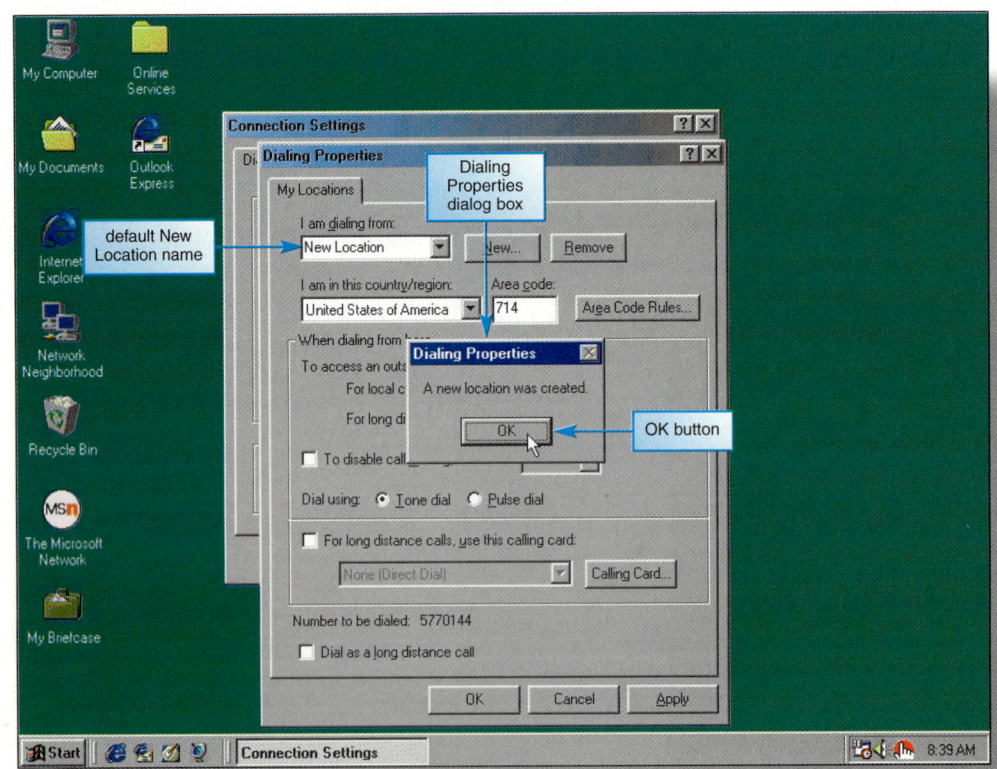

FIGURE 7-17

Microsoft Outlook Express • WIN 7.19

PROJECT 7

6 **Click the OK button. Type** Holiday Motel **in the I am dialing from box, type** 734 **in the Area code text box, type** 8 **in the For local calls, dial text box, and then point to the OK button in the Dialing Properties dialog box.**

The smaller Dialing Properties dialog box closes and the new location (Holiday Motel), new area code (734), and local call dialing prefix (8) display (Figure 7-18).

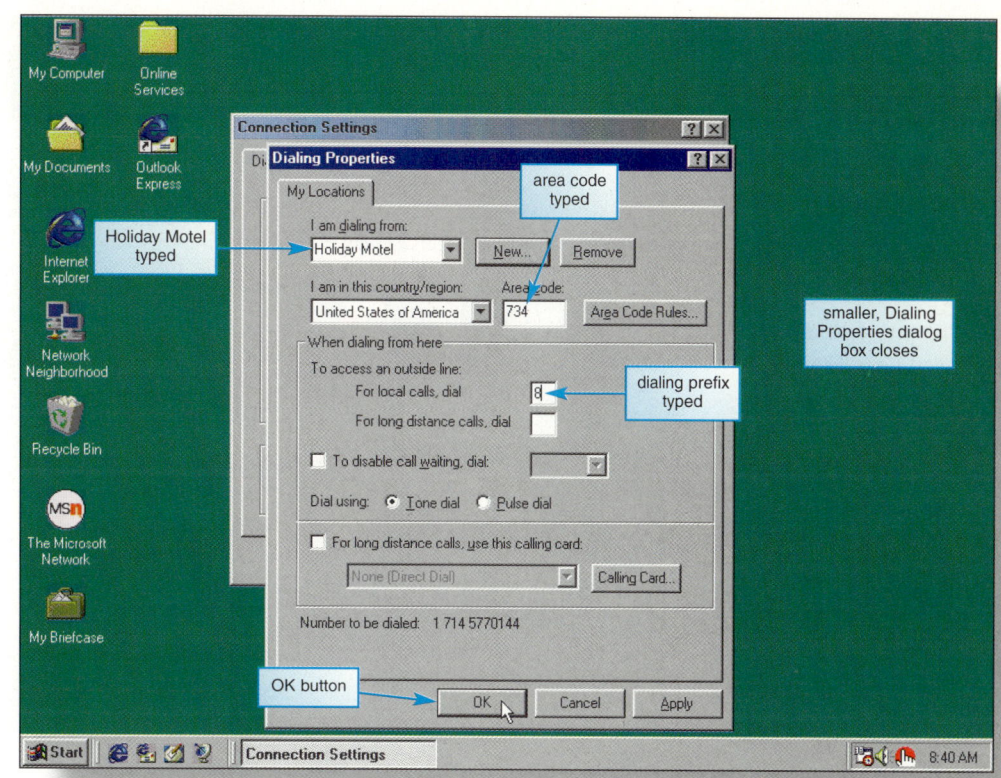

FIGURE 7-18

7 **Click the OK button and then point to the Phone Book button to the right of the Phone number text box.**

The Dialing Properties dialog box closes (Figure 7-19). A long distance dialing prefix (1) and Placentia area code (714) precede the telephone number and backup telephone number to indicate the modem has to dial a long distance number to connect to MSN using the new area code (734).

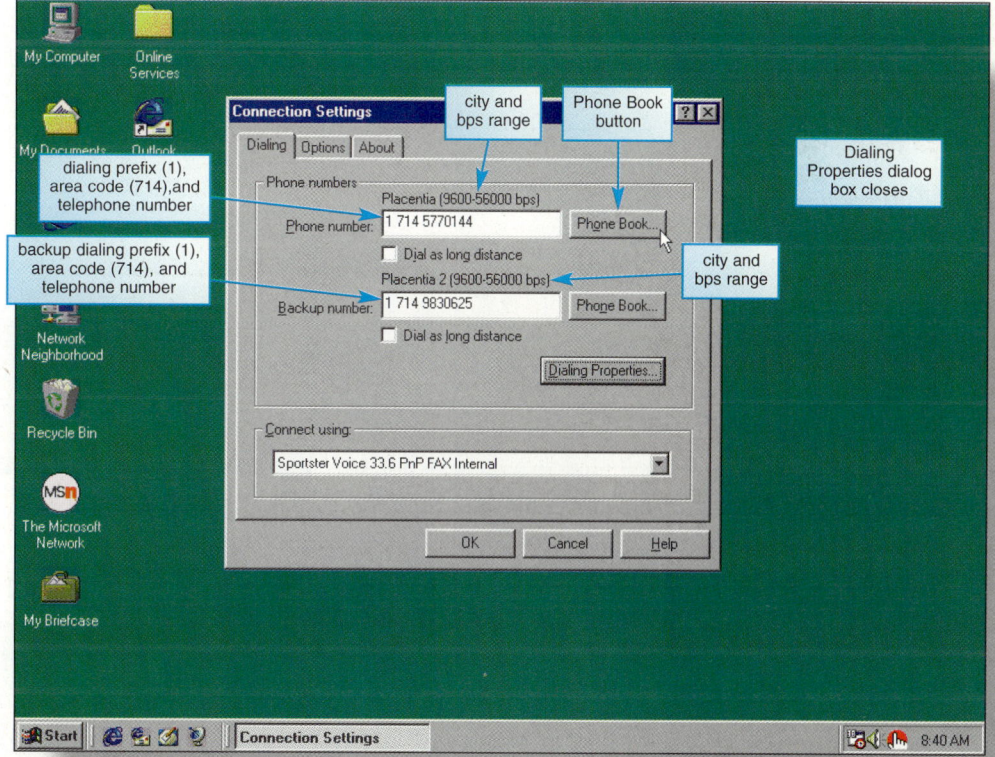

FIGURE 7-19

WIN 7.20 • **Project 7** • **Communicating with Other Computers**

8 **Click the Phone Book button. Click the State or region box arrow, scroll the list to display Michigan, and then point to Michigan.**

The Phone Book dialog box displays (Figure 7-20). The Modem name displays in the Service type box, the country name displays in the Country box, the state name (California) displays in State or region box, and the highlighted Michigan name displays in the State or region list box. A list of California telephone numbers displays in the Access numbers list box.

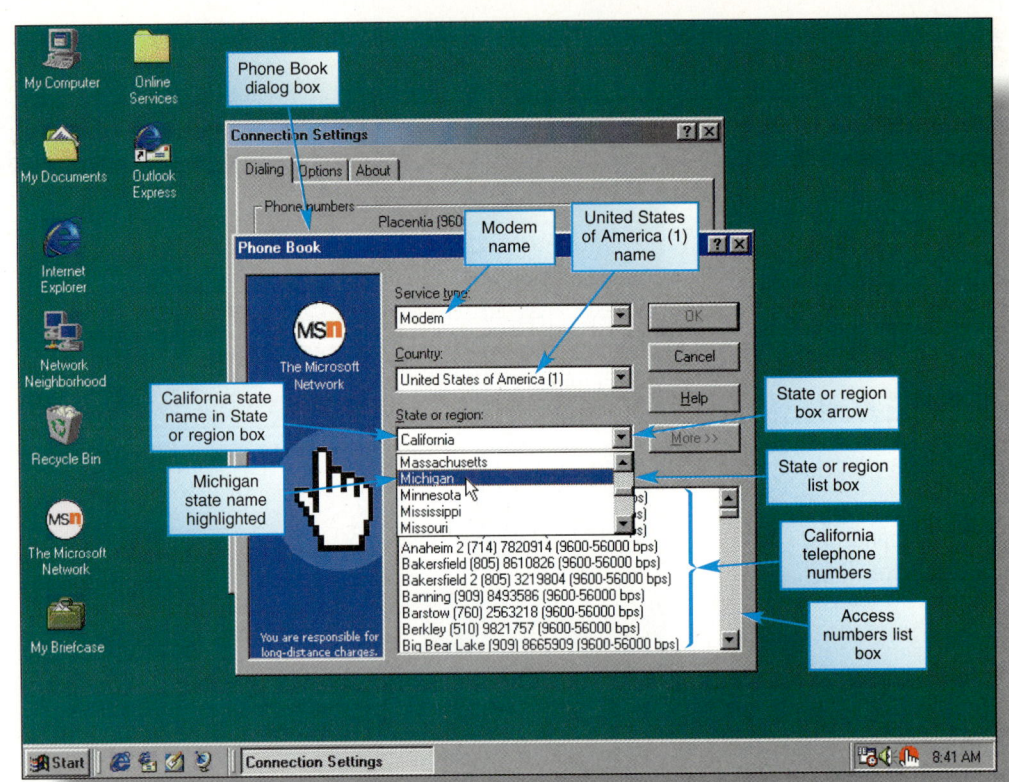

FIGURE 7-20

9 **Click Michigan. Click the first Ann Arbor name in the Access numbers list box and then point to the OK button.**

The word, Michigan, displays in the State or region box and the first Ann Arbor entry in the Access numbers list box is selected (Figure 7-21).

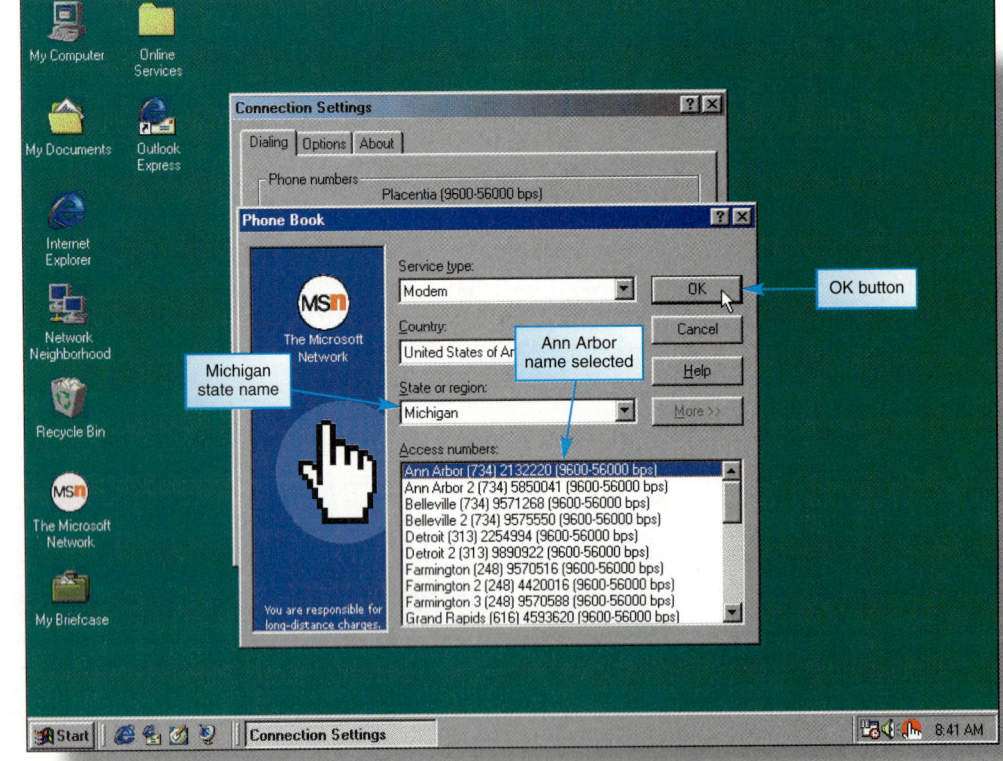

FIGURE 7-21

Click the OK button.

The Phone Book dialog box closes (Figure 7-22) The words, Ann Arbor (9600-56000 bps), display above the Phone number text box and the telephone number, 8 2132220, displays in the text box.

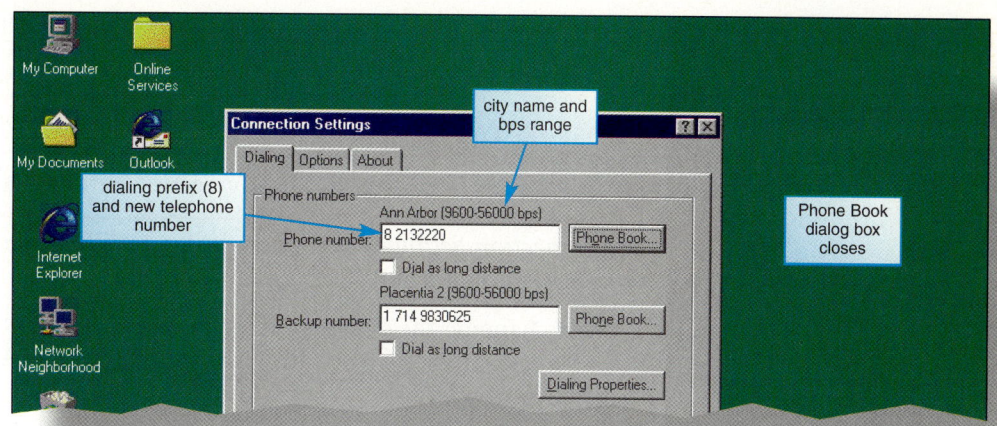

FIGURE 7-22

The dialing properties and the telephone number are changed. Next, change the backup telephone number.

Changing the Backup Telephone Number

After changing the telephone number, you should change the backup telephone number. Perform the following steps to change the backup telephone number.

TO CHANGE THE BACKUP TELEPHONE NUMBER

1. Click the Phone Book button to the right of the Backup number text box.
2. Click the State or region box arrow, scroll the list box to display Michigan, and then click Michigan.
3. Click the second Ann Arbor name (Ann Arbor 2) in the Access numbers list box.
4. Click the OK button in the Phone Book dialog box.

The entry, Ann Arbor 2 (9600-56000 bps), displays above the Backup number text box in the Connection Settings dialog box and the dialing prefix and backup number, 8 5850041, display in the Backup number text box (Figure 7-23).

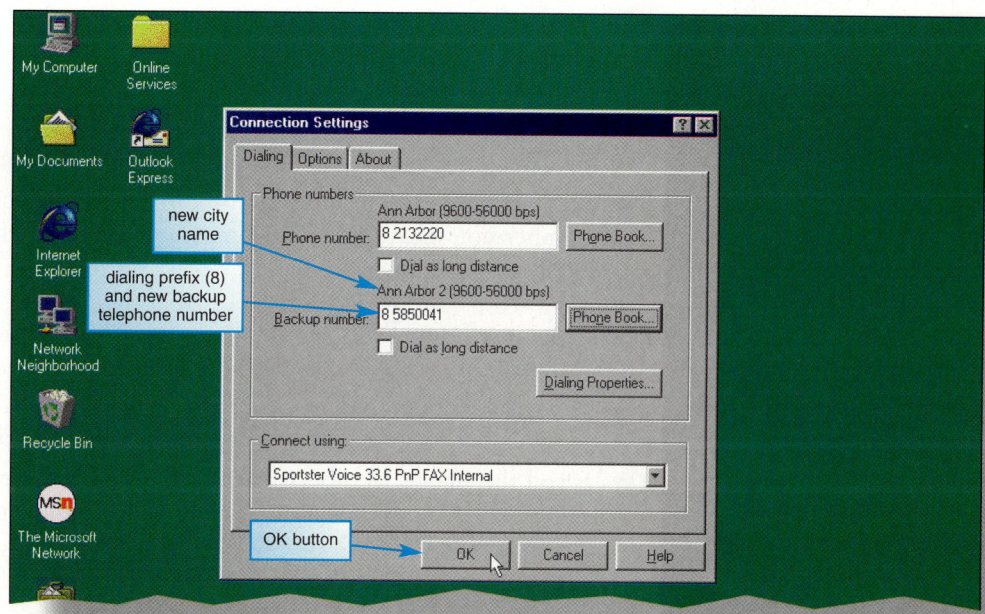

FIGURE 7-23

After changing the backup telephone number, perform the following step to close the Connection Settings dialog box.

TO CLOSE THE CONNECTION SETTINGS DIALOG BOX

1 Click the OK button in the Connection Settings dialog box.

The Connection Settings dialog box closes and the process of changing the connection settings is complete.

After changing the connection settings, you can use the laptop computer to sign in to The Microsoft Network from the motel room in Ann Arbor, Michigan by double-clicking The Microsoft Network icon on the desktop.

Resetting the Connection Settings

After changing the telephone number, backup telephone number, area code, and special instructions for dialing a local telephone number, restore the connection settings to their original settings by performing the following steps.

TO RESTORE THE ORIGINAL CONNECTION SETTINGS

1 Right-click The Microsoft Network icon on the desktop and then click Connection Settings.

2 Click the Dialing Properties button.

3 Verify that Holiday Motel displays in the I am dialing from box.

4 Click the Remove button.

5 Click the Yes button in the Are You Sure? dialog box.

6 Click the OK button in the Dialing Properties dialog box.

7 Click the Phone Book button to the right of the Phone number text box in the Connection Settings dialog box.

8 Locate the paper containing the city name and telephone number, city name and backup telephone number, and state name you wrote down in Step 3 on page WIN 7.18.

9 Click the State or region box arrow, scroll the list box to display the state name you located in Step 8 above, and then click the state name.

10 Scroll the Access numbers list box to display the city name of the telephone number you located in Step 8 above and then click the city name.

11 Click the OK button in the Phone Book dialog box.

12 Click the Phone Book button to the right of the Backup number text box in the Connection Settings dialog box.

13 Click the State or region box arrow, scroll the list box to display the state name you located in Step 8 above, and then click the state name.

14 Scroll the Access numbers list box to display the city name of the backup telephone number you located in Step 8 above and then click the city name.

15 Click the OK button in the Phone Book dialog box.

16 Click the OK button in the Connection Settings dialog box.

The telephone number and backup telephone number, area code, and special instructions for dialing a local telephone call are restored to their original settings.

Connecting to the Internet Using an Internet Service Provider

As mentioned previously, Windows 98 provides two methods to connect to the Internet. You can connect using an online service, such as MSN, or an Internet service provider. An **Internet service provider** (**ISP**) maintains a computer, called a **server**, connected to the Internet. Internet service providers throughout the United States often advertise in the newspaper and commonly offer a flat monthly rate for unlimited use of their service.

To connect to the Internet using an ISP, you need an account with the service provider, a computer with a modem, and the Dial-Up Networking software installed when Windows 98 was setup. **Dial-Up Networking** allows you to connect to another computer using a modem. If you have an ISP account, a modem, and Dial-Up Networking, you can connect to the Internet by creating a **Dial-Up Networking connection** to the ISP. You can create this connection using the Dial-Up Networking software or the Internet Connection wizard.

Setting Up a Connection to an Internet Service Provider

The **Internet Connection wizard** allows you to sign up for an account with an ISP if you do not have an account and create the Dial-Up Networking connection to connect to the Internet.

Assume you do not have an ISP and you want to use the wizard to sign up for an ISP account and create the Dial-Up Networking connection required to connect to the Internet. Because you do not have an ISP account, the Internet Connection wizard will search a geographic area, based on zip code, for an ISP in the area and then display a list of the ISPs.

Once you find a list of Internet service providers, you can review the costs and features of each provider, select a provider you like, and provide the information (name, address, and credit card number) necessary to establish an account. The Internet Connection wizard sets up an account and then creates the Dial-Up Networking connection needed to connect to the Internet using the ISP.

Perform the steps on the next page to sign up for an account with EarthLink, an Internet service provider available in most areas of the United States, and create the Dial-Up Networking connection needed to connect a computer to the Internet. If your computer already has a connection to an ISP, you may not create a Dial-Up Networking connection, or you may not use a credit card to sign up for an account, read the steps on the next page without performing them.

More About

Dial-Up Networking

To determine if Dial-Up Networking is installed on your computer, double-click the My Computer icon on the desktop. If you do not see the Dial-Up Networking folder, then Dial-Up Networking is not installed and can be installed using the Add/Remove Programs icon in the Control Panel window.

More About

Creating a Dial-Up Networking Connection

If after creating a Dial-Up Networking connection the connection does not work, use the Modem Troubleshooter to help you identify and solve problems with the connection.

To Sign Up for an ISP Account Using the Internet Connection Wizard

1 **Click the Start button, point to Programs, point to Internet Explorer, and then point to Connection Wizard on the Internet Explorer submenu.**

The Start menu, Programs submenu, and Internet Explorer submenu display (Figure 7-24). The highlighted Connection Wizard command displays on the Internet Explorer submenu.

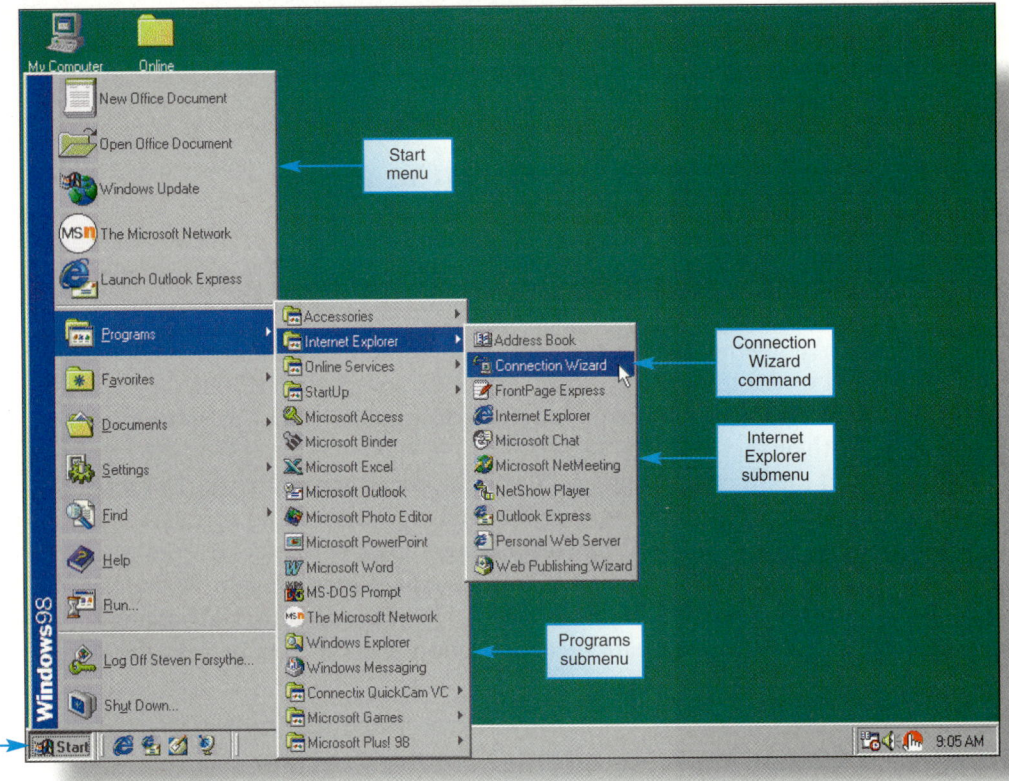

FIGURE 7-24

2 **Click Connection Wizard. If necessary, click the first option button in the Internet Connection Wizard dialog box and then point to the Next button.**

The Internet Connection Wizard dialog box displays (Figure 7-25). The dialog box contains two messages, three option buttons, and the Next and Cancel buttons. The first option button, identified by the words, I want to sign up and configure my computer …, is selected.

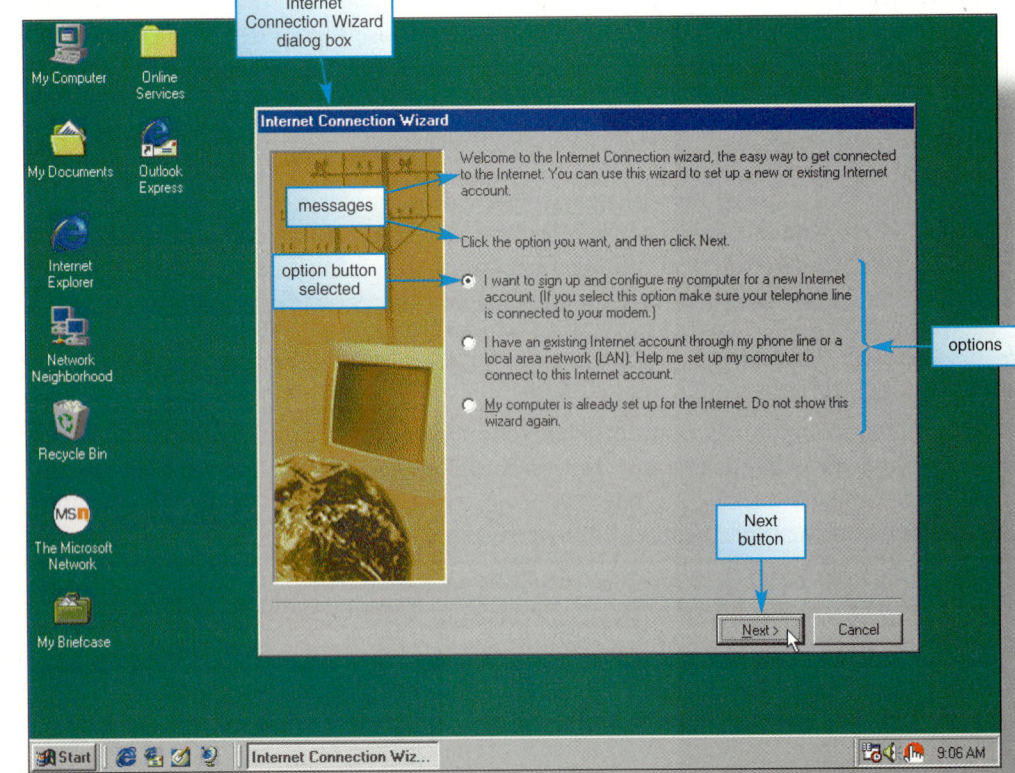

FIGURE 7-25

Connecting to the Internet Using an Internet Service Provider • **WIN 7.25**

③ Click the Next button.

The contents of the dialog box changes and the Internet Connection Wizard dials the Microsoft Referral Service telephone number (1 800 7936675) (Figure 7-26). A message indicates the wizard will connect to the referral service and retrieve a list of Internet service providers in your area. A progress bar indicates the progress of connecting to the service and the Internet connection icon displays in the tray status area while connected to the service.

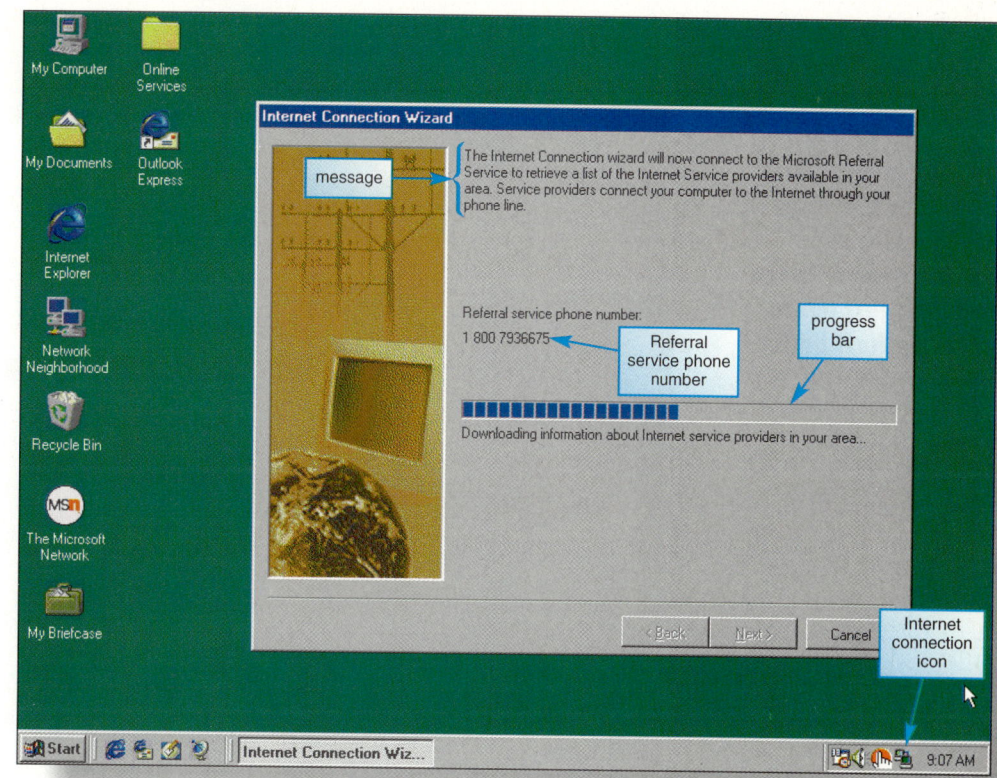

FIGURE 7-26

④ When the contents of the dialog box change, click EarthLink in the Internet service providers list box. Scroll the Provider information list box to read about the EarthLink service.

The contents of the Internet Connection Wizard dialog box changes (Figure 7-27). The dialog box contains two messages, the Internet service providers list box contains a list of ISPs and the selected EarthLink name, and the Provider information list box contains a summary of the EarthLink service.

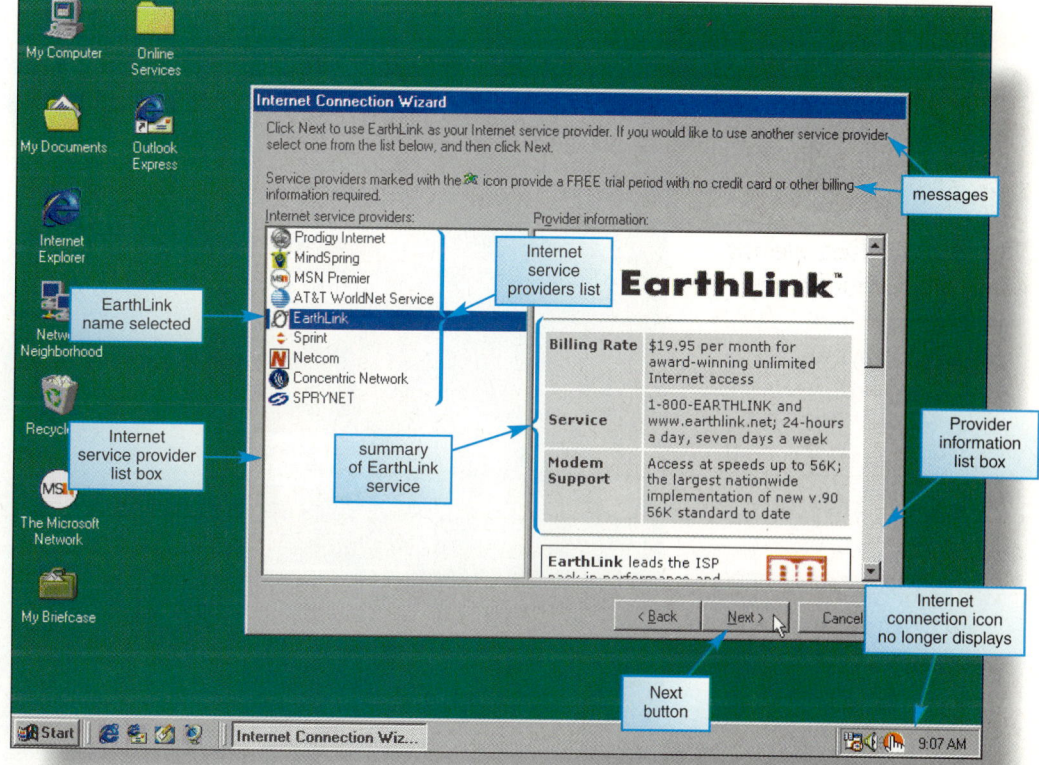

FIGURE 7-27

5 **Click the Next button. When the contents of the dialog box change, type your first name, last name, address, city, state or province, zip or postal code, and telephone number in the appropriate text boxes. Point to the Next button.**

The contents of the Internet Connection Wizard dialog box changes (Figure 7-28). Fictitious information for one of the authors of this book displays in the text boxes.

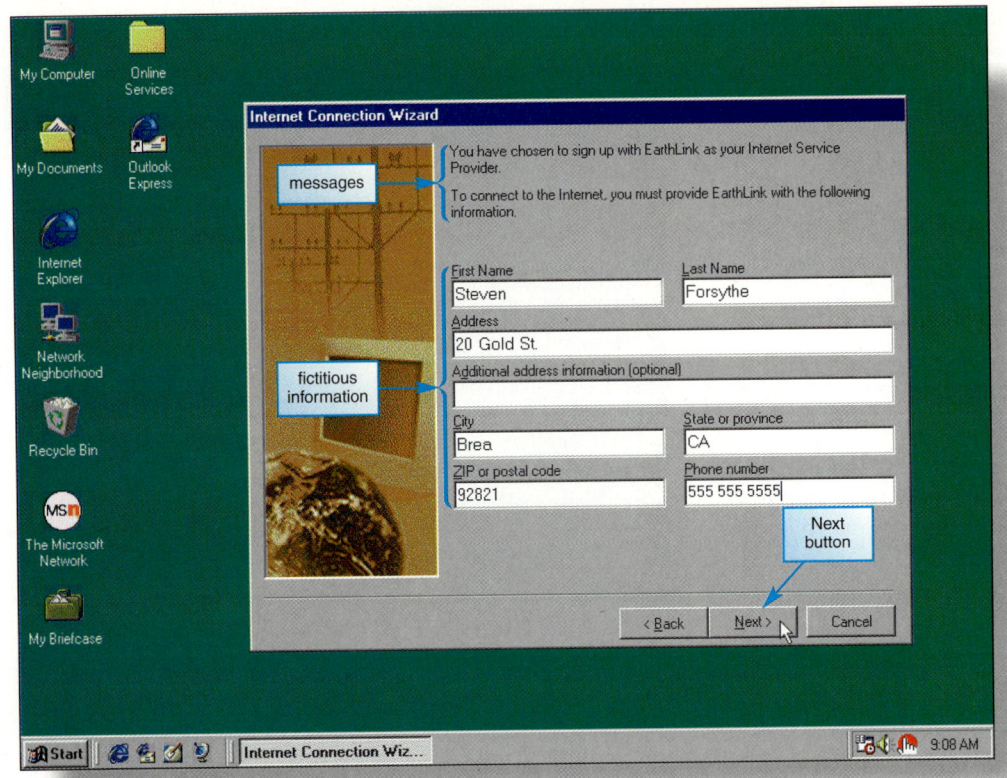

FIGURE 7-28

6 **Click the Next button. If necessary, click the first option button in the Billing Option pane and then point to the Next button.**

The contents of the Internet Connection Wizard dialog box changes (Figure 7-29). A message displays at the top of the dialog box, two billing options display in the Billing Option list box, and the first option is selected.

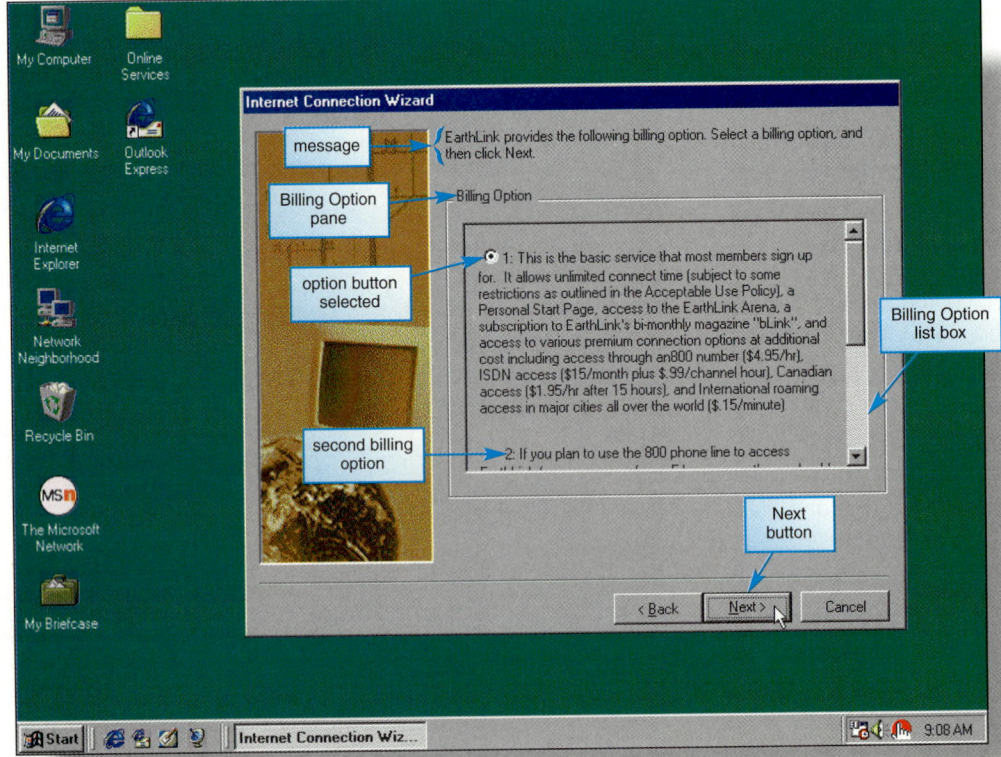

FIGURE 7-29

Connecting to the Internet Using an Internet Service Provider • WIN 7.27

7 **Click the Next button. Select the type of credit card you wish to use and then type your credit card number, expiration month and year, name on your credit card, billing address, and zip or postal code. Point to the Next button.**

The contents of the Internet Connection Wizard dialog box changes (Figure 7-30). Fictitious information for one of the authors of this book displays in the dialog box.

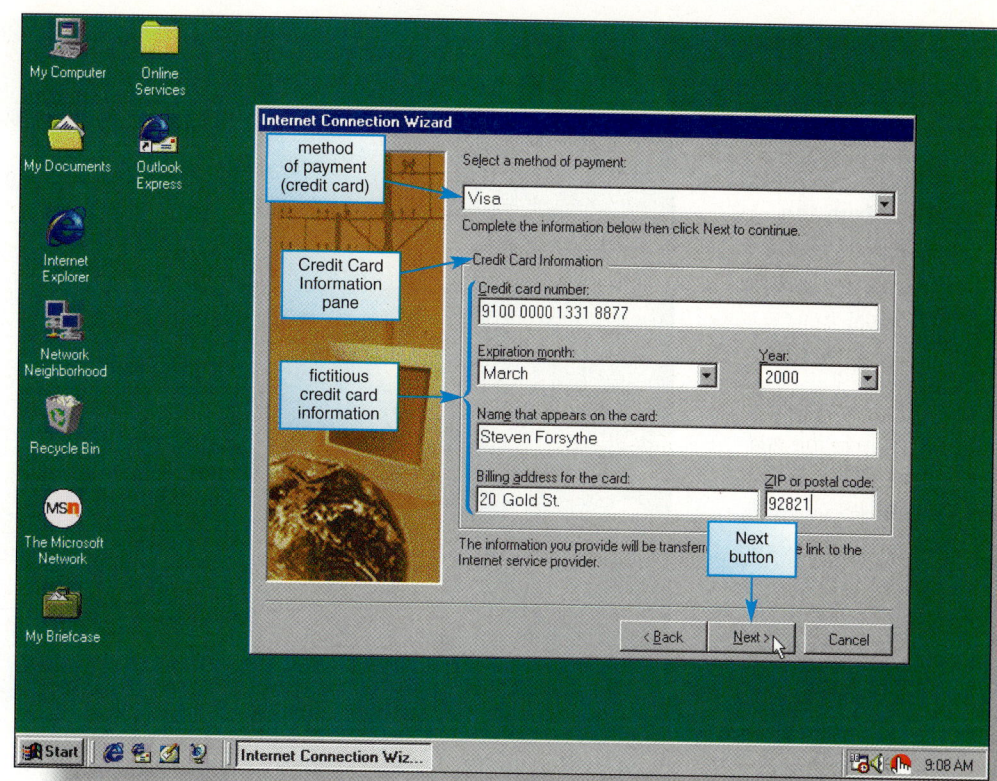

FIGURE 7-30

8 **Click the Next button.**

The contents of the Internet Connection Wizard dialog box change and the Internet Connection Wizard dials the EarthLink telephone number (1 800 972-4916) (Figure 7-31). Messages at the top of the dialog box indicate the wizard will connect to EarthLink and you will receive a User ID and password from EarthLink. Another message indicates the wizard is dialing the EarthLink telephone number.

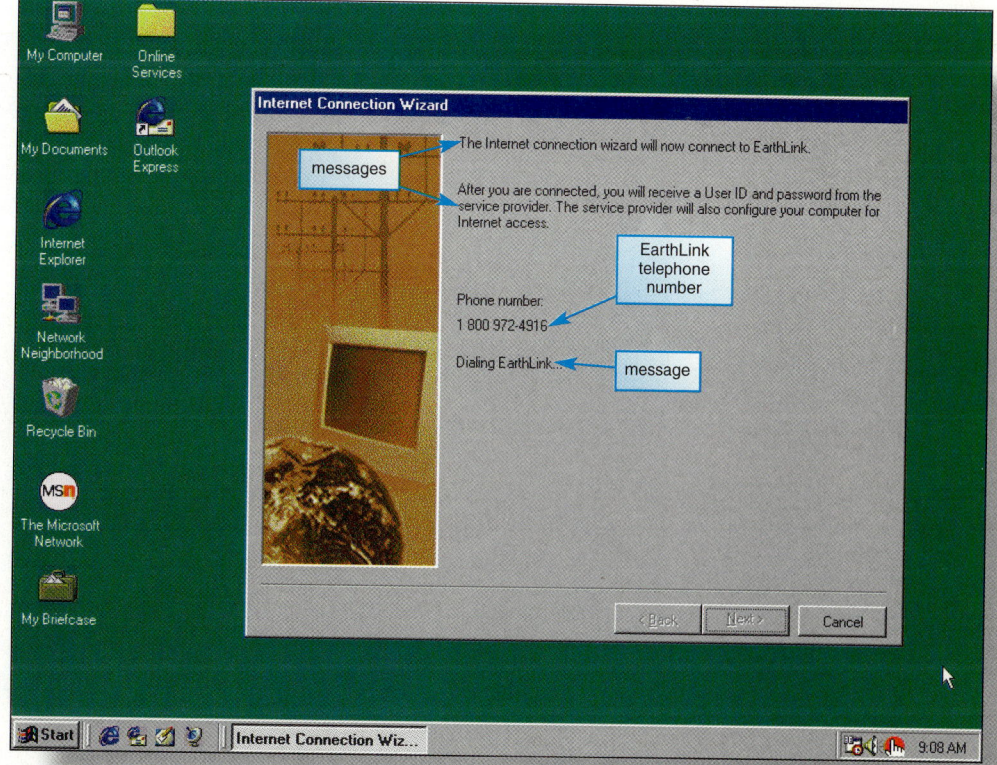

FIGURE 7-31

WIN 7.28 • Project 7 • Communicating with Other Computers

9 Decide upon a user name and password to use to connect to EarthLink. Type the user name in the Username text box and then type the password in the Password text box. Point to the Next button.

A fictitious user name (sgforsythe) and password (goblue) display in the text boxes (Figure 7-32). The Internet connection icon displays in the tray status area.

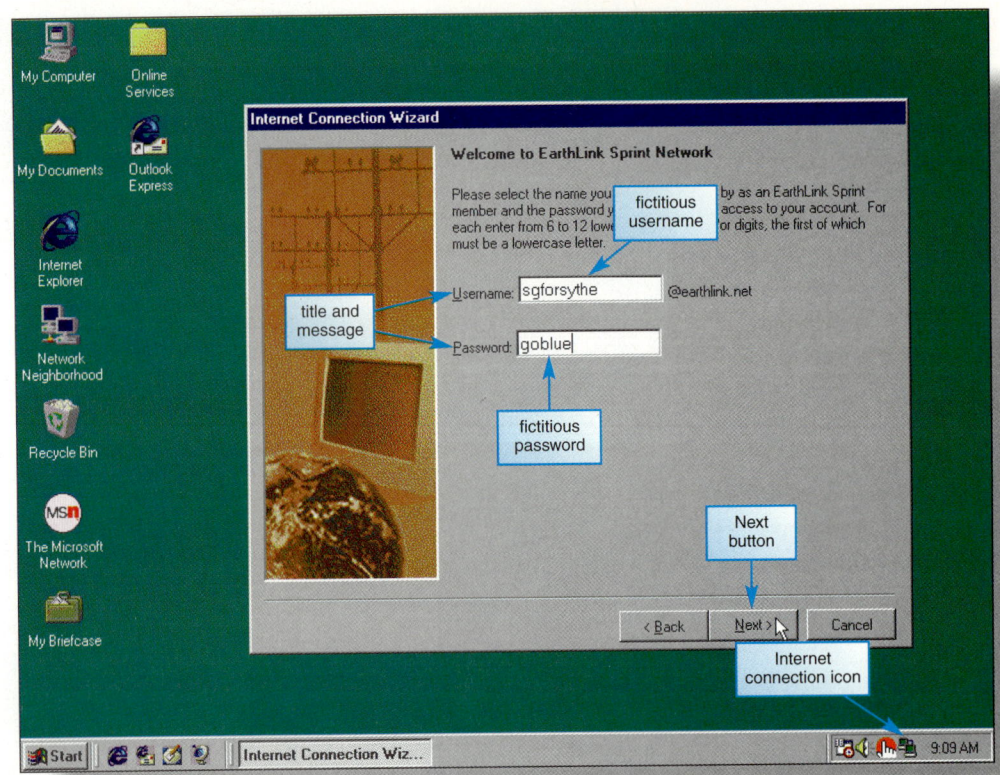

FIGURE 7-32

10 Click the Next button and then point to the box arrow.

The contents of the Internet Connection Wizard dialog box change (Figure 7-33). Messages indicating how to select a free local telephone number and a box containing a telephone number in Anaheim, California display.

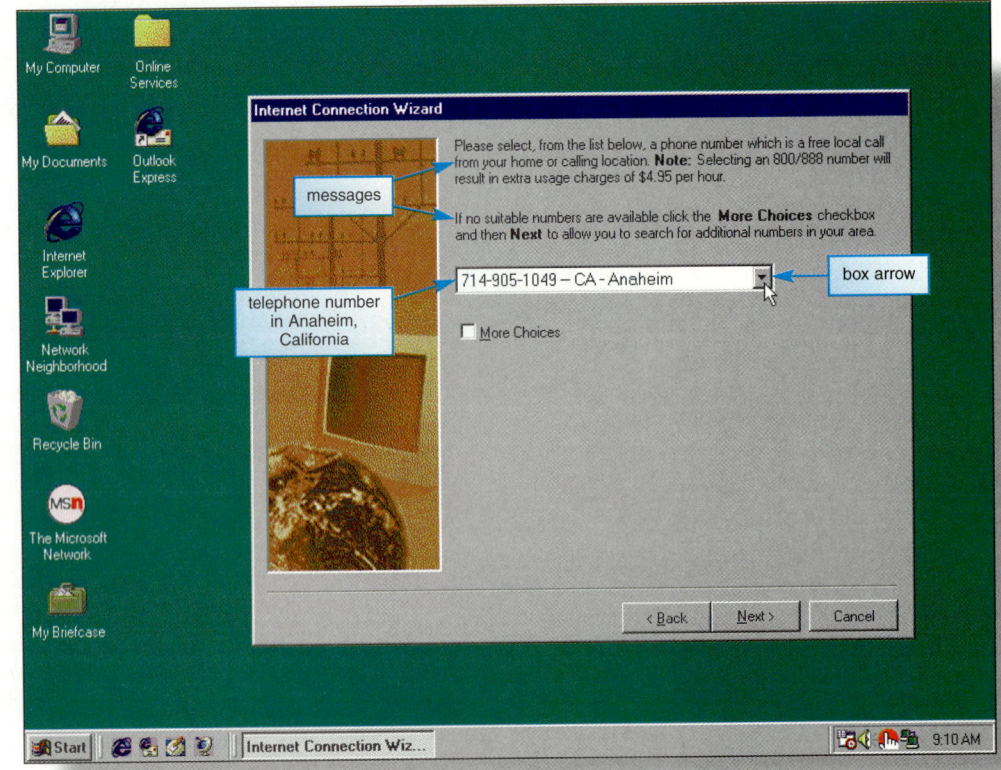

FIGURE 7-33

Connecting to the Internet Using an Internet Service Provider • **WIN 7.29**

PROJECT 7

11 **Click the box arrow and then point to 714-948-3565 — CA - Anaheim in the list box.**

A list box contains a list of local telephone numbers (Figure 7-34). The highlighted telephone number displays in the list.

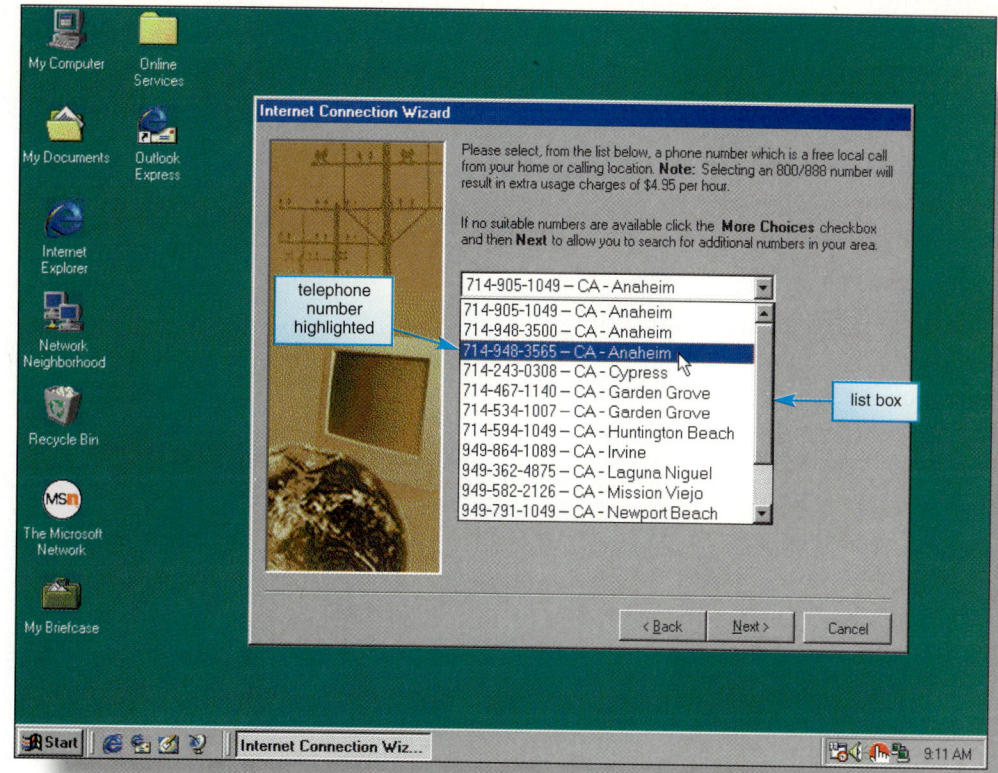

FIGURE 7-34

12 **Click 714-948-3565 — CA - Anaheim and then point to the Next button.**

The list box closes and the selected 714-948-3565 — CA - Anaheim name displays in the box (Figure 7-35).

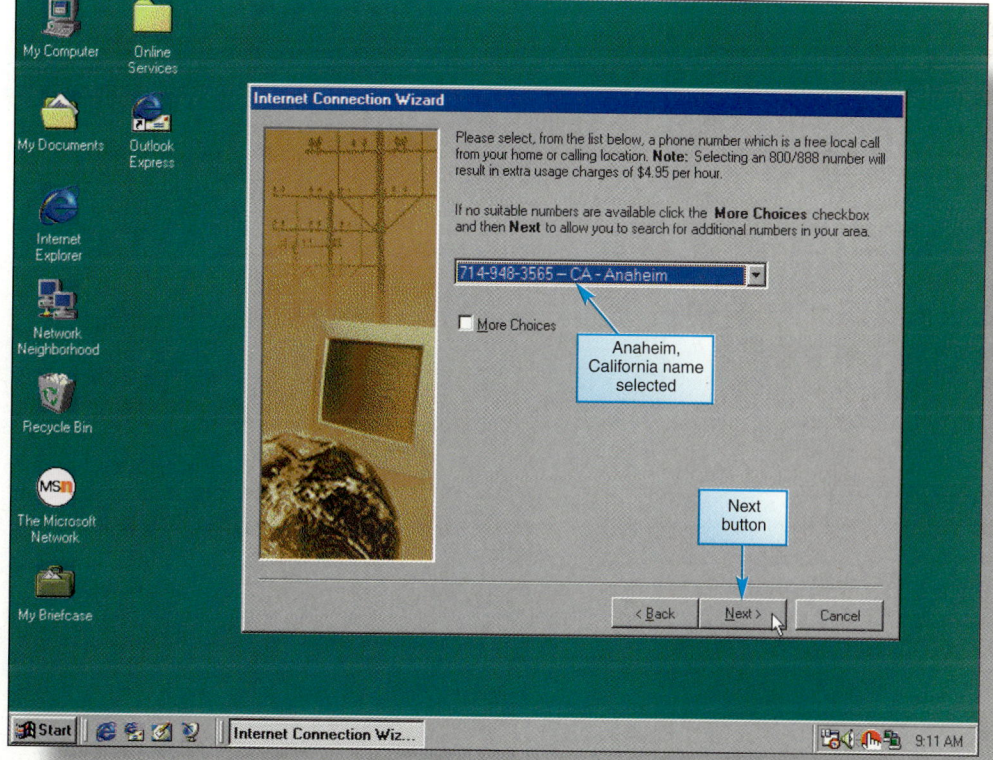

FIGURE 7-35

13 **Click the Next button. Scroll the customer agreement to read the agreement and then click I accept the agreement option button. Point to the Next button.**

The EarthLink Sprint customer agreement displays in a list box and two option buttons display below the list box (Figure 7-36). The I accept the agreement option button is selected.

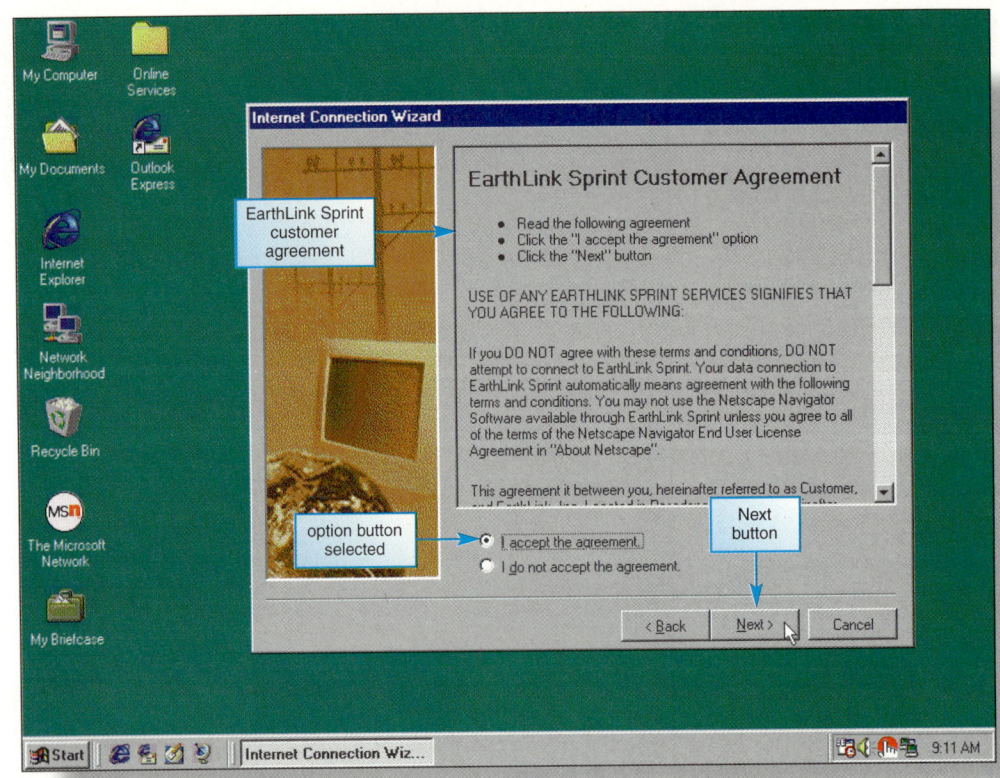

FIGURE 7-36

14 **Click the Next button and then point to the Finish button.**

The contents of the Internet Connection Wizard dialog box change (Figure 7-37). The messages indicate an EarthLink Sprint account was created, there is a Web page and telephone number available to answer questions, and how to complete the wizard and surf the Internet using the Internet Explorer icon.

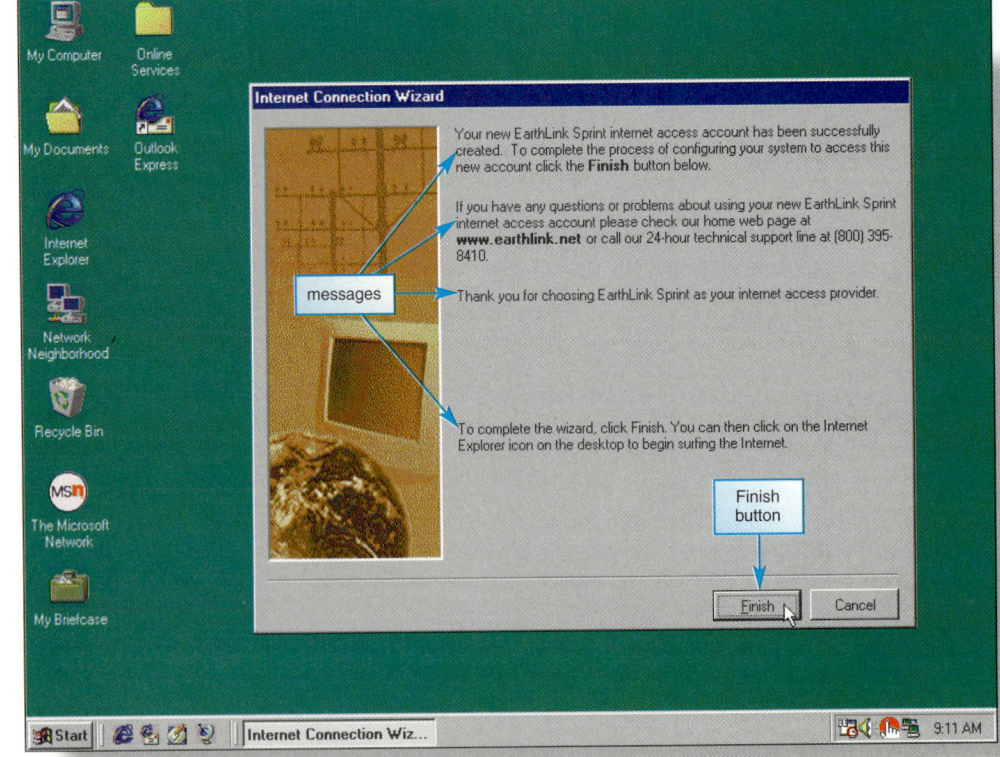

FIGURE 7-37

Click the Finish button. Point to the OK button in the smaller Internet Connection Wizard dialog box.

A second, smaller Internet Connection Wizard dialog box displays (Figure 7-38). The dialog box contains a message to record your account name and password for future use.

 **Click the OK button**

The two Internet Connection Wizard dialog boxes close.

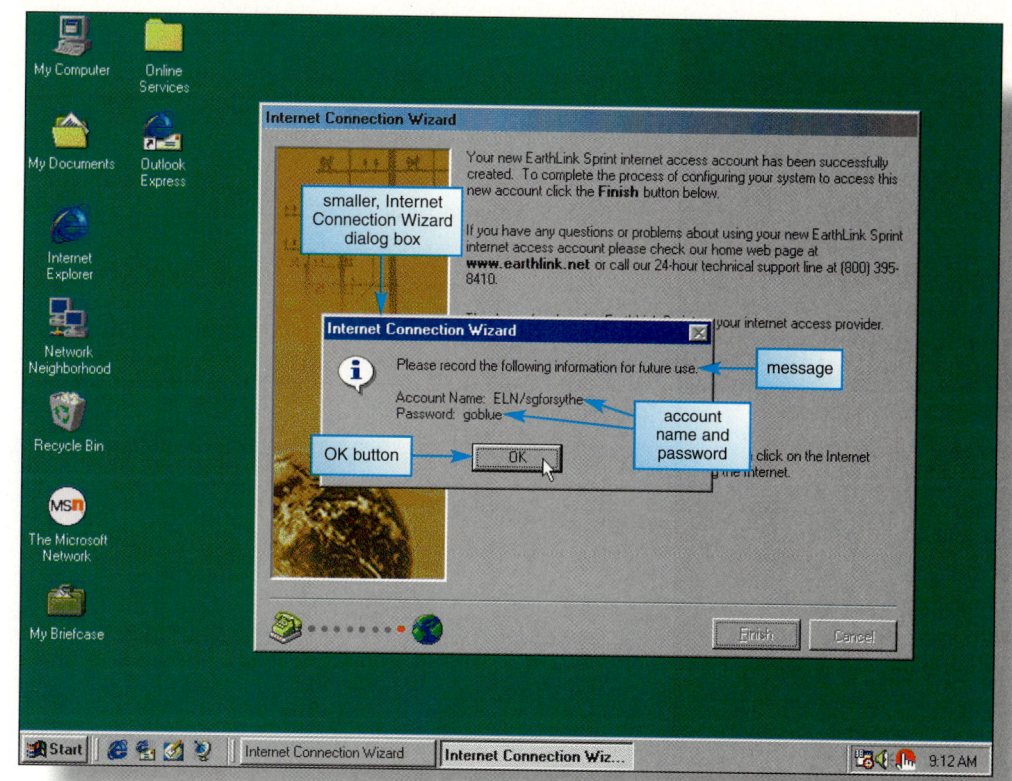

FIGURE 7-38

Creating a Dial-Up Networking Connection for an Existing ISP Account

In the previous example, you used the Internet Connection wizard to select an ISP from a list of providers in your area, sign up for an ISP account, and create a Dial-Up Networking connection. In some cases, you may want to use an ISP that is not contained in the list of ISPs. In this case, you typically contact the ISP to sign up for an account.

The Internet service provider will ask for personal information, including credit card information, and provide you with the information you need to use the Internet Connection wizard to create a Dial-Up Networking connection. This information includes the ISP name, area code and telephone number to connect to the Internet service provider, your user name and password, your e-mail address, and the address of the Internet service provider's mail server.

In addition, the ISP provides you with the primary and alternate IP address of their computer. A unique identifier, called an **Internet Protocol address (IP address)**, identifies each computer on the Internet. An IP address, such as 207.75.124.100, consists of four groups of numbers separated by periods and uniquely identifies a computer. The ISP usually sends this information to you through the mail.

With this information, you can create a Dial-Up Networking connection to the ISP using the Internet Connection wizard.

Other Ways

1. Double-click My Computer icon, double-click Dial-Up Networking icon, double-click Make New Connection icon
2. Right-click Start button, click Explore, click Dial-Up Networking icon, double-click Make New Connection icon

WIN 7.32 • Project 7 • Communicating with Other Computers

Dialing an Internet Service Provider

After creating a Dial-Up Networking connection to EarthLink, use the Internet Explorer icon on the desktop to connect to the ISP and display the EarthLink home page in the Microsoft Internet Explorer window. Perform the following steps to dial the EarthLink service provider. If you do not have a connection to EarthLink or a valid user name and password, read the following steps without performing the steps.

To Dial an Internet Service Provider

1 **Double-click the Internet Explorer icon on the desktop. Type** goblue **in the Password text box in the Dial-up Connection dialog box and then point to the Connect button.**

Internet Explorer launches and the Dial-up Connection dialog box displays (Figure 7-39). The user name (ELN/sgforsythe) displays in the User name text box and the password (goblue) displays as six asterisks in the Password text box.

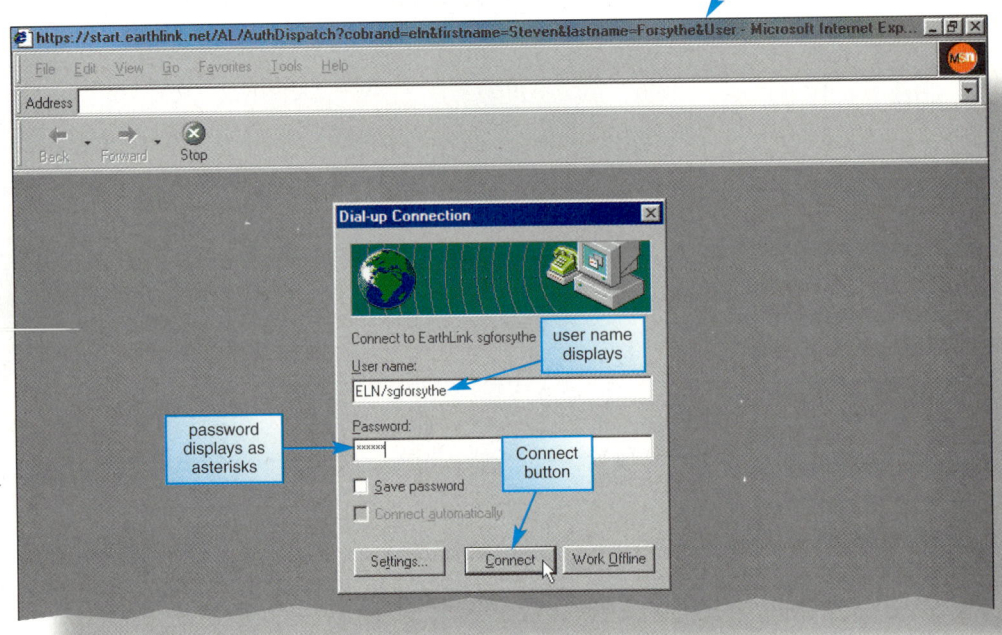

FIGURE 7-39

2 **Click the Connect button.**

The Dialing Progress dialog box replaces the Dial-up Connection dialog box (Figure 7-40). Three messages indicate the modem currently is making the first of five attempts to connect to EarthLink.

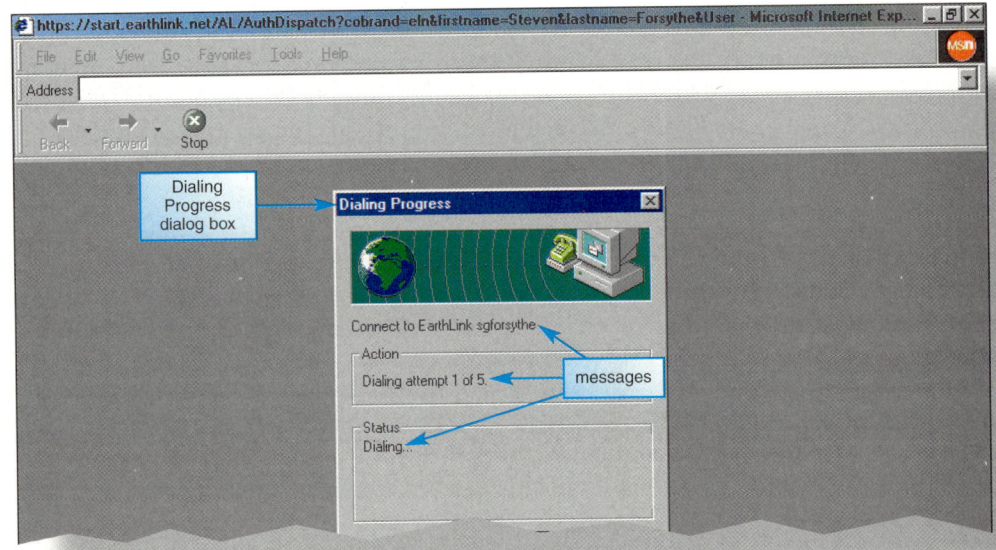

FIGURE 7-40

3 The Dialing Progress dialog box closes, the title in the Microsoft Internet Explorer window changes, the URL for the EarthLink home page displays in the Address box, and the EarthLink home page displays in the window (Figure 7-41).

4 Click the Close button in the EarthLink Home Page - Microsoft Internet Explorer window.

The EarthLink Home Page - Microsoft Internet Explorer window closes.

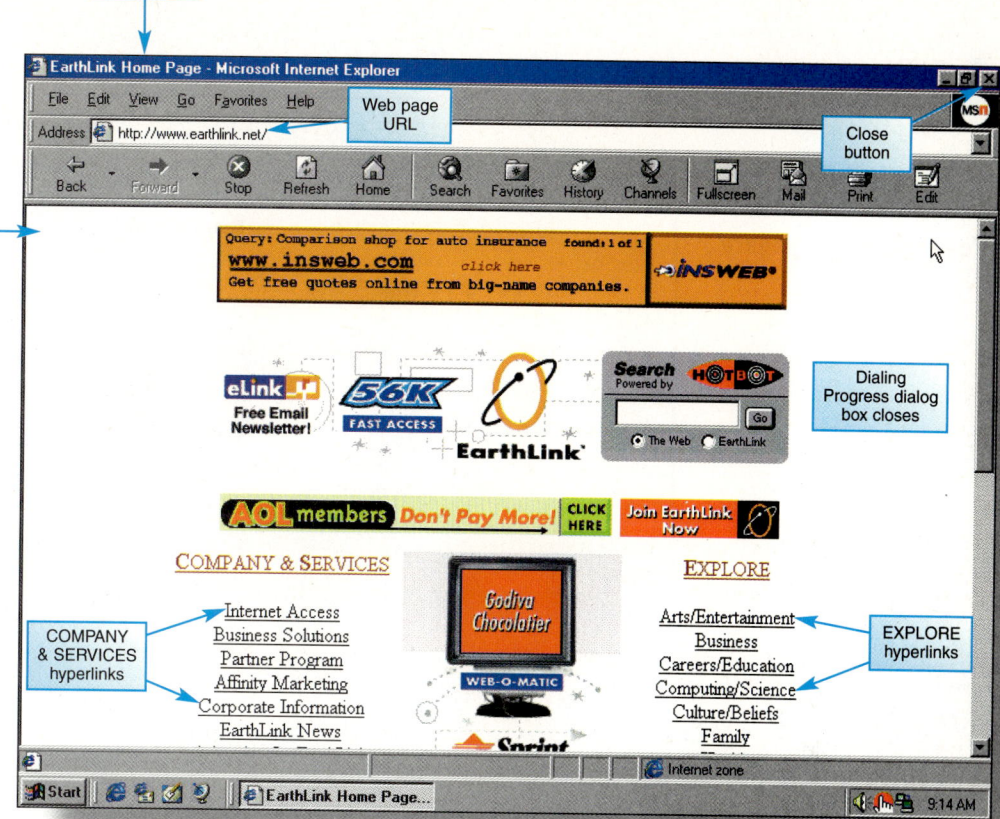

FIGURE 7-41

Hyperlinks to other Web pages display in the window in Figure 7-41. In the future, EarthLink may add new hyperlinks and delete existing hyperlinks from this Web page.

Disconnecting from an Internet Service Provider

When you have finished using the Internet, perform the steps on the next page to disconnect from the EarthLink service provider.

Other Ways

1. Double-click My Computer icon, double-click Dial-Up Networking icon, double-click EarthLink icon
2. Click Start button, point to Programs, point to Accessories, point to Communications, click Dial-Up Networking, double-click EarthLink icon

WIN 7.34 • Project 7 • Communicating with Other Computers

Steps: To Disconnect from an Internet Service Provider

1 Point to the Internet connection icon in the tray status area (Figure 7-42).

FIGURE 7-42

2 Double-click the Internet connection icon and then point to the Disconnect button in the Connected to EarthLink sgforsythe dialog box.

The Connected to EarthLink sgforsythe dialog box displays (Figure 7-43). The dialog box contains information about the current connection to EarthLink and the Disconnect button.

3 Click the Disconnect button and then click the Close button in the Microsoft Internet Explorer window.

The connection to the EarthLink service provider terminates, the Connected to EarthLink dialog box and the Microsoft Internet Explorer window close, and the Internet connection icon no longer displays in the tray status area.

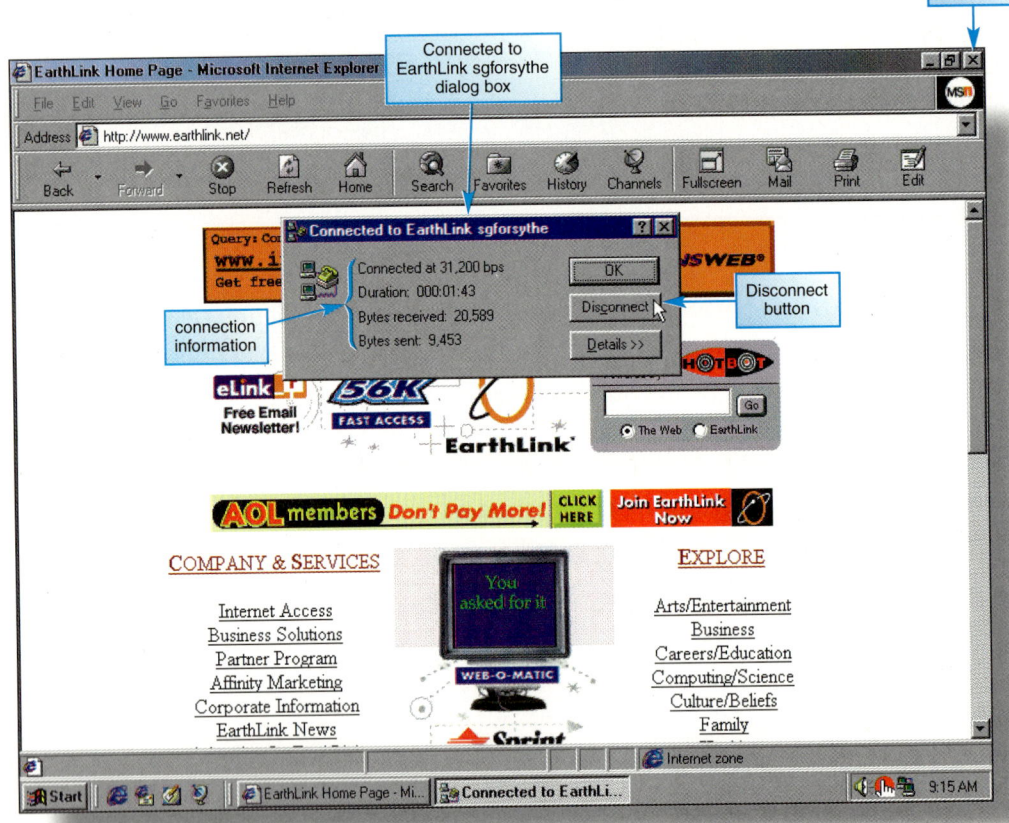

FIGURE 7-43

1. Right-click Internet connection icon, click Disconnect

Viewing a Dial-Up Networking Connection Icon

Whether you sign up for an account with an online service or an Internet service provider, a Dial-Up Networking connection is created and an icon is added to the Dial-Up Networking folder. Perform the following steps to view the EarthLink icon in the Dial-Up Networking folder.

Steps: To View a Dial-Up Networking Connection Icon

 Double-click the My Computer icon on the desktop and then double-click the Dial-Up Networking icon. Point to the Close button in the Dial-Up Networking window.

The Dial-Up Networking window displays (Figure 7-44). The window contains the Make New Connection icon and the EarthLink sgforsythe icon. Different icons may display in the window on your computer.

 **Click the Close button.**

The Dial-Up Networking window closes.

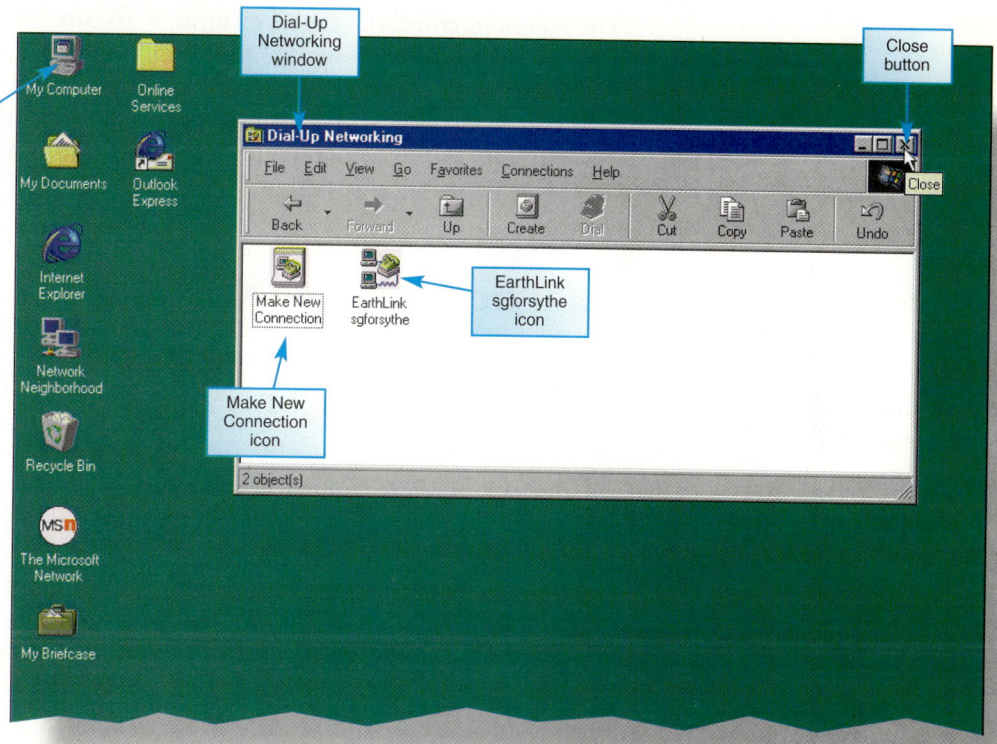

FIGURE 7-44

Removing a Dial-Up Networking Connection Icon

After creating a Dial-Up Networking connection to the EarthLink service provider, remove the Dial-Up Networking icon from the Dial-Up Networking folder by performing the following steps.

TO REMOVE A DIAL-UP NETWORKING CONNECTION ICON

1. Double-click the My Computer icon on the desktop.
2. Double-click the Dial-Up Networking icon in the My Computer window.
3. Right-click the EarthLink icon in the Dial-Up Networking window and then click Delete.
4. Click the Yes button in the Confirm Connection Delete dialog box.
5. Click the Close button in the Dial-Up Networking window.

The EarthLink icon no longer displays in the Dial-Up Networking window and the Dial-Up Networking window closes.

Using a Modem to Communicate Summary

At the beginning of this project, two methods to use a computer to communicate with other computers were given. One method involved using a modem to connect to other computers. On the previous pages, two popular methods to communicate using a modem were shown. These methods involved accessing an online service (The Microsoft Network) and connecting to the Internet using an Internet service provider.

The second method of communicating with other computers is to connect a computer to a network of computers. On the following pages, you will read about networks and network components, set up a computer to connect to a network, and view the computers and workgroups on the network. In addition, you will share computer resources (files, folders, printers, and so on) with other computers on the network and map a network drive.

An Introduction to Networks

A **network** is a communication system, composed of hardware and software, which connects people with computing resources. These resources, such as printers, files, and folders, can be on their desks, in the next room, or on the other side of the world. Computers on a network connect to each other using a cable or telephone line, or through wireless communication. When you connect to a network, you can share the resources on your computer with other computers on the network and use shared resources on other computers.

Local area networks (**LANs**) link computers that are located within a few miles of each other and usually are not more than a thousand feet apart. A LAN enables people in a small geographic area to communicate with each other and share the computer resources connected on the network. **Wide area networks** (**WANs**) link computers that are located over a large geographic area. A network can link many types of computers, including large and powerful mainframe computers, mid-sized minicomputers, and personal computers.

If networking is installed on a computer as a result of setting up Windows 98, the Network Neighborhood icon will display on the desktop and Windows 98 will allow you to create a peer-to-peer network. A **peer-to-peer network** allows any computer to share the software, data, or hardware located on any other computer on the network without identifying one computer as the server. In the next section, you will install a peer-to-peer network using Windows 98.

Network Components

The four **network components** required to use a network include a network adapter, client software, service software, and protocol. A **network adapter** is a hardware device that physically connects a computer to the network. **Client software** enables a computer to use the shared resources located on another computer on the network. The client software is part of the Windows 98 operating system. **Service software** allows you to share computer resources with other computers on the network. Windows 98 includes the service software.

Protocol is the *language* used to communicate with other computers on the network. Among the protocols that Windows 98 supports are NetBEUI, TCP/IP, and IPX/SPX. Computers running the Windows NT and Windows for Workgroups

---

> **More About**
>
> **Peer-to-Peer Networks**
>
> A peer-to-peer network is an easy and inexpensive network to create. Each computer in the network must have a network adapter board and can be connected to the network with cable purchased in any computer store. Using inexpensive network adapter boards, the costs to connect two computers can be under $150.

operating systems and LAN Manager servers use the NetBEUI protocol. Wide area networks and computers that connect to the Internet use the TCP/IP protocol. Computers running the Windows 98 or Windows NT operating systems or on a Novell NetWare network use the IPX/SPX protocol. To connect to a network, you must install all four network components (adapter, client, service, and protocol).

Installing the Network Hardware Component

To install the network hardware component (network adapter), follow the instructions included with the network adapter to install the network adapter physically in the computer and connect the network adapter to the network. You connect a network adapter to a network using a cable. Cables used include telephone wire, coaxial cable, or fiber-optic cables.

After physically installing the network adapter, associate the correct device driver with the adapter using the Add New Hardware wizard. The steps to add a network adapter are similar to the steps to add a USB Device shown in Project 5 (see Figure 5-39 through 5-41 on pages WIN5.31 through WIN 5.32).

The network adapter used in the following steps is an Intel EtherExpress network adapter. If you do not have an Intel EtherExpress network adapter or are not allowed to set up a network adapter on the computer on which you are working, read the following steps without performing them. Perform the following steps to install a network adapter.

> **More About**
>
> **Installing a Network Adapter**
>
> If, after installing a network adapter, the adapter does not work, use the Networking Troubleshooter to identify and solve problems with the adapter.

TO INSTALL A NETWORK ADAPTER

1. Install the Intel EtherExpress network hardware adapter by following the network adapter manufacturer's instructions.
2. Click the Start button, point to Settings, and then click Control Panel.
3. Double-click the Add New Hardware icon in the Control Panel window.
4. When the Add New Hardware Wizard dialog box displays, read the instructions in the dialog box, and then click the Next button.
5. When the instructions in the Add New Hardware Wizard dialog box change, read the instructions in the dialog box, and then click the Next button.
6. When new instructions and the Yes (Recommended) and No option buttons display in the dialog box, read the new instructions. If necessary, click Yes (Recommended) and then click the Next button.
7. When new instructions and a warning display in the dialog box, read the instructions and warning, and then click the Next button to start the detection process. A progress bar indicates the progress of the detection process.
8. When the detection process is complete and the Intel EtherExpress 16 or 16TP ISA device name displays in the Detected list box in the dialog box, click the Finish button. A Copying Files dialog box may display while files required to use the network adapter are copied into the appropriate folder on the hard disk.
9. The System Settings Change dialog box displays to indicate the computer must be restarted to finish setting up the network adapter. Click the Yes button to restart the computer.

Windows 98 adds the Intel EtherExpress network adapter to the computer and restarts the computer. When the computer restarts, you can set up the network software required to connect the computer to the network.

Installing the Network Software Components

After installing and adding a network adapter, you must install the network software components to allow the network adapter to communicate with other computers on the network. The three network software components to install include the client software, protocol, and service software. The client software to install (Microsoft Client for Microsoft Networks) enables a computer to connect to other Windows 98 computers and use their shared files and printers. The protocol (IPX/SPX protocol) enables Windows 98 and Windows NT computers to communicate with each other. The service software to install (File and printer sharing for Microsoft Networks) enables a computer to share files and printers with other Windows NT and Windows 98 computers.

While installing the network components, you assign a computer name to the computer, associate a workgroup name with the computer, and select a password for the computer. The **computer name**, or **user name**, is a unique name that identifies the computer on the network. The **workgroup name** is a name assigned to a group of computers. You assign a computer to a workgroup based upon the workgroup its user is more likely to communicate with and the workgroup with the most computer resources the user would use. The **password** allows you access to the network. Depending upon the network, a person in charge of the network, called a **network administrator**, may assign the computer name, workgroup name, and password.

In this project, the computer name is Forsythe, the workgroup is Editorial, and the password is GoBlue. Contact your instructor to determine your computer name, workgroup, and password and then use them instead of Forsythe, Editorial, and GoBlue.

After installing the network components, you must restart the computer. As part of the restart process you will have to log onto the network. If your computer is not connected to a network or you may not install a network software component on the computer, read the following steps without performing the steps. Otherwise, perform the following steps to install the three network software components (client, protocol, and service).

More About

Installing Network Software Components

Sometimes, when installing a network software component, the component you wish to install already may be installed. Double-click the Network icon in the Control Panel window and check for the component before installing.

 To Install Network Software Components

1 Click the Start button, point to Settings, and then click Control Panel. Point to the Network icon in the Control Panel window.

The Control Panel window with the Network icon displays (Figure 7-45).

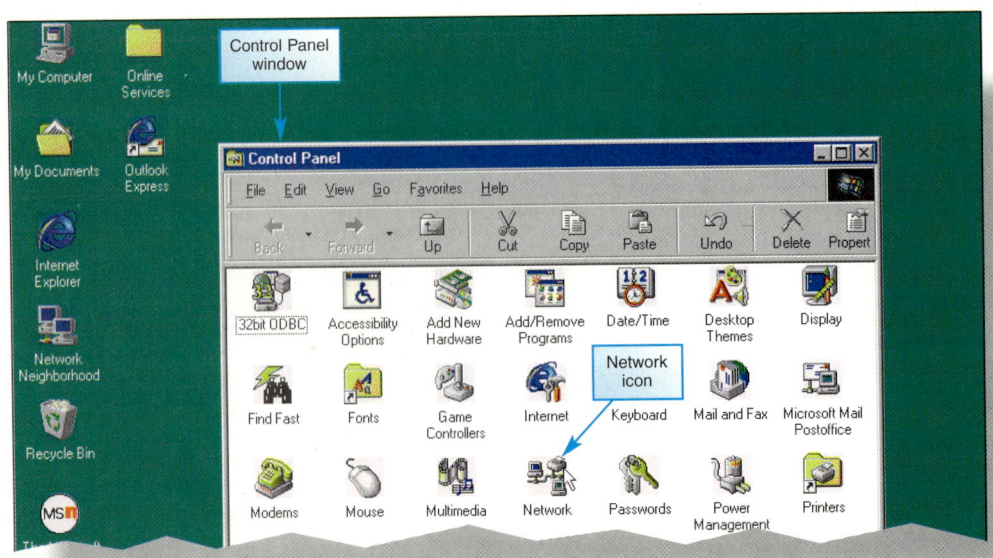

FIGURE 7-45

2 **Double-click the Network icon and then point to the Add button in the Network dialog box.**

One network component (Intel EtherExpress 16 or 16TP ISA) is installed and displays in the list box in the Network dialog box (Figure 7-46). This component was installed when the Intel EtherExpress network adapter was added to the computer. Other components may display in the list box on your computer.

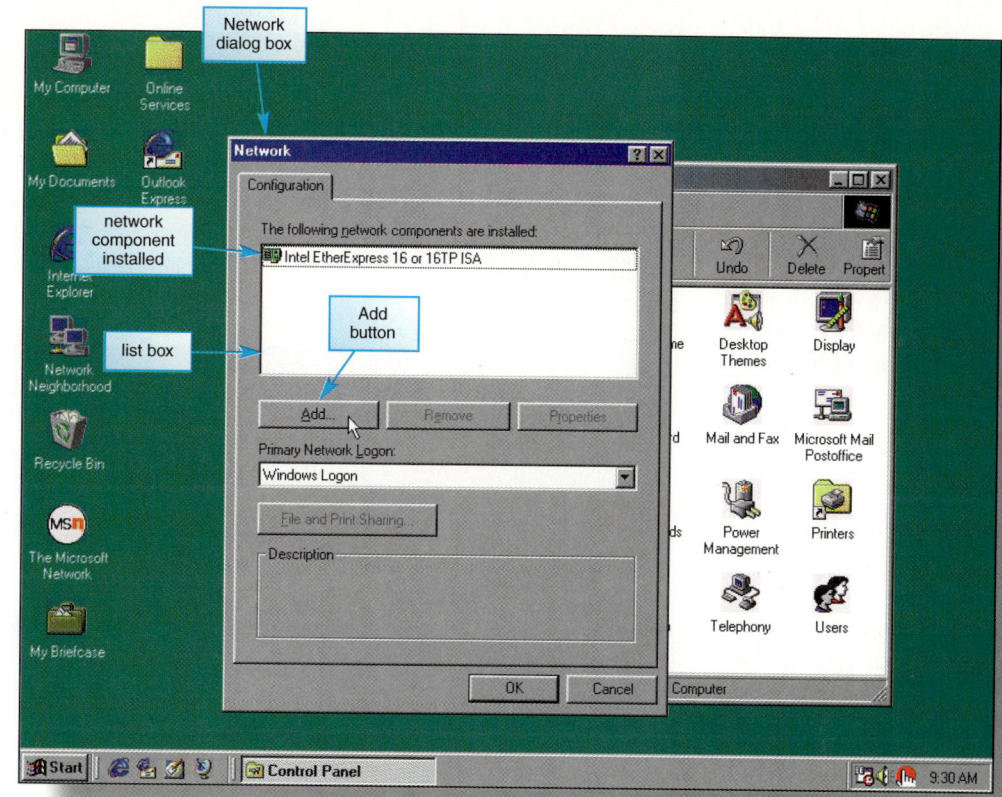

FIGURE 7-46

3 **Click the Add button. Click Client in the list box in the Select Network Component Type dialog box and then point to the Add button.**

The Select Network Component Type dialog box displays and the Client component is selected in the list box (Figure 7-47). A message below the list box explains what a client enables your computer to do.

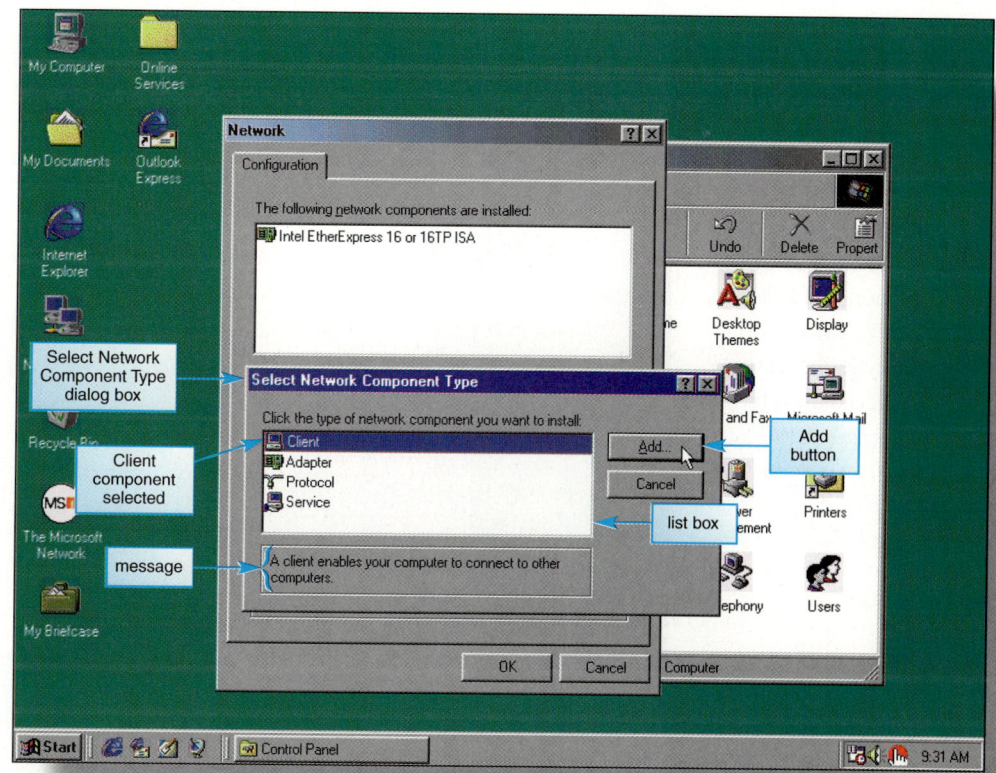

FIGURE 7-47

4 **Click the Add button. When the Select Network Client dialog box displays, click Microsoft in the Manufacturers list box. If necessary, click Client for Microsoft Networks in the Network Clients list box and then point to the OK button.**

The Select Network Client dialog box displays (Figure 7-48). Microsoft is selected in the Manufacturers list box and Client for Microsoft Networks is selected in the Network Clients list box.

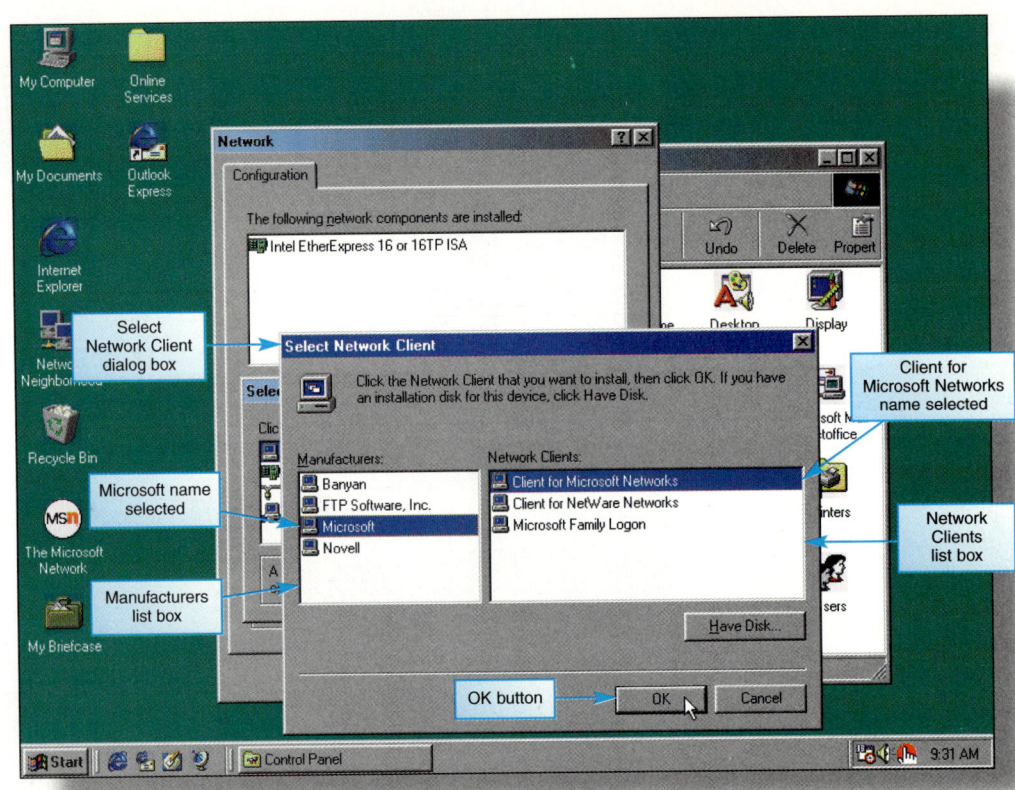

FIGURE 7-48

5 **Click the OK button and then point to the Add button in the Network dialog box.**

The Select Network Client and Select Network Component Type dialog boxes close and two components (Client for Microsoft Networks and TCP/IP) display in the list box in the Network dialog box (Figure 7-49). The TCP/IP protocol installs when the Client for Microsoft Networks client software is installed.

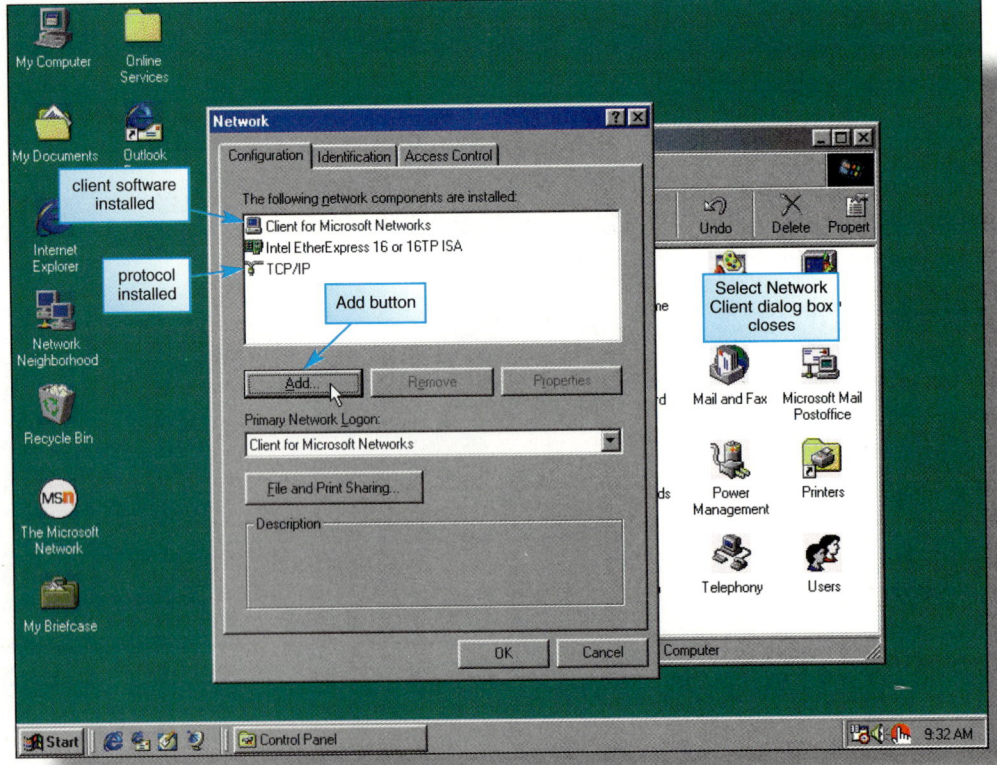

FIGURE 7-49

Network Components • WIN 7.41

6 **Click the Add button. When the Select Network Component Type dialog box displays, click Protocol in the list box, and then point to the Add button.**

The Select Network Component Type dialog box displays and the Protocol component is selected in the list box (Figure 7-50). A message below the list box explains what a protocol is and why computers must use a protocol.

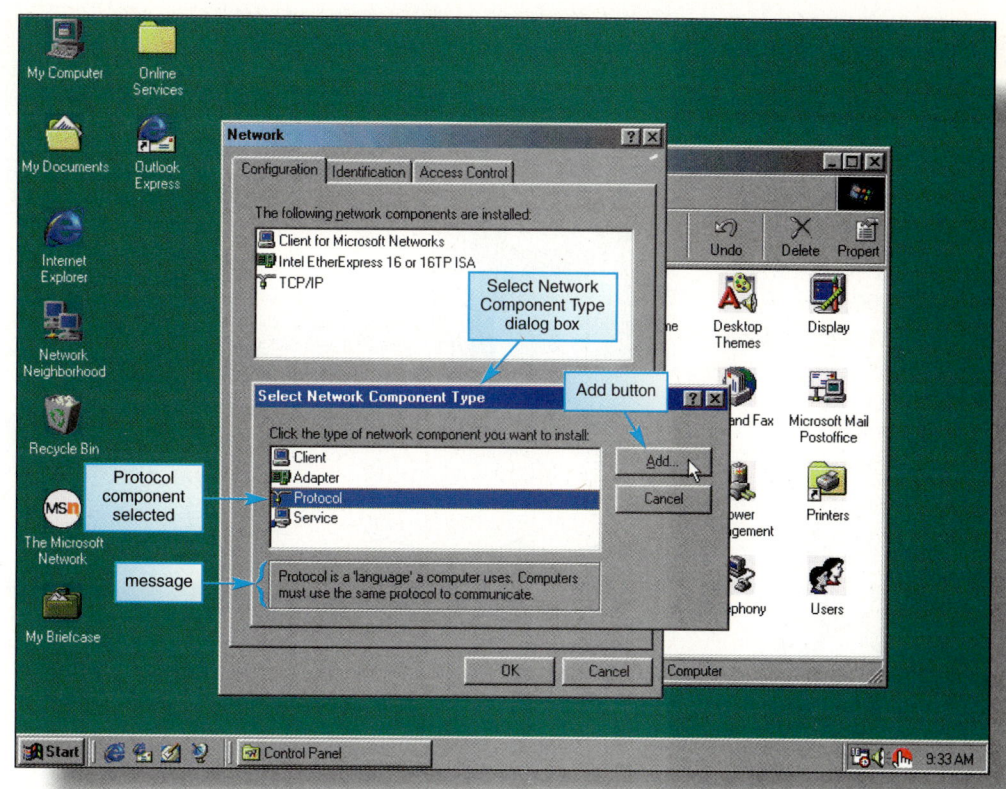

FIGURE 7-50

7 **Click the Add button. When the Select Network Protocol dialog box displays, click Microsoft in the Manufacturers list box, click IPX/SPX-compatible Protocol in the Network Protocols list box, and then point to the OK button.**

The Select Network Protocol dialog box displays, Microsoft is selected in the Manufacturers list box, and IPX/SPX-compatible Protocol is selected in the Network Protocols list box (Figure 7-51).

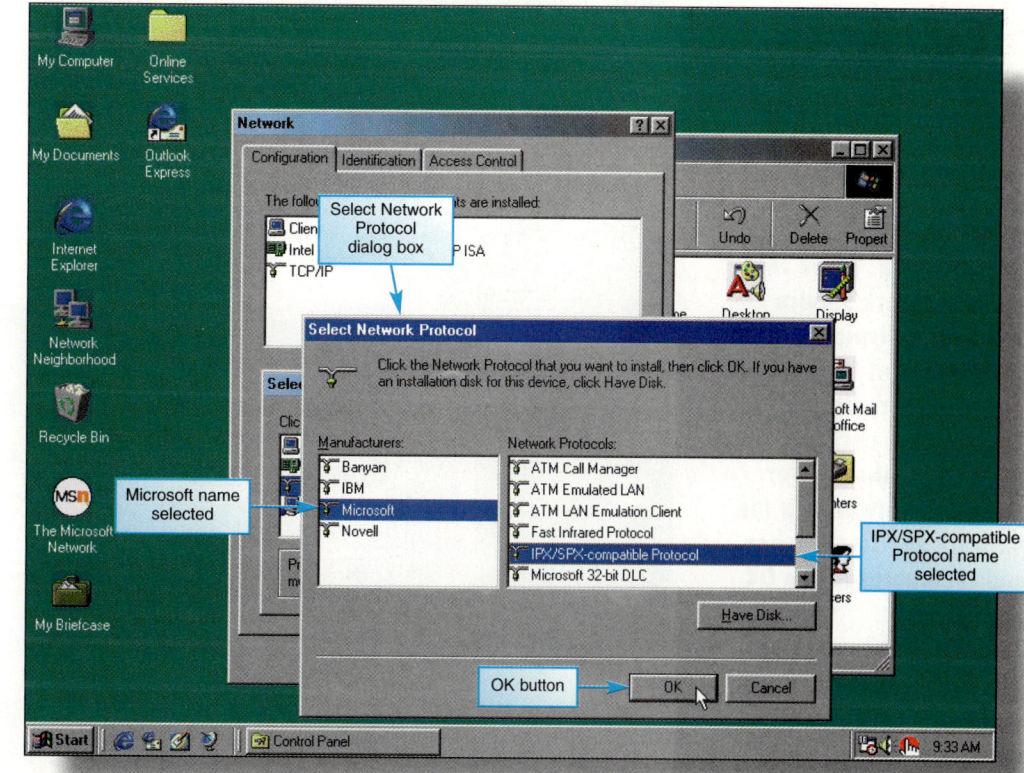

FIGURE 7-51

8 **Click the OK button and then point to the Add button in the Network dialog box.**

The Select Network Protocol and Select Network Component Type dialog boxes close and the IPX/SPX-compatible Protocol component displays in the list box in the Network dialog box (Figure 7-52).

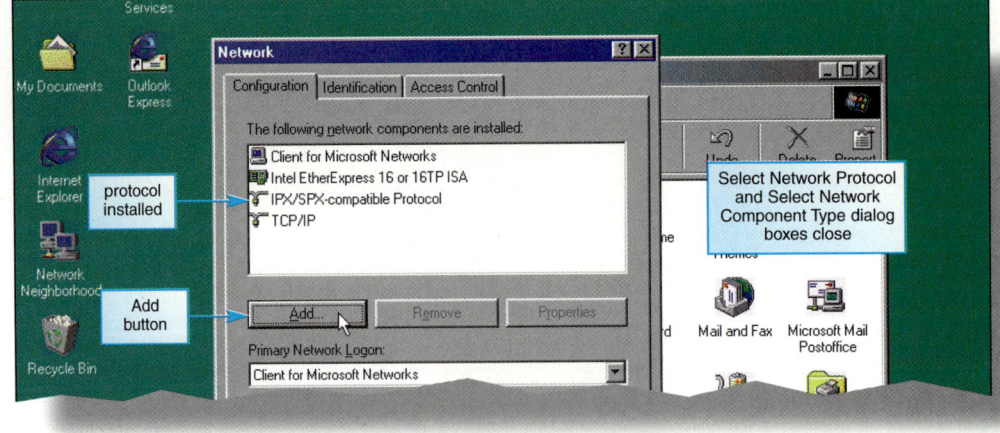

FIGURE 7-52

9 **Click the Add button. Click Service in the Select Network Component Type dialog box and then point to the Add button.**

The Select Network Component Type dialog box displays and the Service component is selected in the list box (Figure 7-53). A message below the list box explains what a service allows a computer to share with other computers.

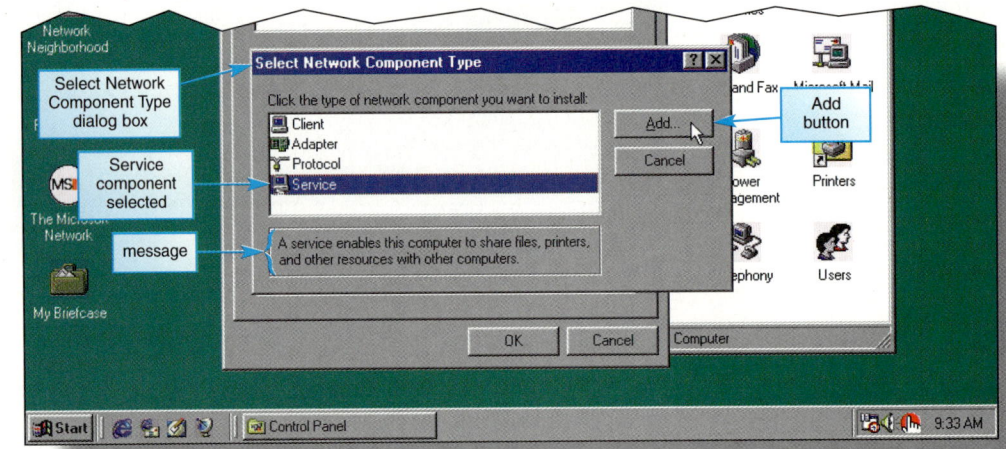

FIGURE 7-53

10 **Click the Add button. When the Select Network Service dialog box displays, click Microsoft in the Manufacturers list box. If necessary, click File and printer sharing for Microsoft Networks in the Network Services list box, and then point to the OK button.**

The Select Network Service dialog box displays, Microsoft is selected in the Manufacturers list box, and File and printer sharing for Microsoft Networks is selected in the Network Services list box (Figure 7-54).

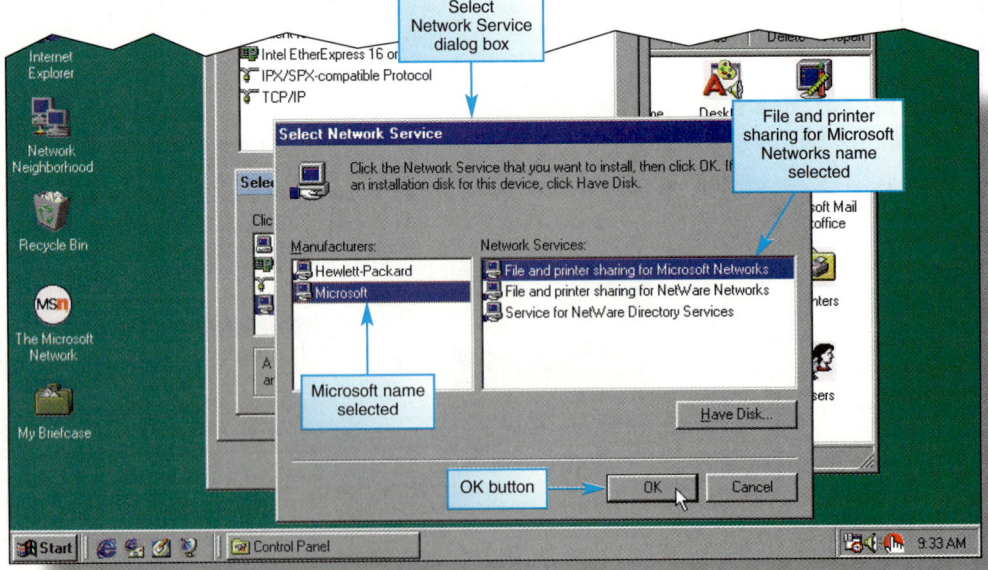

FIGURE 7-54

Network Components • WIN 7.43

11 **Click the OK button and then point to the Identification tab in the Network dialog box.**

The Select Network Service and Select Network Component Type dialog boxes close (Figure 7-55). The File and printer sharing for Microsoft Networks component displays in the list box.

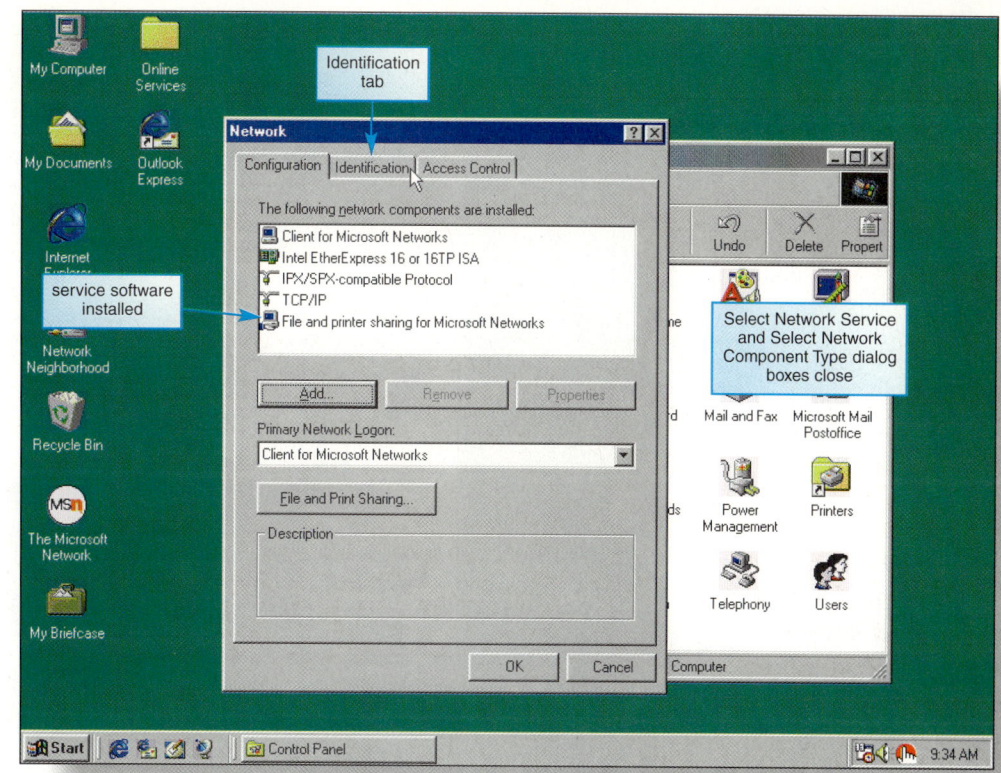

FIGURE 7-55

12 **Click the Identification tab. Type** Forsythe **in the Computer name text box, type** Editorial **in the Workgroup text box, type** Dell Pentium 200 **in the Computer Description text box, and then point to the OK button.**

The Identification sheet displays (Figure 7-56). The computer name displays in the Computer name text box, the workgroup name displays in the Workgroup text box, and the computer description displays in the Computer Description text box.

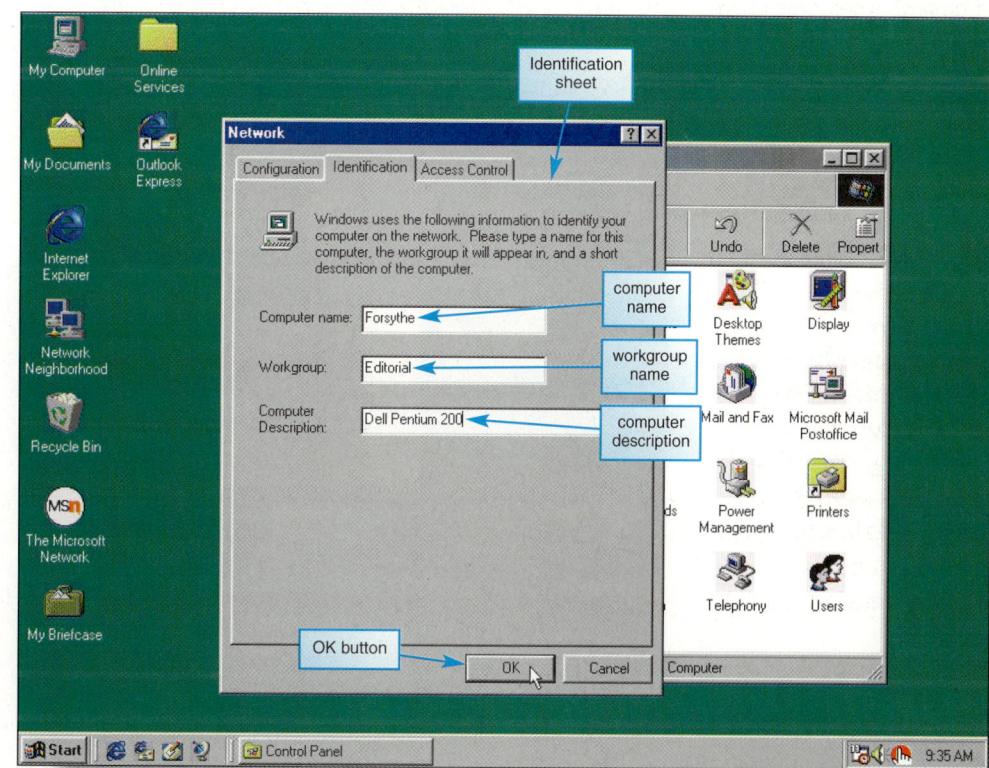

FIGURE 7-56

WIN 7.44 • Project 7 • Communicating with Other Computers

13 **Click the OK button and then point to the Yes button in the System Settings Change dialog box.**

The Network dialog box closes and the System Settings Change dialog box displays (Figure 7-57). A message in the dialog box indicates you must restart your computer for the new settings to take effect.

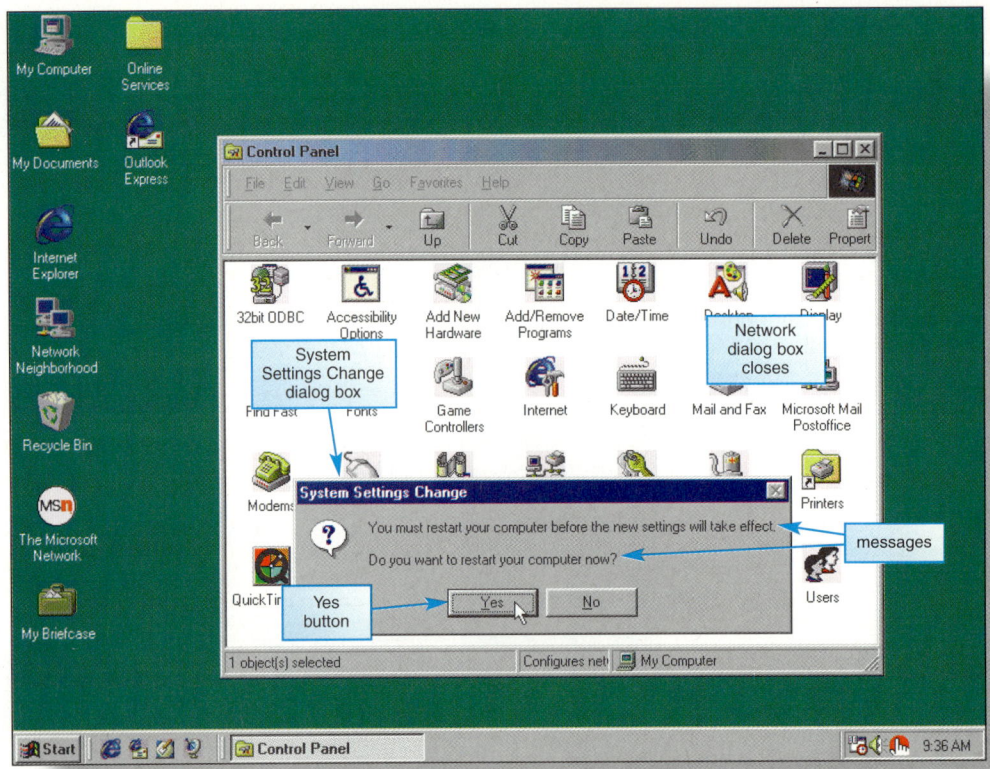

FIGURE 7-57

14 **Click the Yes button to restart the computer.**

Windows 98 restarts the computer, completes the setup of the network components, and displays the Enter Network Password dialog box (Figure 7-58). The dialog box contains a message and the User name and Password text boxes. The User name text box contains an insertion point.

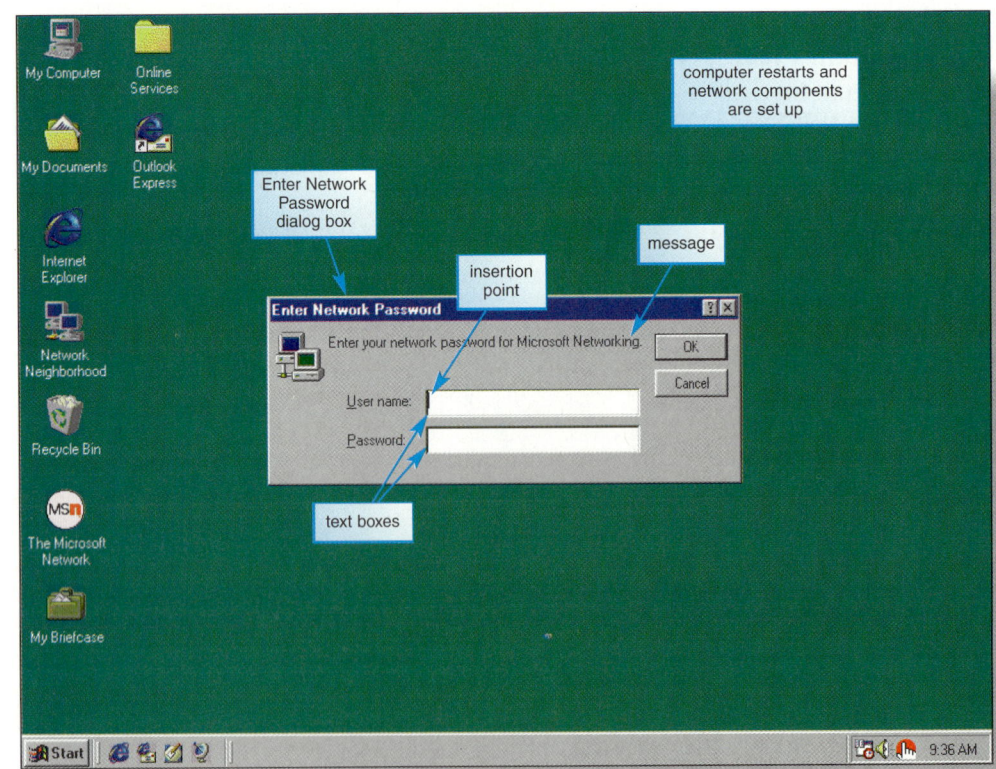

FIGURE 7-58

Type Forsythe **as the user name. Click the Password text box and then type** GoBlue **as the password. Point to the OK button.**

The computer name (Forsythe) displays in the User name text box and an asterisk displays in the Password text box for each character of the password (Figure 7-59).

 **Click the OK button.**

The network verifies the password and logs your computer onto the network.

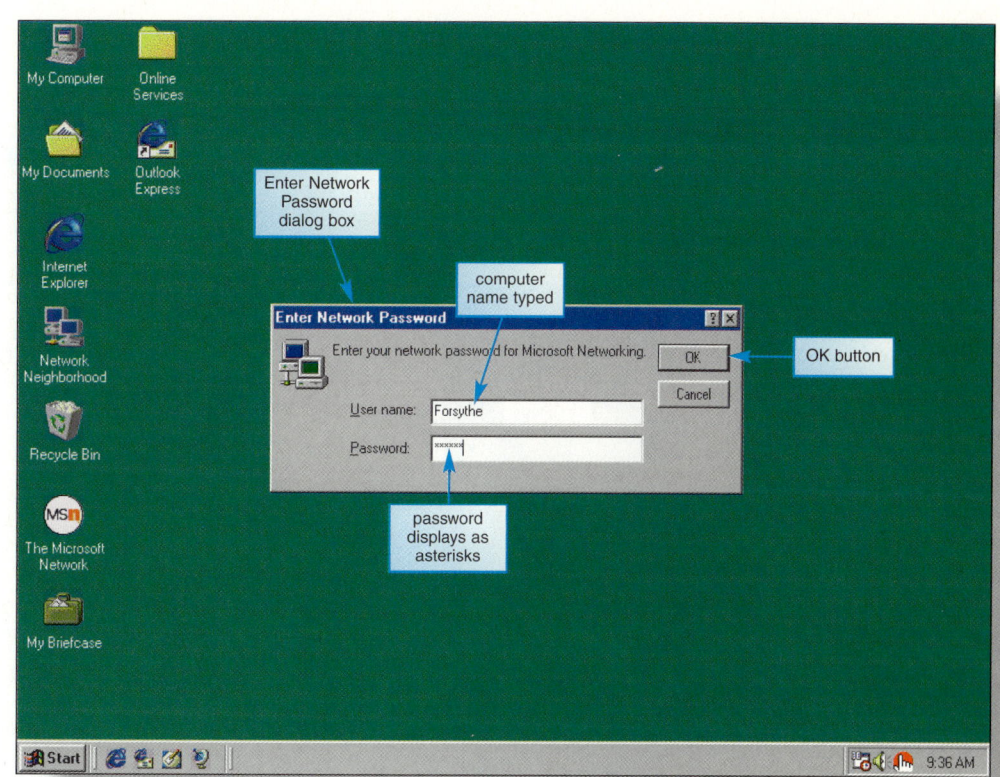

FIGURE 7-59

Viewing Computers and Workgroups on a Network

Once connected to a network, you have many services and computer resources available to you. You can use the Network Neighborhood icon on the desktop to view computers, workgroups, and shared computer resources on other computers on the network. In addition, you can use the Find command, used in previous projects to find files and folders, to locate other computers on the network.

Viewing Computers, Workgroups, and Shared Computer Resources on the Network

Network Neighborhood allows you to locate other computers and workgroups on the network and view the computer resources available on each computer. Perform the steps on the next page to view the computers and workgroups on the network and the shared computer resources on the Lopez computer. If the Lopez computer is not available on your network, use another computer on your network to perform the steps on the next page.

Other Ways

1. Double-click My Computer icon, double-click Control Panel icon, right-click Network icon, click Open
2. Double-click My Computer icon, double-click Control Panel icon, click Network icon, on File menu click Open

More About

Viewing Computers on a Network

When a computer on a network is turned on, it may take a few minutes for the computer icon to display in the Network Neighborhood window on the other computers on the network. To check for the icon without closing the window, click the Refresh command on the View menu.

WIN 7.46 • Project 7 • Communicating with Other Computers

To View the Computers and Workgroups on the Network

1) **Double-click the Network Neighborhood icon on the desktop. Point to the Entire Network name in the Network Neighborhood window.**

The Network Neighborhood window displays and the entries in the window display in List view (Figure 7-60). The first name in the window consists of a network icon and the words, Entire Network. Below this name is a computer icon and computer name for each computer (Forsythe and Lopez) on the network.

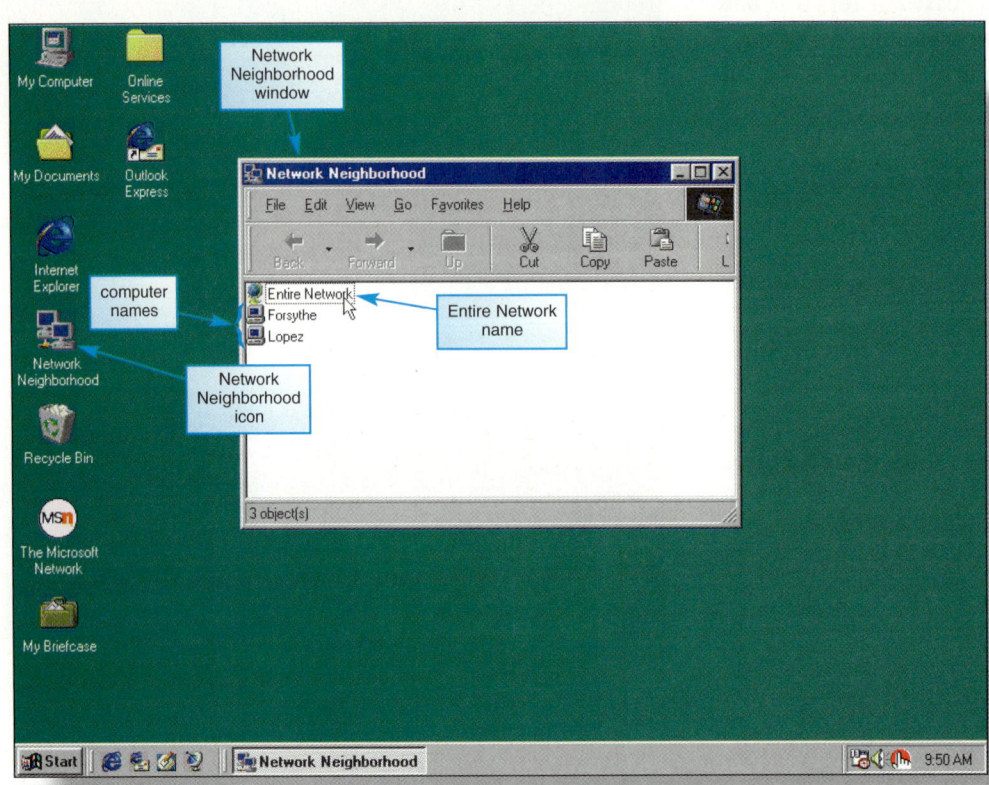

FIGURE 7-60

2) **Double-click Entire Network and then point to the Back button on the toolbar.**

The Entire Network window displays in the same window as the Network Neighborhood window (Figure 7-61). The Editorial workgroup icon displays in Large Icons format in the window.

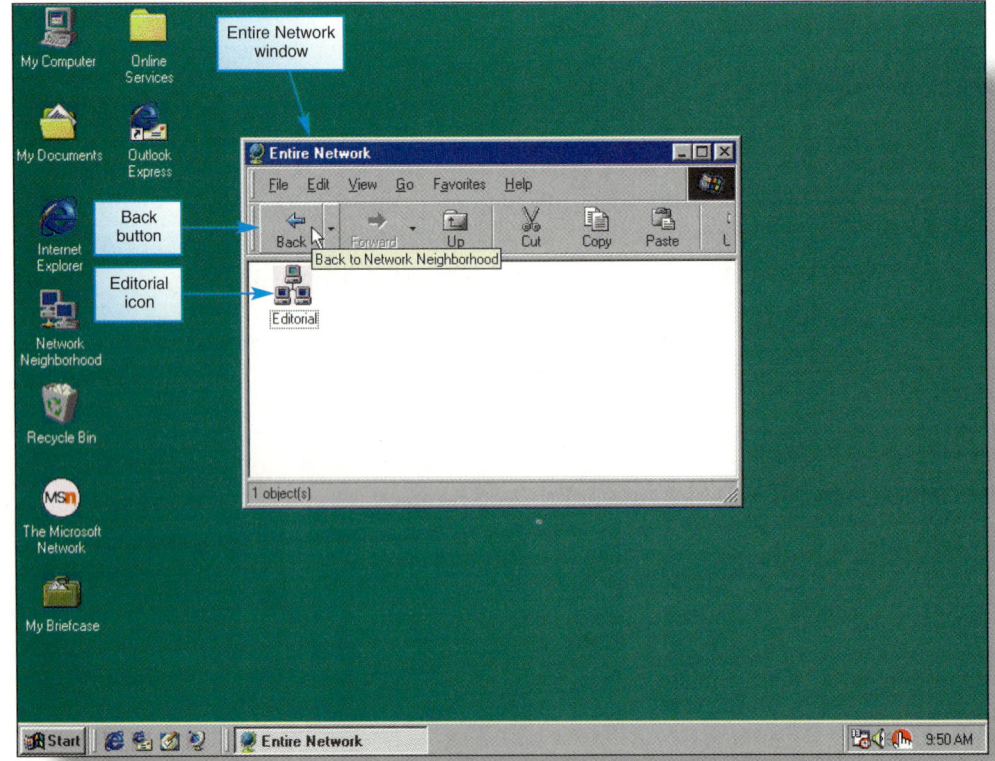

FIGURE 7-61

Viewing Computers and Workgroups on a Network • **WIN 7.47**

③ Click the Back button and then point to the Lopez computer name in the Network Neighborhood window.

The Network Neighborhood window displays (Figure 7-62).

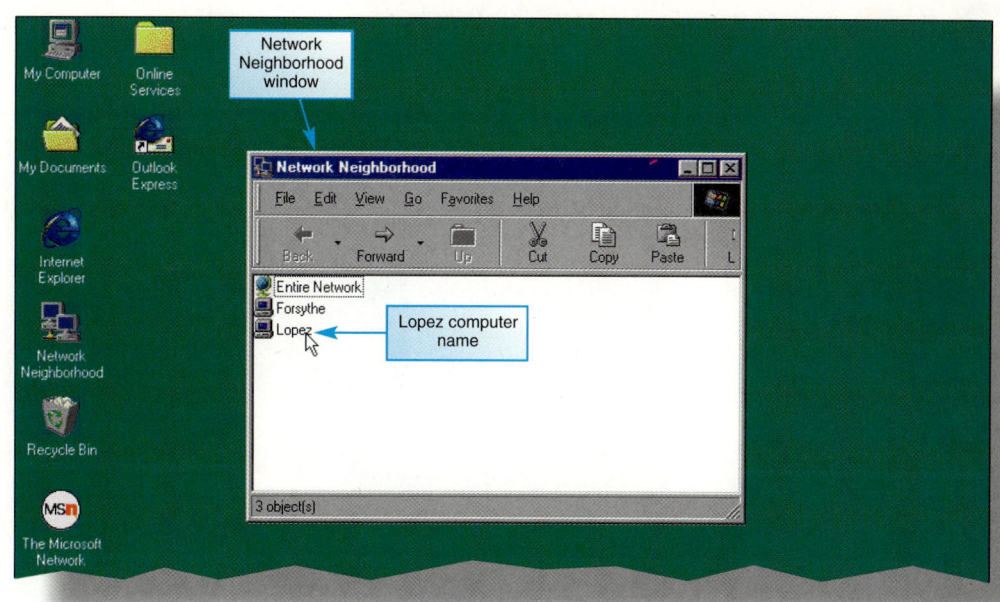

FIGURE 7-62

④ Double-click Lopez.

The Lopez window, containing three shared computer resources, displays in the same window as the Network Neighborhood window (Figure 7-63). The shared resources, consisting of two shared folders (art files and text files) and a shared printer (hp 560c), display in Large Icons format.

⑤ Click the Close button in the Lopez window.

The Lopez window closes.

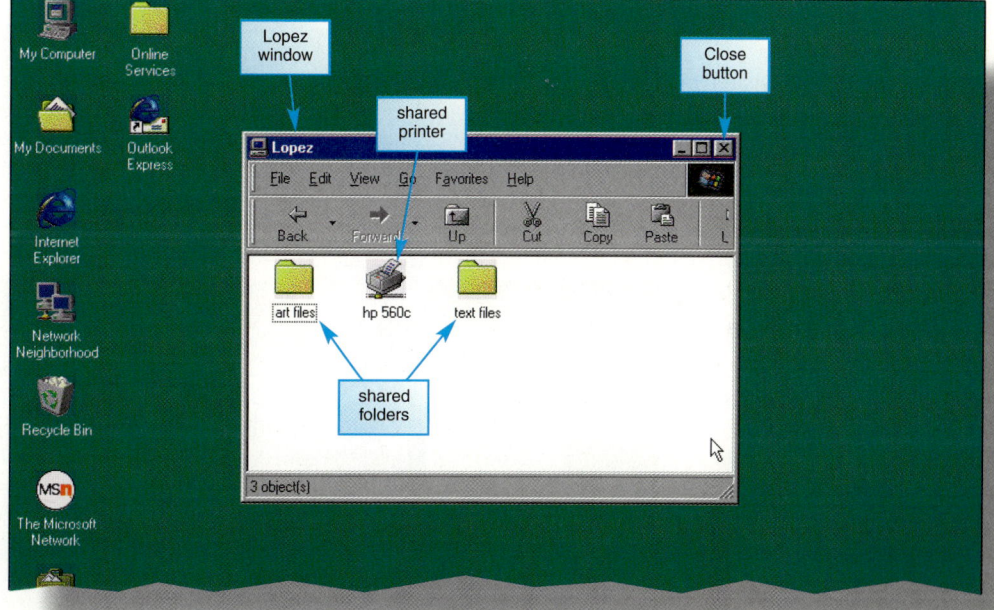

FIGURE 7-63

Locating Computers on the Network Using the Find Command

In previous projects, you used the Find command to search for files and folders on the hard disk and people and information on the Internet. If you know the name of the computer you are looking for, you also can use the Find command to locate a computer on a network. Perform the steps on the next page to locate the Lopez computer on the network. If the Lopez computer is not available on your network, use another computer on your network to perform the steps on the next page.

Other Ways

1. Right-click Network Neighborhood icon, click Explore
2. Right-click My Computer icon, click Explore, click Network Neighborhood
3. Right-click Start button, click Explore, click Network Neighborhood
4. Click Start button, click Find, click Computer, type computer name, click Find Now button

WIN 7.48 • Project 7 • Communicating with Other Computers

Steps: To Locate a Computer on a Network

1 **Click the Start button, point to Find, and then point to Computer.**

The Start menu and Find submenu display (Figure 7-64). The highlighted Computer command displays on the Find submenu.

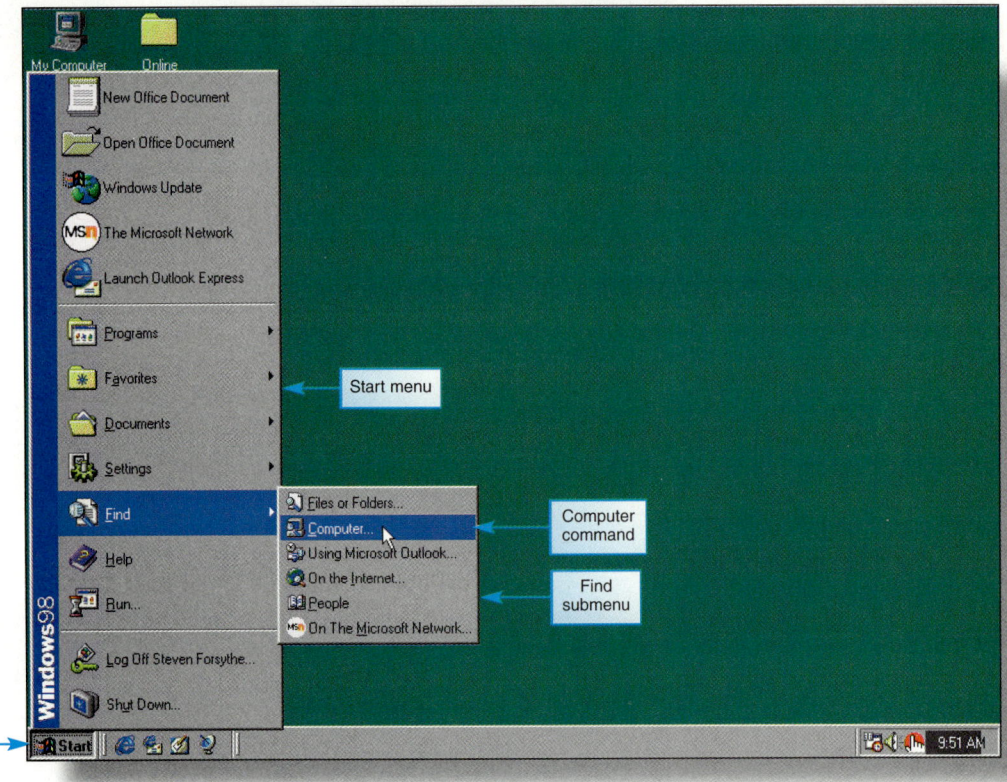

FIGURE 7-64

2 **Click Computer. Type** Lopez **in the Named box in the Find: Computer window and then point to the Find Now button.**

The Find: Computer window displays and Lopez displays in the Named box (Figure 7-65).

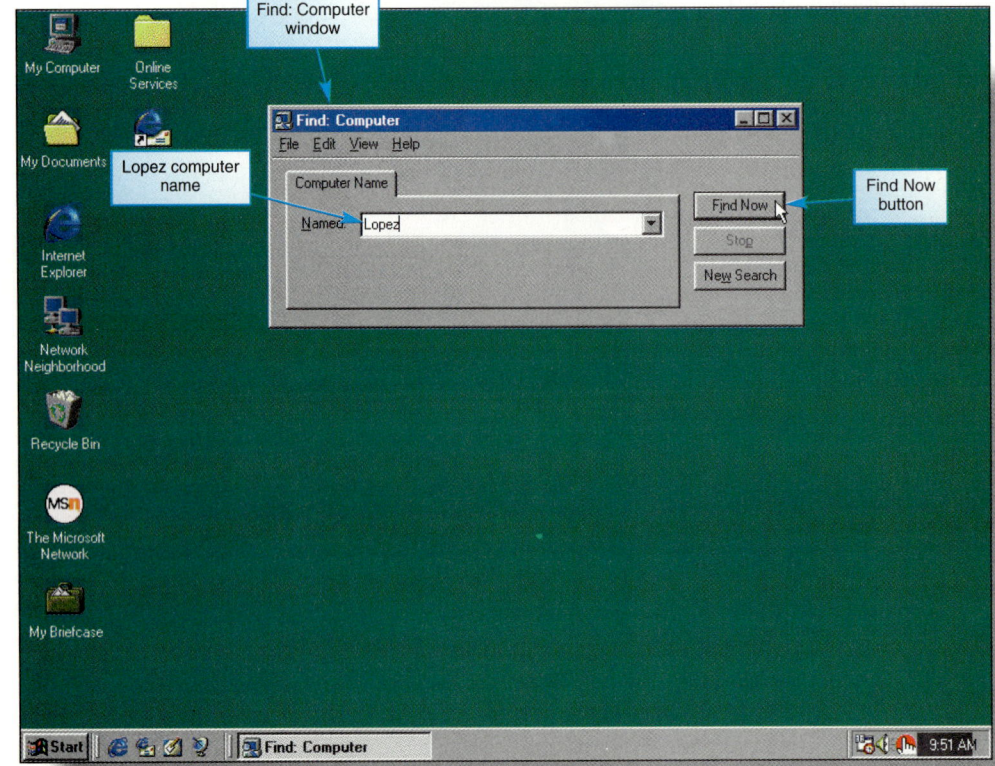

FIGURE 7-65

Click the Find Now button.

Windows 98 searches the network and displays the computer name (Lopez), location of the computer (Network Neighborhood), and comment (Toshiba Satellite 315CDS) in the list box in the expanded Find: Computer window (Figure 7-66).

 **Click the Close button in the Find: Computer window.**

The Find: Computer window closes.

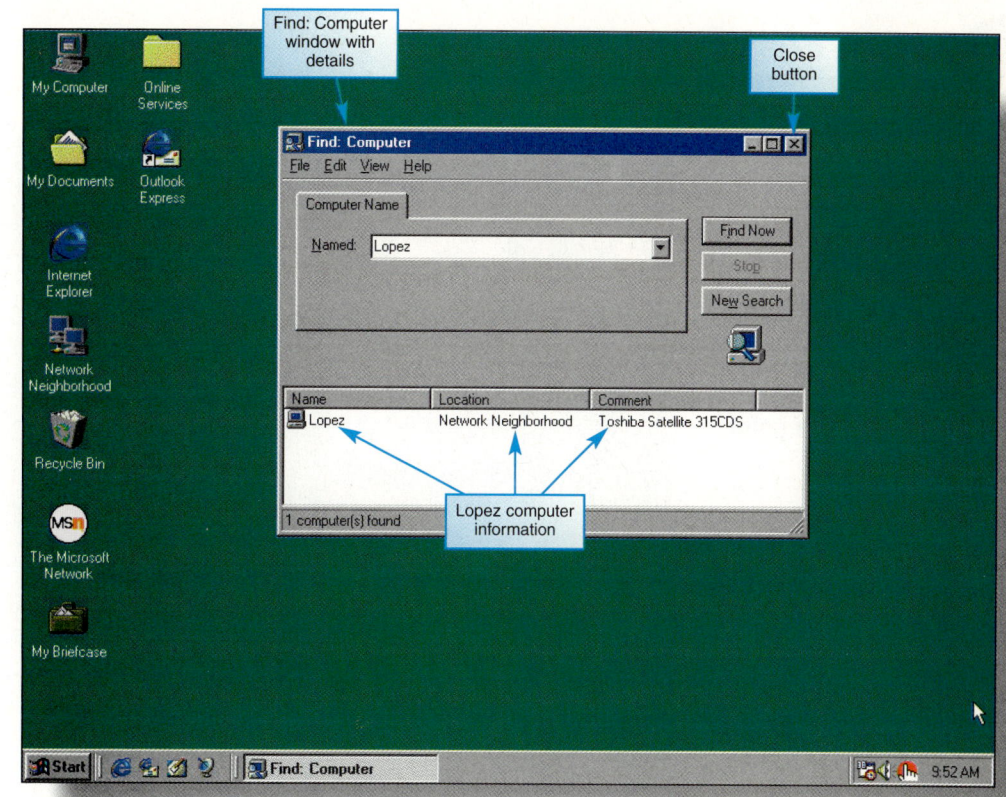

FIGURE 7-66

Sharing Computer Resources on a Network

Previously in this project while installing network components, you installed the service network component (File and printer sharing for Microsoft Networks) to allow file and printer sharing. In a previous section, you used Network Neighborhood to view other computers on the network and the shared computer resources on the computer.

In this section, you will learn to share computer resources on a computer with other network users. **Computer resources** that you can share with other users include programs, documents, files, folders, and printers. In the process of sharing a resource, you have the option of requiring the user to enter a password to access the shared resource.

Sharing a Folder

Assume that you need a folder to contain bitmap images you want to share with other users of the network. You plan to create the folder on the desktop, name the folder Bitmap Files, share the folder by giving full access to the folder, and copying the bitmap graphics image documents to the folder at a later time. **Full access** means another user can open the folder, change the contents of the folder, and change the contents of the documents in the folder. Perform the steps on the next page to create and fully share the Bitmap Files folder without assigning a password to the shared folder.

1. Double-click Network Neighborhood icon

Sharing

Besides Full access, other types of sharing include Read-Only and Depends on Password. Read-Only access allows other users to open and copy documents but not modify or change information in the documents. Depends on Password access allows different types of access for different users.

WIN 7.50 • Project 7 • Communicating with Other Computers

 Steps **To Share a Folder**

1 **Right-click the desktop, point to New, and click Folder. Type** `Bitmap Files` **in the object name text box of the newly created folder and then press the ENTER key. Right-click the Bitmap Files folder icon and then point to Sharing.**

The Bitmap Files folder displays on the desktop and a shortcut menu displays (Figure 7-67).

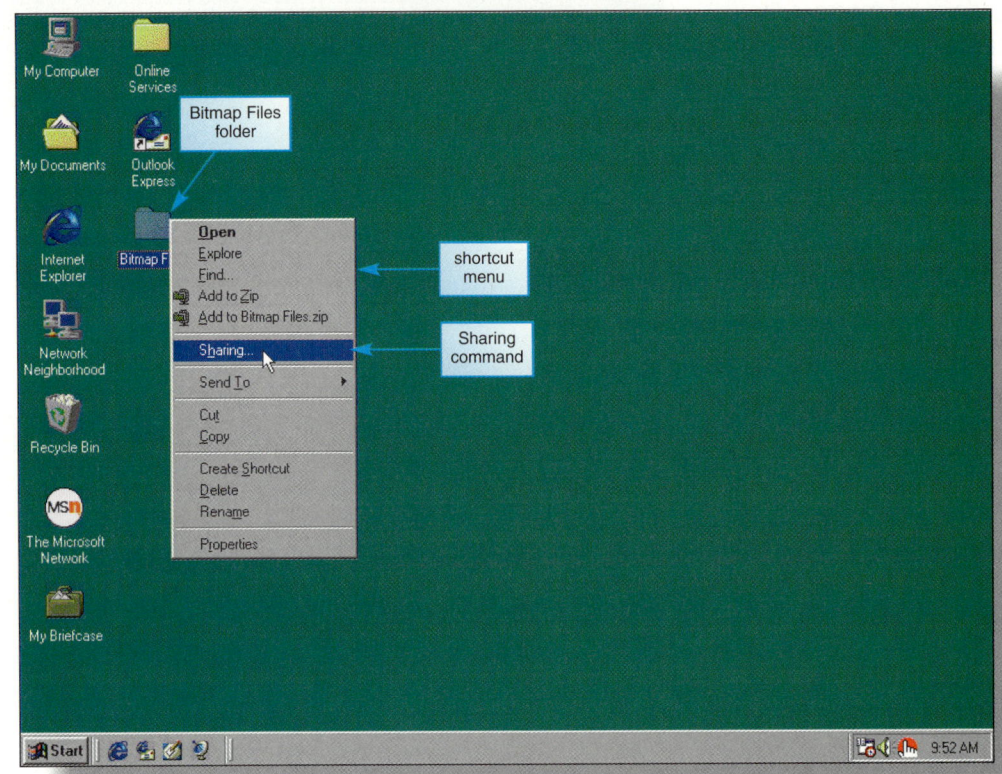

FIGURE 7-67

2 **Click Sharing. If necessary, click the Sharing tab in the Bitmap Files Properties dialog box. Click Shared As, click Full, and then point to the OK button.**

The Sharing sheet displays in the Bitmap Files Properties dialog box and the Shared As option button and Full option button are selected (Figure 7-68). The BITMAP FILES share name displays in the Share Name text box.

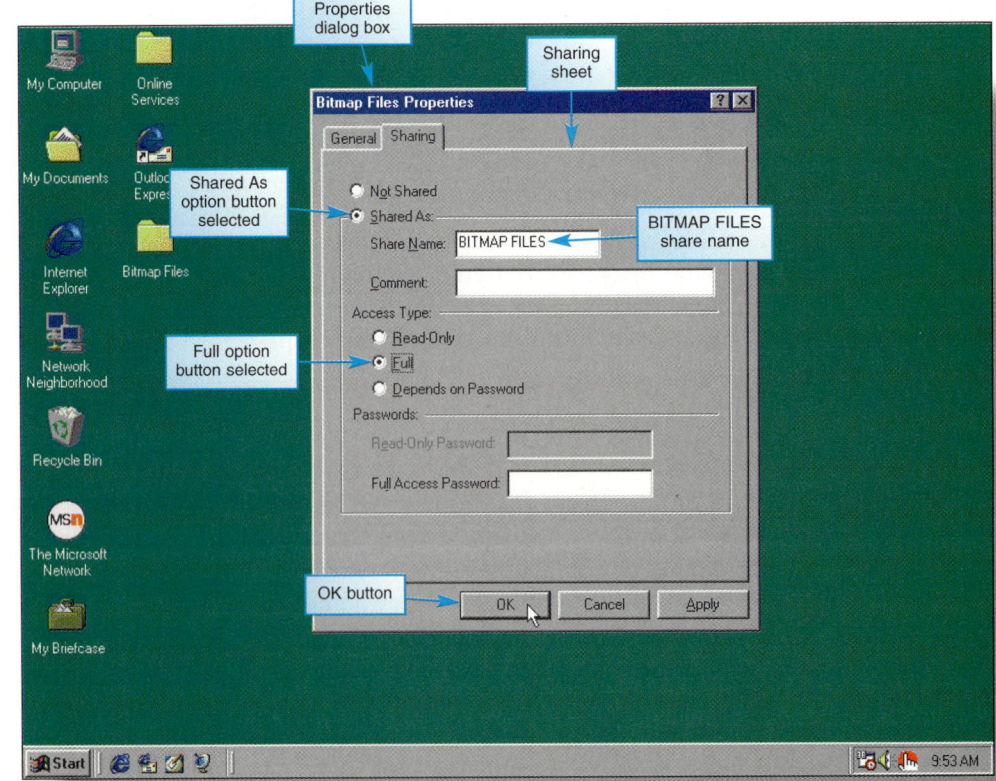

FIGURE 7-68

Click the OK button.

The Bitmap Files Properties dialog box closes and a wrist and hand display on the lower edge of the Bitmap Files folder icon (Figure 7-69). The Bitmap Files folder is accessible fully to other computers on the network.

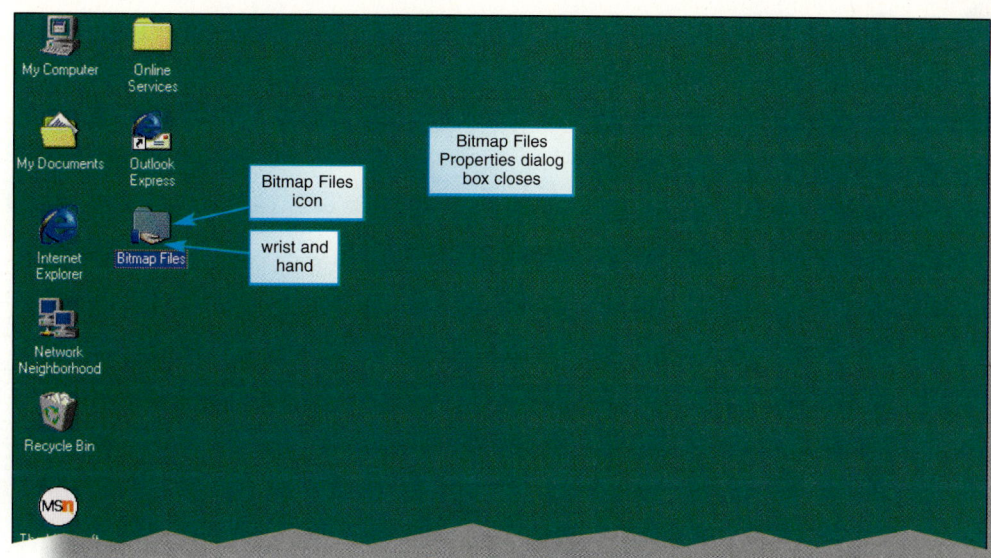

FIGURE 7-69

After sharing the Bitmap Files folder, other users on the network have full access to the folder. To access the folder from another computer, the user locates the computer resources on the computer using the techniques shown earlier using Network Neighborhood or the Find command, and double-clicks the Bitmap Files icon.

Deleting a Shared Folder

After creating the Bitmap Files folder on the desktop and sharing the folder, return the desktop to its original state by deleting the Bitmap Files folder. Perform the following steps to delete the Bitmap Files folder.

TO DELETE A SHARED FOLDER

1. Right-click the Bitmap Files folder icon.
2. Click Delete.
3. Click the Yes button in the Confirm Folder Delete dialog box.

Windows 98 removes the Bitmap Files folder from the desktop.

Sharing a Printer

To allow other users on the network to use a printer connected to a computer, you must share the printer icon in the Printers window. As with a shared folder, you have the option of requiring the user to enter a password to access the printer. Perform the steps on the next page to share the HP LaserJet III printer without assigning a password to the shared printer. If the HP LaserJet III printer icon is not available on your computer, use another printer icon to perform the steps on the next page.

1. Right-click folder icon, click Sharing tab, click Read-Only
2. Right-click folder icon, click Sharing tab, click Depends on Password

Share Names

The share name (BITMAP FILES) in the Share Name text box is based upon the first 12 characters of the folder name. If a folder name is longer than 12 characters, only the first 12 characters display in the Share Name text box.

WIN 7.52 • Project 7 • Communicating with Other Computers

Steps: To Share a Printer

1 Double-click the My Computer icon on the desktop, double-click the Printers icon in the My Computer window, right-click the HP LaserJet III icon in the Printers window, and then point to Sharing on the shortcut menu.

The Printers window displays in the same window as the My Computer window and a shortcut menu displays (Figure 7-70).

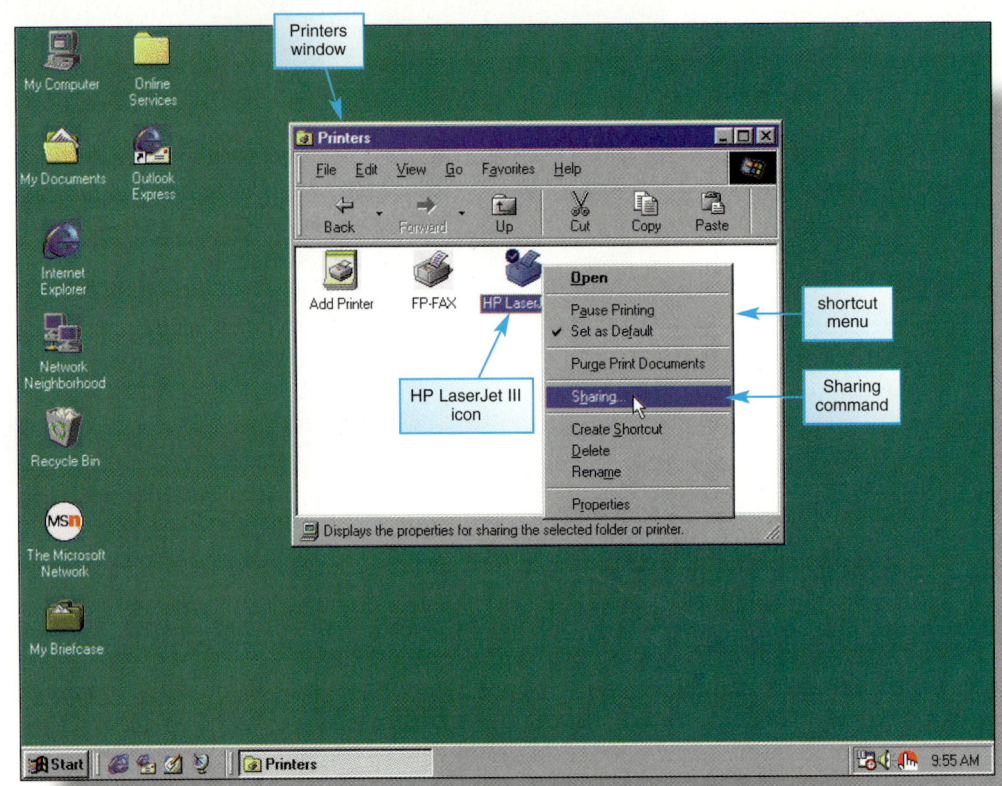

FIGURE 7-70

2 Click Sharing. If necessary, click the Sharing tab in the HP LaserJet III Properties dialog box, click Shared As, type `HP LaserJet` in the Share Name text box, and then point to the OK button.

The Sharing sheet displays in the HP LaserJet III Properties dialog box, the Shared As option button is selected, and HP LaserJet displays in the Share Name text box (Figure 7-71).

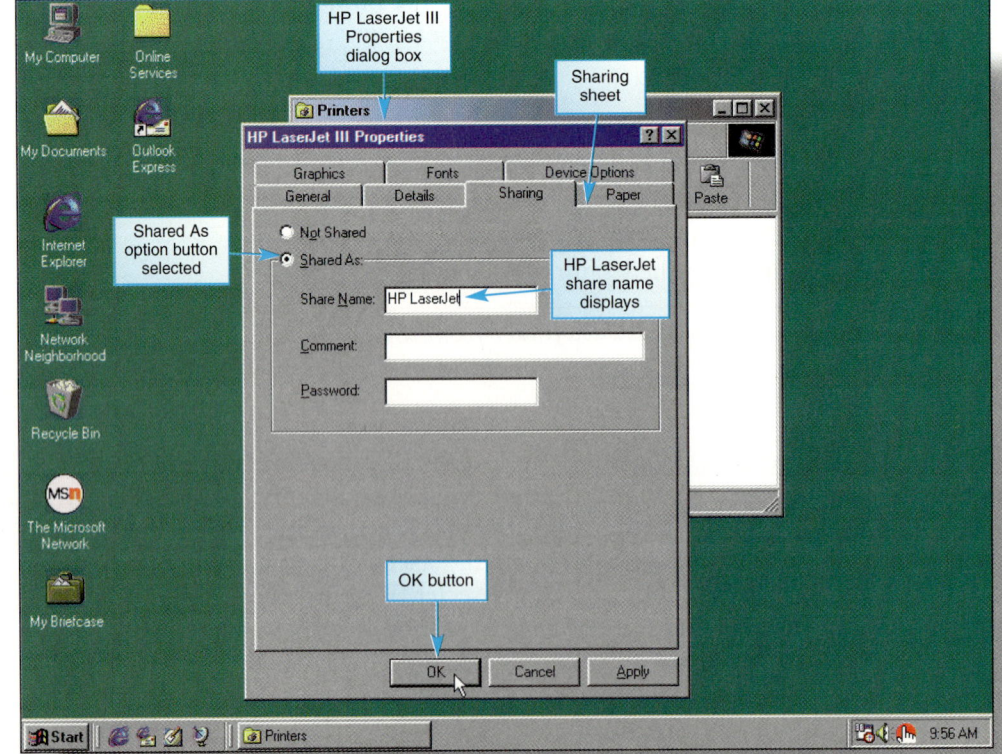

FIGURE 7-71

③ Click the OK button.

The HP LaserJet III Properties dialog box closes and a wrist and hand display on the lower edge of the HP LaserJet III icon (Figure 7-72).

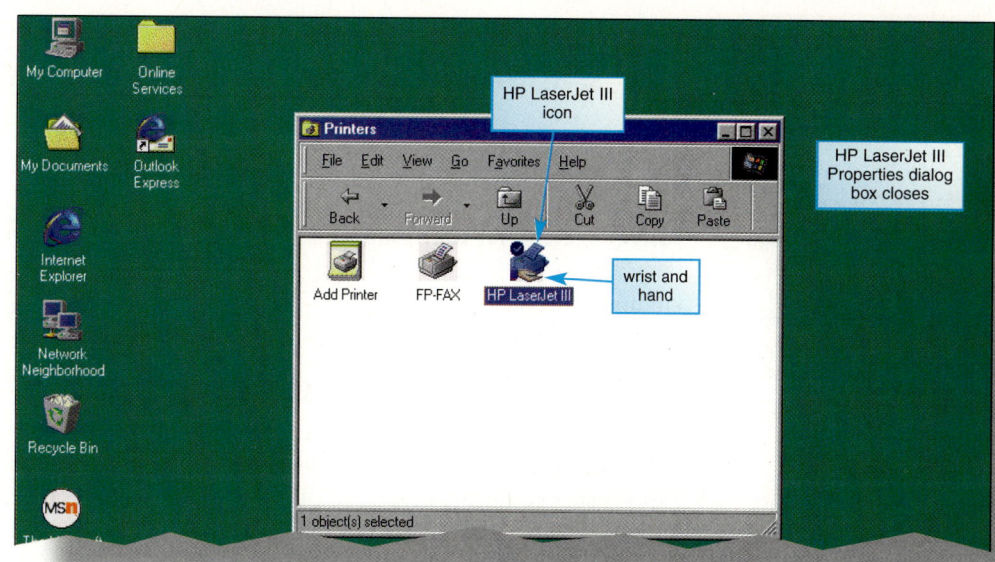

FIGURE 7-72

After sharing the HP LaserJet III printer, other users on the network have full access to the printer. To access the printer from another computer, the user locates the shared HP LaserJet printer icon using the techniques shown earlier using Network Neighborhood or the Find command. Next, the user has several options for using the printer. The user can create a shortcut to the printer on the desktop, move the printer icon to a location on the hard disk, and then drag a document icon to the printer icon to print the document. Or, the user may make the shared HP LaserJet III printer the default printer and be able to print within any Windows 98 application software program.

Removing Sharing from a Printer

After sharing the HP LaserJet III printer, return the printer to its original state by removing sharing from the printer. Perform the following steps to remove sharing from the HP LaserJet III printer.

TO REMOVE SHARING FROM A PRINTER

1. Right-click the HP LaserJet III icon in the Printers folder.
2. Click Sharing.
3. If necessary, click the Sharing tab.
4. Click Not Shared in the Sharing sheet.
5. Click the OK button in the HP LaserJet III Properties dialog box.
6. Click the Close button in the Printers window.

The HP LaserJet III printer is no longer available to other computers on the network.

More About

Mapping a Drive Letter

In addition to folders, you also can map a drive letter to a printer port. For information about how to map a drive letter to a printer port, use Windows Help and the Index tab to look up the mapping printer ports to network drives Help topic.

Mapping a Drive Letter to a Network Resource

If you use a shared computer resource on a network computer frequently, you may want to assign an unused drive letter, such as drive F or drive G, to the resource. The process of assigning a drive letter to a shared computer resource is called **mapping a drive letter**. After mapping a drive letter to a computer resource, you can double-click the drive icon in the My Computer or Windows Explorer window to access the mapped drive.

Mapping a Drive Letter

To map a drive letter to a shared resource, you must know the path of the shared resource. The **path**, which consists of the computer name, location of the resource, and resource name, gives the operating system directions to find the resource on the network. For example, to map a drive letter to the Art Files folder on the Lopez computer, the path would be \\Lopez\Art Files. Perform the following steps to map a drive letter (G) to the Art Files folder on the Lopez computer.

 To Map a Drive Letter

1 **Right-click the Network Neighborhood icon and then point to Map Network Drive.**

A shortcut menu displays (Figure 7-73).

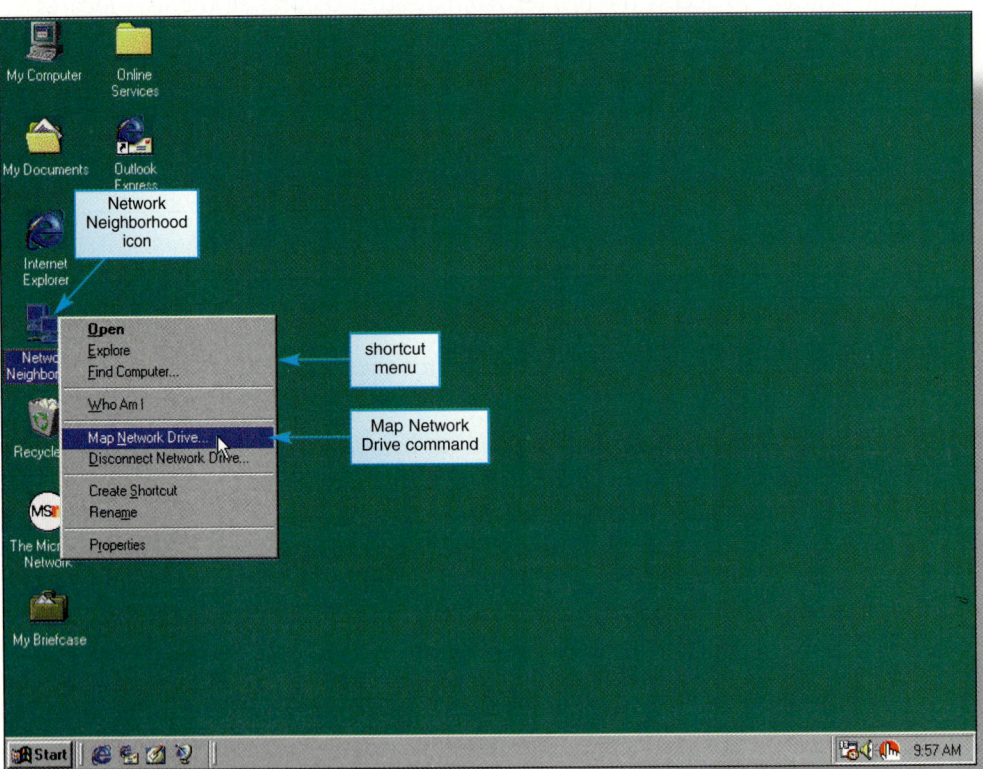

FIGURE 7-73

② **Click Map Network Drive. Click the Path box in the Map Network Drive dialog box and then type** \\Lopez\Art Files **as the path. Point to the OK button.**

The Map Network Drive dialog box displays, the drive icon displays in the Drive box and the path displays in the Path box (Figure 7-74). The drive icon that displays in the Drive box on your computer may be different.

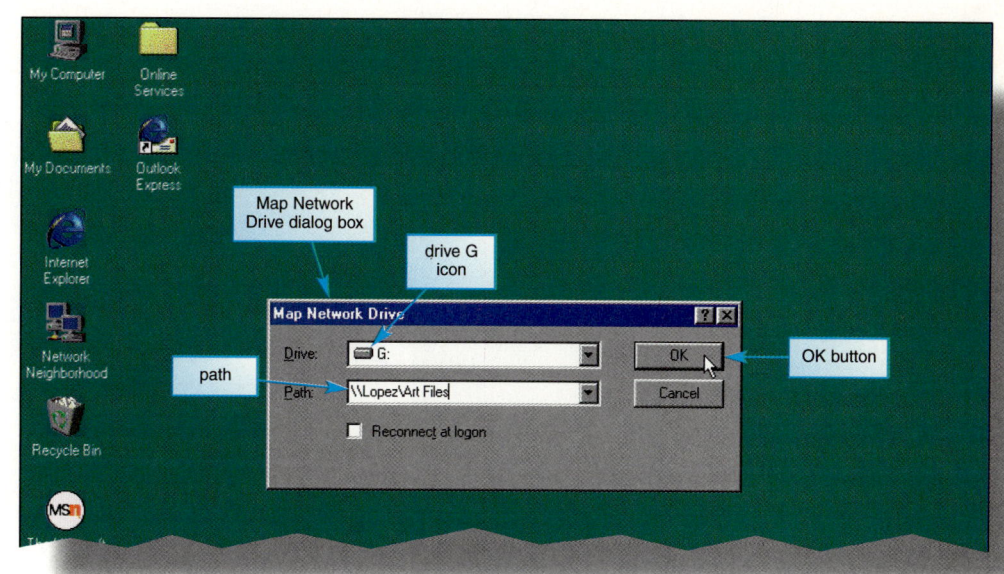

FIGURE 7-74

③ **Click the OK button.**

The Map Network Drive dialog box closes, the Art Files folder is mapped to network drive G, and the Art files on 'Lopez' (G:) window displays (Figure 7-75).

④ **Click the Close button in the Art files on 'Lopez' (G:) window.**

The Art files on 'Lopez' (G:) window closes.

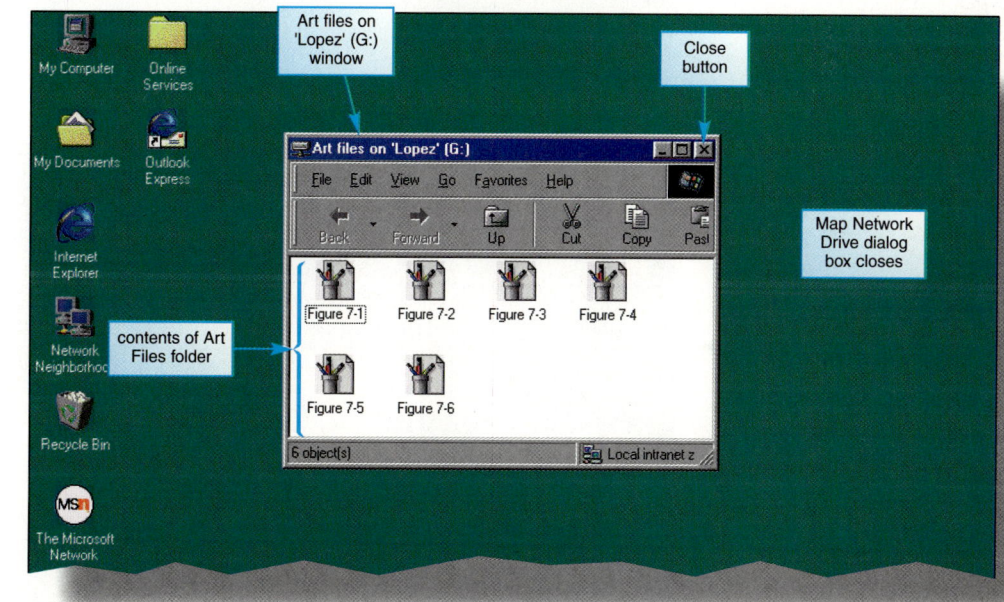

FIGURE 7-75

Accessing a Mapped Network Drive

After mapping a network drive to the Art Files folder on the Lopez computer, you access the mapped folder by double-clicking the drive G icon in the My Computer or Windows Explorer window on your computer. Perform the steps on the next page to access the mapped network drive G.

Other Ways

1. Right-click My Computer icon, click Map Network Drive, click Path box, click path, click OK button

WIN 7.56 • Project 7 • Communicating with Other Computers

 To Access a Mapped Network Drive

1 **Double-click the My Computer icon on the desktop. Point to the Art files on 'Lopez' (G:) icon in the My Computer window.**

The My Computer window, containing the Art files on 'Lopez' (G:) icon, displays (Figure 7-76).

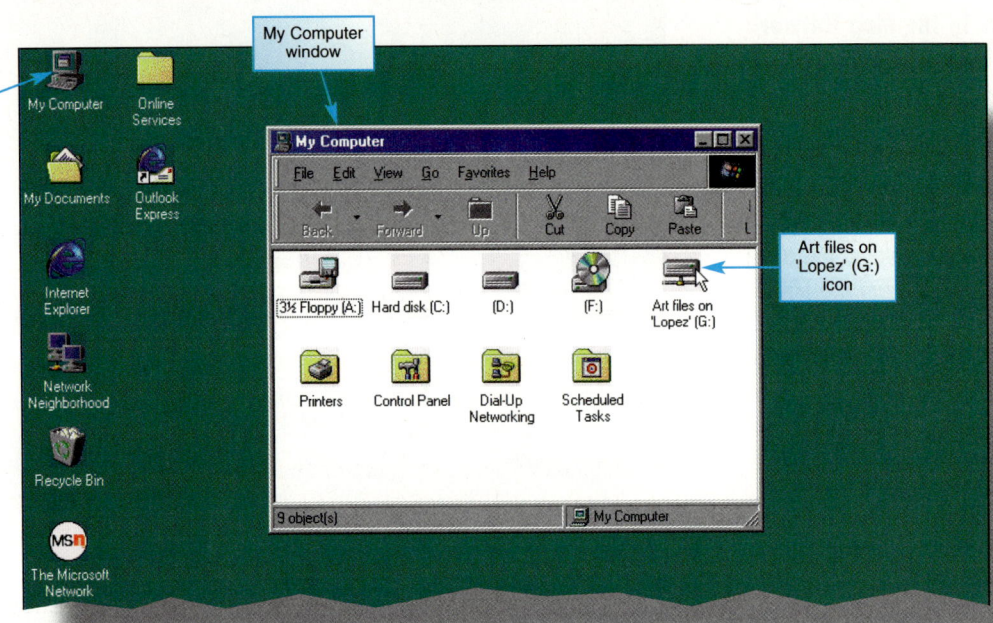

FIGURE 7-76

2 **Double-click the Art files on 'Lopez' (G:) icon.**

The Art files on 'Lopez' (G:) window displays (Figure 7-77). Six documents in the Art Files folder display in the window.

3 **Click the Close button in the Art files on 'Lopez' (G:) window.**

The Art files on 'Lopez' (G:) window closes.

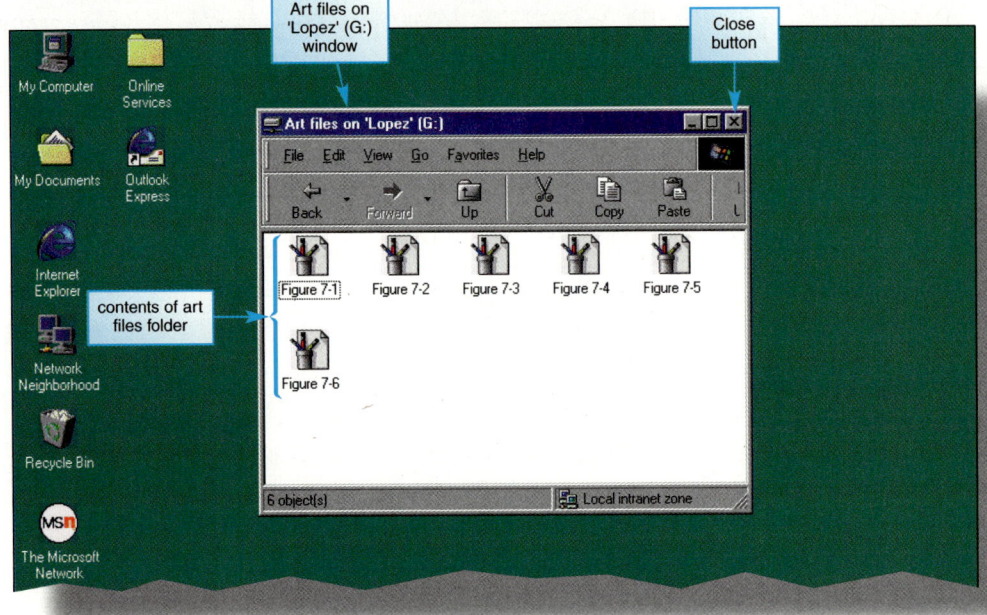

FIGURE 7-77

1. Right-click My Computer icon, click Open, double-click mapped drive icon

Disconnecting a Mapped Network Drive

After mapping a network letter to the Art Files folder on the Lopez computer, return the network drive letters to their original configuration by disconnecting the network drive G. Perform the following steps to disconnect the network drive G.

TO DISCONNECT A MAPPED NETWORK DRIVE

1. Right-click the Network Neighborhood icon.
2. Click Disconnect Network Drive.
3. If necessary, click the drive G icon in the Drive list box in the Disconnect Network Drive dialog box.
4. Click the OK button in the Disconnect Network Drive dialog box.

Windows 98 disconnects the network drive G from the Art Files folder on the Lopez computer.

Project Summary

The purpose of this project is to introduce you to the methods available to use a computer to communicate with other computers. One method shown used a modem to connect to an online service (The Microsoft Network). You checked the MSN connection settings, signed in to MSN, launched Outlook Express, opened and read an e-mail message, replied to an e-mail message, signed out from MSN, and changed the connection settings. Another method explained to use a modem was to connect to an Internet service provider. You used the Internet Connection wizard to sign up for an Internet service provider and create a Dial-Up Networking connection. Next, you dialed the Internet service provider and disconnected from the Internet service provider.

A second method of using a computer to communicate with other computers was to connect the computer to a network. You installed a network adapter, installed network software components (client, protocol, and service), viewed computers and workgroups on the network, searched for a computer on the network, and shared computer resources (folder and printer) with other computers on the network. In addition, you mapped a drive letter to a network resource and accessed the mapped network drive.

What You Should Know

Having completed this project, you now should be able to perform the following tasks:

- Access a Mapped Network Drive *(WIN 7.56)*
- Change the Backup Telephone Number *(WIN 7.21)*
- Change the Connection Settings *(WIN 7.17)*
- Check the MSN Connection Settings *(WIN 7.6)*
- Close the Connection Settings Dialog Box *(WIN 7.22)*
- Delete a Shared Folder *(WIN 7.51)*
- Dial an Internet Service Provider *(WIN 7.32)*
- Disconnect a Mapped Network Drive *(WIN 7.57)*
- Disconnect from an Internet Service Provider *(WIN 7.34)*
- Install a Network Adapter *(WIN 7.37)*
- Install Network Software Components *(WIN 7.38)*
- Launch Outlook Express *(WIN 7.11)*
- Locate a Computer on a Network *(WIN 7.48)*
- Map a Drive Letter *(WIN 7.54)*
- Open an E-mail Message *(WIN 7.13)*
- Remove a Dial-Up Networking Connection Icon *(WIN 7.35)*
- Remove Sharing from a Printer *(WIN 7.53)*
- Reply to an E-mail Message *(WIN 7.14)*
- Restore the Original Connection Settings *(WIN 7.22)*
- Share a Folder *(WIN 7.50)*
- Share a Printer *(WIN 7.52)*
- Sign In to The Microsoft Network *(WIN 7.8)*
- Sign Out from The Microsoft Network *(WIN 7.16)*
- Sign Up for an ISP Account Using the Internet Connection Wizard *(WIN 7.24)*
- View a Dial-Up Networking Connection Icon *(WIN 7.35)*
- View the Computers and Workgroups on a Network *(WIN 7.46)*

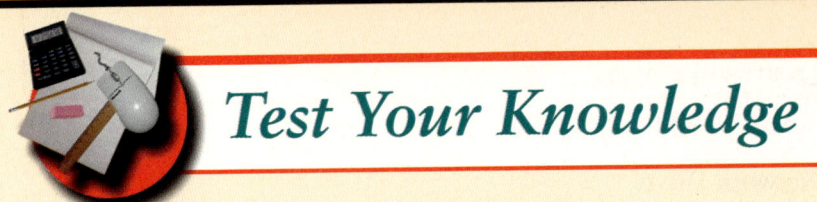

Test Your Knowledge

1 True/False

Instructions: Circle T if the statement is true or F if the statement is false.

T F   1. The Internet is a collection of networks, each of which is composed of a collection of smaller networks.
T F   2. Connecting to The Microsoft Network (MSN) for the first time is called signing in to the network.
T F   3. Connection settings for MSN include a telephone number, backup telephone number, and dialing properties.
T F   4. You can use Outlook Express to check for e-mail messages from MSN members, America Online, and Internet service provider members.
T F   5. You do not need Dial-Up Networking software to connect to MSN.
T F   6. A unique identifier, called a Uniform Resource Locator (URL), identifies each computer on the Internet.
T F   7. Network adapter, client and service software, and protocol are examples of network components.
T F   8. Network Neighborhood allows you to enter a computer name and search the network for the corresponding computer.
T F   9. To allow another network user to use your printer, you must share the printer by connecting a cable between your printer and their computer.
T F 10. When referring to a shared resource, a path consists of the computer name, resource location, and resource name.

2 Multiple Choice

Instructions: Circle the correct response.

1. _____ is a service provided on The Microsoft Network.
   a. Sending and receiving e-mail
   b. Talking to members in a chat room
   c. Access to the latest news, sports, and weather
   d. All of the above

2. A communication system, composed of hardware and software, that allows users to share data and computer resources is called _____.
   a. a network adapter
   b. a network
   c. the Internet
   d. the World Wide Web

3. You send and receive e-mail using _____.
   a. Outlook Express
   b. Inbox
   c. Network Neighborhood
   d. Outbox

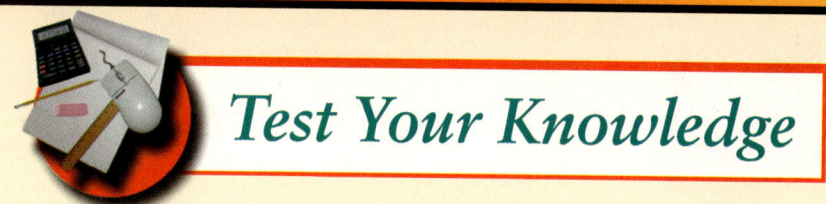

Test Your Knowledge

4. A(n) _____ maintains a computer, called a server, which is connected to the Internet.
   a. network provider
   b. Internet service provider
   c. online service
   d. browser
5. Before dialing an Internet service provider, you must _____.
   a. sign on to the network
   b. surf the World Wide Web
   c. create a Dial-Up Networking connection
   d. none of the above
6. EarthLink is a(n) _____.
   a. protocol
   b. online service
   c. Internet service provider
   d. network provider
7. To create a Dial-Up Networking connection for an existing Internet service provider account, you need a(n) _____.
   a. IP address
   b. user name and password
   c. mail server address
   d. all of the above
8. The _____ enables you to share computer resources on your computer with other computers on a network.
   a. network adapter
   b. client software
   c. service software
   d. protocol
9. A _____ is a name assigned to a group of computers.
   a. computer name
   b. user name
   c. password
   d. workgroup name
10. You view the computers and workgroups on a network using _____.
    a. Network Neighborhood
    b. The Microsoft Network
    c. the Internet
    d. the Find command

WIN 7.60 • Project 7 • Communicating with Other Computers

Test Your Knowledge

3 Opening and Reading an E-mail Message

Instructions: Figure 7-78 illustrates the Inbox - Outlook Express window. In the spaces provided, list the steps to open and read the new e-mail message from Ginny Harvey and send a reply to her. The return e-mail message should contain a subject (Re: New Table of Contents) and a message (The new table of contents looks good. I would, however, switch the last two topics. Please call me with your comments.).

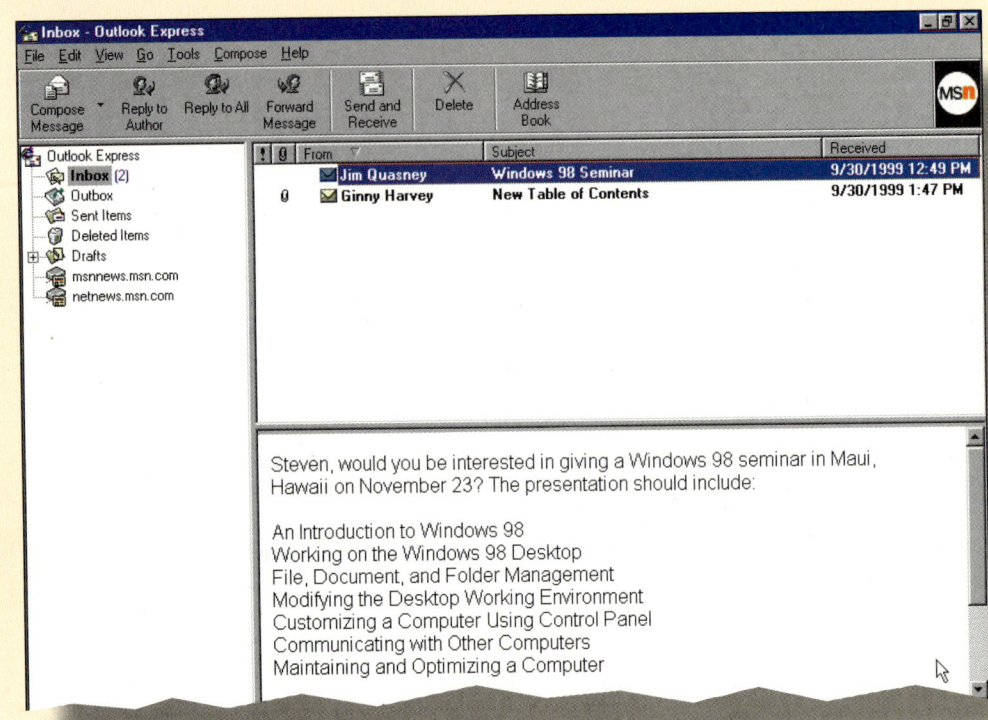

FIGURE 7-78

Step 1: _____
Step 2: _____
Step 3: _____
Step 4: _____
Step 5: _____

4 Sharing a Printer

Instructions: In the spaces provided, list the steps to share the HP 560C printer connected to your computer with the other computers on the network.

Step 1: _____
Step 2: _____
Step 3: _____
Step 4: _____
Step 5: _____
Step 6: _____
Step 7: _____
Step 8: _____

Use Help

1 Using Outlook Express Help

Instructions: Use Help and a computer to perform the following tasks.

1. If necessary, launch Microsoft Windows 98.
2. Click the Launch Outlook Express icon on the Quick Launch toolbar to launch Outlook Express.
3. Click Help on the menu bar of the Inbox - Outlook Express window.
4. Click Contents and Index on the Help menu.
5. Using the Index tab, answer the following questions.
   a. According to the instructions in Outlook Express Help, how do you insert a file into an e-mail message?
   _____
   _____

   b. How do you save a file attached to an e-mail message you receive? _____
   _____

   c. If an e-mail message displays in the preview pane, how do you save a file attached to the e-mail message?
   _____

6. Click the Index tab in the Outlook Express Help window.
7. Using the Contents tab, answer the following questions.
   a. What is a newsgroup? _____
   b. When you find a newsgroup you like, what must you do to display the newsgroup in your Outlook Express folder list? _____
   c. List one method to accomplish this. _____
8. Using the Contents tab, answer the following questions.
   a. What does the Address Book provide? _____
   _____

   b. How do you open the Address Book from the Inbox – Outlook Express window?
   _____

9. Click the Close button in the Outlook Express Help window.
10. Click the Close button in the Inbox – Outlook Express window.

2 Using Windows Help to Troubleshoot Network Problems

Instructions: Use Windows Help and a computer to perform the following tasks.

1. You are having problems finding other computers in the Network Neighborhood list. What is the first thing the Troubleshooter suggests you try? _____
2. You are having problems logging on to the network. What does Troubleshooter say you must do before connecting to a network? _____

(continued)

Use Help

Using Windows Help to Troubleshoot Network Problems *(continued)*

3. You are unable to share a printer on your computer.
   a. What question does Troubleshooter ask you?
   _____
   b. What are the steps given in Help to enable file and print sharing?
   _____
4. Other computers on the network are unable to connect to your computer. What does Troubleshooter ask you to verify? _____
5. You are unable to install a network adapter.
   a. What does the Troubleshooter indicate may not be installed correctly on your computer?
   _____
   b. If this is not installed correctly, what wizard does Troubleshooter suggest you use.
6. Click the Close button in the Windows Help window.

1 Sending E-mail Messages Using The Microsoft Network

Instructions: To familiarize yourself with sending e-mail using The Microsoft Network, you would like to create a document, attach the document to an e-mail message, and send the e-mail to Steven Forsythe (one of the authors of this book). Because the MSN service is evolving constantly, some of the following steps may require you to use Help to find the current method of performing the step. Perform the following steps to send an e-mail message using MSN. If you cannot use MSN to send and receive e-mail, use another online service, an Internet service provider, or the network to which your computer is connected.

Part 1: Creating a Document to Attach to the E-mail

1. If necessary, launch Windows 98.
2. Create a new document on the desktop. The document can be a text document file, Microsoft Word document, WordPad document, WordPerfect document, or whatever other type of document you have available on your computer.
3. Rename the document using your first and last name (example: Steven Forsythe).
4. Open the document and briefly describe your experience using this textbook, or anything else of interest.
5. Click File on the menu bar and then click Save on the File menu to save the document.

In the Lab

6. Click File on the menu bar and then click Print on the File menu to print the document.
7. Click the Close button in the application window.

Part 2: *Signing In to The Microsoft Network and Launching Outlook Express*

1. Double-click The Microsoft Network icon on the desktop.
2. Type your MSN user name and password in the MSN - Sign-In window.
3. Click the Connect button in the MSN - Sign-In window.
4. If the message, You have new messages, displays when you sign in, click the message to launch Outlook Express. If not, launch Outlook Express by clicking the Launch Outlook Express icon on the Quick Launch toolbar.

Part 3: *Creating an E-mail Message*

1. Click the Compose Message button on the toolbar.
2. Type StevenForsythe@msn.com in the To text box. Type Project 7 - In the Lab Assignment 1 - followed by your city and state separated by a comma (example: Brea, California) in the Subject text box.
3. In the message area, type Hello Steven Forsythe - and then press the ENTER key twice. Type Here is the file you requested. as the message and then press the ENTER key twice.

Part 4: *Attaching the Document to the E-mail Message*

1. Click the Insert File button (identified by the paper clip icon) on the toolbar.
2. In the Insert Attachment window, click the Look in box arrow, click Desktop, click the file with your name in the list box, and then click the Attach button. A document icon with your name should display your e-mail message.

Part 5: *Sending the E-mail Message and Signing Out from MSN*

1. Click the Send button on the toolbar.
2. Click the Close button in the Inbox - Outlook Express window.
3. Click the Close button in MSN On Stage - Microsoft Internet Explorer window.
4. Click the Hang-up Now button in the MSN - Disconnect dialog box.
5. Quit Windows 98.

2 Using an Internet Service Provider to Surf the World Wide Web

Instructions: You would like to join in on the surf the World Wide Web craze. You sign up for an Internet service provider account and create a Dial-Up Networking connection to the Internet service provider. You have been watching television and looking in magazines to develop a list of URLs. In addition, you would like to search for Web sites on the Internet. Perform the following steps to dial your Internet service provider and surf the World Wide Web.

(continued)

In the Lab

Using an Internet Service Provider to Surf the World Wide Web *(continued)*

Part 1: *Dialing an Internet Service Provider*
1. If necessary, launch Windows 98.
2. Double-click the Internet Explorer icon on the desktop.
3. Type your user name and password in the MSN Sign-In dialog box. If you are at school, obtain the user name and password from your instructor.
4. Click the Connect button to connect to the Internet service provider.

Part 2: *Entering Uniform Resource Locators*
1. Type http://www.mtv.com in the Address box and then press the ENTER key. Answer the following questions.
    a. What hyperlinks are available on the MTV Online Home page?

    b. What graphic(s) display on the home page?

2. Type http://cnn.com in the Address box and then press the ENTER key. Answer the following question. What news story displays on the CNN Interactive home page?

3. Compare the NBC (http://nbc.com/) and CBS (http://cbs.com/) Web sites. Answer the following questions.
    a. Which Web site is better? Why?

    b. Do the Web sites contain similar information? If so, list common topics?

4. Type http://www.fbi.gov/homepage.htm in the Address box and then press the ENTER key. Answer the following questions.
    a. What emblem displays on the Federal Bureau of Investigation Home Page?

    b. Explore the FBI home page and find the list of ten most wanted men. List them below.

In the Lab

5. Type http://www.microsoft.com in the Address box and then press the ENTER key. Explore the Microsoft Web page for job opportunities at Microsoft Corporation. Are jobs available in the field of Technical Support? If so, list two jobs.

   _____

   _____

6. Type http://www.amazon.com in the Address box and then press the ENTER key. Type Steven Forsythe in the Keyword Search text box and then click the Go! button.
   a. What do you find? _____
   b. What is the price of the Microsoft Windows 98 Complete Concepts and Techniques book?

   _____

   c. Click the hyperlink for this book. What information displays? _____

   _____

Part 3: *Searching the Internet*

1. Type http://www.altavista.digital.com in the Address box and then press the ENTER key. The AltaVista search service starts. Typing a word or words in the Search text box and clicking the Search button searches the Internet for sites containing the word or words you typed.
2. Use the words, community college, to perform a search. Answer the following questions.
   a. How many Web sites were found? _____
      Explore the Web sites by clicking several underlined listings (hyperlinks).
   b. Which site was the best you found? _____
3. Use the word, university, to perform a search. Answer the following questions.
   a. How many Web sites did you find? _____
      Explore the Web sites by clicking several underlined listings (hyperlinks).
   b. Did you find any international universities listed? If so, list two.

   _____

4. Use the words, high school, to perform a search. Answer the following questions.
   a. How many Web sites did you find? _____
      Explore the Web sites by clicking an underlined listing (hyperlink).
   b. Did you find any international high schools listed? If so, list two.

   _____

Part 4: *Disconnecting from the Internet Service Provider*

1. Click the Close button in the window to disconnect from the Internet service provider.
2. If necessary, follow the instructions to disconnect.

In the Lab

3 Using a Network

Name: _____ Computer Name: _____ E-mail Address: _____

Instructions: You and another network user were discussing your favorite CD-ROM video games at lunch. As a result, each of you decides to create a document on your desktop, list your top five video games in the document, and share the documents with each other. Each of you then can copy the other person's list of video games from their shared document into their own document. After copying the list to your document, you decide to e-mail your friend and thank them for their list. At lunch, you obtain your friend's name, computer name, and e-mail address and record the information below. Your friend makes the same decision. Perform the following steps to share video game lists and send an e-mail to the other person.

Part 1: Log On to the Network

1. If necessary, launch Windows 98.
2. Type your computer name in the User name text box.
3. Type your password in the Password text box.
4. Click the OK button.

Part 2: Create a Folder and a Document on the Desktop

1. Create a new folder on the desktop.
2. Use your first name and the words, Video Games List, to name the folder (example: Steven's Video Games List).
3. Create a new text document on the desktop.
4. Name the document using your first and last name (example: Steven Forsythe).
5. Open the document and type five video games.
6. Save the document on the desktop.
7. Print a copy of the document on the printer.
8. Close the document.
9. Drag the document into the Video Games List folder.

Part 3: Share the Folder

1. Right-click the folder icon, click Sharing.
2. If necessary, click the Sharing tab, click Shared As, and click Full.
3. Click the OK button.

Part 4: View the Other Computers on the Network

1. Wait for your friend to create a document, create a folder, and then share the folder.
2. Double-click the Network Neighborhood icon on the desktop.
3. Double-click your friend's computer icon in the Network Neighborhood window.
4. Double-click your friend's shared folder. The folder name is your friend's first and last name.

Part 5: Copying and Pasting the Video Game List into Your Document

1. Open your friend's document.
2. Highlight the list of video games in your friend's document.
3. Copy the list by right-clicking the highlighted list and then clicking Copy.

In the Lab

4. Close the window containing your friend's document.
5. Click the Close button in the window containing your friend's folder.
6. Open your folder, open your document in the folder, and open the document. Your list of five video games should display.
7. Move the insertion point to the end of the document.
8. Right-click an open area of the document and then click Paste. The document now should contain ten video games.
9. Save the document.
10. Print a copy of the document.
11. Close the document and then close the folder.

Part 6: *Sending an E-mail to Your Friend*

1. Launch Outlook Express by clicking the Launch Outlook Express icon on the Quick Launch toolbar.
2. Click the Compose Message button on the toolbar in the Inbox - Outlook Express window.
3. Type your friend's e-mail address in the To text box. Type Thank You in the Subject text box.
4. Type a short message in the message list thanking your friend for sharing the video game list.
5. Click the Send button.

Part 7: *Deleting the E-mail and Folder*

1. Read the e-mail from your friend in your Inbox. Click the Delete button on the toolbar to delete your friend's e-mail.
2. Close the Inbox - Outlook Express window.
3. Drag your folder on the desktop to the Recycle Bin.
4. Quit Windows 98.

Cases and Places

The difficulty of these case studies varies:
▶ are the least difficult; ▶▶ are more difficult; and ▶▶▶ are the most difficult.

1 ▶ Tomorrow, you are leaving on a four-day sales trip. Your itinerary includes a one-day stay in Detroit, a two-day stay in Boston, and a one-day stay in Philadelphia. Before leaving, you want to check the weather forecast for Detroit, Boston, and Philadelphia using The Microsoft Network. Sign in to The Microsoft Network, select the appropriate hyperlink to check the weather, find and record the weather forecast (rain, snow, partly cloudy, and so forth) and temperatures (high and low) for each city on the trip.

Cases and Places

2 ▶ Your company just signed up with a new Internet service provider (NetControl), and your boss asks you to create a Dial-Up Networking connection to the Internet service provider. The Internet service provider supplies you with a telephone number (301-555-3874), company user name (JWCo), password (Sprockets), e-mail address (JWCo@netcontrol.net), Internet mail server (mailer.netcontrol.net), primary IP address (201.124.99.105), and alternate IP address (205.88.14.123). Create the Dial-Up Networking connection. When you are finished, remove the Dial-Up Networking connection to NetControl.

3 ▶ Using computer magazines, advertising brochures, the Internet, or other resources, compile information about the latest version of Microsoft Outlook. In a brief report, compare Microsoft Outlook and Microsoft Outlook Express. Include the differences and similarities, how to obtain the software, the function and features of each program, and so forth. If possible, test Microsoft Outlook and then add your personal comments.

4 ▶▶ Check your local newspaper for advertisements for Internet service providers. Call two Internet service providers in your area and have them send information describing their services. Compare hours and services, costs, availability of technical support, and any additional information of interest about the providers. In a report, describe each Internet service provider, compare their services, and make a recommendation for the Internet service provider to use.

5 ▶▶ In addition to using Windows 98 to network computers, other networks (Novell NetWare, Banyan VINES, Artisoft LANtastic, Artisoft POSConnect, and Windows NT) are available. Using the Internet, magazines, newspapers, or other resources, obtain information about three of these networks. Prepare a report describing the purpose of each network, who the network is designed for, costs of purchasing the network software, and the more interesting features of the software and network.

6 ▶▶▶ Visit a business in your area that uses a network. Interview the network administrator (the person in charge of the network) and several employees who use the network. Determine the type of network being used and identify the network components (network adapters, client and service software, and protocol). Inquire as to any installation problems, if problems currently exist, what problems the network solved, and if ways to improve the network are available. Summarize your findings in a report.

7 ▶▶▶ Prodigy, America Online, and CompuServe often advertise their online services by mailing a copy of an installation disk to prospective customers. These floppy disks commonly contain the installation instructions, temporary member ID, and password required to connect to the service without charge. Obtain a floppy disk from two online services (ask friends, business associates, or instructors for the disks) and follow the instructions to install and connect to each of the online services. Compare the two online services with The Microsoft Network. Consider ease of use, speed, services offered, organization, Internet access, and costs. Summarize your findings in a report.

Microsoft Windows 98

Working with Multimedia and NetMeeting

PROJECT 8

OBJECTIVES

You will have mastered the material in this project when you can:

- Describe multimedia and its components
- Record, play, and embed a voice message
- Change the sound scheme
- Play an audio compact disc
- Create and edit a Play List
- Adjust the volume of a sound device
- Play a digital video disc
- Change the video window view
- Play a multimedia file using Media Player
- Launch Microsoft NetMeeting
- Change the directory information and ILS server
- Filter the users in the directory list
- Place and end a call
- Send a text message using Chat
- Draw and send an image using Whiteboard
- Send a file using File Transfer
- Log off from the ILS server

Microsoft Windows 98

Beware, Multimedia Pirates
Digital Watermarks Provide Security

Have you ever photocopied a chapter from your roommate's textbook? Copied a classmate's homework answers? Installed Windows 98 on your computer using a friend's CD-ROM? Downloaded a copyrighted image from the Internet and pasted it on your home page? If so, you may be guilty of plagiarism, as you have taken the works or ideas belonging to another person and used them as your own.

Not everything you copy can be considered plagiarized, however. Legally, you can use a scanner to digitize your vacation photos and add them to a PowerPoint presentation. You can save your research paper on your hard drive and

Creator: John Smith
Creation Date: June 16, 2000
Authorized Users: Joan Smith
Distributor: Multimedia Corp.

on a floppy disk. You can make a backup copy of most software you have bought and store it in a safe place. What differs with these examples is that you are the rightful owner of these items, termed *intellectual property*.

Software piracy is a worldwide problem, with software companies losing more than $11 billion annually in sales of business applications such as Microsoft Office. The Business Software Alliance (BSA) and the Software Publishers Association (SPA) estimate that 40 percent of the new business programs installed on corporate computers are pirated. Some experts estimate that at least one illegal copy has been made for every legal copy of software being used today.

Computers make duplicating works easy, inexpensive, and quick. But computer gurus have devised a method to prevent the unauthorized duplication of electronic private work; this technology is called *digital watermarking*. A watermark is not a new concept, however. When you hold an expensive piece of stationery up to the light, usually you can see a watermark, such as a company logo or the paper manufacturer's name, embedded in the fibers. In electronic form, a digital watermark can be applied to multimedia, such as the audio and video files you will work with in this project.

Unlike a paper watermark, a digital watermark cannot be seen by the naked eye. Instead, it is embedded in the sound, graphics, text, or World Wide Web HTML file, and it contains information on the file's origin, creation date, creator, authorized users, and distributor. If an unauthorized person tries to copy this file, a warning box displays stating that the image is protected.

Theft of digital media on the Internet is rampant. Often Web surfers copy audio files, such as copyrighted songs or video files, such as footage from blockbuster movies and sports events and place these images on their personal Web pages. Some of these software pirates try to crop or cut the images in an attempt to eliminate or cut the watermarks. Some digital watermark software programs allow the watermark owner to crawl through the Web in search of sites containing the illegal images, and this software is savvy enough to detect the altered files.

The growth of digital multimedia has increased the need to protect files from unscrupulous software pirates. Watermarks are one vehicle for signing the works to verify authenticity and help prevent unauthorized duplication and distribution.

Microsoft Windows 98

Working with Multimedia and NetMeeting

PROJECT 8

CASE PERSPECTIVE

You recently attended a free Microsoft seminar on multimedia. Prior to attending the seminar, you were unsure what multimedia capabilities your personal computer had or how to use those capabilities. At the seminar, you watched an impressive display of multimedia presentations and took extensive notes. You were careful to make a list of the multimedia features you wanted to try on your computer.

Your list included how to play multimedia files, record and embed voice messages in documents, change the sound scheme, and play songs on a compact disc in the order you want. The list also contained a reminder to buy a video camera and try the videoconferencing features of Microsoft NetMeeting.

You thought videoconferencing might be a solution to the high cost of using the telephone to communicate with out-of-town business associates, friends, and family. Your goal is to learn more about the multimedia features of your computer and use Microsoft NetMeeting to place videoconference calls.

Introduction

Movie audiences used to watch silent black and white movies and follow the movie plot by reading text flashed on the movie screen. Today, action-packed movies commonly contain special effects to enhance the movie experience. Bright colors, loud noises, and fast moving props hold the attention of movie audiences.

In business, presentations that used to consist of black text on white backgrounds now involve and entertain their audiences with recorded music, flying graphics, and animation. Audio, video, and animation are commonplace on the Internet. The use of multimedia in education, business, and leisure activities is transforming the way individuals learn, work, and play. In Project 8, you will learn about multimedia and the hardware devices and software supported by Windows 98.

An Introduction to Multimedia

Multimedia is the use of any combination of text, colors, graphics, audio, video, and animation. **Text** is a fundamental component in many multimedia presentations. In addition to ordinary text, which conveys basic information, a variety of textual effects help to emphasize and clarify information. For example, you can emphasize certain words or phrases by changing the font size or style and varying colors for different blocks of text.

The popularity of the Windows 98 graphical user interface demonstrates the importance of graphics in the computer environment. A **still graphic image**, such as a photograph or drawing, contains no movement. You can download graphic images from the Internet, purchase images on compact disc or create your own graphic images using drawing software. You can digitize photographs using a color scanner, use a digital camera to take a photograph, or buy groups of photographs on compact disc.

Animation refers to graphic images that move. Multimedia presentations use animation to convey information more vividly than text and graphics. An animation showing an engine piston valve opening and closing as it moves up and down provides a better understanding of how an internal combustion engine works than a written explanation with still graphic images.

Audio is digitized sound that has been stored in some form for replay. You can capture sounds from a microphone, CD-ROM drive, radio, or any other audio device that transmits sound to a hardware device connected to a computer. You can play audio using a keyboard, synthesizer, or other musical device connected to the computer. As with animation, audio allows you to provide information not possible through any other method of communication in a computer environment. For example, the sound of a human heart beating is conveyed much better using audio.

Video is composed of photographic images that display at speeds of 15 to 30 frames per second and provide the appearance of motion.

An increasingly popular way to use multimedia technology in business and at home is Microsoft NetMeeting. **Microsoft NetMeeting** is a Windows 98 program that allows you to use the Internet to engage in a live videoconference with one or more computer users. NetMeeting allows you to exchange text messages, collaborate on a shared application with other users, and send files to other users.

In Project 8, you will record and play audio, embed and play a recorded audio file in a document, and change the sound scheme on your computer. You will play an audio compact disc, change the order that you play the songs on the compact disc, adjust the volume, and watch a movie recorded on a digital video disc (DVD). In addition, you will use NetMeeting to videoconference with, send text messages to, share an application with, and send a file to another NetMeeting user.

Recording and Playing Audio

Audio is digitized sound that has been stored in some form for replay. Audio allows you to enhance the computer experience and present information in a way that is not possible through any other method of communication in a computer environment.

On a computer, audio is stored in two types of files: Wave (.wav) and MIDI (.mid) files. A **Wave file**, identified by the .wav file extension, is a recording of sounds that you can reproduce on any multimedia computer system. Thus, a voice or instrument sound recorded in a Wave file sounds like a voice or instrument when played on a multimedia computer system. A **Musical Instrument and Digital Interface (MIDI) file** performs the same function as sheet music. MIDI files describe how you should play the music and the instruments you should use to play each part. A MIDI file might sound different on different computer systems.

Many operations you perform in Windows 98 have associated sounds that Windows 98 plays when you perform the operation. For instance, you hear a sound when you launch Windows 98, open a document, maximize a window, close a document, and quit Windows 98. You can change this collection of sounds, called a **sound scheme**, by selecting an existing, or creating a new, sound scheme.

In the following sections, you will record and play a Wave file using a microphone, embed the Wave file in a word processing document, play the recorded Wave file, and change the sound scheme on your computer.

Recording and Playing Sound Files Using Sound Recorder

If your computer has a sound card and speakers, Sound Recorder allows you to record, play, and edit sound files. A **sound card**, or **video card**, is a circuit board containing processors used to provide both audio input and output. Today, most computers sold by retail stores contain a sound card and at least two speakers. If the sound card has a Line-In connector, you can connect a stereo receiver or other sound source to the sound card and record music from the sound source. If the computer has a microphone, you can make your own voice recordings and use them to annotate a document. For example, if you create a spreadsheet and give the spreadsheet to a friend, you also may want to include a voice recording explaining the formulas used or assumptions made while creating the spreadsheet. The length of a voice recording is limited to 60 seconds.

Recording a Voice Message Using Sound Recorder

Assume that your computer has a sound card, speakers, and a microphone and you wish to leave a message for your partner (Frank) to pick you up at a client's house at 4:00 P.M. Because your partner does not know where the client lives, you decide to record the driving directions in a sound file. After recording the message, you embed the sound file in a word processing document and leave the icon for the document on the desktop for your partner to find. Perform the following steps to record these directions. If your computer does not have a sound card, speakers, and a microphone, read the following steps without performing them.

Sound Recorder

If Sound Recorder is not available on your computer, click the Start button, point to Settings, click Control Panel, double-click Add/Remove Programs, click Windows Setup tab, click Multimedia, click the Details button, click the Sound Recorder check box, click the OK button in the Multimedia dialog box, and then click the OK button in the Add/Remove Properties dialog box.

Recording and Playing Audio • **WIN 8.7**

PROJECT 8

 Steps **To Record a Voice Message**

1 **Click the Start button on the taskbar, point to Programs, point to Accessories, point to Entertainment, and then point to Sound Recorder.**

The Start menu, Programs submenu, Accessories submenu, and Entertainment submenu display (Figure 8-1). The highlighted Sound Recorder command displays on the Entertainment submenu.

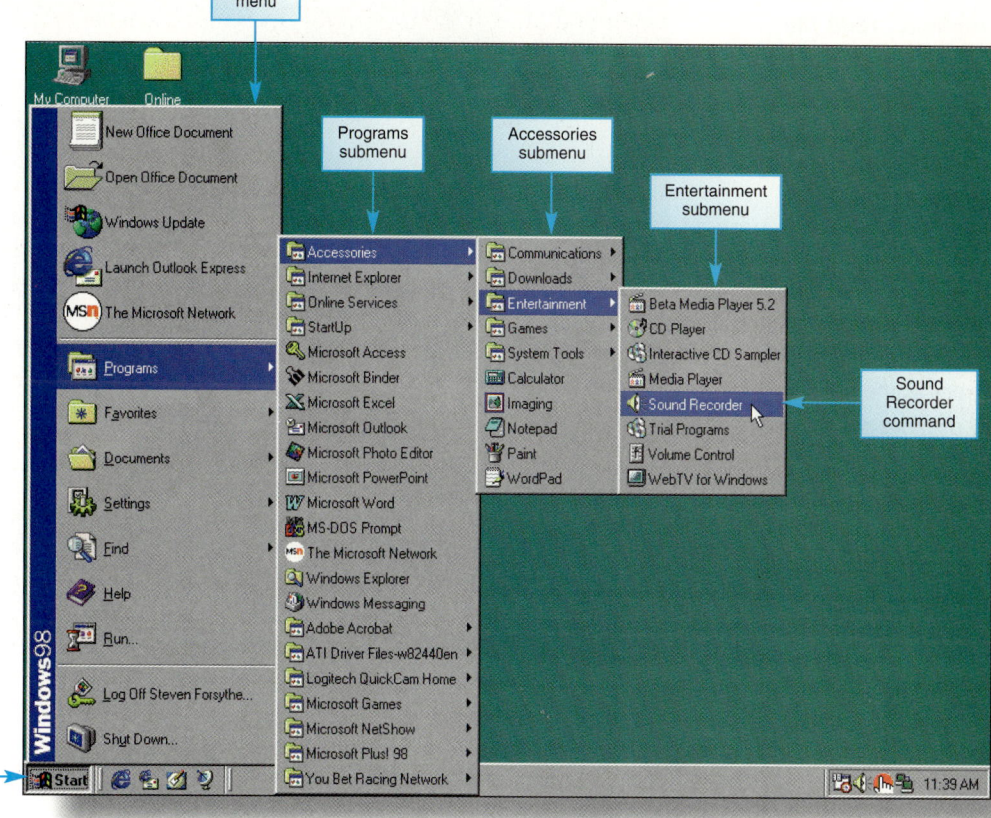

FIGURE 8-1

2 **Click Sound Recorder and then point to the Record button.**

The Sound - Sound Recorder window displays (Figure 8-2). The window contains the Position pane, Sound box, Length pane, slide and slider, and a row of buttons (Seek To Start, Seek To End, Play, Stop, and Record).

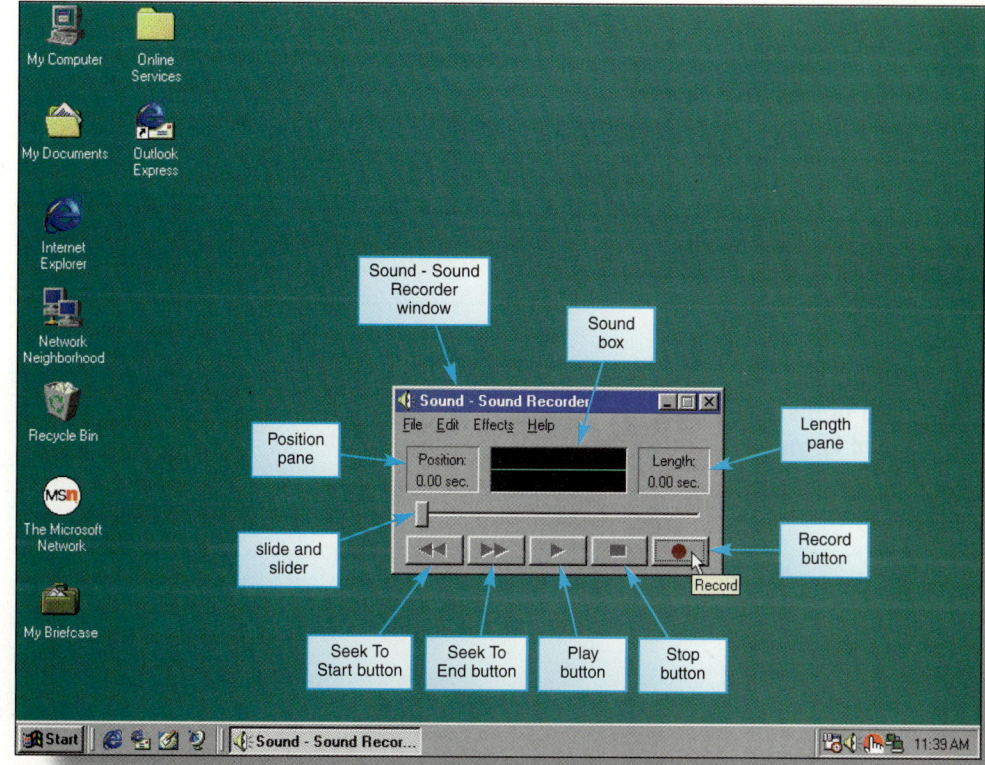

FIGURE 8-2

WIN 8.8 • Project 8 • Working with Multimedia and NetMeeting

Microsoft **Windows 98**

 **Click the Record button. Using the microphone, read the following message:** <u>Go south on Alabama Avenue, turn right on Main Street, turn left on Birch Road, and stop at 201 Birch Road.</u>

As you talk, Sound Recorder records your voice, displays a sound wave in the Sound box, moves the slider to the right, displays the elapsed time of the recording in the Position pane, and displays the maximum length of a recording (60:00 sec.) in the Length pane (Figure 8-3).

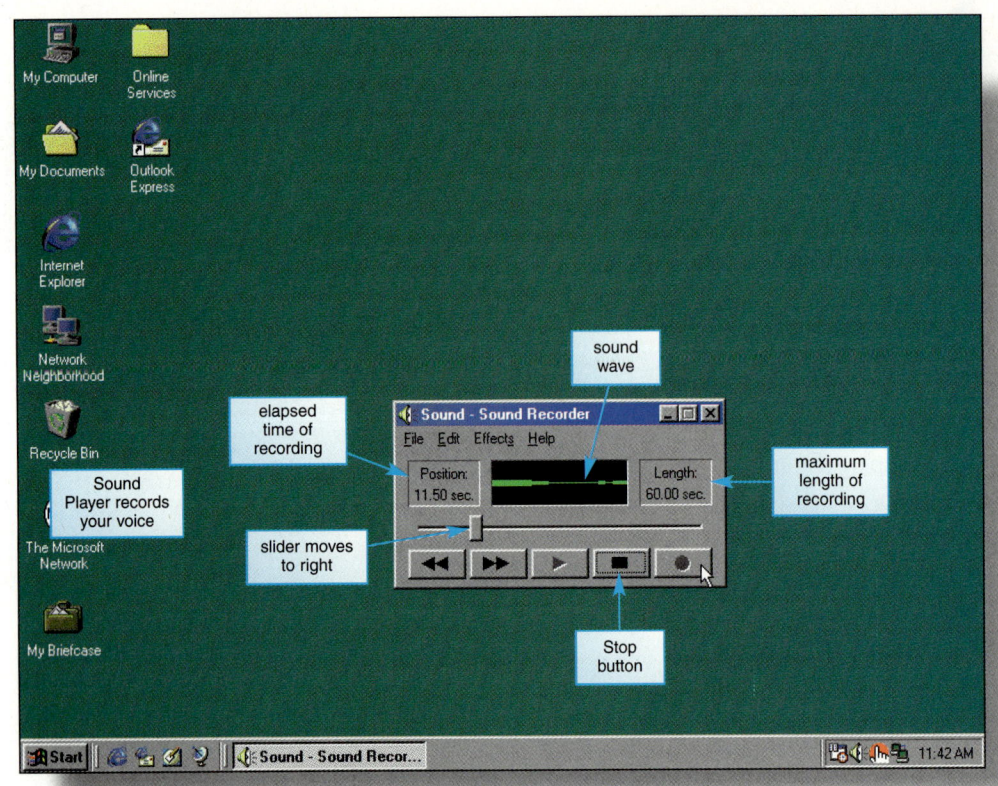

FIGURE 8-3

4 When you have finished reading the message, click the Stop button.

The slider displays at the right end of the slide and the length of the recording displays in the Position pane and Length pane.

Playing a Recorded Voice Message

After recording a voice message using Sound Recorder, you can play the message or save the message as a Wave file on a disk. Perform the following steps to play the voice message.

 To Play a Voice Message

1 Point to the Play button in the Sound - Sound Recorder window (Figure 8-4).

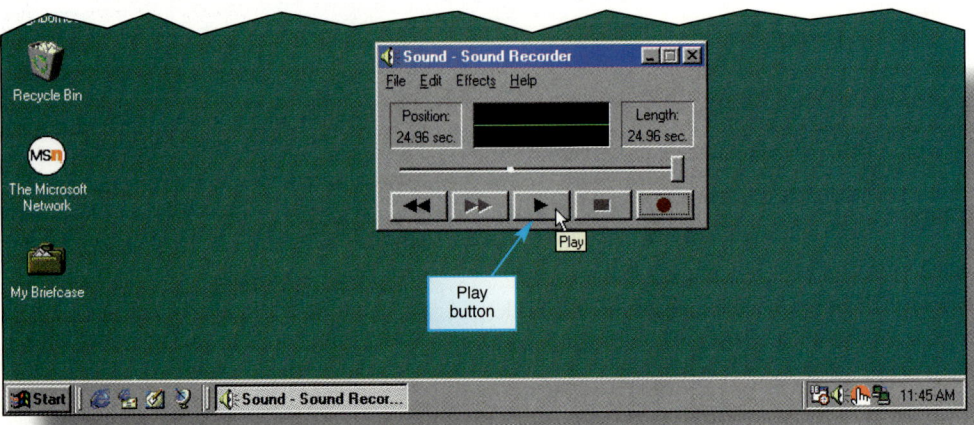

FIGURE 8-4

Click the Play button.

Sound Recorder plays the voice message, displays a sound wave in the Sound box, and moves the slide to the right along the slider (Figure 8-5). The elapsed time displays in the Position pane and the total length of the recording displays in the Length pane.

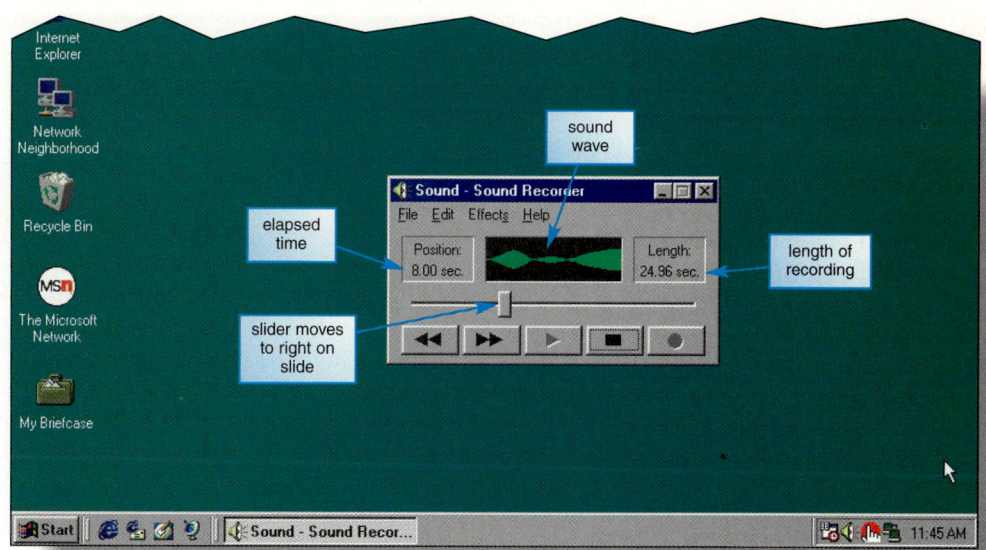

FIGURE 8-5

Embedding a Sound File in a Document

When you **embed an object**, you insert information from one document (**source**) into another document (**object**). To embed an object, you make a copy of the source file using the Copy command and embed the copy into the destination file using the Paste command. To embed the voice message you recorded previously (source), you will create a Microsoft Word document (object) on the desktop and insert the voice message into the Word document. Perform the following steps to embed the sound file in a Word document. If the Word application is not available on your computer, read the following steps without performing them.

 **To Embed a Sound File in a Document**

 Click Edit on the menu bar and then point to Copy.

The Edit menu, containing the highlighted Copy command, displays (Figure 8-6).

More About
Embedding a Sound File

When you embed a sound file (source) in a document (object), a copy of the sound file is made and attached to the document. When you save the document, you save the copy of the sound file with the document. If you change the sound file (source), the copy of the sound file in the document does not change.

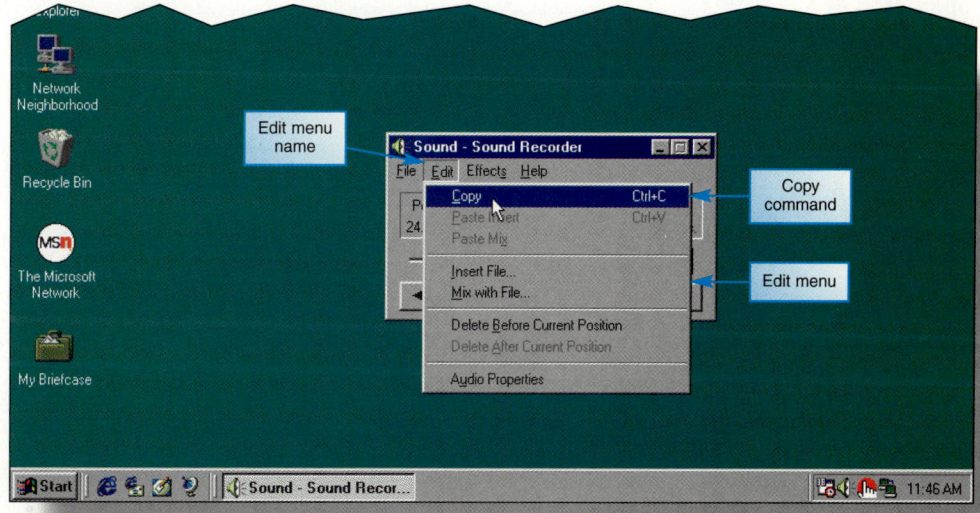

FIGURE 8-6

WIN 8.10 • Project 8 • Working with Multimedia and NetMeeting

2 **Click Copy. Right-click the desktop, point to New, and click Microsoft Word Document. Type** Frank - Read Immediately! **in the icon title text box, press the ENTER key, and then point to the Frank - Read Immediately! icon on the desktop.**

Windows 98 copies the voice message to the Clipboard and the Frank - Read Immediately! document icon displays on the desktop (Figure 8-7).

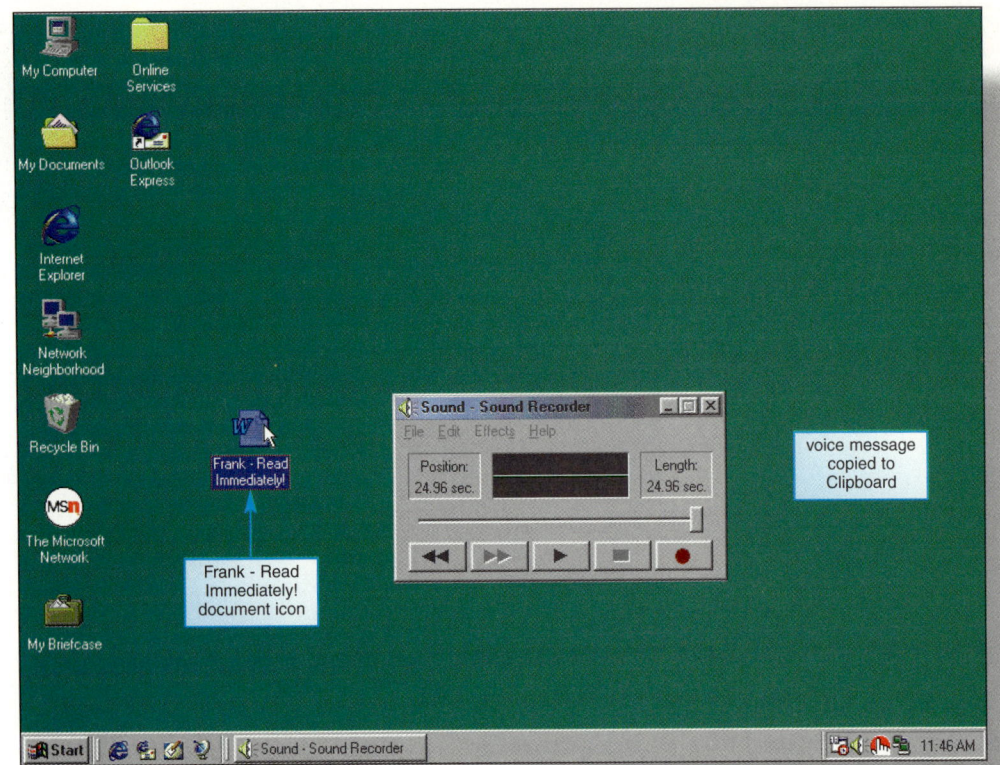

FIGURE 8-7

3 **Double-click the document icon. Type the message (Figure 8-8) in the text area and then press the ENTER key twice. Right-click an open area of the window and then point to Paste.**

Windows 98 launches Word and displays the Microsoft Word - Frank - Read Immediately! window (Figure 8-8). The message is typed, the insertion point displays below the message, a shortcut menu displays, and the highlighted Paste command displays.

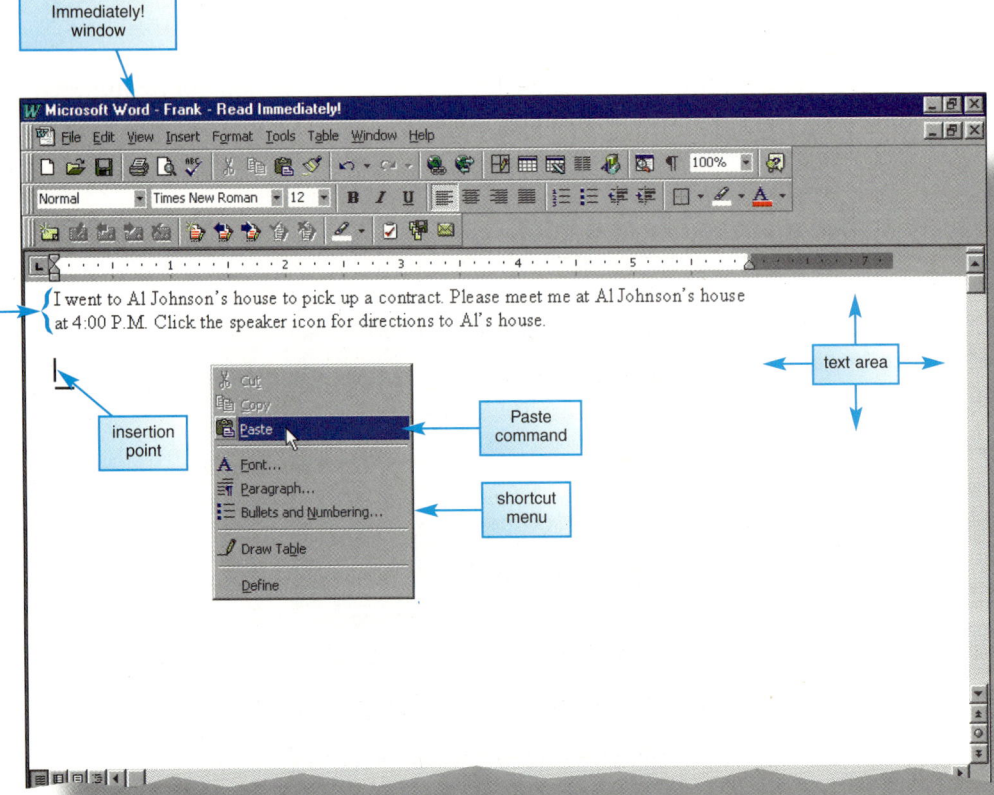

FIGURE 8-8

Click Paste.

The appearance of the Microsoft Word - Frank - Read Immediately! window changes slightly and a speaker icon displays below the message in the document (Figure 8-9).

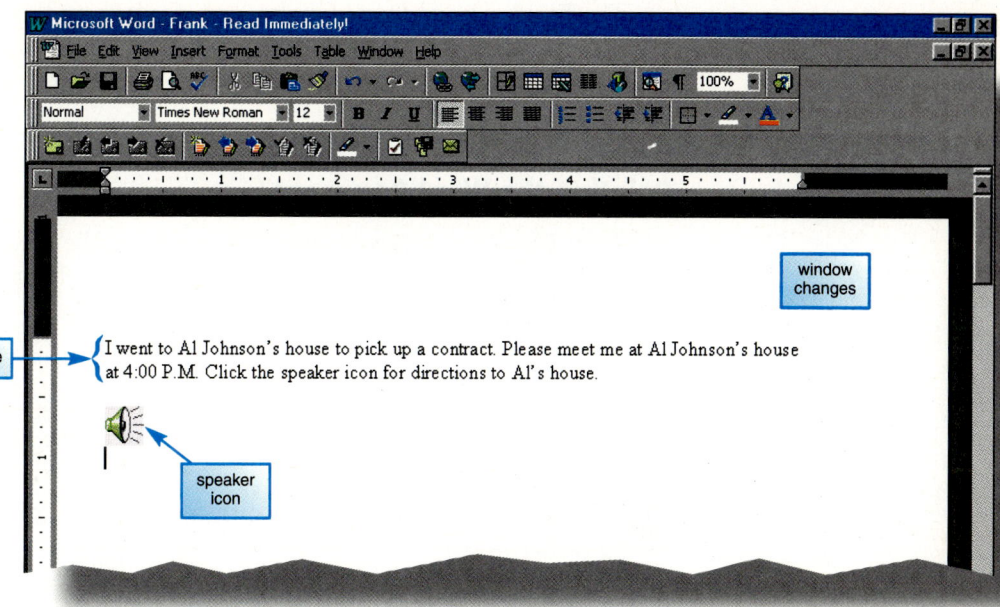

FIGURE 8-9

Playing a Recorded Voice Message

Previously, you recorded a voice message, played the message, and then embedded the message in a Word document. Perform the following steps to listen to the recorded message in the Microsoft Word - Frank - Read Immediately! document.

TO PLAY A RECORDED VOICE MESSAGE

1. Point to the speaker icon in the Microsoft Word - Frank - Read Immediately! document to display a four-headed arrow.
2. Double-click the speaker icon to play the recorded message.

Sound Recorder plays the recorded voice message.

Closing the Word and Sound Recorder Windows

After listening to the recorded voice message in the Microsoft Word - Frank - Read Immediately! document, perform the following steps to close the Word and Sound Recorder windows.

TO CLOSE THE WORD AND SOUND RECORDER WINDOWS

1. Click the Close button in the Microsoft Word - Frank - Read Immediately! window.
2. Click the Yes button in the Microsoft Word dialog box.
3. Click the Close button in the Sound - Sound Recorder window.
4. Click the No button in the Sound Recorder dialog box.

Windows 98 closes the Microsoft Word - Frank - Read Immediately! window and Sound - Sound Recorder window.

Other Ways

1. Press CTRL+C in Sound Recorder, start application, press CTRL+V
2. On Edit menu in Sound Recorder, click Copy, start application, on Edit menu click Paste

The Frank - Read Immediately! icon displays on the desktop. When Frank checks the desktop, he will find the icon on the desktop, double-click the icon, read the message, double-click the speaker icon, listen to the sound file, and know when and where to pick you up.

Deleting the Word Document

After Frank reads the message and listens to the recorded voice message, he should remove the Frank - Read Immediately! icon from the desktop by performing the following steps.

TO DELETE AN ICON FROM THE DESKTOP

1. Drag the Frank - Read Immediately! icon to the Recycle Bin icon on the desktop.
2. Click the Yes button in the Confirm File Delete dialog box.

Windows 98 removes the Frank - Read Immediately! icon from the desktop.

> **More About**
>
> **Sound Schemes**
>
> Not all sound schemes are installed with Windows 98. To install sound schemes on your computer, click the Start button, point to Settings, click Control Panel, double-click Add/Remove Programs, click Windows Setup tab, click Multimedia, click the Details button, click the Multimedia Sound Schemes check box, click the OK button in the Multimedia dialog box, and then click the OK button in the Add/Remove Properties dialog box.

Changing the Sound Scheme

As mentioned earlier, many operations you perform in Windows 98 have associated sounds that Windows 98 plays when you perform the operation. Each operation, referred to as a **program event**, is an action performed by the computer user or a software program. Windows 98 groups program events into categories such as Windows, Windows Explorer, Sound Recorder, Media Player, The Microsoft Network, and Power Management.

Windows 98 allows you to assign a sound to each program event in a category. Each sound is stored in a Wave file on the hard disk. A **sound scheme** is the collection of sounds assigned to all program events in all categories. You can change the sound scheme either by selecting an existing, or creating your own, sound scheme. Perform the following steps to change the sound scheme by selecting an existing sound scheme.

Recording and Playing Audio • WIN 8.13

PROJECT 8

 To Change the Sound Scheme

① **Click the Start button on the taskbar, point to Settings, click Control Panel, and then point to the Sounds icon.**

The Control Panel window with the Sounds icon displays (Figure 8-10).

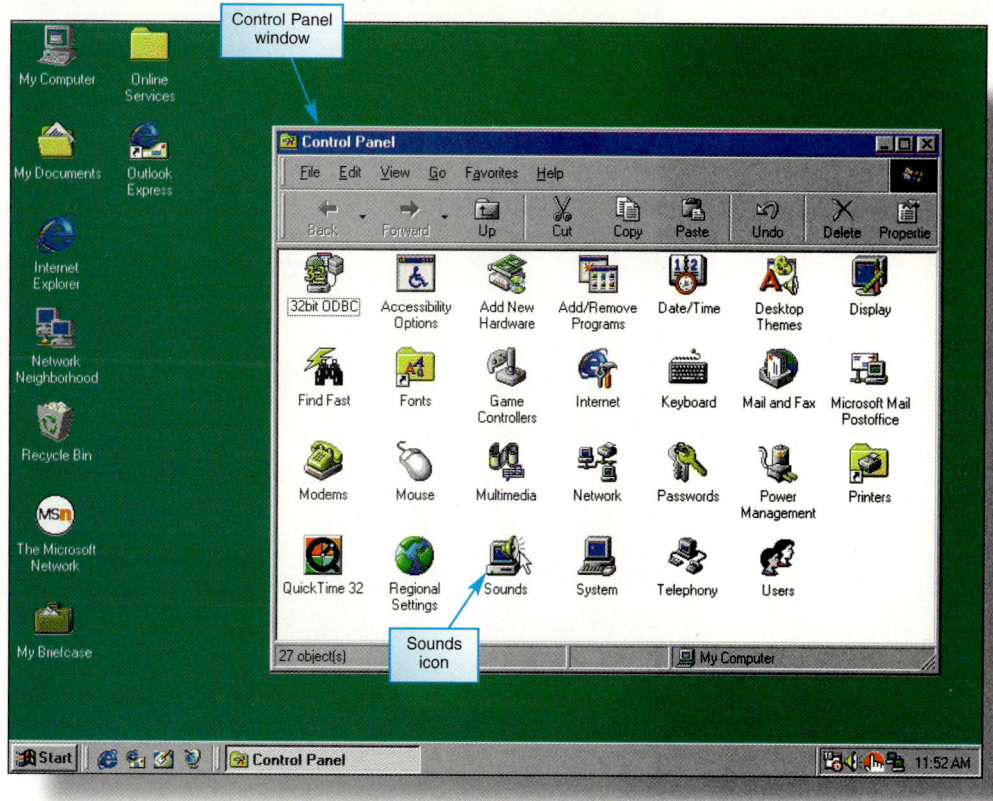

FIGURE 8-10

② **Double-click the Sounds icon and then point to the Schemes box arrow.**

The Sounds Properties dialog box displays (Figure 8-11). The Windows category name and a partial list of the program events in the category display in the Events list box. Other categories that are not visible in the list display below the Windows category. The Schemes box contains the default sound scheme name (Windows Default). A different sound scheme may display on your computer.

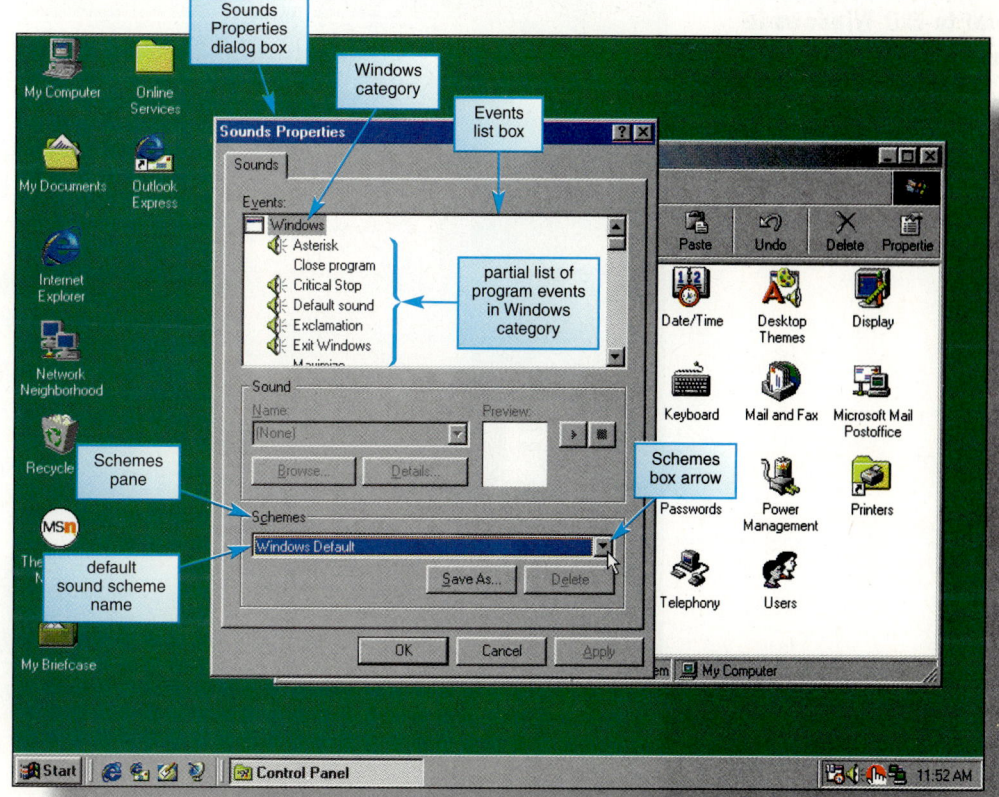

FIGURE 8-11

WIN 8.14 • Project 8 • Working with Multimedia and NetMeeting

③ Click the Schemes box arrow and then point to Musica Sound Scheme.

The highlighted Musica Sound Scheme name displays in the Schemes list box (Figure 8-12).

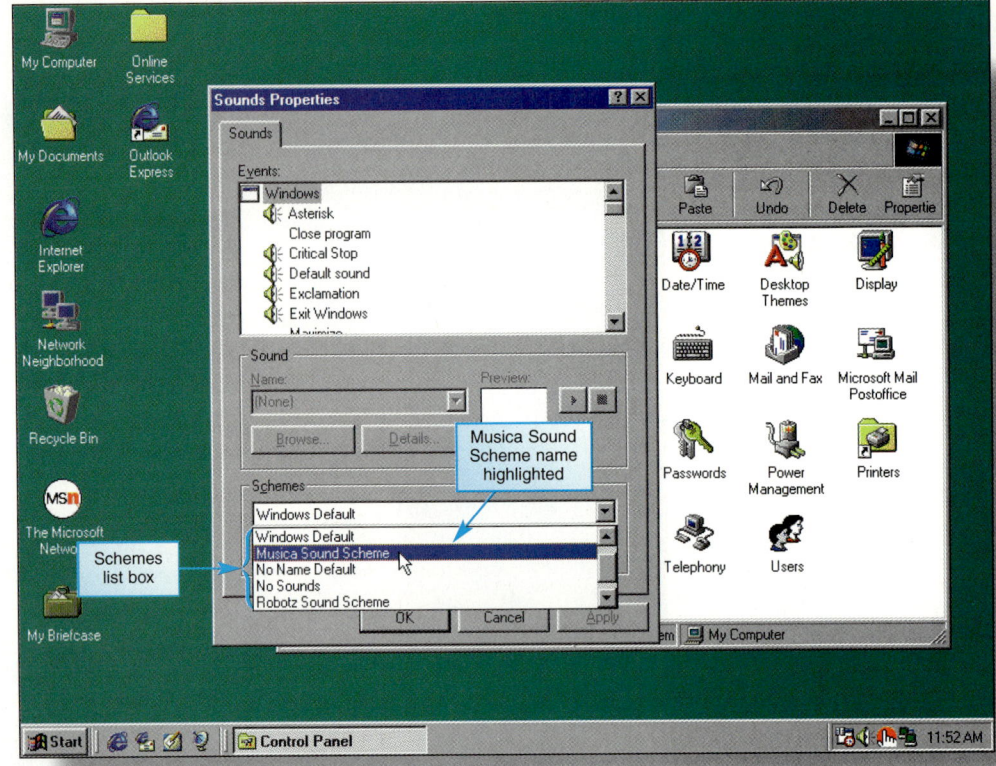

FIGURE 8-12

④ Click Musica Sound Scheme and then point to Exit Windows in the Events list box.

The highlighted Musica Sound Scheme name displays in the Schemes box (Figure 8-13).

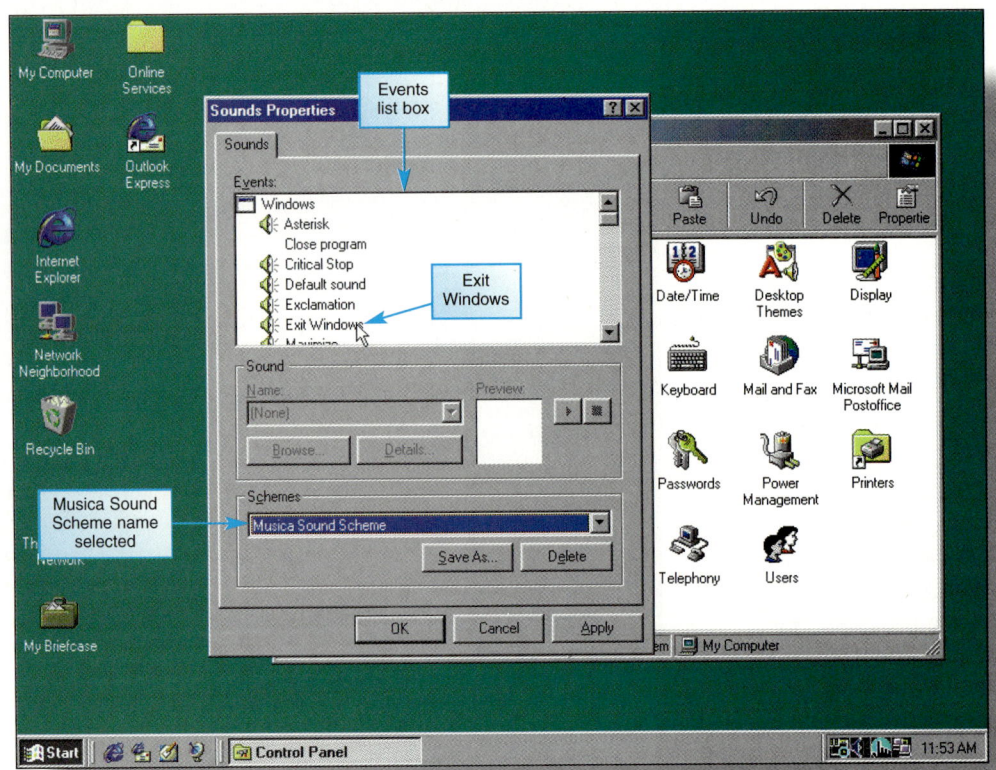

FIGURE 8-13

5 **Click Exit Windows and then point to the Play button in the Sound pane.**

Windows 98 highlights the Exit Windows event, displays the Musica Windows Exit name in the Name box, displays a drum in the Preview pane, and activates the Browse, Details, and Play buttons (Figure 8-14).

6 **Click the Play button. After listening to the program event, click the Cancel button in the Sounds Properties dialog box to cancel the changes made and then click the Close button in the Control Panel window.**

When you click the Play button, the Musica Exit Windows sound plays. The Sounds Properties dialog box and Control Panel window close.

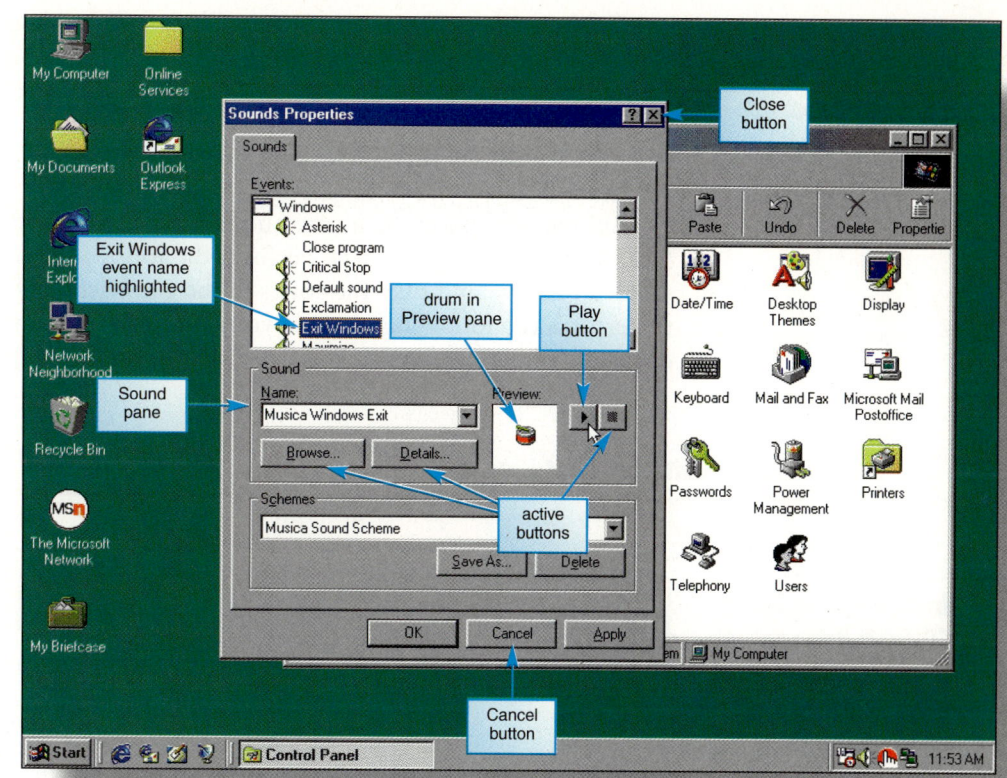

FIGURE 8-14

Playing an Audio Compact Disc

Most new computers contain a CD-ROM drive. A **CD-ROM** (**compact disc read-only memory**) **drive**, also referred to as a **CD drive** or **CD Player**, is a hardware device that reads compact discs. A **compact disc** (**CD**) is the preferred media to deliver and install software (application software, operating system software, game software, and so on) and record and play music.

Whether a CD contains software or songs, one side of the CD contains printed information about the CD and the other side contains the software or songs. An audio CD contains printed information such as the recording company name, artist name, CD title, song titles, and copyright information on one side and the recorded songs on the other side. The number of songs on a CD varies according to the wishes of the recording company and artist. Typically, a single CD contains from eight to twenty songs. Each song occupies a single circular recording area on the CD called a **track**.

One method of listening to the songs on an audio CD is to plug a pair of headphones into the CD-ROM drive. Another method is to use a sound card. As mentioned earlier, a sound card is a circuit board containing processors used to provide both audio input and output. Today, most computers sold by retail stores contain a sound card, at least two speakers, and a CD-ROM drive that plays a single or multiple CDs.

Other Ways

1. Click Start button, point to Settings, click Control Panel, double-click Sounds icon, press TAB, press DOWN ARROW to select music scheme, press TAB three times, press ENTER

More About

CD Player

If CD Player is not available on your computer, click the Start button, point to Settings, click Control Panel, double-click Add/Remove Programs icon, click Windows Setup tab, click Multimedia, click the Details button, click the CD Player check box, click the OK button in the Multimedia dialog box, and then click the OK button in the Add/Remove Properties dialog box.

CD Player is a software program included with Windows 98 that allows you to play a CD and control the operation of the CD-ROM drive. CD Player allows you to pause and resume play of a CD, play the previous or next track (song), play tracks in random order, skip forward or backward while playing a track, and eject the CD from the CD-ROM drive. The next section illustrates how to use CD Player to play an audio CD.

Assume you purchase a new audio CD by your favorite artist and would like to listen to the songs on the CD. Perform the following steps to insert the CD into the CD-ROM drive and play the songs in the recorded order. You will need an audio CD to perform the following steps. If you do not have an audio CD or your computer does not have a CD-ROM drive, read the following step without performing it.

Steps: To Play an Audio Compact Disc

1 **Press the Eject button on the front of the CD-ROM drive to open the CD tray, insert the CD into the tray, and press the Eject button to close the CD tray.**

The CD tray opens, you insert the CD into the tray, and the CD tray closes. The CD Player program launches, the CD Player button displays in the taskbar button area, and the first song on the CD plays (Figure 8-15).

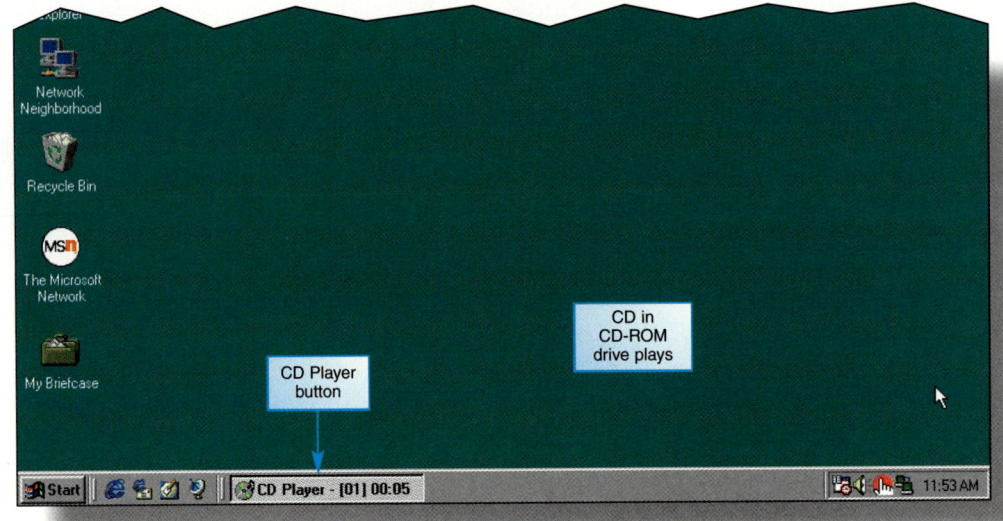

FIGURE 8-15

1. With CD in CD-ROM drive, click CD Player button on taskbar, click Play

AutoPlay is a Windows 98 feature that allows you to play a compact disc when you insert the disc into a compact disc player. When you insert the compact disc, Windows 98 searches for the autorun.inf file on the disc. If Windows 98 finds the file on the compact disc, Windows 98 causes CD Player to play the songs on the disc. If Windows does not find the file, Windows 98 assumes the compact disc contains software and begins the process of installing the software.

More About

Preview Pane in CD Player

In Figure 8-16, the elapsed time displays in the preview pane. You can choose to replace the elapsed track time display with either the track time remaining or disc time remaining. Click View on the menu bar and then click either the Track Time Remaining or Disc Time Remaining command.

Creating a Play List Using CD Player

When you insert a CD into the CD-ROM drive, CD Player launches and starts playing the first song (track) on the CD. CD Player allows you to pause and resume play of a CD, play the previous or next track, play tracks in random order, skip forward or backward within a track, and design a Play List. A **Play List** consists of the CD title, artist name, and song title of each song on the CD. The Play List allows you to choose the songs and the order in which to play. If your computer has a multiple-play CD-ROM drive, CD Player allows you to switch to another CD, randomly play tracks from all CDs, and design a Play List for all song titles on all CDs.

Assume that you wish to design a Play List for your new audio CD. You plan to enter the CD title, artist name, and song titles for all songs on the CD in the Play List. To illustrate how to create a Play List, enter the artist name, CD title, and song titles in the following steps instead of those on the CD you inserted in the CD-ROM drive. Perform the following steps to create a Play List for the CD in the CD-ROM drive.

 To Create a Play List

1 Click the CD Player button on the taskbar and then point to Disc on the menu bar of the CD Player window.

The CD Player window displays (Figure 8-16). The track number (01) and elapsed time (00:26) display in the preview pane. The default artist name (New Artist) and CD-ROM drive letter (F:), default CD title (New Title), and default track name (Track 1) and number (<01>) display in the Artist box, Title text box, and Track box, respectively.

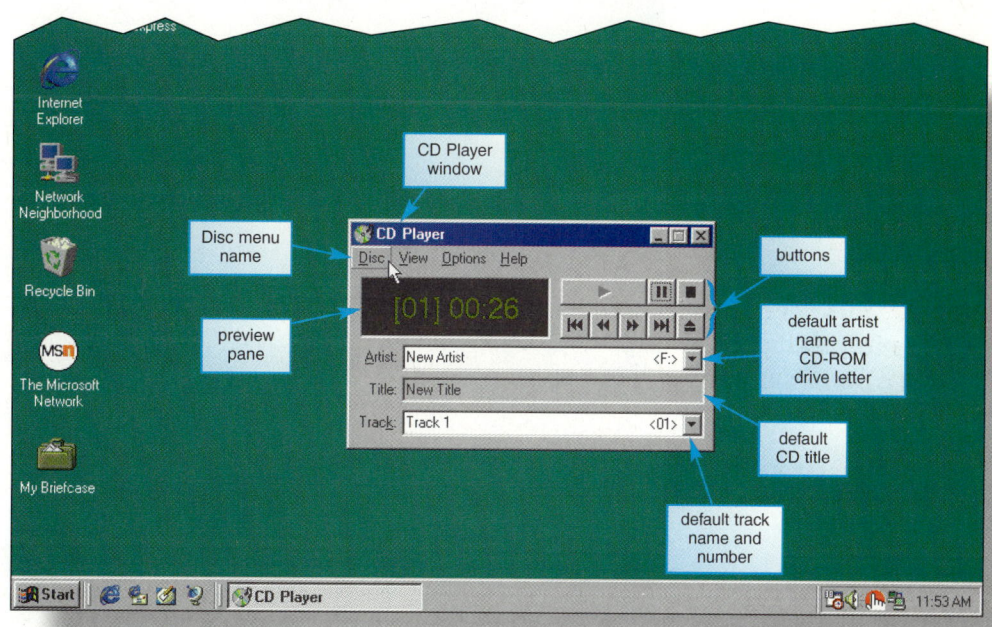

FIGURE 8-16

2 Click Disc and then point to Edit Play List.

The Disc menu, containing the highlighted Edit Play List command, displays (Figure 8-17).

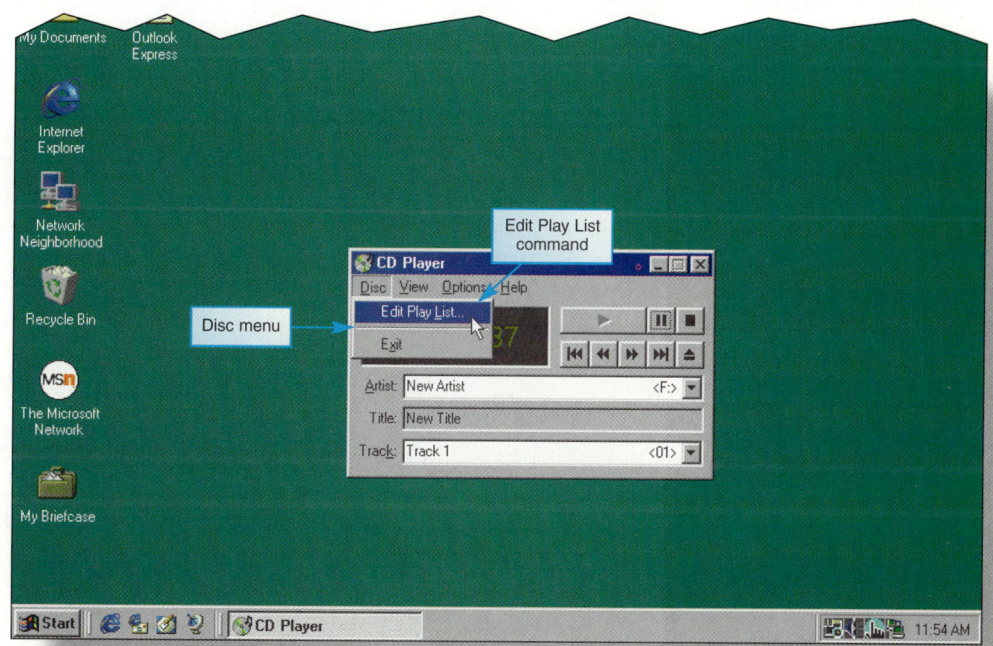

FIGURE 8-17

WIN 8.18 • **Project 8** • Working with Multimedia and NetMeeting

3 **Click Edit Play List.**

The CD Player: Disc Settings dialog box displays (Figure 8-18). The highlighted default artist name (New Artist) displays in the Artist text box and default CD title (New Title) displays in the Title text box. The Play List and Available Tracks list boxes contain a default track name for each track on the CD and the default track name for the first track (Track 1) displays in the Track 01 list box.

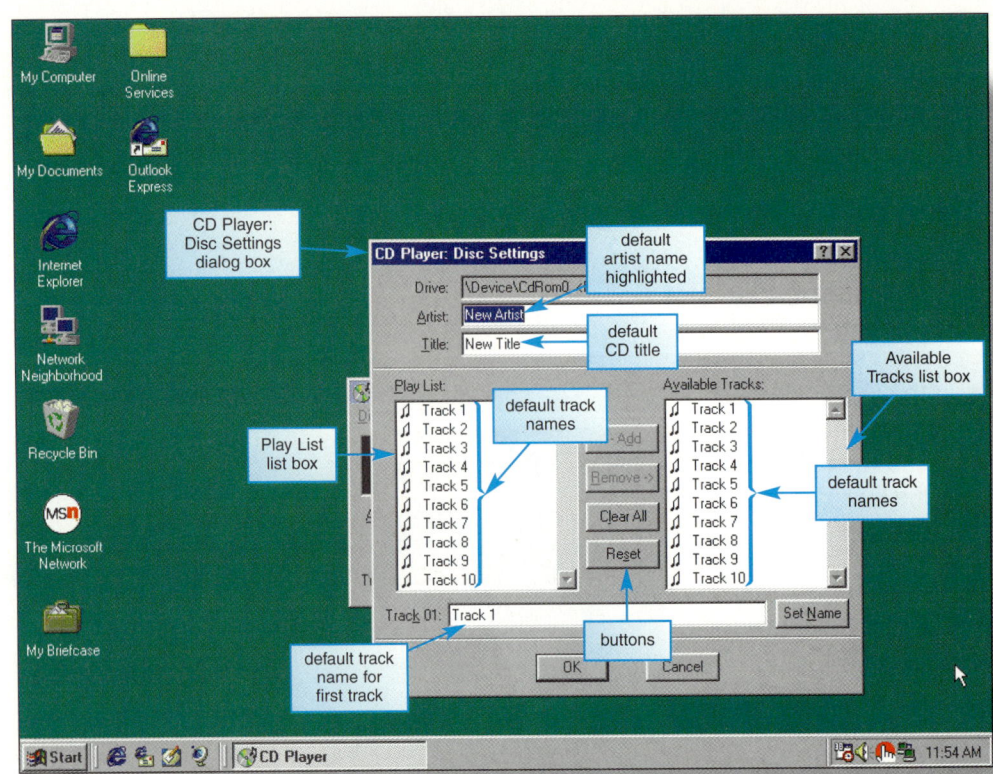

FIGURE 8-18

4 **Type** Johnny Sleep **in the Artist text box and then press the TAB key. Type** A Sleep on the Road **in the Title text box. Click Track 1 in the Available Tracks list box. Type** Here We Go Again **in the Track 01 text box and then point to the Set Name button.**

The artist name displays in the Artist text box, the CD title displays in the Title text box, and the first song title displays in the Track 01 text box (Figure 8-19).

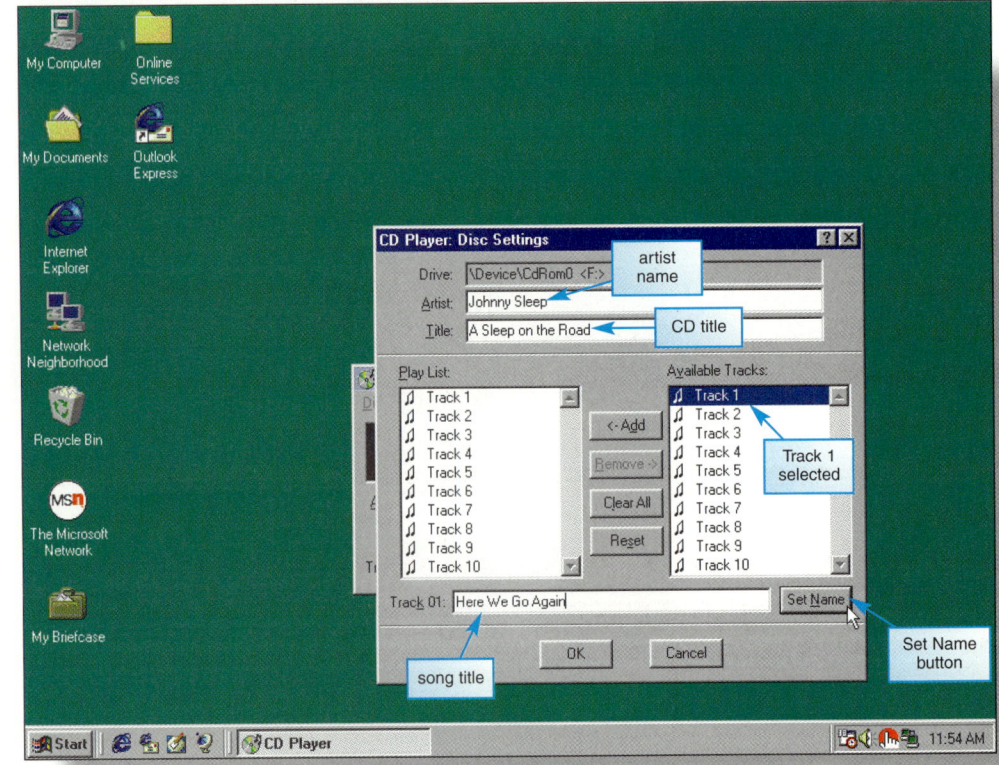

FIGURE 8-19

Click the Set Name button.

The Here We Go Again song title displays in the Play List and Available Tracks list boxes (Figure 8-20). The default track name for the second track (Track 2) is highlighted in the Available Tracks list box and displays in the Track 02 text box.

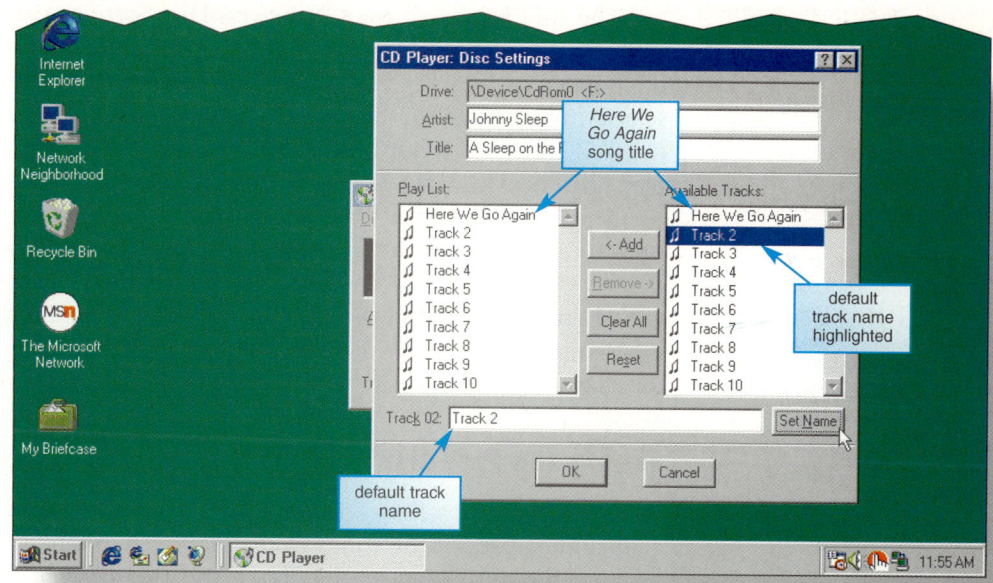

FIGURE 8-20

Complete the entry of the remaining nine song titles (Figure 8-21) by typing the appropriate song title in the Track text box and then clicking the Set Name button.

The Play List and Available Tracks list boxes contain song titles for each track on the CD. (Figure 8-21). The Play List list box contains the Play List indicating the order in which the songs will be played by CD Player.

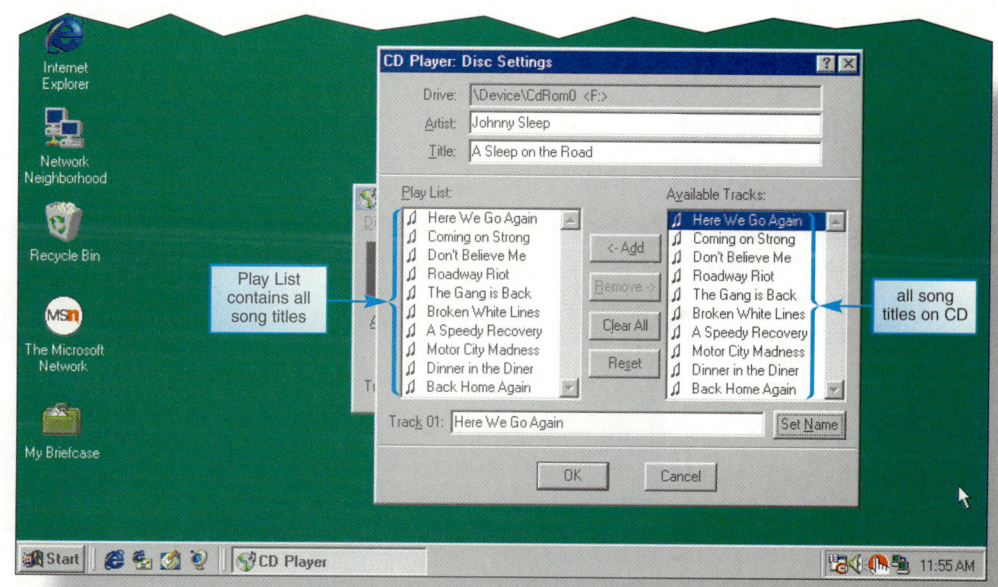

FIGURE 8-21

If, after creating a Play List, you remove the CD from the CD-ROM drive, CD player automatically will recognize the CD the next time you insert the CD into the CD-ROM drive. The Play List associated with the CD will be available for use in CD Player. In addition, you will be able to play a song by clicking the Track box arrow in the CD Player window and selecting a song title in the Track list box (see Figure 8-16 on page WIN 8.17).

The CD Player window shown in Figure 8-16 contains two rows of buttons that allow you to play, pause, stop, play the previous or next track, skip forward or backward within a track, and eject the CD.

1. Press ALT+D, L

WIN 8.20 • Project 8 • Working with Multimedia and NetMeeting

More About

Editing the Play List

You can display a toolbar that contains shortcut buttons that allow you to edit the Play List, change the display in the preview pane, and control how the CD plays (random, continuous, or introductory). Introductory play will cause the first 10 seconds of each song on the CD to play. To display the toolbar, click View on the menu bar and then click Toolbar.

The Add button in the CD Player: Disc Settings dialog box shown in Figure 8-18 on page WIN 8.18 adds a highlighted track name in the Available Tracks list box to the bottom of the Play List in the Play List list box. The Remove button removes the selected track from the Play List. The Clear All button removes all song titles from the Play List. The Reset button restores the Play List to its default setting, which is to play all tracks in order from first to last.

The Available Tracks list box shown in Figure 8-21 on the previous page lists the titles of the songs on the CD. The song titles in the Play List box indicate the order that CD Player will play those songs. Currently, CD Player will play all the songs on the CD in the order they appear on the CD. You can change the order that CD Player plays songs by removing, adding, or changing the position of a song title in the Play List list box. The next section demonstrates how to accomplish this.

Editing the Play List

After creating a Play List for a CD, you can remove a song, add a song, or change the order of the songs in the Play List. Assume that you would prefer not to listen to the sixth song on the Play List, titled *Broken White Lines*, because you have heard that song too many times on the radio. In addition, you would like to listen to the *A Speedy Recovery* song after listening to the *Here We Go Again* song. Perform the following steps to remove the *Broken White Lines* song title and change the position of the *A Speedy Recovery* song title in the Play List.

 To Edit the Play List

1 **Click Broken White Lines in the Play List list box and then point to the Remove button.**

The Broken White Lines song title in the Play List list box is selected (Figure 8-22).

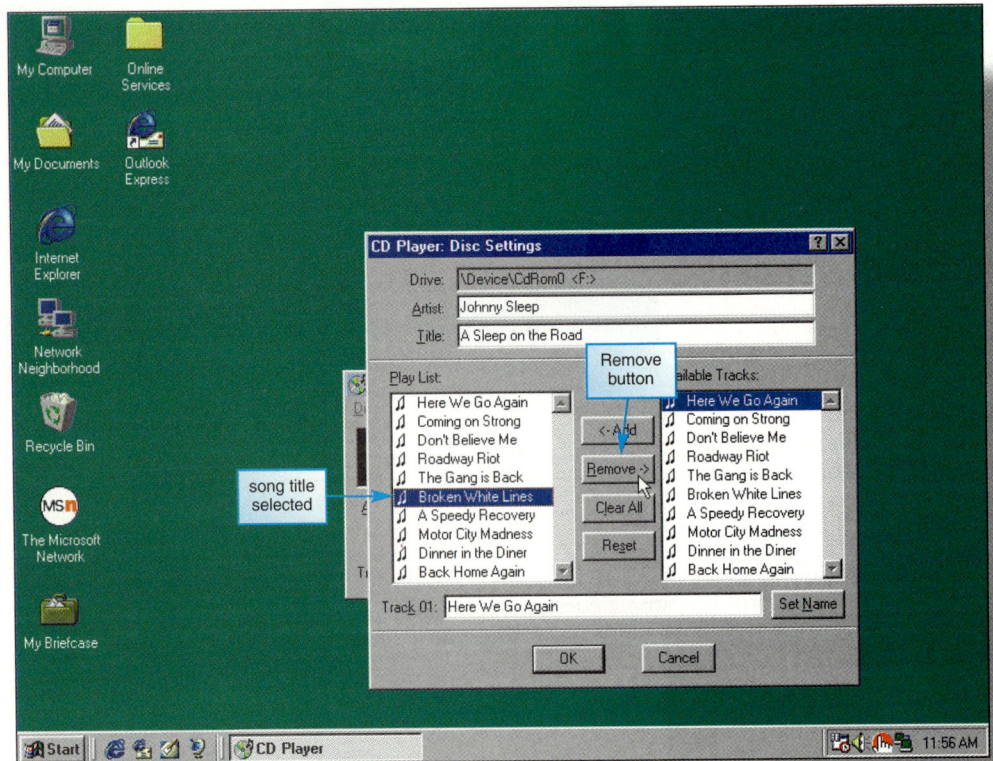

FIGURE 8-22

② **Click the Remove button and then click A Speedy Recovery in the Play List list box.**

CD Player removes the Broken White Lines song title from the Play List list box and selects the A Speedy Recovery song title (Figure 8-23). The song titles in the Available Tracks list box are unchanged.

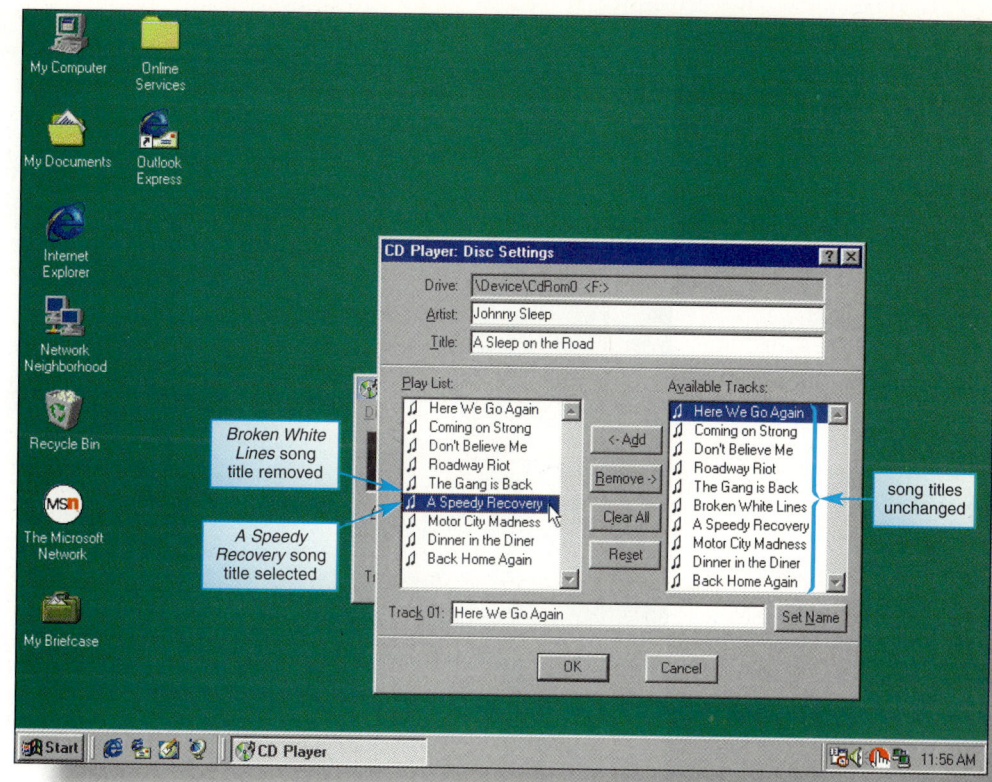

FIGURE 8-23

③ **Point to the musical notes icon to the left of the *A Speedy Recovery* song title in the Play List list box and then hold down the left mouse button.**

A right arrow displays to the left and above the A Speedy Recovery song title in the Play List list box and the mouse pointer changes to contain musical notes (Figure 8-24).

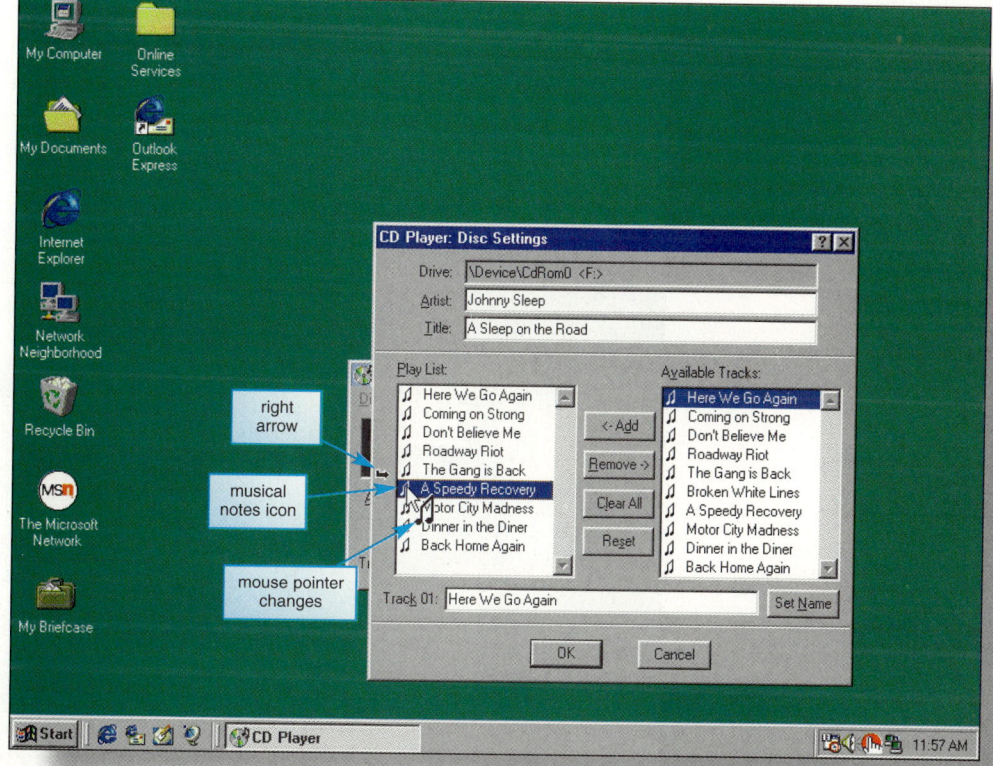

FIGURE 8-24

WIN 8.22 • Project 8 • Working with Multimedia and NetMeeting

4 **Drag the right arrow up until the right arrow displays below the *Here We Go Again* song title.**

The right arrow displays below the Here We Go Again song title (Figure 8-25).

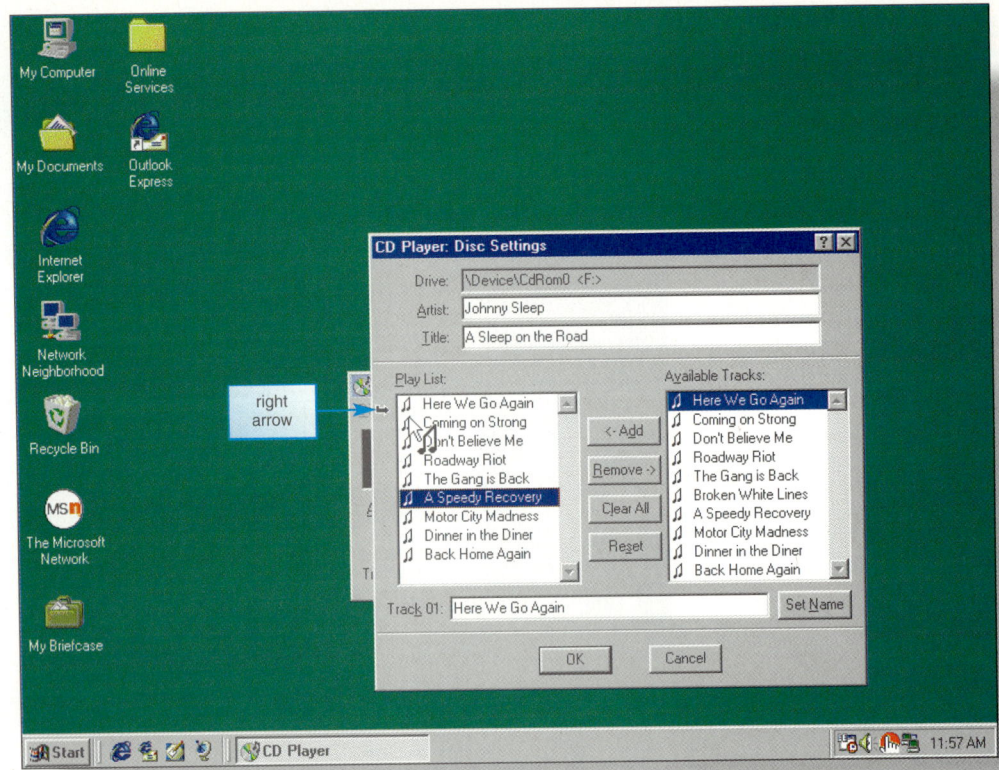

FIGURE 8-25

5 **Release the left mouse button and then point to the OK button.**

The A Speedy Recovery song title displays below the Here We Go Again song title in the Play List list box (Figure 8-26).

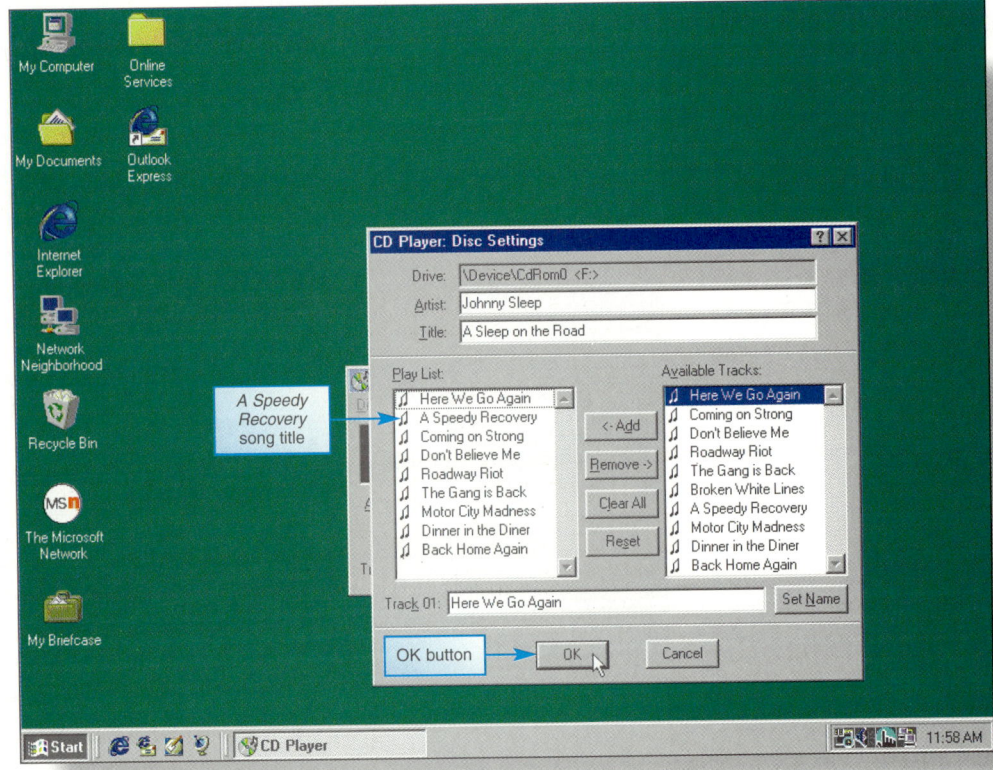

FIGURE 8-26

Recording and Playing Audio • WIN 8.23

6 **Click the OK button.**

The CD Player: Disc Settings dialog box closes (Figure 8-27). The artist name (Johnny Sleep) displays in the Artist box, the CD title (A Sleep on the Road) displays in the Title text box, and the title of the song currently playing displays in the Track box.

FIGURE 8-27

After closing the CD Player: Disc Settings dialog box, use the buttons in the CD Player window to play the CD, pause and resume play, play the previous or next track, and skip forward or backward within a track.

Adjusting the Volume of a Sound Device

Volume Control allows you to adjust the volume of a sound device and the balance between the left and right speakers. The sound devices (Wave, Synthesizer, MIDI, CD Audio, Line-In, Microphone, Auxiliary, Modem, PC Speaker, and so on) available on a computer depend on the type of sound card installed on the computer and whether an internal modem is installed. Computers without sound cards do not have Volume Control. Perform the following steps to adjust the volume for the CD-ROM drive.

To Adjust the Volume of a Sound Device

1 **Click View on the menu bar and then point to Volume Control.**

CD Player displays (Figure 8-28). The View menu contains the Volume Control command.

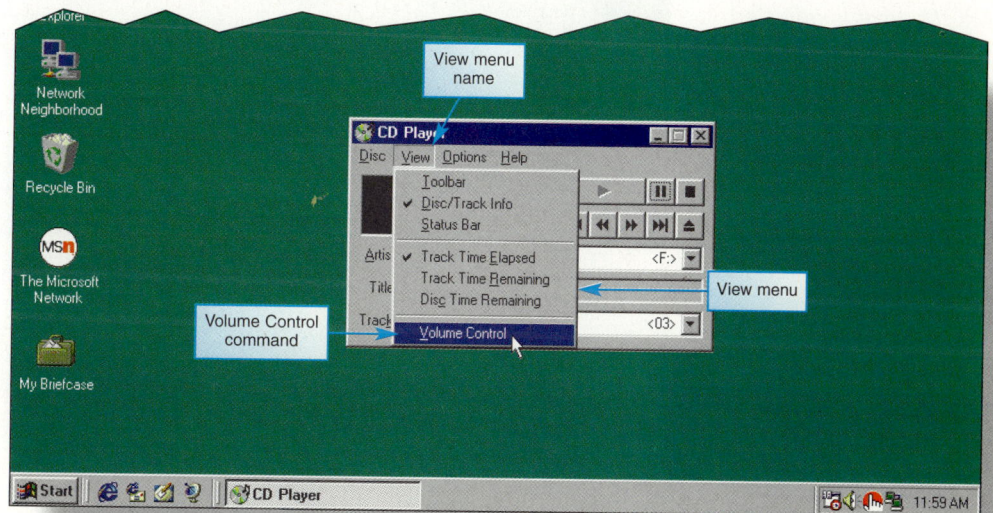

FIGURE 8-28

Other Ways

1. Press ALT+D, L

More About

Volume Control

If Volume Control is not available on your computer, click the Start button, point to Settings, click Control Panel, double-click Add/Remove Programs icon, click Windows Setup tab, click Multimedia, click the Details button, click Volume Control, click the OK button, and then click the OK button.

WIN 8.24 • Project 8 • Working with Multimedia and NetMeeting

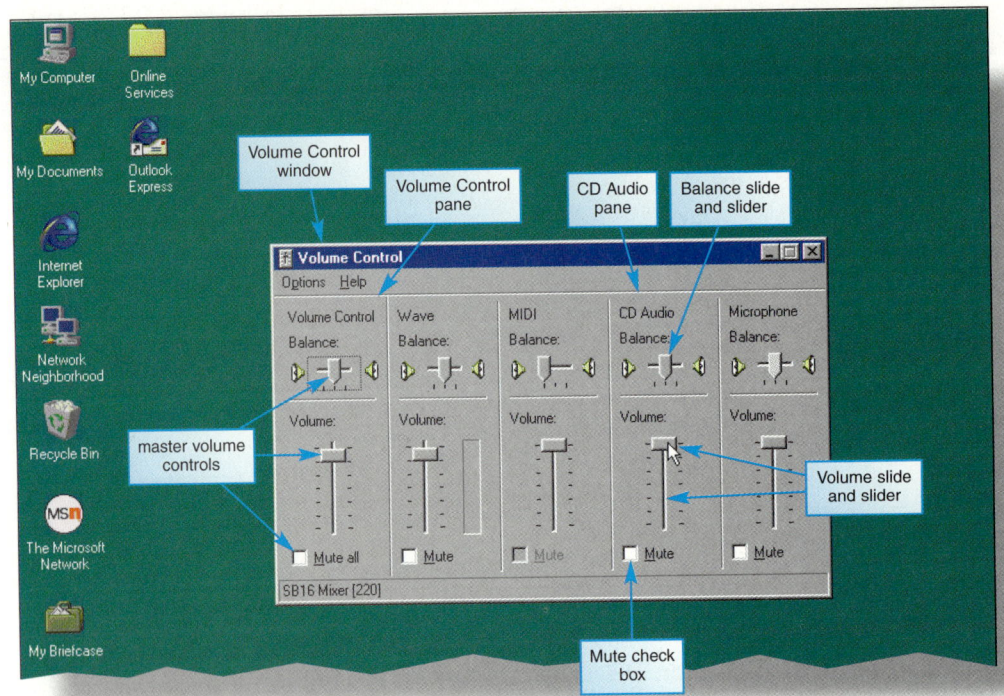

2 **Click Volume Control and then point to the Volume slider in the CD Audio area.**

The Volume Control window contains five areas (Figure 8-29). Each area contains a Balance slide and slider, Volume slide and slider, and Mute check box. The Balance and Volume sliders and Mute check box in the CD Audio area control the volume and balance for the CD-ROM device. The Volume Control area is the master control for all audio devices.

FIGURE 8-29

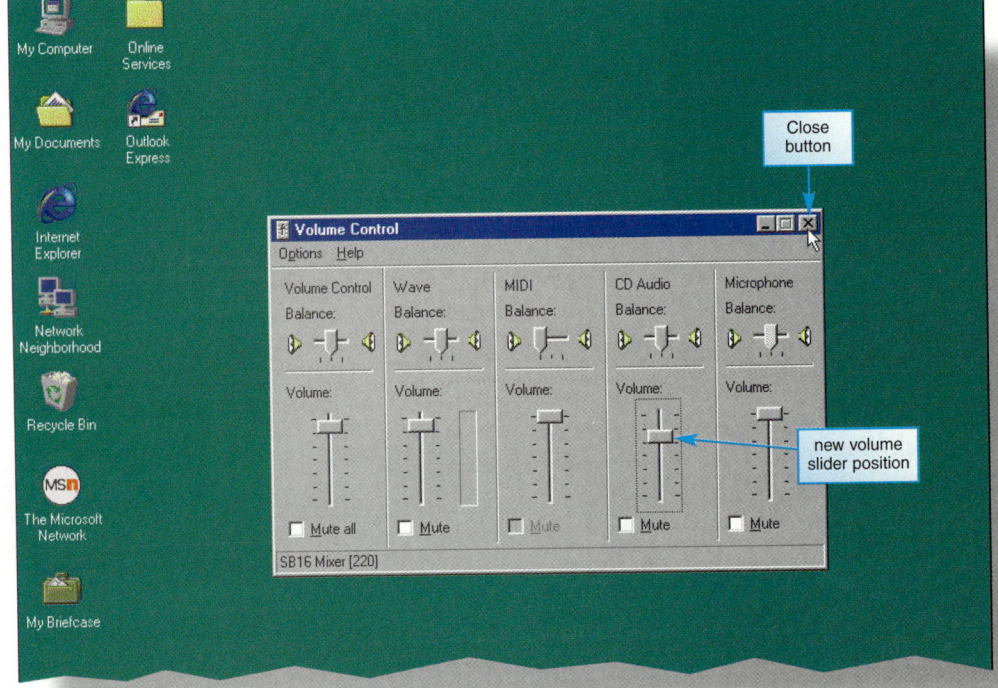

3 **Drag the Volume slider toward the bottom of the slide to reduce the volume. Drag the Volume slider toward the top of the slide to increase the volume. Experiment with the slider until you find the best sound level for you and then point to the Close button.**

The volume for the CD-ROM drive is adjusted (Figure 8-30).

4 **Click the Close button.**

The Volume Control window closes.

FIGURE 8-30

Other Ways

1. Click Start button, point to Programs, point to Accessories, point to Entertainment, click Volume Control
2. Double-click Volume icon in tray status area

The Volume Control area in the Volume Control window in Figure 8-29 lets you adjust the overall balance and volume for all sound devices. If the Volume slider is at the lower end of the slide, adjusting the other Volume sliders in the window will have no effect. In addition, a check mark in the Mute all check box turns off all sound. Other areas in the Volume Control window include the Wave, MIDI, and Microphone areas. The Wave area controls the playing of all Wave (.wav) files, the MIDI area controls all MIDI (.mid) files, and the Microphone controls the volume of the microphone. The areas in the Volume Control window may be different on your computer.

> **More About**
>
> **Volume Control**
>
> Clicking the Speaker icon in the tray status area of the taskbar displays a slide, slider, and Mute check box that are similar to the controls in the Volume Control area in the Volume Control window. Try it!

Ejecting a Compact Disc from the CD-ROM Drive

When you are finished listening to a CD, eject the CD from the CD-ROM drive by performing the following steps.

Steps: To Eject a Compact Disc

  Point to the Eject button in the CD Player window (Figure 8-31).

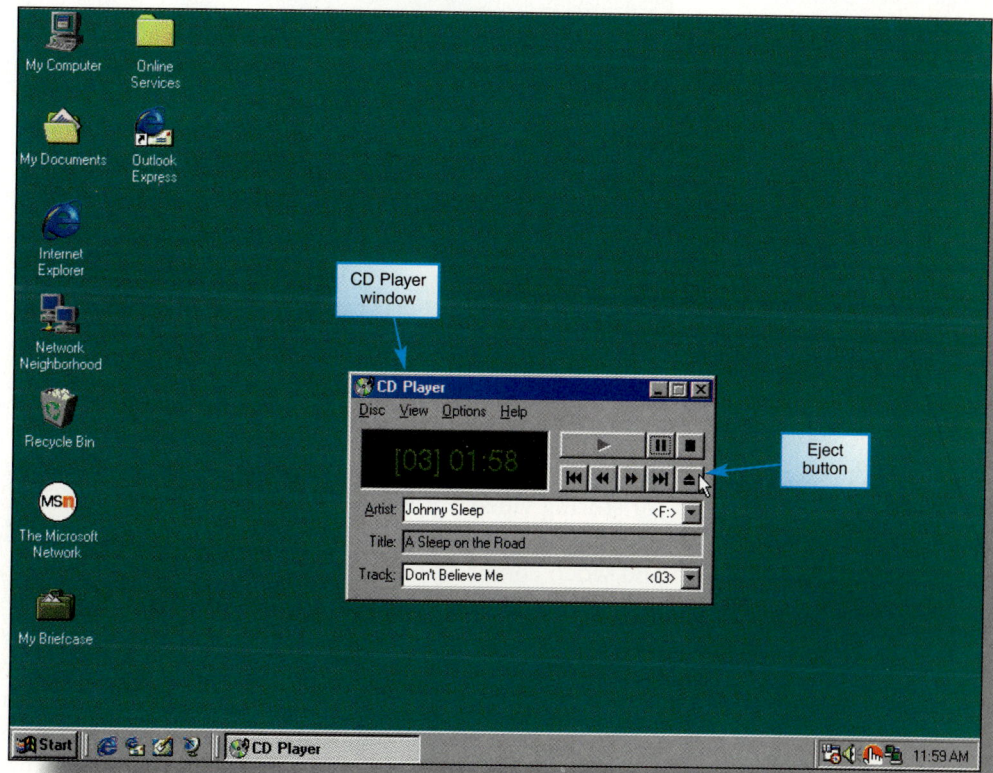

FIGURE 8-31

Click the Eject button.

The CD Player stops playing the CD and the CD tray opens. In the CD Player window, the track number (00) and elapsed time (00:00) display in the preview pane and the contents of the Artist box, Title text box, and Track box change (Figure 8-32).

 **Remove the CD from the tray, click the Eject button in the CD Player window, and then click the Close button.**

You remove the CD from the CD-ROM drive, the CD tray closes, and the CD Player window closes.

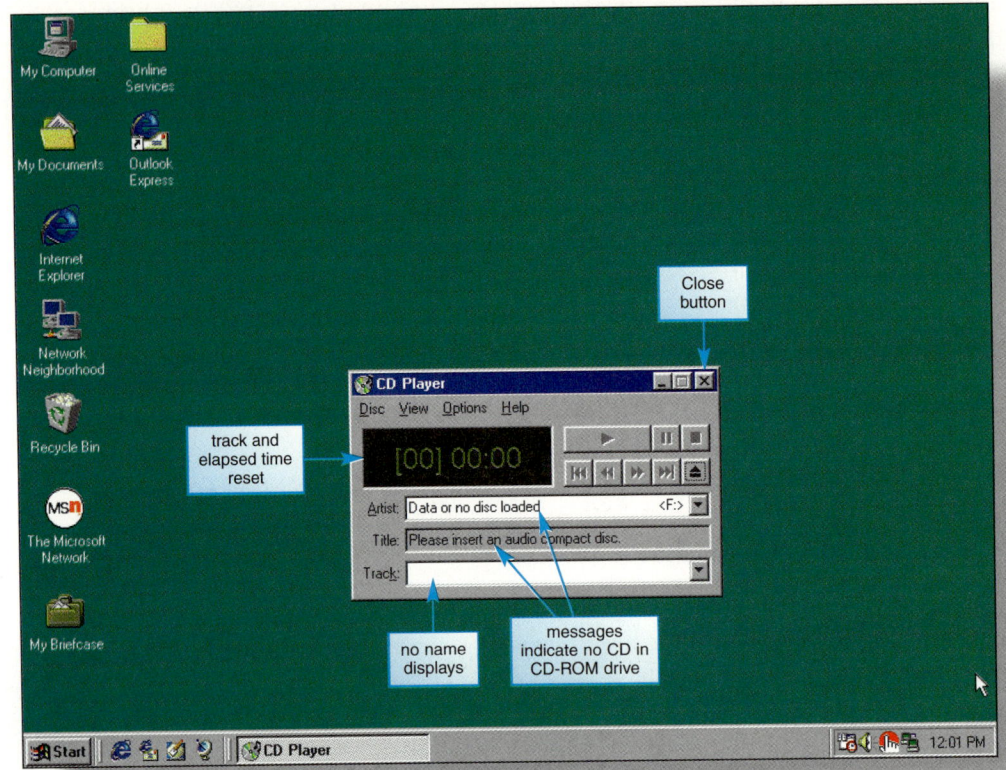

FIGURE 8-32

1. Press Eject button on CD-ROM drive, remove compact disc, press Eject button

More About

DVD Drives

If your computer has a DVD drive when Windows 98 is set up, DVD Player (similarly to CD Player) will be installed. If you install a DVD drive after installing Windows 98, the software included with the DVD drive will replace the DVD Player software.

Recording and Playing Video

Video is composed of photographic images that display at speeds of 15 to 30 frames per second and provide the appearance of motion. The three formats commonly used for storing video are AVI, Apple QuickTime, and MPEG. Because video files tend to be large, the **Moving Pictures Experts Group** (**MPEG**) developed standards for audio and video compression and decompression. MPEG compression methods reduce the size of video files up to 95 percent, while retaining near-television quality.

DirectShow, a component of the Microsoft DirectX software included with Windows 98, enhances the multimedia experience by providing support for digital video discs and the capability of playing high-quality audio and video. In addition, a technique called **streaming** delivers data to your desktop in a continuous flow. This stream of data allows you to begin viewing content immediately before the entire file has been transmitted. This technology makes it possible to listen to audio and view video while using the Internet and to play a digital video disc.

Playing a DVD

Movie studios are beginning to record full-length movies on a **digital video disc** (**DVD**). One side of the DVD contains printed information (copyright information, movie studio name, and movie title, rating, and length) and the other side contains the recorded movie. DVD drives play full-length motion pictures on CD-sized discs and are available for connection to personal computers and televisions. A DVD stores audio and video in such a way as to allow more than two hours of better-than-laser-disc quality video and better-than-CD quality audio. Although you can listen to a DVD using headphones attached to your computer, DVD movies are best when played on a computer (or a television) that has a speaker system. You also can play a CD using a DVD drive.

Prior to playing a DVD, you must purchase and install a DVD drive, a hardware decoder card, and appropriate software. In the following steps, assume that a Creative PC-DVD Encore hardware card and DVD drive manufactured by Creative Technology Limited are installed on your computer. A software program included with the hardware card and DVD drive allow you to play DVDs and control the operation of the DVD drive. Other manufacturers of DVD drives, hardware cards, and software are available.

Perform the following step to insert a DVD into the DVD drive and play the movie stored on the DVD. If your computer does not have a DVD drive, hardware card, or you do not have a DVD disc, read the following step without performing it.

  To Play a Digital Video Disc

1. **Press the Eject button on the front of the DVD drive, insert the DVD into the tray, and then press the Eject button.**

   The DVD tray opens, you insert the DVD into the tray, and the DVD tray closes. A video window and DVD Player display on the desktop, the Creative PC-DVD Video Window button and Creative PC-DVD Player button display in the taskbar button area, and the movie plays in Wide Video view (Figure 8-33).

FIGURE 8-33

The Creative PC-DVD Video window shown in Figure 8-33 contains six buttons and a video window that displays the movie. The six buttons allow you to display the video window in Standard or Wide Video view, change the size of the video window, display the video window in Full Screen view, and obtain Help.

The Creative PC-DVD Player window contains the PC-DVD remote control that allows control of the DVD and DVD drive. The appearance of the video window and remote control will change depending on the manufacturer of the DVD drive.

1. With DVD in DVD drive, click Creative PC-DVD Player button on taskbar, click Play button

Changing the Video Window View to Full Screen View

Although you could watch the movie in Wide Video view, the Full Screen view enlarges and clarifies the image. Perform the following step to change the view to Full Screen view.

To Change the Video Window View

1 **Double-click the video window in the Creative PC-DVD Video window.**

The view changes from Wide Video view to Full Screen view and the movie displays across the desktop (Figure 8-34).

FIGURE 8-34

1. Click Full Screen Video Window button in video window
2. Click Creative Technology Limited icon in upper-left corner of video window, click Full Screen
3. Right-click black area surrounding video window, click Full Screen

To Eject the DVD and Close the Open Windows

When you are finished watching the movie, eject the DVD from the DVD drive and close the Creative PC-DVD Video window and Creative PC-DVD Player window by performing the following steps.

Recording and Playing Video • **WIN 8.29**

PROJECT 8

 To Eject the DVD and Close the Open Windows

1 **Point to the Eject/Close button in the Creative PC-DVD Player window (Figure 8-35).**

FIGURE 8-35

2 **Click the Eject/Close button. Remove the DVD from the tray, click the Eject/Close button in the Creative PC-DVD Player window, and then point to the Close Remote Control button in the Creative PC-DVD Player window.**

The DVD Player stops playing the movie and the DVD tray opens. You remove the DVD from the DVD drive, and the DVD tray closes. The movie no longer displays in the Creative PC-DVD Video Window (Figure 8-36).

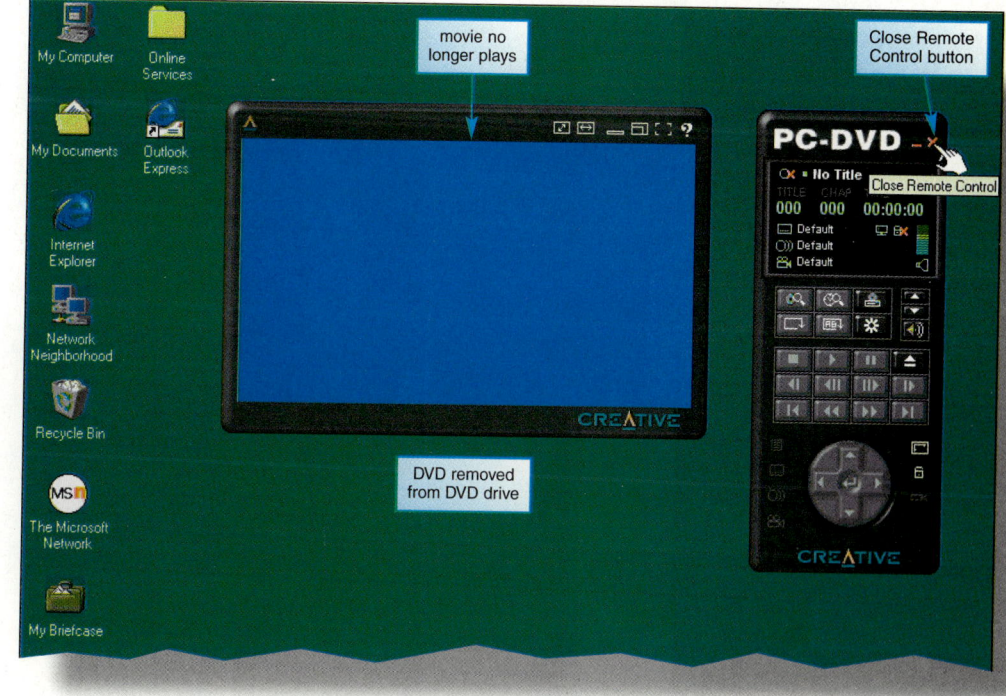

FIGURE 8-36

3 **Click the Close Remote Control button.**

The Creative PC-DVD Video window and Creative PC-DVD Player window close.

1. Press Eject button on DVD drive, remove DVD, press Eject button, click Close Remote Control button in Creative PC-DVD Player window

WIN 8.30 • Project 8 • Working with Multimedia and NetMeeting

More About

Media Player

You can play a compact disc using Media Player. CD Player, however, has controls (Play button, Pause button, Stop button, and so on) that are similar to the buttons on a standard CD player.

Playing Multimedia Files

Media Player, a program included with Windows 98, allows you to play any multimedia file (audio, video, or animation). In most cases, multimedia files are part of a software program, such as an encyclopedia program or a software game. Normally, you play these files in the process of exploring a topic in the encyclopedia or playing a game.

Playing a Multimedia File Using Media Player

Several multimedia files (Wave and MIDI files) are stored in the Media folder on the hard disk when you set up Windows 98. To hear sounds when you play these files, your computer must have a sound card. Perform the following steps to play the Canyon sound (MIDI) file.

To Play a Multimedia File Using Media Player

1 **Click the Start button on the taskbar, point to Programs, point to Accessories, point to Entertainment, and then point to Media Player.**

The Start menu, Programs submenu, Accessories submenu, and Entertainment submenu display (Figure 8-37). The highlighted Media Player command displays on the Entertainment submenu.

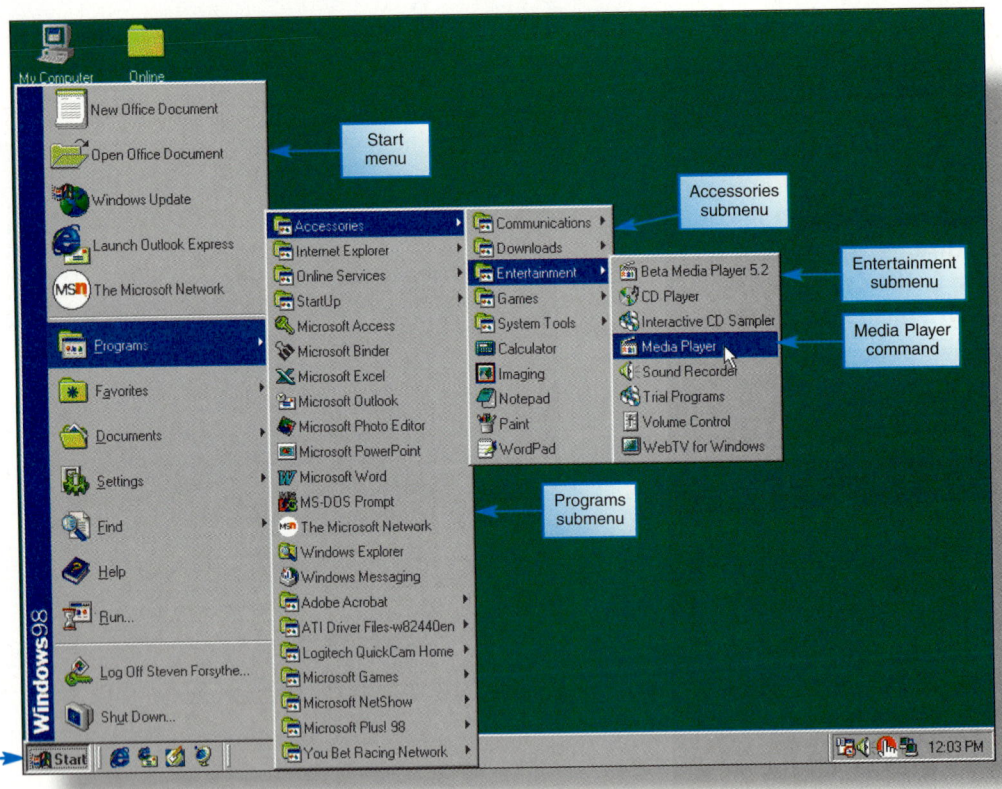

FIGURE 8-37

Playing Multimedia Files • WIN 8.31

2 **Click Media Player.**

The Media Player window displays (Figure 8-38). The window contains a slide and slider and nine dimmed buttons (Play, Stop, Eject, Previous Mark, Rewind, Fast Forward, Next Mark, Start Selection, and End Selection).

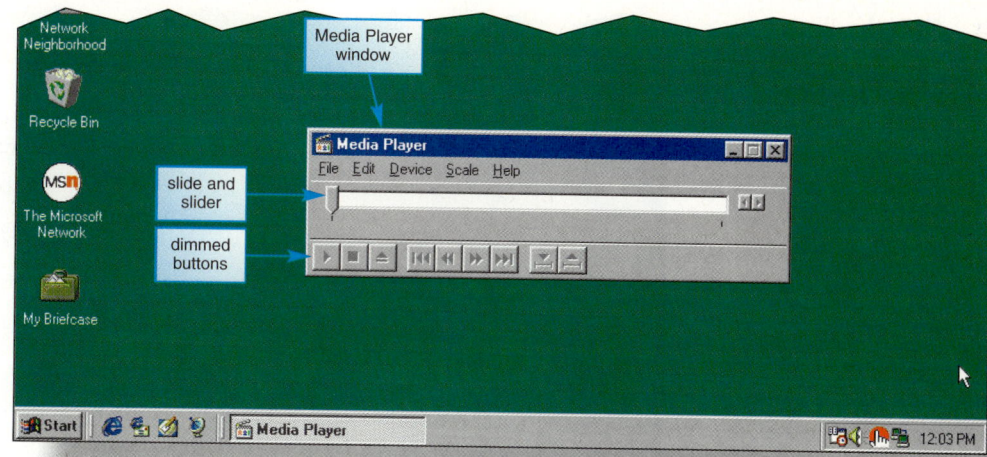

FIGURE 8-38

3 **Click File on the menu bar and then point to Open.**

The File menu, containing the highlighted Open command, displays (Figure 8-39).

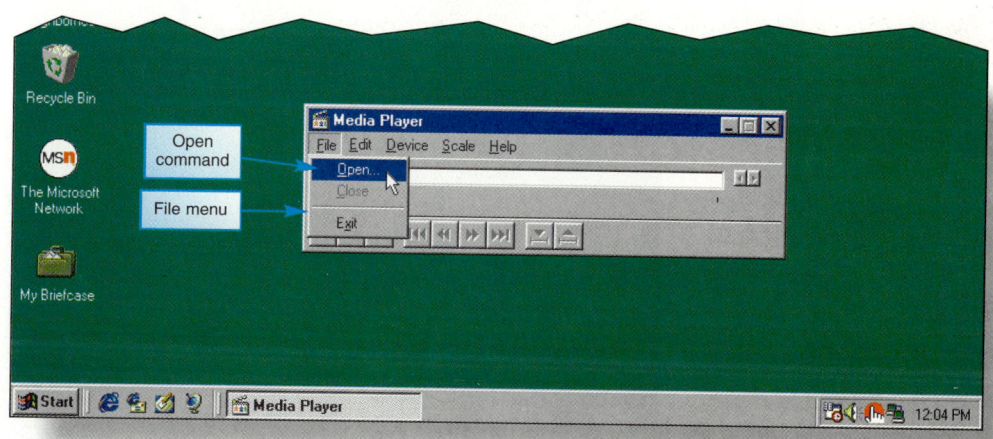

FIGURE 8-39

4 **Click Open. Click the Canyon file name in the list box and then point to the Open button. If this file name does not display in the list box, click another file name.**

The Open dialog box displays (Figure 8-40). The Media folder name displays in the Look in box, a list of MIDI and Wave files display in the list box, and the Canyon file name displays in the File name text box and is selected in the list box.

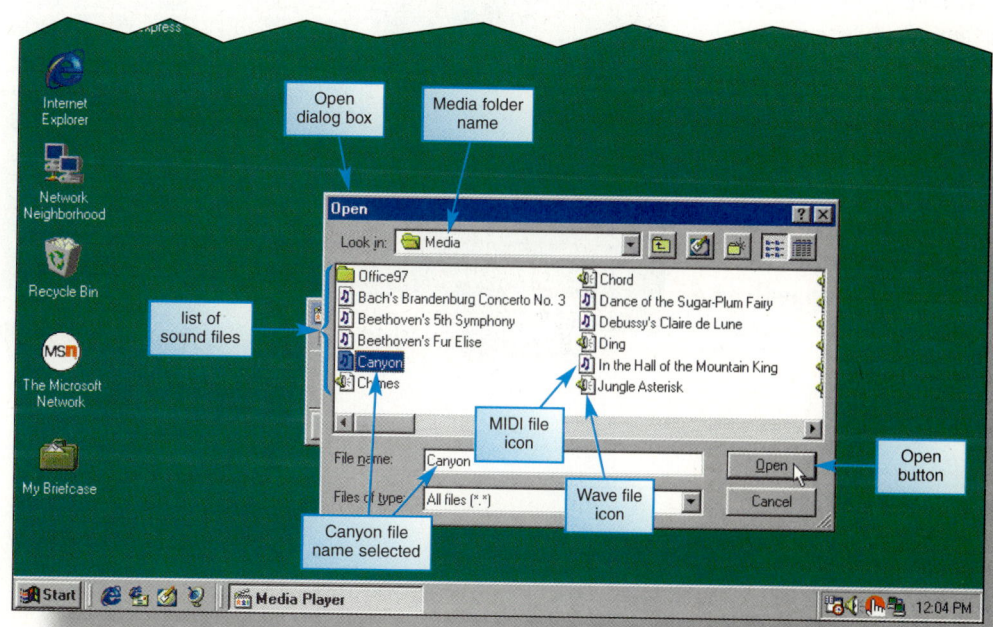

FIGURE 8-40

 **Click the Open button and then point to the Play button.**

The Open dialog box closes, the title of the Media Player window changes to contain the sound file name (Canyon) and the status of the Media Player (stopped), and a box containing the elapsed time (00:00 (min:sec)) displays (Figure 8-41).

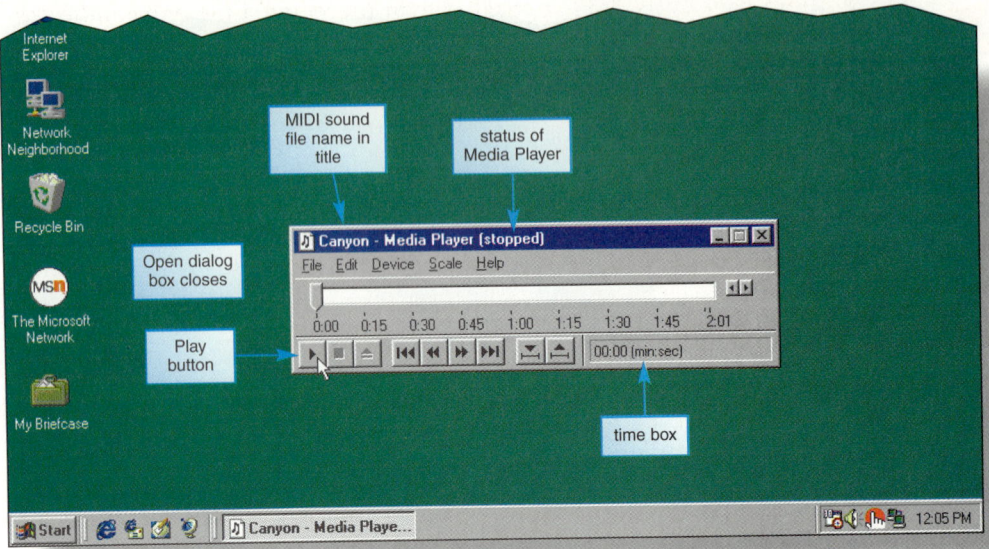

FIGURE 8-41

 **Click the Play button.**

As Media Player plays the sound file, the status in the title changes to (playing), the Pause button replaces the Play button, the slide moves to the right across the slider, and the elapsed time displays in the time box (Figure 8-42). The time at the right end of the slide (2:01) indicates the total time (minutes and seconds) to play the sound file.

 **When Media Player finishes playing the sound file, click the Close button in the Canyon - Media Player (stopped) window.**

The Canyon - Media Player (stopped) window closes.

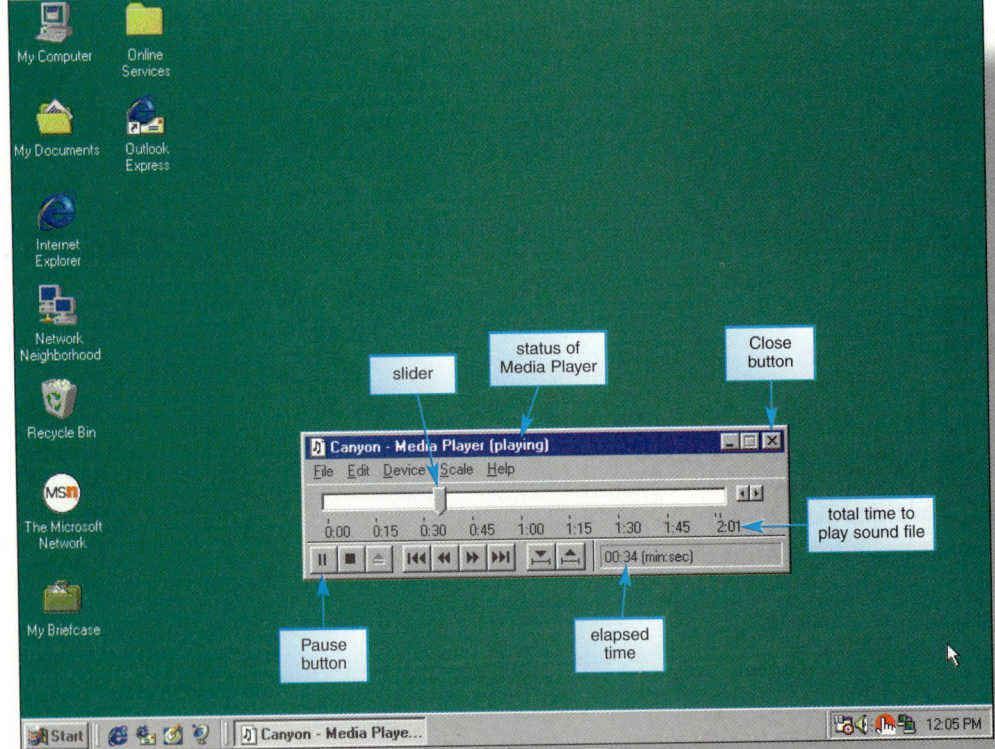

FIGURE 8-42

1. Double-click file name in Open dialog box, click Play button
2. Double-click file name in Media folder

In Figure 8-40 on page WIN 8.31, a speaker icon preceding a file name indicates the file is a Wave file and a musical notes icon preceding a file name indicates the file is a MIDI file.

Summary of Multimedia Operations

You used Sound Recorder to record and play a voice message, embedded and played a sound file in a document, and changed the Windows sound scheme. In addition, you played a compact disc, created and edited a CD Play List, adjusted the volume, played a digital video disc, and used Media Player to play a multimedia file. In the next section, you will learn how to use Microsoft NetMeeting.

Microsoft NetMeeting

An increasingly popular way to use multimedia technology in business and at home is Microsoft NetMeeting. **Microsoft NetMeeting** is a program included with Windows 98 that allows you to use the Internet to engage in a live videoconference with one or more computer users.

NetMeeting allows users to communicate in several ways. One method of communicating with other NetMeeting users is to use Microsoft Chat. **Chat** allows users to send text messages to each other and is especially useful when several users are involved in a meeting. When one person in the meeting types a message, the message displays on the desktop of every other person in the meeting.

A second method of communicating with other users is to use Whiteboard. **Whiteboard** is a drawing program that allows all users to sketch and type simultaneously while viewing the results of the other users. A third method of communicating is to use File Transfer. **File Transfer** allows you to send data files to one or more NetMeeting users.

Using Chat, Whiteboard, or File Transfer to communicate with other NetMeeting users does not require audio devices (microphone, speakers, and headphones) or video devices (video camera). Other methods of communicating require additional devices.

If your computer has a sound card, speakers, and a microphone, NetMeeting allows you to talk and listen to other users without the usual costs associated with long distance telephone calls. If your computer has a video camera, NetMeeting allows you to engage in live, face-to-face meetings by exchanging live video images.

Every computer connected to the Internet has a unique **Internet Protocol address** (**IP address**) that identifies the computer, and every NetMeeting user must have an e-mail address. To communicate with another NetMeeting user, you must know the IP address of their computer or be able to locate their e-mail address on a computer server maintained by an **Internet Locator Service** (**ILS**). The ILS server maintains a **directory list** of personal information (e-mail address, first name, last name, city, state, and personal comments) for each user logged on to the server. Only the e-mail address, first name, and last name are required.

When you log on to an ILS server, the server adds your personal information to its directory list and records the IP address of the computer you are using. If someone wants to contact you, they select your e-mail address from the directory list and the server associates the e-mail address with your computer's IP address, making it possible to contact you. Similarly, when you want to contact another user, you select their e-mail address in the directory list of the ILS server on to which they are logged. The server associates their e-mail address with their IP address and makes the connection. Thus, to place a call to another NetMeeting user, you must know the ILS server the user is logged on to and their e-mail address.

More About

IP addresses

You can determine the IP address of your computer by clicking the Start button, clicking Run, typing winipcfg in the Open box, and then clicking the OK button.

More About

ILS Servers

Internet locator servers (ILSs) will become more prevalent as live conferencing becomes more popular. Use your favorite search engine to locate other ILSs you can use.

WARNING! Not everyone who uses NetMeeting has business purposes in mind and many people who use NetMeeting are open and frank about the type of communication they want. Some areas may contain violent or sexually explicit content. **Content Advisor**, a program available with Internet Explorer that provides a way to help control the types of content your computer can access on the Internet, is not available in NetMeeting. Consequently, you may decide you do not want to use NetMeeting.

Launching Microsoft NetMeeting

Before communicating with other NetMeeting users, you must launch NetMeeting. Perform the following steps to launch NetMeeting and display the Microsoft NetMeeting window.

Steps To Launch NetMeeting

  If necessary, connect to the Internet. Click the Start button on the taskbar, point to Programs, point to Internet Explorer, and then point to Microsoft NetMeeting.

The Start menu, Programs submenu, and Internet Explorer submenu display (Figure 8-43). The highlighted Microsoft NetMeeting command displays on the Internet Explorer submenu.

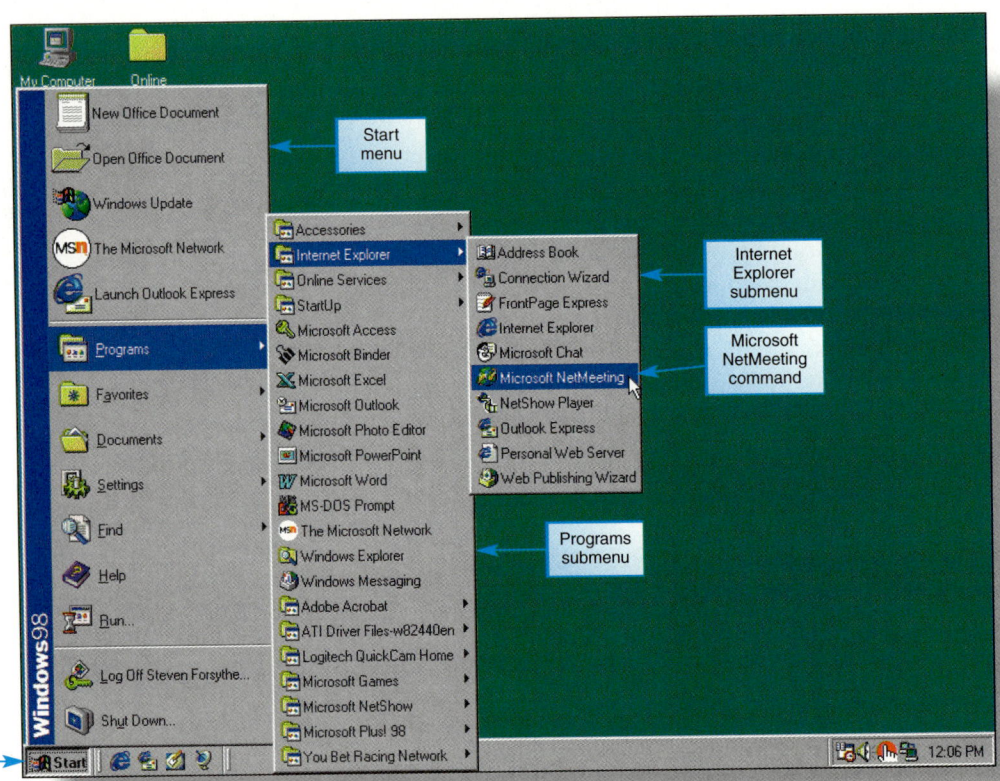

FIGURE 8-43

2 Click Microsoft NetMeeting.

Windows 98 launches NetMeeting and displays the maximized Microsoft NetMeeting - No Connections window (Figure 8-44). The window contains a menu bar, Directory toolbar, Navigation Icons bar, and Directory sheet.

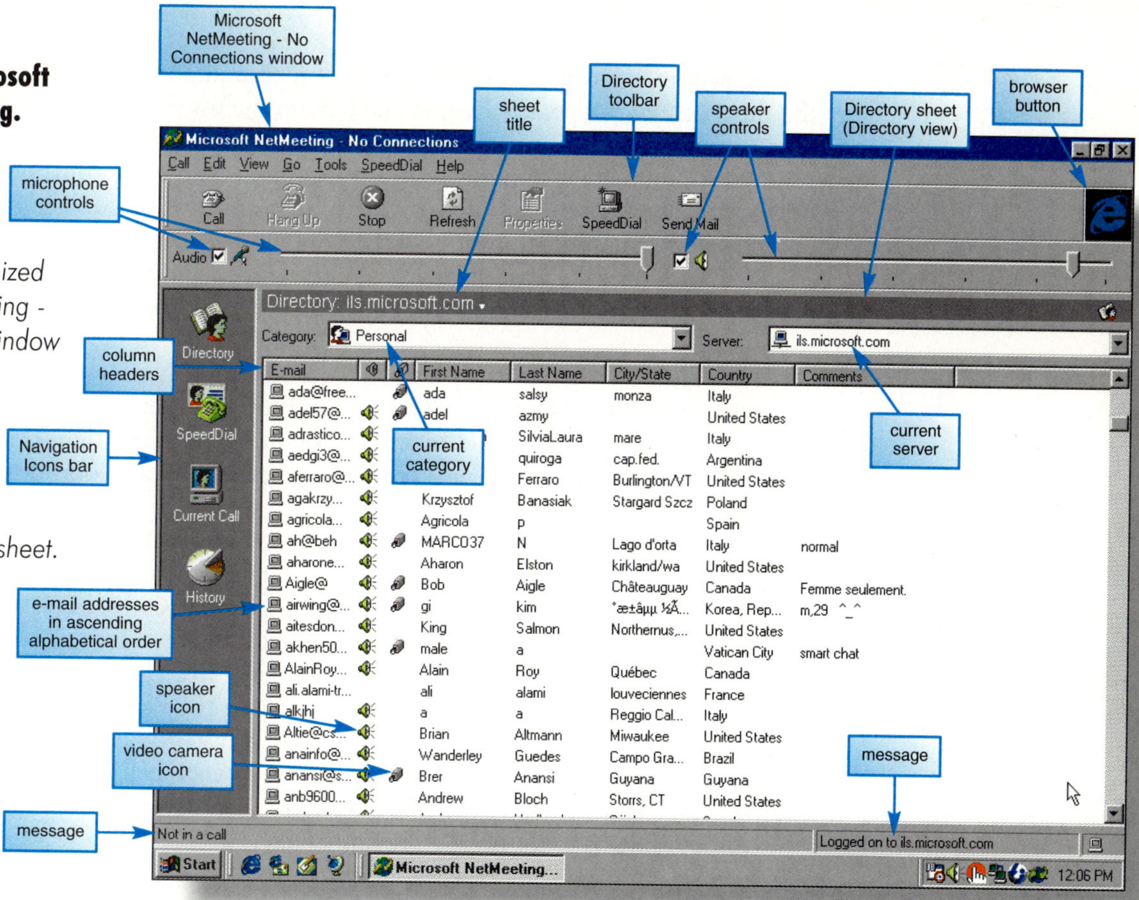

FIGURE 8-44

The Microsoft NetMeeting window shown in Figure 8-44 displays in the default Directory view. In Directory view, the Directory toolbar displays below the menu bar. The **Directory toolbar** contains seven buttons and the browser button. The toolbar buttons change when the view changes. The microphone controls (Audio check box and Microphone Volume slide and slider) indicate the microphone is working and the volume level of the microphone. The speaker controls (Volume check box and Speaker Volume slide and slider) indicate the speakers are working and the volume level of the speakers.

Below the Directory toolbar and slides are the Navigation Icons bar and the Directory sheet. The Navigation Icons bar contains the Directory, SpeedDial, Current Call, and History icons. The **Directory sheet** associated with the Directory icon displays to the right of the Navigation Icons bar. The Directory sheet title (Directory: ils.microsoft.com) indicates the current view is the Directory view and the current ILS server is the ils.microsoft.com server. The current category (Personal) displays in the Category box and the current ILS server name (ils.microsoft.com) displays in the Server box.

The **directory list** contains the personal information for every NetMeeting user logged on to the server specified in the Server box (ils.microsoft.com) who chose the category specified in the Category box (Personal). The directory list displays in ascending alphabetical order based on e-mail addresses.

Eight column markers display at the top of the directory list. The names in the column below the first header (E-mail) indicate the e-mail addresses of the users in the directory list. A computer icon precedes each e-mail address in the E-mail column. If a red star displays on the computer icon, the user is currently in a meeting.

More About

Directory Listings

As you will discover the first time you explore a directory server listing, not everyone who uses NetMeeting has business purposes in mind and many people who use NetMeeting are open and frank about the type of desired communication. NetMeeting does not offer a Content Advisor for its directory listings, so you may decide you do not want to use NetMeeting.

A speaker icon identifies the second header, and a video camera icon identifies the third header. A speaker icon in the column below the second header indicates the user has speakers and a microphone and is able to listen to your communication and respond to it. A video camera icon in the column below the third header indicates the user has a video camera and is able to transmit live video. The names in the columns below the fourth header (First Name), fifth header (Last Name), sixth header (City/State), seventh header (Country), and eighth header (Comments) indicate the first name, last name, city and state, country, and personal comments of each user.

The status bar at the bottom of the NetMeeting - No Connections window contains two messages. The message at the left on the status bar (Not in a call) indicates whether you are currently in a meeting. The message at the right on the status bar (Logged on to ils.microsoft.com) indicates whether you are logged on to a server and the server name.

The icons in the Navigation Icons bar allow you to change the view. Clicking the **SpeedDial icon** changes the view to the SpeedDial view and displays a list of users you would like to be able to call quickly. Clicking the **Current Call icon** changes the view to the Current Call view, which allows you to view a list of the users currently in the meeting. In addition, you can preview your live video transmission and view their live video transmission in this view. Clicking the **History icon** changes the view to the History view, which allows you to view a list of your callers, your response to their calls (Accepted or Ignored), and the time of each call. If the current view is not the Directory view, clicking the **Directory icon** changes the view to the Directory view illustrated in Figure 8-44 on the previous page.

Changing the Directory Information

If more than one person uses the NetMeeting program on your computer, it is important to change the directory information to your personal information before placing a call. After changing the information, your personal information displays in the directory list and is visible to other NetMeeting users. Perform the following steps to change the directory information.

To Change the Directory Information

1. **Click Call on the menu bar and then point to Change My Information.**

The highlighted Change My Information command displays on the Call menu (Figure 8-45). The Log Off command contains the server name on to which you are logged.

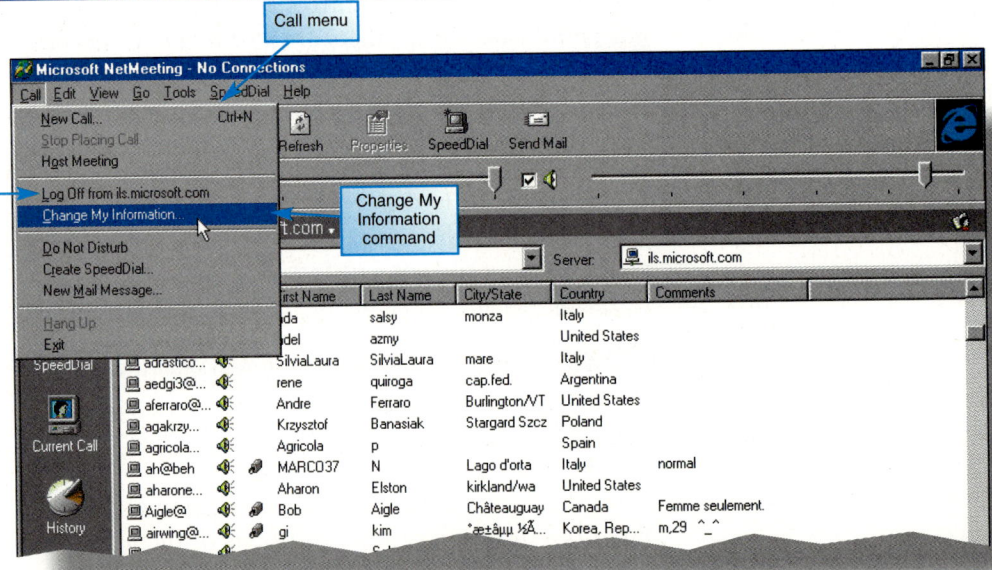

FIGURE 8-45

Microsoft NetMeeting • WIN 8.37

 Click Change My Information.

The My Information sheet displays in the Options dialog box (Figure 8-46). The Information sheet contains five text boxes. One box is for entering comments. The three option buttons categorize your NetMeeting usage for the server. The insertion point displays in the First name text box and the For personal use (suitable for all ages) option button is selected.

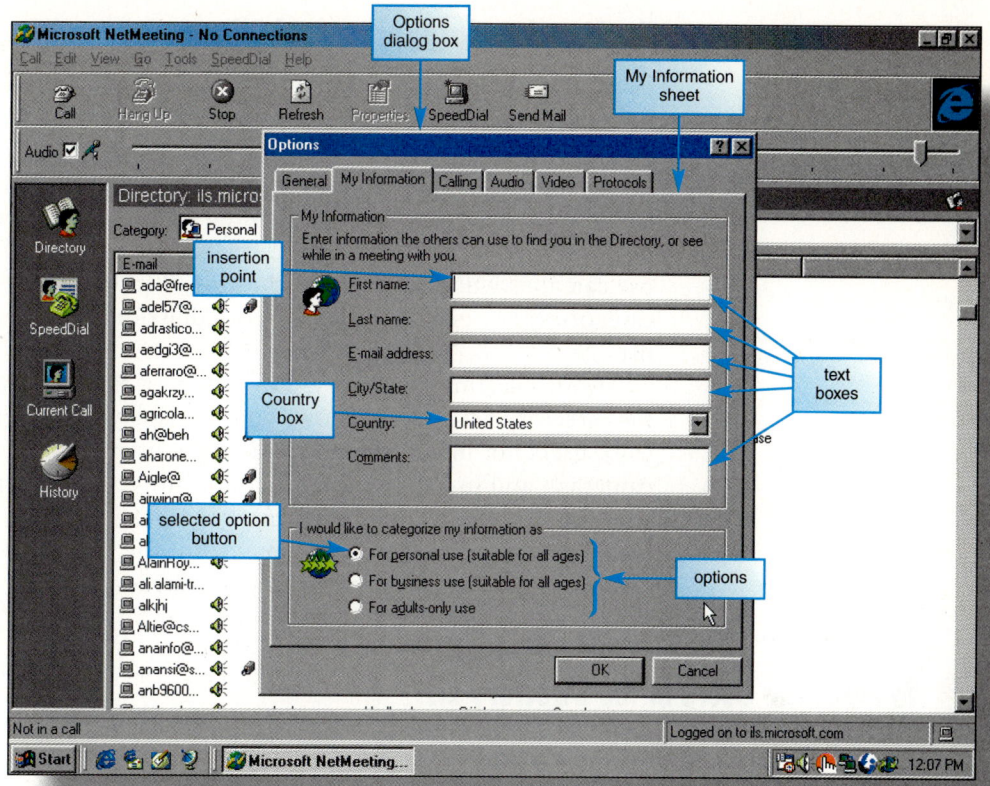

FIGURE 8-46

Type your first name, last name, e-mail address, and city and state in the First name, Last name, E-mail address, and City/State text boxes, respectively. Select your country in the Country box, type a comment in the Comments text box, and then point to the OK button.

The personal information for Steven Forsythe, one of the authors of this book, displays in the My Information sheet (Figure 8-47). Your personal information should display on your computer.

 Click the OK button.

The Options dialog box closes.

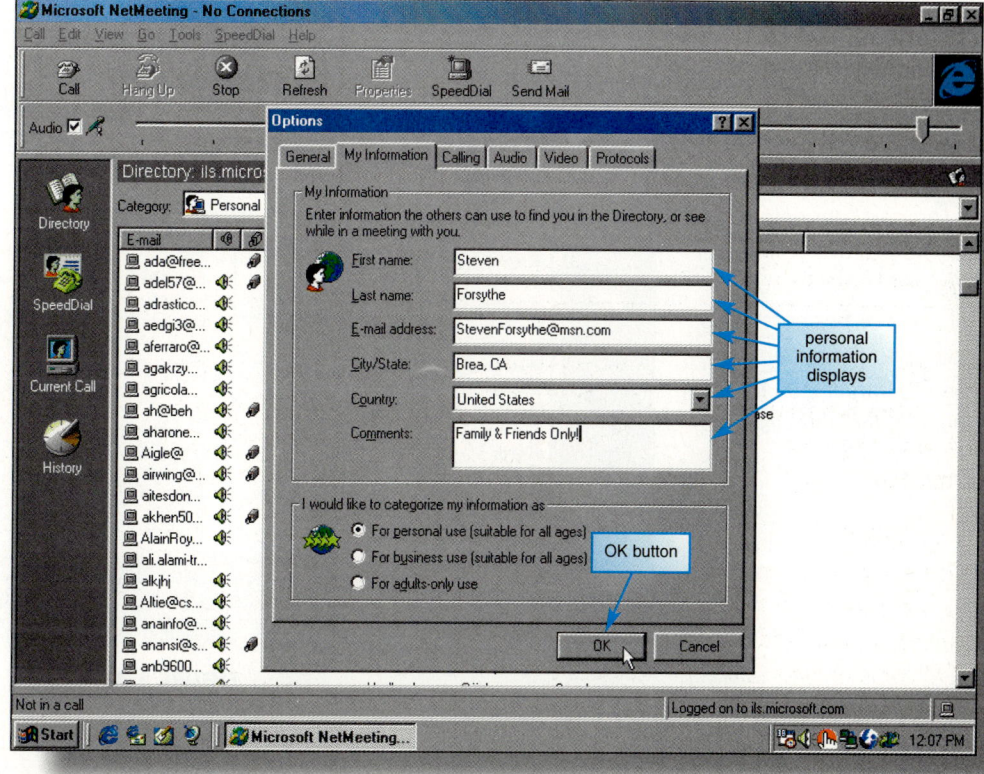

FIGURE 8-47

NetMeeting Categories and Filters

Three categories (For personal use, For business use, and For adults-only use) display in the Options dialog box shown in Figure 8-46 on the previous page. The default category is the For personal use category. When you select a category in the Options dialog box, the directory list you view will contain the personal information of only the users who have chosen the same category. For example, if you select the For business use category, only NetMeeting users who have chosen the For business use category will display in the directory list. Users who select one of the other two categories (For personal use and For adults-only use) will not display in the directory list.

After selecting a category, you can use a filter to categorize further the users in the directory list. A **filter** allows you to display only users currently in a meeting (In a call), users not in a meeting (Not in call), users who have video cameras (With video cameras), and users in your country (In my country). Applying a filter to the directory list reduces the number of users that display in the directory list and displays only users who satisfy the requirement of the filter. Perform the following steps to display only users who have a video camera.

To Filter the Users in the Directory List

1 **Click the Category box arrow in the Directory sheet and then point to With video cameras (Personal) in the Category list box.**

The Category list box displays (Figure 8-48). The first entry (Personal) is the current category. The next four entries are filters. The last two entries (All and Business) allow you to list all users or business users logged on to the current server. A different icon identifies each entry in the list box.

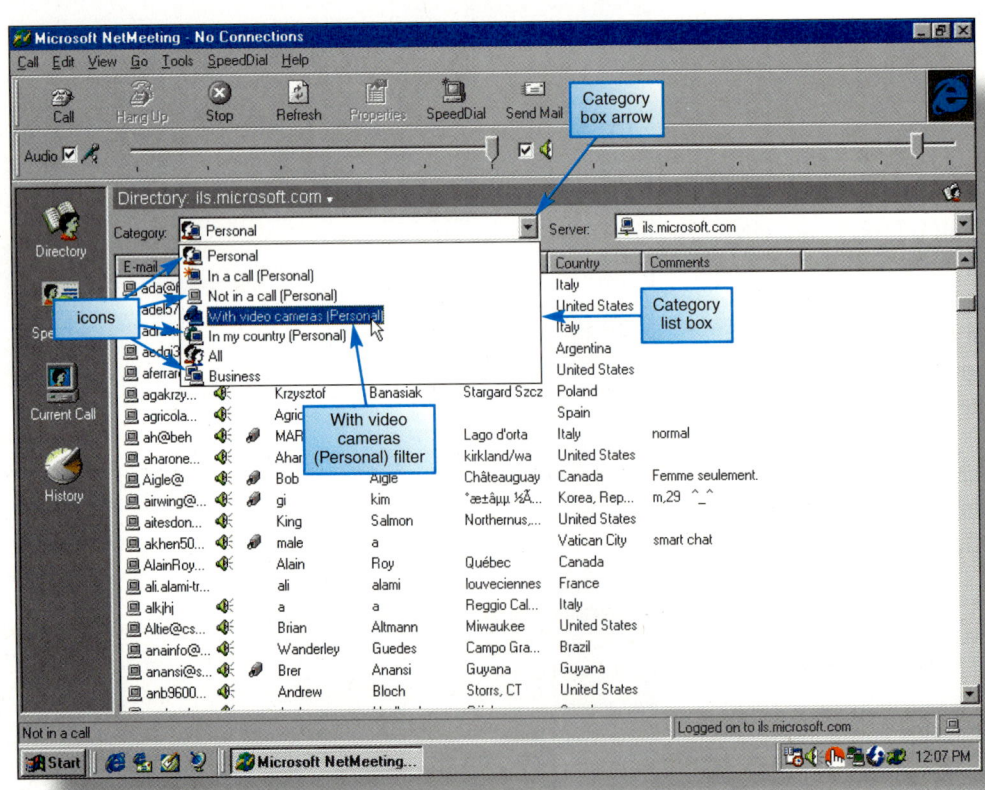

FIGURE 8-48

Click With video cameras (Personal).

The directory list changes to contain only personal users who have video cameras attached to their computers (Figure 8-49). Each name in the directory has a video camera icon in the third column.

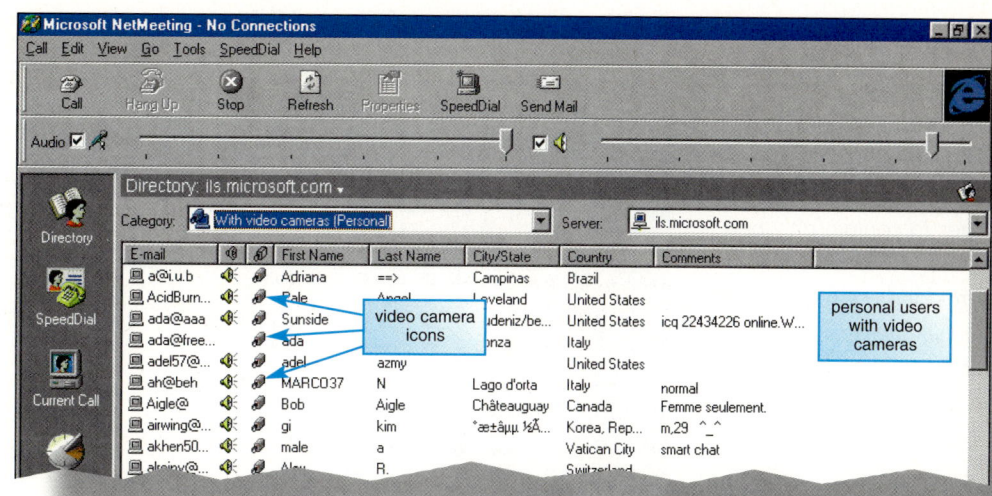

FIGURE 8-49

Changing the ILS Server

Currently, you are logged on to the ils.microsoft.com server. The ils.microsoft.com server name displays in the Server box and a list of all personal users logged on to the ils.microsoft.com server with a video camera displays in the directory list (Figure 8-49). Assume you want to place a call to a relative, Jill, who is out of town on business. Jill always logs on to the ils5.microsoft.com server and uses the jillforsythe@earthlink.net e-mail address.

Before placing the call, you must display the directory list for the ils5.microsoft.com server and locate Jill's e-mail address in the directory list. Perform the following steps to change to the ils5.microsoft.com server.

More About

Logging On to Another ILS Server

To log on to another ILS server, click Call on the menu bar, click Log Off, click Tools on the menu bar, click Options, click Calling, click the Server name box arrow, click the server name, and then click the OK button.

Steps To Change the ILS Server

 Click the Server box arrow in the Directory sheet and then point to ils5.microsoft.com.

The Server list box, containing nine server names, displays (Figure 8-50). The highlighted current server name (ils.microsoft.com) displays in the Server box and the highlighted ils5.microsoft.com server name displays in the Server list box.

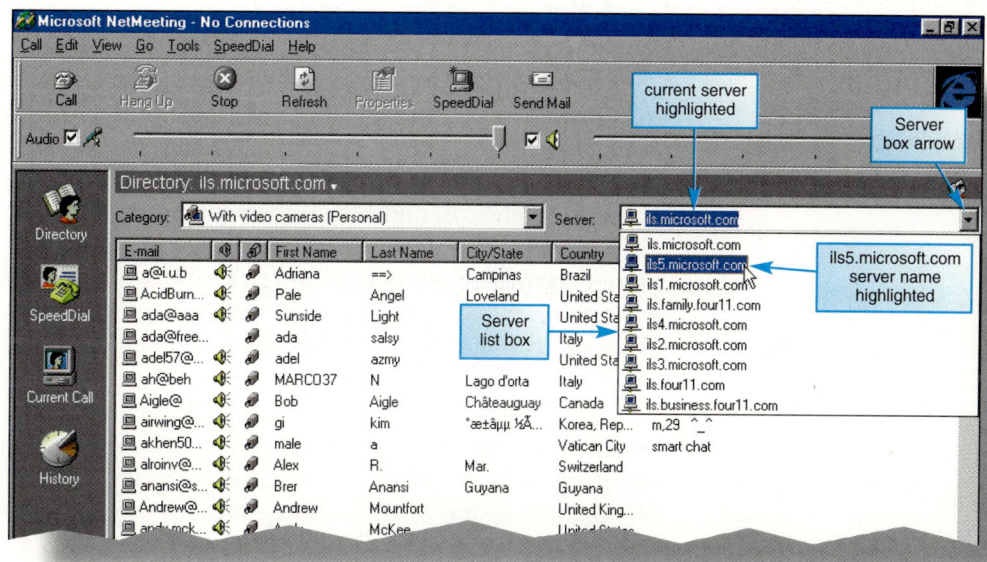

FIGURE 8-50

Click ils5.microsoft.com.

The ils5.microsoft.com server name displays in the Server box and the directory list changes to contain only personal users who have video cameras and are logged on to the ils5.microsoft.com server (Figure 8-51).

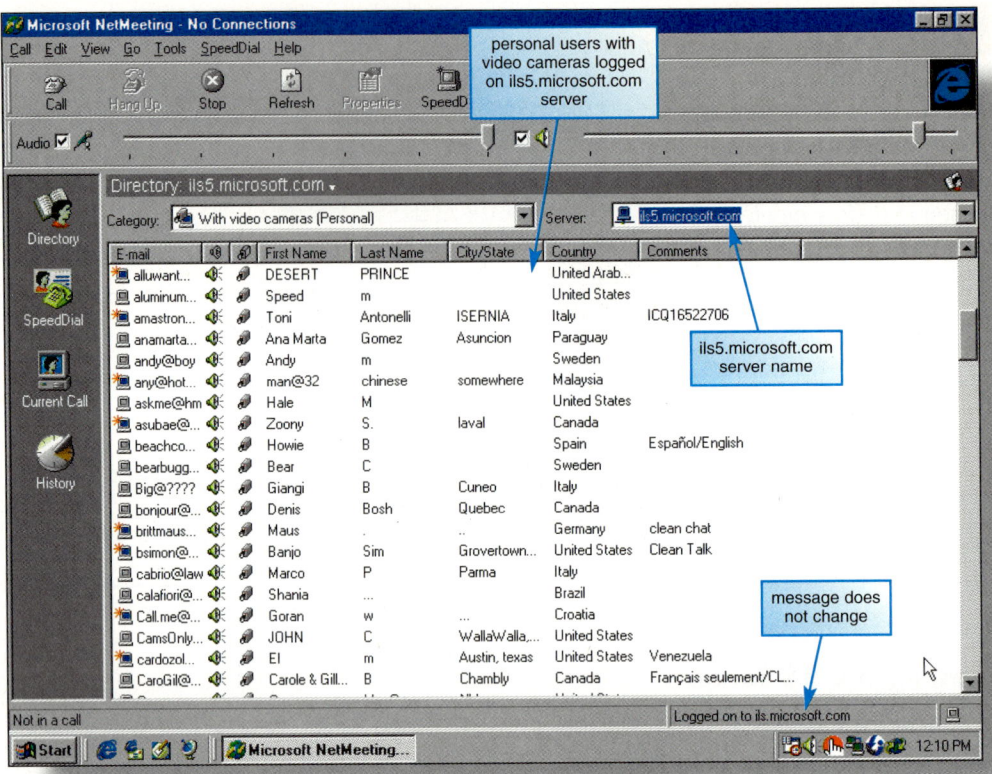

FIGURE 8-51

In Figure 8-51, the server name in the Server box changes to ils5.microsoft.com and the directory list contains the users logged on to the ils5.microsoft.com server. The message at the right on the status bar does not change. The message indicates you are logged on to the ils.microsoft.com server. Changing the current server does not change the server on to which you are logged. Other users can see your name in the directory list by changing their current server to ils.microsoft.com.

Placing a Call

Currently, you are logged on to the ils.microsoft.com server, your personal information displays in the directory list of the ils.microsoft.com server, and the directory list for the ils5.microsoft.com server displays in the Directory sheet. As such, you can place a call to anyone in the directory list and use any of the NetMeeting tools (Chat, Whiteboard, and File Transfer) to communicate with that user.

The following steps show how to place a call to Jill at the e-mail address jillforsythe@earthlink.net. Because Jill will not be there to accept your call when performing these steps, you must substitute the e-mail address of a person you choose to call in each step that contains the jillforsythe@earthlink.net address.

If you are in a computer lab setting, find another student in the computer lab to perform these steps. The person you call must enter their personal information, select the For personal use category, click the Calling tab, select the ils5.microsoft.com server name in the Server list box, and then click the Yes button in the Microsoft NetMeeting dialog box. The Logged on to ils5.microsoft.com message must display at the right on the status bar on their computer.

Perform the following steps to scroll the directory list to display the jillforsythe@earthlink.net address in the E-mail column and then place a call to Jill.

Microsoft NetMeeting • WIN 8.41

Steps: To Place a Call

1 Scroll the directory list to display jillforsythe... in the e-mail column and then point to the jillforsythe... e-mail address.

Jill Forsythe's partial e-mail address displays in the E-mail column (Figure 8-52).

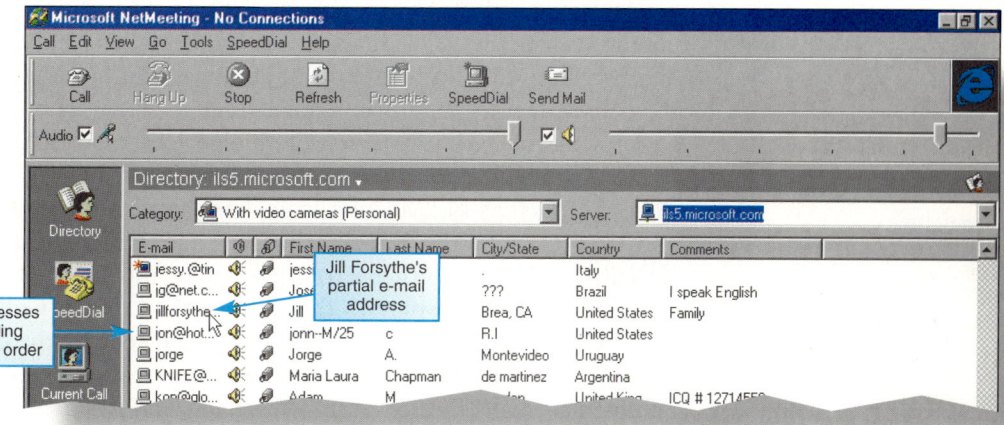

FIGURE 8-52

2 Double-click the Jill Forsythe... e-mail address.

Jill's address is selected in the directory list and two messages display on the status bar while the call is made. When Jill accepts the call, the Current Call toolbar replaces the Directory toolbar, the Current Call sheet displays, two names display in the sheet, and a message displays on the status bar (Figure 8-53). The My Video window and Jill Forsythe window contain the live video transmissions.

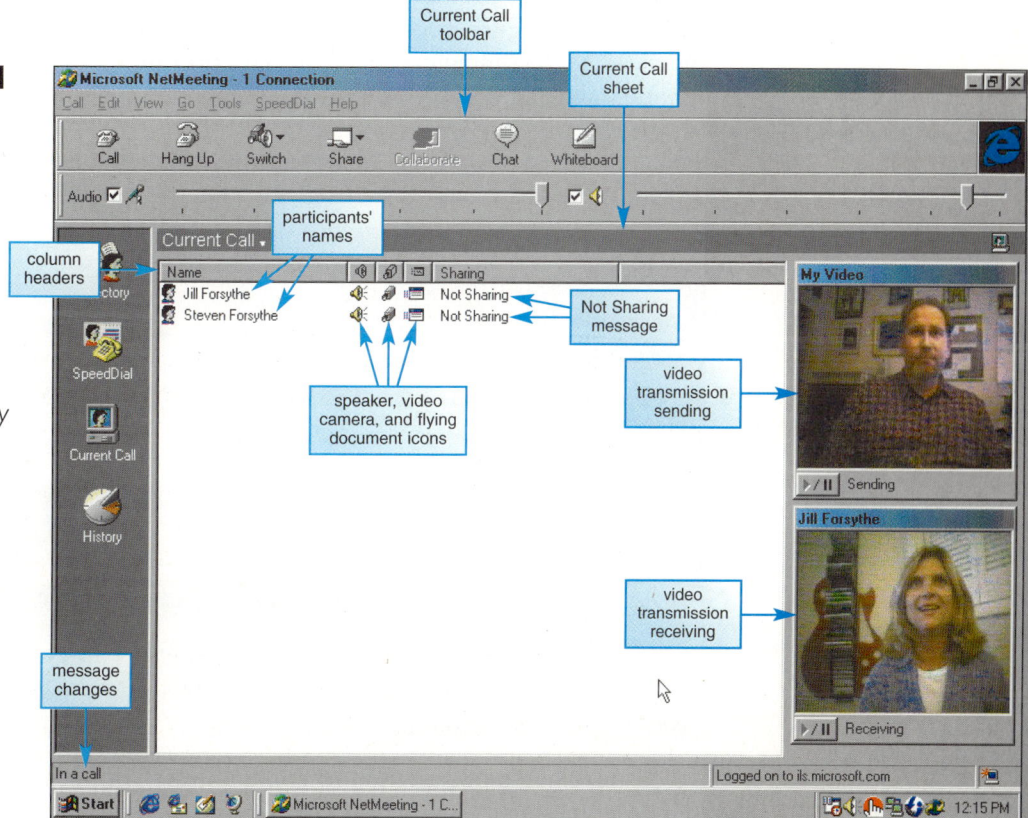

FIGURE 8-53

Other Ways

1. Click e-mail address, click Call button on Directory toolbar, click Call button
2. Click SpeedDial icon, double-click e-mail address
3. Highlight e-mail address, press ALT+C, N, press ENTER

Video Transmission Windows

To change the size of the Sending and Receiving windows that display in the Current Call sheet, click Tools on the menu bar, click Options, click the Video tab, click the desired size option button in the Send Image size pane, and then click the OK button.

Five column markers display at the top of the Current Call list shown in Figure 8-53 on page WIN 8.41. Names in the column below the first header (Name) indicate the first and last names of the callers. A speaker icon identifies the second header and a video camera icon identifies the third header. A speaker icon in the column below the second header indicates the user has a microphone and speakers and is able to talk and listen to communication by others. A video camera icon in the column below the third header indicates the user has a video camera and is able to transmit live video. A flying document icon identifies the fourth header. A flying document icon in the fourth column indicates the user is using a conferencing program, such as NetMeeting, can share applications, and use Chat, Whiteboard, and File Transfer. The Not Sharing message in the column below the fifth header (Sharing) indicates neither participant currently is sharing an application.

Two windows display to the right of the Current Call sheet. The My Video window contains the live video transmission sent by the caller (Steven Forsythe). The Jill Forsythe window contains the live video transmission sent by the person that accepted the call (Jill Forsythe). The two windows are larger than their default sizes to improve how you see the video transmission.

In the previous steps, you successfully placed a call to another person using NetMeeting. The person you placed the call to would see the Microsoft NetMeeting dialog box in Figure 8-54. The dialog box on Jill Forsythe's desktop would contain the message, Incoming call from Steven Forsythe…, and two buttons (Accept and Ignore). Clicking the Accept button accepts the call.

Chat

When several people are in the same meeting, you can choose to send a message to only one of them (called a whisper) by clicking the Send to box arrow, clicking the person's name in the Send to list box, typing the message, and then pressing the ENTER key.

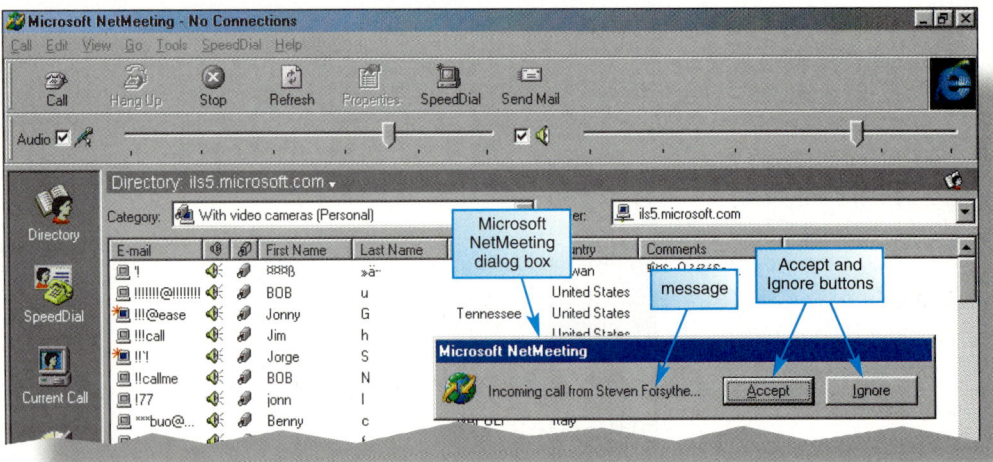

FIGURE 8-54

Sending a Text Message Using Chat

Using Chat is one method to communicate with other users. Chat allows you to send text messages to other NetMeeting users. Chat is useful when several users are involved in a meeting or the sound quality is not adequate for a meeting. When one person in the meeting types and sends a message using Chat, the message displays on the desktop of every other person in the meeting to which the message was sent. Because only two people can use audio and video at a time, Chat is especially useful when several users are involved in the same meeting.

Assume you have a problem with the microphone, and the sound quality is not good enough to continue the meeting. Steven suggests to Jill that they use Chat to complete their meeting. Jill agrees. Perform the following steps to use Chat to send a text message to and receive a text response from Jill.

Audio Quality

Current Internet capabilities cause the quality of the audio connection to be less than you have with a typical telephone conversation. The quality will improve as the technology progresses.

Microsoft NetMeeting • WIN 8.43

 To Send a Text Message Using Chat

1 Point to the Start Chat button on the Current Call toolbar (Figure 8-55).

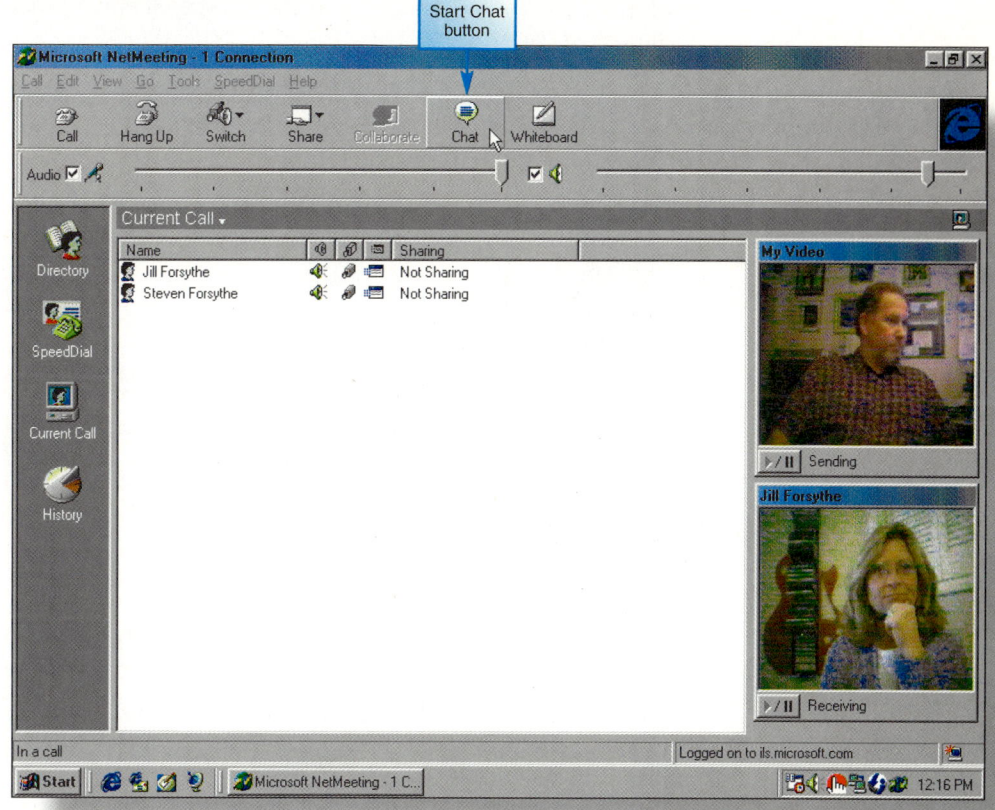

FIGURE 8-55

2 Click the Start Chat button.

The Untitled - Chat - in use by 1 other(s) window displays (Figure 8-56). The window contains a display area, Message text box, Send button, Send to box, and message area. The insertion point displays in the Message text box. A similar Untitled - Chat window displays on the desktop of the other participant.

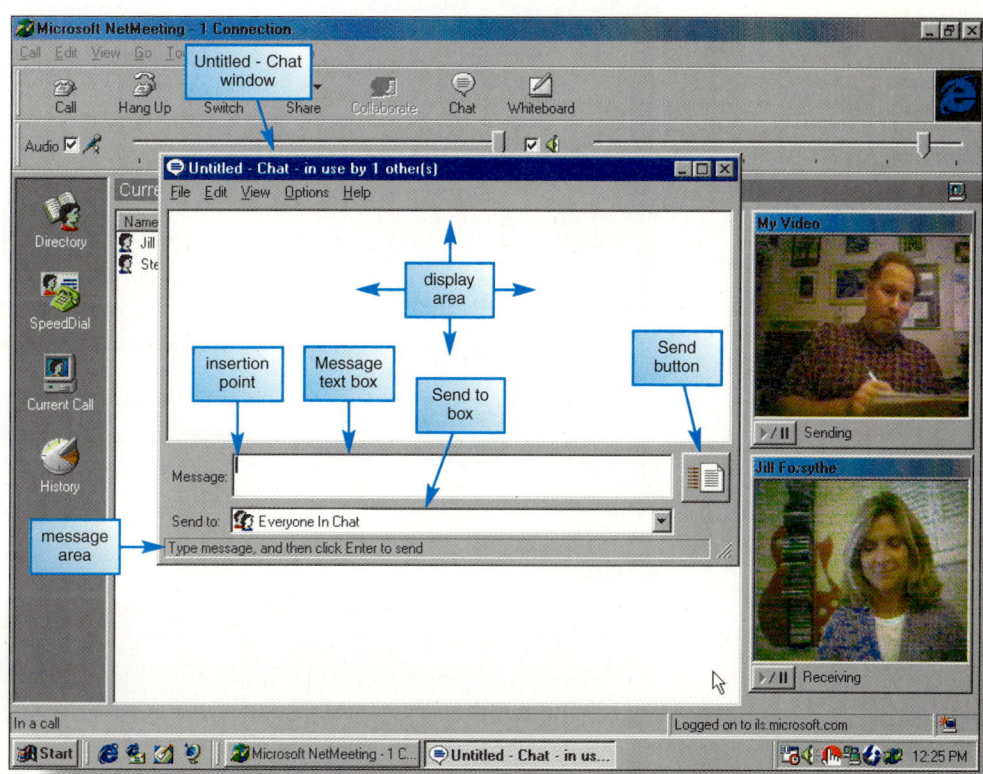

FIGURE 8-56

Type I hope the weather in Michigan is good. Where are you staying? **in the Message text box and then point to the Send button.**

The message displays in the Message text box (Figure 8-57).

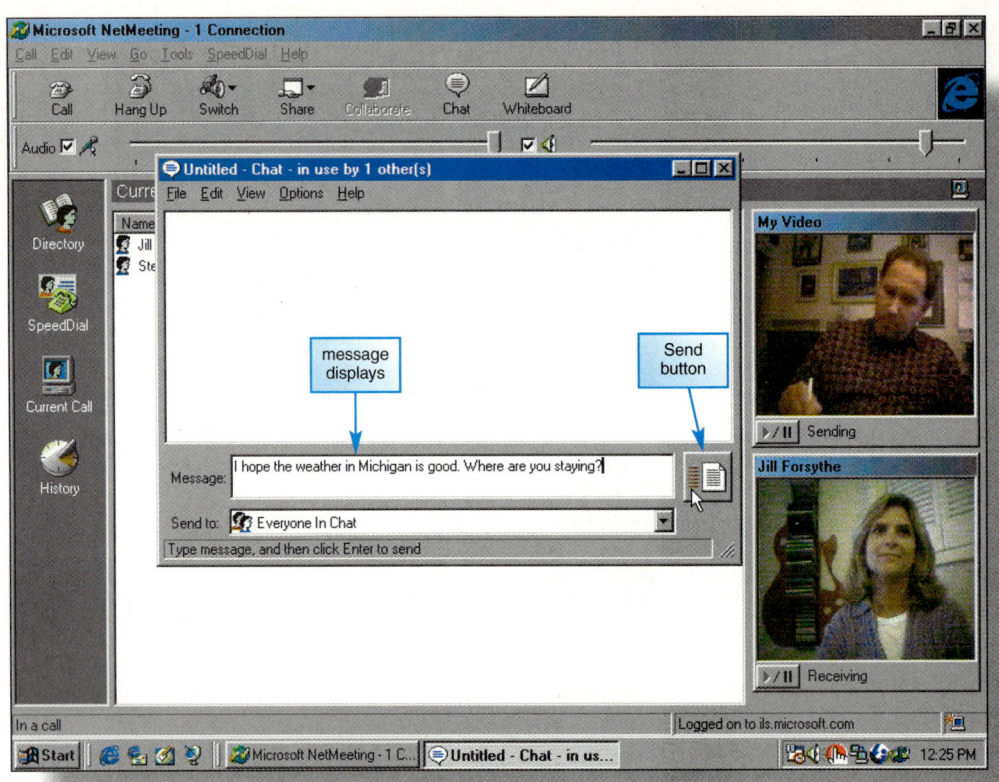

FIGURE 8-57

 Click the Send button.

Chat removes the message in the Message text box, displays your name and the message in the display area, and sends the message to the other participant (Figure 8-58). Your name and message display in the other participant's display area.

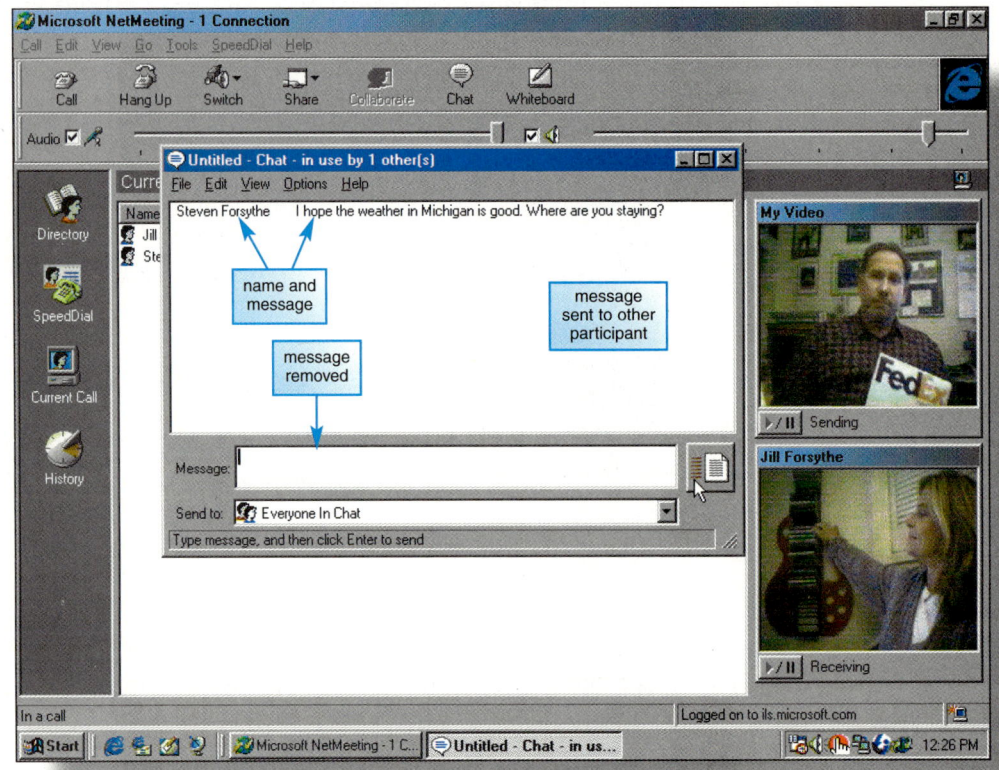

FIGURE 8-58

⑤ **The other participant (Jill Forsythe) sends a response.**

Jill sends a response (I am staying at the Thomas Edison Inn in Port Huron. Do you remember where Port Huron is located?) and Jill's name and message display in the display area in the Untitled - Chat window (Figure 8-59).

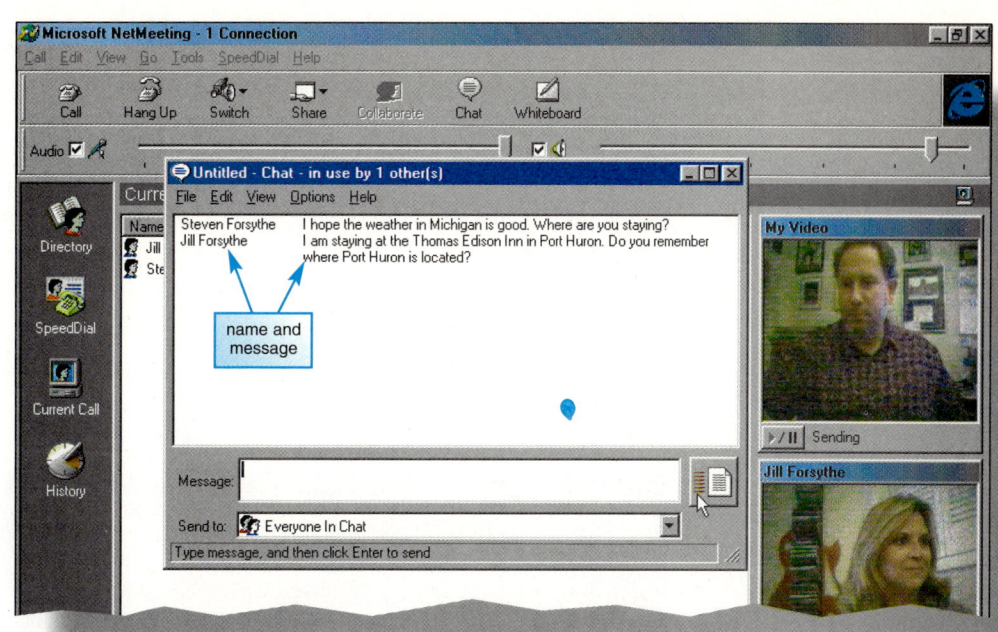

FIGURE 8-59

⑥ **Type** I think so. I will draw a map for you using Whiteboard and show you where I think Port Huron is located. **in the Message text box and then click the Send button.**

NetMeeting sends the message (Figure 8-60). Your name and message display in both your and Jill Forsythe's display area.

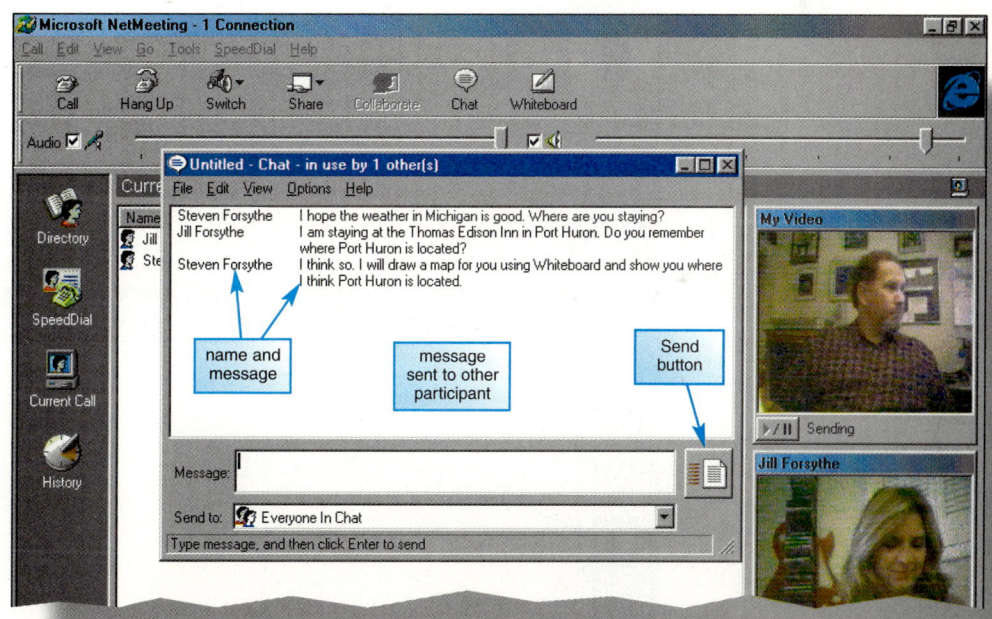

FIGURE 8-60

1. On Tools menu click Chat, type message, click Send
2. Press CTRL+T, type message, press ENTER

You can continue conversing in this manner, reading what the other user has to say, and then typing your response. If you wish to send a message to only one person, select the person's name in the Send to list box and then click the Send button.

Your last message (Figure 8-60) indicated you would use Whiteboard to show where Port Huron is located. You decide to draw a map of the state of Michigan and identify where the city of Port Huron is located on the map.

Drawing a Graphics Image Using Whiteboard

A second method of communicating with other NetMeeting users is to use Whiteboard. Whiteboard is a drawing program that allows all users in a meeting to sketch and type simultaneously while viewing the results of the other users. When one person in the meeting draws an image, the image displays on the desktop of every other person in the meeting. Perform the following steps to use Whiteboard to draw a map of the state of Michigan and place an X on the map where the city of Port Huron is located.

To Draw and Send an Image Using Whiteboard

 Point to the Whiteboard button on the Current Call toolbar (Figure 8-61).

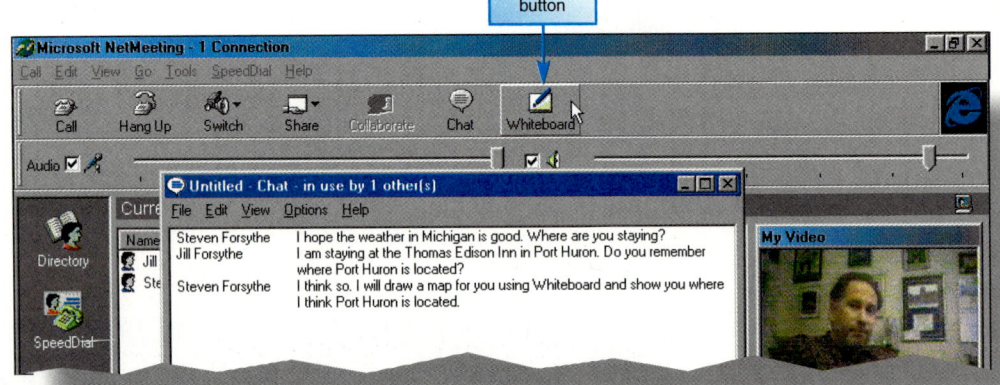

FIGURE 8-61

2 Click the Whiteboard button and then click the Pen tool in the Tool Box. If necessary, maximize the Untitled - Whiteboard - in use by 1 other(s) window.

The maximized Untitled - Whiteboard - in use by 1 other(s) window displays (Figure 8-62). The window contains a **Tool Box** with tools to create images and a **Color box** to select colors for an image. The **Pen tool** in the Tool Box is recessed and the Pen tool displays in the drawing area. A similar window displays on the desktop of the other caller.

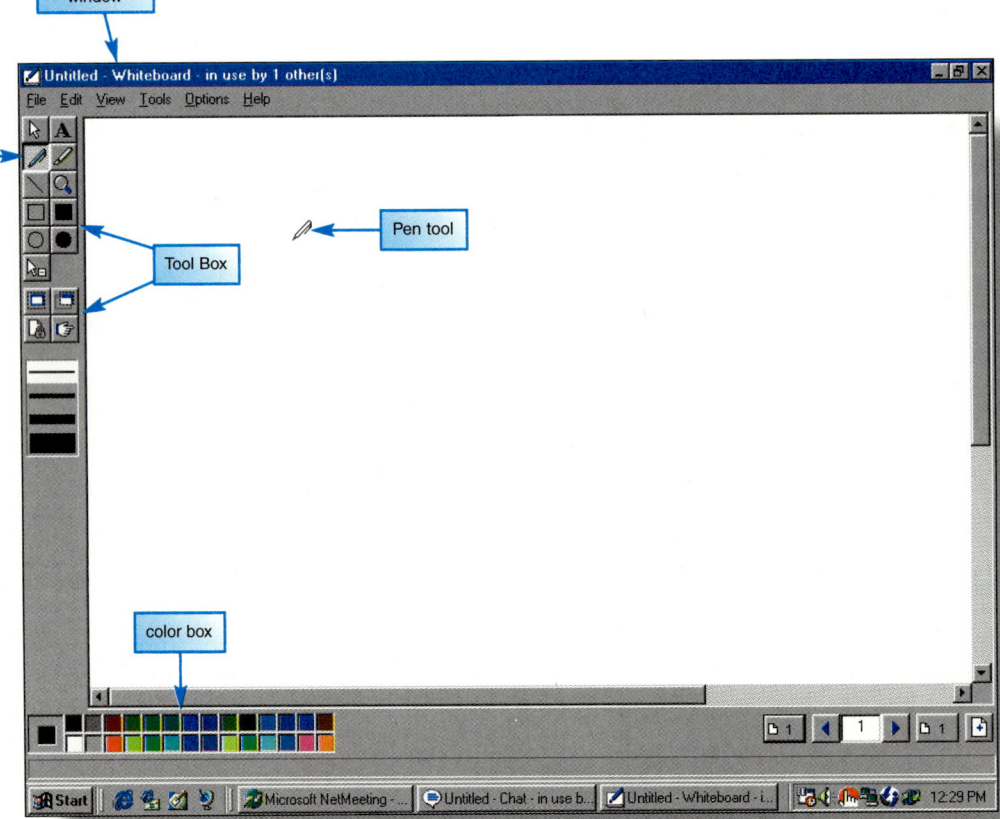

FIGURE 8-62

3 **Using the Pen tool, draw a map of Michigan and place an X where Port Huron is located.**

A map of Michigan is drawn and an X displays in the middle-right area of the map of Michigan (Figure 8-63). As you draw the map and the X, the map and X display in the drawing area of the other caller's Untitled - Whiteboard window.

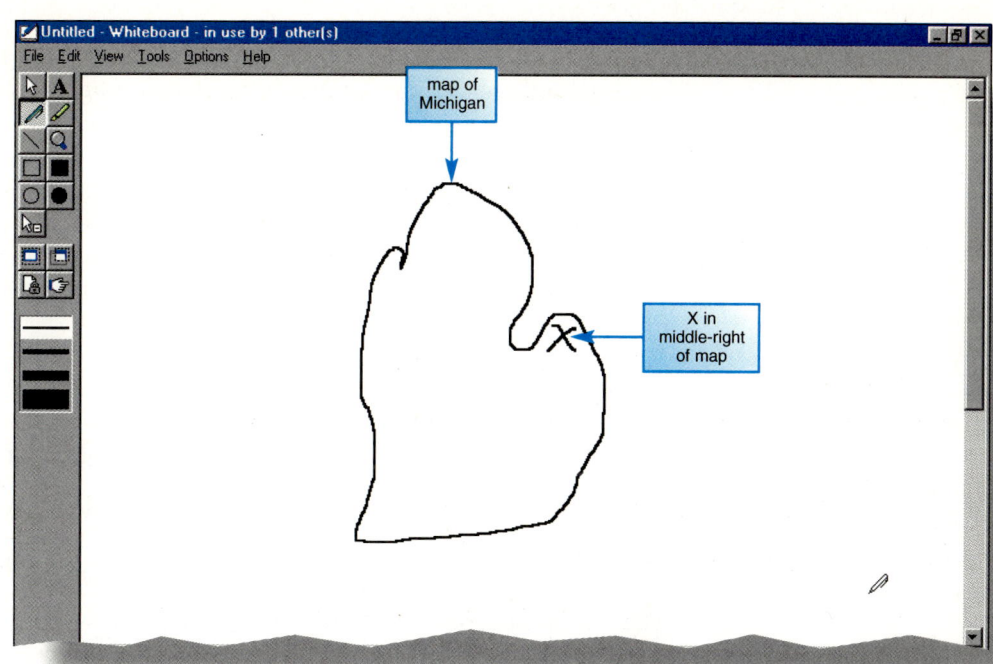

FIGURE 8-63

4 **Jill uses the Eraser tool to erase the X in the incorrect location on the map of Michigan and then uses the Pen tool and the color red to draw a red X in the correct location on the map.**

When Jill changes the image, the changes display in the drawing area in the Untitled - Whiteboard window on your desktop (Figure 8-64).

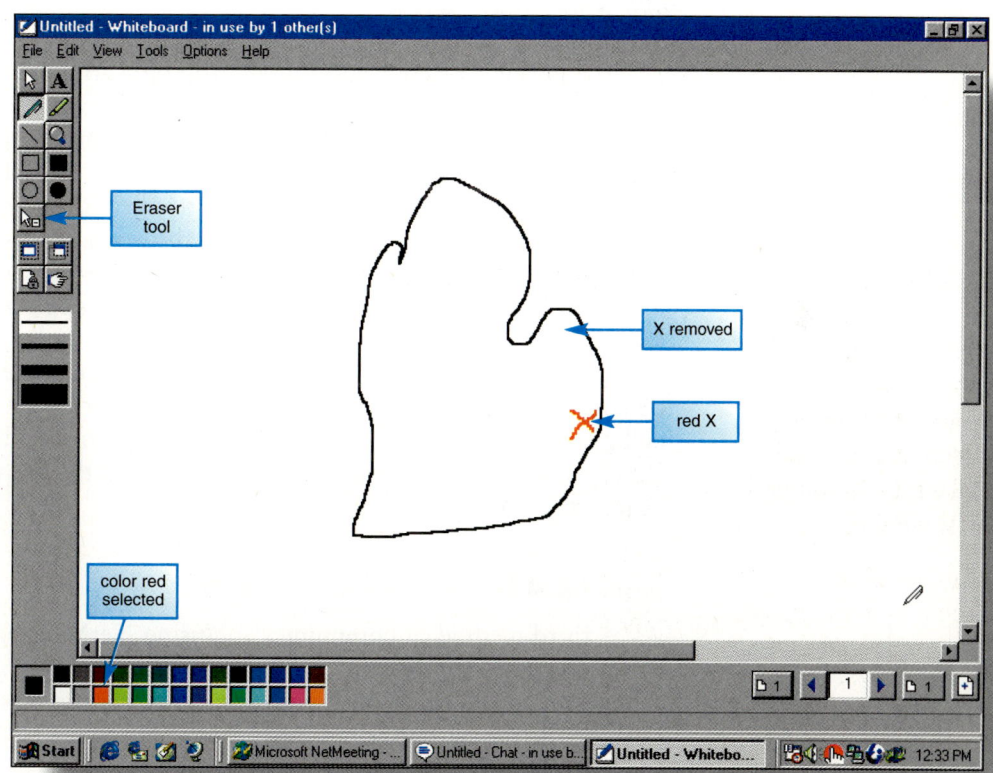

FIGURE 8-64

1. On Tools menu click Whiteboard
2. Press CTRL+W

You can continue drawing in this manner, making additional changes to the image and viewing changes made to the image by the other user. You can save or print the drawing using commands on the File menu. In addition, you can continue to send and receive text messages using Chat.

Closing the Chat and Whiteboard Windows

When you are finished exchanging text messages and drawing images, you should close the Untitled - Whiteboard and Untitled - Chat windows. Perform the following steps to close the windows.

TO CLOSE THE CHAT AND WHITEBOARD WINDOWS

1. Click the Close button in the Untitled - Whiteboard window.
2. Click the No button in the Whiteboard dialog box.
3. Click the Close button in the Untitled - Chat window.
4. Click the No button in the Chat dialog box.

The Untitled - Whiteboard and Untitled - Chat windows close and the text messages and drawing images are not saved.

Sharing an Application

In addition to using the Whiteboard application to allow multiple users to work on the same document simultaneously, you also can share other applications with the users in a meeting. Once a meeting begins, launch the application you wish to share (Notepad, Paint, Word, Internet Explorer, and so on), click the Share button on the Current Call toolbar, and then click the application name of the application you wish to share. Other users will be able to see the application but will not be able to work in the application.

To allow other users to work in your shared application, called **collaborating**, click the Collaborate button on the Current Call toolbar. Any users who also click the Collaborate button will be able to work in the shared application. Only the person who shared the application can save or print the document on which you collaborated. For another user to obtain a copy of the document after collaborating, the person who shared the document must send the file to the user using File Transfer.

Sending a File Using File Transfer

A third method of communicating using NetMeeting is to use File Transfer. File Transfer allows you to send a file to one or more users in a meeting. Assume that Jill would like to use the Clouds.bmp file as the background for her desktop but cannot find the file on her hard disk. Perform the following steps to send the Clouds.bmp file located in the Windows folder on your hard disk to Jill.

Microsoft NetMeeting • **WIN 8.49**

PROJECT 8

 To Send a File Using File Transfer

1 Click Tools on the menu bar, point to File Transfer, and then point to Send File.

The Tools menu and File Transfer submenu display (Figure 8-65).

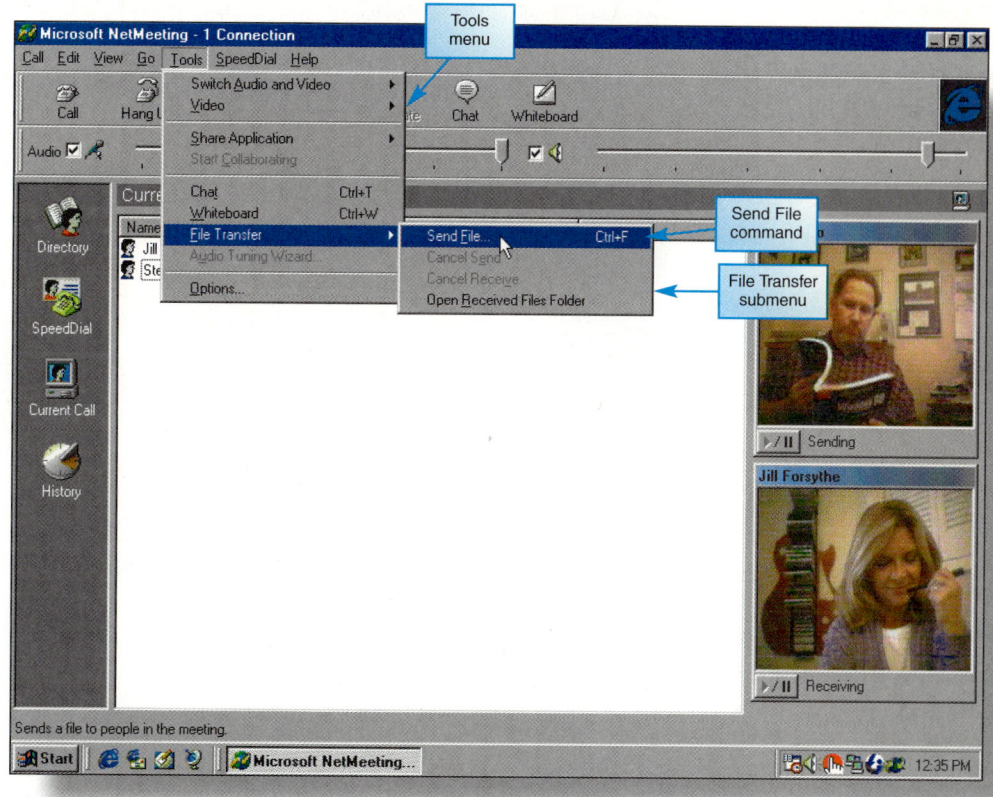

FIGURE 8-65

2 Click Send File and then point to the Windows folder in the list box in the Select a File to Send dialog box.

The Select a File to Send dialog box displays (Figure 8-66).

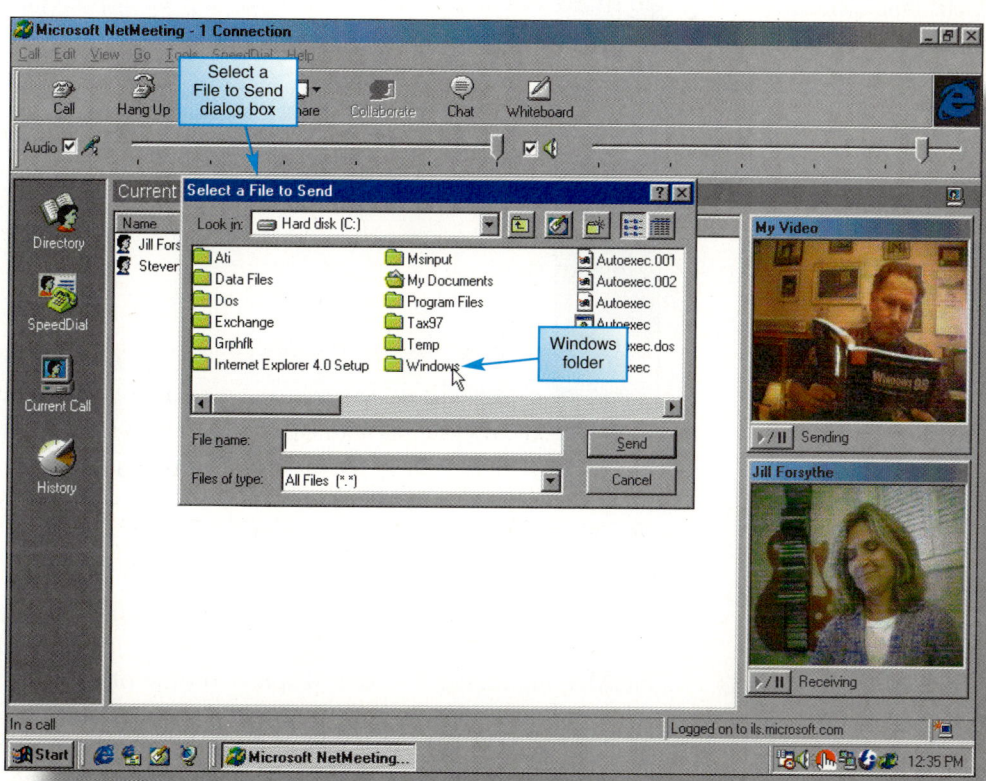

FIGURE 8-66

WIN 8.50 • Project 8 • Working with Multimedia and NetMeeting

3 **Double-click the Windows folder. Scroll the list box to display the Clouds file name, click the Clouds file name in the list box, and then point to the Send button.**

The contents of the Windows folder display in the list box and the selected Clouds file name displays in the list box (Figure 8-67).

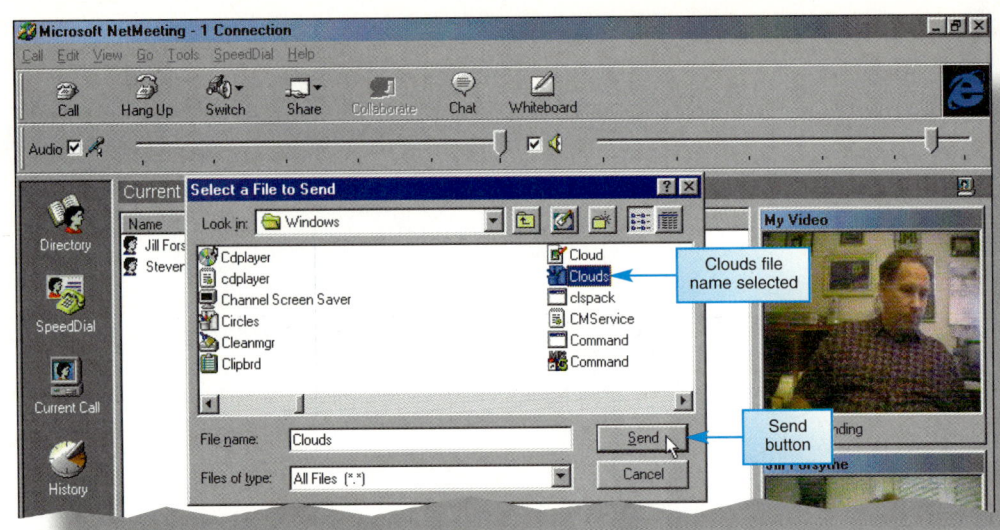

FIGURE 8-67

4 **Click the Send button and then point to the OK button in the Microsoft NetMeeting dialog box.**

NetMeeting sends the file to Jill's computer. The Microsoft NetMeeting dialog box contains the message, ('Clouds.bmp' was sent successfully.), and the OK button (Figure 8-68).

5 **Click the OK button.**

The Microsoft NetMeeting dialog box closes.

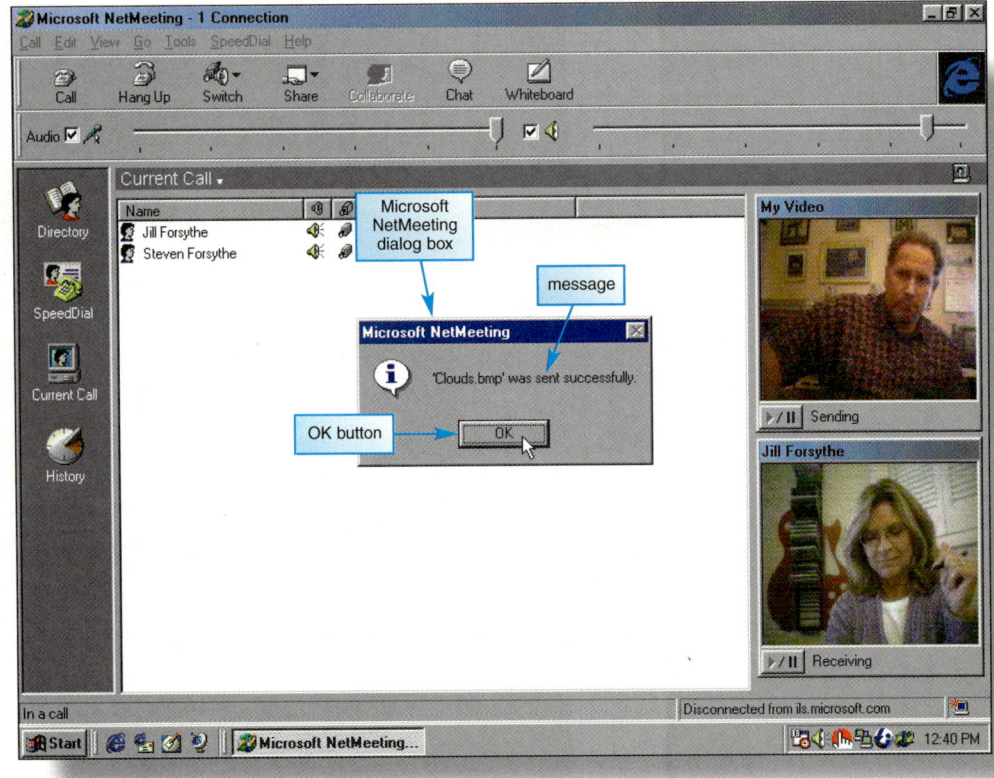

FIGURE 8-68

Other Ways

1. Right-click name in Current Call list, click Send File, select file, click Send
2. Drag file to Current Call list
3. Press CTRL+F, select file, press ENTER

When you send a file to another participant, the file you send is stored automatically in the Received Files folder on the other participant's hard disk. The Microsoft NetMeeting dialog box that displays on the other participant's desktop when you send a file contains buttons that give you the option to open the file, delete the file, or close the dialog box. If you close the dialog box, you can locate a file that was sent to you by clicking Tools on the menu bar, clicking File Transfer, and then clicking Open Received Files Folder.

Microsoft NetMeeting • WIN 8.51

Ending a Call and Quitting NetMeeting

After placing a call, chatting with another NetMeeting participant, collaborating with the participant on a drawing using Whiteboard, and sending a file to the participant, you decide it is time to end the call and the NetMeeting session. Perform the following steps to end the call, log off from the ils.microsoft.com server, and quit NetMeeting.

 To End a Call, Log Off from the Server, and Quit NetMeeting

1 **Point to the Hang Up button on the Current Call toolbar (Figure 8-69).**

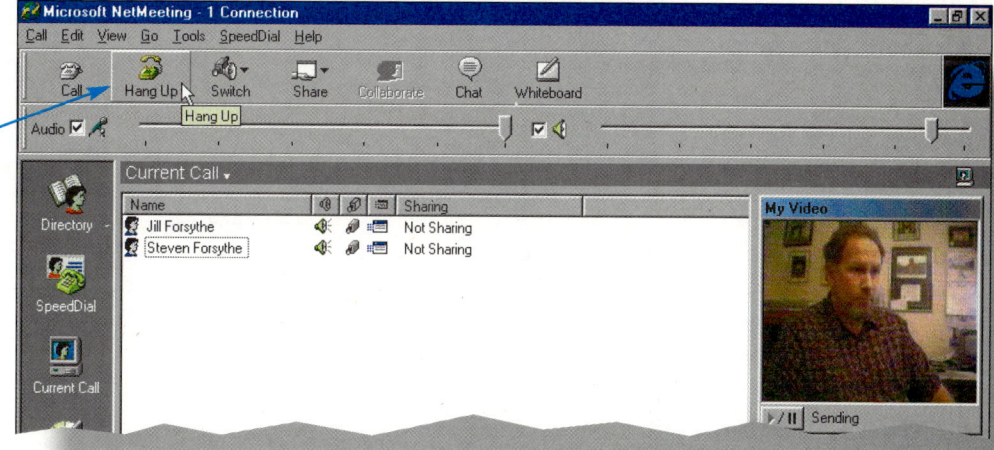

FIGURE 8-69

2 **Click the Hang Up button.**

NetMeeting ends the call, displays a message (Not in a call) at the left on the status bar, and replaces the Current Call sheet with the Directory sheet in the Microsoft NetMeeting window (Figure 8-70).

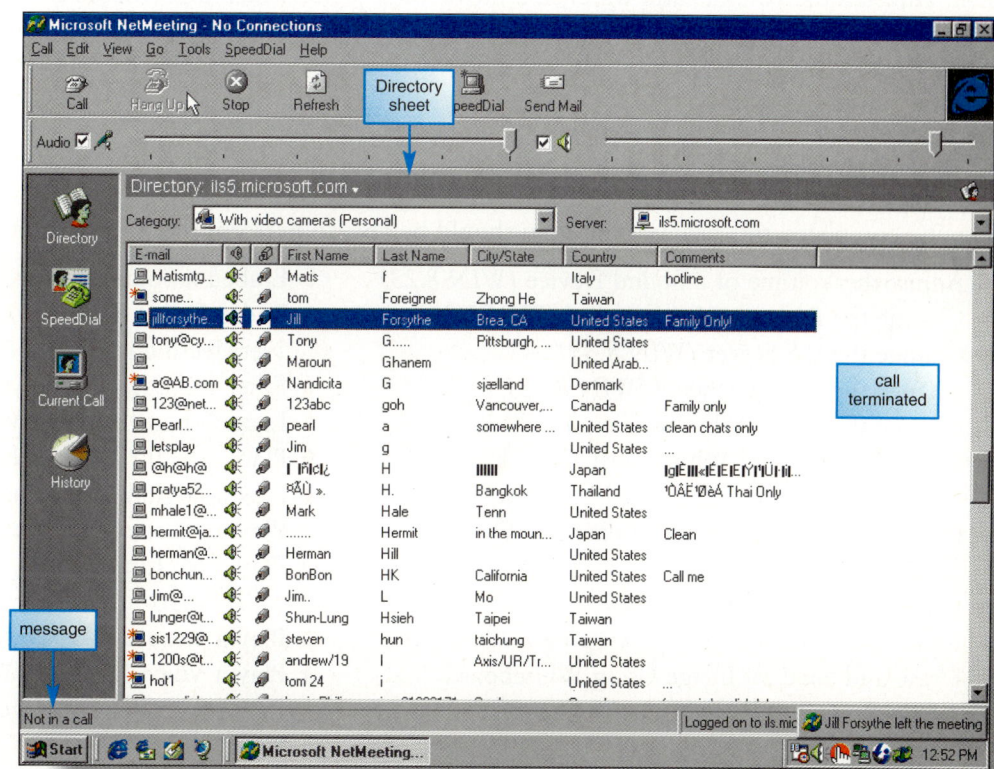

FIGURE 8-70

WIN 8.52 • **Project 8** • **Working with Multimedia and NetMeeting**

3 **Click Call on the menu bar and then point to Log Off from ils.microsoft.com on the Call menu.**

The Call menu displays (Figure 8-71).

4 **Click Log Off from ils.microsoft.com. Click the Close button in the Microsoft NetMeeting window.**

NetMeeting logs off the ils.microsoft.com server and the Microsoft NetMeeting window closes.

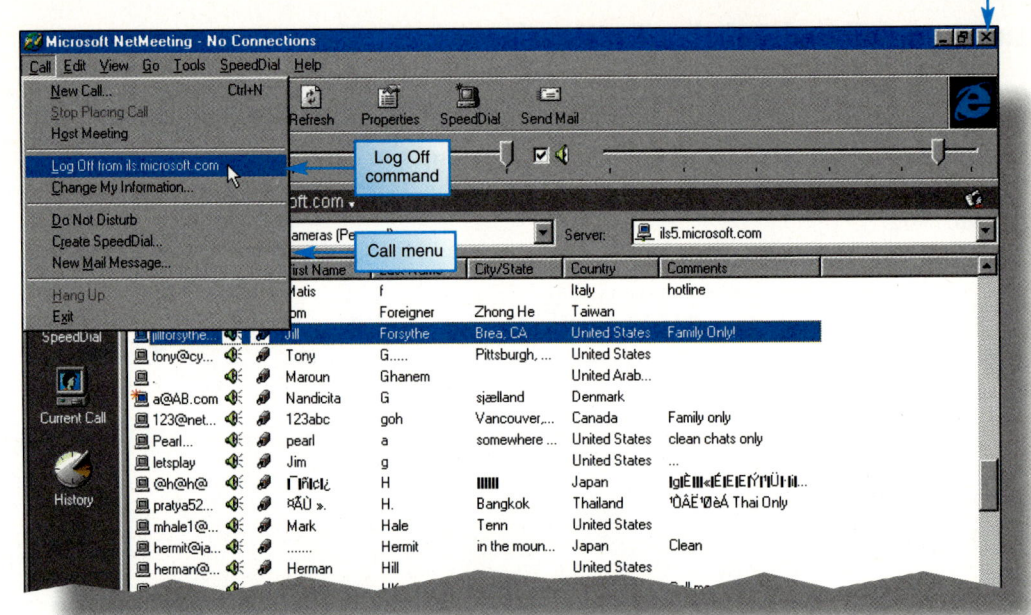

FIGURE 8-71

Project Summary

In this project, you played and recorded sound, embedded and played a recorded audio file in a document, and changed the sound scheme on your computer. You played an audio compact disc, created and edited the Play List, adjusted the volume, and watched a movie on a digital video disc. In addition, you used NetMeeting to videoconference with, send text messages to, share an application with, and send a file to another NetMeeting user.

What You Should Know

Having completed this project, you now should be able to perform the following tasks.

- Adjust the Volume of a Sound Device *(WIN 8.23)*
- Change the Directory Information *(WIN 8.36)*
- Change the ILS Server *(WIN 8.39)*
- Change the Sound Scheme *(WIN 8.13)*
- Change the Video Window View *(WIN 8.28)*
- Close the Chat and Whiteboard Windows *(WIN 8.48)*
- Close the Word and Sound Recorder Windows *(WIN 8.11)*
- Create a Play List *(WIN 8.17)*
- Delete an Icon from the Desktop *(WIN 8.12)*
- Draw and Send an Image Using Whiteboard *(WIN 8.46)*
- Edit the Play List *(WIN 8.20)*
- Eject a Compact Disc *(WIN 8.25)*
- Eject the DVD and Close the Open Windows *(WIN 8.29)*
- Embed a Sound File in a Document *(WIN 8.9)*
- End a Call, Log Off from the Server, and Quit NetMeeting *(WIN 8.51)*
- Filter the Users in the Directory List *(WIN 8.38)*
- Launch NetMeeting *(WIN 8.34)*
- Place a Call *(WIN 8.41)*
- Play a Digital Video Disc *(WIN 8.27)*
- Play an Audio Compact Disc *(WIN 8.16)*
- Play a Multimedia File Using Media Player *(WIN 8.30)*
- Play a Recorded Voice Message *(WIN 8.11)*
- Play a Voice Message *(WIN 8.8)*
- Record a Voice Message *(WIN 8.7)*
- Send a File Using File Transfer *(WIN 8.49)*
- Send a Text Message Using Chat *(WIN 8.43)*

Test Your Knowledge

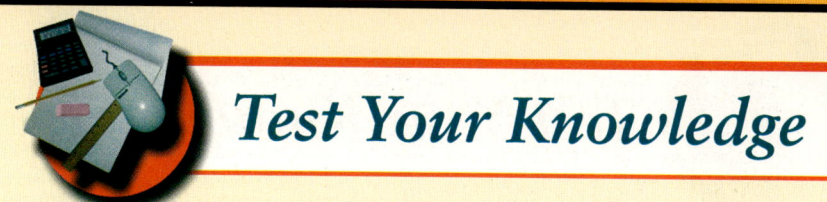

1 True/False

Instructions: Circle T if the statement is true or F if the statement is false.

T F 1. Using text and video in the same presentation is an example of multimedia.
T F 2. Microsoft NetShow allows you to engage in live videoconferences.
T F 3. When embedding a sound file in a word processing document, the sound file is the source.
T F 4. Closing a window and exiting Windows 98 are program events.
T F 5. At least two songs are stored on a single track on a compact disc.
T F 6. You cannot change the order that you play the songs on a compact disc.
T F 7. Chat allows you to send text messages to another NetMeeting user.
T F 8. When another user accepts the NetMeeting call you place, the Current Call sheet replaces the Directory sheet on your computer.
T F 9. A filter allows you to display only users with video cameras.
T F 10. Collaborating is the process of allowing another participant to work in your shared application.

2 Multiple Choice

Instructions: Circle the correct response.

1. _____ is composed of photographic images that provide the appearance of motion.
   a. Text
   b. Audio
   c. Animation
   d. Video

2. Wave files and MIDI files are _____ files.
   a. text
   b. animation
   c. audio
   d. video

3. A(n) _____ file performs the same function as sheet music.
   a. Wave
   b. MIDI
   c. MPEG
   d. AVI

4. _____ is an example of a sound scheme name.
   a. Launching Windows 98
   b. Musica
   c. Exiting Windows 98
   d. Both a and c

(continued)

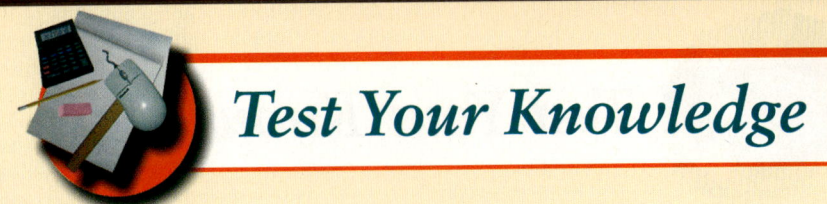

Test Your Knowledge

Multiple Choice *(continued)*

5. Moving Pictures Experts Group (MPEG) allows you to _____.
   a. compress a video file
   b. decompress an audio file
   c. compress and decompress an animation file
   d. compress a MIDI file

6. _____ allows you to play any multimedia file.
   a. DirectX
   b. CD Player
   c. Media Player
   d. Sound Recorder

7. Every computer connected to the Internet has _____.
   a. a unique e-mail address
   b. NetMeeting
   c. an ILS
   d. an IP address

8. The toolbar in the Microsoft NetMeeting - No Connections window changes when you _____.
   a. display another sheet
   b. place a call that is not accepted
   c. change your personal information
   d. change the ILS

9. Clicking the _____ button in the Microsoft NetMeeting - No Connections window displays a list of users you would like to be able to call quickly.
   a. Directory
   b. SpeedDial
   c. Current Call
   d. History

10. When you send a file to another NetMeeting participant, the file is stored in the _____ folder.
    a. Windows
    b. My Documents
    c. Received Files
    d. StartUp

3 Embedding a Sound File in a Document

Instructions: Figure 8-72 illustrates the Sound - Sound Recorder window. In the spaces provided, list the steps to embed the last sound file recorded using Sound Recorder in the Family Recording document. An icon for the Family Recording document displays on the desktop.

Test Your Knowledge • WIN 8.55

PROJECT 8

Test Your Knowledge

FIGURE 8-72

Step 1: _____
Step 2: _____
Step 3: _____
Step 4: _____
Step 5: _____

4 Using a Filter and Changing the ILS While Using NetMeeting

Instructions: In the spaces provided, list the steps to start NetMeeting, display only users who are not in a call, and change the ILS server to the ils.family.four11.com.

Steps to Start NetMeeting:

Step 1: _____
Step 2: _____
Step 3: _____
Step 4: _____

Steps to Display Users Who Are Not in a Call:

Step 1: _____
Step 2: _____

Steps to Change the ILS Server Name:

Step 1: _____
Step 2: _____

Use Help

1 Using Sound Recorder, CD Player, Volume Control, Media Player, and NetMeeting Help

Instructions: Use Help and a computer to perform the following tasks.

1. If necessary, launch Windows 98.
2. Launch Sound Recorder. Use Sound Recorder Help to answer the following questions:
   a. How do you add an echo to a sound file? _____
   b. How do you insert a sound file in another sound file? _____
   _____
3. Close the Sound Recorder Help and Sound Recorder windows.
4. Insert an audio compact disc into the CD-ROM drive. Click the CD Player button on the taskbar. Use CD Player Help to answer the following questions:
   a. How do you play tracks in random order? _____
   b. How do you customize CD Player by displaying a status bar in the CD Player window? _____
   _____
   c. How can you temporarily disable the AutoPlay feature using the SHIFT key? _____
   _____
5. Close the CD Player Help and CD Player windows.
6. Double-click the speaker icon in the tray status area. Use Volume Control Help to answer the following question:
   a. In the Volume Control window, how do you display a recording device that does not display currently in the window? _____
7. Close the Volume Control Help and Volume Control windows.
8. Launch Media Player. Use Media Player Help to answer the following questions.
   a. How do you automatically rewind a multimedia file? _____
   b. How do you copy a multimedia file into a document? _____
9. Close the Media Player Help and Media Player windows.
10. Launch NetMeeting. Use NetMeeting Help to answer the following questions.
    a. When would you want to send a text message to another participant? _____
    _____
    b. Under what two conditions is a user's name added to the SpeedDial list? _____
    _____
    c. How do you manually add a name to your SpeedDial list? _____
    d. How do you find a file sent to you by another participant? _____

In the Lab

1 Recording, Playing, and Embedding Voice Messages

Instructions: You would like to create a sound file containing a Happy Birthday message, attach the sound file to an e-mail message, and send the e-mail to Steven Forsythe (one of the authors of this book). The author will make every attempt to reply to your e-mail message. Perform the following steps to create a sound file containing the Happy Birthday message, save the sound file on the desktop, launch Outlook Express, compose an e-mail message, attach the sound file to the e-mail message, and send the message. To perform this lab assignment, your computer must have a sound card, speakers, and a microphone.

Part 1: Creating a Voice Message to Attach to the E-mail

1. If necessary, launch Windows 98 and connect to the Internet.
2. Click the Start button on the taskbar, point to Programs, point to Accessories, point to Entertainment, and then click Sound Recorder.
3. Click the Record button. Using the microphone, sing the following song: Happy birthday to you, Happy birthday to you, Happy birthday dear Steven, Happy birthday to you.
4. When you have finished singing the song, click the Stop button.
5. Play the message by clicking the Play button in the Sound - Sound Recorder window.

Part 2: Saving the Voice Message on the Desktop

1. Click File on the menu bar and then click Save As.
2. Type Happy Birthday Steven in the File name text box.
3. Click the Save in box arrow and then click Desktop in the Save in list box.
4. Click the Save button.
5. Click the Close button in the Happy Birthday Steven - Sound Recorder window.

Part 3: Launching Outlook Express and Creating an E-mail Message

1. Click the Launch Outlook Express icon on the Quick Launch toolbar.
2. Click the Compose Message button on the toolbar.
3. Type StevenForsythe@msn.com in the To text box. Type Project 8 - In the Lab Assignment 1 - followed by your city and state separated by a comma (example: Brea, California) in the Subject text box.
4. In the message pane, type Happy Birthday Steven. and press the ENTER key twice. Type From and press the SPACEBAR. Type your first and last name and press the ENTER key twice. Type Please double-click the icon below for your birthday surprise: and press the ENTER key twice.

Part 4: Attaching the Sound File to the E-mail Message

1. Click the Insert File button (identified by the paper clip icon) on the toolbar.
2. Click the Look in box arrow, click Desktop, click the Happy Birthday Steven icon, and click the Attach button. A sound icon should display in your e-mail message.

Part 5: Sending the E-mail Message

1. Click the Send button on the toolbar.
2. Click the Close button in the Inbox - Outlook Express window.
3. Drag the Happy Birthday Steven icon from the desktop to the Recycle Bin.
4. Click the Yes button in the Confirm File Delete dialog box.
5. Quit Windows 98.

In the Lab

2 Creating a Customized Sound Scheme for Your Computer

Instructions: You would like to create a personalized sound scheme for your computer. To do so, you decide to record two messages in your own voice and assign each message to a program event. The first message (the window is minimized) is associated with the Minimize program event and the second message (the window is maximized) is associated with the Maximize program event. You name and save the new sound scheme. Perform the following steps to record two voice messages, assign each message to a program event, and save the new sound scheme. To perform this lab assignment, your computer must have a sound card, speakers, and a microphone.

Part 1: Creating and Saving the First Voice Message

1. If necessary, launch Windows 98.
2. Click the Start button on the taskbar, point to Programs, point to Accessories, point to Entertainment, and then click Sound Recorder.
3. Click the Record button. Using the microphone, read the following message: <u>The window is minimized</u>.
4. When you have finished reading the message, click the Stop button.
5. Play the message by clicking the Play button in the Sound - Sound Recorder window.
6. Click File on the menu bar and then click Save As.
7. Type `Minimize Your Window` in the File name text box.
8. Click the Save in box arrow and then click Desktop in the Save in list box.
9. Click the Save button.

Part 2: Creating and Saving the Second Voice Message

1. Click File on the menu bar and then click New.
2. Click the Record button. Using the microphone, read the following message: <u>The window is maximized</u>.
3. When you have finished reading the message, click the Stop button.
4. Play the message by clicking the Play button in the Sound - Sound Recorder window.
5. Click File on the menu bar and then click Save As.
6. Type `Maximize Your Window` in the File name text box.
7. Click the Save button.
8. Click the Close button in the Maximize Your Window - Sound window.

Part 3: Assigning the Recorded Messages to Program Events

1. Click the Start button on the taskbar, point to Settings, and click Control Panel on the Settings submenu.
2. Double-click the Sounds icon.
3. Write down on a piece of paper, the sound scheme name in the Scheme box.
4. Scroll the Events list box to display the Minimize event and then click the Minimize event.
5. Click the Browse button, click the Look in box arrow, click Desktop, click Minimize Your Window in the Look in list box, and then click the OK button.
6. Scroll the Events list box to display the Maximize event and then click the Maximize event.
7. Click the Browse button, click Maximize Your Window in the Look in list box, and then click the OK button.

In the Lab

8. Click the Save As button, type My Sound Scheme in the Save this sound scheme as text box, and then click the OK button.
9. Click the OK button in the Sounds Properties dialog box.

Part 4: *Testing the New Sound Scheme*

1. Maximize the Control Panel window.
2. Restore the Control Panel window.
3. Minimize the Control Panel window.

Part 5: *Removing the New Sound Scheme*

1. Click the Control Panel button in the taskbar button area.
2. Double-click the Sounds icon.
3. Verify My Sound Scheme displays in the Schemes box.
4. Click the Delete button. Click the Yes button in the Scheme dialog box to remove the sound scheme.
5. Click the Schemes box arrow.
6. Click the sound scheme name you wrote down in the Schemes list box in Part 3, Step 3.
7. Click the OK button in the Sounds Properties dialog box. Click the Close button in the Control Panel window.

3 Using NetMeeting

Instructions: You think that NetMeeting is the wave of the future for videoconferencing. You have found NetMeeting easy to use, inexpensive, and entertaining. You decide to use NetMeeting to place a call to various NetMeeting users. If you are in a computer lab environment, you may want to arrange to place a call to another student in the lab. Perform the following steps to launch NetMeeting and place calls to various individuals listed in the directory list.

WARNING! Not everyone who uses NetMeeting has business purposes in mind and many people who use NetMeeting are open and frank about the type of communication they want. Some areas may contain violent or sexually-explicit content. Content Advisor, a program available with Internet Explorer that provides a way to help control the types of content that your computer can access on the Internet, is not available in NetMeeting. Consequently, you may want to discourage children or family members from using NetMeeting.

Part 1: *Launch NetMeeting*

1. If necessary, connect to the Internet.
2. Click the Start button on the taskbar, point to Programs, point to Internet Explorer, and then click Microsoft NetMeeting.

Part 2: *Enter Your Directory Information*

1. Click Call on the menu bar and then click Change My Information.
2. Type your first name in the First name text box. Type your last name in the Last name text box. Type your e-mail address in the E-mail address text box. Type your city and state in the City/State text box.

(continued)

In the Lab

Using NetMeeting *(continued)*

3. Select your country in the Country box. Type a comment in the Comments text box.
4. Click the For personal use (suitable for all ages) option button.
5. Click the OK button in the Options dialog box.

Part 3: *Place a Call to Someone Who Has Computer Speakers*

1. Click the Category box arrow in the Directory sheet and then click Not in a Call.
2. Click the Server box arrow in the Directory sheet and then click ils1.microsoft.com.
3. Scroll the directory list until you find a name for a user who has computer speakers but does not have a video camera.
4. Double-click the name.
5. If the person accepts your call, begin the conversation by explaining who you are, where you live, and why you placed the call.
6. In the spaces provided, record interesting information (name, age, home town, school name and location, hobbies, sisters and brothers, and so on) about the individual to whom you are talking.

_____
_____
_____
_____

7. When finished talking, click the Hang Up button on the Current Call toolbar to end the conversation.

Part 4: *Placing a Call to Someone Who Lives in Your State*

1. Click the Server box arrow in the Directory sheet and then click ils3.microsoft.com.
2. Click the City/State column header button to sort the names in the directory list by city/state.
3. Scroll the directory list until you find an individual who lives in your state.
4. Double-click the name.
5. If the person accepts your call, begin the conversation by explaining who you are, where you live, and why you placed the call.
6. In the spaces provided, record interesting information about the individual to whom you are talking.

_____
_____
_____
_____

7. When finished talking, click the Hang Up button on the Current Call toolbar to end the conversation.

Part 5: *Place a Call to Someone in a Foreign Country*

1. Click the Server box arrow in the Directory sheet and then click ils5.microsoft.com.
2. Click the Country header button to sort the names in the directory list by country.
3. Scroll the directory list until you find an individual who lives in Canada.
4. Double-click the name.

In the Lab

5. If the person accepts your call, begin the conversation by explaining who you are, where you live, and why you placed the call.
6. In the spaces provided, record interesting information about the individual to whom you are talking.

_____
_____
_____

7. When finished talking, click the Hang Up button on the Current Call toolbar to end the conversation.

Part 6: Place a Call to Someone with a Video Camera
1. Click the Category box arrow in the Directory sheet and then click With video cameras (Personal).
2. Click the Server box arrow in the Directory sheet and then click ils.family.four11.com.
3. Scroll the directory list until you find a name that contains an interesting comment.
4. Double-click the name.
5. If the person accepts your call, begin the conversation by explaining who you are, where you live, and why you placed the call.
6. In the spaces provided, record interesting information about the individual to whom you are talking.

_____
_____
_____
_____

7. When finished talking, click the Hang Up button on the Current Call toolbar to end the conversation.
8. Click the Close button in the Microsoft NetMeeting - No Connections window.

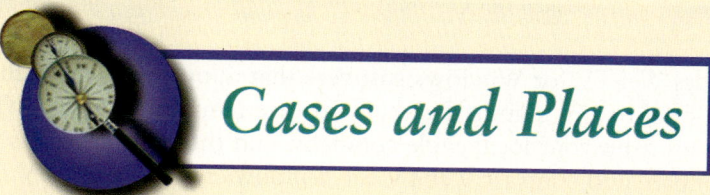

Cases and Places

The difficulty of these case studies varies: ▶ are the least difficult; ▶▶ are more difficult; and ▶▶▶ are the most difficult.

1 ▶ Audio is stored in two types of files (Wave and MIDI) on a computer. Search your hard disk and the Internet for Wave and MIDI files (.wav and .mid file extensions). Create a folder on the desktop and save copies of the files you found in the folder. In a class presentation, explain the difference between the two types of files and then illustrate the difference by playing some of the more interesting files you found. Use Sound Player or Media Player to play the files.

Cases and Places

2 ▶ You can play a compact disc or a digital video disc on a DVD drive but you cannot play a digital video disc on a CD-ROM drive. To understand this statement, investigate how music (audio) is stored on a compact disc and how a movie (audio and video) is stored on a digital video disc. In a brief report, summarize your findings. Include drawings to illustrate how the data is stored and try to answer the question, Why will a digital video disc not play on a CD-ROM drive?

3 ▶▶ Until recently, you could purchase CDs from a retail store (MTS, Inc./Tower Records, Wal-Mart Stores, Inc., and so on) or through the mail (BMG Music Service and The Columbia House Company). Today, you can purchase CDs using the Internet. Using an Internet browser (Microsoft® Internet Explorer or Netscape® Communicator) and a search service (Yahoo!, AltaVista, Infoseek, and so on), search for three Web sites that sell compact discs. Select three audio CDs that you like and compare their prices when purchased from a retail store, mail order company, and Web site. Remember to include shipping and handling charges in the price of a CD. Write a brief report to present your findings.

4 ▶▶ NetMeeting allows you to log on to and display the directory list for nine ILS servers. Microsoft owns and operates six of those servers. Conservative users have expressed concerns that some users try to disguise their identities by displaying false information in the First Name, Last Name, City/State, and Comments columns. In a brief report, summarize the reasons for correctly identifying yourself on the Internet, problems that result when users disguise their identities, who you think is responsible, and what can be done to prevent this problem.

5 ▶▶▶ Visit a music-recording studio to learn how musicians and music producers use computers to play and record music. Explain how musical instruments have changed because of computers and how the process of recording music on CDs has affected music and the music industry. Summarize your findings in a brief report.

6 ▶▶▶ Windows 98 includes WebTV for Windows software that allows you to watch television on your personal computer. In a brief report, summarize the hardware required to use WebTV, the steps to download program listings from your local cable company, and the procedure to select and watch a television program. Compare and contrast WebTV for Windows with the WebTV designed for use with your television set.

7 ▶▶▶ Visit a large company that uses videoconferencing to communicate over long distances. Interview at least two people who use videoconferencing to determine why they use videoconferencing, the videoconferencing software they use, the hardware required, and any problems they have experienced while using the software. Summarize your findings in a brief report.

Microsoft Windows 98

Maintaining and Optimizing Your Computer and System Registry

Objectives

You will have mastered the material in this project when you can:

- Back up files on a disk using Backup
- Restore a backup file
- Explain the Windows 98 file system
- Describe the file allocation table (FAT)
- Scan the hard disk for errors using ScanDisk
- Delete unnecessary files on the hard disk using Disk Cleanup
- Defragment the files on the disk using Disk Defragmenter
- Schedule routine maintenance using the Maintenance wizard
- View the scheduled tasks using Task Scheduler
- Display the Windows Update home page
- Check for and download components using Product Updates
- Make a backup copy of the system registry using Registry Checker
- View and modify the system registry using Registry Editor
- Describe Drive Converter and other system tools

Microsoft **Windows 98**

Won't You Please, Please Help Me?

Registry Checker and Techies Find and Fix Glitches

Go ahead, admit it. You are starting to feel comfortable working with Windows 98, right? You have worked through eight comprehensive projects in this textbook, and you now know the ins and outs of tweaking Microsoft's latest operating system to your specifications. Change the desktop? No problem. Connect to the Net? It's a snap.

Suppose for just a moment, that something goes awry. Your computer will not boot, or the fonts will not display, or you cannot connect to the Internet. After many stressful attempts at using all the skills you have learned thus far to troubleshoot the problems, you settle down with Registry Checker, which is the Windows 98 system maintenance program that finds and fixes registry problems.

The registry contains all the hardware and software settings for your computer, including information about the programs you use and how you have configured your system. You will learn the intricacies of the registry when you work through the exercises in this project.

Each time you start your computer, Windows 98 uses Registry Checker to make a backup file of the entire registry database. If Registry Checker finds a corrupted registry file, it automatically will attempt to use the backup copy or repair itself.

As a last resort, you can modify entries in the registry database using Registry Editor, which is an advanced tool that enables you to change settings in your system registry. *A word of caution:* Do not edit your registry unless it is necessary. An error in your registry can cause your computer to become nonfunctional.

If after taking your best shot at solving the problem and nothing works, your next step may be to contact technical support for some encouragement – and some helpful advice.

Several flavors of tech support exist, and you need to find the service that best matches your timeframe and your wallet. Most computer manufacturers offer free 24-hour support for a limited time after you have bought their systems. This service sometimes ends as early as two months after you have taken delivery, and then you must pay on a per-incident basis. Be prepared to face lengthy hold times and inconsistent levels of technician knowledge and assistance.

Some computer vendors offer services other than traditional telephone support. For example, you can call their fax-on-demand support number and select a ready-made *cheat sheet* of possible glitch fixes. If you can connect to the Internet, their Web sites and forums address common questions, supply downloadable patches and upgrades, and other diagnostic services through your modem.

Finally, you can try third-party technical support services that may charge upwards of $2.50 per minute, or you can visit a neighborhood computer repair shop.

Although you hope the registry will resolve your computer problems, it is helpful to know where to turn for assistance and comforting to recognize that help is on the way.

Microsoft Windows 98

Maintaining and Optimizing Your Computer and System Registry

PROJECT 9

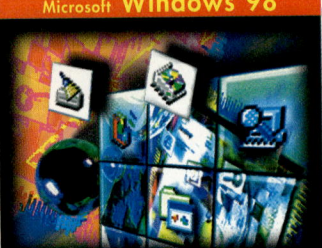

Case Perspective

After upgrading the operating system from Windows 95 to Windows 98, you notice the hard disk seems to work longer when you launch an application or search for a file. A friend of yours recommends that you scan and defragment the hard disk. Being unfamiliar with these terms, you decide to look in the stack of computer magazines that have accumulated in the closet for articles about Windows 98. Of particular interest are the "Maintaining Your Computer", "Optimizing the Performance of Your Computer", and "Understanding the System Registry" articles.

By reading these articles you learn about scheduling routine maintenance, backing up a hard disk, checking for and downloading software upgrades and device drivers, and organizing the system registry. Your goal in this project is to use this information to make the computer run smoother and faster.

Introduction

The importance of maintaining and optimizing the performance of a computer system cannot be overstated. When a computer requires increasingly longer times to perform operations such as starting an application or searching for a file, problems may exist with the hard disk. Problems may develop with the file system that places files on the hard disk, the physical surface of the hard disk, the organization of files on the hard disk, or unnecessary files left on the hard disk.

In this project, you will use several of the Windows 98 system tools to perform maintenance on a computer. These tools allow you to scan the hard disk for errors, delete unnecessary files, and reorganize the files. You will use a wizard to schedule and perform these maintenance operations at regular intervals when the computer is not being used. Also, you will automate the process of updating system files, device drivers, and software components by downloading these components from the Internet when new versions or releases become available.

Central to the operation of the Windows 98 operating system is the system registry. The **system registry** is a central location for information about hardware and software that the operating system requires to operate properly. In this project, you will view the organization of the system registry, back up the system registry, and modify settings in the system registry.

Backing Up and Restoring Files

A frustrating experience while working with a computer is to lose data stored on the hard disk. Almost everyone has heard a story about someone who lost a file and spent hours recovering the lost information. Although Windows 98 cannot prevent accidents from occurring, taking proper steps will ensure you can recover lost information when an accident happens.

Using Backup to Back Up Selected Files on the Hard Disk

Backup, a Windows 98 system tool, allows you to select files, folders, or the entire hard disk, create a backup file to contain the files, and save the backup file on a storage device or another computer on the network. Storage devices include floppy disk, tape drive, hard disk, CD-ROM, or removable hard disk. If a file becomes damaged or lost, you can restore the file using the backup file created by Backup.

In previous projects, you used a wizard to customize a folder, install new hardware, and install a printer. To guide you through the process of backing up files, Windows 98 allows you to use the Backup wizard. The **Backup wizard** assists you in selecting the files to back up, choosing the name and location of the backup file to contain the files, setting the options to perform the backup procedure, and performing the backup procedure.

To illustrate the use of the Backup wizard, you will back up the files in the My Documents folder to a file on the floppy disk in drive A. Perform the following steps to back up the files in the My Documents folder.

More About

Backing Up a Disk

Backup determines which files on a disk to back up by checking the archive attribute of each file on the disk. The archive attribute indicates if a file has changed since the last backup. When Backup detects a file that has changed, Backup backs up the file. You can view the archive attribute of a file in the Properties dialog box of the file.

 To Back Up the Files in a Folder on a Floppy Disk

1 Insert a formatted floppy disk in drive A.

2 Click the Start button, point to Programs, point to Accessories, point to System Tools, and then point to Backup.

The Start menu, Programs submenu, Accessories submenu, and System Tools submenu display (Figure 9-1). The highlighted Backup command displays on the System Tools submenu.

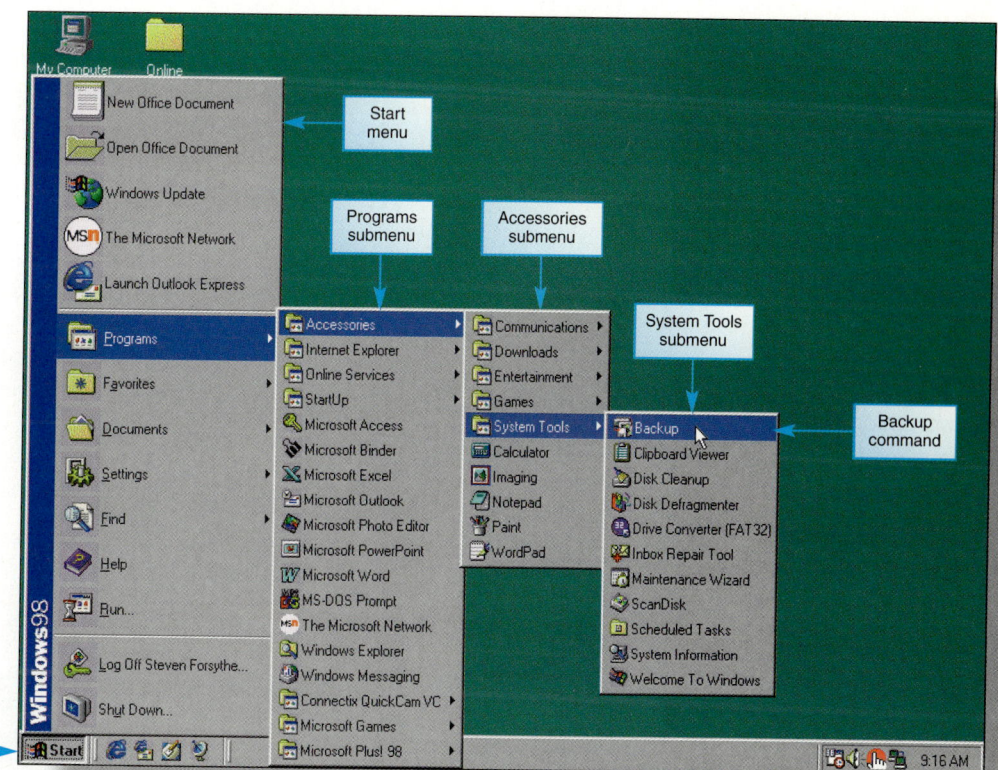

FIGURE 9-1

WIN 9.6 • Project 9 • Maintaining and Optimizing Your Computer and System Registry

3 Click Backup and then point to the OK button in the Microsoft Backup dialog box.

The Microsoft Backup - [Untitled] window and the Microsoft Backup dialog box display (Figure 9-2). The dialog box contains messages and three option buttons. The Create a new backup job option button is selected.

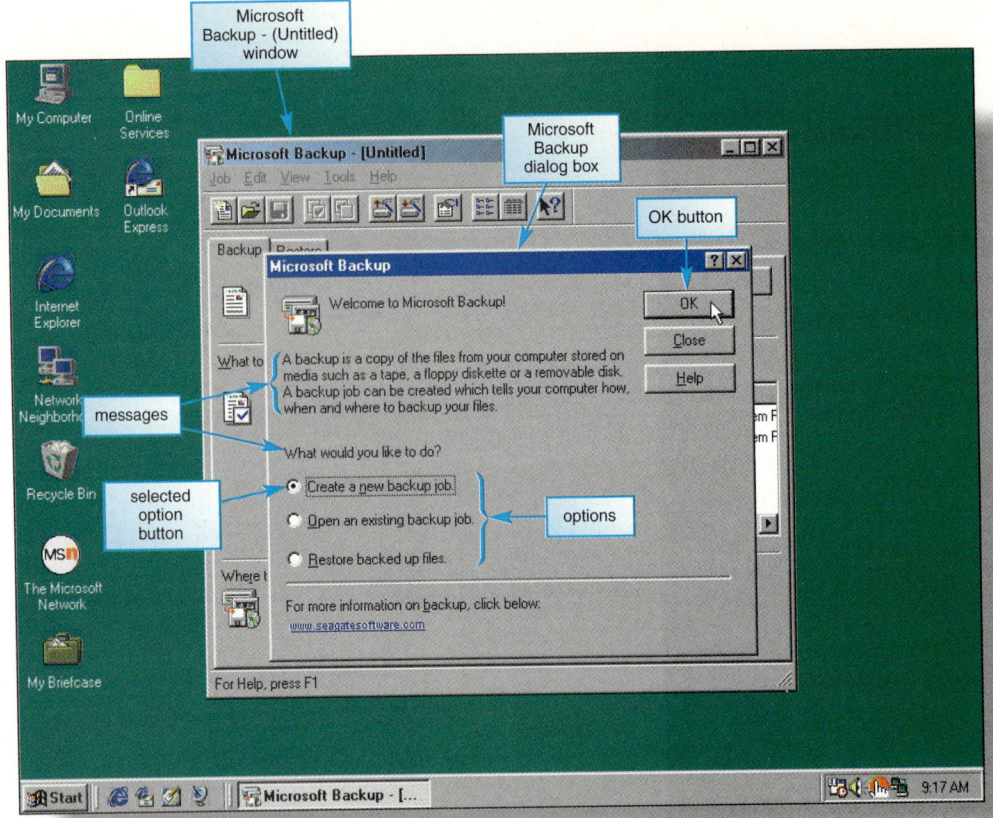

FIGURE 9-2

4 Click the OK button, click Back up selected files, folders and drives, and then point to the Next button in the Backup Wizard dialog box.

The Backup Wizard dialog box displays (Figure 9-3). The dialog box contains a title (What to back up), a message, two option buttons, and four command buttons. The Back up selected files, folders, and drives option button is selected.

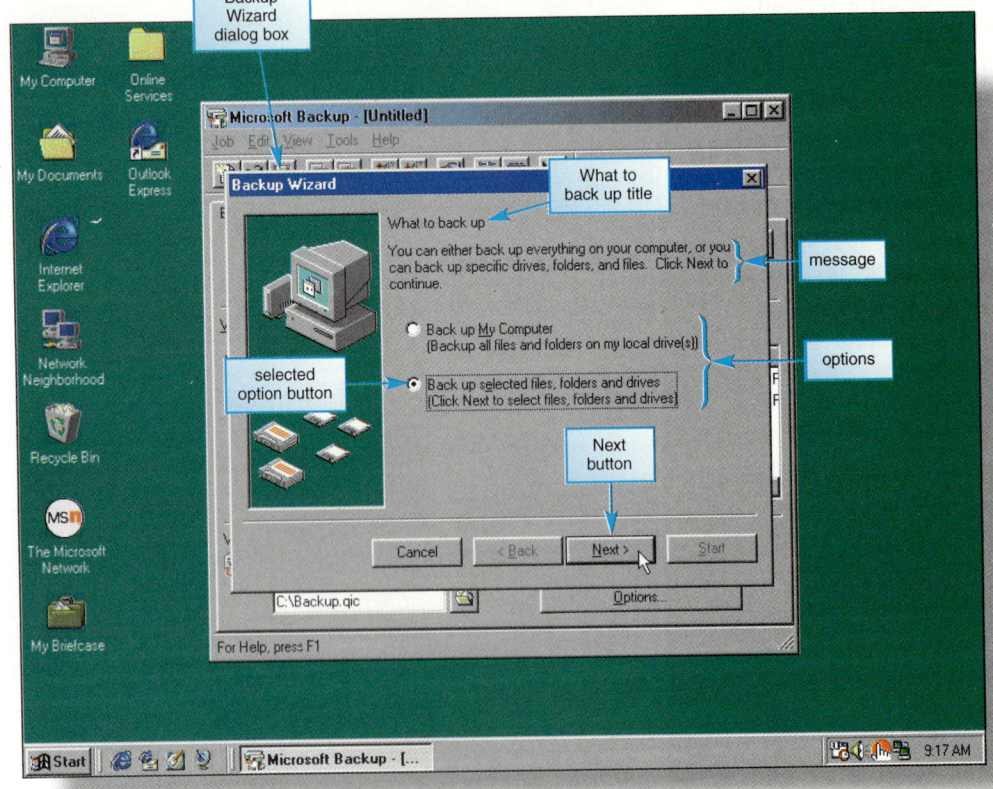

FIGURE 9-3

Backing Up and Restoring Files • WIN 9.7

5 **Click the Next button and then point to the plus sign to the left of C: - [Hard disk] in the left pane of the Backup Wizard dialog box.**

Two panes display in the Backup Wizard dialog box (Figure 9-4). The left pane contains a hierarchy of the items on the computer. Each entry below My Computer consists of a plus sign, check box, icon, and icon name. The right pane contains the contents of the Desktop folder.

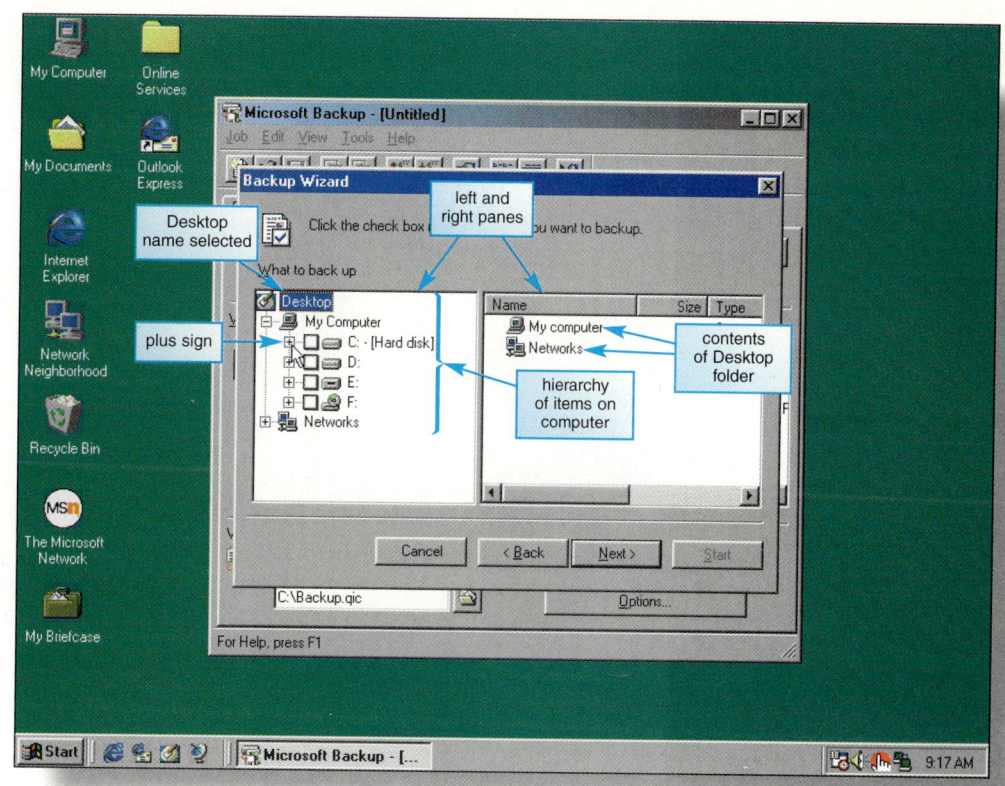

FIGURE 9-4

6 **Click the plus sign, click the check box to the left of the My Documents icon, and then point to the Next button.**

The hierarchy below the C: - [Hard disk] icon expands to display a partial list of the folders on drive C (Figure 9-5). A *blue check mark* in the My Documents check box indicates Backup will back up the entire contents of the folder.

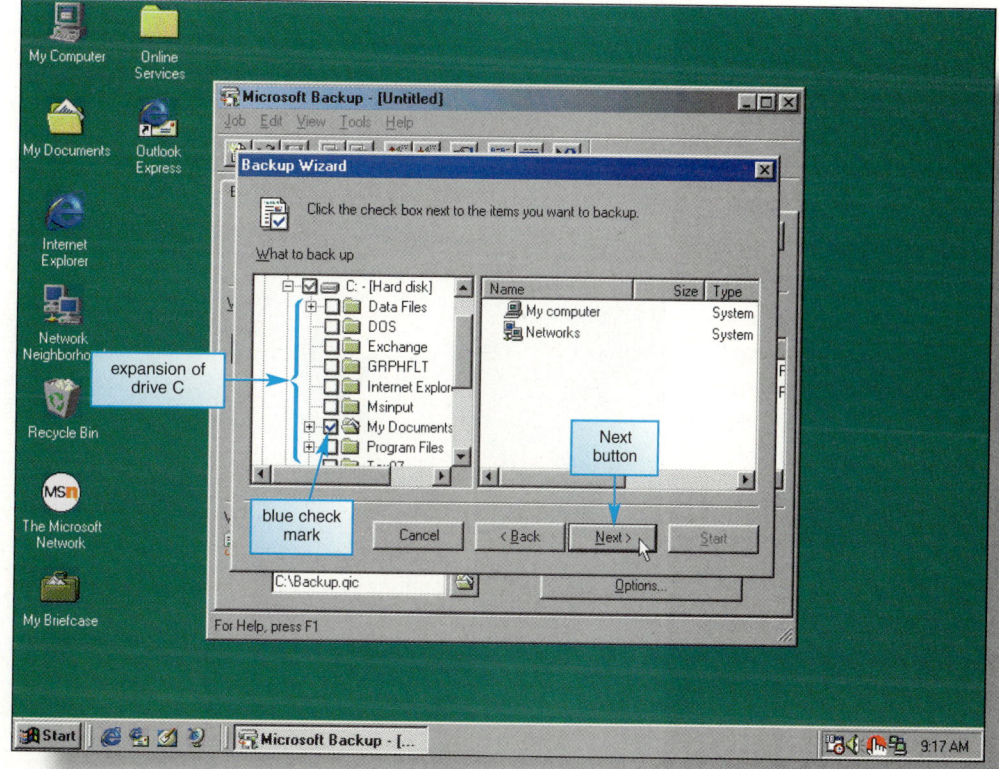

FIGURE 9-5

7 Click the Next button and then point to the Next button in the Backup Wizard dialog box.

A message and two option buttons display in the Backup Wizard dialog box (Figure 9-6). The All selected files option button is selected.

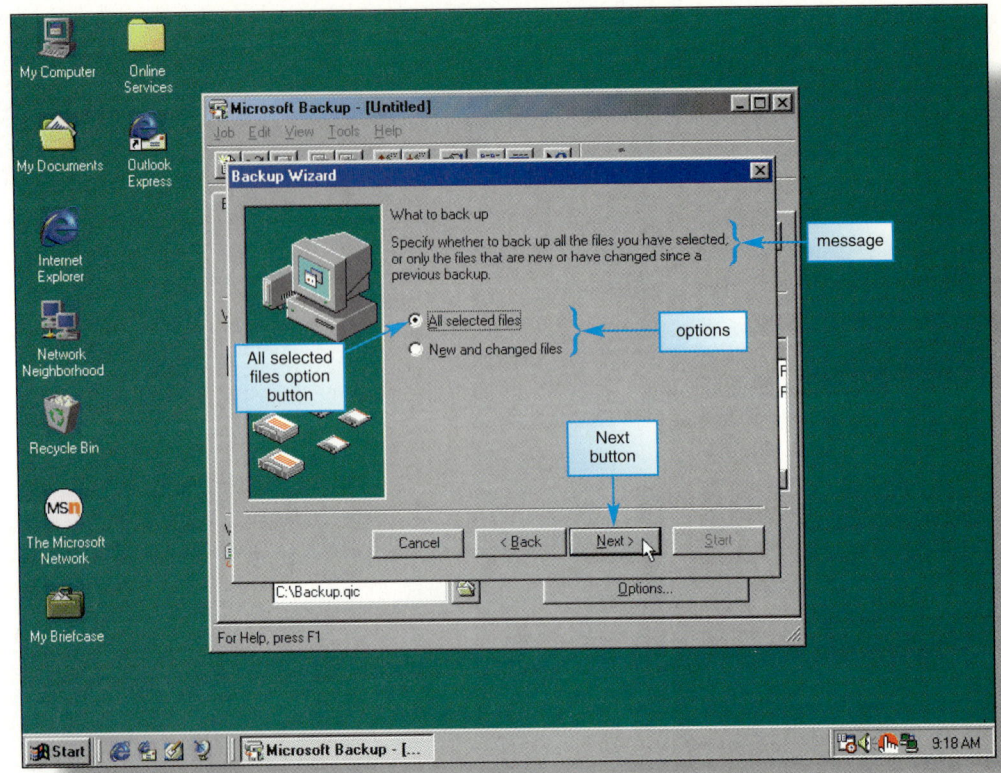

FIGURE 9-6

8 Click the Next button and then point to the Browse button in the Backup Wizard dialog box.

A new title (Where to back up), new message, and the Where to back up box and text box display in the dialog box (Figure 9-7). The Where to back up box contains the destination and the text box contains the location and file name to use to back up the files in the My Document folder. The Browse button displays to the right of the text box.

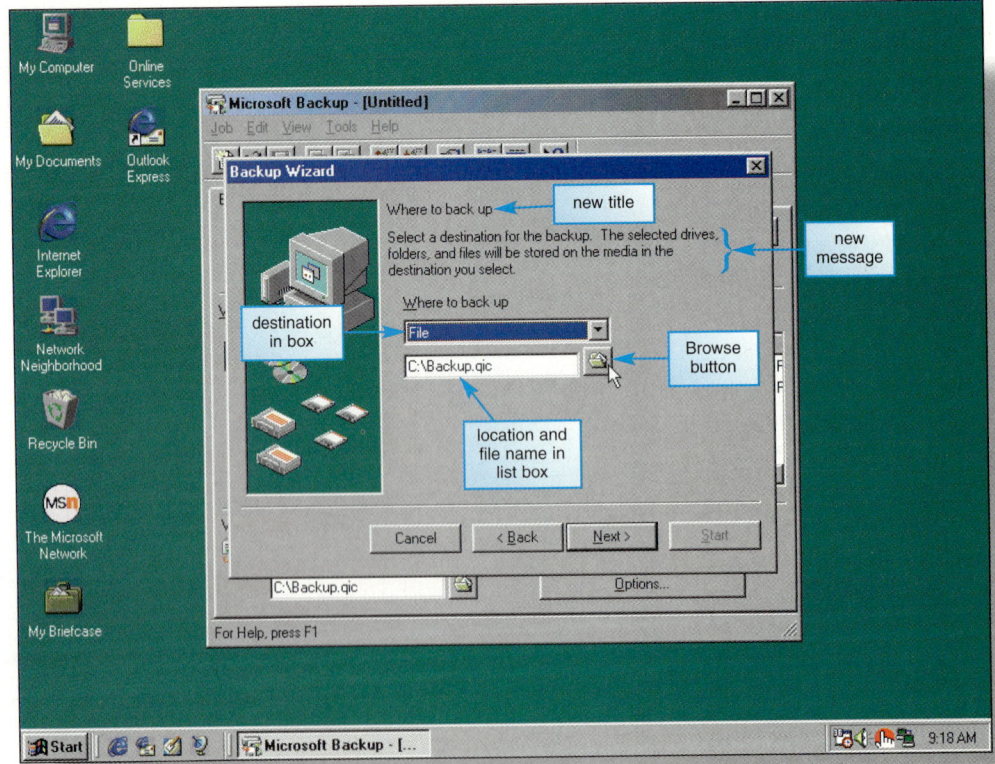

FIGURE 9-7

Backing Up and Restoring Files • WIN 9.9

9 **Click the Browse button, click the Look in box arrow in the Where to back up dialog box, and then point to 3½ Floppy (A:) in the Look in list box.**

The Where to back up dialog box displays (Figure 9-8). The Look in list box contains the highlighted 3½ Floppy (A:) name.

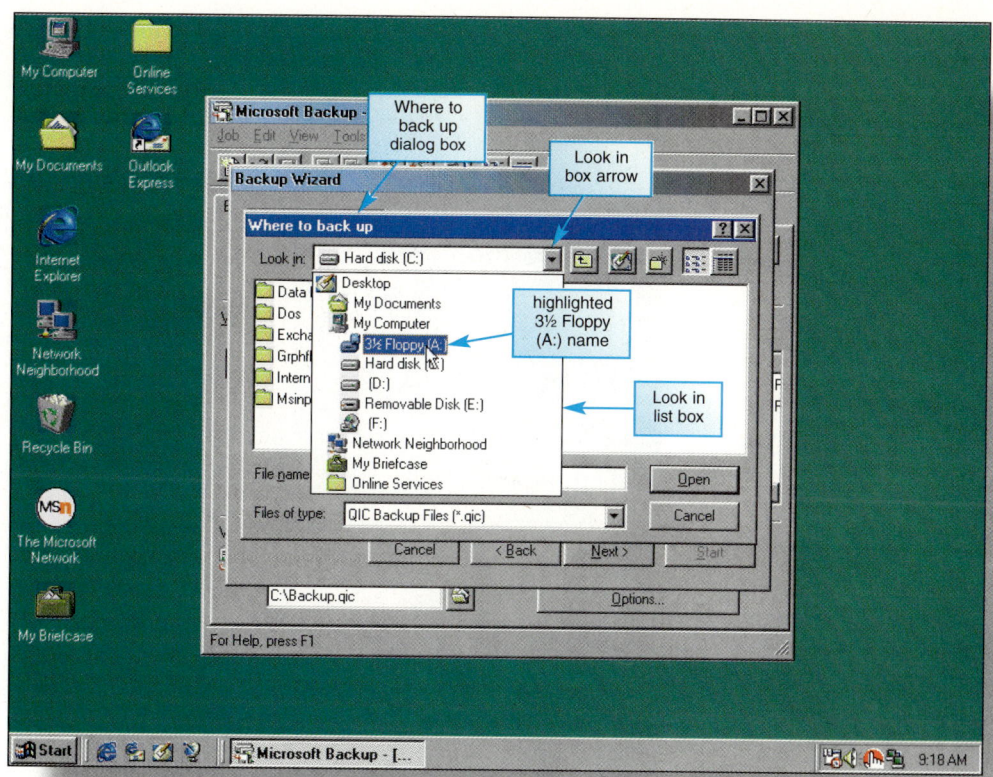

FIGURE 9-8

10 **Click 3½ Floppy (A:), double-click the File name text box, type** My Documents Folder **in the text box, and then point to the Open button.**

The 3½ Floppy (A:) name displays in the Look in box, My Documents Folder file name displays in the File name text box, and QIC Backup Files (*.qic) file type displays in the Files of type box (Figure 9-9). The list box is empty.

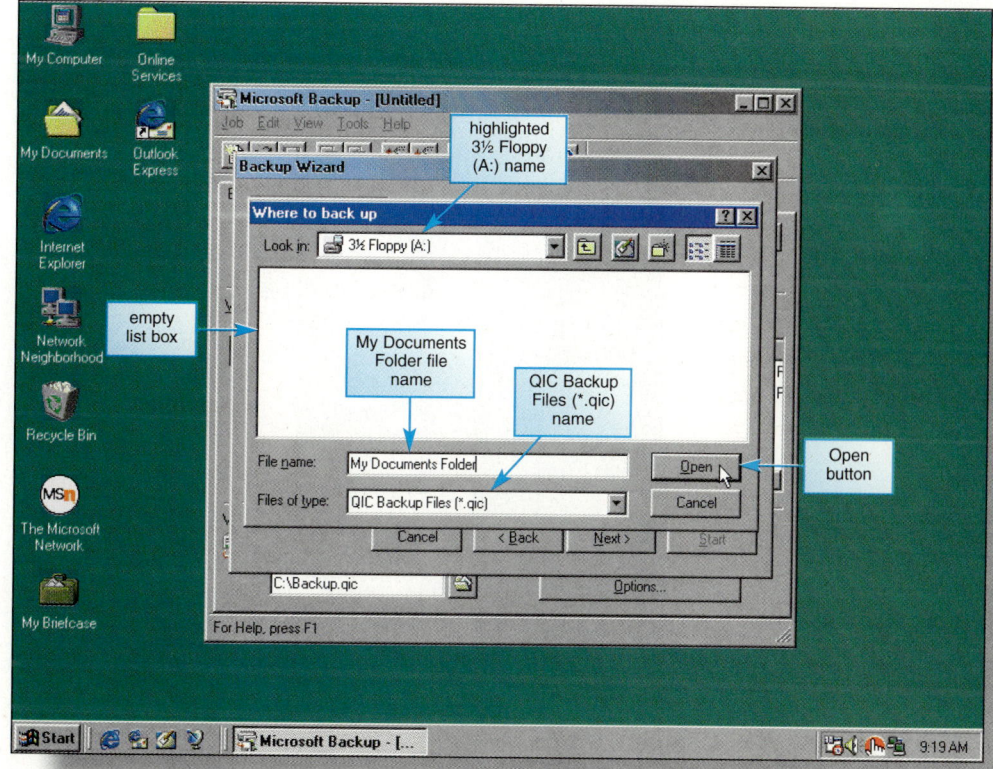

FIGURE 9-9

WIN 9.10 • Project 9 • Maintaining and Optimizing Your Computer and System Registry

11 **Click the Open button and then point to the Next button in the Backup Wizard dialog box.**

The Where to back up dialog box closes (Figure 9-10). The highlighted A:\My Documents Folder.qic name displays in the text box.

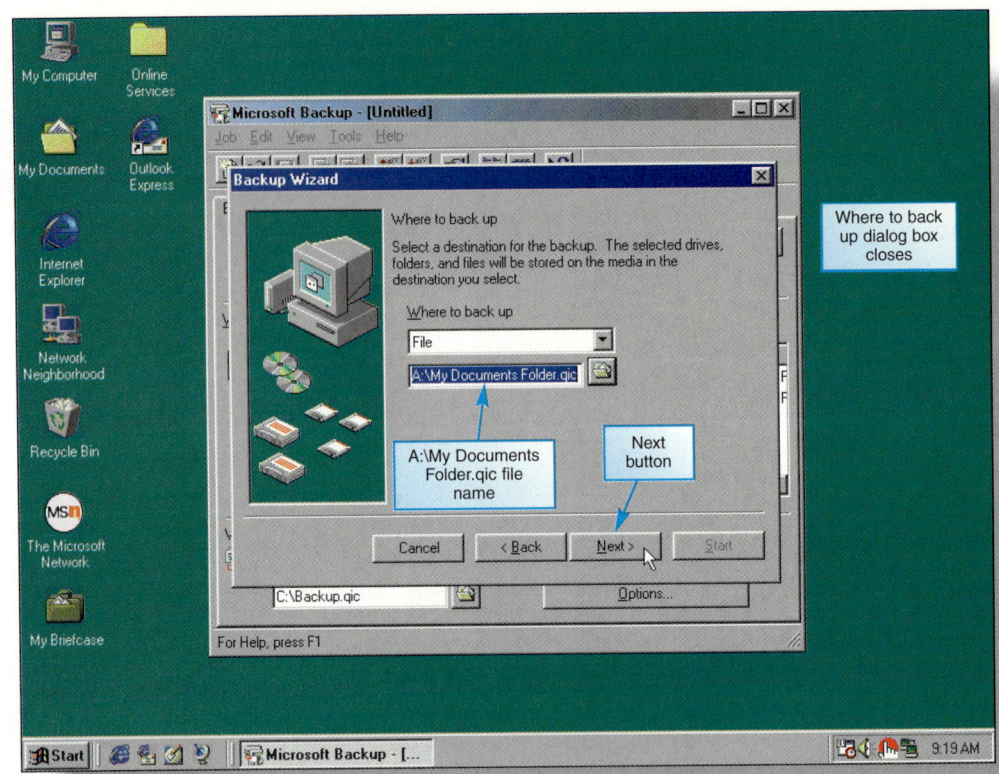

FIGURE 9-10

12 **Click the Next button and then point to the Next button in the Backup Wizard dialog box.**

A new title (How to back up), a new message, and two options display in the dialog box (Figure 9-11). Both check boxes are selected.

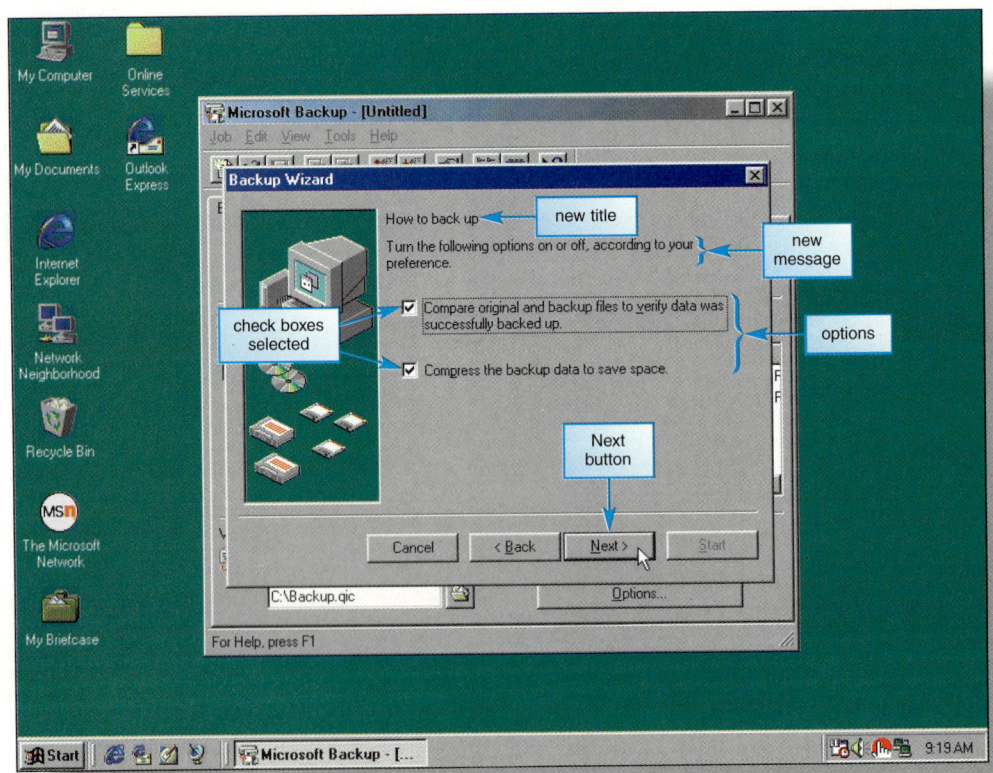

FIGURE 9-11

Backing Up and Restoring Files • **WIN 9.11**

PROJECT 9

 Click the Next button, type My Documents Folder Weekly Backup **in the Type a name for this backup job box, and then point to the Start button in the Backup Wizard dialog box.**

A new title (Name the backup job) displays, the backup job name displays in the Type a name for this backup job box, and a summary of the backup job displays (Figure 9-12).

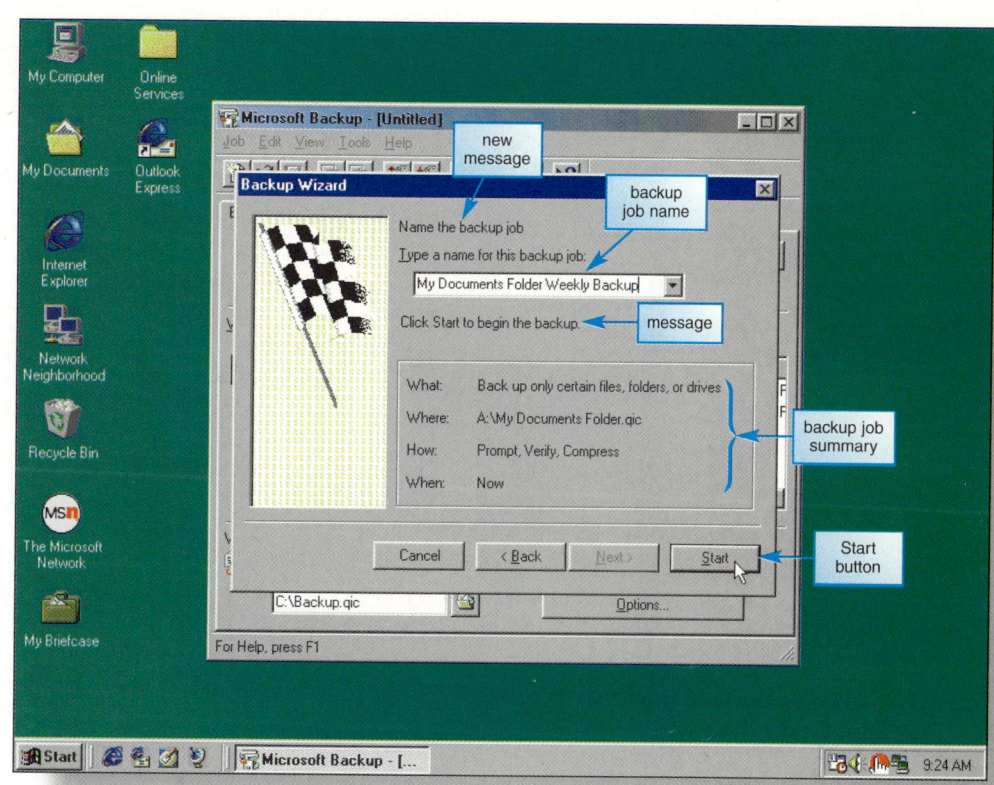

FIGURE 9-12

 Click the Start button.

The Backup Wizard dialog box closes and the Backup Progress window displays while the files in the My Documents folder are backed up (Figure 9-13). The device, media name, and status display along with a Progress indicator, Time text box, Processing indicator, estimated and processed values for number of files and number of bytes, and the compression ratio.

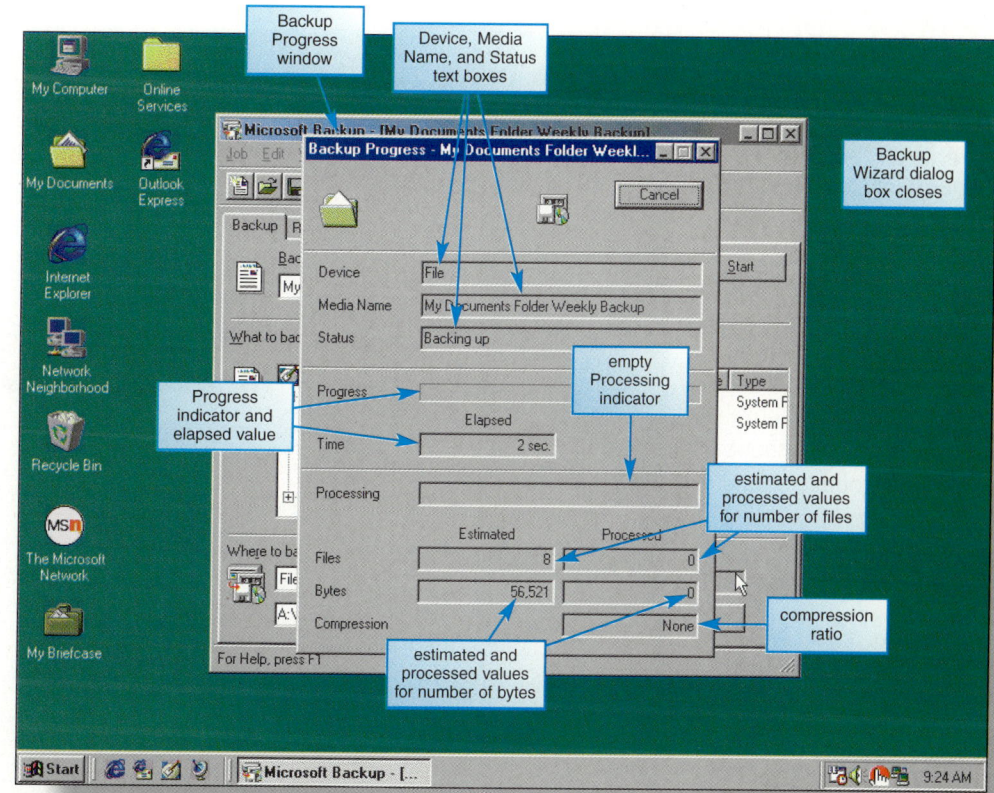

FIGURE 9-13

15 **When the backup procedure is complete, point to the OK button in the Microsoft Backup dialog box.**

The Microsoft Backup dialog box containing a message (Operation completed.) displays (Figure 9-14).

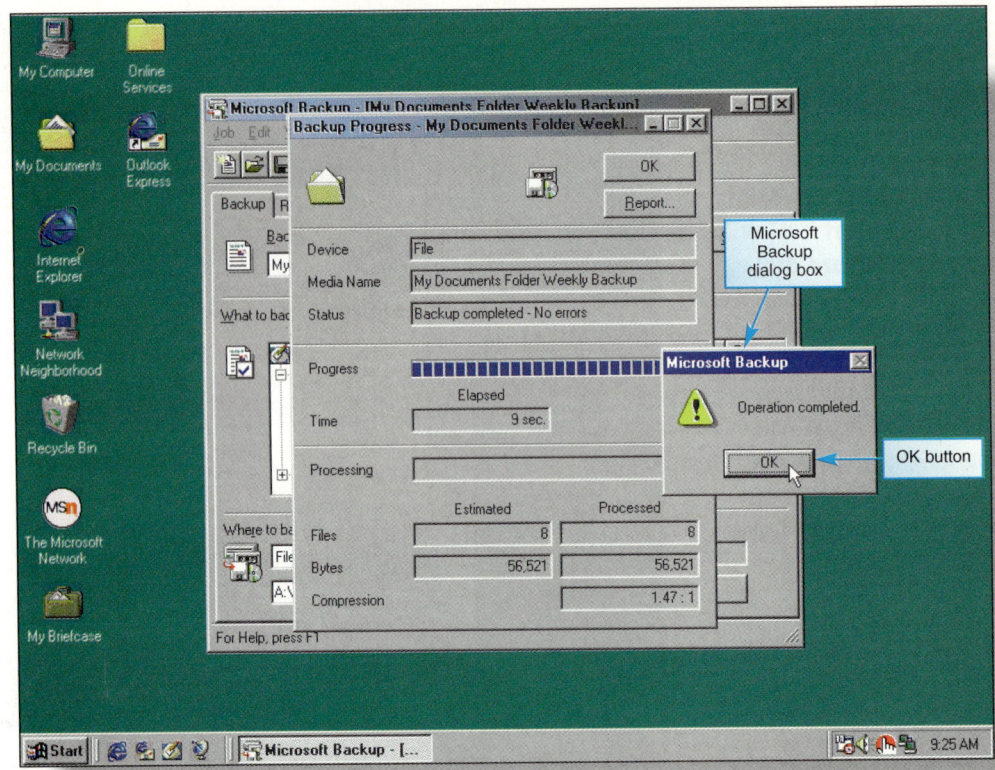

FIGURE 9-14

16 **Click the OK button and then point to the OK button in the Backup Progress - My Documents Folder Weekly Backup Job window.**

The Microsoft Backup dialog box closes and the Backup Progress window is visible (Figure 9-15). A message displays in the Status text box, the Progress indicator shows the backup is complete, and the elapsed time (9 sec.), processed files (8), processed bytes (56,521), and compression ratio (1.47:1) display. These values may be different on your computer.

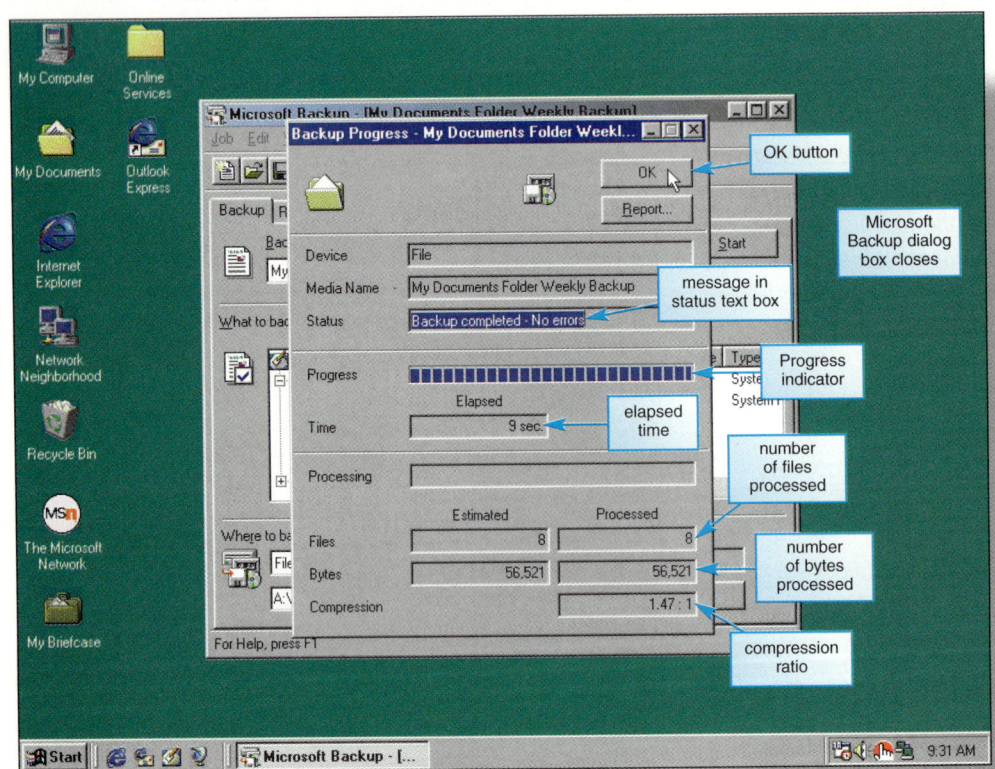

FIGURE 9-15

Backing Up and Restoring Files • WIN 9.13

 Click the OK button and then point to the Close button in the Microsoft Backup - [My Documents Folder Weekly Backup] window.

For the first time, the Microsoft Backup window is visible completely (Figure 9-16). The details of the backup job display in the Backup sheet.

 Click the Close button.

The Microsoft Backup window closes.

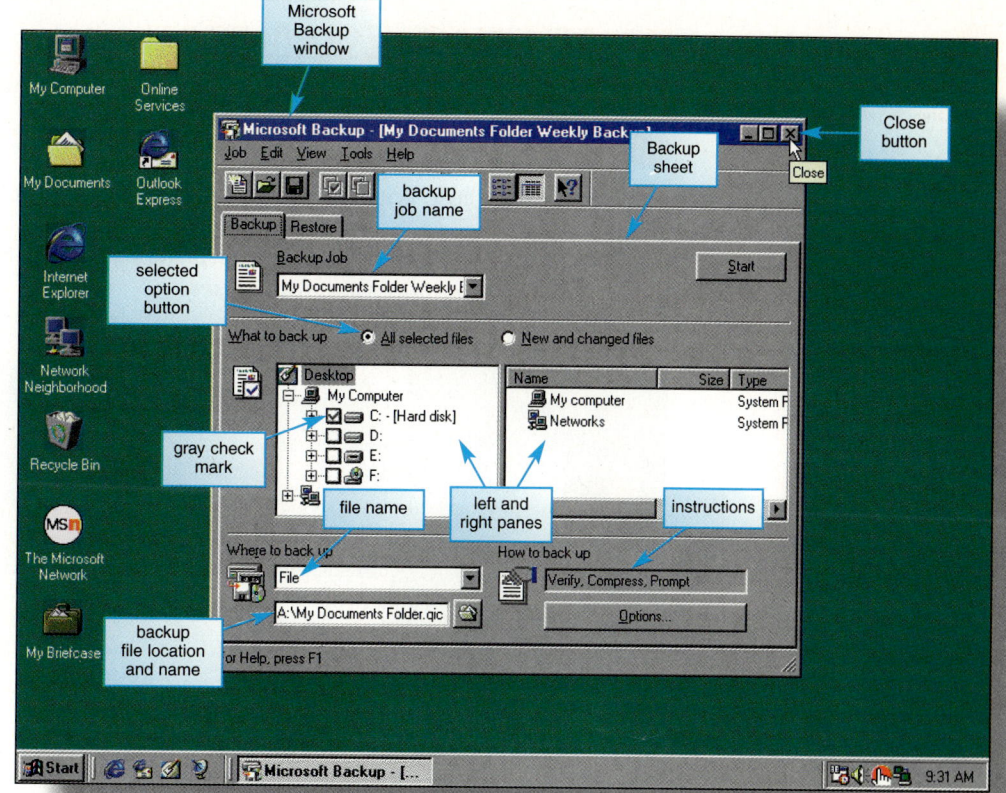

FIGURE 9-16

In the Backup sheet in the Microsoft Backup window shown in Figure 9-16, the backup job name displays in the Backup Job box, the All selected files option button is selected, and two panes display in the window. In the left pane, a **gray check mark** displays in the check box to the left of the C: - [Hard disk] icon. A gray check mark indicates that some, but not all, files on the drive are selected to back up.

The previous steps backed up the files in the My Documents folder on the desktop to the My Documents Folder.qic file on the floppy disk in drive A. Backup also allows you to back up the entire contents of the hard disk. Many times a tape drive is used to back up the contents of a hard disk. In addition, a common strategy for backing up the hard disk is to perform a **full backup** (backing up all files on the hard disk to the tape drive) at regular intervals, such as at the end of the week. Then, perform a **differential backup** (backing up only files that have changed) at regular intervals, such as at the end of each day.

Displaying the Contents on a Floppy Disk

After backing up files using the Backup wizard, you might want to examine the disk in drive A to ensure the backup file was created on the floppy disk. To view the contents of the floppy disk in drive A, complete the steps on the next page.

Other Ways

1. Click Start button on taskbar, click Help, click Index tab, type backup, click Display button, click Click here hyperlink

More About

Backing Up a Disk

Whether you use a floppy disk, tape drive, or some other media to store backed up files, it is a good idea to store the backup media (disk or tape) at a different location than that of the computer. If the original information is destroyed, the backup disks or tapes will not be destroyed and can be used to restore the original information.

TO DISPLAY THE CONTENTS ON A FLOPPY DISK

1 Double-click the My Computer icon on the desktop.

2 Double-click the 3½ Floppy (A:) icon in the My Computer window.

3 Click the Close button in the 3½ Floppy (A:) window.

The My Documents Folder file icon displays in the 3½ Floppy (A:) window (Figure 9-17). The My Computer window closes.

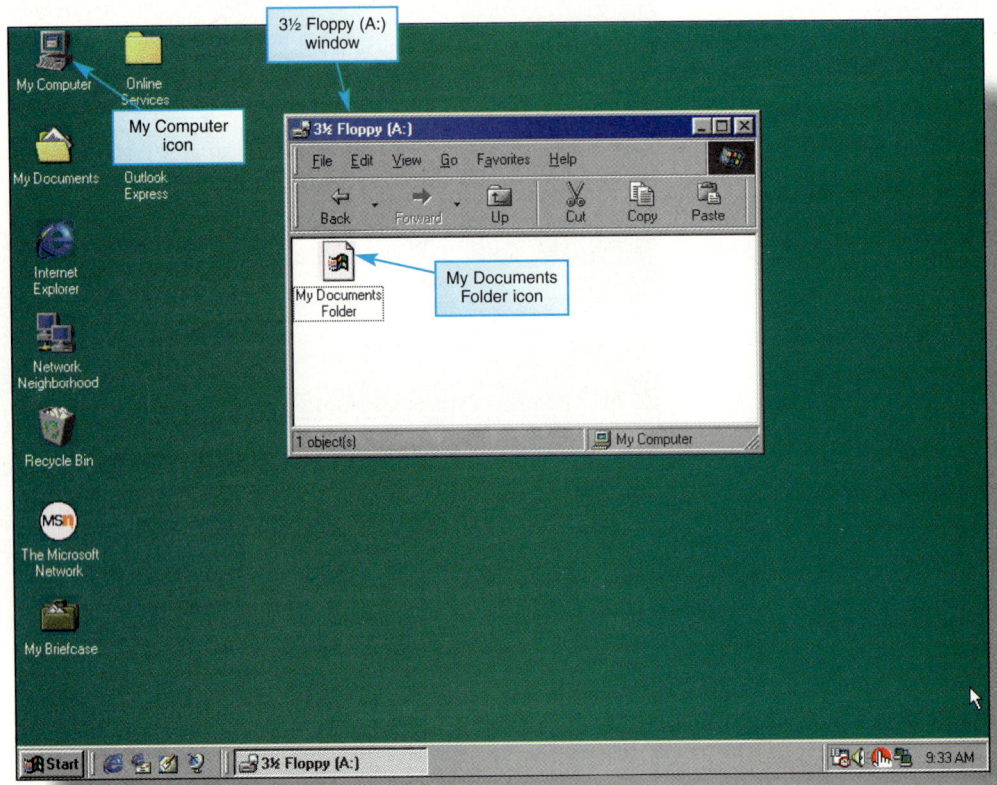

FIGURE 9-17

Restoring the Backup Files to the My Documents Folder

If, after performing a backup, you determine that one of the files in the My Documents folder on the desktop is unusable or corrupted, you can use the Restore wizard to replace the unusable file. The wizard replaces the unusable file in the My Documents folder on the desktop with the copy of the file in the My Documents Folder.qic backup file on drive A. Assume that the Lopez appointments file is contained in the My Documents folder on the desktop and that the contents of the Lopez Appointments file in the My Documents folder is deleted accidentally. Perform the following steps to restore the Lopez appointments file in the My Documents folder. If the My Documents folder on the desktop does not contain the Lopez appointments file, select another file in the folder when performing the following steps.

Backing Up and Restoring Files • WIN 9.15

 To Restore an Unusable File

1 **Click the Start button, point to Programs, point to Accessories, point to System Tools, and then click Backup. Click the Restore backed up files option button in the Microsoft Backup dialog box and then point to the OK button.**

The Microsoft Backup - (Untitled) window and Microsoft Backup dialog box display and the Restore backed up files option button is selected in the Microsoft Backup dialog box (Figure 9-18).

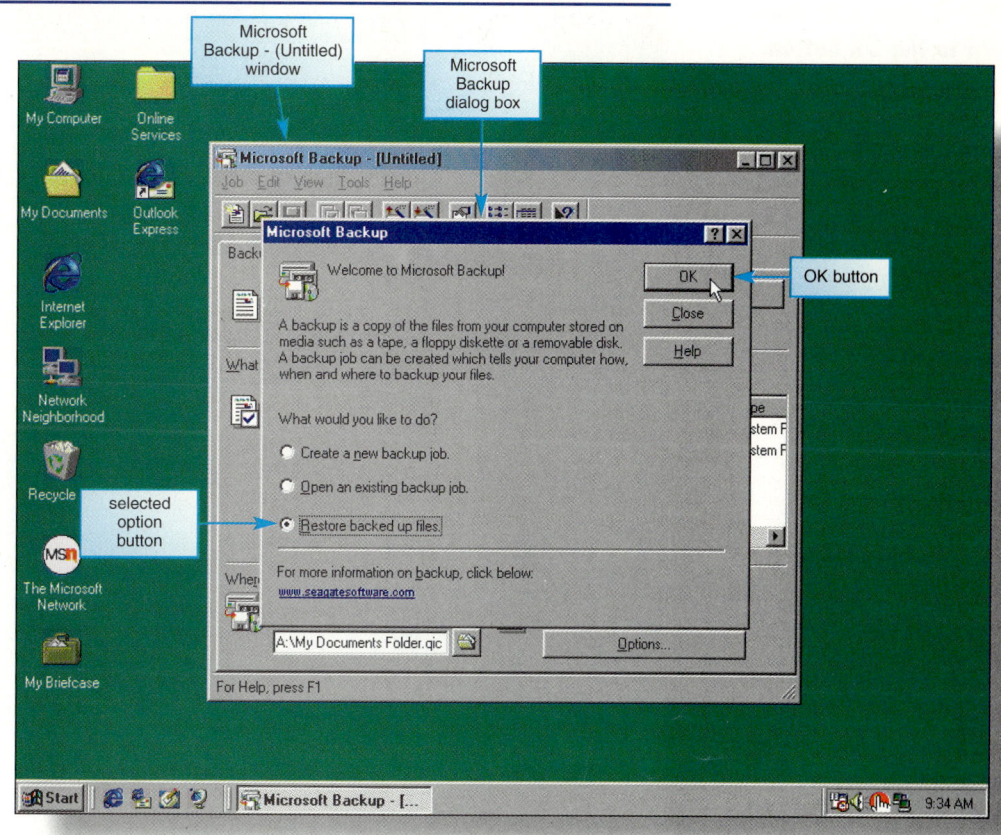

FIGURE 9-18

2 **Click the OK button and then point to the Next button in the Restore Wizard dialog box.**

The Restore Wizard dialog box displays (Figure 9-19). The dialog box contains a title (Restore from), a message, the Restore from box and text box, and a Browse button. The A:\My Documents Folder.qic name displays in the text box.

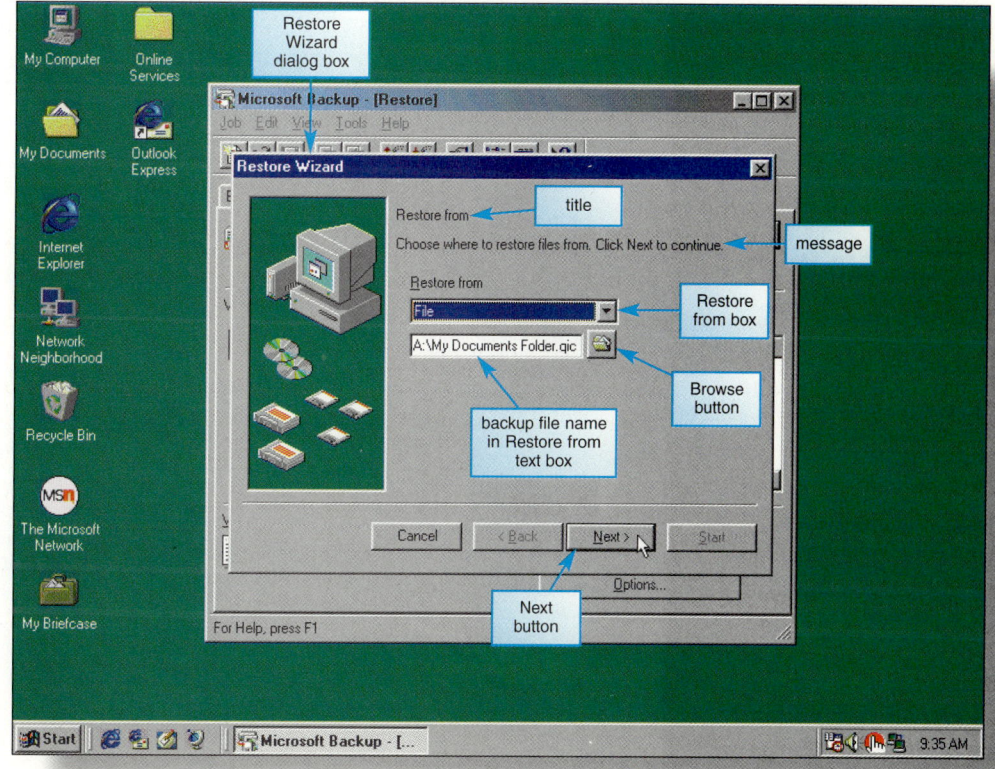

FIGURE 9-19

3 **Click the Next button and then point to the OK button.**

The Select Backup Sets dialog box displays (Figure 9-20). A list box in the dialog box contains a list of the backup files previously created using the Backup wizard. Currently, the highlighted My Documents Folder name displays in the list box.

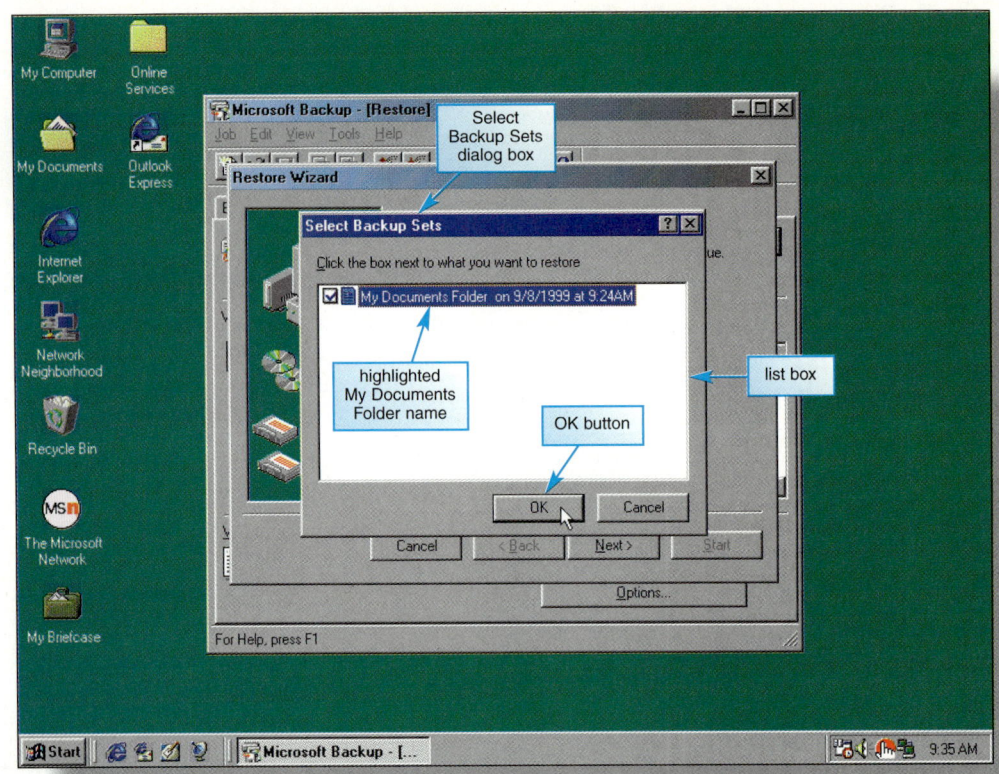

FIGURE 9-20

4 **Click the OK button, click the plus sign preceding C: - [Hard disk], and then click My Documents in the left pane. Point to the check box to the left of the Lopez appointments file name in the right pane. If Lopez appointments does not display, point to another file name.**

The contents of the Restore Wizard dialog box change (Figure 9-21). The hierarchy expands to include the My Documents name and the files in the My Documents folder display in the right pane. The file names in the right pane may be different on your computer. The mouse pointer changes to a check mark when you point to the Lopez appointments file name.

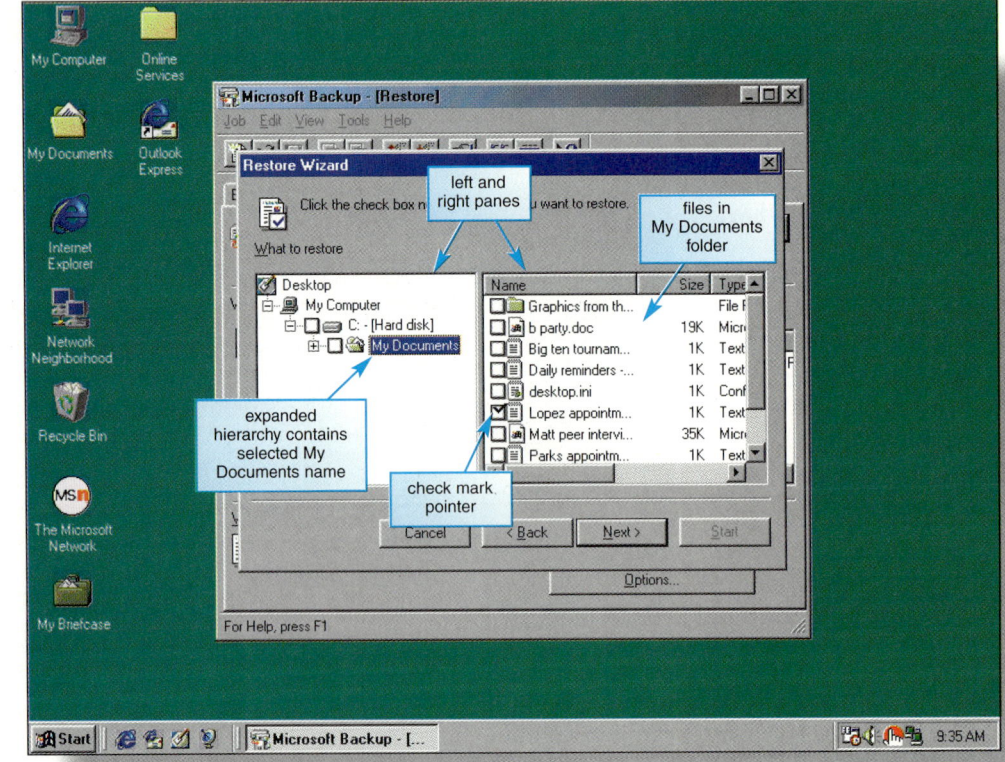

FIGURE 9-21

Backing Up and Restoring Files • WIN 9.17

5 **Click Lopez appointments and then point to the Next button in the Restore Wizard dialog box.**

Gray check marks display in the C: - [Hard disk] and My Documents check boxes in the left pane and a blue check mark displays in the Lopez appointments check box in the right pane (Figure 9-22). The blue check mark indicates the file to be restored. The gray check mark indicates that some, but not all, files in the My Documents folder on the hard disk will be restored.

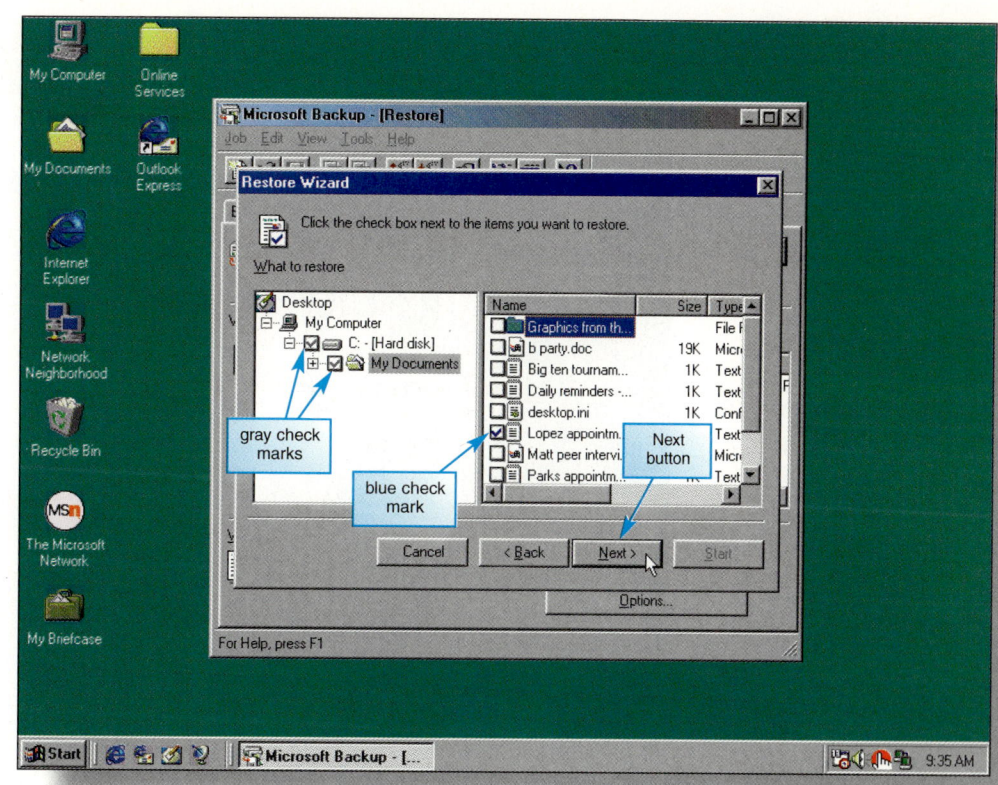

FIGURE 9-22

6 **Click the Next button and then point to the Next button in the Restore Wizard dialog box.**

The contents of the Restore Wizard dialog box change (Figure 9-23). The dialog box contains a new title and the Where to restore box contains the highlighted Original Location name.

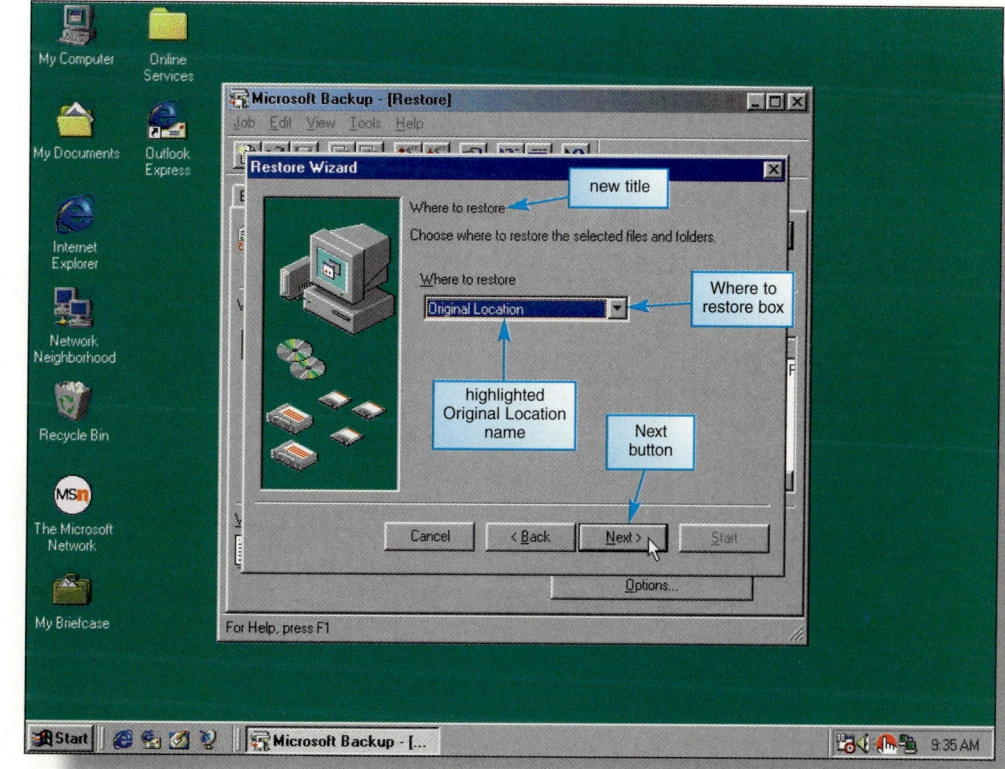

FIGURE 9-23

7 **Click the Next button, click Always replace the file on my computer, and then point to the Start button in the Restore Wizard dialog box.**

The contents of the Restore Wizard dialog box change (Figure 9-24). The dialog box contains a new title, two new messages, and three option buttons. The Always replace the file on my computer option button is selected.

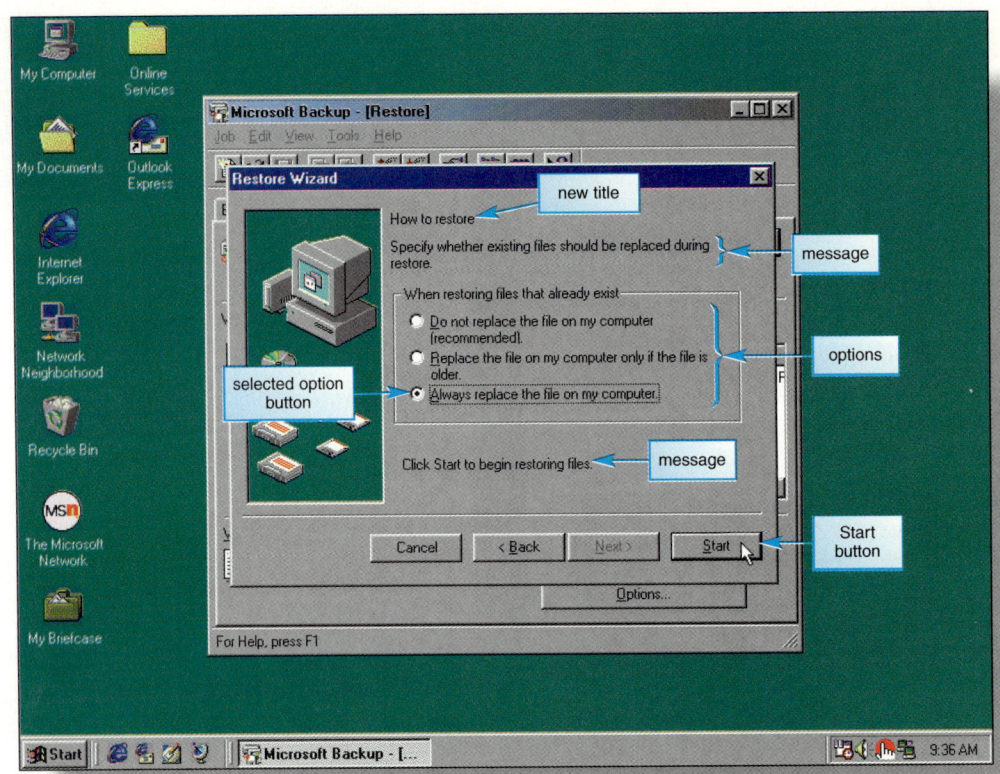

FIGURE 9-24

8 **Click the Start button and then point to the OK button.**

The Media Required dialog box displays (Figure 9-25). The dialog box contains a message and the highlighted My Documents Folder Weekly Backup name in the list box.

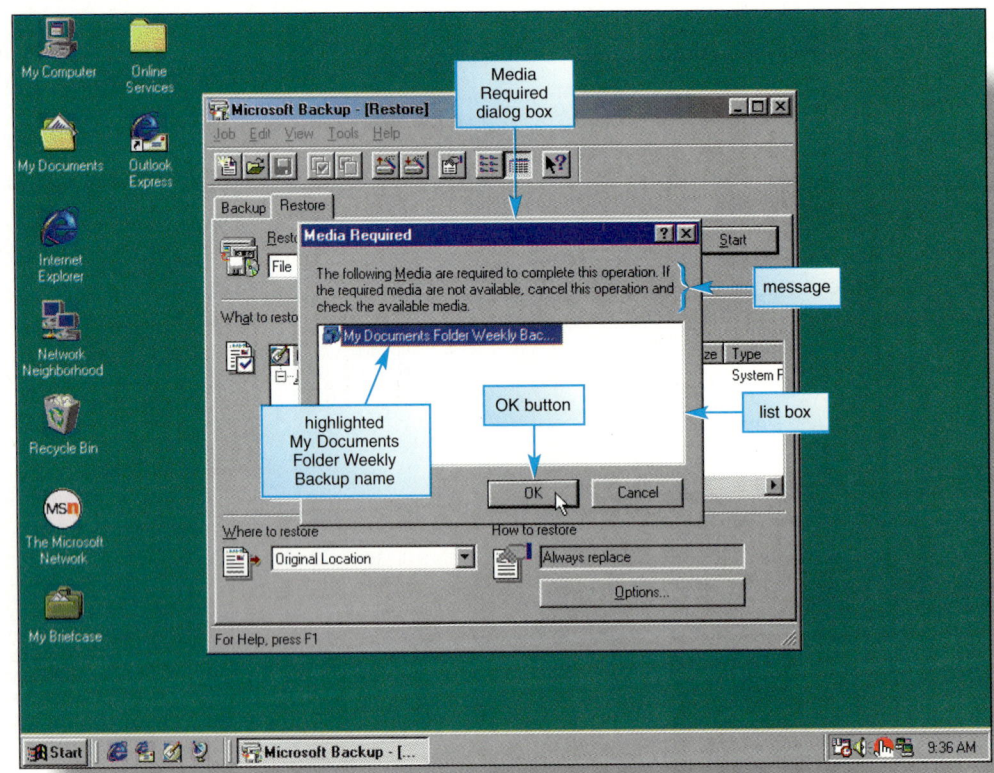

FIGURE 9-25

9 **Click the OK button in the Media Required dialog box and then point to the OK button in the Microsoft Backup dialog box.**

The Media Required dialog box closes and the Restore Progress window, containing a summary of the restore operations, displays while the file in the My Documents folder is restored. When the file is restored, the Microsoft Backup dialog box displays (Figure 9-26).

10 **Click the OK button in the Microsoft Backup dialog box, click the OK button in the Restore Progress window, and then click the Close button in the Microsoft Backup - [Restore] window.**

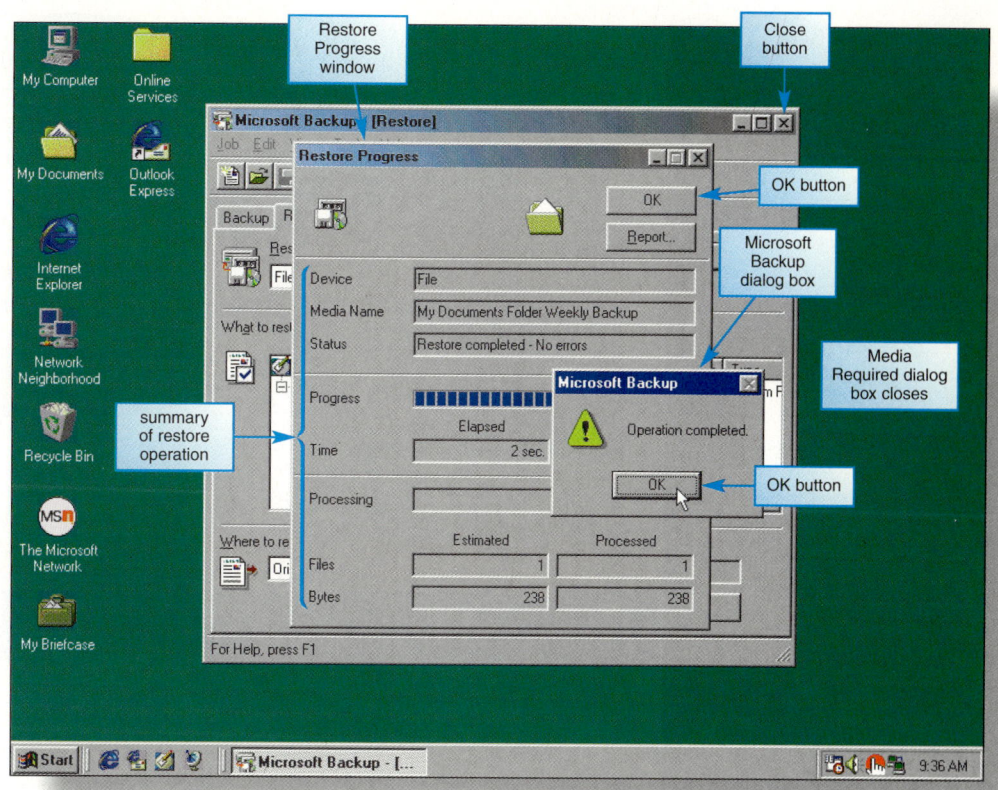

FIGURE 9-26

The Lopez appointments file located in the My Documents folder on the desktop is replaced with the Lopez appointments file located in the My Documents Folder.qic file on the floppy disk in drive A.

7 **Remove the floppy disk from drive A.**

The floppy disk is removed from drive A.

The Lopez appointments file in the My Documents Folder.qic file on the floppy disk in drive A replaces the corrupted Lopez appointments file in the My Document folder on the desktop.

The Windows 98 File System and the File Allocation Table (FAT)

In previous projects, two methods to save a document on the desktop were shown. In each case, a file icon was placed on the desktop and the actual file was stored on the hard disk. When you issue the command to save a file, the file name is checked to ensure the file name is designed according to the rules for naming files, and important identifying information about the file and the file itself are stored physically on the hard disk. Files stored on the hard disk are stored in clusters. A **cluster**, also known as an **allocation unit**, is the smallest storage location that the operating system can allocate to a file. Figure 9-27 on the next page illustrates a hard disk platter containing several clusters, the Business Letters file stored in clusters 1 through 8, and the Business Memos file stored in clusters 9 through 15.

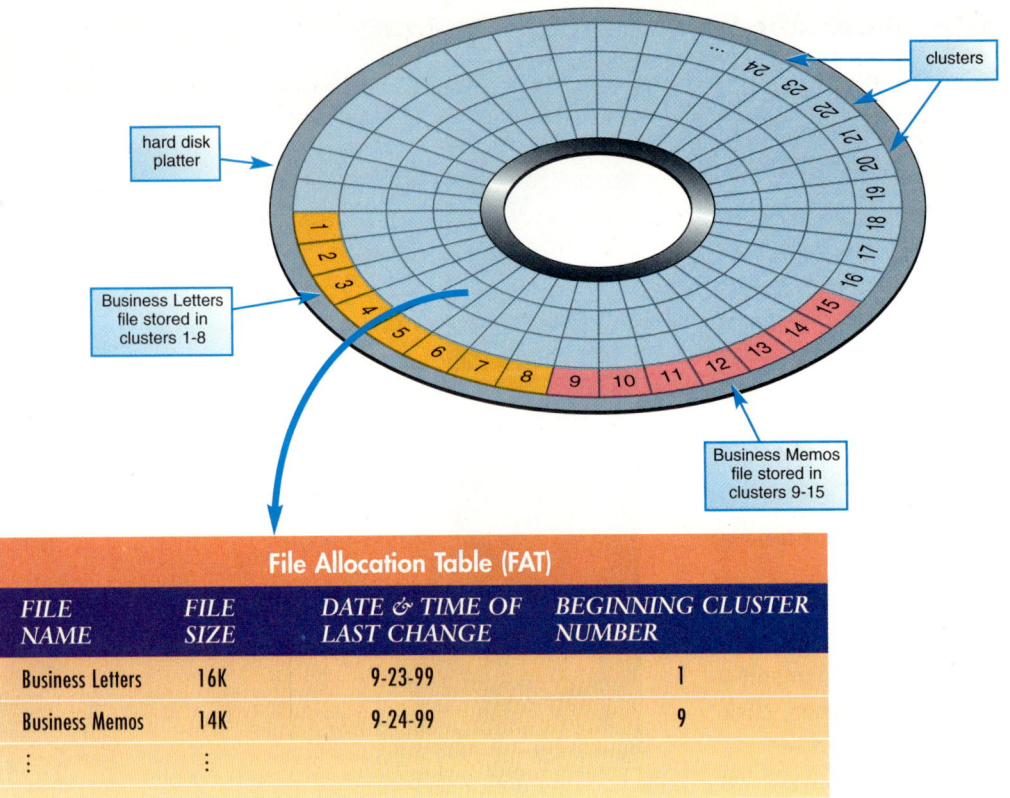

FIGURE 9-27

The Windows 98 **file system** verifies that the file name you use to save a file is valid and assists in the process of physically placing the identifying information and the file on the hard disk. The **file allocation table** (**FAT**) keeps track of the file name, file size, date and time the file was last modified, and the cluster number where the file begins. The operating system uses the file allocation table to look up a file name and find the location of the file on the hard disk. In this sense, the file allocation table is similar to a table of contents in a book. Figure 9-27 also illustrates the file allocation table containing the file name, file size, date and time of last change, and beginning cluster number for the Business Letters and Business Memos files. Additional information about the file allocation table will be explained later in this project.

Maintaining the Hard Disk

For various reasons, problems may develop with the file system, file allocation table, or physical surface of the hard disk. These problems commonly fall into two categories: logical errors and physical errors. A **logical error** involves the organization of files and data on the disk. Logical errors include problems with the file allocation table, long file names, directory structure, compressed disks, and storage of files. A **physical error** is a physical problem with the disk media. These problems can be fixed using ScanDisk.

More About

Scanning the Hard Disk for Errors

ScanDisk starts over the process of scanning a disk every time a software program or operating system program accesses the hard disk. As a result, you should close all open programs before starting ScanDisk and perform the scan when no one is using the computer.

Using ScanDisk to Scan a Hard Disk for Errors

ScanDisk is a system tool included with Windows 98 that allows you to check a hard disk or floppy disk for logical and physical errors and then repair any corrupted or damaged areas of the disk. ScanDisk does not physically repair a damaged area of the disk, but moves data from the bad area into a working area and prevents data from being stored in the bad area. Just as you perform regularly scheduled maintenance on a car or an appliance, you also should use ScanDisk regularly to check the hard disk for problems.

ScanDisk performs either a standard search or a thorough search. A **standard search** checks all files and folders for errors on the disk you select and takes approximately one minute to search a 2.1 GB hard disk. A **thorough search** performs a standard search (all files and folders on the disk) and scans the disk surface for defects. The thorough search takes approximately forty-five minutes to search a 2.1 GB hard disk and longer on larger hard disks. Perform the following steps to conduct a standard search on drive C using ScanDisk.

More About

ScanDisk

When a problem is detected while launching Windows 98, ScanDisk automatically launches and corrects potential errors in the file allocation table (FAT) before continuing the process of launching the operating system.

 **To Scan the Hard Disk for Errors**

1 **Quit all application programs.**

2 **Click the Start button, point to Programs, point to Accessories, point to System Tools, and then point to ScanDisk.**

The Start menu, Programs submenu, Accessories submenu, and System Tools submenu display (Figure 9-28). The highlighted ScanDisk command displays on the System Tools submenu.

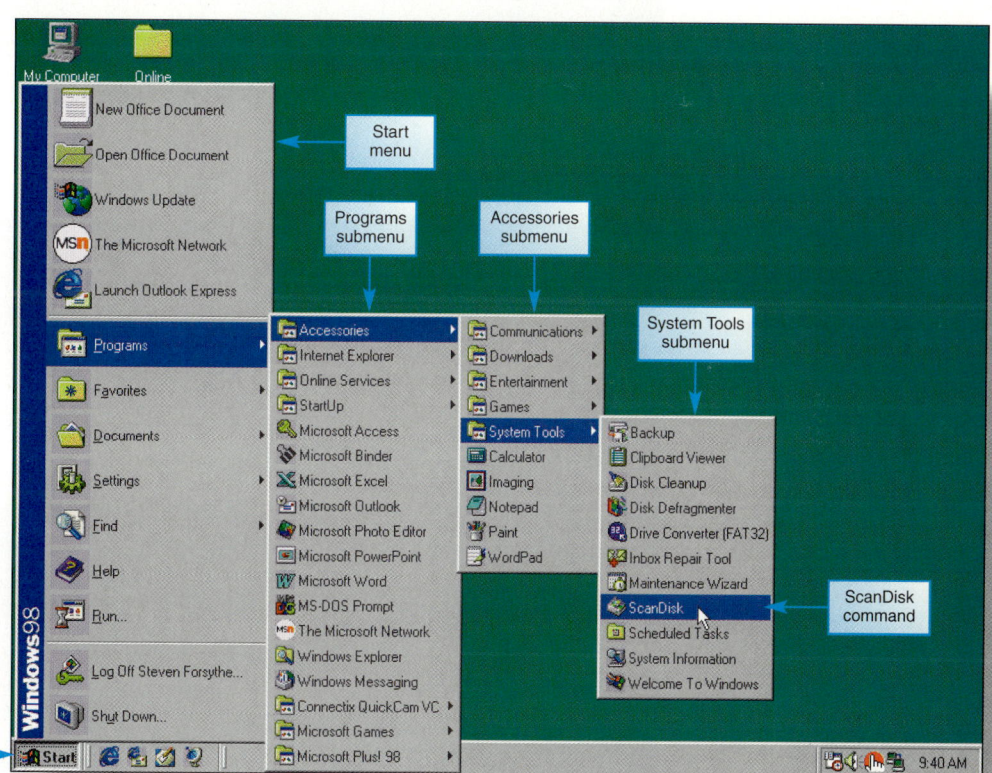

FIGURE 9-28

WIN 9.22 • Project 9 • Maintaining and Optimizing Your Computer and System Registry

3 **Click ScanDisk. If necessary, click Automatically fix errors and then point to the Start button in the ScanDisk - Hard disk (C:) window.**

The ScanDisk - Hard disk (C:) window displays (Figure 9-29). The highlighted Hard disk (C:) name displays in the list box, the Standard option button is selected in the Type of test pane, the Automatically fix errors check box is selected, and the Progress indicator signifies no progress has been made.

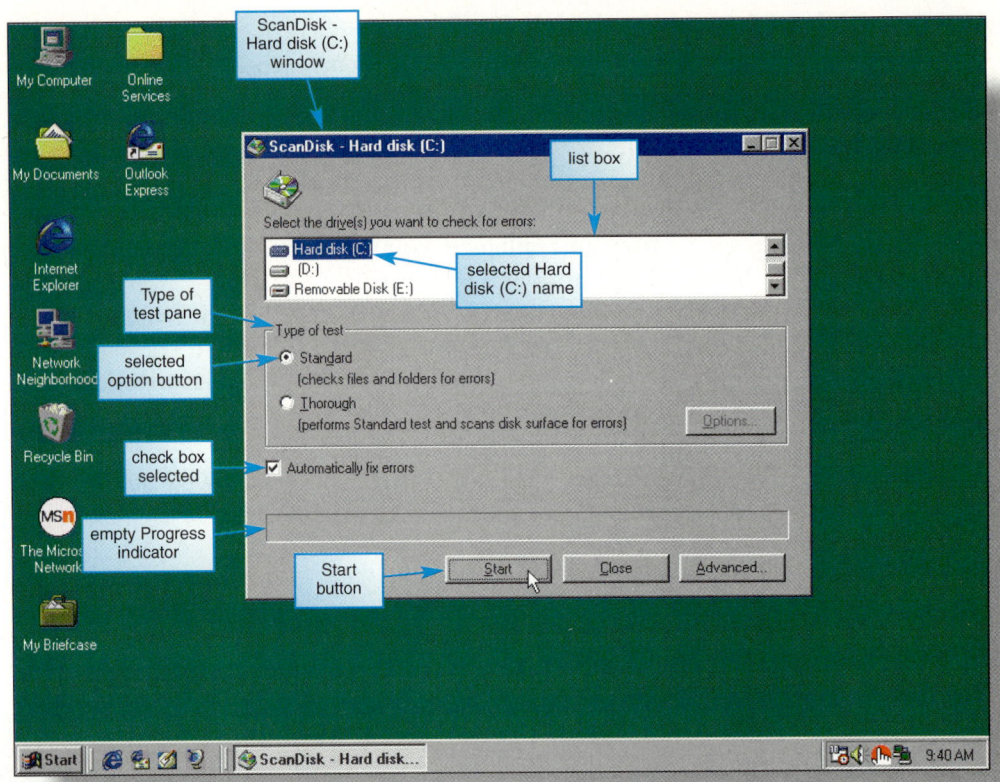

FIGURE 9-29

4 **Click the Start button.**

ScanDisk begins to scan the hard disk in drive C (Figure 9-30). Different messages display below the check box and blue rectangles display in the Progress indicator to indicate the progress of the scan.

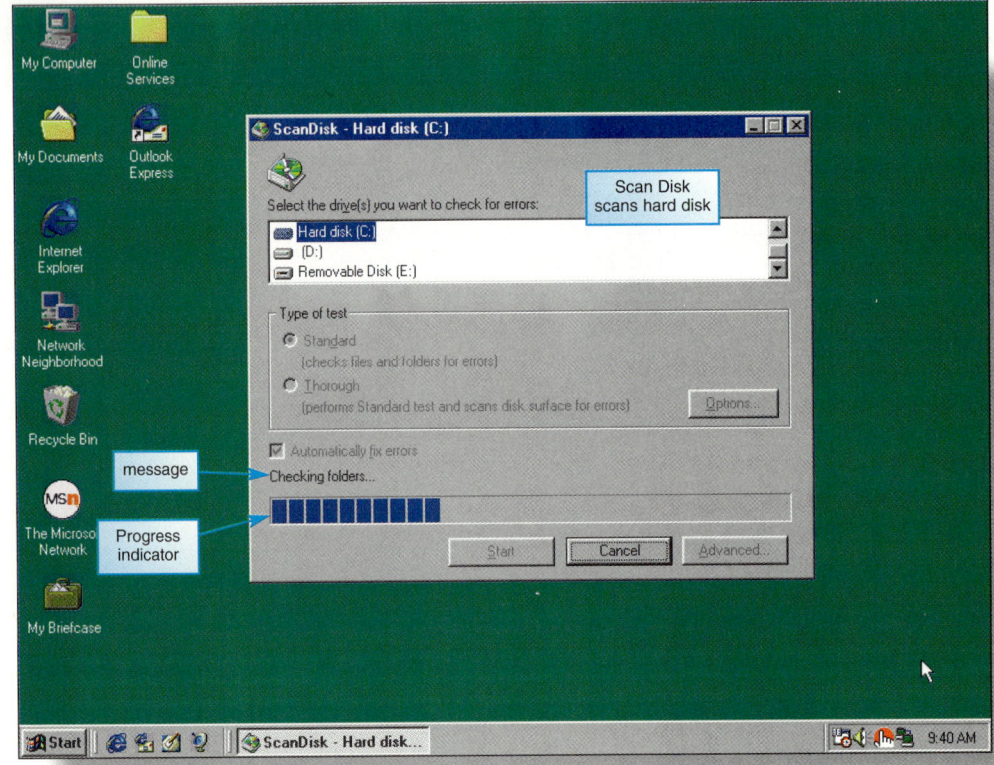

FIGURE 9-30

5 **When the ScanDisk Results - Hard disk (C:) dialog box displays, point to the Close button.**

ScanDisk finishes scanning the hard disk and displays the ScanDisk Results - Hard disk (C:) dialog box (Figure 9-31). A message indicates no errors were found and a summary of the results displays below the message.

6 **Click the Close button in the ScanDisk Results - Hard disk (C:) dialog box and then click the Close button in the ScanDisk - Hard disk (C:) window.**

The ScanDisk Results - Hard disk (C:) dialog box and ScanDisk - Hard disk (C:) window close.

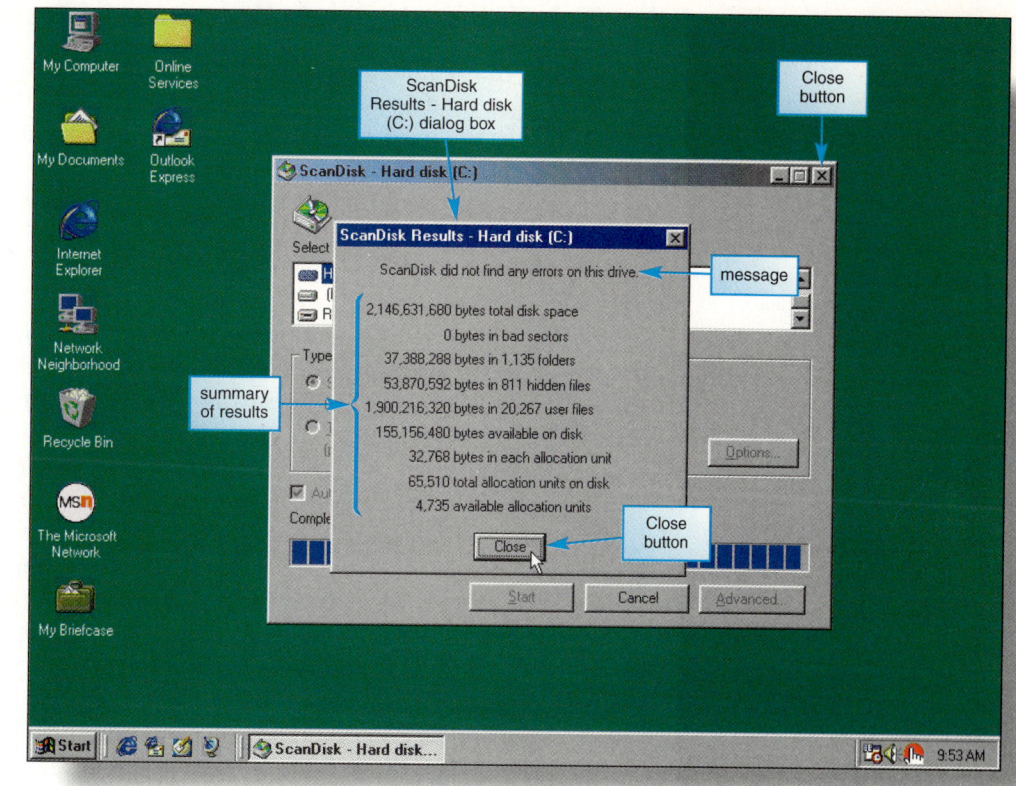

FIGURE 9-31

A standard search, even on the largest hard disks, rarely takes more than a few minutes. A thorough search on a large hard disk, however, could takes several hours. Because the process of scanning a hard disk is slowed down when you use the computer to access information on the hard disk, a thorough search should be performed when the computer is not being used. One alternative is to schedule the search using the Maintenance wizard and perform the search at a time when the computer is not being used, such as at night or early in the morning. More information about the process of scheduling computer maintenance, such as scanning a disk and using the Maintenance wizard, can be found on pages WIN 9.31 through WIN 9.37.

Other Ways

1. Click Start button on taskbar, click Help, click Index tab, type scandskw, click Display button, click Using ScanDisk, click Display button, click Click here hyperlink
2. Click Start button, click Run, type scandisk, click OK button, click Start button
3. Double-click Task Scheduler icon on taskbar, right-click Maintenance-ScanDisk icon, click Run

More About

ScanDisk

In the ScanDisk dialog box in Figure 9-29, you can scan more than one disk by selecting one disk in the list box, holding down the CTRL key, selecting another disk, and releasing the CTRL key.

More About

DiskCleanup

You also can launch DiskCleanup when in a Windows Explorer window by right-clicking the drive icon you want to clean up, click the Properties command on the shortcut menu, and then click the Disk Cleanup button.

Using Disk Cleanup to Delete Unnecessary Files on the Hard Disk

Whenever you launch an application program, delete a file using Recycle Bin, view a Web page, or download a file from a Web site, files are stored on the hard disk. As a result, the hard disk contains many unnecessary files that occupy space on the hard disk and reduce the amount of free space on the hard disk. If the free space falls too low for the operating system, error messages indicating memory problems may display when you run application programs. Removing the unnecessary files and increasing the amount of free space on the hard disk will increase the performance of a computer system.

The easiest method to delete unnecessary files and make more free space available is to use Disk Cleanup. **Disk Cleanup** searches the hard disk, lists the files you can delete safely, allows you to select the type of files to delete, and then deletes the files from the hard disk. Files you can select for deletion include temporary Internet files, downloaded program files, temporary files, and files in the Recycle Bin.

A **temporary Internet file** is a file stored on the hard disk that contains a copy of a Web page that you display in a browser window. If, in the future, you want to display the Web page in the browser window again, the copy of the Web page stored in the temporary Internet file is used instead of retrieving the Web page from the Internet. These files are stored in the Temporary Internet Files folder in the Windows subfolder on the hard disk.

A **downloaded program file** is downloaded, or copied, from a Web page when you display certain Web pages in a browser window and is stored in the Downloaded Program Files folder in the Windows subfolder on the hard disk. These files often are ActiveX and Java applets, which are small programs written specifically to provide interactive content on a Web page.

When you launch an application program, a **temporary file** often is stored in the Temp folder on the hard disk and then deleted when you quit the program. When you quit an application program abnormally or if the computer shuts down or reboots while an application is running, some files may remain in the Temp folder.

In addition to removing temporary Internet files, downloaded program files, and temporary files, Disk Cleanup also allows you to delete the files in the Recycle Bin. Perform the following steps to delete the temporary Internet files, downloaded program files, temporary files, and Recycle Bin files on the hard disk.

Maintaining the Hard Disk • WIN 9.25

 **To Delete Unnecessary Files on the Hard Disk**

1 **Click the Start button, point to Programs, point to Accessories, point to System Tools, and then point to Disk Cleanup.**

The Start menu, Programs submenu, Accessories submenu, and System Tools submenu display (Figure 9-32). The highlighted Disk Cleanup command displays on the System Tools submenu.

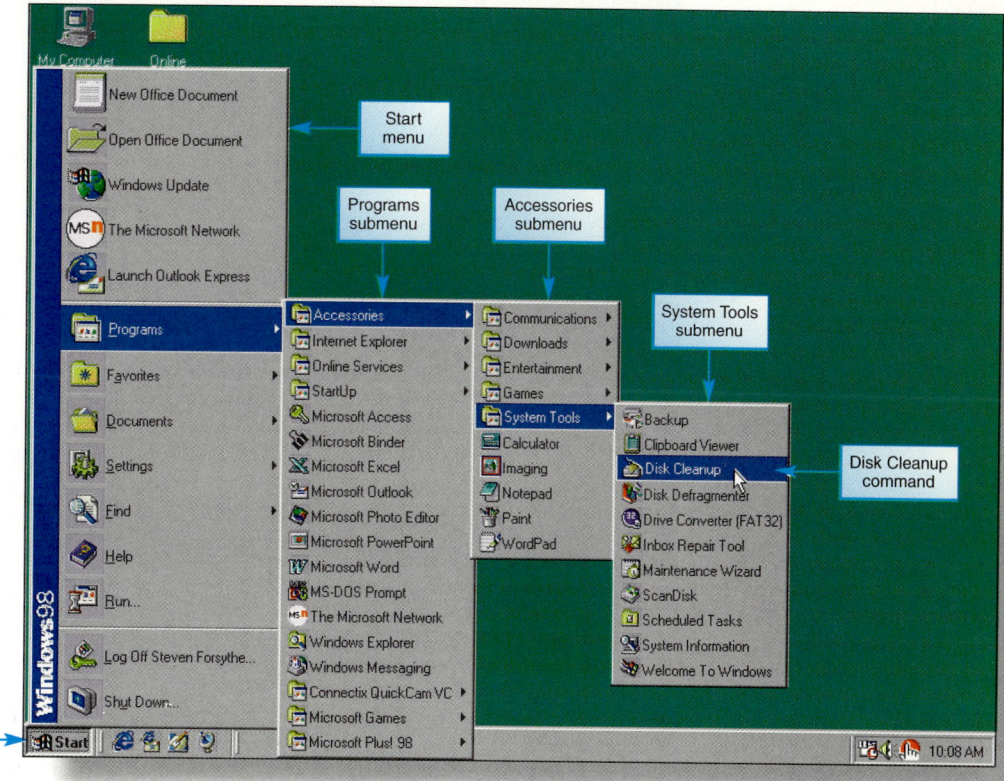

FIGURE 9-32

2 **Click Disk Cleanup and then point to the OK button in the Select Drive dialog box.**

The Select Drive dialog box displays (Figure 9-33). The dialog box contains a message and the Drives box. A drive icon and the HARD DISK (C:) name display in the Drives box.

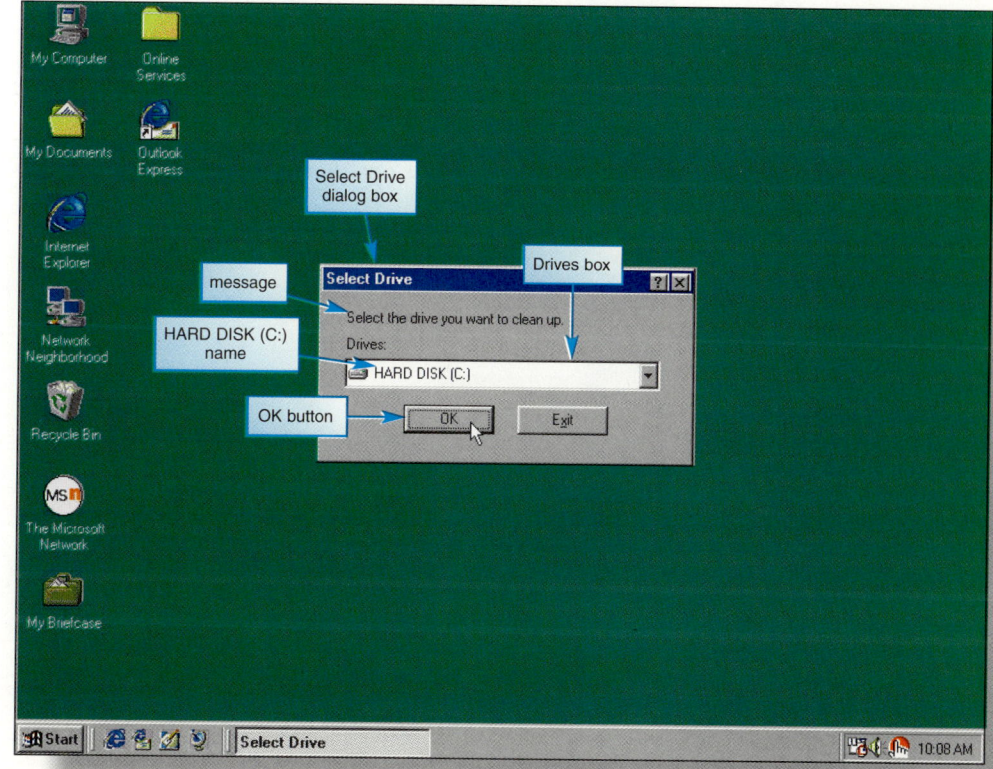

FIGURE 9-33

WIN 9.26 • Project 9 • Maintaining and Optimizing Your Computer and System Registry

3) Click the OK button.

The Disk Cleanup dialog box displays momentarily while the files to be deleted are scanned and the amount of free space is calculated (Figure 9-34). The dialog box contains a message, a Calculating Progress indicator indicating the progress of the scan, and the type of files currently being scanned (Downloaded Program Files).

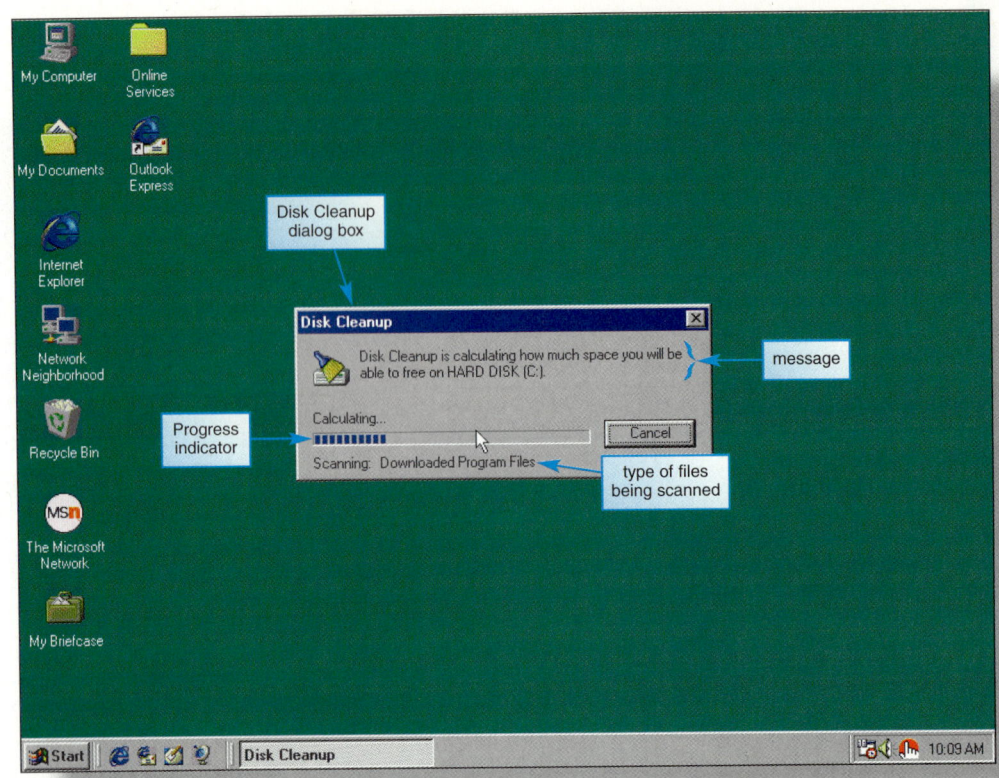

FIGURE 9-34

4) When the Disk Cleanup dialog box closes, point to the OK button.

The Disk Cleanup sheet in the Disk Cleanup for HARD DISK (C:) dialog box contains a message, two list boxes, and the total amount of disk space you can gain (10.17 MB) (Figure 9-35). All check boxes in the first list box are selected, the Temporary Internet Files name is highlighted, and a description of this file type displays in the second list box.

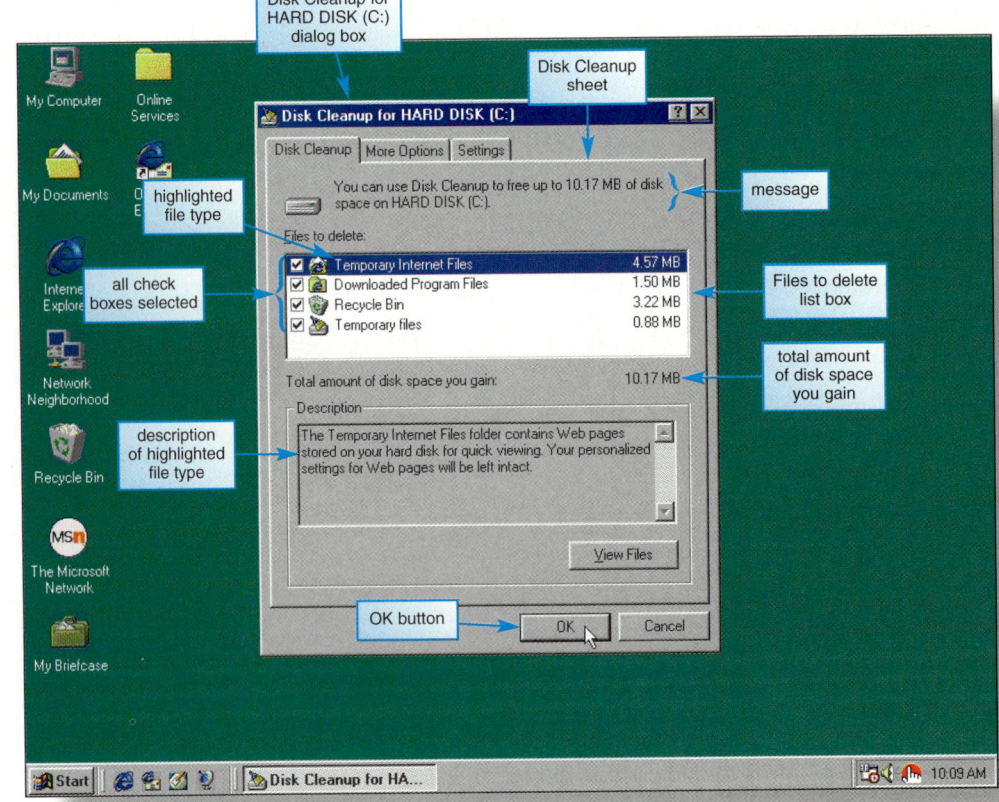

FIGURE 9-35

Maintaining the Hard Disk • **WIN 9.27**

5 **Click the OK button and then point to the Yes button in the smaller Disk Cleanup for HARD DISK (C:) dialog box.**

A smaller Disk Cleanup for HARD DISK (C:) dialog box displays (Figure 9-36). The dialog box contains a message and the Yes and No buttons.

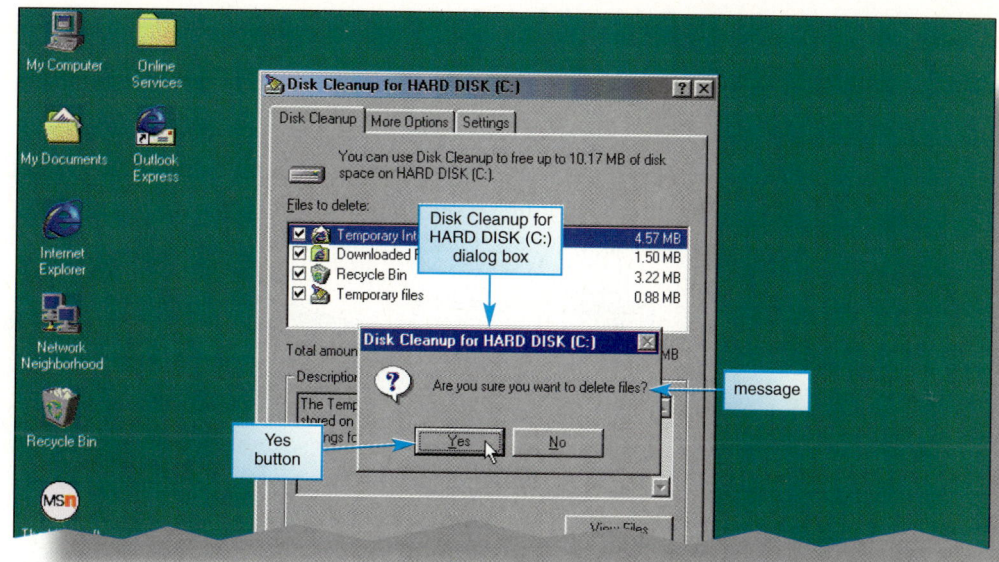

FIGURE 9-36

6 **Click the Yes button.**

The two Disk Cleanup for HARD DISK (C:) dialog boxes close and the Disk Cleanup dialog box displays momentarily while the files are deleted (Figure 9-37). The dialog box contains a message, a Progress indicator, and the type of files currently being cleaned (Downloaded Program Files).

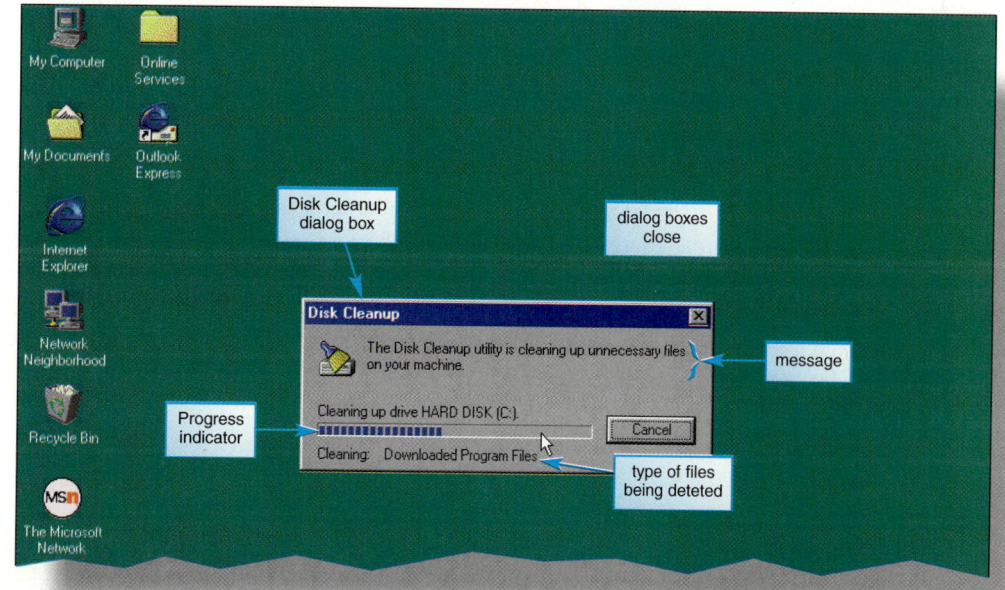

FIGURE 9-37

The Disk Cleanup for HARD DISK (C:) dialog box in Figure 9-35 contains the More Options and Settings tabs. The More Options sheet, accessible by clicking the More Options tab, gives advice on how to free additional disk space by removing optional Windows components and installed programs that are no longer used and converting the hard disk to the FAT32 format. More information about the FAT32 conversion option can be found on page WIN 9.59. The Settings sheet, accessible by clicking the Settings tab, allows you to turn on or turn off the option to launch Disk Cleanup automatically if the disk drive run lows on free space.

Other Ways

1. Click Start button on taskbar, click Help, click Index tab, type `disk cleanup`, click Display button, click Using Disk Cleanup, click Display button, click Click here hyperlink
2. Click Start button, click Run, type `cleanmgr`, click OK button
3. Double-click Task Scheduler icon on taskbar, right-click Maintenance-Disk cleanup icon, click Run

Using Disk Defragmenter to Defragment Files on a Hard Disk

As mentioned earlier, when you issue the command to save a file on disk, the file is stored on the disk in one or more clusters. When you store a file on a hard disk, each file is stored in a set of clusters on the disk. For example, if three files were saved on a hard disk, the operating system might store the first file in clusters 1 through 9, the second file in clusters 10 through 17, and the third file in clusters 18 through 26 (see Figure 9-38a). The three files occupy clusters 1 through 26.

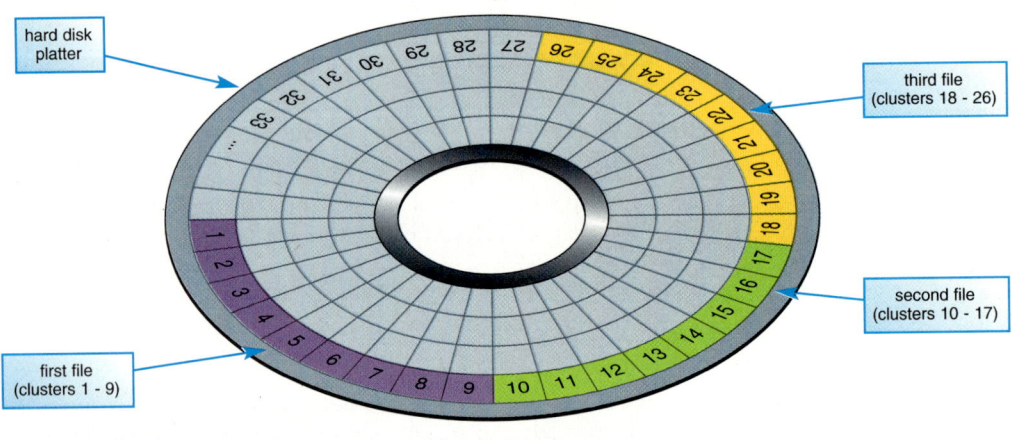

FIGURE 9-38a

When you delete a file from a disk, the clusters used by the deleted file become free disk space on the disk and the next file the operating system stores on the disk may use all or part of those clusters. For example, if you delete the file occupying clusters 10 through 17, 8 clusters become free space and reusable. Assume the next file the operating system stores on the hard disk is 12 clusters (see Figure 9-38b). In this case, the operating system would store the first part of the new file (8 clusters) in clusters 10 through 17 and store the last part of the new file (4 clusters) in clusters 27 through 30.

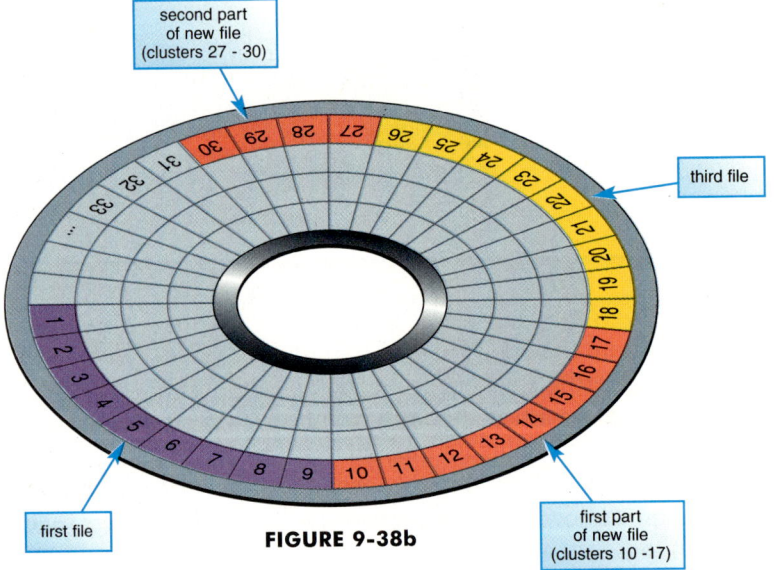

FIGURE 9-38b

The new file that is stored in two blocks of clusters on the hard disk (clusters 10 through 17 and clusters 27 through 30) is referred to as a **fragmented file** because the file occupies two blocks of clusters that are not located next to each other. When this happens, these two blocks of clusters are referred to as **noncontiguous blocks of clusters**. As old files are deleted and new files are added to the hard disk, the number of fragmented files becomes greater, requiring more time for the operating system to add and remove files, and reducing the efficiency of the hard disk.

Disk Defragmenter, a system tool included with Windows 98, rearranges the files on the hard disk in contiguous blocks with no fragmentation. Disk Defragmenter also increases the speed that programs launch using a process called Task Monitor. **Task Monitor** automatically monitors the programs you use, the number of times you use a program, and the process the operating system uses to find and retrieve those programs from the hard disk. This information enables Disk Defragmenter to place more frequently used programs in a special location on the hard disk that minimizes the time to find and retrieve those programs, causing the more frequently used programs to launch more quickly.

The time it takes to run Disk Defragmenter depends on the number of fragmented files on the hard disk and the size of the hard disk. It may take 20 to 30 minutes to run Disk Defragmenter on a small 2.1 GB hard disk and several hours on a larger hard disk. Because the process of defragmenting a hard disk is slowed down when a program accesses the hard disk, Disk Defragmenter only should be run when all application programs are closed, the computer is disconnected from the Internet, and the computer is not being used.

The following steps illustrate how to defragment a hard disk. Before defragmenting a hard disk you should obtain permission to defragment the hard disk and you should be aware that the process may take several hours. Because of these restrictions, **READ** but **DO NOT PERFORM** the following steps.

More About

Disk Defragmenter

Disk Defragmenter starts over the process of defragmenting a disk every time a software program or operating system program accesses the hard disk. As a result, you should close all open programs and start Disk Defragmenter when no one is using the computer.

More About

Disk Defragmenter

After launching Disk Defragmenter, clicking the Show Details button in the Disk Defragmenter dialog box displays the progress of the defragmentation process. You can watch the clusters on the disk as Disk Defragmenter moves them from one location to another location on the disk. Although the display is colorful and interesting to watch, it slows down the defragmentation process.

Steps To Defragment Files on the Hard Disk

1 Quit all application programs.

2 Click the Start button, point to Programs, point to Accessories, point to System Tools, and then point to Disk Defragmenter.

The Start menu, Programs submenu, Accessories submenu, and System Tools submenu display (Figure 9-39). The highlighted Disk Defragmenter command displays on the System Tools submenu.

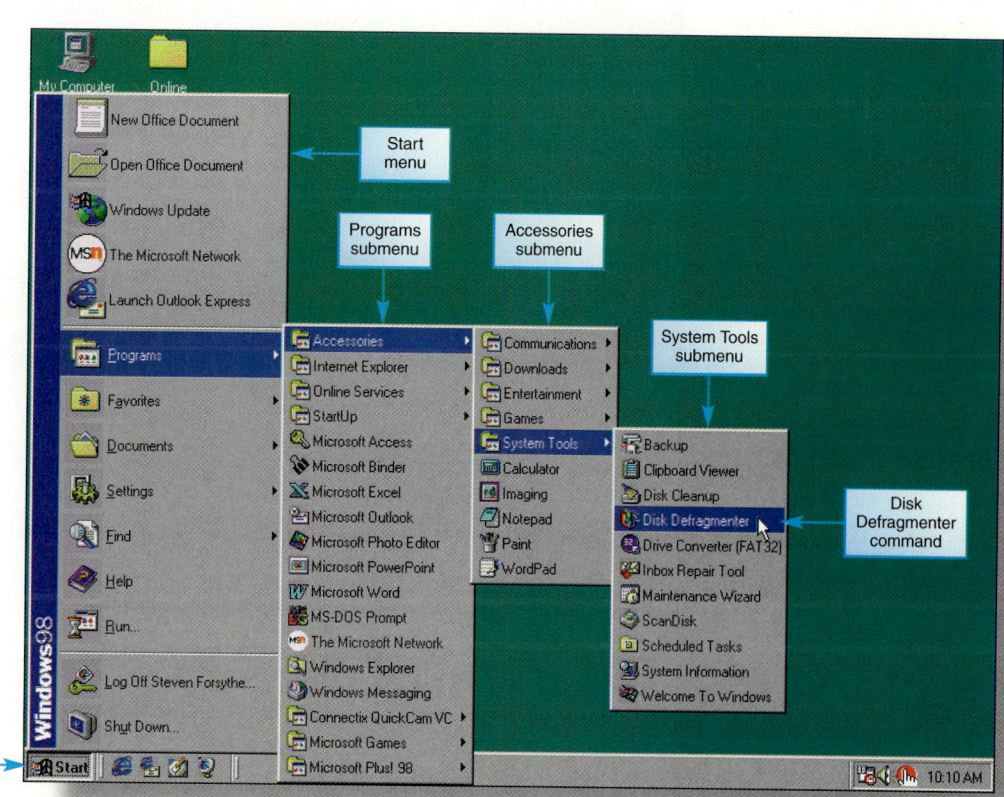

FIGURE 9-39

WIN 9.30 • **Project 9** • Maintaining and Optimizing Your Computer and System Registry

3 **Click Disk Defragmenter and then point to the OK button in the Select Drive dialog box.**

The inactive Disk Defragmenter window and active Select Drive dialog box display (Figure 9-40). The Disk Defragmenter window contains a Progress indicator and a message (0% Complete). The Select Drive dialog box contains a message, Drive box containing the highlighted Drive C name, and copyright notices.

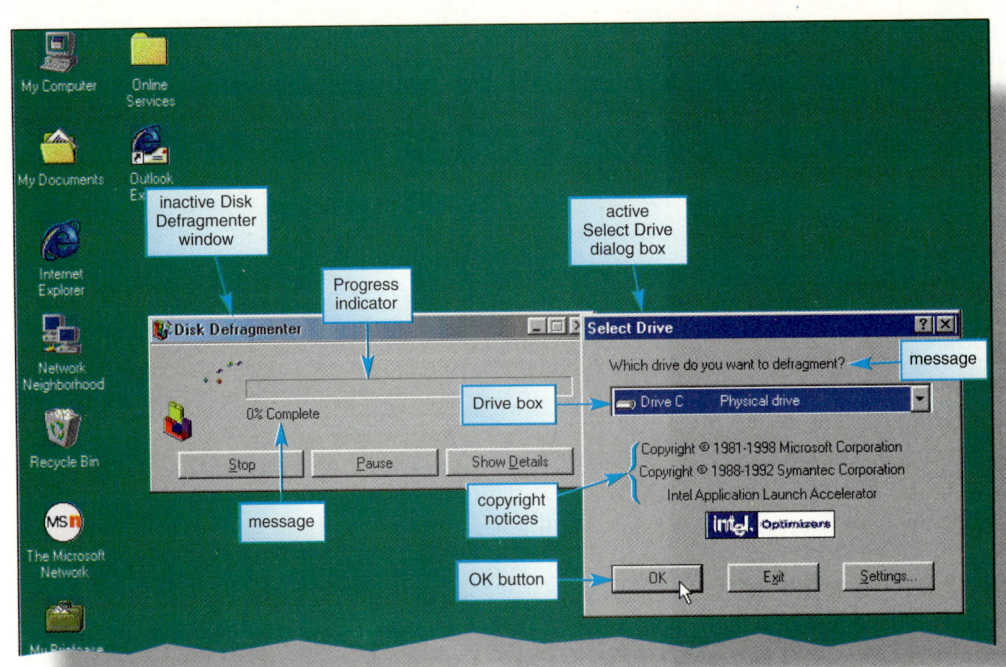

FIGURE 9-40

4 **Click the OK button and then point to the Yes button in the Disk Defragmenter dialog box.**

The Select Drive dialog box closes and the defragmentation of drive C begins. As the defragmentation progresses, blue rectangles display in the Progress indicator and the Complete message indicates the progress. When the defragmentation process is complete, blue rectangles fill the Progress indicator, the 100% Complete message displays, and the Disk Defragmenter dialog box displays (Figure 9-41).

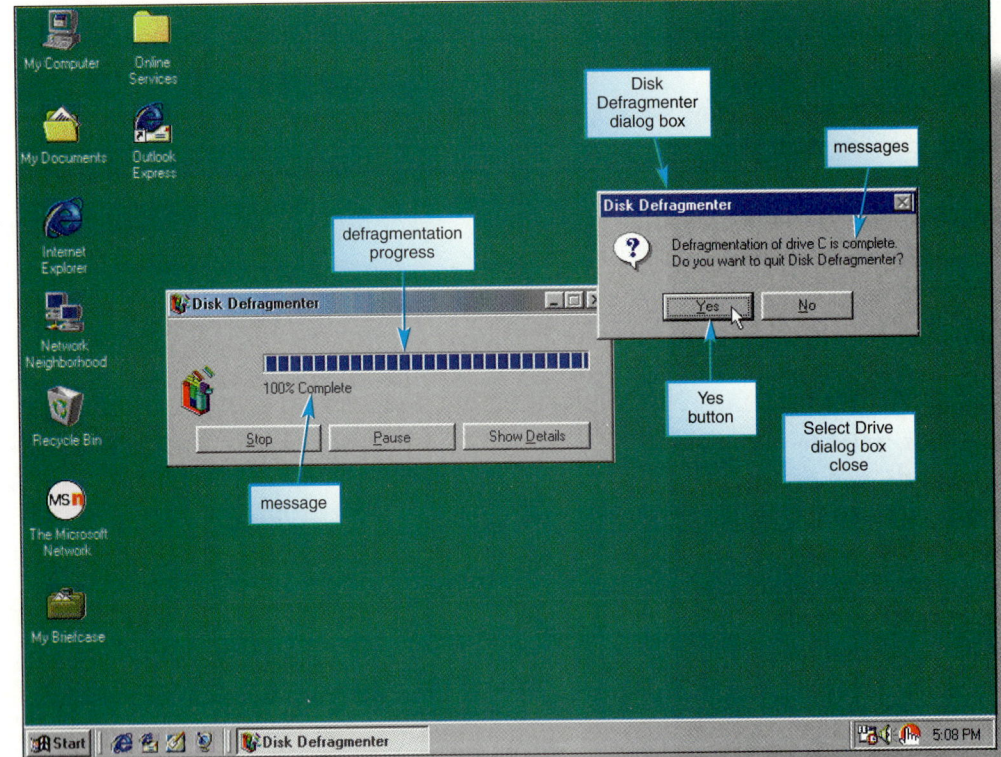

5 **Click the Yes button.**

The Disk Defragmenter window and Disk Defragmenter dialog box close.

FIGURE 9-41

Because defragmenting a hard disk is a relatively slow process, one alternative is to schedule the defragmentation using Maintenance wizard and perform the defragmentation at a time when the computer is not being used, such as at night or early in the morning. The process of scheduling operations, such as defragmenting a disk, using Maintenance wizard is illustrated in the next section.

Scheduling Routine Maintenance Using the Maintenance Wizard

Previously, you used ScanDisk to check the hard disk for logical and physical errors and repair any corrupted or damaged areas of the disk, Disk Cleanup to search for and delete unnecessary files on the hard disk, and Disk Deframentation to defragment the files on the hard disk. All three of these operations should be performed regularly for optimum performance.

One method of scheduling these events is to use Task Scheduler. **Task Scheduler** maintains a list of tasks to be performed, allows you to add a task to the list, change the schedule for or delete an existing task, and then automatically performs the tasks at the scheduled date and time. Task Scheduler allows you to select from a list of more than 50 programs that can be scheduled. Task Scheduler starts each time you start Windows and the Task Scheduler icon displays in the tray status area on the taskbar.

A second method of scheduling these events is to use the Maintenance wizard. The **Maintenance wizard** allows you to select or design a maintenance schedule to make programs run faster (Disk Defragmenter), check a hard disk for problems (ScanDisk), and free hard disk space (Disk Cleanup). Using the Maintenance wizard, you can design a schedule quickly for performing one or more of these three tasks, change the schedule for or turn off an existing task, and customize how a task will run at its scheduled time. The tasks can be scheduled to run daily, weekly, or monthly. Once a schedule is designed, the operations will be performed automatically by Task Scheduler, along with any previously scheduled tasks. Performing maintenance regularly is the best guarantee that a computer system will operate at maximum performance.

Before using the Maintenance wizard, you should decide on the date and time to run the ScanDisk, Disk Defragmenter, and Disk Cleanup programs. The Maintenance wizard allows you to choose a predetermined schedule (Express setup) or design a schedule (Custom setup). You then can select whether the tasks should run during the day (Days – Noon to 3:00 PM), during the evening (Evenings – 8:00 PM to 11:00 PM), or at night (Nights – Midnight to 3:00 AM).

The Maintenance wizard schedules the tasks based upon the time of day you choose to run the tasks (Days, Nights, Evenings, or Custom) and the day of the week you run the Maintenance wizard. Assume you run the Maintenance wizard on Monday and select the Night schedule. In this case, the ScanDisk program will run at 1:00 A.M. on Tuesday (the day after running the wizard) and the Disk Defragmenter program will be run at 1:00 A.M. on Wednesday (two days after running the wizard). The Disk Cleanup program will be run at 12:30 A.M. on the first day of every month.

Assume you want to perform routine maintenance at night (Nights - Midnight and 3:00 AM), scan the disk and defragment the disk on the same day of the week, and scan the disk before defragmenting it. One method of accomplishing this is to choose to design a schedule (Custom schedule), schedule the tasks to run at night, and change the time and day for the Disk Defragmenter program from 1:00 A.M. on Wednesday to 2:00 A.M. on Tuesday. Thus, the ScanDisk program would run at 1:00 A.M. on Tuesday and the Disk Defragmenter program would run at 2:00 A.M. on Tuesday.

Other Ways

1. Click Start button on taskbar, click Help, click Index tab, type disk defragmenter, click Display button, click Using Disk Defragmenter to speed up access to your hard disk, click Display button, click Click here hyperlink
2. Click Start button, click Run, type defrag, click OK button
3. Double-click Task Scheduler icon on taskbar, right-click Disk Defragment Program icon, click Run

WIN 9.32 • Project 9 • Maintaining and Optimizing Your Computer and System Registry

Assume for the purpose of running the Maintenance wizard that the date is Wednesday, September 8, 1999. Perform the following steps to use the Maintenance wizard to schedule the routine maintenance.

Steps: To Schedule Routine Maintenance

  Click the Start button, point to Programs, point to Accessories, point to System Tools, and then point to Maintenance Wizard.

The Start menu, Programs submenu, Accessories submenu, and System Tools submenu display (Figure 9-42). The highlighted Maintenance Wizard command displays on the System Tools submenu.

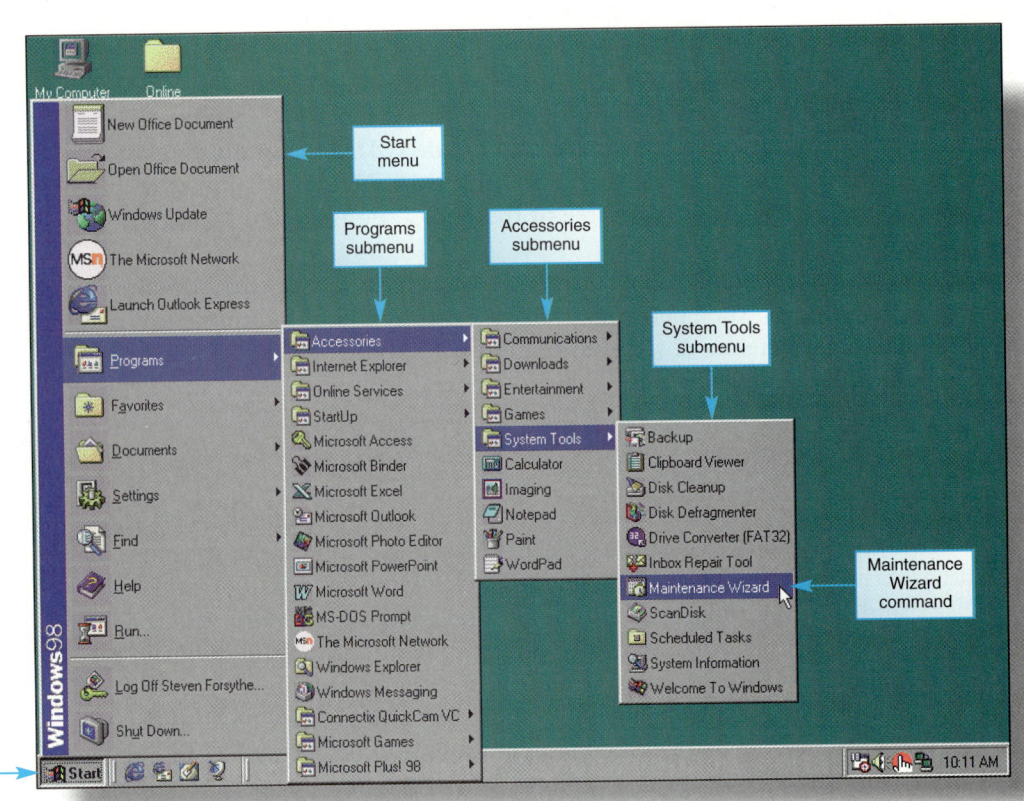

FIGURE 9-42

Click Maintenance Wizard, click Change my maintenance settings or schedule in the Maintenance Wizard dialog box, and then point to the OK button.

The Maintenance Wizard dialog box displays and the Change my maintenance settings or schedule option button is selected (Figure 9-43).

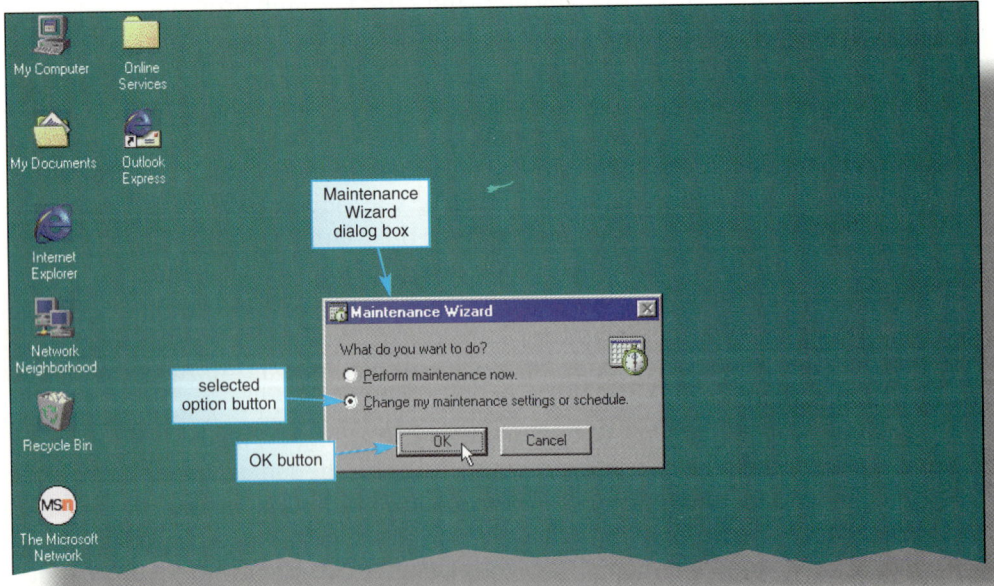

FIGURE 9-43

Scheduling Routine Maintenance Using the Maintenance Wizard • WIN 9.33

3 **Click the OK button, click Custom - Select each maintenance setting myself in the Maintenance Wizard dialog box, and then point to the Next button.**

The smaller Maintenance Wizard dialog box closes and a second, larger Maintenance Wizard dialog box displays (Figure 9-44). The dialog box contains messages, and two option buttons. The Custom - Select each maintenance setting myself option button is selected.

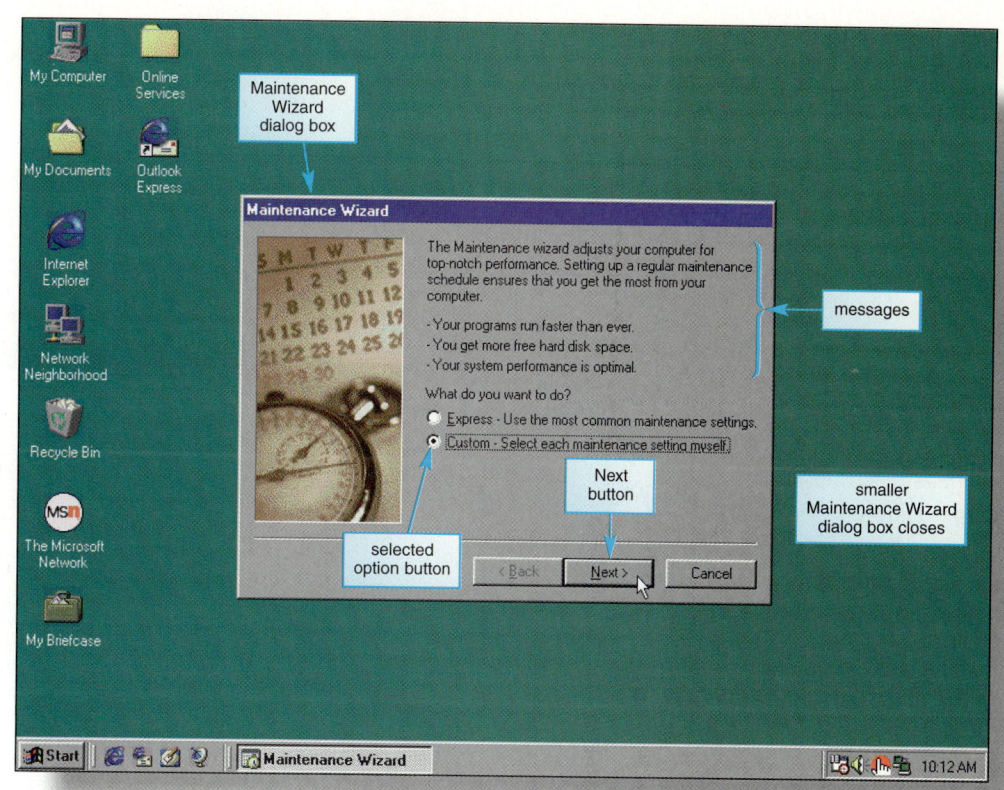

FIGURE 9-44

4 **Click the Next button. If necessary, click Nights - Midnight to 3:00 AM and then point to the Next button.**

The contents of the Maintenance Wizard dialog box change (Figure 9-45). The dialog box contains the Select a Maintenance Schedule title, new messages, and four option buttons. The Nights - Midnight to 3:00 AM option button is selected.

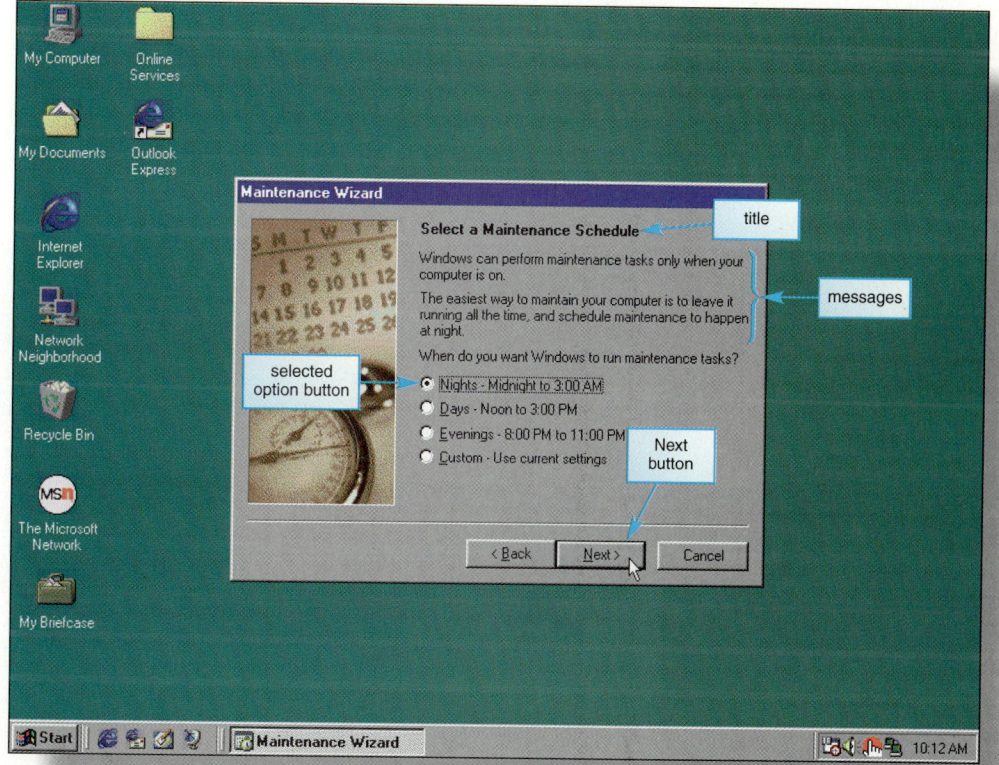

FIGURE 9-45

5 **Click the Next button, deselect each check box in the list box, and then point to the Next button.**

The contents of the Maintenance Wizard dialog box change (Figure 9-46). The dialog box contains the Start Windows More Quickly title, new messages, a list box containing the MSN Quick View check box, and another message. Different check boxes may display in the list box on your computer.

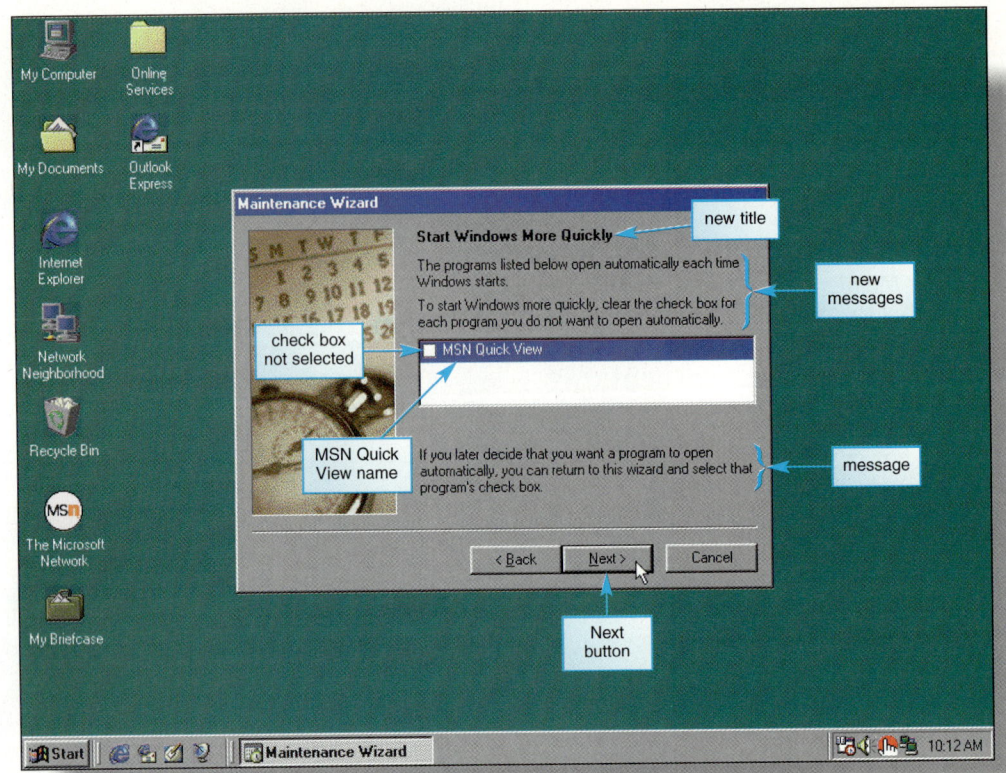

FIGURE 9-46

6 **Click the Next button and then point to the Reschedule button in the Maintenance Wizard dialog box.**

The Maintenance Wizard dialog box contains the Speed Up Programs title, a new message, a pane, and the No option button (Figure 9-47). The pane contains the selected Yes option button, and the current schedule (1:00 AM every Friday every week, starting 9/8/1999) for the Disk Defragmenter.

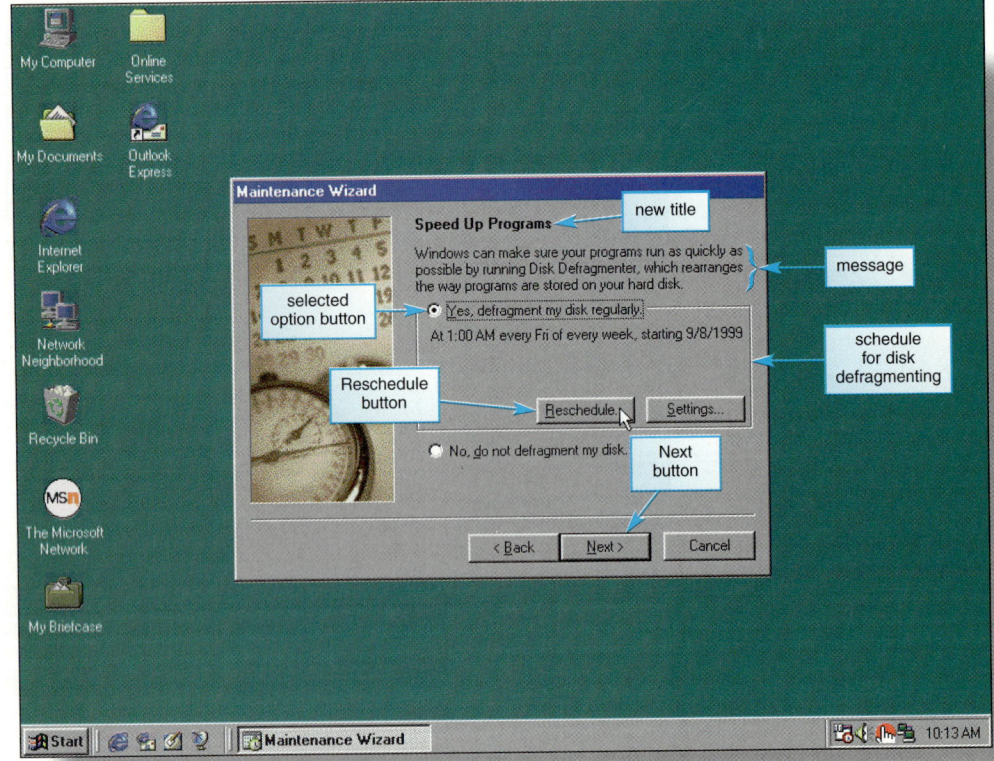

FIGURE 9-47

Scheduling Routine Maintenance Using the Maintenance Wizard • WIN 9.35

7 **Click the Reschedule button, click the Start time box up or down arrow to display 2:00 AM, click the Thu check box, deselect any other check boxes, and then point to the OK button.**

The modified schedule displays at the top of the Reschedule dialog box, the Start time box contains the 2:00 AM time, and a check mark displays in the Thu check box (Figure 9-48).

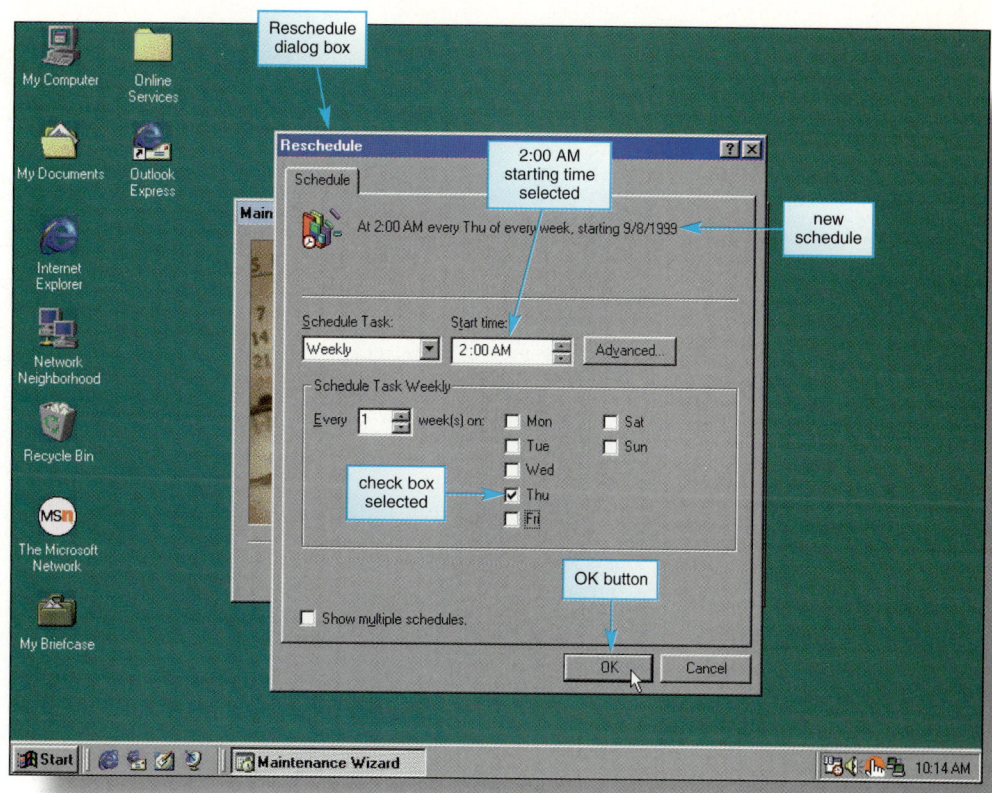

FIGURE 9-48

8 **Click the OK button and then point to the Next button in the Maintenance Wizard dialog box.**

The Reschedule dialog box closes (Figure 9-49). The schedule for defragmenting the disk changes in the Maintenance Wizard dialog box.

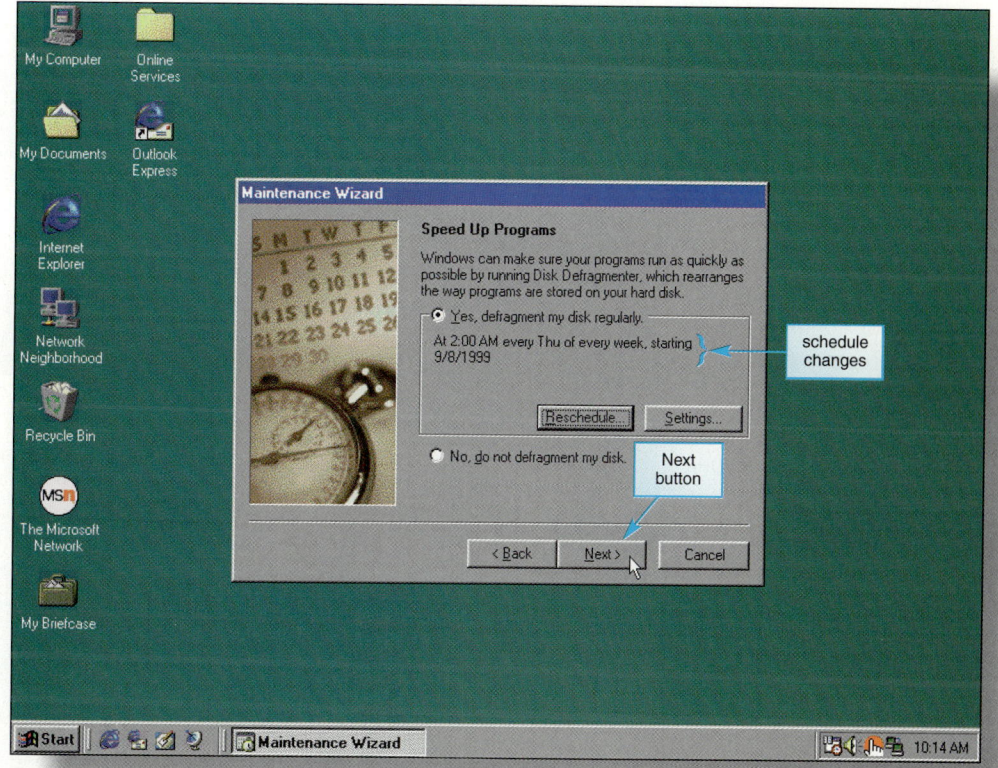

FIGURE 9-49

WIN 9.36 • Project 9 • Maintaining and Optimizing Your Computer and System Registry

9 **Click the Next button and then point to the Next button in the Maintenance Wizard dialog box.**

The contents of the Maintenance Wizard dialog box change (Figure 9-50). The dialog box contains the Scan Hard Disk for Errors title, a new message, a pane, and the No option button. The pane contains the selected Yes option button and the current schedule for scanning the hard disk.

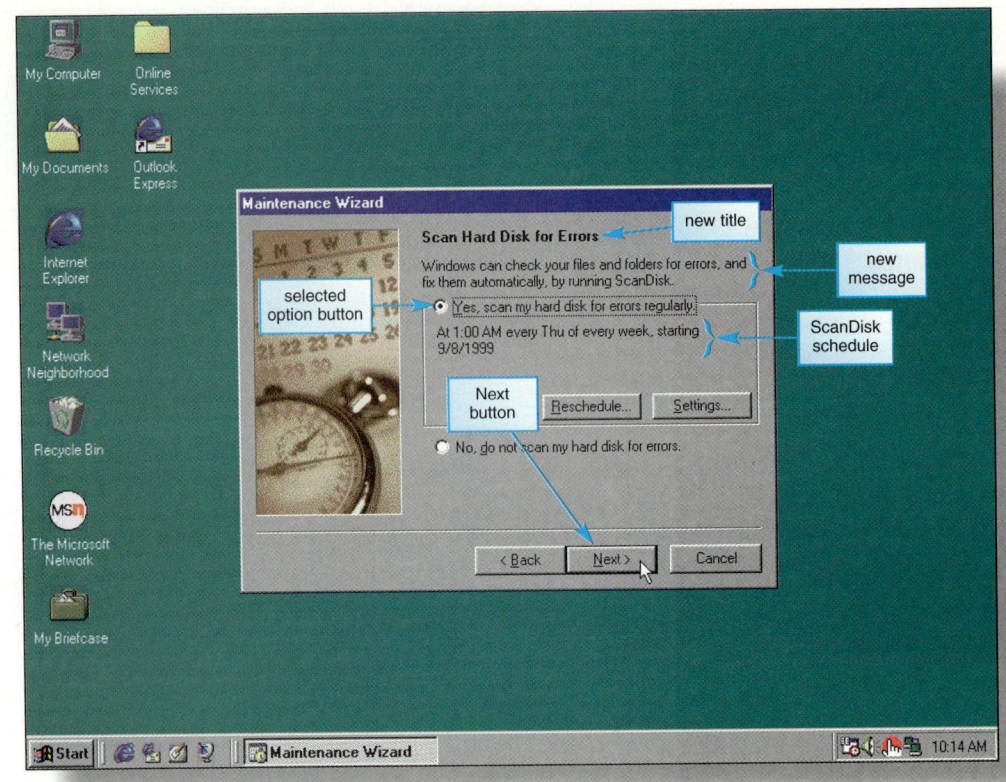

FIGURE 9-50

10 **Click the Next button and then point to the Next button in the Maintenance Wizard dialog box.**

The contents of the Maintenance Wizard dialog box change (Figure 9-51). The dialog box contains the Delete Unnecessary Files title, a new message, a pane, and the unselected No option button. The pane contains the selected Yes option button, the current schedule for deleting files, and a list box containing four file types.

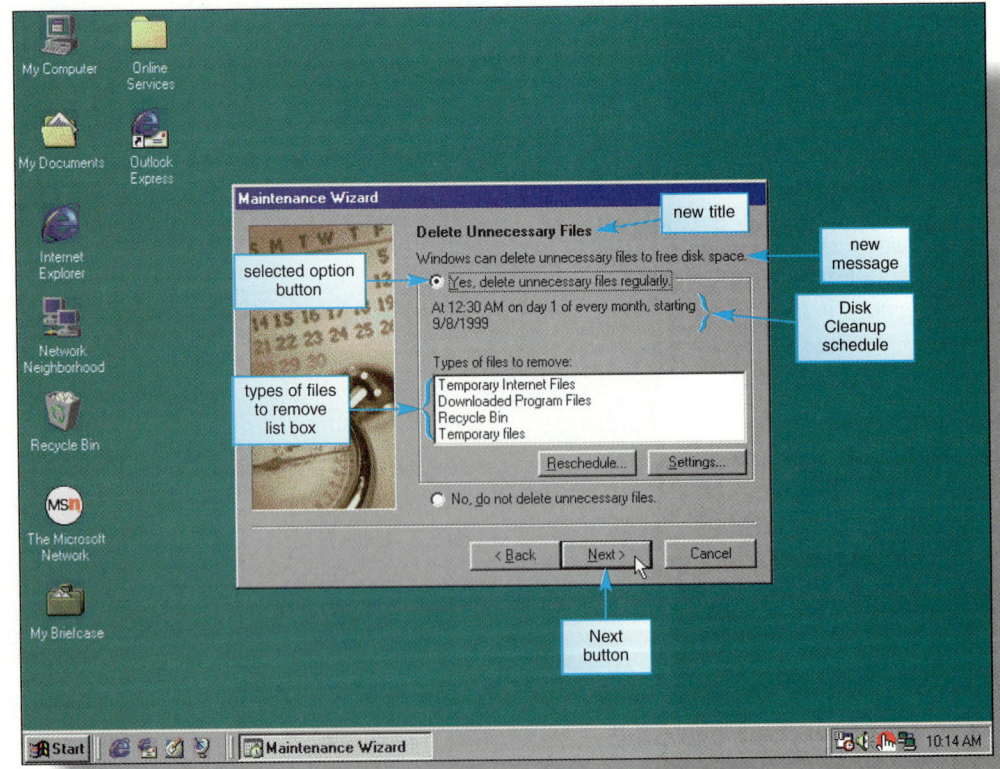

FIGURE 9-51

Scheduling Routine Maintenance Using the Maintenance Wizard • WIN 9.37

  Click the Next button and then point to the Finish button.

The contents of the Maintenance Wizard dialog box change (Figure 9-52). The dialog box contains a new message and a list box containing the schedules for the Disk Defragmenter, ScanDisk, and Disk Cleanup tasks, and a check box.

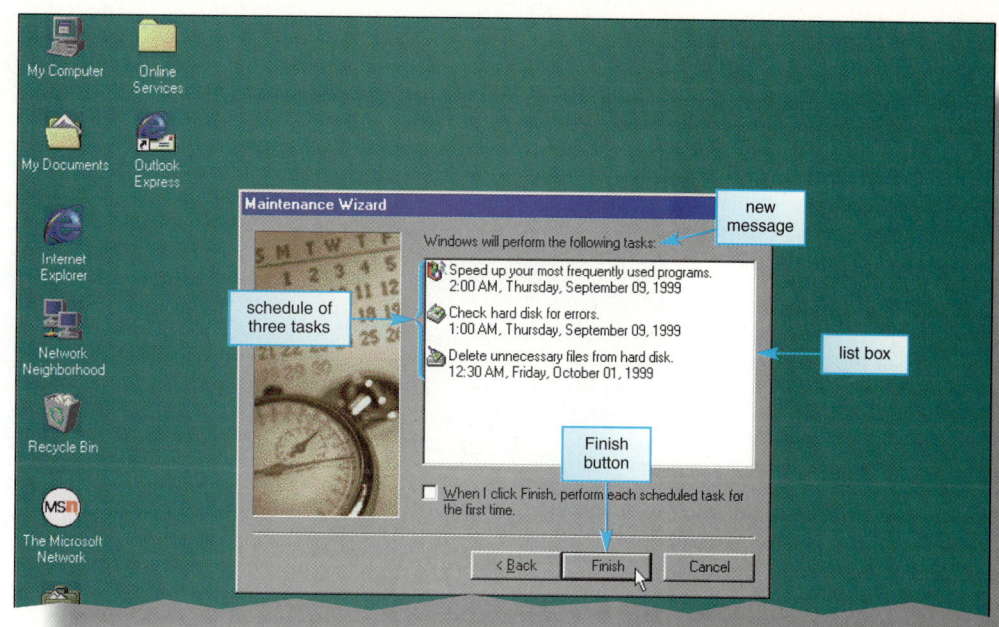

Click the Finish button.

The Maintenance Wizard dialog box closes.

FIGURE 9-52

Currently, the schedule for performing the ScanDisk program is 1:00 AM on Thursday every week, the Disk Cleanup program is 12:30 AM on day 1 of every month, and the Disk Defragmenter is 2:00 AM on Thursday every week. The three tasks will be performed starting September 9, 1999. This date and the day of the week the tasks are performed will be different on your computer.

Viewing the Routine Maintenance Tasks Using Task Scheduler

Previously, you created a schedule to scan the hard disk, defragment the hard disk, and delete unnecessary files on the hard disk using the Maintenance wizard. You can view these three tasks and their schedules by double-clicking the Task Scheduler icon in the tray status area on the taskbar. Perform the following steps to view the tasks and schedules created using the Maintenance wizard.

Other Ways

1. Click Start button on taskbar, click Help, click Index tab, type maintenance wizard, click Display button, click Click here hyperlink
2. Click Start button, click Run, type tuneup, click OK button

More About

Task Scheduler

If you want to turn Task Scheduler off, double-click the My Computer icon, double-click the Task Scheduler icon, click Advanced, and then click Stop Using Task Scheduler.

Steps: To View Tasks and Schedules

 Point to the Task Scheduler icon in the tray status area on the taskbar (Figure 9-53).

FIGURE 9-53

Double-click the Task Scheduler icon and then point to the Close button in the Scheduled Tasks window.

Although not visible in Figure 9-54, the Scheduled Tasks window contains five column headers (Figure 9-54). The list box below the headers contains the Add Scheduled Task name and names for the three tasks. Each name consists of the task, schedule, next run time, last run time, and status.

 **Click the Close button.**

The Scheduled Tasks window closes.

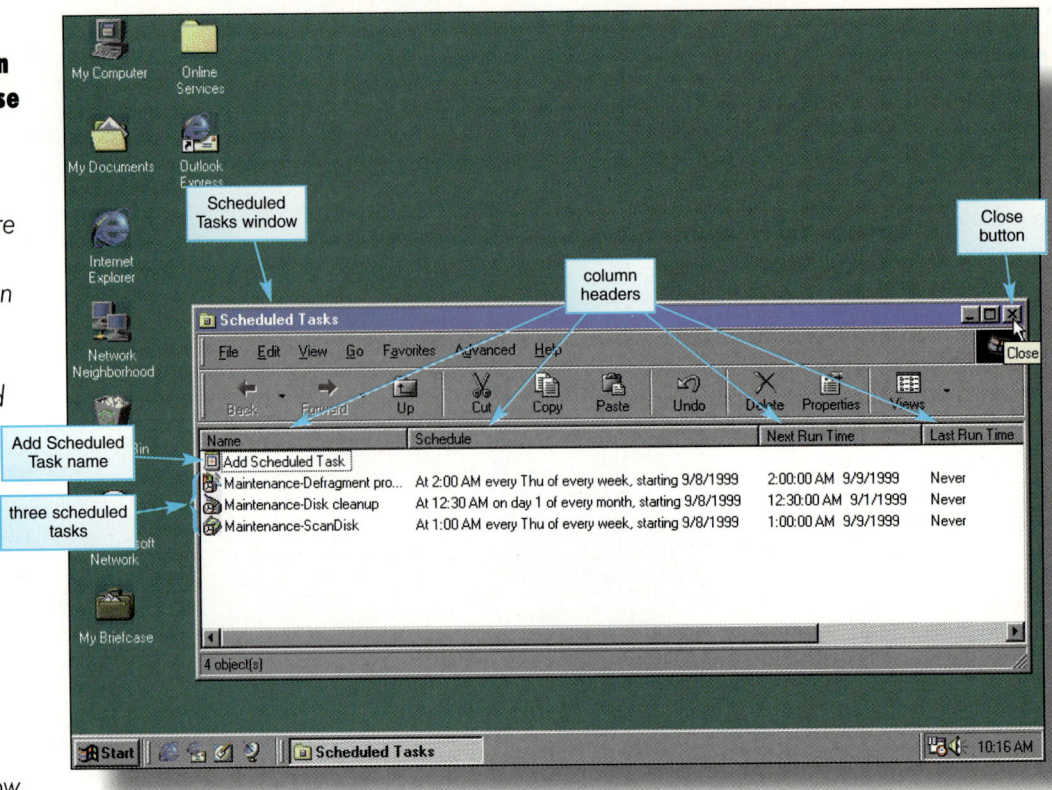

FIGURE 9-54

Other Ways

1. Double-click My Computer icon, double-click Scheduled Tasks icon
2. Double-click Network Neighborhood icon, double-click computer icon, double-click Scheduled Tasks icon

Previously, you used the Maintenance wizard to schedule routine maintenance. The routine maintenance included scanning the hard disk, defragmenting the hard disk, and removing unnecessary files from the hard disk. You scheduled the tasks for late at night. Remember that the computer must be turned on and the Windows 98 operating system launched to allow Task Scheduler to perform the scheduled maintenance.

When Task Scheduler performs the routine maintenance tasks, a series of dialog boxes display while the tasks are performed. After a scheduled task is performed, Task Scheduler changes the name in the Last Run Time column in the Scheduled Tasks window (Figure 9-54) to contain the time and date the maintenance was performed.

Windows Update

Another way to maintain a computer is to update system files, device drivers, and software components when new versions or releases become available. **Windows Update** automates the process of updating system files, device drivers, and software components on a computer and provides up-to-date technical support. Windows Update scans the hard disk on a computer system, generates a list of items that can or should be updated, compares these items to a master database located at the Windows Update Web site, and then downloads and installs the files for the items you select. If, after downloading a new component, the file does not work or you prefer the old file, you have the option of using the Uninstall option to revert to the previous version.

One advantage of the World Wide Web is that the format of a Web page and the information on the Web page can be modified easily. As a result, Web pages and the hyperlinks on a Web page change frequently. Note that the Microsoft Outlook Web page and hyperlinks you view on your computer may look different from the Web page and hyperlinks shown in this book.

Perform the following steps to display the home page for the Windows Update Web site.

 To Display the Windows Update Home Page

1 **If necessary, connect to the Internet. Click the Start button and then point to Windows Update.**

The Start menu displays (Figure 9-55).

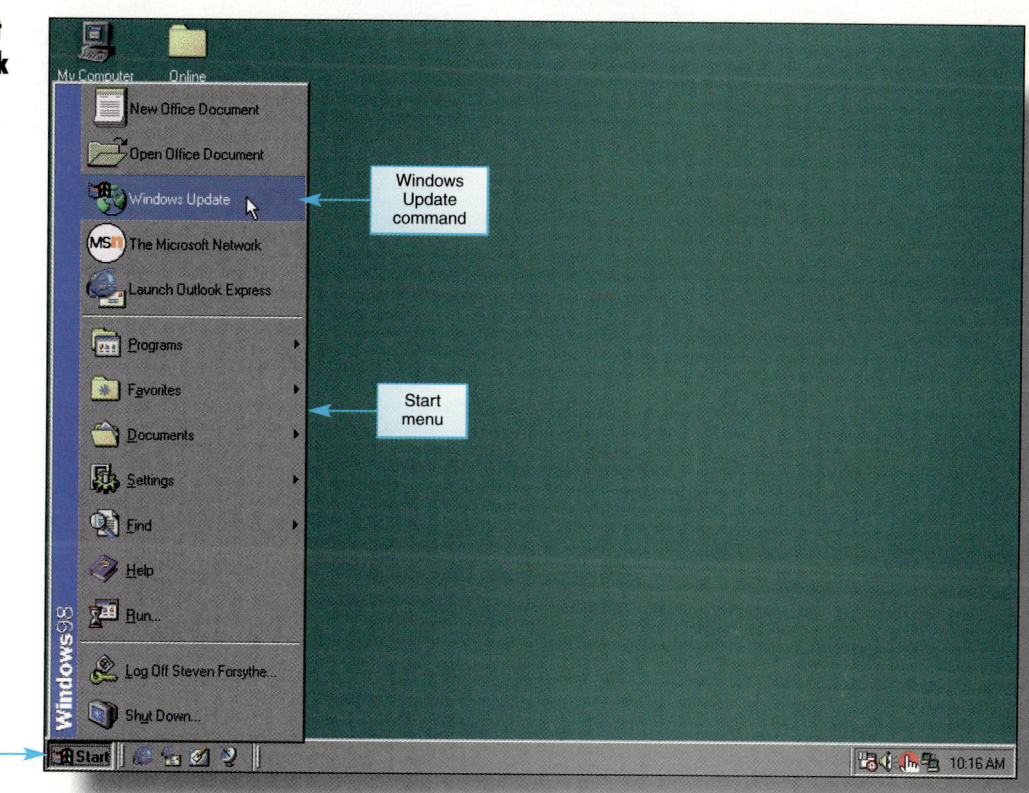

FIGURE 9-55

WIN 9.40 • Project 9 • Maintaining and Optimizing Your Computer and System Registry

 Click Windows Update.

The Microsoft Windows Update - Microsoft Internet Explorer window containing the Windows Update home page displays (Figure 9-56). The navigation bar containing three names displays in the left side of the window. The first name, WINDOWS UPDATE HOME PAGE, is highlighted to indicate the Windows Update home page displays in the window. The right side of the window contains the Welcome to Windows Update title and information about Windows Update.

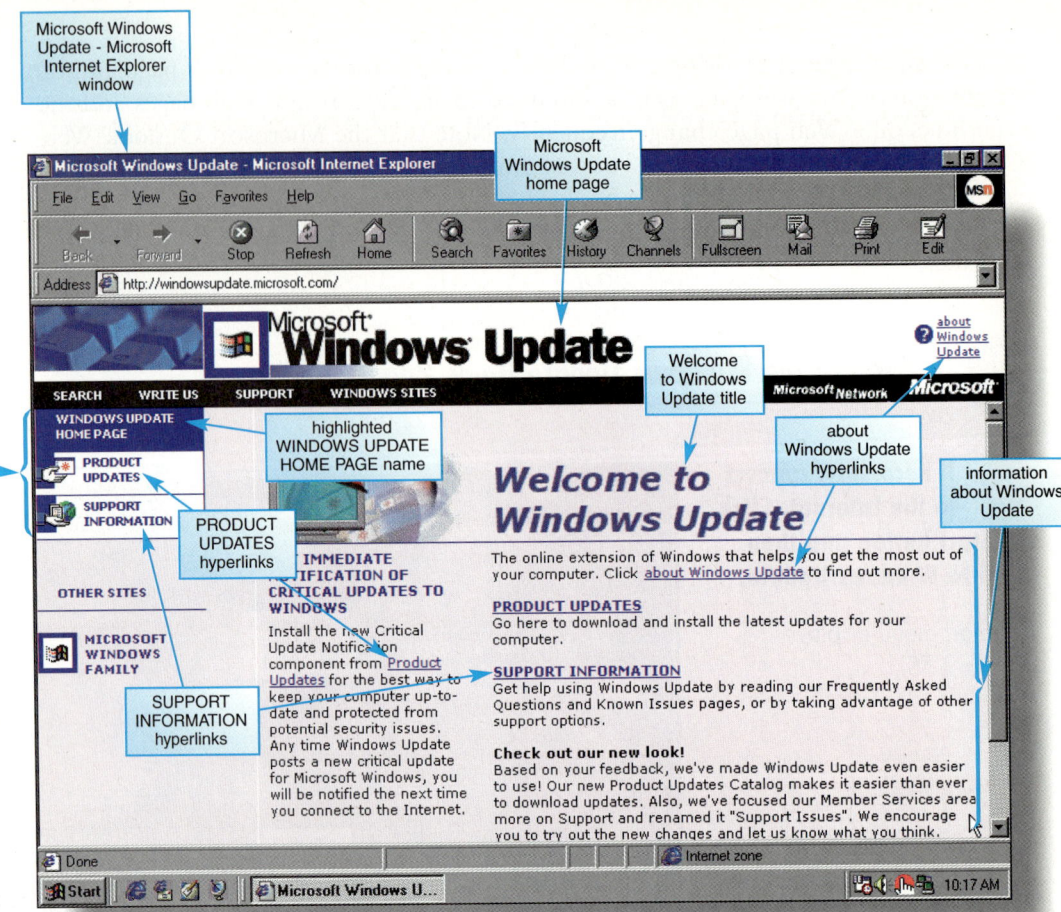

FIGURE 9-56

Other Ways

1. Click Start button on taskbar, point to Settings, click Windows Update
2. Click Start button, click Run, type wupdmgr, click OK button
3. Press CTRL+ESC, W; or CTRL+ESC, S, W

Because you modify Web pages frequently, the Microsoft Windows Update home page that displays on your desktop may be different from the Web page shown in Figure 9-56.

Currently, the Windows Update consists of two areas: the Product Updates area and the Support Information area. Clicking the PRODUCT UPDATES name on the navigation bar or the PRODUCT UPDATES hyperlink in the right side displays the Product Updates area in the right side. Clicking the SUPPORT INFORMATION name on the navigation bar or the SUPPORT INFORMATION hyperlink in the right side displays the Support Information area in the right side. The Support Information area contains hyperlinks to frequently asked questions, known issues you may want information about, and options for obtaining technical support from Microsoft.

Two hyperlinks, labeled about Windows Update, display in the right side of the Windows Update window in Figure 9-56. One hyperlink displays to the right of the Microsoft Windows Update title at the top of the home page and the other hyperlink displays in the text below the Welcome to Windows Update title. Clicking either hyperlink displays the About Microsoft Windows Update - Microsoft Internet Explorer window containing information about Windows Update, the Product Updates area, and the Support Information area.

The Product Updates Area

The **Product Updates area** is a catalog of critical and recommended updates, enhancements to the Windows operating system, and programs that work with Windows 98. In the Product Updates area, you can scroll a list of components, select as many components as you want, and then download and install the selected components on the computer.

When you click the Product Updates hyperlink, the Windows Update dialog box displays that asks you if you want Product Updates to determine what components are installed on the computer and determine whether new components, upgrades, or enhancements are available for the computer. If you agree, Product Updates scans the hard disk for installed programs and displays the recommended list of components to download to the computer. If you do not agree, a complete list of all the components available for download from the Product Updates area displays, including those you already may have installed. You then will have to decide which components, if any, you wish to download to the computer.

When the recommended list or complete list displays, you can browse the list, select the components you want, and download them to the computer. Perform the following steps to check for components you may want to download to the computer.

More About

Product Updates

While checking for components, Product Updates searches the hard disk for components (programs, games, drivers, and so on). In the process, Product Updates accumulates information about the hard disk, determines what software is installed on the hard disk, and what software is used the most. Rest assured - the information Product Updates finds about your computer is not sent to Microsoft or transmitted over the Internet.

 To Check for Components

1 **Point to PRODUCT UPDATES on the navigation bar in the Microsoft Windows Update - Microsoft Internet Explorer window (Figure 9-57).**

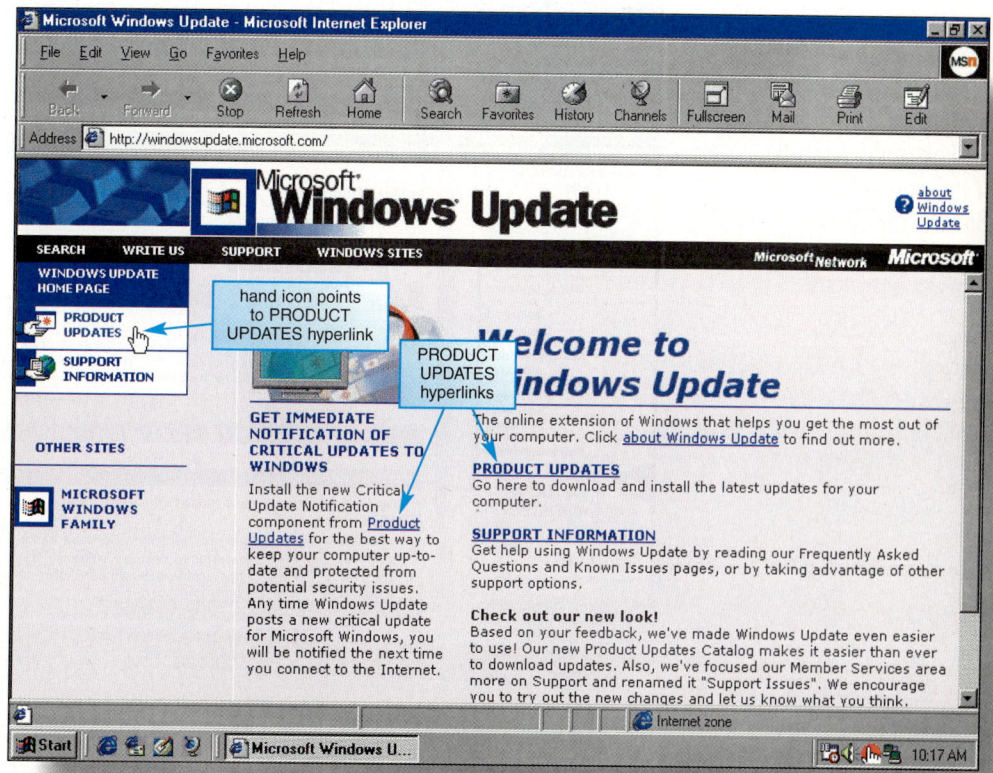

FIGURE 9-57

WIN 9.42 • Project 9 • Maintaining and Optimizing Your Computer and System Registry

 Click PRODUCT UPDATES and then point to the Yes button in the Windows Update dialog box.

The PRODUCT UPDATES hyperlink on the navigator bar is highlighted, six hyperlinks display right-aligned below the PRODUCT UPDATES hyperlink, the contents of the right side change, and the Windows Update dialog box displays on top of the Microsoft Windows Update window (Figure 9-58). The dialog box contains messages and the Yes and No buttons.

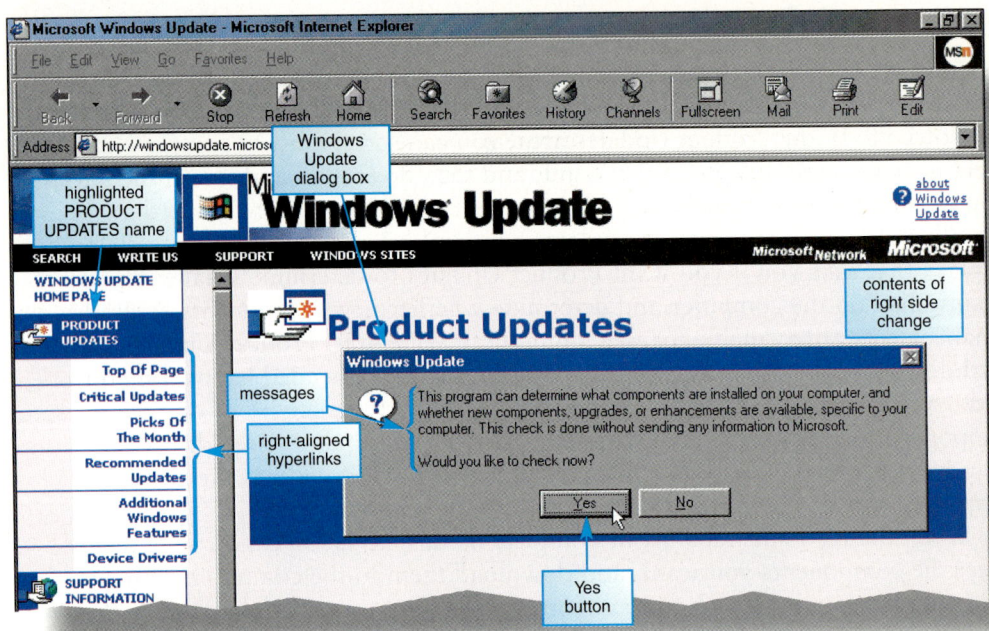

FIGURE 9-58

Click the Yes button.

The Windows Update dialog box closes, Product Updates scans the hard disk for components, a right arrow precedes the Top Of Page hyperlink in the left side, and the contents of the right side change (Figure 9-59).

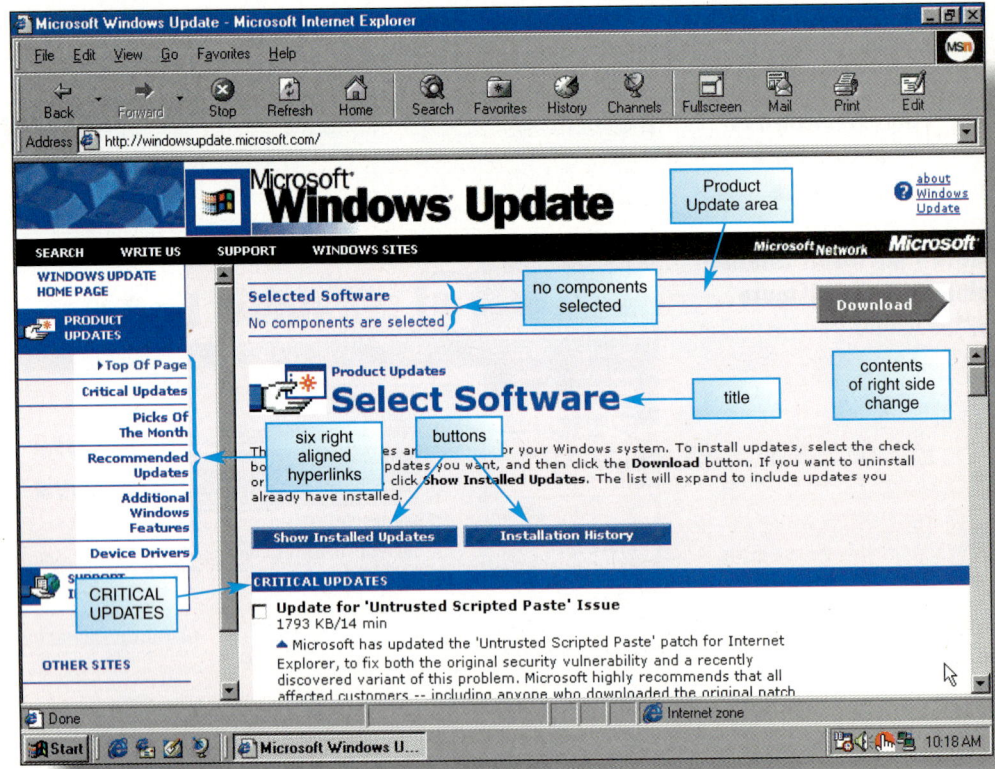

FIGURE 9-59

1. On Help menu, click Product Updates
2. Click PRODUCT UPDATES hyperlink in right side of Microsoft Windows Update window

Currently, six hyperlinks display right-aligned below the PRODUCT UPDATES name in the navigation bar in Figure 9-59. A right arrow precedes the Top Of Page hyperlink to indicate the top of the Product Updates Web page displays in the right side. The first five hyperlinks in the navigation bar represent areas in the Product Updates area in the right side. Clicking one of these hyperlinks will cause the right side to scroll and the beginning of the area associated with the selected hyperlink to display at the top of the right frame. Clicking the sixth hyperlink (Device Drivers) determines the device drivers installed on the computer and determines whether new device drivers are available for the computer.

Currently, the right side in the Windows Update window contains an area to list components that have been selected (no components currently are selected), the Select Software title, two buttons (Show Installed Updates and Installation History), and the top of the CRITICAL UPDATES area. The words, Show Installed Updates, on the Show Installed Updates button indicate the recommended list of components displays in the right side. Clicking the Show Installed Updates button changes the words on the button to Hide Installed Updates and displays the complete list of components. Clicking the Download button displays a history (time, date, and description) of the components you already have downloaded.

> **More About**
>
> **Critical Updates**
>
> Any components listed under the Critical Updates title will fix known problems with the computer and should be downloaded.

Downloading a Component

As indicated by the five hyperlinks below the Top Of Page hyperlink (Figure 9-59) in the navigation bar, the right side of the Microsoft Windows Update home page contains five areas that contain downloadable components. These areas are Critical Updates, Picks Of The Month, Recommended Updates, Additional Windows Features, and Device Drivers. To view the components in each area, you can scroll the right side until the component displays or you can click a hyperlink in the navigation bar and then scroll to view the components in that area.

To illustrate how to download a component to the hard disk, you will download the Wallet 2.1 program from the Commerce area of the Product Updates area to the hard disk. Wallet 2.1 makes shopping at Web sites easier and safer by storing personal and credit card information on the computer. Downloading this component will take approximately two minutes.

Perform the following steps to download the Wallet 2.1 program. If the Wallet 2.1 program is not available on the Product Updates area on your computer, download a desktop theme. If you are not allowed to download software from the Internet to the hard disk on the computer you are working, read the following steps without performing them.

Steps: To Download a Component

1 Scroll the right side to display the Wallet 2.1 check box and then point to the check box.

The right side scrolls and the Wallet 2.1 component displays (Figure 9-60).

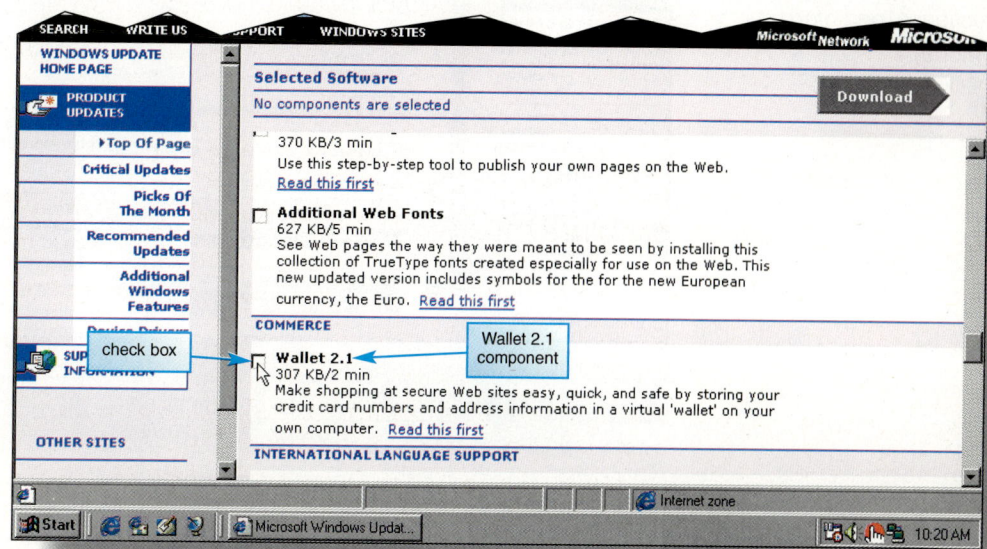

FIGURE 9-60

2 **Click the check box and then point to the Download button.**

The Selected Software area contains the size of the file to be downloaded (307 KB) and the approximate time to download the file (2 minutes) when using a 28.8Kbps modem (Figure 9-61).

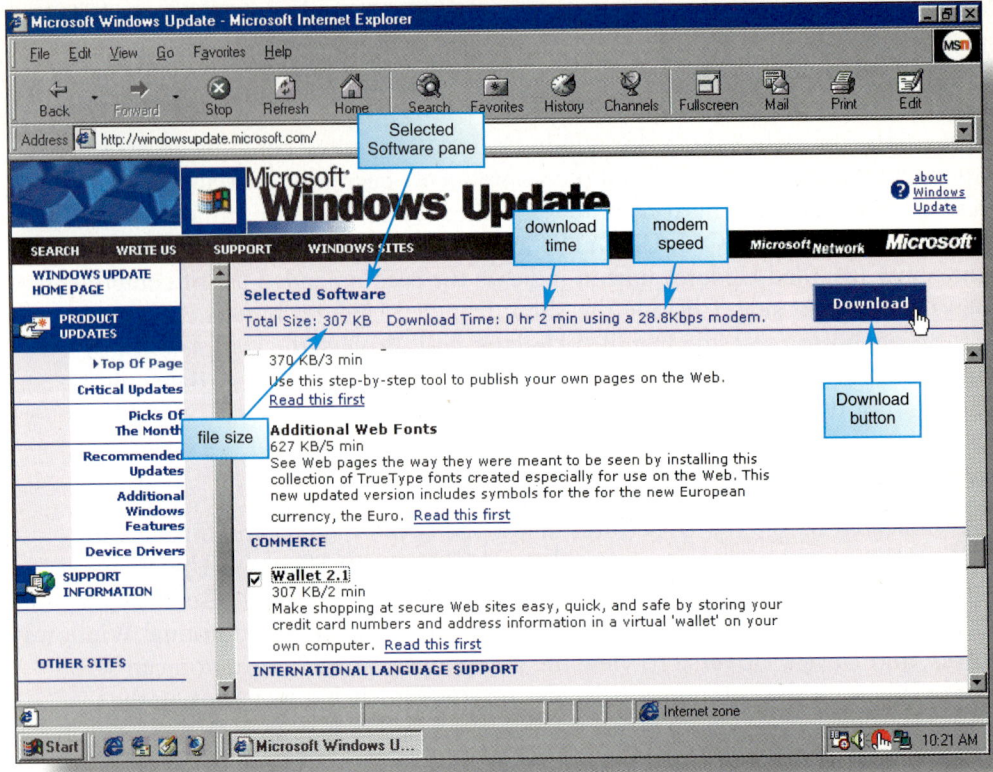

FIGURE 9-61

3 **Click the Download button and then point to the Start Download button.**

The contents of the right side change (Figure 9-62). The Download Checklist title displays, followed by three steps (Confirm Selections, View Instructions?, and Start Download).

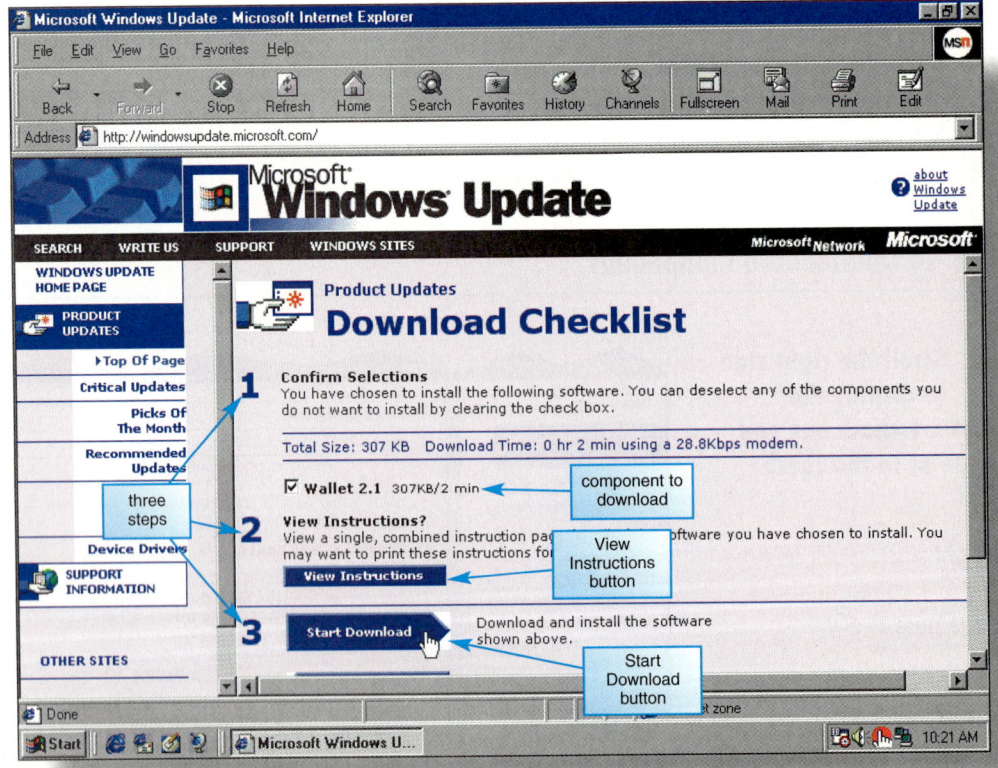

FIGURE 9-62

Windows Update • WIN 9.45

4) Click the Start Download button. If necessary, click the Yes button in the Supplemental End User License Agreement dialog box.

The Windows Update window displays while the component is downloaded on the hard disk (Figure 9-63). The window contains a message, Download progress indicator, Download time remaining message (no message displays), Bytes received (275 KB) and total bytes (307 KB) to download message, Install progress indicator, Percent complete message, and Cancel button.

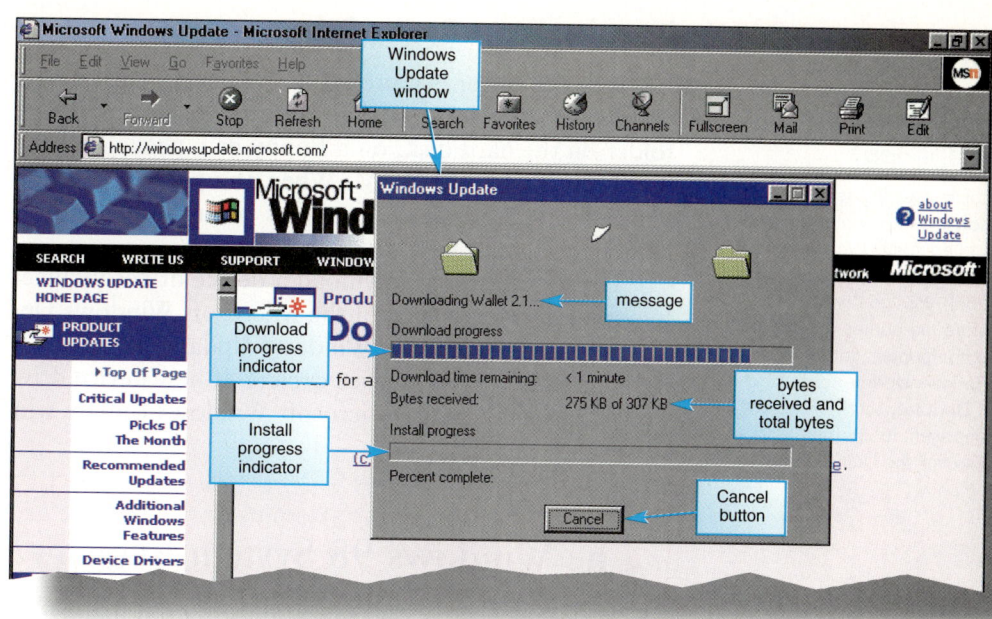

FIGURE 9-63

5) When the Install Complete dialog box displays, point to the OK button.

When the download is complete, the Install Complete dialog box displays (Figure 9-64).

6) Click the OK button and then click the Close button in the Microsoft Windows Update – Microsoft Internet Explorer window.

The Install Complete dialog box and Microsoft Windows Update window close.

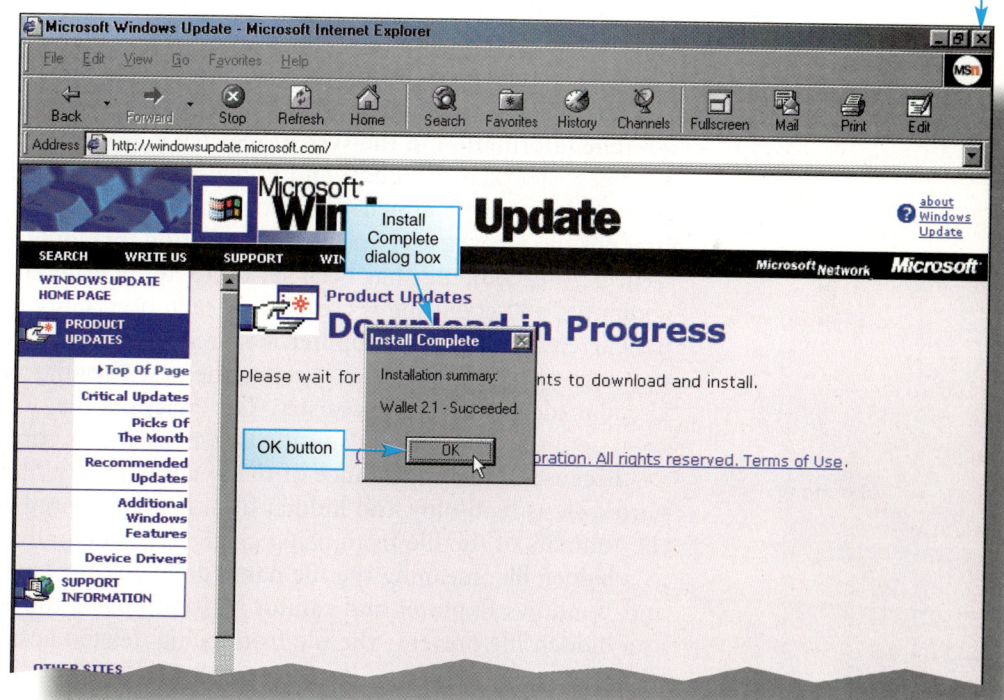

FIGURE 9-64

Wallet 2.1 is downloaded and installed on the hard disk. The first time you visit a Web site that uses Wallet, you will be prompted to type your personal and credit card information. This information will be used to complete any purchases made at this Web site or other sites you visit.

More About

Downloading a Component

After connecting to Windows Update and downloading an updated component (program, game, driver, system tool, and so on), you may want to restore the earlier version of the component. To do so, start Windows Update, click Product Updates, scroll to find the component to uninstall, and then click the Uninstall button.

Downloading a Device Driver

A **device driver** is a program used by the operating system to control a hardware device. Most device drivers for existing hardware devices are located in the Windows folder on the hard disk, on a floppy disk packaged with the hardware device, or on the Windows 98 CD-ROM. When an updated device driver is made available for a hardware device, Microsoft allows you to download the device driver from the Windows Update Web site.

The procedure to download a device driver involves clicking the Device Drivers hyperlink in the left side of the Microsoft Windows Update window and then clicking the Yes button in the Windows Update dialog box to have Windows Update scan the hard disk for new device drivers. If new device drivers are available, click the Install hyperlink in the Microsoft Windows Update window to install the new device driver.

The Windows 98 System Registry

The **system registry** is the central information database for Windows 98. A primary role of the registry is to serve as a central location for information about hardware and software. Everything the operating system needs to know about hardware and software is stored in the system registry. For example, when a new hardware device is installed, Windows 98 checks the system registry for an existing device driver for the device. If a device driver is found, the hardware device is installed. If a device driver is not found, Windows 98 searches all available media for the device driver that best matches the device and adds the device driver to the system registry alongside the other settings for the hardware device.

The information in the system registry is stored in three separate files. These files are the System.dat, User.dat, and Policy.pol. The **System.dat** file records information about the hardware attached to the computer and is the largest of the three files. The **User.dat** file records user specific information including settings you have personalized. If your computer has been set up to allow different individuals to use the same computer, a User.dat file is created for each user. Only the User.dat file of the individual currently using the computer is stored in the system registry. When the current user logs off and a new user logs on, the new User.dat file is substituted for the old User.dat file in the system registry. The **Policy.pol** file, which is an optional component, contains information specific to a network or corporate environment.

Because of the importance of the system registry files, the files are stored on the hard disk as read-only and hidden files. A file is stored as a **read-only file** to prevent the contents of the file from being changed accidentally. In addition, a file is stored as a **hidden file**, meaning the file name does not display when you use My Computer and Windows Explorer and cannot be found using the Find command. Storing a file as a hidden file prevents the file from being deleted accidentally.

Backing Up the System Registry

To protect itself, the operating system automatically creates a backup copy of the system registry files each time you launch Windows 98 successfully. Each set of backup files is compressed to save storage space and stored in a single cabinet file (.cab file extension), which is located in the hidden Sysbckup subfolder of the Windows folder. The number of backup copies made of the system registry, file names of additional files backed up in the process, and the disk location of the resulting cabinet files are determined by settings in the Scanreg.ini file, which is located in the Windows folder. The default setting for the number of backup copies made in this file is set to five.

Making a Backup Copy of the System Registry Using Registry Checker

Each time you launch the Windows 98 operating system, a program called **Registry Checker** scans the system registry for problems. If a problem exists, Registry Checker replaces the corrupted system registry with the most recent backup copy of the system registry. If no backup copies exist, Registry Checker attempts to fix the problem with the existing system registry. If a problem exists, Registry Checker creates a backup copy of the system registry.

In some cases, you may want to run Registry Checker to make a backup copy manually of the system registry. For example, when you install new hardware or software, the new settings for the hardware or software are added to the system registry. If you are satisfied the hardware or software works properly, you may want to make a backup copy of the modified system registry instead of waiting for the next time Windows 98 launches.

To make a backup copy of the system registry, you use Registry Checker, which you launch from the System Information window. **System Information** is a system tool that records system configuration information for the computer and stores it in a central location. While troubleshooting a problem with a computer, support technicians may use System Information to find the data they need to resolve the problem quickly. In addition, you start Registry Checker from the System Information window. Perform the following steps to make a backup copy of the system registry using Registry Checker.

 To Make a Backup Copy of the System Registry

1 **Click the Start button, point to Programs, point to Accessories, point to System Tools, and then point to System Information.**

The Start menu, Programs submenu, Accessories submenu, and System Tools submenu display (Figure 9-65). The highlighted System Information command displays on the System Tools submenu.

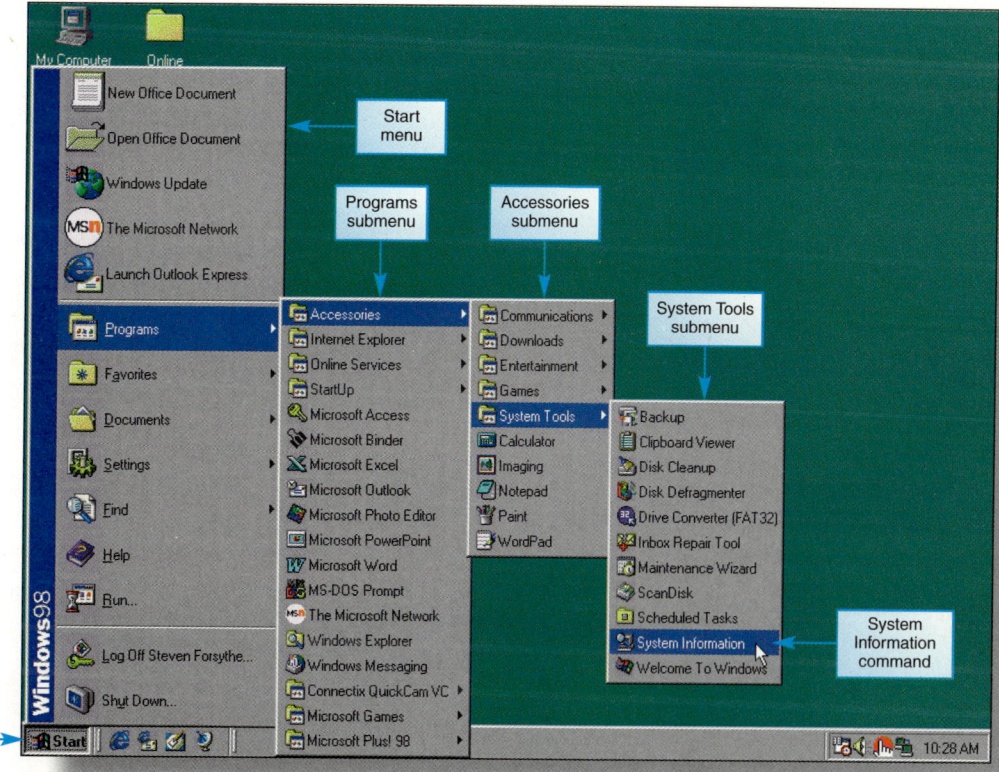

FIGURE 9-65

WIN 9.48 • Project 9 • Maintaining and Optimizing Your Computer and System Registry

2 **Click System Information and then point to Tools on the menu bar.**

The Microsoft System Information window displays and is divided into two panes (Figure 9-66). The left pane contains a hierarchical structure of the System Information (Hardware Resources, Components, and Software Environment). The System Information name is highlighted in the left pane and the right pane contains the system information.

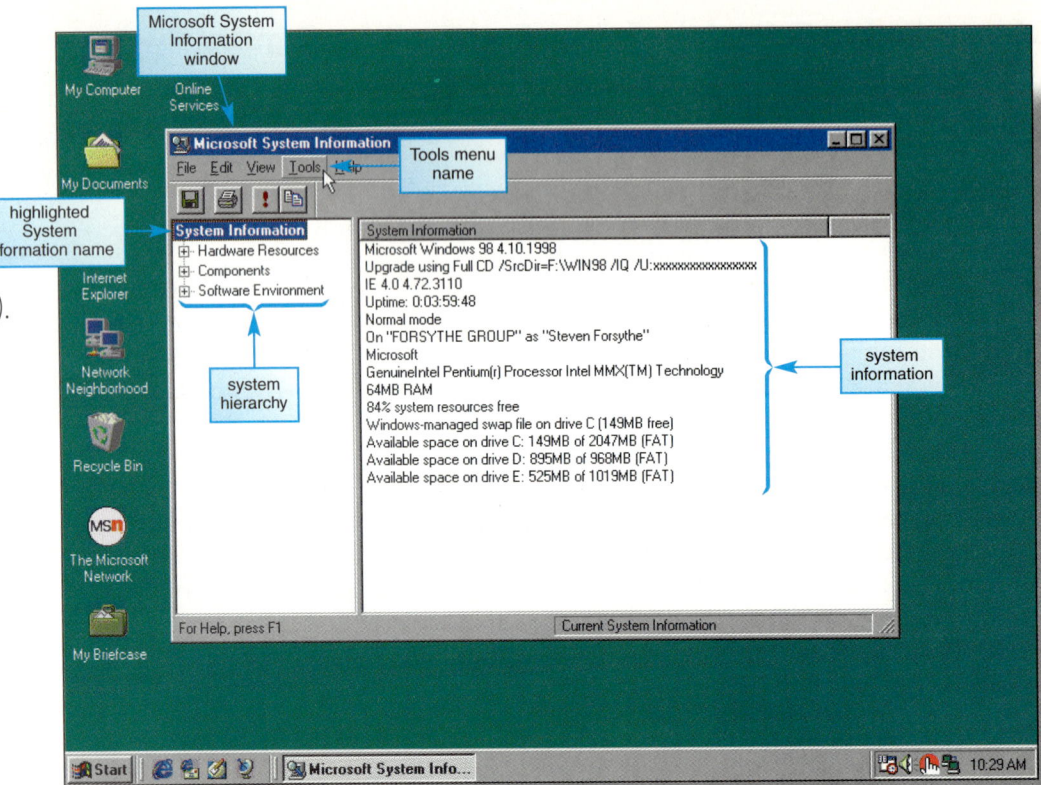

FIGURE 9-66

3 **Click Tools and then point to Registry Checker.**

The Tools menu displays and the Registry Checker command is highlighted (Figure 9-67). The Tools menu contains other system tools, such as Signature Verification Tool, Dr. Watson, and ScanDisk.

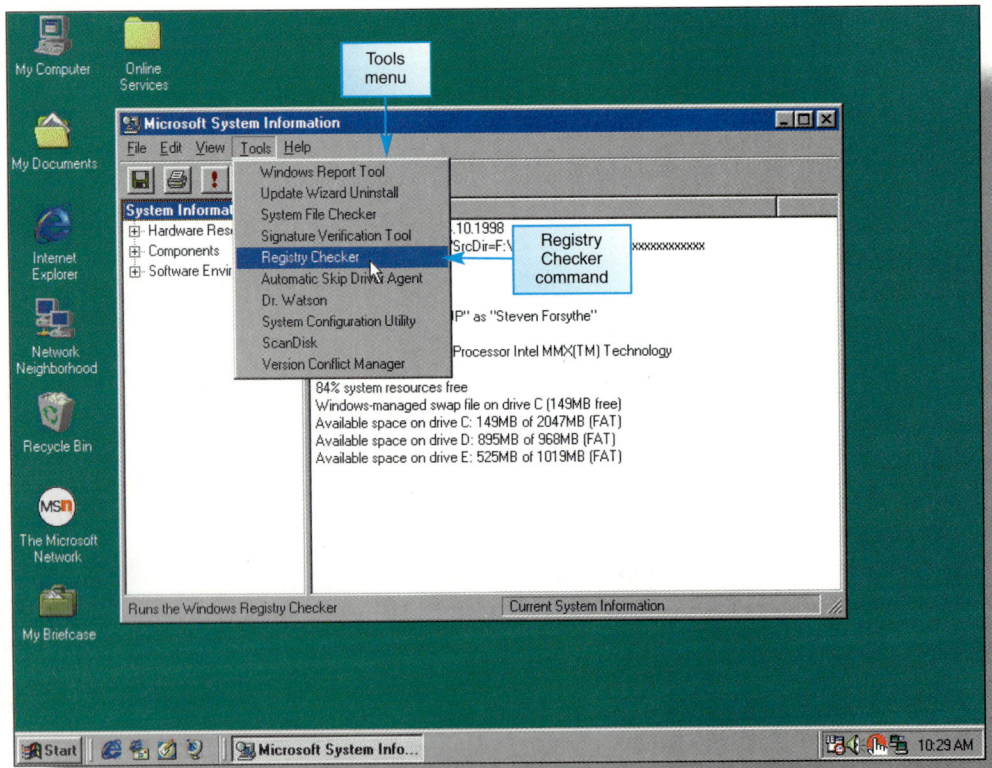

FIGURE 9-67

④ **Click Registry Checker and then point to the Yes button in the Registry Scan Results dialog box.**

The Tools menu closes and the Windows Registry Checker dialog box containing the message, Scanning System Registry, displays while Registry Checker scans the system registry for problems (Figure 9-68). When the scan is complete, the Registry Scan Results dialog box displays on top of the Registry Checker dialog box. The dialog box contains messages.

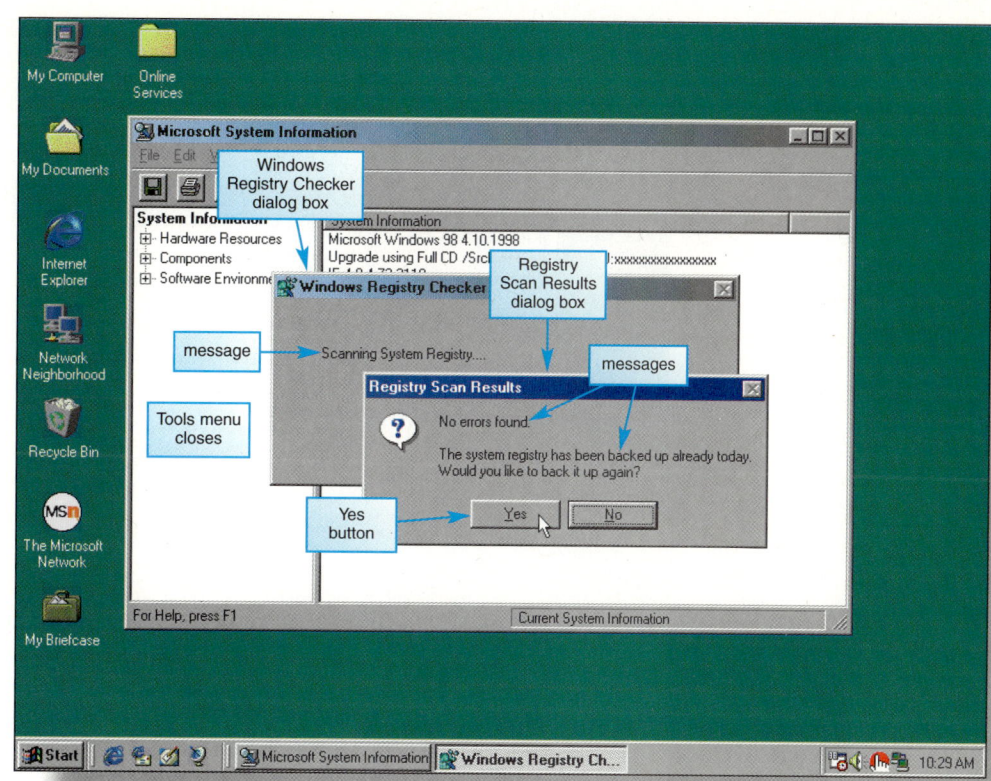

FIGURE 9-68

⑤ **Click the Yes button and then point to the OK button in the smaller Windows Registry Checker dialog box.**

The Registry Scan Results dialog box closes and a smaller Windows Registry Checker dialog box displays (Figure 9-69). The dialog box contains a message and the OK button.

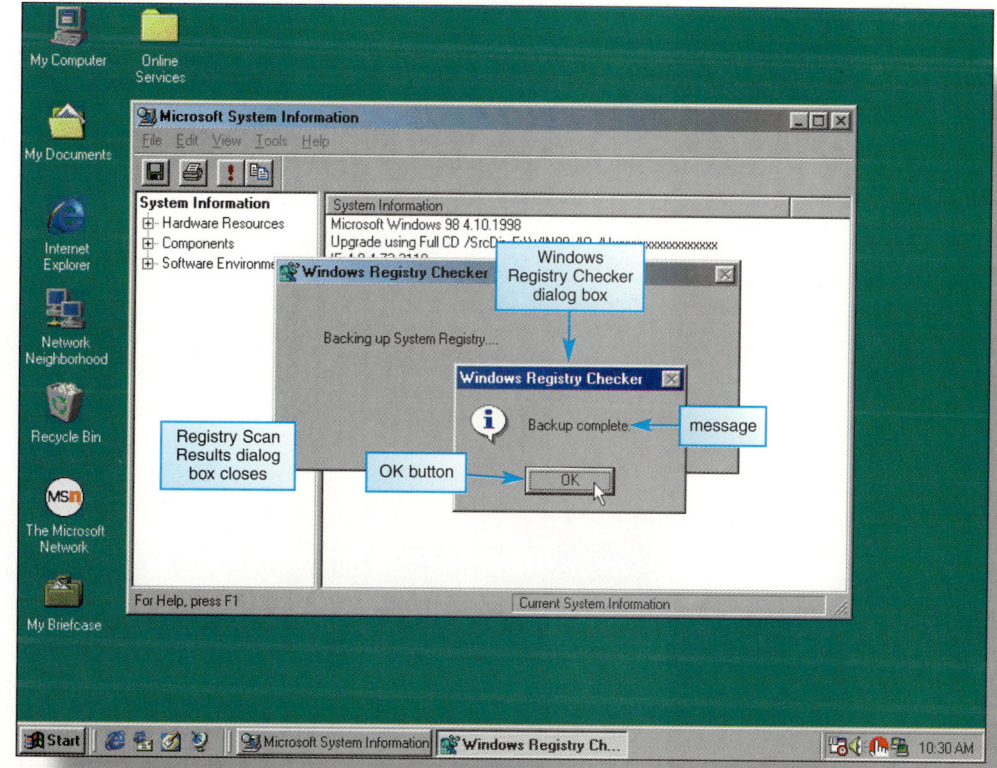

FIGURE 9-69

Click the OK button and then point to the Close button in the Microsoft System Information window.

The Windows Registry Checker dialog boxes close (Figure 9-70).

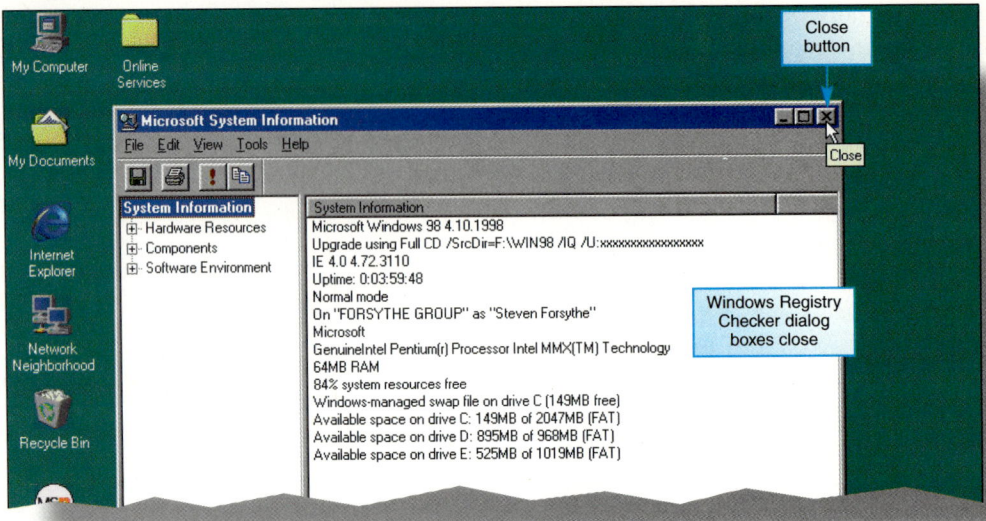

Click the Close button.

The Microsoft System Information window closes.

FIGURE 9-70

Other Ways

1. Click Start button on taskbar, click Help, click Index tab, type system information, click Display button, click Using System Information to display system data, click Display button, click Click here hyperlink
2. Click Start button, click Run, type msinfo32, click OK button

Viewing the System Registry Settings Using Registry Editor

Registry Editor is a tool that enables you to view and change the settings in the system registry. The system registry was designed by Microsoft Corporation for Windows 98 with the intention that only the operating system, application and system software, and experienced computer programmers would make modifications to the system registry settings. The importance of the system registry to the operating system is shown by the elaborate backup system (Registry Checker) that was designed for the system registry.

An operating system student should, however, have an understanding of the system registry and its organization. The system registry is organized into six main units, each unit is called an **HKEY**. Each HKEY is subdivided into **keys**, with each key containing **values**. The HKEYs and keys are organized in a hierarchical structure similar to that used by Windows Explorer to view the contents of the drives, folders, and files on the computer. A plus sign in a small box preceding a key (HKEY or key) indicates the key contains keys that do not display in the hierarchy. Clicking the box with a plus sign preceding the key expands the key and displays additional keys. A minus sign in a small box preceding a key indicates the key contains additional keys and these keys are visible in the hierarchy. The six HKEY names and the type of information they contain are summarized in Table 9-1.

Table 9-1	
HKEY NAME	**INFORMATION CONTAINED IN HKEY**
HKEY_CLASSES_ROOT	Backward compatibility to previous Windows versions, file types and their properties, Quick Viewers
HKEY_CURRENT_USER	Configuration information for the currently logged on user
HKEY_LOCAL_MACHINE	Software and hardware data for the computer
HKEY_USERS	Current user information plus all previously loaded user profiles
HKEY_CURRENT_CONFIG	Points to information in HKEY_LOCAL_MACHINE
HKEY_DYN_DATA	Contains dynamic data from main memory that changes each time Windows launches

The Windows 98 System Registry • WIN 9.51

Associated with each HKEY are keys that contain other subkeys and keys that contain values. For instance, HKEY_CURRENT_USER contains eight keys (AppEvents, C:, Control Panel, InstallLocationsMRU, keyboard layout, Network, RemoteAccess, and Software). These keys are shown in the My Computer folder in the Registry Editor window (see Figure 9-74 on page WIN 9.53). Seven of the keys contain subkeys and only the InstallLocationsMRU key contains values.

The values in the InstallLocationsMRU key are the locations of recently installed application programs. The MRU in the InstallLocationsMRU key name is an abbreviation for words, Most Recently Used. Each time you install an application software program, the location of the hardware device you used to install the program is stored in the InstallLocationsMRU key. Locations you may see in this key include A:\, F:\WIN98, and C:\WINDOWS\SYSTEM. Next time you install an application program, Windows 98 displays the locations from the key in a list box so you can select the location to use to install the program.

Perform the following steps to use the Registry Editor to view the six HKEYs in the system registry, the eight keys in HKEY_CURRENT_USER, and the values in the InstallLocationsMRU key.

Steps) To View the System Registry

1 **Click the Start button and then point to Run on the Start menu.**

The Start menu displays with the Run command highlighted (Figure 9-71).

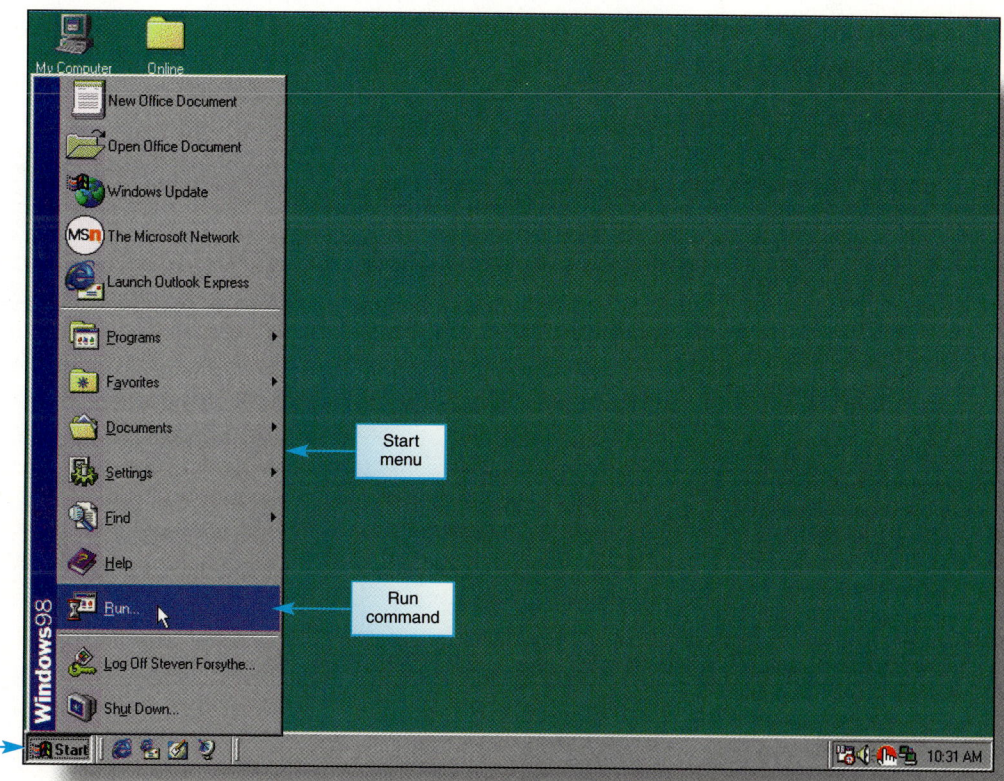

FIGURE 9-71

WIN 9.52 • Project 9 • Maintaining and Optimizing Your Computer and System Registry

2 **Click Run, type** `regedit` **in the Open box in the Run dialog box, and then point to the OK button.**

The Run dialog box, containing a message, Open box, and three command buttons displays (Figure 9-72). The Registry Editor program name, regedit, displays in the Open box.

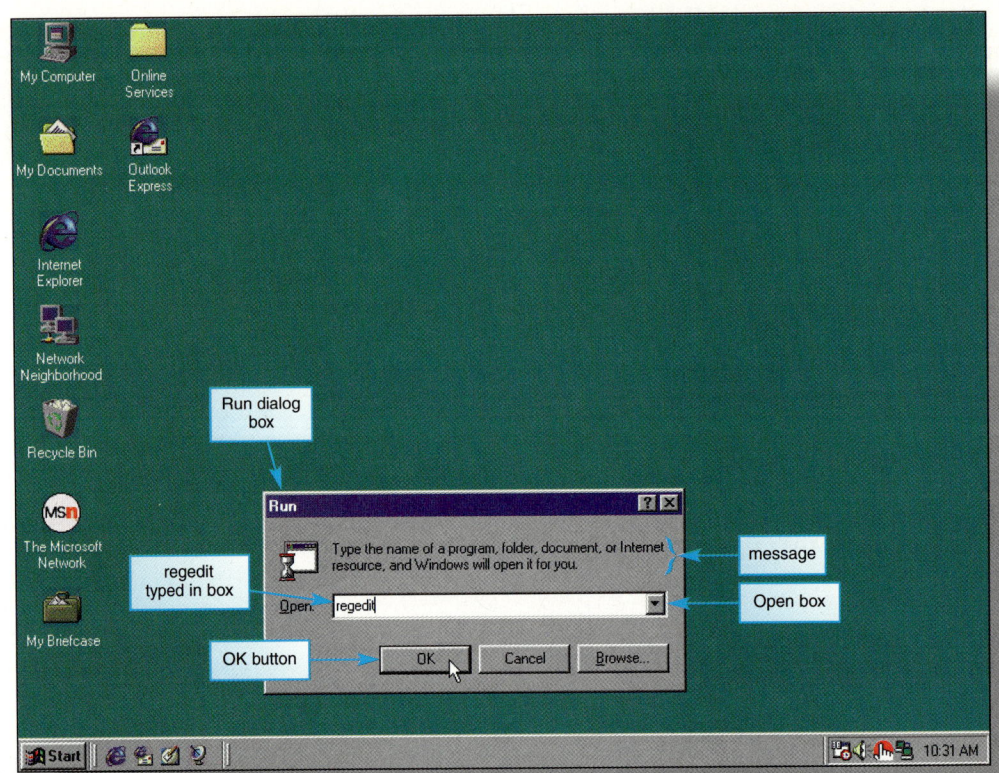

FIGURE 9-72

3 **Click the OK button and then point to the plus sign to the left of HKEY_CURRENT_USER in the left frame of the Registry Editor window.**

The Run dialog box closes and the Registry Editor window containing two panes displays (Figure 9-73). The left pane displays the hierarchical structure of the system registry, highlighted My Computer name, and six HKEYs. The right pane contains two column headers (Name and Data).

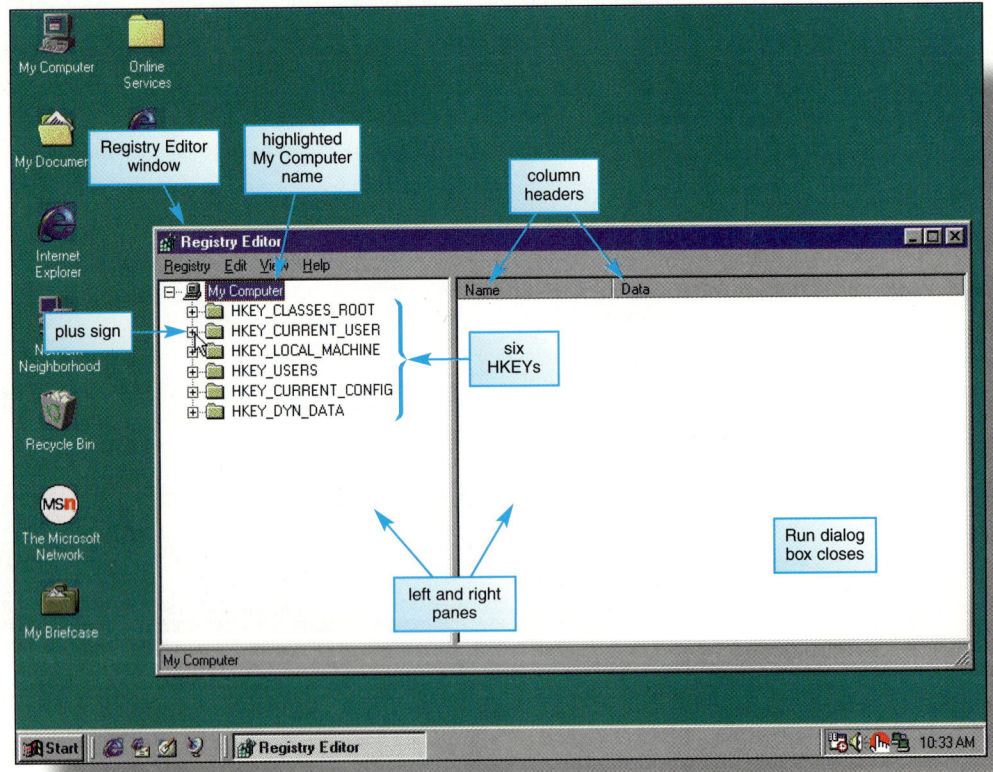

FIGURE 9-73

The Windows 98 System Registry • WIN 9.53

4 **Click the plus sign and then point to InstallLocationsMRU.**

The hierarchy below the HKEY_CURRENT_USER icon expands to display the eight keys in HKEY_CURRENT_USER (Figure 9-74). A dotted vertical line connects the keys. A key that is not preceded by a plus sign does not contain keys. A key preceded by a plus sign contains more keys. The minus sign to the left of HKEY_CURRENT_USER indicates the folder is expanded.

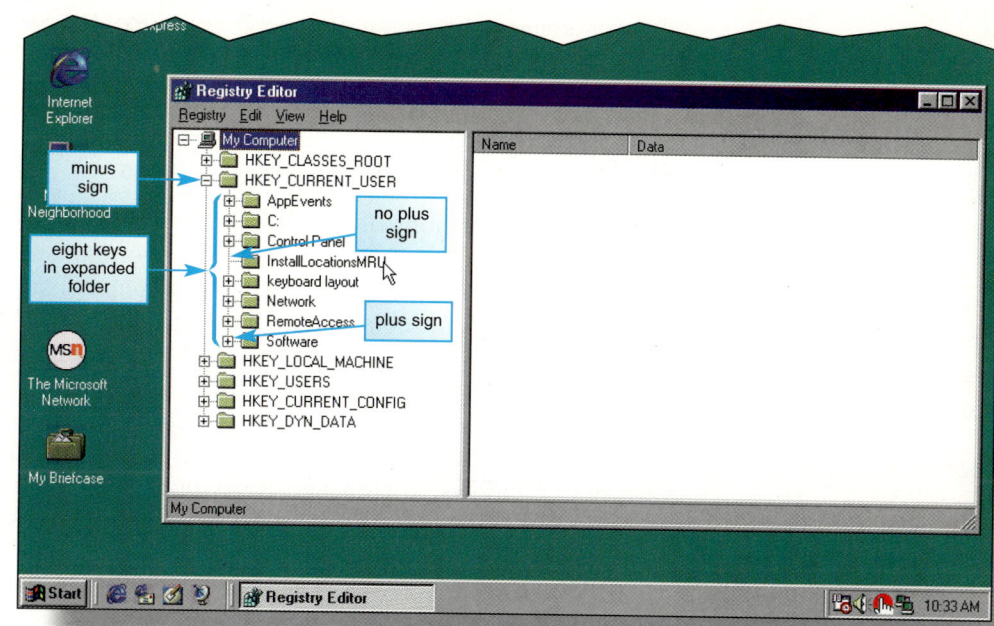

FIGURE 9-74

5 **Click InstallLocationsMRU and then point to the Close button in the Registry Editor window.**

The highlighted InstallLocationsMRU key name displays in the left pane and the values that compose the key display in the right pane (Figure 9-75). An icon, indicating the value's data type and name, displays below the Name column header. The letters, ab, indicate the data type is text. The data associated with each name displays below the Data column header.

6 **Click the Close button.**

The Registry Editor window closes.

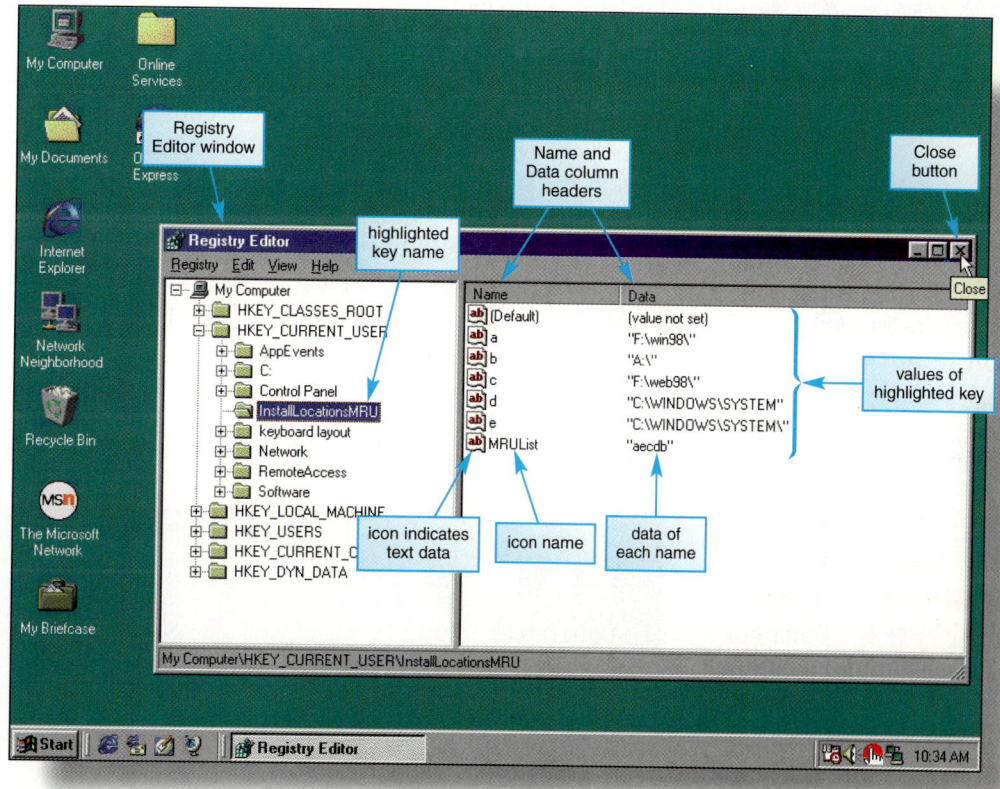

FIGURE 9-75

Other Ways

1. Click Start button on taskbar, click Help, click Index tab, type registry checker, click Display button, click Click here hyperlink

The Registry Editor allows you to view the HKEYs, keys, and the values they contain. The Registry Editor also can be used to modify the values in the system registry.

Modifying the System Registry Settings

In previous versions of Windows, only the operating system, system and application software, and experienced computer programmers could modify the system registry. Indeed, changing a setting in the system registry could render the entire computer system unusable, forcing you to reinstall the Windows operating system.

Although this type of malfunction still is a possibility, major improvements have been made to the system registry to prevent it from happening. One improvement is that Registry Checker creates a backup copy of the system registry each time Windows 98 launches. Five backup copies are maintained at all times. In addition, each time Windows 98 launches, Registry Checker scans the current system registry for problems and automatically replaces a corrupted system registry with the most recent backup copy.

Although very few reasons exist to modify the values in the system registry, only two pieces of information (registered name and registered organization) can be changed using Registry Editor. Often, when you buy a computer from a retail store, the registered name and registered organization are altered by the retail store. For example, buying a computer from ABC Computers may result in the registered name containing the phrase, Preferred Customer of ABC Computers, and the registered organization containing the retail store name, ABC Computers. In addition, if you buy a previously owned computer, you may want to modify the registered organization and name to identify the computer as your property.

To change these values, you must be able to navigate through the HKEYs and keys in the system registry to the CurrentVersion key. The CurrentVersion key contains the registered name and organization. To navigate to this key, click HKEY_LOCAL_MACHINE, click SOFTWARE, click Microsoft, click Windows, and then click CurrentVersion to display the values in the CurrentVersion folder. Perform the following steps to modify the registered name and organization.

Registry Editor

Unlike using the Save button to save a document while using a word processing program, changes you make in Registry Editor take place immediately. When working with Registry Editor, remember these guidelines: (1) Be alert when using Registry Editor. (2) Back up the part of the registry with which you plan to work. (3) Write down any values that you are going to change. (4) Close Registry Editor as soon as the changes are made.

Steps — To Modify a System Registry Value

1 **Click the Start button, click Run on the Start menu, type** regedit **in the Open box in the Run dialog box, click the OK button, and then point to the plus sign in the small box to the left of the HKEY_LOCAL_MACHINE folder.**

The Registry Editor window displays (Figure 9-76). A plus sign displays to the left of HKEY_LOCAL_MACHINE.

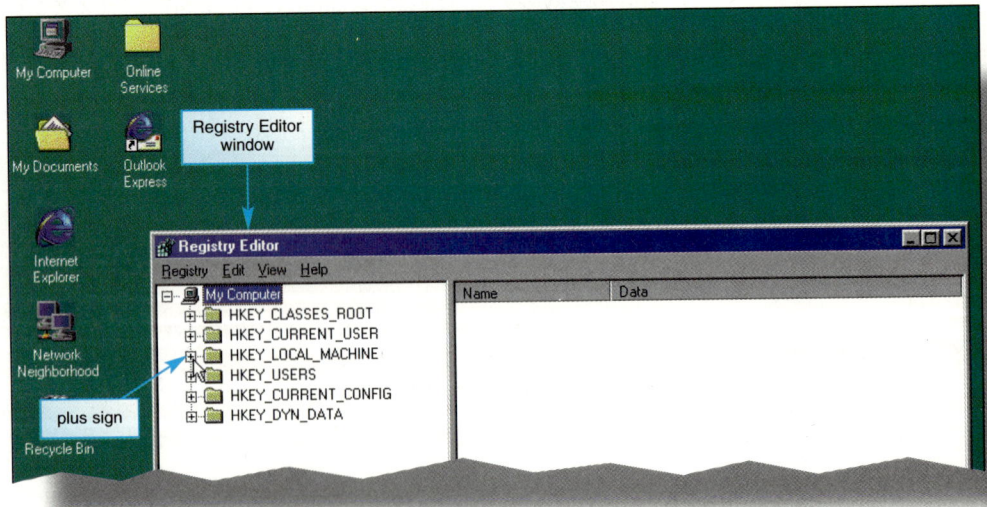

FIGURE 9-76

2 **Click the plus sign and then point to the plus sign in the small box to the left of the SOFTWARE folder.**

The hierarchy below the HKEY_LOCAL_MACHINE folder expands to display nine keys (folders) (Figure 9-77). The keys may be different on your computer. A minus sign displays to the left of the HKEY_LOCAL_MACHINE folder.

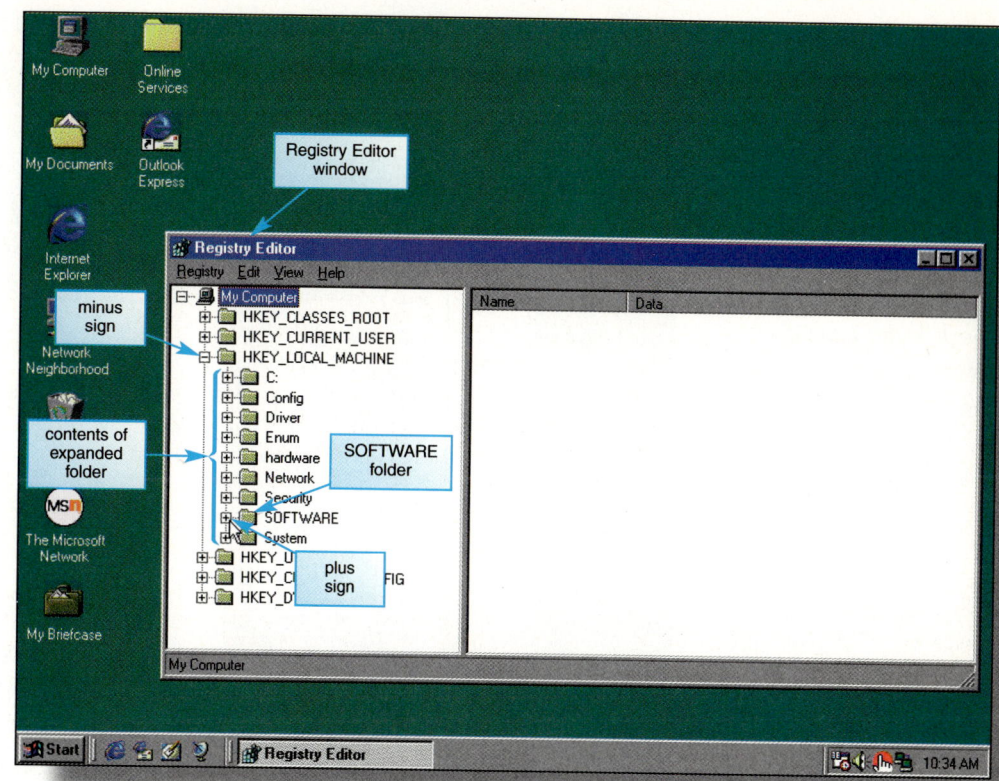

FIGURE 9-77

3 **Click the plus sign. If necessary, scroll the left pane to display the Microsoft folder. Point to the plus sign in the small box to the left of the Microsoft folder.**

The hierarchy below the SOFTWARE folder expands and the left pane scrolls to display the Microsoft folder (Figure 9-78).

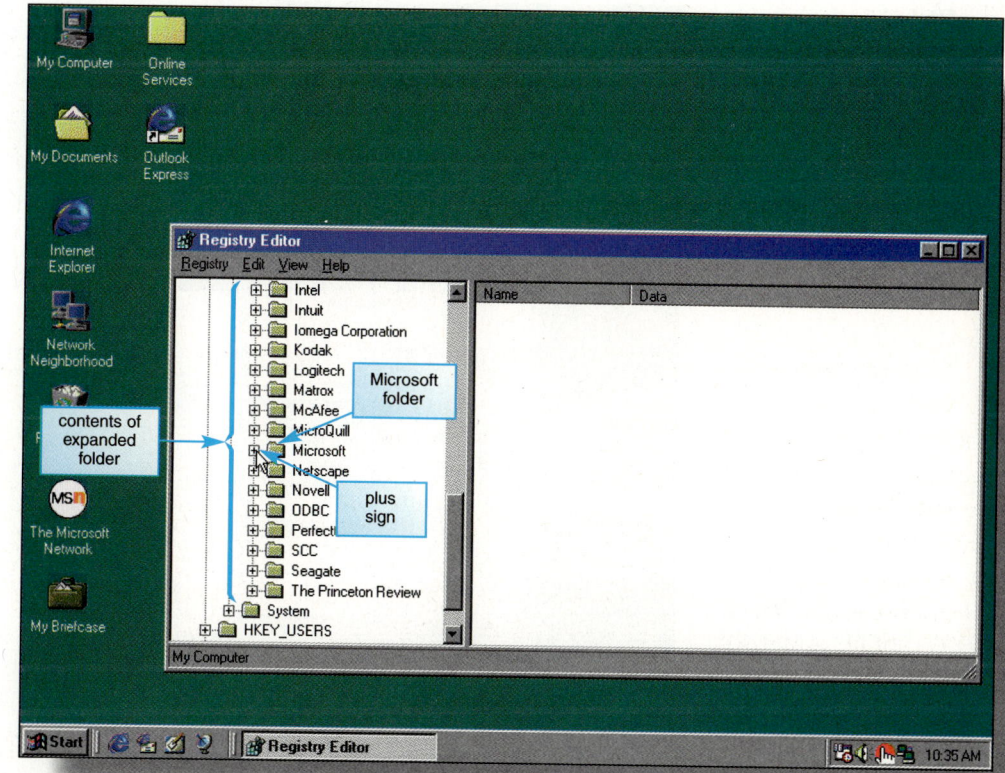

FIGURE 9-78

WIN 9.56 • Project 9 • Maintaining and Optimizing Your Computer and System Registry

4 **Click the plus sign. If necessary, scroll the left pane to display the Windows folder. Point to the plus sign in the small box to the left of the Windows folder.**

The hierarchy below the Microsoft folder expands and the left pane scrolls to display the Windows folder (Figure 9-79).

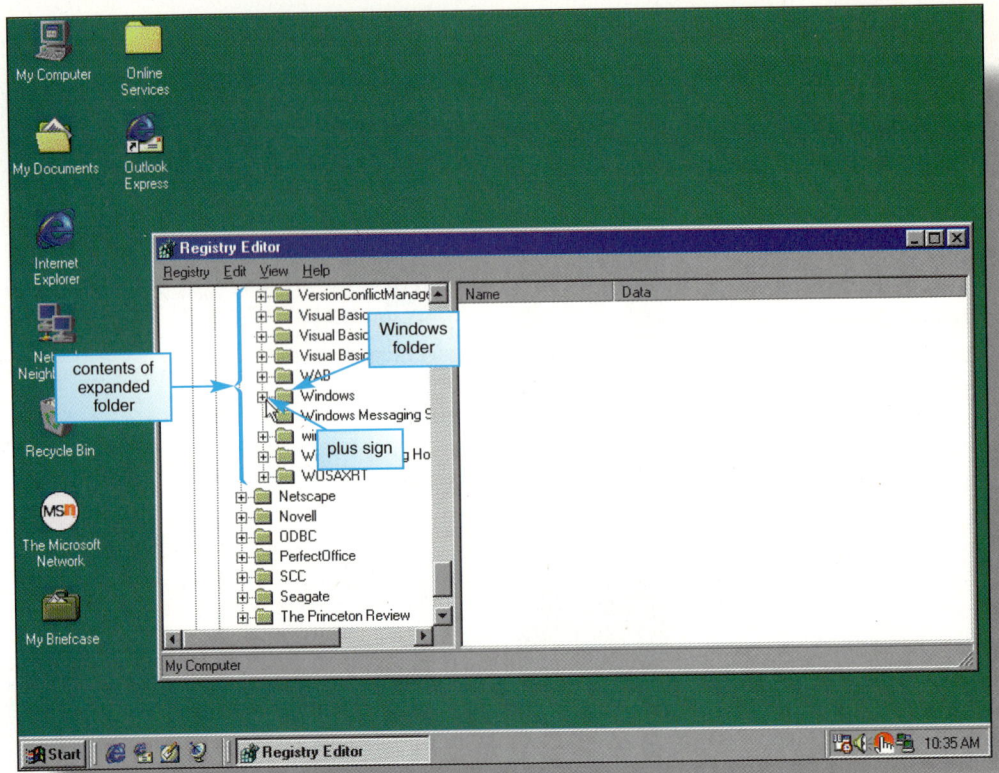

FIGURE 9-79

5 **Click the plus sign and then point to CurrentVersion.**

The hierarchy below the Windows folder expands and the CurrentVersion folder displays (Figure 9-80).

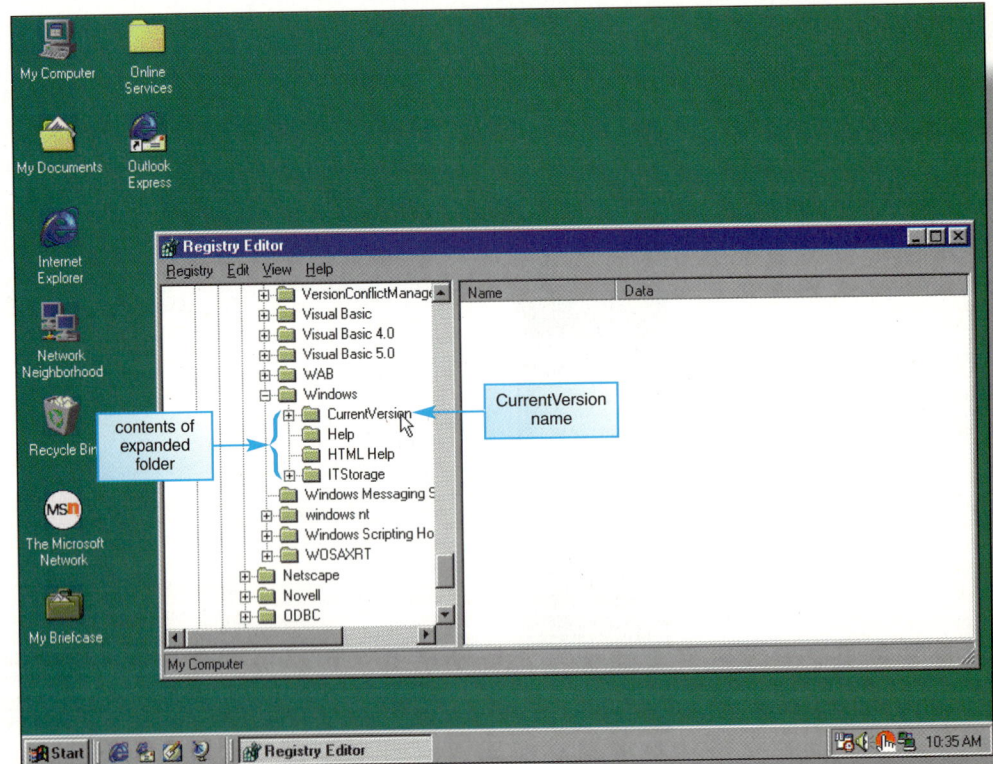

FIGURE 9-80

6 **Click CurrentVersion. If necessary, scroll the right pane to display the RegisteredOrganization and RegisteredOwner names. Point to RegisteredOwner.**

The highlighted Current Version name displays in the left pane and the right pane scrolls to display the RegisteredOrganization and RegisteredOwner names (Figure 9-81).

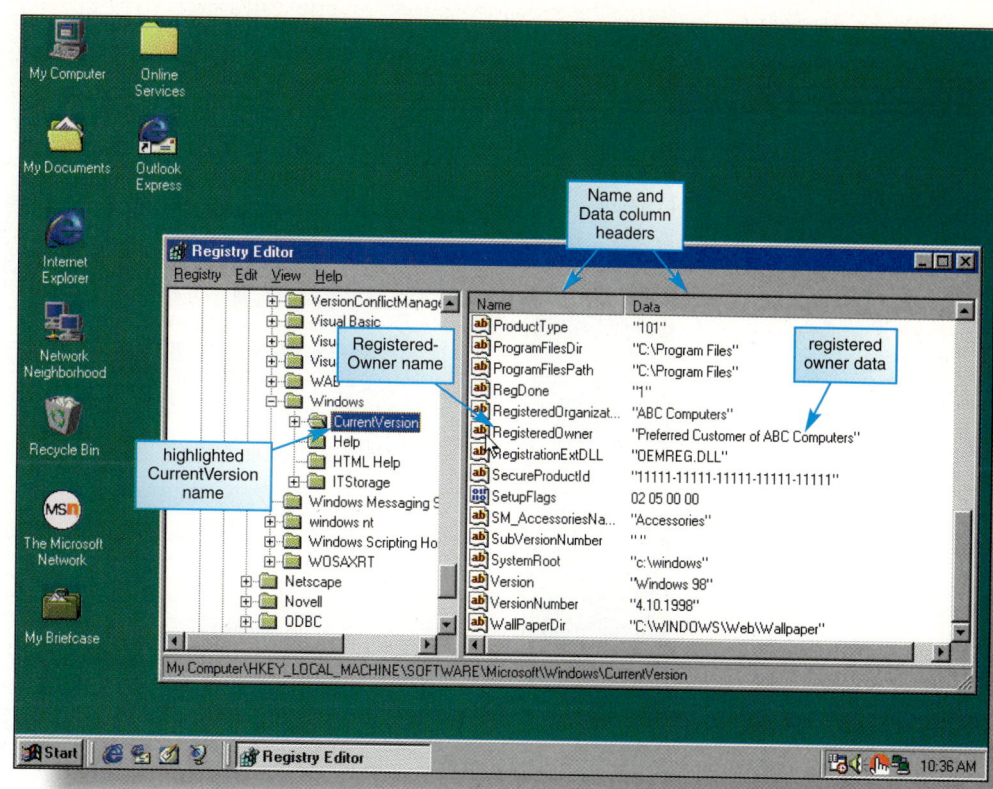

FIGURE 9-81

 **Double-click the RegisteredOwner icon.**

The Edit String dialog box displays (Figure 9-82). The dialog box contains the Value name text box containing the value name (RegisteredOwner) and the Value data text box containing the highlighted value data (Preferred Customer of ABC Computers).

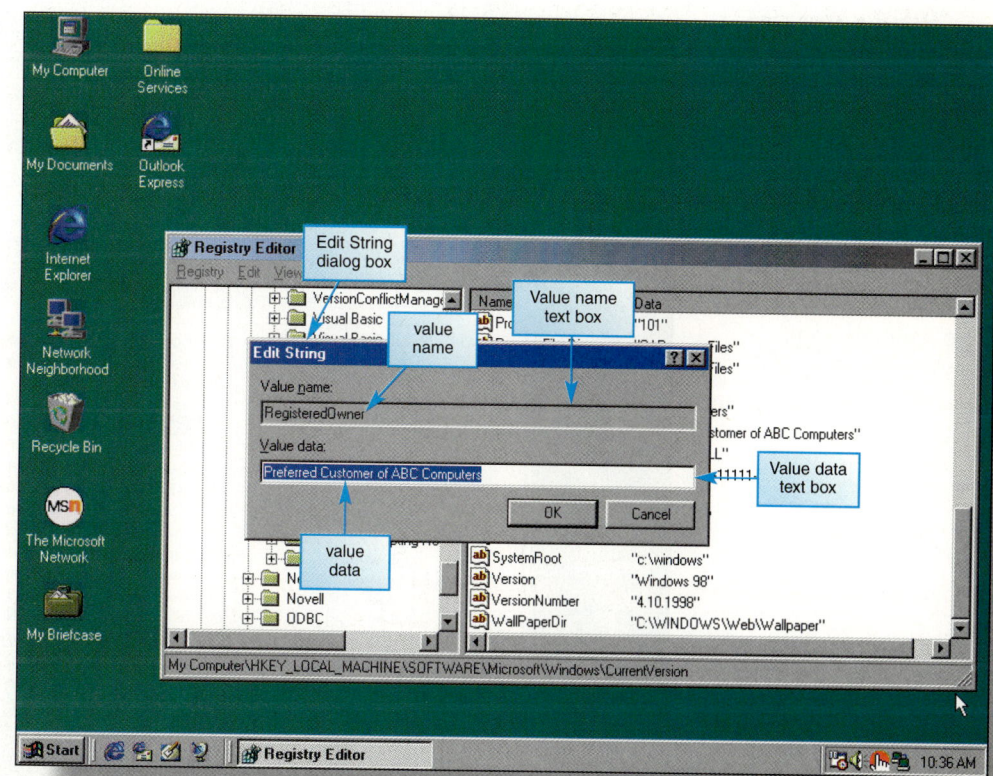

FIGURE 9-82

WIN 9.58 • Project 9 • Maintaining and Optimizing Your Computer and System Registry

8 **Type your name in the Value data text box and then point to the OK button.**

One of the author's names (Steven Forsythe) displays in the Value data text box (Figure 9-83). Your name should display in the text box on your computer.

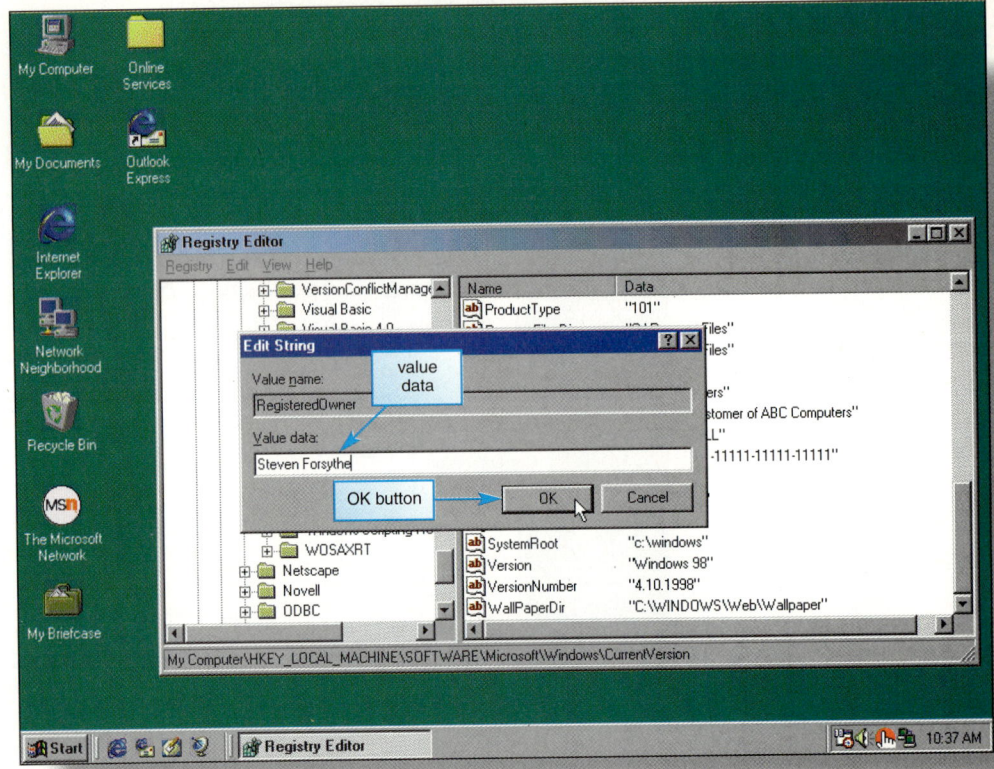

FIGURE 9-83

9 **Click the OK button.**

The Edit String dialog box closes and the RegisteredOwner name is highlighted in the right pane (Figure 9-84). The RegisteredOwner data (Steven Forsythe) is enclosed in quotation marks and displays to the right of the RegisteredOwner name in the Data column.

Other Ways

1. Click Start button on taskbar, click Help, click Index tab, type `registry checker`, click Display button, click Click here hyperlink

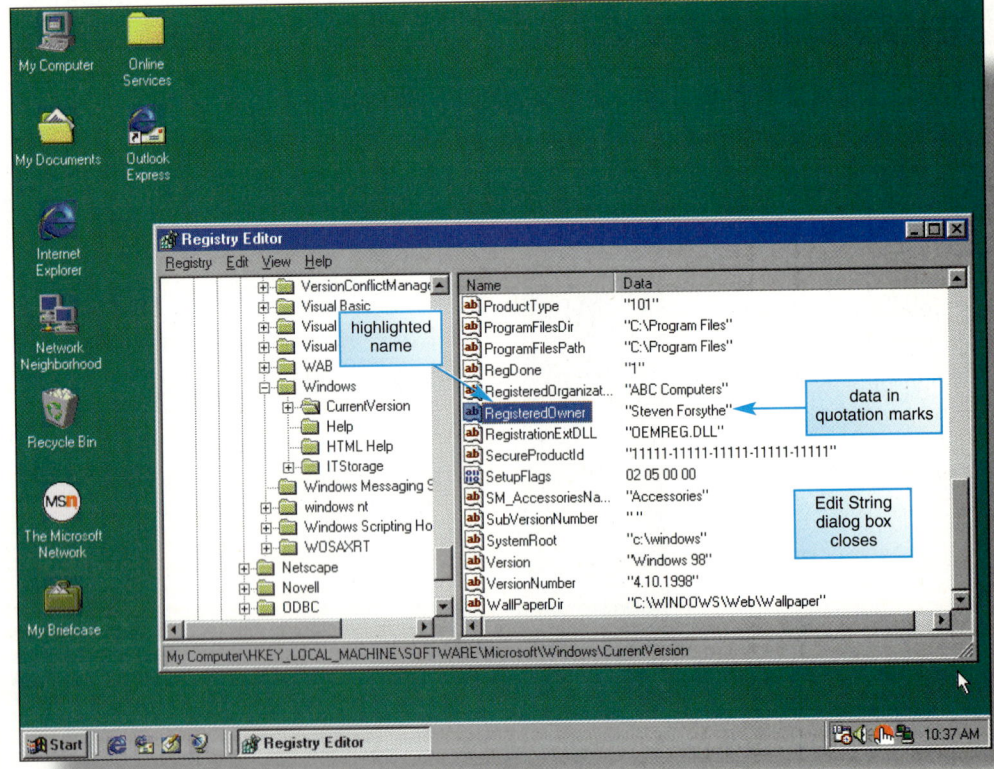

FIGURE 9-84

Modifying the Registered Organization Using Registry Editor

After modifying the registered name, you should modify the registered organization. Perform the following steps to modify the registered organization.

TO MODIFY A SYSTEM REGISTRY VALUE

1. Double-click the RegisteredOrganization icon in the right pane of the Registry Editor window.
2. Type your organization or school name in the Value data text box in the Edit String dialog box.
3. Click the OK button in the Edit String dialog box.
4. Click the Close button in the Registry Editor window.

The RegisteredOrganization name is highlighted in the right pane and the organization name is enclosed in quotation marks and displays to the right of the RegisteredOrganization name in the Data column (Figure 9-85). The Registry Editor window closes.

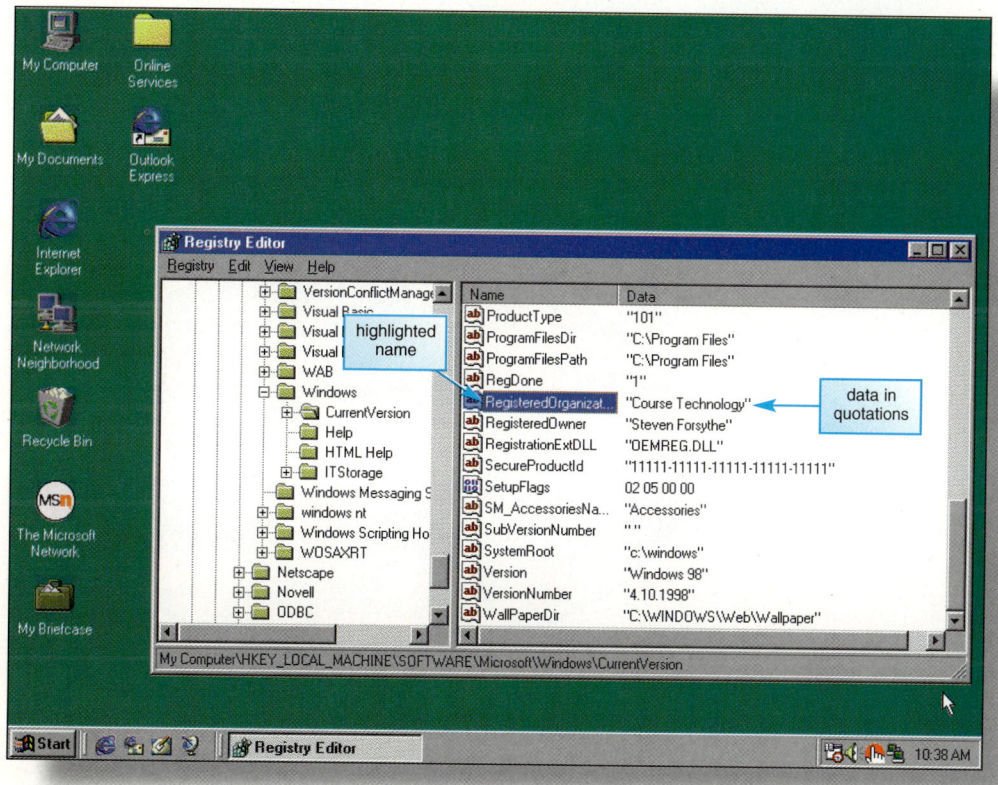

FIGURE 9-85

Drive Converter (FAT32)

As mentioned earlier, files are stored on the hard disk in clusters. A cluster is the smallest storage location that the operating system can allocate to a file. The file allocation table (FAT) keeps track of the file name, file size, time and date the file was last modified, and the cluster number where the file begins. The operating system uses the file allocation table to look up a file name and find the location of the file on the hard disk. The names FAT and FAT16 are used interchangeably.

Microsoft operating systems prior to Windows 98 (Windows 95, Windows 3.1, and DOS) used the FAT16 file system. With the FAT16 file system, the size of each cluster was 32K (32,768 bytes = 32 x 1024). If you saved a file on the hard disk whose file size was 1,000 bytes, FAT16 would store the file in one 32,768 byte cluster (Figure 9-86). As a result, 31,768 bytes in the cluster were left blank and unusable. The FAT16 file system resulted in a large amount of hard disk space that was unusable.

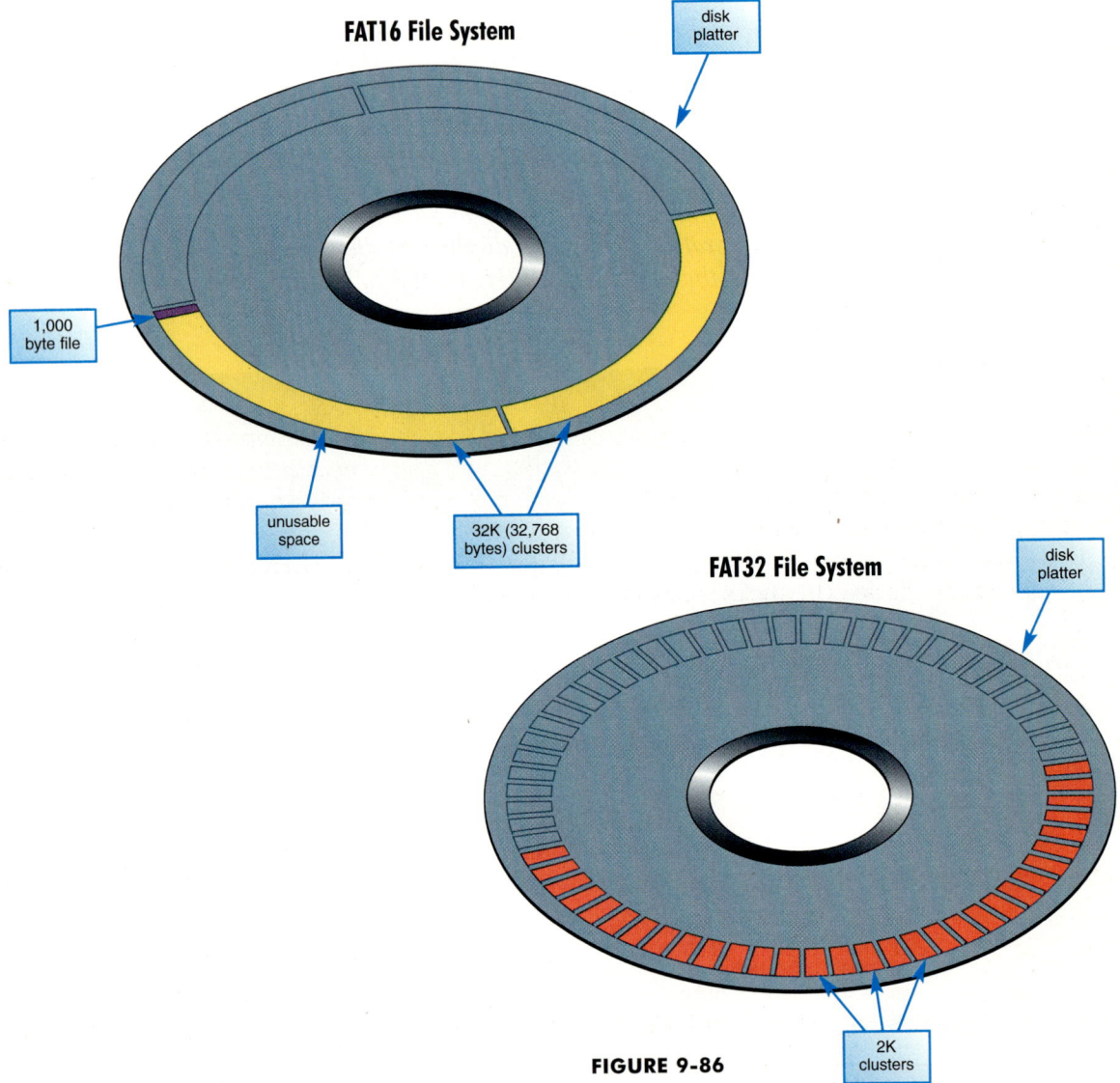

FIGURE 9-86

To fix this problem, the FAT32 file system was used for the first time with the Windows 98 operating system. With the FAT32 file system, the size of each cluster is 2K (2,048 bytes = 2 x 1024). The decrease in the size of the cluster eliminated much of the unusable space on the hard disk.

If you install Windows 98 on a computer system that used one of the previous Microsoft operating system, the system operates with the FAT16 file system. Switching from FAT16 to FAT32 can free several hundred megabytes of disk space on the hard disk. In most cases, the amount of free space of the hard disk will increase by 20% to 30%. In addition, programs load faster and the computer uses fewer system resources.

To determine which file system (FAT16 or FAT32) is being used on a computer, double-click the My Computer icon on the desktop, right-click the hard disk icon, and click Properties.

To convert to FAT32, you use Drive Converter. **Drive Converter** is a system tool included with Windows 98 that converts a hard disk from the FAT or FAT16 to the FAT32 file system. Switching to the FAT32 file system involves several drawbacks. Prior to switching, you should use Windows Help to read about Drive Converter and these drawbacks.

Additional System and Diagnostic Tools

In addition to the system tools illustrated earlier in this project, several other tools are important for monitoring system resources and diagnosing hardware and software problems. These tools include Resource Meter, System Information, System Monitor, Compression Agent, DriveSpace, System File Checker, Device Manager, and Dr. Watson. More information about these tools is available in Windows Help.

Project Summary

This project introduced you to the concept of maintaining a computer and improving system performance. You used several system tools to back up the files in a folder on a floppy disk, restore an unusable file, scan a disk for errors, delete unnecessary files on the hard disk, defragment a hard disk, and then schedule routine maintenance using the Maintenance wizard. You displayed the Windows Update home page and checked for and downloaded software components from the Web site on a hard disk. In addition, you made a backup copy of the system registry, viewed the system registry settings, and then modified those settings.

What You Should Know

Having completed this project, you now should be able to perform the following tasks:

- Back Up the Files in a Folder on a Floppy Disk *(WIN 9.5)*
- Check for Components *(WIN 9.41)*
- Defragment Files on the Hard Disk *(WIN 9.29)*
- Delete Unnecessary Files on the Hard Disk *(WIN 9.25)*
- Display the Contents on a Floppy Disk *(WIN 9.14)*
- Display the Windows Update Home Page *(WIN 9.39)*
- Download a Component *(WIN 9.43)*
- Make a Backup Copy of the System Registry *(WIN 9.47)*
- Modify a System Registry Value *(WIN 9.54, WIN 9.59)*
- Restore an Unusable File *(WIN 9.15)*
- Scan the Hard Disk for Errors *(WIN 9.21)*
- Schedule Routine Maintenance *(WIN 9.32)*
- View Tasks and Schedules *(WIN 9.37)*
- View the System Registry *(WIN 9.51)*

WIN 9.62 • Project 9 • Maintaining and Optimizing Your Computer and System Registry

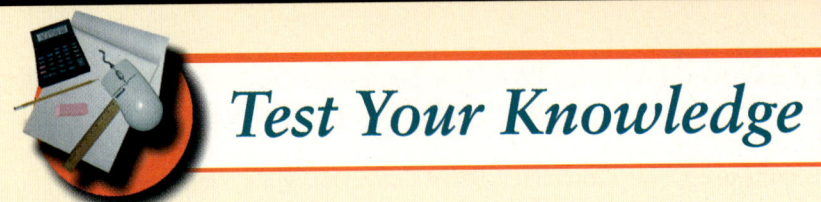

Test Your Knowledge

1 True/False

Instructions: Circle T if the statement is true or F if the statement is false.

T F   1. A cluster is the largest storage location the operating system can allocate to a file.
T F   2. When you save a file on a disk, the file allocation table (FAT) records the file name, file size, modification time and date, and beginning cluster number for the file.
T F   3. A logical error is a problem with the surface of a disk.
T F   4. When you use ScanDisk to scan a disk, the standard search takes less time than the thorough search.
T F   5. A temporary file is a file that contains a copy of a Web page that you displayed in a browser window.
T F   6. When a file occupies blocks of clusters that are not located next to each other, the file is called a fragmented file.
T F   7. You can schedule a task that will perform a disk scan using either Task Scheduler or the Maintenance wizard.
T F   8. Windows Update allows you to download system files, device drivers, and software components from the Internet.
T F   9. Registry Checker allows you to view and modify the system registry.
T F   10. You should never modify the system registry.

2 Multiple Choice

Instructions: Circle the correct response.

1. The _____ system tool allows you to select files, folders, or the entire hard disk, and create one file to contain the files.
   a. ScanDisk
   b. Backup
   c. Disk Defragmenter
   d. Disk Cleanup
2. The smallest storage location the operating system can allocate to a file is called a _____.
   a. file allocation table
   b. noncontiguous block of clusters
   c. temporary file
   d. cluster
3. One difference between a standard search and a thorough search is that the _____.
   a. standard search takes more time than a thorough search
   b. standard search is performed on all files and folder on the disk
   c. thorough search scans the disk surface for defects
   d. thorough search takes less time than a standard search

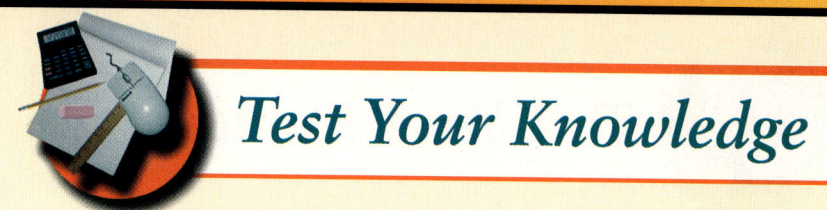

Test Your Knowledge

4. A physical error is a problem with the _____.
    a. disk media
    b. storage of files
    c. file allocation table
    d. directory structure
5. The _____ file is a file stored on the hard disk that contains a copy of a Web page.
    a. temporary
    b. downloaded program
    c. temporary Internet
    d. none of the above
6. A file that is stored on the hard disk in blocks of clusters that are not located next to each other is called a _____ file.
    a. defragmented
    b. contiguous
    c. temporary
    d. fragmented
7. The _____ is the central information database for Windows 98.
    a. file allocation table (FAT)
    b. system registry
    c. Product Updates catalog
    d. allocation unit
8. In the system registry, the _____ file records information about the hardware attached to the computer.
    a. System.dat
    b. User.dat
    c. Policy.pol
    d. Registry.dat
9. The tool that makes a backup copy of the system registry is the _____ tool.
    a. Registry Editor
    b. System Information
    c. Registry Checker
    d. Drive Converter
10. _____ is an hkey and _____ is a key.
    a. HKEY_LOCAL_MACHINE, HKEY_USERS
    b. CurrentVersion, RegisteredOwner
    c. HKEY_CURRENT_USER, InstallLocationsMRU
    d. HKEY_USERS, RegisteredOrganization

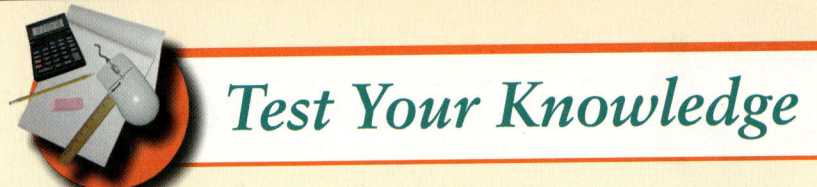

Test Your Knowledge

3 Rescheduling a Task Using the Maintenance Wizard

Instructions: Figure 9-87 shows the Maintenance Wizard dialog box that displays when scheduling the Disk Defragmenter program. In the spaces provided, list the steps to change the schedule from 1:00 A.M. on every Friday of every week, starting 9/8/1999 to 2:00 A.M. every Thursday of every week, starting 9/8/1999.

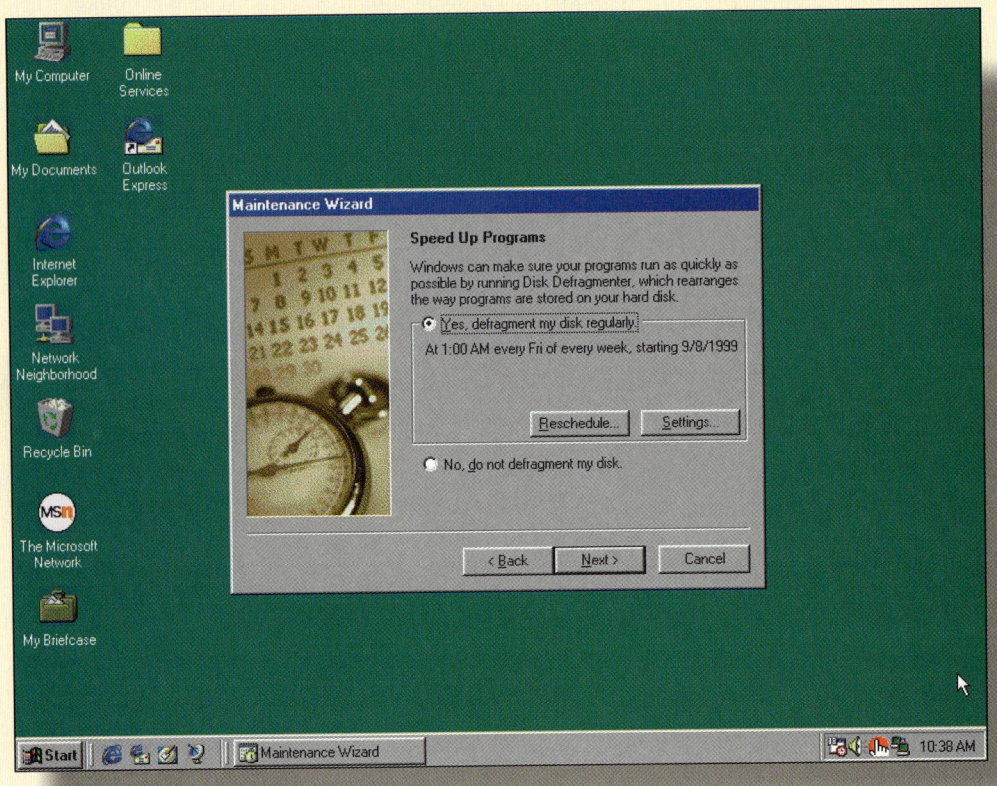

FIGURE 9-87

Step 1: _____
Step 2: _____
Step 3: _____
Step 4: _____
Step 5: _____

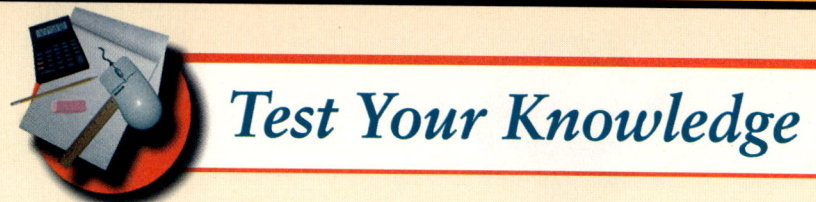

Test Your Knowledge

4 Using Registry Checker to Back Up the System Registry

Instructions: A new application software program is installed on the hard disk. As a result, the system registry should be backed up. In the spaces provided, list the steps to back up the system registry using the Registry Checker.

Step 1: _____

Step 2: _____

Step 3: _____

Step 4: _____

Step 5: _____

Step 6: _____

Use Help

1 Using Windows Help to Identify the Purpose of System Tools and Programs

Instructions: Use Windows Help and a computer to perform the following tasks.

1. If necessary, start Windows 98.
2. Click the Start button. Click Help on the Start menu. If necessary, click the Index tab.
3. Type resource meter in the text box.
4. Double-click Resource Meter in the list box.
   What does the Resource Meter program do? _____
5. Type system monitor in the text box.
6. Double-click System Monitor in the list box.
   What does the System Monitor do? _____
7. Type compression agent in the text box.
8. Double-click Compression Agent in the list box.
   What does the Compression Agent do? _____
9. Type system file checker in the text box.
10. Double-click System File Checker in the list box.
11. Double-click Using System File Checker in the Topics Found dialog box.
    What does the System File Checker do? _____
12. Type windows report tool in the text box.
13. Double-click Windows Report Tool in the list box.
    What does the Windows Report tool do? _____
14. Type version conflict manager in the text box.
15. Double-click Version Conflict Manager in the list box.
    What does the Version Conflict Manager do? _____
16. Type Dr. Watson in the text box.
17. Double-click Dr. Watson in the list box.
18. Double-click Using Dr. Watson to diagnose system faults in the Topics Found dialog box.
    What does Dr. Watson do? _____
19. Type DriveSpace 3 in the text box.
20. Double-click DriveSpace 3 in the list box.
21. Double-click Using DriveSpace 3 to increase disk space in the Topics Found dialog box.
    What does Drive Space 3 do? _____
22. Click the Close button in the Windows Help window.

Use Help

2 Obtaining Help About Using Windows Update

Instructions: Use a computer and the Windows Update Web site to perform the following tasks.

1. If necessary, start Windows 98 and connect to the Internet.
2. Click the Start button. Click Windows Update. The Microsoft Windows Update home page displays.
3. Click the about Windows Update hyperlink in the Microsoft Windows Update window.
   Currently, what two areas comprise Windows Update? _____
4. Click the About Product Updates hyperlink.
   What is the About Product Updates area? _____
5. Scroll to the top of the About Microsoft Windows Update window.
6. Click the Updating device drivers hyperlink.
   List the steps to download and install a device driver.

   Step 1: _____
   Step 2: _____
   Step 3: _____

7. Scroll to the top of the About Microsoft Windows Update window.
8. Click the About Support Information hyperlink.
   a. What is Support Information? _____
   b. What can you do in Support Information? _____
9. Click the Close button in the About Microsoft Windows Update window.
10. Click the Close button in the Microsoft Windows Update window.

In the Lab

1 Scheduling Tasks Using the Maintenance Wizard

Instructions: Use the Maintenance wizard to design a maintenance schedule to perform a standard scan on the hard disk and delete all unnecessary files on the hard disk. When choosing a time to perform the maintenance tasks, use a time that is 15 minutes later than the current time to start the disk scan and 20 minutes later than the current time to start the file deletions. For example, if the current time on your computer is 1:30 P.M., schedule the disk scan to start at 1:45 P.M. and the file deletion to begin at 1:50 P.M. These time settings should allow enough time to schedule the tasks using the Maintenance wizard before Task Scheduler performs the tasks. Perform the following steps to schedule and perform the routine maintenance.

Part 1: *Starting the Maintenance Wizard*

1. If necessary, start Windows 98.
2. Click the Start button on the taskbar.
3. Point to Programs, point to Accessories, point to System Tools, and click Maintenance Wizard.

Part 2: *Customizing the Maintenance Settings*

1. Click Custom - Select each maintenance setting myself in the Maintenance Wizard dialog box.
2. Click the Next button in the Maintenance Wizard dialog box.
3. Click the option button that contains the time interval that is closest to the current time of day.
4. Click the Next button in the Maintenance Wizard dialog box.
5. Click the Next button in the Maintenance Wizard dialog box.
6. Click the No, do not defragment my disk option button.
7. Click the Next button in the Maintenance Wizard dialog box.

Part 3: *Setting the Time and Date for Scanning the Disk*

1. Click the Yes, scan my hard disk for errors regularly dialog box.
2. Click the Reschedule button in the dialog box.
3. Check the tray status area for the current time. What is the current time? _____
4. Set the time to be 15 minutes later than the time you wrote down on the piece of paper in Step 3 above. Use the Start time box to enter this time.
5. Select the check box that corresponds to the current day of the week.
6. Remove the check mark from the other check boxes.
7. Click the Advanced button in the Reschedule dialog box.
8. Click the Start Date box arrow.
9. Click today's date in the monthly calendar.
10. Click the OK button in the Advanced Schedule Options dialog box.
11. Click the OK button in the Reschedule dialog box.
12. Click the Next button in the Maintenance Wizard dialog box.

In the Lab

Part 4: Setting the Time and Day for Deleting Unnecessary Files

1. Click the Reschedule button in the dialog box.
2. Click the Schedule Task box arrow and click Weekly in the list box.
3. Set the time to be 20 minutes later than the time you wrote down on the piece of paper in Step 3 of Part 3. Use the Start time box to enter this time.
4. Select the check box that corresponds to the current day of the week.
5. Deselect the other check boxes.
6. Click the Advanced button in the Reschedule dialog box.
7. Click the Start Date box arrow.
8. Click today's date in the monthly calendar.
9. Click the OK button in the Advanced Schedule Options dialog box.
10. Click the OK button in the Reschedule dialog box.
11. Click the Next button in the Maintenance Wizard dialog box.

Part 5: Capturing and Printing a Copy of the Maintenance Wizard Dialog Box

1. Hold down the ALT key, press the PRINT SCREEN key, and release the ALT key.
2. Click the Start button, point to Programs, point to Accessories, and then click Paint.
3. Click Edit on the menu bar and then click Paste.
4. If a message (The image in the Clipboard is larger than the bitmap. Would you like the bitmap enlarged?) displays in the Paint dialog box, click the Yes button.
5. Click File on the menu bar, click Print, and then click the OK button.
6. Click the Close button in the Paint window. Click the No button in the Paint dialog box.
7. Click the Finish button in the Maintenance Wizard dialog box.

Part 6: Performing the Tasks Using Task Scheduler

1. Wait and watch for the time in the taskbar to match the beginning time of the ScanDisk program.
2. a. Does the ScanDisk program begin? _____
   b. How long does it take to scan the hard disk? _____
3. a. Does the Disk Cleanup program begin? _____
   b. What time is it when the program begins? _____

Part 7: Deleting the Three Files in the Scheduled Tasks Window

1. Double-click the Task Scheduler icon in the tray status area.
2. Select the Maintenance-Defragment programs, Maintenance-Disk Cleanup, and Maintenance-ScanDisk icons in the Scheduled Tasks window (*Hint:* Click the first icon, hold down the SHIFT key, click the last icon, and then release the SHIFT key).
3. Click the Delete button on the Standard Buttons toolbar.
4. Click the Yes button in the Confirm Multiple File Delete dialog box.
5. Click the Close button in the Scheduled Tasks window.

In the Lab

2 Scheduling Tasks Using the Task Scheduler

Instructions: Use Task Scheduler to design a schedule to perform a disk scan on the hard disk and then perform a disk defragmentation of the hard disk. Perform the disk scan every Friday at 10:00 P.M. Perform the disk defragmentation every Friday at 10:30 P.M. Perform the following steps to add the two tasks using the Task Scheduler.

Part 1: Starting Task Scheduler

1. If necessary, start Windows 98.
2. Double-click the My Computer icon on the desktop.
3. Double-click the Scheduled Tasks icon in the My Computer window. The Scheduled Tasks window displays.

Part 2: Adding the Scan the Hard Disk Task

1. Double-click the Add Scheduled Task icon in the Scheduled Tasks window. The Scheduled Task wizard starts.
2. Click the Next button in the Scheduled Task Wizard dialog box.
3. Scroll the list box in the Scheduled Task Wizard dialog box to display the ScanDisk name.
4. Click the ScanDisk name in the list box.
5. Click the Next button in the Scheduled Task Wizard dialog box.
6. Type `Scan the Hard Disk` in the Type a name for this task text box.
7. Click Weekly.
8. Click the Next button in the Scheduled Task Wizard dialog box.
9. Using the Start time text box, enter `10:00 P.M.` as the start time.
10. Click the Friday check box to select it.
11. Click the Next button in the Scheduled Task Wizard dialog box.
12. Click the Finish button in the Scheduled Task Wizard dialog box.
    a. What is the task name listed in the Scheduled Tasks window? _____
    b. What is the schedule? _____
    c. What is the next run time? _____

Part 3: Adding the Defragment the Hard Disk Task

1. Double-click the Add Scheduled Task icon in the Scheduled Tasks window to launch the Scheduled Task wizard.
2. Click the Next button in the Scheduled Task Wizard dialog box.
3. Scroll the list box in the Scheduled Task Wizard dialog box to display the Disk Defragmenter name.
4. Click the Disk Defragmenter name in the list box.
5. Click the Next button in the Scheduled Task Wizard dialog box.
6. Type `Defragment the Hard Disk` in the Type a name for this task text box.
7. Click Weekly.
8. Click the Next button in the Scheduled Task Wizard dialog box.
9. Using the Start time text box, enter `10:30 P.M.` as the start time.
10. Click the Friday check box to select it.
11. Click the Next button in the Scheduled Task Wizard dialog box.

In the Lab

12. Click the Finish button in the Scheduled Task Wizard dialog box.
    a. What is the new task name listed in the Scheduled Tasks window? _____
    b. What is the schedule? _____
    c. What is the next run time? _____

Part 4: *Adding the Launch Outlook Express Task*

1. Double-click the Add Scheduled Task icon in the Scheduled Tasks window to launch the Scheduled Task wizard.
2. Click the Next button in the Scheduled Task Wizard dialog box.
3. Scroll the list box in the Scheduled Task Wizard dialog box to display the Outlook Express name.
4. Click the Outlook Express name in the list box.
5. Click the Next button in the Scheduled Task Wizard dialog box.
6. Type Launch Outlook Express in the Type a name for this task text box.
7. Click When my computer starts.
8. Click the Next button in the Scheduled Task Wizard dialog box.
9. Click the Finish button in the Scheduled Task Wizard dialog box.
    a. What is the new task name listed in the Scheduled Tasks window? _____
    b. What is the schedule? _____
    c. What is the next run time? _____

Part 5: *Deleting the Three Files in the Scheduled Tasks Window*

1. Select the Scan the Hard Disk, Defragment the Hard Disk, and Launch Outlook Express names in the Scheduled Tasks window (*Hint:* Click the first task name in the list, hold down the SHIFT key, click the last task name in the list, and then release the SHIFT key).
2. Click the Delete button on the Standard Buttons toolbar.
3. Click the Yes button in the Confirm Multiple File Delete dialog box.
4. Click the Close button in the Scheduled Tasks window.

3 Exploring the Windows Update Web Site

Instructions: Use a computer to perform the following tasks.

Part 1: *Displaying the Windows Update Home Page*

1. Click the Start button on the taskbar. If necessary, connect to the Internet.
2. Click Windows Update on the Start menu to open the Windows Update window.

Part 2: *Checking for Components Using Product Updates*

1. Click the PRODUCT UPDATES hyperlink in the Microsoft Windows Update window.
2. Click the Yes button in the Windows Update dialog box.
3. Scroll the right side of the window and list all answers in the spaces provided.
    a. List any critical updates.

    _____
    _____

continued)

In the Lab

Exploring the Windows Update Web Site *(continued)*

    b. List any picks of the month.
_____
_____

    c. List any recommended updates.
_____
_____

    d. List four additional Windows features (Internet features).
_____
_____

    e. List four additional Windows features (Fun and Games).
_____
_____

Part 2: Checking for Device Driver Updates

1. Click the Device Drivers hyperlink in the Microsoft Windows Update window.
2. Click the Yes button in the Windows Update Wizard dialog box.
3. List any device driver updates.
   _____   _____
   _____   _____
4. Click the Close button in the Microsoft Windows Update Wizard window.

Part 3: Exploring the Support Information

1. Click the SUPPORT INFORMATION hyperlink in the Microsoft Windows Update window.
2. Click the Frequently Asked Questions hyperlink.
3. List the first four frequently asked questions.
_____
_____
4. Scroll to the top of Web page. Click the Known Issues hyperlink.
5. In the spaces provided, select and summarize two known issues.
_____
_____
6. Click the Close button in the Known Issues window.
7. Scroll to make the SUPPORT OPTIONS visible.
8. List the support options available.
_____
_____
9. Click the Close button in the Microsoft Windows Update window.

Cases and Places

The difficulty of these case studies varies:
❱ are the least difficult; ❱❱ are more difficult; and ❱❱❱ are the most difficult.

1 ❱ To prevent accidental data loss, smart business owners use a backup system. Today, three types of backup systems are in use: full backup, differential backup, and incremental backup. Most businesses use a single system or combination of systems to protect their data. In a brief report, explain the three backup systems and the advantages and disadvantages of each system.

2 ❱ Among the System tools not explained in this project are the Windows Report Tool, System File Checker, Signature Verification Tool, Dr. Watson, and Version Conflict Manager. Using Windows Help, explain the purpose of any three of these tools in a brief report.

3 ❱ Every computer user using Windows 98 should have a Startup disk. Windows 98 allows you to create a Startup disk while installing, or after installing, Windows 98. Determine the reason to have a Startup disk, the contents of the disk, and when you use the disk. Summarize your results in a brief report.

4 ❱❱ Windows 98 contains a hidden message from Microsoft Corporation. To find the message, locate Memphis, Egypt; Memphis, Tennessee; and Redmond, Washington on a world atlas. Double-click the time in the tray status area, click the Time Zone tab, and then hold down the CTRL key. Click Memphis, Egypt and pretend to drag an object to the Memphis, Tennessee. Click Memphis, Egypt and pretend to drag an object to Redmond, Washington. Release the CTRL key. If nothing happens, repeat the previous steps until a list of the Windows 98 developers and a slide show accompanied by music displays in a dialog box.

5 ❱❱ In addition to System tools, Windows 98 also contains several accessories. Some accessories have been explained in previous projects (Notepad and Paint). Using Windows Help, read about the three accessories not explained in this book (Calculator, Imaging, and WordPad). In a presentation to your class, explain the purpose of each accessory and demonstrate them.

Cases and Places

6 ▶▶▶ The FrontPage Express software, included with Windows 98, allows you to create and edit Web pages. Using FrontPage Express Help, retail books about FrontPage, and any other reference material, learn to use FrontPage Express. Create a simple Web page and demonstrate the page to the class. Explain the steps involved in creating the Web page.

7 ▶▶▶ Visit a small, medium, and large business that use Windows 98. Interview two computer users at each business to determine what they like about Windows 98, what they do not like about Windows 98, which System tools they use, and whether they perform routine maintenance, have a backup system, and use NetMeeting. Summarize your findings in a brief report.

Index

Access
  mapped network drive, WIN 7.55-56
  network resources, WIN 7.49
Accessibility features, **WIN 5.20-24**
Accessing online service, WIN 7.5-10
Accessories submenu
  Entertainment, Media Player commands, WIN 8.30
  Entertainment, Sound Recorder commands, WIN 8.7
  Notepad command, WIN 2.6
  System Tools, Backup commands, WIN 9.5
  System Tools, Disk Cleanup commands, WIN 9.25
  System Tools, Disk Defragmenter commands, WIN 9.29
  System Tools, Maintenance Wizard commands, WIN 9.32
  System Tools, ScanDisk commands, WIN 9.21
  System Tools, System Information commands, WIN 9.47
AC power, WIN 6.53
Active content, **WIN 2.47**
Active Desktop™, **WIN 1.37**, WIN 1.39, WIN 4.15
  adding active desktop item to, WIN 2.49-54
  deleting item from, WIN 2.55-57
  turning off, WIN 2.57-58
  turning on, WIN 2.48
  working with, WIN 2.47-58
Active Desktop command (Settings submenu), WIN 2.49, WIN 2.58
Active Desktop command (shortcut menu)
  turning off, WIN 2.58
  viewing as Web page, WIN 2.48, WIN 2.58
Active Desktop gallery, **WIN 2.51**
Active Desktop item, **WIN 1.38**, **WIN 2.4**, **WIN 2.49-54**, **WIN 4.40**
  adding to desktop, WIN 2.49-54
  Web style desktop, WIN 4.49
Active Desktop view, WIN 1.9
Active Web content, **WIN 2.47**
Active window, **WIN 1.17**, WIN 1.18
  changing, WIN 3.17
  Notepad, WIN 2.22
Add New Hardware icon (Control Panel), network hardware, WIN 7.37
Add New Hardware wizard, **WIN 5.33**
Add Printer wizard, **WIN 5.33-38**
Add/Remove button (Install/Uninstall sheet), **WIN 5.46**
Add/Remove Program Properties dialog box, WIN 5.46, WIN 5.49
Add/Remove Programs icon (Control Panel), **WIN 5.46**, WIN 5.48
Address Bar toolbar, **WIN 4.31**
Address Book (Outlook Express), **WIN 7.13**

Address toolbar, **WIN 4.20-21**
  folder contents on, WIN 4.21-22
  searching for Internet information, WIN 4.23-24
  Web page on, WIN 4.21, WIN 4.22-23
Advanced sheet (Find window), **WIN 3.50**, **WIN 6.10-11**
After Dark screen saver, WIN 4.13
Allen, Paul, WIN 1.4-5
All Folders pane (Explorer window), **WIN 3.27**, WIN 3.34
Allocation unit, **WIN 9.19**
Alta-Vista search service, **WIN 6.28-29**
Always on top option (Taskbar Properties dialog box), **WIN 4.19**
America Online, WIN 7.4, WIN 7.5
Animation, **WIN 8.5**
Appearance sheet (Display Properties dialog box), **WIN 4.11-13**
Application-centric approach, **WIN 2.6**
Application program, **WIN 1.7**, **WIN 1.40**, **WIN 2.6**
  launching, creating document by, WIN 2.6-12
  launching after finding, WIN 3.50, WIN 6.5, WIN 6.10
  launching from Explorer, WIN 3.34-35
  launching from window, WIN 3.13-14
  launching using Find command, WIN 6.5
  launching using Run command, WIN 3.50-52
  launching using shortcut, WIN 2.40-41
  launching using Start menu, WIN 1.40-43
  running multiple, WIN 2.23
  sharing, WIN 8.48
  shortcut, WIN 2.34
Area code, dialing properties and, WIN 7.7, WIN 7.19
Areal density, WIN 3.3
Arrange Icons command (shortcut menu), WIN 2.42
as Web Page command (My Computer View menu), WIN 1.17
as Web Page command (My Documents View menu), WIN 4.38
AT&T WorldNet, WIN 7.5
Audio, **WIN 8.5**
  recording and playing, WIN 8.5-26
  compact disc, playing, WIN 8.15-23
Audio CD, **WIN 3.7**
AudioNet Juke Box item, **WIN 1.38**
Audio quality, Internet, WIN 8.42
Auto Arrange command (Arrange Icons submenu), WIN 2.42
AutoPlay, **WIN 8.16**

Back button (Help toolbar), **WIN 1.47**
Back button (Standard Buttons toolbar), WIN 2.32, WIN 3.23-24, **WIN 4.56**

Back button (3½ Floppy (A:) window), **WIN 2.33**
Background
  desktop, WIN 4.6-10
  folder, WIN 4.34-37
Background tab (Display Properties dialog box), WIN 4.6-10
Backup, **WIN 2.30-31**, **WIN 9.5-13**
  differential, WIN 9.13
  files, WIN 9.4-13
  full, WIN 9.13
  hard disk, WIN 3.46
  restoring files, WIN 9.14-19
  system registry, WIN 9.46-50, WIN 9.54
Backup command (System Tools submenu), WIN 9.5
Backup telephone number, WIN 7.21
Backup wizard, **WIN 9.5-11**
Battery power, WIN 6.53
Begin button, Welcome to Windows 98 screen, **WIN 1.9**
Berkeley Software, WIN 4.13
Billing options, Internet connection, WIN 7.26
Bitmap images, **WIN 3.12**
Blind CC: (Outlook Express e-mail), WIN 7.14
Blue check mark (Backup wizard), **WIN 9.7**
Boolean search, **WIN 2.58**
Border, window, see Window border
Browse, searching using, WIN 6.6, WIN 6.7
Browser, see Web browser
Button(s), **WIN 1.14**
  Channel, WIN 1.38, WIN 2.49
  mouse, WIN 1.11
  open window, WIN 1.18
  taskbar area and, WIN 1.9
  window size, WIN 1.19-23
Button name, displaying entire, WIN 2.11
Buttons sheet (Mouse Properties dialog box), WIN 5.13, **WIN 5.20**
by Date command (Arrange Icons submenu), **WIN 2.42**
by Name command (Arrange Icons submenu), **WIN 2.42**
by Size command (Arrange Icons submenu), **WIN 2.42**
by Type command (Arrange Icons submenu), **WIN 2.42**

Call menu (NetMeeting), Change My Information command, WIN 8.36
Call waiting, dialing properties and, WIN 7.7
Cancel button (dialog box), WIN 1.33
Cancel command (shortcut menu), WIN 1.33
Captions, ShowSounds feature and, WIN 5.20
Carbon copy (CC:), WIN 7.14

WIN I.1

WIN I.2 • Index

Cascade windows, **WIN 3.15**-17
Cascading menu, **WIN 1.13**
CC: (Outlook Express e-mail), WIN 7.14
CD drive, **WIN 8.15**
CD Player, **WIN 8.15**-23
CD-ROM (compact disc read-only memory) drive, WIN 3.7, **WIN 8.15**-26
Center setting, desktop image, **WIN 4.7**, WIN 4.10
Change My Information command (NetMeeting Call menu), WIN 8.36
Channel(s)
 subscribing to, WIN 2.49-54
 viewing list of, WIN 1.9
Channel bar
 displaying, WIN 2.51
 Web style desktop, **WIN 1.38**, WIN 2.48, WIN 2.49, WIN 4.49
Channel buttons, **WIN 1.38**, **WIN 2.49**
Channels bar, Explorer, **WIN 4.32**
Chat, **WIN 8.33**, WIN 8.42-48
Chat command (NetMeeting Tools menu), WIN 8.45
Check box, **WIN 1.10**
Chips, storage capacity of, WIN 3.2-3
Classic style desktop, xv, WIN 1.9, **WIN 1.35-36, WIN 4.40**
 choosing, WIN 4.45-49
 folder display and, WIN 4.42
 folder windows and, WIN 4.43
Classic Windows desktop, xv, WIN 1.9, **WIN 1.35-36, WIN 4.40**
Click, **WIN 1.12**-14, WIN 5.13
Client software, **WIN 7.36**, WIN 7.38, WIN 7.39
Clipboard, **WIN 3.21**
Clock, showing, WIN 4.19
Close button (Welcome to Windows 98 screen), WIN 1.9
Close button (window title bar), **WIN 1.23-24**, WIN 2.12
Close command (MSN File menu), WIN 7.16
Close command (shortcut menu), multiple windows, WIN 2.27-28
Closing
 document on desktop, WIN 2.16-17
 folder expansions, WIN 3.35-37
 menu, WIN 1.14, WIN 2.10
 multiple windows, WIN 2.26-28
 Notepad document, WIN 2.11-12
 shortcut menu, WIN 1.16
 Welcome to Windows 98 screen, WIN 1.9, WIN 1.10
 window, WIN 1.23-24, WIN 1.31-32
Clusters, **WIN 9.19**, **WIN 9.28**
 noncontiguous blocks of, WIN 9.29
Collaborating, **WIN 8.48**
Color box, **WIN 3.13**
Color box (Whiteboard), **WIN 8.46**
Color scheme, desktop, WIN 4.12, WIN 5.20, WIN 5.22, WIN 5.24

Command, **WIN 1.13**
Communicating, using Microsoft NetMeeting, WIN 8.33-52
Communicating with other computers, WIN 7.1-57
 using modem, WIN 7.4-36
 using networks, WIN 7.36-57
Communication settings, sets of, WIN 7.7
Compact disc, **WIN 8.15**
 audio, WIN 8.15-23
Components
 checking for, WIN 9.41-43
 downloading, WIN 9.43-45
Compose menu (Outlook Express), Reply to Author command, WIN 7.15
Composing e-mail, WIN 7.13-14
Compression sheet (Hard disk (C:) Properties dialog box), **WIN 3.46**
CompuServe, WIN 7.4, WIN 7.5
Computer(s)
 communicating with other, WIN 7.1-57
 finding on network, WIN 6.5
 maintaining and optimizing performance of, WIN 9.1-61
 power management and, WIN 6.51-53
 viewing on network, WIN 7.45-49
Computer name, network, **WIN 7.38**, WIN 7.43, WIN 7.47
Computer resources, **WIN 5.41**
 sharing on network, WIN 7.42-43, WIN 7.47, **WIN 7.49**-53
Connecting
 to Internet, WIN 1.9
 to Internet service provider, WIN 7.32
 to The Microsoft Network, WIN 1.9, WIN 1.14
Connection settings, MSN, **WIN 7.6**
 changing, WIN 7.16-21
 resetting, WIN 7.22
Connection Settings command (shortcut menu), WIN 7.6, WIN 7.17
Connection Settings dialog box, WIN 7.6, WIN 7.17
Connection status pane (MSN - Sign-In window), WIN 7.8
Connection Wizard, WIN 7.23-31
Connect to the Internet option (Welcome to Windows 98 screen), WIN 1.9
Content Advisor, Microsoft NetMeeting, **WIN 8.34**
Contents pane (Explorer window), **WIN 3.28**
Contents sheet (Help), **WIN 1.44**-47, WIN 5.39
Continuous reinvention, WIN 2.3
Control Panel, WIN 5.1-49
 accessibility properties, WIN 5.20-24
 adding and removing programs, WIN 5.46-48
 changing object properties, WIN 5.4-30
 date/time properties, WIN 5.24-30
 hardware properties, WIN 5.41

 keyboard properties, WIN 5.6-11
 mouse properties, WIN 5.11-20
 network hardware, WIN 7.37
 Network icon, WIN 7.38
 network software, WIN 7.38
 power management, WIN 6.52
 sound schemes, WIN 8.13
 Web style desktop, WIN 1.39
Control Panel command (Settings submenu)
 desktop theme, WIN 4.12
 display, WIN 4.6
 network hardware, WIN 7.37
 network software, WIN 7.38
 object properties, WIN 5.4, WIN 5.5
 power management, WIN 6.52
Control Panel folder, **WIN 1.18**
 object properties, **WIN 5.4**
 opening, WIN 5.5-6
 shortcut to, **WIN 4.27**
Copy and paste method, **WIN 3.21**, WIN 3.23-25
Copy button (Standard Buttons toolbar), WIN 3.23
Copy command (Sound Recorder Edit menu), WIN 8.9
Copy Here command (shortcut menu), **WIN 1.34**, WIN 3.38-39
Copying
 files in Web style, WIN 4.57-60
 files to My Briefcase, WIN 6.35
 files using copy and paste, WIN 3.21-25
 files using right-drag, WIN 3.37-39
 files using Send To command, WIN 2.30-31, WIN 6.17, WIN 6.37
 folder onto disk, WIN 2.30-31
 moving versus, WIN 3.21, WIN 3.25, WIN 3.39
Country, dialing properties and, WIN 7.7
Create Shortcut(s) Here (shortcut menu), **WIN 1.34**, WIN 2.39, WIN 4.28
Creative PC-DVD Video window, WIN 8.27
Credit card, Internet service provider and, WIN 7.27
Currency, regional settings, WIN 5.28
Current Call icon (NetMeeting), **WIN 8.36**
Cursor blink rate, **WIN 5.9**-11
Custom Settings dialog box, xv
Custom style desktop, xv, WIN 1.9, **WIN 1.38, WIN 4.40**
 folder display and, WIN 4.42
 resetting display to, WIN 4.60
Customize this Folder command (My Documents View menu), WIN 4.34
Customize this Folder wizard, **WIN 4.34**-37
Cut button (Standard Buttons toolbar), **WIN 3.25**
Cut command (shortcut menu), folder, WIN 2.20, WIN 2.31

Daily appointments list, WIN 2.4-47
Daily tasks, WIN 1.9
Date
  customizing, WIN 5.24-28
  finding file by, WIN 3.49, WIN 6.8-10
  regional settings, WIN 5.28
Date & Time sheet (Date/Time Properties dialog box), WIN 5.25
Date pane (Date & Time sheet), **WIN 5.25**
Date sheet (Find window), **WIN 3.50,** WIN 6.8-10
Date sheet (Regional Settings Properties dialog box), **WIN 5.30**
Daylight Saving Time (DST), **WIN 5.28**
Default Custom style, **WIN 4.40,** WIN 4.60
Default printer, **WIN 5.34**
Default settings, desktop, **WIN 1.39**
Defragmenting files, WIN 9.28-31
Delete button (Standard Buttons toolbar), **WIN 1.22,** WIN 3.42
Delete command (Explorer File menu), WIN 3.43
Delete command (shortcut menu)
  files, WIN 2.45, WIN 3.25, WIN 3.43
  shortcut, WIN 2.37
Deleted Items folder (Outlook Express), **WIN 7.12**
Deleting
  desktop item, WIN 2.55-57
  Dial-Up Networking Connection icon, WIN 7.35
  e-mail, WIN 7.15
  files and folders in Explorer, WIN 3.42-44
  files, folders, and shortcuts from desktop, WIN 2.44-47
  files, folders, and shortcuts using File, Delete command, WIN 3.25
  files using Send To command, WIN 6.19-20
  icons on desktop, **WIN 2.43**
  restoring from Recycle Bin, WIN 2.44, WIN 6.22-23
  shared folder, WIN 7.51
  shared printer, WIN 7.53
  shortcut, WIN 2.34, WIN 2.37-38, **WIN 2.42-43**
  unnecessary files on hard disk, WIN 9.24-27
  See also Removing
Depends on Password option, locating computers on network and, WIN 7.47, WIN 7.49
Desktop, **WIN 1.8**
  Active™, see Active Desktop™
  appearance, WIN 4.11-13
  arranging icons on, WIN 2.41-42
  background, WIN 4.6-10
  creating document on, WIN 2.12-13
  customizing folders, WIN 4.29-39
  customizing taskbar, WIN 4.15-27

default settings, WIN 1.39
deleting shortcuts, folders, and documents on, WIN 2.42-47
entering data into document on, WIN 2.14-16
High Contrast, WIN 5.20, WIN 5.22
icons, WIN 1.9
modifying, WIN 4.1-61
multiple open windows open on, WIN 3.15-20
My Briefcase on, WIN 6.32-47
naming document on, WIN 2.14
naming folder on, WIN 2.18-19
opening document on, WIN 2.15
opening multiple documents on, WIN 2.23-24
pattern, WIN 4.9-10
properties, WIN 4.4, WIN 4.5-15
saving document on, WIN 2.7-11
screen saver, WIN 4.13-15
shortcut on, WIN 2.39-44
storing documents in folder on, WIN 2.17-20
toolbars, WIN 4.20-29
as work area, WIN 1.11
working on, WIN 2.1-63
Desktop icon (Save As dialog box), WIN 2.9-10
Desktop item, deleting, WIN 2.55-57
Desktop theme, WIN 4.12
Desktop toolbar, **WIN 4.20**
Desktop views, WIN 1.35-39, WIN 4.40-60
  changing, WIN 1.22
  Classic style, xv, WIN 1.9, WIN 1.35-36, WIN 4.40, WIN 4.42, WIN 4.43, WIN 4.45-49
  Custom style, xv, WIN 1.9, WIN 1.38, WIN 4.40, WIN 4.42, WIN 4.60
  folder windows and, WIN 4.43-44
  settings, xv, WIN 1.8
  Web style, WIN 1.9, WIN 1.36, WIN 1.37-39, WIN 2.47-58, WIN 4.40, WIN 4.49-60
Details command (My Briefcase View menu), WIN 6.36
Details command (Recycle Bin View menu), WIN 6.22
Details view, **WIN 3.8**
Device driver, **WIN 5.30,** WIN 5.41
  downloading, **WIN 9.46**
Device Manager sheet (System Properties dialog box), WIN 5.42
Dialing Internet service provider, WIN 7.32-33
Dialing properties, **WIN 7.6**-7
  changing, WIN 7.17-21
Dialing Properties button (Connection Settings dialog box), WIN 7.6, WIN 7.17
Dialing Properties dialog box, WIN 7.7, WIN 7.18-19

Dialog box, **WIN 1.50**
Dial-Up Connection dialog box, WIN 7.32
Dial-Up Networking, **WIN 7.23**
Dial-Up Networking connection, **WIN 7.23**
  existing ISP account, WIN 7.31
Dial-Up Networking Connection icon
  removing, WIN 7.35
  viewing, WIN 7.35
Dial-Up Networking folder, **WIN 1.18**
Dial-Up Networking icon, **WIN 7.8,** WIN 7.31
(D:) icon, **WIN 3.7**
Differential backup, **WIN 9.13**
Digital video disc (DVD), **WIN 8.26**-27
Digital watermark software programs, WIN 8.3
Directory icon (NetMeeting), **WIN 8.36**
Directory information (NetMeeting), WIN 8.36-37
Directory list, ILS server, **WIN 8.33,** **WIN 8.35**
Directory sheet (NetMeeting), **WIN 8.35**
Directory toolbar (NetMeeting), **WIN 8.35**
DirectShow, **WIN 8.26**
Disabilities, customizing for, WIN 5.20-24
Disc menu (CD Player), Edit Play List command, WIN 8.17
Disconnecting
  from Internet service provider, WIN 7.16, WIN 7.33-34
  mapped network drive, WIN 7.56-57
  from MSN, WIN 7.16
Discover Windows 98, WIN 1.10
Disk Cleanup, **WIN 9.24**-27
Disk Cleanup command (Start, Programs, Accessories, System Tools menu), WIN 9.25
Disk Defragmenter, **WIN 9.29**-31
Disk Defragmenter command (System Tools submenu), WIN 9.29
Disk label, **WIN 3.6**
Displaying a folder as a Web page, **WIN 1.38, WIN 4.38**
Display Properties dialog box, WIN 4.5-15
Document(s)
  application-centric approach, WIN 2.6
  closing Notepad, WIN 2.11-12
  creating by launching application program, WIN 2.6-12
  document-centric approach, WIN 2.12
  hypertext, see Hypertext documents
  Notepad, WIN 2.4-47
  opening from Start menu, WIN 2.35-36
  opening from window, WIN 3.12-13
  opening using Documents command, WIN 6.47-48
  opening using shortcut, WIN 2.40-41

printing from within folder, WIN 2.28-29
printing multiple, WIN 2.28-29
printing Notepad, WIN 2.11
removing from Documents submenu, WIN 6.49-50
shortcuts, WIN 2.34-47
viewing using Quick View, WIN 6.15-16
Document-centric approach, **WIN 2.12**
Document icon, on desktop, WIN 2.15
Document in folder, opening and modifying, WIN 2.20-28
Document on desktop
  closing and saving, WIN 2.16-17
  creating, WIN 2.12-13
  entering data into, WIN 2.14-16
  naming, WIN 2.14
  opening, WIN 2.15
  opening multiple, WIN 2.23-24
  saving, WIN 2.7-11
  storing in folder, WIN 2.17-20
Documents command (Start menu)
  opening documents, WIN 6.47-48
  removing list of documents from, WIN 6.49-50
Double-click, **WIN 1.16-17**
Double-click speed, **WIN 5.13-14**
Double-click to open an item (single-click to select) option button (Custom Settings dialog box), **WIN 4.49**
Downloaded program file, **WIN 9.24**
Downloading
  components, WIN 9.43-45
  device driver, WIN 9.46
  program file, **WIN 9.24**
Down scroll arrow, **WIN 1.27-28**
Drafts folder (Outlook Express), **WIN 7.12**
Drawing, Whiteboard and, WIN 8.33, WIN 8.46-48
Drag/dragging, **WIN 1.24-26**
Drive
  copying files from folder to, WIN 3.21-25, WIN 3.37-39
  displaying contents in Explorer, WIN 3.28-29
  expanding in Explorer, WIN 3.29-30
  properties, WIN 3.44-46
  viewing contents of, WIN 3.9-10
Drive converter (FAT32), **WIN 9.59-61**
Drive icons, **WIN 1.18**, WIN 3.6-7
Drive letter, mapping to network resource, WIN 7.54-57
Driver sheet (System Properties dialog box), WIN 5.44
DVD, *see* Digital video disc

EarthLink service, WIN 7.25-35
Editing Play List, WIN 8.20-23
Edit menu (Sound Recorder)
  Copy command, WIN 8.9
  Paste command, WIN 8.10

Edit Play List command (CD Player Disc menu), WIN 8.17
Effects sheet (Display Properties dialog box), WIN 4.15
Electronic mail, *see* E-mail
Ellipsis (...)
  button name followed by, WIN 2.11
  commands followed by, WIN 1.13, WIN 2.8, WIN 2.11
E-mail (electronic mail), **WIN 7.10**
  composing, WIN 7.13-14
  deleted, WIN 7.12
  deleting, WIN 7.15
  incoming, WIN 7.12
  new messages, WIN 7.10-11
  Outlook Express, WIN 7.10-15
  reading messages, WIN 7.12-13
  replying to, WIN 7.13-15
  sent, WIN 7.12
E-mail address, placing call using, WIN 8.40-42
Embed an object, **WIN 8.9**
Embedding sound file in document, WIN 8.9-11
Emptying Recycle Bin, WIN 6.24-25
Enable all web-related content on my desktop option button (Custom Settings dialog box), **WIN 4.52**
Entertainment submenu (Accessories submenu)
  Media Player command, WIN 8.30
  Sound Recorder command, WIN 8.7
Eraser tool (Whiteboard), WIN 8.47
Errors, hard disk, WIN 9.20-23
ESPN SportsZone™ channel, subscribing to, WIN 2.49-54
ESPN SportsZone™ item, **WIN 1.38**
ESPN SportsZone Web page, WIN 4.22-23
Exit command (Notepad File menu), WIN 2.12
Explore command (shortcut menu), **WIN 3.26**, WIN 3.33
Explorer, **WIN 3.26-44**
  copying files, WIN 3.37-39
  deleting files, WIN 3.42-44
  displaying drive contents, WIN 3.28
  displaying files and folders, WIN 3.28
  expanding drive or folder, WIN 3.29-31
  floppy disk contents, WIN 3.39-40
  launching, WIN 3.26-27
  launching program from, WIN 3.34-35
  opening folders, WIN 3.32-33
  renaming files and folders, WIN 3.40-42
Explorer bar, adding to folder, WIN 4.32-34
Explorer Bar command (My Documents View menu), WIN 4.33
Explorer window, WIN 3.27-28
Exploring - My Computer window, WIN 3.27-28

F1 (Help), WIN 1.44, WIN 1.45
Faxes, in Outlook Express folders, WIN 7.12
Favorites bar, **WIN 4.32**
(F:) icon, **WIN 3.7**
File(s)
  backup, WIN 2.30-31, WIN 9.4-13
  copying from folder to drive, WIN 3.21-25, WIN 3.37-39
  copying in Web style, WIN 4.57-60
  copying to My Briefcase, WIN 6.35
  copying using copy and paste, WIN 3.21-25
  copying using right-drag, WIN 3.37-39
  copying using Send To command, WIN 2.30-31, WIN 6.17, WIN 6.37
  date created or modified, WIN 3.49, WIN 6.8-10
  defragmenting, WIN 9.28-31
  deleting from desktop, WIN 2.44-46
  deleting in Explorer, WIN 3.42-44
  deleting unnecessary, WIN 9.24-27
  deleting using File, Delete command, WIN 3.25
  deleting using Send To command, WIN 6.19-20
  displaying in Explorer, WIN 3.28
  finding, WIN 3.48-50, WIN 6.4-15
  fragmented, WIN 9.28
  hidden, WIN 9.46
  icons, WIN 3.11
  MIDI, WIN 8.5
  moving, WIN 3.21, WIN 3.25, WIN 3.39
  network sharing, WIN 7.42-43, WIN 7.47
  opening after finding, WIN 6.10
  Outlook Express folders, WIN 7.12
  path, WIN 3.52
  read-only, WIN 9.46
  renaming, WIN 3.40-42
  restoring, WIN 9.14-19
  sending using File Transfer, WIN 8.48-50
  sizes, WIN 3.49
  sound, WIN 8.5, WIN 8.6-12
  synchronizing in My Briefcase, WIN 6.4347
  system registry, WIN 9.46
  temporary, WIN 9.24
  types, WIN 3.49, WIN 6.10-12
  Wave, WIN 8.5
File allocation table (FAT), **WIN 9.20**, WIN 9.59-61
File extension, WIN 2.8, WIN 2.9
File menu (Explorer)
  Delete command, WIN 3.43
  Properties command, WIN 3.45, WIN 3.47
  Rename command, WIN 3.41
File menu (Find window), Save Search command, WIN 6.14

File menu (Media Player), Open command, WIN 8.31
File menu (MSN), Close command, WIN 7.16
File menu (Network), Open command, WIN 7.45
File menu (Notepad)
 Exit command, WIN 2.12
 Print command, WIN 2.11
 Save As command, WIN 2.8-9, WIN 2.17
 Save command, WIN 2.10, WIN 2.16
File menu (Outlook Express), Open command, WIN 7.13
File menu (Windows), Save command, WIN 2.28
File name, **WIN 2.8-11**
 finding, WIN 3.48-49, WIN 6.5, WIN 6.6
Files or Folders command (Find submenu), WIN 3.48, WIN 6.4-5
File system, **WIN 9.20**
File Transfer (NetMeeting), **WIN 8.33**
 sending file using, WIN 8.48-50
File Transfer command (NetMeeting Tools menu), WIN 8.49
Filter, NetMeeting, **WIN 8.38**
Find command (Start menu), **WIN 3.48**, **WIN 6.4**-15
 computers on network, WIN 7.47-49
 files or folders, WIN 3.48, WIN 6.4-5
 Internet information and, WIN 6.5, WIN 6.27-29
 people on Internet and, WIN 6.5, WIN 6.30-32
Finding files or folders, WIN 3.48-50, WIN 6.4-15
 by date, WIN 3.49, WIN 6.8-10
 by type, WIN 6.10-12
 using saved search, WIN 6.15
 using word or series of words in file, WIN 6.12-13
Floppy disk
 backing up files to, WIN 9.5
 copying files from folder onto, WIN 3.23-25, WIN 3.37-39
 copying files in Web style, WIN 4.57-60
 copying folder onto, WIN 2.30-31
 displaying contents of, WIN 3.39-40
 moving My Briefcase to, WIN 6.36-37
 opening folder on, WIN 2.31-34
 viewing contents of, WIN 9.13-14
Folder(s), **WIN 1.18**
 adding toolbar to, WIN 4.31-32
 background, WIN 4.34-37
 backup, WIN 2.30-31, WIN 9.7-11
 closing expansions, WIN 3.35-37
 contents of, on Address toolbar, WIN 4.21-22
 copying files to drive from, WIN 3.21-25, WIN 3.37-39
 copying onto disk, WIN 2.30-31

customizing, WIN 4.29-39
deleting from desktop, WIN 2.46-47
deleting in Explorer, WIN 3.44
deleting using File, Delete command, WIN 3.25
displaying as Web page, WIN 1.38, WIN 4.38-39, WIN 4.43
displaying in Explorer, WIN 3.28
expanding in Explorer, WIN 3.31
Explorer bar, WIN 4.32-34
finding, WIN 3.48-50, WIN 6.4-15
icons, WIN 3.10-11
mapping drive letter to, WIN 7.54-55
moving document into, on desktop, WIN 2.19-20
naming on desktop, WIN 2.18-19
opening, xv
opening and modifying on desktop, WIN 2.20-28
opening in Explorer, WIN 3.32-33
opening on floppy disk, WIN 2.31-34
opening View menu in, WIN 4.30-31
Outlook Express, WIN 7.12
printing document from within, WIN 2.28-29
Programs, WIN 3.33
properties, WIN 3.46-47
renaming, WIN 3.40-42
sharing, WIN 7.49-51
shortcut, WIN 2.41
storing documents, on desktop, WIN 2.17-20
Temp, WIN 9.24
Web content in, WIN 4.41
Windows, WIN 3.10-11
Folder Options command (Settings submenu), xv, WIN 4.45
Folder Options dialog box, xv, WIN 4.46, WIN 4.47-48, WIN 4.50
Folder window
 desktop view and, WIN 4.43-44
 opening, WIN 3.10-11, WIN 3.22
 Web style desktop, WIN 4.53, WIN 4.55, WIN 4.56-57
Fonts, viewing, WIN 5.22-24
Fonts folder, **WIN 5.22**
Font sizes, viewing, WIN 5.22-24
For all folders with HTML content option button (Custom Settings dialog box), **WIN 4.52**
Forward button (Help toolbar), **WIN 1.47**
Forward button (Standard Buttons toolbar), WIN 2.32, **WIN 4.56**
Fragmented file, **WIN 9.28**
Free Space button (My Computer window), **WIN 3.8**
Full access, **WIN 7.49**
Full backup, **WIN 9.13**

Gates, Bill, WIN 1.4-5, WIN 2.2-3
General sheet (Folder Options dialog box), WIN 4.46, WIN 4.48, WIN 4.50

General sheet (Hard disk (C:) Properties dialog box), **WIN 3.45**
General sheet (System Properties dialog box), **WIN 5.43**
Gigabyte of RAM, **WIN 3.46**
Graphical user interface (GUI), **WIN 1.8**
 history of, WIN 2.2-3
Graphic image
 animated, WIN 8.5
 drawing using Whiteboard, WIN 8.46-48
 still, WIN 8.4
Gray check mark (Backup window), **WIN 9.13**
Green left arrow, synchronizing files and, **WIN 6.45**
Green right arrow, synchronizing files and, **WIN 6.45**
GUI, see Graphical user interface

Hard disk, **WIN 3.6-7**
 backing up, WIN 2.31, WIN 3.46, WIN 9.13
 capacity, WIN 3.3
 compressing, WIN 3.46
 defragmenting files, WIN 9.28-31
 deleting unnecessary files on, WIN 9.24-27
 finding files and folders on, WIN 6.5-15
 maintaining, WIN 9.20-38
 properties, WIN 3.44-46
 Recycle Bin and, WIN 6.21, WIN 6.26
 scanning for errors, WIN 9.21-23
Hard disk (C:) icon, **WIN 3.6**
Hard disk (C:) window, WIN 3.9-10
Hard disk (C:) Properties dialog box, WIN 3.45
Hardware
 adding new, WIN 5.30-38
 device drivers, WIN 5.30, WIN 5.41
 Help Troubleshooter, WIN 5.38-41
 network, WIN 7.37
 operating system control of, WIN 1.6
 power management, WIN 6.51-53
 profiles, WIN 5.45-46
 properties, WIN 5.41-46
 user interface and, WIN 1.7
Hardware Profiles sheet (System Properties dialog box), **WIN 5.45**
Hearing impaired, **WIN 5.20**
Help, WIN 1.43-49
 hardware troubleshooting, WIN 5.38-41
 Microsoft Support Online, WIN 2.58-62
Help command (Start menu), WIN 1.44
 Web Help, WIN 2.59
Help toolbar, WIN 1.47
Help topic, **WIN 1.45**
Help Troubleshooter, hardware, WIN 5.38-41
Hibernation mode, **WIN 6.51**
Hidden file, **WIN 9.46**
Hide button (Help toolbar), **WIN 1.47**

Hiding
  frame in Help window, WIN 1.47
  taskbar, WIN 4.17-19
Hierarchical structure, WIN 3.27,
  WIN 3.28, WIN 6.7
High Contrast feature, WIN 5.20,
  WIN 5.22-24
History bar, WIN 4.32
History icon (NetMeeting), WIN 8.36
HKEY, WIN 9.50
Holographic storage, WIN 3.3
Home page, Internet service provider,
  WIN 7.32
Hourglass icon, WIN 2.10
Hovering, WIN 4.54
Hyperlink, WIN 1.36, WIN 1.37
  Search bar, WIN 4.34
  searching for, WIN 4.23-24, WIN 6.27
Hypermedia, WIN 1.36
Hypertext documents, WIN 1.36

Icons, WIN 1.9
  arranging on desktop, WIN 2.41-42
  Classic Style desktop, WIN 1.36
  Control Panel window, WIN 5.6
  deleting on desktop, WIN 2.43
  document, on desktop, WIN 2.15
  drive, WIN 1.18, WIN 3.6-7
  Explorer window, WIN 3.27
  file, WIN 3.11
  folder, WIN 3.10-11
  hourglass, WIN 2.10
  launching application using desktop,
    WIN 1.42-43
  moving, WIN 1.32-34
  My Computer window, WIN 1.18
  Paint, WIN 3.12
  shortcut, WIN 2.34
  size, WIN 1.17, WIN 3.7, WIN 3.8,
    WIN 3.9, WIN 3.27, WIN 4.19,
    WIN 4.26
  system folder, WIN 3.6
  toolbar, WIN 4.26
  Web style desktop, WIN 1.38,
    WIN 4.49, WIN 4.53-55
Icon title, showing, WIN 4.26
Icon title text box, WIN 2.13
ILS (Internet Locator Service), WIN 8.33
ILS (Internet Locator Service) server,
  WIN 8.33, WIN 8.35, WIN 8.39-40
Image
  animated graphic, WIN 8.5
  drawing using Whiteboard,
    WIN 8.46-48
  still graphic, WIN 8.4
Inbox folder (Outlook Express), WIN 7.12
Inbox - Outlook Express window,
  WIN 7.11-15
Index sheet, Help, WIN 1.47-48
Insertion point, WIN 2.7
  blink rate, WIN 5.9-11

Install button (Install/Uninstall sheet),
  WIN 5.46
Install/Uninstall sheet (Add/Remove
  Program Properties dialog box),
  WIN 5.49
Installing
  Dial-Up Networking, WIN 7.23
  network hardware component,
    WIN 7.37
  network software components,
    WIN 7.38-45
  peer-to-peer network, WIN 7.36-45
Intel, WIN 1.5
Intel EtherExpress 16, WIN 7.39
Intel EtherExpress network hardware
  adapter, WIN 7.37
Intellectual property, WIN 8.3
Internet, WIN 1.36, WIN 7.5
  Active Desktop™ and, WIN 2.47
  audio quality, WIN 8.42
  connecting to, WIN 7.23-35
  finding people on, WIN 6.5,
    WIN 6.30-32
  finding Web content on, WIN 6.5,
    WIN 6.27-29
  Microsoft Support Online and,
    WIN 2.58-62
  searching using Address toolbar,
    WIN 4.23-24
  Windows Update and, WIN 9.39
Internet connection icon, WIN 1.9
Internet Connection wizard, WIN 7.23-31
Internet Explorer (IE), WIN 1.6
  launching from desktop icon, WIN 1.9,
    WIN 4.25
  launching from Explorer, WIN 3.34-35
  launching using Start menu,
    WIN 1.40-43
  searches and, WIN 6.28
Internet Explorer 4 Web browser,
  WIN 1.37
Internet Explorer Channel bar, WIN 2.48,
  WIN 2.49
  position of, WIN 2.50
  removing, WIN 2.57-58
Internet Explorer command (Programs
  submenu), WIN 1.40-41
  Microsoft NetMeeting, WIN 8.34
Internet Explorer icon, WIN 1.9
  connecting to ISP and, WIN 7.32
Internet Explorer window, ISP home page
  in, WIN 7.32
Internet Locator Service, see ILS
Internet newsgroups, WIN 7.10,
  WIN 7.12
Internet Protocol address (IP address),
  WIN 7.31, WIN 8.33
Internet service provider (ISP), WIN 7.4,
  WIN 7.5, WIN 7.23
  connecting to Internet using,
    WIN 7.23-35

  dialing, WIN 7.32-33
  disconnecting from, WIN 7.33-34
Interrupt request (IRQ), WIN 5.41
IP address, see Internet Protocol address
IPX/SPX protocol, WIN 7.37, WIN 7.38,
  WIN 7.41
ISP, see Internet service provider

Keyboard, WIN 1.7, WIN 1.34
  customizing, WIN 5.6-11
  layouts, WIN 5.11
Keyboard icon (Control Panel), WIN 5.6
Keyboard repeat delay, WIN 5.6-8
Keyboard repeat rate, WIN 5.8-9
Keyboard shortcuts, WIN 1.34-35
Keys, WIN 9.50
Keyword search, WIN 2.58, WIN 4.23,
  WIN 4.32, WIN 4.34, WIN 6.27
Kildall, Gary, WIN 2.2-3
Knowledge Database, WIN 2.58

Label name, hard drive, WIN 3.45
Language sheet (Keyboard Properties
  dialog box), WIN 5.11
LAN Manager, WIN 7.37
Laptop computer
  communication settings, WIN 7.7
  connecting settings, WIN 7.16
Large Icons, WIN 1.17, WIN 3.7,
  WIN 3.8, WIN 3.9, WIN 3.27
Large Icons command (View menu),
  WIN 1.17
Launch Internet Explorer Browser icon,
  WIN 1.9
Launch Outlook Express icon, WIN 1.9
Launching
  application program, creating document
    by, WIN 2.6-12
  application program after finding,
    WIN 3.50, WIN 6.5, WIN 6.10
  application program from Explorer,
    WIN 3.34-35
  application program from window,
    WIN 3.13-14
  application program using Find
    command, WIN 6.5
  application programs using Run
    command, WIN 3.50-52
  application program using shortcut,
    WIN 2.40-41
  application program using Start menu,
    WIN 1.40-43
  from Address toolbar, WIN 4.24-25
  Windows 98, WIN 1.8-9
Left-handed button configuration,
  WIN 5.12-13
Left panel, folder as Web page, WIN 4.38
Link, see Hyperlink
Links toolbar, WIN 4.20, WIN 4.31
List view, WIN 3.8
Local area networks (LANs), WIN 7.36

Local calls, dialing properties and, WIN 7.7
Location, dialing, WIN 7.7, WIN 7.17-18
Logical error, **WIN 9.20**
Log Off command (Start menu), WIN 1.14
Long distance calls, dialing properties and, WIN 7.7, WIN 7.19
LPT1 printer port, **WIN 5.34**

Maintain Your Computer, WIN 1.10
Maintaining hard disk, WIN 9.20-38
Maintenance wizard, **WIN 9.31-38**
Maintenance Wizard command (System Tools submenu), WIN 9.32
Map Network Drive command (shortcut menu), WIN 7.54
Mapped network drive, WIN 7.54-57
  accessing, WIN 7.55-56
  disconnecting, WIN 7.56-57
Mapping a drive letter to network resource, **WIN 7.54-57**
Maximize button, **WIN 1.21-22**
Media Player, **WIN 8.30-32**
Megabyte of RAM, **WIN 3.46**
Memory
  user interface and, WIN 1.7
  See also RAM
Menu, **WIN 1.13**
  closing, WIN 1.14, WIN 2.10
  opening, WIN 2.10
  shortcut, see Shortcut menu
Menu bar (My Computer window), **WIN 1.18**
Microsoft Client for Microsoft Networks, WIN 7.38
Microsoft Corporation
  history of, WIN 1.5, WIN 2.2-3
  usability labs, WIN 1.8
Microsoft DirectX software, WIN 8.26
Microsoft IntelliMouse™, **WIN 1.11**, **WIN 5.12**
Microsoft Internet Explorer, see Internet Explorer
Microsoft Internet Explorer 4 Web browser, see Internet Explorer 4 Web browser
Microsoft Network, The
  connecting to, WIN 1.9, WIN 1.14
  finding information on, WIN 6.6, WIN 6.29
  icon, **WIN 1.9**
Microsoft NetMeeting, **WIN 8.5**, **WIN 8.33-52**
Microsoft Network, The (MSN), WIN 7.4, **WIN 7.5**
  connection settings, WIN 7.6-7
  icon, WIN 7.7, WIN 7.8
  signing in to, WIN 7.8-10
  signing out from, WIN 7.15-16
Microsoft Office document, opening, WIN 1.14

Microsoft Referral Service, WIN 7.25
Microsoft Support Online, **WIN 2.58-62**
Microsoft Windows, see Windows
Microsoft Windows 98, see Windows 98
Microsoft Windows Update Web site, **WIN 2.58**
MIDI file, **WIN 8.5**
  playing, WIN 8.30-32
Minimize All Windows command (shortcut menu), WIN 2.26
Minimize button, **WIN 1.19-21**
Minus sign, file and folder structure, **WIN 3.28**, WIN 3.36-37
Mobility impaired, **WIN 5.20**
Modem, **WIN 7.4**
  dialing properties and, WIN 7.7
  Internet connection and, WIN 1.9
  troubleshooting, WIN 7.23
Modified, date file was, WIN 3.49, WIN 6.8-9
Monitor, **WIN 1.7**
Moore, Gordon, WIN 3.2-3
Motion sheet (Mouse Properties dialog box), WIN 5.17-19, **WIN 5.20**
Mouse, **WIN 1.7**, **WIN 1.11**
  customizing, WIN 5.11-20
  double-click speed, WIN 5.13-14
  operations, WIN 1.11-18, WIN 1.24-31
Mouse buttons, WIN 1.11
  changing configuration, WIN 5.12-13
MouseKeys feature, **WIN 5.20-22**
Mouse pointer, **WIN 1.9**
  changing scheme, WIN 5.15-16
  speed, WIN 5.16-18
  trails, WIN 5.18-19
  using numeric keypad to move, WIN 5.20-22
Move Here command (shortcut menu), **WIN 1.34**, WIN 2.19, WIN 2.43-44, WIN 3.25, **WIN 3.39**
Movies, DVD, WIN 8.26-29
Moving
  Active Desktop item, WIN 2.55
  copying versus, WIN 3.21, WIN 3.25, WIN 3.39
  document into folder, WIN 2.19-20
  icon, WIN 1.32-34
  My Briefcase to floppy disk, WIN 6.36-37
  object by dragging, WIN 1.24-25
  taskbar, WIN 4.16
Moving Pictures Experts Group (MPEG), **WIN 8.26**
MPEG (Moving Pictures Experts Group), **WIN 8.26**
MSN, see Microsoft Network, The
MSN On Stage Web page, WIN 7.9, WIN 7.10
MSN - Sign-In window, WIN 7.8-9
Multimedia, **WIN 8.4**
  audio CD, WIN 8.15-23
  introduction to, WIN 8.4-5

Microsoft NetMeeting, WIN 8.5, WIN 8.33-52
  playing files, WIN 8.30-32
  recording and playing audio, WIN 8.5-26
  recording and playing video, WIN 8.26-29
Music, CD, WIN 8.15-23
Musical Instrument and Digital Interface, see MIDI file
My Briefcase, **WIN 6.32-47**
  copying files to, WIN 6.35
  moving to floppy disk, WIN 6.36-37
  synchronizing files, WIN 6.43-47
  viewing contents of, WIN 6.36
My Briefcase icon, **WIN 1.9**
My Computer icon, **WIN 1.9**, **WIN 3.4**
My Computer window
  contents of, WIN 3.4-9
  displaying as Web page, WIN 1.38-39
  elements of, WIN 1.18-19
  icons in, WIN 3.6-9
  mapped network drive, WIN 7.56
  viewing as Web page, WIN 1.17
  Web style, WIN 4.54-55
My Documents folder, **WIN 4.29**
  customizing, WIN 4.29-39
My Documents icon, **WIN 1.9**

Name/naming
  document on desktop, WIN 2.14
  folder on desktop, WIN 2.18-19
  hard drive, WIN 3.45
Name & Location sheet (Find window), WIN 3.49, WIN 6.6, WIN 6.8, WIN 6.12-13
Name button (My Computer window), **WIN 3.8**
Natural language search, **WIN 2.58**, WIN 2.60
NetBEUI protocol, WIN 7.37
NetMeeting, see Microsoft NetMeeting
Network(s), **WIN 7.5**, **WIN 7.36-57**
  components, **WIN 7.36-45**
  hardware component, WIN 7.37
  finding computers on, WIN 6.5
  My Briefcase and, WIN 6.32
  peer-to-peer, WIN 7.36-45
  software components, WIN 7.38-45
  viewing computers and workgroups on, WIN 7.45-49
Network adapter, **WIN 7.36**
  installing, WIN 7.37
Network administrator, **WIN 7.38**
Network components, WIN 7.36-45
Network icon (Control Panel window), WIN 7.38
Network Neighborhood, **WIN 7.45-47**
  finding files using, WIN 6.6
Network Neighborhood icon, **WIN 1.9**, WIN 7.46

Network resource
  mapping drive letter to, WIN 7.54-57
  sharing, WIN 7.42-43, WIN 7.47,
    WIN 7.51-53
New command (shortcut menu),
    WIN 1.15
  folder, WIN 2.18
  Text Document, WIN 2.7, WIN 2.13
Newsgroup, see Internet newsgroups
Noncontiguous blocks of clusters,
    WIN 9.29
Notepad, **WIN 2.4, WIN 2.5**-47
  launching, WIN 2.6-12, WIN 3.3,13-14
Notepad command (Accessories
    submenu), WIN 2.6
Novell NetWare network, WIN 7.37
Numbers, regional settings, WIN 5.28
Numeric keypad, using to move mouse
    pointer, WIN 5.20-22

Object, **WIN 1.9, WIN 8.9**
  embedding, WIN 8.9
  moving by dragging, WIN 1.24-25
  properties of, see Properties of an object
  right-clicking, WIN 1.14-15, WIN 6.16
Online service, **WIN 7.4**-35
  accessing, WIN 7.5-10
  messages from, WIN 7.12
Online Services icon, **WIN 1.9**
Only for folders where I select "as Web
    Page" (View menu) option button
    (Custom Settings dialog box),
    WIN 4.49
Open/opening
  Control Panel folder, WIN 5.5-6
  document from Start menu,
    WIN 2.35-36
  document from window, WIN 3.12-13
  document in folder, WIN 2.20-28
  document using Documents command,
    WIN 6.47-48
  document using shortcut, WIN 2.40-41
  e-mail messages, WIN 7.12-13
  files after finding, WIN 6.10
  folder on floppy disk, WIN 2.31-34
  folder window, WIN 3.10-11, WIN 3.22
  inactive window, WIN 2.24-25
  menu, WIN 2.10
  Microsoft Office document, WIN 1.14
  multiple documents, WIN 2.23-24
  View menu in folder, WIN 4.30-31
  window by double-clicking,
    WIN 1.16-17
  Open command (Media Player File menu),
    WIN 8.31
  Open command (Network File menu),
    WIN 7.45
  Open command (Outlook Express File
    menu), WIN 7.13
  Open command (shortcut menu)
    document, WIN 2.15, WIN 2.22
    folder, WIN 2.21

multiple documents, WIN 2.24
shortcuts, WIN 2.41
Open each folder in its own window
    option button (Custom Settings dialog
    box), **WIN 4.49**
Open each folder in the same window
    option button (Custom Settings dialog
    box), **WIN 4.52**
Open windows, managing, WIN 3.15-20
Operating systems
  history of, WIN 2.2-3
  32-bit, WIN 1.6
Options button (Help toolbar), **WIN 1.47**
Options menu, Web Help command,
    WIN 1.47
Outbox folder (Outlook Express),
    WIN 7.12
Outlook Express, WIN 1.9, WIN 1.14,
    WIN 7.10-15
Outlook Express icon, **WIN 1.9**

Paint icon, **WIN 3.12**
Paint program, **WIN 3.12**-13,
    WIN 3.50-51
Password
  MSN, WIN 7.8, WIN 7.10
  network, WIN 7.38, WIN 7.44
  network resources, WIN 7.49
  online service, **WIN 7.5**
Paste button (Standard Buttons toolbar),
    WIN 3.24
Paste command (shortcut menu), folder,
    WIN 2.20, WIN 2.31
Paste command (Sound Recorder Edit
    menu), WIN 8.10
Path
  file, **WIN 3.52**
  folder, **WIN 4.21**
  shared resource, **WIN 7.54**
Pattern, desktop, **WIN 4.9**-10
Peer-to-peer network, **WIN 7.36**-45
Pen tool (Whiteboard), **WIN 8.46**
People on Internet, finding, WIN 6.5,
    WIN 6.30-32
Performance sheet (System Properties
    dialog box), **WIN 5.46**
Phone Book button (Connection Settings
    dialog box), WIN 7.19
Phone Book dialog box, WIN 7.20
Physical error, **WIN 9.20**
Piracy, software, WIN 8.3
Plagiarism, WIN 8.2
Playing
  audio compact disc, WIN 8.15-23
  digital video disc, WIN 8.26-27
  multimedia files, WIN 8.30-32
  recorded voice message, WIN 8.8-9
Play List, CD, **WIN 8.16**-23
Plug and Play (PNP) technology,
    WIN 5.33
Plus sign, file and folder structure,
    WIN 3.28, WIN 3.30, WIN 6.7

Point, **WIN 1.11**
  hovering and, WIN 4.54
Point and click, WIN 1.11-14
Pointer speed, mouse, WIN 5.16-18
Pointers sheet (Mouse Properties dialog
    box), WIN 5.15, **WIN 5.20**
Pointer trail, **WIN 5.18**-19
Policy.pol file, **WIN 9.46**
Port, WIN 5.31, **WIN 5.34**
Power management, **WIN 6.51**-53
Power scheme, **WIN 6.51**
Presentation graphics program, **WIN 1.40**
Preview button (Screen Saver pane),
    WIN 4.15
Primary mouse button, **WIN 1.11**,
    WIN 5.12
Print command (Notepad File menu),
    WIN 2.11
Print command (shortcut menu),
    WIN 2.11
  multiple documents, WIN 2.29
Printer
  adding, WIN 5.33-38
  network sharing, WIN 7.42-43,
    WIN 7.47, WIN 7.51-53
Printer port, mapping drive letter to,
    WIN 7.54
Printers folder, **WIN 1.18**
Printing
  document from within folder,
    WIN 2.28-29
  multiple documents, WIN 2.28-29
  Notepad document, WIN 2.11
Prodigy, WIN 7.4, WIN 7.5
Product Updates area (Windows Update),
    WIN 9.41-43
Program(s), WIN 1.6, **WIN 1.40, WIN 2.6**
  adding, WIN 5.46-48
  removing, WIN 5.48
  See also Application program
Program event, **WIN 8.12**
Programs folder, **WIN 3.33**
Programs submenu, **WIN 1.13**
  Accessories, Notepad command,
    WIN 2.6
  Explorer command, WIN 3.27
  Internet Explorer command, WIN 1.40
  Internet Explorer submenu, Microsoft
    NetMeeting command, WIN 8.34
Programs window, WIN 3.32-33
Properties
  hardware, WIN 5.41-46
  Start menu, WIN 6.49
Properties, of an object, **WIN 1.9,
    WIN 3.44**
  accessibility, WIN 5.20-24
  date/time, WIN 5.24-30
  desktop, **WIN 4.4**, WIN 4.5-15
  drive, WIN 3.44-46
  folder, WIN 3.46-47
  keyboard, WIN 5.6-11
  mouse, WIN 5.11-20

Recycle Bin, WIN 6.25-27
Standard Buttons toolbar, WIN 1.22
taskbar, WIN 4.17-19, WIN 6.49
using Control Panel to change,
  WIN 5.4-30
Properties button (Standard Buttons
  toolbar), **WIN 1.22**, WIN 3.45
Properties command (Explorer File menu),
  WIN 3.45, WIN 3.47
Properties command (shortcut menu)
  display, WIN 4.5-6
  hiding taskbar, WIN 4.17
  Recycle Bin, WIN 6.25
  removing desktop item, WIN 2.56
  subscribing to channel, WIN 2.49-50
Protocol, network, **WIN 7.36-37**,
  WIN 7.38, WIN 7.40

Quick Launch toolbar, WIN 1.8, **WIN 1.9**
  launching application using,
    WIN 1.41-42
Quick View, **WIN 6.15-16**
Quotation marks, Web search and,
  WIN 4.23

RAM (random-access memory), WIN 1.6,
  WIN 2.7, WIN 3.46
Reading e-mail messages, WIN 7.12-13
Read-only file, **WIN 9.46**
Read-Only option, network resources,
  WIN 7.49
Recording and playing audio, WIN 8.5-26
Recording voice message, WIN 8.7-8
Recycle Bin, **WIN 2.43**, WIN 3.25,
  WIN 9.24
  emptying, WIN 6.24-25
  properties, WIN 6.25-27
  recovery from, WIN 2.44
  restoring deletions, WIN 6.22-23
  Send To menu and, WIN 6.17-21
  viewing contents of, WIN 6.21-22
Recycle Bin icon, **WIN 1.9**
Red down arrow, synchronizing files and,
  WIN 6.45
Refresh command (Network
  Neighborhood View menu), WIN 7.45
Regional settings, **WIN 5.28-30**
Regional Settings icon, **WIN 5.28**
Registry Checker, **WIN 9.47-50**,
  WIN 9.54
Registry Checker command (Microsoft
  System Information Tools menu),
  WIN 9.48
Registry Editor, **WIN 9.50**
Removable Disk (E) command (Send To
  submenu), WIN 2.30
Removable Disk (E:) icon, **WIN 3.7**
Removing
  Internet Explorer Channel bar,
    WIN 2.57-58
  pattern, WIN 4.10
  program, WIN 5.48

shortcut from toolbar, WIN 4.29
toolbar, WIN 4.26
wallpaper, WIN 4.8
See also Deleting
Rename command (Explorer File menu),
  file, WIN 3.41
Rename command (shortcut menu)
  document, WIN 2.14
  file, WIN 3.41
Renaming
  document, WIN 2.14
  files or folders, **WIN 3.40-42**
Replying to e-mail, WIN 7.13-15
Reply to Author button (Outlook
  Express), WIN 7.14
Reply to Author command (Outlook
  Express Compose menu), WIN 7.15
Resizing, *see* Size
Resources sheet (System Properties dialog
  box), **WIN 5.45**
Restore button, window, **WIN 1.21-23**
Restore wizard, WIN 9.14-19
Restoring backup files, WIN 9.14-19
Restoring deletions, from Recycle Bin,
  WIN 6.22-23
Right arrow, following commands,
  WIN 1.13
Right-click, **WIN 1.14-16**, WIN 6.16
Right-drag, **WIN 1.32-34**
  copying files using, WIN 3.37-39
  creating shortcut using, WIN 2.39
  deleting object using, WIN 2.43
Right-handed button configuration,
  WIN 5.12, WIN 5.13
Right panel, folder as Web page,
  WIN 4.38
Run command (Start menu), launching
  programs using, WIN 2.7,
  WIN 3.50-52

Save As command (Notepad File menu),
  WIN 2.8-9, WIN 2.17
Save As dialog box, WIN 2.9-10
Save button (Save As dialog box),
  WIN 2.10
Save command (Notepad File menu),
  WIN 2.10, WIN 2.16
Save command (Windows File menu),
  WIN 2.28
Save Search command (Find window File
  menu), WIN 6.14
Saving
  document on desktop, WIN 2.7-11,
    WIN 2.16-17
  search, WIN 6.14
ScanDisk, **WIN 9.21-23**
ScanDisk command (System Tools
  submenu), WIN 9.21
Scheduled Tasks folder, **WIN 1.18**
Scheme
  desktop, WIN 4.11, WIN 4.12,
    WIN 5.20, WIN 5.22, WIN 5.24

mouse pointer, WIN 5.15-16
power, WIN 6.51
Scorepost: ESPN SportsZone™ channel,
  WIN 2.53-54
Screen saver, **WIN 4.13-15**
Screen Saver tab (Display Properties dialog
  box), WIN 4.14
Scroll arrows, WIN 1.27-28
Scroll bar, WIN 1.27-31
Scroll box, **WIN 1.27**
Scrolling in window, WIN 1.27-31
Search/searching
  files and folders, WIN 3.48, WIN 6.4-15
  for Internet information, WIN 6.5,
    WIN 6.27-29
  Internet using Address toolbar,
    WIN 4.23-24
  Microsoft Support Online, WIN 2.58-59
  for people, WIN 6.5, WIN 6.30-32
  saving, WIN 6.14
  Web using Search bar, WIN 4.32
Search bar, **WIN 4.32**
Search engine, **WIN 4.32**
Search service, **WIN 6.27-29**
Secondary mouse button, **WIN 1.11**,
  WIN 1.14, WIN 5.12
Send To command (shortcut menu),
  WIN 6.16-21
  copying folder, WIN 2.30
  copying multiple files, WIN 4.59
  deleting file, WIN 6.19-20
Send To menu, adding commands to,
  WIN 2.30, WIN 6.17-19
Sent Items folder (Outlook Express),
  WIN 7.12
Server
  ILS, WIN 8.33, WIN 8.35, WIN 8.39-40
  Internet service provider, **WIN 7.23**
Services, MSN, **WIN 7.5**
Service software, **WIN 7.36**, WIN 7.38
Settings button (Screen Saver pane),
  WIN 4.15
Settings command (Start menu)
  Control Panel, network hardware,
    WIN 7.37
  Control Panel, network software,
    WIN 7.38
Settings sheet (Display Properties dialog
  box), WIN 4.15
Settings submenu
  Active Desktop command, WIN 2.49,
    WIN 2.58
  Folder Options command, xv, WIN 4.45
Settings submenu, Control Panel
  command
  desktop theme, WIN 4.12
  display, WIN 4.6
  object properties, WIN 5.4, WIN 5.5
  power management, WIN 6.52
  taskbar, WIN 4.19
Sharing
  application, WIN 8.48

resources on network, WIN 7.42-43, WIN 7.49-53
Shortcut(s), **WIN 2.34**
  Control Panel folder, WIN 4.27
  creating, WIN 1.34, WIN 2.39-40, WIN 4.28
  deleting from Start menu, WIN 2.37-38
  deleting from desktop, **WIN 2.42-43**, WIN 2.46-47
  deleting icon, WIN 2.34
  deleting using File, Delete command, WIN 3.25
  folder, WIN 2.41, WIN 4.27
  keyboard, WIN 1.34-35
  opening document using, WIN 2.40-41
  placing on Start menu, WIN 2.34-35
  Send To menu, WIN 6.17-19
  on toolbar, WIN 4.27-29
  to Web pages, WIN 4.31
Shortcut menu, **WIN 1.15**, WIN 6.16
  closing, WIN 1.16
Show clock option (Taskbar Properties dialog box), **WIN 4.19**
Show Desktop icon (Quick Launch toolbar), **WIN 1.9, WIN 2.25-26**
Show Files hyperlink, WIN 4.58-59
Show small icons in Start menu option (Taskbar Properties dialog box), **WIN 4.19**
ShowSounds feature, **WIN 5.20**
Shut Down command (Start menu), WIN 1.14, **WIN 1.49**-50
Signing in to The Microsoft Network, WIN 7.8-10
Signing out from The Microsoft Network, WIN 7.15-16
Signing up, to online service, **WIN 7.5**
Single-click to open an item (point to select) option button (Custom Settings dialog box), **WIN 4.52**
Single window option, **WIN 3.9**
16TP ISA, WIN 7.39
Size
  icons, WIN 1.17, WIN 3.7, WIN 3.8, WIN 3.9, WIN 3.27, WIN 4.19, WIN 4.26
  taskbar, WIN 4.25-26
  window, WIN 1.19-23, WIN 1.25-26, WIN 1.31
Small Icons, **WIN 3.7, WIN 3.8**, WIN 4.19
Software
  CD, WIN 8.15
  client, WIN 7.36, WIN 7.38, WIN 7.39
  network, WIN 7.38-45
  piracy, WIN 8.3
  service, WIN 7.36, WIN 7.38
  user interface and, WIN 1.7
  See also Application program
Sound, *see* Audio
Sound card, **WIN 8.6**, WIN 8.15
Sound device, volume of, WIN 8.23-25

Sound files
  embedding in document, WIN 8.9-11
  recording and playing, WIN 8.6-12
Sound Recorder, recording and playing sound files using, WIN 8.6-12
Sound scheme, **WIN 8.6, WIN 8.12**
  changing, WIN 8.12-15
Sound Sentry feature, **WIN 5.20**
Source, **WIN 8.9**
Speaker(s)
  NetMeeting and, WIN 8.33, WIN 8.36
  volume, WIN 8.23-25
Speaker icon, **WIN 1.9**
SpeedDial icon (NetMeeting), **WIN 8.36**
Speed sheet (Keyboard Properties dialog box), **WIN 5.7**
Sporting event, displaying additional information about, WIN 2.54-55
Standard Buttons toolbar, **WIN 1.18, WIN 1.22, WIN 3.6**
Standard search, ScanDisk, **WIN 9.21**
Standby mode, **WIN 6.51**
Start button, **WIN 1.9**, WIN 1.12-13
Start menu, **WIN 1.13**
  Documents command, WIN 6.47-50
  Explore, Dial-Up Networking command, WIN 7.31
  Find command, WIN 3.48, WIN 6.4-15, WIN 7.47-49
  Help command, WIN 1.44
  Help command, Web Help, WIN 2.59
  launching application using, WIN 1.40-41
  Log Off command, WIN 1.14
  opening document from, WIN 2.35-36
  placing shortcut on, WIN 2.34-35
  Programs command, WIN 1.13
  Programs command, Accessories, Entertainment, Media Player, WIN 8.30
  Programs command, Accessories, Entertainment, Sound Recorder, WIN 8.7
  Programs command, Accessories, Notepad, WIN 2.6
  Programs command, Accessories, System Tools, Backup, WIN 9.5
  Programs command, Accessories, System Tools, Disk Cleanup, WIN 9.25
  Programs command, Accessories, System Tools, Disk Defragmenter, WIN 9.29
  Programs command, Accessories, System Tools, Maintenance Wizard, WIN 9.32
  Programs command, Accessories, System Tools, ScanDisk, WIN 9.21
  Programs command, Accessories, System Tools, System Information, WIN 9.47
  Programs command, Windows Explorer, WIN 3.27
  Programs command, Internet Explorer, WIN 1.40

Programs command, Internet Explorer, Microsoft NetMeeting, WIN 8.34
removing shortcut from, WIN 2.37-38
Run command, Notepad, WIN 2.7
Run command, Paint, WIN 3.51-52
sections, WIN 1.14
Settings command, Active Desktop, WIN 2.49, WIN 2.58
Settings command, Control Panel, desktop theme, WIN 4.12
Settings command, Control Panel, display, WIN 4.6
Settings command, Control Panel, network hardware, WIN 7.37
Settings command, Control Panel, network software, WIN 7.38
Settings command, Control Panel, object properties, WIN 5.4, WIN 5.5
Settings command, Control Panel, power management, WIN 6.52
Settings command, desktop view, xv, WIN 4.45
Settings command, taskbar, WIN 4.19
Shut Down command, WIN 1.14, WIN 1.49-50
Windows Update command, WIN 9.39
Start Menu Programs sheet (Taskbar Properties dialog box), WIN 6.49
Startup disk, creating, WIN 5.49
Startup Disk sheet (Add/Remove Program Properties dialog box), **WIN 5.49**
State, dialing properties and, WIN 7.20
Status bar, **WIN 1.19**
Still graphic image, **WIN 8.4**
Storage capacity, WIN 3.2-3
Streaming, **WIN 8.26**
Stretch setting, desktop image, **WIN 4.7-8**, WIN 4.10
Subfolders, searching, WIN 6.6
Subject (Outlook Express e-mail), WIN 7.14
Submenu, **WIN 1.13**
Subscribe to channel, **WIN 2.49-54**
Subscription, **WIN 2.49-54**
Switching between windows, WIN 3.15
Synchronizing files, in My Briefcase, **WIN 6.43-47**
System configuration information, WIN 9.47
System.dat file, **WIN 9.46**
System folder icons, WIN 3.6
System icon (Control Panel), **WIN 5.41-46**
System Information, **WIN 9.47**
System Information command (System Tools submenu), WIN 9.47
System menu, **WIN 1.18**
System registry, **WIN 9.4, WIN 9.46-59**
  backing up, WIN 9.46-50, WIN 9.54
  modifying settings, WIN 9.54-58
  viewing settings, WIN 9.50-54
System Settings Change dialog box, WIN 7.37, WIN 7.44

System Tools submenu
 Backup command, WIN 9.5
 Disk Cleanup command, WIN 9.25
 Disk Defragmenter command, WIN 9.29
 Maintenance Wizard command, WIN 9.32
 ScanDisk command, WIN 9.21
 System Information command, WIN 9.47

Tab(s), **WIN 1.44**
Table of contents, Welcome to Windows 98 screen, WIN 1.10
Tape backup, WIN 2.31
Task(s), scheduling, WIN 1.9, WIN 1.18
Taskbar, **WIN 1.9**
 cascading windows and, WIN 3.17
 customizing, WIN 4.15-27
 hiding, WIN 4.17-19
 moving, WIN 4.16
 size, WIN 4.25-26
 toolbars on, WIN 4.20-29
Taskbar & Start Menu command (Settings submenu), WIN 4.19
Taskbar button area, **WIN 1.9**, WIN 1.17, WIN 1.20, WIN 1.21
 opening window from, WIN 2.25
 open window in, WIN 3.14, WIN 3.15
Taskbar Options sheet (Taskbar Properties dialog box), **WIN 4.17-19**
Taskbar Properties dialog box, WIN 4.17-19, WIN 6.49
Task Monitor, **WIN 9.29**
Task Scheduler, **WIN 9.31**, WIN 9.37
Task Scheduler icon, **WIN 1.9**
TCP/IP protocol, WIN 7.37, WIN 7.40
Telephone number
 backup, WIN 7.21
 charge to use, WIN 7.8
 connection settings, WIN 7.17-21
 dialing properties and, WIN 7.7, WIN 7.17-21
 NetMeeting, WIN 8.36
Temporary file, **WIN 9.24**
Temporary Internet file, **WIN 9.24**
Text
 finding file containing specific, WIN 6.12-13
 multimedia, **WIN 8.4**
Text label, **WIN 1.18**
Text message, sending using Chat, WIN 8.42-48
The Microsoft Network, *see* Microsoft Network, The
The Microsoft Network icon, **WIN 1.9**
Theme, desktop, WIN 4.12
32-bit operating system, **WIN 1.6**
Thorough search, ScanDisk, **WIN 9.21**
Tile setting, desktop image, **WIN 4.7**, WIN 4.10
Tile windows, **WIN 3.19-20**

Tile Windows Vertically command (shortcut menu), WIN 3.19
Time
 current, WIN 1.9
 customizing, WIN 5.24-28
 file last modified, WIN 3.49, WIN 6.8-9
 hard disk maintenance, WIN 9.31, WIN 9.35
 regional settings, WIN 5.28
 showing clock, WIN 4.19
Time pane (Date & Time sheet), **WIN 5.25**
Time sheet (Regional Settings Properties dialog box), **WIN 5.29**
Time zone, customizing, WIN 5.24-28
Time Zone sheet (Date/Time Properties dialog box), **WIN 5.27**
Title, window, WIN 1.18
Title bar, **WIN 1.9**
 active window, WIN 3.17
 My Computer window, **WIN 1.18**
To: (Outlook Express e-mail), WIN 7.14
Tone dial, WIN 7.7
Toolbar(s)
 adding to folder, WIN 4.31-32
 customizing, WIN 4.27-29
 icons, WIN 4.26
 removing, WIN 4.26
 shortcut on, WIN 4.27-29
 taskbar, WIN 4.20-29
Toolbars command (My Documents View menu), WIN 4.31
Toolbars command (shortcut menu), WIN 4.20
Toolbar titles, showing, WIN 4.26
Tool box, **WIN 3.13**
Tool Box (Whiteboard), **WIN 8.46**
Tools menu (Microsoft System Information), Registry Checker command, WIN 9.48
Tools menu (NetMeeting)
 Chat command, WIN 8.45
 File Transfer command, WIN 8.49
Track, CD, **WIN 8.15**
Tools sheet (Hard disk (C:) Properties dialog box), **WIN 3.46**
ToolTip, **WIN 1.12**, WIN 1.14
Total Size button (My Computer window), **WIN 3.8**
Tray status area, **WIN 1.9**
TrueType fonts, **WIN 5.23**
Tutorial, WIN 1.10
.txt extension, WIN 2.8, WIN 2.9
Type button (My Computer window), **WIN 3.8**

Underline icon titles consistent with my browser settings option button (Custom Settings dialog box), **WIN 4.52**
Undo button (Standard Buttons toolbar), **WIN 1.22**

Undo Cascade command (shortcut menu), WIN 3.18
Undo Tile command (shortcut menu), WIN 3.20
Uniform Resource Locator (URL), **WIN 1.37**
 Address toolbar, WIN 4.21, WIN 4.22
 Internet service provider, WIN 7.33
 United States setting, **WIN 5.28**
Update, Windows, WIN 9.38-46
Update All button (Standard Buttons toolbar), **WIN 6.43**, WIN 6.45
Updating My Briefcase files, WIN 6.43-47
Up scroll arrow, **WIN 1.27**
URL, *see* Uniform Resource Locator
USB (universal serial bus) device, adding, **WIN 5.31-33**
USB port, **WIN 5.31**
User.dat file, **WIN 9.46**
User name
 MSN, WIN 7.8
 network, **WIN 7.38**, WIN 7.44
 online service, **WIN 7.5**
Use Windows classic desktop option button (Custom Settings dialog box), **WIN 4.49**
User friendly, **WIN 1.8**
User interface, **WIN 1.7-8**

Values, **WIN 9.50**
Video, **WIN 8.5**
 NetMeeting, WIN 8.33, WIN 8.36, WIN 8.39
 recording and playing, WIN 8.26-29
Video card, **WIN 8.6**
Video transmission windows, WIN 8.42
Video window view, WIN 8.28
View, video window, WIN 8.28
View As Web Page command (Active Desktop submenu), WIN 2.48, WIN 2.58
View Channels icon, **WIN 1.9**
View menu, opening in folder, WIN 4.30-31
View menu (CD Player), Volume Control command, WIN 8.23
View menu (My Briefcase), Details command, WIN 6.36
View menu (My Computer window)
 as Web Page command, WIN 1.17
 Large Icons command, WIN 1.17
View menu (My Documents)
 as Web Page command, WIN 4.38
 Customize this Folder command, WIN 4.34
 Explorer Bar command, WIN 4.33
 Toolbars command, WIN 4.31
View menu (Network Neighborhood), Refresh command, WIN 7.45
View menu (Recycle Bin), Details command, WIN 6.22

Views, desktop, *see* Desktop views
Views button (Standard Buttons toolbar), **WIN 1.22**, WIN 3.7
Visually impaired, **WIN 5.20**, WIN 5.22
Voice message, recording and playing, WIN 8.6-12
Volume Control, **WIN 8.23**-25
Volume Control command (CD Player View menu), WIN 8.23
Volume level, WIN 1.9

Wallpaper, **WIN 4.6**-8
Wave file, **WIN 8.5**
  recording and playing, WIN 8.6-12
Web, *see* World Wide Web
Web browser, **WIN 1.37**, WIN 1.40
Web browser program, WIN 1.37, **WIN 1.40**
Web content
  on Internet, finding, WIN 6.5, WIN 6.27-29
  viewing in folder, WIN 4.41
Web Help button (Help toolbar), **WIN 1.47**
Web Help command (Options menu), **WIN 1.47**
Web pages, **WIN 1.36**-37
  Address toolbar, WIN 4.21, WIN 4.22-23
  displaying folder as, WIN 1.38, WIN 4.38-39, WIN 4.43
  receiving active content from, WIN 2.49
  shortcuts to, WIN 4.31
  viewing My Computer window as, WIN 1.17
  Windows Update, WIN 9.39
Web sheet (Display Properties dialog box), WIN 4.15
Web site, **WIN 1.36**-37
  Microsoft Windows Update, WIN 2.58

Web style desktop, WIN 1.9, WIN 1.36, **WIN 1.37-39**, **WIN 4.40**
  choosing, WIN 4.49-52
  Control Panel and, WIN 4.44
  copying files, WIN 4.57-60
  folder windows, WIN 4.53, WIN 4.55, WIN 4.56-57
  icons, WIN 4.53-55
  working with, WIN 2.47-58
Welcome to Windows 98 screen, WIN 1.9-10
Wheel button, **WIN 1.11**, WIN 5.12
Whisper, NetMeeting and, WIN 8.42
Whiteboard, **WIN 8.33**, WIN 8.46-48
Wide area networks (WANs), **WIN 7.36**
Window(s)
  active, *see* Active window
  cascading, WIN 3.15-17
  closing, WIN 1.23-24, WIN 1.31-32
  closing multiple, WIN 2.26-28
  displaying as Web page, WIN 1.38-39
  drive, WIN 3.9
  folder, *see* Folder window
  launching application program from, WIN 3.13-14
  managing open, WIN 3.15-20
  maximizing, WIN 1.21-22, WIN 1.27
  minimizing, WIN 1.19-21, WIN 2.25
  opening by double-clicking, WIN 1.16-17
  opening document from, WIN 3.12-13
  opening inactive, WIN 2.24-25
  redisplaying, WIN 1.20, WIN 1.21-23
  reopening, WIN 1.24
  resizing by dragging, WIN 1.25-26, WIN 1.31
  restoring, WIN 1.21-23
  scrolling in, WIN 1.27-31
  switching between, WIN 3.15
  tiling, WIN 3.19-20
  title, **WIN 1.18**

Window border
  dragging, WIN 1.27
  My Computer window, **WIN 1.18**
Windows, **WIN 1.6**
Windows 98, **WIN 1.6**
  adding components, WIN 5.49
  desktop, *see* Desktop
  file system, WIN 9.19-20
  fundamentals of using, WIN 1.1-51
  Help, WIN 1.43-49
  launching, WIN 1.8-9
  MSN and, WIN 7.5, WIN 7.8
  shutting down, WIN 1.49-50
  startup disk, WIN 5.49
  system registry, WIN 9.4, WIN 9.46-59
  user interface, WIN 1.7-8
Windows 98 Explorer, *see* Explorer
Windows folder, **WIN 3.10**-11
  properties of, WIN 3.46-47
Windows for Workgroups, WIN 7.36-37
Windows NT, WIN 7.36, WIN 7.38
Windows Setup sheet (Add/Remove Program Properties dialog box), **WIN 5.49**
Windows Update, **WIN 2.58**, **WIN 2.59-61**, **WIN 9.38-46**
  launching, WIN 1.14
Windows Update command (Start menu), WIN 9.39
Wizard, **WIN 4.34**, **WIN 5.33**
Word document, embedding sound file in, WIN 8.9-11
Word processing program, **WIN 1.40**, **WIN 2.6**
Work area, desktop as, WIN 1.11
Workgroup(s), viewing on network, WIN 7.45-49
Workgroup name, **WIN 7.38**, WIN 7.43
World Wide Web, **WIN 1.36**

Yahoo! People Search, WIN 6.30-31